African Development Indicators 2003

The World Bank
Washington, D.C.

1818 H Street, NW
Washington, DC 20433
Telephone 202-473-1000
Internet www.worldbank.org
E-mail feedback@worldbank.org

1 2 3 4 05 04 03

Cover photo collage created by Jeeyeon Seo using photos by (C) Gubb, Louise 2002 / from *A Day in The Life of Africa*. Cover design by Naylor Design.

ISBN 0-8213-5453-1
ISSN 1020-2927

Contents

Figures

Table des matières

11. Population active et emploi 267

12. Flux d'aide 284

Graphiques

Foreword

Reducing poverty in Africa and Meeting the Millennium Development Goals by 2015 are raising difficult challenges in most African countries. Nearly half the region's population still lives in extreme poverty. Africa urgently needs rich nations to deliver on their promises of more generous aid and wider trade opportunities to reverse the cruel effects of the HIV/AIDS pandemic, civil wars, and persistent low growth rates. The World Bank's latest annual report on social and economic conditions across the continent, *African Development Indicators (ADI) 2003,* warns that the rapid spread of HIV/AIDS, anemic aid and investment flows, and weak commodity prices threaten to undo the hard-fought gains of recent years.

As in previous years, ADI 2003 assembles economic, social, and environmental data from a variety of sources to present a broad picture of development across Africa. There have been a number of improvements: Macroeconomic and other data lags have been reduced, enabling external debt reporting up to 2001 and updates on the HIPC initiative and HIV/AIDS. Chapter 12 includes for the first time ODA not allocated by country. New tables have been added covering access to ICT and air transport. Chapter 16 contains a new set of standardized household indicators for selected countries.

ADI 2003 depicts a diverse continent. Gross national income (GNI) per head for all Africa averaged $664 in 2001 — with $1668 and $461 in North and Sub-Saharan Africa (SSA) respectively. But it stood at only $300 per head in SSA, excluding South Africa, ranging from under $100 per head in the Democratic Republic of Congo to over $6000 in Seychelles. At 2.9 percent in 2001, GDP growth in SSA barely exceeded the growth of its rapidly urbanizing population (cities grew at close to 5 percent), continuing the overall trend of the 1990s. On average, output per head has stagnated. Yet country performance has diverged widely — sixteen have averaged more than 4 percent growth over the last decade, while several have seen their economies contract, invariably as a result of severe civil conflict. On average, investment and trade trends have been steady, with a slight increase in the overall current account deficit. Net FDI flows to SSA rose to $6.8 billion in 2001, but were heavily concentrated in oil exporting countries and South Africa.

Access to ICT is still limited but increasing. In 2000 there were some nine personal computers per thousand population in SSA, a 10 percent rise over the previous year. In North Africa, computer ownership was somewhat higher, at 16 per thousand. Internet use is rising sharply — but of the 3.7 million recorded Internet users in SSA, 2.4 million were in South Africa (however, these data may not fully account for multiple user access). Air transport, too, has been a high-growth sector, with 31.8 million passengers recorded. But of this total, 21 million are accounted for by North and South Africa.

Net ODA to Africa rose slightly in 2001 because of higher multilateral flows, but on a per capita basis it has halved since 1992, from $40 to $20 (ODA was $21 per head for SSA). As of February 2003, seventeen countries had reached HIPC decision points and five had reached completion points. Total debt service relief represented $30 billion, and pro-poor expenditures had begun to increase in most of the countries. However, ten countries, mostly conflict-affected, had not yet reached the HIPC decision point.

In SSA, death rates have continued to rise because of the HIV/AIDS pandemic, causing life expectancy at birth to fall from 49 in 1985 to 47 in 2000. AIDS-related deaths were 2.2 million in 2001 (for a cumulative total close to 20 million), almost 30 million were infected and 11 million were orphaned, including a million each in Nigeria and Ethiopia. Under-5 mortality stood at 162 per thousand for SSA; in eight countries it exceeded 200 per thousand. Only half of the children in SSA were immunized. Health expenditures averaged only $13 per head in poor countries, and were below $6 per head in several. But these averages in social indicators conceal wide variation between countries: maternal mortality, for example, ranges from as low as 45 per 100,000 births to 2,300. Education trends were somewhat more favorable, with a steady fall in illiteracy, from 50 percent in 1990 to 37 percent in 2001. But there is a lot of catching-up to do: at 79 percent, primary enrollment has barely recovered to its level in 1980. Social indicators were more favorable in North Africa, with life expectancy at 69 in 2000 and immunization rates near 90 percent.

ADI 2003 draws attention to Africa's rich environmental resources, but also to the stress that environment is coming under. Many countries have large numbers of endangered species, and each year 0.7% of forest cover is being lost.

The detailed World Bank Africa Database 2003, including the World Bank's Country at a Glance Tables and electronic copy of ADI, is also being made available on CD ROM, together with a user-friendly interface to facilitate downloading and analysis. Directions for obtaining the CD ROM can be found on the World Bank's external web site (www.worldbank.org). With access to electronic media widening in Africa, ADI is expected to evolve further, with the goal of offering the most useful combination of information in hardcopy and electronic forms. We welcome user feedback and suggestions for improving ADI in future years.

Alan Harold Gelb
Chief Economist, Africa Region

Acknowledgments

This volume was produced by the Operational Quality and Knowledge Services of the Africa Region, in collaboration with the Development Data Group of the Development Economics Vice Presidency.

The volume was prepared by a team led by Tariqul I. Khan and comprising José Delcour, Tosi Mpanu-Mpanu, Rose Mungai, Kadra Nour, Joan Pandit, and Christophe Rockmore. Valuable guidance was provided by the Africa Chief Economist's office. The chapters on national accounts, balance of payments, trade, and government finance draw heavily on the work of World Bank Africa country desks. The chapters on power, communication and transportation, labor force and social indicators tap the World Bank's World Development Indicators database. The chapter on external debt is heavily drawn from DRS (Debt Reporting System) of the World Bank. The chapter on environment was prepared with data from the World Resources Institute. The chapter on privatization of public enterprises was provided by Lucy Fye. The update for the chapter on HIPC initiative was provided by Young Kim and Sarah Lacoche. The HIV/AIDS table was prepared with data from UNAIDS. In addition, many World Bank staff provided information on their countries or their economic or sectoral specialties.

Lawrence Mastri provided assistance in editing and producing the volume, while Chii Akporji, Richard Crabbe, and Cindy Fisher from the World Bank Publications Office coordinated final production of the book. Other staff aided and advised on the design and content of this volume.

ADI 2003 was produced using the new data reporting tool of the Africa Live Database (LDB) system. This tool was programmed to generate automatically all the tables in this volume and can be used for other publications. Using data warehousing technology, the LDB instantly recalculates all indicators and aggregates them once new information is available. This guarantees that the most recent data are reflected in this and future volumes.

Preface

African Development Indicators 2003 continues the data publication series started by the World Bank in 1989 with *African Economic and Financial Data* (published jointly with the United Nations Development Programme), followed by *African Development Indicators 1992, 1994/95, 1996, 1997, 1998/99, 2000, 2001,* and *2002*. These data volumes are intended to provide Africans and those interested in Africa with a consistent and convenient set of data to monitor development programs and aid flows in the region. Each successive volume provides access to more focused information and represents an improvement in the quality and availability of the data.

The data in this volume derive from a variety of sources. In most cases, the original source is national statistical services in Africa. In addition, many international agencies collect or compile data on Africa and organize national data in a standardized framework. This volume draws heavily from such sources. The data have been supplemented by World Bank staff estimates to help address problems of missing or inconsistent data from standard sources. Some of the estimation methods used here differ from methods used in other sources. This volume addresses these differences in methodologies in the chapter introductions and in the technical notes.

In the tradition of the first seven volumes, this data collection is intended to serve as a prime source of information on Africa. Its wide dissemination to African and non-African analysts and policymakers will contribute to a better understanding of Africa and to development on that continent.

John Roome
Director, Operational Quality
and Knowledge Services
Africa Region

Acronyms and Abbreviations

ADB	African Development Bank
ADI	African Development Indicators
AEFD	African Economic and Financial Data (UNDP/World Bank 1989)
AFESD	Arab Fund for Economic and Social Development
BADEA	Arab Bank for Economic Development in Africa
BIS	Bank for International Settlements
CDIAC	Carbon Dioxide Information Analysis Center
CFA	Communauté Financière Africane (franc zone)
CIDA	Canadian International Development Agency
c.i.f.	Cost, insurance, freight
CITES	Convention on International Trade in Endangered Species of Wild Flora and Fauna
CMEA	Council for Mutual Economic Assistance
COMTRADE	Commodity Trade database (United Nations)
CPI	Consumer price index
DAC	Development Assistance Committee of the OECD
DDG	Development Data Group, World Bank
DRS	Debtor Reporting System (World Bank)
ECA	Economic Commission for Africa
FAO	UN Food and Agriculture Organization
f.o.b.	Free on board
GDF	Global Development Finance (formerly World Debt Tables-WDT)
GDI	Gross domestic investment
GDP	Gross domestic product
GDS	Gross domestic savings
GFS	Government Finance Statistics (IMF)
GNFS	Goods and nonfactor services
GNP	Gross national product
GNS	Gross national savings
HIPC	Heavily Indebted Poor Countries
IBRD	International Bank for Reconstruction and Development
ICP	International Comparison Project
IDA	International Development Association
IEA	International Energy Agency
IFAD	International Fund for Agricultural Development
IFS	International Financial Statistics (IMF)
ILO	International Labour Organization
IMF	International Monetary Fund
ISIC	UN International Standard Industrial Classification
ITU	International Telecommunications Union

IUCN	International Union for Conservation of Nature and Natural Resources
LIBOR	London interbank offered rate
LIMIC	Low-income and middle-income countries
MBO	Management employee buyout
METMIN	Metals and Minerals Database (World Bank)
ODA	Official development assistance
OECD	Organization for Economic Cooperation and Development
OPEC	Organization of Petroleum Exporting Countries
ORT	Oral rehydration therapy
PE	Public enterprise
SAF	Structural adjustment facility
SDA	Social dimensions of adjustment
SDR	Special drawing right
SIMA	Statistical Information Management and Analysis Database (World Bank)
SITC	UN Standard International Trade Classification
SNA	System of national accounts
UNAIDS	United Nations Program on HIV/AIDS
UNCTAD	United Nations Conference on Trade and Development
UNDP	United Nations Development Programme
UNECE	United Nations Economic Commission for Europe
UNEP	United Nations Environment Programme
UNESCO	United Nations Education, Scientific, and Cultural Organization
UNHCR	United Nations High Commissioner for Refugees
UNICEF	United Nations Children's Fund
UNIDO	United Nations Industrial Development Organization
UNSO	United Nations Statistical Office
UNSTAT	United Nations Statistical Department
UNTA	United Nations Technical Assistance
WFP	World Food Programme
WHO	World Health Organization
WRI	World Resources Institute
ZIMCO	Zambia Industrial and Mining Corporation

Introduction

The task of monitoring Africa's development progress and aid flows requires basic empirical data that can be readily used by analysts. This publication—which is the seventh in a series that began with the African Economic and Financial Data (AEFD), and was followed by African Development Indicators (ADI) 1992, 1994, 1995, 1996, 1997, 1998/99, 2000, 2001, and 2002—is meant to provide a starting point to fulfill that task.

This volume has been able to extend the work of the previous volumes in this series. In particular:

- Most macroeconomic data (in particular, national accounts, balance of payments, government finance statistics, and trade) reflect data maintained by World Bank country desks, often referred to as operational data. These data are often more up to date and offer better country coverage than the data stored in the Bank's central files, SIMA, which were used in publications before 1998. SIMA is a large database that contains some, but not all, data produced by Bank staff—operational and other—and some, but not all, data produced by UN agencies.
- The coverage of many of the data series has been improved, reflecting improvements in the underlying data series, as well as estimates made by Bank staff.

However, substantial data gaps remain, notably in areas such as public enterprises, gender, and labor. Strengthening the statistical capacity in African countries is an ongoing process and greater efforts and institutional support will be required if substantial improvements are to be made.

This volume presents the available relevant data for 1980–2000, grouped into fourteen chapters: background data; national accounts; prices and exchange rates; money and banking; external sector; external debt and related flows; government finance; agriculture; power, communications, and transportation; public enterprises; labor force and employment; aid flows; social indicators; and environmental indicators. Chapter 14 (environmental indicators) was once again taken from the World Resources Institute's World Resources 2001.

Each chapter begins with a brief introduction on the nature of the data, followed by a set of charts, statistical tables, and technical notes. These define the indicators and identify specific sources.

A companion CD-Rom, known as World Bank Africa Database 2002, provides year-by-year time series of most chapters back to 1980. These series will provide analysts with data needed to help place the most recent years in an historical context.

The data in this volume incorporate numerous revisions to those published previously in the series. There are several reasons for this.

- Many of the data that were based on estimates in the earlier volumes have been replaced with updated actual data or improved estimates. In most cases, these reflect revisions made by the original reporting authorities or sources, but it also includes corrections of errors in previous volumes.
- Data series expressed in constant U.S. dollars and exchange rates use a base year of 1995; previous ADIs were based on 1987 exchange rates and prices; and AEFD used 1980 exchange rate and prices.
- Some series expressed in constant prices have been revised as a result of updated or revised deflators.
- As in the 2000 volume, macroeconomic data reflect country desk information. The difference is most noticeable in the chapter on government finance, as figures reflect consolidated government data instead of only central government data.

Considerable effort has been made to standardize and to harmonize related data sets drawn from diverse sources. Because statistical methods, coverage, practices, and definitions differ widely among sources, full comparability cannot be assured, and the indicators must be interpreted with care. In addition, the statistical systems in many developing economies are still weak, and this affects the availability and reliability of the data they report. Moreover, intercountry and intertemporal comparisons always involve complex technical problems, which have no full and unequivocal solution.

The data are drawn from sources thought to be the most authoritative, but many data sources are subject to considerable margins of error. To provide reasonably timely data required for meaningful monitoring, the World Bank, the International Monetary Fund (IMF), and other agencies sometimes make estimates on the basis of available secondary information to fill critical gaps in national reporting, especially for the most recent years, when data cannot be readily produced by national statistical sources. Nonetheless, data gaps exist for many indicators, and some countries are covered only sporadically.

Readers are urged to take these limitations into account in using the data and interpreting the indicators, particularly when making comparisons across economies. Weaknesses in the data point to the need for strengthened statistical systems throughout the region.

As a visual aid to data interpretation and cross-country comparisons, figures for selected indicators are included. As with time series, the figures should also be interpreted with caution, in particular in cross-country analysis, because countries with missing data are excluded from the charts.

Throughout this volume (except when otherwise stated), the symbol ".." indicates that data are not available or not applicable. A zero (0) indicates either zero value or an insignificant value, that is, less than one-half of the smallest unit shown. The symbol "MR" indicates "most recent year available." In chapter 13, columns headed by a period (for example, 1992–95) show data for the latest available year in the period.

To facilitate cross-country comparisons, values of many national series have been converted from the national currencies to U.S. dollars, using the World Bank Atlas methodology.

Indicators in this volume generally follow standard definitions as far as possible and cover years through 2001, depending on the chapter. Data for 2001 are preliminary and therefore may not be internally consistent within and across accounts, and may not be available for all countries. Because data are continually updated, the statistics here may be different from those in other publications.

Shares and ratios are always calculated using current price series; when gross domestic product GDP is used as the denominator for these calculations, it is always expressed at market prices (except in Figure 2-3).

In all but the last chapter, the data are arranged by indicator to facilitate cross-country comparisons. For country-specific work, data can be arranged to show all indicators together for each country.

In this volume, the statistical tables are usually arranged as time series, by country and by country groups. The largest country group is All Africa, consisting of two subgroups: North Africa and Sub-Saharan Africa (including South Africa). In turn, the Sub-Saharan Africa group is shown excluding South Africa and Nigeria. These two subgroups correspond to the Sub-Saharan Africa and Sub-Saharan Africa excluding Nigeria groups shown in the *AEFD* and *ADI 1992*, where South Africa was listed separately.

Annual data shown for country groups are totals, averages, or medians for the countries included in the group, as indicated on the table. These group aggregates can be either simple arithmetic)—where missing data are not imputed-or gap-filled—where weights are used to adjust group totals for missing countries. In the latter case, when values are missing for a country or a year, estimates are made to maintain the same country composition of the groups through time. However, the implicit estimated values for the countries with missing data are not shown separately in the tables. These gap-fill estimates are made, and the aggregate statistics shown, only if the countries for which data are available for a given year account for at least two-thirds of the full group, as defined by benchmarks in 1995. This procedure is standard for many World Bank statistical publications.

Most group averages are weighted according to the relative importance of the countries in the group total for that indicator, based on simple addition across countries when the indicator is expressed in reasonably comparable units. Group averages for analytical ratios (for example, imports to GDP) can be either weighted or simple (arithmetic). Usually they are calculated from the group totals for both the numerator and the denominator, which is analytically equivalent to calculating weighted averages, where the weight for each country is its share in the group total for the denominator. Sometimes, however, when it is appropriate to treat the experiences of different countries equally in determining a representative value for the group, these group averages are arithmetic—that is, each country has equal weight.

Period averages—shown for 1975–84, 1985–89, and 1990 to most recent year—are calculated from time series (levels, ratios, growth rates, or medians) for both countries and country groups. They are either simple averages or average annual percentage growth rates. These growth rates always use the least-squares method and are usually computed from real-term series. In this publication, the least-squares growth rates are computed using the level for the year before the first year shown in the label. The least-squares growth rate, r, is estimated by fitting a least-squares linear regression trend line to the logarithmic annual values of the variable in the relevant period. More specifically, the regression equation takes the form: $\log X = a + bt + e$, where this is equivalent to the logarithmic transformation of the compound growth rate equation, $X = X\ (1 + r)^t$. In these equations X is the variable, t is time, and $a = \log X$ and $b = \log (1 + r)$ are the parameters to be estimated; e is the error term. If b^* is the least-squares estimate of b, then the annual average growth rate, r, is obtained as [anti log (b^*)] – 1 and multiplied by 100 to express it in percentage terms. The least-squares growth rate dampens the influence of exceptional values, particularly at the end points. Least-square growth rates are calculated only if more than two-thirds of consecutive data—carrying the same sign—are present in the time series.

Throughout this volume, data for Ethiopia include Eritrea up to 1992, except when otherwise indicated. Mauritius data are reported for fiscal years ending June 30. The data are published under the second year of the reporting period—for example, July 2000 to June 2001 is published under 2001. Therefore, in some cases (e.g., Government Finance) data for Mauritius may appear a year off compared to last year's publication, where data were published under the first year of the reporting period.

1

Selected Background Data

The first two tables of the volume provide selected indicators, including a series on population, as background to the data in the rest of the volume. Table 1-1 provides a comparative view, across indicators, of some of the more important indicators for all countries in the most recent year for which relatively complete information is available.

1-1. Basic indicators

	Population mid-2001 (millions)	Land area (thousands of square km.)	GNI per capita: Atlas dollars 2001	GNI per capita: Av. annual percentage growth 1990-01	Life expectancy at birth (years) 2000	School enrollment: Primary 1980	School enrollment: Primary 1995-99	School enrollment: Secondary 1980	School enrollment: Secondary 1995-99	Total net ODA per capita 2001
SUB-SAHARAN AFRICA	674.5	23,626	461	-0.2	47	80	79	15	26	21
excluding South Africa	631.3	22,405	300	0.2	46	80	75	15	20	21
excl. S.Africa & Nigeria	501.4	21,494	303	0.1	46	72	81	14	22	26
Angola	13.5	1,247	500	-0.8	47	175	64	21	15	20
Benin	6.4	111	380	1.9	53	67	86	16	22	42
Botswana	1.7	567	3,100	2.2	39	91	108	19	82	17
Burkina Faso	11.6	274	220	1.9	44	17	43	3	10	34
Burundi	6.9	26	100	-4.1	42	26	62	3	7	19
Cameroon	15.2	465	580	-1.2	50	98	91	18	20	26
Cape Verde	0.4	4	1,340	3.0	69	114	122	8	69	171
Central African Republic	3.8	623	260	-0.6	43	71	56	14	10	20
Chad	7.9	1,259	200	-0.7	48	..	70	..	11	23
Comoros	0.6	2	380	-1.4	61	86	84	22	21	48
Congo, Democratic Rep. of	52.4	2,267	80	0.2	46	92	47	24	18	5
Congo, Republic of	3.1	342	640	-4.1	51	141	84	74	52	24
Côte d'Ivoire	16.4	318	630	0.3	46	75	77	19	22	11
Djibouti	0.6	23	890	0.0	46	37	37	12	15	85
Equatorial Guinea	0.5	28	700	..	51	..	125	..	31	28
Eritrea	4.2	101	160	0.2	52	..	61	..	28	67
Ethiopia	65.8	1,000	100	2.0	42	37	71	9	5	16
Gabon	1.3	258	3,160	-0.5	53	..	151	..	54	7
Gambia, The	1.3	10	320	0.3	53	53	75	11	27	38
Ghana	19.7	228	290	1.8	57	79	78	41	37	33
Guinea	7.6	246	410	1.9	46	36	63	17	14	36
Guinea-Bissau	1.2	28	160	-1.8	45	68	83	6	20	48
Kenya	30.7	569	350	-0.1	47	115	91	20	30	15
Lesotho	2.1	30	530	-0.5	44	103	104	18	28	26
Liberia	3.2	96	140	..	47	48	118	22	23	11
Madagascar	16.0	582	260	-0.4	55	130	102	..	14	22
Malawi	10.5	94	160	1.2	39	60	158	5	45	38
Mali	11.1	1,220	230	0.8	42	26	55	8	15	32
Mauritania	2.7	1,025	360	1.5	52	37	84	11	18	95
Mauritius	1.2	2	3,830	4.0	72	93	108	50	107	18
Mozambique	18.1	784	210	4.0	42	99	85	5	14	52
Namibia	1.8	823	1,960	2.4	47	..	113	..	60	61
Niger	11.2	1,267	180	-1.2	46	25	32	5	7	22
Nigeria	129.9	911	290	0.3	47	109	82	18	30	1
Rwanda	8.7	25	220	-1.9	40	63	122	3	12	33
São Tomé and Principe	0.2	1	280	-0.6	65	..	..	..	..	251
Senegal	9.8	193	490	1.1	52	46	73	11	20	43
Seychelles	0.1	0	6,530	0.4	72	..	..	..	..	164
Sierra Leone	5.1	72	140	-5.6	39	52	65	14	24	65
Somalia	9.1	627	..	0.0	48	21	10	9	6	16
South Africa	43.2	1,221	2,820	0.0	48	90	119	..	90	10
Sudan	31.7	2,376	340	0.0	56	50	55	16	29	5
Swaziland	1.1	17	1,300	0.2	46	103	125	38	60	27
Tanzania	34.4	884	270	0.7	44	93	63	3	5	36
Togo	4.7	54	270	-0.8	49	118	124	33	36	10
Uganda	22.8	197	260	3.8	42	50	141	5	13	34
Zambia	10.3	743	320	-1.8	38	90	79	16	25	36
Zimbabwe	12.8	387	480	-0.3	40	85	97	8	45	12
NORTH AFRICA	140.3	5,738	1,668	1.5	69	84	103	41	69	17
Algeria	30.8	2,382	1,650	-0.2	71	94	114	33	67	6
Egypt, Arab Republic	65.2	995	1,530	2.8	67	73	100	50	84	19
Libya	5.4	1,760	..	0.0	71	125	117	76	79	..
Morocco	29.2	446	1,190	0.8	67	83	90	26	39	18
Tunisia	9.7	155	2,070	3.1	72	102	118	27	75	39
ALL AFRICA	814.8	29,364	664	0.3	50	81	89	20	33	20

Note: 2001 data are preliminary (see page 2). GNI per capita previously called GNP per capita.

1-2. Population

	Millions of people											*Average annual percentage growth*		
	1980	*1992*	*1993*	*1994*	*1995*	*1996*	*1997*	*1998*	*1999*	*2000*	*2001*	*75-84*	*85-89*	*90-MR*
SUB-SAHARAN AFRICA	382.04	538.80	550.69	564.43	579.81	595.97	612.76	628.46	644.02	659.50	674.54	3.0	2.9	2.6
excluding South Africa	354.46	502.11	513.22	526.14	540.69	556.06	572.09	587.06	601.91	616.70	631.30	3.0	2.9	2.7
excl. S.Africa & Nigeria	283.31	400.23	408.33	418.13	429.42	441.57	454.41	466.24	478.02	489.79	501.42	3.0	2.9	2.6
Angola	7.06	10.29	10.64	10.99	11.34	11.69	12.05	12.40	12.76	13.13	13.51	3.0	3.0	3.1
Benin	3.46	5.03	5.19	5.35	5.49	5.64	5.79	5.95	6.11	6.27	6.44	2.7	3.2	2.9
Botswana	0.91	1.36	1.40	1.45	1.50	1.54	1.58	1.61	1.65	1.68	1.70	3.6	3.4	2.8
Burkina Faso	6.96	9.31	9.53	9.76	9.99	10.23	10.47	10.73	11.00	11.27	11.55	2.4	2.4	2.4
Burundi	4.13	5.75	5.89	6.02	6.16	6.29	6.42	6.55	6.68	6.81	6.94	2.5	2.9	2.2
Cameroon	8.72	12.29	12.62	12.95	13.27	13.60	13.92	14.24	14.56	14.88	15.20	2.9	2.9	2.5
Cape Verde	0.29	0.36	0.36	0.37	0.38	0.39	0.40	0.41	0.42	0.43	0.45	1.0	1.9	2.5
Central African Republic	2.31	3.07	3.15	3.24	3.35	3.44	3.53	3.60	3.67	3.72	3.77	2.5	2.4	2.4
Chad	4.48	6.06	6.25	6.46	6.71	6.89	7.09	7.28	7.49	7.69	7.92	2.4	2.4	3.0
Comoros	0.34	0.46	0.47	0.48	0.49	0.50	0.52	0.53	0.54	0.56	0.57	..	2.6	2.6
Congo, Democratic Rep. of	26.91	39.59	40.96	42.38	43.85	45.31	46.75	48.18	49.58	50.95	52.35	3.0	3.3	3.3
Congo, Republic of	1.67	2.37	2.44	2.52	2.60	2.68	2.77	2.85	2.93	3.02	3.10	2.9	3.0	3.1
Côte d'Ivoire	8.19	12.62	13.04	13.46	13.88	14.31	14.73	15.16	15.59	16.01	16.41	3.9	3.7	3.1
Djibouti	0.30	0.53	0.56	0.57	0.58	0.59	0.60	0.61	0.62	0.63	0.64	6.0	4.6	2.9
Equatorial Guinea	0.22	0.37	0.38	0.39	0.40	0.41	0.42	0.43	0.45	0.46	0.47	2.4	3.4	2.6
Eritrea	2.38	3.31	3.39	3.48	3.57	3.67	3.77	3.88	3.99	4.10	4.20	2.6	3.0	2.7
Ethiopia	37.72	54.79	53.30	54.89	56.53	58.23	59.75	61.27	62.78	64.30	65.82	2.8	3.2	2.3
Gabon	0.69	0.99	1.02	1.05	1.08	1.11	1.14	1.17	1.20	1.23	1.26	3.1	3.1	2.8
Gambia, The	0.64	1.01	1.05	1.08	1.12	1.15	1.19	1.22	1.26	1.30	1.34	3.1	4.1	3.4
Ghana	10.74	16.11	16.55	16.95	17.30	17.66	18.05	18.45	18.87	19.31	19.71	2.3	3.7	2.4
Guinea	4.46	6.09	6.26	6.42	6.59	6.76	6.92	7.09	7.25	7.42	7.58	1.7	2.8	2.6
Guinea-Bissau	0.76	1.00	1.03	1.05	1.08	1.10	1.13	1.15	1.17	1.20	1.23	3.0	2.5	2.3
Kenya	16.63	24.68	25.35	26.02	26.69	27.36	28.04	28.73	29.42	30.09	30.74	3.8	3.4	2.6
Lesotho	1.36	1.75	1.79	1.83	1.87	1.91	1.94	1.98	2.01	2.04	2.06	2.2	2.1	1.9
Liberia	1.88	2.54	2.60	2.66	2.73	2.81	2.88	2.96	3.04	3.13	3.21	3.2	2.3	2.5
Madagascar	8.87	12.19	12.54	12.91	13.30	13.72	14.15	14.59	15.05	15.52	15.98	2.6	2.8	3.0
Malawi	6.18	8.78	8.92	9.06	9.21	9.44	9.66	9.88	10.10	10.31	10.53	3.3	3.3	2.0
Mali	6.59	8.93	9.16	9.39	9.62	9.85	10.09	10.33	10.58	10.84	11.09	2.2	2.7	2.5
Mauritania	1.55	2.10	2.15	2.21	2.28	2.34	2.42	2.49	2.58	2.67	2.75	2.6	2.5	2.9
Mauritius	0.97	1.08	1.10	1.11	1.12	1.13	1.15	1.16	1.17	1.19	1.20	1.4	0.8	1.2
Mozambique	12.10	14.69	15.01	15.42	15.82	16.23	16.63	16.97	17.30	17.69	18.07	2.7	1.0	2.2
Namibia	0.99	1.48	1.52	1.56	1.59	1.62	1.65	1.68	1.72	1.76	1.79	1.9	4.2	2.4
Niger	5.62	8.21	8.50	8.80	9.11	9.43	9.77	10.13	10.48	10.83	11.18	3.2	3.2	3.5
Nigeria	71.15	101.88	104.89	108.01	111.27	114.50	117.68	120.82	123.90	126.91	129.87	3.1	3.0	2.8
Rwanda	5.16	7.35	7.54	6.23	6.40	6.73	7.90	8.11	8.31	8.51	8.69	3.3	3.0	2.0
São Tomé and Principe	0.09	0.12	0.13	0.13	0.13	0.14	0.14	0.14	0.14	0.15	0.15	1.5	2.8	2.6
Senegal	5.54	7.66	7.86	8.08	8.30	8.53	8.78	9.03	9.29	9.53	9.77	2.9	2.8	2.7
Seychelles	0.06	0.07	0.07	0.07	0.08	0.08	0.08	0.08	0.08	0.08	0.08	1.4	0.7	1.5
Sierra Leone	3.24	4.19	4.29	4.40	4.51	4.62	4.73	4.83	4.93	5.03	5.13	2.0	2.2	2.3
Somalia	6.49	7.72	7.76	7.63	7.35	7.61	7.89	8.18	8.47	8.78	9.08	6.3	-0.4	2.0
South Africa	27.58	36.69	37.47	38.28	39.12	39.91	40.67	41.40	42.11	42.80	43.24	2.3	2.5	2.0
Sudan	19.32	25.89	26.51	27.20	27.95	28.67	29.35	29.98	30.56	31.10	31.69	3.0	2.2	2.3
Swaziland	0.57	0.82	0.85	0.87	0.90	0.93	0.96	0.99	1.02	1.05	1.07	3.2	3.2	3.1
Tanzania	18.58	27.10	27.94	28.79	29.65	30.49	31.32	32.13	32.92	33.70	34.45	3.2	3.2	2.8
Togo	2.52	3.62	3.71	3.81	3.91	4.02	4.14	4.26	4.39	4.53	4.65	2.5	3.3	2.7
Uganda	12.81	17.47	18.05	18.63	19.22	19.81	20.42	21.04	21.62	22.21	22.79	2.4	2.6	3.1
Zambia	5.74	8.26	8.50	8.74	8.98	9.21	9.44	9.67	9.88	10.09	10.28	3.4	3.0	2.6
Zimbabwe	7.13	10.78	11.03	11.26	11.48	11.70	11.92	12.15	12.39	12.63	12.82	3.4	3.7	2.1
NORTH AFRICA	88.35	119.03	121.53	123.96	126.34	128.63	130.94	133.25	135.59	137.92	140.27	2.7	2.5	1.9
Algeria	18.67	26.27	26.89	27.50	28.06	28.57	29.05	29.51	29.95	30.39	30.84	3.1	2.8	2.0
Egypt, Arab Republic	40.88	54.78	55.93	57.06	58.18	59.27	60.42	61.58	62.77	63.98	65.18	2.5	2.5	2.0
Libya	3.04	4.49	4.58	4.66	4.76	4.85	4.95	5.06	5.17	5.29	5.41	4.5	3.2	2.0
Morocco	19.38	25.00	25.47	25.93	26.39	26.85	27.31	27.78	28.24	28.71	29.17	2.3	2.2	1.8
Tunisia	6.38	8.49	8.66	8.82	8.96	9.09	9.22	9.33	9.46	9.56	9.67	2.6	2.5	1.6
ALL AFRICA	470.39	657.84	672.22	688.39	706.15	724.60	743.70	761.72	779.61	797.42	814.80	2.9	2.8	2.5

Note: 2001 data are preliminary (see page 2).

Figure 1-1. Development diamonds for all African countries, 2001*

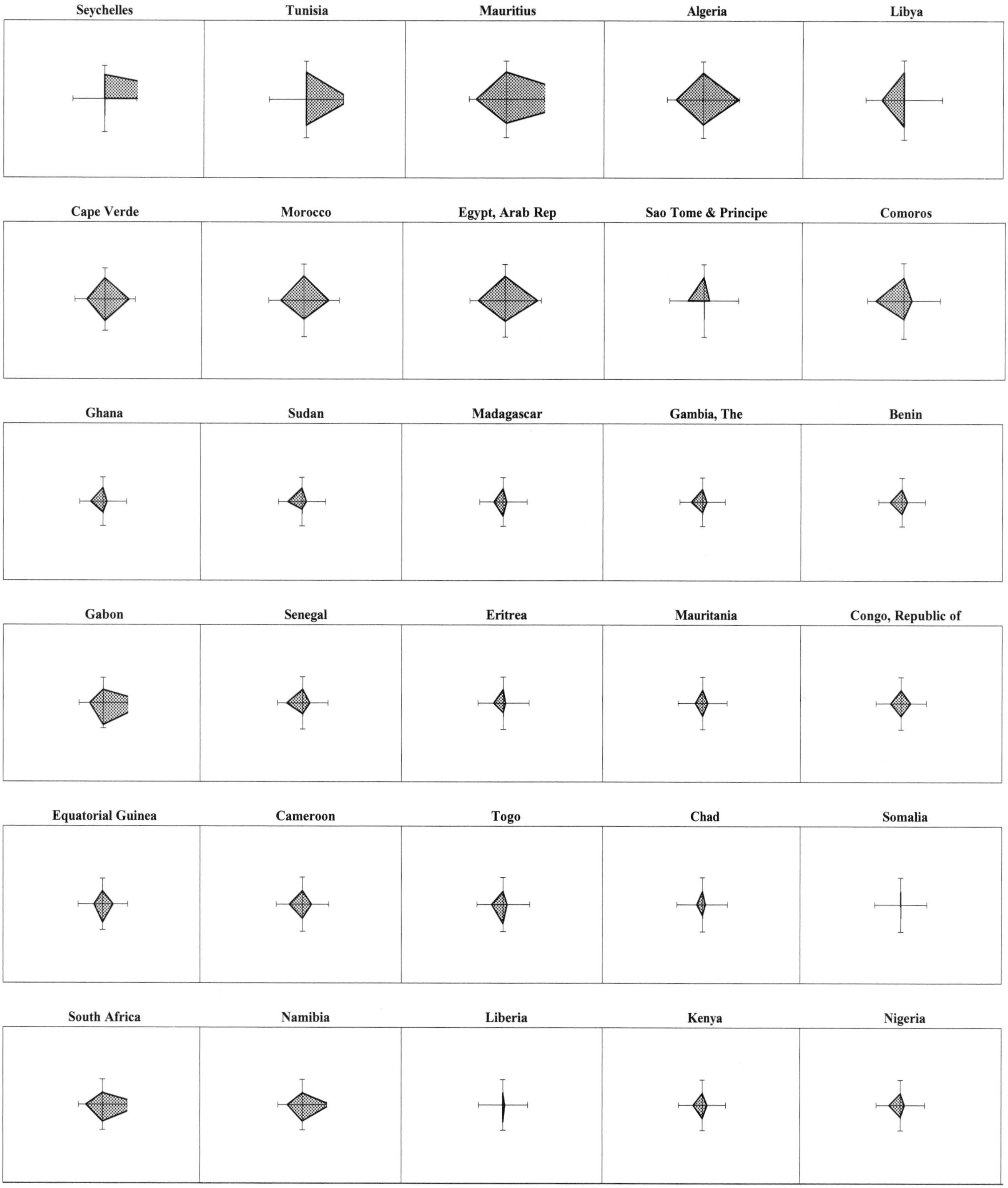

*Or most recent year available

(Graph continued on the following page)

Figure 1-1. *(continued)*

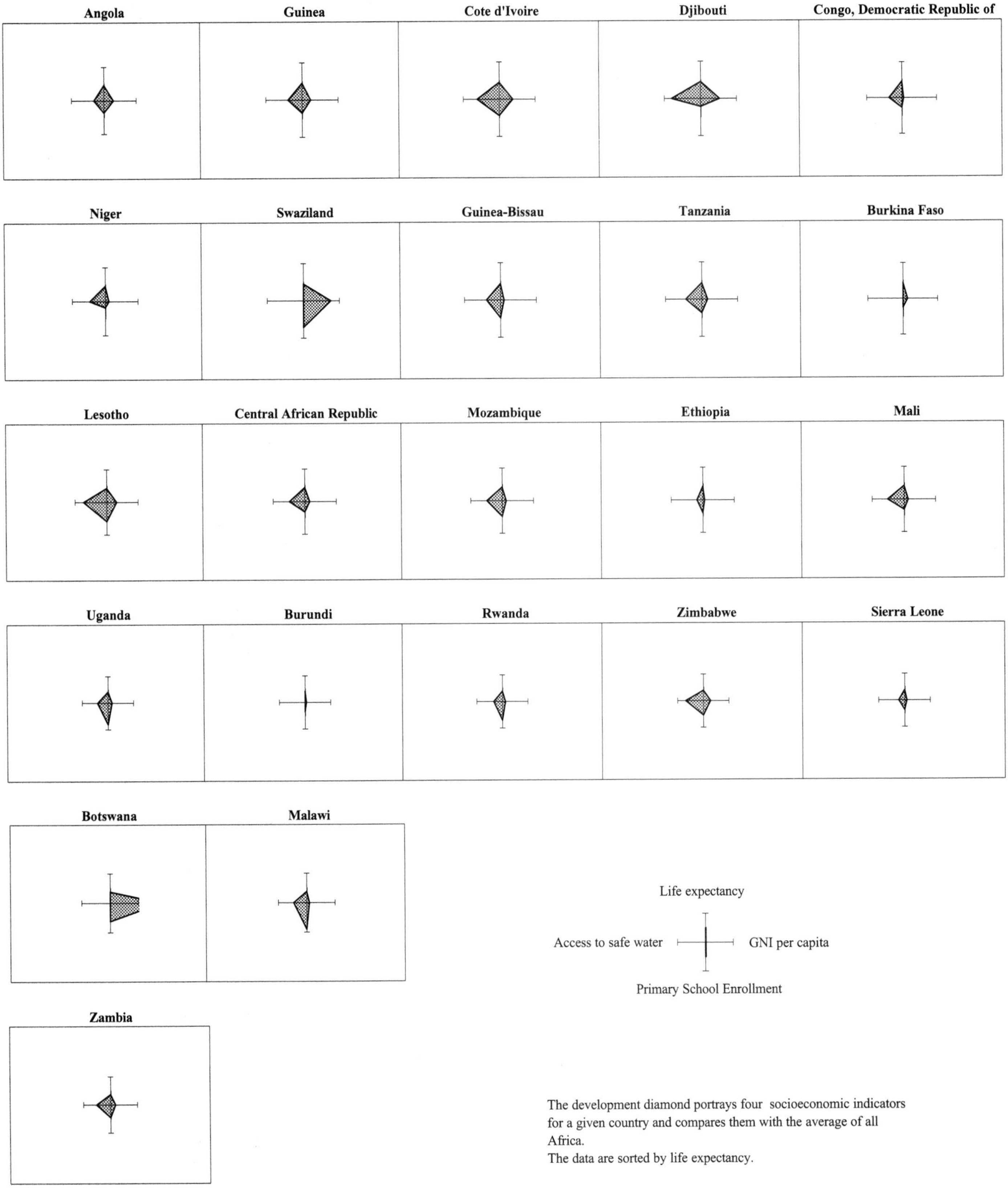

The development diamond portrays four socioeconomic indicators for a given country and compares them with the average of all Africa.
The data are sorted by life expectancy.

Figure 1-2. Selected basic indicators, 2001*

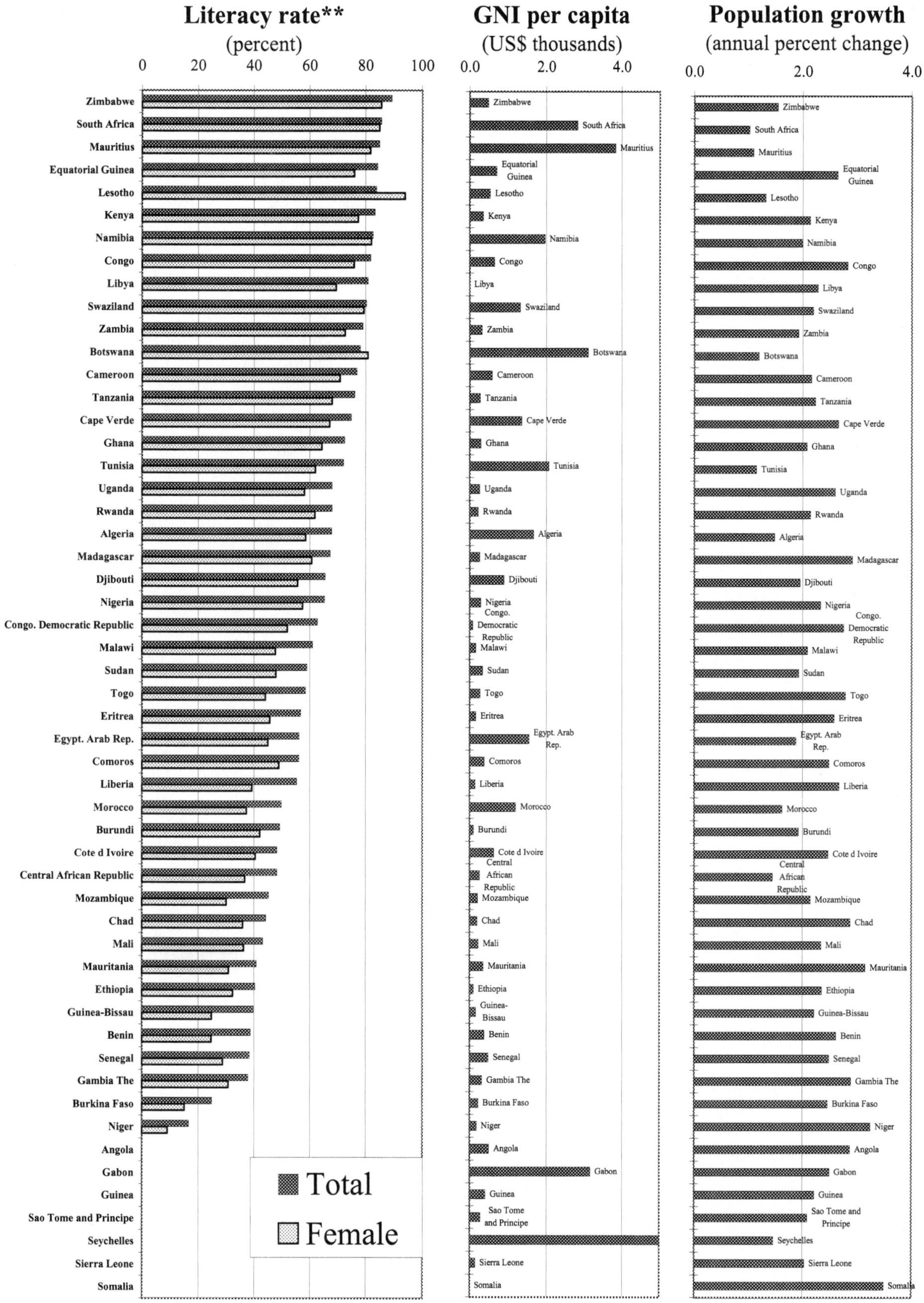

* Or most recent year available.

** Sorted by total literacy rate.

Technical notes

Tables

Table 1-1. Basic indicators. The data for this table are from the World Bank's Statistical Information Management and Analysis Database (SIMA), except for official development assistance (ODA), which are from the OECD, Geographical Distribution of Financial Flows to Developing Countries database (see technical notes to Chapter 12). Regional aggregates for GNP per capita, life expectancy, and education are weighted by population.

Population estimates for mid-2001 are World Bank estimates. These are usually projections from the most recent population censuses or surveys (mostly from 1980–2001). Refugees not permanently settled in the country of asylum are generally considered to be part of the population of their country of origin (see technical notes to Tables 13-1, 13-4, and 13-5).

Land area refers to the land surface area of a country, excluding inland waters.

GNI per capita figures in U.S. dollars are calculated according to the World Bank Atlas method described below. GNI measures the total domestic and foreign value added claimed by residents. It comprises GDP (defined in the note for Table 2-5) plus net factor income from abroad, which is the income residents receive from abroad for factor services (labor and capital) less similar payments made to nonresidents who contributed to the domestic economy. The data are from the Food and Agriculture Organization (FAO).

The *World Bank Atlas* method uses a three-year average of conversion factors to convert GNI data, expressed in different national currencies, to a common denomination, conventionally U.S. dollars. The *Atlas* conversion factor for any year is the average of the official exchange rate (Table 3-4) or alternative conversion factor (Table 3-6) for that year and for the two preceding years, after adjusting them for differences in relative inflation between that country and the United States. This three-year average smoothes fluctuations in prices and exchange rates for each country. The resulting GNI in U.S. dollars is divided by the midyear population for the latest of the three years to derive GNI per capita.

The following formulas describe the procedures for computing the conversion factor for year t:

$$e^*_{t-2,t} = \frac{1}{3}\left[e_{t-2}\left(\frac{P_t}{P_{t-2}} \Big/ \frac{P^\$_t}{P^\$_{t-2}}\right) + e_{t-1}\left(\frac{P_t}{P_{t-1}} \Big/ \frac{P^\$_t}{P^\$_{t-1}}\right) + e_t \right]$$

and for calculating per capita GNI in U.S. dollars for year t:

$$Y^\$_t = (Y_t / N_t) + e^*_{t-2,t}$$

where Y_t = current GNI (local currency) for year t, $P_{t<D\%-2>}$ = GNI deflator for year t, N_t midyear population for year t, and $P^\$_t$ = US GNI deflator for year t.

Growth rates of GNI per capita for this table are shown in real terms. They have been calculated by the least-squares method using constant GNI per capita series in 1995 prices in national currency (World Bank, SIMA). See also technical notes for Table 2-19.

Life expectancy at birth indicates the number of years a newborn infant would live if prevailing patterns of mortality at the time of its birth were to remain the same throughout its life. Figures are World Bank estimates based on data from the UN Population Division, the UN Statistical Office, and national statistical offices.

Primary school enrollment is the ratio of children of all ages enrolled in primary school to the population of children of primary school age. While many countries consider the primary school age to be 6 to 11 years, others use different age groups. These different country practices are also reflected in the ratios. Gross enrollment may be reported in excess of 100 percent if some pupils are younger or older than the country's standard range of primary school age. In practice, enrollment does not necessarily equal attendance, nor does it remain constant throughout the year. Data are from the United Nations Education, Scientific, and Cultural Organization (UNESCO).

Secondary school enrollment is the ratio of children of all ages enrolled in secondary schools to the population of children of secondary school age. The definition of secondary school age differs among countries. It is most commonly considered to be 12 to 17 years. Data are from UNESCO.

Total net ODA per capita consists of net disbursements of loans and grants from all official sources on concessional financial terms, divided by the midyear population for the corresponding year (see the technical notes to Chapter 12).

Table 1-2. Population. Average annual percentage growth shown in this table was calculated using the least-squares method.

Statistical background for the population estimates is available in the UN Population and Vital Statistics Report and the World Bank's World Population Projections (World Bank 1994–95) (see also the technical notes to Chapter 13).

Figures

The following indicators have been used to derive the figures in this chapter.

Figure 1-1. Life expectancy (Table 1-1); access to safe water (Table 13-10); GNI per capita (Table 2-19); primary school enrollment (Table 1-1).

Figure 1-2. Literacy rate (Table 13-13); GNI per capita (Table 2-19); population growth (Table 1-2).

Methodology used for regional aggregations and period averages in chapter 1

	Aggregations [a]						Period averages [b]	
Table	*(1)*	*(2)*	*(3)*	*(4)*	*(5)*	*(6)*	*(2)*	*(3)*
Table 1-1								
Column 1	x							
Column 2	x							
Column 3				x				
Column 4				x				x
Column 5					x			
Column 6					x			
Column 7					x			
Column 8					x			
Column 9					x			
Column 10		x						
Table1-2	x						x	

Note: Regional aggregations are shown in the rows for Sub-Saharan Africa, North Africa, and All Africa. Period averages are shown in column 4 for Table 1-1 and in the last three columns for Table 1-2.. This table shows only the methodologies used in this chapter.

a. Regional aggregations: (1) simple total; (2) simple total of the first indicator divided by the simple total of the second indicator (same country coverage); (3) simple total of the gap-filled indicator; (4) simple total of the gap-filled main indicator divided by the simple total of the gap-filled secondary indicator; (5) simple total of the first gap-filled main indicator less the simple total of the second gap-filled main indicator, all divided by the simple total of the secondary indicator; (6) weighted total (by population); (7) median; (8) no aggregation; (9) simple arithmetic mean.

b. Period averages: (1) arithmetic mean (using the same series as shown in the table i.e., ratio if the rest of the table is shown as ratio, level if the rest of the table is shown as level, growth rate if the rest is shown as growth rate); (2) least-squares growth rate (using main indicator); (3) least-squares growth rate (using main indicator in constant terms, with the rest of the table in current terms).

2

National Accounts

National accounts data provide the broadest picture of a nation's economic performance. National accounts give information on the structure of production in the form of gross domestic product (GDP) and its components by industrial origin, GDP and its components by expenditure, and information on a nation's economic relations with the outside world. These are the key statistics for assessing a nation's economic condition at a given time or the trends in a nation's economic performance over time. National accounts data also provide a quantitative basis for forecasting and policymaking and as such are used widely both by analysts and policymakers.

GDP and its components by industrial origin are compiled following the widely used System of National Accounts (SNA). The SNA methodology accounts for virtually all activities pertinent to the production of goods and the provision of services in an economy by residents and nonresidents, regardless of the allocation to domestic and foreign claims. GDP does not account for the depreciation of fixed capital.

There are three methods of compiling GDP figures: income, expenditure, and production methods. Because of technical and resource constraints, the income method is not used in most developing countries. In this volume, GDP and its components by industrial origin are compiled using the production method. The three components of GDP by industrial origin are value added in agriculture, value added in industry, and value added in services. (See the technical notes at the end of this chapter.) The national accounts are constructed in national currencies and in current prices. Figures reported in this chapter are, however, in U.S. dollars, usually converted from national currency series at the official exchange rate. If the official exchange rate is significantly different from the prevailing market rate or shows extreme volatility, the local currency is converted into U.S. dollars by using an alternative conversion factor. The conversion factors used for this purpose are presented in Table 3-6. Reporting currencies in a common denominator facilitates cross-country comparisons and aggregations in country groups.

In addition, estimates of GDP and its components by industrial origin are converted into constant prices. Reporting figures in constant prices is essential for monitoring real changes in the structure of production and for analyzing relations among prices, production, employment, and so forth.

Constant price series in U.S. dollars use a 1995 base year and are converted from national currency series using 1995 exchange rates. To establish a common base year for all countries, national accounts in national currencies at constant prices based on years other than 1995 have been partly rebased to 1995 by rescaling constant price series of components of GDP.

Using a single base year raises problems when there are profound structural changes or significant changes in relative prices. For example, values expressed in constant U.S. dollars necessarily reflect the exchange rates prevailing during the base year. Where subsequent exchange rate changes have been substantial, as they have for many African countries since 1980, comparisons among countries and aggregate trends will be affected. For this reason alone, the data should be used with considerable caution.

Monitoring resource allocations across sectors in any given point in time requires the use of current prices. Accordingly, in addition to GDP in constant prices, GDP in current prices is provided. Following GDP in current prices are components of GDP by expenditure. Data on consumption, investment, and savings are constructed using the SNA's convention. Conceptually, all income is either consumed or saved, and as such the sum of total consumption and gross domestic saving equals GDP.

When viewed from a production point of view, by definition savings equals investment. Investment measures additions to fixed assets of an economy, whether it represents additions to the stock of capital or merely replenishes depreciated capital stock, plus net changes in the level of inventories. It is financed either through domestic savings or by drawing on the savings of foreigners. Data on gross domestic investment and gross domestic savings thus shed light not only on the nature of the domestic inter-temporal resource allocation but also on the size of the resource gap. Gross national savings, however, indicates the amount of savings generated by a nation's residents.

Although this volume includes a chapter on international trade, the fact that balance of payments is an integral part of the national accounts warrants the inclusion of the resource balance and its components in this chapter. Moreover, a closer examination of the fifth edition of the IMF's Balance of Payments Manual (1993) reflects differences in concepts, definitions, and classifications from the UN's SNA guidelines. For instance, in the SNA, factor services rendered by residents of another country are excluded from goods and services, but this practice is not universally followed. The tables on resource balance, and on values of exports (f.o.b.) and imports (c.i.f.) of goods and nonfactor services in current U.S. dollars provide a comprehensive and systematic framework for macroeconomic analysis in general. Those interested in a more specialized and rigorous study of international trade transactions should use the data provided in Chapter 5.

The rate of growth of real domestic product is an important indicator of economic progress and as such is widely monitored. Because these growth rates are calculated from national series, they are suitable for both cross-country comparisons and trend analysis for individual countries. Aggregate values and trends, however, reflect the choice of the base year, as explained above.

Gross national income per capita, which is GDP per capita adjusted for changes in international terms of trade and which include net factor income from abroad, and total consumption per capita are also widely monitored indicators of economic progress. When expressed in current U.S. dollars to facilitate comparison and aggregation, however, the values for these indicators necessarily reflect exchange rate fluctuations as well as underlying economic and demographic changes. These indicators may be used with caution for cross-country comparison during any single year. They require special attention when used for trend analysis.

Data for Chapter 2 are from the World Bank's country desks. Estimates are based on data obtained from national sources, usually collected by World Bank staff who review the quality of national accounts data and, in some instances, help adjust national series.

2-1. Gross domestic product, real

	Millions of U.S. dollars, constant 1995 prices											Average annual percentage growth		
	1980	1992	1993	1994	1995	1996	1997	1998	1999	2000	2001	75-84	85-89	90-MR
SUB-SAHARAN AFRICA	251,066	296,627	298,983	305,564	316,993	332,648	344,042	351,722	360,445	371,252	382,091	2.2	2.3	2.4
excluding South Africa	123,480	156,330	156,946	158,911	165,785	174,942	182,181	188,666	193,942	199,145	206,179	1.9	3.3	2.8
excl. S.Africa & Nigeria	100,455	129,487	129,504	131,447	137,644	145,597	152,051	157,979	162,927	166,951	172,727	2.5	3.0	2.8
Angola	5,076	5,857	4,410	4,565	5,040	5,604	6,047	6,458	6,674	6,877	7,095	..	4.5	1.3
Benin	1,253	1,778	1,840	1,921	2,009	2,121	2,242	2,345	2,455	2,598	2,728	3.8	1.5	4.7
Botswana	1,394	4,329	4,412	4,572	4,773	5,040	5,386	5,710	6,061	6,585	7,000	11.6	12.2	5.2
Burkina Faso	1,258	1,965	2,060	2,089	2,184	2,347	2,460	2,530	2,677	2,736	2,891	3.6	4.4	4.4
Burundi	728	1,190	1,122	1,079	1,000	917	920	964	955	946	977	3.8	5.1	-1.9
Cameroon	6,319	8,170	7,909	7,711	7,965	8,364	8,790	9,233	9,639	10,044	10,576	8.5	-0.1	1.5
Cape Verde	171	399	427	456	491	510	538	578	627	670	692	13.8	4.5	5.7
Central African Republic	964	994	998	1,047	1,122	1,077	1,134	1,187	1,230	1,258	1,277	0.4	0.7	1.8
Chad	788	1,537	1,296	1,427	1,438	1,473	1,536	1,649	1,665	1,676	1,825	-1.3	5.4	2.3
Comoros	167	229	236	224	232	229	238	241	246	243	248	..	1.3	1.2
Congo, Democratic Rep. of	7,531	6,739	5,831	5,604	5,643	5,592	5,278	5,193	4,964	4,668	4,457	-0.3	1.7	-5.1
Congo, Republic of	1,281	2,154	2,133	2,015	2,116	2,207	2,194	2,275	2,207	2,388	2,457	9.2	-1.0	1.3
Côte d'Ivoire	8,566	9,179	9,162	9,343	9,992	10,762	11,375	11,921	12,112	11,833	11,727	2.2	2.0	2.8
Djibouti	..	546	524	509	498	481	478	481	491	495	..	..	..	-1.4
Equatorial Guinea	..	128	137	144	164	212	363	442	625	731	740	..	1.4	20.0
Eritrea	..	369	410	506	519	566	612	631	635	558	612	..	..	5.3
Ethiopia	..	4,642	5,262	5,446	5,779	6,393	6,725	6,647	6,990	7,364	7,933	..	2.9	4.3
Gabon	3,565	4,377	4,481	4,635	4,958	5,213	5,514	5,628	5,279	5,385	5,520	-0.2	-1.4	2.7
Gambia, The	241	367	378	379	382	390	410	430	457	483	512	4.3	3.3	3.3
Ghana	4,231	5,726	6,004	6,209	6,457	6,755	7,038	7,369	7,694	7,978	8,297	-1.1	5.2	4.2
Guinea	..	3,190	3,325	3,536	3,692	3,862	4,048	4,234	4,386	4,489	4,649	..	4.7	4.1
Guinea-Bissau	134	231	236	243	254	283	302	217	234	251	252	2.1	3.1	1.4
Kenya	5,612	8,413	8,443	8,665	9,047	9,422	9,617	9,773	9,900	9,884	9,993	4.7	5.9	2.0
Lesotho	490	832	863	892	933	1,026	1,109	1,058	1,081	1,116	1,161	6.7	5.6	4.1
Liberia	..	..	..	..	..	..	..	..	..	..	..	..	..	..
Madagascar	3,048	3,045	3,109	3,107	3,160	3,228	3,347	3,479	3,641	3,814	4,043	-0.2	2.3	2.1
Malawi	992	1,243	1,363	1,224	1,429	1,533	1,591	1,644	1,710	1,739	1,714	3.2	1.9	3.6
Mali	2,013	2,351	2,301	2,322	2,466	2,546	2,718	2,811	2,983	3,119	3,084	2.3	0.8	3.5
Mauritania	753	925	976	1,021	1,068	1,127	1,163	1,206	1,255	1,319	1,380	1.6	3.3	4.0
Mauritius	1,686	3,316	3,512	3,671	3,820	4,018	4,254	4,509	4,748	4,871	5,222	..	7.7	5.2
Mozambique	1,938	1,896	2,061	2,216	2,311	2,475	2,750	3,096	3,328	3,382	3,852	..	6.0	6.2
Namibia	2,442	2,927	3,135	3,365	3,503	3,615	3,768	3,892	4,024	4,156	4,270	..	2.2	4.5
Niger	1,833	1,737	1,762	1,833	1,881	1,945	1,999	2,207	2,194	2,163	2,327	2.0	4.2	2.2
Nigeria	22,357	26,806	27,396	27,423	28,109	29,318	30,109	30,675	31,012	32,184	33,440	-0.7	5.0	2.7
Rwanda	1,658	2,092	1,923	957	1,293	1,458	1,660	1,807	1,944	2,061	2,199	6.8	2.9	0.0
São Tomé and Principe	..	43	44	45	45	46	47	48	49	50	52	..	1.8	1.8
Senegal	3,057	4,225	4,131	4,253	4,476	4,704	4,948	5,230	5,498	5,806	6,140	2.1	3.5	3.6
Seychelles	..	485	515	511	508	532	560	579	563	533	490	..	..	1.6
Sierra Leone	1,123	1,017	1,031	1,011	930	987	813	806	741	769	811	2.5	-0.3	-4.3
Somalia	..	..	..	..	..	..	..	..	..	..	..	..	..	..
South Africa	127,410	140,226	141,956	146,547	151,113	157,621	161,793	163,026	166,481	172,074	175,901	2.4	1.4	1.9
Sudan	4,388	6,426	6,720	6,787	7,194	7,620	8,103	8,625	9,182	9,739	10,409	2.6	0.9	6.2
Swaziland	640	1,228	1,272	1,315	1,365	1,418	1,472	1,520	1,573	1,608	1,633	3.3	10.0	3.3
Tanzania	..	4,936	4,996	5,074	5,255	5,495	5,688	5,899	6,104	6,419	6,784	..	..	3.2
Togo	1,175	1,244	1,056	1,214	1,309	1,425	1,486	1,454	1,489	1,461	1,500	2.1	3.4	1.8
Uganda	..	4,478	4,851	5,161	5,756	6,278	6,576	6,944	7,466	7,728	8,086	..	3.4	6.8
Zambia	3,351	3,650	3,898	3,559	3,471	3,699	3,821	3,750	3,834	3,971	4,166	0.2	2.3	0.7
Zimbabwe	4,354	6,432	6,500	7,100	7,111	7,848	8,058	8,291	8,233	7,831	7,172	3.0	4.2	1.9
NORTH AFRICA	106,378	164,327	165,142	171,630	174,245	185,670	190,423	201,480	209,482	216,741	226,068	6.0	3.0	3.4
Algeria	31,384	41,471	40,601	40,235	41,764	43,476	43,955	46,196	47,675	48,819	50,583	5.5	0.8	1.8
Egypt, Arab Republic	29,896	53,746	55,295	57,478	60,159	63,173	66,643	70,361	74,599	78,422	81,009	8.3	4.1	4.5
Libya	..	..	..	..	..	..	..	..	..	..	..	..	..	..
Morocco	21,590	32,322	31,995	35,309	32,986	37,016	36,191	38,969	38,984	39,324	41,880	4.1	4.7	2.5
Tunisia	10,475	16,653	17,018	17,579	17,987	19,256	20,304	21,269	22,559	23,623	24,898	5.3	2.4	4.8
ALL AFRICA	360,106	461,745	464,960	477,831	492,187	519,101	535,396	553,640	570,149	588,147	608,094	3.3	2.5	2.7

Note: 2001 data are preliminary (see page 2).

2-2. Value added in agriculture

	Millions of U.S. dollars, constant 1995 prices											Average annual percentage growth		
	1980	1992	1993	1994	1995	1996	1997	1998	1999	2000	2001	75-84	85-89	90-MR
SUB-SAHARAN AFRICA	42,653	50,101	52,252	53,273	54,286	58,643	60,222	61,197	63,335	65,271	67,441	0.8	4.2	2.6
excluding South Africa	37,094	45,101	45,970	46,471	48,936	51,938	53,421	54,936	56,863	58,546	60,661	0.8	3.6	2.9
excl. S.Africa & Nigeria	..	37,006	37,770	38,061	40,235	42,905	43,990	45,109	46,507	47,621	49,159	..	3.0	2.7
Angola	..	517	276	303	369	423	466	490	496	543	640	..	0.5	-1.3
Benin	361	601	617	673	684	755	798	850	884	941	970	3.0	4.6	5.5
Botswana	165	200	195	189	193	192	190	188	173	169	175	-3.7	11.4	-1.0
Burkina Faso	457	724	734	732	783	850	837	897	930	895	958	1.0	4.6	3.7
Burundi	358	520	499	448	421	427	429	452	438	455	472	2.0	4.1	-0.9
Cameroon	2,131	2,749	2,782	2,868	3,119	3,350	3,603	3,847	4,109	4,294	4,530	4.5	0.6	5.0
Cape Verde	31	60	65	63	67	92	88	90	101	104	106	12.7	22.8	4.3
Central African Republic	391	451	462	468	491	515	547	568	591	628	653	0.6	1.1	3.6
Chad	319	520	406	515	505	519	546	604	585	565	588	-1.0	5.1	3.9
Comoros	63	89	91	87	95	95	102	102	107	123	127	..	3.7	3.0
Congo, Democratic Rep. of	2,076	2,830	2,883	2,859	3,191	3,258	3,169	3,123	2,964	2,882	2,726	1.7	2.5	0.9
Congo, Republic of	159	219	200	207	221	232	234	238	223	235	253	3.4	4.8	1.1
Côte d'Ivoire	2,365	2,627	2,629	2,639	2,880	2,992	3,034	3,207	3,139	3,544	3,488	2.7	3.0	3.1
Djibouti	..	14	15	14	15	15	15	16	16	17	..	..	..	0.6
Equatorial Guinea	..	64	64	73	83	95	115	102	112	122	130	..	0.1	6.5
Eritrea	..	107	86	118	104	98	98	155	143	81	110	..	..	1.2
Ethiopia	..	2,658	2,819	2,716	2,809	3,221	3,331	2,972	3,072	3,140	3,500	..	3.4	2.4
Gabon	431	461	455	448	398	397	417	395	413	428	446	..	0.8	-1.0
Gambia, The	95	96	91	97	99	96	103	112	140	157	176	3.0	-2.4	4.5
Ghana	2,143	2,316	2,370	2,415	2,504	2,634	2,748	2,888	3,000	3,063	3,176	0.2	2.3	3.2
Guinea	..	667	700	735	761	795	835	879	927	918	940	..	3.1	4.1
Guinea-Bissau	59	110	117	123	132	152	165	132	142	147	149	-2.6	3.4	3.7
Kenya	1,660	2,281	2,207	2,275	2,384	2,490	2,520	2,560	2,593	2,541	2,572	4.1	4.4	1.2
Lesotho	136	142	156	152	145	170	171	176	184	181	178	-1.0	4.6	1.3
Liberia	..	..	..	..	..	..	..	..	..	..	..	..	..	..
Madagascar	593	749	773	769	784	803	818	836	864	871	906	0.2	2.8	1.9
Malawi	261	253	387	275	384	482	482	495	550	581	532	2.2	1.2	6.6
Mali	823	1,083	991	1,057	1,082	1,117	1,168	1,175	1,287	1,358	1,195	3.2	8.9	2.5
Mauritania	160	208	235	246	251	251	264	281	306	315	314	2.9	4.5	4.5
Mauritius	275	344	366	339	320	340	360	365	368	282	355	..	2.3	-0.1
Mozambique	..	605	734	686	805	892	968	1,039	1,099	986	1,123	..	7.3	4.3
Namibia	234	312	334	386	376	410	384	407	433	482	480	..	3.6	4.4
Niger	577	673	678	747	756	757	777	941	894	819	940	1.1	5.4	3.0
Nigeria	6,432	8,187	8,298	8,498	8,809	9,169	9,556	9,942	10,457	11,002	11,563	-3.0	6.4	3.6
Rwanda	663	771	640	440	569	682	711	785	853	930	1,008	5.6	1.1	2.7
São Tomé and Principe	..	11	12	12	12	13	13	14	14	15	15	..	3.5	3.7
Senegal	652	831	788	861	881	934	911	882	935	1,043	1,114	-1.2	4.5	2.3
Seychelles	28	22	20	22	21	21	22	22	22	23	23	-3.0	-2.5	-0.8
Sierra Leone	582	396	384	403	363	384	366	376	356	363	377	7.9	0.9	-5.5
Somalia	..	..	..	..	..	..	..	..	..	..	..	..	..	..
South Africa	5,448	4,973	6,166	6,651	5,326	6,603	6,703	6,214	6,425	6,672	6,739	0.2	7.6	0.2
Sudan	..	..	..	..	..	..	..	..	..	..	..	..	..	..
Swaziland	180	173	167	172	168	205	202	205	222	217	220	-1.4	3.0	0.9
Tanzania	..	2,059	2,123	2,167	2,294	2,383	2,441	2,488	2,591	2,679	2,827	..	..	3.4
Togo	285	442	469	468	494	575	601	584	615	587	615	2.8	4.3	3.6
Uganda	..	2,213	2,419	2,462	2,607	2,718	2,748	2,800	2,994	3,115	3,268	..	2.7	3.8
Zambia	346	310	521	423	564	560	531	538	592	600	586	0.5	5.6	3.2
Zimbabwe	684	760	966	1,036	958	1,147	1,184	1,244	1,298	1,337	1,176	-0.1	1.2	3.6
NORTH AFRICA	16,087	21,879	21,536	24,702	21,322	27,210	24,563	27,295	26,752	25,710	..	2.0	5.3	1.9
Algeria	2,484	3,957	3,811	3,468	3,986	4,939	4,275	4,762	4,891	4,646	4,971	3.7	6.4	3.4
Egypt, Arab Republic	6,302	8,631	8,846	9,185	9,451	9,742	10,076	10,452	10,839	11,209	..	2.8	2.7	3.1
Libya	..	..	..	..	..	..	..	..	..	..	..	..	..	..
Morocco	5,032	5,588	5,328	8,599	4,820	8,580	6,309	8,071	6,726	5,639	6,936	0.4	10.0	-0.8
Tunisia	1,504	2,661	2,527	2,275	2,049	2,655	2,734	2,710	3,023	2,993	3,038	1.2	-1.2	3.4
ALL AFRICA	58,680	72,034	73,818	78,061	75,618	85,949	84,814	88,569	90,137	90,995	95,532	1.2	4.5	2.4

Note: 2001 data are preliminary (see page 2).

2-3. Value added in industry

	Millions of U.S. dollars, constant 1995 prices											Average annual percentage growth		
	1980	*1992*	*1993*	*1994*	*1995*	*1996*	*1997*	*1998*	*1999*	*2000*	*2001*	*75-84*	*85-89*	*90-MR*
SUB-SAHARAN AFRICA	82,700	90,980	89,485	90,877	93,816	97,079	100,748	101,681	102,711	106,036	109,136	2.3	1.7	1.5
excluding South Africa	38,884	45,841	44,273	44,511	45,719	48,331	50,793	52,247	53,521	55,750	57,879	1.9	3.0	2.2
excl. S.Africa & Nigeria	24,293	32,582	31,092	31,720	32,777	34,608	36,901	38,630	40,298	41,610	43,562	..	3.4	2.5
Angola	..	3,496	2,670	3,053	3,339	3,638	3,826	4,219	4,491	4,650	4,840	..	8.1	3.4
Benin	134	269	272	285	293	316	328	329	336	365	399	5.4	-1.9	4.5
Botswana	652	2,167	2,147	2,188	2,253	2,371	2,545	2,630	2,749	3,145	3,407	24.7	8.0	3.9
Burkina Faso	246	341	335	342	414	429	467	408	451	487	503	1.6	4.8	4.1
Burundi	142	259	217	203	168	146	145	147	158	164	191	8.9	3.7	-3.8
Cameroon	1,478	2,321	2,221	1,901	1,855	1,939	2,088	2,248	2,389	2,509	2,672	18.3	0.7	-0.9
Cape Verde	28	79	85	88	96	99	96	105	112	125	131	6.3	17.1	5.0
Central African Republic	190	189	191	216	224	199	195	198	206	225	234	1.4	0.6	0.8
Chad	88	206	181	172	206	201	223	263	256	257	289	-2.0	2.5	2.2
Comoros	22	25	27	27	28	27	25	27	27	40	41	..	-9.0	6.5
Congo, Democratic Rep. of	2,464	1,268	1,084	1,062	952	952	759	776	838	824	855	-2.0	0.3	-9.2
Congo, Republic of	483	894	929	901	949	965	1,046	1,104	1,122	1,171	1,148	11.5	-0.3	3.0
Côte d'Ivoire	1,406	1,878	1,891	1,909	1,999	2,187	2,601	2,671	2,714	2,456	2,397	6.5	6.5	3.5
Djibouti	..	100	95	87	67	64	63	61	62	62	..	..	..	-5.3
Equatorial Guinea	..	29	35	35	44	84	236	337	543	652	644	..	6.4	45.6
Eritrea	..	42	60	69	83	114	137	128	131	123	131	..	..	12.8
Ethiopia	..	402	516	552	597	629	674	689	719	732	774	..	-0.1	4.3
Gabon	1,859	2,173	2,264	2,469	2,597	2,655	2,679	2,714	2,752	2,797	2,853	..	-1.7	2.6
Gambia, The	31	47	48	46	44	46	46	51	54	57	62	3.1	10.6	2.4
Ghana	1,356	1,661	1,456	1,508	1,568	1,642	1,747	1,803	1,891	1,962	2,041	-7.5	9.1	2.8
Guinea	..	1,010	1,081	1,102	1,169	1,271	1,328	1,376	1,449	1,519	1,594	..	3.1	4.5
Guinea-Bissau	18	26	28	28	29	30	31	19	19	20	21	3.2	-3.5	-2.2
Kenya	769	1,160	1,162	1,184	1,226	1,268	1,294	1,312	1,325	1,309	1,318	4.7	5.2	1.7
Lesotho	129	235	229	224	243	254	336	285	340	398	429	15.1	7.2	7.4
Liberia	..	..	..	..	..	..	..	..	..	..	..	..	..	..
Madagascar	306	260	269	266	271	276	289	304	317	335	360	-2.9	2.8	2.4
Malawi	173	250	231	237	247	268	268	271	278	277	280	2.7	3.7	2.0
Mali	217	383	398	382	408	435	532	569	578	622	746	1.6	1.4	7.1
Mauritania	169	234	281	288	298	302	287	286	284	303	307	0.6	3.7	2.1
Mauritius	372	931	986	1,032	1,079	1,137	1,200	1,268	1,329	1,406	1,505	..	12.9	5.6
Mozambique	..	347	340	361	410	467	635	925	1,070	1,116	1,497	..	-4.5	13.1
Namibia	776	859	777	847	865	821	875	920	926	920	935	..	1.9	2.2
Niger	368	310	315	317	325	346	358	368	376	384	393	10.4	-4.1	1.9
Nigeria	13,605	13,309	13,210	12,845	13,009	13,791	13,992	13,757	13,406	14,310	14,514	0.0	2.1	1.4
Rwanda	424	460	402	139	207	242	285	314	331	342	368	7.4	0.3	-3.3
São Tomé and Principe	..	9	9	9	9	9	9	9	10	10	10	..	0.9	1.6
Senegal	541	887	865	861	961	1,014	1,071	1,162	1,235	1,326	1,416	3.7	4.9	4.8
Seychelles	49	81	91	94	115	126	153	156	159	163	168	-0.7	3.4	8.9
Sierra Leone	216	246	231	231	193	203	188	177	151	158	167	-3.1	2.2	-3.9
Somalia	..	..	..	..	..	..	..	..	..	..	..	..	..	..
South Africa	43,794	45,127	45,169	46,305	48,025	48,713	49,942	49,458	49,242	50,359	51,352	2.6	0.7	0.8
Sudan	..	..	..	..	..	..	..	..	..	..	..	..	..	..
Swaziland	139	427	438	461	484	494	524	544	556	562	571	4.4	23.4	3.9
Tanzania	..	736	708	719	705	753	803	886	932	1,001	1,066	..	..	3.5
Togo	277	270	190	241	290	306	313	316	315	331	331	1.5	6.2	2.1
Uganda	..	512	555	627	754	879	979	1,092	1,194	1,271	1,339	..	6.4	11.5
Zambia	1,233	1,535	1,413	1,274	1,096	1,102	1,181	1,053	987	1,016	1,109	-0.4	2.7	-3.2
Zimbabwe	1,353	1,793	1,673	1,956	1,828	2,016	2,030	2,008	1,939	1,749	1,578	-1.0	5.4	-0.2
NORTH AFRICA	42,050	61,297	61,314	61,744	64,256	66,620	70,050	73,531	76,421	81,765	..	6.2	1.2	3.4
Algeria	15,236	19,324	19,041	18,601	19,139	19,723	20,454	21,361	22,332	23,298	23,476	5.0	0.9	1.7
Egypt, Arab Republic	9,620	16,886	17,145	17,384	18,195	18,886	20,053	21,479	22,263	25,090	..	11.0	0.1	5.3
Libya	..	..	..	..	..	..	..	..	..	..	..	..	..	..
Morocco	7,171	10,119	10,016	10,416	10,882	11,406	12,038	12,312	12,653	12,973	13,363	3.4	3.1	3.2
Tunisia	2,945	4,650	4,791	4,949	5,224	5,390	5,713	6,001	6,310	6,640	6,985	7.1	2.6	4.6
ALL AFRICA	125,498	151,936	150,362	152,229	157,616	163,215	170,205	174,334	178,033	186,383	191,397	3.5	1.6	2.2

Note: 2001 data are preliminary (see page 2).

2-4. Value added in services

	Millions of U.S. dollars, constant 1995 prices											Average annual percentage growth		
	1980	*1992*	*1993*	*1994*	*1995*	*1996*	*1997*	*1998*	*1999*	*2000*	*2001*	*75-84*	*85-89*	*90-MR*
SUB-SAHARAN AFRICA	107,985	139,100	139,871	143,241	149,517	156,369	161,458	166,051	170,953	175,633	181,502	3.0	2.5	2.6
excluding South Africa	45,981	60,361	60,561	61,616	64,234	67,403	70,299	72,839	74,605	75,805	78,024	2.7	3.3	2.6
excl. S.Africa & Nigeria	42,534	54,861	54,731	55,767	58,260	61,261	63,852	66,292	68,025	69,258	71,126	..	2.9	2.6
Angola	..	1,800	1,448	1,215	1,332	1,535	1,737	1,742	1,692	1,688	1,614	..	1.7	-1.6
Benin	783	907	953	958	1,033	1,040	1,107	1,156	1,227	1,279	1,348	3.8	0.4	4.1
Botswana	387	1,477	1,633	1,835	1,982	2,117	2,267	2,469	2,646	2,726	3,037	0.6	25.1	8.1
Burkina Faso	490	859	967	1,010	937	1,010	1,099	1,116	1,193	1,263	1,321	8.9	4.0	4.6
Burundi	166	315	308	298	285	252	253	259	267	276	286	6.2	4.1	-1.0
Cameroon	2,365	2,473	2,332	2,637	2,793	2,714	2,689	2,669	2,663	2,756	2,880	8.6	-1.4	-0.1
Cape Verde	114	261	279	306	328	326	358	386	419	444	458	10.5	8.2	6.2
Central African Republic	358	299	287	309	347	299	320	345	354	325	308	0.3	1.0	-1.2
Chad	391	764	662	712	696	707	718	739	778	806	895	-0.7	6.3	1.5
Comoros	83	116	118	111	109	107	111	113	112	79	79	..	2.0	-2.2
Congo, Democratic Rep. of	3,286	2,699	1,897	1,715	1,501	1,381	1,363	1,295	1,204	1,024	936	-0.5	2.1	-11.1
Congo, Republic of	629	1,037	1,004	907	945	1,008	918	940	874	992	1,060	9.3	-2.7	-0.1
Côte d'Ivoire	4,859	4,675	4,639	4,807	5,113	5,612	5,778	6,081	6,332	5,783	5,804	1.0	-0.2	2.4
Djibouti	..	371	354	344	355	332	337	349	355	360	..	..	..	-0.5
Equatorial Guinea	..	30	32	32	34	38	43	52	59	65	72	..	6.5	10.0
Eritrea	..	201	238	297	309	330	349	324	334	332	347	..	..	5.0
Ethiopia	..	1,416	1,663	1,794	1,962	2,098	2,246	2,483	2,664	2,916	3,050	..	4.1	6.4
Gabon	1,326	1,756	1,778	1,755	1,963	2,137	2,362	2,447	2,108	2,153	2,213	..	-1.7	3.5
Gambia, The	119	171	190	186	188	197	212	227	226	229	230	4.7	1.9	3.8
Ghana	1,015	1,929	2,184	2,288	2,385	2,482	2,569	2,691	2,819	2,963	3,089	0.1	7.8	5.8
Guinea	..	1,409	1,436	1,561	1,604	1,656	1,713	1,800	1,836	1,903	1,870	..	5.3	3.4
Guinea-Bissau	47	79	76	77	78	87	91	62	67	75	82	10.0	4.7	0.3
Kenya	2,112	3,635	3,714	3,842	4,046	4,256	4,387	4,475	4,548	4,593	4,655	5.9	5.6	3.2
Lesotho	187	347	366	401	424	465	462	470	439	434	431	5.0	5.6	3.7
Liberia	..	..	..	..	..	..	..	..	..	..	..	..	..	..
Madagascar	1,924	1,805	1,844	1,853	1,882	1,922	2,014	2,111	2,226	2,381	2,526	0.1	1.8	2.5
Malawi	441	611	616	579	631	626	678	709	727	732	752	3.1	3.3	2.3
Mali	552	677	699	695	695	754	770	806	842	864	868	1.6	0.0	2.6
Mauritania	353	378	384	398	402	437	487	512	538	569	618	2.1	3.6	4.9
Mauritius	843	1,608	1,700	1,827	1,960	2,079	2,207	2,337	2,482	2,611	2,787	..	6.0	6.3
Mozambique	..	769	774	990	907	929	922	878	852	948	869	..	10.0	2.5
Namibia	1,146	1,634	1,685	1,773	1,861	1,952	2,032	2,074	2,151	2,235	2,322	..	2.6	4.4
Niger	888	754	769	769	800	842	864	898	924	961	995	-0.1	7.6	1.7
Nigeria	3,488	5,580	5,884	5,910	6,049	6,230	6,535	6,651	6,697	6,677	7,018	1.5	7.6	3.3
Rwanda	571	861	881	378	518	534	665	708	761	788	823	7.6	6.4	-0.9
São Tomé and Principe	..	23	23	24	25	24	24	25	25	26	26	..	1.4	0.9
Senegal	1,850	2,504	2,476	2,525	2,634	2,756	2,967	3,192	3,335	3,448	3,621	3.1	2.8	3.7
Seychelles	241	382	403	395	372	384	386	401	382	347	262	-2.4	6.1	-0.4
Sierra Leone	323	347	353	339	311	327	284	281	257	267	279	2.8	-1.8	-3.0
Somalia	..	..	..	..	..	..	..	..	..	..	..	..	..	..
South Africa	61,526	78,147	78,705	80,975	84,598	88,266	90,490	92,563	95,652	99,049	102,649	3.2	2.0	2.5
Sudan	..	..	..	..	..	..	..	..	..	..	..	..	..	..
Swaziland	223	389	413	420	439	446	460	475	496	518	527	5.8	4.1	3.6
Tanzania	..	1,834	1,810	1,816	1,866	1,934	1,994	2,077	2,184	2,315	2,446	..	..	3.0
Togo	619	533	396	506	524	543	571	553	557	541	551	2.0	1.5	-0.1
Uganda	..	1,467	1,571	1,693	1,917	2,082	2,200	2,345	2,514	2,647	2,779	..	3.2	7.7
Zambia	1,596	1,491	1,599	1,429	1,396	1,606	1,670	1,741	1,850	1,931	2,025	0.1	3.0	2.3
Zimbabwe	2,076	3,180	3,200	3,301	3,500	3,776	3,828	3,937	4,016	3,872	3,667	5.4	3.7	2.8
NORTH AFRICA	43,389	73,909	74,875	78,126	80,857	84,239	87,573	92,228	97,209	99,772	..	7.5	4.2	3.5
Algeria	10,209	14,309	14,027	14,443	14,848	15,060	15,394	16,049	16,316	16,586	17,083	6.2	0.8	1.8
Egypt, Arab Republic	12,243	25,010	25,798	27,251	28,682	30,473	32,094	33,819	36,609	37,012	..	11.0	6.8	4.1
Libya	..	..	..	..	..	..	..	..	..	..	..	..	..	..
Morocco	9,925	16,776	16,753	17,075	17,285	17,801	18,147	19,173	19,864	20,681	21,742	5.9	4.0	3.1
Tunisia	6,006	9,287	9,659	10,344	10,714	11,186	11,834	12,547	13,206	13,981	14,879	5.7	3.2	5.3
ALL AFRICA	152,161	213,456	215,166	221,721	230,780	241,049	249,456	258,601	268,374	275,627	285,768	4.3	3.0	2.9

Note: 2001 data are preliminary (see page 2).

2-5. Gross domestic product, nominal

	Millions of U.S. dollars, current prices											Annual Average		
	1980	1992	1993	1994	1995	1996	1997	1998	1999	2000	2001	75-84	85-89	90-MR
SUB-SAHARAN AFRICA	261,582	304,123	287,731	280,072	316,993	333,512	342,885	324,400	328,836	335,441	325,596	202,260	240,457	314,974
excluding South Africa	181,822	173,732	157,347	144,173	165,785	189,926	194,204	190,871	197,737	207,929	213,835	142,053	161,620	183,680
excl. S.Africa & Nigeria	116,443	140,924	136,066	120,496	137,644	154,529	157,873	158,694	162,898	166,691	172,572	99,971	137,905	151,777
Angola	0	5,779	5,286	4,060	5,040	7,526	7,675	6,445	6,090	8,858	9,471	0	7,560	7,390
Benin	1,405	1,624	2,106	1,497	2,009	2,208	2,157	2,335	2,387	2,255	2,372	1,035	1,413	2,056
Botswana	1,061	4,146	4,160	4,340	4,773	4,805	5,191	4,932	5,069	5,362	5,196	815	2,040	4,642
Burkina Faso	1,709	1,996	2,142	1,753	2,184	2,477	2,286	2,522	2,533	2,312	2,486	1,311	2,038	2,354
Burundi	920	1,083	939	925	1,000	900	957	878	714	679	689	778	1,136	922
Cameroon	6,741	11,396	11,891	7,854	7,965	9,109	9,115	8,703	9,399	8,880	8,591	5,630	10,942	9,707
Cape Verde	107	394	363	411	491	502	506	540	588	558	588	86	233	469
Central African Republic	797	1,434	1,299	853	1,122	1,070	1,003	1,047	1,051	953	967	619	1,150	1,141
Chad	1,033	1,882	1,463	1,179	1,438	1,605	1,508	1,693	1,564	1,407	1,603	928	1,236	1,580
Comoros	124	281	278	186	232	230	212	216	223	204	221	113	176	234
Congo, Democratic Rep. of	14,391	8,206	8,975	5,817	5,643	6,068	3,285	6,150	12,136	15,350	..	12,212	8,165	8,188
Congo, Republic of	1,706	2,933	1,919	1,769	2,116	2,541	2,323	1,949	2,354	3,220	2,751	1,452	2,182	2,450
Côte d'Ivoire	10,175	11,153	10,405	7,666	9,992	12,139	11,722	12,782	12,560	10,593	10,411	7,172	9,247	10,893
Djibouti	..	470	471	487	498	494	503	514	536	553	..	..	380	491
Equatorial Guinea	..	154	152	126	164	259	498	456	872	1,341	1,846	104	107	511
Eritrea	..	451	371	469	519	618	649	714	703	627	688	..	..	581
Ethiopia	..	5,568	6,249	4,894	5,779	6,010	6,383	6,516	6,446	6,366	6,240	5,603	7,356	6,051
Gabon	4,279	5,592	4,381	4,191	4,958	5,741	5,428	4,619	4,352	4,932	4,334	3,211	3,609	4,990
Gambia, The	241	347	366	363	382	392	410	417	432	422	410	181	236	381
Ghana	4,445	6,413	5,966	5,441	6,457	6,926	6,884	7,474	7,710	4,978	5,301	3,762	5,150	6,336
Guinea	..	3,285	3,279	3,434	3,692	3,867	3,783	3,589	3,461	3,063	2,985	..	2,230	3,356
Guinea-Bissau	111	226	237	236	254	271	269	206	224	215	199	131	165	236
Kenya	7,265	8,002	4,977	7,148	9,047	9,257	10,612	11,444	10,527	10,449	11,396	5,550	7,641	9,120
Lesotho	432	827	818	837	933	942	1,024	890	911	899	797	310	416	848
Liberia	1,117	..	..	..	..	..	..	..	..	..	..	987	1,143	..
Madagascar	4,042	3,024	3,371	2,977	3,160	3,995	3,546	3,739	3,717	3,878	4,604	3,057	2,724	3,479
Malawi	1,238	1,800	2,071	1,182	1,429	2,432	2,534	1,736	1,810	1,707	1,749	1,018	1,294	1,878
Mali	1,787	2,846	2,678	1,763	2,466	2,619	2,475	2,597	2,570	2,298	2,321	1,285	1,776	2,456
Mauritania	709	1,191	944	1,027	1,068	1,116	1,096	1,002	958	977	1,030	645	867	1,047
Mauritius	1,153	2,974	3,307	3,373	3,820	4,163	4,384	4,146	4,175	4,424	4,500	1,060	1,646	3,706
Mozambique	3,526	1,854	1,981	2,178	2,311	2,841	3,397	3,873	3,985	3,813	3,607	3,457	3,293	2,896
Namibia	2,309	2,867	2,847	3,253	3,503	3,492	3,635	3,399	3,387	3,428	3,100	2,046	1,930	3,198
Niger	2,509	2,345	1,607	1,563	1,881	1,988	1,846	2,077	2,018	1,798	1,954	1,725	2,008	1,990
Nigeria	64,202	32,710	21,353	23,663	28,109	35,299	36,229	32,144	34,776	41,085	41,237	42,093	23,750	31,866
Rwanda	1,163	2,038	1,971	754	1,293	1,382	1,851	1,989	1,931	1,811	1,703	1,091	2,123	1,768
São Tomé and Principe	47	46	48	50	45	45	44	41	47	46	47	41	53	48
Senegal	2,987	6,027	5,431	3,642	4,476	4,651	4,387	4,646	4,752	4,371	4,620	2,364	4,110	4,850
Seychelles	147	434	469	483	508	548	588	604	623	595	570	97	244	514
Sierra Leone	1,101	681	769	994	930	942	850	672	669	636	749	969	807	777
Somalia	604	..	..	..	..	..	..	..	..	..	..	677	989	917
South Africa	80,544	130,533	130,406	135,778	151,113	143,733	148,814	133,768	131,409	127,928	113,274	61,201	79,315	131,583
Sudan	7,617	6,402	7,895	8,170	7,194	8,269	10,642	11,480	10,302	11,249	12,525	7,964	15,971	9,892
Swaziland	545	1,002	1,063	1,146	1,365	1,331	1,437	1,359	1,377	1,401	1,255	432	561	1,211
Tanzania	..	4,601	4,258	4,511	5,255	6,496	7,684	8,383	8,638	9,079	9,341	5,569	4,561	6,455
Togo	1,136	1,693	1,234	983	1,309	1,465	1,499	1,416	1,421	1,221	1,259	813	1,161	1,394
Uganda	1,245	2,858	3,220	3,997	5,756	6,049	6,269	6,535	5,966	5,889	5,675	4,108	5,097	4,987
Zambia	3,884	3,183	3,274	3,347	3,471	3,271	3,911	3,238	3,132	3,239	3,639	3,159	2,781	3,364
Zimbabwe	6,679	6,751	6,564	6,891	7,111	8,553	8,428	5,732	5,494	7,204	9,057	5,993	6,939	7,434
NORTH AFRICA	125,005	152,490	157,899	160,024	174,245	194,559	200,333	211,661	220,001	233,504	237,598	97,452	144,967	187,205
Algeria	42,345	48,003	49,946	42,543	41,764	46,845	47,869	47,357	47,592	53,306	56,689	34,827	60,619	49,140
Egypt, Arab Republic	22,912	41,856	47,197	51,898	60,159	67,651	75,605	82,704	89,207	98,782	97,545	20,312	37,154	66,059
Libya	35,545	..	..	..	..	..	..	..	..	..	..	24,534	22,897	..
Morocco	18,821	28,451	26,801	30,351	32,986	36,639	33,415	35,817	35,277	33,346	34,219	13,499	18,731	31,747
Tunisia	8,743	15,497	14,609	15,626	17,987	19,587	18,900	19,850	20,970	19,462	20,035	6,901	9,465	17,324
ALL AFRICA	386,951	458,632	446,510	440,475	492,187	528,221	543,349	534,513	546,857	566,240	560,050	299,799	386,605	502,085

Note: 2001 data are preliminary (see page 2).

2-6. Total consumption

	Percentage of GDP											Annual Average		
	1980	*1992*	*1993*	*1994*	*1995*	*1996*	*1997*	*1998*	*1999*	*2000*	*2001*	*75-84*	*85-89*	*90-MR*
SUB-SAHARAN AFRICA	77.0	87.3	85.9	83.8	83.9	80.7	83.6	85.5	84.4	81.3	82.6	80.1	81.1	83.8
excluding South Africa	81.6	90.4	89.2	85.1	86.6	80.0	84.2	87.0	85.5	80.7	82.8	82.9	83.5	85.0
excl. S.Africa & Nigeria	89.6	93.7	91.0	86.4	87.7	83.4	86.3	88.4	86.5	84.4	85.0	85.2	84.0	87.2
Angola	..	98.3	90.1	73.9	73.7	51.3	73.3	81.5	58.8	36.9	54.3	..	76.0	70.5
Benin	106.3	100.0	98.9	94.0	93.3	96.6	94.4	93.4	95.2	94.1	93.5	101.7	102.3	95.8
Botswana	73.3	63.0	63.2	63.0	62.5	58.7	57.0	60.2	61.6	61.0	61.8	76.7	55.9	60.8
Burkina Faso	105.8	93.0	94.4	92.1	90.8	90.7	88.7	87.2	91.0	92.7	90.4	101.7	97.6	91.4
Burundi	100.6	105.1	104.7	107.6	104.8	97.5	96.1	102.9	100.5	105.7	104.8	95.9	96.7	103.3
Cameroon	78.3	83.5	82.4	82.1	80.4	82.7	80.9	80.8	82.0	79.7	79.5	76.9	77.1	80.9
Cape Verde	124.0	103.5	96.3	97.2	97.6	108.0	108.4	115.3	117.5	119.0	113.5	119.8	102.9	107.4
Central African Republic	108.9	100.4	98.2	94.0	93.8	99.4	95.6	94.7	89.0	92.2	88.8	101.6	99.2	95.3
Chad	..	106.3	106.2	101.5	101.7	96.7	97.7	95.9	102.2	98.5	99.2	97.6	111.1	100.9
Comoros	110.1	103.1	98.5	106.5	105.3	103.6	109.0	104.7	105.7	101.4	100.2	106.5	102.5	103.8
Congo, Democratic Rep. of	89.9	93.9	96.0	89.4	85.9	72.5	74.1	83.1	82.2	94.6	93.8	89.5	86.7	87.9
Congo, Republic of	64.3	75.6	76.4	84.5	62.3	64.3	62.2	69.7	59.0	42.3	38.9	73.9	76.8	66.1
Côte d'Ivoire	79.6	89.3	90.6	77.6	81.1	79.2	77.2	80.3	78.7	82.7	83.1	75.7	81.6	83.2
Djibouti	..	..	..	..	108.3	106.9	105.7	100.8	105.5	105.3	..	..	..	105.4
Equatorial Guinea	..	110.0	113.7	74.9	72.7	69.3	56.9	80.1	35.2	26.0	9.6	92.4	133.3	70.6
Eritrea	..	238.4	72.6	137.0	136.1	127.6	120.9	131.1	132.8	128.4	119.2	..	..	134.4
Ethiopia	..	97.0	94.4	94.6	92.0	93.0	92.1	92.3	98.6	100.1	97.8	93.6	92.8	95.2
Gabon	39.4	65.3	63.3	54.7	52.7	49.0	49.0	61.0	65.2	71.7	49.7	41.9	67.7	58.7
Gambia, The	94.2	90.7	96.0	97.2	103.9	94.4	95.5	97.2	96.8	97.3	99.1	95.7	92.4	95.6
Ghana	95.1	98.7	94.0	87.5	88.4	78.8	95.8	89.8	96.3	96.7	94.2	93.7	94.5	92.3
Guinea	..	88.8	88.9	87.9	87.2	88.0	84.6	85.7	81.7	83.1	79.6	..	83.6	85.0
Guinea-Bissau	101.0	96.8	93.0	96.1	101.2	98.2	97.0	110.1	101.2	110.5	111.2	103.0	100.1	100.8
Kenya	86.6	86.3	76.2	80.4	88.7	86.8	92.1	92.6	91.1	96.2	95.8	82.6	83.1	87.7
Lesotho	152.0	134.5	145.3	135.9	138.4	129.9	124.5	127.0	124.1	120.2	114.8	168.2	162.7	133.1
Liberia	72.7	..	..	..	..	..	..	..	..	..	..	76.7	83.6	..
Madagascar	101.4	97.1	97.9	96.7	96.6	93.9	95.3	93.0	92.8	92.3	87.7	98.1	94.8	94.8
Malawi	89.2	99.3	100.9	103.0	100.3	96.9	100.7	92.5	100.2	99.5	101.0	84.4	88.2	97.2
Mali	98.9	95.6	93.6	92.5	92.2	92.8	90.0	88.8	89.9	92.7	90.6	99.8	99.9	92.2
Mauritania	103.5	95.2	95.3	83.1	91.1	93.7	92.1	95.0	92.8	83.2	86.0	105.6	89.7	91.1
Mauritius	85.5	74.6	74.8	76.4	76.6	76.2	75.7	75.1	76.2	76.3	74.7	83.1	75.2	75.8
Mozambique	110.6	117.2	122.4	113.9	101.9	101.8	98.9	93.2	90.7	88.1	80.8	110.4	110.2	102.7
Namibia	..	93.0	94.0	87.4	88.8	86.6	91.3	86.6	88.2	87.7	88.1	..	81.9	89.4
Niger	85.4	94.2	96.1	100.0	99.8	96.9	96.8	97.3	96.3	96.7	96.8	91.6	92.1	97.2
Nigeria	68.6	76.5	79.8	79.4	81.6	65.1	75.4	80.4	80.9	66.0	73.1	78.5	82.3	75.0
Rwanda	95.8	97.1	98.6	148.5	107.3	105.8	104.1	102.8	99.8	98.6	98.1	93.2	94.7	104.3
São Tomé and Principe	111.6	128.1	131.6	117.5	111.4	113.7	116.5	107.0	110.3	103.6	98.0	106.6	121.9	116.8
Senegal	105.0	92.6	94.5	88.1	88.9	87.2	87.7	87.1	88.5	89.2	88.0	98.9	96.2	89.7
Seychelles	72.9	82.4	81.6	78.7	76.5	62.2	79.9	77.6	86.0	73.8	91.7	80.4	69.9	79.3
Sierra Leone	99.1	92.6	92.6	88.7	102.1	104.7	104.3	101.9	105.7	108.1	112.3	95.9	85.9	99.7
Somalia	112.9	..	..	..	..	..	..	..	..	..	..	111.4	94.4	112.5
South Africa	68.6	83.9	82.4	82.1	80.9	81.7	82.9	83.4	82.8	82.3	82.5	75.6	78.0	82.5
Sudan	97.9	..	..	..	..	86.0	92.4	99.3	89.9	80.0	88.3	94.2	91.8	89.3
Swaziland	90.4	99.8	102.1	96.5	98.7	94.1	96.7	96.7	96.1	95.5	93.7	85.9	84.5	95.4
Tanzania	..	99.7	104.6	98.4	98.1	96.4	95.1	100.8	96.6	90.8	91.7	89.0	89.4	97.3
Togo	76.8	93.5	100.2	88.7	88.8	92.1	99.5	94.5	92.4	95.9	96.4	78.6	92.4	93.2
Uganda	..	99.6	98.9	95.7	92.6	95.4	90.6	95.9	92.6	93.1	93.9	97.0	97.0	95.6
Zambia	80.7	99.7	91.8	92.6	87.8	94.7	90.6	96.1	101.1	91.7	90.2	81.1	85.1	92.6
Zimbabwe	86.2	89.0	79.0	78.2	83.0	81.3	88.9	84.7	84.3	85.2	91.0	84.8	81.0	84.3
NORTH AFRICA	59.5	77.0	80.0	82.0	82.1	80.9	78.7	80.2	78.2	74.9	75.1	64.7	78.7	78.5
Algeria	56.9	67.8	72.3	73.4	71.9	68.6	67.8	72.9	68.6	55.8	59.1	61.4	76.2	67.8
Egypt, Arab Republic	84.8	84.6	86.8	88.6	87.8	89.2	84.5	84.5	83.1	82.7	82.3	84.6	84.3	85.4
Libya	43.1	..	..	..	..	..	..	..	..	..	..	53.5	..	..
Morocco	86.3	83.5	83.5	84.7	85.9	83.8	82.6	81.9	80.4	81.8	80.7	87.1	82.0	82.7
Tunisia	76.0	72.6	78.3	78.5	79.3	76.5	76.0	76.4	75.4	76.1	75.5	75.8	78.4	76.0
ALL AFRICA	71.6	84.0	83.9	83.2	83.2	80.8	82.0	83.6	82.1	78.9	79.7	75.4	79.9	81.9

Note:2001 is preliminary.Angola's drop is for weakness in nat. acct. stats. Since 1994, Nigeria's ratios are distorted because the off. ex. rt. used by the Govt. for oil exp. and oil val. added is significantly over-valued.

2-7. General government consumption

	Percentage of GDP											Annual Average		
	1980	*1992*	*1993*	*1994*	*1995*	*1996*	*1997*	*1998*	*1999*	*2000*	*2001*	*75-84*	*85-89*	*90-MR*
SUB-SAHARAN AFRICA	15.0	18.9	18.3	17.6	16.5	15.8	16.5	15.8	16.3	16.4	16.8	15.5	16.3	17.0
excluding South Africa	15.6	18.0	16.8	15.0	14.6	13.0	13.9	12.9	14.3	15.3	15.5	15.7	15.2	15.2
excl. S.Africa & Nigeria	17.1	17.8	16.7	15.2	15.4	14.2	15.0	13.5	14.5	14.0	13.1	16.0	15.7	15.3
Angola	..	41.9	41.5	40.1	52.6	39.4	54.4	30.0	60.6	43.9	35.5	..	31.5	43.3
Benin	8.6	10.7	10.3	10.1	11.2	10.7	10.2	9.4	10.0	11.6	11.6	9.9	14.1	10.6
Botswana	21.3	26.4	28.0	28.3	28.5	27.3	26.8	28.9	30.1	30.7	27.2	22.7	24.1	27.5
Burkina Faso	10.4	15.8	14.5	18.1	16.9	15.1	14.8	14.7	13.8	14.2	13.8	12.8	14.2	15.1
Burundi	9.2	10.1	13.3	12.7	13.4	12.6	14.5	13.3	16.1	14.7	13.5	10.3	9.7	13.0
Cameroon	9.7	12.8	12.8	10.0	8.6	8.4	8.2	9.2	9.8	10.2	11.2	9.7	10.8	10.6
Cape Verde	8.2	15.7	17.6	18.3	19.8	17.4	16.2	15.0	19.4	25.3	12.9	10.0	12.3	17.4
Central African Republic	15.1	16.9	15.0	17.5	15.2	9.6	10.9	11.6	11.5	11.3	11.4	15.0	15.9	13.5
Chad	..	9.2	10.0	12.7	11.8	8.7	7.9	5.7	6.7	7.8	8.4	13.0	13.8	9.0
Comoros	30.9	19.5	18.9	23.5	22.3	19.0	17.6	15.7	14.6	13.3	13.5	29.7	27.4	18.8
Congo, Democratic Rep. of	8.4	21.7	15.4	4.4	4.9	6.2	14.5	8.2	6.5	0.9	1.4	9.1	9.7	9.1
Congo, Republic of	17.6	21.1	21.2	16.2	13.0	14.5	20.0	21.4	17.0	9.5	10.7	17.3	20.5	16.6
Côte d'Ivoire	16.9	17.4	16.4	13.0	11.9	10.5	10.0	9.0	9.5	8.8	9.1	16.5	16.2	12.4
Djibouti	..	..	..	..	32.4	27.7	27.8	23.5	26.4	25.2	..	..	..	27.2
Equatorial Guinea	..	29.4	39.3	15.3	16.4	19.8	11.0	21.0	10.3	6.7	4.2	28.3	27.4	20.6
Eritrea	..	23.0	33.4	31.8	46.4	41.0	31.6	54.2	58.5	53.8	39.8	..	..	41.4
Ethiopia	..	10.1	10.6	12.5	11.8	11.7	11.4	13.9	18.5	23.2	17.5	15.3	16.0	14.6
Gabon	13.2	15.5	15.3	12.0	14.1	13.6	13.7	16.9	16.6	10.0	11.1	14.5	20.9	13.9
Gambia, The	31.2	13.9	14.1	14.5	13.7	14.9	13.9	12.7	13.0	13.7	15.4	36.6	17.7	13.9
Ghana	11.2	12.1	14.4	13.7	12.1	12.0	13.6	14.6	13.6	15.3	15.6	9.9	10.1	13.0
Guinea	..	7.5	7.1	6.6	6.2	6.4	6.2	6.1	5.9	3.9	4.8	..	8.9	6.5
Guinea-Bissau	27.6	9.0	7.1	7.1	6.4	6.6	7.0	9.3	10.8	13.9	12.3	23.6	12.5	9.2
Kenya	19.8	16.1	16.7	15.2	14.8	16.0	16.2	16.4	17.0	17.5	16.8	18.4	18.1	16.5
Lesotho	31.2	23.4	23.9	25.5	27.7	25.6	25.9	31.0	29.5	25.5	24.3	23.4	26.6	25.5
Liberia	16.3	..	..	..	..	..	..	..	..	..	..	15.8	19.0	..
Madagascar	12.1	8.2	7.9	6.9	6.7	9.8	7.8	7.8	7.2	6.8	8.0	11.1	8.9	7.8
Malawi	19.3	14.1	13.0	31.6	18.6	12.5	12.6	13.3	12.4	16.7	17.6	16.4	17.7	15.8
Mali	9.8	13.2	12.8	11.3	9.7	10.2	12.0	11.3	12.6	13.3	12.8	9.4	13.5	12.2
Mauritania	45.3	16.4	20.7	16.5	14.1	14.3	13.8	14.5	15.2	17.3	15.6	45.2	25.3	16.9
Mauritius	14.4	12.6	12.7	13.1	13.4	13.4	13.2	12.9	12.9	13.2	13.0	14.7	12.6	13.0
Mozambique	12.2	12.6	11.7	12.9	7.8	8.0	9.2	10.4	9.5	9.9	10.4	14.2	11.3	10.4
Namibia	..	35.1	31.6	28.3	30.0	27.6	30.0	29.4	29.6	26.4	28.6	..	28.9	29.5
Niger	10.4	17.5	15.8	16.0	14.1	11.3	13.8	13.1	14.9	13.0	12.3	11.5	12.9	14.3
Nigeria	12.1	18.4	17.5	14.3	11.1	8.0	9.4	9.7	13.4	20.5	25.2	14.4	12.5	14.6
Rwanda	12.5	14.5	14.3	11.2	10.3	11.5	9.6	10.0	11.0	10.5	11.7	14.7	12.6	11.4
São Tomé and Principe	34.5	31.5	34.5	31.9	27.6	27.2	31.9	25.6	29.8	28.0	29.5	22.1	39.7	30.0
Senegal	20.3	15.4	14.7	12.8	12.4	12.0	10.4	10.3	10.9	10.4	10.1	17.2	15.6	12.3
Seychelles	28.7	30.4	29.8	29.6	29.3	27.0	25.5	31.5	27.8	27.2	34.9	30.8	34.5	29.1
Sierra Leone	8.4	10.3	11.2	10.2	13.1	11.0	9.0	8.9	11.5	14.6	17.2	8.4	7.5	11.2
Somalia	15.6	..	..	..	..	..	..	..	..	..	..	19.8	..	..
South Africa	14.3	20.2	20.1	20.0	18.3	19.4	19.8	19.9	19.2	18.1	19.0	15.7	18.8	19.5
Sudan	16.0	..	..	..	..	7.5	5.4	4.5	4.9	5.9	5.3	12.1	11.9	5.6
Swaziland	26.9	17.2	22.5	21.5	19.2	20.9	24.8	24.2	22.2	19.9	19.6	22.2	19.0	20.7
Tanzania	..	19.6	19.4	17.1	11.5	11.6	8.8	7.8	7.0	6.5	6.3	13.5	14.6	12.7
Togo	22.4	12.4	16.1	13.2	12.1	11.7	10.3	12.2	11.1	10.8	9.3	20.0	15.2	12.6
Uganda	..	9.7	9.8	10.3	9.8	10.3	10.8	10.4	11.5	12.0	12.5	10.8	9.3	10.3
Zambia	25.5	15.0	18.4	13.1	15.5	18.3	17.5	15.8	12.9	9.5	13.0	25.7	19.9	16.7
Zimbabwe	18.5	24.2	14.9	16.7	18.0	16.9	16.3	17.5	15.2	24.2	19.3	16.9	22.1	18.2
NORTH AFRICA	12.5	14.4	14.9	14.8	14.5	14.0	14.0	14.3	14.0	13.0	12.9	14.3	16.8	14.1
Algeria	15.2	16.0	17.3	17.9	16.8	16.4	16.7	18.1	17.1	14.1	14.2	15.2	18.7	16.3
Egypt, Arab Republic	15.7	10.4	10.2	10.3	10.5	10.4	10.2	10.1	10.1	9.7	10.3	19.5	14.9	10.4
Libya	21.8	..	..	..	..	..	..	..	..	..	..	27.8	..	..
Morocco	18.3	16.8	18.1	17.1	17.4	16.9	17.8	18.0	19.2	19.1	17.9	18.9	15.6	17.4
Tunisia	14.5	16.0	16.3	16.5	16.9	15.6	15.8	15.7	15.5	15.7	13.6	15.7	17.1	15.9
ALL AFRICA	13.8	17.5	17.2	16.6	15.8	15.2	15.6	15.2	15.5	15.1	15.2	14.9	16.4	16.0

Note: 2001 data are preliminary (see page 2). Since 1994, Nigeria's ratios are distorted because the official exchange rate used by the Government for oil exports and oil value added is significantly over-valued.

2-8. Gross domestic investment

	Percentage of GDP											Annual Average		
	1980	*1992*	*1993*	*1994*	*1995*	*1996*	*1997*	*1998*	*1999*	*2000*	*2001*	*75-84*	*85-89*	*90-MR*
SUB-SAHARAN AFRICA	20.9	14.6	15.9	17.1	18.4	18.2	17.7	18.6	18.4	17.5	18.4	20.5	15.1	17.0
excluding South Africa	19.8	16.7	17.6	18.7	18.6	19.1	19.0	20.8	21.0	19.1	20.1	20.1	15.4	18.6
excl. S.Africa & Nigeria	18.4	15.4	16.7	18.5	19.1	20.3	19.4	20.1	20.5	18.2	18.3	18.3	15.5	18.2
Angola	..	3.6	11.2	16.6	28.1	34.7	25.5	35.5	46.8	35.4	34.0	..	14.8	24.7
Benin	15.2	13.8	15.4	15.8	19.6	17.1	18.4	17.0	17.5	18.9	19.2	17.7	12.6	16.8
Botswana	40.1	30.4	28.8	26.5	24.6	25.0	28.1	33.5	26.9	17.0	22.0	36.3	24.0	27.8
Burkina Faso	17.0	21.1	19.8	21.8	25.8	27.4	28.5	30.1	26.4	25.5	25.4	20.2	21.7	24.4
Burundi	13.9	15.0	16.3	10.6	9.6	12.1	8.1	8.8	9.1	9.1	6.9	14.3	15.9	11.2
Cameroon	21.0	14.3	16.5	15.3	14.5	15.4	16.2	17.5	18.3	16.4	17.8	25.1	22.6	16.4
Cape Verde	51.6	34.5	39.7	43.4	42.4	24.1	22.0	19.8	20.9	19.3	17.8	49.1	32.3	27.8
Central African Republic	7.0	12.2	10.2	11.7	13.5	4.3	9.8	13.5	14.4	10.8	14.0	10.5	12.5	11.6
Chad	..	7.5	9.8	16.6	10.3	14.9	14.8	17.4	12.6	17.0	42.6	11.9	7.9	15.5
Comoros	33.2	19.5	18.3	20.7	19.5	19.4	15.8	17.9	14.9	13.1	13.1	33.4	24.2	17.0
Congo, Democratic Rep. of	10.0	6.9	1.8	7.9	9.4	27.9	27.9	20.0	21.6	4.2	5.1	12.7	13.7	12.3
Congo, Republic of	35.8	21.6	29.5	31.2	36.6	27.0	22.4	26.7	27.8	21.0	27.2	36.2	22.4	25.6
Côte d'Ivoire	26.5	6.9	8.3	12.5	13.5	12.1	14.4	13.3	13.1	10.6	9.9	23.6	11.8	10.7
Djibouti	..	..	..	..	8.4	9.1	9.4	15.3	8.9	12.9	..	..	..	10.7
Equatorial Guinea	..	24.2	22.0	74.1	76.3	113.6	65.7	91.6	54.7	37.5	15.0	13.9	0.0	53.6
Eritrea	..	-102.9	71.3	20.7	27.9	33.9	38.4	36.9	42.8	35.7	35.3	..	..	24.0
Ethiopia	..	9.2	14.2	15.2	16.4	16.9	17.0	17.2	16.3	15.3	18.0	13.7	14.7	14.8
Gabon	27.5	22.4	22.4	21.9	23.7	23.3	29.6	37.3	28.0	26.1	30.5	42.9	35.7	26.1
Gambia, The	26.7	22.2	21.0	18.1	20.2	21.6	17.2	18.4	17.8	17.0	17.9	19.7	17.1	19.6
Ghana	5.6	12.8	22.2	24.0	20.0	29.2	24.8	23.1	21.0	23.7	24.0	6.9	10.8	21.3
Guinea	..	17.4	17.8	15.4	16.6	17.3	17.6	18.0	23.0	22.1	22.1	..	16.1	18.6
Guinea-Bissau	28.2	48.4	30.9	21.8	22.3	23.0	21.8	11.4	16.8	16.0	21.7	23.8	35.6	24.6
Kenya	24.5	13.7	17.7	16.4	17.5	16.8	15.4	15.3	14.6	13.7	12.8	21.5	20.3	16.1
Lesotho	37.0	66.0	54.6	55.5	60.5	58.5	54.0	47.1	43.3	39.5	36.8	32.4	42.9	52.7
Liberia	27.3	..	..	..	..	..	..	..	..	..	..	23.8	9.2	..
Madagascar	15.0	11.2	11.4	10.9	10.9	11.6	12.8	14.8	14.9	15.0	15.5	10.2	10.9	12.9
Malawi	24.7	19.9	15.2	29.1	17.0	11.6	12.2	13.5	14.8	12.5	10.9	25.3	18.9	16.7
Mali	15.5	21.9	21.8	27.3	22.9	22.9	20.6	20.9	21.2	22.6	22.2	14.8	20.1	22.5
Mauritania	26.3	19.3	20.6	20.7	19.3	18.6	17.6	19.0	17.8	30.3	26.7	26.7	26.6	20.6
Mauritius	25.4	28.9	30.0	30.9	28.8	25.3	27.2	27.6	26.0	25.7	24.4	24.7	25.6	27.9
Mozambique	5.9	15.6	12.7	19.8	22.8	21.8	20.6	24.2	36.9	39.6	41.6	5.8	10.3	23.9
Namibia	..	21.6	16.5	21.7	21.7	23.1	20.7	26.4	24.4	24.0	24.5	..	17.4	22.5
Niger	28.1	6.9	6.4	10.4	7.3	9.7	10.9	11.3	10.2	10.8	11.5	18.2	13.7	9.2
Nigeria	21.3	21.8	23.3	19.6	16.3	14.2	17.4	24.1	23.4	22.7	27.6	22.3	15.1	20.7
Rwanda	16.1	15.6	16.7	10.0	13.4	14.4	13.8	14.8	17.2	17.5	18.4	14.8	15.4	15.0
São Tomé and Principe	16.8	38.8	35.3	41.6	68.1	56.2	49.1	35.8	39.0	43.5	49.9	14.6	14.8	42.5
Senegal	11.7	14.8	14.1	18.6	16.7	18.5	18.0	18.6	19.0	19.8	20.0	13.1	11.8	17.1
Seychelles	..	21.2	28.7	25.4	30.3	49.1	30.7	38.0	30.4	30.6	37.2	21.4	22.7	30.7
Sierra Leone	16.2	8.3	7.7	7.8	5.2	10.0	-2.4	5.3	0.3	8.0	7.9	15.1	9.2	6.5
Somalia	42.4	..	..	..	..	..	..	..	..	..	..	27.1	28.5	15.5
South Africa	23.4	12.0	14.0	15.6	18.2	16.9	16.0	15.4	14.5	14.8	15.0	21.3	14.9	14.7
Sudan	14.7	..	..	..	..	21.9	19.7	15.9	16.3	17.7	17.7	16.0	13.2	18.2
Swaziland	37.3	25.3	23.1	21.5	20.0	31.9	20.6	22.4	18.8	19.8	18.6	31.8	21.6	21.7
Tanzania	..	27.2	25.1	24.6	19.8	16.6	14.9	13.8	15.5	17.6	17.0	..	16.8	20.4
Togo	28.4	15.7	7.5	15.0	16.1	18.8	16.3	20.8	18.9	20.9	20.7	29.8	17.1	17.9
Uganda	6.2	15.9	15.2	14.7	16.4	16.1	16.8	16.2	19.4	19.8	20.0	7.2	9.8	16.5
Zambia	23.3	11.9	15.0	8.2	16.0	12.8	14.6	16.4	17.6	18.7	20.0	22.3	14.7	15.0
Zimbabwe	16.9	20.2	22.8	23.7	19.7	18.5	18.1	17.1	16.1	12.6	7.8	16.7	16.9	17.8
NORTH AFRICA	28.2	25.6	23.4	22.9	22.8	20.6	22.6	25.9	25.8	24.3	24.4	31.1	28.2	24.4
Algeria	39.1	30.8	29.1	31.2	31.8	25.1	23.8	28.7	27.8	23.8	25.8	41.7	30.7	28.2
Egypt, Arab Republic	27.5	18.2	16.2	16.6	17.2	16.6	21.7	25.6	25.5	23.9	22.7	29.9	28.6	21.2
Libya	22.1	..	..	..	..	..	..	..	..	..	..	26.3	..	..
Morocco	24.2	23.2	22.5	21.3	20.7	19.6	20.7	22.2	23.4	24.4	24.6	26.5	23.1	22.5
Tunisia	29.4	34.3	29.2	24.5	24.8	25.1	26.4	27.0	26.8	27.4	28.1	31.2	25.0	28.2
ALL AFRICA	22.6	18.0	18.4	19.1	19.9	19.0	19.4	21.2	21.2	20.1	20.7	23.3	19.7	19.5

Note: 2001 data are preliminary (see page 2). Since 1994, Nigeria's ratios are distorted because the official exchange rate used by the Government for oil exports and oil value added is significantly over-valued.

2-9. Gross public investment

	Percentage of GDP											Annual Average		
	1980	*1992*	*1993*	*1994*	*1995*	*1996*	*1997*	*1998*	*1999*	*2000*	*2001*	*75-84*	*85-89*	*90-MR*
SUB-SAHARAN AFRICA	8.8	6.7	5.6	5.0	5.3	5.2	5.6	6.5	6.1	5.5	5.8	8.6	6.9	5.9
excluding South Africa	..	7.9	6.6	6.0	6.3	5.9	6.5	7.3	7.2	6.4	7.1	..	6.4	6.7
excl. S.Africa & Nigeria	..	6.4	5.9	6.5	6.5	6.1	6.3	6.5	6.5	5.5	5.6	6.1	5.6	6.1
Angola	..	..	..	..	..	..	4.7	5.9	12.9	6.3	5.4	..	..	7.0
Benin	..	6.6	7.1	9.3	10.4	7.5	7.6	6.5	6.9	8.2	7.8	..	8.2	7.7
Botswana	0.0	12.9	12.8	13.0	11.0	11.4	12.4	13.2	13.1	12.3	10.8	0.0	0.0	12.4
Burkina Faso	..	10.1	8.4	8.3	11.0	12.3	14.4	13.7	16.5	13.6	13.2	..	7.6	11.0
Burundi	12.8	11.7	12.9	9.0	8.3	10.4	5.0	5.6	6.2	5.6	3.6	14.0	13.6	8.6
Cameroon	4.4	2.7	1.8	1.3	1.2	0.5	1.0	2.0	2.3	1.4	2.1	4.7	9.0	2.1
Cape Verde	..	26.2	28.2	32.0	27.1	20.5	18.0	21.3	6.5	11.0	7.5	..	19.3	18.4
Central African Republic	3.7	7.5	6.2	7.2	9.8	1.8	3.9	7.1	6.8	7.1	7.4	4.7	6.3	6.4
Chad	..	4.5	5.8	7.3	6.3	3.5	5.6	7.8	9.4	10.3	10.8	2.2	4.8	7.1
Comoros	23.2	10.3	6.8	10.4	6.4	5.8	6.0	7.7	5.4	3.8	4.4	23.3	14.2	6.4
Congo, Democratic Rep. of	5.1	2.8	0.9	0.6	4.4	0.5	0.9	0.1	1.1	0.2	0.1	3.9	4.9	1.5
Congo, Republic of	35.8	4.7	7.1	12.8	9.3	5.2	3.6	4.7	6.1	7.0	10.2	35.5	11.1	6.7
Côte d'Ivoire	11.4	3.8	3.7	4.1	4.2	4.9	5.4	6.0	4.2	2.8	1.2	10.5	4.4	4.0
Djibouti	..	..	..	..	3.6	3.9	4.3	6.6	..	..	..	..	..	4.6
Equatorial Guinea	..	10.1	8.9	4.1	1.9	1.2	4.4	7.5	1.3	0.8	0.4	..	0.0	5.4
Eritrea	..	3.5	15.5	11.4	13.0	16.3	19.1	21.3	30.6	26.2	18.6	..	..	17.5
Ethiopia	..	3.2	5.0	7.1	7.5	7.5	8.3	7.4	7.9	5.3	8.9	..	6.9	6.5
Gabon	5.3	5.3	5.1	5.6	5.1	5.9	9.2	13.4	7.3	4.8	5.6	15.8	5.9	6.4
Gambia, The	..	7.8	7.5	7.0	10.0	12.9	7.9	5.2	4.7	3.8	5.8	13.8	7.6	7.3
Ghana	..	10.3	11.1	13.3	14.0	13.3	12.4	11.3	9.8	9.2	10.6	2.5	7.0	10.9
Guinea	..	6.7	6.2	5.9	6.3	5.4	6.1	4.1	7.2	7.2	7.3	..	7.4	6.5
Guinea-Bissau	..	28.4	24.6	20.4	15.2	14.8	15.6	6.2	10.8	11.7	15.8	..	29.6	17.3
Kenya	10.1	7.1	8.0	8.5	7.4	7.0	6.4	5.0	4.3	4.4	4.1	8.8	7.6	6.8
Lesotho	0.0	15.3	14.8	14.5	15.6	19.6	18.4	12.0	8.7	8.1	10.0	7.5	9.1	14.9
Liberia	..	..	..	..	..	..	..	..	..	..	..	..	..	..
Madagascar	..	7.5	7.8	6.2	5.8	6.7	6.5	7.9	6.9	6.7	7.2	6.4	7.0	6.9
Malawi	17.5	10.2	8.4	15.1	9.4	6.1	7.1	8.7	10.6	10.0	8.1	13.6	8.1	9.2
Mali	..	9.5	9.3	13.7	9.4	9.2	8.2	9.5	9.4	10.4	10.5	..	10.2	10.1
Mauritania	..	3.4	4.3	4.3	3.8	6.1	5.6	5.6	6.0	7.5	8.3	..	7.6	5.4
Mauritius	8.1	8.9	8.5	8.2	8.4	8.6	7.6	6.2	6.3	6.5	6.9	7.9	7.7	7.9
Mozambique	7.6	12.8	12.3	14.0	12.0	10.3	12.1	9.8	11.6	13.3	14.0	10.4	8.6	12.1
Namibia	..	9.9	6.1	5.2	7.1	7.3	8.2	7.9	8.7	8.0	8.3	..	6.1	7.6
Niger	20.4	5.4	4.9	6.6	5.2	4.6	5.8	6.4	6.4	5.9	6.5	13.8	8.5	5.7
Nigeria	..	13.4	10.7	3.6	5.3	5.2	7.1	11.3	10.4	9.8	12.9	..	..	9.3
Rwanda	12.2	10.2	7.7	2.7	8.1	9.3	8.3	6.8	6.3	6.0	6.6	13.7	10.2	7.1
São Tomé and Principe	0.0	23.8	20.3	26.6	33.1	29.2	22.1	19.8	26.0	26.0	33.0	0.0	0.0	23.9
Senegal	5.5	5.2	4.2	5.0	4.4	6.4	6.4	6.5	6.6	6.7	6.7	4.1	4.0	5.6
Seychelles	..	9.4	11.2	7.5	6.8	8.1	8.9	13.4	13.6	14.3	6.0	16.3	7.6	10.0
Sierra Leone	5.3	4.7	5.3	4.0	2.4	3.3	1.5	4.9	2.4	5.2	4.8	5.1	2.9	3.9
Somalia	..	..	..	..	..	..	..	..	..	..	..	..	..	..
South Africa	13.0	5.2	4.4	4.1	4.3	4.4	4.5	5.4	4.7	4.1	3.6	13.0	8.1	4.8
Sudan	6.9	..	..	..	..	..	0.6	0.7	1.2	2.3	3.1	5.6	3.0	1.6
Swaziland	8.6	11.8	9.5	8.6	5.9	5.2	4.9	6.5	7.3	7.5	7.1	10.9	8.8	7.8
Tanzania	..	9.2	7.5	6.0	3.4	3.5	2.9	3.3	3.1	3.4	3.7	..	3.5	5.4
Togo	20.2	3.5	2.3	2.3	3.5	5.0	2.0	4.3	3.4	3.3	2.5	12.2	10.2	3.7
Uganda	..	7.4	6.7	5.4	5.4	5.3	5.4	4.7	5.5	6.4	6.4	..	4.4	6.0
Zambia	4.0	6.7	4.5	4.0	5.1	6.0	5.4	11.3	10.6	10.0	11.8	4.1	4.7	7.5
Zimbabwe	1.8	3.8	3.7	3.1	2.9	2.3	2.8	1.8	4.1	0.0	1.0	2.9	2.6	2.7
NORTH AFRICA	..	8.6	9.4	8.3	7.5	6.8	9.2	9.5	..	..	..	..	11.1	8.5
Algeria	11.0	6.9	8.7	7.9	7.3	6.8	7.3	7.6	5.9	8.0	0.0	12.9	12.7	6.7
Egypt, Arab Republic	..	8.5	7.1	6.1	5.5	5.5	10.6	11.3	9.8	7.5	6.4	..	12.6	8.1
Libya	19.4	..	..	..	..	..	..	..	..	..	..	21.1		..
Morocco	9.8	9.5	11.8	10.1	8.9	6.8	7.1	6.5	..	..	..	13.5	8.8	8.8
Tunisia	15.0	12.0	15.3	13.7	12.3	11.0	11.9	11.6	12.4	12.5	0.0	17.2	11.4	11.2
ALL AFRICA	..	7.3	6.9	6.2	6.1	5.7	6.8	7.6	7.0	6.4	5.0	10.7	8.8	6.6

Note: 2001 data are preliminary (see page 2). Since 1994, Nigeria's ratios are distorted because the official exchange rate used by the Government for oil exports and oil value added is significantly over-valued.

2-10. Gross private investment

	Percentage of GDP											Annual Average		
	1980	1992	1993	1994	1995	1996	1997	1998	1999	2000	2001	75-84	85-89	90-MR
SUB-SAHARAN AFRICA	8.5	9.5	10.8	11.9	11.9	12.3	11.9	12.3	12.4	11.8	12.7	9.7	9.2	11.5
excluding South Africa	..	8.8	11.2	12.7	12.1	12.8	12.1	13.2	13.7	12.7	13.1	7.5	7.9	11.7
excl. S.Africa & Nigeria	..	8.9	11.0	12.0	12.3	13.7	12.5	13.3	13.9	12.6	12.7	9.2	8.3	11.8
Angola	..	0.1	19.8	28.4	21.1	21.7	20.8	29.6	33.9	29.1	28.6	..	9.2	20.4
Benin	..	6.7	7.9	6.2	6.9	9.1	10.8	10.5	10.6	10.7	11.4	..	4.5	8.6
Botswana	34.5	16.7	14.1	12.6	14.6	13.4	12.5	14.2	14.7	12.2	14.4	29.3	26.8	14.7
Burkina Faso	..	13.2	10.3	14.9	14.0	13.9	14.4	16.4	9.9	11.9	12.2	..	13.0	13.4
Burundi	1.1	2.8	3.0	1.6	1.4	1.8	2.2	2.3	1.8	2.4	2.3	1.5	2.7	2.3
Cameroon	15.6	11.6	14.7	14.0	13.3	14.9	15.2	15.5	16.0	15.1	15.7	24.2	12.1	14.2
Cape Verde	20.8	8.2	11.5	11.3	15.3	3.6	4.0	-1.5	14.4	8.3	10.3	10.1	7.7	9.3
Central African Republic	3.2	4.4	3.3	4.5	3.4	2.5	5.9	6.5	7.7	3.7	6.6	4.1	5.3	5.0
Chad	..	0.8	1.1	4.4	5.3	5.9	7.0	6.5	6.7	10.2	34.0	0.3	0.8	7.0
Comoros	5.3	7.1	8.1	9.2	9.1	7.9	7.4	7.0	6.5	6.5	6.2	5.4	5.7	7.3
Congo, Democratic Rep. of	3.7	4.3	1.4	7.0	5.3	26.6	27.0	19.9	20.5	4.0	5.0	5.8	8.3	11.1
Congo, Republic of	0.0	15.9	21.8	16.9	25.0	20.7	18.2	19.6	20.4	12.3	16.4	0.0	11.4	17.8
Côte d'Ivoire	13.0	4.7	4.1	7.0	8.7	9.9	9.1	9.9	10.2	8.2	7.8	12.3	7.1	7.5
Djibouti	..	..	..	..	4.8	5.2	5.1	8.6	..	..	..	..	..	5.9
Equatorial Guinea	..	14.1	13.1	70.0	74.4	112.4	61.3	84.1	29.2	16.7	13.9	..	0.0	44.5
Eritrea	..	-106.4	55.7	9.3	14.9	17.6	19.3	15.6	12.2	9.5	16.8	..	..	6.5
Ethiopia	..	6.0	9.2	8.0	9.0	9.4	8.7	9.8	8.2	8.9	9.2	..	8.9	8.2
Gabon	21.4	16.7	17.8	15.4	17.6	17.3	20.4	23.9	20.8	21.3	24.9	24.0	29.8	19.6
Gambia, The	..	14.4	13.5	11.1	10.2	8.6	9.3	13.2	13.1	13.2	12.1	7.4	9.5	12.3
Ghana	..	2.4	12.7	9.3	7.1	15.9	11.4	11.1	11.8	14.8	13.1	4.4	3.7	10.3
Guinea	..	9.8	10.6	11.1	10.3	11.9	11.6	13.8	14.9	14.0	14.0	..	8.7	11.7
Guinea-Bissau	..	20.0	6.3	1.4	7.1	8.3	6.2	5.2	5.1	1.5	7.9	..	10.0	7.1
Kenya	8.2	6.2	8.9	7.5	9.7	9.2	8.1	9.4	9.3	8.5	8.1	8.7	7.8	8.3
Lesotho	37.0	50.7	39.8	41.0	44.9	38.9	35.5	35.1	34.6	31.4	26.7	25.6	33.9	37.8
Liberia	..	..	..	..	..	..	..	..	..	..	..	..	..	..
Madagascar	..	3.7	3.7	4.7	5.2	5.0	6.3	6.9	8.0	8.3	8.3	2.2	3.9	6.0
Malawi	4.7	6.9	4.6	11.6	7.6	5.4	2.7	2.4	2.3	2.6	2.8	7.0	7.8	5.8
Mali	..	12.4	12.5	13.7	13.5	13.7	12.4	11.4	11.8	12.2	11.7	..	9.9	12.4
Mauritania	..	15.9	16.4	16.4	15.5	12.5	12.0	13.3	11.8	22.8	18.4	..	19.0	15.2
Mauritius	16.1	19.3	19.3	20.6	18.7	16.4	18.4	18.7	19.1	19.1	16.6	15.1	14.2	18.8
Mozambique	-1.7	2.8	0.4	5.8	10.8	11.6	8.5	14.5	25.3	26.3	27.6	-4.5	1.7	11.8
Namibia	..	11.7	10.3	16.5	14.6	15.8	12.5	18.6	15.7	16.0	16.2	..	11.3	15.0
Niger	5.1	1.9	1.9	2.3	1.8	4.7	4.8	4.6	3.6	4.6	4.8	3.6	2.4	3.6
Nigeria	..	8.3	12.5	16.0	11.1	8.9	10.3	12.8	13.0	12.9	14.6	5.2	6.1	11.4
Rwanda	0.0	5.5	9.1	7.3	5.3	5.1	5.5	8.0	10.9	11.6	11.8	0.0	4.7	8.0
São Tomé and Principe	11.4	15.0	15.0	15.0	35.0	27.0	27.0	16.0	14.0	17.5	16.9	11.4	13.7	18.8
Senegal	7.7	9.2	9.7	11.1	10.2	9.9	11.6	11.8	12.4	13.1	13.3	7.9	8.4	10.9
Seychelles	..	11.5	15.6	17.9	23.6	38.9	24.0	24.6	16.8	16.3	31.2	5.4	14.9	20.3
Sierra Leone	9.5	3.6	2.4	3.8	2.8	6.7	-3.9	0.4	-2.1	2.8	3.1	9.0	5.7	2.4
Somalia	..	..	..	..	..	..	..	..	..	..	..	..	..	..
South Africa	12.9	10.4	10.3	11.0	11.6	11.7	11.8	11.2	10.4	10.5	11.9	13.9	11.8	11.2
Sudan	3.8	..	..	..	..	..	11.6	10.3	10.7	10.3	13.4	8.0	8.3	11.3
Swaziland	28.7	13.4	13.5	12.9	14.1	26.7	15.7	15.9	11.4	12.3	11.5	20.7	12.8	14.0
Tanzania	..	17.8	17.4	18.5	16.2	13.0	11.8	10.3	12.3	14.1	13.1	8.6	11.7	14.7
Togo	8.0	12.5	8.6	9.7	10.1	12.2	11.0	12.9	12.6	14.5	17.2	8.0	7.6	12.7
Uganda	..	8.5	8.5	9.2	10.2	11.3	11.7	11.0	13.7	13.1	13.3	..	5.4	10.4
Zambia	17.2	3.8	7.0	7.3	7.3	5.2	7.7	3.5	5.4	7.2	6.8	12.6	4.1	6.0
Zimbabwe	12.3	18.6	19.9	18.3	21.7	15.7	15.3	15.7	10.8	12.4	6.7	13.3	12.4	15.6
NORTH AFRICA	..	16.7	14.7	15.3	15.4	14.1	14.6	15.4	16.2	15.0	19.2	13.0	15.3	16.0
Algeria	22.8	19.8	18.3	20.7	21.9	18.1	17.4	19.0	20.1	13.5	24.6	25.3	16.6	19.2
Egypt, Arab Republic	..	10.5	9.2	10.5	10.7	10.5	12.1	12.3	13.0	14.1	14.4	7.1	13.3	12.3
Libya	1.8	..	..	..	..	..	..	..	..	..	..	3.6	..	..
Morocco	16.7	18.6	18.6	17.2	17.7	16.3	17.3	19.3	20.7	20.7	21.2	18.1	17.6	18.9
Tunisia	13.3	20.3	12.8	13.3	11.9	12.2	12.7	13.2	12.9	13.8	23.7	13.2	12.2	15.6
ALL AFRICA	10.5	11.8	12.1	13.1	13.0	12.9	12.9	13.5	13.8	13.1	15.3	11.4	11.3	13.0

Note: 2001 data are preliminary (see page 2). Since 1994, Nigeria's ratios are distorted because the official exchange rate used by the Government for oil exports and oil value added is significantly over-valued.

2-11. Gross domestic savings

	Percentage of GDP											Annual Average		
	1980	1992	1993	1994	1995	1996	1997	1998	1999	2000	2001	75-84	85-89	90-MR
SUB-SAHARAN AFRICA	23.0	12.7	14.1	16.2	16.1	19.3	16.4	14.5	15.6	18.7	17.4	19.9	18.9	16.2
excluding South Africa	18.4	9.6	10.8	14.9	13.4	20.0	15.8	13.0	14.5	19.3	17.2	17.1	16.5	15.0
excl. S.Africa & Nigeria	10.4	6.3	9.0	13.6	12.3	16.6	13.7	11.6	13.5	15.6	15.0	14.8	16.0	12.8
Angola	..	1.7	9.9	26.1	26.9	48.7	26.7	18.5	41.2	63.1	45.7	..	24.0	29.5
Benin	-6.3	0.0	1.1	6.0	6.7	3.4	5.6	6.6	4.8	5.9	6.5	-1.7	-2.3	4.2
Botswana	26.7	37.0	36.8	37.0	37.5	41.3	43.0	39.8	38.4	39.0	38.2	23.3	44.1	39.2
Burkina Faso	-5.8	7.0	5.6	7.9	9.2	9.3	11.3	12.8	9.0	7.3	9.6	-1.7	2.4	8.6
Burundi	-0.6	-5.1	-4.7	-7.6	-4.8	2.5	3.9	-2.9	-0.5	-5.7	-4.8	4.1	3.3	-3.3
Cameroon	21.7	16.5	17.6	17.9	19.6	17.3	19.1	19.2	18.0	20.3	20.5	23.1	22.9	19.1
Cape Verde	-24.0	-3.5	3.7	2.8	2.4	-8.0	-8.4	-15.3	-17.5	-19.0	-13.5	-19.8	-2.9	-7.4
Central African Republic	-8.9	-0.4	1.8	6.0	6.2	0.6	4.4	5.3	11.0	7.8	11.2	-1.6	0.8	4.7
Chad	..	-6.3	-6.2	-1.4	-1.7	3.3	2.3	4.1	-2.2	1.5	0.8	2.4	-11.1	-0.8
Comoros	-10.1	-3.1	1.5	-6.5	-5.3	-3.6	-9.0	-4.7	-5.7	-1.4	-0.2	-6.5	-2.5	-3.8
Congo, Democratic Rep. of	0.0	0.0	0.0	0.0	0.0	27.5	25.9	16.9	17.8	5.4	6.2	45.3	0.0	8.3
Congo, Republic of	35.7	24.4	23.6	15.5	37.7	35.7	37.8	30.3	41.0	57.7	61.1	26.1	23.2	33.9
Côte d'Ivoire	20.4	10.7	9.4	22.4	18.9	20.8	22.8	19.7	21.3	17.3	16.9	24.3	18.4	16.8
Djibouti	..	..	..	..	-8.3	-6.9	-5.7	-0.8	-5.5	-5.3	..	..	..	-5.4
Equatorial Guinea	..	-10.0	-13.7	25.1	27.3	30.7	43.1	19.9	64.8	74.0	90.4	7.6	-33.3	29.4
Eritrea	..	-138.4	27.4	-37.0	-36.1	-27.6	-20.9	-31.1	-32.8	-28.4	-19.2	..	..	-34.4
Ethiopia	..	3.0	5.6	5.4	8.0	7.0	7.9	7.7	1.4	-0.1	2.2	6.4	7.2	4.8
Gabon	60.6	34.7	36.7	45.3	47.3	51.0	51.0	39.0	34.8	28.3	50.3	58.1	32.3	41.3
Gambia, The	5.8	9.3	4.0	2.8	-3.9	5.6	4.5	2.8	3.2	2.7	0.9	4.3	7.6	4.4
Ghana	4.9	1.3	6.0	12.5	11.6	21.2	4.2	10.2	3.7	3.3	5.8	6.3	5.5	7.7
Guinea	..	11.2	11.1	12.1	12.8	12.0	15.4	14.3	18.3	16.9	20.4	..	16.4	15.0
Guinea-Bissau	-1.0	3.2	7.0	3.9	-1.2	1.8	3.0	-10.1	-1.2	-10.5	-11.2	-3.0	-0.1	-0.8
Kenya	13.4	13.7	23.8	19.6	11.3	13.2	7.9	7.4	8.9	3.8	4.2	17.4	16.9	12.3
Lesotho	-52.0	-34.5	-45.3	-35.9	-38.4	-29.9	-24.5	-27.0	-24.1	-20.2	-14.8	-68.2	-62.7	-33.1
Liberia	27.3	..	..	..	..	..	..	..	..	..	..	23.3	16.4	..
Madagascar	-1.4	2.9	2.1	3.3	3.4	6.1	4.7	7.0	7.2	7.7	12.3	1.9	5.2	5.2
Malawi	10.8	0.7	-0.9	-3.0	-0.3	3.1	-0.7	7.5	-0.2	0.5	-1.0	15.6	11.8	2.8
Mali	1.1	4.4	6.4	7.5	7.8	7.2	10.0	11.2	10.1	7.3	9.4	0.2	0.1	7.8
Mauritania	-3.5	4.8	4.7	16.9	8.9	6.3	7.9	5.0	7.2	18.4	14.0	-5.6	10.3	9.1
Mauritius	14.5	25.4	25.2	23.6	23.4	23.8	24.3	24.9	23.8	23.7	25.3	16.9	24.8	24.2
Mozambique	-10.6	-17.2	-22.4	-13.9	-1.9	-1.8	1.1	6.8	9.3	11.9	19.2	-10.4	-10.2	-2.7
Namibia	..	7.0	6.0	12.6	11.2	13.4	8.7	13.4	11.8	12.3	11.9	..	18.1	10.6
Niger	14.6	5.8	3.9	0.0	0.2	3.1	3.2	2.7	3.7	3.3	3.2	8.4	7.9	2.8
Nigeria	31.4	23.5	20.2	20.6	18.4	34.9	24.6	19.6	19.1	34.0	26.9	21.5	17.7	25.0
Rwanda	4.2	2.9	1.4	-48.5	-7.3	-5.8	-4.1	-2.8	0.2	1.4	1.9	6.8	5.3	-4.3
São Tomé and Principe	-11.6	-28.1	-31.6	-17.5	-11.4	-13.7	-16.5	-7.0	-10.3	-3.6	2.0	-6.6	-21.9	-16.8
Senegal	-5.0	7.4	5.5	11.9	11.1	12.8	12.3	12.9	11.5	10.8	12.0	1.1	3.8	10.3
Seychelles	27.1	17.6	18.4	21.3	23.5	37.8	20.1	22.4	14.0	26.2	8.3	19.6	30.1	20.7
Sierra Leone	..	7.4	7.4	11.3	-2.1	-4.7	-4.3	-1.9	-5.7	-8.1	-12.3	10.9	14.1	0.3
Somalia	-12.9	..	..	..	..	..	..	..	..	..	..	-11.4	5.6	-12.5
South Africa	31.4	16.1	17.6	17.9	19.1	18.3	17.1	16.6	17.2	17.7	17.5	24.4	22.0	17.5
Sudan	2.1	..	..	..	..	14.0	5.8	16.5	12.1	20.0	13.9	5.8	7.9	13.7
Swaziland	9.6	0.2	-2.1	3.5	1.3	5.9	3.3	3.3	3.9	4.5	6.3	14.1	15.5	4.6
Tanzania	..	0.3	-4.6	1.6	1.9	3.6	4.9	-0.8	3.4	9.2	8.3	11.0	7.1	2.7
Togo	23.2	6.5	-0.2	11.3	11.2	7.9	0.5	5.5	7.6	4.1	3.6	21.4	7.6	6.8
Uganda	-0.4	0.4	1.1	4.3	7.4	4.6	9.4	4.1	7.4	6.9	6.1	4.1	3.0	4.4
Zambia	19.3	0.3	8.2	7.4	12.2	5.3	9.4	3.9	-1.1	8.3	9.8	18.9	14.9	7.4
Zimbabwe	13.8	11.0	21.0	21.8	17.0	18.7	11.1	15.3	15.7	14.8	9.8	15.2	19.0	15.8
NORTH AFRICA	40.5	23.0	20.0	18.0	17.9	19.1	21.3	19.8	21.8	25.1	24.9	35.3	21.3	21.5
Algeria	43.1	32.2	27.7	26.6	28.1	31.4	32.2	27.1	31.4	44.2	40.9	38.6	23.8	32.2
Egypt, Arab Republic	15.2	15.4	13.2	11.4	12.2	10.8	15.5	15.5	16.9	17.3	17.7	15.4	15.7	14.6
Libya	56.9	..	..	..	..	..	..	..	..	..	..	46.5	..	..
Morocco	13.7	16.5	16.5	15.3	14.1	16.2	17.4	18.1	19.6	18.2	19.3	12.9	18.0	17.3
Tunisia	24.0	22.3	21.3	22.2	20.4	..	..	..	..	25.3	24.5	22.1	19.1	22.1
ALL AFRICA	28.4	16.0	16.1	16.8	16.8	19.2	18.0	16.4	17.9	21.1	20.3	24.6	20.1	18.1

Note: 2001 data are preliminary (see page 2). Since 1994, Nigeria's ratios are distorted because the official exchange rate used by the Government for oil exports and oil value added is significantly over-valued.

2-12. Gross national savings

	Percentage of GDP											Annual Average		
	1980	*1992*	*1993*	*1994*	*1995*	*1996*	*1997*	*1998*	*1999*	*2000*	*2001*	*75-84*	*85-89*	*90-MR*
SUB-SAHARAN AFRICA	20.7	9.7	10.4	12.5	13.4	16.8	14.3	12.4	12.7	15.3	14.2	18.5	13.9	12.8
excluding South Africa	17.0	6.7	6.3	9.6	10.3	17.7	14.2	11.5	11.8	15.7	14.7	17.1	11.2	11.4
excl. S.Africa & Nigeria	10.4	4.1	5.1	8.9	9.7	14.6	12.1	10.7	11.3	12.7	12.6	15.3	11.0	9.7
Angola	..	20.6	12.5	26.9	6.0	31.8	13.3	5.9	24.6	44.5	30.4	..	19.9	19.2
Benin	0.0	0.0	0.0	0.0	0.0	0.0	11.0	11.3	9.9	11.3	12.5	0.0	0.0	4.7
Botswana	41.4	41.4	43.8	33.2	36.0	39.8	44.1	47.1	38.2	36.5	36.8	39.4	48.6	41.3
Burkina Faso	..	14.9	17.3	14.6	16.3	15.7	17.1	18.9	12.9	19.7	20.7	..	..	16.6
Burundi	4.6	4.2	7.9	9.0	9.2	7.7	8.8	2.9	3.7	3.2	6.4	5.6	7.9	6.1
Cameroon	5.1	12.4	11.3	11.2	13.7	11.2	13.4	15.0	14.3	14.7	16.1	12.9	21.6	13.8
Cape Verde	16.4	29.3	31.7	31.4	29.6	18.7	11.2	6.1	5.2	1.3	25.9	4.7	21.6	19.1
Central African Republic	-2.9	0.1	1.8	11.4	6.3	-1.6	4.1	5.9	11.4	8.6	13.2	6.0	4.2	5.5
Chad	..	-0.1	-4.6	6.1	1.9	6.5	5.4	6.4	-1.3	3.2	1.5	6.9	-3.7	2.6
Comoros	-0.4	6.9	15.2	7.6	0.0	1.8	-2.4	7.7	7.0	10.4	12.7	11.3	18.7	7.2
Congo, Democratic Rep. of	0.0	0.0	0.0	0.0	0.0	21.1	13.6	10.5	9.3	-2.6	-1.8	0.0	0.0	4.2
Congo, Republic of	26.2	10.9	9.4	5.6	19.7	0.0	4.9	-8.8	10.6	29.0	30.9	19.8	16.8	10.0
Côte d'Ivoire	..	-6.3	-1.5	13.2	10.7	9.4	12.6	10.4	11.8	7.2	7.7	15.7	5.1	5.4
Djibouti	..	..	..	..	..	..	..	..	..	..	..	..	..	..
Equatorial Guinea	..	-15.6	-16.2	22.5	23.6	10.1	27.7	9.7	18.4	11.2	-15.4	..	-12.3	5.7
Eritrea	..	-92.0	81.9	29.2	11.6	14.9	40.7	12.1	13.3	19.1	22.9	..	..	15.4
Ethiopia	..	5.9	9.7	9.9	14.9	18.0	10.5	12.1	5.2	10.0	13.7	7.9	9.5	10.3
Gabon	47.8	19.7	22.0	30.7	29.0	32.3	34.5	23.9	18.9	11.5	33.7	48.1	23.5	25.9
Gambia, The	13.2	27.7	28.0	22.1	6.5	14.9	13.4	15.4	13.5	12.2	11.1	11.5	18.6	17.7
Ghana	4.5	3.6	12.8	19.1	17.6	26.1	10.3	18.1	9.6	13.3	17.2	5.9	5.8	13.6
Guinea	..	5.7	7.1	8.8	9.6	8.9	11.8	13.0	16.5	15.5	19.8	..	8.7	12.3
Guinea-Bissau	..	..	..	..	..	..	..	..	..	..	..	-8.5	5.7	..
Kenya	10.7	9.7	18.3	16.2	11.8	15.5	10.4	10.8	12.7	10.6	9.6	14.0	14.0	12.7
Lesotho	-11.4	33.1	23.0	29.2	22.5	23.6	26.1	17.2	18.4	18.2	23.1	-36.9	-0.1	23.5
Liberia	..	..	..	..	..	..	..	..	..	..	..	..	..	..
Madagascar	-2.4	3.9	3.6	1.4	0.4	4.9	5.5	7.1	8.7	8.9	13.2	1.7	5.6	5.6
Malawi	6.6	4.5	0.1	15.9	16.8	7.4	0.2	12.6	6.6	7.4	3.6	13.9	10.3	8.8
Mali	1.9	14.3	14.9	19.1	13.7	12.8	13.0	13.7	12.5	11.2	11.3	1.0	7.5	14.0
Mauritania	-12.8	5.7	0.4	13.1	6.8	4.9	8.1	6.5	9.9	31.7	22.2	-15.5	20.4	10.4
Mauritius	14.0	28.3	28.5	26.0	25.6	25.7	26.0	26.7	25.4	25.1	27.2	14.0	25.5	26.5
Mozambique	-9.9	-26.6	-30.9	-22.8	-9.6	-7.7	-4.2	1.4	4.0	20.8	24.0	-10.9	-15.5	-7.3
Namibia	..	23.4	20.3	24.4	27.4	27.9	23.0	28.8	28.3	29.1	28.9	..	23.9	26.0
Niger	13.0	4.5	2.5	-1.9	-2.5	1.7	1.6	1.6	2.8	2.6	2.7	6.1	7.3	1.3
Nigeria	26.1	17.2	13.2	12.8	12.9	29.6	12.0	15.4	13.9	27.6	23.6	19.0	12.8	18.4
Rwanda	13.3	1.4	-0.5	-48.8	-7.1	-7.0	-6.3	-4.0	-1.1	-0.3	-0.3	15.5	8.8	-4.2
São Tomé and Principe	-5.5	-36.5	-39.9	-21.6	-22.2	-23.0	-25.7	-18.1	-19.0	-8.7	-7.5	-4.1	-28.0	-25.4
Senegal	-7.4	5.8	2.3	11.7	10.1	12.2	14.7	15.4	12.9	13.4	14.2	-2.8	-0.6	10.1
Seychelles	..	19.5	19.6	21.0	21.6	38.3	20.9	21.3	12.6	24.1	10.7	..	..	21.0
Sierra Leone	..	-6.0	-0.7	2.5	-2.6	-0.9	-3.3	-0.9	-2.7	-2.7	-9.6	9.7	10.8	-1.6
Somalia	..	..	..	..	..	..	..	..	..	..	..	..	..	..
South Africa	27.3	13.5	15.1	15.6	16.8	15.6	14.4	13.7	14.1	14.5	13.2	20.2	18.1	14.5
Sudan	3.9	..	..	..	..	6.8	-0.2	10.9	3.8	6.0	6.7	6.9	7.6	5.7
Swaziland	25.1	13.7	5.1	6.0	10.0	15.8	15.5	7.1	9.6	9.5	10.8	25.8	30.8	12.7
Tanzania	..	4.2	4.9	6.6	-1.2	4.2	4.0	-2.1	2.0	10.1	9.4	13.8	21.5	4.3
Togo	26.4	1.1	1.5	9.6	14.2	11.4	3.8	8.8	7.3	6.8	4.8	23.7	9.0	8.4
Uganda	-1.0	2.1	3.0	10.4	12.1	10.8	14.2	12.2	13.4	13.5	13.5	-13.4	3.8	8.9
Zambia	9.3	-10.6	0.7	-0.2	4.6	-1.5	3.7	-3.6	-6.6	3.3	5.4	9.5	0.3	-0.2
Zimbabwe	12.4	11.3	20.6	21.7	16.8	18.0	9.1	12.6	14.0	11.2	7.4	13.1	17.0	14.4
NORTH AFRICA	37.1	19.9	16.8	15.2	15.2	16.5	19.4	18.3	20.1	23.3	26.7	31.7	17.6	19.4
Algeria	..	..	..	..	..	..	..	..	..	40.6	38.1	..	..	39.4
Egypt, Arab Republic	..	..	..	..	..	..	..	..	..	23.0	22.7	..	..	22.8
Libya	53.5	..	..	..	..	..	..	..	..	..	..	39.8	..	..
Morocco	..	..	..	..	..	..	..	21.3	22.5	22.8	23.8	..	..	22.6
Tunisia	25.0	21.4	19.3	20.4	19.3	..	..	..	..	24.7	23.8	22.5	18.9	21.6
ALL AFRICA	26.0	14.5	14.5	15.0	15.5	18.0	17.3	16.0	16.9	19.7	19.2	22.4	16.7	16.5

Note: 2001 data are preliminary (see page 2). Since 1994, Nigeria's ratios are distorted because the official exchange rate used by the Government for oil exports and oil value added is significantly over-valued.

2-13. Resource balance

	Percentage of GDP											Annual Average		
	1980	*1992*	*1993*	*1994*	*1995*	*1996*	*1997*	*1998*	*1999*	*2000*	*2001*	*75-84*	*85-89*	*90-MR*
SUB-SAHARAN AFRICA	2.8	-1.2	-1.7	-1.0	-1.8	1.1	-1.3	-4.1	-2.8	1.2	-1.3	-1.8	0.5	-0.9
excluding South Africa	0.4	-5.2	-6.3	-4.3	-4.2	0.9	-3.2	-7.8	-6.5	0.1	-3.3	-3.7	-2.8	-3.6
excl. S.Africa & Nigeria	-6.1	-6.8	-6.8	-5.3	-5.5	-3.7	-5.6	-8.4	-7.0	-2.6	-3.8	-5.2	-3.7	-5.3
Angola	..	-1.9	-1.3	9.5	-1.2	14.0	1.2	-17.1	-5.6	27.7	11.7	..	9.1	4.8
Benin	-21.5	-13.7	-14.2	-9.8	-12.9	-13.7	-12.8	-10.4	-12.7	-13.0	-12.7	-19.4	-14.8	-12.5
Botswana	-13.4	6.6	8.0	10.5	12.9	16.4	14.9	6.3	11.5	22.1	16.2	-13.0	20.1	11.4
Burkina Faso	-22.9	-14.1	-14.1	-13.9	-16.5	-18.1	-17.2	-17.3	-17.4	-18.2	-15.8	-21.8	-19.3	-15.8
Burundi	-14.5	-20.1	-21.0	-18.2	-14.4	-9.6	-4.2	-11.6	-9.7	-14.7	-11.8	-10.2	-12.6	-14.5
Cameroon	0.8	2.2	1.1	2.6	5.0	2.0	2.9	1.7	-0.3	3.9	2.7	-2.0	0.3	2.7
Cape Verde	-75.6	-38.0	-36.0	-40.5	-40.0	-32.2	-30.4	-35.1	-38.4	-38.3	-31.3	-65.2	-35.2	-35.1
Central African Republic	-15.9	-12.6	-8.3	-5.7	-7.3	-3.7	-5.4	-8.2	-3.4	-3.1	-2.8	-12.0	-11.7	-6.9
Chad	-11.9	-13.7	-16.0	-18.2	-12.0	-11.6	-12.5	-13.3	-14.7	-15.5	-41.8	-10.3	-19.0	-16.4
Comoros	-43.2	-22.6	-16.8	-27.2	-24.8	-23.1	-24.9	-22.6	-20.7	-14.5	-13.3	-39.8	-26.7	-20.8
Congo, Democratic Rep. of	0.1	-0.8	2.2	2.7	4.8	-0.3	-2.0	-3.1	-3.8	1.2	1.1	-2.2	-0.4	-0.1
Congo, Republic of	-0.1	2.8	-5.9	-15.7	1.1	8.8	15.5	3.7	13.2	36.7	34.0	-10.2	0.8	8.3
Côte d'Ivoire	-6.2	3.8	1.1	9.8	5.4	8.7	8.3	6.4	8.2	6.7	7.1	0.7	6.6	6.1
Djibouti	..	..	..	..	-16.7	-16.0	-15.1	-16.1	-14.4	-18.2	..	..	..	-16.1
Equatorial Guinea	..	-34.2	-35.7	-49.0	-49.0	-82.8	-22.5	-71.7	10.3	36.5	25.6	-6.3	-28.6	-28.3
Eritrea	..	-35.5	-43.9	-57.7	-64.0	-61.5	-59.4	-68.0	-75.6	-64.0	-54.5	..	..	-58.4
Ethiopia	..	-6.2	-8.6	-9.8	-8.5	-9.9	-9.1	-9.4	-14.9	-15.3	-15.9	-7.4	-7.5	-9.9
Gabon	33.1	12.3	14.2	23.4	23.6	27.6	21.4	1.7	6.8	2.2	19.8	15.2	-3.4	15.2
Gambia, The	-20.9	-12.9	-17.0	-15.3	-24.1	-15.9	-12.7	-15.6	-14.6	-14.3	-17.0	-15.4	-9.5	-15.2
Ghana	-0.7	-11.5	-16.2	-11.5	-8.4	-8.0	-20.6	-12.9	-17.3	-20.4	-18.2	-0.6	-5.3	-13.5
Guinea	..	-6.2	-6.7	-3.3	-3.8	-5.4	-2.2	-3.7	-4.8	-5.2	-1.7	..	0.2	-3.6
Guinea-Bissau	-29.2	-45.2	-23.8	-17.9	-23.5	-21.3	-18.8	-21.5	-18.0	-26.5	-32.9	-27.2	-35.6	-25.4
Kenya	-11.1	0.0	6.0	3.2	-6.2	-3.6	-7.5	-7.8	-5.7	-9.8	-8.5	-4.1	-3.5	-3.9
Lesotho	-89.1	-100.5	-100.0	-91.4	-98.9	-88.4	-78.4	-74.1	-67.3	-59.7	-51.6	-100.6	-105.6	-85.7
Liberia	0.0	..	..	..	..	..	..	..	..	..	..	-0.5	7.2	..
Madagascar	-16.4	-8.3	-9.3	-7.6	-7.6	-5.5	-8.1	-7.8	-7.7	-7.3	-3.2	-8.2	-5.6	-7.7
Malawi	-14.0	-19.2	-16.1	-32.1	-17.3	-8.5	-12.9	-6.0	-15.0	-12.1	-11.9	-9.7	-7.0	-13.9
Mali	-14.4	-17.4	-15.4	-19.9	-15.1	-15.7	-10.6	-9.7	-11.1	-15.3	-12.9	-14.6	-20.0	-14.7
Mauritania	-29.8	-14.5	-15.9	-3.8	-10.4	-12.3	-9.7	-14.0	-10.6	-13.5	-12.7	-32.3	-16.2	-11.7
Mauritius	-10.9	-3.5	-4.7	-7.4	-5.5	-1.5	-2.9	-2.7	-2.2	-2.0	0.9	-7.9	-0.7	-3.7
Mozambique	-16.5	-32.8	-35.1	-33.7	-24.7	-23.7	-19.5	-17.4	-27.6	-27.7	-22.4	-16.2	-20.5	-26.7
Namibia	..	-14.6	-10.5	-9.1	-10.5	-9.7	-12.0	-13.1	-12.7	-11.7	-12.5	..	0.8	-11.9
Niger	-13.5	-1.1	-2.5	-10.3	-7.2	-6.5	-7.6	-8.6	-6.5	-7.5	-8.2	-9.8	-5.8	-6.5
Nigeria	10.2	1.7	-3.1	1.0	2.1	20.7	7.2	-4.5	-4.2	11.2	-0.7	-0.8	2.6	4.3
Rwanda	-11.9	-12.7	-15.3	-58.5	-20.7	-20.2	-17.9	-17.6	-17.1	-16.1	-16.5	-8.0	-10.1	-19.3
São Tomé and Principe	-28.4	-66.8	-66.9	-59.1	-79.5	-69.9	-65.6	-42.8	-49.3	-47.1	-47.9	-21.2	-36.7	-59.3
Senegal	-16.7	-7.4	-8.6	-6.7	-5.7	-5.7	-5.7	-5.7	-7.6	-9.0	-8.0	-12.0	-8.0	-6.8
Seychelles	-11.2	-3.6	-10.3	-4.0	-6.8	-11.3	-10.6	-15.6	-16.4	-4.4	-28.9	-10.2	6.5	-10.0
Sierra Leone	-15.4	-0.9	-0.3	3.5	-7.4	-14.7	-1.9	-7.2	-6.0	-16.1	-20.2	-9.0	4.9	-6.1
Somalia	-55.3	..	..	..	..	..	..	..	..	..	..	-38.5	-22.9	-28.0
South Africa	8.0	4.0	3.7	2.3	0.9	1.4	1.1	1.2	2.7	2.9	2.5	3.0	7.1	2.8
Sudan	-12.6	..	..	..	..	-8.0	-12.1	-15.2	-6.2	2.2	-6.0	-10.2	-5.0	-7.1
Swaziland	-27.6	-25.1	-25.2	-18.0	-18.6	-26.0	-17.3	-19.1	-14.8	-15.3	-12.3	-17.7	-6.1	-17.1
Tanzania	..	-26.9	-29.7	-23.0	-17.9	-13.0	-10.0	-14.7	-12.2	-8.4	-8.7	-8.5	-15.3	-17.7
Togo	-5.3	-9.2	-7.7	-3.7	-5.0	-10.9	-15.8	-15.3	-11.2	-16.8	-17.1	-8.4	-9.6	-11.1
Uganda	-6.6	-15.5	-14.1	-10.4	-9.0	-11.5	-7.4	-12.1	-12.1	-12.9	-13.9	-3.1	-6.8	-12.1
Zambia	-4.0	-11.6	-6.8	-0.8	-3.8	-7.5	-5.2	-12.5	-18.7	-10.4	-10.2	-3.4	0.3	-7.6
Zimbabwe	-3.2	-9.3	-1.7	-1.9	-2.7	0.2	-7.0	-1.8	-0.4	2.2	1.2	-1.5	2.1	-2.0
NORTH AFRICA	8.2	3.3	2.1	0.5	0.9	4.1	4.3	-1.2	1.0	6.6	6.3	0.6	-3.9	2.6
Algeria	4.0	2.4	-1.4	-4.6	-3.7	6.3	8.4	-1.6	3.5	20.4	15.0	-2.7	0.2	4.1
Egypt, Arab Republic	-12.4	-2.8	-3.0	-5.2	-5.0	-5.8	-6.3	-10.1	-8.6	-6.6	-5.0	-14.5	-12.9	-6.6
Libya	34.8	..	..	..	..	..	..	..	..	..	..	20.1	..	..
Morocco	-10.5	-6.7	-6.0	-6.0	-6.7	-3.4	-3.3	-4.1	-3.8	-6.1	-5.3	-13.6	-5.1	-5.3
Tunisia	-5.4	-6.9	-7.5	-3.0	-4.1	-1.6	-2.5	-3.4	-2.2	-3.5	-3.6	-7.0	-3.4	-4.2
ALL AFRICA	3.9	-0.2	-1.0	-1.0	-1.3	1.7	0.1	-3.5	-1.9	2.6	1.0	-1.5	-1.3	-0.2

Note: 2001 data are preliminary (see page 2). Since 1994, Nigeria's ratios are distorted because the official exchange rate used by the Government for oil exports and oil value added is significantly over-valued.

2-14. Exports of goods and nonfactor services, nominal

	Millions of U.S. dollars, current prices											Annual Average		
	1980	1992	1993	1994	1995	1996	1997	1998	1999	2000	2001	75-84	85-89	90-MR
SUB-SAHARAN AFRICA	80,598	78,175	71,823	77,444	91,110	102,249	102,682	91,355	95,366	112,226	105,464	51,717	58,477	90,022
excluding South Africa	52,489	50,425	43,821	47,382	56,458	66,991	66,174	56,974	61,707	75,725	74,188	34,153	36,024	58,173
excl. S.Africa & Nigeria	31,910	36,575	33,799	37,578	44,078	50,002	49,899	46,242	48,911	54,207	54,351	24,849	30,635	44,287
Angola	..	3,976	2,849	3,465	3,843	6,191	5,294	3,614	5,364	8,176	7,006	..	2,613	4,788
Benin	222	241	291	302	405	349	347	399	385	334	360	168	227	331
Botswana	563	1,998	1,959	2,139	2,432	2,601	2,914	2,537	2,743	3,119	2,643	446	1,372	2,439
Burkina Faso	173	202	237	244	306	276	267	362	287	237	250	126	214	280
Burundi	81	95	88	95	129	51	96	71	62	62	45	86	125	83
Cameroon	1,898	2,342	2,032	1,734	2,045	2,048	2,306	2,306	2,241	2,729	2,736	1,615	2,226	2,271
Cape Verde	19	43	48	61	94	112	129	109	114	131	152	22	39	89
Central African Republic	201	165	182	205	229	185	196	178	117	125	117	145	194	175
Chad	175	209	195	189	321	281	286	319	242	233	241	143	173	248
Comoros	11	48	53	37	46	42	38	26	29	31	35	15	29	39
Congo, Democratic Rep. of	2,371	1,369	1,017	1,316	1,607	1,821	1,054	1,848	2,745	3,048	..	1,691	2,105	1,858
Congo, Republic of	1,024	1,257	849	1,035	1,369	1,746	1,756	1,487	1,702	2,586	2,317	782	996	1,570
Côte d'Ivoire	3,561	3,559	2,991	3,291	4,109	4,989	4,855	5,038	5,067	4,214	4,097	2,701	3,301	4,065
Djibouti	..	..	..	..	203	204	209	244	250	247	..	..	..	226
Equatorial Guinea	..	3	3	70	91	201	502	464	818	1,272	974	34	39	375
Eritrea	..	55	121	138	123	191	203	110	66	97	147	..	..	125
Ethiopia	..	251	521	489	786	787	1,011	1,034	916	984	958	560	640	715
Gabon	2,770	2,577	2,136	2,585	2,851	3,489	3,199	2,119	1,964	1,825	2,619	1,877	1,603	2,555
Gambia, The	103	219	213	159	187	185	185	213	199	202	223	77	117	198
Ghana	376	1,105	1,208	1,374	1,583	2,224	2,231	2,532	2,459	2,448	2,770	336	850	1,837
Guinea	..	637	640	763	766	734	771	770	759	735	830	..	660	747
Guinea-Bissau	14	11	21	39	30	28	56	30	56	68	81	12	16	39
Kenya	2,030	2,149	2,244	2,647	2,948	3,035	2,976	2,845	2,686	2,744	2,966	1,533	1,779	2,639
Lesotho	91	151	171	181	199	224	274	242	216	226	270	52	70	197
Liberia	614	..	..	..	..	..	..	..	..	..	..	508	466	..
Madagascar	539	496	516	656	763	819	775	805	909	1,187	1,316	415	406	770
Malawi	307	418	334	350	424	521	569	563	497	451	455	258	293	462
Mali	263	439	424	406	521	525	646	636	640	575	627	175	290	525
Mauritania	261	448	413	431	525	506	430	399	370	378	391	255	455	438
Mauritius	539	1,818	1,942	1,912	2,219	2,584	2,740	2,653	2,716	2,801	2,868	490	1,002	2,298
Mozambique	383	257	262	304	351	346	385	406	403	469	781	275	155	370
Namibia	..	1,481	1,521	1,579	1,734	1,790	1,743	1,528	1,552	1,633	1,663	..	1,269	1,564
Niger	617	393	251	258	323	337	303	369	321	321	325	397	385	325
Nigeria	18,859	13,816	10,062	9,881	12,449	16,995	16,286	10,776	12,832	21,499	19,908	8,898	5,563	13,920
Rwanda	168	113	102	47	67	83	144	111	113	150	159	144	179	115
São Tomé and Principe	10	10	11	12	9	11	12	12	16	16	18	9	11	12
Senegal	803	1,404	1,204	1,272	1,544	1,588	1,488	1,538	1,443	1,335	1,367	775	1,035	1,416
Seychelles	100	243	257	250	271	315	370	400	422	459	482	90	157	327
Sierra Leone	252	153	165	269	162	164	112	95	92	110	128	180	187	148
Somalia	200	..	..	..	..	..	..	..	..	..	..	142	64	90
South Africa	28,267	27,844	28,025	30,090	34,702	35,307	36,549	34,403	33,699	36,572	31,498	17,752	22,450	31,918
Sudan	806	..	..	..	..	462	516	513	791	1,799	1,692	782	838	908
Swaziland	413	737	778	837	1,020	958	1,087	1,080	1,001	889	865	291	420	883
Tanzania	..	573	766	930	1,089	1,142	1,274	1,144	1,190	1,330	1,456	581	395	995
Togo	580	456	301	300	425	488	434	471	455	398	411	401	498	435
Uganda	242	250	227	349	679	724	838	634	735	656	664	563	483	526
Zambia	1,608	1,158	1,099	1,205	1,253	1,024	1,178	865	701	682	985	1,138	946	1,042
Zimbabwe	1,561	1,838	2,016	2,384	2,719	3,090	3,169	2,632	2,538	2,118	1,977	1,211	1,631	2,380
NORTH AFRICA	47,051	51,289	50,307	49,746	57,218	62,364	64,478	58,396	63,127	78,499	79,247	31,418	33,263	59,296
Algeria	14,541	12,154	10,880	9,966	11,325	14,148	14,665	10,829	13,259	22,579	21,701	10,590	10,182	14,114
Egypt, Arab Republic	6,992	12,150	13,071	11,904	13,506	13,650	14,779	13,442	13,500	15,940	17,072	5,294	6,161	13,162
Libya	23,523	..	..	..	..	..	..	..	..	..	..	13,757	..	..
Morocco	3,273	7,134	6,986	7,555	9,045	9,629	9,510	9,970	10,624	10,409	10,405	2,580	4,515	8,734
Tunisia	3,518	6,127	5,909	7,010	8,031	8,249	8,271	8,529	8,852	8,566	8,864	2,441	3,504	7,420
ALL AFRICA	123,386	126,741	119,024	124,694	145,639	161,881	164,054	146,786	154,974	185,758	179,057	80,494	90,674	146,096

Note: 2001 data are preliminary (see page 2).

2-15. Imports of goods and nonfactor services, nominal

	Millions of U.S. dollars, current prices											Annual Average		
	1980	1992	1993	1994	1995	1996	1997	1998	1999	2000	2001	75-84	85-89	90-MR
SUB-SAHARAN AFRICA	73,373	81,676	76,760	80,357	96,660	98,641	107,282	104,600	104,591	108,276	109,635	54,973	57,379	92,902
excluding South Africa	51,690	59,446	53,781	53,553	63,430	65,348	72,467	71,816	74,564	75,519	81,323	39,322	40,499	64,689
excl. S.Africa & Nigeria	39,063	46,116	43,051	43,948	51,599	55,695	58,796	59,601	60,264	58,612	60,967	30,058	35,777	52,261
Angola	..	4,088	2,915	3,079	3,903	5,140	5,203	4,715	5,705	5,725	5,897	..	1,895	4,318
Benin	524	464	591	448	664	652	623	642	688	627	662	373	439	590
Botswana	705	1,724	1,627	1,682	1,817	1,816	2,143	2,229	2,159	1,936	1,801	535	958	1,888
Burkina Faso	564	483	540	488	666	725	660	798	729	658	643	413	596	653
Burundi	214	312	285	263	273	137	136	174	131	162	126	175	267	221
Cameroon	1,847	2,087	1,904	1,532	1,646	1,867	2,041	2,159	2,268	2,383	2,506	1,696	2,209	2,012
Cape Verde	100	192	179	227	290	273	283	298	340	344	336	77	113	255
Central African Republic	327	346	290	253	311	225	250	264	153	154	144	220	327	260
Chad	298	467	429	403	493	467	475	544	473	451	911	240	404	506
Comoros	64	111	99	88	103	95	91	75	75	60	64	60	75	88
Congo, Democratic Rep. of	2,353	1,438	818	1,157	1,339	1,840	1,118	2,041	3,207	2,864	..	1,916	2,141	1,886
Congo, Republic of	1,026	1,176	962	1,313	1,346	1,523	1,397	1,416	1,391	1,404	1,382	872	963	1,323
Côte d'Ivoire	4,190	3,136	2,874	2,538	3,570	3,935	3,879	4,224	4,041	3,505	3,362	2,714	2,742	3,402
Djibouti	..	..	..	..	286	282	285	327	327	347	..	..	..	309
Equatorial Guinea	..	56	57	132	171	416	614	791	729	782	502	49	72	370
Eritrea	..	214	284	409	455	572	589	596	597	499	523	..	..	474
Ethiopia	..	595	1,059	969	1,276	1,382	1,589	1,648	1,877	1,961	1,948	973	1,191	1,320
Gabon	1,354	1,890	1,513	1,603	1,679	1,904	2,037	2,041	1,669	1,718	1,761	1,338	1,717	1,787
Gambia, The	153	263	275	214	279	248	237	278	262	262	293	108	140	256
Ghana	407	1,845	2,172	2,000	2,126	2,776	3,648	3,493	3,794	3,464	3,736	360	1,124	2,688
Guinea	..	841	860	875	906	942	855	903	924	894	879	..	658	870
Guinea-Bissau	46	113	78	81	89	86	107	74	96	125	147	48	75	99
Kenya	2,837	2,152	1,943	2,420	3,512	3,366	3,770	3,739	3,289	3,770	3,939	1,791	2,063	3,072
Lesotho	475	982	989	946	1,121	1,057	1,077	902	829	763	682	364	508	915
Liberia	614	..	..	..	..	..	..	..	..	..	..	514	387	..
Madagascar	1,202	746	830	881	1,002	1,039	1,062	1,095	1,197	1,471	1,462	692	558	1,030
Malawi	480	764	667	730	672	727	894	667	769	657	664	352	392	707
Mali	520	935	836	756	894	936	910	888	925	927	926	364	635	882
Mauritania	473	620	563	470	636	643	536	539	471	510	522	463	591	560
Mauritius	665	1,923	2,099	2,160	2,428	2,647	2,867	2,767	2,808	2,888	2,828	573	1,020	2,422
Mozambique	965	865	958	1,038	922	1,018	1,047	1,081	1,505	1,526	1,588	836	711	1,115
Namibia	..	1,899	1,820	1,875	2,103	2,128	2,179	1,972	1,980	2,033	2,052	..	1,253	1,943
Niger	957	418	291	420	457	466	444	547	452	455	486	569	495	451
Nigeria	12,324	13,248	10,719	9,646	11,858	9,688	13,677	12,236	14,304	16,884	20,190	8,996	4,898	12,434
Rwanda	307	372	404	488	334	362	475	462	443	441	440	237	397	411
São Tomé and Principe	24	41	42	41	46	42	41	30	40	38	40	19	30	41
Senegal	1,302	1,851	1,668	1,515	1,797	1,852	1,737	1,804	1,803	1,729	1,737	1,070	1,340	1,747
Seychelles	117	259	306	270	306	377	433	495	524	485	647	105	141	382
Sierra Leone	421	159	168	234	231	303	128	143	132	212	279	270	139	194
Somalia	534	..	..	..	..	..	..	..	..	..	..	400	296	346
South Africa	21,838	22,585	23,232	26,965	33,385	33,340	34,879	32,855	30,122	32,842	28,647	15,866	17,053	28,396
Sudan	1,763	..	..	..	..	1,119	1,799	2,258	1,434	1,546	2,441	1,606	1,637	1,672
Swaziland	563	988	1,046	1,043	1,274	1,304	1,335	1,339	1,205	1,104	1,019	383	442	1,094
Tanzania	..	1,811	2,031	1,968	2,029	1,986	2,040	2,375	2,242	2,097	2,273	1,058	1,061	2,010
Togo	640	612	396	337	490	647	672	687	615	603	626	471	609	591
Uganda	324	694	682	763	1,199	1,417	1,304	1,426	1,455	1,413	1,454	625	873	1,114
Zambia	1,764	1,527	1,322	1,232	1,383	1,271	1,381	1,268	1,287	1,018	1,358	1,249	941	1,292
Zimbabwe	1,771	2,463	2,130	2,516	2,910	3,074	3,760	2,737	2,561	1,956	1,872	1,342	1,481	2,527
NORTH AFRICA	36,840	46,264	46,963	48,941	55,715	54,331	55,849	60,920	60,884	63,015	64,212	30,264	38,900	54,169
Algeria	12,847	11,458	11,557	11,940	12,855	11,204	10,636	11,592	11,571	11,709	13,177	11,053	14,352	11,997
Egypt, Arab Republic	9,822	13,325	14,488	14,604	16,544	17,562	19,528	21,812	21,144	22,457	21,963	8,159	10,934	17,564
Libya	11,167	..	..	..	..	..	..	..	..	..	..	8,634	..	..
Morocco	5,247	9,043	8,594	9,377	11,243	10,862	10,627	11,425	11,959	12,459	12,220	4,374	5,397	10,372
Tunisia	3,987	7,201	7,007	7,480	8,766	8,553	8,735	9,194	9,317	9,257	9,584	2,950	3,813	8,103
ALL AFRICA	108,359	127,882	123,456	129,032	152,247	153,006	163,403	165,316	165,272	171,083	173,615	84,105	95,828	146,907

Note: 2001 data are preliminary (see page 2).

2-16. Exports of goods and nonfactor services, real

	Millions of U.S. dollars, constant 1995 prices											Average annual percentage growth		
	1980	1992	1993	1994	1995	1996	1997	1998	1999	2000	2001	75-84	85-89	90-MR
SUB-SAHARAN AFRICA	65,362	79,064	79,425	84,656	90,925	99,386	104,311	108,064	109,915	113,355	118,281	1.0	2.8	4.4
excluding South Africa	41,274	50,390	49,331	53,274	56,273	61,528	64,360	67,255	68,592	68,568	72,132	1.3	2.8	4.1
excl. S.Africa & Nigeria	27,692	40,139	39,481	42,718	43,893	47,681	50,361	52,492	55,738	55,926	58,781	2.8	2.9	4.1
Angola	2,296	5,159	3,082	4,522	3,843	4,370	4,811	5,277	5,338	5,129	5,138	..	1.1	6.0
Benin	502	451	446	425	405	398	430	430	482	521	562	4.0	-7.9	3.7
Botswana	752	2,143	2,124	2,269	2,432	2,698	2,943	2,731	2,790	3,269	3,524	14.2	10.7	4.1
Burkina Faso	335	333	398	287	306	290	307	439	388	350	351	4.7	-0.2	0.8
Burundi	51	146	131	101	129	82	159	153	208	274	328	4.7	0.2	9.5
Cameroon	1,337	2,489	2,078	1,976	2,045	2,270	2,590	2,878	3,249	3,087	3,145	14.0	-1.5	2.4
Cape Verde	31	47	57	68	94	113	137	117	121	157	179	11.5	-5.0	12.7
Central African Republic	144	108	126	239	229	211	293	312	241	309	280	-0.4	0.0	9.7
Chad	190	237	253	258	321	255	289	303	255	289	288	-0.3	5.2	0.9
Comoros	11	46	60	57	46	44	45	32	35	42	47	..	10.2	0.2
Congo, Democratic Rep. of	1,788	1,584	1,443	1,335	1,607	1,855	1,445	1,794	2,681	2,583	2,635	4.2	1.0	-1.1
Congo, Republic of	714	1,120	1,139	1,104	1,369	1,450	1,606	1,717	1,623	1,681	1,765	10.1	2.2	4.2
Côte d'Ivoire	3,073	3,787	3,386	4,093	4,109	4,240	4,575	4,612	4,700	4,385	4,332	8.5	0.7	1.8
Djibouti	..	..	..	..	..	..	..	..	..	..	..	..	..	..
Equatorial Guinea	..	2	2	80	91	164	365	449	520	641	723	..	-1.8	49.9
Eritrea	..	99	153	147	123	194	203	121	74	109	169	..	..	-0.6
Ethiopia	..	329	605	708	786	900	1,225	1,106	1,077	1,331	1,310	..	1.6	7.2
Gabon	1,593	2,477	2,787	2,913	2,851	2,969	3,060	2,889	2,698	2,602	2,647	0.7	0.4	1.7
Gambia, The	127	231	219	165	187	184	185	219	210	231	278	7.3	-3.6	1.3
Ghana	961	1,271	1,488	1,542	1,583	2,256	2,345	2,596	2,910	2,844	2,852	-9.4	11.3	10.0
Guinea	..	643	652	673	766	791	818	923	953	981	1,014	..	6.6	4.3
Guinea-Bissau	24	13	19	38	30	28	55	35	70	93	99	-1.8	5.8	16.8
Kenya	1,562	2,456	3,230	3,193	2,948	3,083	2,637	2,501	2,825	3,077	3,287	-0.2	5.6	2.2
Lesotho	86	160	184	193	199	245	290	262	301	281	394	9.1	12.3	9.6
Liberia	..	..	..	..	..	..	..	..	..	..	..	..	..	..
Madagascar	800	636	671	738	763	796	767	732	845	975	1,033	-4.1	3.9	3.7
Malawi	353	407	386	426	424	496	518	632	537	506	525	2.7	-1.7	4.1
Mali	243	444	458	490	521	536	777	758	866	835	792	8.9	2.7	8.4
Mauritania	366	371	323	456	525	522	427	447	469	525	567	5.8	-0.3	1.6
Mauritius	733	1,924	2,020	2,117	2,219	2,411	2,580	2,732	2,865	2,808	2,961	..	15.8	5.3
Mozambique	314	261	284	324	351	430	467	514	586	674	1,079	..	2.7	15.0
Namibia	..	1,566	1,733	1,562	1,734	1,815	1,838	1,821	1,896	1,952	2,047	..	..	4.5
Niger	388	356	326	291	323	382	376	439	394	..	..	-1.3	-1.3	2.7
Nigeria	12,962	10,337	9,940	10,656	12,449	13,913	14,082	14,846	13,004	12,800	13,515	-2.9	2.3	4.0
Rwanda	185	192	158	61	67	95	123	126	149	163	229	6.5	1.8	-2.4
São Tomé and Principe	..	12	11	11	9	8	10	12	16	17	18	..	13.6	3.4
Senegal	956	1,386	1,353	1,378	1,544	1,568	1,589	1,681	1,782	1,968	2,097	0.5	2.8	3.0
Seychelles	..	300	318	339	271	339	373	345	468	537	554	..	21.7	5.1
Sierra Leone	375	384	333	254	162	132	102	15	11	12	14	-11.1	-2.5	-28.8
Somalia	..	..	..	..	..	..	..	..	..	..	..	..	..	..
South Africa	24,198	28,749	30,141	31,447	34,702	37,913	40,004	40,876	41,395	44,802	46,181	0.7	2.8	5.0
Sudan	..	..	..	..	..	..	..	..	..	..	..	..	..	..
Swaziland	485	903	932	960	1,020	1,020	1,114	1,207	1,144	1,021	1,126	2.7	19.8	2.4
Tanzania	..	567	736	821	1,089	1,094	822	903	1,070	1,267	1,493	..	..	9.8
Togo	532	370	359	352	425	504	465	460	454	450	444	4.6	4.2	0.6
Uganda	..	420	401	528	679	863	1,118	952	1,250	1,241	1,318	..	1.2	13.8
Zambia	1,787	1,333	1,379	1,500	1,253	1,336	1,593	1,671	1,754	1,501	1,937	-2.9	-2.9	3.0
Zimbabwe	965	1,789	2,067	2,455	2,719	2,829	2,996	3,593	3,781	3,156	3,043	5.4	5.5	8.1
NORTH AFRICA	28,716	51,984	53,738	54,440	57,218	58,900	62,473	63,425	67,488	72,483	74,830	3.8	6.5	4.2
Algeria	7,239	11,243	11,029	10,654	11,325	12,175	12,942	13,162	13,951	14,984	14,814	1.9	3.0	3.1
Egypt, Arab Republic	6,537	12,228	13,113	12,477	13,506	13,718	14,051	13,547	14,472	15,961	16,993	5.5	7.1	4.0
Libya	..	..	..	..	..	..	..	..	..	..	..	..	..	..
Morocco	3,401	7,846	8,232	8,846	9,045	9,271	9,983	10,576	11,404	11,909	12,074	4.1	8.2	5.3
Tunisia	3,855	6,757	6,985	7,895	8,031	7,975	8,780	9,169	9,602	10,233	10,926	5.6	10.5	5.1
ALL AFRICA	94,293	128,272	130,084	136,356	145,440	156,026	164,288	169,150	174,456	182,254	189,524	1.8	3.9	4.4

Note: 2001 data are preliminary (see page 2).

2-17. Imports of goods and nonfactor services, real

	Millions of U.S. dollars, constant 1995 prices											Average annual percentage growth		
	1980	1992	1993	1994	1995	1996	1997	1998	1999	2000	2001	75-84	85-89	90-MR
SUB-SAHARAN AFRICA	95,410	82,257	82,570	86,515	96,656	102,535	110,056	114,058	116,763	122,910	132,567	1.7	-1.1	4.9
excluding South Africa	73,904	59,883	58,280	58,171	63,449	66,395	72,001	75,603	81,345	84,839	90,968	1.0	-2.6	4.3
excl. S.Africa & Nigeria	43,560	48,259	46,822	47,571	51,622	53,996	57,971	62,092	65,767	66,654	69,235	..	1.9	3.9
Angola	2,359	4,460	2,427	3,438	3,903	3,885	4,042	3,821	4,243	4,490	4,719	..	-3.6	7.3
Benin	965	695	700	479	664	656	689	736	748	803	848	2.8	-6.0	3.7
Botswana	888	1,748	1,700	1,787	1,817	1,974	2,366	2,681	2,768	2,892	3,118	7.2	13.7	4.3
Burkina Faso	547	706	763	545	666	709	702	921	849	742	749	3.2	4.3	1.8
Burundi	190	287	313	294	273	162	152	275	311	436	411	8.4	-4.1	2.8
Cameroon	1,207	1,580	1,593	1,628	1,646	1,891	2,203	2,493	2,566	2,979	3,327	10.5	-3.7	5.3
Cape Verde	160	214	210	252	290	277	301	319	362	413	395	11.9	-3.1	7.6
Central African Republic	319	329	286	305	311	222	292	298	175	198	186	3.0	2.8	-4.0
Chad	379	584	559	460	493	424	480	451	413	446	1,191	-4.0	7.9	-0.5
Comoros	82	97	92	79	103	97	109	96	101	96	102	..	-3.2	1.6
Congo, Democratic Rep. of	1,872	2,021	1,312	980	1,339	1,265	976	1,628	2,595	3,042	3,347	4.3	9.5	-2.5
Congo, Republic of	1,330	1,228	1,548	1,446	1,346	1,564	1,570	1,592	1,575	1,634	1,646	8.0	-11.9	2.2
Côte d'Ivoire	4,160	3,089	3,030	3,077	3,570	3,438	3,720	3,925	3,862	3,808	3,656	3.2	-0.1	2.5
Djibouti	..	..	..	..	..	..	..	..	..	..	..	..	..	..
Equatorial Guinea	..	31	37	151	171	340	447	767	987	1,063	373	..	12.6	32.8
Eritrea	..	353	351	445	455	560	582	612	638	548	583	..	..	6.5
Ethiopia	..	1,088	1,333	1,174	1,276	1,314	1,556	1,710	2,024	2,152	2,113	..	3.0	5.1
Gabon	1,900	1,960	2,048	1,723	1,679	1,918	2,295	2,297	1,920	1,964	2,008	4.0	-9.2	0.3
Gambia, The	342	278	283	223	279	247	237	286	277	300	366	5.3	-1.0	2.3
Ghana	1,994	1,909	2,231	2,022	2,126	2,777	3,824	4,132	4,584	3,791	3,867	-9.8	9.9	9.9
Guinea	..	879	837	858	906	881	883	959	993	1,028	1,069	..	4.9	1.7
Guinea-Bissau	98	130	98	96	89	84	104	77	98	133	125	0.1	-5.9	-0.5
Kenya	2,115	1,912	2,558	2,989	3,512	3,576	3,670	3,472	3,292	3,887	3,842	-3.9	9.4	6.8
Lesotho	592	983	1,047	1,018	1,121	1,207	1,220	1,082	962	947	993	7.2	4.1	1.1
Liberia	..	..	..	..	..	..	..	..	..	..	..	..	..	..
Madagascar	1,889	855	974	973	1,002	1,041	1,122	1,178	1,250	1,524	1,703	-3.0	-5.4	5.5
Malawi	853	904	834	757	672	737	906	732	836	699	732	-2.1	2.2	-0.6
Mali	506	971	895	835	894	963	1,062	1,069	1,060	1,187	1,113	7.0	2.6	2.7
Mauritania	471	553	517	473	636	609	538	612	605	694	728	2.9	-3.4	2.1
Mauritius	935	2,132	2,240	2,389	2,428	2,531	2,796	3,033	3,215	3,256	3,300	..	20.8	5.0
Mozambique	1,253	822	926	1,194	922	968	1,076	1,162	1,684	1,684	1,735	..	1.2	6.1
Namibia	..	1,869	1,850	1,848	2,103	2,264	2,106	2,110	2,273	2,326	2,476	..	..	3.1
Niger	1,151	447	453	465	457	461	452	529	428	..	..	4.9	-3.1	-3.1
Nigeria	27,928	11,631	11,458	10,640	11,858	12,430	14,036	13,575	15,597	18,099	21,519	5.8	-15.1	5.8
Rwanda	175	391	455	514	334	346	480	524	492	436	453	10.4	-0.1	5.1
São Tomé and Principe	..	45	47	43	46	41	43	35	44	43	54	..	5.3	-0.8
Senegal	1,548	1,901	1,816	1,736	1,797	1,851	1,891	2,096	2,188	2,306	2,426	2.3	1.3	2.0
Seychelles	..	249	325	279	306	390	442	574	615	580	594	..	14.2	10.9
Sierra Leone	454	247	239	229	231	354	132	60	38	71	114	-7.8	4.3	-12.2
Somalia	..	..	..	..	..	..	..	..	..	..	..	..	..	..
South Africa	22,394	22,752	24,599	28,557	33,385	36,294	38,248	38,694	35,814	38,453	41,988	-1.4	2.8	6.5
Sudan	..	..	..	..	..	..	..	..	..	..	..	..	..	..
Swaziland	662	1,211	1,252	1,197	1,274	1,388	1,368	1,497	1,377	1,266	1,326	10.1	8.8	3.4
Tanzania	..	1,793	1,999	1,911	2,029	1,866	1,339	1,887	2,051	2,053	2,219	..	..	1.6
Togo	702	635	430	378	490	624	717	770	704	685	723	6.0	5.7	0.4
Uganda	..	716	692	772	1,199	1,355	1,382	1,425	2,105	2,238	2,254	..	7.3	11.7
Zambia	2,287	1,166	1,080	1,217	1,383	1,322	1,385	1,449	1,473	1,177	1,497	-10.7	3.8	1.0
Zimbabwe	959	2,475	2,198	2,610	2,910	2,823	3,534	3,743	3,830	3,004	2,983	3.7	3.1	7.5
NORTH AFRICA	52,209	51,050	51,292	52,529	55,715	53,159	55,918	61,853	63,302	67,201	70,141	4.9	-5.1	2.8
Algeria	18,603	12,731	11,878	12,603	12,855	11,145	11,413	12,246	12,454	13,326	15,617	5.1	-10.1	-0.6
Egypt, Arab Republic	16,885	14,253	15,385	15,675	16,544	16,801	17,123	18,494	18,804	19,270	18,532	4.5	-5.9	2.7
Libya	..	..	..	..	..	..	..	..	..	..	..	..	..	..
Morocco	5,495	10,289	10,004	9,802	11,243	10,687	11,800	14,334	14,804	15,955	16,319	2.7	6.1	6.2
Tunisia	5,316	7,998	8,217	8,504	8,766	8,507	9,252	9,777	10,074	11,043	11,733	8.5	2.0	4.1
ALL AFRICA	147,283	132,980	133,530	138,771	152,247	155,926	166,292	176,003	180,160	190,177	202,918	2.8	-2.7	4.2

Note: 2001 data are preliminary (see page 2).

2-18. GDP growth

	Percent annual change											Average annual percentage growth		
	1980	1992	1993	1994	1995	1996	1997	1998	1999	2000	2001	75-84	85-89	90-MR
SUB-SAHARAN AFRICA	5.9	-1.2	0.8	2.2	3.7	4.9	3.4	2.2	2.5	3.0	2.9	2.2	2.3	2.4
excluding South Africa	1.7	-0.3	0.4	1.3	4.3	5.5	4.1	3.6	2.8	2.7	3.5	1.9	3.3	2.8
excl. S.Africa & Nigeria	1.0	-0.9	0.0	1.5	4.7	5.8	4.4	3.9	3.1	2.5	3.5	2.5	3.0	2.8
Angola	..	-6.9	-24.7	3.5	10.4	11.2	7.9	6.8	3.3	3.0	3.2	..	4.5	1.3
Benin	6.8	4.0	3.5	4.4	4.6	5.5	5.7	4.6	4.7	5.8	5.0	3.8	1.5	4.7
Botswana	12.0	2.9	1.9	3.6	4.4	5.6	6.9	6.0	6.1	8.6	6.3	11.6	12.2	5.2
Burkina Faso	0.8	2.5	4.9	1.4	4.5	7.5	4.8	2.9	5.8	2.2	5.6	3.6	4.4	4.4
Burundi	1.0	0.7	-5.7	-3.9	-7.3	-8.4	0.4	4.8	-1.0	-0.9	3.2	3.8	5.1	-1.9
Cameroon	-2.0	-3.1	-3.2	-2.5	3.3	5.0	5.1	5.0	4.4	4.2	5.3	8.5	-0.1	1.5
Cape Verde	37.7	3.3	7.1	6.9	7.5	4.0	5.4	7.4	8.6	6.8	3.3	13.8	4.5	5.7
Central African Republic	-4.5	-6.4	0.3	4.9	7.2	-4.0	5.3	4.7	3.6	2.3	1.5	0.4	0.7	1.8
Chad	-6.0	8.0	-15.7	10.1	0.8	2.4	4.3	7.3	1.0	0.6	8.9	-1.3	5.4	2.3
Comoros	..	8.5	3.0	-5.3	3.6	-1.3	4.2	1.2	1.9	-1.1	1.9	..	1.3	1.2
Congo, Democratic Rep. of	2.2	-10.5	-13.5	-3.9	0.7	-0.9	-5.6	-1.6	-4.4	-6.0	-4.5	-0.3	1.7	-5.1
Congo, Republic of	17.6	2.6	-1.0	-5.5	5.0	4.3	-0.6	3.7	-3.0	8.2	2.9	9.2	-1.0	1.3
Côte d'Ivoire	-11.0	-0.2	-0.2	2.0	7.0	7.7	5.7	4.8	1.6	-2.3	-0.9	2.2	2.0	2.8
Djibouti	..	-0.2	-3.9	-2.9	-2.3	-3.3	-0.6	0.5	2.2	0.7	..	..	..	-1.4
Equatorial Guinea	..	10.7	6.3	5.1	14.3	29.1	71.2	21.9	41.4	16.9	1.3	..	1.4	20.0
Eritrea	..	..	11.1	23.4	2.5	9.2	8.0	3.1	0.6	-12.1	9.7	..	..	5.3
Ethiopia	..	-5.1	13.4	3.5	6.1	10.6	5.2	-1.2	5.2	5.4	7.7	..	2.9	4.3
Gabon	2.6	-3.3	2.4	3.4	7.0	5.2	5.8	2.1	-6.2	2.0	2.5	-0.2	-1.4	2.7
Gambia, The	6.3	3.4	3.0	0.2	0.9	2.2	4.9	4.9	6.4	5.6	6.0	4.3	3.3	3.3
Ghana	0.5	3.9	4.8	3.4	4.0	4.6	4.2	4.7	4.4	3.7	4.0	-1.1	5.2	4.2
Guinea	..	2.9	4.2	6.3	4.4	4.6	4.8	4.6	3.6	2.3	3.6	..	4.7	4.1
Guinea-Bissau	-16.0	1.1	2.1	3.2	4.4	11.6	6.5	-28.1	7.8	7.5	0.2	2.1	3.1	1.4
Kenya	5.6	-0.8	0.4	2.6	4.4	4.1	2.1	1.6	1.3	-0.2	1.1	4.7	5.9	2.0
Lesotho	7.4	4.8	3.8	3.4	4.5	10.0	8.1	-4.6	2.2	3.3	4.0	6.7	5.6	4.1
Liberia	..	..	..	..	..	..	..	..	..	..	..	..	..	..
Madagascar	0.8	1.2	2.1	-0.1	1.7	2.1	3.7	3.9	4.7	4.8	6.0	-0.2	2.3	2.1
Malawi	0.4	-7.3	9.7	-10.2	16.7	7.3	3.8	3.3	4.0	1.7	-1.5	3.2	1.9	3.6
Mali	-4.3	8.3	-2.1	0.9	6.2	3.2	6.8	3.4	6.1	4.5	-1.1	2.3	0.8	3.5
Mauritania	3.4	1.7	5.5	4.6	4.6	5.5	3.2	3.7	4.1	5.1	4.6	1.6	3.3	4.0
Mauritius	..	5.4	5.9	4.5	4.1	5.2	5.9	6.0	5.3	2.6	7.2	..	7.7	5.2
Mozambique	..	-8.1	8.7	7.5	4.3	7.1	11.1	12.6	7.5	1.6	13.9	..	6.0	6.2
Namibia	..	8.2	7.1	7.3	4.1	3.2	4.2	3.3	3.4	3.3	2.7	..	2.2	4.5
Niger	-2.2	-6.5	1.4	4.0	2.6	3.4	2.8	10.4	-0.6	-1.4	7.6	2.0	4.2	2.2
Nigeria	4.2	2.9	2.2	0.1	2.5	4.3	2.7	1.9	1.1	3.8	3.9	-0.7	5.0	2.7
Rwanda	9.0	5.9	-8.1	-50.2	35.2	12.7	13.8	8.9	7.6	6.0	6.7	6.8	2.9	0.0
São Tomé and Principe	..	0.7	1.1	2.2	2.0	1.5	1.0	2.5	2.5	3.0	3.0	..	1.8	1.8
Senegal	-3.3	2.2	-2.2	2.9	5.2	5.1	5.2	5.7	5.1	5.6	5.7	2.1	3.5	3.6
Seychelles	..	7.2	6.2	-0.8	-0.6	4.7	5.3	3.4	-2.8	-5.4	-8.1	..	..	1.6
Sierra Leone	4.8	-19.0	1.4	-1.9	-8.0	6.1	-17.6	-0.9	-8.1	3.8	5.4	2.5	-0.3	-4.3
Somalia	..	..	..	..	..	..	..	..	..	..	..	..	..	..
South Africa	9.2	-2.1	1.2	3.2	3.1	4.3	2.6	0.8	2.1	3.4	2.2	2.4	1.4	1.9
Sudan	1.5	6.6	4.6	1.0	6.0	5.9	6.3	6.4	6.5	6.1	6.9	2.6	0.9	6.2
Swaziland	12.4	1.0	3.6	3.4	3.8	3.9	3.8	3.2	3.5	2.2	1.6	3.3	10.0	3.3
Tanzania	..	0.6	1.2	1.6	3.6	4.6	3.5	3.7	3.5	5.2	5.7	..	..	3.2
Togo	14.6	-4.0	-15.1	15.0	7.8	8.8	4.3	-2.1	2.4	-1.9	2.7	2.1	3.4	1.8
Uganda	..	3.4	8.3	6.4	11.5	9.1	4.7	5.6	7.5	3.5	4.6	..	3.4	6.8
Zambia	3.0	-1.7	6.8	-8.7	-2.5	6.6	3.3	-1.9	2.2	3.6	4.9	0.2	2.3	0.7
Zimbabwe	14.4	-9.0	1.1	9.2	0.2	10.4	2.7	2.9	-0.7	-4.9	-8.4	3.0	4.2	1.9
NORTH AFRICA	5.0	2.0	0.5	3.9	1.5	6.6	2.6	5.8	4.0	3.5	4.3	6.0	3.0	3.4
Algeria	0.8	1.8	-2.1	-0.9	3.8	4.1	1.1	5.1	3.2	2.4	3.6	5.5	0.8	1.8
Egypt, Arab Republic	10.0	4.4	2.9	3.9	4.7	5.0	5.5	5.6	6.0	5.1	3.3	8.3	4.1	4.5
Libya	..	..	..	..	..	..	..	..	..	..	..	..	..	..
Morocco	3.6	-4.0	-1.0	10.4	-6.6	12.2	-2.2	7.7	0.0	0.9	6.5	4.1	4.7	2.5
Tunisia	7.4	7.8	2.2	3.3	2.3	7.1	5.4	4.8	6.1	4.7	5.4	5.3	2.4	4.8
ALL AFRICA	5.6	-0.1	0.7	2.8	3.0	5.5	3.1	3.4	3.0	3.2	3.4	3.3	2.5	2.7

Note: 2001 data are preliminary (see page 2).

2-19. Gross national income (GNI) per capita

	U.S. dollars, Atlas method											Annual Average		
	1980	1992	1993	1994	1995	1996	1997	1998	1999	2000	2001	75-84	85-89	90-MR
SUB-SAHARAN AFRICA	662	549	531	510	520	536	544	511	491	476	461	540	508	519
excluding South Africa	526	348	317	285	287	304	319	312	302	297	300	424	369	318
excl. S.Africa & Nigeria	445	364	338	302	306	318	331	326	316	307	303	368	387	334
Angola	..	500	330	210	340	400	510	500	410	430	500	..	810	484
Benin	410	370	380	330	350	350	390	380	380	390	380	314	326	371
Botswana	1,190	3,270	3,320	2,950	3,190	3,100	3,260	3,290	3,040	3,070	3,100	980	1,598	3,117
Burkina Faso	260	290	250	210	220	230	240	230	230	220	220	198	242	246
Burundi	220	210	180	160	150	140	140	140	120	110	100	186	246	158
Cameroon	620	910	890	730	660	610	620	610	610	580	580	598	988	722
Cape Verde	..	1,100	1,100	1,140	1,210	1,270	1,300	1,300	1,350	1,350	1,340	..	940	1,203
Central African Republic	340	470	440	360	340	290	310	290	280	280	260	270	390	355
Chad	240	340	260	230	210	210	220	230	210	200	200	221	238	242
Comoros	..	650	640	500	400	440	450	410	400	380	380	327	420	477
Congo, Democratic Rep. of	630	210	180	150	130	120	80	90	80	90	80	483	244	138
Congo, Republic of	880	1,110	890	710	630	540	570	480	510	590	640	832	1,042	723
Côte d'Ivoire	1,140	790	740	660	650	700	760	780	750	680	630	857	792	723
Djibouti	..	..	..	..	880	870	850	830	850	880	890	..	..	864
Equatorial Guinea	..	400	420	370	390	430	860	1,060	820	710	700	..	337	571
Eritrea	..	140	130	160	160	170	180	180	170	150	160	..	..	160
Ethiopia	..	110	120	110	110	110	110	100	100	100	100	135	162	113
Gabon	4,820	5,170	4,570	4,140	3,930	4,130	4,400	3,980	3,300	3,190	3,160	4,344	4,072	4,176
Gambia, The	380	350	350	340	350	350	350	340	340	340	320	295	280	338
Ghana	430	420	410	370	360	370	390	390	390	330	290	355	400	376
Guinea	..	510	540	560	560	570	560	520	500	450	410	..	445	509
Guinea-Bissau	150	240	230	220	230	240	240	160	170	180	160	184	188	213
Kenya	440	330	250	250	260	320	350	350	360	350	350	339	364	325
Lesotho	490	670	700	710	710	710	720	600	580	560	530	430	474	642
Liberia	620	..	..	..	..	..	100	110	120	140	140	522	470	122
Madagascar	450	240	240	240	240	250	250	260	250	250	260	352	270	245
Malawi	190	220	240	170	170	190	220	220	190	170	160	164	166	199
Mali	270	320	300	250	250	240	260	250	260	250	230	201	226	263
Mauritania	460	540	500	480	460	470	450	420	400	390	360	404	494	461
Mauritius	..	2,780	3,050	3,130	3,360	3,570	3,800	3,760	3,710	3,660	3,830	1,127	1,548	3,290
Mozambique	..	140	130	130	140	150	180	200	220	210	210	240	246	171
Namibia	..	2,100	2,100	2,170	2,310	2,310	2,300	2,170	2,110	2,070	1,960	1,800	1,504	2,125
Niger	430	290	240	210	190	200	200	200	190	180	180	316	290	224
Nigeria	780	290	240	220	210	250	270	260	250	260	290	601	292	257
Rwanda	250	310	260	140	200	200	210	230	240	240	220	207	330	245
São Tomé and Principe	..	410	370	350	340	320	290	270	270	290	280	..	495	338
Senegal	530	780	720	590	550	530	530	520	500	500	490	436	558	595
Seychelles	2,080	5,930	6,330	6,440	6,460	6,960	7,390	7,230	7,080	6,730	6,530	1,644	3,352	6,449
Sierra Leone	340	130	150	170	190	210	170	150	130	130	140	286	212	162
Somalia	100	..	..	..	..	..	..	..	..	..	..	124	150	130
South Africa	2,540	3,320	3,460	3,610	3,740	3,770	3,700	3,330	3,190	3,060	2,820	2,131	2,374	3,328
Sudan	470	340	290	260	260	260	280	310	320	310	340	413	624	343
Swaziland	970	1,300	1,290	1,300	1,510	1,590	1,640	1,400	1,420	1,380	1,300	794	824	1,366
Tanzania	..	170	170	160	160	190	210	230	250	270	270	..	..	204
Togo	450	450	360	330	330	340	360	330	320	290	270	334	342	355
Uganda	..	200	190	190	250	290	320	310	300	280	260	180	328	266
Zambia	630	370	380	350	350	360	370	330	320	310	320	562	330	359
Zimbabwe	950	710	640	630	610	680	680	570	470	440	480	854	776	638
NORTH AFRICA	1,304	1,311	1,255	1,300	1,336	1,439	1,486	1,524	1,565	1,630	1,668	1,068	1,382	1,436
Algeria	2,080	1,960	1,780	1,660	1,590	1,550	1,540	1,560	1,540	1,580	1,650	1,772	2,702	1,743
Egypt, Arab Republic	530	790	800	880	990	1,100	1,200	1,270	1,370	1,490	1,530	483	772	1,084
Libya	10,460	..	..	..	..	..	..	..	..	..	..	7,921	6,190	..
Morocco	970	1,100	1,060	1,170	1,120	1,300	1,250	1,250	1,200	1,180	1,190	733	794	1,163
Tunisia	1,360	1,700	1,690	1,740	1,820	2,000	2,080	2,050	2,090	2,100	2,070	1,093	1,244	1,855
ALL AFRICA	773	689	664	654	667	697	710	687	675	672	664	631	669	681

Note: 2001 data are preliminary (see page 2). Gross National Income (GNI) previously called Gross National Product (GNP).

2-20. Total consumption per capita

	Current U.S. dollars											Annual Average		
	1980	1992	1993	1994	1995	1996	1997	1998	1999	2000	2001	75-84	85-89	90-MR
SUB-SAHARAN AFRICA	527	493	449	416	459	452	468	441	431	414	399	426	416	449
excluding South Africa	418	313	273	233	266	273	286	283	281	272	281	335	310	284
excl. S.Africa & Nigeria	368	330	303	249	281	292	300	301	295	287	293	304	334	303
Angola	..	552	448	273	327	330	467	424	281	249	381	..	642	460
Benin	432	323	402	263	341	378	351	366	372	338	345	305	336	353
Botswana	858	1,919	1,873	1,888	1,995	1,833	1,876	1,840	1,896	1,951	1,895	667	945	1,873
Burkina Faso	260	199	212	166	198	220	194	205	210	190	195	193	239	214
Burundi	224	198	167	165	170	140	143	138	108	105	104	179	219	156
Cameroon	605	774	776	498	482	554	530	494	530	475	450	488	792	595
Cape Verde	458	1,146	961	1,071	1,253	1,385	1,366	1,509	1,633	1,527	1,495	349	741	1,289
Central African Republic	375	469	405	247	314	309	272	275	255	236	228	273	409	331
Chad	..	330	249	185	218	225	208	223	214	180	201	200	254	239
Comoros	406	636	586	412	497	473	447	425	433	371	387	343	450	492
Congo, Democratic Rep. of	481	195	210	123	111	97	52	106	201	285	..	413	211	167
Congo, Republic of	658	936	600	593	507	608	522	476	474	451	344	587	817	619
Côte d'Ivoire	989	789	723	442	584	672	615	677	634	547	527	671	711	649
Djibouti	..	..	..	..	929	897	889	852	913	921	..	..	..	900
Equatorial Guinea	..	460	457	242	299	438	672	844	689	764	379	446	452	498
Eritrea	..	325	79	185	197	215	208	241	234	196	195	..	..	208
Ethiopia	..	99	111	84	94	96	98	98	101	99	93	130	148	100
Gabon	2,435	3,680	2,717	2,185	2,423	2,543	2,340	2,415	2,368	2,874	1,707	1,947	2,854	2,718
Gambia, The	354	313	336	326	356	322	330	331	331	315	303	272	267	322
Ghana	393	393	339	281	330	309	365	364	394	249	253	326	358	336
Guinea	..	479	466	470	489	504	462	434	390	343	313	..	348	431
Guinea-Bissau	146	219	214	215	238	241	231	197	193	199	181	185	184	219
Kenya	378	280	150	221	301	294	349	369	326	334	355	278	299	297
Lesotho	482	635	665	622	691	641	655	572	563	531	444	377	423	598
Liberia	433	..	..	..	..	..	..	..	..	..	..	408	411	..
Madagascar	462	241	263	223	230	273	239	238	229	230	253	341	243	241
Malawi	179	204	234	134	156	250	264	163	180	165	168	140	147	194
Mali	268	305	273	174	236	247	221	223	218	197	190	196	225	234
Mauritania	473	541	418	386	428	446	418	382	345	305	323	440	417	415
Mauritius	1,020	2,052	2,255	2,316	2,609	2,798	2,893	2,686	2,710	2,844	2,800	910	1,188	2,475
Mozambique	322	148	162	161	149	178	202	213	209	190	161	300	259	180
Namibia	..	1,803	1,760	1,826	1,963	1,872	2,015	1,751	1,739	1,710	1,523	..	1,317	1,790
Niger	382	269	182	178	206	204	183	200	185	161	169	279	261	212
Nigeria	619	245	162	174	206	201	232	214	227	214	232	464	223	209
Rwanda	216	269	258	180	217	217	244	252	232	210	192	196	312	240
São Tomé and Principe	588	479	501	452	384	377	369	308	357	325	305	490	613	430
Senegal	566	729	653	397	480	476	438	448	453	409	416	428	579	525
Seychelles	1,667	4,986	5,267	5,137	5,164	4,462	6,074	5,942	6,695	5,414	6,338	1,076	2,480	5,332
Sierra Leone	337	151	166	200	211	213	188	142	143	137	164	319	183	170
Somalia	105	..	..	..	..	..	..	..	..	..	..	128	143	144
South Africa	2,004	2,986	2,866	2,913	3,125	2,943	3,034	2,695	2,584	2,460	2,161	1,655	1,873	2,764
Sudan	386	..	..	..	..	248	335	380	303	290	349	391	631	318
Swaziland	872	1,219	1,283	1,268	1,496	1,349	1,447	1,327	1,297	1,280	1,100	671	655	1,256
Tanzania	..	169	159	154	174	205	233	263	254	245	249	246	178	204
Togo	347	437	333	229	298	336	361	314	299	259	261	253	335	328
Uganda	..	163	176	205	277	291	278	298	256	247	234	189	333	240
Zambia	546	384	353	355	339	336	375	322	321	294	319	455	334	345
Zimbabwe	807	557	470	479	515	594	628	399	374	486	643	711	603	545
NORTH AFRICA	842	986	1,040	1,059	1,132	1,224	1,204	1,274	1,269	1,269	1,272	707	1,074	1,146
Algeria	1,291	1,239	1,342	1,136	1,070	1,125	1,117	1,170	1,091	979	1,087	1,125	1,998	1,190
Egypt, Arab Republic	476	647	732	806	908	1,018	1,058	1,135	1,180	1,277	1,232	417	641	940
Libya	5,040	..	..	..	..	..	..	..	..	..	..	4,321	..	..
Morocco	838	950	879	991	1,074	1,143	1,011	1,056	1,004	950	947	610	675	985
Tunisia	1,041	1,326	1,321	1,392	1,593	1,648	1,559	1,625	1,672	1,550	1,563	820	970	1,460
ALL AFRICA	589	585	557	532	580	589	599	586	576	560	548	481	538	573

Note: 2001 data are preliminary (see page 2).

Figure 2-1. Gross domestic product, 2001*

* Or most recent year available.

** Sorted by GDP level.

Figure 2-2. GDP and export growth rates, average 2000-2001*

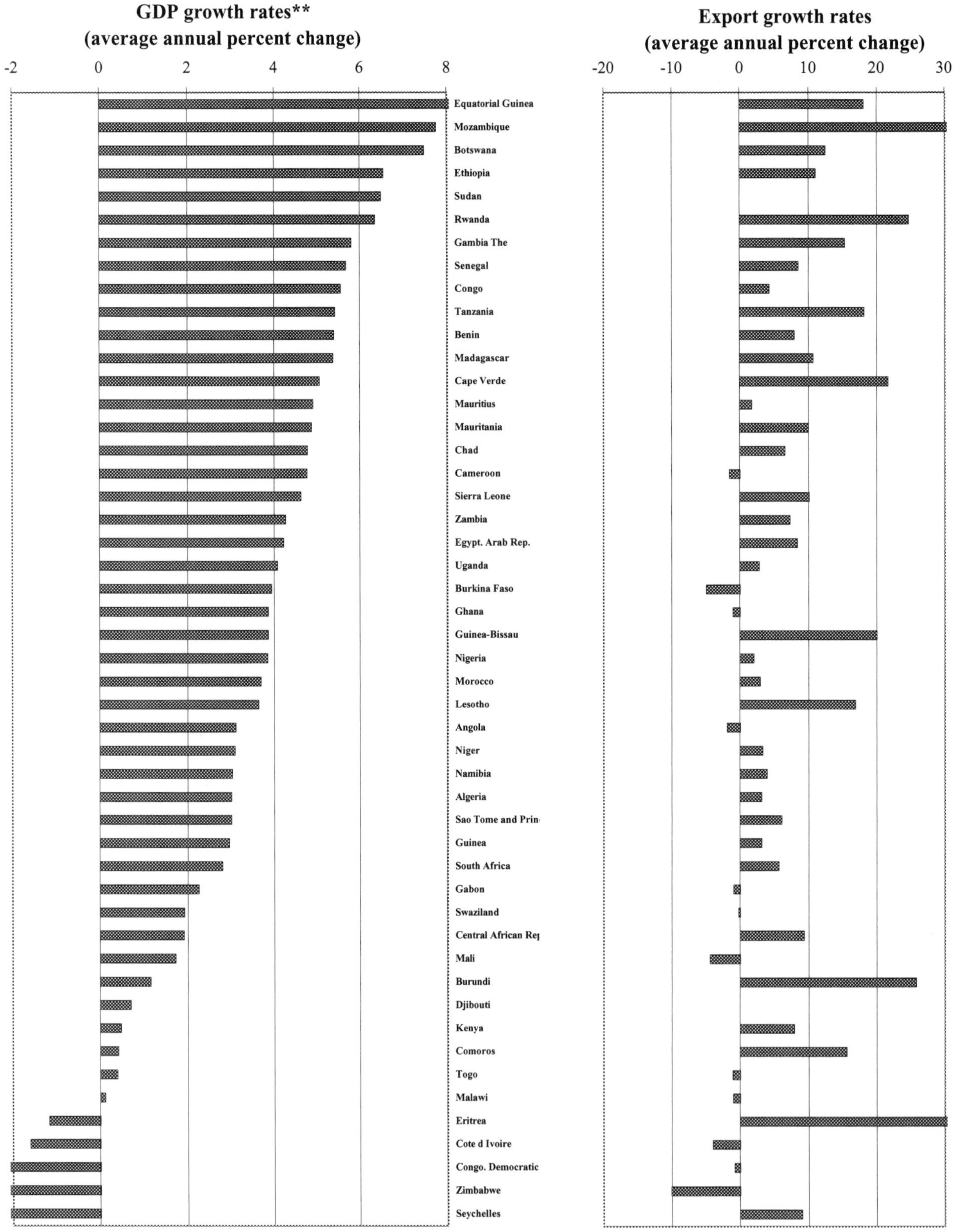

* Or most recent year available.

** Sorted by GDP.

Figure 2-3. Composition of GDP, 2001*

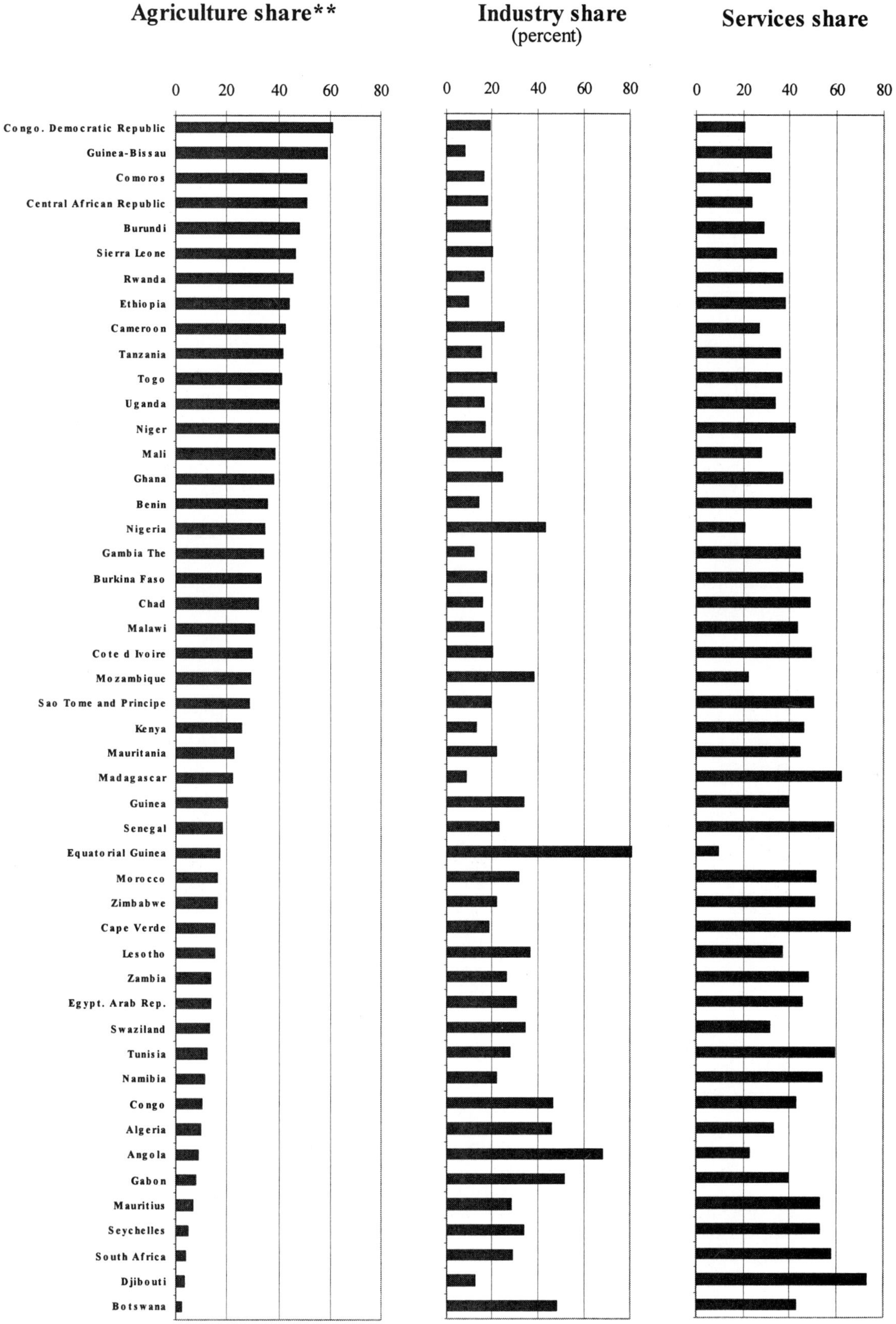

* Or most recent year available.

** Sorted by agriculture share.

Technical notes

Tables

Table 2-1. Gross domestic product, real. Gross domestic product (GDP) measures the total output of goods and services for final use produced by residents and nonresidents, regardless of the allocation to domestic and foreign claims (World Bank country desks). It is calculated without making deductions for depreciation of "manmade" assets or depletion and degradation of natural resources. In this table, GDP figures are shown at market prices (also known as purchaser values) and have been converted to U.S. dollars using constant (1995) exchange rates. For a few countries where the official exchange rate does not reflect effectively the rate applied to actual foreign exchange transactions, an alternative currency conversion factor has been used (Table 3-6). The sum of the components of GDP by industrial origin (presented in this volume in the form of value added) will not normally equal total GDP for several reasons. First, components of GDP by expenditure are individually rescaled and summed to provide a partially rebased series for total GDP. Second, total GDP is shown at purchaser value, while value added components are conventionally reported at producer prices. As explained above, the former excludes net indirect taxes, while the latter includes indirect taxes. Third, certain items, such as imputed bank charges, are added in total GDP.

Table 2-2. Value added in agriculture. Value added in agriculture is shown at factor cost (World Bank country desks). It comprises the gross output of forestry, hunting, and fishing less the value of their intermediate inputs. However, for Botswana, Cameroon, Chad, Congo, Gabon, Guinea, Madagascar, Mali, Morocco, Niger, Rwanda, Senegal, Togo, Zaire, and Zambia it is shown at market prices, that is, including intermediate inputs.

Table 2-3. Value added in industry. Value added in industry is shown at factor cost (World Bank country desks). It comprises the gross output of mining, manufacturing, construction, electricity, water, and gas, less the value of their intermediate inputs. However, for Botswana, Cameroon, Chad, Congo, Gabon, Guinea, Madagascar, Mali, Morocco, Niger, Rwanda, Senegal, Togo, Zaire, and Zambia it is shown at market prices, that is, including intermediate inputs.

Table 2-4. Value added in services. Also shown at factor cost, this table consists of the gross output of all other branches of economic activity, including government, less the value of their intermediate inputs (World Bank country desks). However, for Botswana, Cameroon, Chad, Congo, Gabon, Guinea, Madagascar, Mali, Morocco, Niger, Rwanda, Senegal, Togo, Zaire, and Zambia it is shown at market prices, that is, including intermediate inputs. Other items, such as imputed bank service charges (which are difficult to assess in the same fashion for all countries) and any corrections for statistical discrepancies, are not included.

Table 2-5. Gross domestic product, nominal. This table, presented at market prices, is obtained by converting national currency GDP series in current prices (World Bank country desks) to U.S. dollars at official annual exchange rates (Table 3-4; see also the note for Table 2-1). GDP growth rates are presented in real terms.

Table 2-6. Total consumption. Total consumption is the sum of private consumption (World Bank country desks) and general government consumption (Table 2-7). Private consumption, not separately shown here, is the value of all goods and services purchased or received as income in kind by households and nonprofit institutions. It excludes purchases of dwellings, but includes imputed rent for owner-occupied dwellings. In practice, it includes any statistical discrepancy in the use of resources.

Table 2-7. General government consumption. This indicator includes all current expenditure for purchases of goods and services by all levels of government, including capital expenditure on national defense and security (World Bank country desks). Other capital expenditure by government is included in investment.

Tables 2-8, 2-9, and 2-10. Gross domestic, public, and private investment. Gross domestic investment (GDI) consists of gross domestic fixed capital formation plus net changes in the level of inventories (World Bank country desks). GDI comprises outlays by the public sector (Table 2-9) and the private sector (Table 2-10). Examples include improvements in land, dwellings, machinery, and other equipment. For some countries the sum of gross private investment and gross public investment does not add up to gross domestic investment due to statistical discrepancies.

Table 2-11. Gross domestic savings. Gross domestic savings (GDS) is calculated by deducting total consumption (Table 2-6) from gross domestic product in current prices (Table 2-5).

Table 2-12. Gross national savings. Gross national savings (GNS) is the sum of gross domestic savings (Table 2-11), net factor income from abroad (World Bank country desks) and net private transfers from abroad (Table 5-5). The estimate here also includes net public transfers from abroad (Table 5-6).

Table 2-13. Resource balance. The table indicates the difference between exports f.o.b. (Table 2-14) and imports c.i.f. (Table 2-15) of goods and nonfactor services (or the difference between GDS and GDI). The resource balance is shown as a share of GDP in U.S. dollars at current prices (Table 2-5).

Tables 2-14 and 2-15. Exports and imports of goods and nonfactor services, nominal. Data for exports and imports of goods and nonfactor services are from the World Bank country desks and refer to all goods and nonfactor services (GNFS) provided to, or by, the rest of the world, including merchandise, freight, insurance, travel, and other nonfactor services. The value of factor services, such as investment income, interest, and labor income, is not included. These series are generally estimated on the basis of foreign trade statistics from customs declarations. They are not fully comparable with the series from the balance of payments, which are based on changes in ownership between residents of a country and the rest of the world. Exports, as well as imports of GNFS, are shown in current U.S. dollars.

Tables 2-16 and 2-17. Exports and imports of goods and nonfactor services, real. These are defined as in Tables 2-14 and 2-15, but expressed in constant 1995 U.S. dollars.

Table 2-18. GDP growth. This table (World Bank country desks) provides average annual growth rates calculated from GDP at constant 1995 prices (Table 2-1).

Table 2-19. GNI per capita. Figures presented here (World Bank country desks) are calculated using the *World Bank Atlas* method, as described in the technical notes for Table 1-1; they are similar in concept to GNI per capita in current prices, except that the use of three-year averages of exchange rates smoothes out sharp fluctuations from year to year.

Table 2-20. Total consumption per capita. This table is obtained by dividing total consumption at current U.S. dollars (Table 2-6) by the corresponding midyear population (Table 1-2).

Figures

The following indicators have been used to derive the figures in this chapter.

Figure 2-1. Gross domestic product (Table 2-5); GDP per capita (Tables 1-2 and 2-5).
Figure 2-2. GDP growth (Table 2-1); export growth (Table 2-16).
Figure 2-3. Value added in agriculture (Table 2-2); value added in industry (Table 2-3); value added in services (Table 2-4); gross domestic product (Table 2-1).

Methodology used for regional aggregations and period averages in chapter 2

	Aggregations [a]			*Period averages* [b]	
Table	*(3)*	*(4)*	*(5)*	*(1)*	*(2)*
2-1	x				x
2-2	x				x
2-3	x				x
2-4	x				x
2-5	x			x	
2-6		x		x	
2-7		x		x	
2-8		x		x	
2-9		x		x	
2-10		x		x	
2-11		x		x	
2-12		x		x	
2-13			x	x	
2-14	x			x	
2-15	x			x	
2-16	x				x
2-17	x				x
2-18	x				x
2-19		x		x	
2-20		x		x	

Note : Regional aggregations are shown in the rows for Sub-Saharan Africa, North Africa, and All Africa. Period averages are shown in the last three columns. This table shows only the methodologies used in this chapter.

a. Regional aggregations: (1) simple total; (2) simple total of the first indicator divided by the simple total of the second indicator (same country coverage); (3) simple total of the gap-filled indicator; (4) simple total of the gap-filled main indicator divided by the simple total of the gap-filled secondary indicator; (5) simple total of the first gap-filled main indicator less the simple total of the second gap-filled main indicator, all divided by the simple total of the secondary indicator; (6) weighted total (by population); (7) median; (8) no aggregation; (9) simple arithmetic mean.

b. Period averages: (1) arithmetic mean (using the same series as shown in the table i.e., ratio if the rest of the table is shown as ratio, level if the rest of the table is shown as level, growth rate if the rest is shown as growth rate); (2) least-squares growth rate (using main indicator); (3) least-squares growth rate (using main indicator in constant terms, with the rest of the table in current terms).

3

Prices and Exchange Rates

Information on prices and exchange rates are important in monitoring national economic performance. This chapter provides three sets of price deflators and six exchange rate indicators. The GDP deflator for national currency series shows changes in domestic prices only. The US dollar series GDP deflator includes the effects of both domestic price changes, as reflected in the national currency series GDP implicit deflator, and changes in the exchange rate between national currencies and U.S. dollars. The consumer price index measures the price changes of a selected bundle of consumer goods, which differs among countries.

The US dollar exchange rate (units of national currency per US dollar) is reported because of extensive use of U.S. dollars to denominate international transactions; U.S. dollars are also widely used for statistical comparisons across countries. The SDR exchange rate index (based on SDRs per unit of national currency) is a broader measure of the changes in the international value of domestic currencies because it is based on five major currencies. For Sub-Saharan Africa, it may be more representative of movements in non-dual exchange rates than that expressed in U.S. dollars alone because a large share of the region's foreign trade and debt is not denominated in U.S. dollars. A decrease in the index shows that the currency has depreciated, which indicates that foreign goods have become relatively more expensive than domestic goods. We have included information on the parallel market exchange rate and the ratio of the parallel to the official exchange rates to provide a measure of the premium on the official rate. It is tempting to view the divergence between the official and parallel rates as a measure of the disequilibrium in the official exchange rate. However, this is not necessarily true. Conversion factors are sometimes used in place of official exchange rates when the latter are considered to be especially unrepresentative of rates effectively applied to international transactions.

3-1. GDP deflator (local currency series)

	Index 1995=100											Annual Average		
	1980	*1992*	*1993*	*1994*	*1995*	*1996*	*1997*	*1998*	*1999*	*2000*	*2001*	*75-84*	*85-89*	*90-MR*
SUB-SAHARAN AFRICA	21.3	66.8	71.4	90.7	100.0	110.8	119.2	124.4	132.3	146.1	156.4	21.8	46.5	103.7
excluding South Africa	23.1	65.8	71.4	90.7	100.0	110.9	120.5	123.7	131.6	149.9	159.7	24.1	47.7	104.2
excl. S.Africa & Nigeria	24.8	66.8	71.4	90.9	100.0	110.8	119.2	122.8	129.7	143.2	156.4	25.7	49.3	103.3
Angola	0.0	0.0	0.2	5.0	100.0	5,499.5	10,686.7	14,460.8	93,904.3	477,054.8	1,086,173.3	0.0	0.0	140,657.1
Benin	47.5	64.2	64.9	86.7	100.0	106.7	112.5	117.7	119.9	123.8	127.7	45.9	59.6	95.7
Botswana	21.3	72.9	82.4	91.9	100.0	114.3	126.9	131.7	139.5	149.9	156.4	19.2	46.4	108.3
Burkina Faso	57.5	80.7	80.9	93.4	100.0	108.1	108.7	117.8	116.7	120.5	126.3	56.4	81.3	101.8
Burundi	45.5	75.9	81.3	86.7	100.0	119.0	146.8	163.2	168.8	206.9	234.6	38.2	58.5	127.0
Cameroon	43.0	75.4	77.0	85.4	100.0	105.4	108.2	109.5	110.7	111.9	115.3	42.9	74.0	95.7
Cape Verde	32.6	87.4	89.1	95.9	100.0	105.8	114.1	119.3	125.3	125.6	130.7	30.1	67.1	104.9
Central African Republic	35.0	76.5	73.9	90.7	100.0	101.8	103.2	104.2	105.4	108.0	111.2	35.1	71.6	93.8
Chad	55.5	64.9	64.1	91.9	100.0	111.7	114.8	121.4	115.9	119.8	129.0	54.4	67.6	98.4
Comoros	41.6	86.6	88.9	92.3	100.0	103.2	104.0	105.7	111.8	119.9	130.8	52.2	73.3	101.8
Congo, Democratic Rep. of	0.0	0.0	0.1	17.7	100.0	737.3	1,160.7	2,714.6	13,989.9	102,145.0	497,058.6	0.0	0.0	51,493.7
Congo, Republic of	56.4	72.2	71.4	97.7	100.0	118.0	123.8	101.3	131.6	192.4	164.4	57.2	74.5	110.0
Côte d'Ivoire	50.3	64.4	64.4	91.3	100.0	115.6	120.5	126.7	127.9	127.7	130.4	45.9	69.2	99.8
Djibouti	..	86.1	89.9	95.7	100.0	102.6	105.1	106.9	109.1	111.7	..	..	70.5	97.0
Equatorial Guinea	..	63.7	63.2	97.5	100.0	125.4	160.5	121.9	172.1	261.8	366.1	..	64.5	138.1
Eritrea	..	82.9	82.5	91.1	100.0	109.0	113.3	123.7	133.8	159.7	181.6	..	..	117.8
Ethiopia	..	76.4	86.4	88.7	100.0	101.2	105.2	115.1	118.1	120.1	111.7	41.8	56.4	95.9
Gabon	50.8	67.8	68.5	100.6	100.0	112.8	115.1	97.0	101.7	130.6	115.3	46.6	64.2	96.1
Gambia, The	18.0	88.2	92.7	96.2	100.0	102.9	106.9	108.1	112.8	117.0	125.4	17.6	52.1	100.7
Ghana	0.8	40.8	53.7	69.8	100.0	139.8	167.0	195.5	222.8	283.5	381.6	1.6	14.4	143.5
Guinea	..	93.7	95.0	95.7	100.0	101.4	103.2	105.7	110.4	120.2	126.3	..	37.7	98.9
Guinea-Bissau	0.2	37.6	56.1	69.1	100.0	139.3	186.8	201.0	212.4	219.4	208.3	0.3	4.2	122.2
Kenya	18.7	59.6	66.5	89.9	100.0	109.1	126.0	137.4	145.4	156.6	174.2	19.0	35.9	105.1
Lesotho	18.9	78.2	85.4	91.8	100.0	108.8	117.3	128.2	142.0	154.1	162.9	18.1	41.6	107.8
Liberia	..	..	..	..	..	..	..	..	..	..	..	..	..	..
Madagascar	6.6	43.4	48.6	68.9	100.0	117.8	126.4	137.1	150.4	161.3	175.9	7.7	22.6	100.1
Malawi	6.6	34.1	43.7	55.2	100.0	158.9	171.3	214.8	305.3	382.4	482.1	6.9	16.9	167.1
Mali	37.6	64.3	66.0	84.4	100.0	105.4	106.5	109.2	106.3	105.1	110.5	37.1	59.6	90.2
Mauritania	33.3	86.3	90.0	95.7	100.0	104.7	110.3	120.7	123.2	136.5	143.9	33.3	60.4	105.1
Mauritius	28.0	81.4	87.9	96.1	100.0	105.3	112.8	119.1	125.1	132.8	136.3	33.9	52.4	103.7
Mozambique	0.6	27.3	41.3	65.8	100.0	143.6	157.4	164.6	169.5	189.3	210.7	0.8	4.7	108.4
Namibia	20.3	77.0	81.8	94.6	100.0	114.5	122.6	133.1	141.8	157.8	172.3	24.2	47.0	112.1
Niger	57.9	71.6	71.5	94.9	100.0	104.7	108.0	111.2	113.4	118.6	123.3	55.9	77.7	96.9
Nigeria	3.2	32.9	50.2	64.1	100.0	136.9	138.8	131.1	147.2	184.5	195.6	3.2	8.4	101.2
Rwanda	24.8	49.5	56.4	66.1	100.0	110.9	128.2	131.1	126.5	130.6	130.8	25.0	33.9	93.1
São Tomé and Principe	..	23.8	33.0	57.3	100.0	150.8	302.0	413.9	480.1	517.4	562.1	..	6.7	222.8
Senegal	41.4	75.7	74.6	95.3	100.0	101.3	103.7	105.0	106.6	107.4	110.5	40.8	71.0	94.2
Seychelles	..	96.1	99.1	100.2	100.0	107.6	110.7	115.2	124.2	134.1	143.2	..	..	109.7
Sierra Leone	0.1	44.3	56.0	76.3	100.0	116.3	135.8	172.6	215.8	229.1	243.0	0.2	2.8	118.7
Somalia	..	..	..	..	..	..	..	..	..	..	..	..	..	..
South Africa	13.6	73.2	82.8	90.7	100.0	108.1	116.9	125.1	133.0	142.2	152.8	13.1	36.3	103.6
Sudan	0.2	16.7	32.2	60.0	100.0	233.7	356.3	460.1	487.8	511.3	535.9	0.2	1.7	234.0
Swaziland	18.3	64.2	75.2	85.3	100.0	110.6	123.9	135.2	147.5	165.9	179.9	18.7	39.3	108.1
Tanzania	..	48.3	60.1	78.8	100.0	119.3	143.9	164.3	183.4	197.0	209.9	..	22.5	114.5
Togo	41.0	72.2	66.3	90.0	100.0	105.4	118.0	115.1	117.7	119.2	123.2	42.2	63.5	97.1
Uganda	..	65.8	85.6	91.4	100.0	104.6	108.2	116.0	116.7	123.6	132.7	0.2	8.5	93.8
Zambia	0.1	18.1	44.0	72.9	100.0	123.6	155.7	186.0	225.8	293.6	365.0	0.1	0.8	132.9
Zimbabwe	11.4	61.7	75.4	91.3	100.0	125.8	146.2	188.9	294.9	471.6	802.3	11.8	24.9	203.6
NORTH AFRICA	26.0	81.7	87.5	91.2	100.0	105.9	111.1	114.9	118.1	123.0	126.4	25.4	49.3	99.9
Algeria	10.9	53.0	60.3	77.8	100.0	123.8	131.9	126.3	139.4	172.4	181.6	9.9	17.7	103.2
Egypt, Arab Republic	16.3	76.3	83.9	89.8	100.0	107.1	113.4	117.4	119.6	126.5	130.5	14.4	34.4	98.7
Libya	..	..	..	..	..	..	..	..	..	..	..	..	..	..
Morocco	40.2	88.0	91.2	92.6	100.0	101.0	103.0	103.4	103.9	105.5	108.1	38.8	68.2	96.7
Tunisia	35.7	87.0	91.1	95.1	100.0	104.7	108.8	112.4	116.6	119.4	122.4	36.5	64.3	101.4
ALL AFRICA	21.3	69.7	72.7	90.7	100.0	109.9	117.6	122.8	129.7	139.3	152.8	21.8	46.5	102.6

Note: 2001 data are preliminary (see page 2). Group data are medians of individual country values for each year.

3-2. GDP deflator (U.S. dollar series)

	Index 1995=100											Annual Average		
	1980	*1992*	*1993*	*1994*	*1995*	*1996*	*1997*	*1998*	*1999*	*2000*	*2001*	*75-84*	*85-89*	*90-MR*
SUB-SAHARAN AFRICA	104.2	102.5	96.2	91.7	100.0	100.3	99.7	92.2	91.2	90.4	85.2	82.4	86.3	95.8
excluding South Africa	147.2	111.1	100.3	90.7	100.0	108.6	106.6	101.2	102.0	104.4	103.7	117.6	115.3	105.5
excl. S.Africa & Nigeria	115.9	108.8	105.1	91.7	100.0	106.1	103.8	100.5	100.0	99.8	99.9	99.4	115.1	104.8
Angola	..	98.3	118.0	89.3	100.0	135.0	123.2	113.8	90.7	92.7	96.2	..	131.1	118.4
Benin	112.1	91.4	114.5	77.9	100.0	104.1	95.5	98.4	98.1	99.5	103.8	83.7	88.8	100.5
Botswana	71.7	92.6	99.6	97.1	100.0	103.6	94.0	94.4	100.3	103.1	105.9	57.9	68.3	98.0
Burkina Faso	118.3	88.5	91.6	81.9	100.0	101.7	91.1	93.0	99.1	101.3	104.6	89.5	105.4	101.5
Burundi	127.7	92.2	87.8	85.8	100.0	98.5	104.3	99.0	105.6	107.0	108.4	104.0	113.4	99.2
Cameroon	106.7	139.5	150.4	101.9	100.0	108.9	103.7	94.6	99.2	103.2	105.2	83.4	110.7	115.1
Cape Verde	..	96.6	85.7	86.6	100.0	97.2	94.4	96.5	99.1	101.8	104.2	..	77.4	94.8
Central African Republic	82.6	144.2	130.2	81.5	100.0	99.5	88.7	89.2	91.1	93.3	95.6	62.5	106.6	107.1
Chad	131.2	126.8	117.2	82.6	100.0	109.8	100.9	103.3	106.2	110.0	103.2	100.2	112.0	112.4
Comoros	73.9	116.3	111.8	83.2	100.0	99.8	90.6	91.0	92.7	96.0	98.4	61.8	82.7	100.8
Congo, Democratic Rep. of	..	108.4	137.0	113.7	100.0	93.4	103.0	114.2	117.7	121.1	..	85.5	83.5	110.7
Congo, Republic of	131.8	134.9	89.1	87.0	100.0	112.3	104.4	85.4	93.3	95.4	94.4	101.1	108.2	105.0
Côte d'Ivoire	118.8	121.5	113.6	82.1	100.0	100.2	90.6	92.3	99.6	102.4	104.8	82.9	102.8	103.2
Djibouti	..	85.7	89.5	95.3	100.0	104.1	106.8	..	..	..	..	..	68.5	94.9
Equatorial Guinea	..	120.0	111.4	87.6	100.0	122.3	130.3	..	128.3	133.9	176.4	..	96.1	121.4
Eritrea	..	83.9	80.5	91.5	100.0	103.0	99.1	95.5	..	..	..	..	..	93.4
Ethiopia	..	120.1	118.9	89.9	100.0	93.8	94.0	97.4	90.0	82.6	79.9	118.4	159.2	100.7
Gabon	120.0	127.8	97.7	90.4	100.0	112.3	96.2	101.0	..	..	..	82.9	94.7	109.4
Gambia, The	99.9	94.7	96.9	95.9	100.0	100.4	99.4	98.8	99.0	103.7	106.5	75.8	77.4	98.0
Ghana	105.0	111.9	99.2	87.6	100.0	102.5	97.8	101.9	103.9	104.1	107.0	93.9	112.5	104.0
Guinea	..	105.5	100.9	97.7	100.0	103.1	97.4	85.9	83.9	81.2	82.3	..	84.0	94.7
Guinea-Bissau	82.8	98.0	100.5	96.9	100.0	101.8	95.5	101.7	105.5	104.3	105.8	85.3	87.1	102.9
Kenya	129.5	95.1	59.0	82.5	100.0	97.9	109.9	118.3	113.6	115.1	118.1	104.1	105.7	100.5
Lesotho	88.0	99.4	101.3	97.2	100.0	89.6	91.7	79.3	81.4	83.8	89.5	71.1	71.6	91.8
Liberia	..	..	..	..	..	..	..	..	..	..	..	..	..	..
Madagascar	132.6	98.5	108.4	95.8	100.0	123.8	106.1	107.9	113.7	115.9	117.8	108.3	93.2	106.1
Malawi	119.5	138.7	145.5	91.9	100.0	140.0	147.9	96.1	98.6	99.6	104.1	103.2	107.4	121.7
Mali	90.0	122.6	117.7	79.9	100.0	103.7	91.9	95.3	100.2	103.3	107.3	67.8	90.1	104.2
Mauritania	94.1	128.5	96.6	100.5	100.0	97.8	93.9	81.8	78.6	80.6	82.1	87.4	111.9	99.4
Mauritius	65.1	92.4	87.8	92.5	100.0	102.8	95.0	90.8	92.5	94.8	97.4	54.3	66.8	93.1
Mozambique	175.8	99.6	98.6	98.8	100.0	110.9	120.5	121.9	118.3	120.1	122.8	188.4	197.9	112.7
Namibia	92.1	95.0	90.3	95.3	100.0	92.9	93.9	87.6	81.9	83.6	85.7	81.8	73.8	90.7
Niger	136.8	134.9	91.1	85.3	100.0	102.3	92.3	94.0	101.8	105.2	108.3	100.7	115.4	106.4
Nigeria	287.2	122.0	77.9	86.3	100.0	120.4	131.2	133.7	146.3	154.3	163.9	210.6	116.3	121.3
Rwanda	70.3	97.6	102.7	77.4	100.0	93.6	113.0	114.8	114.4	116.4	118.1	69.8	105.8	106.1
São Tomé and Principe	..	105.4	109.1	111.1	100.0	97.2	94.2	85.4	94.8	93.7	95.5	..	131.1	103.1
Senegal	96.8	141.4	130.2	84.9	100.0	101.3	90.8	91.7	93.7	96.1	99.5	73.8	105.5	108.1
Seychelles	46.9	89.3	91.1	94.4	100.0	95.4	97.1	94.6	82.6	84.8	86.9	39.3	67.4	90.2
Sierra Leone	115.8	74.4	83.0	96.4	100.0	103.6	113.4	88.5	..	..	..	103.1	104.2	90.9
Somalia	..	..	..	..	..	..	..	..	..	..	..	..	..	..
South Africa	70.8	96.5	93.0	94.0	100.0	91.5	92.0	83.2	79.8	81.8	84.1	54.3	61.9	89.0
Sudan	178.4	120.8	142.9	142.1	100.0	96.3	126.1	123.7	..	..	..	177.1	344.5	150.5
Swaziland	98.5	84.0	82.8	86.1	100.0	93.2	96.1	86.9	82.2	85.2	87.0	75.8	64.6	86.5
Tanzania	..	115.4	95.4	87.2	100.0	113.1	131.6	142.6	144.7	147.1	150.9	..	108.4	118.7
Togo	95.8	134.8	117.5	80.2	100.0	102.5	100.1	101.7	108.2	110.5	112.9	76.6	94.2	109.6
Uganda	..	63.8	66.4	77.4	100.0	96.4	95.8	97.6	85.0	81.1	85.1	72.9	147.1	85.8
Zambia	122.9	92.5	89.0	94.3	100.0	88.9	102.9	89.5	81.5	83.4	86.6	98.8	81.3	91.6
Zimbabwe	148.7	101.8	97.7	96.0	100.0	111.6	106.2	73.6	68.6	77.7	80.1	130.8	117.2	96.6
NORTH AFRICA	117.5	92.8	95.6	93.2	100.0	104.8	105.2	105.1	105.0	107.7	105.1	92.8	101.6	100.5
Algeria	134.1	119.4	123.7	105.8	100.0	107.6	108.5	108.9	..	..	..	108.5	147.7	115.5
Egypt, Arab Republic	78.0	79.3	86.9	91.9	100.0	109.0	115.5	113.6	..	..	..	70.4	85.5	95.1
Libya	..	..	..	..	..	..	..	..	..	..	..	..	..	..
Morocco	87.2	88.0	83.8	86.0	100.0	99.2	92.5	..	..	..	..	66.2	66.6	89.3
Tunisia	83.5	93.5	86.2	89.0	100.0	101.7	93.3	103.3	..	..	..	68.3	71.2	92.7
ALL AFRICA	107.5	99.3	96.0	92.2	100.0	101.8	101.5	96.5	95.9	96.3	92.1	85.0	91.4	97.4

Note: 2001 data are preliminary (see page 2). Group data are obtained by dividing GDP in current US$ by GDP in constant US$ series for each group.

3-3. Consumer price index

	Index 1995=100											Average annual percentage growth		
	1980	*1992*	*1993*	*1994*	*1995*	*1996*	*1997*	*1998*	*1999*	*2000*	*2001*	*75-84*	*85-89*	*90-MR*
SUB-SAHARAN AFRICA	15.5	67.6	67.6	89.5	100.0	107.7	115.1	124.8	130.8	135.4	144.8	13.2	13.0	9.4
excluding South Africa	15.6	67.3	67.4	89.3	100.0	108.0	114.9	124.4	130.4	133.6	144.8	12.3	11.7	9.4
excl. S.Africa & Nigeria	16.3	67.6	67.6	89.5	100.0	107.6	114.6	124.1	130.0	131.7	143.8	11.6	9.9	9.2
Angola	..	0.0	0.3	3.6	100.0	4,257.3	13,587.8	28,159.8	98,053.7	416,724.4	1,052,476.0	..	..	634.7
Benin	..	62.8	63.1	87.4	100.0	104.9	108.6	114.8	115.2	120.0	124.7	..	..	7.9
Botswana	20.2	71.6	81.9	90.5	100.0	110.1	119.7	127.7	137.5	149.4	159.2	12.1	9.5	10.3
Burkina Faso	..	74.0	74.4	93.1	100.0	106.2	108.6	114.1	112.9	112.5	118.2	..	0.5	4.9
Burundi	28.9	66.6	73.0	83.8	100.0	126.4	165.8	186.5	192.8	239.7	261.9	13.4	5.4	15.1
Cameroon	32.2	70.1	67.9	91.7	100.0	103.9	108.9	112.4	114.1	111.7	116.8	11.5	6.4	5.6
Cape Verde	..	84.3	89.3	92.2	100.0	106.0	115.1	120.1	125.4	122.3	126.9	..	5.8	5.5
Central African Republic	53.3	69.4	67.4	83.9	100.0	103.7	105.4	103.4	101.9	105.2	109.2	..	-0.7	4.6
Chad	..	70.3	65.3	91.7	100.0	112.4	118.7	133.1	124.1	128.8	144.8	..	-1.3	7.4
Comoros	..	74.1	76.1	93.5	100.0	102.0	105.1	108.7	112.5	117.9	124.9	..	3.9	5.5
Congo, Democratic Rep. of	0.0	0.0	0.1	15.6	100.0	641.9	1,768.5	2,284.0	8,791.2	57,143.6	261,305.8	57.3	63.0	857.1
Congo, Republic of	..	61.3	64.1	91.4	100.0	110.0	..	124.1	130.8	129.7	129.8	..	0.9	8.0
Côte d'Ivoire	38.8	67.9	69.4	87.5	100.0	102.5	106.6	111.6	112.5	115.2	120.2	12.9	6.0	6.4
Djibouti	..	85.7	89.5	95.3	100.0	104.2	106.3	..	..	..	..	..	7.1	5.0
Equatorial Guinea	..	63.6	64.6	89.8	100.0	106.0	109.2	112.5	119.2	126.4	132.9	..	-6.0	7.5
Eritrea	..	78.1	78.9	89.3	100.0	110.3	114.3	125.2	135.7	162.7	186.5	..	..	10.0
Ethiopia	35.3	81.6	84.5	90.9	100.0	94.9	97.2	99.7	107.6	108.3	99.5	10.6	2.2	5.5
Gabon	47.4	66.6	67.0	91.2	100.0	100.7	104.7	106.2	104.2	104.7	..	12.5	1.0	4.1
Gambia, The	15.6	88.2	91.7	95.4	100.0	102.1	105.0	106.1	110.1	111.1	115.6	10.5	24.3	3.9
Ghana	0.9	40.2	50.2	62.7	100.0	146.6	187.4	214.8	241.5	302.3	401.8	67.9	27.7	27.9
Guinea	..	94.9	90.9	94.7	100.0	103.0	105.0	110.3	115.4	123.2	129.9	..	22.8	7.2
Guinea-Bissau	..	40.3	59.7	68.8	100.0	150.7	224.7	239.4	237.7	258.2	266.9	..	..	32.4
Kenya	10.9	52.4	76.4	98.5	100.0	108.9	121.2	129.4	136.8	150.5	159.1	13.6	9.4	15.4
Lesotho	15.5	74.8	84.6	91.5	100.0	109.3	117.3	125.9	138.6	147.1	157.5	14.2	13.7	10.1
Liberia	..	..	..	..	..	..	..	..	..	..	..	..	..	..
Madagascar	7.0	43.9	48.3	67.1	100.0	119.8	125.1	132.9	146.1	163.7	175.0	15.3	15.9	17.3
Malawi	5.3	33.0	40.5	54.5	100.0	137.6	150.2	194.9	282.2	365.6	465.2	..	20.4	32.0
Mali	..	71.8	71.6	88.2	100.0	106.8	106.4	110.7	109.4	108.6	114.3	..	..	4.6
Mauritania	..	82.4	90.1	93.9	100.0	104.7	109.5	118.3	123.1	127.1	133.1	..	6.8	6.0
Mauritius	32.3	79.5	87.9	94.3	100.0	106.6	113.8	121.6	130.0	135.4	142.7	14.9	5.3	7.0
Mozambique	..	27.9	39.7	64.8	100.0	148.5	159.4	161.8	166.4	187.6	204.6	..	67.6	30.6
Namibia	17.0	75.6	82.1	90.9	100.0	108.0	117.5	124.8	135.5	147.7	161.8	..	13.1	9.8
Niger	62.0	67.3	66.5	90.4	100.0	105.3	108.4	113.3	110.7	113.9	118.5	12.6	-3.3	5.1
Nigeria	2.0	23.4	36.9	57.9	100.0	129.3	139.9	154.3	161.7	185.2	209.2	17.7	23.2	29.9
Rwanda	23.0	46.0	50.0	82.0	100.0	108.9	121.6	130.0	126.8	131.7	136.2	11.1	1.9	14.5
São Tomé and Principe	..	45.8	57.5	72.9	100.0	137.5	230.6	348.0	404.8	449.3	493.4	..	27.4	34.4
Senegal	40.7	70.5	70.1	92.7	100.0	102.8	104.4	105.6	106.5	107.2	110.5	9.7	1.7	4.7
Seychelles	68.5	97.2	98.5	100.2	100.0	98.9	99.5	102.1	108.6	115.4	122.2	10.6	1.5	2.1
Sierra Leone	0.1	52.3	63.9	79.4	100.0	123.1	141.5	191.8	257.2	255.1	260.4	22.7	85.1	31.4
Somalia	..	..	..	..	..	..	..	..	..	..	..	..	..	..
South Africa	14.9	77.0	84.5	92.0	100.0	107.4	117.0	124.9	131.2	138.1	144.8	12.9	15.8	8.8
Sudan	0.1	13.7	27.6	59.4	100.0	232.8	341.4	399.8	463.8	481.1	525.5	22.9	40.3	67.4
Swaziland	15.5	69.9	78.3	89.1	100.0	106.4	114.0	123.3	130.8	146.7	155.4	14.4	15.4	9.4
Tanzania	2.1	46.7	58.5	77.9	100.0	121.0	140.4	158.4	170.9	181.0	190.3	19.6	30.7	20.4
Togo	42.7	62.3	61.7	85.9	100.0	104.7	113.3	114.4	114.3	116.5	121.1	11.1	0.5	7.5
Uganda	0.1	79.1	83.9	92.1	100.0	107.2	114.6	114.6	121.9	125.4	127.9	..	159.5	11.3
Zambia	0.1	16.8	48.3	74.1	100.0	143.1	178.0	221.6	280.9	354.1	431.0	14.7	57.0	59.7
Zimbabwe	8.1	52.3	66.7	81.6	100.0	121.4	144.2	190.1	301.3	469.6	829.8	11.9	11.2	30.8
NORTH AFRICA	21.5	79.9	88.7	93.3	100.0	104.0	107.7	111.7	114.7	120.4	123.0	13.3	4.8	6.0
Algeria	11.9	49.5	59.7	77.1	100.0	118.7	125.5	131.7	135.2	135.6	141.4	10.9	8.9	16.5
Egypt, Arab Republic	11.0	71.3	79.9	86.4	100.0	107.2	112.1	116.8	120.4	123.7	126.5	13.2	19.3	8.9
Libya	31.1	79.9	88.7	93.3	100.0	104.0	107.7	111.7	114.7	..	..	9.4	4.8	6.8
Morocco	37.0	85.2	89.6	94.2	100.0	103.0	104.1	106.9	107.7	109.7	110.4	9.9	4.7	3.9
Tunisia	..	86.4	89.9	94.1	100.0	103.7	107.5	110.9	113.9	117.2	119.4	..	7.3	4.4
ALL AFRICA	15.5	69.4	69.4	89.8	100.0	107.2	114.5	123.7	128.4	131.7	142.1	13.8	11.7	9.0

Note: 2001 data are preliminary (see page 2). Group data are medians of individual country values for each year. Some numbers for Angola are shown in scientific notation.

3-4. Official exchange rate

	National currency per U.S. dollar											Annual Average		
	1980	1992	1993	1994	1995	1996	1997	1998	1999	2000	2001	75-84	85-89	90-MR
SUB-SAHARAN AFRICA	..	..	..	..	..	..	..	..	..	..	..	..	..	..
excluding South Africa	..	..	..	..	..	..	..	..	..	..	..	..	..	..
excl. S.Africa & Nigeria	..	..	..	..	..	..	..	..	..	..	..	..	..	..
Angola	0.0	0.0	0.0	0.0	0.0	0.1	0.2	0.4	2.8	10.0	22.1	0.0	0.0	3.0
Benin	211.3	264.7	283.2	555.2	499.1	511.6	583.7	590.0	615.7	712.0	733.0	276.7	342.6	491.9
Botswana	0.8	2.1	2.4	2.7	2.8	3.3	3.7	4.2	4.6	5.1	5.8	0.9	1.9	3.4
Burkina Faso	211.3	264.7	283.2	555.2	499.1	511.6	583.7	590.0	615.7	712.0	733.0	276.7	342.6	491.9
Burundi	90.0	208.3	242.8	252.7	249.8	302.7	352.4	447.8	563.6	720.7	830.4	91.8	131.5	377.0
Cameroon	211.3	264.7	283.2	555.2	499.1	511.6	583.7	590.0	615.7	712.0	733.0	276.7	342.6	491.9
Cape Verde	40.2	68.0	80.4	81.9	76.9	82.6	93.2	98.2	102.7	115.9	123.2	46.6	78.9	88.7
Central African Republic	211.3	264.7	283.2	555.2	499.1	511.6	583.7	590.0	615.7	712.0	733.0	276.7	342.6	491.9
Chad	211.3	264.7	283.2	555.2	499.1	511.6	583.7	590.0	615.7	712.0	733.0	276.7	342.6	491.9
Comoros	211.3	264.7	283.2	416.4	374.4	383.7	437.7	442.5	461.8	534.0	549.8	276.7	342.6	391.9
Congo, Democratic Rep. of	0.0	0.0	0.0	0.0	0.1	0.5	1.3	1.6	4.0	21.8	..	0.0	0.0	2.7
Congo, Republic of	211.3	264.7	283.2	555.2	499.1	511.6	583.7	590.0	615.7	712.0	733.0	276.7	342.6	491.9
Côte d'Ivoire	211.3	264.7	283.2	555.2	499.1	511.6	583.7	590.0	615.7	712.0	733.0	276.7	342.6	491.9
Djibouti	177.7	177.7	177.7	177.7	177.7	177.7	177.7	177.7	177.7	177.7	177.7	177.7	177.7	177.7
Equatorial Guinea	211.3	264.7	283.2	555.2	499.1	511.6	583.7	590.0	615.7	712.0	733.0	276.7	342.6	491.9
Eritrea	..	4.6	6.2	6.2	6.3	6.4	..	..	8.2	9.6	10.9	..	..	7.3
Ethiopia	2.1	2.8	5.0	5.5	6.2	6.4	6.7	7.1	7.9	8.2	8.5	2.1	2.1	5.7
Gabon	211.3	264.7	283.2	555.2	499.1	511.6	583.7	590.0	615.7	712.0	733.0	276.7	342.6	491.9
Gambia, The	1.7	8.9	9.1	9.6	9.5	9.8	10.2	10.6	11.4	12.8	15.7	2.3	6.4	10.4
Ghana	2.8	437.1	649.1	956.7	1,200.4	1,637.2	2,050.2	2,314.1	2,669.3	5,455.1	7,170.8	6.1	153.9	2,102.8
Guinea	19.0	902.0	955.5	976.6	991.4	1,004.0	1,095.3	1,236.8	1,387.4	1,746.9	1,950.6	21.1	370.4	1,138.4
Guinea-Bissau	0.5	106.7	155.1	198.3	278.0	405.7	583.7	590.0	615.7	712.0	733.0	0.6	11.8	372.3
Kenya	7.4	32.2	58.0	56.1	51.4	57.1	58.7	60.4	70.3	76.2	78.6	9.4	17.5	54.1
Lesotho	0.8	2.9	3.3	3.6	3.6	4.3	4.6	5.5	6.1	6.9	8.6	1.0	2.3	4.6
Liberia	1.0	1.0	1.0	1.0	1.0	1.0	1.0	41.5	41.9	41.0	48.6	1.0	1.0	15.1
Madagascar	211.3	1,864.0	1,913.8	3,067.3	4,265.6	4,061.3	5,090.9	5,441.4	6,283.8	6,767.5	6,588.5	297.7	1,083.7	4,056.1
Malawi	0.8	3.6	4.4	8.7	15.3	15.3	16.4	31.1	44.1	59.5	72.2	1.0	2.2	23.0
Mali	211.3	264.7	283.2	555.2	499.1	511.6	583.7	590.0	615.7	712.0	733.0	276.7	342.6	491.9
Mauritania	45.9	87.0	120.8	123.6	129.8	137.2	151.9	188.5	209.5	238.9	255.6	49.0	76.7	150.4
Mauritius	7.7	15.6	17.6	18.0	17.4	17.9	21.1	24.0	25.2	26.2	29.1	8.5	14.1	20.2
Mozambique	33.0	2,566.5	3,951.1	6,158.4	9,203.4	11,517.8	11,772.6	12,110.2	13,028.6	15,447.1	20,703.6	34.7	335.3	9,072.5
Namibia	0.8	2.9	3.3	3.6	3.6	4.3	4.6	5.5	6.1	6.9	8.6	1.0	2.3	4.6
Niger	211.3	264.7	283.2	555.2	499.1	511.6	583.7	590.0	615.7	712.0	733.0	276.7	342.6	491.9
Nigeria	0.5	17.3	22.1	22.0	21.9	21.9	21.9	21.9	92.3	101.7	111.2	0.6	3.7	39.3
Rwanda	92.8	133.4	144.3	220.0	262.2	306.8	301.5	312.3	333.9	389.7	443.0	93.7	85.0	254.6
São Tomé and Principe	34.8	321.3	429.9	732.6	1,420.3	2,203.2	4,552.5	6,883.2	7,119.0	7,978.2	8,842.1	36.5	69.7	3,402.3
Senegal	211.3	264.7	283.2	555.2	499.1	511.6	583.7	590.0	615.7	712.0	733.0	276.7	342.6	491.9
Seychelles	6.4	5.1	5.2	5.1	4.8	5.0	5.0	5.3	5.3	5.7	5.9	6.7	6.0	5.2
Sierra Leone	1.0	499.4	567.5	586.7	755.2	920.7	981.5	1,563.6	1,804.2	2,092.1	1,986.2	1.3	29.5	1,017.0
Somalia	6.3	..	..	..	..	..	..	..	..	..	..	9.1	175.6	..
South Africa	0.8	2.9	3.3	3.6	3.6	4.3	4.6	5.5	6.1	6.9	8.6	1.0	2.3	4.6
Sudan	0.1	9.7	15.9	29.0	58.1	125.1	157.6	200.8	252.6	257.1	258.7	0.1	0.3	113.8
Swaziland	0.8	2.9	3.3	3.6	3.6	4.3	4.6	5.5	6.1	6.9	8.6	1.0	2.3	4.6
Tanzania	8.2	297.7	405.3	509.6	574.8	580.0	612.1	664.7	744.8	800.4	876.4	9.2	71.4	540.0
Togo	211.3	264.7	283.2	555.2	499.1	511.6	583.7	590.0	615.7	712.0	733.0	276.7	342.6	491.9
Uganda	0.1	1,133.8	1,195.0	979.4	968.9	1,046.1	1,083.0	1,240.3	1,454.8	1,644.5	1,755.7	0.7	78.6	1,138.7
Zambia	0.8	172.2	452.8	669.4	864.1	1,207.9	1,314.5	1,862.1	2,388.0	3,110.8	3,610.9	0.9	8.5	1,312.3
Zimbabwe	0.6	5.1	6.5	8.2	8.7	10.0	12.1	23.7	38.3	44.4	55.1	0.8	1.8	18.2
NORTH AFRICA	..	..	..	..	..	..	..	..	..	..	..	..	..	..
Algeria	3.8	21.8	23.3	35.1	47.7	54.7	57.7	58.7	66.6	75.3	77.2	4.3	5.6	45.5
Egypt, Arab Republic	0.7	3.3	3.4	3.4	3.4	3.4	3.4	3.4	3.4	3.5	4.0	0.6	0.7	3.3
Libya	0.3	0.3	0.3	0.3	0.3	0.4	0.4	0.4	0.5	0.5	0.6	0.3	0.3	0.4
Morocco	3.9	8.5	9.3	9.2	8.5	8.7	9.5	9.6	9.8	10.6	11.3	5.2	8.8	9.3
Tunisia	0.4	0.9	1.0	1.0	0.9	1.0	1.1	1.1	1.2	1.4	1.4	0.5	0.9	1.1
ALL AFRICA	..	..	..	..	..	..	..	..	..	..	..	..	..	..

Note: 2001 data are preliminary. Uganda changed its currency in 1987 and Congo Dem. Rep. in 1993. Angola and Congo Dem. Rep. again changed their currency in 1998. Guinea-Bissau joined W.A.M.U. in 1997.

3-5. SDR exchange rate index

	SDRs per unit of national currency, index 1995=100											*Annual Average*		
	1980	*1992*	*1993*	*1994*	*1995*	*1996*	*1997*	*1998*	*1999*	*2000*	*2001*	*75-84*	*85-89*	*90-MR*
SUB-SAHARAN AFRICA	..	..	..	..	..	..	..	..	..	..	..	..	..	..
excluding South Africa	..	..	..	..	..	..	..	..	..	..	..	..	..	..
excl. S.Africa & Nigeria	..	..	..	..	..	..	..	..	..	..	..	..	..	..
Angola	4,972,385	773,106	77,622	6,952	100	4	1	0	0	0	0	5,637,728	5,353,747	697,258
Benin	275	203	192	95	100	102	94	95	90	81	81	245	185	128
Botswana	416	140	124	109	100	88	84	74	66	63	57	402	188	102
Burkina Faso	275	203	192	95	100	102	94	95	90	81	81	245	185	128
Burundi	323	129	112	105	100	86	78	63	49	40	36	354	244	93
Cameroon	275	203	192	95	100	102	94	95	90	81	81	245	185	128
Cape Verde	223	122	104	99	100	97	91	88	83	76	74	240	122	98
Central African Republic	275	203	192	95	100	102	94	95	90	81	81	245	185	128
Chad	275	203	192	95	100	102	94	95	90	81	81	245	185	128
Comoros	207	153	144	95	100	102	94	95	90	81	81	184	139	111
Congo, Democratic Rep. of	6.67E+11	8.16E+06	423,415	3,019	100	14	5	4	2	0	..	1.44E+12	2.28E+10	2.89E+08
Congo, Republic of	275	203	192	95	100	102	94	95	90	81	81	245	185	128
Côte d'Ivoire	275	203	192	95	100	102	94	95	90	81	81	245	185	128
Djibouti	117	108	109	106	100	104	110	112	111	115	119	130	125	110
Equatorial Guinea	275	203	192	95	100	102	94	95	90	81	81	245	185	128
Eritrea	..	..	..	..	..	..	..	..	..	..	..	..	..	..
Ethiopia	347	274	134	120	100	101	101	97	86	86	87	386	373	154
Gabon	275	203	192	95	100	102	94	95	90	81	81	245	185	128
Gambia, The	647	115	114	106	100	102	103	100	93	86	73	568	204	104
Ghana	50,406	296	201	132	100	76	64	57	50	26	20	76,474	1,429	149
Guinea	6,092	119	113	108	100	103	100	90	80	66	61	6,082	1,435	104
Guinea-Bissau	61,655	281	193	148	100	73	52	52	47	43	45	62,731	7,181	208
Kenya	796	170	100	98	100	93	96	94	80	77	77	727	369	120
Lesotho	543	137	121	108	100	89	87	74	66	60	51	510	202	100
Liberia	117	108	109	106	100	104	110	3	3	3	2	130	125	73
Madagascar	2,349	246	241	160	100	110	92	87	75	72	77	2,029	587	153
Malawi	2,199	470	377	211	100	104	103	59	38	31	25	2,087	910	229
Mali	275	203	192	95	100	102	94	95	90	81	81	245	185	128
Mauritania	329	164	117	111	100	99	94	77	69	63	60	345	212	109
Mauritius	264	120	107	103	100	101	91	81	77	76	71	284	155	99
Mozambique	31,525	386	259	154	100	81	84	83	76	67	52	33,843	13,448	258
Namibia	543	137	121	108	100	89	87	74	66	60	51	510	202	100
Niger	275	203	192	95	100	102	94	95	90	81	81	245	185	128
Nigeria	4,669	145	108	106	100	105	110	112	27	25	23	4,415	1,462	118
Rwanda	302	195	181	115	100	82	88	86	80	71	65	333	356	133
São Tomé and Principe	4,681	477	355	210	100	67	36	23	22	20	19	5,055	3,204	270
Senegal	275	203	192	95	100	102	94	95	90	81	81	245	185	128
Seychelles	87	100	100	100	100	100	104	101	99	96	97	92	100	100
Sierra Leone	81,552	159	141	133	100	84	85	53	46	41	44	78,935	8,296	146
Somalia	..	..	..	..	..	..	..	..	..	..	..	..	..	..
South Africa	543	137	121	108	100	89	87	74	66	60	51	510	202	100
Sudan	129,561	857	382	212	100	47	40	31	132	249	256	141,388	23,252	2,284
Swaziland	543	137	121	108	100	89	87	74	66	60	51	510	202	100
Tanzania	8,149	210	156	119	100	103	103	96	86	82	78	8,361	1,975	146
Togo	275	203	192	95	100	102	94	95	90	81	81	245	185	128
Uganda	1,520,277	92	88	105	100	97	99	88	74	68	66	1,025,920	7,512	107
Zambia	126,813	590	210	121	100	75	72	52	40	32	28	127,103	18,640	513
Zimbabwe	1,570	183	145	113	100	91	80	45	25	23	19	1,556	622	125
NORTH AFRICA	..	..	..	..	..	..	..	..	..	..	..	..	..	..
Algeria	1,441	234	221	150	100	91	91	90	79	73	73	1,447	1,103	174
Egypt, Arab Republic	565	110	110	106	100	105	110	112	111	112	102	823	592	123
Libya	136	131	123	115	100	100	100	100	79	78	70	152	147	106
Morocco	253	108	100	98	100	102	99	99	97	92	90	225	121	101
Tunisia	272	115	102	99	100	101	94	93	89	80	78	254	140	99
ALL AFRICA	..	..	..	..	..	..	..	..	..	..	..	..	..	..

Note: 2001 data are preliminary (see page 2). Guinea-Bissau joined the Western African Monetary Union (W.A.M.U) in May, 1997. Some values for Angola and Congo, Dem, Rep. are in scientific notation.

3-6. Currency conversion factor

	Units of national currency per US dollar											*Annual Average*		
	1980	*1992*	*1993*	*1994*	*1995*	*1996*	*1997*	*1998*	*1999*	*2000*	*2001*	*75-84*	*85-89*	*90-MR*
SUB-SAHARAN AFRICA	..	..	..	..	..	..	..	..	..	..	..	..	..	..
excluding South Africa	..	..	..	..	..	..	..	..	..	..	..	..	..	..
excl. S.Africa & Nigeria	..	..	..	..	..	..	..	..	..	..	..	..	..	..
Angola	..	0.0	0.0	0.0	0.0	0.1	0.2	0.4	2.8	10.0	22.1	..	0.0	3.0
Benin	211.3	350.6	283.2	555.2	499.1	511.6	583.7	590.0	615.7	712.0	733.0	276.7	342.6	499.0
Botswana	0.8	2.1	2.4	2.7	2.8	3.3	3.7	4.2	4.6	5.1	5.8	0.9	1.9	3.4
Burkina Faso	211.3	396.6	388.5	555.2	499.1	511.5	583.7	590.0	615.7	712.0	733.0	276.7	342.6	511.6
Burundi	90.0	208.3	242.8	252.7	249.8	302.8	352.4	447.8	563.6	720.7	830.3	91.8	131.5	377.0
Cameroon	209.2	280.4	265.4	435.0	518.5	501.8	541.1	602.1	588.4	656.3	735.7	265.6	356.7	474.5
Cape Verde	40.2	68.0	80.4	81.9	76.9	82.6	93.1	98.2	102.7	115.9	118.2	46.6	78.9	88.3
Central African Republic	211.3	264.7	283.2	555.2	499.1	511.6	582.4	590.0	615.7	712.0	733.0	276.7	342.6	491.8
Chad	211.3	264.7	283.2	555.2	499.1	511.6	583.7	590.0	615.7	712.0	733.0	276.7	342.6	491.9
Comoros	211.3	264.7	283.2	416.4	374.4	383.7	437.8	442.5	461.8	534.0	549.8	274.7	342.6	391.9
Congo, Democratic Rep. of	0.0	0.0	0.0	0.0	0.1	0.5	1.3	1.6	4.0	21.8	..	0.0	0.0	2.7
Congo, Republic of	211.3	264.7	396.1	555.2	499.1	511.6	583.7	590.0	615.7	712.0	733.0	276.7	342.6	501.3
Côte d'Ivoire	211.3	264.7	283.2	555.2	499.1	511.5	583.7	590.0	615.7	712.0	733.0	276.7	342.6	491.9
Djibouti	177.7	177.7	177.7	177.7	177.7	177.7	177.7	177.7	177.7	177.7	177.7	177.7	177.7	177.7
Equatorial Guinea	110.6	264.7	283.2	555.2	499.1	511.6	583.7	590.0	615.7	712.0	733.0	146.9	342.6	491.9
Eritrea	..	4.6	6.2	6.6	6.8	6.7	7.2	7.4	8.2	9.6	10.9	..	..	7.4
Ethiopia	..	3.7	4.3	5.8	5.9	6.3	6.5	6.9	7.5	8.1	8.3	2.1	2.1	5.8
Gabon	211.3	264.7	349.6	555.2	499.1	511.5	583.7	590.0	615.7	712.0	733.0	276.7	342.6	497.4
Gambia, The	1.7	8.9	9.1	9.6	9.5	9.8	10.2	10.6	11.4	12.8	15.0	2.3	6.4	10.3
Ghana	9.6	437.1	649.1	956.7	1,200.4	1,637.2	2,050.2	2,314.1	2,669.3	5,455.1	7,170.8	17.5	157.0	2,102.8
Guinea	19.0	902.0	955.5	976.6	991.4	1,004.0	1,095.3	1,236.8	1,387.4	1,746.9	1,950.6	21.1	373.0	1,138.4
Guinea-Bissau	0.8	106.7	155.1	198.3	278.0	405.7	583.7	590.0	615.7	712.0	733.0	0.8	12.3	372.3
Kenya	7.4	32.2	58.0	56.1	51.4	57.1	58.7	60.4	70.3	76.2	78.6	9.4	17.5	54.1
Lesotho	0.8	2.9	3.3	3.6	3.6	4.3	4.6	5.5	6.1	6.9	8.6	1.0	2.3	4.6
Liberia	1.0	..	..	..	..	..	..	..	..	..	..	1.0	1.0	1.0
Madagascar	211.3	1,864.0	1,913.8	3,067.3	4,265.6	4,061.3	5,090.9	5,441.4	6,283.8	6,767.5	6,588.5	297.7	1,083.7	4,056.1
Malawi	0.8	3.6	4.4	8.7	15.3	15.3	16.4	31.1	44.1	59.5	72.2	1.0	2.2	23.0
Mali	211.3	265.3	283.2	555.2	499.1	511.5	583.7	590.0	615.7	712.0	733.0	276.7	342.6	491.9
Mauritania	45.9	87.0	120.8	123.6	129.8	137.2	151.9	188.5	209.5	238.9	250.0	49.0	76.7	150.0
Mauritius	7.1	15.8	16.3	18.2	17.4	17.7	19.1	22.6	24.8	25.5	27.6	9.8	14.0	19.6
Mozambique	32.4	2,566.5	3,951.1	6,158.4	9,203.4	11,517.8	11,722.6	12,110.2	13,028.6	15,447.1	20,703.6	34.3	328.8	9,068.3
Namibia	0.8	2.9	3.3	3.6	3.6	4.3	4.6	5.5	6.1	6.9	8.6	0.9	2.3	4.6
Niger	211.3	264.7	391.4	555.2	499.1	511.5	583.7	590.0	615.7	712.0	733.0	276.7	342.6	500.9
Nigeria	0.8	19.0	45.3	52.3	70.4	80.0	81.1	88.0	92.3	101.7	111.6	1.1	5.3	63.6
Rwanda	92.8	133.4	144.3	220.0	262.2	306.8	301.5	312.3	333.9	389.7	443.0	93.7	85.0	254.6
São Tomé and Principe	34.8	320.0	429.9	732.6	1,420.3	2,203.2	4,552.5	6,883.2	7,119.0	7,978.2	8,842.1	36.5	69.7	3,402.2
Senegal	211.3	264.7	283.2	555.2	499.1	511.6	583.7	590.0	615.7	712.0	733.0	276.7	342.6	491.9
Seychelles	6.4	5.1	5.2	5.1	4.8	5.0	5.0	5.3	5.3	5.7	5.9	6.7	6.0	5.2
Sierra Leone	1.0	499.4	567.5	586.7	755.2	920.7	981.5	1,563.6	1,804.2	2,092.1	1,985.9	1.3	29.1	1,017.0
Somalia	28.8	..	..	..	..	..	..	..	..	..	..	28.1	236.3	1,896.1
South Africa	0.8	2.9	3.3	3.6	3.6	4.3	4.6	5.5	6.1	6.9	8.6	1.0	2.3	4.6
Sudan	0.1	9.7	15.9	29.0	58.1	125.1	157.6	200.8	252.6	257.1	258.7	0.1	0.3	114.0
Swaziland	0.8	2.9	3.3	3.5	3.6	4.3	4.6	5.5	6.1	6.9	8.5	1.0	2.3	4.5
Tanzania	8.2	297.7	405.3	509.6	574.8	580.0	612.1	664.7	744.8	800.4	876.4	9.2	71.4	540.0
Togo	211.3	264.7	283.2	555.2	499.1	511.6	583.7	590.0	615.7	712.0	733.0	276.7	342.6	491.9
Uganda	1.0	960.8	1,201.8	1,101.0	932.5	1,012.0	1,058.1	1,149.7	1,362.1	1,512.0	1,762.9	2.1	53.2	1,076.9
Zambia	0.8	178.9	452.8	669.4	864.1	1,207.9	1,314.5	1,862.1	2,388.0	3,110.8	3,610.9	0.9	8.5	1,313.2
Zimbabwe	0.6	5.1	6.5	8.1	8.7	10.0	12.1	23.7	38.3	44.4	55.1	0.8	1.8	18.2
NORTH AFRICA	..	..	..	..	..	..	..	..	..	..	..	..	..	..
Algeria	3.8	21.8	23.3	35.1	47.7	54.7	57.7	58.7	66.6	75.3	77.2	4.3	5.6	45.5
Egypt, Arab Republic	0.7	3.3	3.3	3.4	3.4	3.4	3.4	3.4	3.4	3.4	3.7	0.7	1.4	3.3
Libya	0.3	0.3	0.3	0.3	0.3	0.4	0.4	0.4	0.5	0.5	0.6	0.3	0.3	0.4
Morocco	3.9	8.5	9.3	9.2	8.5	8.7	9.5	9.6	9.8	10.6	11.3	5.2	8.8	9.3
Tunisia	0.4	0.9	1.0	1.0	0.9	1.0	1.1	1.1	1.2	1.4	1.4	0.5	0.9	1.1
ALL AFRICA	..	..	..	..	..	..	..	..	..	..	..	..	..	..

Note: Off. exch. rate adjusted for some countries to better reflect the rate at which intl. transactions are carried out. G. Bissau joined W.A.M.U. in 1997.

3-7. Parallel market exchange rate

	National currency per U.S. dollar											Annual Average		
	1980	1989	1990	1991	1992	1993	1994	1995	1996	1997	1998	75-84	85-89	90-MR
SUB-SAHARAN AFRICA	..	..	..	..	..	..	..	..	..	..	..	..	..	..
excluding South Africa	..	..	..	..	..	..	..	..	..	..	..	..	..	..
excl. S.Africa & Nigeria	..	..	..	..	..	..	..	..	..	..	..	..	..	..
Angola	..	..	..	1,266.7	1,087.5	31,740.0	203,137.5	569,573.8	163,370.0	283,138.8	564,250.0	900.0	1,837.5	227,195.5
Benin	209.5	324.8	281.8	289.0	270.1	288.0	586.4	499.3	516.4	593.3	..	304.2	343.9	415.5
Botswana	0.8	2.3	1.9	2.4	2.5	2.8	2.9	2.8	3.4	3.7	4.4	1.2	2.4	3.0
Burkina Faso	209.5	324.8	281.8	17.1	16.8	288.0	586.4	499.3	516.4	593.3	..	304.2	343.9	349.9
Burundi	106.0	214.0	186.1	269.3	310.9	370.7	409.4	340.8	369.6	459.2	568.1	122.3	161.7	364.9
Cameroon	209.5	324.8	281.8	289.0	270.1	288.0	586.4	499.3	516.4	593.3	..	304.2	343.9	415.5
Cape Verde	..	..	..	88.0	79.5	87.0	92.0	89.3	89.5	99.5	0.0	..	..	78.1
Central African Republic	209.5	324.8	281.8	289.0	270.1	288.0	586.4	499.3	516.4	593.3	603.2	304.2	343.9	436.4
Chad	209.5	324.8	281.8	289.0	270.1	288.0	586.4	499.3	516.4	593.3	..	304.2	343.9	415.5
Comoros	209.5	324.8	281.8	289.0	270.1	288.0	446.0	390.6	415.6	467.6	468.3	304.2	343.9	368.6
Congo, Democratic Rep. of	6.4	469.4	738.1	19,318.8	756,558.3	3,112,920.5	1,209.8	7,452.1	52,429.4	160,358.3	69,064.0	14.3	182.6	464,449.9
Congo, Republic of	209.5	324.8	281.8	289.0	270.1	288.0	586.4	499.3	516.4	593.3	..	304.2	343.9	415.5
Côte d'Ivoire	209.5	324.8	281.8	289.0	270.1	288.0	586.4	499.3	516.4	593.3	..	304.2	343.9	415.5
Djibouti	..	217.9	191.8	213.8	205.8	212.0	208.6	198.5	192.1	183.9	184.0	..	207.8	198.9
Equatorial Guinea	209.5	324.8	281.8	289.0	270.1	288.0	586.4	586.4	516.4	593.3	..	304.2	343.9	426.4
Eritrea	..	..	..	..	..	..	..	..	..	..	0.0	..	..	0.0
Ethiopia	2.8	5.9	6.0	6.7	9.5	13.3	12.0	10.7	10.2	7.5	7.2	3.5	5.1	9.2
Gabon	209.5	324.8	281.8	289.0	270.1	288.0	586.4	499.3	516.4	593.3	..	334.6	343.9	415.5
Gambia, The	1.7	7.4	8.3	8.8	11.5	9.1	9.0	10.4	10.8	10.8	11.2	2.5	7.1	10.0
Ghana	15.9	328.8	360.8	382.2	451.6	665.7	976.4	1,224.3	1,663.4	2,080.7	2,334.8	41.7	222.1	1,126.7
Guinea	41.7	580.1	693.3	793.0	1,608.1	1,156.9	1,074.1	1,017.9	1,025.9	1,125.3	1,265.8	102.9	453.8	1,084.5
Guinea-Bissau	..	..	..	4,172.5	6,075.0	9,883.3	14,012.5	19,166.7	26,855.0	..	0.0	..	1,800.0	11,452.1
Kenya	8.2	22.4	23.3	30.0	44.4	91.7	66.8	53.4	59.5	62.1	63.6	11.9	19.0	55.0
Lesotho	..	2.7	2.7	2.9	3.0	3.5	3.8	3.7	4.5	4.7	5.6	1.4	2.5	3.8
Liberia	..	..	..	..	..	40.0	45.0	42.3	45.8	48.5	48.5	..	1.5	45.0
Madagascar	265.0	1,639.1	1,589.2	2,071.3	2,239.2	2,217.9	3,122.9	4,397.5	4,551.7	5,582.1	5,630.6	521.1	1,133.5	3,489.2
Malawi	1.6	3.6	3.3	3.9	4.6	5.9	9.2	16.7	16.5	17.6	33.3	1.7	2.8	12.3
Mali	209.5	324.8	281.8	289.0	270.1	288.0	586.4	499.3	516.4	593.3	..	304.2	343.9	415.5
Mauritania	65.0	..	..	213.3	221.7	247.5	145.0	139.3	144.0	158.9	194.3	93.2	178.0	183.0
Mauritius	..	16.0	15.7	17.1	16.8	18.3	18.4	18.2	19.4	21.4	24.4	..	14.5	18.8
Mozambique	80.0	1,250.0	..	2,100.0	2,800.0	3,950.0	6,875.0	9,865.7	12,172.5	12,533.7	12,851.3	322.2	1,793.8	7,893.5
Namibia	..	..	..	..	..	..	..	..	..	4.9	5.8	..	..	5.3
Niger	209.5	324.8	281.8	289.0	270.1	288.0	586.4	499.3	516.4	593.3	..	304.2	343.9	415.5
Nigeria	0.9	10.7	9.3	6.7	21.9	56.8	71.7	78.3	81.8	84.7	91.5	1.4	6.4	55.9
Rwanda	115.0	109.8	104.2	209.1	238.9	297.4	286.5	268.1	331.8	360.5	642.1	135.4	111.4	304.3
São Tomé and Principe	..	..	..	222.5	360.0	432.5	810.0	1,503.3	2,407.5	7,300.0	0.0	..	..	1,629.5
Senegal	209.5	324.8	281.8	289.0	270.1	288.0	586.4	499.3	516.4	593.3	..	304.2	343.9	415.5
Seychelles	..	..	5.9	5.7	5.5	5.4	5.5	5.5	5.4	5.5	5.7	..	..	5.6
Sierra Leone	1.4	180.9	470.6	535.7	845.1	647.5	618.7	741.3	942.1	1,137.9	2,024.4	2.1	86.5	884.8
Somalia	9.9	398.8	1,982.1	4,675.0	6,095.0	7,456.3	6,961.3	6,549.2	7,789.8	5,919.3	7,850.0	14.7	224.0	6,142.0
South Africa	0.9	2.7	2.7	2.9	3.0	3.5	3.8	3.7	4.5	4.7	5.7	1.2	2.5	3.8
Sudan	1.0	15.9	43.6	105.3	62.4	31.6	45.3	77.5	147.2	171.2	221.6	1.3	8.4	100.6
Swaziland	..	3.0	2.7	3.1	3.3	3.8	3.9	3.9	4.7	4.9	5.8	..	2.5	4.0
Tanzania	21.0	263.5	292.4	348.5	405.9	443.5	523.2	587.3	604.7	656.9	709.8	30.5	175.4	508.0
Togo	209.5	324.8	281.8	289.0	270.1	288.0	586.4	499.3	516.4	593.3	..	304.2	343.9	415.5
Uganda	75.7	597.5	685.8	859.2	1,365.4	1,515.8	1,289.2	1,076.2	1,135.2	1,178.1	1,333.8	203.8	3,681.6	1,159.8
Zambia	1.3	107.8	121.2	133.3	104.2	531.0	805.4	935.6	1,281.8	1,583.0	2,411.7	1.7	33.5	878.6
Zimbabwe	1.1	3.5	3.3	5.3	6.7	7.7	9.4	8.9	10.8	13.9	195.0	1.7	2.8	29.0
NORTH AFRICA	..	..	..	..	..	..	..	..	..	..	..	..	..	..
Algeria	10.9	37.1	29.8	33.8	87.4	106.8	128.7	131.9	127.6	129.8	131.4	13.6	27.2	100.8
Egypt, Arab Republic	0.8	2.6	2.6	3.4	3.4	3.4	3.4	3.4	3.6	3.4	3.4	0.9	2.0	3.3
Libya	0.5	0.9	1.0	1.2	1.6	1.7	1.6	1.3	2.0	2.2	2.5	0.5	1.0	1.7
Morocco	4.1	9.2	9.3	9.2	8.9	9.4	9.4	8.6	8.8	9.7	9.8	6.0	9.1	9.2
Tunisia	0.4	1.0	0.9	1.0	1.0	1.0	1.1	0.9	1.0	1.1	1.2	0.6	0.9	1.0
ALL AFRICA	..	..	..	..	..	..	..	..	..	..	..	..	..	..

Note: Rates are annual avg. of month-end est., based on a sample of transactions. G. Bissau joined the W.A.M.U. in 97. New Ugandan shilling introduced in 1987.

3-8. Ratio of parallel market to official exchange rates

	Ratio of parallel market to official exchange rates											Annual Average		
	1980	1989	1990	1991	1992	1993	1994	1995	1996	1997	1998	75-84	85-89	90-MR
SUB-SAHARAN AFRICA	..	..	..	..	..	..	..	..	..	..	..	..	..	..
excluding South Africa	..	..	..	..	..	..	..	..	..	..	..	..	..	..
excl. S.Africa & Nigeria	..	..	..	..	..	..	..	..	..	..	..	..	..	..
Angola	..	..	..	2.30E+10	4.33E+09	1.19E+10	3.41E+09	2.07E+08	1.28E+06	1.24E+06	1.44E+06	3.01E+10	6.14E+10	5.36E+09
Benin	0.99	1.02	1.04	1.02	1.02	1.02	1.06	1.00	1.01	1.02	..	1.03	1.01	1.02
Botswana	1.03	1.14	1.02	1.19	1.18	1.16	1.08	1.01	1.02	1.01	1.03	1.23	1.27	1.08
Burkina Faso	0.99	1.02	1.04	0.06	0.06	1.02	1.06	1.00	1.01	1.02	..	1.03	1.01	0.78
Burundi	1.18	1.35	1.09	1.48	1.49	1.53	1.62	1.36	1.22	1.30	1.27	1.28	1.22	1.37
Cameroon	0.99	1.02	1.04	1.02	1.02	1.02	1.06	1.00	1.01	1.02	..	1.03	1.01	1.02
Cape Verde	..	..	..	1.23	1.17	1.08	1.12	1.16	1.08	1.07	0.00	..	..	0.99
Central African Republic	0.99	1.02	1.04	1.02	1.02	1.02	1.06	1.00	1.01	1.02	1.02	1.03	1.01	1.02
Chad	0.99	1.02	1.04	1.02	1.02	1.02	1.06	1.00	1.01	1.02	..	1.03	1.01	1.02
Comoros	0.99	1.02	1.04	1.02	1.02	1.02	1.07	1.04	1.08	1.07	1.06	1.03	1.01	1.05
Congo, Democratic Rep. of	6.86E+11	3.69E+11	3.08E+11	3.72E+11	3.52E+11	1.24E+11	1.01E+05	1.06E+05	1.04E+05	1.22E+05	4.30E+04	6.49E+11	3.25E+11	1.28E+11
Congo, Republic of	0.99	1.02	1.04	1.02	1.02	1.02	1.06	1.00	1.01	1.02	..	1.03	1.01	1.02
Côte d'Ivoire	0.99	1.02	1.04	1.02	1.02	1.02	1.06	1.00	1.01	1.02	..	1.03	1.01	1.02
Djibouti	..	1.23	1.08	1.20	1.16	1.19	1.17	1.12	1.08	1.03	1.04	..	1.17	1.12
Equatorial Guinea	0.99	1.02	1.04	1.02	1.02	1.02	1.06	1.17	1.01	1.02	..	1.03	1.01	1.04
Eritrea	..	..	..	..	..	..	..	..	..	..	..	..	..	..
Ethiopia	1.35	2.85	2.90	3.24	3.39	2.66	2.20	1.74	1.61	1.12	1.01	1.70	2.48	2.21
Gabon	0.99	1.02	1.04	1.02	1.02	1.02	1.06	1.00	1.01	1.02	..	1.02	1.01	1.02
Gambia, The	0.99	0.98	1.05	1.00	1.29	1.00	0.94	1.09	1.10	1.06	1.05	1.06	1.10	1.07
Ghana	5.78	1.22	1.11	1.04	1.03	1.03	1.02	1.02	1.02	1.01	1.01	7.98	1.67	1.03
Guinea	2.20	0.98	1.05	1.05	1.78	1.21	1.10	1.03	1.02	1.03	1.02	4.62	3.42	1.14
Guinea-Bissau	..	..	..	74.13	56.95	63.72	70.65	68.94	66.19	..	0.00	..	105.43	57.22
Kenya	1.11	1.09	1.02	1.09	1.38	1.58	1.19	1.04	1.04	1.06	1.05	1.18	1.08	1.16
Lesotho	..	1.03	1.04	1.05	1.05	1.07	1.07	1.02	1.05	1.02	1.02	1.09	1.09	1.04
Liberia	..	..	..	..	..	40.00	45.00	42.30	45.80	48.50	1.17	..	1.50	37.13
Madagascar	1.25	1.02	1.06	1.13	1.20	1.16	1.02	1.03	1.12	1.10	1.03	1.53	1.05	1.09
Malawi	1.97	1.30	1.21	1.39	1.28	1.34	1.05	1.09	1.08	1.07	1.07	1.77	1.25	1.18
Mali	0.99	1.02	1.04	1.02	1.02	1.02	1.06	1.00	1.01	1.02	..	1.03	1.01	1.02
Mauritania	1.42	..	..	2.60	2.55	2.05	1.17	1.07	1.05	1.05	1.03	1.79	2.37	1.57
Mauritius	..	1.05	1.06	1.09	1.08	1.04	1.02	1.05	1.08	1.02	1.01	..	1.03	1.05
Mozambique	2.42	1.65	..	1.44	1.09	1.00	1.12	1.07	1.06	1.06	1.06	8.06	24.05	1.11
Namibia	..	..	..	..	..	..	..	..	..	1.06	1.04	..	..	1.05
Niger	0.99	1.02	1.04	1.02	1.02	1.02	1.06	1.00	1.01	1.02	..	1.03	1.01	1.02
Nigeria	1.65	1.45	1.16	0.68	1.27	2.57	3.26	3.58	3.74	3.87	4.18	2.09	2.24	2.70
Rwanda	1.24	1.37	1.26	1.67	1.79	2.06	1.30	1.02	1.08	1.20	2.06	1.44	1.31	1.49
São Tomé and Principe	..	..	..	1.10	1.12	1.01	1.11	1.06	1.09	1.60	0.00	..	..	1.01
Senegal	0.99	1.02	1.04	1.02	1.02	1.02	1.06	1.00	1.01	1.02	..	1.03	1.01	1.02
Seychelles	..	..	1.11	1.08	1.07	1.04	1.09	1.15	1.09	1.09	1.09	..	..	1.09
Sierra Leone	1.33	3.02	3.11	1.81	1.69	1.14	1.05	0.98	1.02	1.16	1.29	1.42	2.46	1.47
Somalia	1.57	0.81	..	..	..	..	..	..	..	..	..	1.45	1.76	..
South Africa	1.16	1.03	1.04	1.05	1.05	1.07	1.07	1.02	1.05	1.02	1.03	1.12	1.09	1.04
Sudan	20.00	35.33	96.89	151.39	6.40	1.98	1.56	1.33	1.18	1.09	1.10	16.25	23.50	29.21
Swaziland	..	1.14	1.04	1.12	1.16	1.16	1.10	1.08	1.09	1.06	1.05	..	1.11	1.10
Tanzania	2.56	1.84	1.50	1.59	1.36	1.09	1.03	1.02	1.04	1.07	1.07	3.02	3.08	1.20
Togo	0.99	1.02	1.04	1.02	1.02	1.02	1.06	1.00	1.01	1.02	..	1.03	1.01	1.02
Uganda	1,020.63	2.68	1.60	1.17	1.20	1.27	1.32	1.11	1.09	1.09	1.08	535.92	151.70	1.21
Zambia	1.65	7.80	4.00	2.06	0.61	1.17	1.20	1.08	1.06	1.20	1.30	1.69	3.17	1.52
Zimbabwe	1.71	1.65	1.35	1.46	1.31	1.19	1.15	1.03	1.08	1.15	8.23	2.09	1.55	1.99
NORTH AFRICA	..	..	..	..	..	..	..	..	..	..	..	..	..	..
Algeria	2.84	4.88	3.33	1.83	4.00	4.57	3.67	2.77	2.33	2.25	2.24	3.08	4.82	3.00
Egypt, Arab Republic	1.14	3.00	1.68	1.08	1.02	1.01	1.00	1.00	1.06	1.00	1.01	1.42	2.74	1.10
Libya	1.69	3.00	3.53	4.27	5.62	5.57	4.99	3.76	5.53	5.77	6.30	1.64	3.47	5.04
Morocco	1.04	1.08	1.13	1.06	1.04	1.01	1.02	1.01	1.01	1.02	1.02	1.07	1.03	1.03
Tunisia	0.99	1.05	1.02	1.08	1.13	1.00	1.09	0.95	1.03	0.99	1.02	1.02	1.03	1.03
ALL AFRICA	..	..	..	..	..	..	..	..	..	..	..	..	..	..

Note: 2001 data are preliminary (see page 2).Guinea-Bissau joined the WAMU in May,1997.New Ugandan shilling = 100 old Ugandan shilling, introduced in 1987.Values for Angola and Congo, Dem, Rep. are in scientific notation.

3-9. Real effective exchange rate index

	Index 1990=100											*Annual Average*		
	1980	*1992*	*1993*	*1994*	*1995*	*1996*	*1997*	*1998*	*1999*	*2000*	*2001*	*75-84*	*85-89*	*90-MR*
SUB-SAHARAN AFRICA	112.8	92.2	89.5	79.9	79.0	81.5	78.2	82.0	80.3	75.2	75.9	72.6	109.8	84.0
excluding South Africa	110.5	92.2	89.2	75.8	79.0	80.8	77.9	81.3	78.7	74.9	74.9	71.0	110.3	83.3
excl. S.Africa & Nigeria	108.2	92.2	89.5	71.8	78.9	80.1	77.6	80.6	77.2	74.4	74.9	69.1	109.8	82.6
Angola	..	..	..	..	..	..	..	..	..	..	..	..	..	..
Benin	..	102.5	102.3	69.0	79.5	81.5	80.0	86.0	83.0	..	..	..	93.1	88.2
Botswana	165.4	92.2	86.9	79.9	85.9	88.5	72.8	73.8	73.8	74.9	75.9	160.2	127.3	80.9
Burkina Faso	..	..	..	..	..	..	..	..	..	..	..	..	..	..
Burundi	129.8	84.5	81.7	85.1	92.2	97.9	85.6	87.9	90.1	92.7	95.9	159.6	137.1	91.2
Cameroon	88.2	96.4	89.8	57.6	66.4	67.3	66.1	65.7	71.3	68.3	68.3	84.0	98.8	76.1
Cape Verde	88.7	90.2	87.6	88.0	89.6	89.0	92.1	94.2	89.1	85.8	..	97.2	100.1	90.4
Central African Republic	105.9	94.4	89.7	56.0	66.0	67.5	65.2	64.0	64.9	65.6	66.7	100.7	101.7	74.5
Chad	102.3	108.6	111.6	58.7	64.4	66.8	66.9	66.9	63.9	66.1	..	114.4	108.5	79.5
Comoros	..	96.3	97.3	..	..	..	..	..	..	..	..	..	104.9	96.8
Congo, Democratic Rep. of	..	..	..	..	..	..	..	..	..	..	..	..	..	..
Congo, Republic of	102.2	90.0	89.2	69.3	79.0	75.2	77.6	79.9	80.3	75.5	78.8	102.2	102.1	82.0
Côte d'Ivoire	106.1	100.8	99.2	60.9	70.3	70.7	69.5	74.1	72.7	69.4	70.0	90.0	94.5	79.5
Djibouti	..	..	..	..	..	..	..	..	..	..	..	..	..	..
Equatorial Guinea	..	..	..	..	..	..	..	..	..	..	..	..	..	..
Eritrea	..	..	..	..	..	..	..	..	..	..	..	..	..	..
Ethiopia	92.5	98.9	44.5	37.9	38.5	35.4	35.8	35.5	35.2	32.9	32.5	92.5	109.5	53.0
Gabon	112.8	76.4	74.0	49.9	55.1	54.5	53.7	55.5	53.1	49.5	50.2	102.0	99.0	63.1
Gambia, The	100.8	103.2	103.1	95.9	95.3	94.8	99.6	98.2	95.9	91.8	84.2	97.0	81.0	96.6
Ghana	..	90.3	79.4	63.8	73.5	80.1	84.9	91.9	92.3	59.6	58.8	341.2	139.7	81.4
Guinea	..	96.9	100.6	98.5	92.8	95.1	94.4	93.7	80.6	76.6	72.8	..	116.2	92.2
Guinea-Bissau	..	75.8	80.8	71.8	66.4	69.6	78.2	81.3	77.2	80.9	78.5	..	100.0	79.3
Kenya	142.5	102.5	87.2	113.1	117.8	113.4	105.3	106.9	108.9	111.5	111.8	141.2	120.5	106.4
Lesotho	..	..	..	..	..	..	..	..	..	..	..	..	..	..
Liberia	..	..	..	..	..	..	..	..	..	..	..	..	..	..
Madagascar	193.1	92.9	102.7	90.2	81.9	104.1	93.6	94.5	91.9	101.1	109.5	200.0	130.3	95.8
Malawi	..	..	..	..	..	..	..	..	..	..	..	..	..	..
Mali	..	..	..	..	..	..	..	..	..	..	..	..	..	..
Mauritania	120.7	102.6	93.8	86.3	78.9	79.6	79.9	..	..	..	..	139.8	115.1	90.4
Mauritius	..	..	..	..	..	..	..	..	..	..	..	..	..	..
Mozambique	117.6	65.5	63.5	61.4	58.7	67.4	73.7	66.6	67.7	70.0	..	150.1	205.2	70.9
Namibia	..	..	..	..	..	..	..	..	..	..	..	..	..	..
Niger	..	82.8	79.3	55.2	62.1	65.5	65.7	67.2	63.2	61.8	..	..	108.0	71.8
Nigeria	350.6	70.5	77.2	142.8	122.1	167.7	193.1	203.6	193.3	191.4	..	431.4	282.8	140.6
Rwanda	83.3	73.4	85.1	128.7	78.0	85.2	102.2	103.2	104.8	106.4	106.4	60.9	112.9	95.8
São Tomé and Principe	..	..	..	..	..	..	..	..	..	..	..	..	..	..
Senegal	108.2	93.3	91.0	58.8	63.7	64.2	59.9	61.2	59.8	56.2	55.9	98.2	106.9	71.5
Seychelles	90.6	99.5	106.0	104.5	102.1	97.3	101.1	101.1	101.1	122.4	139.4	103.8	109.4	106.1
Sierra Leone	122.8	92.1	102.5	116.6	105.4	117.7	146.3	106.4	108.6	143.5	152.4	173.7	166.9	116.1
Somalia	..	..	..	..	..	..	..	..	..	..	..	..	..	..
South Africa	133.9	107.7	105.5	100.8	97.8	90.2	96.5	87.4	82.7	81.0	78.7	134.6	97.3	94.4
Sudan	45.0	28.2	27.9	33.0	25.4	25.3	26.2	19.9	18.3	20.5	20.5	43.4	47.1	43.5
Swaziland	165.4	92.2	86.9	79.9	85.9	88.5	72.8	73.8	73.8	73.8	73.8	167.5	127.3	80.6
Tanzania	..	86.8	94.0	93.6	97.7	118.3	125.6	135.5	135.5	120.6	121.8	..	138.3	110.7
Togo	..	96.5	93.1	61.9	71.8	73.6	75.7	82.7	76.1	68.7	..	117.5	104.9	81.4
Uganda	..	49.2	50.4	61.0	65.9	64.8	66.2	67.7	58.9	60.0	64.9	..	133.2	64.2
Zambia	148.1	89.5	101.6	97.8	93.6	98.0	117.3	107.2	104.8	106.0	132.1	157.6	93.1	103.4
Zimbabwe	165.4	92.2	86.9	79.9	85.9	88.5	72.8	73.8	..	..	..	167.1	127.3	82.9
NORTH AFRICA	150.7	102.2	103.3	105.4	108.3	109.1	109.5	110.9	112.0	112.7	109.0	148.9	120.0	106.8
Algeria	143.1	60.8	73.9	64.7	53.7	55.8	61.3	64.3	59.2	57.7	59.3	166.3	163.2	64.2
Egypt, Arab Republic	..	101.4	108.7	112.6	118.9	126.9	131.2	156.3	162.2	174.1	171.7	..	104.7	130.0
Libya	..	..	..	..	..	..	..	..	..	..	..	..	..	..
Morocco	156.5	103.0	105.9	109.3	112.8	113.7	114.7	117.5	118.7	122.0	117.0	139.5	109.4	111.4
Tunisia	150.7	104.6	100.7	101.5	103.7	104.4	104.3	104.2	105.3	103.5	100.9	148.9	116.4	103.0
ALL AFRICA	119.2	92.5	89.8	79.9	79.5	85.2	79.9	84.4	80.6	76.1	78.5	77.8	110.4	85.1

Note: 2001 data are preliminary (see page 2).

Figure 3-1. Real effective exchange rate, 2001*

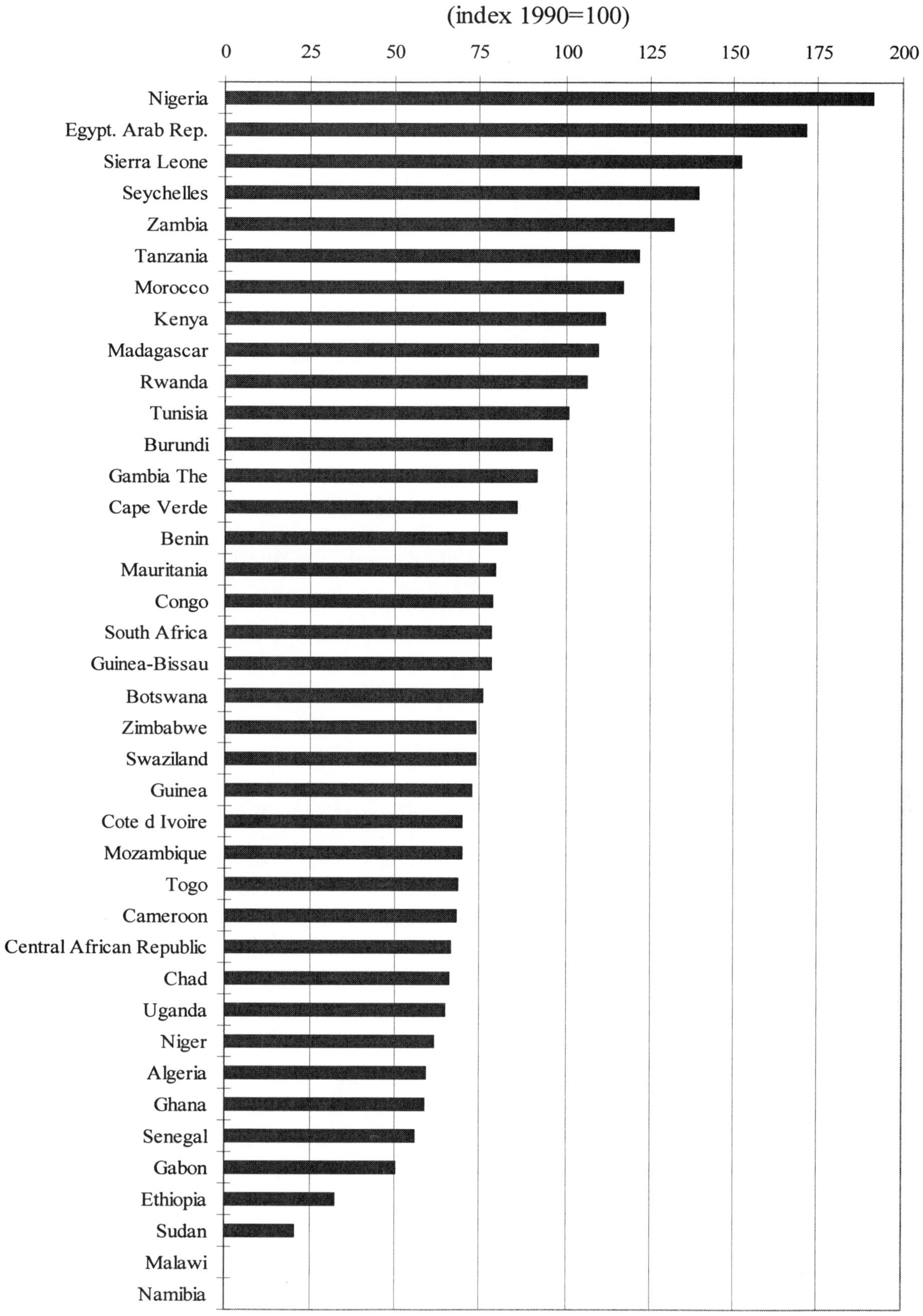

Technical notes

Tables

Table 3-1. GDP deflator (local currency series). The implicit GDP deflator for national currency series is obtained by dividing, for each year of the time series, the value of GDP at current prices (World Bank country desks) by the value of GDP at constant 1995 prices (World Bank country desks), both in national currency.

Table 3-2. GDP deflator (US dollar series). The GDP deflator for US dollar series (with base year 1995 = 100) (World Bank country desks) is obtained by dividing, for each year of the time series, the value of GDP at current U.S. dollars (Table 2-5) by the value of GDP at constant 1995 dollars (Table 2-1). GDP at current U.S. dollars was obtained by converting current national series at single-year exchange rates, while GDP at constant 1995 dollars was obtained by converting constant national series at 1995 prices at a fixed (1995) exchange rate. As a result, the GDP deflator for US dollar series includes both the effects of domestic price changes and the effects of exchange rate variations.

Table 3-3. Consumer price index. Consumer price indexes (IMF, *IFS*, line 64) are generally compiled using the Laspeyres formula: goods in the consumption basket selected according to consumption patterns in the base year, derived from household expenditure surveys, are weighted by their relative prices in the base year. The data often relate only to selected representative income groups in capital cities or major urban areas. Thus, the consumer price indexes shown for some countries may not accurately represent price movements because the underlying consumption basket may not be representative of overall national consumption patterns, and the weights assigned to prices may be outdated.

Table 3-4. Official exchange rate. The official exchange rate (IMF, *IFS*, line rf) is expressed as the annual average of the official market exchange rate in national currency per US dollar.

Table 3-5. SDR exchange rate index. This index is based on the average annual exchange rate for SDRs per unit of national currency (IMF, *IFS*, line rd-zf).

Table 3-6. Currency conversion factor. These are the annual exchange rates used by the World Bank (World Bank country desks) to convert national currency series into U.S. dollars. For most countries, in most years, the conversion factor is identical to the average annual official exchange rate. However, where the official exchange rate is judged to diverge by an exceptionally large margin from the rate effectively applied to international transactions, a more appropriate conversion factor is estimated. An alternative conversion factor is used when there are egregious differences between the official and effective transaction rates, when officially recognized multiple exchange rates have analytically significant spreads, or when exchange rates need to be adjusted to a fiscal year base. The objective in estimating alternative conversion factors is to approximate as closely as possible exchange rates actually used. For example, where multiple exchange rates are maintained, a transaction-weighted rate is calculated.

Note that national statistical compilers sometimes use an official exchange rate to assign a national currency value to international transactions originally denominated in foreign currencies. In these cases, the official rate must be used to convert the same items back to dollars, regardless of whether it was the rate actually applied to the international transactions, even if an alternative conversion factor is used for other components of GDP.

Table 3-7. Parallel market exchange rate. Data reported here are from *Pick's Currency Yearbooks* and *Currency Alerts* (now discontinued) and *Global Currency Report*. They are averages of month-end rates for the period covered, based on a sample of transactions, usually in a capital city or a financial center of the country. They include the rates at the *Bureaux de Change* that have been established in some countries with auction markets as semi-official foreign exchange windows for small transactions. The current table corrects some errors contained in *ADI 1994-95*.

Table 3-8. Ratio of parallel market to official exchange rates. This ratio is obtained by dividing parallel market exchange rates (Table 3-7) by official exchange rates (Table 3-4), to measure the premium on the official exchange rate. The premium is usually high in the presence of an overvalued exchange rate. This table reflects the corrected series for Table 3-7.

Table 3-9. Real effective exchange rate index. This index (World Bank Country Desks) gives a measure of price competitiveness of the country's exports relative to its trading partners. A decline (increase) in the index indicates real depreciation (appreciation) of the exchange rate. The data have been rebased to 1990. The year 1987 coincided with the early period of massive devaluations in the process of adjustment by several Sub-Saharan African countries. As a result, the substantial devaluations that continued to take place after 1987 may not be very pronounced in the data. Relative movements in the inflation rates between a country and the trading partner(s) may diminish the real impact of a devaluation, particularly if inflationary tendencies are stronger domestically than abroad.

Figure

The following indicator has been used to derive the figure in this chapter.

Figure 3-1. Real effective exchange rate (Table 3-9).

Methodology used for regional aggregations and period averages in chapter 3

	Aggregations [a]			*Period averages* [b]	
Table	*(4)*	*(7)*	*(8)*	*(1)*	*(2)*
3-1		X		X	
3-2	X			X	
3-3		X			X
3-4			X	X	
3-5			X	X	
3-6			X	X	
3-7			X	X	
3-8			X	X	
3-9		X		X	

Note: Regional aggregations are shown in the rows for Sub-Saharan Africa, North Africa, and All Africa. Period averages are shown in the last three columns. This table shows only the methodologies used in this chapter.

a. Regional aggregations: (1) simple total; (2) simple total of the first indicator divided by the simple total of the second indicator (same country coverage); (3) simple total of the gap-filled indicator; (4) simple total of the gap-filled main indicator divided by the simple total of the gap-filled secondary indicator; (5) simple total of the first gap-filled main indicator less the simple total of the second gap-filled main indicator, all divided by the simple total of the secondary indicator; (6) weighted total (by population); (7) median; (8) no aggregation; (9) simple arithmetic mean.

b. Period averages: (1) arithmetic mean (using the same series as shown in the table i.e., ratio if the rest of the table is shown as ratio, level if the rest of the table is shown as level, growth rate if the rest is shown as growth rate); (2) least-squares growth rate (using main indicator); (3) least-squares growth rate (using main indicator in constant terms, with the rest of the table in current terms).

4

Money and Banking

Monetary variables directly affect prices and exchange rates and indirectly affect real economic performance. Money plays a vital role in any modern economy. Data in this chapter are concerned with the creation of the types of assets that transactors in the economy wish to hold from the types of liabilities that debtors are willing to incur. However, emphasis here is on the creation of the means of payment, that is, on the more liquid end of the liquidity spectrum for assets.

Money and the institutions that deal in money provide cover against credit risks, limit transactions costs, help mobilize savings, allocate credit, and facilitate investment and hence growth of the economy. Data on money and banking help to assess the prevailing financial conditions of a country and to arrive at a proper evaluation of the financial policy options open to a country for achieving its macroeconomic objectives. The government usually intervenes in finance to control the supply of money and credit. The primary objective of such intervention is to maintain price stability. However, the government may also intervene to finance a budget deficit that in turn may threaten price stability. The government also ensures that financial institutions are properly supervised to ensure continued confidence in the financial system and to avoid destabilizing runs on the banking system. Time series are provided for nine indicators in this section.

4-1. Domestic Credit

	Level	Percentage annual change											Average annual percentage growth		
	1995	1980	1992	1993	1994	1995	1996	1997	1998	1999	2000	2001	75-84	85-89	90-MR
SUB-SAHARAN AFRICA	..	20	11	6	20	11	11	14	11	9	12	11	21	14	11
excluding South Africa	..	19	11	5	20	11	10	13	11	10	12	10	22	14	11
excl. S.Africa & Nigeria	..	18	10	4	20	11	11	14	11	9	12	9	22	14	11
Angola	8	..	..	..	..	..	404	340	156	176	-1,191	-91	..	..	..
Benin	117,710	49	-4	-26	74	21	4	-24	2	6	36	-42	9	..	-8
Botswana	-4,747	-26	14	10	20	-3	16	146	19	0	20	16	..	-54	15
Burkina Faso	66,293	3	-16	-5	4	-14	30	116	9	5	23	5	-32	68	10
Burundi	39,933	20	-6	4	16	-14	52	20	25	34	12	28	-12	..	11
Cameroon	791,344	28	-34	-3	-1	-1	-4	6	9	9	-1	9	-11	13	..
Cape Verde	21,027	39	17	19	23	19	11	21	6	5	32	7	-17	-4	-5
Central African Republic	63,333	39	-18	0	31	-4	-4	-2	11	14	4	11	-11	..	7
Chad	71,325	-1	12	-15	30	-10	28	0	2	8	20	21	-13	..	-12
Comoros	12,449	..	8	-20	9	0	-18	3	-2	20	4	-6	..	2	-9
Congo, Democratic Rep. of	7	22	2,862	1,648	5,299	182	..	..	..	..	..	..	3	84	26
Congo, Republic of	183,036	17	4	-32	3	10	8	14	11	9	-28	37	-2	-13	7
Côte d'Ivoire	1,540,052	23	2	-3	6	12	3	8	5	-1	-4	-2	-20	35	..
Djibouti	45,598	..	8	-2	10	17	7	-3	-4	-31	12	-10	..	-36	15
Equatorial Guinea	20,829	..	-12	-26	47	1	11	16	-15	36	13	-75	..	..	4
Eritrea	..	..	..	..	..	..	..	..	..	..	..	-100	..	..	..
Ethiopia	14,087	18	14	6	9	11	19	8	9	27	16	-3	-4	7	1
Gabon	453,735	11	-7	1	25	15	-4	14	26	-4	-25	46	-13	-27	29
Gambia, The	281	23	-223,914	-17	-13	41	9	35	17	31	16	107	-3	..	..
Ghana	1,462,375	28	43	46	16	53	42	72	21	48	70	..	1	-12	11
Guinea	282,366	..	24	9	18	29	17	-7	-7	..	..	13	..	..	..
Guinea-Bissau	2,171	..	30	52	14	-50	58	234	15	44	47	-29	..	..	-10
Kenya	198,876	13	18	-2	50	37	19	21	9	10	1	3	-6	-13	-10
Lesotho	-270	..	-39	-37	-71	-616	83	52	25	-98	-1,234	59	..	29	..
Liberia	1,692	2	14	11	6	14	11	5	1,783	-9	12	14	7	30	15
Madagascar	2,506,189	50	28	16	29	-3	-2	2	29	10	13	21	1	-27	-2
Malawi	2,646	6	66	16	35	-3	16	12	-3	75	17	74	-17	36	7
Mali	136,883	5	2	12	20	15	0	29	29	18	-9	34	-9	..	12
Mauritania	32,877	13	0	7	-1	-37	-36	-38	-66	-87	-1,182	-120	-16	44	..
Mauritius	46,369	14	19	25	23	13	6	26	22	9	5	15	-9	2	-7
Mozambique	887,600	..	-3	-39	131	28	-40	107	4	192	97	49	..	1	10
Namibia	5,595	..	91	29	28	31	22	-1	9	9	15	14	..	..	-12
Niger	81,241	45	-4	-17	25	-17	10	23	3	3	1	-3	-3	..	..
Nigeria	474,361	23	142	64	56	8	-22	-1	40	23	-25	76	-21	31	-5
Rwanda	44,016	12	33	23	-7	-7	-2	61	13	13	-1	7	4	10	0
São Tomé and Principe	22,360	..	..	..	..	..	22	-110	-783	-7	-45	350	..	..	..
Senegal	538,122	16	-1	-2	7	2	7	2	6	8	16	7	-13	-13	21
Seychelles	1,615	12	11	25	20	15	16	23	31	15	12	11	-3	15	2
Sierra Leone	426,184	35	-8	1	1,076	-12	6	11	7	13	20	7	-3	1	-16
Somalia	..	31	..	..	..	..	..	..	..	..	..	..	-6	16	..
South Africa	333,490	21	..	12	21	12	18	16	17	9	14	20	3	1	-2
Sudan	46,238	22	153	65	48	47	114	18	24	23	43	23	-6	16	-8
Swaziland	328	0	68	109	163	-36	-45	-15	-269	7	37	71	-16	..	..
Tanzania	693,880	24	23	40	11	11	-15	-1	17	23	5	-8	-6	14	-13
Togo	169,769	13	-7	2	21	44	10	7	11	-7	0	-8	-20	..	-30
Uganda	234,994	64	..	-4	-13	-42	34	38	31	15	74	-11	19	..	..
Zambia	1,921,138	17	..	..	123	63	21	0	71	13	60	-5	-8	62	-11
Zimbabwe	20,496	28	43	59	20	19	27	83	41	7	66	84	..	15	1
NORTH AFRICA	..	18	11	7	10	15	6	15	9	12	11	10	20	11	10
Algeria	968,930	17	32	17	4	25	10	10	9	25	-20	28	-3	-13	1
Egypt, Arab Republic	157,300	42	4	7	13	17	14	16	19	12	11	11	-3	3	0
Libya	11,529	-11	1	4	10	8	-4	-16	2	3	2	10	-11	8	-17
Morocco	166,721	18	11	9	11	15	6	49	9	3	11	2	-7	-3	-4
Tunisia	9,746	19	11	5	6	7	0	15	8	14	27	9	-2	-5	4
ALL AFRICA	..	18	11	6	20	11	10	14	10	10	12	10	21	14	11

Note: 2001 data are preliminary (see page 2). Levels for 1995 are expressed in millions of units of national currency. Group data are medians of individual country values in each year or period.

4-2. Credit to the private sector

	Level	Percentage annual change											Average annual percentage growth		
	1995	*1980*	*1992*	*1993*	*1994*	*1995*	*1996*	*1997*	*1998*	*1999*	*2000*	*2001*	*75-84*	*85-89*	*90-MR*
SUB-SAHARAN AFRICA	..	15	7	11	14	17	13	20	14	11	14	11	17	14	14
excluding South Africa	..	15	7	11	14	17	13	22	14	11	13	10	17	13	13
excl. S.Africa & Nigeria	..	15	6	10	13	17	13	20	13	11	13	10	16	13	13
Angola	1	..	..	..	..	..	3,595	241	-1	391	318	298	..	..	..
Benin	80,447	34	-20	-2	11	7	27	-30	40	61	20	-1	-17	..	..
Botswana	1,560	10	36	12	12	-3	4	9	39	43	23	13	-2	1	-6
Burkina Faso	80,590	4	-12	-9	-17	9	13	80	10	3	16	14	-27	5	2
Burundi	30,648	14	7	35	8	-15	31	7	26	29	46	9	-9	57	0
Cameroon	371,390	29	-55	-8	0	1	4	-10	23	12	13	11	-5	..	52
Cape Verde	10,391	-14	20	59	1	37	17	20	12	12	5	15	-10	3	-8
Central African Republic	23,159	50	-37	-5	17	24	0	4	16	-1	11	12	-24	..	-1
Chad	27,790	-2	-1	-33	14	17	8	-3	17	0	1	26	-7	..	..
Comoros	9,525	..	3	-12	-3	10	-29	25	-17	23	10	-3	..	-3	3
Congo, Democratic Rep. of	4	32	4,696	1,889	22,432	474	..	..	..	..	..	..	1	13	89
Congo, Republic of	85,683	23	-1	-46	15	13	14	9	5	41	-31	-8	6	-22	15
Côte d'Ivoire	1,016,035	12	-11	-5	-5	19	2	13	1	-7	4	6	-18	..	..
Djibouti	37,901	..	-1	-6	2	13	3	-1	9	-35	14	-14	..	-32	..
Equatorial Guinea	3,397	..	-37	-74	13	51	82	94	18	51	27	35	..	..	24
Eritrea	..	..	..	..	..	..	..	..	..	..	..	..	..	..	..
Ethiopia	3,706	-30	52	116	47	86	74	24	9	29	6	3	-29	-7	19
Gabon	196,080	16	-28	-3	0	25	-2	41	6	0	10	20	-12	-8	1
Gambia, The	363	19	-24	59	7	-10	0	23	14	20	10	33	-7	-11	-5
Ghana	393,289	18	56	35	46	44	73	70	42	50	56	..	9	-4	1
Guinea	181,518	..	34	22	11	26	4	-1	-13	..	..	7	..	..	..
Guinea-Bissau	6,129	..	27	78	53	-8	20	51	13	-22	23	-63	..	..	-9
Kenya	118,189	20	31	5	28	50	24	25	1	11	4	-4	-8	5	-13
Lesotho	674	-10	16	59	39	-4	0	46	-15	2	3	7	-5	-1	-21
Liberia	191	-39	53	-12	64	-20	-60	36	1,040	-21	-23	25	-10	79	..
Madagascar	1,563,020	26	6	15	26	16	2	14	1	7	24	15	14	-22	-9
Malawi	1,253	8	34	-14	54	6	12	14	99	6	50	5	-13	..	-5
Mali	131,787	8	7	3	-9	52	31	16	27	14	-2	20	-22	..	34
Mauritania	31,417	13	2	3	3	-27	13	8	7	18	24	17	-10	30	1
Mauritius	32,879	9	23	28	20	15	5	26	31	10	13	10	-3	-1	-4
Mozambique	2,374,200	..	45	14	58	54	46	50	27	32	27	-83	..	40	-2
Namibia	4,743	..	30	30	31	34	19	16	9	4	17	16	..	..	-13
Niger	42,004	20	-4	-10	10	-41	3	-18	39	-3	29	7	-21	..	..
Nigeria	201,785	38	141	18	61	42	25	23	18	22	30	41	-19	12	1
Rwanda	28,538	46	26	17	-9	74	1	56	20	11	17	9	-20	-13	2
São Tomé and Principe	6,694	..	..	..	..	..	32	36	88	11	6	10	..	..	..
Senegal	357,834	16	6	2	-17	2	16	4	2	11	28	5	-20	9	17
Seychelles	245	3	5	10	21	17	10	44	19	9	12	14	-6	..	2
Sierra Leone	17,600	28	28	44	12	5	23	25	6	-13	12	25	4	31	-19
Somalia	..	-5	..	..	..	..	..	..	..	..	..	..	17	64	..
South Africa	327,114	26	..	11	18	16	17	14	16	10	15	22	7	4	-2
Sudan	13,068	29	90	69	96	48	144	23	13	-2	64	41	-2	-7	1
Swaziland	928	15	3	9	22	2	6	12	6	6	7	6	-13	63	-14
Tanzania	201,015	11	-12	40	20	-10	-42	43	44	26	10	21	-1	78	-16
Togo	131,241	13	0	-8	-1	28	7	10	4	-10	1	-7	-18	-6	-11
Uganda	246,361	85	..	56	12	28	31	-1	33	22	12	1	5	..	-8
Zambia	253,971	10	..	..	98	81	47	10	3	31	56	10	-10	74	-14
Zimbabwe	15,276	18	42	44	29	28	21	49	37	13	51	61	..	116	-3
NORTH AFRICA	..	13	14	10	11	9	10	12	12	20	11	11	18	9	11
Algeria	103,499	14	-77	1	25	7	33	-21	19	35	41	37	-4	-13	11
Egypt, Arab Republic	66,777	-9	25	19	32	37	26	26	27	20	10	12	-3	-6	6
Libya	3,475	8	7	10	7	8	-17	8	0	28	0	1	-1	..	-9
Morocco	90,906	13	15	11	11	15	10	54	12	9	11	0	-4	..	-5
Tunisia	9,274	22	14	7	8	9	1	12	10	10	24	11	-1	1	0
ALL AFRICA	..	14	7	10	14	16	13	18	14	11	13	11	17	13	13

Note: 2001 data are preliminary (see page 2). Levels for 1995 are expressed in millions of units of national currency. Group data are medians of individual country values in each year or period.

4-3. Credit to the government

	Level	Percentage annual change											Average annual percentage growth		
	1995	*1980*	*1992*	*1993*	*1994*	*1995*	*1996*	*1997*	*1998*	*1999*	*2000*	*2001*	*75-84*	*85-89*	*90-MR*
SUB-SAHARAN AFRICA	..	19	16	5	35	2	9	4	16	11	0	4	21	13	9
excluding South Africa	..	19	16	4	34	3	8	2	15	11	-1	5	22	14	8
excl. S.Africa & Nigeria	..	20	15	2	34	4	9	4	13	11	0	6	24	13	9
Angola	7	..	..	..	..	..	86	538	322	122	-2,024	-44	..	..	..
Benin	36,262	-9	-172	-308	-274	73	-45	8	-125	1,037	-6	95	..	..	..
Botswana	-6,426	15	19	11	19	-3	13	113	23	5	21	16	-10	-25	-1
Burkina Faso	-14,605	46	4	-25	-115	-704	-63	-500	-7	27	76	-36	..	-60	..
Burundi	7,694	9	-27	-58	93	-20	136	64	20	43	-37	78	13	-34	..
Cameroon	410,935	40	16	1	-2	-3	-11	21	-2	8	-15	4	..	..	..
Cape Verde	10,732	188	15	-3	46	6	4	20	0	-1	69	0	-41	26	5
Central African Republic	40,174	26	-3	2	38	-15	-6	-6	8	23	1	10	-6	..	-3
Chad	43,535	0	44	-1	38	-21	40	-1	-9	15	31	20	-10	..	..
Comoros	2,924	..	23	-41	49	-23	17	-41	62	11	-9	-16	..	..	-13
Congo, Democratic Rep. of	2	18	2,786	1,628	3,914	-3	..	..	..	..	..	..	3	143	..
Congo, Republic of	96,501	7	24	-18	-5	8	3	20	17	-16	-24	92	8	..	-5
Côte d'Ivoire	510,099	-52	70	2	35	1	6	0	13	11	-19	-18	-8	..	-22
Djibouti	7,697	..	-165	123	112	37	30	-13	-60	17	-5	21	..	..	..
Equatorial Guinea	17,432	..	26	5	53	-5	-3	-13	-42	11	-18	-458	..	..	..
Eritrea	..	..	..	..	..	..	..	..	..	..	..	29	..	..	..
Ethiopia	9,916	18	15	19	4	-4	-3	-3	10	24	27	-7	-26	16	1
Gabon	246,554	-3	47	7	50	8	-4	-6	52	-9	-63	135	..	..	..
Gambia, The	-82	-43	-112	-476	35	-60	-29	-42	-13	-150	268	922	-20	..	..
Ghana	1,031,892	30	39	49	7	51	35	74	11	47	79	..	-2	22	-1
Guinea	100,355	..	11	-13	35	36	42	-15	4	..	..	19	..	..	..
Guinea-Bissau	-3,959	..	988	-979	324	72	-1	-108	85	1,383	73	-2	..	..	-8
Kenya	69,644	11	0	-10	89	17	7	16	10	-8	-6	22	-2	59	2
Lesotho	-944	329	-120	773	97	44	24	49	2	-51	-25	-12	-19	-4	-21
Liberia	1,498	49	11	15	-1	20	19	4	1,824	-8	13	14	-13	25	18
Madagascar	943,169	81	68	16	33	-24	-7	-21	102	14	-1	31	-17	-23	..
Malawi	1,380	11	117	41	24	-9	20	11	-93	1,741	-33	297	-6	-18	38
Mali	5,096	2	-374	-239	639	-84	-799	-37	16	-15	82	-65	0	..	..
Mauritania	1,411	13	-6	24	-17	-85	-1,118	77	44	30	38	4	1	53	11
Mauritius	13,358	18	10	20	32	11	9	26	-1	-2	-23	44	-25	..	8
Mozambique	-1,486,000	..	335	95	26	75	97	36	36	-4	-10	-269	..	..	-12
Namibia	796	..	-303	27	4	20	49	-79	16	115	-15	-12	..	..	14
Niger	39,237	-59	-6	-39	102	50	17	62	-14	8	-19	-14	-12	16	-6
Nigeria	272,350	6	181	98	55	-8	-56	-57	181	27	-159	-127	-12	38	10
Rwanda	14,249	109	46	27	-8	-51	-6	76	-3	22	-40	-4	..	-28	..
São Tomé and Principe	15,665	..	..	..	..	..	18	-178	-68	83	107	-168	..	..	..
Senegal	179,488	53	-26	-23	174	3	-10	-5	18	4	-15	12	-18	-25	..
Seychelles	1,369	118	13	28	20	15	17	19	33	16	12	10	-8	-9	2
Sierra Leone	408,584	37	-16	-14	1,689	-12	5	10	7	14	18	6	-6	-8	-18
Somalia	..	38	..	..	..	..	..	..	..	..	..	..	-28	-12	..
South Africa	6,376	0	..	51	112	-60	81	79	50	-7	3	-27	-25	..	-18
Sudan	33,177	19	176	65	34	47	101	16	30	34	35	16	-13	19	-8
Swaziland	-600	27	-3	-6	-28	50	34	19	50	6	12	20	..	..	-18
Tanzania	446,034	37	91	46	5	30	3	-12	9	21	2	-25	-15	-9	-30
Togo	38,278	14	66	-57	-278	177	20	-3	32	0	-2	-12	..	..	..
Uganda	-11,367	58	87,960	-21	-28	-105	-26	-1,469	26	-4	302	-24	19	136	..
Zambia	1,667,167	20	..	..	126	60	17	-2	86	11	60	-8	-23	42	-12
Zimbabwe	5,051	41	50	105	6	-4	43	167	53	-5	90	104	..	6	18
NORTH AFRICA	..	21	-2	2	5	8	3	12	3	5	13	9	20	13	5
Algeria	864,285	24	253	20	1	28	7	15	8	24	-27	26	-5	-17	1
Egypt, Arab Republic	86,799	60	-2	2	5	5	5	7	10	5	13	9	-2	8	-9
Libya	8,055	-20	-2	2	11	8	1	-24	3	-12	-3	26	-13	..	-31
Morocco	74,178	21	8	7	10	14	3	12	-1	-11	13	4	-10	3	3
Tunisia	473	2	-13	-14	-12	-16	-22	81	-17	97	65	-8	-1	-26	..
ALL AFRICA	..	19	15	4	32	5	6	7	11	11	1	5	21	13	7

Note: 2001 data are preliminary (see page 2). Levels for 1995 are expressed in millions of units of national currency. Group data are medians of individual country values in each year or period.

4-4. Net foreign assets

	Billions of units of national currency											Annual Average		
	1980	1992	1993	1994	1995	1996	1997	1998	1999	2000	2001	75-84	85-89	90-MR
SUB-SAHARAN AFRICA	..	..	..	..	..	..	..	..	..	..	..	..	..	..
excluding South Africa	..	..	..	..	..	..	..	..	..	..	..	..	..	..
excl. S.Africa & Nigeria	..	..	..	..	..	..	..	..	..	..	..	..	..	..
Angola	..	..	..	..	0	0	0	0	6	31	48	..	..	12
Benin	-23	65	70	160	146	173	215	206	298	354	481	-17	-43	184
Botswana	0	9	11	11	12	19	22	28	30	35	43	0	3	19
Burkina Faso	0	90	106	164	236	220	204	183	170	147	148	6	58	151
Burundi	5	30	35	45	54	47	46	32	33	32	12	3	6	33
Cameroon	-14	-182	-236	-318	-343	-302	-204	-195	-191	10	93	13	-60	-186
Cape Verde	2	5	6	6	5	7	6	6	10	7	10	2	5	6
Central African Republic	3	13	21	85	92	101	90	66	66	68	53	1	14	57
Chad	-4	11	-1	14	48	55	47	35	24	21	34	0	12	28
Comoros	..	7	11	16	16	19	19	15	20	23	36	4	6	16
Congo, Democratic Rep. of	0	0	0	0	0	..	..	..	..	..	..	0	0	0
Congo, Republic of	8	-19	-4	4	15	25	18	-44	-11	199	11	-3	-22	14
Côte d'Ivoire	-223	-511	-515	-72	58	62	100	114	25	73	396	-211	-409	-103
Djibouti	..	35	37	36	34	28	26	24	34	30	38	21	32	34
Equatorial Guinea	..	-7	-7	-14	-10	-7	-7	-1	5	16	61	..	-4	1
Eritrea	..	..	..	..	..	..	..	..	..	1	1	..	..	1
Ethiopia	0	1	3	5	6	5	6	6	5	5	7	0	0	4
Gabon	16	-29	-33	52	9	86	69	-64	-74	146	-39	35	-20	12
Gambia, The	0	1	1	1	1	1	1	1	1	1	1	0	0	1
Ghana	0	-77	-43	217	499	736	981	1,004	261	-1,234	..	-2	-111	201
Guinea	..	105	159	112	97	80	151	176	..	151	200	..	..	131
Guinea-Bissau	..	-4	-5	-6	-4	-3	16	15	14	29	36	..	-1	7
Kenya	2	-6	30	16	24	47	56	54	55	87	94	1	-2	37
Lesotho	0	1	1	1	2	2	3	4	3	4	5	0	0	2
Liberia	0	-1	-1	-1	-1	-1	-1	-28	-25	-27	-31	0	0	-11
Madagascar	-110	-133	-11	1	316	861	1,489	921	1,496	1,919	2,405	-150	-1,458	355
Malawi	0	-1	0	-1	0	2	2	9	9	14	12	0	0	4
Mali	-8	69	74	107	120	184	205	172	126	197	223	-29	-33	131
Mauritania	-2	-32	-30	-33	-25	-11	-2	0	7	24	26	-3	-11	-10
Mauritius	0	16	17	16	19	20	22	20	26	34	36	0	3	21
Mozambique	..	-2,707	-5,671	-3,162	-3,534	-1,627	-861	-243	735	4,348	7,810	-26	-354	-653
Namibia	..	0	0	0	0	0	1	1	2	3	3	..	..	1
Niger	5	28	24	23	22	12	0	-9	-17	3	32	5	16	14
Nigeria	6	35	63	56	108	237	228	235	663	1,275	1,433	3	8	369
Rwanda	14	10	5	3	28	38	46	40	45	67	80	8	9	31
São Tomé and Principe	..	..	..	..	9	19	101	139	156	191	222	..	..	120
Senegal	-97	-172	-207	-130	-70	-46	36	78	119	122	197	-102	-233	-37
Seychelles	0	0	0	0	0	0	0	0	0	0	0	0	0	0
Sierra Leone	0	-188	-204	-339	-396	-159	-169	-220	-322	-180	-202	0	-11	-216
Somalia	0	..	..	..	..	..	..	..	..	..	..	0	-63	..
South Africa	6	-11	-16	-21	-18	-31	-23	-32	2	11	32	2	1	-10
Sudan	0	-37	-59	-122	-202	-444	-494	-687	-724	-677	-697	0	-1	-346
Swaziland	0	1	1	1	1	2	2	2	3	3	4	0	0	2
Tanzania	0	-295	-384	-278	-207	-68	245	275	374	583	898	0	-79	71
Togo	0	54	23	43	33	13	14	8	23	67	66	21	62	40
Uganda	0	-243	-104	64	177	252	392	655	790	1,197	1,519	0	-3	470
Zambia	-1	..	-496	-788	-1,022	-1,287	-1,228	-2,397	-2,572	-3,661	-2,794	-1	-12	-1,491
Zimbabwe	0	-3	-3	-2	-3	-3	-13	-30	-12	-8	-11	0	0	-8
NORTH AFRICA	..	..	..	..	..	..	..	..	..	..	..	..	..	..
Algeria	17	23	20	60	26	134	350	281	170	776	1,311	12	10	265
Egypt, Arab Republic	-1	34	46	51	49	54	49	36	25	23	21	-1	1	34
Libya	4	2	2	2	3	3	2	2	3	6	7	2	2	3
Morocco	0	30	35	40	34	36	40	43	59	54	102	-1	-3	42
Tunisia	0	1	1	1	1	1	2	1	2	1	2	0	0	1
ALL AFRICA	..	..	..	..	..	..	..	..	..	..	..	..	..	..

Note: 2001 data are preliminary (see page 2).

4-5. Growth of money supply

	Level	Percentage annual change											Average annual percentage growth		
	1995	1980	1992	1993	1994	1995	1996	1997	1998	1999	2000	2001	75-84	85-89	90-MR
SUB-SAHARAN AFRICA	..	19	11	12	32	15	14	15	9	16	15	15	14	15	14
excluding South Africa	..	16	11	12	33	15	14	14	8	16	17	14	14	14	14
excl. S.Africa & Nigeria	..	14	11	12	32	15	14	14	7	16	15	14	14	15	14
Angola	3	..	..	..	..	..	3,393	108	40	343	342	168	..	..	..
Benin	161,730	32	10	-13	67	-13	17	2	-5	47	35	10	-5	..	3
Botswana	829	10	-1	15	11	7	15	9	46	17	7	24	-10	16	0
Burkina Faso	213,703	20	1	12	39	25	7	18	-3	-2	5	-3	-8	-8	12
Burundi	38,802	3	10	12	28	-3	12	10	1	42	-1	17	-11	-23	4
Cameroon	319,242	13	-28	-14	35	-12	-2	35	14	11	17	13	-1	3	12
Cape Verde	11,867	26	31	7	8	3	11	22	-2	17	11	3	-11	-14	5
Central African Republic	111,237	32	-4	16	74	8	5	-8	-18	13	3	-3	-10	15	-12
Chad	85,330	-16	-9	-28	32	43	33	-5	-8	-3	18	22	0	-26	..
Comoros	12,040	..	9	5	10	-5	8	-19	-6	16	21	63	..	-4	8
Congo, Democratic Rep. of	19	73	4,114	2,461	5,635	407	..	..	..	..	..	..	31	30	54
Congo, Republic of	134,845	37	6	-20	40	0	14	9	-14	28	68	-23	1	..	11
Côte d'Ivoire	944,519	1	-4	1	62	18	2	12	13	-2	-4	15	-15	..	20
Djibouti	36,998	..	11	4	3	-2	-3	-10	-10	4	-8	3	..	23	..
Equatorial Guinea	9,509	..	35	-29	135	58	50	-4	10	90	35	26	..	..	-3
Eritrea	..	..	..	..	..	..	..	..	..	..	..	..	..	..	..
Ethiopia	9,280	0	15	4	21	3	-2	8	-7	12	11	4	-3	0	-6
Gabon	219,087	10	-27	-3	42	12	26	8	-5	-5	19	4	-17	-6	13
Gambia, The	471	6	11	6	-12	16	-4	39	0	14	37	14	5	-10	5
Ghana	925,287	30	53	28	50	33	31	45	17	3	22	..	1	-1	-7
Guinea	274,125	..	20	19	-3	9	0	21	9	..	..	12	..	..	..
Guinea-Bissau	7,211	..	83	27	58	47	51	236	-12	22	64	8	..	..	-7
Kenya	69,333	-8	47	27	13	4	14	15	3	16	9	6	-2	-23	-9
Lesotho	538	..	12	23	12	11	19	23	25	-3	8	25	..	-13	3
Liberia	653	-4	-6	60	8	42	7	-1	129	15	-12	7	1	-9	2
Madagascar	1,848,007	22	22	12	57	15	17	23	11	20	13	30	8	4	-7
Malawi	2,211	7	19	35	51	44	25	17	57	33	37	9	-2	-9	16
Mali	198,195	5	1	9	48	14	21	6	5	-1	9	30	-7	-34	6
Mauritania	18,202	12	4	4	-5	-8	-11	8	5	6	23	15	-4	-12	3
Mauritius	9,573	21	8	3	19	8	3	8	9	4	11	16	-13	5	-10
Mozambique	3,264,000	..	45	52	51	35	20	25	15	25	22	18	..	44	-9
Namibia	1,822	..	22	46	15	8	54	4	27	22	28	9	..	..	-4
Niger	100,238	13	-10	11	15	9	-10	-19	-18	15	12	35	-4	3	10
Nigeria	207,509	50	63	57	43	16	14	17	19	22	62	26	-24	36	-3
Rwanda	40,658	7	25	11	16	41	12	23	-1	7	7	1	-11	-28	0
São Tomé and Principe	14,225	..	..	..	..	..	66	108	-3	5	23	54	..	..	..
Senegal	316,756	14	2	-9	54	4	8	0	16	11	6	15	-30	7	6
Seychelles	335	38	10	14	-3	3	34	44	20	37	6	13	-7	22	2
Sierra Leone	49,902	20	25	12	10	29	7	57	7	49	4	35	15	9	-15
Somalia	..	19	..	..	..	..	..	..	..	..	..	..	-8	38	..
South Africa	111,844	36	3	7	25	18	32	17	23	22	2	17	19	-18	0
Sudan	40,464	31	101	76	55	67	86	32	29	28	42	16	-3	19	-7
Swaziland	363	22	20	14	7	17	16	16	2	32	0	14	-15	2	-4
Tanzania	428,284	28	34	33	33	30	5	10	10	16	10	10	-21	109	-12
Togo	131,199	5	-27	-18	105	38	-8	2	7	10	22	-9	-19	..	-4
Uganda	408,701	32	61	26	36	15	10	14	19	13	17	13	9	-10	-14
Zambia	227,058	0	..	..	45	61	19	31	17	24	51	34	4	29	-8
Zimbabwe	11,270	37	6	95	18	52	23	54	24	35	53	143	12	8	8
NORTH AFRICA	..	21	9	5	11	7	7	13	8	9	8	10	19	9	8
Algeria	520,286	17	16	19	8	7	13	15	21	9	17	19	-4	-9	1
Egypt, Arab Republic	41,540	56	9	12	11	9	7	9	20	1	5	8	-5	-7	-9
Libya	6,251	29	16	4	13	6	1	5	0	5	4	1	-3	..	-20
Morocco	135,964	8	6	5	11	6	6	16	8	12	8	15	-11	7	-5
Tunisia	3,637	21	7	4	11	10	13	13	8	16	10	10	-2	-23	21
ALL AFRICA	..	19	10	12	25	12	13	14	8	15	12	14	15	14	12

Note: 2001 data are preliminary (see page 2). Levels for 1995 are expressed in millions of units of national currency. Group data are medians of individual country values in each year or period.

4-6. Discount rate

	Percentage											Annual Average		
	1980	*1992*	*1993*	*1994*	*1995*	*1996*	*1997*	*1998*	*1999*	*2000*	*2001*	*75-84*	*85-89*	*90-MR*
SUB-SAHARAN AFRICA	8.5	12.5	11.8	13.0	13.4	13.5	12.5	11.4	11.3	10.7	9.1	8.4	9.7	11.8
excluding South Africa	8.5	12.5	11.5	12.8	13.3	13.3	12.3	10.7	11.2	10.4	8.9	8.4	9.7	11.6
excl. S.Africa & Nigeria	8.5	12.5	11.5	12.0	13.2	13.0	12.0	10.0	10.8	10.0	8.8	8.4	9.6	11.3
Angola	..	..	..	..	160.0	2.0	48.0	58.0	120.0	150.0	150.0	..	..	98.3
Benin	10.5	12.5	10.5	10.0	7.5	6.5	6.0	6.3	5.8	6.5	6.5	9.5	9.6	8.3
Botswana	5.8	14.3	14.3	13.5	13.0	13.0	12.5	12.5	13.3	14.3	14.3	8.3	7.9	12.9
Burkina Faso	10.5	12.5	10.5	10.0	7.5	6.5	6.0	6.3	5.8	6.5	6.5	9.5	9.6	8.3
Burundi	7.0	11.0	10.0	10.0	10.0	10.0	12.0	12.0	12.0	14.0	14.0	6.4	6.6	11.1
Cameroon	8.5	12.0	11.5	7.8	8.6	7.8	7.5	7.0	7.3	7.0	6.5	7.6	8.9	8.7
Cape Verde	..	..	..	..	..	..	..	..	..	..	..	..	..	..
Central African Republic	8.5	12.0	11.5	7.8	8.6	7.8	7.5	7.0	7.6	7.0	6.5	7.6	8.9	8.7
Chad	8.5	12.0	11.5	7.8	8.6	7.8	7.5	7.0	7.6	7.0	6.5	7.7	8.9	8.7
Comoros	..	..	..	..	..	..	..	..	..	..	..	10.0	9.3	..
Congo, Democratic Rep. of	12.0	55.0	95.0	145.0	125.0	238.0	13.0	22.0	120.0	120.0	..	14.7	33.6	93.9
Congo, Republic of	8.5	12.0	11.5	7.8	8.6	7.8	7.5	7.0	7.6	7.0	6.5	7.6	8.9	8.7
Côte d'Ivoire	10.5	12.5	10.5	10.0	7.5	6.5	6.0	6.3	5.8	6.5	6.5	9.5	9.6	8.3
Djibouti	..	..	..	..	..	..	..	..	..	..	..	..	..	..
Equatorial Guinea	..	12.0	11.5	7.8	8.6	7.8	7.5	7.0	7.6	7.0	6.5	..	8.9	8.7
Eritrea	..	..	..	..	..	..	..	..	..	..	..	..	..	..
Ethiopia	..	5.3	12.0	12.0	12.0	..	..	..	..	..	..	..	4.2	7.9
Gabon	8.5	12.0	11.5	7.8	8.6	7.8	7.5	7.0	7.6	7.0	6.5	7.6	8.9	8.7
Gambia, The	8.0	17.5	13.5	13.5	14.0	14.0	14.0	12.0	10.5	10.0	13.0	7.6	18.0	13.7
Ghana	13.5	30.0	35.0	33.0	45.0	45.0	45.0	37.0	27.0	27.0	27.0	12.7	22.9	33.7
Guinea	..	19.0	17.0	17.0	18.0	18.0	15.0	..	..	11.5	16.3	..	10.5	16.6
Guinea-Bissau	..	45.5	41.0	26.0	39.0	54.0	6.0	6.3	5.8	6.5	6.5	..	..	26.7
Kenya	8.0	20.5	45.5	21.5	24.5	26.9	32.3	17.1	26.5	..	..	9.9	14.0	25.4
Lesotho	8.0	15.0	13.5	13.5	15.5	17.0	15.6	19.5	19.0	15.0	13.0	11.8	12.6	15.9
Liberia	..	..	..	..	..	..	..	..	..	..	..	..	..	..
Madagascar	5.5	..	..	..	..	..	..	..	15.0	..	..	8.0	11.5	15.0
Malawi	10.0	20.0	25.0	40.0	50.0	27.0	23.0	43.0	47.0	50.2	46.8	8.5	11.6	33.3
Mali	10.5	12.5	10.5	10.0	7.5	6.5	6.0	6.3	5.8	6.5	6.5	9.5	9.6	8.3
Mauritania	6.0	7.0	..	..	..	..	..	..	..	..	..	5.5	6.6	7.0
Mauritius	10.5	8.3	8.3	13.8	11.4	11.8	10.5	17.2	..	..	..	9.5	10.8	11.6
Mozambique	..	..	..	69.7	57.8	32.0	13.0	10.0	10.0	10.0	10.0	..	..	26.5
Namibia	..	16.5	14.5	15.5	17.5	17.8	16.0	18.8	11.5	11.3	9.3	..	..	15.4
Niger	10.5	12.5	10.5	10.0	7.5	6.5	6.0	6.3	5.8	6.5	6.5	9.5	9.4	8.3
Nigeria	6.0	17.5	26.0	13.5	13.5	13.5	13.5	13.5	18.0	14.0	20.5	5.9	12.8	16.5
Rwanda	9.0	11.0	11.0	11.0	16.0	16.0	10.8	11.4	11.2	11.7	13.0	7.4	9.0	12.6
São Tomé and Principe	..	45.0	30.0	32.0	50.0	35.0	55.0	29.5	17.0	17.0	15.5	..	25.0	33.0
Senegal	10.5	12.5	10.5	10.0	7.5	6.5	6.0	6.3	5.8	6.5	6.5	9.5	9.6	8.3
Seychelles	..	1.0	1.0	1.0	1.0	1.0	1.0	1.0	1.0	1.0	1.0	6.0	6.0	1.0
Sierra Leone	12.0	..	..	..	..	..	..	..	..	..	..	10.2	15.6	55.0
Somalia	..	..	..	..	..	..	..	..	..	..	..	..	..	..
South Africa	6.5	14.0	12.0	13.0	15.0	17.0	16.0	19.3	12.0	12.0	9.5	11.1	12.9	14.6
Sudan	..	..	..	..	..	..	..	..	..	..	..	..	..	..
Swaziland	7.0	12.0	11.0	12.0	15.0	16.8	15.8	18.0	12.0	11.0	9.5	11.1	10.8	13.2
Tanzania	4.8	14.5	14.5	67.5	47.9	19.0	16.2	17.6	20.2	10.7	8.7	4.5	11.1	23.7
Togo	10.5	12.5	10.5	10.0	7.5	6.5	6.0	6.3	5.8	6.5	6.5	9.5	9.6	8.3
Uganda	8.0	41.0	24.0	15.0	13.3	15.9	14.1	9.1	15.8	18.9	8.9	13.7	38.2	22.7
Zambia	6.5	47.0	72.5	20.5	40.2	47.0	17.7	..	32.9	25.7	40.1	7.5	21.3	38.2
Zimbabwe	4.5	29.5	28.5	29.5	29.5	27.0	31.5	39.5	74.4	57.8	57.2	6.3	9.0	36.2
NORTH AFRICA	5.0	11.4	10.2	11.4	13.5	13.0	11.6	7.8	7.0	5.5	5.5	5.7	8.6	10.0
Algeria	2.8	11.5	11.5	21.0	14.0	13.0	11.0	9.5	8.5	6.0	6.0	2.8	5.0	11.2
Egypt, Arab Republic	11.0	18.4	16.5	14.0	13.5	13.0	12.3	12.0	12.0	12.0	11.0	9.7	13.2	14.1
Libya	5.0	5.0	5.0	..	..	..	..	3.0	5.0	5.0	5.0	5.0	5.0	4.8
Morocco	4.9	..	..	7.2	..	..	..	6.0	5.4	5.0	4.7	5.4	8.4	5.7
Tunisia	5.8	11.4	8.9	8.9	8.9	7.9	..	..	..	..	..	6.1	9.7	10.0
ALL AFRICA	8.5	12.5	11.5	13.0	13.5	13.0	12.3	10.0	10.8	10.0	8.8	8.1	9.7	11.5

Note: Group data are medians of individual country values in each year or period.

4-7. Real discount rate

	Percentage											Annual Average		
	1980	*1992*	*1993*	*1994*	*1995*	*1996*	*1997*	*1998*	*1999*	*2000*	*2001*	*75-84*	*85-89*	*90-MR*
SUB-SAHARAN AFRICA	-3.7	2.4	6.0	-4.2	-0.4	2.2	3.5	4.6	6.5	3.9	3.0	-3.8	1.3	2.8
excluding South Africa	-3.6	3.5	6.5	-5.0	-0.4	2.1	3.5	4.3	6.5	3.8	2.8	-4.2	1.6	2.9
excl. S.Africa & Nigeria	-3.7	3.8	7.3	-4.2	-0.4	2.2	3.4	4.6	6.1	3.9	2.6	-4.0	1.3	3.0
Angola	..	..	..	..	-90.6	-97.6	-53.6	-23.8	-36.8	-41.2	-1.0	..	..	-49.2
Benin	..	..	10.0	-20.6	-6.1	1.5	2.4	0.5	5.4	2.2	2.4	..	..	-0.2
Botswana	-6.9	-1.7	-0.1	2.7	2.3	2.6	3.5	5.5	5.1	5.2	7.2	-3.1	-1.5	2.5
Burkina Faso	..	14.8	9.9	-12.1	0.1	0.3	3.6	1.1	6.9	6.8	1.4	5.4	8.6	4.4
Burundi	4.4	9.0	0.3	-4.2	-7.8	-13.0	-14.6	-0.4	8.3	-8.3	4.4	-5.4	0.9	-2.0
Cameroon	-1.0	12.0	15.2	-20.2	-0.4	3.7	2.6	3.7	5.7	9.2	1.9	-3.8	3.1	4.5
Cape Verde	..	..	..	..	..	..	..	..	..	..	..	..	..	..
Central African Republic	..	13.6	14.8	-13.5	-8.9	3.9	5.8	9.1	9.1	3.7	2.6	1.2	8.7	5.4
Chad	..	15.6	20.0	-23.3	-0.4	-4.1	1.8	-4.6	15.5	3.1	-5.3	-9.4	10.4	3.0
Comoros	..	..	..	..	..	..	..	..	..	..	..	..	5.0	..
Congo, Democratic Rep. of	-23.6	-96.3	-90.7	-99.0	-64.9	-47.3	-59.0	-5.5	-42.8	-66.2	..	-25.6	-17.0	-62.3
Congo, Republic of	..	16.3	6.5	-24.4	-0.7	-2.1	..	..	2.1	8.0	6.4	..	7.9	3.3
Côte d'Ivoire	-3.7	7.9	8.2	-12.8	-5.9	3.9	1.9	1.5	4.9	3.9	2.1	-2.1	4.2	3.1
Djibouti	..	..	..	..	..	..	..	..	..	..	..	..	..	..
Equatorial Guinea	..	10.9	9.7	-22.4	-2.5	1.7	4.4	3.9	1.5	0.9	1.2	..	16.6	2.8
Eritrea	..	..	..	..	..	..	..	..	..	..	..	..	..	..
Ethiopia	..	-4.8	8.2	4.1	1.8	..	..	..	..	..	..	..	0.8	-2.8
Gabon	-3.4	23.8	10.9	-20.8	-1.0	7.0	3.4	5.5	9.7	6.5	..	-4.9	7.1	6.7
Gambia, The	1.1	11.0	9.1	9.1	8.8	11.7	10.9	10.8	6.5	9.0	8.7	-4.2	-3.1	8.8
Ghana	-24.4	18.1	8.0	6.5	-9.1	-1.1	13.4	19.5	13.0	1.4	-4.4	-30.2	-2.2	5.3
Guinea	..	-10.1	22.2	12.3	11.7	14.6	12.9	..	..	4.4	10.3	..	-9.9	6.7
Guinea-Bissau	..	-14.2	-4.8	9.4	-4.4	2.2	-28.9	-0.2	6.5	-2.0	3.0	..	..	-3.0
Kenya	-5.1	-5.4	-0.3	-5.7	22.6	16.5	18.8	9.7	19.6	..	..	-3.4	3.7	7.7
Lesotho	-6.7	-1.9	0.3	4.9	5.7	7.0	7.7	11.3	8.1	8.4	5.5	-1.6	-1.0	5.1
Liberia	..	..	..	..	..	..	..	..	..	..	..	..	..	..
Madagascar	-10.8	..	..	..	..	..	..	..	4.6	..	..	-5.3	-4.2	4.6
Malawi	..	-3.0	1.8	4.0	-18.2	-7.7	12.7	10.2	1.5	15.9	15.4	-3.2	-5.9	2.9
Mali	..	20.0	10.8	-10.7	-5.2	-0.3	6.4	2.1	7.0	7.2	1.2	..	11.1	4.8
Mauritania	..	-2.9	..	..	..	..	..	..	..	..	..	..	-0.6	-0.4
Mauritius	-22.2	3.5	-2.0	6.0	5.1	4.9	3.4	9.7	..	..	..	-3.4	4.6	3.7
Mozambique	..	..	..	4.0	2.1	-11.1	5.2	8.3	6.9	-2.5	0.8	..	..	1.7
Namibia	..	-1.0	5.5	4.3	6.8	9.0	6.6	11.8	2.6	2.1	-0.3	..	..	5.0
Niger	0.2	17.8	11.9	-19.1	-2.8	1.2	3.0	1.6	8.2	3.5	2.4	-2.1	12.8	5.0
Nigeria	-3.6	-18.7	-19.8	-27.7	-34.3	-12.2	4.9	2.9	12.6	-0.5	6.7	-11.7	-8.1	-6.1
Rwanda	1.6	1.3	2.2	-32.3	-4.9	6.5	-0.8	4.2	13.9	7.5	9.3	-3.6	7.2	1.0
São Tomé and Principe	..	13.9	3.6	4.2	9.3	-1.8	-7.6	-14.2	0.6	5.4	5.2	..	-14.4	0.5
Senegal	1.6	12.6	11.2	-16.9	-0.3	3.6	4.4	5.0	4.9	5.7	3.3	-1.2	7.0	4.8
Seychelles	..	-2.2	-0.4	-0.7	1.2	2.1	0.4	-1.5	-5.0	-5.0	-4.7	1.2	4.5	-1.6
Sierra Leone	-0.8	..	..	..	..	..	..	..	..	..	..	-11.9	-34.2	-25.0
Somalia	..	..	..	..	..	..	..	..	..	..	..	..	..	..
South Africa	-6.3	0.1	2.1	3.7	5.8	9.0	6.4	11.8	6.6	6.4	4.5	-1.5	-2.4	5.1
Sudan	..	..	..	..	..	..	..	..	..	..	..	..	..	..
Swaziland	-9.8	4.1	-0.9	-1.6	2.4	9.7	8.1	9.1	5.6	-1.1	3.4	-2.4	-3.8	3.5
Tanzania	-19.5	-6.0	-8.6	25.9	15.2	-1.6	0.1	4.3	11.4	4.5	3.4	-13.2	-14.8	4.8
Togo	-1.6	11.0	11.6	-21.0	-7.7	1.7	-2.1	5.2	5.8	4.5	2.5	-0.8	9.4	2.7
Uganda	..	-7.5	16.9	4.8	4.3	8.0	6.7	9.1	8.8	15.6	6.7	-23.2	-42.2	8.4
Zambia	-4.6	-50.6	-40.1	-21.6	3.9	2.7	-5.4	..	4.8	-0.3	15.1	-6.7	-17.2	-10.1
Zimbabwe	-0.9	-8.8	0.7	5.9	5.6	4.6	10.7	5.8	10.0	1.3	-11.0	-5.5	-1.8	1.3
NORTH AFRICA	-6.4	0.1	-0.8	2.9	-1.9	4.0	6.1	3.8	5.2	5.6	4.1	-4.8	0.1	2.0
Algeria	-6.2	-15.3	-7.5	-6.2	-12.2	-4.8	5.0	4.3	5.7	5.6	1.7	-6.8	-3.8	-3.4
Egypt, Arab Republic	-8.0	4.2	3.9	5.4	-1.9	5.4	7.3	7.5	8.7	9.1	8.5	-3.1	-4.7	4.7
Libya	-6.6	-4.0	-5.5	..	..	..	..	-0.7	2.3	..	..	-3.8	0.2	-2.9
Morocco	-4.1	..	..	1.9	..	..	..	3.2	4.7	3.0	4.1	-4.0	2.9	3.4
Tunisia	..	5.2	4.7	4.0	2.5	4.0	..	..	..	..	..	-1.7	2.2	4.1
ALL AFRICA	-4.6	2.4	4.3	-1.6	-0.4	2.4	4.0	4.3	6.1	4.2	3.2	-4.4	1.1	2.8

Note: 2001 data are preliminary (see page 2). Real discount rate in each year is the nominal discount rate deflated by the annual change in the CPI.

4-8. Commercial bank lending rate

	Percentage											Annual Average		
	1980	1992	1993	1994	1995	1996	1997	1998	1999	2000	2001	75-84	85-89	90-MR
SUB-SAHARAN AFRICA	12.0	17.8	17.5	17.5	19.3	22.0	22.0	22.0	21.9	22.0	20.7	12.3	14.0	19.9
excluding South Africa	12.3	17.8	17.5	17.5	20.2	22.0	22.0	22.0	22.0	22.0	20.7	12.2	14.0	20.0
excl. S.Africa & Nigeria	12.5	17.8	17.5	17.5	19.3	22.0	22.0	22.0	22.0	22.0	20.7	12.4	14.0	19.9
Angola	..	..	..	..	206.3	217.9	37.8	45.0	80.3	103.2	96.0	..	..	112.3
Benin	14.5	16.8	..	..	..	..	..	..	..	..	..	13.8	14.0	16.3
Botswana	8.5	14.0	14.9	13.9	14.3	14.5	14.1	13.5	14.6	15.3	15.8	13.5	9.6	13.7
Burkina Faso	14.5	16.8	..	..	..	..	..	..	..	..	..	13.8	14.0	16.3
Burundi	12.0	13.7	13.8	14.2	15.3	..	..	..	15.2	15.8	16.8	12.0	12.0	14.4
Cameroon	13.0	17.8	17.5	17.5	16.0	22.0	22.0	22.0	22.0	22.0	20.7	13.0	13.9	19.7
Cape Verde	6.5	10.0	10.0	10.7	12.0	12.0	12.1	12.5	12.0	11.9	12.8	6.5	10.0	11.3
Central African Republic	10.5	17.8	17.5	17.5	16.0	22.0	22.0	22.0	22.0	22.0	20.7	11.1	12.2	19.7
Chad	11.0	17.8	17.5	17.5	16.0	22.0	22.0	22.0	22.0	22.0	20.7	10.7	11.1	19.7
Comoros	..	..	..	..	..	..	..	..	..	..	..	15.0	14.0	..
Congo, Democratic Rep. of	..	..	..	398.3	293.9	247.0	134.6	29.0	124.6	165.0	..	..	..	198.9
Congo, Republic of	11.0	17.8	17.5	17.5	16.0	22.0	22.0	22.0	22.0	22.0	20.7	11.3	11.8	19.7
Côte d'Ivoire	14.5	16.8	..	..	..	..	..	..	..	..	..	13.8	14.0	16.3
Djibouti	..	..	..	..	..	..	..	..	..	..	11.5	8.5	9.3	11.0
Equatorial Guinea	..	17.8	17.5	17.5	16.0	22.0	22.0	22.0	22.0	22.0	20.7	..	14.8	19.7
Eritrea	..	..	..	..	..	..	..	..	..	..	..	..	..	..
Ethiopia	..	8.0	14.0	14.3	15.1	13.9	10.5	10.5	10.6	10.9	10.9	..	6.8	10.9
Gabon	12.5	17.8	17.5	17.5	16.0	22.0	22.0	22.0	22.0	22.0	20.7	11.8	11.9	19.7
Gambia, The	15.0	26.8	26.1	25.0	25.0	25.5	25.5	25.4	24.0	24.0	..	16.7	25.4	25.5
Ghana	19.0	..	..	..	..	..	..	..	..	..	..	19.3	23.1	..
Guinea	..	27.0	24.5	22.0	21.5	..	..	19.6	19.9	19.4	..	..	15.8	22.2
Guinea-Bissau	..	50.3	63.6	36.3	32.9	51.8	..	..	..	..	..	..	26.1	46.8
Kenya	10.6	21.1	30.0	36.2	28.8	33.8	30.2	29.5	22.4	22.3	19.7	11.8	14.9	26.0
Lesotho	11.0	18.3	15.8	14.3	16.4	17.7	18.0	20.1	19.1	17.1	16.6	15.2	15.3	17.8
Liberia	18.4	..	..	14.5	15.6	..	16.8	21.7	16.7	20.5	22.1	19.9	14.9	18.3
Madagascar	..	25.0	26.0	30.5	37.5	32.8	30.0	27.0	28.0	26.5	25.3	..	22.3	28.2
Malawi	16.7	22.0	29.5	31.0	47.3	45.3	28.3	37.7	53.6	53.1	56.2	17.7	20.4	37.1
Mali	14.5	16.8	..	..	..	..	..	..	..	..	..	13.8	14.0	16.3
Mauritania	12.0	10.0	..	..	..	..	..	..	..	..	..	12.0	11.6	10.0
Mauritius	..	17.1	16.6	18.9	20.8	20.8	18.9	19.9	21.6	20.8	21.1	13.5	14.7	19.4
Mozambique	..	..	..	..	..	..	..	24.4	19.6	19.0	22.6	..	..	21.4
Namibia	..	20.2	18.0	17.1	18.5	19.2	20.2	20.7	18.5	15.3	14.5	..	..	18.7
Niger	14.5	16.8	..	..	..	..	..	..	..	..	..	13.8	14.0	16.3
Nigeria	8.4	24.8	31.6	20.5	20.2	19.8	17.8	18.2	20.3	21.3	..	8.0	14.1	21.8
Rwanda	13.5	16.7	15.0	..	..	..	..	..	..	..	..	13.3	13.0	16.0
São Tomé and Principe	..	37.0	37.0	30.0	52.0	38.0	51.5	55.6	40.3	37.0	37.0	..	20.0	39.4
Senegal	14.5	16.8	..	..	..	..	..	..	..	..	..	13.8	14.0	16.3
Seychelles	..	15.6	15.7	15.7	15.8	16.2	14.9	14.4	12.0	11.4	..	..	15.5	14.8
Sierra Leone	11.0	62.8	50.5	27.3	28.8	32.1	23.9	23.8	26.8	26.3	24.3	12.7	24.1	36.3
Somalia	..	..	..	..	..	..	..	..	..	..	..	..	..	..
South Africa	9.5	18.9	16.2	15.6	17.9	19.5	20.0	21.8	18.0	14.5	13.8	14.1	16.7	18.1
Sudan	..	..	..	..	..	..	..	..	..	..	..	..	..	..
Swaziland	9.5	15.0	14.0	15.0	18.0	19.8	18.8	21.0	15.0	14.0	12.5	13.2	14.2	16.1
Tanzania	11.5	..	31.0	39.0	42.8	34.0	26.3	22.9	21.9	21.6	20.3	11.4	23.8	28.9
Togo	14.5	17.5	..	..	..	..	..	..	..	..	..	13.8	14.4	16.5
Uganda	10.8	..	..	..	20.2	20.3	21.4	20.9	21.5	22.9	22.7	15.2	33.4	24.8
Zambia	9.5	54.6	113.3	70.6	45.5	53.8	46.7	31.8	40.5	38.8	46.2	9.7	20.8	52.4
Zimbabwe	17.5	19.8	36.3	34.9	34.7	34.2	32.5	42.1	55.4	68.2	38.0	20.3	13.8	35.3
NORTH AFRICA	7.1	13.7	12.6	16.0	17.7	17.3	13.1	13.0	11.5	11.6	11.4	7.5	9.0	12.9
Algeria	..	..	..	16.0	19.0	19.0	12.5	11.0	10.0	10.0	9.5	..	..	13.4
Egypt, Arab Republic	13.3	20.3	18.3	16.5	16.5	15.6	13.8	13.0	13.0	13.2	13.3	12.5	16.3	15.7
Libya	7.0	7.0	7.0	..	..	..	..	..	7.0	7.0	7.0	7.0	7.0	7.0
Morocco	7.0	..	..	10.0	..	..	..	13.5	13.5	13.3	13.3	7.0	8.7	11.7
Tunisia	7.3	..	..	..	..	..	..	..	..	..	..	7.9	8.9	..
ALL AFRICA	12.0	17.8	17.5	17.5	18.8	22.0	22.0	22.0	21.6	21.4	20.7	11.9	14.0	19.8

Note: 2001 data are preliminary (see page 2). Group data are medians of individual country values in each year or period.

4-9. Commercial bank deposit rate

	Percentage											Annual Average		
	1980	*1992*	*1993*	*1994*	*1995*	*1996*	*1997*	*1998*	*1999*	*2000*	*2001*	*75-84*	*85-89*	*90-MR*
SUB-SAHARAN AFRICA	6.2	9.3	11.5	11.1	12.5	12.6	9.7	7.6	7.5	7.0	5.8	6.6	7.8	9.3
excluding South Africa	6.2	9.0	10.6	11.0	12.4	12.6	9.5	7.5	7.5	6.7	5.7	6.6	7.6	9.1
excl. S.Africa & Nigeria	6.2	8.4	9.6	10.7	12.2	12.5	9.7	7.3	6.9	6.6	5.7	6.6	7.5	8.8
Angola	..	..	..	..	125.9	147.1	29.3	36.9	36.6	39.6	47.9	..	..	66.2
Benin	6.2	7.8	..	..	..	..	..	3.5	3.5	3.5	3.5	6.5	6.1	5.1
Botswana	5.0	12.5	13.5	10.4	10.0	10.4	9.3	8.7	9.5	10.1	10.2	9.3	7.2	10.2
Burkina Faso	6.2	7.8	..	..	..	..	..	3.5	3.5	3.5	3.5	6.5	6.1	5.1
Burundi	2.5	..	..	..	..	..	..	..	..	..	..	3.4	4.9	..
Cameroon	7.5	7.5	7.8	8.1	5.5	5.4	5.0	5.0	5.0	5.0	5.0	7.3	7.3	6.2
Cape Verde	..	4.0	4.0	4.0	5.0	5.0	5.0	5.3	4.8	4.3	4.7	..	4.0	4.5
Central African Republic	5.5	7.5	7.8	8.1	5.5	5.5	5.0	5.0	5.0	5.0	5.0	6.4	7.4	6.2
Chad	5.5	7.5	7.8	8.1	5.5	5.5	5.0	5.0	5.0	5.0	5.0	5.3	5.0	6.2
Comoros	..	..	..	..	..	..	..	..	..	..	..	7.5	7.0	..
Congo, Democratic Rep. of	..	..	..	60.0	60.0	60.0	..	..	..	..	..	..	..	60.0
Congo, Republic of	6.5	7.5	7.8	8.1	5.5	5.5	5.0	5.0	5.0	5.0	5.0	6.5	8.0	6.2
Côte d'Ivoire	6.2	7.8	..	..	..	..	..	3.5	3.5	3.5	3.5	6.5	6.1	5.1
Djibouti	..	..	..	..	..	..	..	..	..	..	2.8	..	..	2.8
Equatorial Guinea	..	7.5	7.8	8.1	5.5	5.5	5.0	5.0	5.0	5.0	5.0	..	7.3	6.2
Eritrea	..	..	..	..	..	..	..	..	..	..	..	..	..	..
Ethiopia	..	3.6	11.5	11.5	11.5	9.4	7.0	6.0	6.3	6.7	7.0	..	6.5	7.3
Gabon	7.5	7.5	7.8	8.1	5.5	5.5	5.0	5.0	5.0	5.0	5.0	7.4	8.1	6.2
Gambia, The	5.0	13.8	13.0	12.6	12.5	12.5	12.5	12.5	12.5	12.5	..	7.1	13.9	12.6
Ghana	11.5	16.3	23.6	23.1	28.7	34.5	35.8	32.0	23.6	28.6	30.9	12.0	16.7	27.1
Guinea	..	23.0	19.8	18.0	17.5	..	..	6.4	5.7	7.5	8.0	..	17.1	14.9
Guinea-Bissau	..	39.3	53.9	28.7	26.5	47.3	4.6	3.5	3.5	3.5	3.5	..	25.5	23.6
Kenya	5.8	..	..	..	13.6	17.6	16.7	18.4	9.6	8.1	6.6	7.7	11.0	13.0
Lesotho	..	10.6	8.1	8.4	13.3	12.7	11.8	10.7	7.5	4.9	4.8	10.2	10.0	9.9
Liberia	10.3	..	..	6.3	6.4	..	6.4	6.2	6.3	6.2	5.9	10.4	6.9	6.2
Madagascar	..	20.5	19.5	19.5	18.5	19.0	14.4	8.0	15.3	15.0	12.0	..	17.8	16.9
Malawi	7.9	16.5	21.8	25.0	37.3	26.3	10.2	19.1	33.2	33.3	35.0	9.8	13.2	23.5
Mali	6.2	7.8	..	..	..	..	..	3.5	3.5	3.5	3.5	6.5	6.1	5.1
Mauritania	..	5.0	..	..	..	..	..	..	..	..	..	5.5	6.2	5.0
Mauritius	..	10.1	8.4	11.0	12.2	10.8	9.1	9.3	10.9	9.6	9.8	10.7	9.9	10.5
Mozambique	..	..	..	33.4	38.8	18.1	25.4	8.2	7.9	9.7	15.1	..	..	19.6
Namibia	..	11.4	9.6	9.2	10.8	12.6	12.7	12.9	10.8	7.4	6.8	..	..	10.6
Niger	6.2	7.8	..	..	..	..	..	3.5	3.5	3.5	3.5	6.5	6.1	5.1
Nigeria	5.3	18.0	23.2	13.1	13.5	13.1	7.2	10.1	12.8	11.7	..	5.1	11.8	14.3
Rwanda	6.3	7.7	5.0	..	..	10.9	9.5	8.5	7.9	8.9	9.2	5.1	6.3	8.3
São Tomé and Principe	..	35.0	35.0	35.0	35.0	31.0	36.8	38.3	27.0	15.0	15.0	..	16.0	29.5
Senegal	6.2	7.8	..	..	..	..	..	3.5	3.5	3.5	3.5	6.5	6.1	5.1
Seychelles	..	9.6	9.5	8.9	9.2	9.9	9.2	7.5	5.1	4.8	..	9.1	9.8	8.4
Sierra Leone	9.2	54.7	27.0	11.6	7.0	14.0	9.9	7.1	9.5	9.2	7.7	9.2	14.9	20.5
Somalia	..	..	..	..	..	..	..	..	..	..	..	..	..	..
South Africa	5.5	13.8	11.5	11.1	13.5	14.9	15.4	16.5	12.2	9.2	9.4	10.0	13.7	13.6
Sudan	6.0	..	..	..	..	..	..	..	..	..	..	9.2	..	..
Swaziland	4.5	9.0	7.4	8.0	10.3	12.3	11.3	13.4	7.5	6.5	5.7	9.0	7.8	9.3
Tanzania	4.0	..	..	..	24.6	13.6	7.8	7.8	7.8	7.4	4.8	4.0	12.6	10.5
Togo	6.2	7.8	..	..	..	..	..	3.5	3.5	3.5	3.5	6.5	6.1	5.1
Uganda	6.8	35.8	16.3	10.0	7.6	10.6	11.8	11.4	8.7	9.8	8.5	9.9	23.4	16.1
Zambia	7.0	48.5	..	46.1	30.2	42.1	34.5	13.1	20.3	20.2	23.4	6.2	13.8	30.4
Zimbabwe	3.5	28.6	29.4	26.8	25.9	21.6	18.6	29.1	38.5	50.2	13.9	6.6	9.7	25.5
NORTH AFRICA	4.9	8.0	8.0	11.9	13.5	12.5	9.8	8.5	6.9	6.3	5.6	4.7	7.0	9.0
Algeria	3.0	8.0	8.0	12.0	16.0	14.5	9.8	8.5	7.5	7.5	6.3	3.0	4.6	9.5
Egypt, Arab Republic	8.3	12.0	12.0	11.8	10.9	10.5	9.8	9.4	9.2	9.5	9.5	8.0	11.1	10.7
Libya	5.1	5.5	5.5	..	..	..	..	..	3.2	3.0	3.0	4.7	5.5	4.5
Morocco	4.9	..	..	..	..	..	..	7.3	6.4	5.2	5.0	5.6	8.4	6.8
Tunisia	2.5	..	..	..	..	..	..	..	..	..	..	3.4	6.7	..
ALL AFRICA	6.2	9.0	10.6	11.3	12.5	12.6	9.8	7.8	7.5	7.0	5.8	6.5	7.6	9.2

Note: 2001 data are preliminary (see page 2). Group data are medians of individual country values in each year or period.

Figure 4-1. Credit to private and public sectors as a share of GDP, 2001*

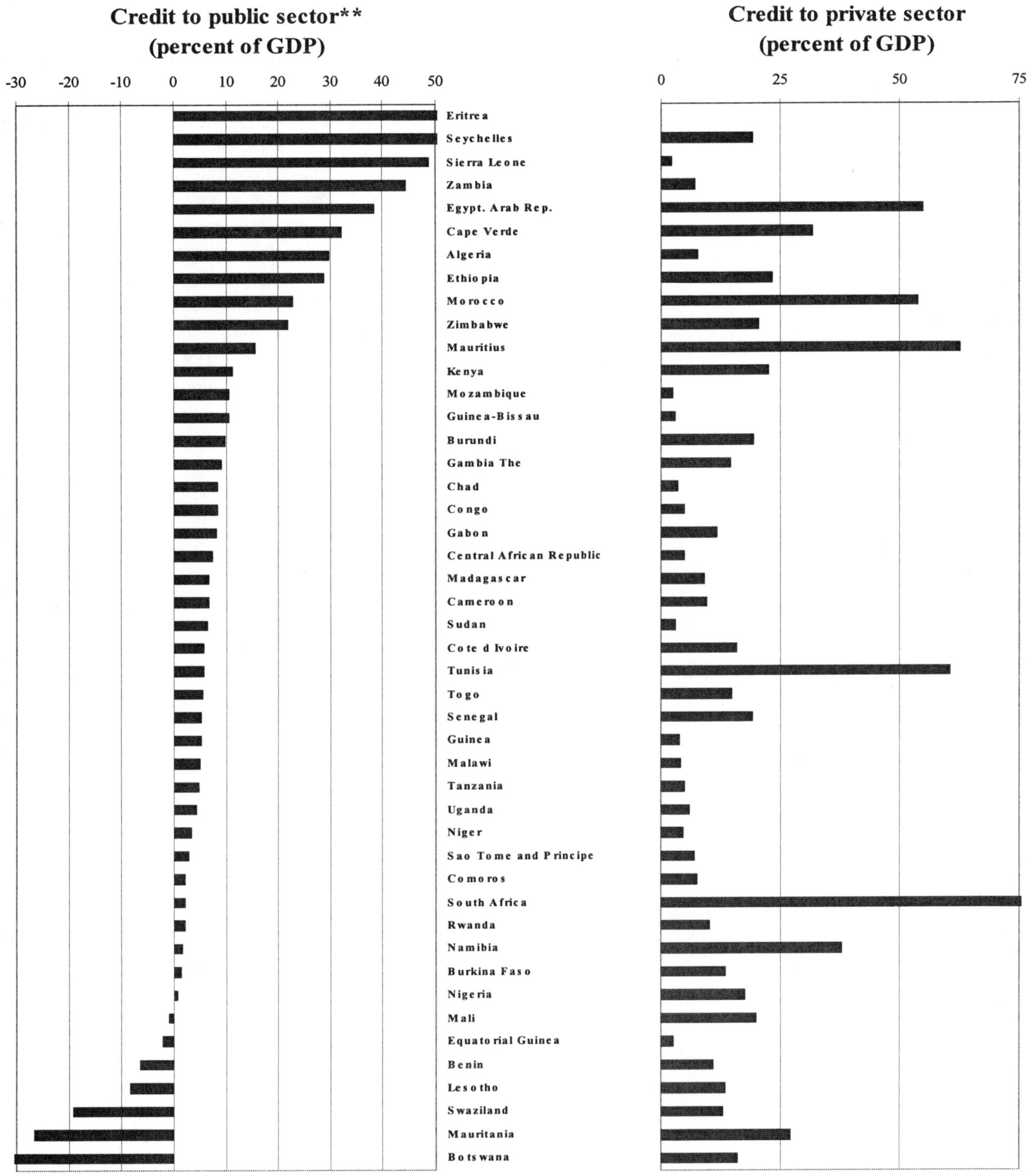

* Or most recent year available.
** Sorted by credit to public sector.

Figure 4-2. Real discount rate, average 1992-2001*

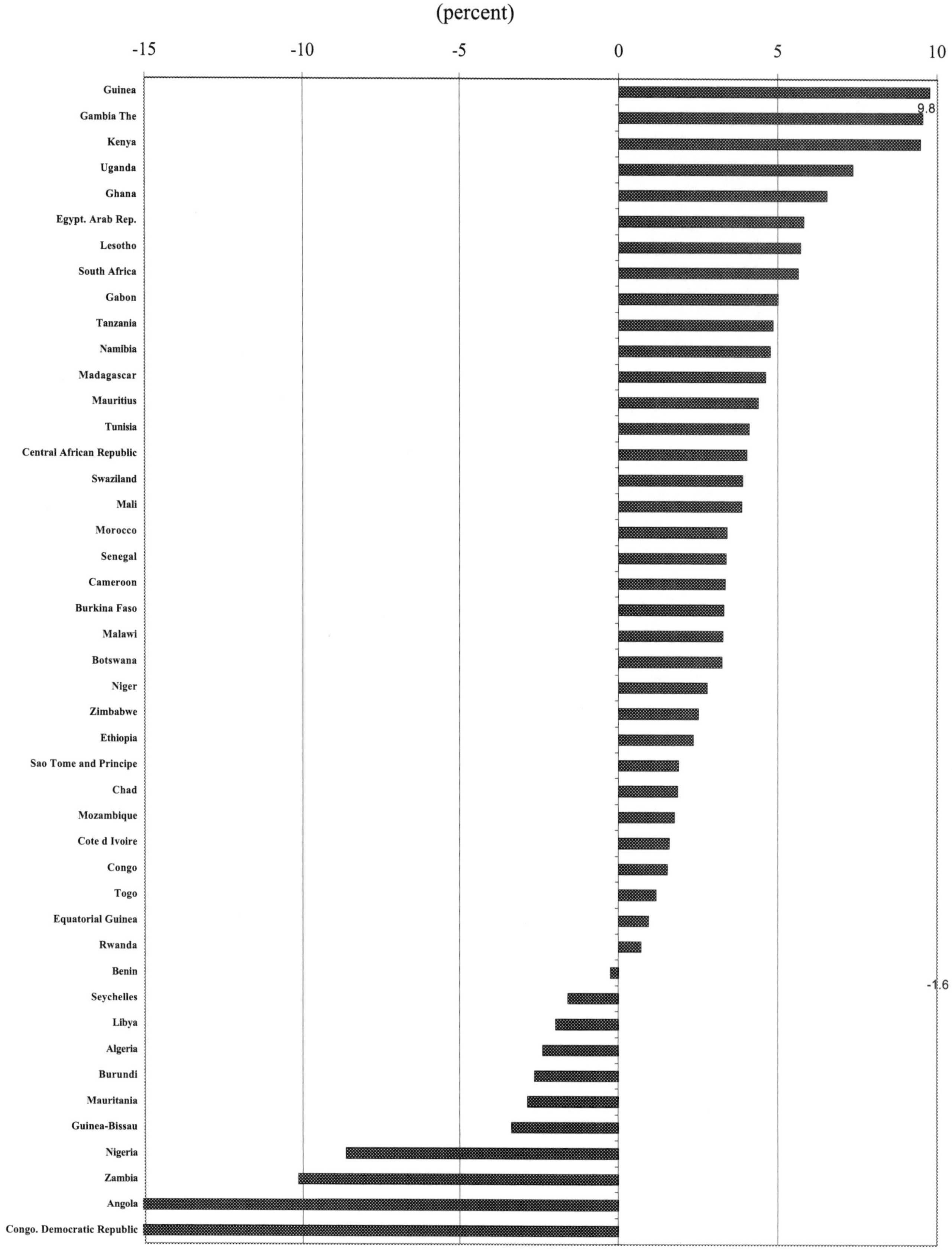

* Or most recent year available.

Technical notes

Tables

Table 4-1. Domestic credit. Domestic credit (IMF, *IFS*, line 32) includes all domestic assets of the banking system. It is the sum of the claims on the central government (net), on official entities, and on the private sector. Domestic credit comprises credit to the private sector (Table 4-2) and credit to the government (Table 4-3).

Table 4-2. Credit to the private sector. Credit to the private sector is taken from IMF, *IFS*, line 32d.

Table 4-3. Credit to the government. Credit to the government sector is taken from IMF, *IFS*, line 32an. Negative numbers for net claims on the central government indicate that government is a net depositor to the banking system. The government's financial position with the monetary system is always presented on a net basis because its recourse to the monetary system cannot always be analyzed meaningfully in terms of liquidity preferences or by considering debtor and creditor positions separately. Movements in net claims on the central government (that is, claims or credits less government deposits) indicate the impact of government operations on the liquidity of the rest of the economy.

Table 4-4. Net foreign assets. Data for net foreign assets are from the IMF, *IFS*, line 31n. As for credit to the government, the financial position of the foreign sector with the monetary system is presented on a net basis for the same reason as noted above. Movements in net foreign assets (that is, foreign assets less foreign liabilities) indicate the direct monetary impact of a country's transactions with the rest of the world.

Table 4-5. Growth of money supply. This table shows the annual percentage change in money (M1), defined as the sum of currency outside of banks and demand deposits other than those of the central government (IMF, *IFS*, line 34). The presentation of the money supply in the form of growth rates rather than levels reflects the importance from the point of view of macroeconomic stability of the rate of growth rather than the stock of money.

Table 4-6. Discount rate. The discount rate reported here is the nominal interest rate at which the monetary authorities lend to (or discount eligible paper from) deposit money banks (IMF, *IFS*, line 60).

Table 4-7. Real discount rate. The real discount rate in each year is the nominal discount rate (Table 4-6) deflated by the annual change in inflation as reflected by the consumer price index (CPI) (Table 3-3). It has been calculated using the formula:

$$\{[l + (i/100)] /[(\pi_t / \pi_{t-1})] - 1\} \, x \, 100$$

where i is nominal interest rate and ð is inflation rate based on the CPI.

Table 4-8. Commercial bank lending rate. The commercial bank lending rate (IMF, *IFS*, line 60p) is the rate charged to borrowers by commercial banks for short- and medium-term use of funds.

Table 4-9. Commercial bank deposit rate. The deposit rate (IMF, IFS, line 60l) is the rate paid to depositors on time savings and demand deposits by deposit money banks and similar financial institutions.

Figures

The following indicators have been used to derive the figures in this chapter.

Figure 4-1. Credit to the private sector (Table 4-2); credit to the public sector (Table 4-3); gross domestic product (Table 2-5).

Figure 4-2. Real discount rate (Table 4-7).

Methodology used for regional aggregations and period averages in chapter 4

	Aggregations [a]		*Period averages* [b]	
Table	*(4)*	*(8)*	*(1)*	*(2)*
4-1	x			x
4-2	x			x
4-3	x			x
4-4		x	x	
4-5	x			x
4-6	x		x	
4-7	x		x	
4-8	x		x	
4-9	x		x	

Note: Regional aggregations are shown in the rows for Sub-Saharan Africa, North Africa, and All Africa. Period averages are shown in the last three columns. This table shows only the methodologies used in this chapter. The definitions of the methodologies used throughout the book are given below.

a. Regional aggregations: (1) simple total; (2) simple total of the first indicator divided by the simple total of the second indicator (same country coverage); (3) simple total of the gap-filled indicator; (4) simple total of the gap-filled main indicator divided by the simple total of the gap-filled secondary indicator; (5) simple total of the first gap-filled main indicator less the simple total of the second gap-filled main indicator, all divided by the simple total of the secondary indicator; (6) weighted total (by population); (7) median; (8) no aggregation; (9) simple arithmetic mean.

b. Period averages: (1) arithmetic mean (using the same series as shown in the table i.e., ratio if the rest of the table is shown as ratio, level if the rest of the table is shown as level, growth rate if the rest is shown as growth rate); (2) least-squares growth rate (using main indicator); (3) least-squares growth rate (using main indicator in constant terms, with the rest of the table in current terms).

5

External Sector

The external sector provides data on economic and financial relations between African countries and the rest of the world, with detailed accounting of commodity trade, one of the principal components of the current account within the balance of payments framework. Commodity trade and price data can also provide a partial basis for analyzing Africa's constraints and performance in the international marketplace, including its terms of trade. Commodity exports are a major source of foreign exchange. Other sources of foreign exchange include receipts from factor and nonfactor services, borrowing from abroad, incoming foreign investment, and foreign transfers and grants.

The balance of payments is a system of accounts, covering a given period, that is intended to record systematically: flows of real resources, including the services of the original factors of production, between the domestic economy of a country and the rest of the world; changes in the country's foreign assets and liabilities that arise from economic transactions; and transfer payments, which are the counterpart of real resources or financial claims provided to, or received from, the rest of the world that carry no provision for repayment.

The tables provide gross entries for goods and services and net entries for unrequited transfers (official and private) and other financial flows; a table for current account balance as traditionally defined (with transfers above the line) is also shown. The information is presented for broad aggregates; fuller detail can be found in the IMF's *Balance of Payments Manual (1993) and Balance of Payments Year Books*.

Unit values for exports (f.o.b.) and imports (c.i.f.) measure changes in the aggregate price level of a country's exports and imports of goods and nonfactor services over time. Unit values reflect average price changes for broad groups of commodities, rather than for any single commodity. The terms of trade indicate relative movements in export and import unit values (here, they are based on goods and nonfactor services from the national accounts). If the prices of exports rise while the prices of imports rise more slowly, stay constant, or decline, the same quantity of exports "buys" a bigger quantity of imports. The effect of such price changes is equivalent to an increase in the real value of output (or increased productivity in value terms) of the export sector. Were import prices to rise more quickly than export prices, the reverse would be true. Export figures for specific commodities show physical quantities rather than value in either current or constant prices. Most of the key nonagricultural primary commodities are exported from a few countries with substantial mineral resources. Variations in export prices and earnings for the five major oil-exporting countries in Sub-Saharan Africa (which in the 1980s accounted for about half of Sub-Saharan export earnings) have dominated trends in this region as a whole.

5-1. Merchandise exports, f.o.b.

	Millions of U.S. dollars (current prices)											Average annual percentage growth		
	1980	1992	1993	1994	1995	1996	1997	1998	1999	2000	2001	75-84	85-89	90-MR
SUB-SAHARAN AFRICA	78,591	66,454	62,704	65,699	78,253	86,195	87,399	75,597	79,639	96,139	89,495	6.9	3.0	3.3
excluding South Africa	52,973	41,987	37,959	39,359	48,183	55,947	56,220	46,464	51,043	64,713	62,969	5.4	0.6	3.8
excl. S.Africa & Nigeria	26,342	30,090	28,034	29,953	36,458	39,814	40,671	36,372	39,131	44,234	44,247	6.0	3.9	3.8
Angola	..	3,833	2,908	3,016	3,730	5,085	5,066	3,491	5,225	7,885	6,703	..	7.0	6.4
Benin	222	371	341	308	235	263	191	239	223	188	210	7.1	6.0	-3.5
Botswana	544	1,744	1,722	1,874	2,160	2,218	2,820	2,061	2,658	2,675	2,314	20.0	24.5	3.6
Burkina Faso	161	238	260	191	237	233	229	323	254	206	221	8.1	11.1	-0.3
Burundi	66	77	74	81	113	40	87	64	56	49	39	9.9	-1.0	-5.3
Cameroon	1,506	1,937	1,652	1,433	1,655	1,605	1,816	1,800	1,682	2,125	2,129	18.2	-5.5	0.3
Cape Verde	9	4	4	20	24	30	38	23	8	24	31	15.2	-8.8	17.5
Central African Republic	147	116	132	162	179	142	155	138	96	111	107	8.6	3.9	-2.1
Chad	71	182	152	135	243	238	237	261	188	181	192	0.8	10.0	1.9
Comoros	11	21	22	11	11	6	6	6	9	14	16	..	15.7	-6.8
Congo, Democratic Rep. of	2,269	1,246	1,144	1,256	1,612	1,652	1,196	1,180	974	892	940	5.9	5.8	-6.6
Congo, Republic of	911	1,179	1,119	959	1,173	1,564	1,587	1,150	1,556	2,449	2,180	22.9	-3.2	5.1
Côte d'Ivoire	3,013	3,189	2,519	2,948	4,304	4,256	4,275	4,432	4,486	3,788	3,668	6.4	0.8	3.9
Djibouti	..	..	..	..	38	40	43	59	69	72	..	..	..	..
Equatorial Guinea	..	52	52	65	86	101	291	460	814	1,363	2,182	..	12.7	43.8
Eritrea	0	15	36	65	81	95	54	28	20	37	20	..	..	-4.2
Ethiopia	459	154	222	280	454	412	599	602	485	486	441	6.3	-0.1	5.7
Gabon	2,531	2,257	2,326	2,365	2,643	3,190	3,043	2,209	2,526	2,750	2,897	8.9	-6.5	2.9
Gambia, The	51	151	141	124	121	114	108	130	120	133	154	3.2	7.9	1.7
Ghana	1,104	986	1,064	1,227	1,431	1,810	1,810	2,091	2,006	1,936	1,893	-3.8	8.5	8.9
Guinea	500	651	672	610	649	610	660	659	646	667	731	4.7	2.5	0.3
Guinea-Bissau	..	6	16	33	24	22	48	26	51	62	47	..	1.3	13.3
Kenya	1,363	1,013	1,103	1,484	1,924	2,083	2,060	2,012	1,755	1,774	1,879	5.8	-2.1	7.3
Lesotho	58	104	132	147	154	182	196	193	189	214	286	10.4	25.8	12.8
Liberia	600	..	..	..	..	..	..	..	..	..	..	1.4	-5.6	..
Madagascar	437	324	332	447	566	522	505	519	582	829	965	2.0	-1.1	9.2
Malawi	281	397	317	327	404	483	530	528	447	406	407	8.8	-0.4	2.5
Mali	205	362	349	337	442	433	561	561	596	547	739	10.9	8.9	7.4
Mauritania	196	400	380	393	479	484	408	360	333	345	345	6.8	7.1	-1.8
Mauritius	406	1,283	1,343	1,334	1,473	1,629	1,727	1,599	1,680	1,523	1,633	..	26.7	3.9
Mozambique	281	139	132	164	174	226	230	245	284	364	704	..	4.5	12.9
Namibia	1,534	1,311	1,293	1,320	1,418	1,463	1,365	1,214	1,227	1,312	1,367	..	8.3	1.3
Niger	576	344	301	225	287	302	272	334	287	283	283	14.6	3.9	-0.4
Nigeria	25,956	11,886	9,924	9,415	11,734	16,117	15,539	10,114	11,927	20,441	18,700	3.8	-7.1	3.7
Rwanda	134	69	68	32	50	62	93	64	62	90	93	5.6	-6.0	-0.9
São Tomé and Principe	17	5	5	6	5	5	5	5	4	3	4	-3.0	-7.7	-3.3
Senegal	480	828	719	791	968	986	905	973	1,028	959	992	2.1	6.0	2.0
Seychelles	6	48	49	52	53	78	115	123	146	195	217	-4.7	32.2	19.0
Sierra Leone	214	150	118	194	102	105	88	65	61	75	77	-1.0	0.0	-8.0
Somalia	133	..	..	..	..	..	..	..	..	..	..	3.6	-2.7	..
South Africa	25,698	24,487	24,750	26,342	30,084	30,285	31,213	29,145	28,625	31,486	26,606	10.3	7.4	2.4
Sudan	566	350	427	462	556	620	594	596	780	1,864	1,635	2.8	-4.4	12.1
Swaziland	368	639	675	746	868	855	853	978	937	909	794	6.3	22.6	5.1
Tanzania	508	414	411	486	593	696	794	588	543	663	776	0.1	1.6	5.8
Togo	476	327	215	226	357	372	352	396	392	327	349	7.1	10.1	0.1
Uganda	319	172	157	254	595	590	684	458	549	453	446	1.3	-6.1	10.3
Zambia	1,457	1,120	994	1,067	1,186	993	1,119	816	756	746	884	-0.9	10.2	-4.1
Zimbabwe	281	1,530	1,610	1,947	2,216	2,496	2,424	1,925	1,924	1,791	1,715	0.0	9.3	1.2
NORTH AFRICA	41,259	33,352	31,134	30,602	37,625	41,279	43,368	38,416	41,314	56,574	56,637	9.7	-5.1	5.5
Algeria	13,652	11,510	10,410	8,892	10,260	13,220	13,820	10,140	12,320	21,700	21,125	14.3	-8.0	4.4
Egypt, Arab Republic	3,854	3,880	3,725	3,337	4,957	4,609	5,345	5,128	4,445	6,388	7,078	9.4	-8.0	6.5
Libya	21,919	..	..	..	..	..	..	..	..	..	..	6.7	-10.5	..
Morocco	2,414	5,024	4,922	5,541	6,871	6,886	7,039	7,144	7,621	7,508	7,256	5.1	14.5	5.4
Tunisia	2,395	4,014	3,746	4,643	5,470	5,519	5,559	5,724	5,873	5,840	6,024	12.0	10.7	6.1
ALL AFRICA	119,714	99,437	93,556	96,400	115,767	127,383	130,378	113,499	120,247	150,548	143,341	8.0	0.2	4.0

Note: 2001 data are preliminary (see page 2).

5-2. Merchandise imports, f.o.b.

	Millions of U.S. dollars (current prices)											Average annual percentage growth		
	1980	1992	1993	1994	1995	1996	1997	1998	1999	2000	2001	75-84	85-89	90-MR
SUB-SAHARAN AFRICA	60,913	59,332	57,230	58,970	71,924	74,306	79,858	77,370	75,816	80,306	81,135	8.3	3.9	4.2
excluding South Africa	42,656	41,173	38,763	37,108	44,518	46,720	51,003	50,136	51,386	53,107	55,791	8.3	2.6	3.9
excl. S.Africa & Nigeria	27,942	32,266	30,455	30,649	36,341	38,515	41,377	40,867	40,850	40,693	41,708	6.5	6.2	3.4
Angola	..	1,988	1,463	1,454	1,852	2,040	2,597	2,079	3,109	3,147	3,325	..	-1.8	7.9
Benin	499	561	539	374	439	444	426	451	474	446	467	8.3	6.9	0.8
Botswana	602	1,557	1,455	1,364	1,605	1,468	1,924	1,983	1,873	1,773	1,604	17.4	18.4	2.4
Burkina Faso	368	516	534	355	485	563	510	634	581	519	510	8.1	10.3	1.3
Burundi	165	182	173	173	176	100	96	124	97	108	108	17.1	-1.8	-5.6
Cameroon	1,452	1,023	1,021	1,017	1,074	1,200	1,347	1,452	1,483	1,538	1,617	12.5	5.5	2.1
Cape Verde	80	167	152	191	219	206	211	208	223	243	227	10.1	6.2	6.5
Central African Republic	185	189	158	151	179	125	145	150	86	83	82	8.7	4.6	-7.5
Chad	55	243	205	212	277	243	246	272	244	243	563	-1.8	12.5	3.1
Comoros	22	58	50	45	54	49	48	42	43	37	40	..	6.1	-1.0
Congo, Democratic Rep. of	1,519	935	614	667	997	1,011	694	775	458	669	702	0.0	10.7	-7.9
Congo, Republic of	545	438	500	613	653	586	649	559	523	596	614	15.2	-5.0	1.9
Côte d'Ivoire	2,614	1,984	1,784	1,608	2,474	2,763	2,712	2,760	2,643	2,321	2,240	6.1	10.4	1.9
Djibouti	..	..	..	..	207	201	204	240	252	271	..	..	..	..
Equatorial Guinea	..	62	52	67	97	127	206	434	440	464	696	..	10.6	26.6
Eritrea	0	278	275	396	404	514	495	527	495	470	490	..	..	6.7
Ethiopia	692	875	1,052	915	1,063	1,144	1,309	1,357	1,558	1,611	1,558	16.4	1.0	5.2
Gabon	829	887	845	777	898	969	1,018	987	841	887	934	4.6	0.0	1.2
Gambia, The	116	204	205	179	209	189	176	207	194	202	233	11.0	7.8	3.8
Ghana	908	1,457	1,728	1,580	1,684	2,295	3,042	2,918	3,252	2,759	2,652	-1.6	11.2	9.9
Guinea	339	589	602	583	583	584	573	577	582	583	562	5.0	5.7	0.1
Guinea-Bissau	..	84	54	54	59	57	73	51	66	86	80	..	1.5	0.6
Kenya	2,585	1,608	1,385	1,761	2,636	2,512	2,944	3,028	2,656	3,045	3,114	8.1	4.3	6.4
Lesotho	424	908	859	869	983	996	1,012	841	793	736	675	14.2	10.1	1.0
Liberia	478	..	..	..	..	..	..	..	..	..	..	1.8	-1.5	..
Madagascar	764	465	510	546	628	643	683	672	749	933	950	5.4	-3.1	7.4
Malawi	308	712	627	536	474	624	783	579	674	563	582	2.7	8.7	1.8
Mali	308	532	502	466	556	552	556	558	632	595	727	9.7	8.3	3.8
Mauritania	321	424	375	304	395	403	355	358	305	330	357	7.0	2.6	-1.2
Mauritius	494	1,474	1,541	1,556	1,875	1,945	2,013	1,972	2,046	2,006	1,912	..	27.8	4.6
Mozambique	720	745	830	881	727	783	760	817	1,200	1,162	1,117	..	11.4	3.5
Namibia	1,094	1,389	1,335	1,406	1,548	1,555	1,644	1,502	1,504	1,560	1,610	..	8.1	3.4
Niger	677	266	259	263	297	306	300	396	317	324	347	11.0	-14.5	3.6
Nigeria	14,735	8,891	8,293	6,470	8,183	8,216	9,630	9,276	10,531	12,392	14,042	12.7	-8.9	5.5
Rwanda	196	241	268	367	194	213	277	256	249	240	255	12.3	6.8	0.3
São Tomé and Principe	15	22	26	24	23	20	19	17	22	22	23	12.5	2.1	-1.5
Senegal	973	1,192	1,102	1,022	1,217	1,268	1,176	1,288	1,375	1,342	1,356	4.3	4.7	2.0
Seychelles	84	180	216	188	214	263	304	352	375	304	415	-0.4	14.2	9.2
Sierra Leone	334	136	130	131	120	185	81	85	68	137	164	1.4	2.6	-3.0
Somalia	402	..	..	..	..	..	..	..	..	..	..	15.0	-6.3	..
South Africa	18,268	18,224	18,518	21,875	27,412	27,599	28,876	27,261	24,477	27,236	25,411	8.7	7.0	4.9
Sudan	1,440	1,002	975	957	1,036	1,547	1,580	1,925	1,412	1,553	1,543	5.6	-0.7	4.9
Swaziland	538	765	772	816	1,064	1,062	1,067	1,099	1,068	1,038	844	16.6	10.0	5.6
Tanzania	1,089	1,444	1,472	1,591	1,510	1,370	1,388	1,376	1,368	1,337	1,492	3.6	9.0	0.6
Togo	524	409	251	229	350	447	508	553	490	486	506	9.4	13.8	2.0
Uganda	318	451	523	672	1,085	1,218	899	966	1,039	978	973	4.5	9.9	7.1
Zambia	1,114	1,302	1,019	1,003	1,194	1,056	1,218	971	871	978	1,253	0.3	6.9	0.9
Zimbabwe	308	1,781	1,512	1,778	2,128	2,247	2,654	2,020	1,675	1,520	1,455	1.4	6.5	1.3
NORTH AFRICA	31,015	36,752	37,896	37,651	45,426	44,783	46,533	46,560	49,505	51,708	52,004	8.0	-0.8	4.0
Algeria	9,596	8,310	7,990	9,154	10,100	9,090	8,130	8,630	8,960	9,300	10,795	5.6	-2.8	0.7
Egypt, Arab Republic	6,814	10,753	12,879	10,377	13,372	14,263	16,718	15,321	16,969	17,861	16,431	10.2	-3.7	5.1
Libya	10,368	..	..	..	..	..	..	..	..	..	..	12.0	-3.1	..
Morocco	3,770	7,450	6,981	7,648	9,353	9,080	8,903	9,463	9,957	10,601	10,494	7.3	8.7	5.1
Tunisia	3,453	6,079	5,757	6,210	7,458	7,280	7,514	7,875	8,015	8,093	8,397	13.2	7.2	5.4
ALL AFRICA	90,970	95,807	94,687	96,267	116,953	118,834	126,233	123,670	124,785	131,499	132,635	7.8	2.0	4.1

Note: 2001 data are preliminary (see page 2).

5-3. Exports of total services (nonfactor and factor)

	Millions of U.S. dollars (current prices)											Average annual percentage growth		
	1980	1992	1993	1994	1995	1996	1997	1998	1999	2000	2001	75-84	85-89	90-MR
SUB-SAHARAN AFRICA	12,232	13,104	13,282	13,372	16,233	17,513	18,133	18,754	18,908	19,731	23,698	6.5	6.0	5.6
excluding South Africa	8,711	8,836	9,319	8,654	10,483	11,415	11,499	12,204	12,300	12,472	12,670	7.9	6.8	4.3
excl. S.Africa & Nigeria	6,249	8,592	9,171	8,490	10,271	11,016	11,121	11,097	11,102	11,243	11,412	8.9	8.2	3.6
Angola	..	159	117	163	129	311	251	158	179	342	352	..	3.5	7.0
Benin	84	143	137	108	162	168	162	191	187	189	160	11.3	8.9	5.3
Botswana	203	731	746	417	744	664	832	923	803	703	716	14.8	16.5	3.8
Burkina Faso	65	83	80	67	80	71	55	53	46	45	43	9.2	5.8	-3.9
Burundi	26	31	25	23	27	17	13	11	8	6	16	21.0	7.4	-10.5
Cameroon	395	436	394	310	405	456	507	521	574	612	597	21.7	-1.7	4.0
Cape Verde	14	46	46	53	68	85	99	89	108	111	135	43.2	11.5	11.7
Central African Republic	58	56	54	45	53	47	43	40	22	16	22	7.0	10.9	-10.1
Chad	0	44	47	28	79	55	54	57	58	56	56	-13.0	10.2	3.3
Comoros	3	33	35	29	38	38	35	22	23	19	22	..	48.4	-1.3
Congo, Democratic Rep. of	135	135	151	66	159	73	64	119	63	88	91	3.1	13.3	-9.5
Congo, Republic of	119	79	68	159	61	63	90	109	146	145	138	7.6	-28.9	12.0
Côte d'Ivoire	587	404	773	536	813	774	619	659	629	473	466	8.4	-3.5	3.6
Djibouti	..	..	..	..	192	188	188	206	196	195	..	..	..	..
Equatorial Guinea	..	4	5	4	4	4	4	7	7	7	7	..	32.3	-17.0
Eritrea	0	73	57	80	99	113	160	94	54	70	137	..	..	3.3
Ethiopia	131	305	291	283	354	413	442	458	460	514	527	5.0	11.5	5.7
Gabon	350	369	344	231	286	298	263	249	261	280	290	12.2	10.1	-1.5
Gambia, The	21	70	77	62	70	75	80	86	82	83	75	10.0	19.7	4.7
Ghana	110	137	156	171	178	461	474	494	498	535	549	-5.8	14.7	21.0
Guinea	54	160	187	153	118	124	111	111	113	68	99	..	20.3	-4.2
Guinea-Bissau	..	5	5	6	6	7	8	4	5	6	7	..	-13.6	2.2
Kenya	835	1,144	1,152	1,184	1,050	974	955	872	964	1,014	1,130	7.1	9.9	-1.3
Lesotho	305	512	479	482	519	505	495	415	372	333	274	14.8	5.8	-3.2
Liberia	13	..	..	..	..	..	..	..	..	..	..	18.0	17.0	..
Madagascar	82	177	187	208	254	303	287	307	346	379	376	2.6	24.1	8.2
Malawi	34	22	18	31	28	44	51	43	59	57	57	-5.4	5.5	8.0
Mali	58	106	99	78	88	103	102	111	99	110	117	10.7	14.1	2.0
Mauritania	73	53	34	40	48	33	23	41	60	93	51	9.6	9.8	0.0
Mauritius	154	631	660	630	757	890	944	908	1,007	1,113	1,211	..	29.8	8.8
Mozambique	171	223	240	246	292	314	342	333	356	405	348	..	9.0	7.4
Namibia	205	78	181	203	348	282	310	292	302	311	298	..	8.8	8.8
Niger	68	56	49	37	41	39	39	54	45	53	63	7.4	10.5	-2.0
Nigeria	2,164	259	171	187	239	427	405	1,129	1,219	1,250	1,284	2.7	-11.0	14.7
Rwanda	49	50	37	22	38	27	60	57	59	74	80	27.2	8.4	3.6
São Tomé and Principe	6	5	5	6	6	6	7	7	13	13	14	20.0	17.7	10.0
Senegal	416	616	577	504	604	630	440	505	500	456	461	9.0	10.8	-2.0
Seychelles	97	198	211	201	224	242	262	280	285	280	291	-0.8	14.2	4.8
Sierra Leone	21	66	70	76	61	61	26	32	33	37	42	42.5	-4.0	-5.5
Somalia	71	..	..	..	..	..	..	..	..	..	..	13.9	-15.9	..
South Africa	3,560	4,281	3,975	4,720	5,756	6,106	6,640	6,559	6,617	7,265	11,015	8.5	4.5	7.9
Sudan	228	74	111	96	134	57	47	30	70	33	30	12.6	-3.4	-11.7
Swaziland	83	78	100	98	152	303	308	290	267	226	153	15.4	18.4	7.0
Tanzania	179	141	206	369	511	472	520	601	695	717	749	-1.1	1.8	19.3
Togo	95	161	115	81	103	162	117	120	104	105	96	17.7	10.9	-4.1
Uganda	11	27	85	90	87	157	192	218	227	245	265	9.2	1.4	25.7
Zambia	168	94	107	123	152	143	228	144	130	147	192	3.7	1.6	6.5
Zimbabwe	34	330	401	443	542	646	696	660	472	358	293	5.2	8.4	3.8
NORTH AFRICA	11,109	18,334	18,463	19,221	21,076	23,231	24,448	23,803	24,938	25,753	27,038	12.2	7.3	5.9
Algeria	978	730	760	798	800	750	1,330	1,110	940	1,300	1,551	7.4	0.9	8.2
Egypt, Arab Republic	2,662	8,189	8,332	8,677	9,556	10,636	11,241	10,455	11,015	11,420	11,696	19.9	11.9	5.4
Libya	1,446	..	..	..	..	..	..	..	..	..	..	12.8	1.9	..
Morocco	896	2,402	2,288	2,238	2,425	2,932	2,643	3,020	3,302	3,281	3,535	8.1	14.5	6.2
Tunisia	1,214	2,107	2,143	2,364	2,657	2,697	2,692	2,848	3,009	2,860	3,022	11.3	14.5	5.7
ALL AFRICA	21,205	29,065	29,363	30,069	34,686	37,818	39,474	39,634	40,715	42,270	47,640	11.7	7.7	5.7

Note: 2001 data are preliminary (see page 2).

5-4. Imports of total services (nonfactor and factor)

	Millions of U.S. dollars (current prices)											Average annual percentage growth		
	1980	1992	1993	1994	1995	1996	1997	1998	1999	2000	2001	75-84	85-89	90-MR
SUB-SAHARAN AFRICA	32,169	37,563	35,614	35,163	40,157	41,859	42,250	43,153	44,861	48,669	48,147	7.8	4.9	3.1
excluding South Africa	24,524	29,393	27,591	26,727	30,221	31,979	31,786	33,184	34,531	37,712	36,712	8.7	5.3	3.1
excl. S.Africa & Nigeria	15,790	24,070	22,794	21,474	24,807	26,739	26,481	26,625	26,972	28,647	28,984	9.9	7.0	2.8
Angola	..	2,922	2,509	2,469	3,446	3,905	3,778	3,779	4,070	4,424	4,230	..	20.3	6.1
Benin	112	219	192	171	226	242	234	236	257	238	228	11.2	4.1	3.7
Botswana	351	790	587	777	960	1,099	1,208	1,037	1,221	1,277	1,193	18.6	18.7	5.2
Burkina Faso	228	238	230	165	204	198	180	190	179	174	166	9.1	5.1	-1.6
Burundi	58	158	133	110	120	57	61	62	45	53	49	20.4	14.1	-10.9
Cameroon	877	1,741	1,626	1,071	1,115	1,270	1,320	1,208	1,267	1,451	1,376	17.7	-16.9	1.8
Cape Verde	8	31	36	40	62	77	88	98	127	118	125	29.4	15.8	15.9
Central African Republic	144	179	155	126	156	124	123	134	80	84	77	7.0	12.3	-6.9
Chad	28	239	240	188	235	246	250	257	249	221	368	-7.6	16.6	1.8
Comoros	12	56	52	45	52	48	45	34	34	25	25	..	2.8	-5.3
Congo, Democratic Rep. of	1,160	1,223	1,092	1,186	1,266	845	753	971	695	641	683	8.5	11.3	-7.6
Congo, Republic of	650	1,115	1,219	1,253	935	1,638	1,497	1,814	1,578	1,762	1,603	16.3	6.0	5.6
Côte d'Ivoire	2,110	2,725	2,484	1,638	2,359	2,383	2,192	2,307	2,257	1,985	1,788	11.6	7.4	-0.8
Djibouti	..	..	..	..	88	90	91	98	80	81	..	..	..	..
Equatorial Guinea	..	41	51	82	95	224	345	411	672	1,204	1,894	..	69.2	41.0
Eritrea	0	0	1	7	44	70	108	77	105	39	46	..	..	46.2
Ethiopia	105	292	314	273	293	318	406	386	397	425	457	-1.9	16.5	4.8
Gabon	1,414	1,781	1,688	1,336	1,679	1,985	1,833	1,511	1,663	1,850	1,916	10.8	-3.3	2.2
Gambia, The	44	80	80	70	79	68	73	81	78	84	74	14.3	15.0	1.5
Ghana	355	513	568	666	588	815	928	932	930	929	964	0.4	8.9	8.8
Guinea	238	408	403	365	407	453	406	455	426	388	410	..	12.3	-0.5
Guinea-Bissau	..	43	39	41	48	48	48	37	45	53	52	..	11.0	2.0
Kenya	872	906	930	1,041	1,222	1,101	989	880	839	847	949	4.9	4.3	-1.0
Lesotho	58	148	160	165	201	180	182	165	132	112	100	12.9	14.5	-0.2
Liberia	97	..	..	..	..	..	..	..	..	..	..	28.2	7.5	..
Madagascar	368	421	457	480	538	535	491	520	519	629	595	10.2	8.7	2.9
Malawi	330	92	82	111	125	149	165	137	146	144	123	11.5	-0.9	11.0
Mali	221	440	356	322	395	446	424	432	417	416	533	7.9	8.8	2.6
Mauritania	172	267	258	221	295	298	233	222	205	190	175	13.2	4.2	-3.3
Mauritius	201	559	602	583	666	723	792	740	799	794	931	..	21.6	6.7
Mozambique	155	355	366	393	416	404	423	509	592	648	784	..	7.0	7.7
Namibia	787	402	380	358	429	456	397	361	351	343	326	..	4.9	-1.2
Niger	339	152	143	193	215	193	180	193	166	164	174	10.7	3.6	-0.1
Nigeria	8,498	5,328	4,806	5,250	5,420	5,251	5,315	6,559	7,550	9,046	7,730	5.3	-0.8	4.1
Rwanda	139	147	154	132	156	169	222	223	213	231	219	13.4	8.8	4.0
São Tomé and Principe	7	23	22	22	28	27	27	18	23	19	21	14.7	11.0	-0.8
Senegal	475	832	787	657	763	743	532	579	606	554	547	12.0	9.6	-3.6
Seychelles	-84	91	104	95	115	133	145	163	183	218	241	..	..	10.0
Sierra Leone	95	204	174	217	135	141	65	75	84	95	111	3.4	1.0	-4.9
Somalia	139	..	..	..	..	..	..	..	..	..	..	9.9	6.1	..
South Africa	7,720	8,231	8,077	8,485	9,987	9,937	10,518	10,030	10,394	11,029	11,495	10.5	4.0	3.2
Sudan	416	1,091	1,146	1,183	1,236	1,039	1,152	1,203	1,476	2,260	1,859	19.8	5.6	4.1
Swaziland	121	89	125	96	194	311	290	336	270	265	217	9.8	18.1	6.8
Tanzania	160	635	723	805	659	759	793	1,168	1,005	900	906	5.7	19.5	7.0
Togo	227	264	201	186	208	272	228	202	205	181	178	14.0	9.9	-3.2
Uganda	132	222	223	241	371	450	460	511	521	603	646	6.2	11.9	12.6
Zambia	872	623	530	566	588	490	622	536	480	505	533	3.1	7.5	-3.5
Zimbabwe	330	961	836	1,016	1,120	1,224	1,415	1,048	993	710	694	8.8	7.5	0.6
NORTH AFRICA	7,995	13,194	12,616	16,132	16,894	16,860	15,468	19,536	17,507	18,664	19,324	12.8	3.7	3.9
Algeria	5,035	4,030	3,510	3,770	4,320	4,710	4,630	4,590	5,070	5,500	5,604	16.1	-5.1	3.8
Egypt, Arab Republic	2,931	3,027	2,620	5,273	4,952	4,688	3,894	7,342	5,069	5,796	6,118	20.4	2.5	6.0
Libya	-10,368	..	..	..	..	..	..	..	..	..	..	..	..	..
Morocco	2,076	2,943	3,045	3,124	3,459	3,280	3,072	3,190	3,175	3,001	3,079	9.0	11.8	1.6
Tunisia	918	1,701	2,012	2,138	2,250	2,274	2,121	2,203	2,212	2,254	2,335	11.5	6.6	5.5
ALL AFRICA	41,848	51,308	48,745	51,544	57,443	59,183	58,298	63,011	62,906	67,940	68,011	6.3	5.0	3.3

Note: 2001 data are preliminary (see page 2).

5-5. Net private transfers

	Millions of U.S. dollars (current prices)											Annual Average		
	1980	*1992*	*1993*	*1994*	*1995*	*1996*	*1997*	*1998*	*1999*	*2000*	*2001*	*75-84*	*85-89*	*90-MR*
SUB-SAHARAN AFRICA	-302	2,563	2,335	2,755	2,611	3,540	4,639	4,647	4,669	5,337	5,369	212	964	3,374
excluding South Africa	-396	2,560	2,342	2,767	2,628	3,563	4,636	4,640	4,666	5,330	5,364	142	873	3,381
excl. S.Africa & Nigeria	-396	1,776	1,550	2,218	1,829	2,619	2,769	3,099	3,041	3,638	3,584	107	880	2,345
Angola	..	26	-5	-4	-34	11	38	79	110	126	137	26	-19	29
Benin	107	95	94	50	68	67	77	72	74	84	82	60	77	78
Botswana	-11	-26	-73	-92	-158	-23	-56	-53	-54	-68	..	-5	-9	-60
Burkina Faso	112	169	153	98	106	84	74	74	65	55	35	75	164	93
Burundi	3	13	17	21	16	11	9	6	6	5	8	6	9	11
Cameroon	19	-72	-95	-41	-23	7	86	80	100	97	85	11	-69	8
Cape Verde	40	70	71	81	93	96	71	79	107	109	81	30	34	81
Central African Republic	0	-27	-31	-10	-11	-10	-10	-9	-6	-8	-8	0	-14	-16
Chad	-4	-15	-23	-8	2	4	4	3	7	2	0	-6	-5	-3
Comoros	2	5	11	7	9	12	14	27	28	24	26	2	6	14
Congo, Democratic Rep. of	-79	-97	-123	-98	-124	0	0	0	0	0	0	-47	-72	-51
Congo, Republic of	-1	-19	-9	60	-2	-4	-4	-11	-6	7	-2	-44	-64	-2
Côte d'Ivoire	-706	-379	-305	-259	-439	-474	-452	-475	-458	-330	-382	-403	-413	-402
Djibouti	..	..	..	..	-11	-10	-9	-5	-7	-9	..	..	..	-9
Equatorial Guinea	..	-4	-3	0	-3	-3	-1	0	0	0	0	0	-1	-1
Eritrea	0	128	165	276	215	244	352	245	244	196	175	0	0	187
Ethiopia	20	316	248	247	311	313	33	88	89	410	379	37	162	234
Gabon	-124	-190	-209	-163	-192	-216	-218	-160	-170	-181	-186	-58	-143	-181
Gambia, The	2	12	13	15	16	17	17	24	20	17	21	2	3	16
Ghana	-3	255	261	271	263	276	393	454	472	496	521	7	136	340
Guinea	-3	-73	-79	-82	-92	-49	-36	-39	-31	-15	-13	-3	-26	-53
Guinea-Bissau	..	1	1	1	3	2	2	16	5	8	16	-10	-1	5
Kenya	27	68	147	148	408	433	497	557	564	837	761	41	76	394
Lesotho	2	133	153	164	179	171	184	143	143	128	118	29	38	142
Liberia	-29	..	..	..	..	..	..	..	..	..	..	-32	-25	..
Madagascar	-21	109	114	46	63	78	102	68	94	102	114	-14	54	86
Malawi	..	101	64	20	-4	-24	-19	-25	9	8	15	15	13	21
Mali	40	74	93	85	96	90	73	68	68	62	54	24	53	78
Mauritania	-28	77	28	14	30	39	54	56	40	48	41	-25	69	36
Mauritius	16	86	92	93	88	101	109	92	86	90	72	21	47	89
Mozambique	0	0	0	0	0	0	0	0	0	0	0	0	0	0
Namibia	0	452	351	327	409	433	452	439	457	456	409	0	0	410
Niger	-57	-40	-34	-41	-23	-25	-22	-6	-5	4	4	-40	-26	-23
Nigeria	..	784	792	549	799	945	1,867	1,541	1,625	1,692	1,779	-137	-18	1,036
Rwanda	0	20	22	45	16	27	25	18	18	11	22	1	7	21
São Tomé and Principe	1	1	2	3	1	1	1	1	1	1	1	1	0	1
Senegal	0	26	40	39	40	40	35	36	83	131	118	7	7	54
Seychelles	0	-3	-6	-7	-5	-6	-6	-11	-7	-6	-6	0	4	-6
Sierra Leone	0	0	0	0	0	0	6	5	7	7	6	1	1	3
Somalia	57	..	..	..	..	..	..	..	..	..	..	43	..	..
South Africa	94	3	-7	-12	-17	-23	3	7	3	7	6	79	91	-7
Sudan	257	138	81	68	60	321	429	490	446	315	412	267	330	251
Swaziland	0	0	0	0	0	2	-1	2	-13	7	-8	1	3	-1
Tanzania	22	194	197	465	18	20	26	18	-38	-38	-32	22	364	100
Togo	1	9	10	9	11	10	9	11	21	29	30	-1	8	14
Uganda	-2	136	108	304	330	421	322	539	375	513	540	7	95	312
Zambia	-176	-33	-19	-19	-20	-17	-16	-27	-16	-18	-20	-86	-35	-24
Zimbabwe	120	40	26	86	120	149	126	128	115	-70	-39	87	23	57
NORTH AFRICA	..	..	..	..	..	..	..	..	..	..	7,092	..	..	7,092
Algeria	..	..	..	..	..	..	..	..	..	0	815	..	..	407
Egypt, Arab Republic	2,791	3,029	3,835	3,232	3,279	2,798	3,256	3,718	3,772	3,747	2,973	2,091	3,289	3,329
Libya	-1,089	..	..	..	..	..	..	..	..	..	..	-1,075	-571	-446
Morocco	1,070	2,325	2,141	2,096	2,261	2,526	2,158	2,293	2,165	2,332	2,522	822	1,419	2,261
Tunisia	348	570	597	688	753	835	766	813	886	807	781	255	435	723
ALL AFRICA	2,818	8,486	8,908	8,771	8,903	9,700	10,819	11,471	11,493	12,223	12,461	2,806	5,536	9,717

Note: 2001 data are preliminary (see page 2). Nigeria's series shows a data break between 1991 and 1992.

5-6. Net official current transfers

	Millions of U.S. dollars (current prices)											Annual Average		
	1980	1992	1993	1994	1995	1996	1997	1998	1999	2000	2001	75-84	85-89	90-MR
SUB-SAHARAN AFRICA	1,229	1,858	1,468	1,611	1,342	1,678	1,184	1,495	990	1,385	1,231	1,368	2,034	1,582
excluding South Africa	1,084	2,227	2,102	2,207	1,970	2,401	1,909	2,243	1,920	2,318	2,302	1,260	1,980	2,228
excl. S.Africa & Nigeria	1,251	2,236	2,048	2,256	2,037	2,469	1,935	2,268	1,900	2,286	2,278	1,334	1,971	2,232
Angola	..	77	171	249	190	214	68	91	102	103	110	..	67	122
Benin	0	20	64	5	6	4	70	52	64	40	84	0	3	37
Botswana	65	95	74	153	119	202	258	293	306	285	0	31	135	176
Burkina Faso	0	79	108	129	59	68	61	81	41	40	44	0	0	83
Burundi	42	102	111	144	136	50	51	50	46	71	94	45	65	90
Cameroon	83	248	76	61	80	28	0	25	17	0	34	47	46	60
Cape Verde	0	58	34	40	45	45	36	42	35	16	3	0	28	35
Central African Republic	0	50	50	32	33	8	23	34	30	27	30	27	41	37
Chad	0	108	49	129	78	57	59	50	21	32	20	0	95	68
Comoros	11	0	0	0	0	0	0	0	0	0	0	20	38	0
Congo, Democratic Rep. of	267	8	7	99	153	103	-1	32	18	136	228	137	113	72
Congo, Republic of	0	0	0	19	21	8	2	6	1	12	6	0	3	8
Côte d'Ivoire	0	-20	46	-31	-27	132	72	81	71	47	45	23	92	60
Djibouti	..	..	..	..	60	57	61	74	68	52	..	..	..	62
Equatorial Guinea	..	1	1	7	7	4	6	4	1	1	2	0	6	4
Eritrea	0	43	17	44	22	27	-3	-3	-4	-3	-2	0	0	12
Ethiopia	60	57	108	87	148	392	226	261	213	291	395	40	57	188
Gabon	33	6	14	15	0	0	0	17	17	17	17	30	16	12
Gambia, The	..	..	0	30	27	25	28	36	31	33	29	1	0	27
Ghana	0	0	256	201	260	206	160	288	148	154	266	0	0	162
Guinea	0	16	16	20	30	13	11	61	27	25	44	0	0	35
Guinea-Bissau	..	29	21	26	30	30	23	7	22	17	16	6	24	24
Kenya	0	0	0	0	0	0	0	0	0	0	0	0	0	0
Lesotho	-90	0	0	0	0	0	0	0	0	0	0	-174	-84	0
Liberia	36	..	..	..	..	..	..	..	..	..	..	57	78	..
Madagascar	0	54	70	44	0	20	17	6	7	12	-15	37	106	41
Malawi	0	0	0	0	0	0	0	0	0	0	0	0	0	0
Mali	-6	214	132	143	97	106	56	47	39	65	58	2	98	105
Mauritania	118	72	86	41	32	104	105	87	105	62	64	119	111	74
Mauritius	0	2	5	7	15	12	3	10	5	6	7	3	13	7
Mozambique	0	0	0	0	0	0	0	0	0	0	0	0	0	0
Namibia	0	0	0	0	0	0	0	0	0	0	0	0	296	0
Niger	154	34	61	0	0	0	0	0	0	0	0	127	104	12
Nigeria	-167	-9	54	-49	-66	-68	-26	-25	20	32	24	-44	8	-4
Rwanda	104	92	78	347	231	196	147	149	180	206	169	92	74	175
São Tomé and Principe	0	3	2	3	5	1	10	9	6	3	7	0	6	6
Senegal	28	8	-26	95	70	18	143	136	77	67	63	-10	-4	55
Seychelles	15	20	22	15	13	16	15	18	11	9	10	13	23	16
Sierra Leone	26	25	21	25	19	57	19	17	31	45	34	11	13	30
Somalia	143	..	..	..	..	..	..	..	..	..	..	111	291	265
South Africa	145	-369	-634	-596	-628	-723	-725	-748	-930	-933	-1,071	96	55	-646
Sudan	0	177	77	55	44	40	23	17	11	4	49	45	335	84
Swaziland	79	0	0	0	0	0	0	0	0	0	0	46	60	0
Tanzania	0	262	266	0	0	0	0	0	0	210	191	42	0	119
Togo	86	56	28	16	26	24	21	22	..	..	..	55	56	37
Uganda	0	0	0	0	0	0	0	0	0	0	0	6	0	0
Zambia	0	0	0	0	0	0	0	0	0	0	0	10	0	0
Zimbabwe	0	0	0	0	0	0	0	0	0	50	70	0	0	10
NORTH AFRICA	..	..	..	..	..	..	..	..	..	..	766	..	..	999
Algeria	0	0	0	0	0	0	0	0	0	0	0	0	0	0
Egypt, Arab Republic	..	1,352	1,902	814	919	724	890	883	1,097	932	769	..	584	1,352
Libya	-46	..	..	..	..	..	..	..	..	..	..	-85	-39	-35
Morocco	47	208	154	173	70	50	48	52	-11	94	-3	15	95	94
Tunisia	42	0	0	0	0	25	25	18	16	18	0	36	7	8
ALL AFRICA	1,230	3,418	3,524	2,598	2,331	2,476	2,146	2,447	2,091	2,430	1,997	1,328	2,441	3,033

Note: 2001 data are preliminary (see page 2).

5-7. Current account balance, excluding net capital grants

	Millions of U.S. dollars (current prices)											Annual Average		
	1980	1992	1993	1994	1995	1996	1997	1998	1999	2000	2001	75-84	85-89	90-MR
SUB-SAHARAN AFRICA	197	-12,943	-12,854	-10,488	-13,491	-7,102	-10,491	-19,741	-16,253	-6,174	-8,916	-8,309	-7,268	-11,320
excluding South Africa	-3,311	-14,890	-14,343	-10,582	-11,287	-5,211	-8,228	-17,413	-15,697	-5,734	-8,567	-7,968	-9,565	-11,138
excl. S.Africa & Nigeria	-7,621	-13,592	-12,186	-8,963	-10,390	-9,164	-11,068	-14,338	-12,407	-7,711	-8,582	-6,201	-7,725	-10,888
Angola	..	-816	-781	-499	-1,284	-323	-953	-2,039	-1,562	885	-253	..	-49	-697
Benin	-197	-151	-95	-73	-194	-185	-159	-133	-183	-183	-159	-174	-84	-142
Botswana	-152	198	427	211	300	494	721	203	618	545	438	-101	301	375
Burkina Faso	-259	-186	-163	-35	-207	-305	-271	-292	-355	-347	-333	-203	-227	-232
Burundi	-86	-117	-79	-15	-4	-39	2	-55	-28	-30	-1	-98	-90	-49
Cameroon	-346	-216	-620	-324	-71	-375	-258	-235	-377	-153	-147	-291	-147	-252
Cape Verde	-25	-20	-33	-38	-51	-27	-55	-74	-93	-100	-101	-38	-14	-52
Central African Republic	-43	-173	-108	-48	-81	-63	-57	-80	-25	-21	-9	-24	-96	-80
Chad	-16	-162	-219	-115	-110	-134	-143	-158	-219	-193	-663	-80	-150	-203
Comoros	-9	-55	-34	-43	-48	-41	-39	-22	-18	-5	-1	-14	-9	-33
Congo, Democratic Rep. of	-87	-866	-528	-530	-465	-28	-188	-415	-98	-194	-126	-366	-514	-434
Congo, Republic of	-167	-315	-541	-670	-335	-593	-471	-1,119	-403	256	104	-258	-230	-405
Côte d'Ivoire	..	-1,515	-1,235	-52	-183	-457	-390	-371	-172	-328	-231	-594	-686	-637
Djibouti	..	..	..	..	-17	-16	-12	-3	-4	-43	..	..	..	-16
Equatorial Guinea	..	-51	-48	-73	-97	-244	-250	-375	-289	-297	-399	6	20	-177
Eritrea	0	-19	0	65	-31	-104	-40	-239	-286	-210	-206	0	0	-89
Ethiopia	-126	-335	-497	-291	-90	68	-416	-333	-708	-335	-272	-176	-376	-332
Gabon	514	-226	-58	336	159	317	237	-183	131	128	168	157	-490	104
Gambia, The	-86	-51	-54	-18	-54	-26	-15	-13	-19	-21	-28	-47	-33	-32
Ghana	-54	-592	-559	-376	-140	-358	-1,132	-522	-1,058	-567	-386	-154	-254	-548
Guinea	-26	-244	-209	-247	-286	-339	-233	-239	-253	-226	-111	-62	-227	-225
Guinea-Bissau	..	-86	-50	-29	-45	-45	-39	-35	-28	-45	-45	..	-49	-45
Kenya	-1,233	-290	88	14	-475	-124	-421	-467	-212	-268	-292	-493	-572	-284
Lesotho	-207	-307	-255	-241	-332	-318	-319	-254	-221	-173	-97	-222	-175	-244
Liberia	46	..	..	..	..	..	..	..	..	..	..	15	-15	..
Madagascar	-635	-222	-263	-280	-284	-254	-262	-292	-238	-240	-106	-264	-142	-241
Malawi	-310	-284	-311	-269	-171	-270	-386	-171	-305	-237	-225	-163	-110	-233
Mali	-232	-216	-185	-145	-228	-265	-187	-203	-247	-227	-291	-168	-216	-211
Mauritania	-133	-90	-105	-37	-102	-40	1	-36	29	29	-30	-133	-22	-51
Mauritius	-117	-31	-44	-75	-208	-35	-22	-103	-65	-69	80	-88	5	-62
Mozambique	-423	-738	-825	-864	-677	-647	-611	-749	-1,152	-1,042	-850	-489	-635	-805
Namibia	-40	50	110	86	199	168	85	81	130	176	139	33	135	113
Niger	-429	-24	-24	-233	-208	-183	-192	-207	-156	-147	-172	-247	-33	-154
Nigeria	4,310	-1,298	-2,158	-1,618	-897	3,953	2,840	-3,075	-3,290	1,977	15	-1,767	-1,841	-250
Rwanda	-48	-157	-218	-53	-15	-70	-175	-190	-143	-90	-110	-23	-157	-112
São Tomé and Principe	1	-31	-33	-28	-35	-34	-23	-12	-22	-22	-18	-6	-19	-26
Senegal	-524	-545	-578	-251	-298	-336	-185	-216	-292	-284	-270	-402	-488	-346
Seychelles	..	-8	-42	-21	-44	-66	-63	-102	-123	-44	-145	..	..	-56
Sierra Leone	-168	-100	-95	-53	-73	-103	-7	-41	-20	-68	-117	-128	-56	-60
Somalia	-136	..	..	..	..	..	..	..	..	..	..	-117	-121	-81
South Africa	3,508	1,947	1,489	94	-2,204	-1,891	-2,263	-2,328	-556	-440	-349	-341	2,297	-181
Sudan	..	-1,354	-1,426	-1,459	-1,479	-1,548	-1,639	-1,996	-1,581	-1,598	-1,276	-411	-603	-1,516
Swaziland	-129	-137	-122	-68	-238	-54	-80	-34	-21	-42	-26	-61	42	-82
Tanzania	-540	-1,068	-1,115	-1,076	-1,047	-942	-842	-1,336	-1,172	-685	-714	-424	-586	-965
Togo	-95	-119	-84	-64	-63	-112	-88	-89	-120	-115	-91	-101	-90	-97
Uganda	-121	-338	-396	-265	-444	-500	-161	-261	-409	-370	-369	-57	-177	-366
Zambia	-538	-743	-467	-398	-464	-427	-509	-574	-481	-608	-730	-377	-308	-525
Zimbabwe	-444	-842	-311	-318	-370	-180	-823	-355	-157	-101	-110	-283	-46	-364
NORTH AFRICA	6,271	2,438	1,301	-2,805	-3,870	421	2,889	-4,207	-2,186	6,621	5,922	-3,616	-3,530	1,151
Algeria	242	1,290	810	-1,839	-2,240	1,050	3,450	-910	20	9,000	7,091	-1,008	-855	1,789
Egypt, Arab Republic	-438	2,670	2,295	410	386	-185	119	-2,479	-1,709	-1,171	-34	-1,765	-1,701	291
Libya	8,259	..	..	..	..	..	..	..	..	..	..	1,034	-408	2,236
Morocco	-1,420	-433	-521	-723	-1,186	35	-87	-144	-55	-387	-263	-1,369	-251	-365
Tunisia	-373	-1,089	-1,283	-654	-830	-479	-593	-675	-443	-821	-873	-507	-314	-750
ALL AFRICA	6,468	-10,506	-11,553	-13,293	-17,361	-6,681	-7,602	-23,948	-18,439	448	-2,994	-11,925	-10,798	-10,169

Note: 2001 data are preliminary (see page 2).

5-8. Current account balance, excluding net capital grants/GDP

	Percentage of GDP											Annual Average		
	1980	1992	1993	1994	1995	1996	1997	1998	1999	2000	2001	75-84	85-89	90-MR
SUB-SAHARAN AFRICA	0.4	-4.3	-4.5	-3.8	-4.3	-2.1	-3.1	-6.1	-5.0	-1.9	-2.9	-4.3	-3.0	-3.7
excluding South Africa	-1.8	-8.7	-9.3	-7.5	-6.9	-2.8	-4.3	-9.3	-8.1	-2.8	-4.3	-6.1	-6.0	-6.3
excl. S.Africa & Nigeria	-8.2	-9.9	-9.2	-7.6	-7.7	-6.0	-7.1	-9.2	-7.8	-4.7	-5.5	-7.3	-5.7	-7.4
Angola	..	-14.1	-14.8	-12.3	-25.5	-4.3	-12.4	-31.6	-25.7	10.0	-2.7	..	-0.6	-11.6
Benin	-14.0	-9.3	-4.5	-4.9	-9.7	-8.4	-7.4	-5.7	-7.6	-8.1	-6.7	-16.6	-5.8	-6.8
Botswana	-14.3	4.8	10.3	4.9	6.3	10.3	13.9	4.1	12.2	10.2	8.4	-12.1	14.1	7.8
Burkina Faso	-15.2	-9.3	-7.6	-2.0	-9.5	-12.3	-11.9	-11.6	-14.0	-15.0	-13.4	-15.6	-11.4	-9.7
Burundi	-9.3	-10.8	-8.4	-1.6	-0.4	-4.4	0.3	-6.2	-3.9	-4.5	-0.1	-9.8	-8.0	-4.9
Cameroon	-5.1	-1.9	-5.2	-4.1	-0.9	-4.1	-2.8	-2.7	-4.0	-1.7	-1.7	-6.0	-1.3	-2.6
Cape Verde	-23.5	-5.2	-9.0	-9.1	-10.3	-5.4	-10.8	-13.7	-15.7	-18.0	-17.2	-42.3	-9.4	-10.4
Central African Republic	-5.4	-12.1	-8.3	-5.6	-7.2	-5.9	-5.6	-7.6	-2.4	-2.2	-0.9	-4.0	-8.2	-6.5
Chad	-1.5	-8.6	-15.0	-9.8	-7.7	-8.4	-9.5	-9.3	-14.0	-13.7	-41.4	-8.6	-12.3	-12.9
Comoros	-7.2	-19.5	-12.4	-23.1	-20.6	-17.7	-18.2	-10.3	-7.9	-2.7	-0.3	-13.0	-6.0	-14.1
Congo, Democratic Rep. of	-0.6	-10.6	-5.9	-9.1	-8.2	-0.5	-5.7	-6.7	-0.8	-1.3	..	-3.4	-6.2	-6.2
Congo, Republic of	-9.8	-10.7	-28.2	-37.8	-15.8	-23.4	-20.3	-57.4	-17.1	7.9	3.8	-21.5	-11.1	-18.9
Côte d'Ivoire	..	-13.6	-11.9	-0.7	-1.8	-3.8	-3.3	-2.9	-1.4	-3.1	-2.2	-8.6	-6.8	-5.8
Djibouti	..	..	..	..	-3.4	-3.3	-2.3	-0.6	-0.8	-7.7	..	..	..	-3.0
Equatorial Guinea	..	-32.8	-31.6	-58.2	-58.9	-94.3	-50.3	-82.2	-33.2	-22.2	-21.6	..	18.7	-40.5
Eritrea	..	-4.3	0.0	13.8	-6.0	-16.9	-6.1	-33.4	-40.6	-33.4	-30.0	..	..	-15.7
Ethiopia	..	-6.0	-8.0	-5.9	-1.6	1.1	-6.5	-5.1	-11.0	-5.3	-4.4	-5.8	-5.1	-5.5
Gabon	12.0	-4.0	-1.3	8.0	3.2	5.5	4.4	-4.0	3.0	2.6	3.9	4.2	-13.9	2.1
Gambia, The	-35.7	-14.7	-14.6	-5.0	-14.2	-6.7	-3.8	-3.0	-4.3	-4.9	-6.8	-22.5	-15.1	-8.8
Ghana	-1.2	-9.2	-9.4	-6.9	-2.2	-5.2	-16.4	-7.0	-13.7	-11.4	-7.3	-3.9	-5.0	-8.6
Guinea	..	-7.4	-6.4	-7.2	-7.7	-8.8	-6.2	-6.7	-7.3	-7.4	-3.7	..	-10.1	-6.7
Guinea-Bissau	..	-37.8	-21.0	-12.4	-17.6	-16.5	-14.7	-16.9	-12.6	-20.7	-22.7	..	-26.4	-19.3
Kenya	-17.0	-3.6	1.8	0.2	-5.3	-1.3	-4.0	-4.1	-2.0	-2.6	-2.6	-8.4	-7.4	-2.9
Lesotho	-47.9	-37.2	-31.1	-28.9	-35.6	-33.8	-31.2	-28.5	-24.3	-19.2	-12.2	-71.8	-42.6	-28.7
Liberia	4.1	..	..	..	..	..	..	..	..	..	..	1.9	-1.2	..
Madagascar	-15.7	-7.3	-7.8	-9.4	-9.0	-6.4	-7.4	-7.8	-6.4	-6.2	-2.3	-7.6	-5.3	-7.2
Malawi	-25.0	-15.8	-15.0	-22.7	-12.0	-11.1	-15.2	-9.8	-16.8	-13.9	-12.9	-15.6	-8.2	-12.8
Mali	-13.0	-7.6	-6.9	-8.3	-9.2	-10.1	-7.6	-7.8	-9.6	-9.9	-12.6	-12.9	-12.6	-8.6
Mauritania	-18.8	-7.6	-11.1	-3.6	-9.5	-3.6	0.1	-3.6	3.0	2.9	-2.9	-19.9	-3.0	-4.8
Mauritius	-10.2	-1.1	-1.3	-2.2	-5.5	-0.9	-0.5	-2.5	-1.6	-1.6	1.8	-7.6	0.2	-1.8
Mozambique	-12.0	-39.8	-41.6	-39.7	-29.3	-22.8	-18.0	-19.3	-28.9	-27.3	-23.6	-14.2	-23.1	-29.3
Namibia	-1.7	1.7	3.9	2.6	5.7	4.8	2.4	2.4	3.8	5.1	4.5	1.8	7.7	3.5
Niger	-17.1	-1.0	-1.5	-14.9	-11.0	-9.2	-10.4	-10.0	-7.7	-8.2	-8.8	-13.6	-3.1	-8.0
Nigeria	6.7	-4.0	-10.1	-6.8	-3.2	11.2	7.8	-9.6	-9.5	4.8	0.0	-4.5	-8.5	-1.5
Rwanda	-4.1	-7.7	-11.0	-7.0	-1.1	-5.1	-9.4	-9.6	-7.4	-5.0	-6.5	-1.6	-7.0	-6.2
São Tomé and Principe	2.1	-67.9	-70.1	-57.4	-76.7	-76.0	-53.1	-30.5	-45.8	-46.3	-38.7	-10.5	-36.8	-55.1
Senegal	-17.5	-9.0	-10.6	-6.9	-6.7	-7.2	-4.2	-4.7	-6.2	-6.5	-5.8	-16.7	-12.4	-7.0
Seychelles	..	-1.7	-9.0	-4.4	-8.7	-12.0	-10.7	-16.8	-19.8	-7.5	-25.4	..	..	-10.1
Sierra Leone	-15.3	-14.6	-12.4	-5.3	-7.9	-10.9	-0.8	-6.2	-3.0	-10.7	-15.6	-11.4	-6.8	-7.8
Somalia	-22.6	..	..	..	..	..	..	..	..	..	..	-17.3	-12.2	-8.8
South Africa	4.4	1.5	1.1	0.1	-1.5	-1.3	-1.5	-1.7	-0.4	-0.3	-0.3	-0.5	3.2	-0.1
Sudan	..	-21.1	-18.1	-17.9	-20.6	-18.7	-15.4	-17.4	-15.3	-14.2	-10.2	-5.3	-3.8	-16.0
Swaziland	-23.8	-13.7	-11.5	-5.9	-17.4	-4.1	-5.6	-2.5	-1.5	-3.0	-2.1	-11.1	5.5	-7.1
Tanzania	..	-23.2	-26.2	-23.8	-19.9	-14.5	-11.0	-15.9	-13.6	-7.5	-7.6	-10.0	-13.5	-16.5
Togo	-8.4	-7.0	-6.8	-6.5	-4.8	-7.6	-5.9	-6.3	-8.5	-9.4	-7.3	-12.2	-7.8	-6.9
Uganda	-9.7	-11.8	-12.3	-6.6	-7.7	-8.3	-2.6	-4.0	-6.9	-6.3	-6.5	-3.1	-3.2	-8.0
Zambia	-13.8	-23.4	-14.3	-11.9	-13.4	-13.1	-13.0	-17.7	-15.3	-18.8	-20.1	-11.9	-13.0	-15.7
Zimbabwe	-6.6	-12.5	-4.7	-4.6	-5.2	-2.1	-9.8	-6.2	-2.9	-1.4	-1.2	-4.0	-0.8	-5.0
NORTH AFRICA	4.9	1.8	0.9	-2.0	-2.5	0.2	1.6	-2.3	-1.1	3.2	2.8	-4.0	-2.4	0.6
Algeria	0.6	2.7	1.6	-4.3	-5.4	2.2	7.2	-1.9	0.0	16.9	12.5	-4.5	-1.4	3.2
Egypt, Arab Republic	-1.9	6.4	4.9	0.8	0.6	-0.3	0.2	-3.0	-1.9	-1.2	0.0	-9.6	-4.7	1.3
Libya	23.2	..	..	..	..	..	..	..	..	..	..	4.8	-2.2	..
Morocco	-7.5	-1.5	-1.9	-2.4	-3.6	0.1	-0.3	-0.4	-0.2	-1.2	-0.8	-10.3	-1.7	-1.2
Tunisia	-4.3	-7.0	-8.8	-4.2	-4.6	-2.4	-3.1	-3.4	-2.1	-4.2	-4.4	-7.4	-3.5	-4.5
ALL AFRICA	2.0	-2.4	-2.7	-3.2	-3.7	-1.3	-1.5	-4.7	-3.6	0.1	-0.6	-4.2	-2.8	-2.2

Note: 2001 data are preliminary (see page 2). Since 1994, Nigeria's ratios are distorted because the official exchange rate used by the Government for oil exports and oil value added is significantly over-valued.

5-9. Net capital grants

	Millions of U.S. dollars (current prices)											Annual Average		
	1980	*1992*	*1993*	*1994*	*1995*	*1996*	*1997*	*1998*	*1999*	*2000*	*2001*	*75-84*	*85-89*	*90-MR*
SUB-SAHARAN AFRICA	1,119	4,941	4,245	3,844	3,933	3,297	3,069	3,450	3,139	3,044	3,438	1,080	2,629	3,653
excluding South Africa	1,119	4,983	4,303	3,778	3,973	3,344	3,263	3,506	3,182	3,103	3,413	1,094	2,624	3,692
excl. S.Africa & Nigeria	1,119	4,983	4,303	3,778	3,973	3,344	3,263	3,506	3,182	3,103	3,413	1,094	2,624	3,692
Angola	0	0	0	0	0	0	0	0	0	0	0	0	0	0
Benin	63	59	63	54	70	56	84	62	67	46	44	63	63	59
Botswana	8	7	9	6	3	5	5	5	5	26	25	6	4	8
Burkina Faso	211	142	98	65	74	53	29	33	38	32	37	151	193	64
Burundi	34	63	53	0	0	0	0	0	0	0	0	38	37	20
Cameroon	0	0	0	0	0	0	0	0	0	0	0	0	0	0
Cape Verde	29	9	19	20	20	13	51	70	29	27	4	20	10	23
Central African Republic	0	82	69	63	56	39	..	..	..	..	..	0	43	62
Chad	28	76	95	70	53	49	53	70	49	67	55	76	107	67
Comoros	0	19	26	19	27	21	19	17	16	9	10	0	0	20
Congo, Democratic Rep. of	0	24	19	41	204	0	0	0	0	0	0	0	108	44
Congo, Republic of	0	0	0	0	0	0	0	0	10	10	5	0	0	2
Côte d'Ivoire	..	86	95	53	70	79	69	68	65	56	48	0	0	62
Djibouti	..	..	..	..	0	0	0	0	0	0	..	..	..	0
Equatorial Guinea	..	26	29	5	3	2	3	3	1	1	2	7	20	12
Eritrea	0	125	52	29	8	4	29	64	110	49	101	0	0	47
Ethiopia	0	375	293	199	280	259	225	229	200	291	395	26	183	260
Gabon	0	0	0	0	0	0	0	0	0	0	0	0	0	0
Gambia, The	..	36	40	35	28	26	28	36	31	33	29	17	41	34
Ghana	83	216	256	201	260	206	159	288	148	154	265	69	144	214
Guinea	17	111	101	104	120	117	114	75	80	72	82	13	56	97
Guinea-Bissau	..	28	37	44	56	41	32	0	21	16	25	16	32	30
Kenya	118	214	94	87	90	125	82	83	62	63	69	84	174	115
Lesotho	..	42	30	31	38	32	23	22	19	17	7	6	16	29
Liberia	..	..	..	..	..	..	..	..	..	..	..	..	..	..
Madagascar	0	72	87	72	85	51	114	100	129	115	113	16	0	78
Malawi	50	153	128	111	152	97	83	157	157	148	98	33	50	120
Mali	78	36	30	57	99	94	92	76	78	123	124	95	62	76
Mauritania	0	21	20	26	30	10	16	25	12	21	21	0	42	20
Mauritius	0	-2	-1	-2	-1	-1	-1	-1	-1	0	-1	0	0	-1
Mozambique	56	499	503	565	339	225	313	313	434	564	469	90	293	431
Namibia	0	0	0	0	0	0	0	0	0	0	0	0	0	0
Niger	0	95	94	134	120	117	113	129	96	85	97	0	55	115
Nigeria	0	0	0	0	0	0	0	0	0	0	0	0	0	0
Rwanda	0	79	87	7	69	68	116	95	71	62	67	10	0	60
São Tomé and Principe	0	4	8	8	18	20	22	4	9	12	14	0	3	11
Senegal	92	328	266	256	272	273	92	108	94	70	89	131	226	198
Seychelles	15	20	22	15	..	..	..	..	..	..	..	13	23	19
Sierra Leone	11	0	0	0	0	3	0	1	4	8	39	5	5	5
Somalia	0	0	0	0	0	0	0	..	..	..	..	0	0	0
South Africa	0	-42	-58	66	-40	-47	-194	-56	-43	-59	25	-16	4	-39
Sudan	..	20	29	15	11	8	4	0	26	18	0	11	0	11
Swaziland	-2	0	0	0	0	0	0	0	0	0	0	-1	0	0
Tanzania	108	809	759	634	525	581	690	682	533	315	343	115	378	579
Togo	..	26	4	7	8	7	13	15	..	..	..	24	34	16
Uganda	38	206	277	228	303	277	307	380	277	358	459	47	72	290
Zambia	23	635	340	338	318	304	198	221	214	185	253	13	95	319
Zimbabwe	58	242	173	181	167	85	85	77	101	53	26	39	68	116
NORTH AFRICA	43	81	104	103	70	46	95	82	73	3	270	195	537	105
Algeria	0	0	0	0	0	0	0	0	0	0	120	0	0	10
Egypt, Arab Republic	2	0	0	0	0	0	0	0	0	0	0	182	461	0
Libya	0	0	0	0	0	0	0	..	..	..	..	0	0	0
Morocco	0	0	0	0	0	0	0	0	0	0	50	0	0	4
Tunisia	42	81	104	103	70	46	95	82	73	3	100	27	75	91
ALL AFRICA	1,162	5,023	4,348	3,947	4,004	3,342	3,164	3,533	3,212	3,047	3,708	1,275	3,165	3,757

Note: 2001 data are preliminary (see page 2).

5-10. Net foreign direct investment

	Millions of U.S. dollars (current prices)											Annual Average		
	1980	1992	1993	1994	1995	1996	1997	1998	1999	2000	2001	75-84	85-89	90-MR
SUB-SAHARAN AFRICA	-708	-357	925	711	736	3,034	5,626	4,535	7,117	5,699	6,852	668	1,807	3,116
excluding South Africa	57	1,576	1,213	1,567	1,992	3,260	4,160	5,754	7,564	5,344	6,352	892	1,941	3,438
excl. S.Africa & Nigeria	796	862	632	979	1,315	2,501	2,621	4,534	6,091	3,970	4,552	736	1,083	2,445
Angola	..	288	302	327	303	181	412	1,114	2,471	878	1,347	346	192	663
Benin	4	26	-7	8	4	-6	19	18	77	75	48	2	1	22
Botswana	109	-12	-296	-24	30	89	100	100	100	30	33	46	64	18
Burkina Faso	0	9	9	25	14	14	8	1	9	24	10	1	0	11
Burundi	1	1	0	0	1	0	0	0	0	6	6	1	1	1
Cameroon	105	206	134	-228	-154	92	100	-50	7	280	170	58	322	68
Cape Verde	..	-1	3	2	26	28	12	9	67	31	23	..	1	17
Central African Republic	5	4	-15	-13	4	12	-5	7	2	3	9	6	4	0
Chad	0	3	21	35	37	43	37	46	46	72	451	11	21	68
Comoros	0	-1	0	0	1	1	0	0	0	0	0	0	3	0
Congo, Democratic Rep. of	0	0	0	0	0	40	0	22	23	74	83	91	9	21
Congo, Republic of	40	49	254	285	27	587	145	299	519	478	218	24	18	228
Côte d'Ivoire	83	35	24	-25	234	223	314	246	196	103	180	51	53	133
Djibouti	..	..	..	..	3	3	2	3	4	9	..	..	..	4
Equatorial Guinea	..	-3	-10	65	93	264	185	366	30	113	230	0	1	116
Eritrea	0	0	0	0	0	37	39	30	83	28	12	0	0	19
Ethiopia	0	0	0	0	0	0	60	7	136	51	52	3	0	26
Gabon	24	-87	-114	-100	-109	-146	-63	-62	129	-15	-33	59	219	-56
Gambia, The	..	11	9	6	7	9	9	12	7	2	6	..	5	8
Ghana	16	22	106	128	83	70	36	45	46	110	106	13	7	66
Guinea	34	56	6	11	25	17	45	49	34	12	12	12	25	27
Guinea-Bissau	..	0	0	0	0	0	0	0	0	0	0	..	0	0
Kenya	78	6	2	4	33	13	40	42	42	127	50	25	27	33
Lesotho	4	26	20	38	30	40	40	42	36	32	30	2	23	37
Liberia	..	..	..	..	..	..	..	..	..	..	..	47	2	..
Madagascar	0	21	15	6	10	10	14	16	58	70	93	-1	3	29
Malawi	10	0	0	0	0	30	24	34	39	27	28	4	0	15
Mali	24	-9	-7	38	30	60	-14	-50	24	18	21	16	1	8
Mauritania	27	5	12	3	7	0	-3	0	0	1	4	1	2	3
Mauritius	0	4	-36	-1	22	31	5	20	19	13	223	1	15	31
Mozambique	0	25	32	35	45	73	64	213	382	139	183	0	3	102
Namibia	..	120	47	104	157	152	83	79	110	145	167	..	..	109
Niger	44	0	0	0	0	0	0	0	2	18	33	17	-5	3
Nigeria	-739	714	581	588	677	760	1,539	1,220	1,473	1,374	1,800	206	857	993
Rwanda	16	6	6	0	2	2	3	7	2	8	5	11	19	4
São Tomé and Principe	..	1	4	2	2	2	0	4	3	4	4	..	1	3
Senegal	61	-53	-48	48	-10	-5	107	53	126	36	1	43	-25	20
Seychelles	6	-3	6	17	27	17	34	42	46	14	22	5	11	20
Sierra Leone	10	5	18	17	-5	0	0	4	2	2	2	4	1	4
Somalia	..	..	..	..	..	..	..	..	..	..	..	-1	..	..
South Africa	-765	-1,933	-288	-856	-1,256	-226	1,466	-1,219	-447	355	500	-178	-134	-322
Sudan	0	0	0	0	0	70	180	670	224	179	98	0	0	118
Swaziland	18	50	31	23	31	28	-3	130	87	6	26	15	35	41
Tanzania	..	15	62	63	104	134	150	172	517	463	372	..	..	172
Togo	42	19	2	6	5	24	19	1	..	..	..	23	13	11
Uganda	0	2	4	5	2	110	110	158	175	169	144	1	22	74
Zambia	62	0	3	40	97	117	207	198	163	122	72	20	0	85
Zimbabwe	-26	15	32	30	98	35	107	436	50	15	10	-18	-5	68
NORTH AFRICA	-78	..	..	..	1,350	1,470	2,409	2,477	2,284	2,886	5,519	72	198	2,341
Algeria	281	30	0	0	0	270	260	500	460	400	1,100	-2	-67	242
Egypt, Arab Republic	541	1,032	1,021	1,285	735	612	723	967	655	1,613	1,613	456	171	957
Libya	-1,136	..	..	..	..	..	..	..	..	..	..	-564	-33	54
Morocco	..	..	..	..	320	327	1,071	313	831	143	2,298	..	..	757
Tunisia	236	487	545	442	295	261	355	697	337	731	509	182	128	417
ALL AFRICA	-786	1,192	2,490	2,437	2,086	4,505	8,035	7,011	9,401	8,585	12,371	776	2,005	5,178

Note: 2001 data are preliminary (see page 2).

5-11. Net long-term borrowing

	Millions of U.S. dollars (current prices)											Annual Average		
	1980	1992	1993	1994	1995	1996	1997	1998	1999	2000	2001	75-84	85-89	90-MR
SUB-SAHARAN AFRICA	7,739	3,844	5,021	4,406	4,007	807	1,559	-628	-224	141	-158	6,158	5,669	2,352
excluding South Africa	7,739	3,844	5,021	2,883	2,528	1,285	1,609	-231	-113	-861	-589	6,158	5,669	2,069
excl. S.Africa & Nigeria	6,229	5,187	5,056	3,031	3,014	2,395	2,135	266	317	77	1,059	5,143	5,467	2,693
Angola	..	501	622	263	218	125	374	-528	-361	-519	-546	234	758	77
Benin	56	65	63	84	77	83	23	32	37	16	76	77	57	62
Botswana	21	22	45	-6	1	-46	-53	-34	-35	-38	-32	28	37	-14
Burkina Faso	55	128	119	80	83	73	40	58	70	58	113	48	73	83
Burundi	35	86	58	31	27	23	7	18	6	27	0	37	85	34
Cameroon	500	520	264	249	-103	-41	-7	-89	-23	18	6	313	237	122
Cape Verde	..	11	6	23	16	19	11	39	47	18	41	18	8	20
Central African Republic	24	41	48	36	30	25	2	-9	-2	9	-9	17	68	31
Chad	3	139	52	61	55	89	68	31	70	18	29	21	41	67
Comoros	13	15	6	10	9	9	5	3	-1	2	11	11	15	6
Congo, Democratic Rep. of	271	54	53	1	0	3	0	0	8	0	0	281	239	54
Congo, Republic of	488	33	383	48	-67	-136	-30	-7	0	-5	-17	222	141	-1
Côte d'Ivoire	1,017	351	278	524	204	64	-580	-225	-577	-294	-289	636	141	30
Djibouti	8	36	19	17	9	15	7	2	-3	-1	5	8	17	14
Equatorial Guinea	18	13	9	4	2	0	1	0	3	0	-1	8	17	4
Eritrea	..	..	..	27	7	7	33	67	108	50	106	..	..	51
Ethiopia	93	263	314	168	141	1	127	78	142	114	424	426	448	196
Gabon	-109	8	58	38	57	-43	-23	-66	-197	-158	-248	52	207	-28
Gambia, The	51	37	7	3	8	43	11	2	11	8	12	18	21	13
Ghana	143	354	324	302	405	694	417	352	126	120	423	69	244	350
Guinea	47	149	245	122	49	85	143	54	30	-21	16	44	132	93
Guinea-Bissau	72	37	22	25	13	23	25	8	-1	4	-14	22	40	18
Kenya	424	175	111	-276	137	-76	-163	-174	-211	57	-70	251	340	29
Lesotho	10	59	52	47	48	58	45	40	26	36	-21	15	32	40
Liberia	61	0	20	-14	0	0	0	0	0	0	0	61	22	-1
Madagascar	333	77	89	51	66	93	217	44	65	76	84	171	153	96
Malawi	120	106	151	74	149	121	129	121	114	88	75	75	72	110
Mali	89	131	58	69	138	110	76	56	57	44	46	78	125	88
Mauritania	108	81	91	82	42	83	26	-7	-12	54	13	100	77	44
Mauritius	79	-1	22	83	255	32	57	-93	38	-269	-62	37	58	20
Mozambique	..	168	152	176	196	222	216	185	92	66	60	300	281	150
Namibia	0	0	50	-45	23	19	20	7	59	..	..	0	-2	13
Niger	223	56	44	35	-3	10	51	49	31	52	53	107	105	36
Nigeria	1,510	-1,343	-35	-148	-486	-1,110	-525	-497	-430	-938	-1,648	1,015	203	-624
Rwanda	25	71	50	20	43	53	62	79	70	27	43	27	71	54
São Tomé and Principe	9	23	14	14	12	10	3	5	14	6	5	6	11	12
Senegal	171	225	100	7	4	66	126	52	-56	-5	145	166	215	65
Seychelles	12	13	6	8	-7	2	2	9	-7	-3	-4	7	7	2
Sierra Leone	50	41	95	45	38	28	33	33	9	67	74	25	14	41
Somalia	106	0	0	0	0	0	0	0	0	0	0	136	83	5
South Africa	..	..	..	1,524	1,478	-478	-51	-396	-111	1,002	431	..	..	425
Sudan	658	94	91	9	36	17	5	-1	-6	-4	-2	495	164	44
Swaziland	19	-10	-9	-5	2	8	39	17	17	1	27	21	-1	5
Tanzania	318	216	142	160	133	63	161	117	153	65	39	290	184	134
Togo	78	39	14	34	19	81	29	52	15	15	21	84	30	36
Uganda	51	202	299	181	161	170	231	104	107	178	306	61	197	190
Zambia	388	136	99	109	110	80	107	-49	192	163	154	205	161	106
Zimbabwe	93	426	322	57	171	33	63	-165	95	-65	-34	164	44	110
NORTH AFRICA	5,063	1,465	579	1,003	1,524	821	-576	-2,077	-2,491	-1,796	-403	5,190	3,669	-11
Algeria	869	470	-453	1,432	1,435	920	-377	-1,554	-1,899	-1,508	-1,830	1,435	836	-317
Egypt, Arab Republic	2,337	-105	183	240	-270	-354	-49	-212	-618	-505	871	2,164	1,481	-24
Libya	110	256	375	-507	77	-14	1	33	-64	..	..	101	316	2
Morocco	1,394	491	196	-293	-183	-202	-806	-174	-439	4	-475	1,118	825	-42
Tunisia	352	352	277	131	465	472	655	-170	529	213	1,031	373	212	370
ALL AFRICA	12,802	5,308	5,599	5,409	5,530	1,628	982	-2,705	-2,715	-1,655	-562	11,349	9,339	2,341

5-12. Other capital flows

	Millions of U.S. dollars (current prices)											Annual Average		
	1980	1992	1993	1994	1995	1996	1997	1998	1999	2000	2001	75-84	85-89	90-MR
SUB-SAHARAN AFRICA	1,896	-3,860	-4,162	-5,612	-2,397	603	-13,620	-1,831	-18,707	-21,489	-3,728	1,628	-1,698	-6,637
excluding South Africa	3,434	-1,953	-5,008	-2,544	-1,044	-522	-5,619	765	-2,801	-24,736	-5,330	1,615	339	-4,085
excl. S.Africa & Nigeria	3,651	-2,710	-2,487	-2,681	-1,635	1,002	-4,842	131	-2,559	-3,852	-4,587	2,633	917	-2,175
Angola	0	373	-550	-443	559	3,845	-368	903	-770	-1,130	-1,433	0	342	88
Benin	116	89	-109	-65	-1	-25	39	27	188	-3	-19	95	83	27
Botswana	125	211	264	-57	-119	-70	-156	-204	-249	-73	-64	104	47	-22
Burkina Faso	..	-144	-24	-29	-1	-34	-6	-66	-58	9	-32	83	46	-53
Burundi	-22	-25	-22	34	-1	-55	-29	-16	-7	-9	-19	-24	-27	-13
Cameroon	705	-216	-100	-201	-329	76	147	0	10	0	-1	614	-485	-42
Cape Verde	..	5	-24	-40	-43	-22	-53	-116	-19	-19	59	4	-7	-22
Central African Republic	24	-67	-10	-47	-75	-31	4	-19	-54	-30	-90	5	-58	-43
Chad	-24	-32	-48	-93	-59	-87	-91	-79	-6	-69	-33	-27	-21	-52
Comoros	-11	27	32	16	-8	28	8	-10	-5	4	-3	-3	0	11
Congo, Democratic Rep. of	652	191	-159	-221	-512	665	772	..	..	496	484	175	-18	182
Congo, Republic of	219	170	463	96	1,091	-1,019	463	1,630	-184	-672	-347	317	389	292
Côte d'Ivoire	626	144	260	-173	-587	-256	-192	439	-223	-103	-659	355	680	-98
Djibouti	..	..	..	..	2	-2	-33	..	-2	25	..	..	..	-2
Equatorial Guinea	..	28	7	-8	6	-32	64	9	279	366	373	15	-63	79
Eritrea	0	-139	-43	-84	-133	-125	30	-91	-1	5	-60	0	0	-54
Ethiopia	-7	-1,277	-856	58	-316	-642	-4,369	-148	-37	-364	-421	-4	-148	-816
Gabon	-337	187	26	-245	-153	-217	-126	-128	-83	-51	-59	-259	-169	-96
Gambia, The	..	-10	1	-36	1	-18	-26	-31	-21	7	-12	..	-27	-16
Ghana	-168	-157	-7	-18	-351	-589	408	-22	574	-612	-491	-20	-28	-101
Guinea	-8	-111	-169	-84	-75	-41	-165	-110	-133	-45	-168	6	28	-117
Guinea-Bissau	..	30	-35	-47	-67	-58	-12	10	15	28	40	-8	-17	-14
Kenya	482	-38	-107	121	199	391	487	570	378	150	369	128	259	197
Lesotho	..	113	216	225	286	249	237	109	47	-19	-9	115	116	121
Liberia	..	..	..	..	..	..	..	..	..	..	..	..	..	..
Madagascar	399	-140	-147	-21	-59	33	-100	-134	-78	-143	-259	68	210	-45
Malawi	62	-3	-12	-8	14	103	144	-97	50	-20	1	31	-9	5
Mali	34	0	0	-10	-43	35	7	-57	7	21	83	38	0	4
Mauritania	-5	-75	27	-107	98	40	-16	8	-34	-170	-59	15	-145	-33
Mauritius	84	177	25	32	60	82	60	7	7	226	-18	46	33	82
Mozambique	-85	-540	-551	-554	-316	-113	-322	-360	-544	-621	-511	-90	-325	-450
Namibia	..	-229	-153	-225	-427	-383	-167	-147	-194	-262	-201	..	..	-241
Niger	0	-185	-125	-36	7	-35	-116	-25	-10	-11	2	0	-115	-54
Nigeria	-217	757	-2,521	137	591	-1,524	-777	634	-242	-20,883	-743	-783	-578	-1,910
Rwanda	1	-11	13	27	-46	-40	27	24	1	-16	-5	-14	49	-3
São Tomé and Principe	-22	0	-1	-9	-15	-23	-22	-8	-11	-8	-14	0	-2	-13
Senegal	-44	-1	0	15	-14	0	4	1	0	-1	0	-14	8	0
Seychelles	..	9	12	-8	30	26	9	27	17	9	9	..	..	9
Sierra Leone	-20	15	-13	-67	7	55	-6	7	-3	18	-4	5	-22	-1
Somalia	..	..	..	..	..	..	..	..	..	..	..	..	..	..
South Africa	-1,538	-1,907	846	-3,068	-1,353	1,125	-8,001	-2,596	-15,907	3,247	1,602	300	-2,038	-2,552
Sudan	504	252	394	501	563	544	394	236	205	425	334	287	518	359
Swaziland	129	182	70	88	288	50	150	-67	-83	64	-15	27	-12	75
Tanzania	..	-68	-14	-289	-279	-490	-711	-547	-618	-662	-239	..	..	-326
Togo	..	..	..	..	..	..	..	..	..	..	..	..	..	..
Uganda	..	-269	-361	-199	-429	-348	-742	-775	-538	-675	-863	-27	-17	-461
Zambia	-123	-895	-552	-295	-380	-331	-229	-439	-404	60	-157	12	-124	-386
Zimbabwe	365	-284	-101	-176	-6	-132	-235	-182	30	21	-75	66	-54	-103
NORTH AFRICA	-573	-2,097	561	2,523	-646	179	86	1,797	163	-3,397	-2,018	152	472	-450
Algeria	201	-1,340	-780	574	-180	-10	-40	0	-950	200	-707	-19	221	-383
Egypt, Arab Republic	0	-333	333	318	-525	237	-138	1,673	-411	-3,152	-1,400	0	-595	-295
Libya	-481	..	..	..	..	..	..	..	..	..	..	161	1,348	-142
Morocco	-101	-673	610	1,377	43	-144	268	240	1,293	-67	89	97	-457	192
Tunisia	-192	249	398	255	16	96	-4	-117	231	-378	0	-22	-45	48
ALL AFRICA	1,323	-5,957	-3,601	-3,089	-3,043	782	-13,534	-34	-18,545	-24,886	-5,746	1,780	-1,227	-7,087

Note: Includes all capital account flows, except changes in reserves, that are not included in the tables on foreign investment or long-term borrowing.

5-13. Use of reserves

	Millions of U.S. dollars (current prices)											Annual Average		
	1980	1992	1993	1994	1995	1996	1997	1998	1999	2000	2001	75-84	85-89	90-MR
SUB-SAHARAN AFRICA	-4,633	1,436	-2,513	-1,437	1,852	-7,429	-1,921	130	4,315	-12,465	-7,063	1,260	-1,470	-2,449
excluding South Africa	-3,818	1,237	216	-2,382	-514	-6,241	-4,277	857	81	-5,521	-2,136	1,072	-1,495	-1,922
excl. S.Africa & Nigeria	727	-778	-509	-2,383	-115	-3,888	-1,216	742	-1,585	-1,562	-1,113	636	-1,353	-1,200
Angola	0	-257	900	46	626	-1,520	183	321	-639	-631	508	33	-40	-39
Benin	19	-92	-30	-75	18	-58	-14	-9	-181	15	-19	10	-5	-56
Botswana	-91	-408	-405	-141	-213	-518	-635	-61	-395	-380	-175	-55	-416	-335
Burkina Faso	-11	-61	-72	-119	-145	1	35	-7	20	27	5	-13	-14	-30
Burundi	8	-13	0	-48	-11	62	19	39	14	17	-7	-1	-37	4
Cameroon	-162	-112	-291	333	-13	-81	-142	39	-4	-242	-169	-38	-108	-65
Cape Verde	0	-15	4	3	9	-22	3	8	-29	21	-5	-1	-4	-1
Central African Republic	-10	-4	-27	-72	-11	-20	18	41	-6	-11	4	-4	3	-6
Chad	5	33	32	-19	-58	13	14	20	33	8	13	-3	-9	8
Comoros	4	0	-14	-10	4	-9	4	3	-4	-9	-21	0	-3	-4
Congo, Democratic Rep. of	-35	-1	14	17	39	-15	21	..	..	87	-11	76	-60	19
Congo, Republic of	-59	27	5	-56	-6	-17	20	69	-60	-169	142	1	2	0
Côte d'Ivoire	112	235	-88	-794	-222	-39	-82	2	117	188	119	92	-75	-39
Djibouti	..	..	..	..	7	-1	12	..	-3	-5	..	..	..	2
Equatorial Guinea	13	8	2	-1	-8	-4	-7	2	-29	-176	-199	2	3	-35
Eritrea	0	-91	-109	-78	58	76	-112	129	22	19	-14	0	0	-8
Ethiopia	40	-46	-112	-256	-253	-104	-163	-134	40	225	13	27	2	-75
Gabon	-93	222	79	-137	42	-83	-39	107	59	-39	-31	-9	-180	5
Gambia, The	..	1	-6	5	-11	-8	-7	-10	-3	-2	14	5	-4	-1
Ghana	96	124	-41	-164	-211	14	-25	-100	102	196	-79	25	-44	-39
Guinea	-25	-3	-49	34	-13	27	-47	5	42	44	-54	-5	-12	-7
Guinea-Bissau	0	-5	9	6	1	-12	2	7	10	-6	4	5	-6	1
Kenya	131	-75	-330	-103	133	-417	13	42	-31	-94	-191	7	-194	-71
Lesotho	-41	51	-92	-119	-109	-112	-89	19	75	78	13	-8	-5	-16
Liberia	41	0	-1	-3	..	..	..	..	..	..	..	27	-3	-1
Madagascar	-83	-17	-20	8	-61	-134	-54	104	-46	-28	-98	6	-44	-19
Malawi	17	0	0	29	-87	-109	53	-77	-31	17	12	16	-1	-16
Mali	-9	-89	-28	-87	-68	-128	3	61	56	19	-28	-6	-38	-46
Mauritania	2	3	-26	11	-131	-67	-61	-19	-23	52	13	9	32	-20
Mauritius	-3	-192	56	53	58	-217	-84	-9	-28	-84	-185	2	-97	-79
Mozambique	32	-40	46	-52	-60	-159	-115	-62	-68	-194	-4	46	-17	-60
Namibia	..	7	-91	-75	-24	-23	-68	-56	-57	-16	-101	..	..	-44
Niger	53	10	-6	-21	9	11	29	1	22	-29	-22	6	5	-2
Nigeria	-4,545	2,015	725	1	-399	-2,353	-3,061	115	1,666	-3,959	-1,023	436	-142	-721
Rwanda	33	41	31	-4	-35	-8	-29	4	10	-10	-11	19	91	-2
São Tomé and Principe	12	0	0	0	-5	0	-8	3	-1	-2	-5	0	0	-2
Senegal	135	-20	112	-240	-82	-55	-147	-61	-86	22	-55	77	-5	-58
Seychelles	-8	-4	-3	6	1	4	-6	2	-8	14	-1	0	-1	-1
Sierra Leone	32	-18	-17	7	18	20	7	16	10	-12	-16	19	-4	2
Somalia	18	..	..	..	..	..	..	..	..	..	..	5	-12	-51
South Africa	-815	199	-2,729	945	2,366	-1,188	2,356	-727	4,234	-6,945	-4,927	188	25	-528
Sudan	177	35	2	1	-23	-13	-23	-25	-36	-90	-91	85	135	-28
Swaziland	-34	-87	63	13	-30	-14	-26	-45	15	22	28	-8	-17	-7
Tanzania	66	-102	123	-107	-46	-81	-208	72	-125	-148	-171	9	-2	-76
Togo	2	86	125	11	-12	12	-35	19	..	..	..	-18	-21	21
Uganda	55	-2	-29	-90	-146	-73	-132	-134	-33	15	-41	25	-10	-52
Zambia	162	-76	-17	-77	1,210	-52	-33	211	-19	-108	-117	152	-85	65
Zimbabwe	125	171	-207	-17	-255	43	739	205	-286	-163	-80	46	-52	25
NORTH AFRICA	-7,615	-4,953	-4,370	-3,944	865	-3,638	-6,982	1,164	2,139	-3,918	-7,760	434	244	-3,113
Algeria	-1,341	330	300	-1,122	740	-2,380	-4,180	1,090	2,350	-7,600	-5,741	-39	337	-1,400
Egypt, Arab Republic	168	-3,999	-4,312	-2,106	-754	-570	-1,912	135	2,117	3,025	685	421	161	-818
Libya	-6,407	-520	-35	..	..	..	..	..	..	..	..	73	-81	-391
Morocco	30	-683	-284	-361	982	-292	-553	-247	-1,639	415	-1,985	0	-117	-589
Tunisia	-65	-82	-39	-355	-103	-397	-336	187	-690	243	-718	-20	-57	-175
ALL AFRICA	-12,248	-3,518	-6,882	-5,381	2,718	-11,067	-8,902	1,294	6,453	-16,383	-14,822	1,694	-1,227	-5,562

Note: Excludes IMF credit transactions, which appear in the table on long-term borrowing.

5-14. Import coverage ratio of reserves

	Reserves in months of imports of goods and services											Annual Average		
	1980	1992	1993	1994	1995	1996	1997	1998	1999	2000	2001	75-84	85-89	90-MR
SUB-SAHARAN AFRICA	4	7	8	8	7	8	7	8	8	8	8	3	5	7
excluding South Africa	5	9	10	10	9	8	9	9	9	9	9	3	6	9
excl. S.Africa & Nigeria	3	10	11	11	9	10	10	11	11	11	11	3	7	10
Angola	..	..	..	..	0	1	1	0	1	2	1	..	..	1
Benin	0	4	4	6	4	5	5	5	7	8	10	1	0	5
Botswana	4	19	24	25	22	24	22	24	24	25	25	4	15	22
Burkina Faso	2	5	6	6	6	5	6	5	5	4	5	2	5	5
Burundi	6	6	7	9	9	11	9	5	4	3	1	5	3	6
Cameroon	1	0	0	0	0	0	0	0	0	1	1	1	1	0
Cape Verde	6	5	4	2	2	1	1	0	1	1	2	6	7	2
Central African Republic	2	3	4	9	9	11	8	6	10	10	9	2	3	7
Chad	2	2	1	2	3	4	3	3	2	3	2	1	2	3
Comoros	2	3	5	6	5	6	5	6	6	8	12	2	3	6
Congo, Democratic Rep. of	2	1	0	1	1	1	..	..	..	..	..	1	2	1
Congo, Republic of	1	0	0	0	0	1	0	0	0	1	0	0	0	0
Côte d'Ivoire	0	0	0	1	1	1	2	2	2	2	3	0	0	1
Djibouti	..	..	..	..	3	3	3	2	3	2	..	..	..	3
Equatorial Guinea	..	2	0	0	0	0	0	0	0	0	0	0	1	0
Eritrea	..	..	..	..	..	..	..	..	..	1	2	..	..	1
Ethiopia	4	3	4	6	7	7	4	4	3	2	3	5	2	4
Gabon	1	0	0	1	1	1	1	0	0	1	0	1	1	1
Gambia, The	0	4	4	5	4	5	5	4	5	5	4	2	2	4
Ghana	3	3	3	4	4	4	2	1	2	1	1	3	5	3
Guinea	..	1	2	1	1	1	1	3	2	2	2	..	..	2
Guinea-Bissau	..	2	2	2	2	1	3	5	4	6	6	..	1	3
Kenya	2	0	2	3	1	3	2	2	3	3	3	2	2	2
Lesotho	1	2	3	4	5	5	6	7	6	6	6	1	1	4
Liberia	0	..	..	..	..	..	..	..	..	..	..	0	0	..
Madagascar	0	1	1	1	1	2	3	2	2	2	3	1	3	2
Malawi	1	1	1	1	2	4	2	5	4	4	4	2	2	3
Mali	1	4	5	3	4	5	5	5	4	5	3	1	1	4
Mauritania	4	1	1	1	2	2	4	4	5	..	..	3	1	2
Mauritius	2	5	4	4	4	4	3	3	3	4	4	1	3	4
Mozambique	..	3	2	2	2	3	5	6	4	5	5	1	2	4
Namibia	..	0	1	1	1	1	1	2	2	2	1	..	..	1
Niger	2	7	6	3	2	2	1	1	1	2	2	2	6	3
Nigeria	5	1	2	2	2	4	6	6	4	6	6	3	2	4
Rwanda	7	2	1	1	3	3	4	4	5	5	5	5	4	3
São Tomé and Principe	..	..	..	..	1	1	3	3	3	3	4	..	..	3
Senegal	0	0	0	1	2	2	3	3	2	2	3	0	0	2
Seychelles	..	1	1	1	1	1	1	1	1	1	1	..	..	1
Sierra Leone	1	1	1	1	2	1	3	3	3	3	2	1	0	2
Somalia	1	..	..	..	..	..	..	..	..	..	..	2	0	..
South Africa	4	1	1	1	1	1	2	2	3	2	2	2	1	2
Sudan	0	0	0	0	1	0	0	0	1	1	0	0	0	0
Swaziland	3	4	4	4	3	2	3	3	3	3	3	3	3	3
Tanzania	0	2	1	2	1	2	3	3	4	5	6	1	0	3
Togo	1	5	4	3	3	1	2	2	2	3	2	3	6	3
Uganda	0	2	2	4	4	4	6	6	6	6	7	1	1	4
Zambia	1	..	1	2	1	2	2	1	0	2	1	1	1	1
Zimbabwe	8	2	3	3	3	3	1	1	2	2	1	3	2	2
NORTH AFRICA	..	7	8	8	8	9	9	8	7	8	10	..	..	8
Algeria	6	3	4	4	3	5	9	8	5	11	14	4	4	6
Egypt, Arab Republic	3	10	11	11	11	12	11	10	8	7	7	2	2	9
Libya	..	..	..	..	..	..	..	..	..	..	..	..	..	..
Morocco	2	4	5	5	4	4	4	4	5	4	8	1	1	5
Tunisia	2	1	1	2	2	2	3	2	3	2	2	2	2	2
ALL AFRICA	4	7	8	8	8	8	8	8	7	8	9	3	4	8

Note: 2001 data are preliminary (see page 2). Based on total reserves, excluding gold, at year-end and on imports of all goods and services at current prices and exchange rates.

5-15. Export unit values

	Index 1995=100											Average annual percentage growth		
	1980	*1992*	*1993*	*1994*	*1995*	*1996*	*1997*	*1998*	*1999*	*2000*	*2001*	*75-84*	*85-89*	*90-MR*
SUB-SAHARAN AFRICA	123.3	98.9	90.4	91.5	100.2	102.9	98.4	84.5	86.8	99.0	89.2	5.9	3.6	-0.5
excluding South Africa	127.2	100.1	88.8	88.9	100.3	108.9	102.8	84.7	90.0	110.4	102.9	4.0	2.8	0.4
excl. S.Africa & Nigeria	115.2	91.1	85.6	88.0	100.4	104.9	99.1	88.1	87.8	96.9	92.5	2.3	1.4	0.0
Angola	..	77.1	92.4	76.6	100.0	141.7	110.0	68.5	100.5	159.4	136.3	..	4.1	0.4
Benin	44.2	53.5	65.3	71.0	100.0	87.6	80.6	92.9	80.0	64.0	64.1	5.9	7.7	0.6
Botswana	74.9	93.2	92.2	94.2	100.0	96.4	99.0	92.9	98.3	95.4	75.0	5.1	12.3	-0.2
Burkina Faso	51.6	60.5	59.6	85.0	100.0	95.3	87.0	82.4	73.9	67.6	71.5	5.1	12.3	-1.0
Burundi	159.5	64.9	67.1	93.8	100.0	61.4	60.0	46.8	29.8	22.7	13.6	6.3	-0.9	-14.0
Cameroon	142.0	94.1	97.8	87.8	100.0	90.2	89.0	80.1	69.0	88.4	87.0	4.8	-3.4	-1.3
Cape Verde	62.3	89.8	85.1	90.0	100.0	98.4	94.2	93.4	93.7	83.3	85.0	9.5	11.8	1.2
Central African Republic	139.5	153.5	144.1	85.7	100.0	87.8	66.8	57.1	48.5	40.5	41.9	8.4	6.4	-12.6
Chad	92.3	88.2	77.1	73.3	100.0	110.2	98.8	105.1	95.0	80.7	83.7	-0.7	3.2	1.2
Comoros	101.4	104.3	87.3	65.4	100.0	96.7	85.1	81.2	84.2	73.0	74.5	..	12.8	-2.5
Congo, Democratic Rep. of	132.6	86.4	70.4	98.6	100.0	98.2	72.9	103.1	102.4	118.0	..	0.9	1.8	3.8
Congo, Republic of	143.5	112.2	74.5	93.8	100.0	120.4	109.3	86.6	104.9	153.8	131.2	9.7	-6.1	1.8
Côte d'Ivoire	115.9	94.0	88.3	80.4	100.0	117.7	106.1	109.2	107.8	96.1	94.6	-1.1	-1.1	2.0
Djibouti	..	..	..	..	..	..	..	..	..	..	..	..	..	..
Equatorial Guinea	..	180.0	133.3	87.6	100.0	122.4	137.5	103.2	157.3	198.4	134.6	..	17.8	-0.5
Eritrea	..	55.0	79.3	94.0	100.0	98.4	100.1	91.0	89.3	89.7	87.3	..	..	2.8
Ethiopia	..	76.3	86.1	69.1	100.0	87.4	82.5	93.5	85.0	73.9	73.1	..	2.0	1.3
Gabon	173.9	104.0	76.6	88.7	100.0	117.5	104.5	73.3	72.8	70.2	99.0	8.8	-4.5	-2.0
Gambia, The	81.3	94.7	96.9	95.9	100.0	100.4	100.0	97.0	94.5	87.3	80.0	3.4	15.8	-0.1
Ghana	39.2	86.9	81.2	89.1	100.0	98.6	95.1	97.5	84.5	86.1	97.1	0.9	8.5	0.8
Guinea	..	99.0	98.1	113.3	100.0	92.8	94.2	83.4	79.7	74.9	81.8	..	0.6	-3.6
Guinea-Bissau	57.5	88.7	109.8	102.2	100.0	102.1	102.3	84.2	79.8	73.4	81.6	14.0	0.9	-3.6
Kenya	130.0	87.5	69.5	82.9	100.0	98.5	112.8	113.7	95.1	89.2	90.2	5.5	-1.8	1.1
Lesotho	105.8	94.4	93.1	93.7	100.0	91.6	94.5	92.6	71.8	80.5	68.6	5.5	5.9	-0.7
Liberia	..	..	..	..	..	..	..	..	..	..	..	..	..	..
Madagascar	67.4	77.9	77.0	88.9	100.0	102.8	101.1	109.8	107.6	121.7	127.4	6.5	-0.1	5.0
Malawi	87.1	102.7	86.5	82.3	100.0	104.9	109.9	89.1	92.6	89.1	86.8	3.8	1.4	-1.3
Mali	108.3	99.0	92.6	82.7	100.0	97.8	83.2	83.9	73.9	68.9	79.2	3.5	6.5	-3.0
Mauritania	71.4	120.5	127.8	94.6	100.0	96.9	100.8	89.2	78.8	71.9	69.0	1.7	7.5	-3.6
Mauritius	73.6	94.5	96.2	90.3	100.0	107.1	106.2	97.1	94.8	99.8	96.9	..	8.9	1.0
Mozambique	122.0	98.5	92.3	93.9	100.0	80.3	82.3	79.0	68.8	69.6	72.4	..	4.8	-4.8
Namibia	..	94.6	87.8	101.1	100.0	98.6	94.9	83.9	81.8	83.7	81.3	..	..	-2.0
Niger	158.9	110.5	77.0	88.7	100.0	88.2	80.6	84.0	81.5	..	..	12.0	6.0	-3.5
Nigeria	145.5	133.7	101.2	92.7	100.0	122.2	115.6	72.6	98.7	168.0	147.3	3.1	10.3	1.6
Rwanda	90.9	59.2	64.7	77.4	100.0	88.1	117.0	88.3	75.7	91.6	69.7	8.0	-8.3	3.0
São Tomé and Principe	..	85.3	94.4	110.0	100.0	127.0	130.5	103.6	102.6	95.1	99.4	..	-14.1	1.6
Senegal	84.0	101.3	89.0	92.3	100.0	101.2	93.6	91.5	81.0	67.8	65.2	2.5	6.8	-2.2
Seychelles	..	81.0	80.9	73.8	100.0	93.1	99.2	116.0	90.1	85.5	87.0	..	-5.3	2.6
Sierra Leone	67.2	39.7	49.6	106.1	100.0	124.7	110.1	647.1	808.3	901.0	926.9	11.6	26.1	32.9
Somalia	..	..	..	..	..	..	..	..	..	..	..	..	..	..
South Africa	116.8	96.9	93.0	95.7	100.0	93.1	91.4	84.2	81.4	81.6	68.2	9.1	5.0	-2.1
Sudan	..	..	..	..	..	..	..	..	..	..	..	..	..	..
Swaziland	85.1	81.6	83.5	87.2	100.0	93.9	97.6	89.4	87.5	87.1	76.8	3.9	2.1	1.7
Tanzania	..	101.0	104.0	113.2	100.0	104.4	155.0	126.7	111.2	104.9	97.5	..	..	0.4
Togo	109.2	123.1	83.9	85.2	100.0	96.8	93.4	102.5	100.3	88.5	92.5	-1.9	5.9	-2.0
Uganda	..	59.6	56.7	66.2	100.0	83.8	74.9	66.6	58.8	52.8	50.4	..	-2.1	-3.5
Zambia	90.0	86.9	79.7	80.3	100.0	76.7	73.9	51.7	40.0	45.4	50.9	2.4	9.3	-6.1
Zimbabwe	161.8	102.8	97.5	97.1	100.0	109.2	105.8	73.3	67.1	67.1	65.0	0.3	3.9	-5.7
NORTH AFRICA	163.8	98.7	93.6	91.4	100.0	105.9	103.2	92.1	93.5	108.3	105.9	6.5	-5.8	0.9
Algeria	200.9	108.1	98.7	93.5	100.0	116.2	113.3	82.3	95.0	150.7	146.5	11.4	-9.6	0.9
Egypt, Arab Republic	106.9	99.4	99.7	95.4	100.0	99.5	105.2	99.2	93.3	99.9	100.5	9.8	-7.5	1.7
Libya	..	..	..	..	..	..	..	..	..	..	..	..	..	..
Morocco	96.2	90.9	84.9	85.4	100.0	103.9	95.3	94.3	93.2	87.4	86.2	1.8	5.8	0.2
Tunisia	91.3	90.7	84.6	88.8	100.0	103.4	94.2	93.0	92.2	83.7	81.1	5.3	1.6	0.7
ALL AFRICA	130.9	98.8	91.5	91.4	100.1	103.8	99.9	86.8	88.8	101.9	94.5	6.6	0.6	-0.1

Note: 2001 data are preliminary (see page 2).

5-16. Import unit values

	Index 1995=100											Average annual percentage growth		
	1980	*1992*	*1993*	*1994*	*1995*	*1996*	*1997*	*1998*	*1999*	*2000*	*2001*	*75-84*	*85-89*	*90-MR*
SUB-SAHARAN AFRICA	76.9	99.3	93.0	92.9	100.0	96.2	97.5	91.7	89.6	88.1	82.7	5.2	7.9	-0.4
excluding South Africa	69.9	99.3	92.3	92.1	100.0	98.4	100.6	95.0	91.7	89.0	89.4	1.8	9.6	0.3
excl. S.Africa & Nigeria	89.7	95.6	91.9	92.4	100.0	103.1	101.4	96.0	91.6	87.9	88.1	..	4.2	0.0
Angola	..	91.7	120.1	89.6	100.0	132.3	128.7	123.4	134.5	127.5	125.0	..	1.4	2.0
Benin	54.3	66.7	84.4	93.6	100.0	99.3	90.4	87.3	92.0	78.1	78.0	6.3	11.7	0.3
Botswana	79.3	98.6	95.7	94.1	100.0	92.0	90.6	83.1	78.0	66.9	57.8	8.1	4.1	-2.2
Burkina Faso	103.1	68.5	70.8	89.5	100.0	102.2	93.9	86.6	85.8	88.7	85.9	5.8	4.3	-0.5
Burundi	112.9	108.6	91.2	89.7	100.0	84.5	89.5	63.1	42.1	37.2	30.5	8.9	7.4	-10.5
Cameroon	153.0	132.1	119.5	94.1	100.0	98.8	92.7	86.6	88.4	80.0	75.3	6.9	-1.1	-3.1
Cape Verde	62.3	89.8	85.1	90.0	100.0	98.4	94.2	93.4	93.7	83.3	85.0	-0.5	11.8	1.2
Central African Republic	102.6	105.1	101.4	83.0	100.0	101.7	85.8	88.6	87.5	78.0	77.7	4.4	4.1	-3.5
Chad	78.6	80.0	76.8	87.7	100.0	110.2	98.9	120.6	114.5	101.0	76.5	2.2	5.8	3.1
Comoros	78.5	114.3	108.5	111.1	100.0	98.2	83.9	77.6	74.9	63.0	63.0	..	11.9	-4.6
Congo, Democratic Rep. of	125.7	71.2	62.3	118.0	100.0	145.4	114.6	125.4	123.6	94.1	..	-2.6	-4.9	7.5
Congo, Republic of	77.1	95.7	62.2	90.8	100.0	97.4	89.0	88.9	88.4	85.9	84.0	5.8	7.4	0.8
Côte d'Ivoire	100.7	101.5	94.9	82.5	100.0	114.5	104.3	107.6	104.6	92.0	92.0	4.4	6.3	0.4
Djibouti	..	..	..	..	..	..	..	..	..	..	..	..	..	..
Equatorial Guinea	..	177.3	156.1	87.7	100.0	122.4	137.3	103.1	73.9	73.6	134.4	..	12.9	-4.3
Eritrea	..	60.8	80.9	92.1	100.0	102.0	101.2	97.5	93.6	90.9	89.7	..	..	2.6
Ethiopia	..	54.7	79.5	82.5	100.0	105.2	102.1	96.4	92.7	91.1	92.2	..	-0.9	3.5
Gabon	71.2	96.4	73.9	93.0	100.0	99.3	88.8	88.8	86.9	87.5	87.7	1.3	10.7	0.0
Gambia, The	44.8	94.7	96.9	95.9	100.0	100.4	100.0	97.0	94.5	87.3	80.0	7.6	11.2	-0.1
Ghana	20.4	96.7	97.4	98.9	100.0	100.0	95.4	84.5	82.8	91.4	96.6	2.0	11.9	-0.1
Guinea	..	95.7	102.8	101.9	100.0	106.9	96.9	94.2	93.0	87.0	82.2	..	5.8	-0.2
Guinea-Bissau	47.0	87.1	79.3	84.3	100.0	102.6	102.7	95.9	98.1	94.2	116.8	8.1	13.0	2.4
Kenya	134.1	112.6	75.9	81.0	100.0	94.1	102.7	107.7	99.9	97.0	102.5	9.6	-0.6	-1.4
Lesotho	80.3	99.8	94.5	92.9	100.0	87.5	88.3	83.4	86.2	80.5	68.6	8.1	6.4	-1.1
Liberia	..	..	..	..	..	..	..	..	..	..	..	..	..	..
Madagascar	63.6	87.3	85.2	90.6	100.0	99.8	94.7	92.9	95.8	96.5	85.8	9.1	6.7	1.5
Malawi	56.3	84.5	80.0	96.4	100.0	98.6	98.7	91.2	91.9	94.1	90.8	6.4	8.7	1.9
Mali	102.9	96.3	93.4	90.5	100.0	97.2	85.7	83.1	87.3	78.1	83.2	1.7	4.9	-0.8
Mauritania	100.4	112.0	109.0	99.4	100.0	105.7	99.6	88.2	77.9	73.4	71.8	5.6	4.9	-3.4
Mauritius	71.1	90.2	93.7	90.4	100.0	104.6	102.5	91.2	87.3	88.7	85.7	..	4.9	0.5
Mozambique	77.0	105.3	103.5	86.9	100.0	105.1	97.4	93.0	89.3	90.6	91.5	..	8.4	-1.1
Namibia	..	101.7	98.4	101.4	100.0	94.0	103.5	93.4	87.1	87.4	82.9	..	..	-0.1
Niger	83.1	93.6	64.1	90.4	100.0	101.1	98.1	103.3	105.6	..	..	1.8	9.3	3.3
Nigeria	44.1	113.9	93.6	90.7	100.0	77.9	97.4	90.1	91.7	93.3	93.8	-3.4	31.6	1.7
Rwanda	175.7	95.2	88.7	94.9	100.0	104.8	98.9	88.0	90.0	101.1	97.0	5.9	6.4	-3.3
São Tomé and Principe	..	90.8	90.3	94.4	100.0	101.9	95.5	84.6	90.0	88.3	75.1	..	3.4	-0.3
Senegal	84.1	97.4	91.9	87.3	100.0	100.1	91.9	86.1	82.4	75.0	71.6	3.8	5.6	-1.3
Seychelles	..	103.8	94.1	96.5	100.0	96.6	97.8	86.2	85.2	83.7	108.9	..	1.8	-1.1
Sierra Leone	92.7	64.4	70.3	102.1	100.0	85.5	97.3	238.6	345.1	299.5	244.4	10.9	1.5	15.7
Somalia	..	..	..	..	..	..	..	..	..	..	..	..	..	..
South Africa	97.5	99.3	94.4	94.4	100.0	91.9	91.2	84.9	84.1	85.4	68.2	10.3	4.2	-2.0
Sudan	..	..	..	..	..	..	..	..	..	..	..	..	..	..
Swaziland	85.1	81.6	83.5	87.2	100.0	93.9	97.6	89.4	87.5	87.1	76.8	4.1	2.1	1.7
Tanzania	..	101.0	101.6	103.0	100.0	106.4	152.3	125.9	109.3	102.1	102.5	..	..	1.7
Togo	91.2	96.3	92.0	89.1	100.0	103.6	93.7	89.3	87.4	88.0	86.7	0.2	7.0	-0.2
Uganda	..	96.9	98.6	98.9	100.0	104.5	94.4	100.1	69.1	63.1	64.5	..	10.9	-4.3
Zambia	77.1	130.9	122.5	101.3	100.0	96.2	99.7	87.5	87.4	86.5	90.7	11.9	3.7	-1.6
Zimbabwe	184.8	99.5	96.9	96.4	100.0	108.9	106.4	73.1	66.9	65.1	62.8	5.7	3.7	-5.8
NORTH AFRICA	70.6	90.6	91.6	93.2	100.0	102.2	99.9	98.5	96.2	93.8	91.5	5.5	8.2	0.5
Algeria	69.1	90.0	97.3	94.7	100.0	100.5	93.2	94.7	92.9	87.9	84.4	5.6	10.3	-0.7
Egypt, Arab Republic	58.2	93.5	94.2	93.2	100.0	104.5	114.0	117.9	112.4	116.5	118.5	8.6	9.7	2.7
Libya	..	..	..	..	..	..	..	..	..	..	..	..	..	..
Morocco	95.5	87.9	85.9	95.7	100.0	101.6	90.1	79.7	80.8	78.1	74.9	3.7	2.7	-1.4
Tunisia	75.0	90.0	85.3	88.0	100.0	100.5	94.4	94.0	92.5	83.8	81.7	5.1	4.4	1.1
ALL AFRICA	73.6	96.2	92.5	93.0	100.0	98.1	98.3	93.9	91.7	90.0	85.6	5.4	8.1	-0.1

Note: 2001 data are preliminary (see page 2).

5-17. Terms of trade

	Index 1995=100											Average annual percentage growth		
	1980	1992	1993	1994	1995	1996	1997	1998	1999	2000	2001	75-84	85-89	90-MR
SUB-SAHARAN AFRICA	160.3	99.6	97.3	98.5	100.2	106.9	101.0	92.2	96.9	112.4	107.8	0.6	-4.0	-0.1
excluding South Africa	181.8	100.8	96.3	96.6	100.4	110.6	102.2	89.2	98.1	124.1	115.0	0.3	-6.2	0.1
excl. S.Africa & Nigeria	128.5	95.4	93.1	95.2	100.5	101.7	97.7	91.8	95.8	110.2	105.0	..	-2.7	0.0
Angola	..	84.1	77.0	85.6	100.0	107.1	85.5	55.5	74.7	125.0	109.1	..	2.6	-1.5
Benin	81.4	80.1	77.3	75.9	100.0	88.2	89.2	106.4	86.9	82.0	82.2	-0.3	-3.6	0.3
Botswana	94.3	94.5	96.4	100.1	100.0	104.8	109.3	111.8	126.1	142.5	129.8	-2.8	8.0	2.0
Burkina Faso	50.0	88.4	84.2	95.0	100.0	93.2	92.7	95.1	86.1	76.2	83.2	-0.7	7.7	-0.6
Burundi	141.3	59.7	73.6	104.6	100.0	72.7	67.1	74.1	70.8	61.1	44.5	-2.4	-7.8	-3.9
Cameroon	92.8	71.2	81.8	93.2	100.0	91.4	96.1	92.5	78.0	110.5	115.5	-1.9	-2.4	1.9
Cape Verde	100.0	100.0	100.0	100.0	100.0	100.0	100.0	100.0	100.0	100.0	100.0	10.1	0.0	0.0
Central African Republic	136.0	146.0	142.1	103.3	100.0	86.4	77.9	64.4	55.4	51.9	53.9	3.9	2.1	-9.5
Chad	117.5	110.3	100.4	83.6	100.0	100.0	99.9	87.1	83.0	79.9	109.5	-2.8	-2.4	-1.8
Comoros	129.2	91.2	80.4	58.8	100.0	98.5	101.4	104.7	112.4	115.9	118.1	..	0.8	2.2
Congo, Democratic Rep. of	105.5	121.4	113.0	83.5	100.0	67.5	63.6	82.2	82.8	125.3	..	3.6	7.0	-3.4
Congo, Republic of	186.0	117.2	119.8	103.2	100.0	123.6	122.9	97.4	118.7	179.0	156.3	3.7	-12.6	1.0
Côte d'Ivoire	115.1	92.6	93.1	97.5	100.0	102.8	101.8	101.5	103.0	104.4	102.8	-5.2	-7.0	1.6
Djibouti	..	..	..	..	..	..	..	..	..	..	..	..	..	..
Equatorial Guinea	..	101.6	85.4	100.0	100.0	100.0	100.2	100.2	213.0	269.6	100.2	..	4.3	3.9
Eritrea	..	90.5	98.0	102.1	100.0	96.5	98.9	93.3	95.4	98.6	97.4	..	..	0.1
Ethiopia	..	139.4	108.3	83.8	100.0	83.1	80.8	97.0	91.7	81.1	79.4	..	2.9	-2.1
Gabon	244.0	107.9	103.7	95.4	100.0	118.4	117.7	82.5	83.7	80.2	112.9	7.5	-13.7	-2.0
Gambia, The	181.6	100.0	100.0	100.0	100.0	100.0	100.0	100.0	100.0	100.0	100.0	-3.9	4.2	0.0
Ghana	191.9	89.9	83.4	90.1	100.0	98.6	99.7	115.3	102.1	94.2	100.5	-1.1	-3.0	0.8
Guinea	..	103.4	95.4	111.2	100.0	86.8	97.2	88.5	85.7	86.1	99.5	..	-5.0	-3.4
Guinea-Bissau	122.2	101.8	138.4	121.3	100.0	99.6	99.6	87.8	81.4	78.0	69.8	5.3	-10.7	-5.8
Kenya	96.9	77.7	91.5	102.4	100.0	104.6	109.8	105.6	95.1	91.9	88.0	-3.8	-1.2	2.5
Lesotho	131.8	94.5	98.5	100.9	100.0	104.7	107.1	111.0	83.3	100.0	100.0	-2.4	-0.4	0.4
Liberia	..	..	..	..	..	..	..	..	..	..	..	..	..	..
Madagascar	105.9	89.2	90.4	98.1	100.0	103.0	106.9	118.2	112.3	126.1	148.4	-2.4	-6.4	3.5
Malawi	154.7	121.5	108.2	85.3	100.0	106.4	111.3	97.7	100.8	94.7	95.6	-2.4	-6.7	-3.2
Mali	105.3	102.8	99.1	91.4	100.0	100.7	97.1	101.0	84.7	88.2	95.2	1.8	1.5	-2.3
Mauritania	71.1	107.6	117.2	95.1	100.0	91.7	101.2	101.1	101.1	98.0	96.2	-3.6	2.5	-0.2
Mauritius	103.4	104.8	102.6	99.9	100.0	102.5	103.6	106.5	108.5	112.5	113.0	..	3.8	0.6
Mozambique	158.4	93.6	89.2	108.0	100.0	76.4	84.5	84.9	77.0	76.8	79.1	..	-3.4	-3.8
Namibia	..	93.1	89.2	99.7	100.0	104.9	91.7	89.8	93.9	95.7	98.0	..	..	-1.9
Niger	191.1	118.1	120.1	98.1	100.0	87.2	82.1	81.3	77.1	..	..	10.1	-3.0	-6.6
Nigeria	329.7	117.3	108.2	102.3	100.0	156.7	118.7	80.5	107.6	180.1	157.0	6.7	-16.2	0.0
Rwanda	51.7	62.2	72.9	81.5	100.0	84.1	118.2	100.3	84.1	90.5	71.8	2.0	-13.8	6.5
São Tomé and Principe	..	94.0	104.6	116.5	100.0	124.6	136.6	122.4	113.9	107.7	132.4	..	-16.9	1.9
Senegal	99.9	104.0	96.9	105.8	100.0	101.2	102.0	106.3	98.3	90.5	91.0	-1.2	1.1	-1.0
Seychelles	..	78.0	86.0	76.5	100.0	96.3	101.4	134.5	105.9	102.2	79.9	..	-7.0	3.7
Sierra Leone	72.4	61.6	70.6	103.9	100.0	145.9	113.2	271.2	234.2	300.8	379.3	0.7	24.3	14.8
Somalia	..	..	..	..	..	..	..	..	..	..	..	..	..	..
South Africa	119.8	97.6	98.5	101.3	100.0	101.4	100.2	99.1	96.8	95.6	100.0	-1.2	0.8	-0.1
Sudan	..	..	..	..	..	..	..	..	..	..	..	..	..	..
Swaziland	100.0	100.0	100.0	100.0	100.0	100.0	100.0	100.0	100.0	100.0	100.0	-0.2	0.0	0.0
Tanzania	..	100.0	102.4	110.0	100.0	98.1	101.7	100.6	101.7	102.7	95.1	..	..	-1.3
Togo	119.7	127.8	91.1	95.6	100.0	93.4	99.7	114.8	114.8	100.6	106.8	-2.1	-1.0	-1.8
Uganda	..	61.5	57.5	66.9	100.0	80.2	79.4	66.6	85.1	83.7	78.1	..	-11.7	0.8
Zambia	116.6	66.4	65.1	79.3	100.0	79.7	74.2	59.1	45.7	52.5	56.1	-8.5	5.4	-4.6
Zimbabwe	87.6	103.3	100.7	100.7	100.0	100.3	99.4	100.2	100.3	103.1	103.6	-5.1	0.1	0.1
NORTH AFRICA	232.2	108.9	102.2	98.1	100.0	103.6	103.3	93.5	97.3	115.5	115.7	1.0	-12.9	0.4
Algeria	290.9	120.1	101.4	98.7	100.0	115.6	121.6	86.9	102.3	171.5	173.6	5.5	-18.1	1.7
Egypt, Arab Republic	183.9	106.3	105.9	102.4	100.0	95.2	92.2	84.1	83.0	85.7	84.8	1.0	-15.6	-1.0
Libya	..	..	..	..	..	..	..	..	..	..	..	..	..	..
Morocco	100.8	103.4	98.8	89.3	100.0	102.2	105.8	118.3	115.3	111.9	115.1	-1.8	3.0	1.6
Tunisia	121.7	100.7	99.2	100.9	100.0	102.9	99.8	98.9	99.7	99.9	99.3	0.2	-2.7	-0.4
ALL AFRICA	177.9	102.7	99.0	98.4	100.1	105.7	101.6	92.4	96.8	113.3	110.4	1.1	-6.9	0.0

Note: 2001 data are preliminary (see page 2).

5-18. Forest products exports

	Thousands of cubic meters											Average annual percentage growth		
	1980	1987	1988	1989	1990	1991	1992	1993	1994	1995	1996	75-84	85-89	90-MR
SUB-SAHARAN AFRICA	8,169	6,803	8,821	7,032	6,931	6,824	7,170	4,764	4,364	3,788	4,289	149.9	2.4	-9.3
excluding South Africa	7,413	5,283	6,044	5,855	5,794	5,632	5,478	4,339	3,960	3,300	3,748	149.8	-1.3	-8.2
excl. S.Africa & Nigeria	7,402	5,266	6,028	5,844	5,757	5,583	5,444	3,908	3,672	3,030	3,499	150.2	-1.1	-9.5
Angola	..	0	0	3	0	..	2	..	..	..	..	..	56.3	..
Benin	..	..	..	..	..	0	0	..	..	..	..	..	..	..
Botswana	..	..	..	..	..	..	..	..	..	..	..	..	..	..
Burkina Faso	..	..	..	..	..	..	..	..	..	..	..	..	..	..
Burundi	..	..	..	..	..	..	..	..	..	..	..	..	..	..
Cameroon	934	521	652	539	837	1,049	816	..	..	..	..	151.6	-4.7	..
Cape Verde	..	..	..	..	..	..	..	..	..	..	..	..	..	..
Central African Republic	177	74	80	113	67	37	36	..	..	..	..	150.6	-5.5	..
Chad	..	..	..	..	..	..	..	..	..	..	..	..	..	..
Comoros	..	..	..	..	1	..	0	..	..	..	..	..	..	..
Congo, Democratic Rep. of	116	147	163	143	142	172	136	113	101	74	91	171.2	0.4	-9.3
Congo, Republic of	385	643	941	937	816	609	530	..	..	..	..	163.8	28.3	..
Côte d'Ivoire	3,394	1,175	1,138	1,084	1,127	967	878	..	..	..	..	150.4	-16.9	..
Djibouti	..	..	..	..	..	..	..	..	..	..	..	..	..	..
Equatorial Guinea	16	133	133	142	129	126	143	400	380	..	5	218.1	12.4	-24.1
Eritrea	..	..	..	..	..	..	..	..	..	..	..	..	..	..
Ethiopia	..	..	..	..	..	..	..	..	..	..	..	..	..	..
Gabon	1,150	1,353	1,343	1,460	1,244	1,392	1,447	1,685	1,729	1,359	1,632	154.9	0.8	2.4
Gambia, The	..	..	..	..	..	0	0	..	..	..	..	..	..	..
Ghana	183	514	531	371	361	390	426	936	735	754	1,018	107.8	26.0	17.3
Guinea	..	8	8	8	13	15	17	45	45	45	45	112.1	-7.6	31.0
Guinea-Bissau	6	5	4	4	6	12	9	5	5	6	8	117.7	22.1	1.3
Kenya	33	4	4	3	4	3	0	82	94	95	27	138.6	-26.5	78.3
Lesotho	..	..	..	..	..	..	..	..	..	..	..	..	..	..
Liberia	524	255	701	729	663	429	642	149	145	206	225	147.3	30.0	-20.0
Madagascar	0	2	1	2	3	26	6	6	10	8	4	111.7	21.2	10.2
Malawi	..	..	1	0	0	0	1	1	1	1	1	153.8	..	20.3
Mali	..	..	..	..	..	0	..	..	..	..	..	..	..	..
Mauritania	..	..	..	..	1	..	..	..	..	..	..	..	..	..
Mauritius	..	..	..	..	..	..	2	..	..	..	..	..	..	..
Mozambique	31	5	10	2	5	4	1	149	137	140	158	68.8	-3.8	115.9
Namibia	..	..	..	..	..	..	..	..	..	..	..	..	..	..
Niger	..	..	..	..	..	..	..	..	..	..	..	..	..	..
Nigeria	11	17	16	11	37	49	34	431	288	269	248	143.7	-32.2	59.9
Rwanda	..	..	..	..	..	0	..	..	..	..	..	..	..	..
São Tomé and Principe	..	..	..	..	0	..	..	0	..	..	..	..	..	..
Senegal	..	..	..	..	..	..	..	..	..	..	..	..	..	..
Seychelles	..	..	..	..	0	..	..	..	..	..	..	..	..	..
Sierra Leone	..	1	1	0	0	0	0	..	..	..	..	..	-8.8	..
Somalia	..	..	..	..	..	..	..	48	..	..	..	..	..	..
South Africa	756	1,520	2,777	1,177	1,137	1,191	1,692	425	405	488	541	150.9	24.9	-15.6
Sudan	..	..	..	..	..	0	..	..	..	..	..	..	..	..
Swaziland	421	355	293	285	254	254	254	241	239	299	270	163.6	-13.1	0.2
Tanzania	5	5	6	3	25	14	8	40	40	37	9	115.7	3.0	16.4
Togo	..	..	..	..	0	..	..	0	0	1	0	..	..	..
Uganda	0	..	..	..	..	..	..	9	11	7	7	45.4	..	..
Zambia	..	..	..	..	0	0	..	..	..	..	..	..	..	..
Zimbabwe	26	65	17	17	56	83	89	..	..	..	..	214.2	-14.1	..
NORTH AFRICA	88	94	117	95	95	77	105	78	84	71	60	160.0	6.1	-5.4
Algeria	..	..	..	..	1	..	..	..	..	..	..	..	..	..
Egypt, Arab Republic	..	..	..	..	0	0	..	3	6	0	..	..	..	..
Libya	..	..	..	..	..	0	0	..	..	..	..	..	..	..
Morocco	74	85	102	88	84	70	98	43	48	50	39	169.1	6.3	-11.4
Tunisia	14	10	16	7	10	8	7	32	29	20	21	135.1	3.4	22.6
ALL AFRICA	8,258	6,897	8,938	7,127	7,026	6,901	7,275	4,842	4,448	3,859	4,349	150.0	2.5	-9.3

5-19. Petroleum exports

	Thousands of metric tons											*Average annual percentage growth*		
	1980	*1991*	*1992*	*1993*	*1994*	*1995*	*1996*	*1997*	*1998*	*1999*	*2000*	*75-84*	*85-89*	*90-MR*
SUB-SAHARAN AFRICA	118,522	132,768	138,295	147,612	146,068	148,560	163,546	174,930	177,405	172,521	184,156	-4.5	4.7	3.8
excluding South Africa	118,522	132,768	138,217	147,309	145,872	148,476	163,544	174,089	176,749	171,097	183,983	-4.5	4.7	3.8
excl. S.Africa & Nigeria	21,791	52,600	55,211	55,114	56,614	61,159	67,007	70,526	72,654	73,430	74,792	3.8	9.0	4.6
Angola	6,334	23,255	25,706	23,497	25,315	28,654	31,441	33,410	35,108	35,171	35,031	-0.2	21.6	5.4
Benin	..	200	138	157	131	97	84	65	62	45	38	..	63.1	-14.9
Botswana	..	..	..	..	..	..	..	..	..	..	..	..	..	..
Burkina Faso	..	..	..	..	..	..	..	..	..	..	..	..	..	..
Burundi	..	..	..	..	..	..	..	..	..	..	..	..	..	..
Cameroon	3,407	6,456	6,097	6,091	5,278	5,014	5,354	5,532	6,200	5,503	5,797	81.7	-0.7	-2.2
Cape Verde	..	..	..	..	..	..	..	..	..	..	..	..	..	..
Central African Republic	..	..	..	..	..	..	..	..	..	..	..	..	..	..
Chad	..	..	..	..	..	..	..	..	..	..	..	..	..	..
Comoros	..	..	..	..	..	..	..	..	..	..	..	..	..	..
Congo, Democratic Rep. of	859	1,125	1,027	1,019	1,141	1,138	1,133	1,136	1,138	1,052	1,309	0.3	-0.8	0.1
Congo, Republic of	3,432	7,496	8,358	9,201	8,725	9,047	10,272	11,809	12,549	13,500	13,606	12.2	6.6	6.2
Côte d'Ivoire	122	..	95	126	315	137	1,049	719	514	476	430	..	-34.8	23.5
Djibouti	..	..	..	..	..	..	..	..	..	..	..	..	..	..
Equatorial Guinea	..	..	..	..	..	..	..	..	..	..	..	..	..	..
Eritrea	..	..	..	..	..	..	..	..	..	..	..	..	..	..
Ethiopia	0	0	0	0	0	0	0	0	0	..	..	..	..	..
Gabon	7,637	14,068	13,790	15,023	15,710	17,072	17,676	17,855	17,083	15,980	14,963	-4.5	1.9	4.1
Gambia, The	..	..	..	..	..	..	..	..	..	..	..	..	..	..
Ghana	..	..	..	..	..	..	..	..	..	..	..	..	..	..
Guinea	..	..	..	..	..	..	..	..	..	..	..	..	..	..
Guinea-Bissau	..	..	..	..	..	..	..	..	..	..	..	..	..	..
Kenya	..	..	..	..	..	..	..	..	..	..	..	..	..	..
Lesotho	..	..	..	..	..	..	..	..	..	..	..	..	..	..
Liberia	..	..	..	..	..	..	..	..	..	..	..	..	..	..
Madagascar	..	..	..	..	..	..	..	..	..	..	..	..	..	..
Malawi	..	..	..	..	..	..	..	..	..	..	..	..	..	..
Mali	..	..	..	..	..	..	..	..	..	..	..	..	..	..
Mauritania	..	..	..	..	..	..	..	..	..	..	..	..	..	..
Mauritius	..	..	..	..	..	..	..	..	..	..	..	..	..	..
Mozambique	..	..	..	..	..	..	..	..	..	..	..	..	..	..
Namibia	..	..	..	..	..	..	..	..	..	..	..	..	..	..
Niger	..	..	..	..	..	..	..	..	..	..	..	..	..	..
Nigeria	96,731	80,168	83,006	92,194	89,258	87,317	96,537	103,563	104,095	97,667	109,191	-6.8	2.2	3.3
Rwanda	..	..	..	..	..	..	..	..	..	..	..	..	..	..
São Tomé and Principe	..	..	..	..	..	..	..	..	..	..	..	..	..	..
Senegal	..	..	..	..	..	..	..	..	..	..	..	..	..	..
Seychelles	..	..	..	..	..	..	..	..	..	..	..	..	..	..
Sierra Leone	..	..	..	..	..	..	..	..	..	..	..	..	..	..
Somalia	..	..	..	..	..	..	..	..	..	..	..	..	..	..
South Africa	..	..	78	303	196	84	2	841	656	1,425	172	..	..	23.3
Sudan	..	..	..	..	..	..	..	..	..	1,702	3,620	..	..	..
Swaziland	..	..	..	..	..	..	..	..	..	..	..	..	..	..
Tanzania	..	..	..	..	..	..	..	..	..	..	..	..	..	..
Togo	..	..	..	..	..	..	..	..	..	..	..	..	..	..
Uganda	..	..	..	..	..	..	..	..	..	..	..	..	..	..
Zambia	..	..	..	..	..	..	..	..	..	..	..	..	..	..
Zimbabwe	..	..	..	..	..	..	..	..	..	..	..	..	..	..
NORTH AFRICA	146,129	115,378	115,283	111,512	100,666	99,749	102,319	98,237	100,246	92,090	99,752	-3.6	-0.6	-1.4
Algeria	39,182	33,002	32,299	33,246	33,254	33,108	36,722	35,499	37,040	36,802	39,652	-5.4	1.2	1.7
Egypt, Arab Republic	17,146	18,461	20,413	19,924	8,480	8,503	6,836	6,241	2,836	2,865	7,190	20.7	-2.8	-16.4
Libya	85,054	60,403	58,463	54,893	55,661	54,573	55,365	53,633	57,443	49,067	49,725	-6.4	-0.4	-0.5
Morocco	..	..	..	..	..	..	..	..	..	..	..	..	..	..
Tunisia	4,747	3,512	4,109	3,449	3,271	3,566	3,397	2,863	2,927	3,356	3,185	-0.5	-3.9	-1.2
ALL AFRICA	264,651	248,146	253,578	259,124	246,734	248,309	265,865	273,167	277,651	264,611	283,908	-4.0	2.0	1.7

5-20. Copper exports

	Thousands of metric tons											Average annual percentage growth		
	1980	*1989*	*1990*	*1991*	*1992*	*1993*	*1994*	*1995*	*1996*	*1997*	*1998*	*75-84*	*85-89*	*90-MR*
SUB-SAHARAN AFRICA	1,286	1,074	973	792	714	598	495	418	392	393	316	5.2	-3.1	-12.8
excluding South Africa	1,164	958	883	688	581	517	421	339	318	322	248	4.6	-3.4	-14.0
excl. S.Africa & Nigeria	1,164	958	883	688	581	517	421	339	318	322	248	4.6	-3.4	-14.0
Angola	0	0	0	0	0	0	0	0	0	0	0	..	..	..
Benin	0	0	0	0	0	0	0	0	0	0	0	..	..	..
Botswana	20	19	19	20	19	22	20	18	23	18	20	..	1.0	0.4
Burkina Faso	0	0	0	0	0	0	0	0	0	0	0	..	..	..
Burundi	0	0	0	0	0	0	0	0	0	0	0	..	..	..
Cameroon	0	0	0	0	0	0	0	0	0	0	0	..	..	..
Cape Verde	0	0	0	0	0	0	0	0	0	0	0	..	..	..
Central African Republic	0	0	0	0	0	0	0	0	0	0	0	..	..	..
Chad	0	0	0	0	0	0	0	0	0	0	0	..	..	..
Comoros	0	0	0	0	0	0	0	0	0	0	0	..	..	..
Congo, Democratic Rep. of	461	439	374	252	116	28	14	5	0	..	..	16.8	-2.7	-55.3
Congo, Republic of	1	0	0	0	0	0	0	0	0	..	..	..	..	..
Côte d'Ivoire	0	0	0	0	0	0	0	0	0	0	0	..	..	..
Djibouti	0	0	0	0	0	0	0	0	0	0	0	..	..	..
Equatorial Guinea	0	0	0	0	0	0	0	0	0	0	0	..	..	..
Eritrea	0	0	0	0	0	0	0	0	0	0	0	..	..	..
Ethiopia	0	0	0	0	0	0	0	0	0	0	0	..	..	..
Gabon	0	0	0	0	0	0	0	0	0	0	0	..	..	..
Gambia, The	0	0	0	0	0	0	0	0	0	0	0	..	..	..
Ghana	0	0	0	0	0	0	0	0	0	0	0	..	..	..
Guinea	0	0	0	0	0	0	0	0	0	0	0	..	..	..
Guinea-Bissau	0	0	0	0	0	0	0	0	0	0	0	..	..	..
Kenya	0	0	0	0	0	0	0	0	0	0	0	..	..	..
Lesotho	0	0	0	0	0	0	0	0	0	0	0	..	..	..
Liberia	0	0	0	0	0	0	0	0	0	0	0	..	..	..
Madagascar	0	0	0	0	0	0	0	0	0	0	0	..	..	..
Malawi	0	0	0	0	0	0	0	0	0	0	0	..	..	..
Mali	0	0	0	0	0	0	0	0	0	0	0	..	..	..
Mauritania	1	0	0	0	0	0	0	0	0	..	..	..	..	..
Mauritius	0	0	0	0	0	0	0	0	0	0	0	..	..	..
Mozambique	0	0	0	0	0	0	0	0	0	0	0	..	..	..
Namibia	41	33	30	34	35	30	26	25	18	..	..	1.9	-7.0	-6.8
Niger	0	0	0	0	0	0	0	0	0	0	0	..	..	..
Nigeria	0	0	0	0	0	0	0	0	0	0	0	..	..	..
Rwanda	0	0	0	0	0	0	0	0	0	0	0	..	..	..
São Tomé and Principe	0	0	0	0	0	0	0	0	0	0	0	..	..	..
Senegal	0	0	0	0	0	0	0	0	0	0	0	..	..	..
Seychelles	0	0	0	0	0	0	0	0	0	0	0	..	..	..
Sierra Leone	0	0	0	0	0	0	0	0	0	0	0	..	..	..
Somalia	0	0	0	0	0	0	0	0	0	0	0	..	..	..
South Africa	121	115	90	104	132	81	74	79	74	71	68	13.2	-0.8	-5.7
Sudan	0	0	0	0	0	0	0	0	0	0	0	..	..	..
Swaziland	0	0	0	0	0	0	0	0	0	0	0	..	..	..
Tanzania	0	0	0	0	0	0	0	0	0	0	0	..	..	..
Togo	0	0	0	0	0	0	0	0	0	0	0	..	..	..
Uganda	0	0	0	0	0	0	0	0	0	..	..	..	..	..
Zambia	617	456	460	382	412	437	361	292	276	304	228	-1.8	-3.4	-7.0
Zimbabwe	23	10	0	0	0	0	0	0	0	..	..	3.8	-16.6	..
NORTH AFRICA	6	12	16	16	17	13	19	16	16	0	0	..	-13.1	2.5
Algeria	0	0	0	0	0	0	0	0	0	..	..	..	..	..
Egypt, Arab Republic	0	0	0	0	0	0	0	0	0	0	0	..	..	..
Libya	0	0	0	0	0	0	0	0	0	0	0	..	..	..
Morocco	6	12	16	16	17	13	19	16	16	..	..	..	-12.9	2.5
Tunisia	0	0	0	0	0	0	0	0	0	0	0	..	..	..
ALL AFRICA	1,292	1,086	989	807	730	611	514	434	408	393	316	5.4	-3.3	-12.9

5-21. Iron exports

	Thousands of metric tons											Average annual percentage growth		
	1980	1987	1988	1989	1990	1991	1992	1993	1994	1995	1996	75-84	85-89	90-MR
SUB-SAHARAN AFRICA	28,215	20,447	22,981	24,956	21,057	17,509	15,778	18,986	19,465	21,397	19,545	..	-0.4	-1.3
excluding South Africa	17,482	14,903	15,734	15,780	9,988	7,474	6,114	6,276	6,722	7,196	7,000	..	-2.3	-8.7
excl. S.Africa & Nigeria	17,482	14,903	15,734	15,780	9,988	7,474	6,114	6,276	6,722	7,196	7,000	..	-2.3	-8.7
Angola	0	0	0	0	0	0	0	0	0	0	0	..	..	..
Benin	0	0	0	0	0	0	0	0	0	0	0	..	..	..
Botswana	0	0	0	0	0	0	0	0	0	0	0	..	..	..
Burkina Faso	0	0	0	0	0	0	0	0	0	0	0	..	..	..
Burundi	0	0	0	0	0	0	0	0	0	0	0	..	..	..
Cameroon	0	0	0	0	0	0	0	0	0	0	0	..	..	..
Cape Verde	0	0	0	0	0	0	0	0	0	0	0	..	..	..
Central African Republic	0	0	0	0	0	0	0	0	0	0	0	..	..	..
Chad	0	0	0	0	0	0	0	0	0	0	0	..	..	..
Comoros	0	0	0	0	0	0	0	0	0	0	0	..	..	..
Congo, Democratic Rep. of	0	0	0	0	0	0	0	0	0	0	0	..	..	..
Congo, Republic of	0	0	0	0	0	0	0	0	0	0	0	..	..	..
Côte d'Ivoire	0	0	0	0	0	0	0	0	0	0	0	..	..	..
Djibouti	0	0	0	0	0	0	0	0	0	0	0	..	..	..
Equatorial Guinea	0	0	0	0	0	0	0	0	0	0	0	..	..	..
Eritrea	0	0	0	0	0	0	0	0	0	0	0	..	..	..
Ethiopia	0	0	0	0	0	0	0	0	0	0	0	..	..	..
Gabon	0	0	0	0	0	0	0	0	0	0	0	..	..	..
Gambia, The	0	0	0	0	0	0	0	0	0	0	0	..	..	..
Ghana	0	0	0	0	0	0	0	0	0	0	0	..	..	..
Guinea	0	0	0	0	0	0	0	0	0	0	0	..	..	..
Guinea-Bissau	0	0	0	0	0	0	0	0	0	0	0	..	..	..
Kenya	0	0	0	0	0	0	0	0	0	0	0	..	..	..
Lesotho	0	0	0	0	0	0	0	0	0	0	0	..	..	..
Liberia	11,695	9,052	9,231	8,540	2,607	670	853	0	0	0	0	..	-5.4	..
Madagascar	0	0	0	0	0	0	0	0	0	0	0	..	..	..
Malawi	0	0	0	0	0	0	0	0	0	0	0	..	..	..
Mali	0	0	0	0	0	0	0	0	0	0	0	..	..	..
Mauritania	5,673	5,851	6,503	7,240	7,381	6,804	5,261	6,276	6,722	7,196	7,000	..	3.0	-0.3
Mauritius	0	0	0	0	0	0	0	0	0	0	0	..	..	..
Mozambique	0	0	0	0	0	0	0	0	0	0	0	..	..	..
Namibia	0	0	0	0	0	0	0	0	0	0	0	..	..	..
Niger	0	0	0	0	0	0	0	0	0	0	0	..	..	..
Nigeria	0	0	0	0	0	0	0	0	0	0	0	..	..	..
Rwanda	0	0	0	0	0	0	0	0	0	0	0	..	..	..
São Tomé and Principe	0	0	0	0	0	0	0	0	0	0	0	..	..	..
Senegal	0	0	0	0	0	0	0	0	0	0	0	..	..	..
Seychelles	0	0	0	0	0	0	0	0	0	0	0	..	..	..
Sierra Leone	0	0	0	0	0	0	0	0	0	0	0	..	..	..
Somalia	0	0	0	0	0	0	0	0	0	0	0	..	..	..
South Africa	10,733	5,544	7,247	9,176	11,069	10,035	9,664	12,710	12,743	14,201	12,545	..	4.0	5.4
Sudan	0	0	0	0	0	0	0	0	0	0	0	..	..	..
Swaziland	114	0	0	0	0	0	0	0	0	0	0	..	..	..
Tanzania	0	0	0	0	0	0	0	0	0	0	0	..	..	..
Togo	0	0	0	0	0	0	0	0	0	0	0	..	..	..
Uganda	0	0	0	0	0	0	0	0	0	0	0	..	..	..
Zambia	0	0	0	0	0	0	0	0	0	0	0	..	..	..
Zimbabwe	0	0	0	0	0	0	0	0	0	0	0	..	..	..
NORTH AFRICA	784	6	48	62	47	50	55	58	42	21	4	..	-11.3	-24.3
Algeria	699	6	0	10	9	10	20	25	25	5	4	..	-41.9	-6.9
Egypt, Arab Republic	0	0	0	0	0	0	0	0	0	0	0	..	..	..
Libya	0	0	0	0	0	0	0	0	0	0	0	..	..	..
Morocco	85	0	48	52	38	40	35	33	17	16	0	..	..	-17.4
Tunisia	0	0	0	0	0	0	0	0	0	0	0	..	..	..
ALL AFRICA	28,999	20,453	23,029	25,018	21,104	17,559	15,833	19,044	19,507	21,418	19,549	..	-0.6	-1.4

5-22. Phosphate exports

	Thousands of metric tons											Average annual percentage growth		
	1980	1988	1989	1990	1991	1992	1993	1994	1995	1996	1997	75-84	85-89	90-MR
SUB-SAHARAN AFRICA	4,277	5,983	5,877	4,995	5,544	4,617	3,747	4,154	4,919	4,496	4,290	0.4	6.9	-3.1
excluding South Africa	4,274	4,715	4,783	3,778	4,378	3,272	2,550	2,881	3,511	3,522	2,990	-0.6	4.6	-4.3
excl. S.Africa & Nigeria	4,274	4,715	4,783	3,778	4,378	3,272	2,550	2,881	3,511	3,522	2,990	-0.6	4.6	-4.3
Angola	0	0	0	0	0	0	0	0	0	0	0	..	..	..
Benin	0	0	0	0	0	0	0	0	0	0	0	..	..	..
Botswana	0	0	0	0	0	0	0	0	0	0	0	..	..	..
Burkina Faso	0	0	0	0	0	0	0	0	0	0	0	..	..	..
Burundi	0	0	0	0	0	0	0	0	0	0	0	..	..	..
Cameroon	0	0	0	0	0	0	0	0	0	0	0	..	..	..
Cape Verde	0	0	0	0	0	0	0	0	0	0	0	..	..	..
Central African Republic	0	0	0	0	0	0	0	0	0	0	0	..	..	..
Chad	0	0	0	0	0	0	0	0	0	0	0	..	..	..
Comoros	0	0	0	0	0	0	0	0	0	0	0	..	..	..
Congo, Democratic Rep. of	0	0	0	0	0	0	0	0	0	0	0	..	..	..
Congo, Republic of	0	0	0	0	0	0	0	0	0	0	0	..	..	..
Côte d'Ivoire	0	0	0	0	0	0	0	0	0	0	0	..	..	..
Djibouti	0	0	0	0	0	0	0	0	0	0	0	..	..	..
Equatorial Guinea	0	0	0	0	0	0	0	0	0	0	0	..	..	..
Eritrea	0	0	0	0	0	0	0	0	0	0	0	..	..	..
Ethiopia	0	0	0	0	0	0	0	0	0	0	0	..	..	..
Gabon	0	0	0	0	0	0	0	0	0	0	0	..	..	..
Gambia, The	0	0	0	0	0	0	0	0	0	0	0	..	..	..
Ghana	0	0	0	0	0	0	0	0	0	0	0	..	..	..
Guinea	0	0	0	0	0	0	0	0	0	0	0	..	..	..
Guinea-Bissau	0	0	0	0	0	0	0	0	0	0	0	..	..	..
Kenya	0	0	0	0	0	0	0	0	0	0	0	..	..	..
Lesotho	0	0	0	0	0	0	0	0	0	0	0	..	..	..
Liberia	0	0	0	0	0	0	0	0	0	0	0	..	..	..
Madagascar	0	0	0	0	0	0	0	0	0	0	0	..	..	..
Malawi	0	0	0	0	0	0	0	0	0	0	0	..	..	..
Mali	0	0	0	0	0	0	0	0	0	0	0	..	..	..
Mauritania	0	0	0	0	0	0	0	0	0	0	0	..	..	..
Mauritius	0	0	0	0	0	0	0	0	0	0	0	..	..	..
Mozambique	0	0	0	0	0	0	0	0	0	0	0	..	..	..
Namibia	0	0	0	0	0	0	0	0	0	0	0	..	..	..
Niger	0	0	0	0	0	0	0	0	0	0	0	..	..	..
Nigeria	0	0	0	0	0	0	0	0	0	0	0	..	..	..
Rwanda	0	0	0	0	0	0	0	0	0	0	0	..	..	..
São Tomé and Principe	0	0	0	0	0	0	0	0	0	0	0	..	..	..
Senegal	1,378	1,847	1,435	1,356	1,304	1,187	983	648	859	836	598	-3.9	4.4	-10.1
Seychelles	0	0	0	0	0	0	0	0	0	0	0	..	..	..
Sierra Leone	0	0	0	0	0	0	0	0	0	0	0	..	..	..
Somalia	0	0	0	0	0	0	0	0	0	0	0	..	..	..
South Africa	4	1,268	1,094	1,217	1,166	1,344	1,197	1,273	1,408	974	1,300	39.6	20.6	0.6
Sudan	0	0	0	0	0	0	0	0	0	0	0	..	..	..
Swaziland	0	0	0	0	0	0	0	0	0	0	0	..	..	..
Tanzania	0	0	0	0	0	0	0	0	0	0	0	..	..	..
Togo	2,896	2,868	3,347	2,422	3,074	2,086	1,567	2,234	2,652	2,686	2,392	1.9	4.5	-2.1
Uganda	0	0	0	0	0	0	0	0	0	0	0	..	..	..
Zambia	0	0	0	0	0	0	0	0	0	0	0	..	..	..
Zimbabwe	0	0	0	0	0	0	0	0	0	0	0	..	..	..
NORTH AFRICA	18,932	16,560	14,700	13,297	10,537	11,068	10,096	11,523	11,466	12,422	13,390	-1.1	-2.3	-0.6
Algeria	768	877	970	735	804	800	449	575	671	993	474	5.6	8.5	-4.3
Egypt, Arab Republic	258	268	246	297	164	180	134	114	48	65	..	12.4	3.8	-21.0
Libya	0	0	0	0	0	0	0	0	0	0	0	..	..	..
Morocco	16,457	14,260	12,407	11,672	9,143	9,132	8,398	9,527	9,420	10,141	11,669	-0.8	-3.1	-0.9
Tunisia	1,449	1,156	1,077	593	426	956	1,114	1,308	1,327	1,224	1,247	-6.9	-0.8	9.3
ALL AFRICA	23,210	22,543	20,576	18,292	16,080	15,684	13,843	15,678	16,385	16,918	17,680	-0.8	-0.2	-1.3

5-23. Cocoa exports

	Thousands of metric tons											Average annual percentage growth		
	1980	1991	1992	1993	1994	1995	1996	1997	1998	1999	2000	75-84	85-89	90-MR
SUB-SAHARAN AFRICA	870	1,369	1,190	1,469	1,271	1,342	1,995	1,688	1,659	1,952	1,956	0.4	5.3	3.5
excluding South Africa	869	1,364	1,180	1,456	1,260	1,334	1,985	1,678	1,650	1,944	1,949	0.4	5.3	3.5
excl. S.Africa & Nigeria	719	1,203	1,069	1,296	1,113	1,195	1,803	1,531	1,515	1,736	1,803	1.0	5.2	3.8
Angola	0	0	0	0	0	0	0	0	0	0	0	-20.0	..	..
Benin	5	0	0	0	0	0	0	0	0	0	0	6.2	-63.8	..
Botswana	0	0	0	0	0	0	0	0	0	0	0	..	128.8	-0.7
Burkina Faso	0	0	0	0	0	0	0	0	0	0	0	..	..	..
Burundi	0	0	0	0	0	0	0	0	0	0	0	..	..	..
Cameroon	105	98	68	112	82	120	142	110	118	127	101	0.1	3.8	2.2
Cape Verde	0	0	0	0	0	0	0	0	0	0	0	..	..	..
Central African Republic	0	0	0	0	0	0	0	0	0	0	0	-21.8	..	..
Chad	0	0	0	0	0	0	0	0	0	0	0	..	..	..
Comoros	0	0	0	0	0	0	0	0	0	0	0	-14.3	..	..
Congo, Democratic Rep. of	4	4	3	3	6	2	3	3	3	2	2	-0.2	2.8	-8.2
Congo, Republic of	2	0	0	0	0	0	1	1	1	1	1	-5.1	-18.7	6.3
Côte d'Ivoire	332	793	724	872	744	795	1,138	1,090	1,020	1,253	1,257	9.1	5.4	4.6
Djibouti	0	0	0	0	0	0	0	0	0	0	0	..	..	..
Equatorial Guinea	7	6	5	3	3	3	6	4	6	3	4	-0.2	0.4	-3.1
Eritrea	0	0	0	0	0	0	0	0	0	0	0	..	..	..
Ethiopia	0	0	0	0	0	0	0	0	0	0	0	..	..	..
Gabon	4	1	2	1	1	1	1	1	1	1	1	-4.2	2.6	-11.3
Gambia, The	0	0	0	0	0	0	0	0	0	0	0	..	..	..
Ghana	218	265	243	278	252	253	478	288	333	319	405	-7.7	9.0	2.2
Guinea	4	2	2	4	4	3	6	7	8	0	2	4.3	-6.2	4.8
Guinea-Bissau	0	0	0	0	0	0	0	0	0	0	0	..	..	..
Kenya	0	0	1	1	1	0	0	0	0	0	0	-8.2	46.3	16.2
Lesotho	0	0	0	0	0	0	0	0	0	0	0	..	..	..
Liberia	4	2	0	0	0	0	1	1	2	2	3	9.1	-15.1	0.0
Madagascar	2	4	3	4	3	2	2	1	1	1	4	5.8	7.6	-5.0
Malawi	0	0	0	0	0	0	0	0	0	0	0	-21.2	..	..
Mali	0	0	0	0	0	0	0	0	0	0	0	..	..	..
Mauritania	0	0	0	0	0	0	0	0	0	0	0	..	..	..
Mauritius	0	0	0	0	0	0	0	0	0	0	0	..	..	6.3
Mozambique	0	0	0	0	0	0	0	0	0	0	0	..	..	..
Namibia	0	0	0	0	0	0	0	0	0	0	0	..	..	..
Niger	0	0	0	0	0	0	0	0	0	0	0	..	..	..
Nigeria	151	161	111	161	148	139	182	147	135	208	145	-2.6	4.2	1.3
Rwanda	0	0	0	0	0	0	0	0	0	0	0	..	..	..
São Tomé and Principe	7	5	4	4	3	5	4	3	3	4	4	-5.6	0.6	-1.3
Senegal	0	0	0	0	0	0	0	0	0	0	0	65.7	-28.8	39.3
Seychelles	0	0	0	0	0	0	0	0	0	0	0	..	..	3.4
Sierra Leone	8	13	5	4	3	3	4	3	3	3	2	6.0	-4.6	-11.0
Somalia	0	0	0	0	0	0	0	0	0	0	0	..	..	..
South Africa	0	6	10	13	11	8	10	10	9	8	7	-8.5	34.0	7.4
Sudan	0	0	0	0	0	0	0	0	0	0	0	..	..	..
Swaziland	0	0	0	0	0	0	0	6	8	7	10	..	..	..
Tanzania	1	2	2	2	2	3	3	3	2	3	2	9.0	9.7	0.2
Togo	15	6	6	5	6	4	11	10	5	8	6	-1.7	-11.9	-0.2
Uganda	0	1	1	1	1	1	1	1	2	2	2	2.5	5.5	13.0
Zambia	0	0	0	0	0	0	0	0	0	0	0	..	..	..
Zimbabwe	0	0	0	0	0	0	0	0	0	0	0	-14.6	-4.1	11.6
NORTH AFRICA	0	2	1	0	0	1	1	1	1	1	1	6.1	25.6	1.0
Algeria	0	0	0	0	0	0	0	0	0	0	0	..	..	..
Egypt, Arab Republic	0	2	0	0	0	0	1	1	0	1	0	-22.9	81.9	-2.2
Libya	0	0	0	0	0	0	0	0	0	0	0	..	..	..
Morocco	0	0	0	0	0	0	0	0	0	0	0	..	-17.2	1.2
Tunisia	0	0	0	0	0	0	0	0	0	0	0	..	17.4	-0.9
ALL AFRICA	870	1,372	1,191	1,469	1,272	1,343	1,996	1,689	1,659	1,953	1,957	0.4	5.3	3.5

5-24. Coffee exports

	Thousands of metric tons											Average annual percentage growth		
	1980	1991	1992	1993	1994	1995	1996	1997	1998	1999	2000	75-84	85-89	90-MR
SUB-SAHARAN AFRICA	819	828	847	830	758	788	959	910	822	769	902	-2.3	0.0	-1.6
excluding South Africa	818	827	846	830	758	787	958	906	816	767	901	-2.4	-0.1	-1.6
excl. S.Africa & Nigeria	816	827	846	829	758	786	957	905	815	766	901	-2.4	-0.1	-1.6
Angola	47	5	5	2	0	2	3	3	3	3	3	-17.7	-19.0	-5.6
Benin	0	0	0	0	0	0	0	0	0	0	0	18.1	-21.6	..
Botswana	0	0	0	0	0	0	0	0	0	0	0	3.8	56.4	-9.3
Burkina Faso	..	..	..	..	..	..	..	..	..	..	..	..	..	..
Burundi	19	41	40	23	29	29	13	32	42	24	22	3.0	-0.2	-4.6
Cameroon	92	113	104	67	54	63	74	59	53	86	89	0.0	4.4	-5.6
Cape Verde	0	0	0	0	0	0	0	0	0	0	0	..	..	..
Central African Republic	11	9	6	8	8	14	5	12	12	12	6	2.2	10.4	-6.5
Chad	..	..	..	..	..	..	..	..	..	..	..	..	..	..
Comoros	0	0	0	0	0	0	0	0	0	0	0	-17.4	..	..
Congo, Democratic Rep. of	74	84	104	55	63	60	49	23	38	23	29	0.3	2.7	-15.3
Congo, Republic of	2	0	0	0	0	2	1	0	0	0	0	8.4	-28.7	17.2
Côte d'Ivoire	207	199	203	226	122	135	145	233	215	106	308	-2.6	-7.4	0.7
Djibouti	..	..	..	..	..	..	..	..	..	..	..	..	..	..
Equatorial Guinea	0	0	0	0	0	0	0	0	0	0	0	-10.7	-18.2	-19.1
Eritrea	..	..	..	..	..	..	..	..	..	..	..	..	..	..
Ethiopia	..	..	..	70	89	77	110	119	115	109	119	..	..	3.3
Gabon	1	0	0	0	0	0	0	0	0	0	0	26.9	12.9	-18.5
Gambia, The	0	0	0	0	0	0	0	0	0	0	0	..	..	..
Ghana	0	1	2	3	1	2	1	3	6	6	5	-21.1	12.5	16.9
Guinea	3	4	5	6	12	19	8	20	22	0	12	0.4	105.1	8.8
Guinea-Bissau	..	..	..	..	..	..	..	..	..	..	..	..	..	..
Kenya	80	83	78	88	80	89	114	68	51	70	87	2.9	-2.7	-3.3
Lesotho	..	..	..	..	..	..	..	..	..	..	..	..	..	..
Liberia	13	0	0	0	0	0	0	0	0	0	0	6.3	-10.9	..
Madagascar	69	41	50	51	37	35	40	26	30	13	5	-2.5	2.6	-15.3
Malawi	0	6	9	6	5	5	5	4	4	4	3	25.2	12.9	-3.9
Mali	0	0	0	0	0	0	0	0	0	0	0	..	..	..
Mauritania	..	..	..	..	..	..	..	..	..	..	..	..	..	..
Mauritius	0	0	0	0	0	0	0	0	0	0	0	..	..	..
Mozambique	0	0	0	0	0	0	0	0	0	0	0	..	..	..
Namibia	0	0	0	0	0	0	0	0	0	0	0	..	..	..
Niger	0	0	0	0	0	0	0	0	0	0	0	..	..	..
Nigeria	2	0	0	1	0	1	1	1	1	1	0	-1.8	41.6	20.6
Rwanda	22	38	34	30	2	8	18	14	0	0	0	1.4	1.4	-52.7
São Tomé and Principe	0	0	0	0	0	0	0	0	0	0	0	-9.5	-26.4	20.6
Senegal	1	0	0	0	0	0	0	0	0	0	0	0.9	-2.6	..
Seychelles	0	0	0	0	0	0	0	0	0	0	0	..	..	..
Sierra Leone	10	6	4	3	4	5	2	3	3	1	2	-0.7	12.2	-12.5
Somalia	..	..	..	..	..	..	..	..	..	..	..	..	..	..
South Africa	0	1	1	0	0	1	1	4	6	2	2	24.9	26.1	12.0
Sudan	..	..	..	..	..	..	..	..	..	..	..	..	..	..
Swaziland	0	0	0	0	0	0	0	0	0	0	0	..	..	..
Tanzania	43	52	51	59	37	48	62	41	39	45	45	0.8	-2.2	-2.4
Togo	9	9	19	13	9	13	5	19	10	19	13	-6.2	28.6	-1.3
Uganda	110	127	119	114	202	169	289	211	163	236	143	-2.8	3.8	1.2
Zambia	0	0	1	1	0	1	2	2	2	2	4	..	59.2	18.3
Zimbabwe	3	9	10	4	4	10	11	12	8	7	6	13.2	-9.3	-5.7
NORTH AFRICA	0	0	0	0	0	0	0	0	0	0	0	-34.0	..	-24.8
Algeria	0	0	0	0	0	0	0	0	0	0	0	..	..	..
Egypt, Arab Republic	0	0	0	0	0	0	0	0	0	0	0	..	..	-37.9
Libya	..	..	..	..	..	..	..	..	..	..	..	..	..	..
Morocco	0	0	0	0	0	0	0	0	0	0	0	..	..	-1.5
Tunisia	0	0	0	0	0	0	0	0	0	0	0	..	..	1.5
ALL AFRICA	819	828	847	830	759	788	959	910	822	769	902	-2.4	0.0	-1.6

5-25. Cotton exports

	Thousands of metric tons											Average annual percentage growth		
	1980	1991	1992	1993	1994	1995	1996	1997	1998	1999	2000	75-84	85-89	90-MR
SUB-SAHARAN AFRICA	459	654	682	705	736	779	823	949	972	1,048	1,177	1.2	7.6	1.8
excluding South Africa	459	651	678	705	736	779	823	945	965	1,043	1,171	1.3	7.4	1.9
excl. S.Africa & Nigeria	459	650	677	702	733	777	801	913	956	1,035	1,171	1.3	7.4	1.7
Angola	0	0	0	0	0	0	0	0	0	0	0	-27.7	10.4	..
Benin	8	43	58	60	74	99	89	112	107	163	134	-0.6	13.3	10.6
Botswana	0	0	0	1	1	1	1	1	1	1	0	..	..	4.3
Burkina Faso	28	55	55	60	38	55	43	60	118	61	74	10.8	14.3	2.6
Burundi	1	0	0	2	2	1	0	0	0	0	0	-0.4	2.0	..
Cameroon	26	23	42	51	59	54	66	51	61	73	73	15.1	19.5	5.3
Cape Verde	0	0	0	0	0	0	..	..	..	..	..	..	..	..
Central African Republic	14	13	6	8	5	12	15	9	15	10	10	-4.0	-12.8	2.5
Chad	35	65	85	40	32	62	50	72	68	37	68	-2.4	-0.4	-0.9
Comoros	0	0	0	0	0	0	..	..	..	..	..	..	..	..
Congo, Democratic Rep. of	2	0	0	0	1	1	1	0	0	0	0	..	..	-25.8
Congo, Republic of	0	0	0	0	0	0	..	..	..	..	..	..	..	..
Côte d'Ivoire	39	97	67	96	100	88	75	94	122	131	161	14.7	15.3	4.4
Djibouti	0	0	0	0	0	0	..	..	..	..	..	..	..	..
Equatorial Guinea	0	0	0	0	0	0	..	..	..	..	..	..	..	..
Eritrea	0	0	0	0	0	0	..	..	..	..	..	..	..	..
Ethiopia	..	..	..	0	0	8	1	0	1	5	0	..	..	43.8
Gabon	0	0	0	0	0	0	..	..	..	..	..	..	..	..
Gambia, The	0	2	1	1	1	1	1	0	0	0	0	..	10.6	-20.2
Ghana	0	0	0	2	7	1	0	0	1	7	10	..	..	11.5
Guinea	0	1	4	10	6	7	5	4	5	0	4	..	..	5.7
Guinea-Bissau	0	1	0	1	1	1	1	1	1	1	1	..	25.4	7.0
Kenya	4	1	6	8	7	1	0	0	0	0	0	-18.6	-73.2	-42.0
Lesotho	0	0	0	0	0	0	..	..	..	..	..	..	..	..
Liberia	0	0	0	0	0	0	0	0	0	0	0	..	..	..
Madagascar	1	3	0	0	1	1	1	0	0	0	0	22.2	-16.8	-12.1
Malawi	3	6	3	0	0	0	0	9	5	3	7	-20.5	-0.6	10.0
Mali	53	114	113	133	90	105	130	140	160	138	164	9.9	14.2	1.4
Mauritania	0	0	0	0	0	0	..	..	..	..	..	..	..	..
Mauritius	0	0	0	0	0	0	0	0	0	0	0	..	..	..
Mozambique	6	6	11	13	16	13	16	16	17	10	12	-8.0	1.1	7.1
Namibia	0	0	0	0	0	0	..	..	..	..	..	..	..	..
Niger	0	0	1	1	0	5	2	2	1	2	2	-12.4	80.4	3.5
Nigeria	0	1	0	3	3	2	22	32	9	7	0	..	..	15.1
Rwanda	0	0	0	0	0	0	..	..	..	..	..	..	..	..
São Tomé and Principe	0	0	0	0	0	0	..	..	..	..	..	..	..	..
Senegal	6	12	16	20	15	9	11	15	14	5	7	2.1	-6.4	-2.3
Seychelles	0	0	0	0	0	0	..	..	..	..	..	..	..	..
Sierra Leone	0	0	0	0	0	0	..	..	..	..	..	..	..	..
Somalia	0	0	0	0	0	0	0	0	0	0	0	..	..	..
South Africa	0	3	5	0	0	0	0	4	7	5	6	-30.6	269.4	4.5
Sudan	132	80	65	58	119	84	94	88	77	194	232	0.0	1.2	3.3
Swaziland	4	10	6	7	4	3	4	2	0	0	0	4.8	40.8	-30.1
Tanzania	31	39	73	61	60	71	82	69	23	30	26	-3.9	17.8	-6.9
Togo	5	36	39	42	43	61	56	48	67	45	30	27.3	22.1	-5.9
Uganda	2	8	8	8	4	6	10	10	1	14	14	-21.5	-25.3	3.3
Zambia	5	2	2	1	1	3	5	17	12	25	3	15.9	12.7	11.6
Zimbabwe	54	34	16	18	47	27	44	91	78	80	140	4.2	-0.2	9.5
NORTH AFRICA	167	16	16	20	114	68	23	42	67	112	63	0.1	-17.0	8.9
Algeria	0	0	0	0	0	0	0	0	0	0	0	..	..	..
Egypt, Arab Republic	164	13	16	18	113	67	23	42	66	112	63	0.2	-18.9	10.0
Libya	0	0	0	0	0	0	..	..	..	..	..	..	..	..
Morocco	3	3	1	2	1	0	0	0	1	0	0	3.4	..	-20.1
Tunisia	0	0	0	0	0	0	0	0	0	0	0	..	..	..
ALL AFRICA	627	670	699	726	851	847	847	990	1,039	1,160	1,240	0.9	3.6	2.3

5-26. Groundnut exports

	Thousands of metric tons											Average annual percentage growth		
	1980	1991	1992	1993	1994	1995	1996	1997	1998	1999	2000	75-84	85-89	90-MR
SUB-SAHARAN AFRICA	605	342	336	276	396	281	391	406	398	311	385	-8.9	15.7	-1.9
excluding South Africa	560	309	312	249	337	244	353	348	365	285	354	-8.7	15.2	-1.8
excl. S.Africa & Nigeria	559	309	310	249	330	244	348	326	351	280	354	-8.2	15.1	-2.0
Angola	1	0	0	0	0	0	0	0	0	0	0	-4.9	..	..
Benin	2	0	0	0	0	0	0	0	0	0	0	-27.0	..	..
Botswana	0	0	0	0	0	0	0	0	0	0	0	-10.2	29.0	-7.9
Burkina Faso	1	1	1	0	0	0	0	0	1	1	2	-43.9	152.2	0.8
Burundi	0	0	0	0	0	0	0	0	0	0	0	..	..	..
Cameroon	1	0	0	0	0	0	0	0	0	0	1	-39.5	15.8	22.8
Cape Verde	0	0	0	0	0	0	0	0	0	0	0	..	..	..
Central African Republic	0	0	0	0	1	1	0	1	1	1	1	..	..	-5.2
Chad	0	0	0	1	2	0	1	0	0	0	0	..	..	9.9
Comoros	..	..	..	..	..	..	..	..	..	..	..	..	..	..
Congo, Democratic Rep. of	0	0	0	0	0	0	0	0	0	0	0	..	..	..
Congo, Republic of	0	0	0	0	0	0	0	0	0	0	0	-10.6	..	..
Côte d'Ivoire	0	0	0	0	0	1	0	0	0	1	1	-8.4	..	..
Djibouti	..	..	..	..	..	..	..	..	..	..	..	..	..	..
Equatorial Guinea	..	..	..	..	..	..	..	..	..	..	..	..	..	..
Eritrea	..	..	..	..	..	..	..	..	..	..	..	..	..	..
Ethiopia	..	..	..	0	0	0	0	0	0	0	0	..	..	..
Gabon	0	0	0	0	0	0	0	0	0	0	0	..	..	..
Gambia, The	67	17	18	28	26	38	32	38	37	20	28	-7.7	-11.7	3.0
Ghana	2	0	0	0	0	0	0	0	0	0	1	..	..	..
Guinea	0	0	0	0	0	0	0	0	0	0	0	..	..	..
Guinea-Bissau	8	0	0	0	0	0	0	0	0	0	0	-4.4	-17.9	-11.6
Kenya	0	0	0	1	0	0	0	0	0	0	0	-24.6	23.1	12.4
Lesotho	..	..	..	..	..	..	..	..	..	..	..	..	..	..
Liberia	..	..	..	..	..	..	..	..	..	..	..	..	..	..
Madagascar	4	1	0	0	0	0	0	1	0	0	1	-44.9	..	1.5
Malawi	28	1	0	0	1	1	1	3	4	1	0	-17.8	23.7	9.6
Mali	15	10	11	12	17	16	15	15	12	13	11	-11.7	9.3	-0.5
Mauritania	0	0	0	0	0	0	0	0	0	0	0	..	..	..
Mauritius	0	0	0	0	0	0	0	0	0	0	0	..	..	36.1
Mozambique	10	0	0	0	0	1	0	0	0	0	0	-8.5	22.4	-13.6
Namibia	0	0	0	0	0	0	0	0	0	0	0	..	..	..
Niger	1	1	1	0	0	1	2	3	4	2	2	-38.0	182.2	1.7
Nigeria	1	0	1	0	7	1	4	22	13	5	0	-37.9	..	24.8
Rwanda	0	0	0	0	0	0	0	0	0	0	0	..	..	..
São Tomé and Principe	..	..	..	..	..	..	..	..	..	..	..	..	..	..
Senegal	175	215	219	119	164	98	207	88	103	155	238	-9.1	21.2	-4.2
Seychelles	..	..	..	..	..	..	..	..	..	..	..	..	..	..
Sierra Leone	..	..	..	..	..	..	..	..	..	..	..	..	..	..
Somalia	0	0	0	0	0	0	0	0	0	0	0	..	..	..
South Africa	45	32	24	27	59	36	38	58	33	26	31	-12.5	23.7	-2.0
Sudan	238	39	51	84	110	82	84	168	159	72	56	-6.0	15.7	-0.3
Swaziland	0	0	0	0	0	0	0	3	11	8	7	..	..	..
Tanzania	1	16	7	0	0	0	1	1	1	1	1	..	181.1	-16.1
Togo	0	0	0	0	0	0	2	0	0	0	0	-36.2	296.1	17.9
Uganda	0	0	0	1	0	0	0	0	0	0	0	..	..	-14.4
Zambia	0	5	1	0	0	0	0	0	0	1	0	-26.0	..	0.6
Zimbabwe	3	3	1	3	7	3	1	5	15	2	3	-19.6	107.4	-2.9
NORTH AFRICA	13	5	5	21	16	15	10	19	24	14	26	-7.3	-19.9	9.5
Algeria	0	0	0	0	0	0	0	0	0	0	0	..	..	..
Egypt, Arab Republic	13	2	4	12	9	10	6	11	15	4	3	-7.3	-19.9	4.7
Libya	0	4	1	8	4	5	5	8	9	9	23	..	..	20.9
Morocco	0	0	0	0	0	0	0	0	0	0	0	..	..	..
Tunisia	0	0	0	0	3	0	0	0	0	0	0	..	..	..
ALL AFRICA	618	347	341	297	413	296	401	425	422	325	411	-8.9	15.5	-1.6

5-27. Oil palm products exports

	Thousands of metric tons											Average annual percentage growth		
	1980	*1990*	*1991*	*1992*	*1993*	*1994*	*1995*	*1996*	*1997*	*1998*	*1999*	*75-84*	*85-89*	*90-MR*
SUB-SAHARAN AFRICA	280	233	194	269	319	247	187	221	180	207	191	-12.2	9.5	-1.9
excluding South Africa	280	232	194	267	317	244	187	220	179	205	189	-12.2	9.4	-2.0
excl. S.Africa & Nigeria	184	223	186	264	315	237	175	203	169	194	179	-9.3	6.3	-0.9
Angola	..	..	..	..	..	..	..	..	..	..	..	..	..	..
Benin	13	6	1	2	3	7	9	8	13	17	15	-12.5	8.9	22.6
Botswana	..	..	0	0	..	..	0	..	..	..	..	..	..	..
Burkina Faso	..	..	..	..	..	..	..	..	..	..	..	..	..	..
Burundi	..	..	..	..	..	..	1	1	0	0	0	..	..	..
Cameroon	21	28	10	27	27	30	8	41	13	15	15	-7.7	12.3	-4.9
Cape Verde	..	..	..	..	..	..	..	..	..	..	..	..	..	..
Central African Republic	..	..	..	..	..	..	0	0	0	0	0	..	..	..
Chad	..	..	..	..	..	..	..	..	..	..	..	..	..	..
Comoros	..	..	..	..	..	..	..	..	..	..	..	..	..	..
Congo, Democratic Rep. of	10	4	1	1	1	3	1	1	1	1	..	-23.7	-21.9	-17.6
Congo, Republic of	0	..	..	..	..	..	..	..	..	..	..	-17.6	..	..
Côte d'Ivoire	99	166	158	186	207	153	121	103	76	103	106	-7.9	9.5	-3.9
Djibouti	..	..	0	..	..	..	..	..	..	..	..	..	..	..
Equatorial Guinea	..	..	..	..	..	..	..	..	..	..	..	..	..	..
Eritrea	..	..	..	..	..	..	..	..	..	..	..	..	..	..
Ethiopia	..	..	..	..	..	..	..	..	..	..	..	..	..	..
Gabon	..	4	2	5	1	..	3	6	9	3	6	..	9.6	4.2
Gambia, The	1	..	..	..	..	..	..	..	..	..	..	-19.8	..	..
Ghana	..	7	3	8	9	11	12	21	19	10	11	..	39.0	10.7
Guinea	15	1	1	1	7	1	0	4	4	1	1	-3.6	1.5	1.0
Guinea-Bissau	6	2	5	3	2	3	1	3	1	2	2	2.0	5.1	-7.6
Kenya	0	..	1	25	53	14	13	10	26	31	12	-52.7	..	43.8
Lesotho	..	..	..	..	..	..	..	..	..	..	..	..	..	..
Liberia	6	5	4	5	5	5	5	5	5	6	6	24.9	12.7	-0.6
Madagascar	..	..	..	0	0	0	0	0	0	0	0	..	..	44.3
Malawi	..	..	..	..	..	..	..	..	..	..	..	..	..	..
Mali	..	..	..	..	..	..	..	..	..	..	..	..	..	..
Mauritania	..	..	..	..	..	..	..	..	..	..	..	..	..	..
Mauritius	..	..	0	0	0	0	0	0	0	0	..	..	..	29.1
Mozambique	..	..	..	..	..	..	..	..	..	..	..	..	..	..
Namibia	..	..	..	..	..	..	..	..	..	..	..	..	..	..
Niger	..	..	..	..	..	..	..	..	..	0	0	..	..	..
Nigeria	96	9	8	3	2	6	11	17	10	11	11	-16.9	17.5	-2.0
Rwanda	..	..	..	..	..	..	..	..	..	..	..	..	..	..
São Tomé and Principe	0	..	..	..	..	..	..	..	..	..	..	-19.1	..	..
Senegal	0	..	..	..	0	0	0	0	2	2	2	-55.4	18.6	62.6
Seychelles	..	0	0	..	..	..	..	..	..	..	..	..	..	..
Sierra Leone	1	0	0	0	..	11	0	0	0	0	0	-11.4	-48.9	-15.4
Somalia	..	..	..	..	..	..	..	..	..	..	..	..	..	..
South Africa	..	0	1	2	2	3	0	1	1	3	1	..	..	43.1
Sudan	..	..	..	..	..	..	..	..	..	..	..	..	..	..
Swaziland	..	..	..	..	..	..	..	..	..	0	..	..	..	..
Tanzania	1	..	0	..	..	..	..	..	1	0	0	..	..	..
Togo	10	0	0	2	0	0	..	..	..	..	..	-13.6	-15.9	..
Uganda	..	..	..	..	..	..	..	..	..	3	2	..	..	..
Zambia	..	..	..	0	..	..	..	..	..	..	..	..	..	..
Zimbabwe	..	0	0	0	..	..	..	..	..	..	..	..	..	..
NORTH AFRICA	..	0	0	..	0	0	0	0	0	0	0	..	..	-12.9
Algeria	..	..	..	..	..	..	..	..	..	..	..	..	..	..
Egypt, Arab Republic	..	..	0	..	0	0	0	0	0	0	0	..	..	-15.1
Libya	..	..	..	..	..	..	..	..	..	..	..	..	..	..
Morocco	..	0	..	..	..	..	0	..	..	0	0	..	..	..
Tunisia	..	..	..	..	..	..	..	0	0	0	..	..	..	..
ALL AFRICA	280	233	195	269	319	247	187	221	181	207	191	-12.2	9.5	-1.9

5-28. Sisal exports

	Thousands of metric tons											Average annual percentage growth		
	1980	1991	1992	1993	1994	1995	1996	1997	1998	1999	2000	75-84	85-89	90-MR
SUB-SAHARAN AFRICA	109	42	44	42	41	47	36	36	34	33	29	-9.6	-8.7	-7.0
excluding South Africa	109	42	43	42	41	47	36	36	34	33	29	-9.7	-8.7	-7.0
excl. S.Africa & Nigeria	109	42	43	42	41	47	36	36	34	33	29	-9.7	-8.7	-7.0
Angola	3	0	0	0	0	0	0	0	0	0	0	-30.8	..	..
Benin	0	0	0	0	0	0	0	0	..	..	..	..	..	..
Botswana	0	0	0	0	0	0	0	0	0	0	0	..	..	..
Burkina Faso	0	0	0	0	0	0	0	0	..	..	..	..	..	..
Burundi	0	0	0	0	0	0	0	0	..	..	..	..	..	..
Cameroon	0	0	0	0	0	0	0	0	..	..	..	..	..	..
Cape Verde	0	0	0	0	0	0	0	0	..	..	..	..	..	..
Central African Republic	0	0	0	0	0	0	0	0	0	0	0	..	..	..
Chad	0	0	0	0	0	0	0	0	..	..	..	..	..	..
Comoros	0	0	0	0	0	0	0	0	0	0	0	..	..	..
Congo, Democratic Rep. of	0	0	0	0	0	0	0	0	0	0	0	..	..	..
Congo, Republic of	0	0	0	0	0	0	0	0	..	..	..	..	..	..
Côte d'Ivoire	0	0	0	0	0	0	0	0	0	0	0	..	..	-2.2
Djibouti	0	0	0	0	0	0	0	0	..	..	..	..	..	..
Equatorial Guinea	0	0	0	0	0	0	0	0	..	..	..	..	..	..
Eritrea	0	0	0	0	0	0	0	0	..	..	..	..	..	..
Ethiopia	0	0	0	0	0	0	0	0	..	..	..	..	..	..
Gabon	0	0	0	0	0	0	0	0	..	..	..	..	..	..
Gambia, The	0	0	0	0	0	0	0	0	..	..	..	..	..	..
Ghana	0	0	0	0	0	0	0	0	..	..	..	..	..	..
Guinea	0	0	0	0	0	0	0	0	..	..	..	..	..	..
Guinea-Bissau	0	0	0	0	0	0	0	0	..	..	..	..	..	..
Kenya	40	28	32	27	26	25	17	19	18	17	17	-1.3	-4.8	-7.3
Lesotho	0	0	0	0	0	0	0	0	..	..	..	..	..	..
Liberia	0	0	0	0	0	0	0	0	..	..	..	..	..	..
Madagascar	10	10	7	9	8	10	10	4	3	5	5	-5.9	-8.1	-8.1
Malawi	0	0	0	0	0	0	0	0	0	0	0	..	..	..
Mali	0	0	0	0	0	0	0	0	..	..	..	..	..	..
Mauritania	0	0	0	0	0	0	0	0	..	..	..	..	..	..
Mauritius	0	0	0	0	0	0	0	0	..	..	..	..	..	..
Mozambique	7	0	0	0	0	0	0	0	0	0	0	-14.5	1.7	-11.5
Namibia	0	0	0	0	0	0	0	0	..	..	..	..	..	..
Niger	0	0	0	0	0	0	0	0	..	..	..	..	..	..
Nigeria	0	0	0	0	0	0	0	0	..	..	..	..	..	..
Rwanda	0	0	0	0	0	0	0	0	..	..	..	..	..	..
São Tomé and Principe	0	0	0	0	0	0	0	0	..	..	..	..	..	..
Senegal	0	0	0	0	0	0	0	0	0	0	0	38.6	..	..
Seychelles	0	0	0	0	0	0	0	0	..	..	..	..	..	..
Sierra Leone	0	0	0	0	0	0	0	0	..	..	..	..	..	..
Somalia	0	0	0	0	0	0	0	0	0	0	0	..	..	..
South Africa	0	0	0	0	0	0	0	0	0	0	0	-4.4	-7.3	-12.5
Sudan	0	0	0	0	0	0	0	0	..	..	..	..	..	..
Swaziland	0	0	0	0	0	0	0	0	0	0	0	..	..	..
Tanzania	48	5	4	5	7	11	9	13	14	12	7	-12.1	-16.9	5.9
Togo	0	0	0	0	0	0	0	0	..	..	..	..	..	..
Uganda	0	0	0	0	0	0	0	0	0	0	0	..	..	..
Zambia	0	0	0	0	0	0	0	0	..	..	..	..	..	..
Zimbabwe	0	0	0	0	0	0	0	0	..	..	..	..	..	..
NORTH AFRICA	0	0	0	0	0	0	0	0	0	0	0	..	..	32.9
Algeria	0	0	0	0	0	0	0	0	..	..	..	..	..	..
Egypt, Arab Republic	0	0	0	0	0	0	0	0	0	0	0	..	..	..
Libya	0	0	0	0	0	0	0	0	..	..	..	..	..	..
Morocco	0	0	0	0	0	0	0	0	0	0	0	..	..	26.5
Tunisia	0	0	0	0	0	0	0	0	0	0	0	..	..	-8.5
ALL AFRICA	109	42	44	42	41	47	36	36	34	33	29	-9.6	-8.7	-7.0

5-29. Tea exports

	Thousands of metric tons											Average annual percentage growth		
	1980	*1991*	*1992*	*1993*	*1994*	*1995*	*1996*	*1997*	*1998*	*1999*	*2000*	*75-84*	*85-89*	*90-MR*
SUB-SAHARAN AFRICA	182	277	271	298	263	337	339	309	381	362	377	3.8	4.9	2.1
excluding South Africa	180	275	270	297	262	336	338	308	378	357	367	3.7	4.8	2.0
excl. S.Africa & Nigeria	180	275	270	297	262	335	338	308	378	357	367	3.7	4.8	2.0
Angola	0	0	0	0	0	0	0	0	0	0	0	..	..	..
Benin	0	0	0	0	0	0	0	0	..	..	..	..	..	..
Botswana	0	0	0	0	0	0	0	0	0	0	0	21.8	-48.8	27.2
Burkina Faso	0	0	0	0	0	0	0	0	0	0	0	-6.7	..	..
Burundi	1	5	6	5	7	7	4	6	6	7	3	12.3	2.6	-3.2
Cameroon	1	0	0	0	0	0	0	0	0	0	0	23.2	-32.4	-36.1
Cape Verde	0	0	0	0	0	0	0	0	..	..	..	..	..	..
Central African Republic	0	0	0	0	0	0	0	0	0	0	0	..	..	..
Chad	0	0	0	0	0	0	0	0	0	0	0	..	..	..
Comoros	0	0	0	0	0	0	0	0	0	0	0	..	..	..
Congo, Democratic Rep. of	1	2	1	2	2	1	2	1	1	1	1	-8.5	-4.9	-5.9
Congo, Republic of	0	0	0	0	0	0	0	0	0	0	0	..	..	..
Côte d'Ivoire	0	0	0	0	0	0	0	0	0	0	0	..	..	..
Djibouti	0	0	0	0	0	0	0	0	2	0	0	..	..	..
Equatorial Guinea	0	0	0	0	0	0	0	0	..	..	..	..	..	..
Eritrea	0	0	0	0	0	0	0	0	..	..	..	..	..	..
Ethiopia	..	..	..	0	0	0	0	0	0	0	0	..	..	-11.8
Gabon	0	0	0	0	0	0	0	0	..	..	..	..	..	..
Gambia, The	0	0	0	0	0	0	0	0	0	0	0	..	..	..
Ghana	0	0	0	0	0	0	0	0	0	0	0	..	..	..
Guinea	0	0	0	0	0	0	0	0	..	..	..	..	..	..
Guinea-Bissau	0	0	0	0	0	0	0	0	..	..	..	..	..	..
Kenya	84	176	172	199	177	259	261	199	264	246	217	6.7	8.4	3.3
Lesotho	0	0	0	0	0	0	0	0	..	..	..	..	..	..
Liberia	0	0	0	0	0	0	0	0	0	0	0	..	..	..
Madagascar	0	0	0	0	0	0	0	0	0	0	0	..	-54.8	38.1
Malawi	31	37	37	35	35	32	32	40	41	30	70	3.8	-0.2	1.5
Mali	0	0	0	0	0	0	0	0	0	0	0	..	..	..
Mauritania	0	0	0	0	0	0	0	0	..	..	..	..	..	..
Mauritius	4	4	5	4	4	3	1	0	0	0	0	8.2	-7.0	-37.6
Mozambique	30	1	1	0	0	0	0	0	0	0	0	-0.2	-48.5	-9.0
Namibia	0	0	0	0	0	0	0	0	0	0	0	..	..	..
Niger	0	0	0	0	0	0	0	0	0	0	0	..	..	..
Nigeria	0	0	0	0	0	0	0	0	0	0	0	..	..	16.7
Rwanda	7	13	13	12	5	3	3	10	12	10	12	8.5	8.0	-3.2
São Tomé and Principe	0	0	0	0	0	0	0	0	..	..	..	..	..	..
Senegal	0	0	0	0	0	0	0	0	0	0	0	-8.6	281.6	..
Seychelles	0	0	0	0	0	0	0	0	0	0	0	-7.6	..	-1.9
Sierra Leone	0	0	0	0	0	0	0	0	..	..	..	..	..	..
Somalia	0	0	0	0	0	0	0	0	0	0	0	..	..	..
South Africa	2	1	1	1	1	1	1	1	3	5	10	44.8	13.6	18.7
Sudan	0	0	0	0	0	0	0	0	..	..	..	..	..	..
Swaziland	0	0	0	0	0	0	0	0	0	0	0	..	..	..
Tanzania	13	18	20	20	22	22	22	19	21	22	17	2.6	1.2	3.2
Togo	0	0	0	0	0	0	0	0	0	0	0	..	..	..
Uganda	1	7	8	10	0	0	0	17	19	22	26	-28.0	11.3	16.4
Zambia	0	0	0	0	0	0	0	0	0	1	1	..	..	50.2
Zimbabwe	6	11	6	8	10	9	12	13	11	16	17	10.5	5.4	1.0
NORTH AFRICA	0	0	0	0	0	0	0	0	0	0	1	..	87.0	20.7
Algeria	0	0	0	0	0	0	0	0	0	0	0	..	..	..
Egypt, Arab Republic	0	0	0	0	0	0	0	0	0	0	1	..	..	31.3
Libya	0	0	0	0	0	0	0	0	0	0	0	..	..	..
Morocco	0	0	0	0	0	0	0	0	0	0	0	..	..	53.8
Tunisia	0	0	0	0	0	0	0	0	0	0	0	..	..	-35.0
ALL AFRICA	182	277	271	298	263	337	339	309	381	362	378	3.8	4.9	2.1

5-30. Sugar exports

	Thousands of metric tons											Average annual percentage growth		
	1980	1991	1992	1993	1994	1995	1996	1997	1998	1999	2000	75-84	85-89	90-MR
SUB-SAHARAN AFRICA	2,148	2,068	1,627	1,259	1,742	1,605	2,356	2,689	2,861	2,720	3,557	0.8	2.6	4.3
excluding South Africa	1,362	1,356	1,343	1,118	1,423	1,215	1,523	1,684	1,629	1,582	2,083	3.1	0.5	2.4
excl. S.Africa & Nigeria	1,362	1,356	1,343	1,118	1,423	1,215	1,523	1,684	1,629	1,582	2,082	3.1	0.3	2.4
Angola	0	0	0	0	0	0	0	0	0	0	0	..	..	..
Benin	0	0	0	0	0	0	0	0	0	0	0	..	..	..
Botswana	0	0	0	0	0	0	1	1	0	0	0	-14.0	65.9	22.5
Burkina Faso	2	0	0	0	0	0	0	0	0	0	3	91.6	..	..
Burundi	0	0	10	0	0	0	4	0	1	2	5	..	..	38.2
Cameroon	9	2	0	1	0	1	7	1	1	1	0	42.1	-24.4	-9.0
Cape Verde	0	0	0	0	0	0	0	0	0	0	0	..	..	..
Central African Republic	0	0	0	0	0	0	0	0	0	0	0	..	..	-4.2
Chad	0	0	0	0	0	0	0	0	0	0	0	..	..	..
Comoros	0	0	0	0	0	0	0	0	..	..	..	..	..	..
Congo, Democratic Rep. of	0	0	0	0	0	0	0	0	0	0	0	..	..	..
Congo, Republic of	0	23	29	18	11	14	7	37	21	25	33	-1.3	-14.0	5.2
Côte d'Ivoire	11	40	23	39	33	12	28	41	12	25	71	142.4	-18.9	2.9
Djibouti	0	0	0	0	0	0	0	0	10	50	52	..	..	..
Equatorial Guinea	0	0	0	0	0	0	0	0	..	..	..	..	..	..
Eritrea	..	..	..	0	0	0	0	0	0	0	0	..	..	..
Ethiopia	..	..	..	15	5	0	0	0	0	0	65	..	..	..
Gabon	2	8	7	0	0	0	0	0	0	0	0	9.3	..	..
Gambia, The	0	0	0	0	..	..	..	..	..	..	..	..	..	..
Ghana	0	0	0	0	0	0	1	0	0	2	4	..	..	..
Guinea	0	0	0	0	0	0	0	0	0	0	0	..	..	..
Guinea-Bissau	0	0	0	0	0	0	0	0	0	0	0	..	..	..
Kenya	56	0	104	50	112	13	52	31	2	5	4	19.0	-15.5	31.7
Lesotho	0	0	0	0	0	0	0	0	..	..	..	..	..	..
Liberia	0	0	0	0	0	0	0	0	0	0	0	8.1	..	..
Madagascar	26	21	17	11	24	15	7	1	1	7	1	-1.1	19.9	-30.4
Malawi	92	51	22	26	34	66	55	30	72	48	48	13.9	-5.4	1.8
Mali	0	0	0	0	0	0	0	0	0	0	0	..	..	..
Mauritania	0	0	0	0	0	0	0	0	..	..	..	..	..	..
Mauritius	618	551	598	535	519	524	773	575	602	534	424	-0.7	4.4	-0.8
Mozambique	64	25	52	0	52	54	25	59	20	20	69	-12.8	-8.1	2.6
Namibia	0	0	0	0	0	0	0	0	0	0	5	..	..	..
Niger	0	0	0	0	0	0	0	0	1	0	2	..	..	5.8
Nigeria	0	0	0	0	0	0	0	0	0	0	1	..	..	16.5
Rwanda	0	0	0	0	0	0	0	0	0	0	0	..	..	..
São Tomé and Principe	0	0	0	0	0	0	0	0	..	..	..	..	..	..
Senegal	0	0	0	0	0	0	0	0	0	0	0	-34.3	244.7	-8.0
Seychelles	0	0	0	0	0	0	0	0	0	0	0	..	..	..
Sierra Leone	0	0	0	0	0	0	0	0	0	0	0	..	..	..
Somalia	0	0	0	0	0	0	0	0	0	0	0	..	..	..
South Africa	786	712	284	141	318	390	833	1,005	1,233	1,138	1,474	-2.7	6.2	8.8
Sudan	0	49	54	39	136	20	49	154	224	183	60	..	..	7.4
Swaziland	300	492	379	363	279	275	241	466	345	395	859	9.2	1.5	0.4
Tanzania	13	0	11	11	11	11	12	4	18	25	18	33.4	0.9	1.5
Togo	0	0	0	0	0	0	0	0	0	0	3	..	..	30.4
Uganda	0	0	0	0	1	1	0	1	1	5	2	..	..	18.1
Zambia	0	4	26	11	7	50	69	63	89	90	76	60.8	-21.0	42.8
Zimbabwe	169	89	12	0	201	160	192	219	207	165	278	3.9	-7.3	15.2
NORTH AFRICA	23	25	1	1	7	6	4	1	33	31	0	-29.0	53.1	-1.7
Algeria	0	13	0	0	0	0	0	0	0	0	0	..	..	..
Egypt, Arab Republic	10	8	1	1	7	6	4	0	2	0	0	-12.4	134.0	-19.8
Libya	0	0	0	0	0	0	0	0	31	31	0	..	..	..
Morocco	0	0	0	0	0	0	0	0	0	0	0	..	-17.5	25.6
Tunisia	13	4	0	0	0	0	0	0	0	0	0	-28.6	-44.5	-7.3
ALL AFRICA	2,171	2,093	1,628	1,260	1,749	1,611	2,360	2,690	2,894	2,751	3,557	0.4	2.7	4.4

5-31. Tobacco exports

	Hundreds of metric tons											Average annual percentage growth		
	1980	1991	1992	1993	1994	1995	1996	1997	1998	1999	2000	75-84	85-89	90-MR
SUB-SAHARAN AFRICA	1,777	2,529	2,835	3,204	4,439	3,150	3,678	3,491	3,777	3,178	3,587	3.0	0.4	4.9
excluding South Africa	1,705	2,439	2,754	3,110	4,269	3,038	3,590	3,370	3,633	3,019	3,444	3.2	0.2	4.7
excl. S.Africa & Nigeria	1,705	2,438	2,749	3,108	4,265	3,037	3,582	3,367	3,631	3,017	3,444	3.2	0.2	4.7
Angola	16	0	0	0	0	0	0	0	0	0	0	-4.7	..	..
Benin	0	0	0	0	0	0	0	0	0	0	0	-36.9	..	..
Botswana	1	0	0	0	0	0	1	1	1	1	0	32.5	-1.9	16.0
Burkina Faso	0	0	0	0	0	0	0	0	0	2	0	..	..	..
Burundi	0	11	11	10	4	0	2	0	1	0	0	..	89.6	-43.2
Cameroon	21	7	7	6	1	3	0	1	3	1	2	-7.9	-11.6	-14.5
Cape Verde	0	0	0	0	0	0	0	0	..	..	..	..	..	..
Central African Republic	8	1	1	1	1	2	1	1	1	1	2	-8.6	-2.0	5.6
Chad	0	0	0	0	0	0	0	0	0	0	0	..	..	..
Comoros	0	0	0	0	0	0	0	0	..	..	..	..	..	..
Congo, Democratic Rep. of	0	35	18	40	30	14	15	12	3	1	2	..	..	-20.1
Congo, Republic of	1	0	0	0	0	0	0	0	0	0	0	-23.6	-46.4	..
Côte d'Ivoire	0	0	0	0	0	2	1	2	2	3	3	-2.6	..	20.3
Djibouti	0	0	0	0	0	0	0	0	..	..	..	..	..	..
Equatorial Guinea	0	0	0	0	0	0	0	0	..	..	..	..	..	..
Eritrea	0	0	0	0	0	0	0	0	..	..	..	..	..	..
Ethiopia	..	..	..	0	0	0	0	0	0	0	0	..	..	..
Gabon	0	0	0	0	0	0	0	0	..	..	..	..	..	..
Gambia, The	0	0	0	0	0	1	0	0	0	0	0	..	..	..
Ghana	0	3	2	3	5	2	7	4	2	3	2	-33.6	-12.6	2.1
Guinea	0	0	0	0	0	0	0	0	0	0	0	..	..	..
Guinea-Bissau	0	0	0	0	0	0	0	0	0	0	0	..	..	..
Kenya	0	19	48	56	29	30	76	51	50	44	53	9.8	31.8	28.0
Lesotho	0	0	0	0	0	0	0	0	..	..	..	..	..	..
Liberia	0	0	0	0	0	0	0	0	0	0	0	3.3	..	..
Madagascar	1	0	0	0	0	4	4	1	0	0	0	-11.2	-6.9	-0.1
Malawi	611	982	973	957	983	980	1,121	1,168	1,296	956	903	8.4	-3.3	2.6
Mali	0	0	0	0	0	0	0	0	0	0	0	-53.9	..	..
Mauritania	0	0	0	0	0	0	0	0	..	..	..	..	..	..
Mauritius	0	0	0	0	0	0	0	0	0	0	0	..	..	..
Mozambique	0	0	0	0	0	0	0	0	0	0	0	..	..	..
Namibia	0	0	0	0	0	0	0	0	0	0	0	..	..	..
Niger	3	0	0	0	1	4	6	5	4	1	1	39.9	..	-14.0
Nigeria	0	1	5	2	4	2	9	3	2	2	0	..	..	14.9
Rwanda	0	0	0	0	0	0	0	0	..	..	..	..	..	..
São Tomé and Principe	0	0	0	0	0	0	0	0	..	..	..	..	..	..
Senegal	0	0	0	1	1	1	1	2	2	4	8	..	..	12.0
Seychelles	0	0	0	0	0	0	0	0	..	..	..	..	..	..
Sierra Leone	0	2	7	2	2	2	2	2	2	1	5	..	23.3	2.0
Somalia	0	0	0	0	0	0	0	0	0	0	0	..	..	..
South Africa	72	90	81	94	169	112	88	121	145	159	143	-1.8	7.0	8.5
Sudan	0	0	0	0	0	0	0	0	0	0	1	..	..	..
Swaziland	2	0	0	1	1	1	1	0	0	0	0	-17.4	-22.6	-20.3
Tanzania	83	80	127	106	154	171	249	355	214	263	473	-7.4	6.4	14.2
Togo	0	0	0	0	0	0	0	0	0	0	0	4.7	..	..
Uganda	3	25	23	41	34	51	21	83	72	47	153	-8.6	-20.7	19.6
Zambia	26	13	25	41	30	9	34	31	38	51	64	-13.6	0.0	14.2
Zimbabwe	930	1,261	1,505	1,843	2,989	1,760	2,042	1,650	1,941	1,639	1,771	3.9	2.3	4.4
NORTH AFRICA	15	11	7	7	9	12	4	6	5	3	2	6.5	-7.2	-11.9
Algeria	0	0	0	0	0	0	0	0	0	0	0	..	..	..
Egypt, Arab Republic	0	0	0	0	0	0	0	0	0	0	0	..	..	-39.8
Libya	0	0	0	0	0	0	0	0	0	0	0	..	..	..
Morocco	0	0	3	3	1	0	0	0	0	0	0	..	..	..
Tunisia	15	11	4	4	8	12	4	6	5	3	2	26.9	-5.4	-9.1
ALL AFRICA	1,792	2,540	2,843	3,211	4,448	3,162	3,683	3,498	3,782	3,181	3,589	3.0	0.4	4.8

5-32. Meat exports

	Hundreds of metric tons											Average annual percentage growth		
	1980	1991	1992	1993	1994	1995	1996	1997	1998	1999	2000	75-84	85-89	90-MR
SUB-SAHARAN AFRICA	1,436	839	928	1,281	1,153	1,418	1,321	1,063	1,238	1,241	1,014	-6.8	-8.8	2.9
excluding South Africa	895	754	837	1,133	1,068	1,115	979	922	1,045	1,049	794	-7.2	-8.8	1.5
excl. S.Africa & Nigeria	895	754	836	1,133	1,068	1,115	979	922	1,045	1,049	794	-7.2	-8.8	1.5
Angola	0	0	0	0	0	0	0	0	0	0	0	..	..	..
Benin	0	0	0	0	0	0	0	0	0	1	9	..	..	..
Botswana	249	256	240	279	250	241	201	228	262	173	212	-0.8	-8.6	-0.6
Burkina Faso	3	0	0	0	0	0	0	0	1	0	0	-4.6	-52.2	..
Burundi	0	0	0	0	0	0	0	0	0	0	0	..	..	..
Cameroon	0	0	0	0	0	0	0	0	0	0	0	-53.6	-61.3	-0.5
Cape Verde	0	0	0	0	0	0	0	0	0	0	0	..	..	..
Central African Republic	20	0	0	0	0	0	0	0	0	0	0	-19.8	..	..
Chad	0	2	2	2	2	2	2	2	2	2	2	-37.5	14.5	-1.6
Comoros	0	0	0	0	0	0	1	0	0	0	0	..	..	..
Congo, Democratic Rep. of	0	0	0	0	0	0	0	0	0	0	0	..	..	..
Congo, Republic of	0	0	0	0	1	0	0	0	0	0	0	..	..	7.2
Côte d'Ivoire	2	0	0	0	0	0	0	1	0	0	1	11.9	..	21.7
Djibouti	0	0	0	0	0	0	0	0	0	0	0	..	..	..
Equatorial Guinea	0	0	0	0	0	0	0	0	..	..	..	..	..	..
Eritrea	0	0	0	0	0	0	0	0	..	..	..	..	..	..
Ethiopia	..	..	..	0	2	6	6	18	25	19	12	..	..	60.8
Gabon	0	0	0	0	0	0	0	0	0	0	0	..	..	49.5
Gambia, The	0	0	0	0	0	0	0	0	0	0	0	..	..	..
Ghana	0	0	0	0	0	0	0	0	0	0	2	..	..	..
Guinea	0	0	0	0	0	0	0	0	0	0	0	..	..	..
Guinea-Bissau	0	0	0	0	0	0	0	0	0	0	0	..	..	..
Kenya	16	28	6	10	11	8	11	12	12	12	7	-11.6	-54.6	-1.1
Lesotho	0	0	0	0	0	0	0	0	0	0	0	..	..	..
Liberia	0	0	0	0	0	0	0	0	0	0	0	..	..	..
Madagascar	72	5	17	22	30	49	24	8	1	0	1	-16.0	-61.1	-11.8
Malawi	0	0	0	0	0	0	0	0	0	0	0	..	-61.0	..
Mali	0	0	0	0	0	0	0	0	0	0	0	-24.4	..	..
Mauritania	0	0	0	0	0	0	0	0	0	0	0	..	..	..
Mauritius	0	4	16	32	65	69	45	52	32	11	5	13.7	44.6	-6.8
Mozambique	0	0	0	0	0	0	0	0	0	0	0	9.6	..	..
Namibia	306	350	360	438	459	425	391	265	372	513	151	5.1	5.8	-2.5
Niger	0	0	0	0	0	0	0	0	0	1	1	-20.1	..	12.8
Nigeria	0	0	1	0	0	0	0	0	0	0	0	..	..	..
Rwanda	0	0	0	0	0	0	0	0	..	..	..	..	..	..
São Tomé and Principe	0	0	0	0	0	0	0	0	..	..	..	..	..	..
Senegal	3	0	1	1	1	0	0	1	1	1	1	3.1	-18.2	-3.1
Seychelles	0	0	0	0	0	0	0	0	0	0	0	..	..	..
Sierra Leone	0	0	0	0	0	0	0	0	0	0	0	..	..	..
Somalia	10	0	0	0	0	0	0	0	0	0	0	-40.8	..	..
South Africa	542	85	91	148	84	304	342	141	193	192	220	-7.0	-9.2	11.2
Sudan	0	0	7	61	40	65	134	174	148	83	109	-12.0	..	30.0
Swaziland	35	15	4	10	10	9	10	16	21	22	75	-5.1	-53.1	19.7
Tanzania	2	0	0	0	0	0	0	1	2	4	4	-37.0	..	..
Togo	0	0	0	0	0	0	0	0	0	1	3	..	..	28.1
Uganda	0	0	0	0	0	1	0	0	0	0	0	..	..	-13.4
Zambia	0	1	0	1	1	1	1	1	1	1	1	-11.8	51.9	1.2
Zimbabwe	175	91	183	275	195	238	151	143	164	205	200	-16.5	-19.4	-5.1
NORTH AFRICA	34	12	45	39	24	17	13	19	20	18	17	-2.2	19.8	-7.2
Algeria	0	0	0	0	0	0	0	0	0	0	0	-58.2	..	..
Egypt, Arab Republic	1	11	43	37	21	14	10	14	11	7	8	-0.4	60.4	-11.6
Libya	0	0	0	0	0	0	0	0	0	0	0	..	..	..
Morocco	32	0	0	1	2	2	2	3	3	5	3	-2.5	-19.9	56.3
Tunisia	1	1	2	1	2	1	1	2	5	6	6	-6.5	-9.8	20.0
ALL AFRICA	1,471	851	973	1,320	1,177	1,435	1,334	1,082	1,258	1,259	1,032	-6.7	-8.5	2.6

5-33. Manufactured goods exports

	Millions of U.S. dollars (current prices)											*Annual Average*		
	1980	*1992*	*1993*	*1994*	*1995*	*1996*	*1997*	*1998*	*1999*	*2000*	*2001*	*75-84*	*85-89*	*90-MR*
SUB-SAHARAN AFRICA	4,315	9,764	10,127	11,387	14,354	14,406	15,250	15,647	15,597	18,398	10,280	3,254	7,356	12,956
excluding South Africa	767	4,112	4,155	4,593	5,850	6,201	5,795	5,477	5,579	5,881	5,724	654	2,998	5,126
excl. S.Africa & Nigeria	767	4,076	4,115	4,546	5,779	6,154	5,755	5,337	5,553	5,850	5,679	654	2,984	5,069
Angola	..	66	63	72	78	105	101	62	75	132	111	..	89	81
Benin	..	0	0	0	0	0	..	..	..	..	..	0	0	0
Botswana	..	..	48	144	336	299	368	305	198	111	30	..	..	204
Burkina Faso	..	..	..	..	..	..	..	..	..	..	..	..	..	..
Burundi	1	11	9	5	7	4	1	0	1	1	1	3	8	4
Cameroon	96	241	227	204	259	302	291	423	399	381	351	81	232	309
Cape Verde	..	1	1	2	6	0	0	0	0	0	0	..	1	1
Central African Republic	..	0	0	0	0	0	0	0	0	0	0	..	0	0
Chad	..	1	0	0	1	2	1	27	29	..	..	5	4	6
Comoros	..	0	0	0	0	0	0	0	0	0	0	0	0	0
Congo, Democratic Rep. of	..	163	93	140	225	305	..	..	..	97	129	..	..	181
Congo, Republic of	0	25	20	13	23	17	16	10	12	12	12	6	40	18
Côte d'Ivoire	..	1,037	956	1,012	1,294	1,329	1,210	1,179	1,309	1,299	1,277	672	841	1,170
Djibouti	..	..	..	..	26	27	29	39	46	46	50	..	..	38
Equatorial Guinea	..	0	0	0	0	0	0	0	0	0	0	0	0	0
Eritrea	..	1	16	21	31	41	20	6	8	4	9	..	..	16
Ethiopia	..	0	0	0	0	0	0	0	0	0	0	..	0	0
Gabon	..	0	0	0	0	0	0	0	0	0	0	0	0	0
Gambia, The	..	..	..	..	..	..	..	..	..	..	..	..	..	..
Ghana	..	..	..	..	..	..	..	..	..	..	..	..	..	..
Guinea	..	0	0	0	0	0	0	0	0	0	0	..	0	0
Guinea-Bissau	..	..	..	..	..	..	..	..	..	..	..	..	..	..
Kenya	177	144	230	224	298	290	283	220	238	252	274	128	127	230
Lesotho	..	..	..	..	..	..	..	..	27	7	6	..	..	13
Liberia	..	..	..	..	..	..	..	..	..	..	..	..	..	..
Madagascar	..	158	175	191	296	318	346	356	398	618	557	42	61	307
Malawi	..	28	32	39	49	69	74	63	56	56	60	..	40	48
Mali	..	..	..	..	..	..	..	..	..	..	..	..	..	..
Mauritania	..	..	..	..	..	..	..	..	..	..	..	0	..	..
Mauritius	108	804	861	887	1,004	1,104	1,098	1,034	1,135	1,171	1,177	117	415	976
Mozambique	..	14	7	3	5	8	20	14	14	14	15	0	0	15
Namibia	158	318	256	302	320	343	223	237	289	297	301	169	236	278
Niger	..	0	0	0	0	0	0	0	..	..	..	0	0	0
Nigeria	..	36	40	47	70	47	40	140	27	30	45	..	34	56
Rwanda	..	2	7	2	4	5	18	10	16	42	48	4	4	13
São Tomé and Principe	..	..	..	..	..	..	..	..	..	..	..	..	..	..
Senegal	136	190	164	201	254	250	254	258	242	241	250	171	157	225
Seychelles	..	13	11	17	18	34	57	60	63	67	71	0	5	36
Sierra Leone	..	0	0	0	0	0	0	0	0	0	0	0	0	0
Somalia	..	..	..	..	..	..	..	..	..	..	..	..	..	..
South Africa	3,548	5,653	5,972	6,794	8,504	8,205	9,455	10,170	10,018	12,517	4,556	2,600	4,358	7,830
Sudan	..	..	..	..	..	..	..	..	..	108	..	31	30	59
Swaziland	..	26	56	52	66	87	81	76	69	67	65	..	20	55
Tanzania	91	64	52	77	109	123	111	30	22	34	56	54	56	68
Togo	..	128	75	60	86	78	74	78	79	65	73	66	92	91
Uganda	..	..	..	..	..	..	..	..	..	..	..	..	..	..
Zambia	..	62	103	129	155	168	180	194	189	163	203	101	47	138
Zimbabwe	..	579	652	750	829	846	900	655	640	567	552	319	495	677
NORTH AFRICA	1,292	6,719	6,332	7,178	9,189	8,761	8,824	9,693	10,271	10,927	11,432	1,039	2,851	8,414
Algeria	..	213	68	28	30	31	40	42	46	81	124	7	105	99
Egypt, Arab Republic	..	1,461	1,167	1,127	1,655	1,314	1,302	1,685	2,080	2,845	3,187	..	868	1,691
Libya	..	..	..	..	..	..	..	..	..	..	..	..	..	..
Morocco	387	2,612	2,710	3,010	3,754	3,673	3,802	3,932	4,087	3,997	3,822	320	1,093	3,335
Tunisia	905	2,432	2,387	3,012	3,750	3,742	3,680	4,033	4,058	4,005	4,300	718	1,133	3,290
ALL AFRICA	5,607	16,483	16,459	18,565	23,543	23,167	24,074	25,340	25,868	29,325	21,712	4,292	10,207	21,370

5-34. Manufactured goods exports, growth

	Percent											Average annual percentage growth		
	1980	1992	1993	1994	1995	1996	1997	1998	1999	2000	2001	75-84	85-89	90-MR
SUB-SAHARAN AFRICA	388.6	-5.3	1.8	14.2	7.7	11.4	3.4	-2.2	6.7	4.8	1.1	38.0	42.4	4.9
excluding South Africa	388.6	-5.3	1.8	14.2	7.7	11.4	3.4	-2.2	6.7	4.8	1.1	38.0	38.4	4.9
excl. S.Africa & Nigeria	388.6	-4.2	1.7	14.2	7.4	11.9	3.5	-3.9	8.8	4.8	0.9	38.0	38.1	5.0
Angola	..	-6.4	28.4	11.7	-4.6	4.7	-0.6	-20.1	8.2	1.8	0.0	..	9.4	-0.3
Benin	..	..	..	..	..	..	..	..	..	..	..	..	..	..
Botswana	..	..	..	189.3	120.8	-6.2	32.0	-14.0	-34.8	-42.7	-71.7	..	..	-3.8
Burkina Faso	..	..	..	..	..	..	..	..	..	..	..	..	..	..
Burundi	..	185.4	-19.2	-39.1	19.1	-36.3	-87.7	3.0	2.2	6.2	6.1	..	0.3	-22.3
Cameroon	21.3	1.1	-0.4	-4.6	-5.5	21.1	5.6	2.7	20.0	5.0	8.0	13.0	0.7	3.1
Cape Verde	..	..	..	..	..	..	..	..	..	..	..	..	..	..
Central African Republic	..	..	..	..	..	..	..	..	..	..	..	..	..	..
Chad	..	-2.9	-4.5	-0.8	22.6	14.0	0.0	5.0	6.1	..	..	..	..	4.7
Comoros	..	..	..	..	..	..	..	100.0	50.0	..	..	..	..	..
Congo, Democratic Rep. of	..	..	..	..	..	..	..	..	..	..	..	..	..	..
Congo, Republic of	..	0.3	-33.3	0.0	0.0	0.0	0.0	0.0	0.0	0.0	0.0	..	..	-3.9
Côte d'Ivoire	..	5.5	-7.3	19.7	1.2	11.5	2.0	6.0	7.1	7.1	3.6	..	0.7	5.1
Djibouti	..	..	..	..	..	-0.2	1.1	31.4	14.9	-2.9	5.6	..	..	9.5
Equatorial Guinea	..	..	..	..	..	..	..	..	..	..	..	..	..	..
Eritrea	..	..	..	..	..	..	..	..	..	..	..	..	..	..
Ethiopia	..	..	..	..	..	..	..	..	..	..	..	..	..	..
Gabon	..	..	..	..	..	..	..	..	..	..	..	..	..	..
Gambia, The	..	..	..	..	..	..	..	..	..	..	..	..	..	..
Ghana	..	..	..	..	..	..	..	..	..	..	..	..	..	..
Guinea	..	..	..	..	..	..	..	..	..	..	..	..	..	..
Guinea-Bissau	..	..	..	..	..	..	..	..	..	..	..	..	..	..
Kenya	..	-8.3	7.0	10.2	9.4	18.8	5.2	2.9	7.7	5.9	8.8	..	-9.1	7.8
Lesotho	..	..	..	..	..	..	..	..	..	-73.2	-4.7	..	..	..
Liberia	..	..	..	..	..	..	..	..	..	..	..	..	..	..
Madagascar	..	7.3	11.1	13.1	64.3	2.3	1.2	-1.3	11.6	52.3	-11.1	..	22.1	16.8
Malawi	..	..	..	..	..	..	..	..	..	..	..	..	..	..
Mali	..	..	..	..	..	..	..	..	..	..	..	..	..	..
Mauritania	..	..	..	..	..	..	..	..	..	..	..	..	..	..
Mauritius	..	-0.5	4.8	0.8	8.1	9.5	5.8	-0.4	12.0	4.3	4.0	..	..	5.6
Mozambique	..	-66.6	-49.5	-55.5	43.4	67.8	159.7	-28.3	-2.2	0.0	8.8	..	..	22.5
Namibia	..	26.2	-19.4	13.7	-2.1	9.8	-33.3	9.2	24.9	5.5	4.0	..	3.0	0.5
Niger	..	..	..	..	..	..	..	..	..	..	..	..	..	..
Nigeria	..	-59.7	11.6	14.4	38.3	-30.6	-10.0	260.3	-81.2	11.0	45.4	..	..	-3.0
Rwanda	..	16.5	-25.9	-38.8	175.0	-15.5	2.8	-46.9	61.9	93.7	14.2	..	-22.1	2.4
São Tomé and Principe	..	..	..	..	..	..	..	..	..	..	..	..	..	..
Senegal	..	-48.3	12.7	14.0	-9.0	10.0	4.8	2.2	4.0	5.0	-9.7	..	0.8	-1.0
Seychelles	..	47.0	27.7	-61.0	33.2	-55.0	-100.0	..	..	..	..	..	..	-8.6
Sierra Leone	..	..	..	..	..	..	..	..	..	..	..	..	..	..
Somalia	..	..	..	..	..	..	..	..	..	..	..	..	..	..
South Africa	..	..	..	..	..	..	..	..	..	..	..	..	..	..
Sudan	..	..	..	..	..	..	..	..	..	..	..	..	..	..
Swaziland	..	92.5	113.9	-10.4	19.9	38.6	0.1	-2.6	-8.3	0.4	0.4	..	..	23.8
Tanzania	..	-100.0	-19.0	48.1	41.8	12.5	-9.4	-73.2	-27.9	59.1	64.3	..	..	-49.9
Togo	..	-164.5	192.4	-22.7	88.5	-94.3	1,063.5	29.6	..	..	..	..	..	..
Uganda	..	..	..	..	..	..	..	..	..	..	..	..	..	..
Zambia	..	28.9	67.3	19.9	11.3	13.5	12.5	12.2	-2.8	-11.5	26.1	..	38,646.5	14.5
Zimbabwe	..	1.3	8.8	20.2	-4.6	5.1	14.9	-25.1	0.2	-9.1	2.2	..	..	1.1
NORTH AFRICA	2.2	6.6	-6.7	13.6	16.9	-8.1	7.4	22.4	10.4	-33.7	7.5	11.8	22.9	4.3
Algeria	..	8.7	-23.6	-57.6	-1.5	7.6	27.3	4.6	9.2	..	..	..	100.0	-13.0
Egypt, Arab Republic	..	22.0	-21.9	-5.5	40.1	-20.9	-15.0	69.5	25.9	39.2	14.4	..	..	7.8
Libya	..	..	..	..	..	..	..	..	..	..	..	..	..	..
Morocco	2.2	5.5	4.0	7.1	15.6	2.5	8.6	5.4	6.8	0.4	0.2	5.5	23.6	6.8
Tunisia	..	-1.6	-4.0	34.9	8.5	-10.0	16.4	21.0	5.7	..	..	..	1.2	9.1
ALL AFRICA	80.8	1.6	-3.3	13.9	13.0	-0.3	5.6	11.7	9.0	-19.3	4.4	22.3	31.1	4.6

5-35. Food Imports

	Millions of U.S. dollars (current prices)											Annual Average		
	1980	1992	1993	1994	1995	1996	1997	1998	1999	2000	2001	75-84	85-89	90-MR
SUB-SAHARAN AFRICA	5,433	6,267	5,685	6,181	7,769	7,559	7,867	7,941	7,359	8,055	8,352	3,682	4,907	7,020
excluding South Africa	4,499	5,319	4,735	4,765	5,813	5,718	6,217	6,309	5,774	6,052	6,798	2,848	3,935	5,566
excl. S.Africa & Nigeria	1,339	4,512	3,964	4,027	4,753	4,789	4,997	4,913	4,258	4,291	4,754	941	3,033	4,429
Angola	..	244	203	215	205	275	365	..	..	..	..	..	263	231
Benin	..	117	113	85	134	136	130	138	128	135	202	80	141	125
Botswana	109	347	315	288	305	292	297	306	305	297	335	121	140	298
Burkina Faso	..	90	0	0	70	86	71	111	..	..	..	..	..	70
Burundi	18	11	19	30	29	11	11	10	11	11	12	19	14	15
Cameroon	82	189	161	189	123	138	155	173	169	162	181	70	134	169
Cape Verde	..	75	53	65	79	75	78	50	53	55	58	..	33	60
Central African Republic	..	30	25	23	29	22	20	23	23	18	14	20	26	24
Chad	..	0	6	25	22	21	18	4	4	..	..	..	16	12
Comoros	..	13	10	9	18	12	20	18	18	9	6	8	8	13
Congo, Democratic Rep. of	..	..	..	..	..	..	..	..	..	..	..	..	..	..
Congo, Republic of	0	34	36	15	16	18	19	20	21	23	24	10	23	24
Côte d'Ivoire	435	377	431	317	523	496	529	630	560	433	444	389	441	475
Djibouti	..	..	..	..	70	67	69	72	75	78	81	..	..	73
Equatorial Guinea	..	..	..	..	..	..	..	..	..	..	..	..	..	..
Eritrea	..	35	32	69	68	85	83	62	92	117	154	..	..	80
Ethiopia	..	131	167	126	181	103	17	28	100	116	241	126	219	120
Gabon	..	174	166	166	181	191	189	166	138	142	149	142	151	163
Gambia, The	..	53	52	46	55	50	57	82	64	0	0	..	7	40
Ghana	..	38	..	..	..	..	..	..	..	..	..	39	48	39
Guinea	..	49	53	76	77	76	77	79	82	87	93	..	12	64
Guinea-Bissau	..	32	25	17	26	25	31	17	31	34	30	16	14	25
Kenya	109	156	145	173	117	199	401	312	189	278	326	89	123	214
Lesotho	..	..	..	..	..	..	..	..	..	..	..	..	..	..
Liberia	..	..	..	..	..	..	..	..	..	..	..	..	..	..
Madagascar	89	58	51	79	67	60	49	54	46	77	84	87	42	59
Malawi	..	63	5	65	82	43	32	77	32	30	34	..	3	40
Mali	103	97	97	86	111	113	111	123	105	111	118	113	88	109
Mauritania	..	137	104	95	128	103	117	103	98	120	113	76	107	114
Mauritius	143	201	219	235	287	330	350	320	339	299	291	137	131	271
Mozambique	..	..	..	..	44	29	30	32	47	87	72	..	..	49
Namibia	..	297	286	301	331	333	352	321	322	334	344	..	..	312
Niger	..	22	22	16	18	19	27	36	..	..	..	..	30	26
Nigeria	3,161	807	771	738	1,060	929	1,219	1,397	1,516	1,761	2,044	1,906	902	1,137
Rwanda	..	29	59	218	56	51	54	57	35	47	52	27	31	60
São Tomé and Principe	..	6	7	7	7	6	5	5	5	5	5	8	7	6
Senegal	210	363	348	310	394	395	336	348	336	305	359	246	243	351
Seychelles	..	40	46	42	47	63	88	85	75	76	79	17	25	59
Sierra Leone	..	58	57	52	66	110	41	36	28	66	72	39	49	56
Somalia	..	..	..	..	..	..	..	..	..	..	..	..	..	..
South Africa	933	948	950	1,416	1,956	1,842	1,650	1,632	1,585	2,003	1,554	835	972	1,454
Sudan	..	166	205	181	215	232	238	264	276	340	311	219	189	244
Swaziland	42	110	135	136	202	172	170	169	164	160	155	32	49	147
Tanzania	..	25	58	97	97	54	57	169	200	176	169	96	86	100
Togo	..	131	82	75	96	149	209	212	..	..	..	118	137	141
Uganda	..	..	..	..	..	..	..	..	..	..	..	..	..	..
Zambia	..	258	50	55	98	25	12	108	0	9	10	24	16	58
Zimbabwe	..	257	121	43	78	119	84	90	88	54	135	77	28	128
NORTH AFRICA	3,100	5,431	5,364	5,541	7,766	7,034	7,192	7,746	6,142	5,735	6,319	2,484	4,242	6,204
Algeria	1,992	2,127	2,092	2,206	2,762	2,601	2,544	2,657	2,609	2,465	2,704	1,558	2,102	2,400
Egypt, Arab Republic	..	1,979	1,878	1,982	2,760	2,513	2,885	3,194	1,799	1,395	1,473	..	1,999	2,165
Libya	..	..	..	..	..	..	..	..	..	..	..	..	..	..
Morocco	720	895	978	817	1,373	1,298	1,072	1,191	1,177	1,338	1,370	594	512	1,057
Tunisia	388	430	417	537	871	622	691	705	557	538	772	333	428	582
ALL AFRICA	8,533	11,698	11,049	11,722	15,535	14,593	15,059	15,688	13,501	13,791	14,671	6,166	9,149	13,224

5-36. Food imports, growth

	Percent											Average annual percentage growth		
	1980	1992	1993	1994	1995	1996	1997	1998	1999	2000	2001	75-84	85-89	90-MR
SUB-SAHARAN AFRICA	61.3	20.6	-6.0	1.2	12.3	-0.6	10.4	-31.0	-3.9	-0.7	7.7	21.7	-2.8	0.4
excluding South Africa	61.3	20.6	-6.0	1.2	12.3	-0.6	10.4	-31.0	-3.9	-0.7	7.7	21.7	-3.6	0.4
excl. S.Africa & Nigeria	76.5	25.2	-6.8	4.6	8.0	3.9	4.1	-11.0	-3.9	-0.7	7.7	25.4	9.8	2.5
Angola	..	340.6	-12.6	2.5	-13.2	34.2	47.1	..	..	..	..	..	-12.7	7.3
Benin	..	..	..	..	..	..	..	..	..	..	..	..	..	..
Botswana	..	..	..	-11.8	0.0	0.7	9.3	7.0	0.0	-0.6	18.4	..	..	3.0
Burkina Faso	..	..	..	..	..	..	..	..	..	..	..	..	..	..
Burundi	..	-0.3	75.5	61.3	-4.0	-62.2	2.8	-9.6	4.0	4.6	4.6	..	3.3	-0.8
Cameroon	0.8	-6.8	-17.2	9.5	-27.6	-3.8	20.6	9.5	-10.1	1.6	9.8	-0.9	20.2	-0.9
Cape Verde	..	78.5	-27.7	11.9	12.5	-8.4	11.0	-35.0	3.5	3.1	5.4	..	..	1.7
Central African Republic	..	1.4	-16.9	-11.4	19.4	-26.5	-7.7	9.4	-3.9	-21.1	-25.4	..	..	-7.7
Chad	..	-89.5	500.0	25.0	-12.8	-0.3	-1.9	2.8	1.2	..	..	..	..	-0.3
Comoros	..	1.5	-12.6	32.7	77.9	-30.5	1.0	1.5	2.0	..	..	..	5.3	6.2
Congo, Democratic Rep. of	..	..	..	..	62.8	50.1	..	..	..	..	..	..	..	..
Congo, Republic of	..	-16.5	32.2	10.9	-1.1	-0.7	9.6	7.6	3.0	3.5	3.2	..	-6.5	4.2
Côte d'Ivoire	..	-25.8	13.0	-26.1	52.6	1.5	7.1	5.0	4.0	-2.0	1.0	..	..	1.6
Djibouti	..	..	..	..	..	-7.3	-1.5	0.9	1.5	-0.1	2.3	..	..	-0.3
Equatorial Guinea	..	..	..	..	..	..	..	..	..	..	..	..	..	..
Eritrea	..	..	..	..	..	..	..	..	..	..	..	..	..	..
Ethiopia	..	..	..	..	..	..	..	..	..	..	..	..	-11.2	..
Gabon	..	..	..	..	..	..	..	..	..	..	..	..	..	..
Gambia, The	..	310.4	-3.5	-12.8	15.5	-12.3	9.1	41.0	-23.6	..	..	..	..	20.6
Ghana	..	4.3	5.5	4.2	5.4	7.7	-0.7	7.3	6.0	4.1	6.0	..	8.4	4.6
Guinea	..	513.8	12.8	38.7	-7.4	0.0	-2.0	5.3	5.8	5.2	5.0	..	7.8	18.8
Guinea-Bissau	..	43.8	-21.4	-15.6	61.3	-7.9	20.2	-44.9	87.3	11.4	-9.6	..	..	6.5
Kenya	..	112.6	-41.6	186.6	-59.6	66.3	97.6	-20.7	-3.2	-1.5	-0.5	..	22.4	10.4
Lesotho	..	..	..	..	..	..	..	..	..	..	..	..	..	..
Liberia	..	..	..	..	..	..	..	..	..	..	..	..	..	..
Madagascar	..	61.7	-17.5	53.4	-26.2	-19.9	-8.8	22.0	-22.2	-9.1	20.5	..	-17.0	-2.7
Malawi	..	354.3	-90.5	967.9	23.5	-47.9	-30.5	56.2	-8.6	-1.7	83.0	..	..	20.1
Mali	2.1	-20.9	1.9	-8.7	13.3	11.3	7.5	11.4	-10.2	23.5	8.3	6.7	-17.6	4.4
Mauritania	..	12.3	-22.4	-5.1	-19.4	4.6	-6.1	11.9	-9.0	52.0	-7.3	..	-3.0	-1.9
Mauritius	..	..	..	..	..	..	..	..	..	..	..	..	..	..
Mozambique	..	..	..	..	..	-39.4	4.3	..	..	..	..	..	..	..
Namibia	..	12.2	-2.5	-2.7	10.0	-5.0	0.0	-13.6	-5.3	-1.9	-2.4	..	..	-1.6
Niger	..	..	..	..	..	..	..	..	..	..	..	..	..	..
Nigeria	59.2	5.3	-3.0	-11.7	31.3	-17.1	39.8	..	..	..	..	20.0	-27.0	7.9
Rwanda	..	1.5	0.9	5.1	8.1	12.2	-10.8	-12.7	-3.8	-6.6	9.1	..	-11.6	0.4
São Tomé and Principe	..	-1.9	23.6	-14.2	2.9	-24.9	-14.6	25.7	-17.2	-4.7	5.1	..	20.0	-5.3
Senegal	..	-2.1	0.7	-15.3	-0.5	1.4	-5.8	5.6	0.7	3.9	3.0	..	0.5	-0.3
Seychelles	..	14.4	27.2	-16.4	10.4	38.5	40.6	3.0	1.5	1.5	2.0	..	6.3	11.6
Sierra Leone	..	6.9	5.4	-11.6	16.3	64.9	-60.1	-5.5	-25.8	131.1	11.3	..	..	0.7
Somalia	..	..	..	..	..	..	..	..	..	..	..	..	..	..
South Africa	..	..	..	..	..	..	..	..	..	..	..	..	..	..
Sudan	..	..	..	..	..	..	..	..	..	..	..	..	10.1	..
Swaziland	..	13.2	21.4	0.4	47.6	-15.4	-1.8	-1.2	16.4	-1.4	-1.4	..	..	6.5
Tanzania	..	..	..	..	..	-64.1	..	..	..	..	..	..	..	..
Togo	..	..	..	..	..	..	..	..	..	..	..	..	2.6	..
Uganda	..	..	..	..	..	..	..	..	..	..	..	..	..	..
Zambia	..	..	-80.3	0.7	64.0	-75.9	-47.3	864.4	-100.0	9.12E+14	10.6	..	-14.5	-51.7
Zimbabwe	..	3.2	-51.0	-65.7	71.9	59.4	-26.4	13.5	0.8	-40.8	135.9	..	-12.7	-1.4
NORTH AFRICA	5.8	16.2	-3.6	-1.0	16.5	-12.5	-0.6	18.0	-11.9	-36.1	-2.6	9.9	16.6	-2.3
Algeria	..	8.6	-10.5	7.5	-12.0	-7.0	-10.6	12.4	-2.5	..	..	..	10.0	-3.8
Egypt, Arab Republic	..	9.8	-4.8	2.0	27.8	-15.3	14.1	21.1	-35.3	-13.3	1.0	..	..	-0.9
Libya	..	..	..	..	..	..	..	..	..	..	..	..	..	..
Morocco	5.8	49.5	10.9	-22.9	53.6	-10.6	-12.2	23.1	18.4	17.8	-5.2	3.6	-3.8	8.7
Tunisia	..	21.9	2.3	21.1	35.2	-30.8	18.3	6.3	-9.7	..	..	..	-4.4	1.8
ALL AFRICA	43.1	17.8	-4.5	-0.2	15.0	-8.3	3.6	-1.9	-9.6	-25.3	1.6	16.5	9.3	-1.3

5-37. Nonfood consumer goods imports

	Millions of U.S. dollars (current prices)											Annual Average		
	1980	*1992*	*1993*	*1994*	*1995*	*1996*	*1997*	*1998*	*1999*	*2000*	*2001*	*75-84*	*85-89*	*90-MR*
SUB-SAHARAN AFRICA	9,829	13,057	12,142	14,483	18,384	18,012	17,231	15,954	9,686	10,243	9,213	7,298	10,133	13,564
excluding South Africa	1,623	6,198	5,270	5,428	7,054	7,128	7,499	6,329	6,367	6,048	5,960	1,114	4,346	6,151
excl. S.Africa & Nigeria	1,623	6,198	5,270	5,428	7,054	7,128	7,499	6,329	6,367	6,048	5,960	1,114	4,346	6,151
Angola	..	1,009	778	712	1,069	1,119	1,263	..	..	..	..	..	328	897
Benin	..	126	121	92	144	146	140	148	137	145	217	..	97	135
Botswana	146	394	451	459	511	475	539	559	632	616	694	158	197	513
Burkina Faso	..	215	0	0	170	192	176	160	..	..	..	..	..	144
Burundi	53	45	33	28	28	8	19	49	-4	10	10	43	38	25
Cameroon	136	68	89	76	64	74	179	244	402	432	428	222	262	191
Cape Verde	..	60	57	65	85	91	81	45	48	49	51	..	41	61
Central African Republic	..	27	26	29	11	32	51	15	-13	-31	-27	30	45	17
Chad	..	102	131	85	103	109	116	120	117	..	..	..	108	112
Comoros	..	49	41	36	35	28	22	17	17	15	15	25	29	29
Congo, Democratic Rep. of	..	..	..	..	..	..	..	..	..	..	..	..	..	..
Congo, Republic of	0	3	3	5	5	7	9	28	36	82	99	26	212	23
Côte d'Ivoire	629	534	491	454	743	675	669	762	681	532	545	466	475	577
Djibouti	..	..	..	..	35	34	34	36	38	39	41	..	..	37
Equatorial Guinea	..	33	25	22	29	50	43	39	49	49	51	21	27	37
Eritrea	..	198	109	95	28	59	3	3	2	1	2	..	..	50
Ethiopia	..	174	189	183	176	254	272	256	365	293	192	116	140	225
Gabon	..	252	241	71	77	78	79	67	61	65	68	330	236	124
Gambia, The	..	31	29	26	34	30	34	36	40	0	0	..	0	22
Ghana	..	306	..	..	..	..	..	..	..	..	..	80	125	231
Guinea	..	313	318	320	389	313	355	378	405	436	467	..	259	364
Guinea-Bissau	..	7	5	6	7	7	9	9	10	10	9	11	9	8
Kenya	152	537	376	689	1,008	980	987	1,123	1,036	1,042	904	130	599	830
Lesotho	..	..	..	..	..	..	..	..	..	..	..	..	..	..
Liberia	..	..	..	..	..	..	..	..	..	..	..	..	..	..
Madagascar	..	188	209	236	299	309	353	387	417	479	571	89	90	313
Malawi	..	57	54	39	31	45	58	30	44	33	35	..	42	43
Mali	181	182	188	176	159	182	168	154	147	165	191	163	95	165
Mauritania	..	29	16	12	18	17	23	22	25	-22	5	23	32	18
Mauritius	46	145	159	163	186	204	179	181	188	188	181	36	69	168
Mozambique	..	..	..	..	140	137	137	147	216	175	174	..	..	161
Namibia	..	183	176	185	204	205	217	198	198	206	212	..	..	192
Niger	..	94	92	117	112	154	130	147	..	..	..	..	113	114
Nigeria	..	..	..	..	..	..	..	..	..	..	..	..	..	..
Rwanda	..	92	88	158	69	71	120	105	133	91	122	31	46	98
São Tomé and Principe	..	10	11	9	7	8	6	6	..	..	..	15	9	8
Senegal	151	212	192	170	199	203	191	203	207	198	219	139	166	203
Seychelles	..	29	39	33	33	40	51	50	51	53	55	8	16	40
Sierra Leone	..	15	19	16	11	11	4	7	6	19	142	18	34	23
Somalia	..	..	..	..	..	..	..	..	..	..	..	..	..	..
South Africa	8,206	6,859	6,872	9,055	11,330	10,884	9,731	9,625	3,319	4,195	3,253	6,185	5,787	7,412
Sudan	..	3	8	15	17	64	64	72	72	43	25	120	88	50
Swaziland	127	58	78	46	32	39	41	43	42	41	39	86	75	45
Tanzania	..	274	293	237	355	268	323	272	357	376	..	71	117	280
Togo	..	27	16	22	27	29	28	14	..	..	..	61	89	23
Uganda	..	..	..	..	..	..	..	..	..	..	..	..	..	..
Zambia	..	..	..	167	199	200	125	121	128	125	139	..	..	151
Zimbabwe	..	121	119	173	205	183	203	77	76	93	84	303	198	129
NORTH AFRICA	2,714	5,738	6,125	7,969	7,761	5,877	7,122	7,454	8,469	11,000	7,696	2,083	4,160	7,136
Algeria	1,785	1,617	1,373	2,027	1,757	1,037	1,095	1,314	1,422	1,386	1,507	1,333	2,029	1,519
Egypt, Arab Republic	..	813	1,448	2,159	1,531	121	1,167	785	1,621	4,087	435	..	1,252	1,269
Libya	..	..	..	..	..	..	..	..	..	..	..	..	..	..
Morocco	334	1,414	1,366	1,525	1,853	2,037	2,134	2,418	2,481	2,701	2,649	288	580	1,929
Tunisia	595	1,895	1,938	2,258	2,621	2,683	2,726	2,937	2,945	2,825	3,105	462	799	2,419
ALL AFRICA	12,543	18,795	18,267	22,452	26,146	23,889	24,352	23,408	18,155	21,242	16,909	9,381	14,293	20,700

5-38. Nonfood consumer goods imports, growth

	Percent											Average annual percentage growth		
	1980	*1992*	*1993*	*1994*	*1995*	*1996*	*1997*	*1998*	*1999*	*2000*	*2001*	*75-84*	*85-89*	*90-MR*
SUB-SAHARAN AFRICA	-1.2	17.3	-0.3	12.1	8.1	8.5	9.6	-18.5	2.6	2.7	4.9	35.7	21.2	4.4
excluding South Africa	-1.2	17.3	-0.3	12.1	8.1	8.5	9.6	-18.5	2.6	2.7	4.9	35.7	18.0	4.4
excl. S.Africa & Nigeria	-1.2	17.3	-0.3	12.1	8.1	8.5	9.6	-18.5	2.6	2.7	4.9	35.7	18.0	4.4
Angola	..	54.2	-19.0	-11.5	36.7	4.7	25.1	..	..	..	..	..	52.1	12.3
Benin	..	..	..	..	..	..	..	..	..	..	..	..	..	..
Botswana	..	..	..	-1.8	5.1	-2.2	22.0	7.7	13.4	-0.6	18.4	..	..	7.9
Burkina Faso	..	..	..	..	..	..	..	..	..	..	..	..	..	..
Burundi	..	9.2	-33.2	-46.6	0.2	-101.6	-5,796.8	259.1	-130.0	-120.4	-0.8	..	-9.7	-18.4
Cameroon	-40.2	58.8	-25.5	69.5	-22.2	40.4	21.7	16.6	3.4	5.0	5.0	-3.7	-3.0	14.2
Cape Verde	..	8.2	-4.5	-6.5	20.1	14.7	-8.7	-44.4	1.5	1.9	1.9	..	..	-1.3
Central African Republic	..	29.9	-1.4	8.2	-64.1	166.4	66.9	-72.7	-186.3	133.1	-16.1	..	..	-8.3
Chad	..	9.5	-20.4	-96.4	-313.0	183.6	-5.4	4.2	1.9	..	..	..	..	..
Comoros	..	14.6	-9.5	27.5	-11.0	20.0	1.0	1.5	2.0	..	..	..	-6.6	6.5
Congo, Democratic Rep. of	..	..	..	..	..	..	..	..	..	..	..	..	..	..
Congo, Republic of	..	-16.5	32.2	10.9	-1.1	140.8	-22.9	-22.1	8.7	-3.1	-6.4	..	2.9	7.2
Côte d'Ivoire	..	22.8	-8.2	-8.4	48.7	5.0	4.7	4.5	4.0	-2.0	1.0	..	..	6.1
Djibouti	..	..	..	..	..	-7.1	-1.5	0.9	2.4	-0.1	1.3	..	..	-0.2
Equatorial Guinea	..	-6.6	13.5	-8.5	18.6	71.3	57.6	157.1	-59.7	-27.2	-8.5	..	1.5	15.8
Eritrea	..	..	..	..	..	..	..	..	..	..	..	..	..	..
Ethiopia	..	..	..	..	..	..	..	..	..	..	..	..	..	..
Gabon	..	..	..	..	..	..	..	..	..	..	..	..	..	..
Gambia, The	..	2,941.6	-8.3	-12.3	25.2	-15.2	11.0	3.5	6.7	..	..	..	..	55.5
Ghana	..	28.6	69.6	-30.7	4.8	10.3	0.9	7.3	6.1	4.1	6.0	..	11.8	9.4
Guinea	..	-9.3	6.2	-3.0	10.6	-20.2	18.6	4.0	4.4	4.8	4.8	..	12.1	1.0
Guinea-Bissau	..	-32.3	-36.5	15.8	13.8	10.9	12.2	2.8	9.3	9.2	-9.0	..	..	-2.3
Kenya	..	20.9	-25.3	70.4	-0.9	-19.5	7.1	4.6	0.3	0.2	2.7	..	9.0	3.4
Lesotho	..	..	..	..	..	..	..	..	..	..	..	..	..	..
Liberia	..	..	..	..	..	..	..	..	..	..	..	..	..	..
Madagascar	..	..	..	..	..	..	..	..	..	..	..	..	..	..
Malawi	..	7.3	-5.4	-32.3	-35.3	66.0	45.9	-19.2	-8.9	18.0	6.8	..	..	-2.2
Mali	2.5	9.6	7.7	-9.5	-19.0	17.8	10.4	-119.4	-455.4	148.9	-40.3	-3.4	9.9	2.5
Mauritania	..	2.8	-46.9	-12.1	23.2	7.7	-7.1	4.3	-42.3	666.1	57.9	..	-10.9	3.4
Mauritius	..	..	..	..	..	..	..	..	..	..	..	..	..	..
Mozambique	..	..	..	..	..	-1.5	4.3	..	..	..	..	..	..	..
Namibia	..	8.4	-3.6	1.6	1.6	3.0	8.5	-6.3	2.7	6.4	5.8	..	..	2.1
Niger	..	..	..	..	..	..	..	..	..	..	..	..	..	..
Nigeria	..	..	..	..	..	..	..	..	..	..	..	..	..	..
Rwanda	..	3.9	-6.3	3.3	-45.0	-83.6	552.5	15.0	55.2	-67.5	54.1	..	0.1	-6.0
São Tomé and Principe	..	7.8	13.3	-20.2	-31.9	17.6	5.1	-57.9	152.8	27.8	-48.6	..	-9.4	-1.9
Senegal	..	-6.0	-8.8	-15.1	8.6	7.2	-1.2	7.9	5.2	-2.0	6.4	..	7.7	-0.6
Seychelles	..	18.3	47.0	-25.4	-1.6	34.6	24.0	3.0	1.5	1.5	1.5	..	21.0	8.3
Sierra Leone	..	-4.8	34.3	-17.7	-38.2	4.1	-58.2	66.6	-8.0	189.4	647.6	..	..	4.6
Somalia	..	..	..	..	..	..	..	..	..	..	..	..	..	..
South Africa	..	..	..	..	..	..	..	..	..	..	..	..	..	..
Sudan	..	..	..	..	..	..	..	..	..	..	..	..	..	..
Swaziland	..	35.1	33.7	-41.0	-31.7	20.7	4.1	3.9	12.9	2.0	2.0	..	..	-1.0
Tanzania	..	..	..	..	..	13.1	..	..	..	..	..	..	..	..
Togo	..	..	..	..	..	..	..	..	..		..	..	10.7	..
Uganda	..	..	..	..	..	..	..	..	..	..	..	..	..	..
Zambia	..	..	..	..	10.2	4.9	-33.9	0.0	6.0	0.4	12.7	..	..	-3.8
Zimbabwe	..	3.2	2.2	40.9	11.7	-6.2	15.5	-59.5	0.8	25.3	-5.4	..	-19.5	-1.1
NORTH AFRICA	1.5	-1.4	16.2	31.0	-5.4	-23.3	17.7	2.8	21.9	2.2	-27.0	7.8	-0.7	4.9
Algeria	..	-21.9	-9.3	73.2	17.3	-16.7	-27.0	5.5	7.7	..	..	..	-20.3	0.2
Egypt, Arab Republic	..	1.8	78.6	44.1	-34.9	-92.6	858.0	-26.3	137.3	182.5	-39.2	..	..	20.4
Libya	..	..	..	..	..	..	..	..	..	..	..	..	..	..
Morocco	1.5	1.3	-3.1	7.7	12.6	15.2	9.9	15.5	5.4	11.8	2.8	-4.9	21.0	9.2
Tunisia	..	11.7	8.3	11.6	3.1	0.3	8.0	6.8	1.9	..	..	..	4.9	6.3
ALL AFRICA	-0.4	8.1	7.1	21.2	1.1	-7.1	12.9	-9.5	11.8	2.5	-11.7	21.7	8.6	4.7

5-39. Fuel imports

	Millions of U.S. dollars (current prices)											Annual Average		
	1980	1992	1993	1994	1995	1996	1997	1998	1999	2000	2001	75-84	85-89	90-MR
SUB-SAHARAN AFRICA	10,344	9,696	9,697	11,501	13,346	14,601	15,796	15,257	7,199	9,357	8,192	7,181	8,164	11,231
excluding South Africa	2,789	3,306	3,296	3,353	3,887	4,604	4,746	4,328	4,322	5,720	5,373	1,720	2,686	4,183
excl. S.Africa & Nigeria	2,448	3,257	3,250	3,267	3,769	4,515	4,602	4,205	4,170	5,542	5,177	1,450	2,629	4,076
Angola	..	0	0	0	0	0	0	..	..	..	..	..	0	0
Benin	..	40	39	27	43	54	48	64	59	80	120	34	29	53
Botswana	90	102	133	93	98	110	127	125	107	104	117	91	68	112
Burkina Faso	..	53	0	0	52	73	69	72	..	..	..	..	..	54
Burundi	25	26	24	29	27	18	14	14	19	20	21	30	27	22
Cameroon	187	8	7	7	139	151	136	149	12	24	63	96	13	60
Cape Verde	..	8	6	5	10	9	9	7	11	20	26	..	5	11
Central African Republic	..	16	15	11	17	13	15	14	13	16	17	17	18	16
Chad	..	4	4	12	12	14	18	22	24	28	26	20	28	18
Comoros	..	7	6	6	8	4	4	4	5	7	6	5	4	6
Congo, Democratic Rep. of	..	..	..	..	..	..	..	..	..	49	43	..	..	46
Congo, Republic of	0	104	162	367	187	215	225	216	221	229	237	2	9	207
Côte d'Ivoire	557	511	459	396	470	651	508	446	534	838	720	433	355	553
Djibouti	..	..	..	..	14	14	14	11	11	12	12	..	..	13
Equatorial Guinea	..	4	3	3	3	5	11	11	13	13	14	5	5	7
Eritrea	..	2	1	2	8	6	7	6	4	5	3	..	..	4
Ethiopia	..	120	198	222	169	148	147	143	111	213	265	183	125	162
Gabon	..	12	11	161	173	221	217	216	162	177	187	44	33	130
Gambia, The	..	27	28	30	45	40	29	23	25	0	0	..	9	22
Ghana	..	162	158	176	194	266	240	220	342	533	257	168	156	244
Guinea	..	69	73	69	82	87	90	86	93	99	107	..	55	82
Guinea-Bissau	..	5	3	6	8	9	9	6	7	10	9	9	7	8
Kenya	852	412	407	333	401	448	519	532	527	850	721	456	343	500
Lesotho	..	..	..	..	..	..	..	..	..	..	..	..	..	..
Liberia	..	..	..	..	..	..	..	..	..	..	..	..	..	..
Madagascar	159	72	85	72	81	106	117	101	124	212	168	123	60	110
Malawi	..	47	40	25	49	59	79	56	66	75	68	..	38	56
Mali	120	84	74	52	85	102	105	88	112	166	147	99	67	97
Mauritania	..	36	37	36	51	43	69	50	61	100	92	43	34	55
Mauritius	84	132	126	116	123	146	169	159	135	151	236	85	76	144
Mozambique	..	..	..	..	68	78	78	84	124	44	41	..	..	74
Namibia	..	82	79	83	91	92	97	88	89	92	95	..	..	86
Niger	..	22	23	20	35	32	28	23	..	..	..	..	19	25
Nigeria	340	49	46	86	118	89	143	123	152	178	197	270	58	107
Rwanda	..	37	35	24	22	27	37	35	46	94	73	49	52	43
São Tomé and Principe	..	3	2	2	3	4	4	3	4	4	4	..	0	3
Senegal	276	150	124	142	138	176	191	156	197	280	283	272	170	179
Seychelles	..	33	34	32	30	43	50	47	45	47	49	26	23	40
Sierra Leone	..	24	22	29	24	23	15	25	21	29	36	45	25	26
Somalia	..	..	..	..	..	..	..	..	..	..	..	..	..	..
South Africa	7,555	6,390	6,401	8,148	9,460	9,997	11,050	10,929	2,877	3,636	2,819	5,461	5,478	7,049
Sudan	..	225	249	230	225	306	293	256	184	137	99	351	230	234
Swaziland	99	108	91	42	78	135	149	126	122	119	116	57	71	105
Tanzania	..	142	101	124	186	189	194	129	104	95	106	247	175	144
Togo	..	37	26	22	41	34	42	38	..	..	..	33	25	36
Uganda	..	72	58	55	64	90	92	84	108	143	170	91	69	91
Zambia	..	53	47	56	41	51	87	42	115	177	220	144	85	91
Zimbabwe	..	207	260	150	176	222	250	229	216	250	202	213	143	211
NORTH AFRICA	2,065	2,679	2,820	2,270	2,554	2,856	3,934	3,616	3,222	5,424	5,775	1,237	2,014	3,359
Algeria	259	147	141	150	115	110	132	110	127	106	112	149	183	127
Egypt, Arab Republic	..	959	1,267	542	721	854	1,909	2,188	1,228	2,451	3,233	..	1,237	1,433
Libya	..	..	..	..	..	..	..	..	..	..	..	..	..	..
Morocco	1,006	1,124	957	1,113	1,177	1,285	1,296	922	1,326	2,039	2,026	745	776	1,286
Tunisia	799	449	455	466	541	607	597	396	541	827	403	387	313	514
ALL AFRICA	12,408	12,375	12,517	13,771	15,901	17,457	19,729	18,873	10,421	14,780	13,967	8,418	10,178	14,590

5-40. Fuel imports, growth

	Percent											Average annual percentage growth		
	1980	1992	1993	1994	1995	1996	1997	1998	1999	2000	2001	75-84	85-89	90-MR
SUB-SAHARAN AFRICA	15.6	-8.9	22.2	-19.4	17.3	8.4	13.5	8.7	0.2	-11.3	2.0	8.3	6.0	4.2
excluding South Africa	15.6	-8.9	22.2	-19.4	17.3	8.4	13.5	8.7	0.2	-11.3	2.0	8.3	2.1	4.2
excl. S.Africa & Nigeria	60.4	-9.3	22.6	-21.6	16.8	10.7	11.8	13.5	0.2	-11.3	2.0	22.3	2.5	4.4
Angola	..	-20.0	-25.0	-33.3	-50.0	..	..	..	..	..	..	..	..	..
Benin	..	..	..	..	..	..	..	..	..	..	..	..	..	..
Botswana	..	..	..	-32.5	-0.5	18.0	24.1	2.2	-14.1	-0.6	18.4	..	..	2.6
Burkina Faso	..	..	..	..	..	..	..	..	..	..	..	..	..	..
Burundi	..	-8.5	2.4	29.0	-15.1	-42.3	-19.8	50.0	20.0	-3.8	2.9	..	-0.3	-1.6
Cameroon	9.7	-63.5	379.3	-38.3	40.6	-12.9	101.9	-4.4	-44.7	255.0	10.0	-42.7	10.1	15.2
Cape Verde	..	-0.6	-10.2	-15.1	91.5	-9.9	-1.1	-18.2	13.5	12.0	4.8	..	..	3.9
Central African Republic	..	-3.7	-5.9	-28.1	46.2	-25.4	18.6	-12.5	-9.0	15.4	6.8	..	..	-4.7
Chad	..	-61.0	-21.0	190.0	35.4	20.5	9.3	124.3	135.4	..	..	..	..	18.7
Comoros	..	8.2	-5.7	42.0	13.8	-47.9	2.0	2.5	2.9	..	..	..	-14.2	2.8
Congo, Democratic Rep. of	..	..	..	..	..	..	..	..	..	..	..	..	..	..
Congo, Republic of	..	-16.5	32.2	10.9	-1.1	-3.6	12.7	9.4	2.1	3.1	3.2	..	-2.6	4.2
Côte d'Ivoire	..	-3.1	1.8	27.1	9.8	9.5	6.2	4.8	3.5	-5.7	-2.0	..	..	5.5
Djibouti	..	..	..	..	..	-7.2	-1.7	-25.8	2.4	-0.5	1.3	..	..	-6.7
Equatorial Guinea	..	24.3	-2.4	-4.5	15.8	23.9	126.9	5.3	24.7	1.9	3.9	..	22.7	12.8
Eritrea	..	..	..	..	..	..	..	..	..	..	..	..	..	..
Ethiopia	..	20.0	119.9	..	..	..	..	..	..	..	..	..	-10.4	..
Gabon	..	..	..	..	..	..	..	..	..	..	..	..	..	..
Gambia, The	..	2,526.8	1.3	4.1	45.1	-13.5	-29.4	-21.7	3.7	..	..	..	..	11.7
Ghana	..	-7.1	3.2	19.0	3.9	9.9	17.9	22.7	11.9	4.4	6.0	..	9.3	8.5
Guinea	..	1.4	14.1	0.1	10.2	11.1	1.5	7.7	5.4	6.5	6.1	..	-3.4	7.2
Guinea-Bissau	..	-49.1	-39.3	137.1	44.3	14.9	4.0	-33.1	15.0	47.3	-8.2	..	..	5.1
Kenya	..	-9.5	2.8	-18.7	12.8	11.7	16.0	2.5	-2.4	-0.5	1.4	..	-10.2	3.4
Lesotho	..	..	..	..	..	..	..	..	..	..	..	..	..	..
Liberia	..	..	..	..	..	..	..	..	..	..	..	..	..	..
Madagascar	..	1.2	33.7	-14.4	3.8	11.6	16.9	27.3	-12.1	8.7	1.5	..	-4.5	7.8
Malawi	..	-12.6	-2.8	-33.5	78.2	2.7	41.8	31.5	1.2	19.7	-6.1	..	..	10.4
Mali	3.0	2.5	-14.1	12.9	28.3	14.8	20.2	70.0	-10.6	-6.6	3.1	0.7	2.7	11.4
Mauritania	..	-7.3	17.2	-2.6	158.8	3.3	-6.1	15.0	17.1	-23.4	6.7	..	6.2	13.0
Mauritius	..	..	..	..	..	..	..	..	..	..	..	..	..	..
Mozambique	..	..	..	..	..	5.4	-62.5	..	..	..	..	..	..	..
Namibia	..	15.3	8.5	11.7	1.7	-15.5	-11.1	-23.2	-15.8	-12.8	-13.2	..	..	-5.6
Niger	..	..	..	..	..	..	..	..	..	..	..	..	..	..
Nigeria	-35.3	14.8	5.3	98.6	26.6	-36.1	70.8	..	..	..	..	-10.6	-9.8	16.3
Rwanda	..	0.0	-8.2	-5.4	8.0	3.5	26.4	60.5	-14.5	-3.4	3.1	..	-6.9	4.4
São Tomé and Principe	..	16.7	-21.7	-1.9	36.5	6.2	40.8	-12.3	17.2	-35.0	4.4	..	..	3.4
Senegal	..	24.5	-8.9	32.2	-14.3	8.2	4.5	15.3	10.1	-11.9	-1.9	..	4.9	3.4
Seychelles	..	0.8	8.2	-3.4	-14.2	44.7	17.7	11.1	1.8	1.8	1.8	..	3.2	6.5
Sierra Leone	..	-10.4	-0.6	27.3	-25.5	-1.1	-28.4	69.4	-18.4	38.1	24.3	..	..	-0.3
Somalia	..	..	..	..	..	..	..	..	..	..	..	..	..	..
South Africa	..	..	..	..	..	..	..	..	..	..	..	..	..	..
Sudan	..	..	..	..	..	..	..	..	..	..	..	..	-15.0	..
Swaziland	..	22.0	-10.0	-49.9	97.3	85.6	18.4	-9.3	-29.8	-37.3	-37.3	..	..	2.4
Tanzania	..	..	..	..	..	-5.2	..	..	..	..	..	..	..	..
Togo	..	..	..	..	..	..	..	..	..	..	..	..	5.3	..
Uganda	..	..	..	..	..	..	..	..	..	..	..	..	..	..
Zambia	..	-35.0	0.1	25.2	-31.7	4.6	82.1	-29.5	98.0	-0.4	44.3	..	0.5	3.6
Zimbabwe	..	6.4	42.3	-39.1	8.5	6.3	19.4	34.8	-31.3	-25.5	-8.4	..	-0.9	2.3
NORTH AFRICA	19.0	10.4	9.6	-4.5	4.8	-5.4	23.2	23.7	-14.9	-5.3	1.9	5.3	17.3	4.5
Algeria	..	8.0	-13.6	5.9	1.3	-12.8	-9.9	30.0	3.6	..	..	..	-8.7	1.4
Egypt, Arab Republic	..	-0.7	41.4	-53.2	31.9	4.1	80.0	65.9	-41.9	34.2	0.5	..	..	9.2
Libya	..	..	..	..	..	..	..	..	..	..	..	..	..	..
Morocco	19.0	15.5	-3.9	23.3	-2.1	-8.2	7.4	4.4	4.0	-1.5	2.9	3.8	4.7	3.7
Tunisia	..	15.0	16.5	9.8	7.1	-4.7	5.8	-12.0	25.5	..	..	..	2.6	4.6
ALL AFRICA	17.6	2.2	14.4	-10.5	9.3	0.0	19.1	17.7	-9.3	-7.7	1.9	6.7	12.7	4.4

5-41. Primary intermediate goods imports

	Millions of U.S. dollars (current prices)											Annual Average		
	1980	1992	1993	1994	1995	1996	1997	1998	1999	2000	2001	75-84	85-89	90-MR
SUB-SAHARAN AFRICA	4,325	3,749	3,625	4,313	5,114	4,867	5,805	5,540	5,546	6,588	5,750	2,851	3,313	4,917
excluding South Africa	141	1,515	1,388	1,661	2,228	2,379	2,298	2,071	1,950	2,043	2,227	173	1,343	1,948
excl. S.Africa & Nigeria	141	1,515	1,388	1,661	2,228	2,379	2,298	2,071	1,950	2,043	2,227	173	1,343	1,948
Angola	..	223	89	129	157	0	0	..	..	..	..	..	292	151
Benin	..	..	..	..	..	..	..	..	..	..	..	..	..	..
Botswana	22	106	163	159	177	176	205	211	203	198	223	25	41	169
Burkina Faso	..	28	0	0	42	42	40	68	..	..	..	..	..	30
Burundi	0	0	0	0	0	0	0	0	0	0	0	0	0	0
Cameroon	55	72	61	60	69	77	94	76	69	70	71	61	76	72
Cape Verde	..	..	..	..	..	16	16	17	18	21	29	..	..	19
Central African Republic	..	53	40	44	58	44	39	45	54	56	59	..	53	51
Chad	..	0	0	0	0	0	0	0	0	..	..	..	0	0
Comoros	..	3	4	4	4	2	0	0	0	0	0	2	2	2
Congo, Democratic Rep. of	..	..	..	..	..	..	..	..	..	..	..	..	..	..
Congo, Republic of	0	28	28	72	78	98	89	101	108	117	126	0	6	75
Côte d'Ivoire	..	..	..	..	..	..	..	..	..	..	..	..	..	..
Djibouti	..	..	..	..	7	7	7	7	7	8	8	..	..	7
Equatorial Guinea	..	..	..	..	..	..	..	..	..	..	..	..	..	..
Eritrea	..	1	5	7	10	17	9	6	9	6	4	..	..	7
Ethiopia	..	17	21	15	21	29	27	28	27	21	25	35	28	24
Gabon	..	10	10	10	10	10	11	5	5	5	6	..	10	8
Gambia, The	..	2	2	2	3	6	3	2	3	0	0	..	45	13
Ghana	..	..	..	..	..	..	..	..	..	..	..	..	..	..
Guinea	..	0	0	0	0	0	0	0	0	0	0	..	0	0
Guinea-Bissau	..	..	..	..	..	12	15	4	19	19	18	..	.	14
Kenya	..	59	47	51	71	75	67	60	54	56	402	42	47	88
Lesotho	..	..	..	..	..	..	..	..	..	..	..	..	..	..
Liberia	..	..	..	..	..	..	..	..	..	..	..	..	..	..
Madagascar	..	..	..	..	..	..	..	..	..	..	..	..	..	..
Malawi	..	85	81	58	46	67	87	46	66	50	53	..	119	65
Mali	..	..	..	..	..	..	..	..	..	..	..	..	..	..
Mauritania	..	0	0	0	0	0	0	0	0	0	0	..	0	0
Mauritius	0	0	0	0	0	0	0	0	0	0	0	0	0	0
Mozambique	..	..	..	..	124	140	140	151	221	169	172	..	..	160
Namibia	..	159	153	161	178	178	189	172	172	179	185	..	..	167
Niger	..	..	..	..	..	..	..	..	..	..	..	..	..	..
Nigeria	..	..	..	..	..	..	..	..	..	..	..	..	..	..
Rwanda	..	0	0	0	0	0	0	0	0	0	0	0	0	0
São Tomé and Principe	..	0	0	0	0	0	0	0	0	0	0	..	0	0
Senegal	..	..	..	..	..	..	..	..	..	..	..	..	..	..
Seychelles	..	0	0	0	0	0	0	29	29	30	32	..	0	10
Sierra Leone	..	14	13	11	18	29	14	12	12	20	20	..	..	15
Somalia	..	..	..	..	..	..	..	..	..	..	..	..	..	..
South Africa	4,184	2,233	2,237	2,653	2,886	2,487	3,507	3,469	3,596	4,545	3,524	2,678	1,970	2,970
Sudan	..	57	113	117	134	234	190	157	114	208	233	172	195	149
Swaziland	64	117	132	197	283	235	200	223	217	211	205	41	34	184
Tanzania	..	132	116	113	255	381	284	123	207	200	..	134	232	220
Togo	..	..	..	..	..	..	..	..	..	..	..	..	..	..
Uganda	..	..	..	..	..	..	..	..	..	..	..	..	..	..
Zambia	..	48	20	72	80	80	50	54	2	13	15	..	45	43
Zimbabwe	..	300	292	379	404	424	522	476	332	386	344	39	163	367
NORTH AFRICA	1,106	1,796	1,601	1,818	1,903	1,432	1,391	1,402	1,368	1,345	1,938	930	1,308	1,621
Algeria	606	981	942	999	831	539	520	603	607	580	516	535	652	744
Egypt, Arab Republic	..	..	..	..	..	..	..	..	..	..	..	..	..	..
Libya	..	..	..	..	..	..	..	..	..	..	..	..	..	..
Morocco	501	816	659	819	1,072	893	871	799	761	765	755	395	656	822
Tunisia	..	..	..	..	..	..	..	..	..	..	668	..	..	668
ALL AFRICA	5,431	5,545	5,226	6,132	7,017	6,299	7,196	6,943	6,914	7,933	7,689	3,781	4,621	6,539

5-42. Primary intermediate goods imports, growth

	Percent											Average annual percentage growth		
	1980	*1992*	*1993*	*1994*	*1995*	*1996*	*1997*	*1998*	*1999*	*2000*	*2001*	*75-84*	*85-89*	*90-MR*
SUB-SAHARAN AFRICA	17.2	-20.2	-3.5	17.9	17.7	-8.7	11.1	-5.1	-14.4	5.8	2.4	32.3	40.2	1.6
excluding South Africa	17.2	-20.2	-3.5	17.9	17.7	-8.7	11.1	-5.1	-14.4	5.8	2.4	32.3	35.6	1.6
excl. S.Africa & Nigeria	17.2	-20.2	-3.5	17.9	17.7	-8.7	11.1	-5.1	-14.4	5.8	2.4	32.3	35.6	1.6
Angola	..	-9.4	-58.0	40.2	10.8	..	..	..	..	..	..	..	-3.2	-15.8
Benin	..	..	..	..	..	..	..	..	..	..	..	..	..	..
Botswana	..	..	..	-5.9	5.1	4.6	25.2	6.9	-3.5	-0.6	18.4	..	..	6.4
Burkina Faso	..	..	..	..	..	..	..	..	..	..	..	..	..	..
Burundi	..	..	..	..	..	..	..	..	..	..	..	..	..	..
Cameroon	17.2	15.9	-16.5	-19.4	2.6	-8.7	12.6	-7.3	-4.0	1.3	2.0	15.3	0.6	-3.6
Cape Verde	..	..	..	..	..	..	..	..	..	..	..	..	..	..
Central African Republic	..	-8.3	-25.0	8.5	19.4	-26.5	-7.7	9.4	17.5	-0.2	3.5	..	..	-3.2
Chad	..	..	..	..	..	..	..	..	..	..	..	..	..	..
Comoros	..	-5.0	16.6	64.2	-1.4	-46.7	..	..	..	..	..	..	-12.8	15.2
Congo, Democratic Rep. of	..	..	..	..	..	..	..	..	..	..	..	..	..	..
Congo, Republic of	..	..	..	..	..	..	..	..	..	..	..	..	..	..
Côte d'Ivoire	..	..	..	..	..	..	..	..	..	..	..	..	..	..
Djibouti	..	..	..	..	..	-6.6	-2.3	1.9	2.4	1.8	2.0	..	..	0.3
Equatorial Guinea	..	..	..	..	..	..	..	..	..	..	..	..	..	..
Eritrea	..	..	..	..	..	..	..	..	..	..	..	..	..	..
Ethiopia	..	..	..	..	..	..	..	..	..	..	..	..	..	..
Gabon	..	..	..	..	..	..	..	..	..	..	..	..	..	..
Gambia, The	..	-97.0	-13.1	-10.3	53.0	98.7	-57.0	-22.8	38.4	..	..	..	..	-28.0
Ghana	..	..	..	..	..	..	..	..	..	..	..	..	..	..
Guinea	..	..	..	..	..	..	..	..	..	..	..	..	..	..
Guinea-Bissau	..	..	..	..	..	..	..	..	..	..	..	..	..	..
Kenya	..	1.6	-17.6	5.1	50.3	-10.8	14.7	38.5	0.5	0.1	1.1	..	0.8	7.4
Lesotho	..	..	..	..	..	..	..	..	..	..	..	..	..	..
Liberia	..	..	..	..	..	..	..	..	..	..	..	..	..	..
Madagascar	..	..	..	..	..	..	..	..	..	..	..	..	..	..
Malawi	..	7.3	-5.4	-32.3	-35.3	66.0	45.9	-19.2	-8.9	18.0	6.8	..	..	-5.9
Mali	..	..	..	..	..	..	..	..	..	..	..	..	..	..
Mauritania	..	..	..	..	..	..	..	..	..	..	..	..	..	..
Mauritius	..	..	..	..	..	..	..	..	..	..	..	..	..	..
Mozambique	..	..	..	..	..	3.7	4.3	..	..	..	..	..	..	..
Namibia	..	8.4	-3.6	1.6	1.6	3.0	8.5	-6.3	2.7	6.4	5.8	..	..	2.1
Niger	..	..	..	..	..	..	..	..	..	..	..	..	..	..
Nigeria	..	..	..	..	..	..	..	..	..	..	..	..	..	..
Rwanda	..	..	..	..	..	..	..	..	..	..	..	..	..	..
São Tomé and Principe	..	..	..	..	..	..	..	..	..	..	..	..	..	..
Senegal	..	..	..	..	..	..	..	..	..	..	..	..	..	..
Seychelles	..	..	..	..	..	..	..	..	..	..	..	..	..	..
Sierra Leone	..	35.4	-6.4	-14.1	52.7	54.4	-45.4	-8.3	-7.1	64.8	-1.9	..	..	4.6
Somalia	..	..	..	..	..	..	..	..	..	..	..	..	..	..
South Africa	..	..	..	..	..	..	..	..	..	..	..	..	..	..
Sudan	..	..	..	..	..	..	..	..	..	..	..	..	..	..
Swaziland	..	7.6	12.3	43.6	35.8	-12.7	-8.5	15.8	-1.8	0.6	0.6	..	..	9.2
Tanzania	..	..	..	..	..	43.8	..	..	..	..	..	..	..	..
Togo	..	..	..	..	..	..	..	..	..	..	..	..	..	..
Uganda	..	..	..	..	..	..	..	..	..	..	..	..	..	..
Zambia	..	51.0	-52.3	222.6	0.1	-13.5	-37.5	5.1	-95.8	19.6	17.8	..	52.5	-22.4
Zimbabwe	..	3.2	1.1	25.6	0.2	10.4	28.2	-2.9	-28.8	11.6	-5.2	..	42.1	5.2
NORTH AFRICA	4.3	3.7	-22.7	9.4	13.5	-11.2	1.9	21.5	-2.5	-37.2	7.8	8.1	-0.7	-2.0
Algeria	..	8.0	-13.6	10.1	1.3	-10.8	-10.6	25.6	4.9	..	..	..	-2.7	-2.2
Egypt, Arab Republic	..	..	..	..	..	..	..	..	..	..	..	..	..	..
Libya	..	..	..	..	..	..	..	..	..	..	..	..	..	..
Morocco	4.3	1.4	-27.9	8.9	21.8	-11.4	9.0	19.5	-6.1	-2.8	7.8	4.7	0.9	1.7
Tunisia	..	..	..	..	..	..	..	..	..	..	..	..	..	..
ALL AFRICA	5.1	-8.4	-14.3	13.6	15.6	-9.9	6.8	6.8	-8.3	-17.5	4.6	9.6	9.8	-0.2

5-43. Manufactured goods imports

	Millions of U.S. dollars (current prices)											Annual Average		
	1980	*1992*	*1993*	*1994*	*1995*	*1996*	*1997*	*1998*	*1999*	*2000*	*2001*	*75-84*	*85-89*	*90-MR*
SUB-SAHARAN AFRICA	2,016	4,332	4,303	4,347	5,371	6,275	7,218	7,024	8,236	9,083	8,249	1,425	3,094	6,189
excluding South Africa	1,057	3,450	3,418	3,191	3,994	4,739	5,082	4,912	4,400	4,234	4,491	718	2,444	4,164
excl. S.Africa & Nigeria	1,057	3,450	3,418	3,191	3,994	4,739	5,082	4,912	4,400	4,234	4,491	718	2,444	4,164
Angola	..	135	72	71	94	343	400	..	..	..	..	..	154	170
Benin	..	..	..	..	..	..	..	..	..	..	..	206	..	..
Botswana	54	175	179	153	166	152	241	249	189	184	207	59	86	305
Burkina Faso	..	..	..	..	..	..	..	..	..	..	..	..	..	..
Burundi	40	55	57	55	62	38	33	35	41	44	48	46	49	50
Cameroon	605	367	378	370	363	398	385	407	424	438	458	511	569	420
Cape Verde	..	..	..	..	..	10	10	12	13	14	16	..	..	12
Central African Republic	..	..	..	..	..	..	..	..	..	..	..	..	..	..
Chad	..	127	156	136	92	108	109	82	81	..	..	..	87	110
Comoros	..	2	2	2	2	2	3	3	3	3	3	0	2	2
Congo, Democratic Rep. of	..	60	61	45	52	82	..	..	..	..	..	..	..	60
Congo, Republic of	..	142	141	86	94	118	141	148	156	164	172	141	128	136
Côte d'Ivoire	..	..	..	..	..	..	..	..	..	..	..	..	..	..
Djibouti	..	..	..	..	28	27	26	37	39	40	41	..	..	34
Equatorial Guinea	..	..	..	..	..	..	..	..	..	..	..	..	..	..
Eritrea	..	41	63	102	117	177	94	87	78	76	75	..	..	91
Ethiopia	..	113	95	129	183	200	332	321	312	212	246	117	140	201
Gabon	..	103	89	30	32	286	289	388	401	422	443	..	85	222
Gambia, The	..	43	46	36	34	29	16	21	22	..	..	..	45	38
Ghana	..	..	..	..	..	..	..	..	..	..	..	..	..	..
Guinea	..	211	196	151	173	159	174	194	215	227	247	..	140	198
Guinea-Bissau	..	..	..	..	..	5	6	2	8	8	8	..	..	6
Kenya	..	291	307	293	487	443	465	413	402	361	437	186	268	371
Lesotho	..	..	..	..	..	..	..	..	..	..	..	..	..	..
Liberia	..	..	..	..	..	..	..	..	..	..	..	..	..	..
Madagascar	..	..	..	..	..	..	..	..	..	..	..	..	..	..
Malawi	..	226	214	176	122	169	230	106	160	153	159	..	29	169
Mali	193	156	136	122	150	150	148	159	189	209	216	174	93	159
Mauritania	..	137	133	113	138	200	97	148	86	54	86	..	101	123
Mauritius	..	..	..	..	..	..	..	..	..	..	..	..	..	..
Mozambique	..	..	..	..	185	229	221	237	348	257	262	..	..	248
Namibia	..	208	200	210	232	233	246	225	225	233	241	..	..	218
Niger	..	..	..	..	..	..	..	..	..	..	..	..	..	..
Nigeria	..	..	..	..	..	..	..	..	..	..	..	..	..	..
Rwanda	..	92	91	23	41	55	71	66	48	43	44	82	100	66
São Tomé and Principe	..	..	..	..	..	..	..	..	..	..	..	..	..	..
Senegal	..	..	..	..	..	..	..	..	..	..	..	..	..	..
Seychelles	..	..	..	..	..	..	..	44	63	64	62	..	..	58
Sierra Leone	..	19	15	15	7	15	6	8	6	9	11	..	..	12
Somalia	..	..	..	..	..	..	..	..	..	..	..	..	..	..
South Africa	959	883	884	1,156	1,377	1,536	2,136	2,112	3,836	4,848	3,759	707	650	2,026
Sudan	..	200	293	255	307	324	353	636	276	333	355	160	122	299
Swaziland	165	169	211	229	321	275	333	318	309	300	292	91	104	258
Tanzania	..	21	12	10	15	17	27	18	15	14	..	6	7	16
Togo	..	102	60	48	80	72	63	75	..	..	..	67	74	82
Uganda	..	..	..	..	..	..	..	..	..	..	..	..	..	..
Zambia	..	..	..	40	54	55	116	108	103	116	129	..	..	90
Zimbabwe	..	256	212	290	364	369	447	365	189	257	232	166	184	287
NORTH AFRICA	3,492	4,151	3,882	4,342	4,740	4,035	3,774	4,108	3,892	3,930	6,005	3,057	3,154	4,226
Algeria	2,593	2,306	2,212	2,347	2,390	1,788	1,564	1,732	1,665	1,681	1,828	2,341	2,073	1,982
Egypt, Arab Republic	..	..	..	..	..	..	..	..	..	..	..	..	..	..
Libya	..	..	..	..	..	..	..	..	..	..	..	..	..	..
Morocco	899	1,846	1,670	1,994	2,350	2,247	2,210	2,376	2,227	2,249	2,358	716	1,081	2,093
Tunisia	..	..	..	..	..	..	..	..	..	..	1,819	..	..	1,819
ALL AFRICA	5,508	8,484	8,185	8,689	10,111	10,310	10,992	11,132	12,127	13,013	14,254	4,482	6,247	10,415

5-44. Manufactured goods imports, growth

	Percent											Average annual percentage growth		
	1980	*1992*	*1993*	*1994*	*1995*	*1996*	*1997*	*1998*	*1999*	*2000*	*2001*	*75-84*	*85-89*	*90-MR*
SUB-SAHARAN AFRICA	18.5	-3.7	11.1	-3.8	24.6	10.1	16.7	-16.7	-7.7	1.0	4.5	29.8	12.0	3.6
excluding South Africa	18.5	-3.7	11.1	-3.8	24.6	10.1	16.7	-16.7	-7.7	1.0	4.5	29.8	11.2	3.6
excl. S.Africa & Nigeria	18.5	-3.7	11.1	-3.8	24.6	10.1	16.7	-16.7	-7.7	1.0	4.5	29.8	11.2	3.6
Angola	..	53.5	-43.9	-5.0	20.5	264.7	29.4	..	..	..	..	..	-15.4	11.9
Benin	..	..	..	..	..	..	..	..	..	..	..	..	..	..
Botswana	..	..	..	-17.5	2.5	-3.7	70.4	7.3	-23.9	-0.6	18.4	..	..	5.6
Burkina Faso	..	..	..	..	..	..	..	..	..	..	..	..	..	..
Burundi	..	-21.6	1.9	-6.4	4.3	-36.1	-7.9	9.0	15.7	6.1	6.1	..	-4.2	-4.4
Cameroon	16.5	-17.1	31.5	-12.3	10.6	2.4	0.8	8.1	2.3	10.0	5.2	-3.9	3.5	2.5
Cape Verde	..	..	..	..	..	..	..	..	..	..	..	..	..	..
Central African Republic	..	..	..	..	..	..	..	..	..	..	..	..	..	..
Chad	..	19.2	-13.0	27.0	21.5	18.3	-0.6	7.0	3.6	..	..	..	..	7.0
Comoros	..	31.2	-1.4	24.3	3.3	6.7	2.0	2.0	2.0	..	..	..	17.6	11.4
Congo, Democratic Rep. of	..	..	..	..	..	..	..	..	..	..	..	..	..	..
Congo, Republic of	..	-16.5	32.2	10.9	-1.1	35.9	35.9	-31.0	8.5	4.6	4.5	..	4.7	6.4
Côte d'Ivoire	..	..	..	..	..	..	..	..	..	..	..	..	..	..
Djibouti	..	..	..	..	..	-7.3	-4.5	33.9	2.4	-0.1	1.3	..	..	5.4
Equatorial Guinea	..	..	..	..	..	..	..	..	..	..	..	..	..	..
Eritrea	..	..	..	..	..	..	..	..	..	..	..	..	..	..
Ethiopia	..	..	..	..	..	..	..	..	..	..	..	..	..	..
Gabon	..	..	..	..	..	..	..	..	..	..	..	..	..	..
Gambia, The	..	-47.3	4.5	-22.2	-9.6	-17.2	-47.4	26.8	6.0	..	..	..	..	-13.4
Ghana	..	..	..	..	..	..	..	..	..	..	..	..	..	..
Guinea	..	-8.6	-2.0	-25.6	3.2	-7.5	8.1	9.4	7.9	2.9	6.2	..	2.8	-1.0
Guinea-Bissau	..	..	..	..	..	..	..	..	..	..	..	..	..	..
Kenya	..	-1.5	9.6	-7.7	86.9	-12.3	0.5	-9.8	-2.1	-0.1	-1.0	..	1.3	4.7
Lesotho	..	..	..	..	..	..	..	..	..	..	..	..	..	..
Liberia	..	..	..	..	..	..	..	..	..	..	..	..	..	..
Madagascar	..	..	..	..	..	..	..	..	..	..	..	..	..	..
Malawi	..	29.2	-3.9	-18.3	-42.3	60.6	48.2	-18.4	-8.9	17.0	5.6	..	..	8.4
Mali	4.5	4.7	-5.0	-13.6	10.2	3.5	4.7	3.8	18.4	8.4	3.0	4.6	0.0	4.2
Mauritania	..	-13.4	-2.2	-6.3	-20.3	-3.8	0.8	26.6	-23.3	-50.5	55.5	..	-2.7	-7.0
Mauritius	..	..	..	..	..	..	..	..	..	..	..	..	..	..
Mozambique	..	..	..	..	..	13.5	-3.3	..	..	..	..	..	..	..
Namibia	..	8.4	-3.6	1.6	1.6	3.0	8.5	-6.3	2.7	6.4	5.8	..	..	2.1
Niger	..	..	..	..	..	..	..	..	..	..	..	..	..	..
Nigeria	..	..	..	..	..	..	..	..	..	..	..	..	..	..
Rwanda	..	3.9	-6.3	3.3	62.1	36.6	39.3	-5.3	-25.5	-4.1	9.0	..	-0.3	8.5
São Tomé and Principe	..	..	..	..	..	..	..	..	..	..	..	..	..	..
Senegal	..	..	..	..	..	..	..	..	..	..	..	..	..	..
Seychelles	..	..	..	..	..	..	..	..	..	..	..	..	..	..
Sierra Leone	..	12.0	-14.2	-2.4	-59.6	120.8	-54.9	47.5	-33.2	43.4	33.8	..	..	-8.0
Somalia	..	..	..	..	..	..	..	..	..	..	..	..	..	..
South Africa	..	..	..	..	..	..	..	..	..	..	..	..	..	..
Sudan	..	..	..	..	..	..	..	..	..	..	..	..	..	..
Swaziland	..	-1.7	24.0	4.9	32.1	-9.9	30.2	-0.8	-1.8	0.6	0.6	..	..	7.5
Tanzania	..	..	..	..	..	-29.3	..	..	..	..	..	..	..	..
Togo	..	..	..	..	..	..	..	..	..	..	..	..	..	..
Uganda	..	..	..	..	..	..	..	..	..	..	..	..	..	..
Zambia	..	..	..	..	54.3	55.7	130.3	-0.1	-9.4	15.4	12.6	..	..	-4.0
Zimbabwe	..	3.2	-13.7	32.5	18.1	6.4	26.2	-13.1	-47.0	39.4	-5.4	..	-2.9	3.3
NORTH AFRICA	-2.7	2.5	-11.7	10.5	5.0	-5.6	-3.5	7.7	0.5	-44.2	9.9	6.6	-6.9	-3.4
Algeria	..	8.1	-13.6	6.7	1.3	-11.1	-10.6	5.5	5.8	..	..	..	-12.3	-3.8
Egypt, Arab Republic	..	..	..	..	..	..	..	..	..	..	..	..	..	..
Libya	..	..	..	..	..	..	..	..	..	..	..	..	..	..
Morocco	-2.7	-3.9	-9.3	15.2	9.2	0.2	3.2	9.6	-3.7	3.7	9.9	-1.2	8.0	3.4
Tunisia	..	..	..	..	..	..	..	..	..	..	..	..	..	..
ALL AFRICA	7.2	-0.4	-1.5	3.3	14.2	2.5	7.7	-6.9	-3.9	-21.0	6.3	12.4	-0.6	0.3

5-45. Capital goods imports

	Millions of U.S. dollars (current prices)											Annual Average		
	1980	1992	1993	1994	1995	1996	1997	1998	1999	2000	2001	75-84	85-89	90-MR
SUB-SAHARAN AFRICA	3,057	9,072	8,042	7,995	10,705	11,475	11,136	10,866	21,705	24,666	22,205	1,846	6,194	12,874
excluding South Africa	3,057	9,072	8,042	7,995	10,705	11,475	11,136	10,866	9,876	9,713	9,789	1,846	6,194	9,607
excl. S.Africa & Nigeria	3,057	9,072	8,042	7,995	10,705	11,475	11,136	10,866	9,876	9,713	9,789	1,846	6,194	9,607
Angola	..	378	322	327	327	303	354	..	..	..	..	..	263	314
Benin	..	215	207	156	246	249	239	253	234	247	371	..	120	230
Botswana	195	536	542	485	657	521	850	875	760	740	834	197	348	676
Burkina Faso	..	131	0	0	151	169	155	196	..	..	..	..	..	116
Burundi	33	78	78	81	88	49	45	49	52	59	66	45	67	68
Cameroon	388	319	325	314	315	362	399	403	407	412	416	359	480	376
Cape Verde	..	98	71	98	121	114	117	95	99	106	106	..	48	95
Central African Republic	..	64	53	43	63	14	20	54	62	82	88	73	67	55
Chad	..	97	125	124	126	149	158	174	154	..	..	52	67	129
Comoros	..	..	..	..	..	..	13	11	14	4	9	..	..	10
Congo, Democratic Rep. of	..	683	464	553	788	862	..	..	..	..	..	..	..	670
Congo, Republic of	0	188	203	113	336	1,105	510	371	321	525	496	20	249	382
Côte d'Ivoire	1,102	481	417	410	584	576	638	725	720	447	439	663	512	520
Djibouti	..	..	..	..	54	53	54	77	81	96	101	..	..	74
Equatorial Guinea	..	26	24	42	64	192	300	384	205	108	83	10	15	126
Eritrea	..	12	62	114	173	162	161	141	122	80	91	..	..	112
Ethiopia	..	320	382	239	334	411	516	582	643	755	589	449	396	465
Gabon	..	335	320	320	339	355	388	343	311	327	344	188	245	341
Gambia, The	..	48	48	39	37	32	37	43	40	0	0	..	4	27
Ghana	..	277	..	..	..	..	..	..	..	..	..	200	171	250
Guinea	..	98	92	72	88	78	83	85	106	120	132	..	62	96
Guinea-Bissau	..	24	14	15	15	10	18	26	-10	4	7	12	13	13
Kenya	409	411	328	503	995	869	844	894	680	730	604	287	455	672
Lesotho	..	..	..	..	..	..	..	..	..	..	..	..	..	..
Liberia	..	..	..	..	..	..	..	..	..	..	..	..	..	..
Madagascar	333	129	140	143	141	164	146	139	140	149	144	160	109	149
Malawi	..	278	272	199	164	259	326	250	305	223	217	..	91	249
Mali	225	201	182	193	246	226	221	231	252	257	280	214	146	223
Mauritania	..	121	114	73	93	72	79	64	59	78	61	85	115	82
Mauritius	89	384	378	381	529	412	493	548	498	653	465	72	186	458
Mozambique	..	..	..	..	166	170	154	166	243	410	396	..	..	244
Namibia	..	461	443	466	514	516	545	498	499	518	534	..	..	484
Niger	..	85	80	67	87	56	68	87	..	..	..	..	107	87
Nigeria	..	..	..	..	..	..	..	..	..	..	..	..	..	..
Rwanda	..	69	72	36	50	54	62	60	55	53	51	50	84	56
São Tomé and Principe	..	9	11	12	12	7	7	8	11	12	13	1	10	11
Senegal	158	175	159	154	180	186	184	221	234	246	283	137	141	201
Seychelles	..	40	60	48	67	166	75	90	91	96	101	16	35	77
Sierra Leone	..	25	23	27	11	24	12	9	5	18	22	54	40	20
Somalia	..	..	..	..	..	..	..	..	..	..	..	..	..	..
South Africa	..	..	..	..	..	..	..	..	11,830	14,952	12,416	..	..	13,066
Sudan	..	355	336	259	322	387	443	541	490	492	520	348	266	400
Swaziland	126	193	172	213	249	284	286	280	272	264	257	95	107	235
Tanzania	..	639	628	597	602	461	503	733	693	638	755	458	472	614
Togo	..	102	58	41	75	105	101	97	..	..	..	51	95	92
Uganda	..	..	..	..	..	..	..	..	..	..	..	..	..	..
Zambia	..	349	328	296	396	361	388	284	253	284	460	118	243	336
Zimbabwe	..	640	508	743	901	930	1,148	784	773	480	458	345	440	710
NORTH AFRICA	4,871	8,101	7,841	7,905	9,775	10,634	10,607	12,193	13,795	13,108	14,066	4,580	5,295	10,482
Algeria	3,324	1,894	1,835	2,118	2,934	3,023	2,831	2,907	3,155	2,983	4,128	3,054	2,444	2,732
Egypt, Arab Republic	..	2,610	2,545	2,349	3,108	4,101	4,114	4,801	5,575	5,639	5,583	..	2,001	3,910
Libya	..	..	..	..	..	..	..	..	..	..	..	..	..	..
Morocco	806	2,019	1,946	2,003	2,186	1,948	1,939	2,567	2,833	2,388	2,237	808	1,009	2,152
Tunisia	742	1,578	1,515	1,434	1,547	1,562	1,724	1,918	2,233	2,099	2,118	719	642	1,689
ALL AFRICA	7,928	17,173	15,883	15,900	20,480	22,110	21,743	23,059	35,501	37,774	36,271	6,426	11,490	23,356

5-46. Capital goods imports, growth

	Percent											Average annual percentage growth		
	1980	1992	1993	1994	1995	1996	1997	1998	1999	2000	2001	75-84	85-89	90-MR
SUB-SAHARAN AFRICA	39.2	-5.3	2.9	3.2	24.2	10.4	8.7	-5.1	-1.2	-0.6	7.3	25.6	13.0	5.3
excluding South Africa	39.2	-5.3	2.9	3.2	24.2	10.4	8.7	-5.1	-1.2	-0.6	7.3	25.6	13.0	5.3
excl. S.Africa & Nigeria	39.2	-5.3	2.9	3.2	24.2	10.4	8.7	-5.1	-1.2	-0.6	7.3	25.6	13.0	5.3
Angola	..	45.1	-10.5	-1.7	-9.0	-7.3	29.4	..	..	..	..	..	-19.2	6.3
Benin	..	..	..	..	..	..	..	..	..	..	..	..	..	..
Botswana	..	..	..	-13.6	27.9	-16.6	75.3	6.9	-12.9	-0.6	18.4	..	..	9.0
Burkina Faso	..	..	..	..	..	..	..	..	..	..	..	..	..	..
Burundi	..	-16.8	6.9	0.2	-3.3	-42.7	2.8	12.0	7.0	10.9	10.9	..	-3.0	-3.6
Cameroon	-7.4	-1.9	2.3	-15.3	13.2	21.9	6.3	6.0	4.0	45.0	5.0	-5.6	8.2	7.0
Cape Verde	..	49.3	-27.7	36.1	21.4	-8.3	0.1	-21.2	4.3	5.8	-0.6	..	..	4.5
Central African Republic	..	2.9	-17.2	-21.1	34.1	-79.1	47.6	162.6	11.9	28.5	4.6	..	..	-2.2
Chad	..	-7.0	-8.0	-2.0	29.6	18.9	5.9	0.4	1.1	..	..	..	..	2.3
Comoros	..	..	..	..	..	..	..	..	..	..	..	..	..	..
Congo, Democratic Rep. of	..	..	..	..	..	..	..	..	..	..	..	..	..	..
Congo, Republic of	..	-16.5	32.2	10.9	-1.1	199.4	-58.4	19.1	2.6	1.2	1.2	..	7.6	7.2
Côte d'Ivoire	..	52.6	-13.5	-2.6	29.4	23.7	8.5	7.5	8.0	6.5	7.5	..	..	10.2
Djibouti	..	..	..	..	..	-4.9	-2.5	37.1	3.0	14.6	1.7	..	..	9.4
Equatorial Guinea	..	-58.9	-4.3	67.5	39.0	189.2	62.3	22.4	-48.3	-48.7	-25.5	..	3.3	20.1
Eritrea	..	..	..	..	..	..	..	..	..	..	..	..	..	..
Ethiopia	..	..	..	..	..	..	..	..	..	..	..	..	..	..
Gabon	..	..	..	..	..	..	..	..	..	..	..	..	..	..
Gambia, The	..	4,501.8	-1.0	-20.8	-7.9	-15.7	11.1	13.2	-8.6	-100.0	..	..	..	31.1
Ghana	..	7.2	14.7	6.0	9.1	24.8	-17.1	13.8	9.8	7.6	8.5	..	-3.1	8.0
Guinea	..	-6.7	-0.5	-24.3	9.4	5.2	7.2	23.5	21.2	11.1	7.1	..	1.9	4.5
Guinea-Bissau	..	58.5	-40.9	26.2	13.8	-37.4	74.0	38.2	-138.9	-140.2	100.0	..	..	-6.8
Kenya	..	-23.4	-15.9	50.3	102.4	-12.6	-2.9	8.9	-2.0	1.1	-1.7	..	-3.7	8.4
Lesotho	..	..	..	..	..	..	..	..	..	..	..	..	..	..
Liberia	..	..	..	..	..	..	..	..	..	..	..	..	..	..
Madagascar	..	-25.4	13.9	-2.1	-9.9	20.1	-3.3	2.8	5.5	10.6	10.8	..	3.4	1.4
Malawi	..	-5.4	-1.8	-28.7	-20.4	59.8	29.5	-8.1	1.6	-46.6	-4.5	..	..	1.3
Mali	3.0	3.0	-5.0	2.2	15.5	-8.0	8.9	8.7	9.0	0.1	8.1	-1.1	3.2	3.9
Mauritania	..	48.8	-4.9	-31.0	46.9	-26.3	-15.9	-0.1	-24.0	56.5	-22.2	..	-14.3	-3.3
Mauritius	..	..	..	..	..	..	..	..	..	..	..	..	..	..
Mozambique	..	..	..	..	..	-14.2	-9.6	..	..	..	..	..	..	..
Namibia	..	8.4	-3.6	1.6	1.6	3.0	8.5	-6.3	2.7	6.4	5.8	..	..	2.1
Niger	..	..	..	..	..	..	..	..	..	..	..	..	..	..
Nigeria	..	..	..	..	..	..	..	..	..	..	..	..	..	..
Rwanda	..	3.9	-6.3	3.3	25.8	11.5	23.3	-0.8	6.1	1.6	8.0	..	6.4	6.8
São Tomé and Principe	..	-32.4	20.8	3.9	-6.4	-38.0	0.2	51.7	5.6	7.1	7.9	..	18.8	-2.8
Senegal	..	-15.2	-8.7	-6.8	8.4	8.4	3.6	22.8	8.7	7.6	10.8	..	4.3	2.9
Seychelles	..	8.8	52.2	-12.7	32.7	125.5	-46.4	25.0	2.0	2.0	3.0	..	23.4	11.6
Sierra Leone	..	-35.1	-3.2	16.1	-61.4	106.6	-47.0	-21.1	-46.8	273.4	19.6	..	..	-9.6
Somalia	..	..	..	..	..	..	..	..	..	..	..	..	..	..
South Africa	..	..	..	..	..	..	..	..	..	..	..	..	..	..
Sudan	..	..	..	..	..	..	..	..	..	..	..	..	20.1	..
Swaziland	..	9.3	-11.9	19.8	10.4	19.9	8.3	1.7	-1.8	0.6	0.6	..	..	5.8
Tanzania	..	..	..	..	..	-22.7	..	..	..	..	..	..	..	..
Togo	..	..	..	..	..	..	..	..	..	..	..	..	6.7	..
Uganda	..	..	..	..	..	..	..	..	..	..	..	..	..	..
Zambia	..	17.4	-5.8	-13.0	23.7	-4.8	13.1	-23.9	-11.3	15.3	64.6	..	16.6	-0.5
Zimbabwe	..	3.2	-17.3	41.4	14.0	8.5	28.5	-27.2	0.8	-36.2	0.0	..	3.4	2.5
NORTH AFRICA	-13.0	-12.2	-1.8	-6.5	10.6	13.5	5.6	23.8	12.5	-36.0	0.5	8.6	-3.3	2.1
Algeria	..	-13.1	-10.5	7.6	7.0	8.9	-1.0	25.3	-1.0	..	..	..	-20.6	0.3
Egypt, Arab Republic	..	-24.1	-4.7	-9.6	26.2	31.5	6.6	23.4	18.4	2.9	1.1	..	..	8.2
Libya	..	..	..	..	..	..	..	..	..	..	..	..	..	..
Morocco	-13.0	3.0	-3.4	-0.7	1.1	-6.6	4.4	35.0	13.4	-13.4	-1.8	-2.0	6.8	3.3
Tunisia	..	9.1	20.7	-23.7	-4.2	-1.0	17.1	10.3	17.2	..	..	..	-13.2	3.6
ALL AFRICA	6.0	-9.5	0.1	-2.4	16.7	12.1	7.0	9.9	6.9	-22.5	3.8	13.0	2.0	3.5

5-47. Direction of trade matrix, imports, 1991

Exporters		DZA	AGO	BEN	BFA	BWA	BDI	CMR	CPV	CAF	TCD	COM	ZAR	COG	CIV	DJI	EGY
		Importers							*Percentage of total imports*								
Algeria	DZA	**	0.0	0.0	0.0	0.0	0.0	0.0	0.0	0.0	0.0	0.0	0.0	0.0	0.9	0.0	0.1
Angola	AGO	0.0	**	0.0	0.0	0.0	0.0	0.0	0.7	0.0	0.0	0.0	0.0	0.3	0.1	0.0	0.0
Benin	BEN	0.0	0.0	**	0.0	0.0	0.0	0.0	0.0	0.0	0.0	0.0	0.0	0.0	0.1	0.0	0.0
Burkina Faso	BFA	0.0	0.0	0.0	**	0.0	0.0	0.2	0.0	0.0	0.0	0.0	0.0	0.0	3.1	0.0	0.0
Botswana	BWA	..	..	..	..	**	..	..	..	..	..	..	..	..	..	..	..
Burundi	BDI	0.0	0.0	0.0	0.0	0.0	**	0.0	0.0	0.0	0.0	0.0	0.1	0.0	0.0	0.1	0.0
Cameroon	CMR	0.0	0.0	0.1	0.0	0.0	0.0	**	0.0	0.0	0.3	0.0	0.0	0.0	0.3	0.0	0.0
Cape Verde	CPV	0.0	0.0	0.0	0.0	0.0	0.0	0.0	**	0.0	0.0	0.0	0.0	0.0	0.3	0.0	0.0
Central African Republic	CAF	0.0	0.0	0.0	0.0	0.0	0.0	0.7	0.0	**	0.6	0.0	0.2	0.2	0.0	0.0	0.0
Chad	TCD	0.0	0.0	0.0	0.0	0.0	0.0	0.7	0.0	0.0	**	0.0	0.0	0.0	0.1	0.0	0.0
Comoros	COM	0.0	0.0	0.0	0.0	0.0	0.0	0.0	0.0	0.0	0.0	**	0.0	0.0	0.0	0.0	0.0
Congo, Dem. Rep. Of	ZAR	0.0	0.0	0.0	0.0	0.0	1.3	0.1	0.0	0.2	0.0	0.0	**	0.2	0.7	0.0	0.0
Congo, Republic of	COG	0.0	0.0	0.6	0.0	0.0	0.0	0.0	0.0	0.0	0.0	0.0	0.2	**	0.0	0.0	0.0
Cote d'Ivoire	CIV	0.0	0.0	1.1	0.7	0.0	0.1	0.3	6.0	0.0	0.1	0.0	0.1	0.0	**	0.0	0.0
Djibouti	DJI	0.0	0.0	0.0	0.0	0.0	0.0	0.0	0.0	0.0	0.0	0.0	0.0	0.0	0.0	**	0.0
Egypt	EGY	0.0	0.0	0.0	0.0	0.0	0.0	0.0	0.0	0.0	0.0	0.0	0.3	0.0	0.0	0.3	**
Equatorial Guinea	GNQ	0.0	0.0	0.0	0.0	0.0	0.0	1.6	0.0	0.0	0.0	0.0	0.0	0.0	0.0	0.0	0.0
Eritrea	ERI	..	..	..	..	..	..	..	..	..	..	..	..	..	..	..	..
Ethiopia	ETH	0.0	0.0	0.0	0.0	0.0	0.0	0.0	0.0	0.0	0.0	0.0	0.0	0.0	0.0	20.9	0.0
Gabon	GAB	0.0	0.0	0.0	0.0	0.0	0.0	1.9	0.0	0.1	0.0	0.0	0.0	0.0	3.2	0.0	0.0
Gambia, The	GMB	0.0	0.0	0.0	0.0	0.0	0.0	0.0	0.0	0.0	0.0	0.0	0.0	0.0	0.3	0.0	0.0
Ghana	GHA	0.0	0.0	0.0	0.0	0.0	0.0	0.0	0.0	0.0	0.0	0.0	0.0	0.0	0.1	0.0	0.0
Guinea	GIN	0.0	0.0	0.0	0.0	0.0	0.0	0.0	0.0	0.0	0.0	0.0	0.0	0.0	2.5	0.0	0.0
Guinea-Bissau	GNB	0.0	0.0	0.0	0.0	0.0	0.0	0.0	3.7	0.0	0.0	0.0	0.0	0.0	0.1	0.0	0.0
Kenya	KEN	0.0	0.0	0.0	0.0	0.0	0.1	0.0	0.0	0.0	0.0	0.0	0.1	0.0	0.0	0.1	0.1
Lesotho	LSO	..	..	..	..	..	..	..	..	..	..	..	..	..	..	..	..
Liberia	LBR	0.0	0.0	0.0	0.0	0.0	0.0	0.0	0.0	0.0	0.0	0.0	0.0	0.0	0.5	0.0	0.2
Libya	LBY	0.1	0.0	0.0	0.0	0.0	0.0	0.0	0.0	0.0	0.0	0.0	0.0	0.0	0.1	0.0	1.8
Madagascar	MDG	0.0	0.0	0.0	0.0	0.0	0.0	0.0	0.0	0.0	0.0	1.0	0.0	0.0	0.1	0.0	0.0
Malawi	MWI	0.0	0.0	0.0	0.0	1.2	0.0	0.0	0.0	0.0	0.0	0.0	0.0	0.0	0.0	0.0	0.0
Mali	MLI	0.0	0.0	0.0	0.9	0.0	0.0	0.0	0.0	0.0	0.0	0.0	0.0	0.0	4.6	0.0	0.0
Mauritania	MRT	0.2	0.0	0.0	0.0	0.0	0.0	0.0	0.0	0.0	0.0	0.0	0.0	0.0	0.2	0.0	0.0
Mauritius	MUS	0.0	0.0	0.0	0.6	0.0	0.0	0.0	0.0	0.0	0.0	0.2	0.0	0.0	0.4	0.0	0.0
Morocco	MAR	0.4	0.0	13.4	0.3	0.0	0.0	2.0	0.0	51.1	4.4	0.5	0.0	1.3	0.6	0.0	0.7
Mozambique	MOZ	0.0	0.0	0.0	0.0	0.1	0.0	0.0	0.0	0.0	0.0	0.0	0.0	0.0	0.0	0.0	0.0
Namibia	NAM	..	..	..	..	..	..	..	..	..	..	..	..	..	..	..	..
Niger	NER	0.1	0.0	2.6	1.3	0.0	0.0	0.0	0.0	0.0	0.0	0.0	0.0	0.0	0.9	0.0	0.0
Nigeria	NGA	0.0	0.0	1.6	0.2	0.0	0.0	0.1	0.0	0.0	1.9	0.0	0.0	0.0	0.2	0.0	0.0
Reunion	REU	0.0	0.0	0.0	0.0	3.3	0.0	0.0	0.0	0.0	0.0	0.0	0.0	0.5	0.2	0.0	0.0
Rwanda	RWA	0.0	0.0	0.0	0.0	0.0	1.9	0.0	0.0	0.0	0.0	0.0	0.1	0.0	0.0	0.0	0.2
Sao Tome and Principe	STP	0.0	0.0	0.0	0.0	0.0	0.0	0.0	0.0	0.0	0.0	0.0	0.0	0.0	0.0	0.0	0.0
Senegal	SEN	0.0	0.0	0.2	0.0	0.0	0.0	3.2	0.0	0.0	0.0	0.0	0.0	0.0	1.8	0.0	0.0
Seychelles	SYC	0.0	0.0	0.0	0.0	0.0	0.0	0.0	0.0	0.0	0.0	0.0	0.0	0.0	0.0	0.0	0.0
Sierra Leone	SLE	0.0	0.0	0.0	0.0	0.0	0.0	0.0	0.0	0.0	0.0	0.0	0.0	0.0	0.7	0.0	0.0
Somalia	SOM	0.0	0.0	0.0	0.0	0.0	0.0	0.0	0.0	0.0	0.0	0.0	0.0	0.0	0.0	24.5	0.0
South Africa	ZAF	0.0	0.0	..	..	..	0.0	0.0	0.0	0.0	0.0	0.0	0.0	0.3	0.4	..	0.0
Sudan	SDN	0.0	0.0	0.0	0.0	0.0	0.0	0.0	0.0	1.4	0.1	0.0	0.0	0.0	0.0	0.0	0.6
Swaziland	SWZ	..	..	..	..	..	..	..	..	..	..	..	..	..	..	..	..
Tanzania	TZA	0.1	0.0	0.0	0.0	0.2	0.1	0.0	0.0	0.0	0.0	0.0	0.0	0.0	0.1	0.0	0.1
Togo	TGO	0.0	0.0	3.3	1.0	0.0	0.0	0.6	0.0	0.0	0.0	0.0	0.0	0.0	0.5	0.0	0.0
Tunisia	TUN	0.6	0.0	0.0	1.1	0.3	0.3	0.1	0.0	0.4	0.5	0.8	0.1	0.0	0.2	0.0	0.4
Uganda	UGA	0.0	0.0	0.0	0.0	0.0	0.7	0.0	0.0	0.0	0.0	0.0	0.0	0.0	0.0	0.0	0.0
Zambia	ZMB	0.2	0.0	0.0	0.0	0.9	0.1	0.0	0.0	0.0	0.0	0.0	0.3	0.0	0.0	0.0	0.0
Zimbabwe	ZWE	0.0	0.0	0.0	0.0	19.1	0.4	0.0	0.0	0.0	0.0	0.0	0.0	0.0	0.0	0.0	0.0
Sub-Saharan Africa	SSA	0.6	0.1	9.6	4.6	24.8	4.7	9.6	10.4	1.8	3.0	1.2	2.9	1.5	21.3	45.7	1.3
European Community	EU	72.8	33.3	39.0	45.4	29.4	80.8	73.9	88.8	38.6	60.0	62.5	66.0	56.3	59.0	6.0	60.6
North America	NNA	17.7	57.4	20.2	0.4	4.1	8.3	7.5	0.0	0.3	0.2	31.3	20.1	35.5	7.9	0.0	5.1
Rest of World	ROW	8.9	9.2	31.2	49.6	41.7	6.2	9.0	0.8	59.3	36.9	5.0	11.0	6.7	11.8	48.3	33.0
World	WLD	100.0	100.0	100.0	100.0	100.0	100.0	100.0	100.0	100.0	100.0	100.0	100.0	100.0	100.0	100.0	100.0

Note: ** means "not applicable."

South Africa's data for 1991 is taken from partner countries' data

Source: International Monetary Fund's Direction of Trade database

(Table continues on the following page)

5-47. Direction of trade matrix, imports, 1991 (continued)

Exporters		GNQ	ERI	ETH	GAB	GMB	GHA	GIN	GNB	KEN	LSO	LBR	LBY	MDG	MWI	MLI	MRT	MUS	MAR	MOZ	NAM	NER
		Importers									*Percentage of total imports*											
Algeria	DZA	0.0	..	0.0	0.1	0.0	0.0	0.0	0.0	0.0	0.0	0.0	0.0	0.0	0.0	5.6	0.0	0.0	1.1	0.0	0.0	0.0
Angola	AGO	0.0	..	0.0	0.0	0.0	0.0	0.0	0.0	0.0	0.0	0.0	0.0	0.0	0.0	0.0	0.0	0.0	0.1	0.0	0.0	0.0
Benin	BEN	0.0	..	0.0	0.0	0.0	0.0	0.0	0.0	0.0	0.0	0.0	0.0	0.0	0.0	0.0	0.3	0.0	0.0	0.0	0.0	0.0
Burkina Faso	BFA	0.0	..	0.0	0.0	0.0	0.4	0.0	0.0	0.0	0.0	0.0	0.0	0.0	0.0	0.6	0.0	0.0	0.0	0.0	0.0	0.0
Botswana	BWA	..	..	..	..	..	..	..	..	..	..	..	..	..	..	..	..	..	..	..	..	..
Burundi	BDI	0.0	..	0.0	0.0	0.0	0.0	0.0	0.0	0.5	0.0	0.0	0.0	0.0	0.6	0.0	0.0	0.0	0.0	0.0	0.0	0.0
Cameroon	CMR	0.0	..	0.0	0.1	0.0	0.0	4.5	0.0	0.1	0.0	0.0	0.0	0.0	0.0	0.0	1.7	0.1	0.1	0.0	0.0	0.0
Cape Verde	CPV	0.0	..	0.0	0.0	0.0	0.0	0.0	0.0	0.0	0.0	0.0	0.0	0.0	0.0	0.0	0.0	0.0	0.0	0.0	0.0	0.0
Central African Republic	CAF	0.0	..	0.0	0.1	0.0	0.0	0.0	0.0	0.0	0.0	0.0	0.0	0.0	0.0	0.0	0.0	0.0	0.0	0.0	0.1	0.0
Chad	TCD	0.0	..	0.0	0.0	0.0	0.0	0.0	0.0	0.0	0.0	0.0	0.0	0.0	0.0	0.0	0.0	0.0	0.0	0.0	0.0	0.0
Comoros	COM	0.0	..	0.0	0.0	0.0	0.0	0.0	0.0	0.1	0.0	0.0	0.0	0.5	0.0	0.0	0.0	0.2	0.0	0.0	0.0	0.0
Congo, Dem. Rep. Of	ZAR	0.0	..	0.0	0.0	0.0	0.0	0.0	0.0	0.4	0.0	0.0	0.0	0.0	0.3	0.0	0.0	0.0	0.1	0.0	0.0	0.0
Congo, Republic of	COG	0.0	..	0.0	0.0	0.0	0.0	0.0	0.0	0.0	0.0	0.0	0.0	0.0	0.0	0.0	0.7	0.0	0.1	0.1	0.0	0.0
Cote d'Ivoire	CIV	0.0	..	0.0	0.1	0.0	0.5	0.9	6.5	0.1	0.0	0.0	0.0	0.0	0.0	1.0	3.7	0.0	0.1	0.4	0.0	2.9
Djibouti	DJI	0.0	..	5.7	0.0	0.0	0.0	0.0	0.0	0.1	0.0	0.0	0.0	0.0	0.0	0.0	0.0	0.0	0.0	0.0	0.0	0.0
Egypt	EGY	0.0	..	0.0	0.0	0.0	0.0	0.0	0.0	2.9	0.0	0.0	0.2	0.0	2.1	0.0	0.2	0.0	0.1	0.0	0.0	0.0
Equatorial Guinea	GNQ	**	..	0.0	0.0	0.0	0.0	0.0	0.0	0.0	0.0	0.0	0.0	0.0	0.0	0.0	0.0	0.0	0.0	0.0	0.0	0.0
Eritrea	ERI	..	**	..	..	..	..	..	..	..	..	..	..	..	..	..	..	..	..	..	..	..
Ethiopia	ETH	0.0	..	**	0.0	0.0	0.0	0.0	0.0	1.5	0.0	0.0	0.0	0.0	0.0	0.0	0.0	0.0	0.0	0.0	0.0	0.0
Gabon	GAB	0.0	..	0.0	**	0.0	0.0	0.0	0.0	0.0	0.0	0.0	0.0	0.0	0.1	0.0	0.0	0.0	0.2	0.0	0.0	0.0
Gambia, The	GMB	0.0	..	0.0	0.0	**	0.0	0.1	0.2	0.0	0.0	0.0	0.0	0.0	0.0	0.0	0.0	0.0	0.0	0.0	0.0	0.0
Ghana	GHA	0.0	..	0.0	0.0	0.0	**	0.0	0.0	0.0	0.0	0.0	0.0	0.0	0.0	0.0	0.0	0.0	0.0	0.0	0.0	0.0
Guinea	GIN	0.0	..	0.0	0.0	0.0	0.0	**	0.1	0.0	0.0	0.0	0.0	0.0	0.0	0.0	0.0	0.0	0.1	0.0	0.0	0.0
Guinea-Bissau	GNB	0.0	..	0.0	0.0	0.2	0.0	0.0	**	0.0	0.0	0.0	0.0	0.0	0.0	0.0	0.0	0.0	0.0	0.0	0.0	0.0
Kenya	KEN	0.0	..	0.0	0.0	0.0	0.0	0.0	0.0	**	0.0	0.2	0.0	0.0	0.0	0.0	0.0	0.2	0.0	0.3	0.0	0.0
Lesotho	LSO	..	..	..	..	..	..	..	..	..	**	..	..	..	..	..	..	..	..	..	..	..
Liberia	LBR	0.0	..	0.0	0.0	0.0	0.0	0.0	0.0	0.0	0.0	**	0.0	0.0	0.0	0.0	0.6	0.0	0.0	0.0	0.0	0.0
Libya	LBY	0.6	..	0.0	0.0	0.0	0.1	0.0	0.0	0.0	0.0	0.0	**	0.0	0.0	0.0	0.0	0.0	3.3	0.0	0.0	0.0
Madagascar	MDG	0.0	..	0.0	0.0	0.0	0.0	0.0	0.0	0.1	0.0	0.0	0.0	**	0.0	0.0	0.0	0.1	0.0	0.0	0.0	0.0
Malawi	MWI	0.0	..	0.0	0.0	0.0	0.0	0.0	0.0	0.1	0.3	0.0	0.0	0.0	**	0.0	0.0	0.0	0.0	0.6	0.0	0.0
Mali	MLI	0.0	..	0.0	0.0	0.0	0.0	0.0	0.0	0.0	0.0	0.0	0.0	0.0	0.0	**	0.0	0.0	0.1	0.0	0.0	0.1
Mauritania	MRT	0.0	..	0.0	0.0	0.0	0.0	0.0	0.0	0.0	0.0	0.0	0.0	0.0	0.0	0.0	**	0.0	0.1	0.0	0.0	0.0
Mauritius	MUS	0.0	..	0.0	0.0	0.0	0.0	0.0	0.0	0.7	0.0	0.0	0.0	3.8	0.0	0.0	0.0	**	0.0	0.0	0.0	0.0
Morocco	MAR	0.0	..	0.0	0.7	0.0	0.1	0.1	0.0	0.0	0.0	0.0	1.2	0.2	0.8	0.0	0.1	0.0	**	0.1	0.0	0.0
Mozambique	MOZ	0.0	..	0.0	0.0	0.0	0.0	0.0	0.0	0.2	0.2	0.0	0.0	0.0	0.2	0.0	0.0	0.0	0.0	**	0.1	0.0
Namibia	NAM	..	..	..	..	..	..	..	..	..	..	..	..	..	..	..	..	..	..	..	**	..
Niger	NER	0.0	..	0.0	0.0	0.0	0.3	0.0	0.0	0.0	0.0	0.0	0.0	0.0	0.0	0.3	0.1	0.0	0.0	0.0	0.0	**
Nigeria	NGA	0.0	..	0.0	0.0	0.0	0.0	0.1	0.0	0.0	0.0	0.0	0.0	0.1	0.0	0.5	0.0	0.0	0.2	0.0	1.8	1.9
Reunion	REU	0.0	..	0.0	0.2	0.0	0.0	0.0	0.0	0.9	0.0	0.0	0.0	4.3	0.0	0.0	0.0	1.7	0.0	0.0	0.0	0.0
Rwanda	RWA	0.0	..	0.0	0.0	0.0	0.0	0.0	0.0	3.1	0.0	0.0	0.0	0.0	0.0	0.0	0.0	0.0	0.0	0.0	0.0	0.0
Sao Tome and Principe	STP	0.0	..	0.0	0.0	0.0	0.0	0.0	0.0	0.0	0.0	0.0	0.0	0.0	0.0	0.0	0.0	0.0	0.0	0.0	0.0	0.0
Senegal	SEN	0.0	..	0.0	0.8	0.5	0.0	0.1	0.1	0.0	0.0	0.0	0.0	0.0	0.1	0.1	0.0	0.0	0.1	0.0	0.0	0.0
Seychelles	SYC	0.0	..	0.0	0.0	0.0	0.0	0.0	0.0	0.2	0.0	0.0	0.0	0.0	0.0	0.0	0.0	0.3	0.0	0.2	0.0	0.0
Sierra Leone	SLE	0.0	..	0.0	0.0	0.0	0.0	0.0	0.0	0.0	0.0	0.1	0.0	0.0	0.1	0.0	0.0	0.0	0.0	0.0	0.0	0.0
Somalia	SOM	0.0	..	0.0	0.0	0.0	0.0	0.0	0.0	0.9	0.0	0.0	0.0	0.0	0.0	0.0	0.0	0.0	0.0	0.1	0.0	0.0
South Africa	ZAF	..	..	0.0	0.0	0.0	0.0	0.0	0.0	0.3	0.0	0.0	0.0	0.2	6.9	0.0	..	0.4	0.0	1.2	0.0	0.0
Sudan	SDN	0.0	..	0.0	0.0	0.0	0.0	0.0	0.0	1.7	0.0	0.0	1.4	0.0	0.0	0.0	0.0	0.0	0.0	0.0	0.0	0.0
Swaziland	SWZ	..	..	..	..	..	..	..	..	..	..	..	..	..	..	..	..	..	..	..	..	..
Tanzania	TZA	0.0	..	0.0	0.0	0.0	0.0	0.0	0.0	2.9	0.0	0.0	0.0	0.0	0.2	0.0	0.0	0.0	0.1	0.1	0.0	0.0
Togo	TGO	0.0	..	0.0	0.1	0.0	0.5	0.0	0.2	0.0	0.0	0.0	0.0	0.0	0.0	0.1	0.5	0.2	0.0	0.0	0.0	0.2
Tunisia	TUN	0.0	..	0.1	0.0	0.3	0.0	0.0	0.0	0.2	1.6	0.0	0.3	0.1	0.0	2.0	0.1	0.2	1.2	0.0	0.0	1.7
Uganda	UGA	0.0	..	0.0	0.0	0.0	0.0	0.0	0.0	3.9	0.0	0.0	0.0	0.0	0.0	0.0	0.0	0.0	0.0	0.0	0.0	0.0
Zambia	ZMB	0.0	..	0.0	0.0	0.0	0.0	0.0	0.0	0.2	0.2	0.0	0.0	0.0	1.0	0.0	0.0	0.0	0.0	0.3	0.2	0.0
Zimbabwe	ZWE	0.0	..	0.0	0.0	0.0	0.0	0.0	0.0	0.5	0.5	0.0	0.0	0.1	0.6	0.0	0.0	0.6	0.0	1.2	0.1	0.0
Sub-Saharan Africa	SSA	0.0	..	0.1	1.5	0.7	1.7	5.7	7.2	19.1	1.1	0.4	1.4	13.0	46.0	2.5	7.8	18.4	1.5	3.4	2.2	5.1
European Community	EU	94.7	..	43.8	49.2	68.4	68.9	57.2	23.7	54.3	44.1	54.5	84.1	55.1	46.4	33.0	56.1	80.5	67.5	21.1	43.9	87.9
North America	NNA	0.7	..	6.8	27.6	1.2	14.4	25.2	0.3	6.5	51.4	1.7	0.0	12.5	17.1	3.0	2.3	12.0	4.0	8.7	12.1	4.1
Rest of World	ROW	4.6	..	49.4	21.7	29.6	15.0	11.9	68.8	20.2	3.5	43.3	14.5	19.4	-9.5	61.4	33.9	-11.0	27.0	66.8	41.7	2.9
World	WLD	100.0	..	100.0	100.0	100.0	100.0	100.0	100.0	100.0	100.0	100.0	100.0	100.0	100.0	100.0	100.0	100.0	100.0	100.0	100.0	100.0

Note: ** means "not applicable."

South Africa's data for 1991 is taken from partner countries' data

Source: International Monetary Fund's Direction of Trade database

(Table continues on the following page)

5-47. Direction of trade matrix, imports, 1991 (continued)

Importers — *Percentage of total imports*

Exporters		NGA	REU	RWA	STP	SEN	SYC	SLE	SOM	ZAF	SDN	SWZ	TZA	TGO	TUN	UGA	ZMB	ZWE	SSA	EU	NNA	ROW	WLD
Algeria	DZA	0.0	0.0	0.0	0.0	0.0	0.0	0.0	0.0	0.0	0.0	0.0	0.0	0.0	2.6	0.0	0.0	0.0	0.1	0.3	0.2	0.1	0.2
Angola	AGO	0.0	0.0	0.0	0.0	0.0	0.0	0.0	0.0	0.0	0.0	0.0	0.0	0.0	0.0	0.0	0.1	0.5	0.0	0.1	0.0	0.0	0.1
Benin	BEN	0.0	0.0	0.0	0.0	0.2	0.0	0.0	0.0	0.0	0.0	0.0	0.0	0.2	0.0	0.0	0.0	0.0	0.0	0.0	0.0	0.0	0.0
Burkina Faso	BFA	0.1	0.0	0.0	0.0	1.1	0.0	0.0	0.0	0.0	0.0	0.0	0.0	4.9	0.0	0.0	0.0	0.0	0.2	0.0	0.0	0.0	0.0
Botswana	BWA	..	..	..	..	..	..	..	..	..	..	..	..	..	..	..	..	..	..	..	..	..	..
Burundi	BDI	0.0	0.0	0.7	0.0	0.0	0.0	0.0	0.0	0.0	0.0	0.0	0.9	0.0	0.0	0.0	0.6	0.3	0.0	0.0	0.0	0.0	0.0
Cameroon	CMR	0.1	0.0	0.0	0.0	2.4	0.0	0.0	0.0	0.0	0.0	0.0	0.0	0.1	0.2	0.0	0.0	0.1	0.1	0.1	0.0	0.0	0.0
Cape Verde	CPV	0.0	0.0	0.0	0.0	0.0	0.0	0.0	0.0	0.0	0.0	0.0	0.0	0.0	0.0	0.0	0.0	0.1	0.0	0.0	0.0	0.0	0.0
Central African Republic	CAF	0.0	0.0	0.0	0.0	0.1	0.0	0.0	0.0	0.0	0.0	0.0	0.0	0.0	0.0	0.0	0.0	0.0	0.0	0.0	0.0	0.0	0.0
Chad	TCD	0.1	0.0	0.0	0.0	0.1	0.0	0.0	0.0	0.0	0.0	0.0	0.0	0.0	0.0	0.0	0.0	0.0	0.0	0.0	0.0	0.0	0.0
Comoros	COM	0.0	1.4	0.0	0.0	0.0	0.0	0.0	0.0	0.0	0.0	0.0	0.0	0.0	0.0	0.0	0.0	0.0	0.0	0.0	0.0	0.0	0.0
Congo, Dem. Rep. Of	ZAR	0.3	0.0	0.3	0.0	0.1	0.0	0.0	0.0	0.2	0.0	0.0	0.2	0.0	0.0	0.0	0.3	0.6	0.2	0.0	0.0	0.0	0.0
Congo, Republic of	COG	0.0	0.0	0.0	0.0	0.8	0.0	0.0	0.0	0.0	0.0	0.1	0.0	0.3	0.0	0.0	0.0	0.1	0.0	0.0	0.0	0.0	0.0
Cote d'Ivoire	CIV	3.2	0.0	0.0	0.0	3.2	1.0	0.8	0.0	0.0	0.0	0.5	0.1	0.2	0.1	0.0	0.0	0.5	0.9	0.1	0.0	0.0	0.1
Djibouti	DJI	0.0	0.0	0.0	0.0	0.0	0.0	0.0	0.1	0.0	0.0	0.0	0.1	0.0	0.0	0.0	0.0	0.0	0.0	0.0	0.0	0.0	0.0
Egypt	EGY	0.0	0.0	0.0	0.0	0.0	0.0	0.2	0.7	0.0	0.8	0.4	0.3	0.0	0.1	1.4	0.0	2.4	0.2	0.2	0.2	0.2	0.2
Equatorial Guinea	GNQ	0.0	0.0	0.0	0.0	0.0	0.0	0.0	0.0	0.0	0.0	0.0	0.0	0.0	0.0	0.0	0.0	0.0	0.1	0.0	0.0	0.0	0.0
Eritrea	ERI	..	..	..	..	..	..	..	..	..	..	..	..	..	..	..	..	..	..	..	..	..	..
Ethiopia	ETH	0.0	0.0	0.0	0.0	0.0	0.0	0.0	0.0	0.0	0.0	0.0	0.0	0.0	0.0	0.0	0.0	0.0	0.0	0.0	0.0	0.0	0.0
Gabon	GAB	0.2	0.0	0.0	0.0	0.3	0.0	0.0	0.0	0.0	0.0	0.0	0.0	0.2	0.1	0.0	0.0	0.0	0.3	0.0	0.0	0.0	0.0
Gambia, The	GMB	0.0	0.0	0.0	0.0	1.4	0.0	0.0	0.0	0.0	0.0	0.0	0.0	0.0	0.0	0.0	0.0	0.0	0.0	0.0	0.0	0.0	0.0
Ghana	GHA	0.3	0.0	0.0	0.0	0.0	0.0	0.0	0.0	0.0	0.0	0.0	0.0	0.2	0.0	0.0	0.0	0.0	0.1	0.0	0.0	0.0	0.0
Guinea	GIN	0.1	0.0	0.0	0.0	0.8	0.0	0.0	0.3	0.0	0.0	0.0	0.0	0.1	0.1	0.0	0.0	0.0	0.2	0.0	0.0	0.0	0.0
Guinea-Bissau	GNB	0.0	0.0	0.0	0.0	0.4	0.0	0.0	0.0	0.0	0.0	0.0	0.0	0.0	0.2	0.0	0.0	0.0	0.0	0.0	0.0	0.0	0.0
Kenya	KEN	0.0	0.0	0.0	0.0	0.0	0.0	0.0	0.0	0.1	0.0	0.0	1.8	0.0	0.1	0.8	0.9	0.9	0.1	0.1	0.0	0.1	0.1
Lesotho	LSO	..	..	..	..	..	..	..	..	..	..	..	..	..	..	..	..	..	..	..	..	..	..
Liberia	LBR	0.0	0.0	0.0	0.0	0.0	0.0	0.0	0.0	0.0	0.0	0.0	0.0	0.0	0.0	0.0	0.0	0.0	0.0	0.0	0.0	0.3	0.1
Libya	LBY	0.0	0.0	0.0	0.0	0.0	0.0	0.4	0.0	0.0	1.1	0.0	0.0	0.0	3.0	0.0	0.0	0.2	0.0	0.2	0.0	0.1	0.1
Madagascar	MDG	0.0	0.4	0.0	0.0	0.0	0.0	0.0	0.0	0.1	0.0	0.1	0.0	0.0	0.0	0.0	0.0	0.2	0.0	0.0	0.0	0.0	0.0
Malawi	MWI	0.0	0.0	0.0	0.0	0.0	0.0	0.0	0.0	1.2	0.0	0.6	0.4	0.0	0.0	0.0	1.1	2.9	0.4	0.0	0.0	0.0	0.0
Mali	MLI	0.0	0.0	0.0	0.0	3.5	0.0	0.0	0.0	0.0	0.0	0.0	0.0	0.3	0.0	0.0	0.0	0.0	0.3	0.0	0.0	0.0	0.0
Mauritania	MRT	0.0	0.0	0.0	0.0	0.0	0.0	0.0	0.0	0.0	0.0	0.0	0.0	0.0	0.1	0.0	0.0	0.0	0.0	0.0	0.0	0.0	0.0
Mauritius	MUS	0.0	0.7	0.0	0.0	0.0	1.8	0.0	0.0	1.1	0.0	0.7	0.9	0.0	0.0	0.0	0.0	0.1	0.4	0.0	0.0	0.1	0.0
Morocco	MAR	0.1	0.0	0.0	0.0	0.0	0.0	0.0	0.0	0.0	0.0	0.0	0.0	0.8	0.9	0.0	0.1	0.4	0.5	0.3	0.1	0.2	0.2
Mozambique	MOZ	0.0	0.0	0.0	0.0	0.0	0.0	0.0	0.0	0.0	0.0	6.0	0.3	0.0	0.0	0.0	0.0	3.9	0.2	0.0	0.0	0.0	0.0
Namibia	NAM	..	..	..	..	..	..	..	..	..	..	..	..	..	..	..	..	..	..	..	..	..	..
Niger	NER	0.4	0.0	0.0	0.0	0.0	0.0	0.0	0.0	0.0	0.0	0.0	0.0	0.4	0.0	0.0	0.0	0.0	0.2	0.0	0.0	0.0	0.0
Nigeria	NGA	**	0.0	0.0	0.0	0.2	0.0	0.0	0.0	0.0	0.0	0.0	0.0	4.1	0.0	0.0	0.0	0.0	0.1	0.2	0.1	0.1	0.1
Reunion	REU	0.0	**	0.0	0.0	0.0	0.0	0.0	0.0	0.3	0.0	0.0	0.0	0.0	0.0	0.0	0.0	0.0	0.2	0.1	0.0	0.0	0.1
Rwanda	RWA	0.0	0.0	**	0.0	0.0	0.0	0.0	0.0	0.2	0.0	0.0	2.8	0.0	0.0	0.0	0.0	0.0	0.1	0.0	0.0	0.0	0.0
Sao Tome and Principe	STP	0.0	0.0	0.0	**	0.0	0.0	0.0	0.0	0.0	0.0	0.0	0.0	0.0	0.0	0.0	0.0	0.0	0.0	0.0	0.0	0.0	0.0
Senegal	SEN	0.6	0.0	0.0	0.0	**	0.0	0.1	0.0	0.0	0.0	0.0	0.0	0.1	0.0	0.0	0.0	0.0	0.4	0.0	0.0	0.0	0.0
Seychelles	SYC	0.0	0.0	0.0	0.0	0.0	**	0.0	0.0	0.1	0.0	0.0	0.0	0.0	0.0	0.0	0.0	0.0	0.0	0.0	0.0	0.0	0.0
Sierra Leone	SLE	0.0	0.0	0.0	0.0	0.1	0.0	**	0.0	0.0	0.0	0.0	0.0	0.0	0.0	0.0	0.0	0.0	0.1	0.0	0.0	0.0	0.0
Somalia	SOM	0.0	0.0	0.0	0.0	0.0	0.0	0.0	**	0.0	0.1	0.0	0.3	0.0	0.0	0.0	0.0	0.0	0.0	0.0	0.0	0.0	0.0
South Africa	ZAF	0.0	0.3	..	0.0	0.0	0.0	0.0	0.0	**	0.0	0.0	0.0	0.0	0.2	0.0	0.4	8.0	0.3	0.5	0.4	0.2	0.4
Sudan	SDN	0.0	0.0	0.0	0.0	0.0	0.0	0.0	0.0	0.0	**	0.0	0.7	0.0	0.1	0.0	0.0	0.1	0.1	0.0	0.0	0.0	0.0
Swaziland	SWZ	..	..	..	..	..	..	..	..	..	..	**	..	..	..	..	..	..	..	..	..	..	..
Tanzania	TZA	0.0	0.0	0.0	0.0	0.0	0.0	0.0	0.5	0.0	0.0	0.7	**	0.0	0.0	0.5	0.9	0.2	0.1	0.0	0.0	0.0	0.0
Togo	TGO	0.1	0.0	0.0	0.0	0.2	0.0	0.0	0.0	0.0	0.0	0.0	0.0	**	0.0	0.0	0.0	0.0	0.1	0.0	0.0	0.0	0.0
Tunisia	TUN	0.0	0.3	0.0	0.0	0.4	0.0	0.0	0.0	0.0	0.4	0.0	0.0	1.2	**	0.9	0.1	0.3	0.1	0.3	0.1	0.1	0.2
Uganda	UGA	0.0	0.0	0.0	0.0	0.0	0.0	0.0	0.1	0.0	0.0	0.0	1.1	0.0	0.1	**	0.0	0.1	0.1	0.0	0.0	0.0	0.0
Zambia	ZMB	0.0	0.0	0.0	0.0	0.0	0.0	0.0	0.0	1.0	0.0	1.1	0.3	4.4	0.0	0.0	**	2.7	0.4	0.0	0.0	0.0	0.0
Zimbabwe	ZWE	0.0	0.0	0.0	0.0	0.0	0.1	0.0	0.0	3.2	0.0	2.3	0.6	0.0	0.0	0.1	0.9	**	1.0	0.1	0.0	0.0	0.1
Sub-Saharan Africa	SSA	5.4	43.8	27.0	0.1	14.9	21.3	1.0	1.0	7.6	0.1	12.4	10.4	15.7	1.2	1.5	18.1	44.9	8.8	1.8	0.8	1.3	1.5
European Community	EU	44.9	94.5	77.9	90.4	58.8	57.6	70.3	18.0	51.6	32.0	42.9	50.5	35.9	78.8	75.1	28.1	45.5	50.7	66.6	22.9	28.1	43.4
North America	NNA	43.5	0.8	6.6	0.0	2.2	0.9	21.8	2.5	11.6	4.1	12.7	4.0	11.5	1.2	11.7	3.4	6.0	22.0	7.5	30.4	22.6	17.7
Rest of World	ROW	6.3	-39.1	-11.5	9.6	24.0	20.2	6.9	78.5	29.2	63.9	32.0	35.1	36.9	18.8	11.7	50.4	3.7	18.5	24.1	46.0	48.1	37.4
World	WLD	100.0	100.0	100.0	100.0	100.0	100.0	100.0	100.0	100.0	100.0	100.0	100.0	100.0	100.0	100.0	100.0	100.0	100.0	100.0	100.0	100.0	100.0

Note: ** means "not applicable." Note: ** means "not applicable."

South Africa's data for 1991 is taken fr South Africa's data for 1991 is taken from partner countries' data

Source: International Monetary Fund's Source: International Monetary Fund's Direction of Trade database

5-48. Direction of trade matrix, imports, 1996

Exporters		DZA	AGO	BEN	BFA	BWA	BDI	CMR	CPV	CAF	TCD	COM	ZAR	COG	CIV	DJI	EGY
		Importers								Percentage of total imports							
Algeria	DZA	**	0.0	0.0	0.0	0.0	0.2	0.3	0.2	0.1	0.0	0.0	0.0	0.0	0.5	0.0	0.6
Angola	AGO	0.0	**	0.0	0.0	0.0	0.0	0.1	0.5	0.0	0.0	0.0	0.0	0.4	0.2	0.0	0.0
Benin	BEN	0.0	0.1	**	0.0	0.0	0.0	0.1	0.0	0.0	0.0	0.0	0.0	0.0	0.5	0.0	0.0
Burkina Faso	BFA	0.0	0.0	0.2	**	0.0	0.0	0.2	0.0	0.0	0.0	0.0	0.0	0.0	2.0	0.0	0.0
Botswana	BWA	..	..	..	..	**	..	..	..	..	..	..	..	..	..	..	..
Burundi	BDI	0.0	0.0	0.0	0.0	0.0	**	0.0	0.0	0.0	0.0	0.0	0.1	0.0	0.0	0.1	0.0
Cameroon	CMR	0.0	0.0	0.1	0.0	0.0	0.0	**	0.0	0.0	0.0	0.0	0.0	0.1	0.3	0.0	0.0
Cape Verde	CPV	0.0	0.1	0.0	0.0	0.0	0.0	0.0	**	0.0	0.0	0.0	0.0	0.0	0.0	0.0	0.0
Central African Republic	CAF	0.0	0.0	0.0	0.0	0.0	0.0	0.8	0.0	**	1.1	0.0	0.1	0.1	0.6	0.0	0.0
Chad	TCD	0.0	0.0	0.0	0.0	0.0	0.0	0.5	0.0	0.3	**	0.0	0.0	0.0	0.0	0.0	0.0
Comoros	COM	0.0	0.0	0.0	0.0	0.0	0.0	0.0	0.0	0.0	0.0	**	0.0	0.0	0.0	0.0	0.0
Congo, Dem. Rep. Of	ZAR	0.0	0.0	0.0	0.0	0.0	0.1	0.1	0.0	3.7	0.0	0.0	**	0.4	0.5	0.0	0.0
Congo, Republic of	COG	0.0	0.1	0.1	0.0	0.0	0.0	1.0	0.0	0.5	0.0	0.0	0.1	**	0.2	0.0	0.0
Cote d'Ivoire	CIV	0.0	0.0	0.1	0.3	0.0	0.0	0.0	0.0	7.5	0.0	0.0	0.0	0.1	**	0.0	0.0
Djibouti	DJI	0.0	0.0	0.0	0.0	0.0	0.0	0.0	0.0	0.0	0.0	0.0	0.0	0.0	0.0	**	0.0
Egypt	EGY	0.0	0.0	0.0	0.1	0.0	0.0	0.0	0.0	4.0	0.1	0.0	0.2	0.0	0.0	0.0	**
Equatorial Guinea	GNQ	0.0	0.0	0.0	0.0	0.0	0.0	1.5	0.0	0.0	0.0	0.0	0.0	0.0	0.0	0.0	0.0
Eritrea	ERI	..	..	..	..	..	..	..	..	..	..	..	..	..	..	..	..
Ethiopia	ETH	0.0	0.0	0.0	0.0	0.0	0.0	0.0	0.0	0.0	0.0	0.0	0.0	0.0	0.0	26.0	0.2
Gabon	GAB	0.0	0.0	0.1	0.0	0.0	0.0	0.5	0.2	0.0	0.0	0.0	0.0	0.1	0.3	0.0	0.0
Gambia, The	GMB	0.0	0.0	0.0	0.0	0.0	0.0	0.0	1.0	0.0	0.0	0.0	0.0	0.0	0.4	0.0	0.0
Ghana	GHA	0.0	0.0	0.0	3.5	0.0	0.0	0.0	0.1	0.0	0.0	0.0	0.0	0.0	2.8	0.0	0.0
Guinea	GIN	0.0	0.0	0.0	0.0	0.0	0.0	0.0	0.0	0.0	0.0	0.0	0.0	0.0	2.0	0.0	0.0
Guinea-Bissau	GNB	0.0	0.0	0.0	0.0	0.0	0.0	0.0	2.5	0.0	0.0	0.0	0.0	0.0	0.1	0.0	0.0
Kenya	KEN	0.0	0.0	0.0	0.0	0.0	0.1	0.0	0.0	0.0	0.0	0.0	0.0	0.0	0.0	0.2	0.1
Lesotho	LSO	..	..	..	..	..	..	..	..	..	..	..	..	..	..	..	..
Liberia	LBR	0.0	0.0	0.0	0.0	0.0	0.0	0.0	0.0	0.0	0.0	0.0	0.0	0.0	0.2	0.0	0.0
Libya	LBY	0.0	0.0	0.0	0.0	0.0	0.0	0.0	0.0	0.0	0.0	0.0	0.0	0.0	0.0	0.0	0.9
Madagascar	MDG	0.0	0.0	0.0	0.0	0.0	0.0	0.0	0.0	0.0	0.0	0.1	0.0	0.0	0.0	0.0	0.0
Malawi	MWI	0.0	0.0	0.0	0.0	0.0	0.0	0.0	0.0	0.0	0.0	0.0	0.0	0.0	0.0	0.0	0.0
Mali	MLI	0.0	0.0	0.0	1.4	0.0	0.0	0.1	0.0	0.0	0.0	0.0	0.0	0.0	4.1	0.0	0.0
Mauritania	MRT	0.0	0.0	0.0	0.0	0.0	0.0	0.0	0.0	0.0	0.0	0.0	0.0	0.0	0.1	0.0	0.0
Mauritius	MUS	0.0	0.0	0.0	7.7	0.0	0.0	0.0	0.0	0.0	0.0	0.0	0.0	0.0	0.0	0.0	0.0
Morocco	MAR	0.7	0.0	9.5	0.2	0.0	0.0	0.4	0.0	0.0	0.0	0.0	0.0	0.2	0.5	0.0	0.2
Mozambique	MOZ	0.0	0.0	0.0	0.0	0.0	0.0	0.0	0.0	0.0	0.0	0.0	0.0	0.0	0.0	0.0	0.0
Namibia	NAM	..	..	..	..	..	..	..	..	..	..	..	..	..	..	..	..
Niger	NER	0.0	0.0	1.4	0.7	0.0	0.0	0.0	0.0	0.0	0.0	0.0	0.0	0.0	0.6	0.0	0.0
Nigeria	NGA	0.1	0.0	2.0	0.1	0.0	0.0	0.8	0.0	0.0	2.1	0.0	0.0	0.0	1.5	0.0	0.0
Reunion	REU	0.0	0.0	0.0	0.0	2.2	0.0	0.6	4.9	0.0	0.0	1.0	0.0	0.3	0.0	0.0	0.0
Rwanda	RWA	0.0	0.0	0.0	0.0	0.0	3.8	0.0	0.0	0.0	0.0	0.0	0.3	0.0	0.0	0.0	0.0
Sao Tome and Principe	STP	0.0	0.0	0.0	0.0	0.0	0.0	0.0	0.0	0.0	0.0	0.0	0.0	0.0	0.0	0.0	0.0
Senegal	SEN	0.0	0.0	0.0	0.0	0.0	0.0	0.3	0.3	0.0	0.0	0.0	0.0	0.0	0.7	0.0	0.0
Seychelles	SYC	0.0	0.0	0.0	0.0	0.0	0.0	0.0	0.0	0.0	0.0	0.0	0.0	0.0	0.0	0.0	0.0
Sierra Leone	SLE	0.0	0.0	0.0	0.0	0.0	0.0	0.0	0.0	0.0	0.0	0.0	0.0	0.0	0.6	0.0	0.0
Somalia	SOM	0.0	0.0	0.0	0.0	0.0	0.0	0.0	0.0	0.0	0.0	0.0	0.0	0.0	0.0	50.7	0.0
South Africa	ZAF	0.0	1.1	3.0	0.1	..	0.0	0.3	0.0	0.5	3.0	0.0	7.1	0.0	0.9	..	0.5
Sudan	SDN	0.0	0.0	0.0	0.0	0.0	0.0	0.0	0.0	0.1	0.2	0.0	0.0	0.0	0.0	0.0	0.4
Swaziland	SWZ	..	..	..	..	..	..	..	..	..	..	..	..	..	..	..	..
Tanzania	TZA	0.0	0.0	0.0	0.0	0.3	4.2	0.0	0.0	0.0	0.0	0.0	0.1	0.0	0.0	0.0	0.0
Togo	TGO	0.0	0.0	2.0	0.4	0.0	0.0	0.1	0.1	0.0	0.0	0.0	0.0	0.0	0.5	0.0	0.0
Tunisia	TUN	0.9	0.0	0.0	0.1	0.0	0.0	0.4	2.0	0.4	0.1	0.2	0.0	0.0	0.5	0.0	0.5
Uganda	UGA	0.0	0.0	0.0	0.0	0.0	0.1	0.0	0.0	0.0	0.0	0.0	0.0	0.0	0.0	0.0	0.0
Zambia	ZMB	0.0	0.0	0.0	0.0	1.0	0.0	0.0	0.0	0.0	0.0	0.0	0.7	0.0	0.0	0.0	0.1
Zimbabwe	ZWE	0.0	0.0	0.0	0.0	11.2	0.2	0.0	0.0	0.0	0.0	0.0	0.0	0.0	0.0	0.0	0.0
Sub-Saharan Africa	SSA	0.1	7.8	6.7	17.8	14.7	12.9	7.3	15.2	12.6	4.0	147.1	16.3	2.3	18.7	77.3	1.4
European Community	EU	61.9	19.3	29.7	29.7	34.8	74.1	77.6	83.5	71.6	66.2	53.5	62.6	56.1	58.4	3.4	55.5
North America	NNA	20.4	59.8	7.2	2.5	8.2	2.2	3.1	1.8	0.5	5.7	40.6	17.2	16.8	9.4	0.0	11.1
Rest of World	ROW	17.6	13.1	56.4	50.1	42.3	10.8	12.0	-0.5	15.3	24.1	-141.2	3.9	24.8	13.6	19.2	32.0
World	WLD	100.0	100.0	100.0	100.0	100.0	100.0	100.0	100.0	100.0	100.0	100.0	100.0	100.0	100.0	100.0	100.0

Note: ** means "not applicable."

(Table continues on the following page)

South Africa's data for 1996 is taken from partner countries' data

Source: International Monetary Fund's Direction of Trade database

5-48. Direction of trade matrix, imports, 1996 (continued)

Exporters		Importers GNQ	ERI	ETH	GAB	Percentage of total imports GMB	GHA	GIN	GNB	KEN	LSO	LBR	LBY	MDG	MWI	MLI	MRT	MUS	MAR	MOZ	NAM	NER
Algeria	DZA	0.0	..	1.1	0.1	0.0	0.0	0.2	0.0	0.0	0.0	0.0	0.0	2.3	0.0	0.0	0.3	0.0	0.5	0.0	0.0	0.2
Angola	AGO	0.0	..	0.0	0.0	0.0	0.7	0.0	0.0	0.0	0.0	0.0	0.0	0.0	0.0	0.0	0.0	0.0	0.1	0.2	0.0	0.0
Benin	BEN	0.0	..	0.0	0.3	0.1	1.1	0.0	0.1	0.0	0.0	0.0	0.0	0.0	0.0	0.0	0.0	0.0	0.0	0.0	0.0	0.0
Burkina Faso	BFA	0.0	..	0.0	0.0	0.0	0.3	0.0	0.0	0.0	0.0	0.0	0.0	0.0	0.0	0.5	0.1	0.0	0.0	0.0	0.0	0.3
Botswana	BWA	..	..	..	..	..	..	..	..	..	..	..	..	..	..	..	..	..	..	..	..	..
Burundi	BDI	0.0	..	0.0	0.0	0.0	0.0	0.0	0.0	0.2	0.0	0.0	0.0	0.0	0.0	0.0	0.0	0.0	0.0	0.0	0.0	0.0
Cameroon	CMR	21.1	..	0.0	0.1	0.0	0.0	3.5	1.3	0.0	0.0	0.0	0.0	0.0	0.0	0.0	1.3	0.0	0.1	0.0	0.1	0.0
Cape Verde	CPV	0.0	..	0.0	0.0	0.0	0.0	0.0	0.0	0.0	0.0	0.0	0.0	0.0	0.0	0.0	0.0	0.0	0.0	0.0	0.0	0.0
Central African Republic	CAF	0.0	..	0.0	0.0	0.0	0.0	0.0	0.0	0.0	0.0	0.0	0.0	0.0	0.0	0.0	0.0	0.0	0.0	0.0	0.1	0.0
Chad	TCD	0.0	..	0.0	0.0	0.0	0.0	0.0	0.0	0.0	0.0	0.0	0.0	0.0	0.0	0.0	0.0	0.0	0.0	0.0	0.0	0.0
Comoros	COM	0.0	..	0.0	0.0	0.0	0.0	0.0	0.0	0.1	0.0	0.0	0.0	0.2	0.0	0.0	0.0	0.1	0.0	0.0	0.0	0.0
Congo, Dem. Rep. Of	ZAR	0.0	..	0.0	0.2	0.0	0.0	0.0	0.0	1.6	0.0	0.0	0.0	0.0	0.1	0.0	0.0	0.0	0.1	0.1	0.0	0.0
Congo, Republic of	COG	0.0	..	0.0	0.2	0.0	0.4	0.0	0.0	0.0	0.0	0.0	0.0	0.0	0.0	0.0	0.8	0.0	0.1	0.0	0.0	0.0
Cote d'Ivoire	CIV	0.0	..	0.0	0.0	0.0	0.3	0.8	0.3	0.1	0.0	0.0	0.0	0.0	0.0	1.5	3.2	0.0	0.1	0.0	0.0	0.0
Djibouti	DJI	0.0	..	7.6	0.0	0.0	0.0	0.0	0.0	0.1	0.0	0.0	0.0	0.0	0.0	0.0	0.0	0.0	0.0	0.0	0.0	0.0
Egypt	EGY	0.0	..	2.9	0.0	0.0	0.2	0.0	0.0	2.8	0.0	0.0	0.7	0.0	2.3	0.0	0.0	0.0	0.1	0.0	0.0	0.0
Equatorial Guinea	GNQ	**	..	0.0	0.0	0.0	0.0	0.0	0.0	0.0	0.0	0.0	0.0	0.0	0.0	0.0	0.1	0.0	0.0	0.0	0.0	0.0
Eritrea	ERI	..	**	..	..	..	..	..	..	..	..	..	..	..	..	..	..	..	..	..	..	..
Ethiopia	ETH	0.0	..	**	0.0	0.0	0.0	0.0	0.0	1.4	0.0	0.0	0.0	0.0	0.0	0.0	0.0	0.0	0.0	0.0	0.0	0.0
Gabon	GAB	0.0	..	0.0	**	0.0	0.0	0.0	0.0	0.0	0.0	0.0	0.0	0.0	0.1	0.0	0.1	0.0	0.1	0.0	0.0	0.0
Gambia, The	GMB	0.0	..	0.0	0.0	**	0.0	0.0	0.1	0.0	0.0	0.0	0.0	0.0	0.3	0.0	0.0	0.0	0.0	0.0	0.0	0.0
Ghana	GHA	0.0	..	0.0	0.0	0.3	**	0.0	0.0	0.1	0.0	0.0	0.0	0.0	0.0	0.0	0.2	0.0	0.2	0.0	0.0	6.2
Guinea	GIN	0.0	..	0.0	0.4	0.3	0.0	**	0.1	0.0	0.0	0.0	0.0	0.1	0.0	0.0	0.0	0.0	0.0	0.0	0.0	0.0
Guinea-Bissau	GNB	0.0	..	0.0	0.0	0.2	0.0	0.0	**	0.0	0.0	0.0	0.0	0.0	0.0	0.0	0.0	0.0	0.0	0.0	0.0	0.0
Kenya	KEN	0.0	..	0.0	0.0	0.0	0.0	0.0	0.0	**	0.0	0.0	0.2	0.0	0.0	0.0	0.1	0.1	0.0	0.0	0.1	0.0
Lesotho	LSO	..	..	..	..	..	..	..	..	..	**	..	..	..	..	..	..	..	..	..	..	..
Liberia	LBR	0.0	..	0.0	0.0	0.0	0.0	0.4	0.0	0.0	0.0	**	0.0	0.0	0.0	0.0	1.3	0.0	0.0	0.0	0.0	0.0
Libya	LBY	0.2	..	0.0	0.0	0.0	0.0	0.0	0.0	0.0	0.0	0.0	**	0.0	0.0	0.0	0.0	0.0	1.8	0.0	0.0	0.0
Madagascar	MDG	0.0	..	0.0	0.0	0.0	0.0	0.0	0.0	0.0	0.0	0.0	0.0	**	0.0	0.0	0.0	0.3	0.0	0.1	0.0	0.0
Malawi	MWI	0.0	..	0.0	0.0	0.1	0.0	0.0	0.0	0.2	0.0	0.0	0.0	0.0	**	0.0	0.0	0.3	0.0	0.6	0.0	0.0
Mali	MLI	0.0	..	0.0	0.0	0.0	0.0	0.0	0.0	0.0	0.0	0.0	0.0	0.0	0.0	**	0.1	0.0	0.1	0.0	0.0	0.2
Mauritania	MRT	0.0	..	0.0	0.0	0.0	0.0	0.0	0.0	0.0	0.0	0.0	0.0	0.0	0.0	0.0	**	0.0	0.1	0.0	0.0	0.0
Mauritius	MUS	0.0	..	0.0	0.0	0.0	0.0	0.0	0.0	0.6	0.0	0.0	0.0	3.8	1.1	0.0	0.0	**	0.0	0.0	0.0	0.0
Morocco	MAR	0.2	..	0.0	0.6	0.0	0.0	1.1	0.0	0.0	0.0	0.0	1.2	0.2	0.0	0.8	0.1	0.0	**	0.3	0.0	0.0
Mozambique	MOZ	0.0	..	0.0	0.0	0.0	0.0	0.0	0.0	0.1	0.0	0.0	0.0	0.0	2.1	0.0	0.0	0.0	0.0	**	0.0	0.0
Namibia	NAM	..	..	..	..	..	..	..	..	..	..	..	..	..	..	..	..	..	..	..	**	..
Niger	NER	0.0	..	0.0	0.0	0.0	0.2	0.0	0.0	0.0	0.0	0.0	0.0	0.0	0.0	0.1	0.0	0.0	0.0	0.0	0.0	**
Nigeria	NGA	0.0	..	0.0	0.0	0.0	3.9	0.0	0.0	0.2	0.0	0.0	0.0	0.0	0.0	0.7	0.0	0.0	0.1	0.0	2.4	32.1
Reunion	REU	0.0	..	0.1	0.0	0.0	0.0	0.0	0.0	0.6	0.0	0.0	0.0	4.0	0.0	0.0	0.0	2.2	0.0	0.0	1.4	0.0
Rwanda	RWA	0.0	..	0.0	0.0	0.0	0.0	0.0	0.0	1.6	0.0	0.0	0.0	0.0	0.0	0.0	0.0	0.1	0.0	0.0	0.0	0.0
Sao Tome and Principe	STP	0.0	..	0.0	0.0	0.0	0.0	0.0	0.0	0.0	0.0	0.0	0.0	0.0	0.0	0.0	0.0	0.0	0.0	0.0	0.0	0.0
Senegal	SEN	0.0	..	0.0	0.5	0.0	0.0	0.0	0.0	0.0	0.0	0.0	0.0	0.0	0.1	0.2	0.0	0.0	0.1	0.0	0.0	0.0
Seychelles	SYC	0.0	..	0.0	0.0	0.0	0.0	0.0	0.0	0.2	0.0	0.0	0.0	0.0	0.0	0.0	0.0	0.2	0.0	0.0	0.0	0.0
Sierra Leone	SLE	0.0	..	0.0	0.0	0.0	0.0	0.0	0.0	0.0	0.0	0.2	0.0	0.0	0.0	0.0	0.0	0.0	0.0	0.0	0.0	0.0
Somalia	SOM	0.0	..	0.0	0.0	0.0	0.0	0.0	0.0	1.9	0.0	0.0	0.0	0.0	0.0	0.0	0.0	0.0	0.0	0.0	0.0	0.0
South Africa	ZAF	..	..	0.0	0.1	0.0	0.2	0.0	0.5	1.8	0.0	0.0	0.0	0.3	13.6	3.7	0.0	0.8	0.0	17.9	0.0	0.0
Sudan	SDN	0.0	..	0.0	0.0	0.0	0.0	0.0	0.0	1.1	0.0	0.0	2.1	0.0	0.0	0.0	0.0	0.0	0.0	0.0	0.0	0.0
Swaziland	SWZ	..	..	..	..	..	..	..	..	..	..	..	..	..	..	..	..	..	..	..	..	..
Tanzania	TZA	0.0	..	0.0	0.0	0.0	0.0	0.0	0.0	11.1	0.0	0.0	0.0	0.0	1.3	0.0	0.0	0.3	0.0	1.8	0.0	0.0
Togo	TGO	0.0	..	0.0	0.1	0.0	0.6	0.0	0.0	0.0	0.0	0.0	0.0	0.0	0.0	0.0	3.9	0.0	0.0	0.0	0.0	0.1
Tunisia	TUN	0.0	..	0.1	0.1	0.0	0.0	0.2	0.1	0.1	0.0	0.0	2.1	0.3	0.3	1.7	0.4	0.0	0.8	0.8	0.0	0.0
Uganda	UGA	0.0	..	0.0	0.0	0.0	0.0	0.0	0.0	14.3	0.0	0.0	0.0	0.0	0.2	0.0	0.0	0.0	0.0	0.0	0.0	0.0
Zambia	ZMB	0.0	..	0.0	0.0	0.0	0.0	0.0	0.0	0.3	0.1	0.0	0.0	0.0	2.0	0.0	0.0	0.0	0.0	0.1	0.7	0.0
Zimbabwe	ZWE	0.0	..	0.0	0.0	0.1	0.0	0.0	0.0	0.1	0.0	0.0	0.0	0.0	4.7	0.0	0.0	0.9	0.0	5.0	2.6	0.1
Sub-Saharan Africa	SSA	22.0	..	0.8	2.2	1.4	11.6	5.0	2.4	44.6	0.2	0.9	2.3	20.6	60.3	8.9	11.4	21.1	1.8	118.1	7.4	39.3
European Community	EU	18.3	..	53.5	13.7	81.7	61.8	49.8	68.1	40.3	40.9	61.0	79.8	69.7	35.4	32.9	54.6	75.2	71.4	43.4	73.4	17.1
North America	NNA	41.4	..	7.7	63.7	1.2	10.8	18.9	0.0	5.4	58.6	2.4	0.0	7.7	15.9	2.6	1.2	14.8	4.5	11.4	14.0	10.9
Rest of World	ROW	18.3	..	38.0	20.4	15.7	15.8	26.3	29.6	9.6	0.3	35.8	17.9	2.0	-11.6	55.6	32.9	-11.2	22.3	-72.9	5.2	32.7
World	WLD	100.0	..	100.0	100.0	100.0	100.0	100.0	100.0	100.0	100.0	100.0	100.0	100.0	100.0	100.0	100.0	100.0	100.0	100.0	100.0	100.0

Note: ** means "not applicable."

(Table continues on the following page)

South Africa's data for 1996 is taken from partner countries' data

Source: International Monetary Fund's Direction of Trade database

5-48. Direction of trade matrix, imports, 1996 (continued)

Exporters		Importers NGA	REU	RWA	STP	SEN	SYC	SLE	SOM	ZAF	SDN	SWZ	TZA	TGO	TUN	UGA	ZMB	ZWE	SSA	EU	NNA	ROW	World
Algeria	DZA	0.0	0.0	0.0	0.0	0.0	0.0	0.0	0.0	0.0	0.0	0.0	0.1	0.0	1.4	1.4	0.0	0.0	0.1	0.3	0.1	0.1	0.2
Angola	AGO	0.0	0.0	0.0	0.0	0.0	0.0	0.0	0.0	1.4	0.0	0.0	0.0	0.0	0.0	0.0	0.1	0.4	0.5	0.1	0.0	0.0	0.0
Benin	BEN	0.0	0.0	0.0	0.0	2.7	0.0	0.0	0.0	0.0	0.0	0.0	0.0	0.3	0.0	0.0	0.0	0.0	0.1	0.0	0.0	0.0	0.0
Burkina Faso	BFA	0.2	0.0	0.0	0.0	0.6	0.0	0.0	0.0	0.0	0.0	0.0	0.0	2.2	0.0	0.0	0.0	0.0	0.2	0.0	0.0	0.0	0.0
Botswana	BWA	..	..	..	..	..	..	..	..	..	..	..	..	..	..	..	..	..	..	..	..	..	..
Burundi	BDI	0.0	0.0	0.2	0.0	0.0	0.0	0.0	0.0	0.0	0.0	0.0	0.5	0.0	0.0	0.0	0.4	0.1	0.0	0.0	0.0	0.0	0.0
Cameroon	CMR	0.7	0.0	0.0	0.0	1.9	0.0	0.0	0.0	0.0	0.0	0.0	0.0	0.9	0.2	0.0	0.0	0.0	0.3	0.0	0.0	0.0	0.0
Cape Verde	CPV	0.0	0.0	0.0	0.0	0.7	0.0	0.0	0.0	0.0	0.0	0.0	0.0	0.0	0.0	0.0	0.0	0.0	0.0	0.0	0.0	0.0	0.0
Central African Republic	CAF	0.0	0.0	0.0	0.0	0.0	0.0	0.0	0.0	0.0	0.0	0.0	0.0	0.0	0.0	0.0	0.0	0.0	0.1	0.0	0.0	0.0	0.0
Chad	TCD	0.1	0.0	0.0	0.0	0.3	0.0	0.0	0.0	0.0	0.0	0.0	0.0	0.0	0.0	0.0	0.0	0.0	0.0	0.0	0.0	0.0	0.0
Comoros	COM	0.0	1.2	0.0	0.0	0.0	0.0	0.0	0.0	0.1	0.0	0.0	0.0	0.0	0.0	0.0	0.0	0.0	0.0	0.0	0.0	0.0	0.0
Congo, Dem. Rep. Of	ZAR	0.3	0.0	0.5	0.0	0.0	0.0	0.0	0.0	0.9	0.0	0.0	0.2	0.0	0.0	0.0	4.1	0.3	0.5	0.0	0.0	0.0	0.0
Congo, Republic of	COG	0.0	0.0	0.0	0.0	0.7	0.0	0.0	0.0	0.1	0.0	0.0	0.0	0.0	0.0	0.0	0.0	0.0	0.1	0.1	0.0	0.0	0.0
Cote d'Ivoire	CIV	3.0	0.0	0.0	0.0	3.2	0.0	0.0	0.0	0.1	0.0	0.0	0.0	1.3	0.1	0.0	0.0	0.0	0.8	0.1	0.0	0.0	0.1
Djibouti	DJI	0.0	0.0	0.0	0.0	0.0	0.0	0.0	0.1	0.0	0.0	0.0	0.1	0.0	0.0	0.0	0.0	0.0	0.1	0.0	0.0	0.0	0.0
Egypt	EGY	0.0	0.0	0.0	0.0	0.0	0.0	0.1	0.3	0.1	3.9	0.0	0.3	0.0	0.4	0.8	0.0	0.4	0.2	0.2	0.3	0.2	0.2
Equatorial Guinea	GNQ	0.0	0.0	0.0	0.0	0.0	0.0	0.0	0.0	0.0	0.0	0.0	0.0	0.0	0.0	0.0	0.0	0.0	0.0	0.0	0.0	0.0	0.0
Eritrea	ERI	..	..	..	..	..	..	..	..	..	..	..	..	..	..	..	..	..	..	..	..	..	..
Ethiopia	ETH	0.0	0.2	0.0	0.0	0.0	0.0	0.0	0.0	0.0	0.1	0.0	0.0	0.0	0.0	0.0	0.0	0.0	0.0	0.0	0.0	0.0	0.0
Gabon	GAB	0.0	0.0	0.0	0.1	1.1	0.0	0.0	0.0	0.0	0.0	0.0	0.0	0.3	0.0	0.0	0.0	0.0	0.1	0.0	0.0	0.0	0.0
Gambia, The	GMB	0.0	0.0	0.0	0.0	1.1	0.0	0.4	0.0	0.0	0.0	0.0	0.0	0.0	0.0	0.0	0.0	0.0	0.0	0.0	0.0	0.0	0.0
Ghana	GHA	2.4	0.0	0.0	0.0	0.1	0.0	0.0	0.0	0.2	0.0	0.0	0.1	0.9	0.1	0.0	0.0	0.1	0.8	0.1	0.0	0.0	0.1
Guinea	GIN	0.1	0.0	0.0	0.1	1.4	0.0	0.1	0.0	0.0	0.0	0.0	0.0	1.1	0.0	0.0	0.0	0.0	0.2	0.0	0.0	0.0	0.0
Guinea-Bissau	GNB	0.0	0.0	0.0	0.0	1.1	0.0	0.0	0.0	0.0	0.0	0.0	0.0	0.0	0.0	0.0	0.0	0.0	0.0	0.0	0.0	0.0	0.0
Kenya	KEN	0.0	0.0	0.1	0.0	0.0	0.1	0.0	0.0	0.8	0.0	0.0	1.8	0.0	0.0	0.1	0.4	0.0	0.3	0.1	0.0	0.1	0.1
Lesotho	LSO	..	..	..	..	..	..	..	..	..	..	..	..	..	..	..	..	..	..	..	..	..	..
Liberia	LBR	0.0	0.0	0.0	0.0	0.0	0.0	0.0	0.0	0.0	0.0	0.0	0.0	0.0	0.0	0.0	0.0	0.0	0.0	0.0	0.0	0.1	0.1
Libya	LBY	0.0	0.0	0.0	0.0	0.0	0.0	0.0	0.0	0.0	1.2	0.0	0.0	0.0	3.8	0.0	0.0	0.0	0.0	0.2	0.0	0.1	0.1
Madagascar	MDG	0.0	0.4	0.0	0.0	0.0	1.2	0.0	0.0	0.3	0.0	0.0	0.3	0.0	0.0	0.0	0.0	0.0	0.1	0.0	0.0	0.0	0.0
Malawi	MWI	0.0	0.0	0.0	0.0	0.0	0.0	0.0	0.0	0.9	0.0	0.0	0.3	0.0	0.0	0.0	4.9	3.2	0.5	0.0	0.0	0.0	0.0
Mali	MLI	0.0	0.0	0.0	0.0	7.4	0.0	0.0	0.0	0.1	0.0	0.0	0.0	0.1	0.0	0.0	0.0	0.0	0.3	0.0	0.0	0.0	0.0
Mauritania	MRT	0.0	0.0	0.0	0.0	2.4	0.0	0.0	0.0	0.0	0.0	0.0	0.0	0.0	0.0	0.0	0.0	0.0	0.0	0.0	0.0	0.0	0.0
Mauritius	MUS	0.0	1.0	0.0	0.0	0.0	0.2	0.0	0.0	1.0	0.0	1.3	0.0	0.0	0.0	0.0	0.0	0.2	0.4	0.0	0.0	0.0	0.0
Morocco	MAR	1.2	0.0	0.0	0.0	0.1	0.2	0.0	0.0	0.1	0.0	0.0	0.0	0.6	0.0	0.0	0.0	0.1	0.4	0.2	0.1	0.2	0.2
Mozambique	MOZ	0.0	0.0	0.0	0.0	0.0	0.0	0.0	0.0	1.0	0.0	0.0	0.0	0.0	0.0	0.0	0.0	1.5	0.4	0.0	0.0	0.0	0.0
Namibia	NAM	..	..	..	..	..	..	..	..	..	..	..	..	..	..	..	..	..	..	..	..	..	..
Niger	NER	0.2	0.0	0.0	0.0	0.2	0.0	0.0	0.0	0.0	0.0	0.0	0.0	0.9	0.0	0.0	0.0	0.0	0.1	0.0	0.0	0.0	0.0
Nigeria	NGA	**	0.0	0.0	0.0	1.2	0.0	0.0	0.0	0.2	0.0	0.1	0.0	0.0	0.1	0.0	0.0	0.1	0.3	0.2	0.1	0.1	0.1
Reunion	REU	0.0	**	0.0	0.0	0.0	2.5	0.0	0.0	0.2	0.0	0.8	0.0	0.0	0.0	0.0	0.0	0.3	0.2	0.1	0.0	0.0	0.0
Rwanda	RWA	0.0	0.0	**	0.0	0.0	0.0	0.0	0.0	0.0	0.0	0.0	5.8	0.0	0.0	0.2	0.1	0.1	0.1	0.0	0.0	0.0	0.0
Sao Tome and Principe	STP	0.0	0.0	0.0	**	0.0	0.0	0.0	0.0	0.0	0.0	0.0	0.0	0.0	0.0	0.0	0.0	0.0	0.0	0.0	0.0	0.0	0.0
Senegal	SEN	0.4	0.0	0.0	0.0	**	0.0	0.0	0.0	0.0	0.0	0.0	0.0	0.1	0.0	0.0	0.0	0.0	0.2	0.0	0.0	0.0	0.0
Seychelles	SYC	0.0	0.0	0.0	0.0	0.0	**	0.0	0.0	0.2	0.0	0.1	0.0	0.0	0.0	0.0	0.0	0.0	0.1	0.0	0.0	0.0	0.0
Sierra Leone	SLE	0.0	0.0	0.0	0.0	0.3	0.0	**	0.0	0.0	0.0	0.0	0.0	0.0	0.0	0.0	0.0	0.0	0.1	0.0	0.0	0.0	0.0
Somalia	SOM	0.0	0.0	0.0	0.0	0.0	0.0	0.0	**	0.0	0.1	0.0	0.4	0.0	0.0	0.0	0.0	0.0	0.1	0.0	0.0	0.0	0.0
South Africa	ZAF	0.0	0.1	0.0	0.0	0.2	1.4	0.0	0.0	**	0.1	0.0	0.6	6.8	0.2	0.1	3.9	15.1	1.0	0.6	0.4	0.4	0.5
Sudan	SDN	0.0	0.0	0.0	0.0	0.0	0.0	0.0	0.0	0.1	**	0.0	0.8	0.0	0.0	0.0	0.0	0.1	0.1	0.0	0.0	0.0	0.0
Swaziland	SWZ	..	..	..	..	..	..	..	..	..	..	**	..	..	..	..	..	..	..	..	..	..	..
Tanzania	TZA	0.0	0.0	0.0	0.0	0.0	0.0	0.0	0.6	0.5	0.0	2.0	**	0.0	0.0	0.3	1.1	0.3	0.5	0.0	0.0	0.0	0.0
Togo	TGO	0.1	0.0	0.0	0.0	0.5	0.0	0.0	0.0	0.0	0.0	0.0	0.0	**	0.0	0.0	0.0	0.0	0.1	0.0	0.0	0.0	0.0
Tunisia	TUN	0.0	0.0	0.0	0.0	0.3	0.0	0.0	0.0	0.0	1.1	0.0	0.0	0.0	**	0.0	0.0	0.0	0.1	0.3	0.0	0.1	0.1
Uganda	UGA	0.0	0.0	0.0	0.0	0.0	0.0	0.0	0.2	0.1	0.0	0.0	1.3	0.0	0.0	**	0.1	0.1	0.5	0.0	0.0	0.0	0.0
Zambia	ZMB	0.0	0.0	0.0	0.0	0.0	0.0	0.0	0.0	1.1	0.0	3.2	1.7	0.0	0.0	0.0	**	3.4	0.5	0.0	0.0	0.0	0.0
Zimbabwe	ZWE	0.0	0.0	0.0	3.7	0.0	0.0	0.0	0.4	4.2	0.0	4.5	0.3	0.0	0.0	0.2	1.3	**	1.5	0.0	0.0	0.1	0.1
Sub-Saharan Africa	SSA	7.8	32.8	2.8	18.1	27.4	62.8	4.5	1.3	13.6	3.8	12.0	31.2	11.1	0.6	5.0	38.8	65.4	14.5	1.6	0.7	1.2	1.5
European Community	EU	34.9	95.9	31.6	79.4	53.4	51.6	75.5	11.7	35.4	26.8	56.5	32.2	25.8	83.5	73.3	15.3	41.0	40.3	60.6	18.2	23.5	36.3
North America	NNA	36.3	0.0	5.7	6.1	1.0	5.4	16.9	0.1	10.4	3.7	11.6	2.7	14.5	1.5	4.3	6.2	7.9	20.4	8.5	31.6	21.9	18.7
Rest of World	ROW	21.0	-28.8	59.8	-3.7	18.2	-19.7	3.0	86.9	40.6	65.7	19.8	33.9	48.7	14.4	17.4	39.7	-14.3	24.7	29.3	49.5	53.4	43.6
World	WLD	100.0	100.0	100.0	100.0	100.0	100.0	100.0	100.0	100.0	100.0	100.0	100.0	100.0	100.0	100.0	100.0	100.0	100.0	100.0	100.0	100.0	100.0

Note: ** means "not applicable." Note: ** means "not applicable."

South Africa's data for 1996 is taken fr South Africa's data for 1996 is taken from partner countries' data

Source: International Monetary Fund's Source: International Monetary Fund's Direction of Trade database

5-49. Direction of trade matrix, imports, 2001

Exporters		*Importers*						*Percentage of total imports*									
		DZA	AGO	BEN	BFA	BWA	BDI	CMR	CPV	CAF	TCD	COM	ZAR	COG	CIV	DJI	EGY
Algeria	DZA	**	0.0	0.0	0.0	0.0	0.0	0.0	0.0	0.0	0.0	0.0	0.0	0.1	0.5	0.0	0.2
Angola	AGO	0.0	**	0.0	0.0	0.0	0.0	0.7	0.1	0.0	0.0	0.0	0.0	0.5	0.0	0.0	0.0
Benin	BEN	0.0	0.0	**	0.1	0.0	0.0	0.1	0.0	0.0	0.1	0.0	0.0	0.0	0.8	0.0	0.0
Burkina Faso	BFA	0.0	0.0	0.6	**	0.0	0.0	0.0	0.0	0.0	0.0	0.0	0.0	0.0	3.3	0.0	0.0
Bostwana	BWA	..	..	..	..	**	..	..	..	..	..	..	..	..	..	..	..
Burundi	BDI	0.0	0.0	0.0	0.0	0.0	**	0.0	0.0	0.0	0.0	0.0	0.1	0.0	0.0	0.0	0.0
Cameroon	CMR	0.0	0.0	0.2	0.0	0.0	0.0	**	0.0	0.0	0.1	0.0	0.0	0.2	0.5	0.0	0.1
Cape Verde	CPV	0.0	0.0	0.0	0.0	0.0	0.0	0.0	**	0.0	0.0	0.0	0.0	0.0	0.0	0.0	0.0
Central African Republic	CAF	0.0	0.0	0.0	0.0	0.0	0.0	0.2	0.0	**	2.8	0.0	0.1	0.2	0.0	0.0	0.0
Chad	TCD	0.0	0.0	0.6	0.0	0.0	0.0	0.5	0.0	0.1	**	0.0	0.0	0.0	0.0	0.0	0.0
Comoros	COM	0.0	0.0	0.0	0.0	0.0	0.0	0.0	0.0	0.0	0.0	**	0.0	0.0	0.0	0.0	0.0
Congo, Dem. Rep. Of	ZAR	0.0	0.0	0.0	0.0	0.0	0.4	1.3	0.0	1.5	0.0	0.0	**	0.5	0.0	0.0	0.0
Congo, Republic of	COG	0.0	0.1	0.1	0.0	0.0	0.3	0.9	0.0	0.2	0.0	0.0	0.1	**	0.0	0.0	0.0
Cote d'Ivoire	CIV	0.0	0.0	0.2	0.5	0.0	0.0	0.1	0.0	0.0	0.0	0.0	0.0	0.0	**	0.0	0.0
Djibouti	DJI	0.0	0.0	0.0	0.0	0.0	0.0	0.0	0.0	0.0	0.0	0.0	0.0	0.0	0.0	**	0.0
Egypt	EGY	0.0	0.0	0.0	0.0	0.0	0.0	0.0	0.0	0.0	0.2	0.0	0.0	0.0	0.0	0.0	**
Equatorial Guinea	GNQ	0.0	0.0	0.0	0.0	0.0	0.0	0.5	0.0	0.0	0.0	0.0	0.0	0.0	0.0	0.0	0.0
Eritrea	ERI	..	..	..	..	..	..	..	..	..	..	..	..	..	..	..	..
Ethiopia	ETH	0.0	0.0	0.0	0.0	0.0	0.0	0.0	0.0	0.0	0.0	0.0	0.0	0.0	0.0	3.5	0.0
Gabon	GAB	0.0	0.0	0.1	0.0	0.0	0.0	0.7	0.0	0.0	0.0	0.0	0.0	0.1	0.5	0.0	0.0
Gambia, The	GMB	0.0	0.0	0.0	0.0	0.0	0.0	0.0	0.0	0.0	0.0	0.0	0.0	0.0	0.3	0.0	0.0
Ghana	GHA	0.0	0.0	0.0	7.3	0.0	0.0	0.0	0.0	0.0	0.1	0.0	0.0	0.0	4.4	0.0	0.1
Guinea	GIN	0.0	0.0	0.0	0.0	0.0	0.0	0.0	0.0	0.0	0.0	0.0	0.0	0.2	1.5	0.0	0.0
Guinea-Bissau	GNB	0.0	0.0	0.0	0.0	0.0	0.0	0.0	0.0	0.0	0.0	0.0	0.0	0.0	0.0	0.0	0.0
Kenya	KEN	0.0	0.0	0.0	0.0	0.0	6.6	0.0	0.0	0.0	0.0	0.0	0.0	0.0	0.0	0.0	0.4
Lesotho	LSO	..	..	..	..	..	..	..	..	..	..	..	..	..	..	..	..
Liberia	LBR	0.0	0.0	0.0	0.0	0.0	0.0	0.0	0.0	0.0	0.0	0.0	0.0	0.0	0.8	0.0	0.0
Libya	LBY	0.0	0.0	0.0	0.0	0.0	0.0	0.0	0.0	0.0	0.0	0.0	0.0	0.0	0.0	0.0	0.9
Madagascar	MDG	0.0	0.0	0.0	0.0	0.0	0.0	0.0	0.0	0.0	0.0	0.1	0.0	0.0	0.0	0.0	0.0
Malawi	MWI	0.0	0.0	0.0	0.0	0.0	0.0	0.0	0.0	0.0	0.0	0.0	0.0	0.0	0.0	0.0	0.0
Mali	MLI	0.0	0.0	0.5	2.5	0.0	0.0	0.0	0.0	0.0	0.0	0.0	0.0	0.0	5.4	0.0	0.0
Mauritania	MRT	0.1	0.0	0.0	0.0	0.0	0.0	0.0	0.4	0.0	0.0	0.0	0.0	0.0	0.1	0.0	0.0
Mauritius	MUS	0.0	0.0	0.4	3.3	0.0	0.0	0.0	0.0	0.0	0.0	0.0	0.0	0.0	0.0	0.0	0.1
Morocco	MAR	0.9	0.0	3.4	3.0	0.0	0.0	0.4	0.0	0.2	3.8	0.0	0.0	0.2	0.4	0.0	0.8
Mozambique	MOZ	0.0	0.0	0.0	0.0	0.0	0.0	0.0	0.0	0.0	0.0	0.0	0.0	0.0	0.0	0.0	0.0
Namibia	NAM	..	..	..	..	..	..	..	..	..	..	..	..	..	..	..	..
Niger	NER	0.0	0.0	3.2	5.3	0.0	0.0	0.0	0.0	0.0	0.0	0.0	0.0	0.0	1.1	0.0	0.0
Nigeria	NGA	0.2	0.0	0.3	0.0	0.0	0.0	0.6	0.0	0.0	4.7	0.0	0.0	0.0	1.4	0.0	0.1
Reunion	REU	0.0	0.0	0.0	0.0	0.0	0.0	0.0	0.0	0.0	0.0	0.0	0.0	0.0	0.0	0.0	0.0
Rwanda	RWA	0.0	0.0	0.0	0.0	0.0	5.5	0.0	0.0	0.0	0.0	0.0	0.5	0.0	0.0	0.0	0.0
Sao Tome and Principe	STP	0.0	0.0	0.0	0.0	0.0	0.0	0.0	0.1	0.0	0.0	0.0	0.0	0.0	0.0	0.0	0.0
Senegal	SEN	0.0	0.0	0.6	0.0	0.0	0.0	0.3	0.6	0.0	0.0	0.1	0.0	0.2	1.9	0.0	0.1
Seychelles	SYC	0.0	0.0	0.0	0.0	0.0	0.0	0.0	0.0	0.0	0.0	0.0	0.0	0.0	0.0	0.0	0.0
Sierra Leone	SLE	0.0	0.0	0.0	0.0	0.0	0.0	0.0	0.0	0.0	0.0	0.0	0.0	0.0	0.5	0.0	0.0
Somalia	SOM	0.0	0.0	0.0	0.0	0.0	0.0	0.0	0.0	0.0	0.0	0.0	0.0	0.0	0.0	44.7	0.0
South Africa	ZAF	0.0	0.0	1.2	0.0	0.0	0.2	0.1	0.0	0.0	0.0	0.0	0.2	0.1	0.3	0.0	0.1
Sudan	SDN	0.0	0.0	0.0	0.0	0.0	0.0	0.0	0.0	0.2	0.5	0.0	0.0	0.0	0.0	0.0	0.6
Swaziland	SWZ	..	..	..	..	..	..	..	..	..	..	..	..	..	..	..	..
Tanzania	TZA	0.0	0.0	0.0	0.0	0.1	0.1	0.0	0.0	0.0	0.0	0.0	0.0	0.0	0.0	0.0	0.1
Togo	TGO	0.0	0.0	1.7	0.6	0.0	0.0	0.0	0.0	0.0	0.0	0.0	0.0	0.0	0.5	0.0	0.0
Tunisia	TUN	0.4	0.0	0.5	0.2	0.0	0.0	0.4	0.0	0.2	1.9	0.0	0.0	0.0	0.4	0.0	0.9
Uganda	UGA	0.0	0.0	0.0	0.0	0.0	2.0	0.0	0.0	0.0	0.0	0.0	0.0	0.0	0.0	0.0	0.0
Zambia	ZMB	0.0	0.0	0.0	0.0	0.4	0.0	0.0	0.0	0.0	0.0	0.0	0.0	0.0	0.0	0.2	0.0
Zimbabwe	ZWE	0.0	0.0	0.0	0.0	1.9	0.0	0.0	0.0	0.0	0.0	0.0	7.5	0.0	0.0	0.0	0.0
Sub-Saharan Africa	SSA	0.3	0.2	9.6	19.9	2.4	15.1	6.2	1.2	2.2	8.3	0.2	8.6	1.9	23.5	48.6	2.1
European Community	EU	66.4	26.4	29.0	42.7	91.8	52.6	69.5	86.4	76.9	60.2	47.4	72.4	15.0	49.7	26.4	50.6
North America	NNA	17.2	48.4	0.6	3.9	1.2	7.3	5.4	10.6	1.3	7.6	27.4	12.9	21.5	9.6	0.5	16.8
Rest of World	ROW	16.2	25.0	60.8	33.5	4.6	25.0	19.0	1.8	19.6	23.9	25.1	6.1	61.7	17.2	24.5	30.6
World	World	100.0	100.0	100.0	100.0	100.0	100.0	100.0	100.0	100.0	100.0	100.0	100.0	100.0	100.0	100.0	100.0

Note: ** means "not applicable."

South Africa's data for 2001 is taken from partner countries' data

Source: International Monetary Fund's Direction of Trade database

(Table continues on the following page)

5-49. Direction of trade matrix, imports, 2001 (continued)

Exporters		GNQ	ERI	ETH	GAB	GMB	GHA	GIN	GNB	KEN	LSO	LBR	LBY	MDG	MWI	MLI	MRT	MUS	MAR	MOZ	NAM	NER
		Importers																				
Algeria	DZA	0.0	..	2.2	0.1	0.0	0.1	0.3	0.0	0.0	0.0	0.0	0.0	0.0	0.0	0.0	0.4	0.0	0.1	0.0	0.0	0.1
Angola	AGO	0.0	..	0.0	0.0	0.0	1.2	0.0	0.0	0.0	0.0	0.0	0.0	0.0	0.0	0.0	0.0	0.0	0.1	0.1	0.0	0.0
Benin	BEN	0.0	..	0.0	0.0	0.2	1.9	0.0	0.0	0.0	0.0	0.0	0.0	0.0	0.0	0.0	0.0	0.0	0.0	0.0	0.0	0.7
Burkina Faso	BFA	0.0	..	0.0	0.0	0.0	0.5	0.0	0.0	0.0	0.0	0.0	0.1	0.0	0.0	1.5	0.1	0.0	0.1	0.0	0.0	0.4
Bostwana	BWA	..	..	..	..	..	..	..	..	..	..	..	..	..	..	..	..	..	..	..	..	..
Burundi	BDI	0.0	..	0.0	0.0	0.0	0.0	0.0	0.0	0.4	0.0	0.0	0.0	0.0	0.1	0.0	0.0	0.0	0.0	0.0	0.0	0.0
Cameroon	CMR	2.2	..	0.0	0.1	0.0	0.0	3.7	0.7	0.0	0.0	0.0	0.0	0.0	0.0	0.0	2.9	0.0	0.0	0.0	0.3	0.0
Cape Verde	CPV	0.0	..	0.0	0.0	0.0	0.0	0.0	0.0	0.0	0.0	0.0	0.0	0.0	0.0	0.0	0.0	0.0	0.0	0.0	0.0	0.0
Central African Republic	CAF	0.0	..	0.0	0.0	0.0	0.0	0.0	0.0	0.0	0.0	0.0	0.0	0.0	0.0	0.0	0.0	0.0	0.0	0.0	0.0	0.0
Chad	TCD	0.0	..	0.0	0.0	0.0	0.0	0.0	0.0	0.0	0.0	0.0	0.0	0.0	0.0	0.0	0.0	0.0	0.0	0.0	0.0	0.3
Comoros	COM	0.0	..	0.0	0.0	0.0	0.0	0.0	0.0	0.2	0.0	0.0	0.0	0.1	0.0	0.0	0.0	0.1	0.0	0.0	0.0	0.0
Congo, Dem. Rep. Of	ZAR	0.0	..	0.0	0.3	0.0	0.0	0.0	0.0	1.8	0.0	0.0	0.0	0.0	0.2	0.0	0.0	0.0	0.0	0.0	0.0	0.0
Congo, Republic of	COG	0.0	..	0.0	0.2	0.0	0.7	0.0	0.0	0.1	0.0	0.0	0.0	0.0	0.0	0.0	1.3	0.0	0.1	0.0	0.0	0.0
Cote d'Ivoire	CIV	0.0	..	0.0	0.0	0.0	0.5	1.1	0.5	0.0	0.0	0.2	0.0	0.0	0.0	1.5	3.8	0.0	0.1	0.0	0.0	0.0
Djibouti	DJI	0.0	..	15.3	0.0	0.0	0.0	0.0	0.0	0.1	0.0	0.0	0.0	0.0	0.0	0.0	0.0	0.0	0.0	0.0	0.0	0.0
Egypt	EGY	0.0	..	0.9	0.0	0.0	0.1	0.0	0.0	4.0	0.0	0.0	0.3	0.0	5.6	0.4	0.4	0.0	0.2	0.2	0.0	0.0
Equatorial Guinea	GNQ	**	..	0.0	0.0	0.0	0.0	0.0	0.0	0.0	0.0	0.0	0.0	0.0	0.0	0.0	0.1	0.0	0.1	0.0	0.0	0.0
Eritrea	ERI	..	**	..	..	..	..	..	..	..	..	..	..	..	..	..	..	..	..	..	..	..
Ethiopia	ETH	0.0	..	**	0.0	0.0	0.0	0.0	0.0	1.0	0.0	0.0	0.0	0.0	0.0	0.0	0.0	0.0	0.0	0.0	0.0	0.0
Gabon	GAB	0.0	..	0.0	**	0.0	0.0	0.0	0.0	0.0	0.0	0.0	0.0	0.0	0.1	0.0	0.1	0.0	0.1	0.0	0.0	0.0
Gambia, The	GMB	0.0	..	0.0	0.0	**	0.1	0.0	0.1	0.0	0.0	0.0	0.0	0.0	0.0	0.0	0.0	0.0	0.0	0.0	0.0	0.0
Ghana	GHA	0.0	..	0.0	0.0	0.7	**	0.0	0.0	0.0	0.0	0.1	0.0	0.0	0.0	0.0	0.4	0.0	0.1	0.0	0.0	0.8
Guinea	GIN	0.0	..	0.0	0.1	1.6	0.0	**	0.0	0.0	0.0	0.0	0.0	0.0	0.0	0.0	0.0	0.0	0.1	0.0	0.0	0.0
Guinea-Bissau	GNB	0.0	..	0.0	0.0	1.1	0.0	0.0	**	0.0	0.0	0.0	0.0	0.0	0.0	0.0	0.0	0.0	0.0	0.0	0.0	0.0
Kenya	KEN	0.0	..	0.4	0.0	0.0	0.0	0.0	0.0	**	0.0	1.2	0.0	0.1	0.0	0.0	0.0	0.2	0.0	0.1	0.0	0.0
Lesotho	LSO	..	..	..	..	..	..	..	..	..	**	..	..	..	..	..	..	..	..	..	..	..
Liberia	LBR	0.0	..	0.0	0.0	0.0	0.0	1.1	0.0	0.0	0.0	**	0.0	0.0	0.0	0.0	2.4	0.0	0.0	0.0	0.0	0.0
Libya	LBY	0.0	..	0.0	0.0	0.0	0.0	0.0	0.0	0.0	0.0	0.0	**	0.0	0.0	0.0	0.0	0.0	0.8	0.0	0.0	0.1
Madagascar	MDG	0.0	..	0.0	0.0	0.0	0.0	0.0	0.0	0.0	0.0	0.0	0.0	**	0.0	0.0	0.0	0.7	0.0	0.0	0.0	0.0
Malawi	MWI	0.0	..	0.0	0.0	0.0	0.0	0.0	0.0	0.4	0.0	0.0	0.0	0.0	**	0.0	0.0	0.1	0.0	1.6	0.0	0.0
Mali	MLI	0.0	..	0.0	0.0	0.1	0.0	0.0	0.0	0.0	0.0	0.0	0.0	0.0	0.0	**	0.1	0.0	0.2	0.0	0.0	0.1
Mauritania	MRT	0.0	..	0.0	0.0	0.4	0.0	0.0	0.0	0.0	0.0	0.0	0.0	0.0	0.0	0.0	**	0.0	0.2	0.0	0.0	0.0
Mauritius	MUS	0.0	..	0.0	0.0	0.0	0.0	0.0	0.0	0.1	0.0	0.0	0.0	3.4	0.3	6.6	0.0	**	0.0	0.3	0.0	0.0
Morocco	MAR	0.2	..	0.5	0.5	0.0	0.1	0.9	0.0	0.0	0.0	0.2	0.6	0.1	0.2	1.2	0.0	0.0	**	0.0	0.0	0.0
Mozambique	MOZ	0.0	..	0.0	0.0	0.0	0.0	0.0	0.0	0.0	0.0	0.0	0.0	0.0	0.2	0.0	0.0	0.0	0.0	**	0.4	0.0
Namibia	NAM	..	..	..	..	..	..	..	..	..	..	..	..	..	..	..	..	..	..	..	**	..
Niger	NER	0.0	..	0.0	0.0	0.0	0.4	0.0	0.0	0.0	0.0	0.0	0.0	0.0	0.0	0.6	0.0	0.0	0.0	0.0	0.0	**
Nigeria	NGA	0.0	..	0.0	0.0	0.0	5.6	0.8	0.0	0.2	0.0	0.0	0.0	0.0	0.0	2.0	0.0	0.0	0.2	0.0	1.6	24.4
Reunion	REU	0.0	..	0.0	0.0	0.0	0.0	0.0	0.0	0.0	0.0	0.0	0.0	0.0	0.0	0.0	0.0	0.0	0.0	0.0	0.0	0.0
Rwanda	RWA	0.0	..	0.2	0.0	0.0	0.0	0.0	0.0	2.7	0.0	0.0	0.0	0.0	0.0	0.0	0.0	0.1	0.0	0.0	0.0	0.0
Sao Tome and Principe	STP	0.0	..	0.0	0.0	0.0	0.0	0.0	0.0	0.0	0.0	0.0	0.0	0.0	0.0	0.0	0.0	0.0	0.0	0.0	0.0	0.0
Senegal	SEN	0.0	..	0.0	0.1	0.6	0.2	0.0	0.0	0.0	0.0	0.1	0.0	0.0	0.0	0.0	0.0	0.0	0.2	0.0	0.0	0.0
Seychelles	SYC	0.0	..	0.0	0.0	0.0	0.0	0.0	0.0	0.1	0.0	0.0	0.0	0.0	0.0	0.0	0.0	0.4	0.0	0.0	0.0	0.0
Sierra Leone	SLE	0.0	..	0.0	0.0	0.1	0.0	0.0	0.0	0.0	0.0	0.3	0.0	0.0	0.1	0.0	0.0	0.0	0.0	0.0	0.0	0.0
Somalia	SOM	0.0	..	0.0	0.0	0.0	0.0	0.0	0.0	1.9	0.0	0.0	0.0	0.0	0.0	0.0	0.0	0.0	0.0	0.0	0.0	0.0
South Africa	ZAF	0.0	..	0.1	1.9	4.0	0.2	0.1	0.0	0.5	0.0	0.1	0.0	0.2	9.1	1.1	0.0	1.2	0.0	3.9	0.0	0.0
Sudan	SDN	0.0	..	0.1	0.0	0.0	0.0	0.0	0.0	2.7	0.0	0.0	0.0	0.0	0.0	0.0	0.0	0.0	0.0	0.0	0.0	0.0
Swaziland	SWZ	..	..	..	..	..	..	..	..	..	..	..	..	..	..	..	..	..	..	..	..	..
Tanzania	TZA	0.0	..	0.8	0.0	1.9	0.0	0.0	0.0	4.3	0.0	0.0	0.0	0.0	0.5	0.0	0.0	0.2	0.0	0.0	0.0	0.0
Togo	TGO	0.0	..	0.0	0.0	0.0	0.5	0.0	0.0	0.0	0.0	0.0	0.0	0.0	0.0	0.0	1.4	0.0	0.0	0.0	0.0	0.0
Tunisia	TUN	0.0	..	0.0	0.0	0.0	0.1	0.0	0.0	0.1	0.0	0.1	2.6	0.2	0.2	0.8	0.4	0.0	0.8	0.0	0.0	0.0
Uganda	UGA	0.0	..	0.0	0.0	0.0	0.0	0.0	0.0	17.9	0.0	0.0	0.0	0.0	0.4	0.0	0.0	0.1	0.0	0.0	0.0	0.0
Zambia	ZMB	0.0	..	0.0	0.0	0.1	0.0	0.0	0.0	0.1	0.0	0.0	0.0	0.1	0.6	0.0	0.0	0.3	0.0	1.3	0.2	0.0
Zimbabwe	ZWE	0.0	..	0.0	0.0	0.0	0.0	0.0	0.0	0.1	0.0	0.0	0.0	0.0	0.6	0.1	0.0	0.7	0.0	11.1	0.5	0.0
Sub-Saharan Africa	SSA	2.2	..	1.6	2.9	10.9	11.8	6.8	1.3	34.6	0.0	2.0	0.2	3.9	12.4	13.6	12.8	4.2	1.8	18.4	3.1	26.8
European Community	EU	36.9	..	36.7	27.9	65.6	54.5	53.8	2.8	34.4	5.3	70.2	82.4	50.4	36.9	26.8	64.6	71.1	68.4	69.1	89.2	47.4
North America	NNA	30.2	..	8.6	45.9	9.7	14.3	13.5	0.0	6.1	76.8	4.8	0.0	26.7	19.0	7.2	0.1	18.7	6.2	1.0	4.2	2.3
Rest of World	ROW	30.7	..	53.1	23.2	13.8	19.4	25.9	95.9	24.9	17.9	22.9	17.4	19.0	31.7	52.4	22.5	6.0	23.6	11.5	3.5	23.5
World	World	100.0	..	100.0	100.0	100.0	100.0	100.0	100.0	100.0	100.0	100.0	100.0	100.0	100.0	100.0	100.0	100.0	100.0	100.0	100.0	100.0

Note: ** means "not applicable." Note: ** means "not applicable."

(Table continues on the following page)

South Africa's data for 2001 is taken frSouth Africa's data for 2001 is taken from partner countries' data

Source: International Monetary Fund's Source: International Monetary Fund's Direction of Trade database

5-49. Direction o
5-49. Direction of trade matrix, imports, 2001 (continued)

Exporters		NGA	REU	RWA	STP	SEN	SYC	SLE	SOM	ZAF	SDN	SWZ	TZA	TGO	TUN	UGA	ZMB	ZWE	SSA	EU	NNA	ROW	World
		Importers																					
Algeria	DZA	0.0	..	0.0	0.0	0.1	0.0	0.0	0.0	0.1	0.0	0.0	0.0	0.0	1.2	3.1	0.0	0.0	0.1	0.3	0.1	0.1	0.2
Angola	AGO	0.0	..	0.0	0.0	0.0	0.0	0.0	0.0	1.0	0.0	0.0	0.1	0.0	0.0	0.0	0.1	0.1	0.4	0.1	0.0	0.0	0.1
Benin	BEN	0.1	..	0.1	0.0	0.8	0.0	0.0	0.0	0.0	0.0	0.3	0.0	13.3	0.0	0.0	0.0	0.0	0.1	0.0	0.0	0.0	0.0
Burkina Faso	BFA	0.1	..	0.0	0.0	0.4	0.0	0.0	0.0	0.0	0.0	0.0	0.0	8.2	0.0	0.0	0.0	0.0	0.2	0.0	0.0	0.0	0.0
Bostwana	BWA	..	..	..	..	..	..	..	..	..	..	..	..	..	..	..	..	..	..	..	..	..	..
Burundi	BDI	0.0	..	0.5	0.0	0.0	0.0	0.0	0.0	0.0	0.0	0.0	1.4	0.0	0.0	0.0	0.1	0.2	0.0	0.0	0.0	0.0	0.0
Cameroon	CMR	1.1	..	0.0	0.0	1.2	0.0	0.0	0.0	0.1	0.0	0.0	0.0	0.6	0.1	0.0	0.0	0.1	0.4	0.0	0.0	0.0	0.0
Cape Verde	CPV	0.0	..	0.0	0.0	0.1	0.0	0.0	0.0	0.0	0.0	0.0	0.0	0.0	0.0	0.0	0.0	0.0	0.0	0.0	0.0	0.0	0.0
Central African Republic	CAF	0.0	..	0.0	0.0	0.1	0.0	0.0	0.0	0.0	0.0	0.0	0.0	0.0	0.0	0.0	0.0	0.0	0.0	0.0	0.0	0.0	0.0
Chad	TCD	0.1	..	0.0	0.0	0.2	0.0	0.0	0.0	0.0	0.0	0.0	0.0	0.5	0.0	0.0	0.0	0.0	0.0	0.0	0.0	0.0	0.0
Comoros	COM	0.0	..	0.0	0.0	0.0	0.0	0.0	0.0	0.0	0.0	0.0	0.0	0.0	0.0	0.0	0.0	0.0	0.0	0.0	0.0	0.0	0.0
Congo, Dem. Rep. Of	ZAR	0.4	..	1.2	0.0	0.0	0.0	0.0	0.0	0.4	0.0	0.0	1.3	0.0	0.0	0.0	0.0	0.2	0.3	0.0	0.0	0.0	0.0
Congo, Republic of	COG	0.0	..	0.0	0.0	0.7	0.0	0.0	0.0	0.1	0.0	0.0	0.0	0.4	0.1	0.0	0.0	0.0	0.1	0.0	0.0	0.0	0.0
Cote d'Ivoire	CIV	2.1	..	0.0	0.0	2.6	0.0	0.3	0.0	0.1	0.0	0.0	0.0	0.1	0.1	0.0	0.0	0.0	0.6	0.1	0.0	0.0	0.0
Djibouti	DJI	0.0	..	0.0	0.0	0.0	0.0	0.0	0.4	0.0	0.0	0.0	0.0	0.0	0.1	0.0	0.0	0.0	0.1	0.0	0.0	0.0	0.0
Egypt	EGY	0.0	..	0.0	0.1	0.0	0.0	0.0	0.5	0.1	3.3	0.0	0.4	0.8	0.2	0.8	6.0	0.1	0.3	0.2	0.2	0.2	0.2
Equatorial Guinea	GNQ	0.0	..	0.0	0.0	0.0	0.0	0.0	0.0	0.0	0.0	0.0	0.0	0.0	0.0	0.0	0.0	0.0	0.0	0.0	0.0	0.0	0.0
Eritrea	ERI	..	..	..	..	..	..	..	..	..	..	..	..	..	..	..	..	..	..	..	..	..	..
Ethiopia	ETH	0.0	..	0.0	0.0	0.0	0.0	0.0	0.0	0.0	0.1	0.0	0.1	0.0	0.0	0.0	0.0	0.0	0.0	0.0	0.0	0.0	0.0
Gabon	GAB	0.0	..	0.0	0.1	0.6	0.0	0.0	0.0	0.0	0.0	0.0	0.0	0.2	0.0	0.0	0.0	0.0	0.1	0.1	0.0	0.0	0.0
Gambia, The	GMB	0.0	..	0.0	0.0	4.0	0.0	0.6	0.0	0.0	0.0	0.0	0.0	0.0	0.0	0.0	0.0	0.0	0.1	0.0	0.0	0.0	0.0
Ghana	GHA	2.9	..	0.0	0.0	0.3	0.0	0.0	0.1	0.3	0.0	0.0	0.0	17.7	0.0	0.0	1.0	0.1	1.0	0.0	0.0	0.0	0.0
Guinea	GIN	0.0	..	0.0	0.0	1.5	0.0	0.0	0.0	0.0	0.0	0.0	0.0	0.5	0.0	0.0	0.0	0.0	0.1	0.0	0.0	0.0	0.0
Guinea-Bissau	GNB	0.0	..	0.0	0.0	1.6	0.0	0.0	0.0	0.0	0.0	0.0	0.0	0.0	0.0	0.0	0.0	0.0	0.0	0.0	0.0	0.0	0.0
Kenya	KEN	0.0	..	0.2	0.0	0.0	0.0	0.0	0.1	0.7	0.1	0.0	5.6	0.0	0.0	0.4	0.7	0.2	0.3	0.0	0.1	0.1	0.1
Lesotho	LSO	..	..	..	..	..	..	..	..	..	..	..	..	..	..	..	..	..	..	..	..	..	..
Liberia	LBR	0.0	..	0.0	0.0	1.1	0.0	0.0	0.0	0.0	0.0	0.0	0.0	0.1	0.0	0.0	0.0	0.0	0.1	0.1	0.0	0.1	0.1
Libya	LBY	0.0	..	0.0	0.0	0.0	0.0	0.0	0.0	0.0	0.0	0.0	0.0	0.0	4.0	0.0	0.0	0.0	0.0	0.1	0.0	0.0	0.1
Madagascar	MDG	0.0	..	0.0	0.0	0.0	0.0	0.0	0.0	0.2	0.0	0.2	0.0	0.0	0.0	0.0	0.3	0.0	0.1	0.0	0.0	0.0	0.0
Malawi	MWI	0.0	..	0.0	0.0	0.0	0.0	0.0	0.0	0.7	0.0	0.0	1.6	0.0	0.0	0.0	9.8	0.6	0.4	0.0	0.0	0.0	0.0
Mali	MLI	0.0	..	0.0	0.0	6.1	0.0	0.0	0.0	0.1	0.0	0.0	0.0	0.6	0.0	0.0	0.0	0.0	0.3	0.0	0.0	0.0	0.0
Mauritania	MRT	0.0	..	0.0	0.0	2.1	0.0	0.0	0.0	0.0	0.0	0.0	0.0	0.0	0.0	0.0	0.0	0.0	0.0	0.0	0.0	0.0	0.0
Mauritius	MUS	0.0	..	0.0	0.0	0.0	0.4	0.0	0.0	0.8	0.0	1.8	0.1	0.0	0.0	0.0	0.0	0.0	0.3	0.0	0.0	0.0	0.0
Morocco	MAR	0.0	..	0.0	0.0	0.2	0.0	1.5	0.0	0.4	0.0	0.0	0.0	1.4	0.7	0.4	0.0	0.1	0.2	0.3	0.1	0.1	0.2
Mozambique	MOZ	0.0	..	0.0	0.0	0.0	0.0	0.0	0.0	2.2	0.0	3.2	0.1	0.0	0.0	0.0	0.1	0.2	0.7	0.0	0.0	0.0	0.0
Namibia	NAM	..	..	..	..	..	..	..	..	..	..	..	..	..	..	..	..	..	..	..	..	..	..
Niger	NER	0.1	..	0.0	0.0	0.1	0.0	0.0	0.0	0.0	0.0	0.0	0.0	2.8	0.1	0.0	0.0	0.0	0.1	0.0	0.0	0.0	0.0
Nigeria	NGA	**	..	0.1	0.0	0.4	0.0	0.0	0.0	0.7	0.0	0.1	0.0	1.5	0.0	0.0	0.0	0.1	0.5	0.2	0.1	0.2	0.2
Reunion	REU	0.0	**	0.0	0.0	0.0	0.0	0.0	0.0	0.0	0.0	0.0	0.0	0.0	0.0	0.0	0.0	0.0	0.0	0.0	0.0	0.0	0.0
Rwanda	RWA	0.0	..	**	0.0	0.0	0.0	0.0	0.0	0.0	0.0	0.0	0.6	0.0	0.0	0.7	0.5	0.0	0.1	0.0	0.0	0.0	0.0
Sao Tome and Principe	STP	0.0	..	0.0	**	0.0	0.0	0.0	0.0	0.0	0.0	0.0	0.0	0.0	0.0	0.0	0.0	0.0	0.0	0.0	0.0	0.0	0.0
Senegal	SEN	1.4	..	0.0	0.0	**	0.0	0.0	0.0	0.1	0.0	0.0	0.0	0.3	0.2	0.0	0.0	0.0	0.4	0.0	0.0	0.0	0.0
Seychelles	SYC	0.0	..	0.0	0.0	0.0	**	0.0	0.0	0.1	0.0	0.1	0.0	0.0	0.0	0.0	0.0	0.0	0.0	0.0	0.0	0.0	0.0
Sierra Leone	SLE	0.1	..	0.0	0.0	0.5	0.0	**	0.0	0.0	0.0	0.0	0.0	0.0	0.0	0.0	0.0	0.0	0.0	0.0	0.0	0.0	0.0
Somalia	SOM	0.0	..	0.0	0.0	0.0	0.0	0.0	**	0.0	0.0	0.0	0.1	0.0	0.0	0.0	0.0	0.0	0.0	0.0	0.0	0.0	0.0
South Africa	ZAF	1.1	..	9.6	0.0	0.0	1.8	4.8	0.0	**	0.0	0.0	0.6	2.3	0.1	0.6	7.4	11.5	0.7	0.5	0.3	0.4	0.4
Sudan	SDN	0.0	..	0.0	0.0	0.0	0.0	0.0	0.0	0.1	**	0.0	0.1	0.0	0.0	0.1	0.0	0.1	0.1	0.0	0.0	0.0	0.0
Swaziland	SWZ	..	..	..	..	..	..	..	..	..	..	**	..	..	..	..	..	..	..	..	..	..	..
Tanzania	TZA	0.0	..	0.2	0.0	0.0	0.0	0.0	0.0	0.6	0.0	3.9	**	0.0	0.0	1.8	0.4	0.1	0.3	0.0	0.0	0.0	0.0
Togo	TGO	0.0	..	0.0	0.0	0.7	0.0	0.0	0.0	0.0	0.0	0.0	0.0	**	0.0	0.0	0.0	0.0	0.1	0.0	0.0	0.0	0.0
Tunisia	TUN	0.0	..	0.0	0.0	0.3	0.0	0.2	0.0	0.0	0.3	0.0	0.0	0.1	**	0.1	0.0	0.1	0.1	0.3	0.0	0.1	0.1
Uganda	UGA	0.0	..	0.0	0.0	0.0	0.0	0.0	0.5	0.2	0.0	0.0	3.7	0.0	0.0	**	0.3	0.0	0.5	0.0	0.0	0.0	0.0
Zambia	ZMB	0.0	..	0.0	0.1	0.0	0.0	0.1	0.0	1.9	0.0	1.5	4.2	0.0	0.0	0.0	**	0.8	0.7	0.0	0.0	0.0	0.0
Zimbabwe	ZWE	0.0	..	0.0	0.1	0.0	0.0	0.0	0.0	2.4	0.0	2.9	0.0	0.0	0.0	0.0	2.0	**	1.1	0.0	0.0	0.0	0.0
Sub-Saharan Africa	SSA	9.6	..	11.8	0.3	25.1	2.3	5.7	0.8	13.1	0.3	14.0	19.7	49.1	0.9	3.7	22.6	14.5	10.6	1.5	0.7	1.1	1.3
European Community	EU	25.7	..	50.3	57.8	46.9	73.7	68.5	3.0	40.6	11.8	35.8	36.5	17.1	81.6	61.8	22.0	43.5	38.7	59.0	18.7	23.4	35.1
North America	NNA	41.4	..	7.5	9.6	11.9	10.2	12.0	0.3	14.9	0.2	19.2	3.7	4.5	2.0	6.4	2.3	6.3	22.9	11.5	35.6	25.3	22.2
Rest of World	ROW	23.3	..	30.4	32.3	16.2	13.9	13.7	95.9	31.4	87.7	31.0	40.0	29.2	15.5	28.1	53.1	35.7	27.8	27.9	44.9	50.2	41.3
World	World	100.0	..	100.0	100.0	100.0	100.0	100.0	100.0	100.0	100.0	100.0	100.0	100.0	100.0	100.0	100.0	100.0	100.0	100.0	100.0	100.0	100.0

Note: ** means "not applicable." Note: ** means "not applicable."

South Africa's data for 2001 is taken fr South Africa's data for 2001 is taken from partner countries' data

Source: International Monetary Fund's Source: International Monetary Fund's Direction of Trade database

5-50. Direction of trade matrix, exports, 1991

Importers — *Percentage of total exports*

Exporters		DZA	AGO	BEN	BFA	BWA	BDI	CMR	CPV	CAF	TCD	COM	ZAR	COG	CIV	DJI	EGY
Algeria	DZA	**	0.0	0.0	0.0	0.0	0.0	0.0	0.0	0.0	0.0	0.0	0.0	0.0	0.0	0.0	0.1
Angola	AGO	0.0	**	0.0	0.0	0.0	0.0	0.0	0.9	0.0	0.0	0.0	0.0	0.1	0.0	0.0	0.0
Benin	BEN	0.0	0.0	**	0.2	0.0	0.0	0.0	0.0	0.0	0.0	0.0	0.0	0.1	0.0	0.0	0.0
Burkina Faso	BFA	0.0	0.0	0.0	**	0.0	0.0	0.0	0.0	0.0	0.0	0.0	0.0	0.0	0.6	0.0	0.0
Bostwana	BWA	..	..	..	..	**	..	..	..	..	..	..	..	..	..	..	..
Burundi	BDI	0.0	0.0	0.0	0.0	0.0	**	0.0	0.0	0.0	0.0	0.0	0.1	0.0	0.0	0.0	0.0
Cameroon	CMR	0.1	0.0	0.1	0.1	0.0	0.0	**	0.0	13.2	8.2	0.0	0.2	2.3	0.1	0.0	0.0
Cape Verde	CPV	0.0	0.0	0.0	0.0	0.0	0.0	0.0	**	0.0	0.0	0.0	0.0	0.0	0.0	0.0	0.0
Central African Republic	CAF	0.0	0.0	0.0	0.0	0.0	0.0	0.0	0.0	**	0.0	0.0	0.0	0.1	0.0	0.0	0.0
Chad	TCD	0.0	0.0	0.0	0.0	0.0	0.0	0.0	0.0	0.4	**	0.0	0.0	0.0	0.0	0.0	0.0
Comoros	COM	0.0	0.0	0.0	0.0	0.0	0.0	0.0	0.0	0.0	0.0	**	0.0	0.0	0.0	0.0	0.0
Congo, Dem. Rep. Of	ZAR	0.0	0.0	0.1	0.0	0.0	1.1	0.0	0.0	2.0	0.0	0.0	**	0.5	0.0	0.0	0.0
Congo, Republic of	COG	0.0	0.2	0.2	0.0	0.0	0.0	0.0	0.0	0.0	0.0	0.0	0.3	**	0.0	0.0	0.0
Cote d'Ivoire	CIV	0.2	0.2	3.4	27.7	0.0	0.1	0.9	6.1	0.3	1.3	0.0	2.5	1.1	**	0.0	0.0
Djibouti	DJI	0.0	0.0	0.0	0.0	0.0	0.1	0.0	0.0	0.0	0.0	0.0	0.0	0.0	0.0	**	0.0
Egypt	EGY	0.1	0.0	0.0	0.0	0.0	0.0	0.0	0.0	0.0	0.0	0.0	0.0	0.0	0.0	0.5	**
Equatorial Guinea	GNQ	0.0	0.0	0.0	0.0	0.0	0.0	0.0	0.0	0.0	0.0	0.0	0.0	0.0	0.0	0.0	0.0
Eritrea	ERI	..	..	..	..	..	..	..	..	..	..	..	..	..	..	..	..
Ethiopia	ETH	0.0	0.0	0.0	0.0	0.0	0.0	0.0	0.0	0.0	0.0	0.0	0.0	0.0	0.0	2.0	0.0
Gabon	GAB	0.0	0.0	0.0	0.0	0.0	0.0	0.1	0.0	1.5	0.0	0.0	0.0	0.0	0.1	0.0	0.0
Gambia, The	GMB	0.0	0.0	0.0	0.0	0.0	0.0	0.0	0.0	0.0	0.0	0.0	0.0	0.0	0.0	0.0	0.0
Ghana	GHA	0.0	0.0	0.0	0.1	0.0	0.0	0.0	0.0	0.0	0.0	0.0	0.0	0.0	0.3	0.0	0.0
Guinea	GIN	0.0	0.0	0.0	0.0	0.0	0.0	2.5	0.0	0.0	0.0	0.0	0.0	0.0	0.3	0.0	0.0
Guinea-Bissau	GNB	0.0	0.0	0.0	0.0	0.0	0.0	0.0	0.0	0.0	0.0	0.0	0.0	0.0	0.1	0.0	0.0
Kenya	KEN	0.0	0.0	0.0	0.0	0.0	2.4	0.0	0.2	0.0	0.0	0.9	0.5	0.0	0.0	0.8	0.3
Lesotho	LSO	..	..	..	..	..	..	..	..	..	..	..	..	..	..	..	..
Liberia	LBR	0.0	0.0	0.0	0.0	0.0	0.0	0.0	0.0	0.0	0.0	0.0	0.0	0.0	0.0	0.0	0.0
Libya	LBY	0.0	0.0	0.0	0.0	0.0	0.0	0.0	0.0	0.0	0.0	0.0	0.0	0.0	0.0	0.0	0.2
Madagascar	MDG	0.0	0.0	0.0	0.0	0.0	0.0	0.0	0.0	0.0	0.0	1.6	0.0	0.0	0.0	0.0	0.0
Malawi	MWI	0.0	0.0	0.0	0.0	0.7	1.6	0.0	0.0	0.0	0.0	0.0	0.2	0.0	0.0	0.0	0.1
Mali	MLI	0.2	0.0	0.0	0.4	0.0	0.0	0.0	0.0	0.0	0.0	0.0	0.0	0.0	0.1	0.0	0.0
Mauritania	MRT	0.0	0.0	0.4	0.0	0.0	0.0	0.8	0.0	0.0	0.0	0.0	0.0	0.6	1.1	0.0	0.0
Mauritius	MUS	0.0	0.0	0.0	0.0	0.0	0.0	0.0	0.0	0.0	0.0	1.5	0.0	0.0	0.0	0.0	0.0
Morocco	MAR	0.9	0.3	0.5	0.1	0.0	0.0	0.6	0.0	0.3	0.0	0.5	0.4	0.7	0.4	0.0	0.0
Mozambique	MOZ	0.0	0.0	0.0	0.0	0.0	0.0	0.0	0.0	0.0	0.0	0.0	0.0	0.0	0.0	0.0	0.0
Namibia	NAM	..	..	..	..	..	..	..	..	..	..	..	..	..	..	..	..
Niger	NER	0.0	0.0	0.7	0.2	0.0	0.0	0.0	0.0	0.0	0.2	0.0	0.0	0.0	0.1	0.0	0.0
Nigeria	NGA	0.0	0.0	0.3	0.0	0.0	0.0	6.8	0.0	0.0	5.4	0.1	4.1	0.0	16.3	0.0	0.0
Reunion	REU	0.0	0.0	0.0	0.0	0.0	0.0	0.0	0.0	0.0	0.0	1.5	0.0	0.0	0.0	0.1	0.0
Rwanda	RWA	0.0	0.0	0.0	0.0	0.0	0.5	0.0	0.0	0.0	0.0	0.0	0.0	0.0	0.0	0.0	0.0
Sao Tome and Principe	STP	0.0	0.0	0.0	0.0	0.0	0.0	0.0	0.0	0.0	0.0	0.0	0.0	0.0	0.0	0.0	0.0
Senegal	SEN	0.0	0.0	1.1	0.5	0.0	0.0	1.5	0.0	0.2	0.4	0.0	0.1	0.8	0.0	0.0	0.0
Seychelles	SYC	0.0	0.0	0.0	0.0	0.0	0.0	0.0	0.0	0.0	0.0	0.0	0.0	0.0	0.0	0.0	0.0
Sierra Leone	SLE	0.0	0.0	0.0	0.0	0.0	0.0	0.0	0.0	0.0	0.0	0.0	0.0	0.0	0.0	0.0	0.0
Somalia	SOM	0.0	0.0	0.0	0.0	0.0	0.0	0.0	0.0	0.0	0.0	0.0	0.0	0.0	0.0	0.0	0.0
South Africa	ZAF	0.0	0.0	0.0	..	..	0.0	0.0	0.0	0.2	0.0	0.0	3.1	0.5	0.4	0.0	0.0
Sudan	SDN	0.0	0.0	0.0	0.0	0.0	0.0	0.0	0.0	0.0	0.0	0.0	0.0	0.0	0.0	0.0	0.0
Swaziland	SWZ	..	..	..	..	..	..	..	..	..	..	..	..	..	..	..	..
Tanzania	TZA	0.0	0.0	0.0	0.0	0.2	2.1	0.0	0.0	0.0	0.0	0.0	0.2	0.0	0.0	0.1	0.0
Togo	TGO	0.0	0.0	1.1	1.3	0.0	0.0	0.0	0.0	0.0	0.0	0.0	0.0	0.1	0.0	0.0	0.0
Tunisia	TUN	1.0	0.0	0.1	0.0	0.0	0.0	0.2	0.0	0.0	0.0	0.0	0.0	0.0	0.3	0.0	0.1
Uganda	UGA	0.0	0.0	0.0	0.0	0.0	0.0	0.0	0.0	0.0	0.0	0.0	0.0	0.0	0.0	0.0	0.0
Zambia	ZMB	0.0	0.1	0.0	0.0	2.4	3.1	0.0	0.0	0.0	0.0	0.0	0.4	0.0	0.0	0.0	0.0
Zimbabwe	ZWE	0.0	0.4	0.0	0.0	26.7	1.4	0.0	0.6	0.0	0.0	0.0	0.9	0.0	0.0	0.0	0.0
Sub-Saharan Africa	SSA	0.6	0.9	7.4	30.6	30.0	12.3	12.8	7.9	17.8	15.5	5.7	9.6	6.3	20.2	3.0	0.5
European Community	EU	69.0	68.3	54.9	53.8	37.8	62.3	66.7	76.3	66.4	68.1	81.0	61.0	65.3	59.7	43.2	43.8
North America	NNA	11.6	11.3	6.3	6.5	10.3	1.2	5.4	3.4	0.9	9.5	0.0	7.4	6.9	4.7	3.6	22.4
Rest of World	ROW	18.7	19.6	31.4	9.2	21.9	24.2	15.0	12.5	15.0	6.9	13.2	22.0	21.4	15.4	50.2	33.3
World	World	100.0	100.0	100.0	100.0	100.0	100.0	100.0	100.0	100.0	100.0	100.0	100.0	100.0	100.0	100.0	100.0

Note: ** means "not applicable."

South Africa's data for 1991 is taken from partner countries' data

Source: International Monetary Fund's Direction of Trade database

(Table continues on the following page)

5-50. Direction of trade matrix, exports, 1991 (continued)

Exporters		GNQ	ERI	ETH	GAB	GMB	GHA	GIN	GNB	KEN	LSO	LBR	LBY	MDG	MWI	MLI	MRT	MUS	MAR	MOZ	NAM	NER
		Importers																				
Algeria	DZA	0.0	..	0.0	0.0	0.0	0.0	0.0	0.0	0.0	0.0	0.0	0.1	0.0	0.0	0.0	6.9	0.0	0.7	0.0	0.0	0.0
Angola	AGO	0.0	..	0.0	0.0	0.0	0.0	0.0	0.0	0.0	0.0	0.0	0.0	0.0	0.0	0.0	0.0	0.0	0.0	0.0	0.0	0.0
Benin	BEN	0.0	..	0.0	0.0	0.0	0.0	0.0	0.0	0.0	0.0	0.0	0.0	0.0	0.0	0.0	0.0	0.0	0.0	0.0	0.0	0.2
Burkina Faso	BFA	0.0	..	0.0	0.0	0.0	0.0	0.0	0.0	0.0	0.0	0.0	0.0	0.0	0.0	0.3	0.0	0.0	0.0	0.0	0.0	0.1
Bostwana	BWA	..	..	..	..	..	..	..	..	..	..	..	..	..	..	..	..	..	..	..	..	..
Burundi	BDI	0.0	..	0.0	0.0	0.0	0.0	0.0	0.0	0.3	0.0	0.0	0.0	0.0	0.0	0.0	0.0	0.0	0.0	0.0	0.0	0.0
Cameroon	CMR	33.3	..	0.0	3.6	0.0	0.0	0.1	0.0	0.1	0.0	0.0	0.0	0.0	0.0	0.0	0.0	0.0	0.6	0.0	0.0	0.1
Cape Verde	CPV	0.0	..	0.0	0.0	0.0	0.0	0.0	0.2	0.0	0.0	0.0	0.0	0.0	0.0	0.0	0.0	0.0	0.0	0.0	0.0	0.0
Central African Republic	CAF	0.0	..	0.0	0.0	0.0	0.0	0.0	0.0	0.0	0.0	0.0	0.0	0.0	0.0	0.0	0.0	0.0	0.0	0.0	0.0	0.0
Chad	TCD	0.0	..	0.0	0.0	0.0	0.0	0.0	0.0	0.0	0.0	0.0	0.0	0.0	0.0	0.0	0.0	0.0	0.1	0.0	0.0	0.0
Comoros	COM	0.0	..	0.0	0.0	0.0	0.0	0.0	0.0	0.0	0.0	0.0	0.0	0.1	0.0	0.0	0.0	0.0	0.0	0.0	0.0	0.0
Congo, Dem. Rep. Of	ZAR	0.0	..	0.0	0.1	0.0	0.0	0.0	0.0	0.1	0.0	0.0	0.0	0.0	0.0	0.0	0.0	0.0	0.0	0.0	0.0	0.0
Congo, Republic of	COG	0.0	..	0.0	0.0	0.0	0.0	0.0	0.0	0.0	0.0	0.0	0.0	0.0	0.0	0.0	0.0	0.0	0.0	0.0	0.0	0.0
Cote d'Ivoire	CIV	0.4	..	0.0	10.4	3.4	3.9	11.6	4.3	0.0	0.0	0.3	0.0	0.1	0.0	29.5	1.2	0.9	0.2	2.4	0.0	12.3
Djibouti	DJI	0.0	..	2.2	0.0	0.0	0.0	0.0	0.0	0.0	0.0	0.0	0.0	0.0	0.0	0.0	0.0	0.0	0.0	0.0	0.0	0.0
Egypt	EGY	0.0	..	0.2	0.0	0.0	0.0	0.0	0.0	0.1	0.1	0.2	2.2	0.0	0.0	0.0	0.0	0.0	0.3	0.0	0.0	0.0
Equatorial Guinea	GNQ	**	..	0.0	0.0	0.0	0.0	0.0	0.0	0.0	0.0	0.0	0.0	0.0	0.0	0.0	0.0	0.0	0.0	0.0	0.0	0.0
Eritrea	ERI	..	**	..	..	..	..	..	..	..	..	..	..	..	..	..	..	..	..	..	..	..
Ethiopia	ETH	0.0	..	**	0.0	0.0	0.0	0.0	0.0	0.0	0.0	0.0	0.0	0.0	0.0	0.0	0.0	0.0	0.0	0.0	0.0	0.0
Gabon	GAB	0.0	..	0.0	**	0.0	0.0	0.0	0.0	0.0	0.0	0.0	0.0	0.0	0.0	0.0	0.1	0.0	0.2	0.0	0.0	0.0
Gambia, The	GMB	0.0	..	0.0	0.0	**	0.0	1.1	0.2	0.0	0.0	0.0	0.0	0.0	0.0	0.0	0.0	0.0	0.0	0.0	0.0	0.0
Ghana	GHA	0.0	..	0.0	0.0	0.0	**	0.0	0.0	0.0	0.0	0.0	0.0	0.0	0.0	0.0	0.0	0.0	0.0	0.0	0.0	0.0
Guinea	GIN	0.0	..	0.0	0.0	0.0	0.0	**	0.1	0.0	0.0	0.0	0.0	0.0	0.0	0.0	0.0	0.0	0.0	0.0	0.0	0.0
Guinea-Bissau	GNB	0.0	..	0.0	0.0	0.0	0.0	0.0	**	0.0	0.0	0.0	0.0	0.0	0.0	0.0	0.0	0.0	0.0	0.0	0.0	0.0
Kenya	KEN	0.0	..	1.1	0.0	0.0	0.0	0.0	0.0	**	0.0	0.0	0.0	0.0	0.4	0.0	0.0	0.3	0.0	0.2	0.0	0.0
Lesotho	LSO	..	..	..	..	..	..	..	..	..	**	..	..	..	..	..	..	..	..	..	..	..
Liberia	LBR	0.0	..	0.0	0.0	0.0	0.0	0.0	0.0	0.0	0.0	**	0.0	0.0	0.0	0.0	0.0	0.0	0.0	0.0	0.0	0.0
Libya	LBY	0.0	..	0.0	0.0	0.0	0.0	0.0	0.0	0.0	0.0	0.0	**	0.0	0.0	0.0	0.1	0.0	1.7	0.0	0.0	0.0
Madagascar	MDG	0.0	..	0.0	0.0	0.0	0.0	0.0	0.0	0.0	0.0	0.0	0.0	**	0.0	0.0	0.0	1.0	0.0	0.0	0.0	0.0
Malawi	MWI	0.0	..	0.0	0.0	0.0	0.0	0.0	0.0	0.0	0.0	0.0	0.0	0.0	**	0.0	0.0	0.0	0.0	0.2	0.0	0.0
Mali	MLI	0.0	..	0.0	0.0	0.0	0.0	0.0	0.0	0.0	0.0	0.0	0.0	0.0	0.0	**	0.0	0.0	0.0	0.0	0.0	0.1
Mauritania	MRT	0.2	..	0.0	0.0	0.0	0.0	0.0	0.0	0.0	0.0	0.1	0.0	0.0	0.0	0.0	**	0.0	0.0	0.0	0.0	0.0
Mauritius	MUS	0.0	..	0.0	0.0	0.0	0.0	0.0	0.0	0.1	0.0	0.0	0.0	1.9	0.0	0.0	0.0	**	0.0	0.0	0.0	0.0
Morocco	MAR	0.2	..	0.0	0.9	0.1	0.1	1.0	0.1	0.0	0.0	0.0	3.6	0.1	0.0	1.1	1.3	0.1	**	0.1	0.0	0.2
Mozambique	MOZ	0.0	..	0.0	0.0	0.0	0.0	0.0	0.0	0.0	0.0	0.0	0.0	0.0	2.6	0.0	0.0	0.1	0.0	**	0.0	0.0
Namibia	NAM	..	..	..	..	..	..	..	..	..	..	..	..	..	..	..	..	..	..	..	**	..
Niger	NER	0.0	..	0.0	0.0	0.0	0.0	0.0	0.0	0.0	0.0	0.0	0.1	0.0	0.0	0.1	0.0	0.0	0.0	0.0	0.0	**
Nigeria	NGA	0.0	..	0.0	2.2	0.2	13.0	2.1	0.0	0.1	0.0	0.0	0.0	0.1	0.0	0.1	0.0	0.0	0.1	0.0	0.0	1.0
Reunion	REU	0.0	..	0.0	0.0	0.0	0.0	0.0	0.0	0.0	0.0	0.0	0.0	1.5	0.0	0.0	0.0	0.3	0.0	0.0	0.0	0.0
Rwanda	RWA	0.0	..	0.0	0.0	0.0	0.0	0.0	0.0	0.0	0.0	0.0	0.0	0.0	0.0	0.0	0.0	0.0	0.0	0.0	0.0	0.0
Sao Tome and Principe	STP	0.0	..	0.0	0.0	0.0	0.0	0.0	0.0	0.0	0.0	0.0	0.0	0.0	0.0	0.0	0.0	0.0	0.0	0.0	0.0	0.0
Senegal	SEN	0.0	..	0.0	0.2	3.6	0.0	0.8	2.7	0.0	0.0	0.0	0.0	0.0	0.0	5.1	0.0	0.0	0.0	0.3	0.0	0.1
Seychelles	SYC	0.0	..	0.0	0.0	0.0	0.0	0.0	0.0	0.0	0.0	0.0	0.0	0.0	0.0	0.0	0.0	0.0	0.0	0.0	0.0	0.0
Sierra Leone	SLE	0.0	..	0.0	0.0	0.0	0.0	0.0	0.0	0.0	0.0	0.0	0.0	0.0	0.0	0.0	0.0	0.0	0.0	0.0	0.0	0.0
Somalia	SOM	0.0	..	0.0	0.0	0.0	0.0	0.1	0.0	0.0	0.0	0.0	0.0	0.0	0.0	0.0	0.0	0.0	0.0	0.0	0.0	0.0
South Africa	ZAF	..	..	0.0	0.0	0.0	0.0	0.0	0.0	0.6	0.0	0.0	0.0	4.7	45.4	0.0	0.0	14.1	0.1	0.0	0.0	0.0
Sudan	SDN	0.0	..	0.0	0.0	0.0	0.0	0.0	0.0	0.0	0.0	0.0	0.1	0.0	0.0	0.0	0.0	0.0	0.0	0.0	0.0	0.0
Swaziland	SWZ	..	..	..	..	..	..	..	..	..	..	..	..	..	..	..	..	..	..	..	..	..
Tanzania	TZA	0.0	..	0.0	0.0	0.0	0.0	0.0	0.0	0.4	0.0	0.0	0.0	0.0	0.2	0.0	0.0	0.3	0.0	0.1	0.0	0.0
Togo	TGO	0.0	..	0.0	0.1	0.0	0.2	0.0	0.0	0.0	0.0	0.0	0.0	0.0	0.0	0.2	0.0	0.0	0.0	0.0	0.0	1.3
Tunisia	TUN	0.4	..	0.9	0.5	0.1	0.3	0.6	5.8	0.0	2.0	0.0	3.9	0.0	0.0	0.0	0.4	0.0	0.4	0.0	0.0	0.0
Uganda	UGA	0.0	..	0.0	0.0	0.0	0.0	0.0	0.0	0.1	0.0	0.0	0.0	0.0	0.0	0.0	0.0	0.0	0.0	0.0	0.0	0.0
Zambia	ZMB	0.0	..	0.0	0.0	0.0	0.0	0.0	0.0	1.7	0.0	0.0	0.0	0.0	2.8	0.0	0.0	0.0	0.0	0.0	4.8	0.0
Zimbabwe	ZWE	0.0	..	0.0	0.0	0.0	0.1	0.0	0.0	0.7	1.2	0.0	0.0	0.0	9.9	0.0	0.0	0.1	0.0	4.6	2.1	0.0
Sub-Saharan Africa	SSA	33.9	..	1.1	16.5	7.2	17.4	15.9	7.5	3.9	1.2	0.4	0.2	4.0	23.2	35.4	1.3	3.3	1.3	8.6	6.9	15.3
European Community	EU	44.6	..	43.3	60.1	47.2	47.4	52.5	56.6	46.5	64.1	12.5	64.5	58.3	35.7	47.9	70.0	34.7	66.0	37.6	62.4	67.8
North America	NNA	14.3	..	25.0	9.4	4.0	12.0	14.0	1.4	5.0	4.1	1.0	0.9	4.2	13.1	4.5	6.6	1.3	8.1	14.8	24.7	4.8
Rest of World	ROW	7.2	..	30.6	13.9	41.6	23.3	17.6	34.4	44.6	30.6	86.1	34.3	33.6	27.9	12.3	22.1	60.7	24.7	39.0	6.1	12.2
World	World	100.0	..	100.0	100.0	100.0	100.0	100.0	100.0	100.0	100.0	100.0	100.0	100.0	100.0	100.0	100.0	100.0	100.0	100.0	100.0	100.0

Note: ** means "not applicable."
Note: ** means "not applicable."

(Table continues on the following page)

South Africa's data for 1991 is taken fr
South Africa's data for 1991 is taken from partner countries' data

Source: International Monetary Fund's
Source: International Monetary Fund's Direction of Trade database

5-50. Direction of trade matrix, exports, 1991 (continued)

Exporters		NGA	REU	RWA	STP	SEN	SYC	SLE	SOM	ZAF	SDN	SWZ	TZA	TGO	TUN	UGA	ZMB	ZWE	SSA	EU	NNA	ROW	World
		Importers																					
Algeria	DZA	0.0	0.0	0.0	0.0	0.0	0.0	0.0	0.0	0.0	0.0	0.0	1.1	0.0	2.0	0.0	0.0	0.0	0.1	0.6	0.3	0.1	0.3
Angola	AGO	0.0	0.0	0.0	0.0	0.0	0.0	0.0	0.0	0.0	0.0	0.0	0.0	0.1	0.0	0.0	0.0	0.0	0.0	0.1	0.3	0.0	0.1
Benin	BEN	0.0	0.0	0.0	0.0	0.0	0.0	0.0	0.0	0.0	0.0	0.0	0.0	0.2	0.0	0.0	0.0	0.0	0.0	0.0	0.0	0.0	0.0
Burkina Faso	BFA	0.0	0.0	0.0	0.0	0.0	0.0	0.0	0.0	0.0	0.0	0.0	0.0	0.4	0.0	0.0	0.0	0.0	0.0	0.0	0.0	0.0	0.0
Bostwana	BWA	..	..	..	..	..	..	..	..	..	..	..	..	..	..	..	..	..	..	..	..	..	..
Burundi	BDI	0.0	0.0	0.8	0.0	0.0	0.0	0.0	0.0	0.0	0.0	0.0	0.0	0.0	0.0	0.2	0.0	0.1	0.0	0.0	0.0	0.0	0.0
Cameroon	CMR	0.5	0.1	0.0	0.9	0.2	0.0	0.0	0.0	0.0	0.0	0.0	0.0	0.2	0.1	0.0	0.0	0.0	0.3	0.1	0.0	0.0	0.1
Cape Verde	CPV	0.0	0.0	0.0	0.0	0.0	0.0	0.0	0.0	0.0	0.0	0.0	0.0	0.0	0.0	0.0	0.0	0.0	0.0	0.0	0.0	0.0	0.0
Central African Republic	CAF	0.0	0.0	0.0	0.0	0.0	0.0	0.0	0.0	0.0	0.3	0.0	0.0	0.0	0.0	0.0	0.0	0.0	0.0	0.0	0.0	0.0	0.0
Chad	TCD	0.0	0.0	0.0	0.0	0.0	0.0	0.0	0.0	0.0	0.0	0.0	0.0	0.0	0.0	0.0	0.0	0.0	0.0	0.0	0.0	0.0	0.0
Comoros	COM	0.0	0.0	0.0	0.0	0.0	0.0	0.0	0.0	0.0	0.0	0.0	0.0	0.0	0.0	0.0	0.0	0.0	0.0	0.0	0.0	0.0	0.0
Congo, Dem. Rep. Of	ZAR	0.0	0.0	1.1	0.0	0.0	0.0	0.0	0.0	0.0	0.0	0.0	0.0	0.0	0.0	0.0	0.9	0.0	0.0	0.1	0.1	0.0	0.0
Congo, Republic of	COG	0.6	0.2	0.0	0.0	0.1	0.0	0.0	0.0	0.0	0.0	0.0	0.0	0.1	0.0	0.0	0.0	0.0	0.1	0.0	0.1	0.0	0.0
Cote d'Ivoire	CIV	0.5	0.3	0.0	0.0	5.6	0.0	11.2	0.0	0.1	0.0	0.0	0.2	5.6	0.3	0.0	0.0	0.0	1.6	0.1	0.0	0.0	0.1
Djibouti	DJI	0.0	0.0	0.0	0.0	0.0	0.0	0.0	17.3	0.0	0.0	0.0	0.0	0.0	0.0	0.0	0.0	0.0	0.1	0.0	0.0	0.0	0.0
Egypt	EGY	0.0	0.0	0.0	0.0	0.0	0.0	0.0	0.1	0.0	2.0	0.0	0.2	0.0	0.3	0.0	0.0	0.0	0.1	0.1	0.0	0.1	0.1
Equatorial Guinea	GNQ	0.0	0.0	0.0	0.0	0.0	0.0	0.0	0.0	0.0	0.0	0.0	0.0	0.0	0.0	0.0	0.0	0.0	0.0	0.0	0.0	0.0	0.0
Eritrea	ERI	..	..	..	..	..	..	..	..	..	..	..	..	..	..	..	..	..	..	..	..	..	..
Ethiopia	ETH	0.0	0.0	0.0	0.0	0.0	0.0	0.0	0.0	0.0	0.0	0.0	0.0	0.0	0.0	0.0	0.0	0.0	0.0	0.0	0.0	0.0	0.0
Gabon	GAB	0.0	0.3	0.0	0.1	2.0	0.0	0.0	0.0	0.0	0.0	0.0	0.0	0.4	0.0	0.0	0.0	0.0	0.1	0.1	0.1	0.0	0.1
Gambia, The	GMB	0.0	0.0	0.0	0.0	0.1	0.0	0.0	0.0	0.0	0.0	0.0	0.0	0.0	0.0	0.0	0.0	0.0	0.0	0.0	0.0	0.0	0.0
Ghana	GHA	0.1	0.0	0.0	0.0	0.0	0.0	0.1	0.0	0.0	0.0	0.0	0.0	2.1	0.0	0.0	0.0	0.0	0.0	0.0	0.0	0.0	0.0
Guinea	GIN	0.0	0.0	0.0	0.0	0.0	0.0	0.0	0.0	0.0	0.0	0.0	0.0	0.0	0.0	0.0	0.0	0.0	0.1	0.0	0.0	0.0	0.0
Guinea-Bissau	GNB	0.0	0.0	0.0	0.0	0.0	0.0	0.0	0.0	0.0	0.0	0.0	0.0	0.0	0.0	0.0	0.0	0.0	0.0	0.0	0.0	0.0	0.0
Kenya	KEN	0.0	0.2	5.1	0.0	0.0	0.5	0.1	8.2	0.0	1.5	0.0	2.9	0.0	0.0	12.4	0.4	0.3	0.3	0.0	0.0	0.0	0.0
Lesotho	LSO	..	..	..	..	..	..	..	..	..	..	..	..	..	..	..	..	..	..	..	..	..	..
Liberia	LBR	0.0	0.0	0.0	0.0	0.0	0.0	0.2	0.0	0.0	0.0	0.0	0.0	0.0	0.0	0.0	0.0	0.0	0.0	0.0	0.0	0.0	0.0
Libya	LBY	0.0	0.0	0.0	0.0	0.0	0.0	0.0	0.0	0.0	11.7	0.0	0.0	0.0	1.9	0.0	0.0	0.0	0.3	0.6	0.0	0.1	0.3
Madagascar	MDG	0.0	0.8	0.0	0.0	0.0	0.2	0.0	0.0	0.0	0.0	0.0	0.0	0.0	0.0	0.0	0.0	0.0	0.1	0.0	0.0	0.0	0.0
Malawi	MWI	0.0	0.0	0.0	0.0	0.0	0.0	0.2	0.0	0.2	0.0	0.0	0.2	0.0	0.0	0.0	0.7	0.2	0.1	0.0	0.0	0.0	0.0
Mali	MLI	0.0	0.0	0.0	0.0	0.0	0.0	0.0	0.0	0.0	0.0	0.0	0.0	0.0	0.1	0.0	0.0	0.0	0.0	0.0	0.0	0.0	0.0
Mauritania	MRT	0.0	0.0	0.0	0.0	0.0	0.0	0.0	0.0	0.0	0.0	0.0	0.0	0.4	0.0	0.0	0.0	0.0	0.1	0.0	0.0	0.0	0.0
Mauritius	MUS	0.0	1.2	1.0	0.0	0.0	6.8	0.0	0.0	0.0	0.0	0.2	0.0	0.0	0.0	0.0	0.0	0.2	0.1	0.1	0.0	0.0	0.0
Morocco	MAR	0.2	0.1	0.0	0.0	0.5	0.0	0.2	0.0	0.0	0.0	0.0	0.3	0.5	1.2	0.0	0.0	0.0	0.2	0.2	0.0	0.1	0.1
Mozambique	MOZ	0.0	0.0	0.0	0.0	0.0	0.2	0.0	0.0	0.0	0.0	0.0	0.0	0.0	0.0	0.0	0.5	0.6	0.1	0.0	0.0	0.0	0.0
Namibia	NAM	..	..	..	..	..	..	..	..	..	..	..	..	..	..	..	..	..	..	..	..	..	..
Niger	NER	0.8	0.0	0.0	0.0	0.0	0.0	0.0	0.0	0.0	0.0	0.0	0.0	0.2	0.0	0.0	0.0	0.0	0.1	0.0	0.0	0.0	0.0
Nigeria	NGA	**	0.0	0.1	0.0	0.0	0.0	3.0	0.0	0.0	0.0	0.0	0.0	0.3	0.0	0.0	0.0	0.0	1.2	0.2	0.6	0.0	0.2
Reunion	REU	0.0	**	0.0	0.0	0.0	0.2	0.0	0.0	0.0	0.0	0.0	0.0	0.0	0.0	0.0	0.0	0.0	0.0	0.0	0.0	0.0	0.0
Rwanda	RWA	0.0	0.0	**	0.0	0.0	0.0	0.0	0.0	0.0	0.0	0.0	0.0	0.0	0.0	0.0	0.0	0.0	0.0	0.0	0.0	0.0	0.0
Sao Tome and Principe	STP	0.0	0.0	0.0	**	0.0	0.0	0.0	0.0	0.0	0.0	0.0	0.0	0.0	0.0	0.0	0.0	0.0	0.0	0.0	0.0	0.0	0.0
Senegal	SEN	0.0	0.0	0.0	0.0	**	0.0	0.2	0.0	0.0	0.0	0.0	0.0	0.2	0.0	0.0	0.0	0.0	0.2	0.0	0.0	0.0	0.0
Seychelles	SYC	0.0	0.0	0.0	0.0	0.0	**	0.0	0.0	0.0	0.0	0.0	0.0	0.0	0.0	0.0	0.0	0.0	0.0	0.0	0.0	0.0	0.0
Sierra Leone	SLE	0.0	0.0	0.0	0.0	0.0	0.0	**	0.0	0.0	0.0	0.0	0.0	0.0	0.0	0.0	0.0	0.0	0.0	0.0	0.0	0.0	0.0
Somalia	SOM	0.0	0.0	0.0	0.0	0.0	0.0	0.0	**	0.0	0.0	0.0	0.0	0.0	0.0	0.0	0.0	0.0	0.0	0.0	0.0	0.0	0.0
South Africa	ZAF	0.0	2.9	18.1	0.0	0.0	13.3	0.0	0.0	**	0.0	0.0	0.0	0.1	0.0	0.0	25.6	35.3	2.3	0.6	0.3	0.4	0.5
Sudan	SDN	0.0	0.0	0.0	0.0	0.0	0.0	0.0	0.2	0.0	**	0.0	0.0	0.0	0.0	0.0	0.0	0.0	0.0	0.0	0.0	0.0	0.0
Swaziland	SWZ	..	..	..	..	..	..	..	..	..	..	**	..	..	..	..	..	..	..	..	..	..	..
Tanzania	TZA	0.0	0.0	6.4	0.0	0.0	0.0	0.0	0.9	0.0	0.2	0.0	**	0.0	0.0	1.2	0.2	0.2	0.1	0.0	0.0	0.0	0.0
Togo	TGO	0.3	0.0	0.0	0.0	0.0	0.0	0.0	0.0	0.0	0.0	0.0	0.0	**	0.0	0.0	0.0	0.0	0.1	0.0	0.0	0.0	0.0
Tunisia	TUN	0.0	0.0	0.0	0.0	0.1	0.0	0.0	0.0	0.1	0.3	0.0	0.0	0.5	**	0.5	0.0	0.0	0.1	0.2	0.0	0.1	0.1
Uganda	UGA	0.0	0.0	0.0	0.0	0.0	0.0	0.0	0.0	0.0	0.0	0.0	0.1	0.0	0.0	**	0.0	0.0	0.0	0.0	0.0	0.0	0.0
Zambia	ZMB	0.0	0.0	0.0	0.0	0.0	0.0	0.0	0.0	0.0	0.0	0.2	0.8	0.0	0.0	0.1	**	3.0	0.2	0.0	0.0	0.0	0.0
Zimbabwe	ZWE	0.0	0.1	0.1	0.0	0.0	0.5	0.1	0.0	1.0	0.1	1.1	0.3	0.0	0.0	0.5	7.1	**	0.7	0.0	0.0	0.0	0.0
Sub-Saharan Africa	SSA	2.9	3.3	14.6	1.0	8.2	8.2	15.2	9.2	1.5	2.2	1.5	4.7	10.2	0.9	14.4	10.4	13.8	6.1	1.6	1.6	0.7	1.3
European Community	EU	53.7	83.5	51.3	75.8	63.8	32.3	53.3	41.3	55.2	41.1	30.1	40.0	48.1	77.4	47.0	39.8	43.7	50.6	66.0	17.5	27.2	42.6
North America	NNA	12.1	0.1	2.8	14.3	8.5	1.1	12.8	5.4	16.7	7.9	6.6	4.3	3.4	4.4	4.1	4.2	4.4	9.6	7.9	29.5	18.4	15.7
Rest of World	ROW	31.2	13.1	31.2	8.8	19.6	58.3	18.7	44.1	26.6	48.7	61.9	51.1	38.3	17.3	34.5	45.6	38.1	33.7	24.6	51.4	53.7	40.4
World	World	100.0	100.0	100.0	100.0	100.0	100.0	100.0	100.0	100.0	100.0	100.0	100.0	100.0	100.0	100.0	100.0	100.0	100.0	100.0	100.0	100.0	100.0

Note: ** means "not applicable." Note: ** means "not applicable."

South Africa's data for 1991 is taken fr South Africa's data for 1991 is taken from partner countries' data

Source: International Monetary Fund's Source: International Monetary Fund's Direction of Trade database

5-51. Direction of trade matrix, exports, 1996

Importers — *Percentage of total exports*

Exporters		DZA	AGO	BEN	BFA	BWA	BDI	CMR	CPV	CAF	TCD	COM	ZAR	COG	CIV	DJI	EGY
Algeria	DZA	**	0.0	0.0	0.0	0.0	0.0	0.0	0.0	0.0	0.0	0.0	0.0	0.0	0.0	0.0	0.0
Angola	AGO	0.0	**	0.4	0.0	0.0	0.0	0.0	0.9	0.0	0.0	0.0	0.0	0.3	0.0	0.0	0.0
Benin	BEN	0.0	0.0	**	0.1	0.0	0.0	0.0	0.0	0.0	0.0	0.0	0.0	0.0	0.0	0.0	0.0
Burkina Faso	BFA	0.0	0.0	0.0	**	0.0	0.0	0.0	0.0	0.0	0.0	0.0	0.0	0.0	0.8	0.0	0.0
Bostwana	BWA	..	..	..	..	**	..	..	..	..	..	..	..	..	..	..	..
Burundi	BDI	0.0	0.0	0.0	0.0	0.0	**	0.0	0.0	0.0	0.0	0.0	0.0	0.0	0.0	0.0	0.0
Cameroon	CMR	0.0	0.1	0.2	0.2	0.0	0.0	**	0.0	11.7	6.0	0.0	0.2	1.5	0.3	0.0	0.0
Cape Verde	CPV	0.0	0.0	0.0	0.0	0.0	0.0	0.0	**	0.0	0.0	0.0	0.0	0.0	0.0	0.0	0.0
Central African Republic	CAF	0.0	0.0	0.0	0.0	0.0	0.0	0.1	0.0	**	0.3	0.0	0.5	0.1	0.0	0.0	0.0
Chad	TCD	0.0	0.0	0.0	0.0	0.0	0.0	0.0	0.0	0.9	**	0.0	0.0	0.0	0.0	0.0	0.0
Comoros	COM	0.0	0.0	0.0	0.0	0.0	0.0	0.0	0.0	0.0	0.0	**	0.0	0.0	0.0	0.0	0.0
Congo, Dem. Rep. Of	ZAR	0.0	0.0	0.0	0.0	0.0	0.8	0.0	0.0	0.7	0.0	0.0	**	0.1	0.0	0.0	0.0
Congo, Republic of	COG	0.0	0.4	0.0	0.0	0.0	0.0	0.1	0.0	0.0	0.0	0.0	0.6	**	0.1	0.0	0.0
Cote d'Ivoire	CIV	0.1	0.4	4.6	22.1	0.0	0.0	0.0	0.4	18.0	1.1	0.0	1.9	0.8	**	0.0	0.0
Djibouti	DJI	0.0	0.0	0.0	0.0	0.0	0.1	0.0	0.0	0.0	0.0	0.0	0.0	0.0	0.0	**	0.0
Egypt	EGY	0.2	0.0	0.0	0.0	0.0	0.1	0.0	0.0	0.0	0.1	0.0	0.0	0.0	0.1	0.2	**
Equatorial Guinea	GNQ	0.0	0.0	0.0	0.0	0.0	0.0	3.1	0.0	0.0	0.0	0.0	0.0	0.0	0.0	0.0	0.0
Eritrea	ERI	..	..	..	..	..	..	..	..	..	..	..	..	..	..	..	..
Ethiopia	ETH	0.0	0.0	0.0	0.0	0.0	0.0	0.0	0.0	0.0	0.0	0.0	0.0	0.0	0.0	11.0	0.0
Gabon	GAB	0.0	0.0	0.1	0.0	0.0	0.0	0.1	0.0	0.0	0.0	0.0	0.5	0.4	0.0	0.0	0.0
Gambia, The	GMB	0.0	0.0	0.0	0.0	0.0	0.0	0.0	0.0	0.0	0.0	0.0	0.0	0.0	0.0	0.0	0.0
Ghana	GHA	0.0	0.5	1.9	1.0	0.0	0.0	0.0	0.0	0.0	0.0	0.0	0.0	0.5	0.2	0.0	0.0
Guinea	GIN	0.0	0.0	0.0	0.0	0.0	0.0	1.5	0.0	0.0	0.0	0.0	0.0	0.0	0.0	0.0	0.0
Guinea-Bissau	GNB	0.0	0.0	0.0	0.0	0.0	0.0	0.1	0.0	0.0	0.0	0.0	0.0	0.0	0.0	0.0	0.0
Kenya	KEN	0.0	0.0	0.0	0.1	0.0	5.7	0.0	0.0	0.0	0.0	2.1	2.7	0.0	0.0	0.5	0.4
Lesotho	LSO	..	..	..	..	..	..	..	..	..	..	..	..	..	..	..	..
Liberia	LBR	0.0	0.0	0.0	0.0	0.0	0.0	0.0	0.0	0.0	0.0	0.0	0.0	0.0	0.0	0.0	0.0
Libya	LBY	0.0	0.0	0.0	0.0	0.0	0.0	0.0	0.0	0.0	0.0	0.0	0.0	0.0	0.0	0.0	0.4
Madagascar	MDG	0.0	0.0	0.0	0.0	0.0	0.0	0.0	0.0	0.0	0.0	1.1	0.0	0.0	0.0	0.0	0.0
Malawi	MWI	0.0	0.0	0.0	0.0	0.0	0.0	0.0	0.0	0.0	0.0	0.0	0.0	0.0	0.0	0.0	0.1
Mali	MLI	0.0	0.0	0.0	0.3	0.0	0.0	0.0	0.0	0.0	0.0	0.0	0.0	0.0	0.2	0.0	0.0
Mauritania	MRT	0.0	0.0	0.0	0.1	0.0	0.0	0.6	0.0	0.0	0.0	0.0	0.0	0.3	0.7	0.0	0.0
Mauritius	MUS	0.0	0.0	0.0	0.0	0.0	0.0	0.0	0.0	0.0	0.0	1.3	0.0	0.0	0.0	0.0	0.0
Morocco	MAR	0.5	0.2	0.3	0.3	0.0	0.0	0.2	0.0	0.2	0.0	0.3	0.6	0.3	0.7	0.0	0.0
Mozambique	MOZ	0.0	0.0	0.0	0.0	0.0	0.0	0.0	0.0	0.0	0.0	0.0	0.0	0.0	0.0	0.0	0.0
Namibia	NAM	..	..	..	..	..	..	..	..	..	..	..	..	..	..	..	..
Niger	NER	0.0	0.0	0.4	0.4	0.0	0.0	0.0	0.0	0.0	0.0	0.0	0.0	0.0	0.4	0.0	0.0
Nigeria	NGA	0.0	0.0	0.8	5.3	0.0	0.0	9.9	0.0	0.5	7.9	0.1	4.7	0.2	18.0	0.0	0.0
Reunion	REU	0.0	0.0	0.0	0.0	0.0	0.0	0.0	0.0	0.0	0.0	1.3	0.0	0.0	0.0	0.0	0.0
Rwanda	RWA	0.0	0.0	0.0	0.0	0.0	0.2	0.0	0.0	0.0	0.0	0.0	0.1	0.0	0.0	0.0	0.0
Sao Tome and Principe	STP	0.0	0.0	0.0	0.0	0.0	0.0	0.0	0.0	0.0	0.0	0.0	0.0	0.0	0.0	0.0	0.0
Senegal	SEN	0.0	0.0	1.8	0.8	0.0	0.0	1.5	1.4	0.2	1.4	0.0	0.0	0.3	0.7	0.0	0.0
Seychelles	SYC	0.0	0.0	0.0	0.0	0.0	0.0	0.0	0.0	0.0	0.0	0.0	0.0	0.0	0.0	0.0	0.0
Sierra Leone	SLE	0.0	0.0	0.0	0.0	0.0	0.0	0.0	0.0	0.0	0.0	0.0	0.0	0.0	0.0	0.0	0.0
Somalia	SOM	0.0	0.0	0.0	0.0	0.0	0.0	0.0	0.0	0.0	0.0	0.0	0.0	0.0	0.0	0.1	0.0
South Africa	ZAF	0.0	20.0	0.2	1.2	..	4.0	0.9	0.3	0.3	0.4	16.0	19.4	1.2	0.6	0.1	0.2
Sudan	SDN	0.0	0.0	0.0	0.0	0.0	0.0	0.0	0.0	0.0	0.0	0.0	0.0	0.0	0.0	0.0	0.1
Swaziland	SWZ	..	..	..	..	..	..	..	..	..	..	..	..	..	..	..	..
Tanzania	TZA	0.0	0.0	0.0	0.0	0.3	3.2	0.0	0.0	0.0	0.0	0.0	0.3	0.0	0.0	0.2	0.0
Togo	TGO	0.0	0.0	1.0	1.4	0.0	0.0	0.0	0.0	0.0	0.1	0.0	0.0	0.0	0.0	0.0	0.0
Tunisia	TUN	1.3	0.0	0.2	0.1	0.0	0.9	0.4	0.0	0.0	0.0	0.0	0.0	0.0	0.3	0.0	0.2
Uganda	UGA	0.1	0.0	0.0	0.0	0.0	0.0	0.0	0.0	0.0	0.0	0.0	0.0	0.0	0.0	0.0	0.0
Zambia	ZMB	0.0	0.0	0.0	0.0	1.0	2.4	0.0	0.0	0.0	0.0	0.0	3.3	0.0	0.0	0.0	0.1
Zimbabwe	ZWE	0.0	0.4	0.0	0.0	17.0	1.0	0.1	0.0	0.0	0.0	0.0	0.5	0.0	0.0	0.0	0.0
Sub-Saharan Africa	SSA	0.4	5.0	12.2	31.8	18.3	13.3	17.7	2.8	32.7	19.3	5.9	24.7	4.5	23.1	11.8	1.0
European Community	EU	67.5	50.8	46.0	52.5	31.6	57.3	63.5	67.8	48.0	67.7	69.9	37.5	85.1	54.6	38.9	41.6
North America	NNA	12.3	14.4	3.3	2.7	9.4	3.7	6.4	22.7	2.7	2.1	0.0	6.5	4.5	5.7	2.7	18.9
Rest of World	ROW	19.8	29.9	38.6	13.0	40.6	25.7	12.4	6.7	16.6	10.8	24.2	31.4	5.9	16.7	46.7	38.4
World	World	100.0	100.0	100.0	100.0	100.0	100.0	100.0	100.0	100.0	100.0	100.0	100.0	100.0	100.0	100.0	100.0

Note: ** means "not applicable."

South Africa's data for 1996 is taken from partner countries' data

Source: International Monetary Fund's Direction of Trade database

(Table continues on the following page)

5-51. Direction of trade matrix, exports, 1996 (continued)

Importers — *Percentage of total exports*

Exporters		GNQ	ERI	ETH	GAB	GMB	GHA	GIN	GNB	KEN	LSO	LBR	LBY	MDG	MWI	MLI	MRT	MUS	MAR	MOZ	NAM	NER
Algeria	DZA	0.0	..	0.0	0.0	0.0	0.0	0.2	0.0	0.0	0.0	0.1	0.0	0.0	0.0	0.0	0.0	0.0	1.2	0.0	0.0	0.1
Angola	AGO	0.0	..	0.0	0.0	0.0	0.0	0.0	0.0	0.0	0.0	0.0	0.0	0.0	0.0	0.0	0.0	0.0	0.0	0.0	0.0	0.0
Benin	BEN	0.0	..	0.0	0.0	0.0	0.0	0.0	0.0	0.0	0.0	0.0	0.0	0.0	0.0	0.0	0.0	0.0	0.2	0.0	0.0	1.0
Burkina Faso	BFA	0.0	..	0.0	0.0	0.0	0.2	0.0	0.0	0.0	0.0	0.0	0.0	0.0	0.0	0.3	0.0	0.5	0.0	0.0	0.0	0.7
Bostwana	BWA	..	..	..	..	..	..	..	..	..	..	..	..	..	..	..	..	..	..	..	..	..
Burundi	BDI	0.0	..	0.0	0.0	0.0	0.0	0.0	0.0	0.0	0.0	0.0	0.0	0.0	0.0	0.0	0.0	0.0	0.0	0.0	0.0	0.0
Cameroon	CMR	22.1	..	0.0	3.9	0.0	0.0	0.4	0.0	0.0	0.0	0.0	0.0	0.0	0.0	0.2	0.0	0.0	0.0	0.0	0.0	0.0
Cape Verde	CPV	0.0	..	0.0	0.0	0.1	0.0	0.0	0.4	0.0	0.0	0.0	0.0	0.0	0.0	0.0	0.0	0.0	0.0	0.0	0.0	0.0
Central African Republic	CAF	0.0	..	0.0	0.0	0.0	0.0	0.0	0.0	0.0	0.0	0.0	0.0	0.0	0.0	0.0	0.0	0.0	0.0	0.0	0.0	0.0
Chad	TCD	0.0	..	0.0	0.0	0.0	0.0	0.0	0.0	0.0	0.0	0.0	0.0	0.0	0.0	0.0	0.0	0.0	0.0	0.0	0.0	0.0
Comoros	COM	0.0	..	0.0	0.0	0.0	0.0	0.0	0.0	0.0	0.0	0.0	0.0	0.0	0.0	0.0	0.0	0.0	0.0	0.0	0.0	0.0
Congo, Dem. Rep. Of	ZAR	0.0	..	0.0	0.0	0.0	0.0	0.0	0.0	0.0	0.0	0.0	0.0	0.0	0.0	0.0	0.0	0.0	0.0	0.0	0.0	0.0
Congo, Republic of	COG	0.0	..	0.0	0.1	0.0	0.0	0.0	0.0	0.0	0.0	0.0	0.0	0.0	0.0	0.0	0.0	0.0	0.0	0.0	0.0	0.0
Cote d'Ivoire	CIV	0.2	..	0.0	2.0	5.8	4.2	10.4	2.6	0.0	0.0	0.3	0.0	0.0	0.1	25.0	1.0	0.0	0.2	0.0	0.0	11.0
Djibouti	DJI	0.0	..	1.9	0.0	0.0	0.0	0.0	0.0	0.0	0.0	0.0	0.0	0.0	0.0	0.0	0.0	0.0	0.0	0.0	0.0	0.0
Egypt	EGY	0.0	..	0.2	0.0	0.0	0.0	0.0	0.0	0.0	0.0	0.0	1.0	0.0	0.0	0.0	0.0	0.0	0.1	0.0	0.0	0.0
Equatorial Guinea	GNQ	**	..	0.0	0.0	0.0	0.0	0.0	0.0	0.0	0.0	0.0	0.0	0.0	0.0	0.0	0.0	0.0	0.0	0.0	0.0	0.0
Eritrea	ERI	..	**	..	..	..	..	..	..	..	..	..	..	..	..	..	..	..	..	..	..	..
Ethiopia	ETH	0.0	..	**	0.0	0.0	0.0	0.0	0.0	0.0	0.0	0.0	0.0	0.0	0.0	0.0	0.0	0.0	0.0	0.0	0.0	0.0
Gabon	GAB	0.8	..	0.0	**	0.3	0.0	3.0	0.0	0.0	0.0	0.0	0.0	0.0	0.0	0.0	0.0	0.0	0.2	0.0	0.0	0.0
Gambia, The	GMB	0.0	..	0.0	0.0	**	0.0	0.0	0.3	0.0	0.0	0.0	0.0	0.0	0.0	0.0	0.0	0.0	0.0	0.0	0.0	0.0
Ghana	GHA	0.0	..	0.0	0.0	0.0	**	0.0	0.0	0.0	0.0	0.0	0.0	0.0	0.0	0.0	0.0	0.0	0.0	0.0	0.0	1.2
Guinea	GIN	0.0	..	0.0	0.0	0.0	0.0	**	0.0	0.0	0.0	0.1	0.0	0.0	0.0	0.0	0.0	0.0	0.0	0.0	0.0	0.0
Guinea-Bissau	GNB	0.0	..	0.0	0.0	0.0	0.0	0.0	**	0.0	0.0	0.0	0.0	0.0	0.0	0.0	0.0	0.0	0.0	0.0	0.0	0.0
Kenya	KEN	0.0	..	2.9	0.0	0.0	0.1	0.0	0.0	**	0.0	0.0	0.0	0.4	1.0	0.0	0.0	0.5	0.0	0.4	0.0	0.0
Lesotho	LSO	..	..	..	..	..	..	..	..	..	**	..	..	..	..	..	..	..	..	..	..	..
Liberia	LBR	0.0	..	0.0	0.0	0.0	0.0	0.0	0.0	0.0	0.0	**	0.0	0.0	0.0	0.0	0.0	0.0	0.0	0.0	0.0	0.0
Libya	LBY	0.0	..	0.0	0.0	0.0	0.0	0.0	0.0	0.5	0.0	0.0	**	0.0	0.0	0.0	0.1	0.0	1.4	0.0	0.0	0.2
Madagascar	MDG	0.0	..	0.0	0.0	0.0	0.0	0.0	0.0	0.0	0.0	0.0	0.0	**	0.0	0.0	0.0	0.6	0.0	0.0	0.0	0.0
Malawi	MWI	0.0	..	0.0	0.0	0.5	0.0	0.0	0.1	0.0	0.0	0.0	0.0	0.0	**	0.0	0.0	0.3	0.0	0.9	0.0	0.0
Mali	MLI	0.0	..	0.0	0.0	0.0	0.0	0.0	0.0	0.0	0.0	0.0	0.0	0.0	0.0	**	0.0	0.0	0.0	0.0	0.0	0.1
Mauritania	MRT	0.2	..	0.0	0.0	0.0	0.0	0.0	0.0	0.0	0.0	0.2	0.0	0.0	0.0	0.1	**	0.0	0.0	0.0	0.0	0.0
Mauritius	MUS	0.0	..	0.0	0.0	0.0	0.0	0.0	0.0	0.1	0.0	0.0	0.0	8.1	0.7	0.0	0.0	**	0.0	0.0	0.0	0.0
Morocco	MAR	1.1	..	0.1	1.0	0.2	0.4	0.8	0.0	0.0	0.0	0.0	2.5	0.1	0.0	1.1	1.7	0.1	**	0.0	0.0	0.3
Mozambique	MOZ	0.0	..	0.0	0.0	0.0	0.0	0.0	0.0	0.0	0.0	0.0	0.0	0.0	0.3	0.0	0.0	0.0	0.0	**	0.0	0.0
Namibia	NAM	..	..	..	..	..	..	..	..	..	..	..	..	..	..	..	..	..	..	..	**	..
Niger	NER	0.0	..	0.0	0.0	0.0	0.3	0.0	0.0	0.0	0.0	0.0	0.0	0.0	0.0	0.0	0.0	0.0	0.0	0.0	0.0	**
Nigeria	NGA	0.0	..	0.0	0.7	0.1	13.2	1.2	0.0	0.0	0.0	0.0	0.0	0.0	0.0	0.1	0.0	0.0	2.2	0.0	0.0	8.8
Reunion	REU	0.0	..	0.0	0.0	0.0	0.0	0.0	0.0	0.0	0.0	0.0	0.0	0.1	0.0	0.0	0.0	0.1	0.0	0.0	0.0	0.0
Rwanda	RWA	0.0	..	0.0	0.0	0.0	0.0	0.0	0.0	0.0	0.0	0.0	0.0	0.0	0.0	0.0	0.0	0.0	0.0	0.0	0.0	0.0
Sao Tome and Principe	STP	0.0	..	0.0	0.0	0.0	0.0	0.0	0.0	0.0	0.0	0.0	0.0	0.0	0.0	0.0	0.0	0.0	0.0	0.0	0.0	0.0
Senegal	SEN	0.0	..	0.0	0.7	4.3	0.0	1.2	7.1	0.0	0.0	0.0	0.0	0.0	0.0	6.5	2.9	0.0	0.0	0.0	0.0	0.3
Seychelles	SYC	0.0	..	0.0	0.0	0.0	0.0	0.0	0.0	0.0	0.0	0.0	0.0	0.0	0.0	0.0	0.0	0.0	0.0	0.0	0.2	0.0
Sierra Leone	SLE	0.0	..	0.0	0.0	0.0	0.0	0.0	0.0	0.0	0.0	0.0	0.0	0.0	0.0	0.0	0.0	0.0	0.0	0.0	0.0	0.0
Somalia	SOM	0.0	..	0.0	0.0	0.0	0.0	0.0	0.0	0.0	0.0	0.0	0.0	0.0	0.0	0.0	0.0	0.0	0.0	0.0	0.0	0.0
South Africa	ZAF	1.1	..	0.2	1.1	0.1	2.2	0.1	0.3	7.2	0.0	0.2	0.0	13.4	46.7	2.5	0.3	14.1	0.4	25.4	0.0	0.1
Sudan	SDN	0.0	..	0.0	0.0	0.0	0.0	0.0	0.0	0.0	0.0	0.0	0.1	0.0	0.0	0.0	0.0	0.0	0.0	0.0	0.0	0.0
Swaziland	SWZ	..	..	..	..	..	..	..	..	..	..	..	..	..	..	..	..	..	..	..	..	..
Tanzania	TZA	0.0	..	0.0	0.0	0.0	0.0	0.0	0.0	0.4	0.0	0.0	0.0	0.3	0.4	0.0	0.0	0.0	0.0	0.0	0.0	0.0
Togo	TGO	0.0	..	0.0	0.1	0.0	0.1	0.0	0.0	0.0	0.0	0.0	0.0	0.0	0.0	0.0	0.0	0.0	0.0	0.0	0.0	0.2
Tunisia	TUN	0.0	..	0.0	0.1	0.1	0.1	0.0	0.0	0.0	0.0	0.0	3.9	0.0	0.0	0.1	0.1	0.0	0.4	0.0	0.0	0.2
Uganda	UGA	0.0	..	0.0	0.0	0.0	0.0	0.0	0.0	0.0	0.0	0.0	0.0	0.0	0.0	0.0	0.0	0.0	0.0	0.0	0.0	0.0
Zambia	ZMB	0.0	..	0.0	0.0	0.0	0.0	0.0	0.0	0.1	0.0	0.0	0.0	0.0	9.6	0.0	0.0	0.0	0.0	0.6	2.2	0.0
Zimbabwe	ZWE	0.0	..	0.0	0.1	0.0	0.1	0.0	0.0	0.4	0.4	0.0	0.0	0.0	11.7	0.0	0.0	0.1	0.0	7.3	12.5	0.0
Sub-Saharan Africa	SSA	23.3	..	3.0	8.3	11.3	18.5	16.3	10.9	2.7	0.4	0.7	0.1	9.3	37.1	33.7	3.9	2.8	3.2	13.3	14.9	23.3
European Community	EU	56.0	..	40.8	68.7	37.1	43.6	47.4	59.7	38.1	41.5	16.7	62.9	52.5	15.7	47.1	68.4	37.5	66.0	19.5	60.4	48.9
North America	NNA	11.8	..	11.8	7.2	3.1	11.9	12.2	7.3	4.4	4.8	1.7	1.9	1.9	3.7	3.4	2.9	1.4	6.9	3.2	11.8	11.5
Rest of World	ROW	8.9	..	44.5	15.9	48.5	26.0	24.0	22.1	54.9	53.2	80.9	35.1	36.2	43.4	15.8	24.7	58.3	23.9	63.9	12.9	16.4
World	World	100.0	..	100.0	100.0	100.0	100.0	100.0	100.0	100.0	100.0	100.0	100.0	100.0	100.0	100.0	100.0	100.0	100.0	100.0	100.0	100.0

Note: ** means "not applicable."
Note: ** means "not applicable."

South Africa's data for 1996 is taken fr South Africa's data for 1996 is taken from partner countries' data

Source: International Monetary Fund's Source: International Monetary Fund's Direction of Trade database

(Table continues on the following page)

5-51. Direction of trade matrix, exports, 1996 (continued)

Exporters		NGA	REU	RWA	STP	SEN	SYC	SLE	SOM	ZAF	SDN	SWZ	TZA	TGO	TUN	UGA	ZMB	ZWE	SSA	EU	NNA	ROW	World
		Importers										Percentage of total exports											
Algeria	DZA	0.1	0.0	0.0	0.0	0.0	0.0	0.0	0.0	0.0	0.0	0.0	0.0	0.0	1.4	0.0	0.0	0.0	0.0	0.3	0.2	0.1	0.2
Angola	AGO	0.0	0.0	0.0	0.0	0.0	0.0	0.0	0.0	0.2	0.0	0.0	0.0	0.0	0.0	0.0	0.0	0.0	0.1	0.0	0.3	0.0	0.1
Benin	BEN	0.1	0.0	0.0	0.0	0.0	0.0	0.0	0.0	0.0	0.0	0.0	0.0	0.5	0.0	0.0	0.0	0.0	0.0	0.0	0.0	0.0	0.0
Burkina Faso	BFA	0.0	0.0	0.0	0.0	0.0	0.0	0.0	0.0	0.0	0.0	0.0	0.0	1.0	0.0	0.0	0.0	0.0	0.1	0.0	0.0	0.0	0.0
Bostwana	BWA	..	..	..	..	..	..	..	..	..	..	..	..	..	..	..	..	..	..	..	..	..	..
Burundi	BDI	0.0	0.0	1.3	0.0	0.0	0.0	0.0	0.0	0.0	0.0	0.0	0.3	0.0	0.0	0.0	0.0	0.0	0.0	0.0	0.0	0.0	0.0
Cameroon	CMR	0.3	0.6	0.0	0.0	0.4	0.0	0.0	0.0	0.0	0.0	0.0	0.0	0.2	0.1	0.0	0.0	0.0	0.2	0.1	0.0	0.0	0.0
Cape Verde	CPV	0.0	0.0	0.0	0.0	0.0	0.0	0.0	0.0	0.0	0.0	0.0	0.0	0.0	0.0	0.0	0.0	0.0	0.0	0.0	0.0	0.0	0.0
Central African Republic	CAF	0.0	0.0	0.0	0.0	0.0	0.0	0.0	0.0	0.0	0.0	0.0	0.0	0.1	0.0	0.0	0.0	0.0	0.0	0.0	0.0	0.0	0.0
Chad	TCD	0.0	0.0	0.0	0.0	0.0	0.0	0.0	0.0	0.0	0.0	0.0	0.0	0.0	0.0	0.0	0.0	0.0	0.0	0.0	0.0	0.0	0.0
Comoros	COM	0.0	0.0	0.0	0.0	0.0	0.0	0.0	0.0	0.0	0.0	0.0	0.0	0.0	0.0	0.0	0.0	0.0	0.0	0.0	0.0	0.0	0.0
Congo, Dem. Rep. Of	ZAR	0.0	0.0	1.4	0.0	0.0	0.0	0.0	0.0	0.5	0.0	0.0	0.0	0.0	0.0	0.0	1.1	0.0	0.2	0.0	0.0	0.0	0.0
Congo, Republic of	COG	0.0	0.2	0.0	0.0	0.0	0.0	0.0	0.0	0.0	0.0	0.0	0.0	0.0	0.0	0.0	0.0	0.0	0.0	0.1	0.0	0.0	0.0
Cote d'Ivoire	CIV	1.1	0.0	0.0	0.0	3.7	0.0	9.4	0.0	0.2	0.0	0.0	0.0	10.4	0.3	0.0	0.0	0.0	1.3	0.2	0.0	0.0	0.1
Djibouti	DJI	0.0	0.0	0.0	0.0	0.0	0.0	0.0	22.7	0.0	0.0	0.0	0.0	0.0	0.0	0.0	0.0	0.0	0.1	0.0	0.0	0.0	0.0
Egypt	EGY	0.0	0.0	0.1	0.1	0.0	0.0	0.1	0.0	0.1	1.7	0.0	0.0	0.0	0.3	0.1	0.0	0.0	0.1	0.1	0.0	0.1	0.1
Equatorial Guinea	GNQ	0.0	0.0	0.0	0.0	0.0	0.0	0.0	0.0	0.0	0.0	0.0	0.0	0.0	0.0	0.0	0.0	0.0	0.1	0.0	0.0	0.0	0.0
Eritrea	ERI	..	..	..	..	..	..	..	..	..	..	..	..	..	..	..	..	..	..	..	..	..	..
Ethiopia	ETH	0.0	0.0	0.0	0.0	0.0	0.0	0.0	0.0	0.0	0.0	0.0	0.0	0.0	0.0	0.0	0.0	0.0	0.0	0.0	0.0	0.0	0.0
Gabon	GAB	0.0	0.0	0.0	2.0	0.2	0.0	0.0	0.0	0.0	0.0	0.0	0.0	0.3	0.0	0.0	0.0	0.0	0.1	0.0	0.2	0.0	0.1
Gambia, The	GMB	0.0	0.0	0.0	0.0	0.0	0.0	0.0	0.0	0.0	0.0	0.0	0.0	0.0	0.0	0.0	0.0	0.0	0.0	0.0	0.0	0.0	0.0
Ghana	GHA	0.8	0.0	0.0	0.0	0.0	0.0	0.0	0.0	0.0	0.0	0.0	0.0	1.4	0.0	0.0	0.0	0.0	0.2	0.0	0.0	0.0	0.0
Guinea	GIN	0.0	0.0	0.0	0.0	0.0	0.0	0.1	0.0	0.0	0.0	0.0	0.0	0.0	0.0	0.0	0.0	0.0	0.0	0.0	0.0	0.0	0.0
Guinea-Bissau	GNB	0.0	0.0	0.0	0.0	0.0	0.0	0.0	0.0	0.0	0.0	0.0	0.0	0.0	0.0	0.0	0.0	0.0	0.0	0.0	0.0	0.0	0.0
Kenya	KEN	0.1	0.5	13.6	0.1	0.0	1.3	0.1	17.4	0.2	1.9	0.0	15.4	0.0	0.0	40.2	0.4	0.2	1.1	0.0	0.0	0.0	0.0
Lesotho	LSO	..	..	..	..	..	..	..	..	..	..	..	..	..	..	..	..	..	..	..	..	..	..
Liberia	LBR	0.0	0.0	0.0	0.0	0.0	0.0	0.3	0.0	0.0	0.0	0.0	0.0	0.0	0.0	0.0	0.0	0.0	0.0	0.0	0.0	0.0	0.0
Libya	LBY	0.0	0.0	0.0	0.0	0.0	0.0	0.0	0.0	0.0	19.4	0.0	0.0	0.0	3.0	0.0	0.0	0.0	0.3	0.4	0.0	0.1	0.2
Madagascar	MDG	0.0	1.1	0.0	0.0	0.0	0.0	0.0	0.0	0.0	0.0	0.0	0.0	0.0	0.0	0.0	0.0	0.0	0.1	0.0	0.0	0.0	0.0
Malawi	MWI	0.0	0.0	0.0	0.0	0.0	0.0	0.1	0.0	0.3	0.0	0.0	0.4	0.0	0.0	0.1	0.9	0.9	0.2	0.0	0.0	0.0	0.0
Mali	MLI	0.0	0.0	0.0	0.0	0.0	0.0	0.0	0.0	0.0	0.0	0.0	0.0	0.0	0.1	0.0	0.0	0.0	0.0	0.0	0.0	0.0	0.0
Mauritania	MRT	0.0	0.0	0.0	0.0	0.0	0.0	0.0	0.0	0.0	0.0	0.0	0.0	3.3	0.0	0.0	0.0	0.0	0.1	0.0	0.0	0.0	0.0
Mauritius	MUS	0.0	1.4	0.5	0.0	0.0	0.8	0.0	0.0	0.1	0.0	0.0	0.3	0.0	0.0	0.0	0.0	0.4	0.2	0.1	0.0	0.0	0.0
Morocco	MAR	0.2	0.0	0.0	0.0	1.0	0.0	0.5	0.0	0.0	0.0	0.0	0.0	0.3	0.8	0.0	0.0	0.0	0.2	0.2	0.0	0.1	0.1
Mozambique	MOZ	0.0	0.0	0.0	0.0	0.0	0.0	0.0	0.0	0.2	0.0	0.0	0.3	0.0	0.0	0.0	0.0	0.4	0.1	0.0	0.0	0.0	0.0
Namibia	NAM	..	..	..	..	..	..	..	..	..	..	..	..	..	..	..	..	..	..	..	..	..	..
Niger	NER	0.8	0.0	0.0	0.0	0.0	0.0	0.0	0.0	0.0	0.0	0.0	0.0	0.1	0.0	0.0	0.0	0.0	0.1	0.0	0.0	0.0	0.0
Nigeria	NGA	**	0.0	0.0	0.0	4.3	0.0	3.4	0.0	0.0	0.0	0.0	0.0	1.5	0.0	0.0	0.0	0.0	1.7	0.3	0.6	0.2	0.3
Reunion	REU	0.0	**	0.0	0.0	0.0	0.0	0.0	0.0	0.0	0.0	0.0	0.0	0.0	0.0	0.0	0.0	0.0	0.0	0.0	0.0	0.0	0.0
Rwanda	RWA	0.0	0.0	**	0.0	0.0	0.0	0.0	0.0	0.0	0.0	0.0	0.0	0.0	0.0	0.0	0.0	0.0	0.0	0.0	0.0	0.0	0.0
Sao Tome and Principe	STP	0.0	0.0	0.0	**	0.0	0.0	0.0	0.0	0.0	0.0	0.0	0.0	0.0	0.0	0.0	0.0	0.0	0.0	0.0	0.0	0.0	0.0
Senegal	SEN	0.1	0.0	0.0	0.0	**	0.0	0.7	0.0	0.0	0.0	0.0	0.0	0.8	0.0	0.0	0.0	0.0	0.2	0.0	0.0	0.0	0.0
Seychelles	SYC	0.0	0.1	0.0	0.0	0.0	**	0.0	0.0	0.0	0.0	0.0	0.0	0.0	0.0	0.0	0.0	0.0	0.0	0.0	0.0	0.0	0.0
Sierra Leone	SLE	0.0	0.0	0.0	0.0	0.0	0.0	**	0.0	0.0	0.0	0.0	0.0	0.0	0.0	0.0	0.0	0.0	0.0	0.0	0.0	0.0	0.0
Somalia	SOM	0.0	0.0	0.0	0.0	0.0	0.0	0.0	**	0.0	0.0	0.0	0.1	0.0	0.0	0.0	0.0	0.0	0.0	0.0	0.0	0.0	0.0
South Africa	ZAF	0.7	2.2	1.3	3.3	0.2	13.5	3.1	0.0	**	1.6	0.0	9.1	1.1	0.0	3.4	30.3	47.9	5.0	0.5	0.3	0.5	0.5
Sudan	SDN	0.0	0.0	0.0	0.0	0.0	0.0	0.0	0.2	0.0	**	0.0	0.0	0.0	0.1	0.0	0.0	0.0	0.0	0.0	0.0	0.0	0.0
Swaziland	SWZ	..	..	..	..	..	..	..	..	..	..	**	..	..	..	..	..	..	..	..	..	..	..
Tanzania	TZA	0.0	0.0	16.6	0.0	0.0	0.0	0.0	1.2	0.0	0.5	0.0	**	0.0	0.0	1.3	1.3	0.1	0.1	0.0	0.0	0.0	0.0
Togo	TGO	0.0	0.0	0.0	3.0	0.0	0.0	0.0	0.0	0.1	0.0	0.0	0.0	**	0.0	0.0	0.0	0.0	0.1	0.0	0.0	0.0	0.0
Tunisia	TUN	0.1	0.0	0.0	0.1	0.2	0.0	0.0	0.0	0.0	0.0	0.0	0.0	0.1	**	0.0	0.0	0.0	0.1	0.2	0.0	0.0	0.1
Uganda	UGA	0.0	0.0	0.5	0.0	0.0	0.0	0.0	0.0	0.0	0.0	0.0	0.1	0.0	0.0	**	0.0	0.0	0.0	0.0	0.0	0.0	0.0
Zambia	ZMB	0.0	0.0	0.4	0.0	0.0	0.0	0.0	0.0	0.2	0.0	1.3	0.7	0.0	0.0	0.1	**	2.2	0.3	0.0	0.0	0.0	0.0
Zimbabwe	ZWE	0.0	0.2	0.5	0.2	0.0	1.5	0.0	0.0	1.3	0.1	2.9	0.3	0.0	0.0	0.2	9.4	**	1.0	0.0	0.0	0.0	0.0
Sub-Saharan Africa	SSA	3.5	4.2	34.9	5.3	8.9	4.0	14.1	18.8	3.3	2.7	4.2	18.2	22.4	0.8	42.1	17.7	17.5	8.6	1.7	1.7	0.9	1.4
European Community	EU	47.3	88.0	33.0	81.1	64.9	25.2	51.9	8.6	45.1	29.9	41.4	25.0	36.7	77.2	29.6	21.9	22.5	44.5	65.6	16.4	26.3	39.1
North America	NNA	13.8	0.2	15.1	0.7	4.7	33.9	11.0	1.9	13.1	4.6	3.0	4.0	3.1	3.1	3.2	5.2	4.7	9.0	7.1	30.8	16.4	15.5
Rest of World	ROW	35.4	7.7	17.0	12.9	21.5	36.9	23.0	70.7	38.5	62.8	51.3	52.7	37.9	18.9	25.2	55.1	55.3	37.8	25.6	51.2	56.4	43.9
World	World	100.0	100.0	100.0	100.0	100.0	100.0	100.0	100.0	100.0	100.0	100.0	100.0	100.0	100.0	100.0	100.0	100.0	100.0	100.0	100.0	100.0	100.0

Note: ** means "not applicable." Note: ** means "not applicable."
South Africa's data for 1996 is taken fr South Africa's data for 1996 is taken from partner countries' data
Source: International Monetary Fund's Source: International Monetary Fund's Direction of Trade database

5-52. Direction of trade matrix, exports, 2001

Exporters		Importers DZA	AGO	BEN	BFA	BWA	BDI	CMR	CPV	CAF	TCD	COM	ZAR	COG	CIV	DJI	EGY
		Percentage of total exports															
Algeria	DZA	**	0.0	0.1	0.0	0.0	0.0	0.0	0.0	0.0	0.0	0.0	0.0	0.0	0.0	0.0	0.0
Angola	AGO	0.0	**	0.0	0.0	0.0	0.0	0.1	0.2	0.0	0.0	0.0	0.0	0.6	0.0	0.0	0.0
Benin	BEN	0.0	0.0	**	0.2	0.0	0.0	0.0	0.0	0.0	0.3	0.0	0.0	0.0	0.0	0.0	0.0
Burkina Faso	BFA	0.0	0.0	0.0	**	0.0	0.0	0.0	0.0	0.0	0.0	0.0	0.0	0.0	0.0	0.0	0.0
Botswana	BWA	..	..	..	..	**	..	..	..	..	..	..	..	..	..	..	..
Burundi	BDI	0.0	0.0	0.0	0.0	0.0	**	0.0	0.0	0.0	0.0	0.0	0.0	0.0	0.0	0.0	0.0
Cameroon	CMR	0.0	0.5	0.1	0.0	0.0	0.0	**	0.0	5.5	3.3	0.0	3.9	2.2	0.1	0.0	0.0
Cape Verde	CPV	0.0	0.0	0.0	0.0	0.0	0.0	0.0	**	0.0	0.0	0.0	0.0	0.0	0.0	0.0	0.0
Central African Republic	CAF	0.0	0.0	0.0	0.0	0.0	0.0	0.0	0.0	**	0.1	0.0	0.4	0.0	0.0	0.0	0.0
Chad	TCD	0.0	0.0	0.0	0.0	0.0	0.0	0.0	0.0	2.3	**	0.0	0.0	0.0	0.0	0.0	0.0
Comoros	COM	0.0	0.0	0.0	0.0	0.0	0.0	0.0	0.0	0.0	0.0	**	0.0	0.0	0.0	0.0	0.0
Congo, Dem. Rep. Of	ZAR	0.0	0.0	0.0	0.0	0.0	0.5	0.0	0.0	1.7	0.0	0.0	**	0.2	0.0	0.0	0.0
Congo, Republic of	COG	0.0	0.4	0.0	0.0	0.0	0.0	0.2	0.0	0.0	0.0	0.0	1.6	**	0.0	0.0	0.0
Cote d'Ivoire	CIV	0.2	0.0	2.2	27.5	0.0	0.0	1.6	3.4	0.0	0.0	0.0	0.0	0.0	**	0.0	0.0
Djibouti	DJI	0.0	0.0	0.0	0.0	0.0	0.1	0.0	0.0	0.0	0.0	0.0	0.0	0.0	0.0	**	0.0
Egypt	EGY	0.1	0.0	0.0	0.0	0.0	0.1	0.1	0.0	0.0	0.0	0.0	0.2	0.0	0.2	0.0	**
Equatorial Guinea	GNQ	0.0	0.0	0.0	0.0	0.0	0.0	1.9	0.0	0.0	0.0	0.0	0.0	0.0	0.0	0.0	0.0
Eritrea	ERI	..	..	..	..	..	..	..	..	..	..	..	..	..	..	..	..
Ethiopia	ETH	0.1	0.0	0.0	0.0	0.0	0.0	0.0	0.0	0.0	0.0	0.0	0.0	0.0	0.0	10.7	0.0
Gabon	GAB	0.0	0.0	0.0	0.0	0.0	0.0	0.2	0.0	0.0	0.0	0.0	1.4	0.9	0.0	0.0	0.0
Gambia, The	GMB	0.0	0.0	0.0	0.0	0.0	0.0	0.0	0.0	0.0	0.0	0.0	0.0	0.0	0.0	0.0	0.0
Ghana	GHA	0.0	0.5	1.9	1.6	0.0	0.0	0.0	0.0	0.0	0.0	0.0	0.0	1.2	0.3	0.0	0.0
Guinea	GIN	0.0	0.0	0.0	0.0	0.0	0.0	1.6	0.0	0.0	0.0	0.0	0.0	0.0	0.4	0.0	0.0
Guinea-Bissau	GNB	0.0	0.0	0.0	0.0	0.0	0.0	0.1	0.0	0.0	0.0	0.0	0.0	0.0	0.0	0.0	0.0
Kenya	KEN	0.0	0.0	0.0	0.0	0.0	6.6	0.0	0.0	0.0	0.0	6.2	5.7	0.2	0.0	0.6	0.5
Lesotho	LSO	..	..	..	..	..	..	..	..	..	..	..	..	..	..	..	..
Liberia	LBR	0.0	0.0	0.0	0.0	0.0	0.0	0.0	0.0	0.0	0.0	0.0	0.0	0.0	0.1	0.0	0.0
Libya	LBY	0.0	0.0	0.0	3.3	0.0	0.0	0.0	0.0	0.0	0.0	0.0	0.0	0.0	0.0	0.0	0.2
Madagascar	MDG	0.0	0.0	0.0	0.0	0.0	0.0	0.0	0.0	0.0	0.0	1.0	0.0	0.0	0.0	0.0	0.0
Malawi	MWI	0.0	0.0	0.0	0.0	0.0	0.4	0.0	0.0	0.0	0.0	0.0	0.1	0.0	0.0	0.0	0.1
Mali	MLI	0.0	0.0	0.0	0.5	0.0	0.0	0.0	0.0	0.0	0.0	0.0	0.0	0.0	0.1	0.0	0.0
Mauritania	MRT	0.0	0.0	0.0	0.1	0.0	0.0	0.7	0.0	0.0	0.0	0.0	0.0	0.7	0.7	0.0	0.0
Mauritius	MUS	0.0	0.0	0.0	0.0	0.3	0.0	0.0	0.0	0.0	0.0	1.4	0.0	0.0	0.0	0.0	0.0
Morocco	MAR	0.1	0.2	0.2	0.9	0.0	0.0	0.3	0.2	0.2	0.0	1.0	0.4	0.9	0.6	0.0	0.1
Mozambique	MOZ	0.0	0.0	0.0	0.0	0.0	0.0	0.0	0.0	0.0	0.0	0.0	0.0	0.0	0.0	0.0	0.0
Namibia	NAM	..	..	..	..	..	..	..	..	..	..	..	..	..	..	..	..
Niger	NER	0.0	0.0	0.1	0.2	0.0	0.0	0.0	0.0	0.0	0.2	0.0	0.0	0.0	0.1	0.0	0.0
Nigeria	NGA	0.0	0.0	0.7	4.2	0.0	0.0	12.1	0.0	1.2	5.5	0.0	12.7	0.4	17.2	0.0	0.0
Reunion	REU	0.0	0.0	0.0	0.0	0.0	0.0	0.0	0.0	0.0	0.0	0.0	0.0	0.0	0.0	0.0	0.0
Rwanda	RWA	0.0	0.0	0.0	0.0	0.0	0.3	0.0	0.0	0.0	0.0	0.0	0.2	0.0	0.0	0.0	0.0
Sao Tome and Principe	STP	0.0	0.0	0.0	0.0	0.0	0.0	0.0	0.0	0.0	0.0	0.0	0.0	0.0	0.0	0.0	0.0
Senegal	SEN	0.0	0.0	0.4	0.7	0.0	0.0	0.5	0.3	0.5	0.4	0.0	0.0	0.6	0.8	0.0	0.0
Seychelles	SYC	0.0	0.0	0.0	0.0	0.0	0.0	0.0	0.0	0.0	0.0	0.0	0.0	0.0	0.0	0.0	0.0
Sierra Leone	SLE	0.0	0.0	0.0	0.0	0.0	0.0	0.0	0.0	0.0	0.0	0.0	0.0	0.0	0.0	0.0	0.0
Somalia	SOM	0.0	0.0	0.0	0.0	0.0	0.0	0.0	0.0	0.0	0.0	0.0	0.0	0.0	0.0	0.1	0.0
South Africa	ZAF	0.3	10.0	0.6	0.7	0.0	2.1	1.4	0.6	0.6	0.6	12.6	15.4	3.5	1.4	1.2	0.2
Sudan	SDN	0.0	0.0	0.0	0.0	0.0	0.0	0.0	0.0	0.0	0.0	0.0	0.0	0.0	0.0	0.0	0.3
Swaziland	SWZ	..	..	..	..	..	..	..	..	..	..	..	..	..	..	..	..
Tanzania	TZA	0.0	0.0	0.0	0.0	0.0	7.9	0.0	0.0	0.0	0.0	0.1	1.4	0.0	0.0	0.0	0.0
Togo	TGO	0.0	0.0	2.7	5.1	0.0	0.0	0.0	0.0	0.0	0.4	0.0	0.0	0.1	0.0	0.0	0.0
Tunisia	TUN	0.7	0.0	0.1	0.6	0.0	0.0	0.1	0.0	0.0	0.1	0.4	0.0	0.4	0.3	1.3	0.2
Uganda	UGA	0.1	0.0	0.0	0.0	0.0	0.0	0.0	0.0	0.0	0.0	0.0	0.0	0.0	0.0	0.0	0.0
Zambia	ZMB	0.0	0.0	0.0	0.0	1.1	0.6	0.0	0.0	0.0	0.0	0.0	0.0	0.0	0.0	0.0	0.2
Zimbabwe	ZWE	0.0	0.0	0.0	0.0	4.3	0.2	0.0	0.0	0.0	0.0	0.0	0.4	0.0	0.0	0.0	0.1
Sub-Saharan Africa	SSA	0.8	11.5	8.8	40.9	5.8	18.6	20.3	4.6	11.9	10.8	21.3	43.2	10.8	21.3	12.6	1.5
European Community	EU	64.3	39.9	35.3	45.7	58.7	57.1	56.4	84.7	63.6	41.9	46.2	35.8	55.0	49.0	32.1	35.0
North America	NNA	11.8	9.1	2.7	1.7	15.9	4.2	10.4	3.1	4.1	39.9	2.2	3.1	11.2	4.3	3.4	22.1
Rest of World	ROW	23.1	39.6	53.2	11.6	19.6	20.0	12.9	7.6	20.4	7.5	30.3	17.9	23.0	25.4	51.9	41.4
World	World	100.0	100.0	100.0	100.0	100.0	100.0	100.0	100.0	100.0	100.0	100.0	100.0	100.0	100.0	100.0	100.0

Note: ** means "not applicable."

(Table continues on the following page)

South Africa's data for 2001 is taken from partner countries' data

Source: International Monetary Fund's Direction of Trade database

5-52. Direction of trade matrix, exports, 2001 (continued)

Exporters		GNQ	ERI	ETH	GAB	GMB	GHA	GIN	GNB	KEN	LSO	LBR	LBY	MDG	MWI	MLI	MRT	MUS	MAR	MOZ	NAM	NER
		Importers																				
Algeria	DZA	0.0	..	0.0	0.0	0.0	0.0	0.0	0.0	0.0	0.0	0.0	0.0	0.0	0.0	0.0	4.0	0.0	1.6	0.0	0.0	0.3
Angola	AGO	0.0	..	0.0	0.0	0.0	0.1	0.0	0.0	0.0	0.0	0.0	0.0	0.0	0.0	0.0	0.0	0.0	0.0	0.0	0.0	0.0
Benin	BEN	0.0	..	0.0	0.0	0.0	0.0	0.0	0.0	0.0	0.0	0.0	0.0	0.0	0.0	0.1	0.0	0.0	0.1	0.0	0.0	1.4
Burkina Faso	BFA	0.0	..	0.0	0.0	0.0	0.4	0.0	0.0	0.0	0.0	0.0	0.0	0.0	0.0	0.4	0.0	0.2	0.0	0.0	0.0	1.7
Botswana	BWA	..	..	..	..	..	..	..	..	..	..	..	..	..	..	..	..	..	..	..	..	..
Burundi	BDI	0.0	..	0.0	0.0	0.0	0.0	0.0	0.0	0.1	0.0	0.0	0.0	0.0	0.0	0.0	0.0	0.0	0.0	0.0	0.0	0.0
Cameroon	CMR	3.6	..	0.0	1.2	0.0	0.0	0.0	0.0	0.0	0.0	0.0	0.0	0.0	0.0	0.0	0.0	0.0	0.1	0.0	0.0	2.7
Cape Verde	CPV	0.0	..	0.0	0.0	0.0	0.0	0.0	0.0	0.0	0.0	0.0	0.0	0.0	0.0	0.0	0.0	0.0	0.0	0.0	0.0	0.0
Central African Republic	CAF	0.0	..	0.0	0.0	0.0	0.0	0.0	0.0	0.0	0.0	0.0	0.0	0.0	0.0	0.0	0.0	0.0	0.0	0.0	0.0	0.0
Chad	TCD	0.0	..	0.0	0.0	0.0	0.0	0.0	0.0	0.0	0.0	0.0	0.0	0.0	0.0	0.0	0.0	0.0	0.0	0.0	0.0	0.0
Comoros	COM	0.0	..	0.0	0.0	0.0	0.0	0.0	0.0	0.0	0.0	0.0	0.0	0.0	0.0	0.0	0.0	0.0	0.0	0.0	0.0	0.0
Congo, Dem. Rep. Of	ZAR	0.0	..	0.0	0.0	0.0	0.0	0.0	0.0	0.0	0.0	0.0	0.0	0.0	0.0	0.0	0.0	0.0	0.0	0.0	0.0	0.0
Congo, Republic of	COG	0.0	..	0.0	0.1	0.0	0.0	0.6	0.0	0.0	0.0	0.0	0.0	0.0	0.0	0.0	0.0	0.0	0.0	0.0	0.0	0.0
Cote d'Ivoire	CIV	0.0	..	0.0	1.4	3.4	6.1	8.1	0.5	0.0	0.0	0.8	0.0	0.0	0.0	25.3	0.9	0.0	0.1	0.0	0.0	9.9
Djibouti	DJI	0.0	..	0.7	0.0	0.0	0.0	0.0	0.0	0.0	0.0	0.0	0.0	0.0	0.0	0.0	0.0	0.0	0.0	0.0	0.0	0.0
Egypt	EGY	0.0	..	0.2	0.0	0.4	0.1	0.4	0.0	0.6	0.0	0.0	1.2	0.1	0.0	0.1	0.3	0.3	0.2	0.1	0.0	0.0
Equatorial Guinea	GNQ	**	..	0.0	0.0	0.0	0.0	0.0	0.0	0.0	0.0	0.0	0.0	0.0	0.0	0.0	0.0	0.0	0.0	0.0	0.0	0.0
Eritrea	ERI	..	**	..	..	..	..	..	..	..	..	..	..	..	..	..	..	..	..	..	..	..
Ethiopia	ETH	0.0	..	**	0.0	0.0	0.0	0.0	0.0	0.1	0.0	0.0	0.0	0.0	0.0	0.0	0.0	0.0	0.0	0.0	0.0	0.0
Gabon	GAB	0.6	..	0.0	**	0.0	0.0	0.6	0.0	0.0	0.0	0.0	0.0	0.0	0.0	0.0	0.0	0.0	0.2	0.0	0.0	0.0
Gambia, The	GMB	0.0	..	0.0	0.0	**	0.0	0.1	0.4	0.0	0.0	0.0	0.0	0.0	0.0	0.0	0.0	0.0	0.0	0.0	0.0	0.0
Ghana	GHA	0.0	..	0.0	0.0	0.2	**	0.0	0.0	0.0	0.0	0.0	0.0	0.0	0.0	0.0	0.0	0.0	0.0	0.0	0.0	1.4
Guinea	GIN	0.0	..	0.0	0.0	0.0	0.0	**	0.0	0.0	0.0	0.2	0.0	0.0	0.0	0.0	0.0	0.0	0.1	0.0	0.0	0.0
Guinea-Bissau	GNB	0.0	..	0.0	0.0	0.0	0.0	0.0	**	0.0	0.0	0.0	0.0	0.0	0.0	0.0	0.0	0.0	0.0	0.0	0.0	0.0
Kenya	KEN	0.0	..	3.2	0.0	0.0	0.0	0.0	0.0	**	0.0	0.0	0.0	0.1	1.6	0.1	0.0	0.1	0.0	0.0	0.0	0.0
Lesotho	LSO	..	..	..	..	..	..	..	..	..	**	..	..	..	..	..	..	..	..	..	..	..
Liberia	LBR	0.0	..	0.0	0.0	0.0	0.0	0.0	0.0	0.3	0.0	**	0.0	0.0	0.0	0.0	0.0	0.0	0.0	0.0	0.0	0.0
Libya	LBY	0.0	..	0.0	0.0	0.0	0.0	0.0	0.0	0.0	0.0	0.0	**	0.0	0.0	0.0	0.0	0.0	0.6	0.0	0.0	0.2
Madagascar	MDG	0.0	..	0.0	0.0	0.0	0.0	0.0	0.0	0.0	0.0	0.0	0.0	**	0.0	0.0	0.0	0.8	0.0	0.0	0.0	0.0
Malawi	MWI	0.0	..	0.0	0.0	0.0	0.0	0.0	0.2	0.0	0.0	0.0	0.0	0.0	**	0.0	0.0	0.1	0.0	0.1	0.0	0.0
Mali	MLI	0.0	..	0.0	0.0	0.0	0.0	0.0	0.0	0.0	0.0	0.0	0.0	0.0	0.0	**	0.0	0.5	0.0	0.0	0.0	0.2
Mauritania	MRT	0.2	..	0.0	0.0	0.0	0.1	0.0	0.0	0.0	0.0	0.3	0.0	0.0	0.0	0.1	**	0.0	0.0	0.0	0.0	0.0
Mauritius	MUS	0.0	..	0.0	0.0	0.0	0.0	0.0	0.0	0.1	0.9	0.0	0.0	7.7	0.3	0.0	0.0	**	0.0	0.1	0.0	0.0
Morocco	MAR	1.5	..	0.0	0.6	1.0	0.1	1.1	0.9	0.0	0.0	0.1	1.5	0.1	0.0	1.6	2.9	0.1	**	0.0	0.0	0.2
Mozambique	MOZ	0.0	..	0.0	0.0	0.0	0.0	0.0	0.0	0.0	0.0	0.0	0.0	0.0	2.6	0.0	0.0	0.0	0.0	**	0.0	0.0
Namibia	NAM	..	..	..	..	..	..	..	..	..	..	..	..	..	..	..	..	..	..	..	**	..
Niger	NER	0.0	..	0.0	0.0	0.0	0.1	0.0	0.0	0.0	0.0	0.0	0.0	0.0	0.0	0.0	0.0	0.0	0.0	0.0	0.0	**
Nigeria	NGA	0.0	..	0.0	0.6	0.1	21.8	0.6	0.0	0.0	0.0	0.0	0.0	0.0	0.0	0.1	0.0	0.0	0.1	0.0	0.0	7.2
Reunion	REU	0.0	..	0.0	0.0	0.0	0.0	0.0	0.0	0.0	0.0	0.0	0.0	0.0	0.0	0.0	0.0	0.0	0.0	0.0	0.0	0.0
Rwanda	RWA	0.0	..	0.0	0.0	0.0	0.0	0.0	0.0	0.0	0.0	0.0	0.0	0.0	0.0	0.0	0.0	0.0	0.0	0.0	0.0	0.0
Sao Tome and Principe	STP	0.0	..	0.0	0.0	0.0	0.0	0.0	0.0	0.0	0.0	0.0	0.0	0.0	0.0	0.0	0.0	0.0	0.0	0.0	0.0	0.0
Senegal	SEN	0.1	..	0.0	0.4	9.1	0.1	1.7	16.7	0.0	0.0	0.2	0.0	0.0	0.0	6.1	2.9	0.0	0.0	0.0	0.1	0.1
Seychelles	SYC	0.0	..	0.0	0.0	0.0	0.0	0.0	0.0	0.0	0.0	0.0	0.0	0.0	0.0	0.0	0.0	0.0	0.0	0.0	0.0	0.0
Sierra Leone	SLE	0.0	..	0.0	0.0	0.0	0.0	0.0	0.0	0.0	0.0	0.0	0.0	0.0	0.0	0.0	0.0	0.0	0.0	0.0	0.0	0.0
Somalia	SOM	0.0	..	0.0	0.0	0.0	0.0	0.0	0.0	0.0	0.0	0.0	0.0	0.0	0.0	0.0	0.0	0.0	0.0	0.0	0.0	0.0
South Africa	ZAF	0.4	..	1.2	1.1	1.9	3.2	0.8	0.2	6.5	0.0	0.0	0.0	4.9	47.7	2.4	0.6	12.0	0.9	58.6	0.0	0.7
Sudan	SDN	0.0	..	0.2	0.0	0.0	0.0	0.0	0.0	0.1	0.0	0.0	0.0	0.0	0.0	0.0	0.0	0.0	0.0	0.0	0.0	0.0
Swaziland	SWZ	..	..	..	..	..	..	..	..	..	..	..	..	..	..	..	..	..	..	..	..	..
Tanzania	TZA	0.0	..	0.1	0.0	0.0	0.0	0.0	0.0	1.3	0.4	0.0	0.0	0.0	2.6	0.0	0.0	0.0	0.0	0.2	0.0	0.1
Togo	TGO	0.0	..	0.0	0.1	0.0	1.8	0.2	0.0	0.0	0.0	0.0	0.0	0.0	0.0	0.2	0.0	0.0	0.0	0.0	0.0	2.3
Tunisia	TUN	0.3	..	0.0	0.1	0.1	0.1	0.2	0.0	0.0	0.0	0.0	6.3	0.2	0.0	0.2	0.3	0.0	0.4	0.0	0.0	1.3
Uganda	UGA	0.0	..	0.0	0.0	0.0	0.0	0.0	0.0	0.0	0.0	0.0	0.0	0.0	0.0	0.0	0.0	0.0	0.0	0.0	0.0	0.0
Zambia	ZMB	0.0	..	0.0	0.0	0.0	0.2	0.0	0.0	0.1	0.0	0.0	0.0	0.0	13.7	0.0	0.0	0.0	0.0	0.0	0.2	0.0
Zimbabwe	ZWE	0.0	..	0.0	0.0	0.0	0.0	0.0	0.0	0.1	1.1	0.0	0.0	0.0	1.9	0.0	0.0	0.0	0.0	0.3	2.0	0.0
Sub-Saharan Africa	SSA	5.0	..	4.8	5.1	14.8	34.0	12.9	18.0	8.9	2.4	1.6	0.0	12.7	70.6	34.9	4.5	13.8	1.7	59.3	2.4	27.7
European Community	EU	59.5	..	35.7	79.6	35.4	31.3	46.0	47.8	26.0	12.2	35.2	67.4	35.4	10.8	46.2	58.5	37.2	64.0	15.6	30.7	42.4
North America	NNA	29.8	..	6.6	5.9	2.5	9.0	12.0	1.1	17.8	0.8	1.0	0.5	2.0	4.2	4.4	4.6	1.5	4.2	3.6	49.8	15.7
Rest of World	ROW	5.7	..	53.0	9.3	47.3	25.7	29.1	33.1	47.3	84.6	62.2	32.1	49.9	14.5	14.5	32.4	47.4	30.1	21.5	17.1	14.2
World	World	100.0	..	100.0	100.0	100.0	100.0	100.0	100.0	100.0	100.0	100.0	100.0	100.0	100.0	100.0	100.0	100.0	100.0	100.0	100.0	100.0

Note: ** means "not applicable." Note: ** means "not applicable."

(Table continues on the following page)

South Africa's data for 2001 is taken fro South Africa's data for 2001 is taken from partner countries' data

Source: International Monetary Fund's I Source: International Monetary Fund's Direction of Trade database

5-52. Direction of trade matrix, exports, 2001 (continued)

Exporters		NGA	REU	RWA	STP	SEN	SYC	SLE	SOM	ZAF	SDN	SWZ	TZA	TGO	TUN	UGA	ZMB	ZWE	SSA	EU	NNA	ROW	World
		Importers																					
Algeria	DZA	0.3	..	0.0	0.0	0.0	0.0	0.0	0.0	0.0	0.0	0.0	0.0	0.0	0.8	0.0	0.0	0.0	0.1	0.6	0.3	0.1	0.3
Angola	AGO	0.0	..	0.0	0.0	0.0	0.0	0.0	0.0	0.0	0.0	0.0	0.0	0.0	0.0	0.0	0.0	0.0	0.0	0.1	0.2	0.1	0.1
Benin	BEN	0.0	..	0.0	0.0	0.1	0.0	0.0	0.0	0.0	0.0	0.0	0.0	0.4	0.0	0.0	0.0	0.0	0.0	0.0	0.0	0.0	0.0
Burkina Faso	BFA	0.0	..	0.0	0.0	0.0	0.0	0.0	0.0	0.0	0.0	0.0	0.0	0.1	0.0	0.0	0.0	0.0	0.0	0.0	0.0	0.0	0.0
Botswana	BWA	..	..	..	..	..	..	..	..	..	..	..	..	..	..	..	..	..	..	..	..	..	..
Burundi	BDI	0.0	..	1.1	0.0	0.0	0.0	0.0	0.0	0.0	0.0	0.0	0.0	0.0	0.0	0.1	0.0	0.0	0.0	0.0	0.0	0.0	0.0
Cameroon	CMR	0.1	..	0.0	0.0	0.4	0.0	0.0	0.0	0.0	0.0	0.0	0.0	0.4	0.1	0.0	0.0	0.0	0.2	0.1	0.0	0.0	0.0
Cape Verde	CPV	0.0	..	0.0	0.0	0.0	0.0	0.0	0.0	0.0	0.0	0.0	0.0	0.0	0.0	0.0	0.0	0.0	0.0	0.0	0.0	0.0	0.0
Central African Republic	CAF	0.0	..	0.0	0.0	0.0	0.0	0.0	0.0	0.0	0.0	0.0	0.0	0.0	0.0	0.0	0.0	0.0	0.0	0.0	0.0	0.0	0.0
Chad	TCD	0.0	..	0.0	0.0	0.0	0.0	0.0	0.0	0.0	0.0	0.0	0.0	0.0	0.0	0.0	0.0	0.0	0.0	0.0	0.0	0.0	0.0
Comoros	COM	0.0	..	0.0	0.0	0.0	0.0	0.0	0.0	0.0	0.0	0.0	0.0	0.0	0.0	0.0	0.0	0.0	0.0	0.0	0.0	0.0	0.0
Congo, Dem. Rep. Of	ZAR	0.0	..	3.0	0.0	0.0	0.0	0.0	0.0	0.0	0.0	0.0	0.0	0.0	0.0	0.0	0.0	7.2	0.1	0.0	0.0	0.0	0.0
Congo, Republic of	COG	0.0	..	0.0	0.0	0.2	0.0	0.0	0.0	0.0	0.0	0.0	0.0	0.0	0.0	0.0	0.0	0.0	0.0	0.0	0.0	0.1	0.0
Cote d'Ivoire	CIV	0.5	..	0.0	0.0	3.8	0.0	5.3	0.0	0.0	0.0	0.0	0.0	10.9	0.1	0.0	0.0	0.0	1.2	0.1	0.0	0.0	0.1
Djibouti	DJI	0.0	..	0.0	0.0	0.0	0.0	0.0	30.7	0.0	0.0	0.0	0.0	0.0	0.0	0.0	0.0	0.0	0.1	0.0	0.0	0.0	0.0
Egypt	EGY	0.1	..	0.0	0.0	0.2	0.0	0.5	0.0	0.0	2.0	0.0	0.3	0.0	0.2	0.1	0.1	0.0	0.1	0.1	0.0	0.1	0.1
Equatorial Guinea	GNQ	0.0	..	0.0	0.0	0.0	0.0	0.0	0.0	0.0	0.0	0.0	0.0	0.0	0.0	0.0	0.0	0.0	0.0	0.0	0.0	0.0	0.0
Eritrea	ERI	..	..	..	..	..	..	..	..	..	..	..	..	..	..	..	..	..	..	..	..	..	..
Ethiopia	ETH	0.0	..	0.3	0.0	0.0	0.0	0.0	0.0	0.0	0.0	0.0	0.2	0.0	0.0	0.0	0.0	0.0	0.0	0.0	0.0	0.0	0.0
Gabon	GAB	0.0	..	0.0	2.3	0.2	0.0	0.0	0.0	0.3	0.0	0.0	0.0	0.1	0.0	0.0	0.0	0.0	0.1	0.0	0.1	0.0	0.1
Gambia, The	GMB	0.0	..	0.0	0.0	0.0	0.0	0.0	0.0	0.0	0.0	0.0	0.0	0.0	0.0	0.0	0.0	0.0	0.0	0.0	0.0	0.0	0.0
Ghana	GHA	0.7	..	0.0	0.0	0.2	0.0	0.0	0.0	0.0	0.0	0.0	0.0	0.8	0.0	0.0	0.0	0.0	0.2	0.0	0.0	0.0	0.0
Guinea	GIN	0.1	..	0.0	0.0	0.0	0.0	0.0	0.0	0.0	0.0	0.0	0.0	0.0	0.0	0.0	0.0	0.0	0.1	0.0	0.0	0.0	0.0
Guinea-Bissau	GNB	0.0	..	0.0	0.0	0.0	0.0	0.0	0.0	0.0	0.0	0.0	0.0	0.0	0.0	0.0	0.0	0.0	0.0	0.0	0.0	0.0	0.0
Kenya	KEN	0.0	..	28.2	0.0	0.0	0.7	0.0	13.9	0.0	3.5	0.0	6.4	0.0	0.0	44.0	0.3	0.2	1.0	0.0	0.0	0.0	0.0
Lesotho	LSO	..	..	..	..	..	..	..	..	..	..	..	..	..	..	..	..	..	..	..	..	..	..
Liberia	LBR	0.0	..	0.0	0.0	0.1	0.0	0.3	0.0	0.0	0.0	0.0	0.0	0.0	0.0	0.0	0.0	0.0	0.0	0.0	0.0	0.0	0.0
Libya	LBY	0.0	..	0.0	0.0	0.0	0.0	0.0	0.0	0.0	0.1	0.0	0.0	0.0	3.3	0.0	0.0	0.0	0.0	0.4	0.0	0.1	0.2
Madagascar	MDG	0.0	..	0.0	0.0	0.0	0.0	0.0	0.0	0.0	0.0	0.0	0.0	0.0	0.0	0.0	0.0	0.0	0.0	0.0	0.0	0.0	0.0
Malawi	MWI	0.0	..	0.0	0.0	0.0	0.0	0.1	0.0	0.1	0.0	0.0	0.1	0.0	0.0	0.2	0.3	0.2	0.1	0.0	0.0	0.0	0.0
Mali	MLI	0.0	..	0.0	0.0	0.0	0.0	0.0	0.0	0.0	0.0	0.0	0.0	0.0	0.0	0.0	0.0	0.0	0.0	0.0	0.0	0.0	0.0
Mauritania	MRT	0.0	..	0.0	0.0	0.0	0.0	0.0	0.0	0.0	0.0	0.0	0.0	0.9	0.0	0.0	0.0	0.0	0.1	0.0	0.0	0.0	0.0
Mauritius	MUS	0.0	..	0.9	0.0	0.0	1.3	0.0	0.0	0.1	0.0	0.0	0.2	0.0	0.0	0.1	0.0	0.8	0.2	0.0	0.0	0.0	0.0
Morocco	MAR	0.2	..	0.0	0.0	0.8	0.0	0.4	0.0	0.0	0.0	0.0	0.0	0.3	0.6	0.0	0.0	0.0	0.2	0.2	0.0	0.1	0.1
Mozambique	MOZ	0.0	..	0.0	0.0	0.0	0.0	0.0	0.0	0.1	0.0	0.7	0.0	0.0	0.0	0.0	0.0	6.7	0.2	0.0	0.0	0.0	0.0
Namibia	NAM	..	..	..	..	..	..	..	..	..	..	..	..	..	..	..	..	..	..	..	..	..	..
Niger	NER	0.5	..	0.0	0.0	0.0	0.0	0.0	0.0	0.0	0.0	0.0	0.0	0.0	0.0	0.0	0.0	0.0	0.1	0.0	0.0	0.0	0.0
Nigeria	NGA	**	..	0.0	0.0	14.1	0.0	3.7	0.0	0.9	0.0	0.0	0.0	0.6	0.0	0.0	0.0	0.0	2.5	0.2	0.6	0.2	0.3
Reunion	REU	0.0	**	0.0	0.0	0.0	0.0	0.0	0.0	0.0	0.0	0.0	0.0	0.0	0.0	0.0	0.0	0.0	0.0	0.0	0.0	0.0	0.0
Rwanda	RWA	0.0	..	**	0.0	0.0	0.0	0.0	0.0	0.0	0.0	0.0	0.0	0.0	0.0	0.0	0.0	0.0	0.0	0.0	0.0	0.0	0.0
Sao Tome and Principe	STP	0.0	..	0.0	**	0.0	0.0	0.0	0.0	0.0	0.0	0.0	0.0	0.0	0.0	0.0	0.0	0.0	0.0	0.0	0.0	0.0	0.0
Senegal	SEN	0.0	..	0.0	0.0	**	0.0	1.0	0.0	0.0	0.0	0.0	0.0	0.7	0.0	0.0	0.0	0.0	0.3	0.0	0.0	0.0	0.0
Seychelles	SYC	0.0	..	0.0	0.0	0.0	**	0.0	0.0	0.0	0.0	0.0	0.0	0.0	0.0	0.0	0.0	0.0	0.0	0.0	0.0	0.0	0.0
Sierra Leone	SLE	0.0	..	0.0	0.0	0.0	0.0	**	0.0	0.0	0.0	0.0	0.0	0.0	0.0	0.0	0.0	0.0	0.0	0.0	0.0	0.0	0.0
Somalia	SOM	0.0	..	0.0	0.0	0.0	0.0	0.0	**	0.0	0.0	0.0	0.0	0.0	0.0	0.1	0.0	0.0	0.0	0.0	0.0	0.0	0.0
South Africa	ZAF	1.9	..	4.4	0.4	1.1	5.5	1.4	0.1	**	1.2	0.0	12.4	1.2	0.1	6.5	67.6	51.2	4.8	0.4	0.2	0.3	0.4
Sudan	SDN	0.0	..	0.0	0.0	0.0	0.0	0.0	0.3	0.0	**	0.0	0.0	0.0	0.1	0.0	0.0	0.0	0.0	0.0	0.0	0.1	0.0
Swaziland	SWZ	..	..	..	..	..	..	..	..	..	..	**	..	..	..	..	..	..	..	..	..	..	..
Tanzania	TZA	0.0	..	2.3	0.0	0.0	0.0	0.0	0.2	0.0	0.0	0.3	**	0.0	0.0	3.1	1.2	0.0	0.2	0.0	0.0	0.0	0.0
Togo	TGO	0.0	..	0.0	0.1	0.0	0.0	0.0	0.0	0.0	0.0	0.0	0.0	**	0.0	0.0	0.0	0.0	0.2	0.0	0.0	0.0	0.0
Tunisia	TUN	0.0	..	0.0	0.0	0.6	0.0	0.0	0.0	0.0	0.0	0.0	0.0	0.2	**	0.0	0.0	0.0	0.1	0.2	0.0	0.0	0.1
Uganda	UGA	0.0	..	1.0	0.0	0.0	0.0	0.0	0.0	0.0	0.0	0.0	0.4	0.0	0.0	**	0.0	0.0	0.0	0.0	0.0	0.0	0.0
Zambia	ZMB	0.0	..	1.4	0.0	0.0	0.0	0.0	0.0	0.2	0.0	0.6	1.9	0.0	0.0	0.2	**	1.0	0.2	0.0	0.0	0.0	0.0
Zimbabwe	ZWE	0.0	..	0.0	0.0	0.0	0.0	0.0	0.0	0.5	0.1	0.0	0.1	0.0	0.0	0.1	1.3	**	0.2	0.0	0.0	0.1	0.0
Sub-Saharan Africa	SSA	4.1	..	42.6	2.8	20.0	7.5	11.9	14.4	2.4	5.0	1.7	21.9	16.1	0.6	54.4	70.9	67.4	12.1	1.3	1.4	1.0	1.3
European Community	EU	43.6	..	28.9	65.0	51.4	26.7	62.0	8.0	43.7	33.2	14.8	25.3	38.2	79.2	20.0	12.7	16.6	40.6	62.9	17.7	24.9	37.4
North America	NNA	9.9	..	8.9	22.1	6.0	37.7	7.7	3.0	12.0	3.3	12.2	4.9	4.0	3.5	3.9	2.2	2.7	9.3	7.6	29.6	16.8	16.2
Rest of World	ROW	42.4	..	19.6	10.2	22.6	28.1	18.4	74.7	41.8	58.6	71.3	47.9	41.6	16.7	21.7	14.1	13.3	38.0	28.1	51.3	57.3	45.1
World	World	100.0	..	100.0	100.0	100.0	100.0	100.0	100.0	100.0	100.0	100.0	100.0	100.0	100.0	100.0	100.0	100.0	100.0	100.0	100.0	100.0	100.0

Note: ** means "not applicable." Note: ** means "not applicable."

South Africa's data for 2001 is taken fr South Africa's data for 2001 is taken from partner countries' data

Source: International Monetary Fund's Source: International Monetary Fund's Direction of Trade database

5-53. Direction of trade matrix, current U.S. dollars, 1991

Importers — *Millions of current US dollars*

Exporters		DZA	AGO	BEN	BFA	BWA	BDI	CMR	CPV	CAF	TCD	COM	ZAR	COG	CIV	DJI	EGY
Algeria	DZA	**	0	0	0	0	0	0	0	0	0	0	0	0	0	0	11
Angola	AGO	0	**	0	0	0	0	0	1	0	0	0	0	1	0	0	0
Benin	BEN	1	0	**	1	0	0	0	0	0	0	0	0	1	1	0	0
Burkina Faso	BFA	0	0	0	**	0	0	0	0	0	0	0	0	0	12	0	0
Bostwana	BWA	..	..	..	..	**	..	..	..	..	..	..	..	..	..	..	..
Burundi	BDI	0	0	0	0	0	**	0	0	0	0	0	1	0	0	0	0
Cameroon	CMR	7	0	0	0	0	0	**	0	19	13	0	1	15	2	0	0
Cape Verde	CPV	0	0	0	0	0	0	0	**	0	0	0	0	0	0	0	0
Central African Republic	CAF	0	0	0	0	0	0	0	0	**	0	0	0	0	0	0	0
Chad	TCD	0	0	0	0	0	0	0	0	1	**	0	0	0	0	0	0
Comoros	COM	0	0	0	0	0	0	0	0	0	0	**	0	0	0	0	0
Congo, Dem. Rep. Of	ZAR	0	0	0	0	0	2	0	0	3	0	0	**	3	1	0	4
Congo, Republic of	COG	0	4	1	0	0	0	0	0	0	0	0	3	**	0	0	0
Cote d'Ivoire	CIV	20	3	16	118	0	0	11	8	0	2	0	22	7	**	0	0
Djibouti	DJI	0	0	0	0	0	0	0	0	0	0	0	0	0	0	**	0
Egypt	EGY	7	0	0	0	0	0	0	0	0	0	0	0	0	1	2	**
Equatorial Guinea	GNQ	0	0	0	0	0	0	0	0	0	0	0	0	0	0	0	0
Eritrea	ERI	..	..	..	..	..	..	..	..	..	..	..	..	..	..	..	..
Ethiopia	ETH	0	0	0	0	0	0	0	0	0	0	0	0	0	0	7	0
Gabon	GAB	3	0	0	0	0	0	1	0	2	0	0	0	0	2	0	1
Gambia, The	GMB	0	0	0	0	0	0	0	0	0	0	0	0	0	0	0	0
Ghana	GHA	0	0	0	0	0	0	0	0	0	0	0	0	0	5	0	0
Guinea	GIN	0	0	0	0	0	0	29	0	0	0	0	0	0	6	0	0
Guinea-Bissau	GNB	0	0	0	0	0	0	0	0	0	0	0	0	0	2	0	0
Kenya	KEN	0	0	0	0	0	4	1	0	0	0	1	5	0	0	3	34
Lesotho	LSO	..	..	..	..	..	..	..	..	..	..	..	..	..	..	..	..
Liberia	LBR	0	0	0	0	0	0	0	0	0	0	0	0	0	0	0	0
Libya	LBY	1	0	0	0	0	0	0	0	0	0	0	0	0	0	0	19
Madagascar	MDG	0	0	0	0	0	0	0	0	0	0	2	0	0	0	0	0
Malawi	MWI	0	0	0	0	2	3	0	0	0	0	0	2	0	0	0	9
Mali	MLI	15	0	0	2	0	0	0	0	0	0	0	0	0	3	0	0
Mauritania	MRT	0	0	2	0	0	0	9	0	0	0	0	0	4	19	0	1
Mauritius	MUS	0	0	0	0	0	0	0	0	0	0	2	0	0	1	0	0
Morocco	MAR	74	5	2	0	0	0	7	0	0	0	1	3	5	7	0	3
Mozambique	MOZ	0	0	0	0	0	0	0	0	0	0	0	0	0	0	0	0
Namibia	NAM	..	..	..	..	..	..	..	..	..	..	..	..	..	..	..	..
Niger	NER	2	0	4	1	0	0	0	0	0	0	0	0	0	2	0	0
Nigeria	NGA	0	0	1	0	0	0	78	0	0	8	0	38	0	298	0	0
Reunion	REU	0	0	0	0	0	0	0	0	0	0	2	0	0	0	0	0
Rwanda	RWA	0	0	0	0	0	1	0	0	0	0	0	0	0	0	0	0
Sao Tome and Principe	STP	0	0	0	0	0	0	0	0	0	0	0	0	0	0	0	0
Senegal	SEN	0	0	5	2	0	0	18	0	0	1	0	1	5	0	0	0
Seychelles	SYC	0	0	0	0	0	0	0	0	0	0	0	0	0	0	0	0
Sierra Leone	SLE	0	0	0	0	0	0	0	0	0	0	0	0	0	0	0	0
Somalia	SOM	0	0	0	0	0	0	0	0	0	0	0	0	0	0	0	1
South Africa	ZAF	0	0	0	..	..	0	0	0	0	0	0	28	3	7	0	0
Sudan	SDN	0	0	0	0	0	0	0	0	0	0	0	0	0	0	0	3
Swaziland	SWZ	..	..	..	..	..	..	..	..	..	..	..	..	..	..	..	..
Tanzania	TZA	0	0	0	0	1	4	0	0	0	0	0	2	0	0	0	1
Togo	TGO	0	0	5	6	0	0	0	0	0	0	0	0	1	1	0	0
Tunisia	TUN	78	0	0	0	0	0	2	0	0	0	0	0	0	5	0	11
Uganda	UGA	0	0	0	0	0	0	0	0	0	0	0	0	0	0	0	2
Zambia	ZMB	0	1	0	0	7	5	0	0	0	0	0	3	0	0	0	0
Zimbabwe	ZWE	0	7	0	0	83	2	0	1	0	0	0	8	0	1	0	6
Sub-Saharan Africa	SSA	48	16	35	130	93	21	148	11	25	24	6	88	41	369	11	63
European Community	EU	5,556	1,189	259	229	117	106	771	102	95	105	88	557	418	1,092	158	5,496
North America	NAM	938	196	30	28	32	2	63	4	1	15	0	67	44	86	13	2,812
Rest of World	ROW	1,507	341	148	39	68	41	174	17	21	11	14	201	137	282	183	4,174
World	WLD	8,049	1,741	473	426	310	171	1,155	134	143	155	108	913	640	1,829	365	12,545

Note: ** means "not applicable."

(Table continues on the following page)

South Africa's data for 1991 is taken from partner countries' data

Source: International Monetary Fund's Direction of Trade database

5-53. Direction of trade matrix, current U.S. dollars, 1991 (continued)

Millions of current US dollars

Exporters		GNQ	ERI	ETH	GAB	GMB	GHA	GIN	GNB	KEN	LSO	LBR	LBY	MDG	MWI	MLI	MRT	MUS	MAR	MOZ	NAM	NER
Algeria	DZA	0	0	0	0	0	0	0	0	0	0	0	7	0	0	0	30	0	51	0	0	0
Angola	AGO	0	0	0	0	0	0	0	0	0	0	0	0	0	0	0	0	0	0	0	0	0
Benin	BEN	0	0	0	0	0	0	0	0	0	0	0	0	0	0	0	0	0	2	0	0	0
Burkina Faso	BFA	0	0	0	0	0	1	0	0	0	0	0	0	0	0	1	0	0	0	0	0	0
Bostwana	BWA	..	..	..	..	..	..	..	..	..	..	..	..	..	..	..	..	..	..	..	..	..
Burundi	BDI	0	0	0	0	0	0	0	0	6	0	0	0	0	0	0	0	0	0	0	0	0
Cameroon	CMR	28	0	0	34	0	0	1	0	3	0	0	0	0	0	0	0	0	39	0	0	0
Cape Verde	CPV	0	0	0	0	0	0	0	0	0	0	0	0	0	0	0	0	0	0	0	0	0
Central African Republic	CAF	0	0	0	0	0	0	0	0	0	0	0	0	0	0	0	0	0	0	0	0	0
Chad	TCD	0	0	0	0	0	0	0	0	0	0	0	0	0	0	0	0	0	4	0	0	0
Comoros	COM	0	0	0	0	0	0	0	0	0	0	0	0	0	0	0	0	0	0	0	0	0
Congo, Dem. Rep. Of	ZAR	0	0	0	1	0	0	0	0	2	0	0	0	0	0	0	0	0	0	0	0	0
Congo, Republic of	COG	0	0	0	0	0	0	0	0	0	0	0	0	0	0	0	0	0	0	0	0	0
Cote d'Ivoire	CIV	0	0	0	99	9	57	76	5	1	0	15	0	1	0	139	5	12	13	19	0	31
Djibouti	DJI	0	0	20	0	0	0	0	0	0	0	0	0	0	0	0	0	0	0	0	0	0
Egypt	EGY	0	0	2	0	0	0	0	0	3	0	8	119	0	0	0	0	0	20	0	0	0
Equatorial Guinea	GNQ	**	0	0	0	0	0	0	0	0	0	0	0	0	0	0	0	0	0	0	0	0
Eritrea	ERI	..	**	..	..	..	..	..	..	..	..	..	..	..	..	..	..	..	..	..	..	..
Ethiopia	ETH	0	0	**	0	0	0	0	0	1	0	0	0	0	0	0	0	0	0	0	0	0
Gabon	GAB	0	0	0	**	0	0	0	0	0	0	0	0	0	0	0	0	0	17	0	0	0
Gambia, The	GMB	0	0	0	0	**	0	7	0	0	0	0	0	0	0	0	0	0	0	0	0	0
Ghana	GHA	0	0	0	0	0	**	0	0	0	0	0	2	0	0	0	0	0	0	0	0	0
Guinea	GIN	0	0	0	0	0	0	**	0	0	0	0	0	0	0	0	0	0	0	0	0	0
Guinea-Bissau	GNB	0	0	0	0	0	0	0	**	0	0	0	0	0	0	0	0	0	0	0	0	0
Kenya	KEN	0	0	10	0	0	0	0	0	**	0	0	0	0	2	0	0	4	0	2	0	0
Lesotho	LSO	..	..	..	..	..	..	..	..	..	**	..	..	..	..	..	..	..	..	..	..	..
Liberia	LBR	0	0	0	0	0	0	0	0	1	0	**	0	0	0	0	0	0	0	0	0	0
Libya	LBY	0	0	0	0	0	0	0	0	0	0	0	**	0	0	0	0	0	122	0	0	0
Madagascar	MDG	0	0	0	0	0	0	0	0	0	0	0	0	**	0	0	0	13	0	0	0	0
Malawi	MWI	0	0	0	0	0	0	0	0	0	0	0	0	0	**	0	0	0	3	2	0	0
Mali	MLI	0	0	0	0	0	0	0	0	0	0	0	0	0	0	**	0	0	0	0	0	0
Mauritania	MRT	0	0	0	0	0	0	0	0	0	0	3	0	0	0	0	**	0	0	0	0	0
Mauritius	MUS	0	0	0	0	0	0	0	0	1	0	0	0	7	0	0	0	**	0	0	0	0
Morocco	MAR	0	0	0	8	0	2	6	0	0	0	0	196	0	0	5	6	2	**	1	0	0
Mozambique	MOZ	0	0	0	0	0	0	0	0	0	0	0	0	0	11	0	0	1	0	**	0	0
Namibia	NAM	..	..	..	..	..	..	..	..	..	..	..	..	..	..	..	..	..	..	..	**	..
Niger	NER	0	0	0	0	0	1	0	0	0	0	0	3	0	0	1	0	0	0	0	0	**
Nigeria	NGA	0	0	0	21	0	190	14	0	2	0	1	0	0	0	0	0	0	5	0	0	3
Reunion	REU	0	0	0	0	0	0	0	0	0	0	0	0	5	0	0	0	4	0	0	0	0
Rwanda	RWA	0	0	0	0	0	0	0	0	0	0	0	0	0	0	0	0	0	0	0	0	0
Sao Tome and Principe	STP	0	0	0	0	0	0	0	0	0	0	0	0	0	0	0	0	0	0	0	0	0
Senegal	SEN	0	0	0	2	9	0	5	3	0	0	0	0	0	0	24	0	0	0	2	0	0
Seychelles	SYC	0	0	0	0	0	0	0	0	0	0	0	0	0	0	0	0	0	0	0	0	0
Sierra Leone	SLE	0	0	0	0	0	0	0	0	0	0	0	0	0	0	0	0	0	0	0	0	0
Somalia	SOM	0	0	0	0	0	0	0	0	0	0	0	0	0	0	0	0	0	0	0	0	0
South Africa	ZAF	..	0	0	0	0	0	0	0	11	0	0	0	17	196	0	0	183	5	0	0	0
Sudan	SDN	0	0	0	0	0	0	0	0	0	0	0	4	0	0	0	0	0	0	0	0	0
Swaziland	SWZ	..	..	..	..	..	..	..	..	..	..	..	..	..	..	..	..	..	..	..	..	..
Tanzania	TZA	0	0	0	0	0	0	0	0	7	0	0	0	0	1	0	0	4	0	1	0	0
Togo	TGO	0	0	0	1	0	3	0	0	0	0	0	0	0	0	1	0	0	2	0	0	3
Tunisia	TUN	0	0	8	4	0	5	4	6	0	2	0	217	0	0	0	2	0	27	0	0	0
Uganda	UGA	0	0	0	0	0	0	0	0	1	0	0	0	0	0	0	0	0	0	0	0	0
Zambia	ZMB	0	0	0	0	0	0	0	0	35	0	0	0	0	12	0	0	0	0	0	7	0
Zimbabwe	ZWE	0	0	0	0	0	2	0	0	13	1	0	2	0	43	0	0	1	0	35	3	0
Sub-Saharan Africa	SSA	29	0	10	158	19	254	104	8	79	1	19	12	14	100	167	6	43	88	66	10	38
European Community	EU	38	0	394	574	126	691	342	60	947	56	581	3,542	207	154	226	304	451	4,629	289	90	169
North America	NAM	12	0	228	90	11	174	91	2	102	4	48	50	15	57	21	28	16	567	114	36	12
Rest of World	ROW	6	0	279	133	111	340	114	36	907	27	4,005	1,884	119	121	58	96	790	1,735	300	9	30
World	WLD	84	0	912	954	267	1,459	651	105	2,034	88	4,653	5,488	356	432	472	434	1,300	7,019	768	144	249

Note: ** means "not applicable." Note: ** means "not applicable."

(Table continues on the following page)

South Africa's data for 1991 is taken fr South Africa's data for 1991 is taken from partner countries' data

Source: International Monetary Fund's Source: International Monetary Fund's Direction of Trade database

5-53. Direction of trade matrix, current U.S. dollars, 1991 (continued)

Millions of current US dollars

Exporters		NGA	REU	RWA	STP	SEN	SYC	SLE	SOM	ZAF	SDN	SWZ	TZA	TGO	TUN	UGA	ZMB	ZWE	SSA	EU	NNA	ROW	World
Algeria	DZA	0	0	0	0	0	0	0	0	0	0	0	13	0	101	0	0	0	43	8,733	2,038	976	11,790
Angola	AGO	0	0	0	0	0	0	0	0	0	0	0	0	1	0	0	0	0	3	1,034	1,788	272	3,097
Benin	BEN	0	0	0	0	0	0	0	0	0	0	0	0	1	0	0	0	0	5	9	1	32	46
Burkina Faso	BFA	0	0	0	0	0	0	0	0	0	0	0	0	3	0	0	0	0	17	15	0	74	106
Bostwana	BWA	..	..	..	..	..	..	..	..	..	..	..	..	..	..	..	..	..	..	..	..	..	..
Burundi	BDI	0	0	1	0	0	0	0	0	0	0	0	0	0	0	1	0	2	12	38	18	24	92
Cameroon	CMR	35	1	0	0	3	0	0	0	0	0	0	0	1	3	0	0	0	157	1,546	52	155	1,909
Cape Verde	CPV	0	0	0	0	0	0	0	0	0	0	0	0	0	0	0	0	0	1	4	0	0	5
Central African Republic	CAF	0	0	0	0	0	0	0	0	0	4	0	0	0	0	0	0	0	5	62	1	41	109
Chad	TCD	2	0	0	0	0	0	0	0	0	0	0	0	0	0	0	0	0	3	56	0	35	94
Comoros	COM	0	0	0	0	0	0	0	0	0	0	0	0	0	0	0	0	0	0	18	9	1	28
Congo, Dem. Rep. Of	ZAR	0	0	2	0	0	0	0	0	0	0	0	0	0	2	0	6	0	21	1,059	323	197	1,600
Congo, Republic of	COG	43	4	0	0	1	0	0	0	4	0	0	0	1	0	0	0	0	60	523	368	161	1,112
Cote d'Ivoire	CIV	37	5	0	0	61	0	22	0	13	0	0	2	41	15	0	0	0	839	1,533	138	273	2,782
Djibouti	DJI	0	0	0	0	0	0	0	23	0	0	0	0	0	0	0	0	0	43	6	0	46	95
Egypt	EGY	2	0	0	0	0	0	0	0	0	25	0	2	0	15	0	0	0	45	1,578	285	1,751	3,659
Equatorial Guinea	GNQ	0	0	0	0	0	0	0	0	0	0	0	0	0	0	0	0	0	0	35	0	2	37
Eritrea	ERI	..	..	..	..	..	..	..	..	..	..	..	..	..	..	..	..	..	..	..	..	..	..
Ethiopia	ETH	0	0	0	0	0	0	0	0	0	0	0	0	0	0	0	0	0	1	112	8	68	189
Gabon	GAB	1	5	0	0	22	0	0	0	0	0	0	0	3	1	0	0	0	37	1,246	699	543	2,525
Gambia, The	GMB	0	0	0	0	1	0	0	0	0	0	0	0	0	0	0	0	0	9	108	2	48	166
Ghana	GHA	4	0	0	0	0	0	0	0	0	0	0	0	15	0	0	0	0	26	524	8	59	617
Guinea	GIN	1	0	0	0	0	0	0	0	0	0	0	0	0	0	0	0	0	37	373	165	78	653
Guinea-Bissau	GNB	0	0	0	0	0	0	0	0	0	0	0	0	0	0	0	0	0	2	7	0	21	31
Kenya	KEN	2	4	9	0	0	1	0	11	4	20	0	34	0	1	46	2	4	167	517	48	282	1,014
Lesotho	LSO	..	..	..	..	..	..	..	..	..	..	..	..	..	..	..	..	..	..	..	..	..	..
Liberia	LBR	0	0	0	0	0	0	0	0	0	0	0	0	0	0	0	0	0	2	264	8	214	488
Libya	LBY	0	0	0	0	0	0	0	0	0	153	0	0	0	96	0	0	0	154	9,668	0	1,390	11,212
Madagascar	MDG	0	16	0	0	1	0	0	0	1	0	0	0	0	0	0	0	0	33	150	43	78	305
Malawi	MWI	0	0	0	0	0	0	0	0	32	0	0	2	0	0	0	4	3	51	194	72	164	482
Mali	MLI	1	0	0	0	0	0	0	0	0	0	0	0	0	5	0	0	0	6	87	8	165	267
Mauritania	MRT	0	0	0	0	0	0	0	0	0	0	0	0	3	1	0	0	1	40	291	12	181	524
Mauritius	MUS	0	23	2	0	0	11	0	0	5	0	0	0	0	0	0	0	4	56	944	147	48	1,195
Morocco	MAR	13	2	0	0	5	0	0	0	0	0	0	3	4	62	0	0	0	89	2,709	132	1,798	4,728
Mozambique	MOZ	0	0	0	0	0	0	0	0	5	0	0	0	0	0	0	3	10	30	68	22	33	153
Namibia	NAM	..	..	..	..	..	..	..	..	..	..	..	..	..	..	..	..	..	..	..	..	..	..
Niger	NER	59	0	0	0	0	0	0	0	0	0	0	0	2	0	0	0	0	70	152	0	56	278
Nigeria	NGA	**	0	0	0	0	0	6	0	0	0	0	0	2	0	0	0	0	664	3,055	3,649	359	7,726
Reunion	REU	0	**	0	0	0	0	0	0	0	0	0	0	0	0	0	0	0	11	122	0	18	151
Rwanda	RWA	0	0	**	0	0	0	0	0	0	0	0	0	0	0	0	0	0	1	66	6	19	91
Sao Tome and Principe	STP	0	0	0	**	0	0	0	0	0	0	0	0	0	0	0	0	0	0	3	0	18	21
Senegal	SEN	1	0	0	0	**	0	0	0	0	0	0	0	1	2	0	0	0	81	333	12	225	651
Seychelles	SYC	0	0	0	0	0	**	0	0	0	0	0	0	0	0	0	0	0	0	15	0	1	16
Sierra Leone	SLE	0	0	0	0	0	0	**	0	0	0	0	0	0	0	0	0	0	0	80	47	18	145
Somalia	SOM	0	0	0	0	0	0	0	**	0	0	0	1	0	0	0	0	0	1	18	2	77	98
South Africa	ZAF	0	54	31	0	0	22	0	0	**	0	0	0	1	0	0	165	517	1,236	8,401	1,893	4,744	16,274
Sudan	SDN	0	0	0	0	0	0	0	0	0	**	0	0	0	1	0	0	0	0	118	15	233	366
Swaziland	SWZ	..	..	..	..	..	..	..	..	..	..	**	..	..	..	..	..	..	..	..	..	..	..
Tanzania	TZA	0	0	11	0	0	0	0	1	0	3	0	**	0	0	4	1	3	42	203	16	152	413
Togo	TGO	19	0	0	0	0	0	0	0	0	0	0	0	**	2	0	0	0	40	75	39	113	267
Tunisia	TUN	0	0	0	0	1	0	0	0	8	4	0	0	4	**	2	0	0	59	2,966	28	1,033	4,085
Uganda	UGA	0	0	0	0	0	0	0	0	0	0	0	1	0	2	**	0	0	3	132	20	20	175
Zambia	ZMB	0	0	0	0	0	0	0	0	5	0	0	10	0	0	0	**	44	131	382	24	540	1,077
Zimbabwe	ZWE	0	2	0	0	0	1	0	0	132	2	1	4	0	0	2	46	**	389	548	79	272	1,288
Sub-Saharan Africa	SSA	208	61	25	0	90	14	30	12	200	29	1	54	75	43	54	67	202	3,253	23,432	10,054	8,886	45,626
European Community	EU	3,792	1,566	89	24	702	54	104	56	7,313	536	21	466	355	3,900	177	257	640	26,978	992,313	107,395	359,791	######
North America	NAM	858	2	5	5	93	2	25	7	2,206	103	5	50	25	222	15	27	64	5,120	118,688	180,721	243,388	547,915
Rest of World	ROW	2,208	245	54	3	216	98	37	59	3,518	635	43	595	283	874	130	294	559	17,952	369,859	315,275	709,308	######
World	WLD	7,066	1,875	173	32	1,101	168	195	135	13,237	1,303	69	1,166	738	5,039	375	646	1,465	53,303	######	613,445	######	######

Note: ** means "not applicable." Note: ** means "not applicable."

South Africa's data for 1991 is taken fr South Africa's data for 1991 is taken from partner countries' data

Source: International Monetary Fund's Source: International Monetary Fund's Direction of Trade database

5-54. Direction of trade matrix, current U.S. dollars, 1996

Importers — *Millions of current US dollars*

Exporters		DZA	AGO	BEN	BFA	BWA	BDI	CMR	CPV	CAF	TCD	COM	ZAR	COG	CIV	DJI	EGY
Algeria	DZA	**	0	0	0	0	0	0	0	0	0	0	0	0	0	0	3
Angola	AGO	0	**	3	0	0	0	0	3	0	0	0	0	4	0	0	0
Benin	BEN	0	0	**	0	0	0	0	0	0	0	0	0	0	1	0	0
Burkina Faso	BFA	0	0	0	**	0	0	0	0	0	0	0	0	0	22	0	0
Bostwana	BWA	..	..	..	..	**	..	..	..	..	..	..	..	..	..	..	..
Burundi	BDI	0	0	0	0	0	**	0	0	0	0	0	0	0	0	0	0
Cameroon	CMR	0	1	2	1	0	0	**	0	16	10	0	3	21	8	0	0
Cape Verde	CPV	0	0	0	0	0	0	0	**	0	0	0	0	0	0	0	0
Central African Republic	CAF	0	0	0	0	0	0	2	0	**	1	0	6	1	0	0	0
Chad	TCD	0	0	0	0	0	0	0	0	1	**	0	0	0	0	0	0
Comoros	COM	0	0	0	0	0	0	0	0	0	0	**	0	0	0	0	0
Congo, Dem. Rep. Of	ZAR	0	0	0	0	0	1	0	0	1	0	0	**	1	0	0	3
Congo, Republic of	COG	0	7	0	0	0	0	1	0	0	0	0	7	**	1	0	0
Cote d'Ivoire	CIV	8	8	40	101	0	0	0	1	25	2	0	24	10	**	0	0
Djibouti	DJI	0	0	0	0	0	0	0	0	0	0	0	0	0	0	**	0
Egypt	EGY	16	1	0	0	0	0	0	0	0	0	0	0	0	2	1	**
Equatorial Guinea	GNQ	0	0	0	0	0	0	38	0	0	0	0	0	0	0	0	0
Eritrea	ERI	..	..	..	..	..	..	..	..	..	..	..	..	..	..	..	..
Ethiopia	ETH	0	0	0	0	0	0	0	0	0	0	0	0	0	0	36	3
Gabon	GAB	4	1	1	0	0	0	1	0	0	0	0	6	5	1	0	0
Gambia, The	GMB	0	0	0	0	0	0	0	0	0	0	0	0	0	0	0	0
Ghana	GHA	0	10	17	5	0	0	0	0	0	0	0	0	7	5	0	2
Guinea	GIN	1	0	0	0	0	0	18	0	0	0	0	0	0	0	0	0
Guinea-Bissau	GNB	0	0	0	0	0	0	1	0	0	0	0	0	0	0	0	0
Kenya	KEN	1	1	0	0	0	6	0	0	0	0	3	33	0	1	2	75
Lesotho	LSO	..	..	..	..	..	..	..	..	..	..	..	..	..	..	..	..
Liberia	LBR	0	0	0	0	0	0	0	0	0	0	0	0	0	0	0	0
Libya	LBY	1	0	0	0	0	0	0	0	0	0	0	0	0	0	0	70
Madagascar	MDG	3	0	0	0	0	0	0	0	0	0	1	0	0	0	0	0
Malawi	MWI	0	0	0	0	0	0	0	0	0	0	0	1	0	0	0	10
Mali	MLI	0	0	0	1	0	0	0	0	0	0	0	0	0	4	0	0
Mauritania	MRT	2	0	0	0	0	0	7	0	0	0	0	0	4	18	0	0
Mauritius	MUS	0	0	0	0	0	0	0	0	0	0	2	0	0	0	0	0
Morocco	MAR	35	4	3	1	0	0	3	0	0	0	0	7	4	20	0	4
Mozambique	MOZ	0	0	0	0	0	0	0	0	0	0	0	0	0	0	0	0
Namibia	NAM	..	..	..	..	..	..	..	..	..	..	..	..	..	..	..	..
Niger	NER	3	1	3	2	0	0	0	0	0	0	0	0	0	12	0	0
Nigeria	NGA	0	0	7	24	0	0	120	0	1	13	0	58	2	484	0	2
Reunion	REU	0	0	0	0	0	0	0	0	0	0	2	0	0	0	0	0
Rwanda	RWA	0	0	0	0	0	0	0	0	0	0	0	1	0	0	0	0
Sao Tome and Principe	STP	0	0	0	0	0	0	0	0	0	0	0	0	0	0	0	0
Senegal	SEN	0	0	16	4	0	0	18	4	0	2	0	0	5	18	0	0
Seychelles	SYC	0	0	0	0	0	0	0	0	0	0	0	0	0	0	0	0
Sierra Leone	SLE	0	0	0	0	0	0	0	0	0	0	0	0	0	0	0	0
Somalia	SOM	0	0	0	0	0	0	0	0	0	0	0	0	0	0	0	0
South Africa	ZAF	3	380	2	6	..	4	11	1	0	1	23	241	17	17	0	27
Sudan	SDN	0	0	0	0	0	0	0	0	0	0	0	0	0	0	0	19
Swaziland	SWZ	..	..	..	..	..	..	..	..	..	..	..	..	..	..	..	..
Tanzania	TZA	0	0	0	0	1	4	0	0	0	0	0	4	0	0	1	2
Togo	TGO	0	0	9	6	0	0	0	0	0	0	0	0	0	0	0	0
Tunisia	TUN	96	0	1	1	0	1	5	0	0	0	0	0	0	7	0	27
Uganda	UGA	8	0	0	0	0	0	0	0	0	0	0	0	0	0	0	4
Zambia	ZMB	0	1	0	0	5	3	0	0	0	0	0	41	0	0	0	20
Zimbabwe	ZWE	0	7	0	0	83	1	1	0	0	0	0	6	0	0	0	2
Sub-Saharan Africa	SSA	31	94	107	146	90	15	214	8	46	31	8	307	62	621	39	180
European Community	EU	5,077	963	404	241	155	63	769	203	67	109	99	466	1,181	1,469	129	7,155
North America	NNA	921	272	29	12	46	4	78	68	4	3	0	80	63	153	9	3,249
Rest of World	ROW	1,489	566	339	60	199	28	150	20	23	17	34	390	82	449	155	6,598
World	WLD	7,518	1,895	879	458	490	110	1,211	299	140	161	142	1,243	1,388	2,691	332	17,183

Note: ** means "not applicable."

(Table continues on the following page)

South Africa's data for 1996 is taken from partner countries' data

Source: International Monetary Fund's Direction of Trade database

5-54. Direction of trade matrix, current U.S. dollars, 1996 (continued)

Exporters		Importers GNQ	ERI	ETH	GAB	GMB	GHA	GIN	GNB	KEN	LSO	LBR	LBY	MDG	MWI	MLI	MRT	MUS	MAR	MOZ	NAM	NER
Algeria	DZA	0	0	0	0	0	0	1	0	0	0	2	2	0	0	0	0	0	106	0	0	0
Angola	AGO	0	0	0	0	0	1	0	0	0	0	0	0	0	0	0	0	0	0	0	0	0
Benin	BEN	0	0	0	0	0	0	0	0	0	0	0	0	0	0	0	0	0	22	0	0	3
Burkina Faso	BFA	0	0	0	0	0	5	0	0	0	0	0	0	0	0	2	0	9	0	0	0	2
Bostwana	BWA	..	..	..	..	..	..	..	..	..	..	..	..	..	..	..	..	..	..	..	..	..
Burundi	BDI	0	0	0	0	0	0	0	0	1	0	0	0	0	0	0	0	0	0	0	0	0
Cameroon	CMR	32	0	0	32	0	0	3	0	0	0	0	0	0	0	1	0	0	4	0	0	0
Cape Verde	CPV	0	0	0	0	0	0	0	0	0	0	0	0	0	0	0	0	0	0	0	0	0
Central African Republic	CAF	0	0	0	0	0	0	0	0	0	0	0	0	0	0	0	0	0	0	0	0	0
Chad	TCD	0	0	0	0	0	0	0	0	0	0	0	0	0	0	0	0	0	0	0	0	0
Comoros	COM	0	0	0	0	0	0	0	0	0	0	0	0	0	0	0	0	0	0	0	0	0
Congo, Dem. Rep. Of	ZAR	0	0	0	0	0	0	0	0	1	0	0	0	0	0	0	0	0	0	0	0	0
Congo, Republic of	COG	0	0	0	1	0	0	0	0	0	0	0	0	0	0	0	0	0	4	0	0	0
Cote d'Ivoire	CIV	0	0	0	17	17	123	80	2	0	0	11	0	0	1	184	5	0	22	0	0	34
Djibouti	DJI	0	0	27	0	0	0	0	0	0	0	0	0	0	0	0	0	0	0	0	0	0
Egypt	EGY	0	0	3	0	0	1	0	0	1	0	0	52	0	0	0	0	0	8	0	0	0
Equatorial Guinea	GNQ	**	0	0	0	0	0	0	0	0	0	0	0	0	0	0	0	0	0	0	0	0
Eritrea	ERI	..	**	..	..	..	..	..	..	..	..	..	..	..	..	..	..	..	..	..	..	..
Ethiopia	ETH	0	0	**	0	0	0	0	0	1	0	0	0	0	0	0	0	0	0	0	0	0
Gabon	GAB	1	0	0	**	1	0	23	0	0	0	0	0	0	0	0	0	0	17	0	0	0
Gambia, The	GMB	0	0	0	0	**	0	0	0	0	0	0	0	0	0	0	0	0	0	0	0	0
Ghana	GHA	0	0	0	0	0	**	0	0	0	0	0	0	0	0	0	0	0	1	0	0	4
Guinea	GIN	0	0	0	0	0	0	**	0	0	0	3	0	0	0	0	0	0	2	0	0	0
Guinea-Bissau	GNB	0	0	0	0	0	0	0	**	0	0	0	0	0	0	0	0	0	0	0	0	0
Kenya	KEN	0	1	40	0	0	2	0	0	**	0	0	0	3	5	0	0	10	0	4	0	0
Lesotho	LSO	..	..	..	..	..	..	..	..	..	**	..	..	..	..	..	..	..	..	..	..	..
Liberia	LBR	0	0	0	0	0	0	0	0	0	0	**	0	0	0	0	0	0	0	0	0	0
Libya	LBY	0	0	0	0	0	0	0	0	16	0	0	**	0	0	0	1	0	127	0	0	1
Madagascar	MDG	0	0	0	0	0	0	0	0	0	0	0	0	**	0	0	0	12	0	0	0	0
Malawi	MWI	0	0	0	0	1	0	0	0	0	0	0	0	0	**	0	0	5	0	9	0	0
Mali	MLI	0	0	0	0	0	0	0	0	0	0	0	0	0	0	**	0	0	2	0	0	0
Mauritania	MRT	0	0	0	0	0	1	0	0	0	0	7	0	0	0	0	**	0	0	0	0	0
Mauritius	MUS	0	0	0	0	0	0	0	0	4	0	0	0	51	4	0	0	**	0	0	0	0
Morocco	MAR	2	0	1	8	0	11	6	0	0	0	0	125	1	0	8	9	2	**	0	0	1
Mozambique	MOZ	0	0	0	0	0	0	0	0	0	0	0	0	0	1	0	0	0	0	**	0	0
Namibia	NAM	..	..	..	..	..	..	..	..	..	..	..	..	..	..	..	..	..	..	..	**	..
Niger	NER	0	0	0	0	0	9	0	0	0	0	0	0	0	0	0	0	0	0	0	0	**
Nigeria	NGA	0	0	0	6	0	388	9	0	1	0	1	0	0	0	0	0	0	197	0	0	28
Reunion	REU	0	0	0	0	0	0	0	0	0	0	0	0	1	0	0	0	1	0	0	0	0
Rwanda	RWA	0	0	0	0	0	0	0	0	0	0	0	0	0	0	0	0	0	0	0	0	0
Sao Tome and Principe	STP	0	0	0	0	0	0	0	0	0	0	0	0	0	0	0	0	0	0	0	0	0
Senegal	SEN	0	0	0	6	12	1	9	7	0	0	0	0	0	0	48	15	0	1	0	0	1
Seychelles	SYC	0	0	0	0	0	0	0	0	1	0	0	0	0	0	0	0	0	0	0	0	0
Sierra Leone	SLE	0	0	0	0	0	0	0	0	0	0	0	0	0	0	0	0	0	0	0	0	0
Somalia	SOM	0	0	0	0	0	0	0	0	0	0	0	0	0	0	0	0	0	0	0	0	0
South Africa	ZAF	2	0	3	9	0	66	1	0	209	0	7	0	84	242	19	2	273	32	270	0	0
Sudan	SDN	0	0	0	0	0	0	0	0	0	0	0	6	0	0	0	0	0	0	0	0	0
Swaziland	SWZ	..	..	..	..	..	..	..	..	..	..	..	..	..	..	..	..	..	..	..	..	..
Tanzania	TZA	0	0	0	0	0	0	0	0	13	0	0	0	2	2	0	0	0	0	0	0	0
Togo	TGO	0	0	0	0	0	2	0	0	0	0	0	0	0	0	0	0	0	3	0	0	1
Tunisia	TUN	0	0	0	1	0	3	0	0	0	0	0	196	0	0	1	1	0	38	0	0	1
Uganda	UGA	0	0	0	0	0	0	0	0	0	0	0	0	0	0	0	0	0	0	0	0	0
Zambia	ZMB	0	0	0	0	0	0	0	0	2	0	0	0	0	50	0	0	0	0	6	4	0
Zimbabwe	ZWE	0	0	0	1	0	3	0	0	10	0	0	0	0	61	0	0	3	1	78	24	0
Sub-Saharan Africa	SSA	33	1	42	69	32	540	125	10	78	0	23	7	59	192	248	21	54	280	142	29	73
European Community	EU	80	0	569	574	106	1,276	363	57	1,113	24	581	3,198	330	81	347	362	726	5,851	208	118	153
North America	NNA	17	14	164	60	9	350	93	7	128	3	58	95	12	19	25	16	28	611	34	23	36
Rest of World	ROW	13	-15	621	133	138	761	184	21	1,603	31	2,811	1,783	227	225	117	130	1,127	2,122	679	25	51
World	WLD	143	0	1,396	836	285	2,927	765	96	2,922	58	3,473	5,083	628	518	738	528	1,935	8,864	1,064	195	313

Note: ** means "not applicable." Note: ** means "not applicable."

South Africa's data for 1996 is taken frc South Africa's data for 1996 is taken from partner countries' data

Source: International Monetary Fund's I Source: International Monetary Fund's Direction of Trade database

(Table continues on the following page)

5-54. Direction of trade matrix, current U.S. dollars, 1996 (continued)

Exporters		Importers NGA	REU	RWA	STP	SEN	SYC	SLE	SOM	ZAF	SDN	SWZ	TZA	TGO	TUN	UGA	ZMB	ZWE	SSA	EU	NNA	ROW	World
Algeria	DZA	7	0	0	0	0	0	0	0	0	0	0	0	0	102	0	0	0	11	6,659	2,106	2,323	11,099
Angola	AGO	0	0	0	0	0	0	0	0	57	0	0	0	0	0	0	0	0	68	876	2,717	883	4,544
Benin	BEN	5	0	0	0	0	0	0	0	8	0	0	0	3	0	0	0	0	22	61	0	179	262
Burkina Faso	BFA	0	0	0	0	0	0	0	0	0	0	0	0	7	1	0	0	0	48	45	1	94	189
Bostwana	BWA	..	..	..	..	..	..	..	..	..	..	..	..	..	..	..	..	..	..	..	..	..	..
Burundi	BDI	0	0	3	0	0	0	0	0	0	0	0	4	0	0	0	0	0	9	7	0	21	37
Cameroon	CMR	18	13	0	0	6	0	0	0	6	0	0	0	2	8	0	0	0	176	1,371	42	194	1,782
Cape Verde	CPV	0	1	0	0	0	0	0	0	0	0	0	0	0	0	0	0	0	2	14	0	1	17
Central African Republic	CAF	0	0	0	0	0	0	0	0	1	0	0	0	0	0	0	0	0	11	111	0	0	122
Chad	TCD	3	0	0	0	0	0	0	0	4	0	0	0	0	0	0	0	0	8	78	7	24	117
Comoros	COM	0	0	0	0	0	0	0	0	0	0	0	0	0	0	0	0	0	0	8	6	1	14
Congo, Dem. Rep. Of	ZAR	0	0	4	0	0	0	0	0	115	0	0	1	0	0	0	11	0	134	915	251	163	1,464
Congo, Republic of	COG	0	4	0	0	0	0	0	0	1	0	0	0	0	0	0	0	0	23	1,022	306	501	1,852
Cote d'Ivoire	CIV	67	0	0	0	54	0	25	0	43	0	0	0	70	18	0	0	0	947	3,135	358	557	4,996
Djibouti	DJI	0	0	0	0	0	0	0	53	0	0	0	0	0	0	0	0	0	80	4	0	33	116
Egypt	EGY	1	0	0	0	1	0	0	0	35	21	0	1	0	24	1	0	0	70	1,613	464	1,388	3,534
Equatorial Guinea	GNQ	0	0	0	0	0	0	0	0	0	0	0	0	0	0	0	0	0	38	33	75	35	180
Eritrea	ERI	..	..	..	..	..	..	..	..	..	..	..	..	..	..	..	..	..	..	..	..	..	..
Ethiopia	ETH	0	1	0	0	0	0	0	0	0	0	0	0	0	0	0	0	0	1	213	30	197	441
Gabon	GAB	0	0	0	1	3	0	0	0	4	0	0	0	2	1	0	0	0	50	362	2,015	718	3,146
Gambia, The	GMB	0	0	0	0	0	0	0	0	0	0	0	0	0	0	0	0	0	2	16	0	4	22
Ghana	GHA	52	0	0	0	0	0	0	0	3	0	0	0	9	0	0	0	0	112	898	165	379	1,554
Guinea	GIN	0	0	0	0	0	0	0	0	0	0	0	0	0	1	0	0	0	23	296	251	44	614
Guinea-Bissau	GNB	0	0	0	0	0	0	0	0	0	0	0	0	0	0	0	0	0	1	41	0	18	60
Kenya	KEN	3	12	35	0	0	4	0	40	42	23	0	239	0	1	306	3	5	826	688	67	424	2,005
Lesotho	LSO	..	..	..	..	..	..	..	..	..	..	..	..	..	..	..	..	..	..	..	..	..	..
Liberia	LBR	0	0	0	0	0	0	1	0	0	0	0	0	0	0	0	0	0	2	628	25	375	1,029
Libya	LBY	0	0	0	0	0	0	0	0	0	235	0	0	0	213	0	0	0	253	8,084	0	1,818	10,155
Madagascar	MDG	0	25	0	0	0	0	0	0	2	0	0	0	0	0	0	0	1	41	189	13	81	324
Malawi	MWI	0	0	0	0	0	0	0	0	68	0	0	6	0	1	1	9	22	123	161	73	104	460
Mali	MLI	2	0	0	0	1	0	0	0	12	0	0	0	0	5	0	0	0	20	94	7	170	292
Mauritania	MRT	0	0	0	0	0	0	0	0	0	0	0	0	22	2	0	0	0	62	306	7	191	566
Mauritius	MUS	0	33	1	0	0	3	0	0	13	0	0	5	0	0	0	0	9	124	1,335	252	89	1,800
Morocco	MAR	9	1	0	0	15	0	1	0	3	0	0	0	2	59	0	0	0	123	2,918	201	1,885	5,128
Mozambique	MOZ	0	0	0	0	0	0	0	0	44	0	0	4	0	0	0	0	10	60	78	27	61	226
Namibia	NAM	..	..	..	..	..	..	..	..	..	..	..	..	..	..	..	..	..	..	..	..	..	..
Niger	NER	47	0	0	0	0	0	0	0	0	0	0	0	1	0	0	0	0	75	98	0	46	219
Nigeria	NGA	**	0	0	0	64	0	9	0	9	0	0	0	10	0	0	0	1	1,236	5,584	5,838	3,493	16,151
Reunion	REU	0	**	0	0	0	0	0	0	0	0	0	0	0	0	0	0	0	4	145	0	16	165
Rwanda	RWA	0	0	**	0	0	0	0	0	0	0	0	0	0	0	0	0	0	1	47	8	112	169
Sao Tome and Principe	STP	0	0	0	**	0	0	0	0	0	0	0	0	0	0	0	0	0	0	6	0	1	8
Senegal	SEN	7	0	0	0	**	0	2	0	1	0	0	0	6	2	0	0	0	183	290	2	249	724
Seychelles	SYC	0	2	0	0	0	**	0	0	1	0	0	0	0	0	0	0	0	4	38	53	74	169
Sierra Leone	SLE	0	0	0	0	0	0	**	0	0	0	0	0	0	0	0	0	0	0	29	2	16	47
Somalia	SOM	0	0	0	0	0	0	0	**	0	0	0	1	0	0	0	0	1	2	21	0	169	192
South Africa	ZAF	45	50	3	1	3	41	8	0	**	19	0	142	7	1	26	293	1,141	3,670	9,512	2,789	10,930	26,902
Sudan	SDN	0	0	0	0	0	0	0	0	1	**	0	0	0	6	0	0	0	2	133	18	343	496
Swaziland	SWZ	..	..	..	..	..	..	..	..	..	..	**	..	..	..	..	..	..	..	..	..	..	..
Tanzania	TZA	0	0	43	0	0	0	0	3	5	6	0	**	0	0	10	13	2	109	234	19	401	764
Togo	TGO	0	0	0	1	0	0	0	0	18	0	0	0	**	0	0	0	0	39	31	33	135	239
Tunisia	TUN	3	1	0	0	3	0	0	0	9	0	0	0	1	**	0	0	0	40	4,418	77	985	5,519
Uganda	UGA	0	0	1	0	0	0	0	0	0	0	0	2	0	0	**	0	1	6	416	25	122	568
Zambia	ZMB	0	0	1	0	0	0	0	0	43	0	1	12	0	0	1	**	53	223	178	29	609	1,039
Zimbabwe	ZWE	2	5	1	0	0	4	0	0	312	1	2	5	0	1	2	91	**	706	740	145	651	2,242
Sub-Saharan Africa	SSA	216	96	90	2	130	12	37	43	814	33	3	283	150	58	321	172	417	6,341	32,141	16,126	21,491	76,099
European Community	EU	2,908	2,018	86	29	953	77	137	20	11,172	363	30	389	246	5,439	226	212	536	32,656	######	158,137	610,498	######
North America	NNA	847	4	39	0	69	104	29	4	3,259	56	2	63	20	215	24	50	111	6,590	138,303	297,345	380,856	823,095
Rest of World	ROW	2,176	176	44	5	315	113	61	163	9,548	761	37	818	254	1,330	192	533	1,316	27,754	496,518	494,528	######	######
World	WLD	6,147	2,294	259	35	1,467	305	264	231	24,793	1,213	72	1,552	671	7,042	763	966	2,380	73,341	######	966,136	######	######

Note: ** means "not applicable." Note: ** means "not applicable."

South Africa's data for 1996 is taken frSouth Africa's data for 1996 is taken from partner countries' data

Source: International Monetary Fund's Source: International Monetary Fund's Direction of Trade database

5-55. Direction of trade matrix, current U.S. dollars, 2001

Importers — *Millions of current US dollars*

Exporters		DZA	AGO	BEN	BFA	BWA	BDI	CMR	CPV	CAF	TCD	COM	ZAR	COG	CIV	DJI	EGY
Algeria	DZA	**	0	1	0	0	0	0	0	0	0	0	0	0	1	0	3
Angola	AGO	0	**	0	0	0	0	1	0	0	0	0	0	5	0	0	0
Benin	BEN	0	0	**	1	0	0	0	0	0	1	0	0	0	0	0	0
Burkina Faso	BFA	0	0	0	**	0	0	0	0	0	0	0	0	0	1	0	0
Bostwana	BWA	..	..	..	..	**	..	..	..	..	..	..	..	..	..	..	..
Burundi	BDI	0	0	0	0	0	**	0	0	0	0	0	0	0	0	0	0
Cameroon	CMR	0	15	1	0	0	0	**	0	5	12	0	27	19	3	0	0
Cape Verde	CPV	0	0	0	0	0	0	0	**	0	0	0	0	0	0	0	0
Central African Republic	CAF	0	0	0	0	0	0	0	0	**	0	0	3	0	0	0	0
Chad	TCD	0	0	0	0	0	0	0	0	2	**	0	0	0	0	0	0
Comoros	COM	0	0	0	0	0	0	0	0	0	0	**	0	0	0	0	0
Congo, Dem. Rep. Of	ZAR	0	0	0	0	0	1	0	0	2	0	0	**	1	0	0	0
Congo, Republic of	COG	2	11	0	0	0	0	4	0	0	0	0	11	**	0	0	0
Cote d'Ivoire	CIV	19	0	31	123	0	0	30	8	0	0	0	0	0	**	0	0
Djibouti	DJI	0	0	0	0	0	0	0	0	0	0	0	0	0	0	**	0
Egypt	EGY	12	1	0	0	0	0	3	0	0	0	0	1	0	5	0	**
Equatorial Guinea	GNQ	0	0	0	0	0	0	36	0	0	0	0	0	0	0	0	0
Eritrea	ERI	..	..	..	..	..	..	..	..	..	..	..	..	..	..	..	..
Ethiopia	ETH	9	0	0	0	0	0	0	0	0	0	0	0	0	0	59	3
Gabon	GAB	2	1	0	0	0	0	3	0	0	0	0	10	8	0	0	0
Gambia, The	GMB	0	0	0	0	0	0	0	0	0	0	0	0	0	0	0	0
Ghana	GHA	2	17	26	7	0	0	1	0	0	0	0	0	10	7	0	1
Guinea	GIN	3	0	0	0	0	0	31	0	0	0	0	0	0	9	0	0
Guinea-Bissau	GNB	0	0	0	0	0	0	1	0	0	0	0	0	0	1	0	0
Kenya	KEN	0	0	0	0	0	8	0	0	0	0	4	39	1	0	3	86
Lesotho	LSO	..	..	..	..	..	..	..	..	..	..	..	..	..	..	..	..
Liberia	LBR	0	0	0	0	0	0	0	0	0	0	0	0	0	2	0	0
Libya	LBY	2	0	0	15	0	0	0	0	0	0	0	0	0	0	0	36
Madagascar	MDG	0	0	0	0	0	0	0	0	0	0	1	0	0	0	0	0
Malawi	MWI	0	0	0	0	0	0	0	0	0	0	0	1	0	0	0	23
Mali	MLI	0	0	0	2	0	0	0	0	0	0	0	0	0	2	0	0
Mauritania	MRT	2	0	0	0	0	0	14	0	0	0	0	0	6	19	0	2
Mauritius	MUS	0	0	0	0	1	0	0	0	0	0	1	0	0	0	0	0
Morocco	MAR	9	7	3	4	0	0	5	0	0	0	1	3	8	15	0	24
Mozambique	MOZ	0	1	0	0	0	0	0	0	0	0	0	0	0	0	0	2
Namibia	NAM	..	..	..	..	..	..	..	..	..	..	..	..	..	..	..	..
Niger	NER	0	0	2	1	0	0	0	0	0	1	0	0	0	2	0	0
Nigeria	NGA	2	0	10	19	0	0	235	0	1	19	0	88	3	435	0	0
Reunion	REU	0	0	0	0	0	0	0	0	0	0	0	0	0	0	0	0
Rwanda	RWA	0	0	0	0	0	0	0	0	0	0	0	1	0	0	0	0
Sao Tome and Principe	STP	0	0	0	0	0	0	0	0	0	0	0	0	0	0	0	0
Senegal	SEN	0	0	6	3	0	0	9	1	1	1	0	0	5	21	0	0
Seychelles	SYC	0	0	0	0	0	0	0	0	0	0	0	0	0	0	0	0
Sierra Leone	SLE	0	0	0	0	0	0	0	0	0	0	0	0	0	0	0	0
Somalia	SOM	0	0	0	0	0	0	0	0	0	0	0	0	0	0	0	0
South Africa	ZAF	32	305	8	3	0	3	28	2	1	2	9	107	30	36	7	31
Sudan	SDN	1	0	0	0	0	0	0	0	0	0	0	0	0	0	0	58
Swaziland	SWZ	..	..	..	..	..	..	..	..	..	..	..	..	..	..	..	..
Tanzania	TZA	0	0	0	0	0	10	0	0	0	0	0	10	0	0	0	3
Togo	TGO	0	0	37	23	0	0	1	0	0	1	0	0	1	1	0	0
Tunisia	TUN	76	0	2	3	0	0	3	0	0	0	0	0	4	8	7	33
Uganda	UGA	10	0	0	0	0	0	0	0	0	0	0	0	0	0	0	2
Zambia	ZMB	0	0	0	0	3	1	0	0	0	0	0	0	0	0	0	39
Zimbabwe	ZWE	1	1	0	0	12	0	0	0	0	0	0	3	0	0	0	14
Sub-Saharan Africa	SSA	86	352	122	182	16	24	397	11	11	38	15	301	92	538	70	267
European Community	EU	6,704	1,220	488	203	165	74	1,099	209	60	146	32	249	468	1,237	177	6,181
North America	NNA	1,234	279	37	8	45	5	203	8	4	139	2	22	96	107	19	3,899
Rest of World	ROW	2,410	1,211	736	52	55	26	251	19	19	26	21	125	195	641	287	7,306
World	WLD	10,434	3,062	1,384	445	281	129	1,950	246	94	349	70	696	851	2,523	553	17,654

Note: ** means "not applicable."

South Africa's data for 2001 is taken from partner countries' data

Source: International Monetary Fund's Direction of Trade database

(Table continues on the following page)

5-55. Direction of trade matrix, current U.S. dollars, 2001 (continued)

Exporters		Importers GNQ	ERI	ETH	GAB	GMB	GHA	GIN	GNB	KEN	LSO	LBR	LBY	MDG	MWI	MLI	MRT	MUS	MAR	MOZ	NAM	NER
Algeria	DZA	0	0	0	0	0	0	0	0	0	0	0	0	0	0	0	23	0	175	0	0	1
Angola	AGO	0	0	0	1	0	1	0	0	0	0	0	0	0	0	0	0	0	0	0	0	0
Benin	BEN	0	0	0	0	0	0	0	0	0	0	0	0	0	0	1	0	1	6	0	0	6
Burkina Faso	BFA	0	0	0	0	0	10	0	0	0	0	0	0	0	0	3	0	4	4	0	0	7
Bostwana	BWA	..	..	..	..	..	..	..	..	..	..	..	..	..	..	..	..	..	..	..	..	..
Burundi	BDI	0	0	0	0	0	0	0	0	3	0	0	0	0	0	0	0	0	0	0	0	0
Cameroon	CMR	10	0	0	16	0	0	0	0	0	0	0	0	0	0	0	0	0	8	0	0	11
Cape Verde	CPV	0	0	0	0	0	0	0	0	0	0	0	0	0	0	0	0	0	0	0	0	0
Central African Republic	CAF	0	0	0	0	0	0	0	0	0	0	0	0	0	0	0	0	0	0	0	0	0
Chad	TCD	0	0	0	0	0	0	0	0	0	0	0	0	0	0	0	0	0	3	0	0	0
Comoros	COM	0	0	0	0	0	0	0	0	0	0	0	0	0	0	0	0	0	0	0	0	0
Congo, Dem. Rep. Of	ZAR	0	0	0	0	0	0	0	0	0	0	0	0	0	0	0	0	0	0	0	0	0
Congo, Republic of	COG	0	0	0	2	0	0	4	0	0	0	0	0	0	0	0	0	0	4	0	0	0
Cote d'Ivoire	CIV	0	0	0	18	12	165	56	0	0	0	31	0	0	0	203	5	0	12	0	0	41
Djibouti	DJI	0	0	7	0	0	0	0	0	0	0	0	0	0	0	0	0	0	0	0	0	0
Egypt	EGY	0	0	3	0	1	4	3	0	20	0	0	45	1	0	1	1	5	26	1	0	0
Equatorial Guinea	GNQ	**	0	0	0	0	0	0	0	0	0	0	0	0	0	0	0	0	3	0	0	0
Eritrea	ERI	..	**	..	..	..	..	..	..	..	..	..	..	..	..	..	..	..	..	..	..	..
Ethiopia	ETH	0	0	**	0	0	0	0	0	5	0	0	0	0	0	0	0	0	2	0	0	0
Gabon	GAB	2	0	0	**	0	0	4	0	0	0	0	0	1	0	0	0	0	19	0	0	0
Gambia, The	GMB	0	0	0	0	**	0	0	0	0	0	0	0	0	0	0	0	0	0	0	0	0
Ghana	GHA	0	0	0	0	1	**	0	0	0	0	0	0	0	0	0	0	0	1	0	0	6
Guinea	GIN	0	0	0	0	0	0	**	0	0	0	9	0	0	0	0	0	0	8	0	0	0
Guinea-Bissau	GNB	0	0	0	0	0	0	0	**	0	0	0	0	0	0	0	0	0	0	0	0	0
Kenya	KEN	0	5	33	0	0	0	0	0	**	0	0	0	1	8	0	0	2	0	0	0	0
Lesotho	LSO	..	..	..	..	..	..	..	..	..	**	..	..	..	..	..	..	..	..	..	..	..
Liberia	LBR	0	0	0	0	0	0	0	0	10	0	**	0	0	0	0	0	0	1	0	0	0
Libya	LBY	0	0	0	0	0	0	0	0	0	0	0	**	0	0	0	0	0	63	0	0	1
Madagascar	MDG	0	0	0	0	0	0	0	0	1	0	0	0	**	0	0	0	16	1	0	0	0
Malawi	MWI	0	0	0	0	0	0	0	0	0	0	0	0	0	**	0	0	1	1	1	0	0
Mali	MLI	0	0	0	0	0	0	0	0	0	0	0	0	0	0	**	0	9	2	0	0	1
Mauritania	MRT	1	0	0	0	0	2	0	0	0	0	12	0	0	0	1	**	0	0	0	0	0
Mauritius	MUS	0	0	0	0	0	0	0	0	4	1	0	0	84	1	0	0	**	0	1	0	0
Morocco	MAR	4	0	0	8	4	4	8	1	1	0	3	58	1	0	13	17	3	**	0	0	1
Mozambique	MOZ	0	0	0	0	0	0	0	0	1	0	0	0	0	12	0	0	0	0	**	0	0
Namibia	NAM	..	..	..	..	..	..	..	..	..	..	..	..	..	..	..	..	..	..	..	**	..
Niger	NER	0	0	0	0	0	2	0	0	0	0	0	0	0	0	0	0	0	0	0	0	**
Nigeria	NGA	0	0	0	8	0	588	4	0	1	0	2	0	0	0	1	0	0	6	0	0	30
Reunion	REU	0	0	0	0	0	0	0	0	0	0	0	0	0	0	0	0	0	0	0	0	0
Rwanda	RWA	0	0	0	0	0	0	0	0	0	0	0	0	0	0	0	0	0	0	0	0	0
Sao Tome and Principe	STP	0	0	0	0	0	0	0	0	0	0	0	0	0	0	0	0	0	0	0	0	0
Senegal	SEN	0	0	0	5	32	3	12	13	0	0	9	0	0	0	49	17	0	1	0	0	1
Seychelles	SYC	0	0	0	0	0	0	0	0	0	0	0	0	0	0	0	0	1	0	0	0	0
Sierra Leone	SLE	0	0	0	0	0	0	0	0	0	0	0	0	0	0	0	0	0	1	0	0	0
Somalia	SOM	0	0	0	0	0	0	0	0	0	0	0	0	0	0	0	0	0	0	0	0	0
South Africa	ZAF	1	2	13	15	7	87	6	0	218	0	1	0	53	219	19	4	244	95	664	0	3
Sudan	SDN	0	0	2	0	0	0	0	0	2	0	0	0	0	0	0	0	0	0	0	0	0
Swaziland	SWZ	..	..	..	..	..	..	..	..	..	..	..	..	..	..	..	..	..	..	..	..	..
Tanzania	TZA	0	0	1	0	0	0	0	0	42	0	0	0	0	12	0	0	0	0	2	0	0
Togo	TGO	0	0	0	1	0	49	1	0	0	0	0	0	0	0	2	0	0	2	0	0	10
Tunisia	TUN	1	0	0	2	1	2	1	0	0	0	0	249	2	0	2	2	0	41	0	0	6
Uganda	UGA	0	0	0	0	0	0	0	0	1	0	0	0	0	0	0	0	0	1	0	0	0
Zambia	ZMB	0	0	0	0	0	6	0	0	5	0	0	0	0	63	0	0	0	0	0	1	0
Zimbabwe	ZWE	0	0	0	0	0	1	0	0	3	1	0	0	0	9	0	0	0	0	3	10	0
Sub-Saharan Africa	SSA	14	7	49	66	53	915	89	14	297	2	64	1	140	324	281	26	281	182	673	12	116
European Community	EU	164	0	365	1,036	127	844	317	38	869	11	1,413	2,643	389	50	371	340	758	6,830	177	158	177
North America	NNA	82	22	68	77	9	243	83	1	595	1	38	21	22	19	35	27	31	450	41	256	65
Rest of World	ROW	16	..	543	121	169	693	200	26	1,580	75	2,494	1,258	548	66	116	189	965	3,211	244	88	59
World	WLD	276	..	1,025	1,301	358	2,695	689	79	3,340	89	4,010	3,923	1,098	459	803	582	2,034	10,674	1,134	514	417

Note: ** means "not applicable." Note: ** means "not applicable."

(Table continues on the following page)

South Africa's data for 2001 is taken fro South Africa's data for 2001 is taken from partner countries' data

Source: International Monetary Fund's I Source: International Monetary Fund's Direction of Trade database

5-55. Direction of trade matrix, current U.S. dollars, 2001 (continued)

Exporters		Importers NGA	REU	RWA	STP	SEN	SYC	SLE	SOM	ZAF	SDN	SWZ	TZA	TGO	TUN	UGA	ZMB	ZWE	SSA	EU	NNA	ROW	World
Algeria	DZA	35	0	0	0	0	0	0	0	0	0	0	0	0	75	0	0	0	62	12,962	3,357	3,156	19,537
Angola	AGO	0	0	0	0	0	0	0	0	1	0	0	0	0	0	0	0	0	11	1,641	3,009	1,559	6,220
Benin	BEN	1	0	0	0	1	0	0	0	2	0	0	0	3	1	0	0	0	17	52	1	110	181
Burkina Faso	BFA	0	0	0	0	0	0	0	0	0	0	0	0	1	0	0	0	0	26	56	5	74	162
Bostwana	BWA	..	..	..	..	..	..	..	..	..	..	..	..	..	..	..	..	..	..	..	..	..	..
Burundi	BDI	0	0	2	0	0	0	0	0	0	0	0	0	0	0	1	0	0	6	21	0	11	39
Cameroon	CMR	13	0	0	0	7	0	0	0	1	0	0	0	3	9	0	0	0	143	1,211	43	351	1,749
Cape Verde	CPV	0	0	0	0	0	0	0	0	0	0	0	0	0	0	0	0	0	0	8	2	0	10
Central African Republic	CAF	0	0	0	0	0	0	0	0	0	0	0	0	0	0	0	0	0	4	132	2	34	172
Chad	TCD	4	0	0	0	0	0	0	0	0	0	0	0	0	1	0	0	0	7	47	6	19	78
Comoros	COM	0	0	0	0	0	0	0	0	0	0	0	0	0	0	0	0	0	0	17	10	9	37
Congo, Dem. Rep. Of	ZAR	0	0	6	0	0	0	0	0	2	0	0	0	0	0	0	0	87	100	848	152	76	1,177
Congo, Republic of	COG	0	0	0	0	3	0	0	0	2	0	0	0	0	1	0	0	0	38	335	481	1,432	2,286
Cote d'Ivoire	CIV	51	0	0	0	71	0	20	0	12	0	0	0	85	12	0	0	0	962	1,685	275	719	3,642
Djibouti	DJI	0	0	0	0	0	0	0	88	0	0	0	0	0	0	0	0	0	96	52	1	49	197
Egypt	EGY	7	0	0	0	5	0	2	0	5	33	0	4	0	22	1	1	1	109	1,301	355	2,376	4,140
Equatorial Guinea	GNQ	0	0	0	0	0	0	0	0	0	0	0	0	0	0	0	0	0	37	618	504	514	1,672
Eritrea	ERI	..	..	..	..	..	..	..	..	..	..	..	..	..	..	..	..	..	..	..	..	..	..
Ethiopia	ETH	0	0	1	0	0	0	0	0	0	0	0	3	0	0	0	0	0	10	141	33	242	426
Gabon	GAB	0	0	0	1	4	0	0	0	66	0	0	0	1	2	0	0	0	101	961	1,579	1,049	3,690
Gambia, The	GMB	0	0	0	0	0	0	0	0	1	0	0	1	0	0	0	0	0	3	18	3	4	27
Ghana	GHA	78	0	0	0	3	0	0	0	3	0	0	0	7	1	0	0	0	166	763	200	409	1,538
Guinea	GIN	7	0	0	0	0	0	0	0	0	0	0	0	0	0	0	0	0	57	453	114	221	845
Guinea-Bissau	GNB	0	0	0	0	0	0	0	0	0	0	0	0	0	0	0	0	0	2	4	0	134	140
Kenya	KEN	3	0	59	0	0	3	0	40	10	59	0	93	0	2	386	3	2	763	742	131	569	2,205
Lesotho	LSO	..	..	..	..	..	..	..	..	..	..	..	..	..	..	..	..	..	..	..	..	..	..
Liberia	LBR	0	0	0	0	1	0	1	0	1	0	0	0	0	0	0	0	0	16	611	42	200	869
Libya	LBY	4	0	0	0	0	0	0	0	0	2	0	0	0	295	0	0	0	22	9,253	0	1,976	11,250
Madagascar	MDG	0	0	0	0	0	0	0	0	2	0	0	0	0	2	0	0	0	20	496	263	169	948
Malawi	MWI	0	0	0	0	0	0	0	0	38	0	0	2	0	1	2	2	3	51	152	78	134	415
Mali	MLI	3	0	0	0	0	0	0	0	2	0	0	0	0	1	0	0	0	19	37	10	79	146
Mauritania	MRT	0	0	0	0	0	0	0	0	0	0	0	0	7	2	0	0	0	63	318	1	118	499
Mauritius	MUS	0	0	2	0	0	6	0	0	18	0	0	3	0	0	1	0	10	134	1,060	279	89	1,562
Morocco	MAR	18	0	0	0	16	0	2	0	1	0	0	0	2	52	0	0	0	150	5,162	317	1,488	7,117
Mozambique	MOZ	0	0	0	0	0	0	0	0	29	0	1	0	0	0	0	0	82	125	512	7	163	808
Namibia	NAM	..	..	..	..	..	..	..	..	..	..	..	..	..	..	..	..	..	..	..	..	..	..
Niger	NER	57	0	0	0	0	0	0	0	0	0	0	0	0	0	0	0	0	65	62	1	26	154
Nigeria	NGA	**	0	0	0	266	0	14	0	234	0	0	1	5	0	0	0	0	1,965	5,274	8,483	4,881	20,603
Reunion	REU	0	**	0	0	0	0	0	0	0	0	0	0	0	0	0	0	0	0	0	0	0	0
Rwanda	RWA	0	0	**	0	0	0	0	0	9	0	0	0	0	0	0	0	0	11	46	7	65	129
Sao Tome and Principe	STP	0	0	0	**	0	0	0	0	0	0	0	0	0	0	0	0	0	0	7	1	4	11
Senegal	SEN	3	0	0	0	**	0	4	0	0	0	0	0	6	3	0	0	0	202	370	96	180	848
Seychelles	SYC	0	0	0	0	0	**	0	0	4	0	0	0	0	0	0	0	0	5	162	22	30	219
Sierra Leone	SLE	0	0	0	0	0	0	**	0	2	0	0	0	0	0	0	0	0	3	35	6	10	53
Somalia	SOM	0	0	0	0	0	0	0	**	0	0	0	0	0	0	0	0	0	1	3	0	90	93
South Africa	ZAF	198	0	9	0	20	26	5	0	**	20	0	180	9	5	57	568	625	3,808	8,724	2,518	6,558	21,608
Sudan	SDN	0	0	0	0	0	0	0	1	0	**	0	0	0	6	0	0	0	6	207	4	1,552	1,769
Swaziland	SWZ	..	..	..	..	..	..	..	..	..	..	**	..	..	..	..	..	..	..	..	..	..	..
Tanzania	TZA	0	0	5	0	0	0	0	1	4	0	0	**	0	0	28	10	0	129	274	28	293	723
Togo	TGO	4	0	0	0	1	0	0	0	6	0	0	0	**	0	0	0	0	139	21	5	56	220
Tunisia	TUN	2	0	0	0	11	0	0	0	7	0	0	0	2	**	0	0	0	60	5,277	68	1,204	6,609
Uganda	UGA	0	0	2	0	0	0	0	0	2	0	0	6	0	0	**	0	0	12	193	20	88	312
Zambia	ZMB	0	0	3	0	0	0	0	0	48	0	1	28	0	0	2	**	13	174	142	15	338	669
Zimbabwe	ZWE	2	0	0	0	0	0	0	0	127	1	0	2	0	0	0	11	**	189	568	63	1,461	2,281
Sub-Saharan Africa	SSA	425	0	88	1	378	35	45	41	627	82	2	319	126	50	478	596	823	9,588	29,028	18,500	24,120	81,236
European Community	EU	4,534	0	60	32	969	125	233	23	11,197	551	15	367	298	7,119	175	107	202	32,142	1,406,859	234,519	622,628	2,296,148
North America	NNA	1,026	0	18	11	113	177	29	9	3,084	55	13	72	31	318	35	19	33	7,390	170,848	392,715	421,251	992,205
Rest of World	ROW	4,412	0	41	5	427	132	69	215	10,704	973	74	696	325	1,501	190	119	162	30,114	628,911	680,207	1,432,729	2,771,961
World	WLD	10,397	0	207	49	1,887	469	376	289	25,612	1,661	103	1,454	780	8,988	878	841	1,220	79,205	2,235,647	1,325,941	2,500,757	6,141,550

Note: ** means "not applicable." Note: ** means "not applicable."

South Africa's data for 2001 is taken fr South Africa's data for 2001 is taken from partner countries' data

Source: International Monetary Fund's Source: International Monetary Fund's Direction of Trade database

Figure 5-1. Terms of trade gains and losses, average 1992-2001*

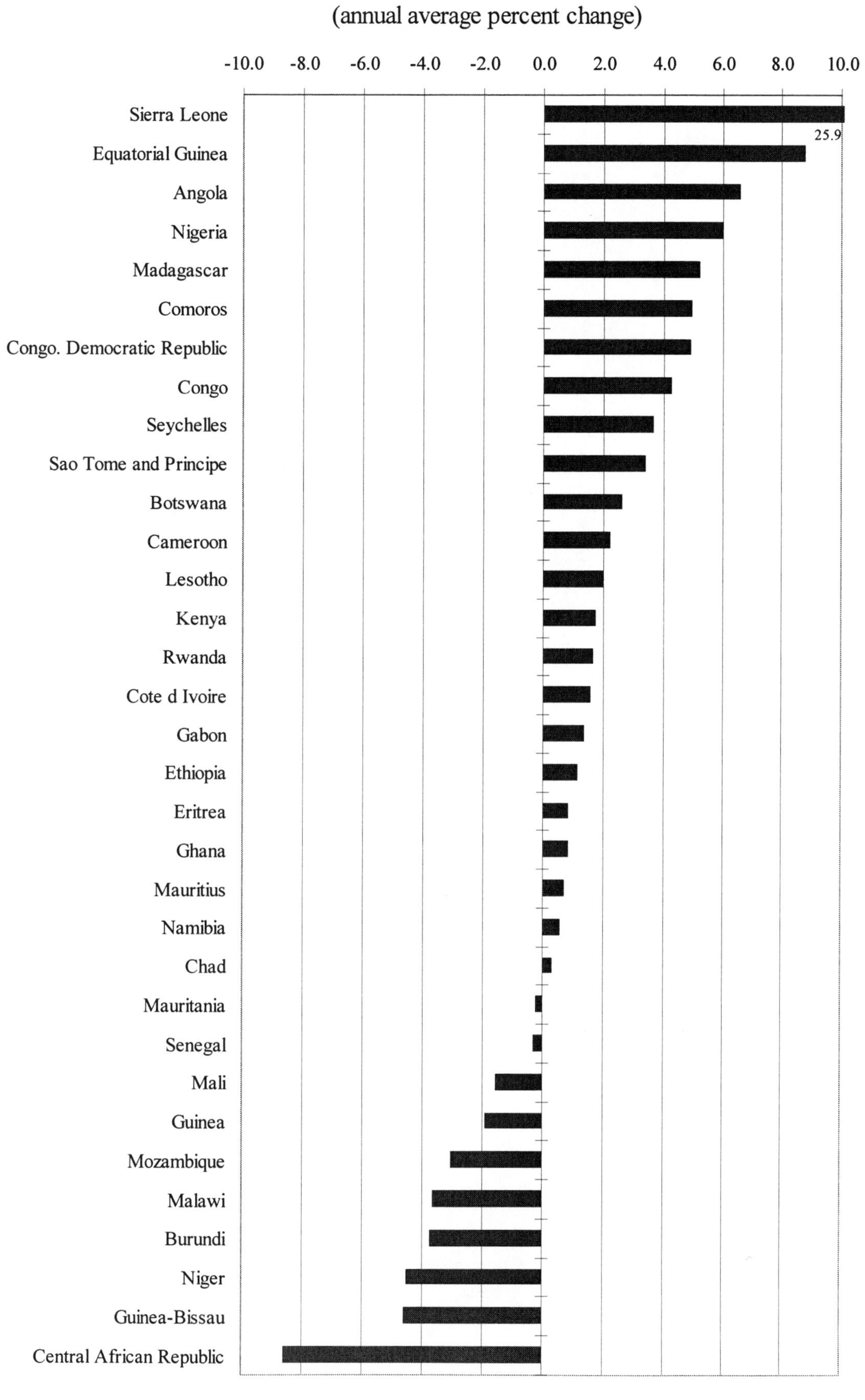

Technical notes

Tables

Tables 5-1 and 5-2. Merchandise exports and merchandise imports, f.o.b. Merchandise exports and imports (World Bank country desks) are both valued f.o.b. and comprise all transactions involving a change of ownership of goods, including nonmonetary gold, between residents of a country and the rest of the world. These transactions include those in which ownership changes even though goods do not cross customs borders. The few types of goods not covered by the merchandise account include travelers' purchases abroad, which are included in travel, and purchases of goods by diplomatic and military personnel, which are classified under other official goods, services, and income.

Tables 5-3 and 5-4. Exports and imports of total services. Service exports and imports (World Bank country desks) include total nonfactor and factor services, based on transactions involving ownership changes as explained above for goods. Nonfactor services comprise shipment, passenger and other transport services, and travel, as well as current account transactions not separately reported (that is, not classified as merchandise, nonfactor services, or transfers). These include transactions with nonresidents by government agencies and their personnel abroad, as well as transactions by private residents with foreign governments and government personnel stationed in the reporting country. Factor services comprise services of labor and capital, thus covering income from direct investment abroad, interest, dividends, and property and labor income. Net interest is recorded on an accrual basis; that is, interest obligations are included whether payments are made or not.

Table 5-5. Net private transfers. Net private transfers (World Bank country desks) are inflows (from private sources to either private or public recipients) less outflows from private sources to either private or public recipients that carry no provisions for repayments. They include workers' remittances; transfers by migrants; gifts, dowries, and inheritances; and alimony and other support remittances.

Table 5-6. Net official current transfers. Net official transfers (World Bank country desks) are the official sources counterpart of Table 5-5. They include transfers on both current and capital accounts, including government grants of real resources and financial items such as subsidies to current budgets, grants of technical assistance, and government contributions to international organizations for administrative expenses.

Table 5-7. Current account balance, excluding net capital grants. Current account balance (World Bank country desks), as presented here, is the difference between exports of goods and all services plus inflows of unrequited current transfers (official and private) and imports of goods and all services plus outflows of unrequited transfers to the rest of the world. Other common presentations exclude or include both current and capital official transfers. Data in previous volumes included both.

Table 5-8. Current account balance, excluding net capital grants, as a percentage of GDP. It is defined as the ratio of figures presented in Table 5-7 to GDP in current prices (Table 2-5).

Table 5-9. Net capital grants. These grants (World Bank country desks) are unrequited transfers, often used to finance balance of payments deficits.

Table 5-10. Net foreign direct investment. Net foreign direct investment (World Bank country desks) is the net amount invested or reinvested by nonresidents to acquire a lasting interest in enterprises in which they exercise significant managerial control. Investment includes equity capital, reinvested earnings, and other capital. The net figures subtract the value of direct investment abroad by residents of the reporting country.

Table 5-11. Net long-term borrowing. Net long-term borrowing is calculated as disbursements less the repayment of principal (amortization) of public, publicly guaranteed, and private nonguaranteed borrowings that have an original or extended maturity of more than one year and that are repayable in foreign currencies, goods, or services. These data are as reported in the World Bank's Debtor Reporting System (DRS) and are in accord with the data on external debt discussed in Chapter 6.

Table 5-12. Other capital flows. Other capital flows comprise the net balance of inflows and outflows of capital not elsewhere included. It covers, for example, changes in the stock of short-term debt, arrears, and other liabilities (all adjusted for valuation changes resulting from exchange rate changes and other factors), and errors and omissions. This table incorporates corrections to data in *ADI 1992*.

Table 5-13. Use of reserves. This table (World Bank country desks) shows the variation from year to year of the net balance of international reserve assets and is valued throughout at year-end London prices (for example, US$37.37 an ounce in 1980 and US$484.10 an ounce in 1987). Positive numbers represent a decrease or use of reserves; negative numbers represent an increase in reserves. This table incorporates corrections to data in ADI 1996.

Table 5-14. Import coverage ratio of reserves. This ratio gives the number of months, at current import levels, that can adequately be covered by available foreign exchange reserves (World Bank country desks). It is obtained by dividing the stock of reserves by imports divided by 12.

Tables 5-15 and 5-16. Export and import unit values. The indexes for total export and import unit values (World Bank country desks) are based on exports and imports of goods and nonfactor services from the national accounts. These indexes are calculated by dividing the values of exports and imports expressed in current U.S. dollars (Tables 2-14 and 2-15) by the volume of exports (f.o.b.) and imports (c.i.f.) expressed in constant 1995 U.S. dollars (Tables 2-16 and 2-17). Because of the way these trade unit value indexes are calculated (Paasche indexes, with changing weights), they reflect the composition of exports and imports in each year and may not give a reliable trend in unit values when trade composition changes dramatically. By contrast, this index reflects more accurately shifts in a country's actual composition of trade than would an index using weights based on trade shares in a single year. Data may differ from those in ADI 1992 and ADI 1994–95 because a different source was used for this volume.

Table 5-17. Terms of trade. Terms of trade measure the relative movement of export and import prices. This series is calculated as the ratio of a country's export unit values or prices (Table 5-15) to its import unit values or prices (Table 5-16). It shows changes over a base year (1995) in the level of export unit values as a percentage of import unit values. Data may differ from those in *ADI 1992* and *ADI 1994–95* because a different source was used for this volume.

Table 5-18. Forest products exports. Exports of forest production (FAO data) are given as an aggregate including all wood from trees and forests (coniferous and nonconiferous), whether in natural form or partially processed (SITC 245, 246, and 247);

sawwood and sleepers (SITC 248); and wood-based panels and fiberwood, compressed or noncompressed (SITC 634 and 641).

Table 5-19. Petroleum exports. This table contains the volumes of crude petroleum exported (World Bank, IEABAL). Data may differ from *ADI 1992* and *ADI 1994–95* because a different source was used for this volume.

Table 5-20. Copper exports. The table presents the unweighted sum of the metal content weights of copper ore and concentrate and of unrefined plus refined copper, metal, and alloys, unwrought (World Bank, METMIN). Data may differ from ADI 1992 and ADI 1994–95 because a different source was used for this volume.

Table 5-21. Iron exports. These are exports measured in metal content weight of iron ore (World Bank, METMIN).

Table 5-22. Phosphates exports. These are the volume of phosphates exports, expressed as the weight of mineral content in phosphate rock (World Bank, METMIN).

Table 5-23. Cocoa exports. Cocoa exports include cocoa beans, cocoa powder and cake, cocoa paste, cocoa butter, and chocolate products not elsewhere specified (FAO data).

Table 5-24. Coffee exports. Coffee exports are shown for green and roasted beans (FAO data).

Table 5-25. Cotton exports. Cotton exports refer to cotton lint only (FAO data).

Table 5-26. Groundnut exports. Groundnut exports include the weight of groundnuts in shelled equivalent (using a conversion factor of 70 percent), groundnut oil, and groundnut cake (FAO data).

Table 5-27. Oil palm products exports. Exports of oil palm products consist of palm oil and palm kernels (FAO data).

Table 5-28. Sisal exports. Only sisal fiber exports are included (FAO data).

Table 5-29. Tea exports. Tea exports figures are for processed tea (FAO data).

Table 5-30. Sugar exports. Sugar exports are shown in terms of raw sugar equivalent. The conversion factor to express refined sugar in raw sugar equivalent is 1.087 for all countries (FAO data).

Table 5-31. Tobacco exports. Only tobacco leaves are included (FAO data).

Table 5-32. Meat exports. Meat exports are defined as fresh, chilled, or frozen meat (SITC category 011) (FAO data).

Tables 5-33 and 5-34. Manufactured goods exports. Data reported in these tables follow the classification of manufacturing industries as reported in the UN *International Standard Industrial Classification of All Economic Activities* (ISIC), Revision 2 (World Bank country desks). First table is expressed in current prices; second table shows growth.

Tables 5-35 and 5-36. Food imports. Data refer to the sum of food, beverages, tobacco, oilseeds and oleaginous fruits, animal and vegetable oils, and fats (SITC sections 0, 1, and 4 and division 22) (World Bank country desks). First table is expressed in current prices; second table shows growth.

Tables 5-37 and 5-38. Nonfood consumer goods imports. Data reported in these tables show consumer goods imports other than food. Data are calculated as total merchandise imports less food, fuel, intermediate goods, and capital goods imports (World Bank country desks). First table is expressed in current prices; second table shows growth.

Tables 5-39 and 5-40. Fuel imports. Figures are defined as SITC section 3 (sum of Canada, Mexico, and United States) (World Bank country desks). First table presents data in current prices; second table shows growth.

Tables 5-41 and 5-42. Primary intermediate goods imports. Data on these tables comprise minerals, ores, and metals imports (the sum of SITC divisions 27, 28, and 68 and item 522.56) and agricultural raw materials imports (the sum of SITC section 2, less divisions 22, 27, and 28 and groups 233, 244, 266, and 267). Synthetics are excluded (World Bank country desks). First table presents data in current prices; second table shows growth.

Tables 5-43 and 5-44. Manufactured goods imports. Data reported on these tables follow the classification of manufacturing industries as reported in the UN *International Standard Industrial Classification of All Economic Activities* (ISIC), Revision 2 (World Bank country desks). First table presents data in current prices; second table shows growth.

Tables 5-45 and 5-46. Capital goods imports. Data shown here are for machinery and transport equipment (SITC section 7) (World Bank country desks). First table presents data in current prices; second table shows growth.

Tables 5-47, 5-48, and 5-49. Direction of trade matrix, imports. These tables show, for each importing country, the percentage of the value of its total imports that originates from each of the exporting countries for 1990, 1995, and 2000, respectively. They are calculated from Tables 5-53 to 5-55, below.

In these tables data posted under South Africa are for South Africa Customs Union, which comprises Botswana, Lesotho, Namibia, South Africa, and Swaziland.

Tables 5-50, 5-51, and 5-52. Direction of trade matrix, exports. As with the foregoing, for each exporter, these tables show the percentage of the value of total exports, f.o.b., that goes to each of its trade partners for 1990, 1995, and 2000, respectively. These are calculated from Tables 5-53 to 5-55, below.

In these tables data posted under South Africa are for South Africa Customs Union, which comprises Botswana, Lesotho, Namibia, South Africa, and Swaziland.

Tables 5-53, 5-54, and 5-55. Direction of trade matrix, current U.S. dollars. These are the value of trade in goods and services to or from the countries indicated. Matrices are shown for 1991, 1996, and 2001. They form the basis for the calculations in the previous six tables. Data for South Africa are for the South Africa Customs Union, which comprises Botswana, Lesotho, Namibia, South Africa, and Swaziland. The source of the data is the International Monetary Fund's Direction of Trade database. IMF staff have estimated some of these numbers in order to have a consistent time series.

Figure

The following indicator has been used to derive the figures in this chapter.

Figure 5-1. Terms of trade gains or losses (Table 5-17).

Methodology used for regional aggregations and period averages in chapter 5

	Aggregations [a]				*Period averages* [b]	
Table	*(1)*	*(3)*	*(4)*	*(6)*	*(2)*	*(3)*
5-1		X				X
5-2		X				X
5-3		X				X
5-4		X				X
5-5	X				X	
5-6	X				X	
5-7	X				X	
5-8				X	X	
5-9	X				X	
5-10	X				X	
5-11	X				X	
5-12	X				X	
5-13	X				X	
5-14				X	X	
5-15			X		X	
5-16			X		X	
5-17			X		X	
5-18	X					X
5-19	X					X
5-20	X					X
5-21	X					X
5-22	X					X
5-23	X					X
5-24	X					X
5-25	X					X
5-26	X					X
5-27	X					X
5-28	X					X
5-29	X					X
5-30	X					X
5-31	X					X
5-32	X				X	
5-33	X				X	
5-34	X					X
5-35	X				X	
5-36	X					X
5-37	X				X	
5-38	X					X
5-39	X				X	
5-40	X					X
5-41	X				X	
5-42	X					X
5-43	X				X	
5-44	X					X
5-45	X				X	
5-46	X					X
5-47	X					
5-48	X					
5-49	X					
5-50	X					
5-51	X					
5-52	X					
5-53	X					
5-54	X					
5-55	X					

Note: Regional aggregations are shown in the rows for Sub-Saharan Africa, North Africa, and All Africa. Period averages are shown in the last three columns. This table shows only the methodologies used in this chapter.

a. Regional aggregations: (1) simple total; (2) simple total of the first indicator divided by the simple total of the second indicator (same country coverage); (3) simple total of the gap-filled indicator; (4) simple total of the gap-filled main indicator divided by the simple total of the gap-filled secondary indicator; (5) simple total of the first gap-filled main indicator less the simple total of the second gap-filled main indicator, all divided by the simple total of the secondary indicator; (6) weighted total (by population); (7) median; (8) no aggregation; (9) simple arithmetic mean.

b. Period averages: (1) arithmetic mean (using the same series as shown in the table i.e., ratio if the rest of the table is shown as ratio, level if the rest of the table is shown as level, growth rate if the rest is shown as growth rate); (2) least-squares growth rate (using main indicator); (3) least-squares growth rate (using main indicator in constant terms, with the rest of the table in current terms).

6

External Debt and Related Flows

The tables in this chapter provide a consistent presentation of the structure and terms of external debt and debt servicing. No data are presented on debt owed to domestic lenders. The aggregates and ratios provide various measures of a country's external debt situation. These measures include the size of debt and its servicing requirements, the amount of debt relative to GDP, the ratio of debt-servicing payments to exports, and the interest rate and terms of the stock of debt (including grace period, maturity, and grant element).

These tables follow the presentation in the *Global Development Finance (GDF—formerly World Debt Tables)* and therefore show IMF purchases, repurchases, charges, and net purchases separately from long- and short-term lending, repayments, interests, or net lending. While IMF purchases and repurchases are not strictly lending (they are swaps of currency), they do add to, or subtract from, the resources available for consumption or investment and do impose a liability against future income streams. For this reason, IMF transactions are included here.

Data on debt and related flows are drawn largely from the World Bank's Debtor Reporting System (DRS), to which member countries submit detailed accounts on the annual status, transactions, and terms of debt and related flows. World Bank and IMF staff estimates based on other sources of data supplement DRS data, especially for recent years, on debt not guaranteed by debtor governments and on short-term debt. The figures in this chapter are based mostly on data supplied by debtor countries. Other data series on debt, on which the World Bank may base some of its estimates, are maintained by the Organization for Economic Cooperation and Development (OECD) and the Bank for International Settlements (BIS) from data provided by creditor governments and agencies. No figures are given for Libya and Namibia, which do not report debt information to the DRS. However, totals do include estimates for these countries.

The following definitions apply throughout the chapter. Long-term loans have an original or extended maturity of more than one year, while the maturity on short-term loans is one year or less. Official and private refer to the source of the foreign loans. Official loans are from multilateral organizations (excluding the IMF) and from foreign governments; these loans are either made directly to the government of the borrowing country or guaranteed by it, or its agencies, when made to a third party. Private loans are from the private sector, including foreign parent companies and their affiliates, suppliers, financial markets (such as commercial banks), and other sources. These private loans may or may not be guaranteed by creditor or debtor governments and agencies. "Public and publicly guaranteed" loans, as defined by the DRS, refer to loans from both official and private foreign sources that are made to, or guaranteed by, the debtor government or its agencies. Almost all loans from foreign official sources are public or publicly guaranteed. Some loans from foreign private sources are made to, or guaranteed by, the debtor government or its agencies (these are labeled *private guaranteed* by the DRS). Some loans from foreign private sources are not public or publicly guaranteed (these are labeled *private nonguaranteed* by DRS).

Concessional loans carry a grant element of 25 percent or more (based on a standard 10 percent discount rate), which is consistent with the Development Assistance Committee of the OECD (DAC) definition of ODA (see Chapter 12). Nonconcessional loans carry a grant element of less than 25 percent. In this chapter, private loans are shown separately from official nonconcessional loans.

Additional information, definitions, and methodology are available in the World Bank, *Global Development Finance 2001* (formerly *World Debt Tables*).

6-1. Gross disbursements: official concessional long-term loans

	Millions of U.S. dollars (current prices)											Annual Average		
	1980	1992	1993	1994	1995	1996	1997	1998	1999	2000	2001	75-84	85-89	90-MR
SUB-SAHARAN AFRICA	2,547	4,815	4,861	4,869	4,691	4,241	3,976	3,561	3,352	3,352	3,556	2,652	4,435	4,223
excluding South Africa	2,547	4,815	4,861	4,869	4,691	4,241	3,976	3,561	3,352	3,352	3,556	2,652	4,435	4,223
excl. S.Africa & Nigeria	2,499	4,779	4,793	4,792	4,593	4,146	3,879	3,416	3,271	3,284	3,536	2,627	4,413	4,145
Angola	0	40	31	73	63	43	36	80	68	34	19	3	38	52
Benin	35	76	79	101	96	104	49	50	70	61	108	33	66	83
Botswana	9	21	40	37	57	15	13	9	4	9	7	11	18	23
Burkina Faso	41	133	131	105	110	102	70	90	108	87	125	36	75	105
Burundi	38	105	76	52	45	34	19	30	20	36	12	32	95	50
Cameroon	143	380	311	372	64	155	220	161	171	216	103	118	115	196
Cape Verde	0	14	6	28	16	17	20	32	57	29	40	3	11	23
Central African Republic	19	45	50	44	32	27	5	3	6	16	0	15	65	36
Chad	5	69	58	69	58	97	80	43	86	33	39	16	43	68
Comoros	13	18	8	12	10	10	6	4	1	3	12	11	14	8
Congo, Democratic Rep. of	131	66	58	1	0	3	0	0	8	0	0	127	234	39
Congo, Republic of	49	17	8	194	14	2	3	0	0	0	38	61	71	35
Côte d'Ivoire	42	366	473	767	548	395	150	312	141	131	10	62	91	319
Djibouti	1	43	26	26	18	24	12	5	3	8	11	7	23	21
Equatorial Guinea	4	15	10	4	2	2	3	1	4	2	0	3	17	5
Eritrea	0	0	0	27	7	5	32	64	98	50	108	0	0	32
Ethiopia	70	184	348	211	199	223	95	115	206	180	523	395	438	224
Gabon	16	9	19	53	64	27	96	13	21	0	0	11	36	37
Gambia, The	27	48	22	22	23	58	24	16	21	21	23	13	26	27
Ghana	114	318	342	324	407	392	404	416	317	320	324	66	251	353
Guinea	56	156	228	125	123	84	173	118	76	60	91	57	176	134
Guinea-Bissau	49	40	23	26	21	28	30	15	2	14	6	16	32	23
Kenya	160	229	309	197	527	289	157	167	100	285	173	117	223	266
Lesotho	7	54	28	43	28	24	29	28	28	28	20	11	27	33
Liberia	39	0	33	0	0	0	0	0	0	0	0	34	20	3
Madagascar	153	102	104	72	88	116	214	102	125	140	132	95	169	131
Malawi	45	137	187	107	211	161	162	147	128	115	117	44	86	147
Mali	75	162	79	120	188	153	118	99	121	96	105	73	140	129
Mauritania	96	73	142	111	101	114	80	53	46	102	77	82	106	87
Mauritius	16	48	42	25	22	12	30	13	19	26	21	14	34	33
Mozambique	0	187	173	221	219	272	239	221	130	124	122	74	255	182
Namibia	..	..	..	..	..	..	..	..	..	..	..	..	..	..
Niger	59	81	67	68	28	41	85	85	48	68	78	40	108	64
Nigeria	49	36	67	77	99	94	97	145	81	68	20	25	21	78
Rwanda	27	80	61	22	54	62	70	88	82	40	64	27	80	64
São Tomé and Principe	8	24	15	15	13	11	5	7	12	6	7	4	11	13
Senegal	113	241	85	98	150	181	199	190	67	119	230	88	279	158
Seychelles	6	4	3	1	2	4	6	6	6	8	4	4	6	5
Sierra Leone	33	42	96	61	94	73	40	34	14	77	83	18	19	54
Somalia	74	0	0	0	0	0	0	0	0	0	0	101	83	5
South Africa	0	0	0	0	0	0	0	0	0	0	0	0	0	0
Sudan	270	93	95	10	27	2	0	0	0	0	0	313	203	45
Swaziland	7	5	1	14	13	5	4	4	11	2	15	8	10	7
Tanzania	159	336	191	230	201	198	245	195	251	203	178	186	196	226
Togo	35	47	17	41	26	99	57	58	38	25	33	37	70	49
Uganda	13	227	328	265	219	211	270	170	171	217	338	33	149	236
Zambia	243	212	205	218	309	205	210	59	194	245	142	100	122	194
Zimbabwe	1	231	190	183	97	66	120	115	198	51	-1	29	85	119
NORTH AFRICA	2,079	1,479	1,619	1,539	1,570	1,439	1,093	951	1,062	901	899	1,746	1,088	1,308
Algeria	79	227	352	388	645	387	212	145	341	182	106	78	69	286
Egypt, Arab Republic	1,064	517	543	437	342	418	383	369	180	154	92	1,085	565	424
Libya	..	..	..	..	..	..	..	..	..	..	..	..	..	..
Morocco	731	433	497	439	405	471	359	294	251	196	332	406	265	357
Tunisia	204	301	227	277	178	164	138	144	290	369	370	177	189	241
ALL AFRICA	4,626	6,293	6,480	6,408	6,262	5,680	5,069	4,512	4,414	4,253	4,455	4,398	5,523	5,531

6-2. Gross disbursements: official nonconcessional long-term loans

	Millions of U.S. dollars (current prices)											Annual Average		
	1980	1992	1993	1994	1995	1996	1997	1998	1999	2000	2001	75-84	85-89	90-MR
SUB-SAHARAN AFRICA	1,692	2,064	1,666	1,452	1,192	1,064	970	756	557	514	320	1,464	2,027	1,253
excluding South Africa	1,692	2,064	1,666	1,452	1,192	1,064	970	756	520	423	316	1,464	2,027	1,242
excl. S.Africa & Nigeria	1,618	1,569	1,190	931	858	850	752	625	426	337	268	1,284	1,487	933
Angola	..	53	5	0	56	11	0	1	0	0	6	14	103	25
Benin	24	5	2	4	5	5	1	11	3	0	0	8	7	4
Botswana	16	63	32	19	9	12	8	10	3	1	1	16	46	19
Burkina Faso	18	10	7	2	2	1	1	0	0	1	14	11	14	5
Burundi	1	3	1	1	0	1	0	0	0	0	0	3	8	1
Cameroon	108	148	84	68	44	21	25	16	18	17	31	71	142	96
Cape Verde	..	4	5	1	1	1	0	23	7	0	0	11	0	4
Central African Republic	6	1	0	0	1	0	1	0	0	0	0	3	8	1
Chad	0	75	1	0	0	2	0	0	0	0	9	2	2	8
Comoros	0	0	0	0	0	0	0	0	0	0	0	1	1	0
Congo, Democratic Rep. of	70	17	0	0	0	0	0	0	0	0	0	61	82	25
Congo, Republic of	60	0	0	137	1	2	21	0	0	0	0	38	54	15
Côte d'Ivoire	189	285	151	151	121	70	34	77	50	18	2	178	234	154
Djibouti	4	0	0	0	0	0	0	0	0	0	0	1	0	0
Equatorial Guinea	11	0	0	0	0	0	0	0	0	0	0	3	2	0
Eritrea	..	..	..	0	0	2	1	3	11	1	0	..	..	2
Ethiopia	7	29	21	21	33	49	54	17	24	4	10	11	62	30
Gabon	19	99	71	79	157	62	30	22	6	9	4	36	71	58
Gambia, The	2	7	3	1	0	0	0	0	0	0	0	2	2	1
Ghana	106	67	26	21	21	123	37	22	13	30	39	38	39	44
Guinea	9	43	47	44	47	42	39	24	19	10	4	12	11	31
Guinea-Bissau	6	1	0	3	0	1	0	0	0	0	0	3	6	2
Kenya	73	100	20	59	39	69	15	27	20	23	0	100	134	40
Lesotho	1	23	41	19	27	20	15	8	9	40	4	3	9	19
Liberia	26	0	0	0	0	0	0	0	0	0	0	23	11	0
Madagascar	59	15	19	10	1	21	103	0	4	11	8	49	50	18
Malawi	60	7	6	4	4	1	5	9	13	3	0	26	21	6
Mali	10	1	5	1	5	3	0	0	0	1	0	5	6	2
Mauritania	16	60	25	28	11	16	9	3	2	8	1	24	26	19
Mauritius	20	15	23	11	17	37	45	37	29	22	5	18	37	25
Mozambique	..	10	9	8	11	10	20	4	2	4	12	58	18	9
Namibia	..	..	..	..	..	..	..	..	..	..	..	..	..	..
Niger	33	1	34	5	0	1	0	0	0	0	0	27	10	4
Nigeria	73	495	476	522	334	214	218	131	94	85	47	180	540	308
Rwanda	0	0	0	0	0	0	2	0	0	0	0	0	0	0
São Tomé and Principe	2	0	0	0	0	0	0	0	5	3	1	2	1	1
Senegal	74	73	68	34	7	0	1	15	4	6	8	63	28	21
Seychelles	6	6	7	8	7	7	5	8	3	1	0	2	3	5
Sierra Leone	9	10	3	3	1	2	0	13	2	0	0	4	1	3
Somalia	13	0	0	0	0	0	0	0	0	0	0	19	2	0
South Africa	..	..	..	0	0	0	0	0	38	91	4	..	..	17
Sudan	297	15	6	2	24	15	5	0	0	0	0	138	23	6
Swaziland	20	1	7	1	4	23	18	27	22	14	12	15	7	12
Tanzania	86	12	4	14	17	3	7	21	2	0	2	81	26	12
Togo	12	1	2	0	0	2	0	11	0	0	0	15	4	2
Uganda	5	21	62	3	11	14	21	4	3	2	2	15	42	14
Zambia	68	38	25	42	18	19	12	5	7	6	10	91	67	23
Zimbabwe	77	252	370	130	137	172	209	210	113	79	34	31	64	159
NORTH AFRICA	1,690	3,560	3,054	2,780	2,571	2,790	2,256	1,571	1,602	1,426	1,359	1,769	3,004	2,517
Algeria	487	1,202	812	1,134	947	1,191	993	606	389	608	298	489	673	940
Egypt, Arab Republic	840	434	444	461	242	220	242	88	50	81	153	702	826	268
Libya	..	..	..	..	..	..	..	..	..	..	..	..	..	..
Morocco	135	882	785	602	950	858	491	562	661	427	265	229	616	686
Tunisia	119	442	614	583	433	521	518	315	502	311	644	131	320	503
ALL AFRICA	3,382	5,624	4,721	4,232	3,763	3,854	3,226	2,328	2,159	1,940	1,679	3,233	5,031	3,769

6-3. Gross disbursements: private long-term loans

	Millions of U.S. dollars (current prices)											Annual Average		
	1980	1992	1993	1994	1995	1996	1997	1998	1999	2000	2001	75-84	85-89	90-MR
SUB-SAHARAN AFRICA	6,290	1,912	1,969	4,664	5,202	4,337	6,609	3,359	4,316	4,846	5,161	4,469	3,517	3,906
excluding South Africa	6,290	1,912	1,969	1,146	1,654	2,045	1,979	1,313	1,621	1,326	1,562	4,469	3,517	1,752
excl. S.Africa & Nigeria	4,660	1,908	1,969	1,146	1,654	2,045	1,979	1,313	1,621	1,326	1,562	3,071	2,734	1,712
Angola	..	553	649	344	431	723	1,154	709	875	1,011	1,066	233	712	700
Benin	4	0	0	0	0	0	0	0	0	0	0	44	1	0
Botswana	3	0	30	0	0	0	0	0	11	4	0	6	4	4
Burkina Faso	6	0	0	0	0	0	0	0	0	0	0	8	1	0
Burundi	0	0	0	0	0	0	0	1	0	0	0	5	2	0
Cameroon	364	141	104	8	0	25	14	10	56	39	0	230	354	55
Cape Verde	..	0	0	0	4	5	2	0	0	0	10	0	0	2
Central African Republic	0	0	0	0	0	0	0	0	0	0	0	2	1	0
Chad	0	0	0	0	0	0	0	0	0	0	0	5	1	0
Comoros	0	0	0	0	0	0	0	0	0	0	0	0	0	0
Congo, Democratic Rep. of	263	0	0	0	0	0	0	0	0	0	0	176	16	0
Congo, Republic of	412	114	451	1	0	0	0	0	0	0	0	207	272	63
Côte d'Ivoire	1,508	202	190	317	75	411	52	56	56	0	0	791	219	155
Djibouti	5	0	0	0	0	0	0	0	0	0	0	1	0	0
Equatorial Guinea	5	0	0	0	0	0	0	0	0	0	0	3	0	0
Eritrea	..	..	..	0	0	0	0	0	0	0	0	..	..	0
Ethiopia	33	113	10	4	0	22	30	10	1	2	0	45	98	42
Gabon	135	0	3	2	0	0	20	10	33	21	11	174	174	13
Gambia, The	22	0	0	0	0	0	0	0	1	0	0	5	0	0
Ghana	0	103	77	123	178	384	208	164	67	45	212	12	64	142
Guinea	57	0	11	0	0	17	20	7	0	0	0	29	13	5
Guinea-Bissau	21	0	0	0	0	0	0	0	0	0	0	5	5	0
Kenya	387	173	87	6	132	72	48	36	139	56	74	224	284	125
Lesotho	5	2	3	2	16	33	24	29	15	2	2	4	8	12
Liberia	11	0	0	0	0	0	0	0	0	0	0	23	0	0
Madagascar	163	0	0	0	1	0	0	0	0	0	0	64	10	0
Malawi	48	14	1	10	0	0	1	0	1	0	0	29	7	3
Mali	10	0	0	0	0	0	0	0	0	0	0	6	1	0
Mauritania	14	0	0	0	0	25	0	0	0	0	0	24	4	2
Mauritius	61	63	39	150	369	91	118	11	97	85	45	28	45	101
Mozambique	..	4	8	4	36	0	6	0	0	0	0	61	46	9
Namibia	..	..	..	..	..	..	..	..	..	..	..	..	..	..
Niger	190	0	0	0	0	0	0	0	0	0	0	91	45	4
Nigeria	1,630	4	0	0	0	0	0	0	0	0	0	1,399	782	40
Rwanda	0	0	0	0	0	0	0	0	0	0	0	3	1	0
São Tomé and Principe	0	0	0	0	0	0	0	0	0	0	0	1	0	0
Senegal	141	8	1	1	1	0	21	2	1	1	58	74	29	10
Seychelles	0	15	8	9	0	1	0	10	1	0	0	1	6	5
Sierra Leone	42	0	0	0	0	0	0	0	0	0	0	24	1	0
Somalia	27	0	0	0	0	0	0	0	0	0	0	25	1	0
South Africa	..	..	..	3,518	3,549	2,291	4,630	2,046	2,695	3,520	3,599	..	..	3,231
Sudan	145	0	0	0	0	0	0	0	0	0	0	100	0	0
Swaziland	0	0	0	0	0	0	33	0	0	0	14	3	3	4
Tanzania	122	35	45	17	42	6	0	0	7	10	1	63	48	15
Togo	50	0	0	0	0	0	0	0	0	0	0	63	0	0
Uganda	65	6	18	0	0	0	0	0	0	0	3	36	60	6
Zambia	289	33	11	35	25	13	50	20	50	10	60	154	62	33
Zimbabwe	55	329	172	115	338	209	167	225	178	41	6	167	128	194
NORTH AFRICA	5,014	7,529	6,566	4,561	3,756	2,574	2,158	1,993	2,232	2,617	3,774	4,872	6,440	4,225
Algeria	2,832	6,118	5,363	3,268	2,092	1,308	438	399	394	425	577	2,743	4,206	2,532
Egypt, Arab Republic	776	375	168	260	40	33	265	289	353	352	1,725	780	1,318	440
Libya	..	..	..	..	..	..	..	..	..	..	..	..	..	..
Morocco	1,119	569	755	762	734	428	462	732	622	1,001	589	906	519	617
Tunisia	288	467	281	199	777	648	824	189	638	840	883	306	318	526
ALL AFRICA	11,304	9,441	8,535	9,225	8,958	6,910	8,767	5,351	6,548	7,463	8,935	9,341	9,957	8,131

6-4. Disbursements: long-term loans and IMF purchases

	Millions of U.S. dollars (current prices)											Annual Average		
	1980	1992	1993	1994	1995	1996	1997	1998	1999	2000	2001	75-84	85-89	90-MR
SUB-SAHARAN AFRICA	11,746	9,317	9,643	11,903	14,079	10,294	12,078	8,481	8,742	9,212	9,581	9,553	10,788	10,246
excluding South Africa	11,746	9,317	8,785	8,384	10,531	8,003	7,449	6,435	6,009	5,600	5,978	9,553	10,788	8,009
excl. S.Africa & Nigeria	9,993	8,782	8,241	7,786	10,098	7,695	7,134	6,159	5,834	5,447	5,911	7,950	9,444	7,583
Angola	0	647	685	417	550	778	1,190	790	943	1,045	1,090	102	853	777
Benin	71	81	103	130	115	128	57	62	83	70	119	86	76	98
Botswana	28	84	102	56	66	27	21	19	17	14	7	34	69	46
Burkina Faso	70	143	151	132	139	112	89	108	125	96	161	56	90	124
Burundi	45	126	77	53	45	35	19	31	20	36	12	44	112	53
Cameroon	626	669	499	478	121	230	296	260	306	340	154	427	634	375
Cape Verde	0	18	10	29	21	24	22	55	63	29	50	8	11	28
Central African Republic	40	46	50	59	33	27	6	15	17	16	11	27	82	41
Chad	5	143	58	83	70	123	92	54	98	47	66	26	51	86
Comoros	13	18	8	14	10	10	6	4	1	3	12	12	15	8
Congo, Democratic Rep. of	603	83	58	1	0	3	0	0	8	0	0	482	461	64
Congo, Republic of	526	132	459	350	15	24	24	10	0	14	38	310	399	118
Côte d'Ivoire	1,777	853	813	1,405	924	1,014	236	613	247	148	12	1,114	599	699
Djibouti	10	43	26	26	18	28	14	8	8	11	16	9	24	23
Equatorial Guinea	38	15	14	7	2	2	3	1	4	2	0	12	21	6
Eritrea	..	..	..	27	7	7	33	67	108	51	108	..	..	51
Ethiopia	119	346	409	256	232	315	179	162	231	185	577	470	606	309
Gabon	171	108	93	198	279	121	168	46	59	47	15	222	308	125
Gambia, The	56	55	26	23	23	58	24	21	26	30	31	26	35	32
Ghana	249	488	509	468	648	940	649	713	457	429	642	184	495	592
Guinea	129	210	286	182	200	143	265	180	106	70	122	103	212	183
Guinea-Bissau	75	41	23	28	24	31	36	18	5	22	6	24	44	27
Kenya	714	502	447	294	698	467	219	231	259	409	247	515	722	458
Lesotho	15	86	82	69	70	76	68	65	53	69	34	19	47	67
Liberia	109	0	33	0	0	0	0	0	0	0	0	113	31	3
Madagascar	444	117	123	82	90	156	336	102	147	200	169	234	264	164
Malawi	190	158	194	147	227	184	178	173	152	126	117	120	129	168
Mali	109	177	98	164	238	186	147	114	144	105	128	95	157	153
Mauritania	155	145	179	163	133	176	108	55	57	118	102	141	150	121
Mauritius	143	127	105	186	409	140	193	60	145	132	71	87	128	158
Mozambique	0	265	211	254	267	300	300	259	161	187	145	122	331	229
Namibia	..	..	..	..	..	..	..	..	..	..	..	..	..	..
Niger	290	83	100	89	28	56	111	111	48	79	89	164	180	81
Nigeria	1,752	535	544	598	433	308	314	276	175	153	67	1,603	1,344	426
Rwanda	34	81	61	22	68	62	92	104	111	65	76	31	81	75
São Tomé and Principe	10	24	15	15	13	11	5	7	16	11	8	7	13	14
Senegal	395	322	153	201	241	216	270	255	92	145	325	261	399	225
Seychelles	12	25	18	18	8	12	11	23	10	8	5	7	16	14
Sierra Leone	104	52	100	200	115	90	47	62	36	91	143	63	26	81
Somalia	135	0	0	0	0	0	0	0	0	0	0	158	101	5
South Africa	0	0	858	3,518	3,549	2,291	4,630	2,046	2,732	3,611	3,603	0	0	2,237
Sudan	921	108	101	12	51	17	5	0	0	0	0	655	226	51
Swaziland	29	7	8	15	18	28	55	31	33	16	41	29	20	23
Tanzania	433	473	240	261	260	244	336	264	341	266	232	353	295	296
Togo	119	59	19	56	59	101	72	84	38	25	33	124	89	61
Uganda	161	308	409	320	285	288	351	224	209	231	354	135	287	301
Zambia	690	282	241	294	2,606	236	286	84	264	287	308	482	276	451
Zimbabwe	132	1,034	799	504	652	447	496	604	522	170	39	257	277	516
NORTH AFRICA	9,124	12,786	11,240	9,722	8,372	7,546	5,971	4,858	5,201	4,944	6,033	8,612	10,892	8,388
Algeria	3,398	7,547	6,526	5,631	4,157	3,629	2,107	1,494	1,429	1,215	980	3,310	5,069	4,048
Egypt, Arab Republic	2,743	1,445	1,155	1,157	624	671	890	746	584	586	1,970	2,627	2,740	1,149
Libya	..	..	..	..	..	..	..	..	..	..	..	..	..	..
Morocco	2,262	1,910	2,037	1,802	2,089	1,757	1,313	1,587	1,534	1,624	1,186	1,704	1,557	1,668
Tunisia	611	1,283	1,122	1,059	1,389	1,333	1,480	648	1,430	1,520	1,896	616	877	1,293
ALL AFRICA	20,870	22,102	20,882	21,625	22,451	17,840	18,049	13,339	13,943	14,156	15,613	18,164	21,680	18,634

Note: In 1995, Zambia was able to clear its arrears to the IMF after completing a 3 year Rights Arrangement Program.

6-5. Amortization: official concessional long-term loans

	Millions of U.S. dollars (current prices)											Annual Average		
	1980	1992	1993	1994	1995	1996	1997	1998	1999	2000	2001	75-84	85-89	90-MR
SUB-SAHARAN AFRICA	243	589	773	718	878	884	1,026	1,731	1,638	1,377	1,525	238	534	1,028
excluding South Africa	243	589	773	718	878	884	1,026	1,731	1,638	1,377	1,525	238	534	1,028
excl. S.Africa & Nigeria	229	588	611	717	876	883	954	1,410	1,635	1,373	1,507	225	524	978
Angola	0	3	2	9	3	8	8	363	406	217	321	0	2	112
Benin	1	8	12	12	15	14	18	19	22	38	29	2	4	17
Botswana	0	9	13	14	11	15	30	14	18	18	15	1	5	14
Burkina Faso	4	9	11	18	20	23	25	27	30	24	20	2	8	19
Burundi	1	14	15	16	14	6	8	9	12	9	12	1	10	12
Cameroon	13	20	37	12	12	14	49	75	47	60	53	12	23	35
Cape Verde	0	5	2	3	4	3	7	6	4	7	6	0	1	4
Central African Republic	0	2	1	5	2	2	4	10	6	7	9	1	2	4
Chad	3	3	1	6	2	7	6	7	12	12	18	1	2	6
Comoros	0	2	2	2	0	1	1	1	2	1	1	0	0	1
Congo, Democratic Rep. of	3	5	4	0	0	0	0	0	0	0	0	5	10	2
Congo, Republic of	11	0	1	8	7	22	0	0	0	1	5	10	4	4
Côte d'Ivoire	18	88	78	56	65	81	68	106	216	131	70	15	35	93
Djibouti	2	7	6	9	9	9	5	3	6	8	7	1	5	7
Equatorial Guinea	0	0	0	0	0	1	1	1	1	1	1	0	0	0
Eritrea	0	0	0	0	0	0	0	0	0	0	1	0	0	0
Ethiopia	7	14	16	19	25	35	26	38	48	37	76	9	53	31
Gabon	4	23	7	8	12	9	39	28	45	16	80	5	4	23
Gambia, The	0	9	8	9	8	9	10	12	9	10	9	1	5	9
Ghana	14	33	32	56	55	56	54	83	99	109	63	20	33	59
Guinea	44	19	16	26	86	44	29	31	43	38	57	36	42	41
Guinea-Bissau	0	1	1	2	4	3	5	6	3	3	11	0	2	5
Kenya	6	33	39	67	69	68	59	64	80	85	55	8	25	58
Lesotho	0	5	9	6	11	11	12	10	11	13	31	1	3	10
Liberia	1	0	1	1	0	0	0	0	0	0	0	4	2	1
Madagascar	18	20	12	13	10	21	55	39	40	59	43	19	13	28
Malawi	2	10	9	10	16	19	21	19	15	18	33	2	4	16
Mali	4	23	23	39	45	42	38	40	58	49	55	4	17	37
Mauritania	3	26	40	33	37	37	39	41	36	34	47	3	28	34
Mauritius	2	31	23	22	25	27	47	23	23	23	28	2	10	25
Mozambique	0	13	12	17	24	29	33	24	21	26	35	2	18	21
Namibia	..	..	..	..	..	..	..	..	..	..	..	..	..	..
Niger	16	4	12	6	6	7	18	12	11	12	16	5	8	9
Nigeria	14	1	162	1	2	1	72	321	3	5	17	13	10	49
Rwanda	0	8	11	2	11	8	9	8	10	11	21	1	7	10
São Tomé and Principe	0	1	0	0	1	1	1	1	2	2	3	0	1	1
Senegal	7	32	31	68	72	64	47	89	89	90	99	5	28	65
Seychelles	0	4	4	3	4	2	2	4	6	5	4	0	1	4
Sierra Leone	2	5	3	9	7	6	6	10	3	6	5	3	3	5
Somalia	2	0	0	0	0	0	0	0	0	0	0	2	2	0
South Africa	0	0	0	0	0	0	0	0	0	0	0	0	0	0
Sudan	14	8	5	3	9	0	0	0	0	2	1	16	48	3
Swaziland	1	6	7	7	8	10	8	7	6	8	6	1	3	7
Tanzania	19	36	38	40	38	54	35	48	64	82	88	14	32	50
Togo	2	5	4	4	7	15	13	13	16	10	11	8	6	9
Uganda	2	10	16	23	22	23	37	44	48	30	29	2	5	25
Zambia	3	4	10	21	47	34	33	27	15	40	23	2	3	22
Zimbabwe	2	32	38	35	58	47	51	48	53	20	13	1	9	37
NORTH AFRICA	294	512	576	739	701	777	988	1,101	1,167	1,364	1,578	264	374	875
Algeria	73	86	84	62	54	110	128	175	234	274	288	72	97	140
Egypt, Arab Republic	119	99	56	68	151	225	288	432	458	577	615	111	120	282
Libya	..	..	..	..	..	..	..	..	..	..	..	..	..	..
Morocco	62	168	282	343	289	227	361	269	266	291	458	41	48	254
Tunisia	41	158	154	266	207	216	211	225	209	223	218	39	109	198
ALL AFRICA	537	1,101	1,349	1,457	1,579	1,661	2,014	2,832	2,804	2,742	3,103	502	908	1,902

6-6. Amortization: official nonconcessional long-term loans

	Millions of U.S. dollars (current prices)											Annual Average		
	1980	1992	1993	1994	1995	1996	1997	1998	1999	2000	2001	75-84	85-89	90-MR
SUB-SAHARAN AFRICA	424	1,448	1,431	1,908	2,119	2,444	1,956	1,782	1,841	2,048	2,440	336	1,127	1,935
excluding South Africa	424	1,448	1,431	1,908	2,119	2,444	1,956	1,782	1,841	2,048	2,440	336	1,127	1,935
excl. S.Africa & Nigeria	392	1,117	1,103	1,478	1,652	1,718	1,446	1,354	1,385	1,139	927	302	859	1,317
Angola	..	38	21	25	21	26	40	71	28	52	28	1	31	39
Benin	1	7	6	9	10	11	10	10	14	7	4	2	5	9
Botswana	6	50	43	46	48	49	40	35	34	27	23	3	22	40
Burkina Faso	4	6	9	9	10	7	7	6	9	6	5	2	4	7
Burundi	1	6	3	5	3	6	4	4	2	0	0	0	4	4
Cameroon	16	61	101	119	134	180	177	147	113	104	75	18	60	114
Cape Verde	..	3	2	3	2	2	3	8	11	2	2	1	2	3
Central African Republic	0	2	1	2	0	0	0	2	1	0	0	1	4	1
Chad	0	1	4	2	1	3	7	5	3	3	1	0	1	3
Comoros	0	1	0	0	0	0	0	0	0	0	0	0	0	1
Congo, Democratic Rep. of	100	19	0	0	0	0	0	0	0	0	0	36	52	6
Congo, Republic of	10	1	0	119	25	104	53	7	0	4	49	11	16	36
Côte d'Ivoire	37	202	216	299	414	429	261	248	268	152	121	30	103	248
Djibouti	1	0	0	0	0	0	0	0	0	0	0	0	0	0
Equatorial Guinea	1	2	1	0	0	2	0	0	0	0	0	1	2	1
Eritrea	..	..	..	0	0	0	0	0	0	1	1	..	..	0
Ethiopia	4	15	13	13	19	26	18	18	28	25	22	6	30	20
Gabon	15	61	24	55	78	71	104	67	187	144	142	14	16	82
Gambia, The	0	6	6	6	7	5	3	2	2	3	2	0	1	4
Ghana	22	44	36	45	62	45	55	56	54	62	32	15	22	46
Guinea	20	23	17	12	20	14	21	46	23	52	22	9	18	25
Guinea-Bissau	0	2	0	1	4	3	1	1	0	7	9	0	1	2
Kenya	25	141	139	183	201	195	170	187	182	104	146	22	96	162
Lesotho	0	8	6	6	7	5	8	10	10	14	9	1	4	8
Liberia	2	0	12	13	0	0	0	0	0	0	0	6	6	3
Madagascar	1	12	14	14	9	18	43	18	23	14	11	8	36	20
Malawi	3	26	21	23	27	18	15	14	12	11	9	5	20	22
Mali	0	7	3	14	11	5	4	5	6	4	4	0	2	6
Mauritania	1	25	36	24	32	36	22	19	22	19	16	6	25	28
Mauritius	4	53	34	36	36	31	31	30	30	33	33	4	19	33
Mozambique	..	13	15	35	34	25	12	11	8	5	9	1	7	16
Namibia	..	..	..	..	..	..	..	..	..	..	..	..	..	..
Niger	2	3	20	8	1	2	2	0	4	2	2	5	12	4
Nigeria	31	331	328	429	468	727	510	428	456	910	1,513	34	269	618
Rwanda	0	0	0	0	0	1	1	1	1	2	0	0	0	1
São Tomé and Principe	1	1	1	1	0	1	0	1	1	1	0	1	1	1
Senegal	12	27	19	47	55	41	42	48	33	39	35	8	45	41
Seychelles	0	4	3	3	3	3	5	5	6	2	1	0	2	3
Sierra Leone	2	7	2	9	22	41	1	4	3	3	5	2	2	9
Somalia	5	0	0	0	0	0	0	0	0	0	0	3	1	0
South Africa	..	..	..	0	0	0	0	0	0	0	0	..	..	0
Sudan	32	6	4	0	6	0	0	1	6	2	1	24	14	4
Swaziland	4	9	9	12	8	10	8	6	11	6	8	3	13	11
Tanzania	7	50	49	45	62	69	33	33	20	46	26	8	47	45
Togo	8	4	2	2	0	6	9	4	7	0	0	8	28	6
Uganda	9	27	61	49	38	25	22	24	18	9	7	6	21	28
Zambia	34	97	80	105	132	83	75	53	36	39	29	28	37	81
Zimbabwe	3	50	71	81	109	121	139	142	170	125	21	5	30	95
NORTH AFRICA	287	2,801	2,558	2,954	2,829	2,398	2,962	2,624	2,515	2,186	2,343	533	1,960	2,643
Algeria	171	1,108	1,080	598	618	560	917	801	883	782	993	157	760	881
Egypt, Arab Republic	32	409	336	306	391	347	350	272	256	280	277	54	357	371
Libya	..	..	..	..	..	..	..	..	..	..	..	..	..	..
Morocco	52	677	806	1,128	1,354	1,115	1,305	1,041	872	637	597	57	353	869
Tunisia	32	307	312	342	432	376	373	386	444	458	430	44	185	358
ALL AFRICA	711	4,249	3,989	4,861	4,948	4,842	4,919	4,406	4,356	4,234	4,782	869	3,087	4,578

6-7. Amortization: private long-term loans

	Millions of U.S. dollars (current prices)											Annual Average		
	1980	1992	1993	1994	1995	1996	1997	1998	1999	2000	2001	75-84	85-89	90-MR
SUB-SAHARAN AFRICA	2,123	2,909	1,271	3,953	4,082	5,507	7,013	4,791	4,971	5,126	5,200	1,853	2,648	4,063
excluding South Africa	2,123	2,909	1,271	1,959	2,012	2,738	2,333	2,349	2,127	2,517	2,028	1,853	2,648	2,181
excl. S.Africa & Nigeria	1,926	1,363	1,182	1,643	1,563	2,047	2,075	2,325	1,981	2,341	1,844	1,312	1,785	1,798
Angola	..	106	39	120	308	619	768	884	870	1,295	1,288	19	62	549
Benin	3	0	0	0	0	0	0	0	0	0	0	4	8	0
Botswana	0	3	1	2	6	9	5	5	1	7	2	2	6	5
Burkina Faso	2	0	0	0	0	0	0	0	0	0	0	2	5	0
Burundi	3	2	1	1	1	1	0	0	0	0	0	2	6	1
Cameroon	85	67	98	67	65	49	39	54	108	90	0	76	292	75
Cape Verde	..	0	0	0	0	0	1	2	1	2	3	0	0	1
Central African Republic	1	1	0	0	0	0	0	0	0	0	0	1	1	0
Chad	0	0	1	0	0	0	0	0	1	1	1	1	1	0
Comoros	0	0	0	0	0	0	0	0	0	0	0	0	0	0
Congo, Democratic Rep. of	90	5	0	0	0	0	0	0	0	0	0	42	32	3
Congo, Republic of	12	97	75	157	50	15	0	0	0	0	0	62	236	73
Côte d'Ivoire	667	212	242	356	60	302	487	316	339	159	110	350	264	256
Djibouti	0	0	0	0	0	0	0	0	0	0	0	1	2	0
Equatorial Guinea	0	0	0	0	0	0	0	0	0	0	0	1	0	0
Eritrea	..	..	..	0	0	0	0	0	0	0	0	..	..	0
Ethiopia	7	33	37	36	48	231	8	8	13	10	10	10	68	49
Gabon	260	17	4	33	75	51	25	17	24	29	41	149	55	31
Gambia, The	0	5	4	4	0	0	0	0	0	1	0	1	1	2
Ghana	42	58	52	66	85	105	124	110	118	103	57	11	56	84
Guinea	11	8	8	9	15	0	40	17	0	0	0	8	8	11
Guinea-Bissau	3	0	0	0	0	0	0	0	0	0	0	1	0	0
Kenya	165	153	126	287	290	243	153	154	207	118	116	161	181	182
Lesotho	3	7	6	5	4	3	3	4	7	7	7	2	5	5
Liberia	12	0	0	0	0	0	0	0	0	0	0	9	0	0
Madagascar	23	8	8	5	5	5	2	1	1	0	2	10	28	5
Malawi	28	16	13	14	23	4	3	1	0	0	0	17	19	8
Mali	2	3	1	1	0	0	0	0	0	0	0	1	3	1
Mauritania	13	2	0	0	0	0	2	2	2	2	3	21	5	1
Mauritius	14	43	26	45	93	50	58	101	54	346	72	17	28	79
Mozambique	..	7	10	5	13	6	5	4	10	31	30	0	14	13
Namibia	..	..	..	..	..	..	..	..	..	..	..	..	..	..
Niger	40	20	24	24	24	24	14	24	2	2	6	40	38	21
Nigeria	197	1,546	89	316	448	690	258	25	146	177	184	540	863	383
Rwanda	2	1	0	0	0	0	0	0	0	0	0	1	4	0
São Tomé and Principe	0	0	0	0	0	0	0	0	0	0	0	0	0	0
Senegal	137	39	4	10	27	11	7	17	7	3	17	46	49	18
Seychelles	0	4	5	4	9	5	3	5	6	4	4	0	5	5
Sierra Leone	29	0	0	0	28	0	0	0	0	0	0	16	2	2
Somalia	0	0	0	0	0	0	0	0	0	0	0	3	0	0
South Africa	..	..	..	1,994	2,070	2,770	4,680	2,442	2,844	2,609	3,172	..	..	2,823
Sudan	7	0	0	0	0	0	0	0	0	0	0	16	1	0
Swaziland	3	2	2	2	0	0	0	0	0	0	0	2	5	1
Tanzania	23	80	11	16	27	22	22	17	23	21	29	18	7	24
Togo	9	0	0	0	0	0	6	0	0	0	0	16	10	1
Uganda	21	14	32	15	9	7	1	2	2	1	1	15	27	11
Zambia	175	46	51	60	62	39	57	52	8	19	6	111	51	42
Zimbabwe	34	305	301	256	234	246	244	525	170	91	39	58	195	230
NORTH AFRICA	3,139	7,790	7,527	4,185	2,843	2,807	2,133	2,866	3,704	3,219	2,560	2,399	4,529	4,549
Algeria	2,284	5,883	5,816	2,698	1,577	1,297	975	1,728	1,905	1,667	1,530	1,646	3,255	3,054
Egypt, Arab Republic	192	921	579	544	352	454	302	255	488	234	207	238	751	503
Libya	..	..	..	..	..	..	..	..	..	..	..	..	..	..
Morocco	477	548	754	624	630	617	453	451	835	692	607	325	174	579
Tunisia	186	393	378	320	285	268	241	208	248	627	217	157	320	343
ALL AFRICA	5,262	10,699	8,798	8,139	6,925	8,314	9,146	7,658	8,675	8,346	7,761	4,252	7,177	8,612

6-8. Amortization: long-term loans and IMF repurchases

	Millions of U.S. dollars (current prices)											Annual Average		
	1980	1992	1993	1994	1995	1996	1997	1998	1999	2000	2001	75-84	85-89	90-MR
SUB-SAHARAN AFRICA	3,174	5,476	3,929	7,045	9,451	9,432	11,061	9,416	9,039	9,092	9,916	2,712	5,454	7,863
excluding South Africa	3,174	5,476	3,929	5,051	7,380	6,663	5,958	6,557	6,195	6,483	6,744	2,712	5,454	5,911
excl. S.Africa & Nigeria	2,932	3,598	3,350	4,305	6,462	5,245	5,118	5,784	5,591	5,393	5,030	2,124	4,313	4,860
Angola	0	146	63	153	332	652	817	1,318	1,304	1,564	1,636	8	95	700
Benin	6	15	18	21	26	27	32	35	45	58	47	7	20	30
Botswana	6	62	57	62	65	73	75	53	52	52	40	6	32	59
Burkina Faso	11	15	20	27	29	31	33	35	44	40	39	7	20	30
Burundi	4	24	23	28	27	21	20	21	21	14	16	5	24	22
Cameroon	131	203	282	204	217	248	277	292	285	273	130	112	381	241
Cape Verde	0	7	4	6	6	5	10	16	16	11	10	0	3	8
Central African Republic	7	7	3	13	10	8	12	25	12	8	9	6	17	11
Chad	5	4	8	10	10	16	24	23	21	16	23	4	7	14
Comoros	0	3	2	2	0	1	1	2	2	1	2	0	0	2
Congo, Democratic Rep. of	277	29	4	5	1	37	0	1	1	0	0	123	279	31
Congo, Republic of	41	98	77	287	84	140	56	18	4	5	56	86	259	116
Côte d'Ivoire	722	594	585	787	625	860	838	670	832	481	368	405	550	657
Djibouti	2	8	6	9	9	9	5	3	7	11	9	2	7	8
Equatorial Guinea	2	2	1	1	1	3	4	4	4	4	4	2	6	3
Eritrea	..	..	..	0	0	0	0	0	0	1	2	..	..	0
Ethiopia	17	62	66	68	91	292	52	68	98	84	121	30	177	106
Gabon	279	137	71	119	216	137	172	135	281	198	274	169	75	158
Gambia, The	0	22	21	24	22	22	20	20	15	14	11	4	15	20
Ghana	106	198	186	248	308	331	398	389	346	311	217	57	248	282
Guinea	76	51	44	54	129	67	100	104	73	98	92	56	77	84
Guinea-Bissau	3	3	1	4	9	7	6	7	4	10	20	2	4	8
Kenya	205	410	366	552	600	567	449	467	529	350	340	217	411	457
Lesotho	3	20	20	18	25	22	27	29	33	39	51	4	13	26
Liberia	18	0	13	15	0	0	0	1	1	1	1	23	10	4
Madagascar	44	56	48	43	38	60	118	72	76	79	57	43	123	71
Malawi	35	72	49	53	76	56	55	60	50	38	49	30	70	60
Mali	9	38	35	63	62	54	49	55	75	70	81	8	43	54
Mauritania	26	61	82	63	79	82	70	69	70	67	79	35	72	73
Mauritius	19	128	83	103	154	108	136	153	107	402	132	30	99	144
Mozambique	0	34	44	67	85	92	64	64	71	91	101	2	39	66
Namibia	..	..	..	..	..	..	..	..	..	..	..	..	..	..
Niger	58	36	66	48	41	44	49	50	22	18	26	50	74	45
Nigeria	242	1,878	579	746	918	1,418	840	773	605	1,091	1,715	588	1,141	1,050
Rwanda	3	10	11	2	11	10	13	11	20	24	32	3	13	14
São Tomé and Principe	1	1	1	1	1	2	2	2	3	2	3	1	2	2
Senegal	165	142	81	154	195	160	158	215	161	154	177	67	183	165
Seychelles	0	12	12	10	16	10	10	14	18	11	9	1	8	12
Sierra Leone	50	17	13	99	60	50	7	14	19	35	85	28	16	35
Somalia	11	0	0	0	0	0	0	0	0	0	0	9	20	0
South Africa	0	0	0	1,994	2,070	2,769	5,103	2,859	2,844	2,609	3,172	0	0	1,952
Sudan	131	14	9	3	54	36	42	59	44	59	54	90	63	33
Swaziland	8	17	17	20	16	21	16	13	17	15	14	6	24	18
Tanzania	81	172	104	116	146	166	121	136	136	174	165	59	101	142
Togo	19	19	14	13	18	32	40	29	32	20	22	33	61	26
Uganda	45	79	119	111	97	105	117	132	119	89	78	35	129	105
Zambia	269	183	211	206	2,067	156	165	132	59	98	270	193	130	330
Zimbabwe	40	387	410	372	401	423	459	763	455	306	82	67	306	383
NORTH AFRICA	3,942	11,480	11,152	8,246	6,755	6,298	6,502	7,077	7,796	6,873	6,608	3,276	7,188	8,421
Algeria	2,528	7,243	7,309	3,553	2,419	2,102	2,370	3,139	3,382	2,815	2,951	1,875	4,112	4,274
Egypt, Arab Republic	446	1,470	971	939	989	1,111	955	959	1,202	1,091	1,099	450	1,278	1,188
Libya	..	..	..	..	..	..	..	..	..	..	..	..	..	..
Morocco	678	1,535	1,997	2,246	2,373	2,006	2,123	1,761	1,972	1,620	1,662	454	849	1,785
Tunisia	290	887	850	928	939	907	875	867	951	1,347	896	243	615	947
ALL AFRICA	7,116	16,955	15,081	15,292	16,206	15,730	17,563	16,492	16,835	15,966	16,525	5,988	12,641	16,284

Note: In 1995, Zambia was able to clear its arrears to the IMF after completing a 3 year Rights Arrangement Program.

6-9. Interest payments: official concessional long-term loans

	Millions of U.S. dollars (current prices)											Annual Average		
	1980	1992	1993	1994	1995	1996	1997	1998	1999	2000	2001	75-84	85-89	90-MR
SUB-SAHARAN AFRICA	237	805	762	601	614	794	739	933	766	632	584	172	354	706
excluding South Africa	237	805	762	601	614	794	739	933	766	632	584	172	354	706
excl. S.Africa & Nigeria	229	444	506	599	613	791	671	798	761	626	564	164	350	606
Angola	0	3	3	7	7	3	6	4	2	6	4	0	1	4
Benin	1	7	8	9	10	9	11	12	13	11	11	1	5	10
Botswana	1	5	6	3	3	9	7	6	5	5	5	1	2	5
Burkina Faso	2	6	6	7	9	11	13	13	15	13	12	2	6	10
Burundi	1	9	9	10	9	6	7	7	6	4	5	1	8	7
Cameroon	15	16	24	19	54	36	61	62	55	66	30	13	24	40
Cape Verde	0	1	1	2	2	1	2	2	2	3	3	0	1	2
Central African Republic	0	6	2	6	3	3	2	5	4	4	4	0	4	4
Chad	0	4	4	5	3	7	5	6	6	6	5	0	2	5
Comoros	0	1	1	1	1	1	1	0	1	1	1	0	1	1
Congo, Democratic Rep. of	47	10	7	0	0	0	0	0	0	0	0	11	13	4
Congo, Republic of	12	5	4	93	9	35	1	1	0	1	4	6	7	16
Côte d'Ivoire	14	29	30	32	47	77	75	145	118	57	47	13	13	59
Djibouti	1	2	2	2	2	3	2	2	2	2	1	1	2	2
Equatorial Guinea	0	1	0	1	0	1	1	1	1	1	1	0	0	1
Eritrea	0	0	0	0	0	0	0	4	3	2	5	0	0	1
Ethiopia	7	10	12	16	19	19	21	25	30	31	48	7	26	22
Gabon	3	20	4	15	40	39	36	24	27	9	43	2	2	22
Gambia, The	0	3	4	4	3	3	5	5	5	5	3	0	2	4
Ghana	11	32	38	39	28	51	43	64	58	51	34	13	19	41
Guinea	12	20	23	27	29	22	23	24	25	22	21	10	12	24
Guinea-Bissau	0	1	2	2	3	3	3	4	5	2	7	0	2	3
Kenya	9	28	39	47	59	57	47	50	47	31	26	10	23	42
Lesotho	0	6	5	4	5	5	5	5	5	9	6	0	2	5
Liberia	2	0	1	0	0	0	0	0	0	0	0	2	2	0
Madagascar	4	19	14	11	11	12	42	36	34	17	16	7	11	21
Malawi	4	11	13	13	19	17	18	16	13	15	15	4	6	14
Mali	2	14	38	19	19	57	18	16	19	17	16	3	11	21
Mauritania	8	11	20	22	18	18	19	18	15	15	16	8	13	16
Mauritius	1	16	16	17	18	17	15	15	14	12	11	1	6	14
Mozambique	0	22	31	16	19	25	27	23	32	18	9	0	14	20
Namibia	..	..	..	..	..	..	..	..	..	..	..	..	..	..
Niger	2	4	7	6	7	5	8	7	7	7	7	2	7	6
Nigeria	9	361	256	2	2	3	68	136	5	6	20	8	4	100
Rwanda	1	5	4	2	8	6	7	6	8	8	9	1	6	6
São Tomé and Principe	0	1	1	1	1	1	2	1	1	1	2	0	0	1
Senegal	7	19	7	25	22	79	30	37	33	39	34	4	30	32
Seychelles	0	2	1	1	2	1	1	1	1	1	1	0	1	1
Sierra Leone	0	7	3	4	5	4	4	5	3	4	4	1	1	4
Somalia	2	0	0	0	0	0	0	0	0	0	0	2	3	0
South Africa	0	0	0	0	0	0	0	0	0	0	0	0	0	0
Sudan	28	10	6	0	1	0	0	0	0	2	1	13	17	3
Swaziland	1	2	2	2	2	3	2	2	2	2	1	0	1	2
Tanzania	15	22	49	28	28	55	27	76	51	42	34	14	15	38
Togo	1	7	6	5	5	13	8	8	7	5	6	1	6	7
Uganda	1	10	13	18	23	25	25	22	24	26	19	1	6	18
Zambia	14	19	22	36	32	29	20	23	41	41	33	5	8	27
Zimbabwe	1	19	19	23	26	23	22	20	21	12	8	2	12	19
NORTH AFRICA	289	577	671	781	906	945	798	776	781	713	847	237	261	701
Algeria	35	26	26	55	89	144	117	124	128	124	117	32	20	83
Egypt, Arab Republic	153	392	422	467	567	551	413	377	377	369	356	121	131	382
Libya	..	..	..	..	..	..	..	..	..	..	..	..	..	..
Morocco	70	81	145	153	161	166	190	200	204	151	303	55	44	157
Tunisia	30	78	78	107	89	84	78	75	72	69	72	29	66	79
ALL AFRICA	526	1,382	1,434	1,382	1,521	1,739	1,538	1,709	1,548	1,344	1,431	409	615	1,407

6-10. Interest payments: official nonconcessional long-term loans

	Millions of U.S. dollars (current prices)											Annual Average		
	1980	1992	1993	1994	1995	1996	1997	1998	1999	2000	2001	75-84	85-89	90-MR
SUB-SAHARAN AFRICA	453	1,425	1,187	1,427	1,404	1,874	1,352	1,124	1,161	1,221	1,047	384	1,311	1,464
excluding South Africa	453	1,425	1,187	1,427	1,404	1,874	1,352	1,124	1,161	1,219	1,035	384	1,311	1,463
excl. S.Africa & Nigeria	399	959	873	1,092	1,082	1,362	1,055	884	921	709	424	325	910	959
Angola	..	12	5	3	5	24	15	11	6	30	5	1	16	13
Benin	1	4	4	10	11	7	7	9	7	3	4	1	3	6
Botswana	6	28	26	26	22	61	18	15	14	9	7	6	26	24
Burkina Faso	2	9	10	8	9	4	3	3	2	2	2	2	6	5
Burundi	0	4	3	3	2	3	2	1	1	0	0	0	4	2
Cameroon	27	71	106	116	99	185	113	98	125	132	26	22	59	105
Cape Verde	..	2	1	1	1	1	1	1	1	1	1	1	2	1
Central African Republic	0	1	1	2	0	0	0	1	1	0	0	1	4	1
Chad	0	2	4	2	1	6	4	5	4	3	1	0	0	3
Comoros	0	1	0	0	0	0	0	0	0	0	0	0	0	0
Congo, Democratic Rep. of	59	16	1	0	0	0	0	0	0	0	0	33	74	9
Congo, Republic of	13	1	0	85	11	141	40	6	0	6	22	8	25	30
Côte d'Ivoire	64	210	188	236	206	252	194	224	194	132	65	48	160	192
Djibouti	0	0	0	0	0	0	0	0	0	0	0	0	0	0
Equatorial Guinea	0	1	0	0	0	0	0	0	0	0	0	0	1	0
Eritrea	..	..	..	0	0	0	0	0	0	0	0	..	..	0
Ethiopia	8	10	9	15	13	19	21	20	21	17	11	6	10	14
Gabon	17	182	25	59	133	180	192	110	194	109	113	11	28	120
Gambia, The	0	3	2	2	2	1	1	1	1	1	0	0	1	1
Ghana	13	30	31	24	24	27	36	26	22	24	8	10	19	25
Guinea	9	13	13	12	14	21	19	19	19	19	11	7	13	16
Guinea-Bissau	0	2	0	1	2	1	0	0	0	8	4	0	1	2
Kenya	45	83	87	114	108	106	70	61	40	21	32	37	99	78
Lesotho	0	6	6	7	8	7	9	8	7	8	5	1	3	6
Liberia	5	0	8	0	0	0	0	0	0	0	0	6	7	1
Madagascar	3	11	10	7	4	5	51	15	42	11	13	6	50	22
Malawi	6	15	12	10	16	9	7	6	4	3	2	8	17	10
Mali	1	2	2	5	4	3	2	2	2	1	1	1	2	2
Mauritania	1	8	23	16	14	11	14	12	12	7	8	4	15	13
Mauritius	6	24	19	18	17	16	14	13	12	11	10	5	18	17
Mozambique	..	17	40	36	52	21	14	5	0	3	1	0	8	17
Namibia	..	..	..	..	..	..	..	..	..	..	..	..	..	..
Niger	5	1	7	3	0	1	2	2	3	3	0	5	19	2
Nigeria	54	466	314	335	322	512	297	240	240	510	611	59	401	504
Rwanda	0	0	0	0	0	0	0	0	0	0	0	0	0	0
São Tomé and Principe	0	0	0	0	0	0	0	0	0	0	0	0	1	0
Senegal	15	20	14	36	43	36	44	51	24	18	19	13	57	32
Seychelles	0	2	2	2	3	2	3	3	3	1	0	0	2	2
Sierra Leone	2	4	10	17	16	9	3	6	3	5	5	2	1	7
Somalia	0	0	0	0	0	3	0	0	0	0	0	0	2	0
South Africa	..	..	..	0	0	0	0	0	0	1	12	..	..	2
Sudan	16	1	2	0	2	0	0	2	7	1	0	13	9	2
Swaziland	6	5	4	4	3	9	5	5	10	9	8	4	9	6
Tanzania	19	29	48	33	48	35	10	25	10	13	9	15	24	26
Togo	11	3	1	1	2	11	5	2	1	0	0	8	30	5
Uganda	1	11	14	14	9	13	13	4	8	5	1	2	14	10
Zambia	39	59	54	75	83	39	33	25	31	35	18	31	34	57
Zimbabwe	1	58	79	90	95	95	93	85	89	56	8	6	40	71
NORTH AFRICA	401	1,739	1,846	2,037	2,364	2,646	2,296	2,306	2,177	1,967	1,858	420	1,278	2,024
Algeria	124	350	343	346	733	1,106	1,008	1,072	1,061	1,007	898	104	285	711
Egypt, Arab Republic	68	448	462	540	550	425	276	256	248	199	214	162	480	370
Libya	..	..	..	..	..	..	..	..	..	..	..	..	..	..
Morocco	66	700	780	865	762	722	639	579	465	401	385	66	352	623
Tunisia	44	211	231	256	279	286	261	253	258	226	189	37	124	234
ALL AFRICA	854	3,164	3,033	3,464	3,767	4,520	3,648	3,430	3,338	3,188	2,904	804	2,589	3,488

6-11. Interest payments: private long-term loans

	Millions of U.S. dollars (current prices)											Annual Average		
	1980	1992	1993	1994	1995	1996	1997	1998	1999	2000	2001	75-84	85-89	90-MR
SUB-SAHARAN AFRICA	1,694	1,628	753	1,947	1,971	2,161	1,582	1,761	1,598	1,521	1,437	1,262	1,646	1,630
excluding South Africa	1,694	1,628	753	1,330	1,116	1,238	732	868	784	780	589	1,262	1,646	1,085
excl. S.Africa & Nigeria	1,228	624	461	591	581	710	554	723	611	606	416	853	980	621
Angola	..	34	18	41	67	266	127	187	126	127	186	7	52	112
Benin	1	0	0	0	0	0	0	0	0	0	0	3	7	0
Botswana	1	2	1	1	3	9	2	2	2	1	1	1	3	2
Burkina Faso	3	0	0	0	0	0	0	0	0	0	0	1	1	0
Burundi	1	0	0	0	0	0	0	0	0	0	0	1	2	0
Cameroon	78	65	26	21	21	14	16	19	22	17	0	56	93	28
Cape Verde	..	0	0	0	0	0	1	1	0	1	0	0	0	0
Central African Republic	0	0	0	0	0	0	0	0	0	0	0	1	0	0
Chad	0	0	0	0	0	0	0	0	0	0	0	0	0	0
Comoros	0	0	0	0	0	0	0	0	0	0	0	0	0	0
Congo, Democratic Rep. of	99	1	0	0	0	0	0	0	0	0	0	61	40	2
Congo, Republic of	13	22	17	50	40	3	0	0	0	0	0	36	64	18
Côte d'Ivoire	513	171	163	159	138	145	145	246	231	273	102	343	341	187
Djibouti	0	0	0	0	0	0	0	0	0	0	0	0	0	0
Equatorial Guinea	0	0	0	0	0	0	0	0	0	0	0	0	0	0
Eritrea	..	..	..	0	0	0	0	0	0	0	0	..	..	0
Ethiopia	2	22	3	9	29	15	4	3	5	4	3	4	25	12
Gabon	100	36	6	29	44	12	10	8	9	7	10	52	26	19
Gambia, The	0	1	0	0	0	0	0	0	0	0	0	0	1	1
Ghana	7	19	17	21	8	31	48	63	57	42	28	4	16	30
Guinea	2	0	1	2	1	0	3	0	0	0	0	2	2	1
Guinea-Bissau	1	0	0	0	0	0	0	0	0	0	0	0	0	0
Kenya	110	90	82	129	97	82	73	55	46	37	25	69	82	75
Lesotho	1	1	1	1	3	4	6	9	10	7	6	1	1	4
Liberia	16	0	0	0	0	0	0	0	0	0	0	5	0	0
Madagascar	19	3	1	1	1	2	0	0	0	0	1	12	12	2
Malawi	25	4	2	2	4	2	1	0	0	0	0	13	7	2
Mali	1	0	0	0	0	0	0	0	0	0	0	1	1	0
Mauritania	4	0	0	0	0	0	2	2	2	2	2	3	2	1
Mauritius	15	13	8	11	21	38	34	35	31	29	17	11	11	21
Mozambique	..	5	4	2	4	1	1	8	8	0	0	1	6	4
Namibia	..	..	..	..	..	..	..	..	..	..	..	..	..	..
Niger	58	8	7	6	6	5	3	2	0	0	1	30	26	5
Nigeria	466	1,004	292	739	535	528	178	145	173	174	173	409	667	464
Rwanda	0	0	0	0	0	0	0	0	0	0	0	0	1	0
São Tomé and Principe	0	0	0	0	0	0	0	0	0	0	0	0	0	0
Senegal	46	8	2	2	4	2	1	1	1	0	4	22	22	5
Seychelles	0	1	2	3	2	1	1	2	1	1	0	0	2	1
Sierra Leone	11	5	4	5	0	0	0	0	0	0	0	7	4	2
Somalia	0	0	0	0	0	0	0	0	0	0	0	1	0	0
South Africa	..	..	..	617	855	923	850	892	814	741	849	..	..	818
Sudan	5	0	0	0	0	0	0	0	0	0	0	15	9	0
Swaziland	2	1	0	0	0	0	0	7	7	6	3	1	1	2
Tanzania	13	6	5	1	5	6	3	3	12	3	1	9	3	4
Togo	8	0	0	0	0	0	0	0	0	0	0	7	6	0
Uganda	1	5	3	1	2	0	0	2	0	0	2	2	4	2
Zambia	63	20	15	15	9	8	12	7	5	4	3	43	23	12
Zimbabwe	9	81	72	79	74	65	59	60	32	45	21	30	83	63
NORTH AFRICA	2,118	3,257	1,972	1,678	1,604	1,458	1,268	1,183	1,187	1,058	879	1,389	2,066	1,653
Algeria	1,280	1,443	1,338	1,098	918	771	818	683	533	422	324	837	1,283	939
Egypt, Arab Republic	129	189	170	137	130	97	71	69	54	46	114	128	272	135
Libya	..	..	..	..	..	..	..	..	..	..	..	..	..	..
Morocco	515	1,516	354	345	437	447	232	239	399	396	274	319	370	434
Tunisia	154	109	109	99	118	137	140	168	173	194	167	88	141	140
ALL AFRICA	3,812	4,884	2,724	3,625	3,575	3,619	2,850	2,943	2,785	2,579	2,316	2,651	3,712	3,283

6-12. Interest payments: long-term loans and IMF charges

	Millions of U.S. dollars (current prices)											Annual Average		
	1980	*1992*	*1993*	*1994*	*1995*	*1996*	*1997*	*1998*	*1999*	*2000*	*2001*	*75-84*	*85-89*	*90-MR*
SUB-SAHARAN AFRICA	2,488	4,044	2,840	4,144	4,548	4,952	3,774	3,883	3,580	3,412	3,098	1,947	3,666	3,961
excluding South Africa	2,488	4,044	2,840	3,489	3,643	3,990	2,891	2,975	2,765	2,670	2,238	1,947	3,666	3,400
excl. S.Africa & Nigeria	1,958	2,213	1,978	2,414	2,784	2,947	2,347	2,454	2,347	1,980	1,433	1,471	2,594	2,331
Angola	0	48	26	51	79	293	148	202	135	163	195	3	69	129
Benin	3	11	13	19	22	17	19	22	20	15	16	5	14	17
Botswana	8	36	33	31	28	78	28	23	21	15	12	8	31	32
Burkina Faso	6	14	16	15	18	16	16	16	17	16	14	5	13	15
Burundi	3	14	12	13	11	9	9	8	6	5	5	2	14	10
Cameroon	121	160	159	157	176	238	192	181	204	217	58	92	177	178
Cape Verde	0	3	2	3	3	3	4	4	3	5	4	1	3	3
Central African Republic	1	7	4	9	5	4	3	7	5	4	4	3	10	6
Chad	1	6	8	8	5	14	11	11	11	9	7	1	3	8
Comoros	0	3	1	1	1	1	1	0	1	1	1	0	1	1
Congo, Democratic Rep. of	220	35	10	2	16	5	0	0	2	0	0	118	179	22
Congo, Republic of	38	29	21	228	62	181	41	7	1	7	27	50	97	64
Côte d'Ivoire	590	436	399	437	398	478	416	618	547	465	217	417	560	451
Djibouti	1	2	2	2	2	3	2	2	2	3	2	1	3	2
Equatorial Guinea	0	1	1	1	1	1	1	1	1	1	1	0	2	1
Eritrea	..	..	..	0	0	0	1	4	3	3	5	..	..	2
Ethiopia	19	42	24	40	61	54	46	49	56	52	63	20	65	48
Gabon	120	246	41	106	223	236	244	148	235	128	170	66	60	168
Gambia, The	1	7	6	6	5	5	6	6	6	6	4	2	6	6
Ghana	35	102	100	95	69	116	132	156	139	119	72	30	100	107
Guinea	24	33	37	41	44	44	45	44	45	42	32	20	29	42
Guinea-Bissau	1	3	2	4	6	4	3	5	5	10	12	1	3	5
Kenya	171	212	212	292	265	247	191	166	134	90	83	126	237	201
Lesotho	2	13	12	11	16	16	20	22	22	23	18	2	6	16
Liberia	24	1	9	0	2	2	0	0	2	0	0	17	11	2
Madagascar	28	37	27	20	17	19	93	51	77	29	31	29	85	47
Malawi	37	33	28	26	40	29	27	23	17	18	17	28	39	29
Mali	4	18	42	25	23	60	21	19	22	20	18	5	19	25
Mauritania	15	20	43	38	33	30	36	33	29	23	26	16	33	31
Mauritius	26	53	42	45	56	71	63	62	56	52	38	24	47	53
Mozambique	0	43	76	55	76	48	42	36	42	22	10	1	27	42
Namibia	..	..	..	..	..	..	..	..	..	..	..	..	..	..
Niger	65	15	23	16	14	11	14	11	11	10	9	37	57	15
Nigeria	529	1,831	862	1,075	859	1,043	544	521	418	690	804	476	1,072	1,069
Rwanda	2	6	5	2	8	7	8	7	9	10	10	1	7	7
São Tomé and Principe	0	1	1	1	1	1	2	1	1	1	3	0	1	1
Senegal	70	53	26	66	72	121	78	91	59	59	57	45	126	74
Seychelles	0	5	5	6	7	5	5	6	6	3	2	0	5	5
Sierra Leone	16	18	18	64	21	14	8	12	7	11	11	12	9	17
Somalia	2	0	0	0	1	3	0	0	1	0	0	5	11	1
South Africa	0	0	0	656	905	962	884	908	815	743	860	0	0	561
Sudan	63	13	11	1	15	12	15	3	13	3	2	57	52	9
Swaziland	9	7	6	6	5	12	7	14	19	17	11	5	12	10
Tanzania	54	58	103	62	82	97	42	104	75	60	47	41	46	70
Togo	19	12	9	6	8	24	14	10	9	5	6	17	47	13
Uganda	7	29	32	35	36	40	40	30	34	33	23	13	44	34
Zambia	141	167	151	167	544	86	71	60	83	85	59	102	85	154
Zimbabwe	10	163	179	203	209	194	184	175	152	123	39	41	150	160
NORTH AFRICA	2,838	5,719	4,591	4,566	4,975	5,142	4,465	4,371	4,228	3,698	3,489	2,083	3,706	4,461
Algeria	1,440	1,888	1,749	1,530	1,810	2,097	2,036	1,977	1,799	1,644	1,415	972	1,592	1,803
Egypt, Arab Republic	367	1,042	1,066	1,153	1,257	1,076	760	702	679	615	684	422	890	894
Libya	..	..	..	..	..	..	..	..	..	..	..	..	..	..
Morocco	663	2,341	1,311	1,375	1,367	1,337	1,062	1,018	1,068	947	961	466	844	1,233
Tunisia	229	417	436	477	503	519	488	503	507	492	428	155	341	466
ALL AFRICA	5,326	9,763	7,431	8,710	9,524	10,094	8,240	8,253	7,808	7,110	6,586	4,030	7,372	8,422

6-13. Total external debt service payments: long-term loans and IMF credits

	Millions of U.S. dollars (current prices)											*Annual Average*		
	1980	*1992*	*1993*	*1994*	*1995*	*1996*	*1997*	*1998*	*1999*	*2000*	*2001*	*75-84*	*85-89*	*90-MR*
SUB-SAHARAN AFRICA	5,662	9,520	6,769	11,190	13,999	14,385	14,835	13,298	12,619	12,559	13,083	4,659	9,120	11,834
excluding South Africa	5,662	9,520	6,769	8,540	11,024	10,653	8,848	9,532	8,960	9,207	9,051	4,659	9,120	9,321
excl. S.Africa & Nigeria	4,890	5,811	5,328	6,718	9,247	8,192	7,465	8,238	7,937	7,426	6,532	3,595	6,907	7,202
Angola	..	195	89	204	411	945	965	1,521	1,438	1,726	1,831	29	164	829
Benin	9	26	31	40	48	44	51	56	65	72	62	13	34	46
Botswana	14	98	90	93	92	152	103	76	73	68	52	13	64	91
Burkina Faso	17	29	36	42	47	47	49	51	61	56	53	11	33	45
Burundi	7	38	35	40	38	30	29	29	27	18	21	8	38	32
Cameroon	252	363	441	361	393	486	470	473	489	490	188	203	559	419
Cape Verde	..	10	6	9	9	8	14	19	20	16	13	3	6	12
Central African Republic	8	14	7	21	15	12	15	32	17	13	13	9	27	17
Chad	6	10	16	18	15	30	35	34	32	25	29	5	10	22
Comoros	0	6	2	3	1	1	2	2	3	2	2	1	1	3
Congo, Democratic Rep. of	497	64	15	6	18	42	0	1	3	0	0	241	458	53
Congo, Republic of	78	127	98	515	146	321	96	25	5	13	83	136	355	181
Côte d'Ivoire	1,312	1,030	984	1,224	1,023	1,338	1,254	1,288	1,379	946	585	822	1,110	1,107
Djibouti	3	10	9	11	11	12	7	5	10	13	11	3	10	10
Equatorial Guinea	2	3	1	2	2	4	5	5	4	5	4	3	7	4
Eritrea	..	..	..	0	0	0	1	4	3	3	7	..	..	2
Ethiopia	36	104	90	107	153	346	99	117	154	136	184	51	242	154
Gabon	399	383	112	225	439	373	415	283	515	326	444	235	134	326
Gambia, The	1	29	27	30	27	27	26	25	20	20	15	5	21	26
Ghana	141	300	286	343	378	447	530	544	485	430	289	87	348	389
Guinea	100	83	81	94	173	110	145	147	118	140	123	76	105	126
Guinea-Bissau	4	6	3	7	15	11	9	12	9	20	32	2	7	13
Kenya	376	621	579	843	866	814	640	633	663	440	423	343	648	658
Lesotho	5	34	33	30	41	38	48	52	55	62	69	6	19	42
Liberia	43	1	22	15	2	2	0	1	3	1	1	41	21	6
Madagascar	72	93	75	63	55	79	211	123	153	108	88	72	208	118
Malawi	71	105	78	79	116	85	82	83	67	56	65	58	109	89
Mali	13	56	77	87	85	115	70	74	98	89	99	13	62	80
Mauritania	40	81	124	102	112	112	105	102	98	90	104	51	104	104
Mauritius	44	180	125	148	210	179	199	215	163	453	170	54	146	197
Mozambique	..	78	119	123	161	140	107	100	113	113	111	6	66	109
Namibia	..	..	..	..	..	..	..	..	..	..	..	..	..	..
Niger	122	51	88	64	55	56	62	61	33	28	35	87	130	60
Nigeria	772	3,709	1,441	1,822	1,777	2,461	1,383	1,294	1,023	1,781	2,519	1,064	2,213	2,119
Rwanda	4	15	16	3	20	17	21	19	30	34	42	4	20	21
São Tomé and Principe	1	2	2	3	2	3	3	4	4	3	6	1	3	3
Senegal	235	196	107	220	267	281	236	306	220	213	235	112	309	239
Seychelles	0	17	17	16	23	15	14	20	23	14	10	1	13	17
Sierra Leone	66	35	31	163	82	65	15	25	26	46	95	39	25	52
Somalia	13	0	0	0	1	3	0	0	1	0	0	14	31	1
South Africa	..	..	..	2,650	2,976	3,732	5,987	3,766	3,659	3,352	4,033	..	..	3,769
Sudan	194	27	20	3	69	48	58	61	57	61	56	147	115	42
Swaziland	17	24	23	26	21	32	23	28	35	31	25	12	36	29
Tanzania	135	229	207	178	229	263	163	241	211	234	211	100	146	211
Togo	38	32	23	19	26	56	54	39	41	25	28	50	108	39
Uganda	52	108	151	146	133	145	157	162	152	122	101	48	172	138
Zambia	410	350	362	374	2,611	242	236	193	141	183	329	295	216	484
Zimbabwe	50	550	590	574	610	617	642	938	607	429	120	107	456	543
NORTH AFRICA	6,780	17,198	15,743	12,812	11,730	11,439	10,967	11,447	12,023	11,031	10,636	5,359	10,894	12,965
Algeria	3,968	9,131	9,058	5,083	4,228	4,199	4,406	5,117	5,181	4,460	4,366	2,848	5,704	6,077
Egypt, Arab Republic	813	2,512	2,037	2,092	2,245	2,187	1,715	1,661	1,881	1,706	1,783	871	2,168	2,082
Libya	..	..	..	..	..	..	..	..	..	..	..	..	..	..
Morocco	1,341	3,876	3,308	3,622	3,740	3,343	3,184	2,779	3,040	2,567	2,623	921	1,693	3,018
Tunisia	518	1,305	1,285	1,405	1,442	1,426	1,363	1,371	1,458	1,839	1,325	398	956	1,412
ALL AFRICA	12,442	26,718	22,512	24,002	25,729	25,824	25,802	24,746	24,642	23,590	23,719	10,018	20,013	24,799

Note: In 1995, Zambia was able to clear its arrears to the IMF after completing a 3 year Rights Arrangement Program.

6-14. Interest payments: short-term loans

	Millions of U.S. dollars (current prices)											Annual Average		
	1980	*1992*	*1993*	*1994*	*1995*	*1996*	*1997*	*1998*	*1999*	*2000*	*2001*	*75-84*	*85-89*	*90-MR*
SUB-SAHARAN AFRICA	1,025	553	523	631	819	885	1,053	1,158	1,160	1,101	703	540	688	825
excluding South Africa	1,025	553	523	379	404	380	498	536	529	592	380	540	688	507
excl. S.Africa & Nigeria	646	513	473	329	348	333	465	499	489	528	337	304	519	464
Angola	..	54	66	55	53	49	46	45	45	26	34	6	35	47
Benin	11	2	1	1	2	2	4	5	5	5	3	5	7	3
Botswana	2	0	0	0	0	0	1	0	1	1	1	0	0	1
Burkina Faso	5	5	2	2	2	2	3	3	3	1	3	2	4	3
Burundi	2	1	1	1	1	0	0	1	2	3	2	1	2	1
Cameroon	28	31	30	24	39	24	40	55	59	72	34	17	54	40
Cape Verde	..	0	0	0	1	0	0	0	1	0	1	0	0	0
Central African Republic	2	2	2	2	1	1	1	1	2	1	0	1	2	1
Chad	0	1	1	0	1	0	1	1	1	1	1	0	0	1
Comoros	0	0	0	0	0	0	0	0	0	1	0	0	0	0
Congo, Democratic Rep. of	45	13	13	9	8	7	12	18	18	25	18	18	27	15
Congo, Republic of	31	35	30	20	35	18	16	16	20	30	10	12	45	27
Côte d'Ivoire	95	130	110	20	23	37	105	96	70	74	34	47	80	84
Djibouti	1	2	2	1	1	0	1	0	0	0	0	1	2	1
Equatorial Guinea	1	0	0	1	0	0	1	2	1	0	0	1	0	0
Eritrea	..	..	..	0	0	0	0	0	0	0	0	..	..	0
Ethiopia	9	5	5	4	1	1	1	1	2	1	1	4	7	3
Gabon	33	50	45	43	17	11	18	25	23	28	12	13	31	30
Gambia, The	3	1	1	2	1	1	1	1	1	1	1	1	2	1
Ghana	18	19	22	26	28	36	29	38	38	38	27	12	12	27
Guinea	9	4	3	3	5	3	10	12	11	15	8	4	5	7
Guinea-Bissau	1	0	0	0	0	1	1	0	0	1	1	1	2	1
Kenya	58	49	53	38	36	30	30	39	40	41	41	24	39	44
Lesotho	1	0	0	0	0	0	0	0	0	0	0	0	0	0
Liberia	11	0	0	0	0	0	0	0	0	0	0	4	3	0
Madagascar	29	3	3	2	3	4	1	2	6	9	4	9	4	4
Malawi	16	4	1	1	3	4	3	1	2	3	1	5	5	2
Mali	3	2	2	1	2	2	15	8	8	8	3	2	4	5
Mauritania	7	6	4	4	5	4	8	8	7	10	5	5	7	7
Mauritius	8	3	4	10	16	19	23	27	27	32	31	3	3	17
Mozambique	..	5	3	1	1	1	3	4	6	11	10	0	8	6
Namibia	..	..	..	..	..	..	..	..	..	..	..	..	..	..
Niger	19	2	2	2	1	1	2	1	1	1	1	7	7	3
Nigeria	379	40	50	50	56	48	33	38	41	64	43	236	169	44
Rwanda	3	6	6	1	1	1	2	2	2	2	1	1	3	3
São Tomé and Principe	0	0	1	0	0	0	0	0	0	1	0	0	0	0
Senegal	24	15	15	14	14	7	11	15	17	15	6	13	21	15
Seychelles	37	2	1	1	1	1	1	1	2	4	3	5	2	2
Sierra Leone	0	0	0	0	1	1	1	0	1	0	0	0	0	0
Somalia	0	0	0	0	0	0	0	0	0	0	0	0	0	0
South Africa	..	..	..	251	415	504	555	622	631	509	322	..	..	476
Sudan	70	0	0	0	0	0	0	0	0	0	0	39	38	2
Swaziland	2	0	0	0	0	0	8	2	2	4	2	1	1	2
Tanzania	26	5	4	5	4	6	6	7	8	10	6	12	19	6
Togo	14	5	4	4	3	2	2	2	4	5	5	6	6	4
Uganda	5	5	3	3	2	3	4	4	5	4	4	2	3	4
Zambia	0	1	1	2	1	9	10	10	8	3	7	0	0	5
Zimbabwe	15	45	33	28	35	44	44	43	41	42	16	22	25	39
NORTH AFRICA	869	570	385	333	316	289	428	336	352	193	223	589	736	392
Algeria	116	200	36	33	22	13	13	15	10	10	9	150	125	53
Egypt, Arab Republic	422	168	164	130	132	133	262	227	231	113	150	246	351	186
Libya	..	..	..	..	..	..	..	..	..	..	..	..	..	..
Morocco	105	15	18	18	24	9	6	3	9	8	4	57	71	13
Tunisia	26	37	67	52	38	39	49	60	77	61	30	9	21	48
ALL AFRICA	1,895	1,123	908	964	1,135	1,174	1,481	1,494	1,512	1,294	926	1,129	1,424	1,217

6-15. Net flows: long- and short-term loans, including IMF

	Millions of U.S. dollars (current prices)											Annual Average		
	1980	1992	1993	1994	1995	1996	1997	1998	1999	2000	2001	75-84	85-89	90-MR
SUB-SAHARAN AFRICA	10,026	4,981	4,977	2,548	7,615	3,232	4,512	-1,482	-978	-1,009	-1,489	7,901	7,193	2,820
excluding South Africa	10,026	4,981	4,977	1,024	4,202	2,552	4,890	-1,185	-280	-2,195	-722	7,901	7,193	2,431
excl. S.Africa & Nigeria	7,245	5,689	4,505	1,684	4,761	3,886	5,552	-906	104	-1,498	695	6,151	5,968	2,967
Angola	..	905	294	305	-90	76	418	-348	-564	-767	270	234	1,029	142
Benin	42	39	87	112	105	101	114	-24	74	-36	85	82	52	71
Botswana	8	22	45	-6	2	-44	-19	-67	-23	-42	-27	28	37	-12
Burkina Faso	56	105	109	117	124	81	71	66	127	37	101	49	76	95
Burundi	40	101	45	25	26	4	3	10	46	14	11	39	89	35
Cameroon	538	380	134	305	64	-188	676	65	-82	-38	-216	343	283	155
Cape Verde	..	12	6	25	35	-5	13	39	60	11	48	18	8	21
Central African Republic	31	39	54	32	25	14	-4	-13	25	-14	-5	21	67	30
Chad	-8	120	51	72	61	109	77	27	78	29	41	22	47	72
Comoros	13	15	7	11	11	7	9	-1	4	4	4	12	15	6
Congo, Democratic Rep. of	278	-28	0	-140	61	-91	242	-13	13	20	2	368	234	23
Congo, Republic of	541	-35	310	97	166	-451	96	-66	154	-52	-336	230	189	-24
Côte d'Ivoire	1,257	627	726	-1,002	935	2,117	413	-1,064	-904	-617	-517	741	351	205
Djibouti	9	30	36	-10	13	18	11	3	-1	-2	7	9	22	12
Equatorial Guinea	41	13	13	17	-8	0	19	12	-21	-12	-2	10	12	4
Eritrea	..	..	..	27	7	7	33	67	103	61	106	..	..	51
Ethiopia	94	233	314	188	133	21	130	93	134	90	453	441	435	196
Gabon	-122	-193	19	-18	14	-84	260	-172	-112	-345	-272	72	295	-54
Gambia, The	58	35	26	-20	-8	44	-5	4	19	21	19	26	15	14
Ghana	75	306	370	323	410	658	272	366	103	-17	399	128	242	341
Guinea	23	143	228	120	98	72	403	-43	68	-41	-10	49	149	104
Guinea-Bissau	73	23	19	27	13	30	27	7	0	22	-17	27	33	19
Kenya	718	114	154	-322	104	-185	21	-229	-336	99	-276	318	346	3
Lesotho	20	67	62	51	46	54	41	35	20	31	-17	16	33	41
Liberia	95	-1	10	-14	0	11	-21	3	1	-5	-5	91	23	-3
Madagascar	476	50	65	22	59	60	210	100	165	45	108	195	128	100
Malawi	154	106	107	95	183	181	48	112	127	86	45	88	58	106
Mali	99	118	62	92	200	135	283	-30	71	-18	2	91	111	99
Mauritania	139	-49	85	96	68	103	158	-84	-12	41	36	111	86	50
Mauritius	104	56	22	260	312	110	134	-16	38	-75	44	56	27	85
Mozambique	..	235	99	189	193	197	335	193	203	32	151	300	309	172
Namibia	..	..	..	..	..	..	..	..	..	..	..	..	..	..
Niger	286	48	26	27	-9	14	98	33	29	54	49	115	110	30
Nigeria	2,780	-708	472	-660	-559	-1,334	-663	-279	-385	-696	-1,417	1,750	1,225	-535
Rwanda	36	73	50	-11	53	52	114	79	95	25	42	31	70	60
São Tomé and Principe	7	26	15	8	13	5	5	5	20	9	3	6	14	12
Senegal	246	177	70	-29	74	-14	143	100	-34	-170	202	210	214	56
Seychelles	-390	-1	-3	6	-17	-2	9	33	-9	39	8	-2	10	7
Sierra Leone	54	36	86	102	55	38	24	56	13	57	65	35	10	46
Somalia	138	0	0	0	0	0	-7	5	0	-7	2	153	74	5
South Africa	..	..	..	1,524	3,412	681	-377	-297	-698	1,186	-767	..	..	583
Sudan	839	272	91	9	0	-119	-157	-14	-191	-97	-183	640	73	-9
Swaziland	29	-10	-8	-4	6	-1	195	-113	41	12	35	22	-1	9
Tanzania	405	303	112	165	92	146	226	137	214	136	-14	341	157	156
Togo	108	32	-57	56	39	72	12	52	87	-43	25	94	48	28
Uganda	130	236	244	223	184	206	244	95	97	136	277	100	164	198
Zambia	360	82	29	88	435	169	-84	25	85	159	135	305	236	93
Zimbabwe	148	793	283	28	437	142	213	-369	46	-369	-184	220	-16	130
NORTH AFRICA	5,825	635	-1,808	1,535	1,967	1,615	7	-2,206	-2,132	-2,750	-1,567	6,046	3,846	-489
Algeria	1,261	-142	-875	2,014	1,361	1,597	-428	-1,622	-1,943	-1,574	-1,994	1,442	973	-362
Egypt, Arab Republic	2,465	-608	-330	146	74	-464	579	1,059	-584	-694	140	2,598	1,409	-134
Libya	..	..	..	..	..	..	..	..	..	..	..	..	..	..
Morocco	1,624	555	-34	-532	-306	-172	-876	-292	-265	-25	-484	1,346	640	-118
Tunisia	267	576	221	448	654	692	568	-718	976	-456	772	382	303	372
ALL AFRICA	15,851	5,616	3,169	4,083	9,582	4,847	4,519	-3,688	-3,110	-3,759	-3,056	13,947	11,039	2,331

6-16. Net flows: long-term loans, including IMF

	Millions of U.S. dollars (current prices)											Annual Average		
	1980	*1992*	*1993*	*1994*	*1995*	*1996*	*1997*	*1998*	*1999*	*2000*	*2001*	*75-84*	*85-89*	*90-MR*
SUB-SAHARAN AFRICA	8,572	3,841	4,855	4,857	4,628	862	1,017	-935	-335	14	-333	6,841	5,334	2,300
excluding South Africa	8,572	3,841	4,855	3,334	3,150	1,340	1,490	-122	-187	-900	-763	6,841	5,334	2,097
excl. S.Africa & Nigeria	7,062	5,184	4,890	3,482	3,635	2,450	2,016	375	243	38	885	5,826	5,132	2,721
Angola	..	501	623	263	218	126	374	-528	-361	-519	-546	234	758	77
Benin	66	65	85	109	89	101	24	27	38	13	72	79	56	68
Botswana	21	22	45	-6	1	-46	-53	-34	-35	-38	-32	28	37	-14
Burkina Faso	59	128	131	105	110	81	56	73	81	56	122	50	70	94
Burundi	41	102	54	25	18	14	-1	9	-1	23	-5	39	89	31
Cameroon	495	466	217	275	-96	-18	19	-32	20	67	23	316	253	134
Cape Verde	..	11	6	23	16	19	11	39	47	18	41	18	8	20
Central African Republic	33	39	46	47	23	19	-5	-11	5	8	2	21	65	30
Chad	0	139	50	74	60	107	68	31	76	31	43	22	43	73
Comoros	13	15	6	12	9	9	4	3	-2	2	10	11	15	6
Congo, Democratic Rep. of	326	54	53	-3	-1	-33	0	-1	7	0	0	359	182	34
Congo, Republic of	485	33	383	63	-69	-116	-32	-8	-4	9	-18	224	141	2
Côte d'Ivoire	1,055	259	229	618	299	154	-602	-57	-585	-333	-356	709	49	42
Djibouti	8	36	19	17	9	19	9	5	1	1	7	8	17	16
Equatorial Guinea	36	13	13	6	1	-1	-2	-3	0	-2	-3	10	15	3
Eritrea	..	..	..	27	7	7	33	67	108	50	106	..	..	51
Ethiopia	102	283	343	188	141	23	127	94	133	101	456	440	429	203
Gabon	-109	-29	22	79	62	-16	-4	-89	-221	-150	-259	53	233	-33
Gambia, The	55	34	5	-1	1	36	4	1	12	15	20	22	20	12
Ghana	143	290	323	220	339	609	251	325	111	119	424	127	246	310
Guinea	54	160	242	128	71	76	165	77	33	-29	30	47	136	99
Guinea-Bissau	72	37	22	25	14	25	30	11	1	12	-14	23	40	20
Kenya	509	92	81	-257	98	-100	-230	-236	-270	59	-93	298	310	1
Lesotho	12	66	62	51	46	54	41	35	20	31	-17	15	33	40
Liberia	91	0	20	-15	0	0	0	-1	-1	-1	-1	89	20	-1
Madagascar	401	60	75	39	51	96	218	30	71	121	112	191	141	93
Malawi	156	87	145	94	151	128	123	113	102	88	68	90	59	108
Mali	100	139	63	101	176	132	98	58	69	36	48	87	114	99
Mauritania	129	84	97	100	55	94	39	-14	-13	51	23	107	79	48
Mauritius	124	-1	22	83	255	32	57	-93	38	-269	-62	56	29	15
Mozambique	..	231	168	187	182	208	236	195	90	96	44	300	292	163
Namibia	..	..	..	..	..	..	..	..	..	..	..	..	..	..
Niger	233	46	35	41	-13	12	62	61	25	62	63	114	106	36
Nigeria	1,510	-1,343	-35	-148	-486	-1,110	-525	-497	-430	-938	-1,648	1,015	203	-624
Rwanda	31	71	50	20	56	52	80	93	91	41	45	28	68	62
São Tomé and Principe	9	23	14	14	12	10	3	4	13	9	5	6	11	13
Senegal	230	180	72	47	46	56	112	40	-70	-9	148	195	216	60
Seychelles	12	13	6	8	-7	2	2	9	-8	-3	-4	6	7	2
Sierra Leone	54	36	86	102	55	40	40	49	17	56	58	35	10	46
Somalia	125	0	0	0	0	0	0	0	0	0	0	149	81	4
South Africa	..	..	..	1,524	1,478	-478	-473	-813	-148	914	431	..	..	304
Sudan	790	94	91	9	-3	-18	-38	-59	-44	-59	-54	565	163	17
Swaziland	22	-10	-9	-5	2	8	39	17	16	1	27	22	-4	5
Tanzania	352	301	136	145	113	78	215	128	205	92	68	294	194	154
Togo	101	40	5	43	41	69	32	56	6	6	11	91	28	35
Uganda	116	229	289	209	188	183	233	92	90	141	276	100	159	196
Zambia	421	100	29	88	539	80	121	-49	206	190	38	289	146	121
Zimbabwe	93	647	389	132	250	24	37	-160	67	-136	-43	190	-29	133
NORTH AFRICA	5,182	1,306	88	1,476	1,617	1,249	-531	-2,219	-2,595	-1,964	-715	5,336	3,704	-47
Algeria	869	304	-782	2,078	1,739	1,527	-263	-1,646	-1,953	-1,601	-1,971	1,435	957	-225
Egypt, Arab Republic	2,297	-25	183	218	-365	-440	-65	-212	-618	-505	871	2,177	1,462	-39
Libya	..	..	..	..	..	..	..	..	..	..	..	..	..	..
Morocco	1,584	375	40	-445	-284	-250	-810	-174	-439	4	-475	1,250	708	-117
Tunisia	321	396	272	131	450	426	605	-220	479	173	1,000	373	262	347
ALL AFRICA	13,754	5,147	4,943	6,333	6,245	2,111	486	-3,154	-2,929	-1,950	-1,048	12,177	9,038	2,252

6-17. Net transfers: long- and short-term loans, including IMF

	Millions of U.S. dollars (current prices)											Annual Average		
	1980	1992	1993	1994	1995	1996	1997	1998	1999	2000	2001	75-84	85-89	90-MR
SUB-SAHARAN AFRICA	6,512	383	2,471	-2,227	2,247	-2,605	-315	-6,096	-5,576	-5,461	-5,399	5,414	2,840	-1,851
excluding South Africa	6,512	383	1,613	-2,844	155	-1,819	1,501	-4,686	-3,469	-5,484	-3,449	5,414	2,840	-1,477
excl. S.Africa & Nigeria	4,641	2,962	2,054	-1,058	1,629	607	2,740	-3,849	-2,626	-4,033	-1,185	4,376	2,855	170
Angola	0	802	202	200	-222	-266	223	-595	-743	-955	41	88	926	-34
Benin	27	26	73	92	81	82	91	-44	48	-51	71	72	31	53
Botswana	-1	-14	12	-36	-26	-123	-49	-90	-45	-59	-40	20	5	-44
Burkina Faso	45	86	91	100	104	63	53	32	95	22	77	43	59	74
Burundi	36	85	32	12	15	-5	-6	2	38	6	9	36	74	24
Cameroon	389	189	-55	123	-151	-450	444	-228	-388	-377	-325	234	51	-77
Cape Verde	0	9	4	21	30	-8	9	35	56	6	43	7	5	18
Central African Republic	28	31	49	21	19	9	-8	-19	13	-19	-19	17	55	21
Chad	-9	113	42	63	55	95	65	4	56	6	20	21	44	59
Comoros	13	12	7	10	11	6	9	-2	4	2	3	11	13	5
Congo, Democratic Rep. of	13	-76	-23	-151	38	-103	229	-31	-5	-4	-16	232	28	-14
Congo, Republic of	473	-99	258	-152	69	-650	39	-76	144	-104	-387	168	47	-116
Côte d'Ivoire	572	61	217	-1,459	514	1,602	-109	-1,764	-1,410	-1,094	-759	277	-290	-313
Djibouti	7	26	31	-13	11	15	9	-3	-8	-6	3	8	16	8
Equatorial Guinea	40	11	12	15	-9	-1	17	13	-20	-11	-1	9	10	4
Eritrea	..	..	..	27	7	7	33	64	100	58	101	..	..	49
Ethiopia	67	186	285	144	70	-35	83	23	101	50	359	417	363	144
Gabon	-275	-489	-67	-167	-226	-331	-2	-343	-369	-532	-466	-7	205	-256
Gambia, The	55	27	18	-27	-14	38	-12	2	11	13	15	23	7	7
Ghana	22	185	248	202	312	506	111	173	-98	-210	265	86	130	198
Guinea	-11	106	188	76	49	25	348	-121	2	-98	-76	25	116	51
Guinea-Bissau	71	20	17	23	7	26	23	2	-5	11	-28	26	28	14
Kenya	489	-147	-112	-652	-197	-462	-199	-433	-494	-66	-401	168	70	-243
Lesotho	18	54	49	39	30	38	20	12	-2	8	-44	13	27	24
Liberia	60	-1	1	-14	-2	10	-21	3	-1	-5	-5	69	9	-5
Madagascar	419	10	35	0	39	37	116	60	75	-38	46	157	38	43
Malawi	101	69	78	69	141	148	18	87	109	75	26	55	14	76
Mali	92	98	19	67	175	73	247	-57	59	-26	-15	84	87	73
Mauritania	117	-74	39	54	30	69	114	-126	-46	20	-2	90	47	13
Mauritius	70	-1	-24	204	241	21	47	-105	-46	-159	-25	30	-23	15
Mozambique	0	187	20	133	116	148	290	177	155	-31	148	119	274	125
Namibia	..	..	..	..	..	..	..	..	..	..	..	..	..	..
Niger	202	31	1	9	-24	2	83	9	23	35	29	70	46	10
Nigeria	1,872	-2,579	-440	-1,785	-1,474	-2,425	-1,239	-838	-843	-1,451	-2,264	1,038	-16	-1,648
Rwanda	31	61	39	-14	44	45	104	52	54	0	30	28	60	45
São Tomé and Principe	7	25	13	7	12	3	4	4	19	7	3	6	12	11
Senegal	151	109	28	-110	-13	-143	54	-6	-110	-245	149	151	67	-32
Seychelles	-427	-7	-10	-2	-25	-7	4	25	-16	33	3	-7	3	0
Sierra Leone	39	17	68	37	32	22	16	29	6	45	39	23	1	26
Somalia	135	0	0	0	-1	-3	-7	5	-1	-7	2	148	62	4
South Africa	0	0	858	617	2,092	-786	-1,816	-1,410	-2,107	23	-1,950	0	0	-373
Sudan	707	259	81	9	-15	-131	-173	41	-166	-46	-133	544	-17	-3
Swaziland	18	-17	-15	-10	1	-13	180	-129	21	-9	22	16	-14	-3
Tanzania	324	241	5	98	6	44	179	69	161	39	-96	288	93	81
Togo	74	15	-70	47	28	45	-4	37	84	-45	24	70	-5	13
Uganda	118	202	209	185	146	163	201	68	39	122	259	84	117	163
Zambia	219	-86	-124	-81	-111	74	-165	-45	-5	70	100	203	151	-63
Zimbabwe	122	585	70	-202	193	-96	-15	-586	-146	-464	-230	158	-191	-62
NORTH AFRICA	2,117	-5,651	-6,783	-3,364	-3,325	-3,815	-4,887	-7,233	-6,711	-6,640	-5,107	3,374	-596	-5,353
Algeria	-294	-2,230	-2,660	450	-471	-513	-2,477	-3,984	-3,753	-3,229	-3,278	320	-745	-2,237
Egypt, Arab Republic	1,676	-1,816	-1,559	-1,137	-1,315	-1,672	-443	130	-1,494	-1,422	-694	1,930	168	-1,213
Libya	..	..	..	..	..	..	..	..	..	..	..	..	..	..
Morocco	857	-1,801	-1,363	-1,925	-1,696	-1,517	-1,943	-1,313	-1,341	-980	-1,450	822	-275	-1,363
Tunisia	12	122	-282	-81	113	133	30	-1,232	393	-1,009	345	218	-59	-135
ALL AFRICA	8,630	-5,268	-4,312	-5,591	-1,078	-6,420	-5,201	-13,329	-12,287	-12,101	-10,506	8,789	2,244	-7,204

6-18. Net transfers: long-term loans, including IMF

	Millions of U.S. dollars (current prices)											Annual Average		
	1980	1992	1993	1994	1995	1996	1997	1998	1999	2000	2001	75-84	85-89	90-MR
SUB-SAHARAN AFRICA	6,084	-203	2,873	713	80	-4,091	-2,757	-4,391	-3,772	-3,320	-3,543	4,894	1,669	-1,545
excluding South Africa	6,084	-203	2,015	-155	-493	-2,650	-1,400	-3,087	-2,846	-3,579	-3,114	4,894	1,669	-1,304
excl. S.Africa & Nigeria	5,103	2,971	2,912	1,068	851	-497	-331	-2,069	-1,998	-1,952	-661	4,355	2,537	389
Angola	0	452	597	213	139	-167	225	-730	-495	-682	-741	90	689	-52
Benin	63	54	72	91	67	84	6	11	17	2	60	74	42	53
Botswana	14	-13	12	-36	-27	-124	-81	-57	-56	-53	-44	20	6	-45
Burkina Faso	53	114	115	90	92	66	40	42	52	42	100	45	57	76
Burundi	38	87	41	12	7	5	-10	2	-7	18	-5	36	75	22
Cameroon	374	306	58	118	-272	-256	-173	-270	-227	-200	-51	224	75	-58
Cape Verde	0	8	4	20	13	16	7	35	44	13	37	7	5	17
Central African Republic	32	32	43	38	18	15	-8	-16	-7	4	-13	18	55	24
Chad	-1	134	42	66	55	93	57	9	54	8	22	21	40	60
Comoros	13	12	6	11	9	8	4	2	-2	1	9	11	14	5
Congo, Democratic Rep. of	106	18	43	-5	-18	-39	0	0	6	0	0	241	2	12
Congo, Republic of	448	4	362	-166	-131	-296	-73	-2	6	-13	-58	174	44	-63
Côte d'Ivoire	465	-177	-171	181	-99	-324	-1,018	-662	-1,021	-737	-564	292	-511	-392
Djibouti	7	33	17	15	7	16	7	0	-5	-3	3	7	14	13
Equatorial Guinea	36	11	12	5	0	-3	-3	-1	2	-1	-1	9	13	3
Eritrea	..	..	..	27	7	7	33	64	105	48	101	..	..	49
Ethiopia	83	241	319	148	79	-31	81	25	101	62	361	419	364	154
Gabon	-228	-275	-19	-27	-160	-252	-247	-236	-455	-310	-441	-13	174	-204
Gambia, The	54	27	-2	-7	-4	31	-2	0	5	9	17	21	14	6
Ghana	108	188	223	125	270	493	119	169	-52	-37	317	96	147	195
Guinea	30	127	204	88	27	32	119	10	-23	-71	-29	27	107	52
Guinea-Bissau	71	35	20	21	9	21	27	6	-4	2	-25	22	37	15
Kenya	338	-119	-132	-549	-168	-347	-421	-402	-388	-65	-177	172	74	-201
Lesotho	10	53	50	39	30	38	21	12	-2	8	-44	13	28	24
Liberia	67	-1	11	-15	-2	-2	0	0	-2	0	0	72	10	-2
Madagascar	373	24	48	19	35	77	125	-7	-12	47	53	162	56	41
Malawi	119	54	117	68	111	99	96	90	85	80	50	63	20	80
Mali	96	121	22	76	153	72	76	39	65	35	33	82	94	77
Mauritania	115	64	55	62	22	63	3	-47	-39	40	-10	90	46	17
Mauritius	98	-53	-21	37	199	-39	-7	-155	-19	-321	-99	33	-19	-39
Mozambique	0	188	92	132	106	160	193	183	48	44	50	119	265	121
Namibia	..	..	..	..	..	..	..	..	..	..	..	..	..	..
Niger	168	32	12	25	-26	1	49	38	21	42	44	77	49	19
Nigeria	981	-3,174	-897	-1,223	-1,344	-2,153	-1,069	-1,018	-848	-1,628	-2,452	540	-869	-1,693
Rwanda	29	65	45	19	48	45	72	68	52	18	33	27	62	49
São Tomé and Principe	9	22	13	12	11	8	2	3	12	8	5	6	10	12
Senegal	160	127	46	-19	-26	-65	34	-51	-128	-69	101	150	90	-13
Seychelles	12	8	0	2	-14	-3	-3	3	-13	-5	-6	6	3	-3
Sierra Leone	39	17	68	37	33	25	32	21	10	44	32	23	1	27
Somalia	122	0	0	0	-1	-3	0	0	-1	0	0	144	70	4
South Africa	0	0	858	868	573	-1,441	-1,357	-1,304	-926	260	-430	0	0	-242
Sudan	727	81	81	9	-18	-31	-53	-4	-19	-7	-3	509	111	25
Swaziland	13	-18	-16	-10	-3	-4	32	3	-2	-16	15	17	-16	-5
Tanzania	297	243	33	83	31	-19	173	66	159	5	-8	253	149	86
Togo	81	28	-3	37	33	45	18	42	7	10	16	74	-19	24
Uganda	109	200	257	174	152	143	193	69	37	132	261	87	115	165
Zambia	280	-68	-122	-80	-6	-6	50	-109	123	103	9	187	60	-31
Zimbabwe	82	484	209	-71	42	-170	-147	-335	-84	-188	-72	150	-179	-20
NORTH AFRICA	2,344	-4,410	-4,503	-3,090	-3,359	-3,892	-4,996	-6,910	-6,822	-5,627	-3,892	3,253	-2	-4,505
Algeria	-570	-1,584	-2,531	548	-71	-570	-2,298	-3,993	-3,752	-3,245	-3,245	463	-635	-2,047
Egypt, Arab Republic	1,930	-1,065	-883	-935	-1,622	-1,515	-824	-914	-1,297	-1,120	187	1,755	572	-932
Libya	..	..	..	..	..	..	..	..	..	..	..	..	..	..
Morocco	922	-1,966	-1,271	-1,820	-1,650	-1,586	-1,871	-1,192	-1,506	-943	-1,437	784	-136	-1,350
Tunisia	92	-22	-163	-346	-53	-93	117	-673	-28	-319	603	218	-79	-112
ALL AFRICA	8,428	-4,614	-1,630	-2,377	-3,279	-7,982	-7,753	-11,301	-10,595	-8,946	-7,435	8,147	1,666	-6,051

6-19. Long-term debt: official concessional

	Millions of U.S. dollars (current prices)											Annual Average		
	1980	*1992*	*1993*	*1994*	*1995*	*1996*	*1997*	*1998*	*1999*	*2000*	*2001*	*75-84*	*85-89*	*90-MR*
SUB-SAHARAN AFRICA	16,381	66,261	69,882	76,182	81,076	83,062	83,307	89,822	84,404	82,668	79,462	16,447	42,937	76,506
excluding South Africa	16,381	66,261	69,882	76,182	81,076	83,062	83,307	89,822	84,404	82,668	79,462	16,447	42,937	76,506
excl. S.Africa & Nigeria	15,942	65,289	68,789	74,892	79,699	81,709	81,984	88,240	82,680	81,211	78,123	16,079	42,520	75,256
Angola	..	1,302	1,315	1,405	1,490	2,152	2,212	2,385	2,004	1,791	1,567	18	423	1,675
Benin	166	1,105	1,165	1,270	1,253	1,293	1,265	1,333	1,359	1,342	1,407	166	539	1,237
Botswana	59	235	265	299	345	328	295	301	283	262	241	86	126	272
Burkina Faso	221	820	916	908	1,004	1,088	1,079	1,215	1,298	1,161	1,249	177	493	1,005
Burundi	104	890	946	1,012	1,047	1,040	989	1,048	1,023	1,003	950	107	570	964
Cameroon	873	2,350	2,484	3,503	4,101	4,152	4,233	4,555	4,265	4,210	3,850	690	1,335	3,450
Cape Verde	..	105	107	133	147	154	162	193	257	269	304	32	78	168
Central African Republic	59	629	674	723	765	768	724	745	741	714	678	64	354	690
Chad	171	538	592	674	692	760	803	872	927	903	895	141	218	713
Comoros	43	170	167	181	192	196	195	203	197	193	213	44	153	186
Congo, Democratic Rep. of	862	3,257	3,265	3,453	3,563	3,412	3,175	3,471	3,311	3,139	3,014	829	2,002	3,297
Congo, Republic of	404	1,756	1,690	1,884	1,984	2,003	1,854	1,886	1,730	1,647	1,627	373	885	1,801
Côte d'Ivoire	438	3,504	3,696	3,883	4,563	4,806	4,503	4,943	4,418	4,126	3,880	411	1,770	4,068
Djibouti	15	217	229	253	267	278	252	263	248	237	234	19	123	236
Equatorial Guinea	32	132	139	142	148	145	139	144	142	137	132	31	84	137
Eritrea	..	..	..	29	37	42	73	140	236	281	382	..	..	152
Ethiopia	562	7,858	8,184	8,483	8,715	8,693	8,632	8,810	4,798	4,811	5,057	1,352	5,913	7,438
Gabon	113	448	408	579	708	747	898	953	825	1,365	1,282	87	230	760
Gambia, The	68	298	310	336	361	394	388	417	418	421	423	59	185	357
Ghana	775	2,574	2,895	3,343	3,741	4,006	4,077	4,620	4,822	4,746	4,656	683	1,447	3,665
Guinea	678	1,977	2,157	2,329	2,457	2,426	2,479	2,649	2,618	2,536	2,485	734	1,256	2,299
Guinea-Bissau	87	439	475	534	565	675	666	698	668	607	569	63	238	558
Kenya	684	2,788	3,090	3,394	3,879	3,938	3,762	4,123	4,131	4,089	3,950	650	1,741	3,520
Lesotho	44	371	382	440	470	468	435	448	454	448	425	48	183	414
Liberia	211	573	599	622	635	610	585	599	582	568	556	221	540	592
Madagascar	467	1,958	1,952	2,118	2,242	2,132	2,681	2,913	2,918	2,875	2,763	499	1,249	2,352
Malawi	258	1,310	1,502	1,681	1,897	1,946	1,973	2,184	2,475	2,452	2,407	275	743	1,842
Mali	613	2,691	2,693	2,464	2,660	2,688	2,627	2,648	2,632	2,492	2,456	592	1,652	2,557
Mauritania	526	1,327	1,521	1,598	1,688	1,739	1,700	1,717	1,809	1,857	1,639	507	1,174	1,600
Mauritius	65	385	384	417	441	403	345	354	316	299	274	65	209	364
Mozambique	..	2,634	2,864	3,239	2,936	3,204	3,185	4,054	3,517	3,485	2,069	269	1,910	2,972
Namibia	..	..	..	..	..	..	..	..	..	..	..	..	..	..
Niger	155	879	932	978	1,017	1,033	1,051	1,160	1,178	1,185	1,193	173	611	1,022
Nigeria	439	972	1,094	1,290	1,377	1,354	1,322	1,582	1,724	1,457	1,339	368	417	1,249
Rwanda	141	787	835	903	961	977	985	1,114	1,158	1,145	1,162	126	487	952
São Tomé and Principe	20	145	158	177	221	218	219	236	284	278	277	16	65	204
Senegal	400	2,080	2,111	2,104	2,239	2,286	2,393	2,775	2,673	2,579	2,620	412	1,598	2,315
Seychelles	19	70	66	67	68	67	67	70	68	68	67	13	55	69
Sierra Leone	176	385	493	591	701	737	732	783	778	815	858	157	267	626
Somalia	546	1,540	1,546	1,576	1,596	1,557	1,503	1,531	1,516	1,487	1,461	564	1,304	1,537
South Africa	..	..	..	0	0	0	0	0	0	0	0	..	..	0
Sudan	1,730	4,597	4,671	4,775	4,838	4,750	4,636	4,704	4,654	4,569	4,504	1,697	3,727	4,646
Swaziland	82	134	124	141	153	140	126	127	124	113	118	60	113	133
Tanzania	2,692	3,845	4,017	4,373	4,455	4,483	5,111	5,524	5,858	5,542	5,260	2,556	3,031	4,625
Togo	318	801	811	892	912	971	961	1,052	1,046	1,005	987	228	456	909
Uganda	254	1,806	2,130	2,456	2,766	2,876	2,973	3,137	2,824	2,901	3,044	222	792	2,499
Zambia	797	2,484	2,616	3,087	3,294	3,502	3,488	3,648	3,532	3,578	3,557	672	1,561	3,112
Zimbabwe	15	1,092	1,209	1,443	1,464	1,407	1,356	1,493	1,565	1,476	1,381	81	628	1,313
NORTH AFRICA	13,488	26,577	27,757	30,680	32,771	36,750	34,493	35,625	34,525	32,335	30,548	11,996	22,083	31,003
Algeria	1,269	1,062	1,318	2,054	3,076	3,287	3,145	3,303	3,415	3,102	2,698	1,031	599	2,356
Egypt, Arab Republic	8,116	17,152	17,997	19,532	20,285	23,969	22,524	23,405	22,480	21,063	19,973	7,117	13,201	19,794
Libya	..	..	..	..	..	..	..	..	..	..	..	..	..	..
Morocco	2,717	5,467	5,532	6,012	6,371	6,659	6,285	6,419	6,046	5,580	5,283	2,597	5,982	6,084
Tunisia	1,386	2,896	2,910	3,082	3,039	2,836	2,539	2,497	2,584	2,589	2,595	1,251	2,301	2,769
ALL AFRICA	29,869	92,837	97,640	106,862	113,846	119,812	117,800	125,447	118,929	115,002	110,010	28,443	65,020	107,508

6-20. Long-term debt: official nonconcessional

	Millions of U.S. dollars (current prices)											Annual Average		
	1980	1992	1993	1994	1995	1996	1997	1998	1999	2000	2001	75-84	85-89	90-MR
SUB-SAHARAN AFRICA	9,293	51,639	50,302	54,964	56,657	52,638	47,652	48,639	43,897	51,976	48,102	8,334	34,247	50,760
excluding South Africa	9,293	51,639	50,302	54,964	56,657	52,638	47,652	48,639	43,866	51,832	47,980	8,334	34,247	50,735
excl. S.Africa & Nigeria	8,740	34,284	33,149	36,443	37,542	35,348	31,963	32,552	28,940	26,714	23,389	7,601	25,170	32,358
Angola	..	637	608	688	736	716	658	1,016	976	912	871	32	390	758
Benin	50	214	203	213	226	150	128	135	110	100	93	30	85	163
Botswana	76	351	340	334	306	248	203	187	152	118	89	76	309	253
Burkina Faso	39	154	148	130	130	70	58	63	50	46	57	34	112	98
Burundi	6	52	49	48	47	40	33	30	25	24	23	9	55	41
Cameroon	364	2,658	2,555	2,789	3,011	3,030	2,944	3,150	2,974	2,850	1,941	299	961	2,680
Cape Verde	..	29	31	31	32	30	26	38	42	39	22	29	32	32
Central African Republic	40	81	78	62	71	68	64	63	52	49	46	37	106	68
Chad	34	126	116	78	137	134	115	115	101	91	83	24	28	100
Comoros	0	7	7	8	8	9	8	9	9	9	8	2	13	9
Congo, Democratic Rep. of	1,747	4,852	4,679	4,981	5,195	5,002	4,620	4,845	4,447	4,245	4,082	1,327	3,725	4,747
Congo, Republic of	200	1,236	1,192	1,949	2,059	1,797	1,598	1,551	1,422	1,346	1,251	158	815	1,504
Côte d'Ivoire	809	5,093	4,906	4,760	4,654	3,981	3,403	3,359	2,837	2,543	2,319	694	3,117	3,957
Djibouti	7	2	2	2	2	1	1	1	1	1	1	4	5	2
Equatorial Guinea	14	66	61	62	65	61	56	58	52	50	48	13	62	60
Eritrea	..	..	..	0	0	2	3	7	17	17	16	..	..	8
Ethiopia	76	380	399	433	464	437	442	456	437	399	375	82	208	414
Gabon	203	1,976	1,929	2,848	3,069	3,081	2,637	2,755	2,337	1,964	1,664	173	807	2,361
Gambia, The	5	39	35	32	24	18	13	17	13	15	13	5	34	25
Ghana	259	448	435	427	400	442	395	375	327	275	453	181	309	406
Guinea	183	382	398	460	448	458	454	448	414	375	330	149	378	428
Guinea-Bissau	10	224	212	200	202	180	172	176	165	108	58	15	145	178
Kenya	523	1,172	1,060	1,459	1,373	1,168	982	884	670	570	548	490	1,311	1,040
Lesotho	2	66	97	116	137	134	131	120	116	133	91	5	38	104
Liberia	148	314	303	306	319	301	285	295	275	276	266	131	299	300
Madagascar	105	1,399	1,277	1,333	1,380	1,344	1,149	1,152	1,411	1,382	958	251	1,408	1,309
Malawi	184	193	177	170	157	126	106	106	102	85	67	132	256	147
Mali	15	81	89	79	77	75	66	179	168	163	160	13	44	107
Mauritania	57	410	363	383	385	361	316	271	309	274	210	74	343	341
Mauritius	89	252	241	233	223	212	209	227	225	201	166	74	242	232
Mozambique	..	1,857	1,832	1,888	2,227	2,127	2,008	1,905	1,116	1,054	151	153	796	1,593
Namibia	..	..	..	..	..	..	..	..	..	..	..	..	..	..
Niger	101	286	278	290	313	298	272	284	246	228	177	90	302	272
Nigeria	554	17,355	17,153	18,521	19,115	17,291	15,689	16,087	14,926	25,117	24,592	733	9,077	18,377
Rwanda	1	1	1	1	7	6	7	4	2	1	0	1	2	3
São Tomé and Principe	3	23	23	23	11	8	7	7	6	12	12	5	21	15
Senegal	253	800	829	840	868	816	699	484	433	371	331	272	916	671
Seychelles	6	28	31	38	42	41	39	44	40	37	34	6	24	36
Sierra Leone	71	321	305	296	265	218	201	220	198	185	154	51	154	229
Somalia	21	322	316	323	329	325	315	320	310	305	302	60	299	319
South Africa	..	..	..	0	0	0	0	0	31	145	122	..	..	37
Sudan	1,564	2,911	2,870	2,990	3,083	3,026	2,886	2,962	2,851	2,760	2,699	1,201	2,537	2,927
Swaziland	79	66	63	56	56	66	70	94	100	99	96	57	113	77
Tanzania	348	1,601	1,386	1,354	1,337	1,217	682	662	594	495	411	341	1,376	1,111
Togo	236	284	267	287	322	289	253	274	239	225	216	180	423	275
Uganda	37	366	354	320	212	197	318	176	139	122	225	63	311	263
Zambia	688	1,672	1,462	1,854	1,793	1,697	1,600	1,572	946	839	807	621	1,794	1,508
Zimbabwe	86	852	1,144	1,273	1,345	1,321	1,295	1,421	1,293	1,169	1,153	86	464	1,130
NORTH AFRICA	9,190	28,964	29,156	33,654	38,259	35,037	33,353	34,466	32,486	30,438	30,058	9,205	28,681	31,863
Algeria	2,226	5,471	5,188	8,869	12,580	14,874	15,102	16,124	15,051	14,341	13,375	1,739	3,884	10,965
Egypt, Arab Republic	4,507	7,525	7,448	8,202	8,510	3,549	3,205	3,343	3,064	2,744	3,276	4,824	15,536	5,615
Libya	..	..	..	..	..	..	..	..	..	..	..	..	..	..
Morocco	802	10,121	9,955	10,114	10,144	9,305	7,934	7,836	7,111	6,452	5,853	983	5,535	8,620
Tunisia	575	3,012	3,338	3,804	4,361	4,644	4,447	4,562	3,830	3,441	3,533	518	1,675	3,700
ALL AFRICA	18,483	80,603	79,458	88,619	94,915	87,675	81,005	83,104	76,383	82,414	78,161	17,539	62,927	82,623

6-21. Long-term debt: private

	Millions of U.S. dollars (current prices)											Annual Average		
	1980	*1992*	*1993*	*1994*	*1995*	*1996*	*1997*	*1998*	*1999*	*2000*	*2001*	*75-84*	*85-89*	*90-MR*
SUB-SAHARAN AFRICA	20,830	33,097	33,121	46,914	48,644	44,849	41,849	40,416	38,770	37,111	35,949	17,630	37,739	40,084
excluding South Africa	20,830	33,097	33,121	33,879	33,872	30,514	27,919	27,108	25,709	21,948	20,375	17,630	37,739	30,653
excl. S.Africa & Nigeria	16,454	24,615	24,626	25,424	25,923	23,428	22,004	21,047	19,752	18,287	16,910	13,134	23,760	22,822
Angola	..	6,200	6,781	7,031	7,318	6,511	5,813	5,666	5,667	5,282	5,005	557	3,853	6,069
Benin	118	5	4	4	4	4	3	4	3	3	3	142	295	5
Botswana	8	21	48	50	47	36	28	24	32	28	19	15	43	32
Burkina Faso	20	5	4	4	5	4	4	4	4	3	3	18	34	7
Burundi	8	4	3	2	2	1	1	1	1	1	1	10	22	3
Cameroon	1,014	1,525	1,397	1,189	1,186	1,069	751	658	727	647	155	727	1,386	1,061
Cape Verde	..	2	2	2	6	12	12	10	9	8	15	0	3	7
Central African Republic	48	20	21	18	18	14	14	33	33	33	33	40	23	23
Chad	54	7	6	6	2	17	17	17	16	15	14	42	31	11
Comoros	0	0	0	0	0	0	0	0	0	0	0	0	0	0
Congo, Democratic Rep. of	1,462	852	836	860	878	861	834	899	504	496	488	1,393	879	772
Congo, Republic of	652	883	1,232	941	913	866	832	814	782	764	753	546	1,408	902
Côte d'Ivoire	5,091	5,263	5,125	5,210	5,345	4,429	4,592	4,330	4,039	3,876	3,764	3,507	5,570	4,746
Djibouti	5	0	0	0	0	0	0	0	0	0	0	3	3	0
Equatorial Guinea	7	16	15	16	17	16	14	15	13	12	12	9	18	15
Eritrea	..	..	..	0	0	0	0	0	0	0	0	..	..	0
Ethiopia	49	765	704	652	594	354	350	348	127	117	100	103	565	456
Gabon	955	626	596	268	199	143	131	125	129	117	84	766	850	317
Gambia, The	24	9	5	1	0	0	0	0	1	2	2	16	25	4
Ghana	131	332	345	419	525	799	851	919	840	755	811	132	291	598
Guinea	159	91	104	98	82	98	76	30	29	29	29	133	133	73
Guinea-Bissau	36	30	25	28	32	1	1	1	1	1	0	17	45	15
Kenya	1,286	1,769	1,696	1,266	1,153	953	805	834	742	696	542	898	1,235	1,221
Lesotho	11	28	24	22	35	61	77	93	91	76	58	9	19	53
Liberia	156	195	200	208	208	199	192	199	205	197	189	115	186	198
Madagascar	346	112	87	86	84	77	45	41	40	39	73	256	272	79
Malawi	192	64	50	49	28	24	21	20	19	18	10	128	72	38
Mali	36	6	4	2	2	0	0	0	0	0	0	30	37	3
Mauritania	131	88	19	9	8	25	24	22	20	19	17	118	125	37
Mauritius	165	306	275	448	751	783	787	702	733	453	412	94	148	517
Mozambique	..	227	162	1,743	1,815	1,872	1,930	1,770	1,759	1,728	1,553	70	768	1,310
Namibia	..	..	..	..	..	..	..	..	..	..	..	..	..	..
Niger	432	206	182	157	133	110	96	72	70	68	62	267	368	146
Nigeria	4,376	8,482	8,496	8,455	7,949	7,086	5,915	6,061	5,958	3,661	3,466	4,496	13,979	7,831
Rwanda	8	2	1	2	2	2	1	1	1	1	1	7	9	2
São Tomé and Principe	0	1	1	1	0	0	0	0	0	4	5	1	2	1
Senegal	461	162	156	153	127	53	66	33	23	21	61	301	303	108
Seychelles	0	33	35	43	36	30	25	31	24	20	16	2	27	28
Sierra Leone	157	457	522	509	92	92	91	91	90	6	2	168	375	235
Somalia	28	35	34	36	37	36	34	35	34	33	32	86	58	35
South Africa	..	..	..	13,035	14,772	14,334	13,930	13,309	13,061	15,163	15,573	..	..	14,147
Sudan	854	1,972	1,949	2,131	2,355	2,090	1,973	2,055	1,843	1,813	1,782	872	1,730	2,016
Swaziland	24	4	2	1	0	0	31	26	24	20	22	14	15	12
Tanzania	341	415	418	416	461	433	298	283	267	236	110	263	488	359
Togo	415	51	50	51	52	50	0	0	0	0	0	247	64	30
Uganda	244	260	115	93	87	81	80	66	26	24	37	149	301	125
Zambia	726	372	333	259	224	193	183	141	106	96	149	671	559	242
Zimbabwe	594	1,193	1,051	935	1,052	1,009	906	618	603	532	489	561	1,113	897
NORTH AFRICA	21,909	30,263	28,409	27,251	25,745	22,433	20,237	19,664	18,545	16,301	16,980	17,043	31,982	24,517
Algeria	13,545	19,221	18,588	17,514	15,647	13,124	10,465	9,054	7,430	5,890	4,713	9,882	17,164	13,514
Egypt, Arab Republic	2,070	3,732	2,915	2,520	2,066	1,484	1,206	1,258	1,039	1,116	2,612	2,132	6,587	2,676
Libya	..	..	..	..	..	..	..	..	..	..	..	..	..	..
Morocco	4,505	5,646	5,373	5,661	5,901	5,600	5,745	6,155	5,750	5,657	5,580	3,534	6,064	5,782
Tunisia	1,429	1,502	1,372	1,319	1,817	2,086	2,531	2,621	3,852	3,639	4,075	1,069	1,832	2,327
ALL AFRICA	42,738	63,360	61,530	74,165	74,389	67,282	62,086	60,080	57,315	53,412	52,929	34,673	69,722	64,601

6-22. Total external debt

	Millions of U.S. dollars (current prices)											Annual Average		
	1980	1992	1993	1994	1995	1996	1997	1998	1999	2000	2001	75-84	85-89	90-MR
SUB-SAHARAN AFRICA	60,707	182,487	188,531	221,592	235,733	231,611	221,130	228,754	215,290	211,442	201,582	54,950	136,779	208,218
excluding South Africa	60,707	182,487	188,531	199,921	210,375	205,561	195,857	204,001	191,382	186,581	177,532	54,950	136,779	191,891
excl. S.Africa & Nigeria	51,785	153,468	157,795	166,828	176,283	174,155	167,402	173,707	162,257	155,226	146,413	46,435	110,855	160,586
Angola	..	10,070	10,586	11,295	11,502	10,548	9,950	10,752	10,233	9,309	9,600	695	5,137	10,120
Benin	424	1,373	1,447	1,589	1,614	1,592	1,627	1,651	1,686	1,600	1,665	408	1,078	1,539
Botswana	147	613	661	694	709	618	566	520	487	423	370	182	481	570
Burkina Faso	330	1,040	1,119	1,131	1,270	1,296	1,299	1,454	1,575	1,406	1,490	269	708	1,240
Burundi	166	1,022	1,062	1,123	1,158	1,127	1,066	1,119	1,131	1,100	1,065	153	697	1,070
Cameroon	2,588	7,426	7,387	8,270	9,385	9,582	9,334	9,917	9,440	9,243	7,146	1,976	4,445	8,392
Cape Verde	..	142	148	176	214	202	207	247	327	327	360	62	118	218
Central African Republic	195	814	875	888	946	933	883	919	909	858	822	181	557	862
Chad	284	723	768	828	900	994	1,023	1,091	1,141	1,115	1,104	227	323	903
Comoros	44	190	189	202	214	218	219	227	228	232	246	48	176	211
Congo, Democratic Rep. of	4,773	10,972	11,273	12,322	13,239	12,830	12,337	13,203	12,048	11,692	11,392	4,319	7,993	11,867
Congo, Republic of	1,526	4,770	5,081	5,413	6,004	5,241	5,071	5,119	5,033	4,887	4,496	1,227	3,849	5,075
Côte d'Ivoire	7,462	18,546	19,071	17,395	18,898	19,524	15,609	14,852	13,170	12,138	11,582	5,644	12,570	16,351
Djibouti	32	235	264	263	282	296	274	288	275	262	262	33	163	261
Equatorial Guinea	76	255	264	288	292	282	283	306	271	248	239	71	185	269
Eritrea	..	..	..	29	37	44	76	151	253	311	410	..	..	164
Ethiopia	824	9,341	9,703	10,063	10,308	10,078	10,077	10,347	5,544	5,483	5,697	1,656	6,850	8,699
Gabon	1,514	3,850	3,861	4,171	4,360	4,310	4,278	4,425	3,979	3,911	3,409	1,231	2,393	4,063
Gambia, The	137	403	426	423	426	452	425	460	465	483	489	116	301	434
Ghana	1,402	4,508	4,887	5,469	5,936	6,443	6,347	6,969	7,017	6,658	6,759	1,313	2,974	5,771
Guinea	1,134	2,634	2,848	3,110	3,242	3,240	3,519	3,546	3,522	3,388	3,254	1,119	1,949	3,117
Guinea-Bissau	140	761	787	852	898	937	921	966	934	804	668	110	465	831
Kenya	3,387	6,898	7,111	7,202	7,412	6,931	6,603	6,881	6,487	6,295	5,833	2,646	5,254	6,847
Lesotho	72	494	542	623	684	701	674	688	682	671	592	69	249	600
Liberia	686	1,922	1,956	2,056	2,154	2,107	2,012	2,103	2,077	2,032	1,987	620	1,550	2,017
Madagascar	1,248	3,911	3,805	4,096	4,322	4,146	4,109	4,394	4,755	4,701	4,160	1,187	3,267	4,168
Malawi	830	1,709	1,826	2,025	2,243	2,315	2,228	2,444	2,751	2,716	2,602	659	1,263	2,174
Mali	727	2,899	2,903	2,695	2,958	3,007	3,143	3,198	3,183	2,964	2,890	699	1,879	2,909
Mauritania	840	2,088	2,141	2,223	2,349	2,412	2,456	2,357	2,528	2,500	2,165	805	1,844	2,292
Mauritius	467	1,051	1,008	1,382	1,757	1,818	1,837	1,856	1,847	1,720	1,724	359	768	1,502
Mozambique	..	5,130	5,212	7,272	7,458	7,566	7,632	8,301	6,978	7,052	4,466	513	3,803	6,370
Namibia	..	..	..	..	..	..	..	..	..	..	..	..	..	..
Niger	863	1,517	1,542	1,525	1,587	1,538	1,572	1,654	1,641	1,638	1,555	640	1,481	1,582
Nigeria	8,921	29,019	30,736	33,092	34,093	31,407	28,455	30,294	29,126	31,355	31,119	8,515	25,924	31,305
Rwanda	190	857	909	952	1,028	1,043	1,111	1,226	1,292	1,271	1,283	158	540	1,041
São Tomé and Principe	24	190	210	223	245	234	237	257	320	315	313	22	97	238
Senegal	1,473	3,666	3,764	3,658	3,841	3,663	3,663	3,858	3,709	3,372	3,461	1,269	3,396	3,663
Seychelles	84	164	157	171	159	148	149	187	172	209	215	127	140	172
Sierra Leone	470	1,390	1,556	1,558	1,250	1,242	1,200	1,314	1,298	1,228	1,188	443	949	1,308
Somalia	660	2,447	2,500	2,616	2,678	2,643	2,561	2,635	2,606	2,561	2,532	785	1,939	2,550
South Africa	..	..	..	21,671	25,358	26,050	25,272	24,753	23,907	24,861	24,050	..	..	24,490
Sudan	5,177	15,450	15,836	16,918	17,603	16,972	16,326	16,843	16,132	15,741	15,348	4,807	10,945	16,097
Swaziland	206	210	196	206	220	208	385	275	301	295	308	146	263	257
Tanzania	5,324	6,669	6,784	7,239	7,412	7,370	7,181	7,653	8,049	7,386	6,676	4,883	6,280	7,120
Togo	1,122	1,353	1,294	1,456	1,476	1,488	1,346	1,472	1,521	1,432	1,406	757	1,127	1,406
Uganda	687	2,926	3,028	3,371	3,575	3,677	3,878	3,912	3,492	3,494	3,733	610	1,733	3,371
Zambia	3,244	6,709	6,485	6,816	6,966	7,068	6,668	6,879	5,868	5,731	5,671	2,954	5,982	6,562
Zimbabwe	786	4,060	4,285	4,524	5,007	4,976	4,919	4,707	4,577	4,022	3,780	982	2,671	4,295
NORTH AFRICA	53,517	93,748	90,886	97,761	103,426	101,642	95,922	97,888	93,522	82,856	79,583	46,420	96,530	94,261
Algeria	19,365	27,343	26,267	30,233	33,042	33,645	30,892	30,678	27,997	25,273	22,503	14,323	23,729	28,709
Egypt, Arab Republic	19,131	31,129	30,567	32,379	33,337	31,366	29,927	32,268	30,877	29,027	29,234	18,167	42,402	31,313
Libya	..	..	..	..	..	..	..	..	..	..	..	..	..	..
Morocco	9,259	22,061	21,459	22,158	22,665	21,889	20,196	20,526	19,191	17,945	16,962	8,335	19,338	20,948
Tunisia	3,527	8,543	8,694	9,614	10,820	11,379	11,230	10,850	11,880	10,610	10,884	3,002	6,284	10,037
ALL AFRICA	114,224	276,235	279,416	319,353	339,159	333,253	317,051	326,641	308,812	294,298	281,165	101,370	233,310	302,479

6-23. Structure of external debt

	Millions of U.S. dollars (current prices)													
	Bilateral				Multilateral				Private		Short-term		IMF	
	Concessional		Nonconcessional		Concessional		Nonconcessional							
	1980	2001	1980	2001	1980	2001	1980	2001	1980	2001	1980	2001	1980	2001
SUB-SAHARAN AFRICA	12,445	33,213	5,694	39,723	3,936	46,249	3,599	8,380	20,830	35,949	11,170	32,043	3,033	6,338
excluding South Africa	12,445	33,213	5,694	39,723	3,936	46,249	3,599	8,258	20,830	20,375	11,170	23,688	3,033	6,338
excluding South Africa & Nigeria	12,043	32,612	5,674	17,272	3,899	45,511	3,066	6,118	16,454	16,910	7,617	21,966	3,033	6,338
Angola	..	1,314	..	842	..	253	..	29	..	5,005	..	2,157	0	0
Benin	82	437	31	75	84	971	20	18	118	3	73	85	16	77
Botswana	28	77	23	2	32	164	53	87	8	19	4	21	0	0
Burkina Faso	89	212	30	23	133	1,037	9	35	20	3	35	64	15	117
Burundi	49	117	1	0	55	832	5	23	8	1	12	89	36	2
Cameroon	663	2,901	142	1,531	210	949	222	410	1,014	155	278	956	59	244
Cape Verde	..	71	..	14	..	233	..	8	..	15	..	19	0	0
Central African Republic	17	138	28	36	42	540	12	11	48	33	25	34	24	31
Chad	97	87	34	50	75	808	0	33	54	14	12	23	14	89
Comoros	21	51	0	0	21	162	0	8	0	0	1	24	0	1
Congo, Democratic Rep. of	667	1,525	1,620	3,508	194	1,489	127	573	1,462	488	329	3,431	373	377
Congo, Republic of	355	1,378	132	966	49	250	69	285	652	753	247	826	22	39
Côte d'Ivoire	369	2,257	355	1,195	69	1,622	454	1,124	5,091	3,764	1,059	1,155	65	464
Djibouti	14	92	5	0	1	142	1	1	5	0	6	12	0	16
Equatorial Guinea	30	50	13	41	2	82	1	7	7	12	7	45	16	2
Eritrea	..	153	..	10	..	229	..	6	..	0	..	12	..	0
Ethiopia	281	2,132	18	202	282	2,925	58	174	49	100	57	60	79	106
Gabon	103	1,256	173	1,308	10	26	30	357	955	84	228	304	15	75
Gambia, The	33	87	0	5	36	336	5	8	24	2	23	26	16	26
Ghana	636	1,058	119	329	139	3,599	140	125	131	811	131	555	105	284
Guinea	615	1,060	116	167	63	1,425	67	163	159	29	80	287	35	123
Guinea-Bissau	58	213	5	50	29	356	5	9	36	0	5	18	1	23
Kenya	414	1,351	159	389	270	2,599	364	159	1,286	542	640	695	254	99
Lesotho	4	41	2	11	40	383	0	80	11	58	8	4	6	15
Liberia	179	366	50	74	33	191	98	193	156	189	81	694	89	281
Madagascar	319	970	71	900	148	1,794	34	57	346	73	244	239	87	127
Malawi	111	405	112	7	147	2,001	72	60	192	10	116	46	80	73
Mali	451	950	6	146	163	1,506	9	15	36	0	24	103	39	171
Mauritania	420	748	38	107	106	890	18	103	131	17	65	195	62	105
Mauritius	39	218	37	32	25	56	53	135	165	412	47	872	102	0
Mozambique	..	927	..	102	..	1,142	..	49	..	1,553	..	499	0	196
Namibia	..	..	..	..	..	..	..	..	..	..	..	..	..	..
Niger	42	231	70	155	112	963	30	22	432	62	159	42	16	81
Nigeria	401	601	21	22,452	38	738	533	2,140	4,376	3,466	3,553	1,723	0	0
Rwanda	51	147	1	0	91	1,014	0	0	8	1	26	36	14	84
São Tomé and Principe	9	112	4	8	11	165	0	4	0	5	0	17	0	2
Senegal	221	846	169	201	179	1,775	84	130	461	61	219	201	140	248
Seychelles	16	43	4	6	3	24	2	28	0	16	59	98	0	0
Sierra Leone	138	257	47	140	39	602	23	14	157	2	7	22	59	152
Somalia	400	785	9	286	147	676	13	16	28	32	47	596	18	141
South Africa	..	0	..	0	..	0	..	122	..	15,573	..	8,355	0	0
Sudan	1,361	2,795	1,298	2,509	368	1,710	266	190	854	1,782	598	5,811	431	551
Swaziland	65	50	34	12	17	67	45	84	24	22	15	72	6	0
Tanzania	2,388	2,061	89	377	305	3,199	259	35	341	110	1,771	554	171	341
Togo	228	248	210	202	90	740	26	14	415	0	120	146	33	57
Uganda	191	282	21	167	63	2,763	16	58	244	37	63	152	89	275
Zambia	778	1,259	314	670	19	2,298	374	137	726	149	586	175	447	982
Zimbabwe	15	858	83	252	0	523	3	901	594	489	90	495	0	262
NORTH AFRICA	11,435	26,432	7,177	17,478	2,053	4,116	2,013	12,580	21,909	16,980	8,063	4,500	868	1,518
Algeria	1,255	2,288	1,956	9,863	14	410	270	3,512	13,545	4,713	2,325	199	0	1,518
Egypt, Arab Republic	6,231	17,780	3,767	1,788	1,885	2,194	741	1,487	2,070	2,612	4,027	3,373	411	0
Libya	..	..	..	..	..	..	..	..	..	..	..	..	..	..
Morocco	2,638	4,295	158	1,345	79	988	644	4,509	4,505	5,580	778	247	457	0
Tunisia	1,311	2,070	218	460	75	525	357	3,073	1,429	4,075	136	682	0	0
ALL AFRICA	23,880	59,645	12,871	57,201	5,989	50,365	5,612	20,960	42,738	52,929	19,233	36,544	3,901	7,856

6-24. Structure of external debt service payments

	Millions of U.S. dollars (current prices)													
	Bilateral				*Multilateral*				*Private*		*Short-term*		*IMF*	
	Concessional		*Nonconcessional*		*Concessional*		*Nonconcessional*							
	1980	*2001*	*1980*	*2001*	*1980*	*2001*	*1980*	*2001*	*1980*	*2001*	*1980*	*2001*	*1980*	*2001*
SUB-SAHARAN AFRICA	422	1,140	452	2,198	59	969	425	1,289	3,818	6,638	1,025	703	487	807
excluding South Africa	422	1,140	452	2,198	59	969	425	1,277	3,818	2,617	1,025	380	487	807
excluding South Africa & Nigeria	400	1,117	437	522	58	955	354	828	3,154	2,260	646	337	487	807
Angola	..	322	..	26	..	3	..	7	..	1,473	..	34	0	0
Benin	1	11	1	3	1	29	1	5	4	0	11	3	0	15
Botswana	1	10	2	2	0	10	10	27	1	3	2	1	0	0
Burkina Faso	3	7	4	1	3	25	2	6	5	0	5	3	0	14
Burundi	1	1	0	0	0	15	1	0	4	0	2	2	1	4
Cameroon	25	59	18	4	4	24	24	97	163	0	28	34	19	4
Cape Verde	..	2	..	1	..	6	..	1	..	3	..	1	0	0
Central African Republic	0	3	0	0	0	10	0	0	1	0	2	0	7	0
Chad	1	7	0	0	2	16	0	3	0	1	0	1	3	3
Comoros	0	0	0	0	0	2	0	0	0	0	0	0	0	1
Congo, Democratic Rep. of	48	0	136	0	2	0	22	0	189	0	45	18	101	0
Congo, Republic of	22	0	13	0	1	10	11	71	25	0	31	10	8	2
Côte d'Ivoire	29	105	55	25	3	12	46	161	1,180	212	95	34	0	69
Djibouti	2	6	1	0	0	2	0	0	0	0	1	0	0	2
Equatorial Guinea	0	0	1	0	0	1	0	1	0	0	1	0	0	3
Eritrea	..	4	..	0	..	3	..	1	..	0	..	0	..	0
Ethiopia	11	63	1	1	2	61	10	32	9	13	9	1	2	13
Gabon	6	123	28	182	0	0	4	73	359	51	33	12	1	15
Gambia, The	0	4	0	0	0	9	0	2	0	0	3	1	1	0
Ghana	24	25	22	15	1	72	13	25	48	85	18	27	33	67
Guinea	55	31	7	6	0	47	21	27	14	0	9	8	2	12
Guinea-Bissau	0	7	0	11	0	11	0	2	4	0	1	1	0	1
Kenya	13	21	22	117	2	59	47	60	274	141	58	41	17	24
Lesotho	0	26	0	2	0	12	0	11	4	13	1	0	0	4
Liberia	3	0	0	0	0	0	7	0	27	0	11	0	5	1
Madagascar	21	14	2	12	1	45	3	12	42	3	29	4	3	2
Malawi	4	8	7	0	2	40	3	10	53	0	16	1	3	7
Mali	4	27	0	2	1	45	0	3	3	0	3	3	4	22
Mauritania	8	17	0	6	3	46	2	18	17	4	7	5	11	14
Mauritius	2	34	4	14	0	5	6	28	29	89	8	31	3	0
Mozambique	..	14	..	0	..	30	..	9	..	30	..	10	0	28
Namibia	..	..	..	..	..	..	..	..	..	..	..	..	..	..
Niger	3	2	5	1	16	22	2	2	98	8	19	1	0	2
Nigeria	22	24	15	1,675	1	14	70	449	663	357	379	43	0	0
Rwanda	0	6	0	0	1	25	0	0	3	0	3	1	0	12
São Tomé and Principe	0	1	1	0	0	4	0	0	0	0	0	0	0	0
Senegal	13	70	19	33	1	63	8	20	183	21	24	6	12	28
Seychelles	0	5	0	1	0	1	0	1	0	4	37	3	0	0
Sierra Leone	2	0	2	9	0	8	2	1	41	0	0	0	19	78
Somalia	3	0	0	0	1	0	5	0	0	0	0	0	4	0
South Africa	..	0	..	0	..	0	..	12	..	4,021	..	322	0	0
Sudan	37	0	30	0	5	2	18	1	12	0	70	0	92	53
Swaziland	2	5	6	4	0	2	4	12	5	3	2	2	0	0
Tanzania	32	33	2	11	2	90	23	24	36	30	26	6	39	24
Togo	2	0	17	0	1	17	2	0	16	0	14	5	0	11
Uganda	3	4	8	0	1	44	2	8	22	3	5	4	16	43
Zambia	16	23	21	12	0	33	51	35	238	10	0	7	84	218
Zimbabwe	3	20	0	11	0	0	3	17	43	60	15	16	0	11
NORTH AFRICA	571	2,030	428	1,935	11	395	261	2,266	5,256	3,439	869	223	253	249
Algeria	107	320	226	1,199	2	85	69	692	3,564	1,854	116	9	0	217
Egypt, Arab Republic	265	860	50	185	7	111	51	307	320	321	422	150	121	0
Libya	..	..	..	..	..	..	..	..	..	..	..	..	..	..
Morocco	130	617	24	200	1	144	94	782	992	880	105	4	100	0
Tunisia	70	234	28	134	1	56	47	485	340	384	26	30	33	32
ALL AFRICA	994	3,171	880	4,132	70	1,364	685	3,554	9,074	10,077	1,895	926	739	1,057

Note: In 1995, Zambia was able to clear its arrears to the IMF after completing a 3 year Rights Arrangement Program.

6-25. Terms of long-term external financing, 2001

	Concessional terms				Nonconcessional terms				Structure of financing (percentage of total)	
	Interest (percent)	Grace period (years)	Maturity (years)	Grant element (percent)	Interest (percent)	Grace period (years)	Maturity (years)	Grant element (percent)	Concessional loans	Nonconcessional loans
SUB-SAHARAN AFRICA	1.0	10.5	37.8	76.6	5.8	3.1	9.7	15.5	63.8	36.2
excluding South Africa	1.0	10.5	37.8	76.6	5.8	3.1	9.7	15.5	79.7	20.3
excl. S. Africa & Nigeria	1.0	10.5	37.8	76.4	6.3	3.6	10.9	15.7	79.3	20.7
Angola	..	..	..	..	..	..	..	..	..	..
Benin	0.9	13.2	38.3	77.7	..	..	..	..	100.0	..
Botswana	0.0	20.4	29.0	90.2	..	..	..	..	99.7	0.3
Burkina Faso	0.9	10.5	38.8	78.7	2.0	0.4	7.4	23.9	95.9	4.1
Burundi	0.8	10.1	39.6	80.4	..	..	..	..	100.0	..
Cameroon	1.8	10.3	31.3	65.3	7.6	5.3	13.6	11.9	86.9	13.1
Cape Verde	1.3	6.1	26.1	60.1	..	..	..	..	67.8	32.2
Central African Republic	0.8	10.0	39.5	80.3	..	..	..	..	100.0	..
Chad	0.8	11.2	40.7	81.2	5.8	4.8	12.3	22.0	64.4	35.6
Comoros	0.8	10.1	39.6	80.4	..	..	..	..	100.0	..
Congo, Democratic Rep. of	..	..	..	..	..	..	..	..	..	..
Congo, Republic of	0.8	10.3	39.8	80.7	..	..	..	..	100.0	..
Côte d'Ivoire	..	..	..	..	..	..	..	..	..	..
Djibouti	0.8	10.3	39.8	80.6	..	..	..	..	100.0	..
Equatorial Guinea	..	..	..	..	..	..	..	..	..	..
Eritrea	1.2	9.2	34.6	69.8	..	..	..	..	100.0	..
Ethiopia	0.8	11.7	40.9	80.8	..	..	..	..	100.0	..
Gabon	4.4	5.3	19.8	36.6	..	..	..	..	100.0	..
Gambia, The	1.4	7.6	33.1	67.7	..	..	..	..	100.0	..
Ghana	0.8	11.9	41.1	81.3	..	..	..	..	88.3	11.7
Guinea	0.8	10.4	39.9	80.7	..	..	..	..	100.0	..
Guinea-Bissau	..	..	..	..	..	..	..	..	..	..
Kenya	0.6	10.2	36.6	80.5	..	..	..	..	74.5	25.5
Lesotho	0.8	13.4	42.9	82.8	..	..	..	..	100.0	..
Liberia	..	..	..	..	..	..	..	..	..	..
Madagascar	0.8	10.9	40.4	81.0	..	..	..	..	100.0	..
Malawi	0.8	11.7	41.2	81.6	..	..	..	..	1.2	98.8
Mali	0.9	10.0	36.4	76.4	..	..	..	..	100.0	0.0
Mauritania	1.6	10.6	36.2	71.2	..	..	..	..	100.0	0.0
Mauritius	3.9	3.9	14.0	33.5	..	..	..	..	68.0	32.0
Mozambique	0.8	10.0	39.5	80.3	..	..	..	..	100.0	..
Namibia	..	..	..	..	..	..	..	..	..	..
Niger	0.8	9.5	38.8	78.4	..	..	..	..	100.0	..
Nigeria	0.8	11.3	38.8	80.4	4.0	1.3	4.8	14.5	88.8	11.2
Rwanda	0.8	10.9	39.6	80.2	..	..	..	..	100.0	..
São Tomé and Principe	0.8	11.3	40.8	81.1	..	..	..	..	100.0	..
Senegal	1.2	7.7	31.5	69.3	..	..	..	..	100.0	..
Seychelles	..	..	..	..	..	..	..	..	..	..
Sierra Leone	0.7	11.8	40.1	81.7	..	..	..	..	100.0	..
Somalia	..	..	..	..	..	..	..	..	..	..
South Africa	0.8	10.3	34.8	78.8	..	..	..	..	0.3	99.7
Sudan	..	..	..	..	..	..	..	..	..	..
Swaziland	5.0	10.0	29.0	40.0	..	..	..	..	72.2	27.8
Tanzania	0.7	9.9	38.7	79.5	0.0	1.4	1.4	12.6	99.7	0.3
Togo	2.5	7.4	24.9	56.4	..	..	..	..	99.7	0.3
Uganda	0.8	11.6	41.1	81.3	..	..	..	..	100.0	..
Zambia	0.9	15.1	43.2	81.4	..	..	..	..	100.0	..
Zimbabwe	..	..	..	..	7.1	1.6	8.1	9.9	0.0	100.0
NORTH AFRICA	3.6	4.9	21.9	42.5	5.2	2.4	8.5	15.4 ..	40.3	59.7
Algeria	4.2	4.9	18.6	36.5	3.7	1.3	3.9	12.9	27.5	72.5
Egypt, Arab Republic	0.8	10.3	49.8	83.2	..	..	..	..	0.3	99.7
Libya	0.0	0.0	0.0	0.0	..	..	..	..	..	..
Morocco	3.5	6.4	23.1	45.8	4.8	2.5	3.6	12.9	84.1	15.9
Tunisia	3.6	3.0	20.8	39.0	6.4	2.7	19.2	20.8	52.7	47.3
ALL AFRICA	1.7	9.1	33.7	67.7	5.4	2.7	8.9	15.4	55.4	44.6

Note: No data indicates no commitment for the year 2001.

6-26. External debt and debt service ratios, 2001

	Debt-GDP ratio		Total external debt per capita (US dollars)	Percentage of debt disbursed	Debt-export ratio		Present value of debt-export ratio, 2001	Debt service-export ratio (Ex post)
	Concessional	Non-concessional			Concessional	Non-concessional		
SUB-SAHARAN AFRICA	24	37	300	89	71	109	143	12
excluding South Africa	39	46	282	89	107	132	184	13
excl. S. Africa & Nigeria	49	38	293	88	144	126	195	12
Angola	17	9	710	89	22	111	129	26
Benin	59	4	259	81	310	57	185	14
Botswana	5	2	218	92	8	4	10	2
Burkina Faso	50	2	129	74	410	79	235	18
Burundi	138	3	153	88	1,718	208	1,172	42
Cameroon	45	23	470	91	141	121	181	8
Cape Verde	52	4	806	61	123	23	94	6
Central African Republic	70	5	218	92	526	112	416	10
Chad	56	5	139	76	342	80	240	11
Comoros	97	4	430	96	332	51	276	4
Congo, Democratic Rep. of	..	28	218	96	292	813	1,029	2
Congo, Republic of	59	45	1,449	95	70	124	183	4
Côte d'Ivoire	37	22	706	92	94	186	258	15
Djibouti	..	0	407	84	..	..	..	..
Equatorial Guinea	7	3	509	88	6	5	9	0
Eritrea	55	2	97	21	93	7	57	2
Ethiopia	81	6	87	91	522	66	301	19
Gabon	30	38	2,704	90	40	67	105	14
Gambia, The	103	3	365	85	167	26	105	6
Ghana	88	9	343	84	189	85	160	13
Guinea	83	11	429	85	298	92	208	16
Guinea-Bissau	286	29	545	91	1,063	186	792	60
Kenya	35	5	190	86	131	63	147	15
Lesotho	53	11	287	78	75	30	72	12
Liberia	..	..	618	99	..	..	..	..
Madagascar	60	21	260	89	206	104	153	7
Malawi	138	4	247	81	495	40	306	14
Mali	106	7	261	82	270	48	155	11
Mauritania	159	20	788	88	371	119	319	25
Mauritius	6	4	1,437	78	9	48	55	7
Mozambique	57	4	247	82	197	228	87	11
Namibia	..	..	..	..	..	..	..	..
Niger	61	9	139	81	328	99	282	10
Nigeria	3	60	240	94	7	149	155	13
Rwanda	68	0	148	80	670	70	387	25
São Tomé and Principe	589	26	2,068	83	1,545	201	559	34
Senegal	57	7	354	81	161	52	148	15
Seychelles	12	6	2,606	73	13	29	41	3
Sierra Leone	115	21	231	96	725	278	704	81
Somalia	..	..	279	89	..	..	..	..
South Africa	0	0	556	89	0	64	62	12
Sudan	36	22	484	94	271	651	874	3
Swaziland	9	8	288	73	12	20	31	3
Tanzania	56	4	194	83	345	93	88	14
Togo	78	17	302	86	208	88	211	7
Uganda	54	4	164	87	429	97	162	15
Zambia	98	22	551	92	331	196	375	31
Zimbabwe	15	13	295	75	69	119	174	7
NORTH AFRICA	15	24	590	88	45	72	106	15
Algeria	5	24	730	82	11	84	92	19
Egypt, Arab Republic	20	3	449	94	92	43	115	9
Libya	..	..	..	..	..	..	..	..
Morocco	15	17	582	83	41	90	113	20
Tunisia	13	18	1,125	73	26	84	110	14
ALL AFRICA	20	31	348	88	61	95	129	13

Figure 6-1. Debt service ratio (ex post), 2001

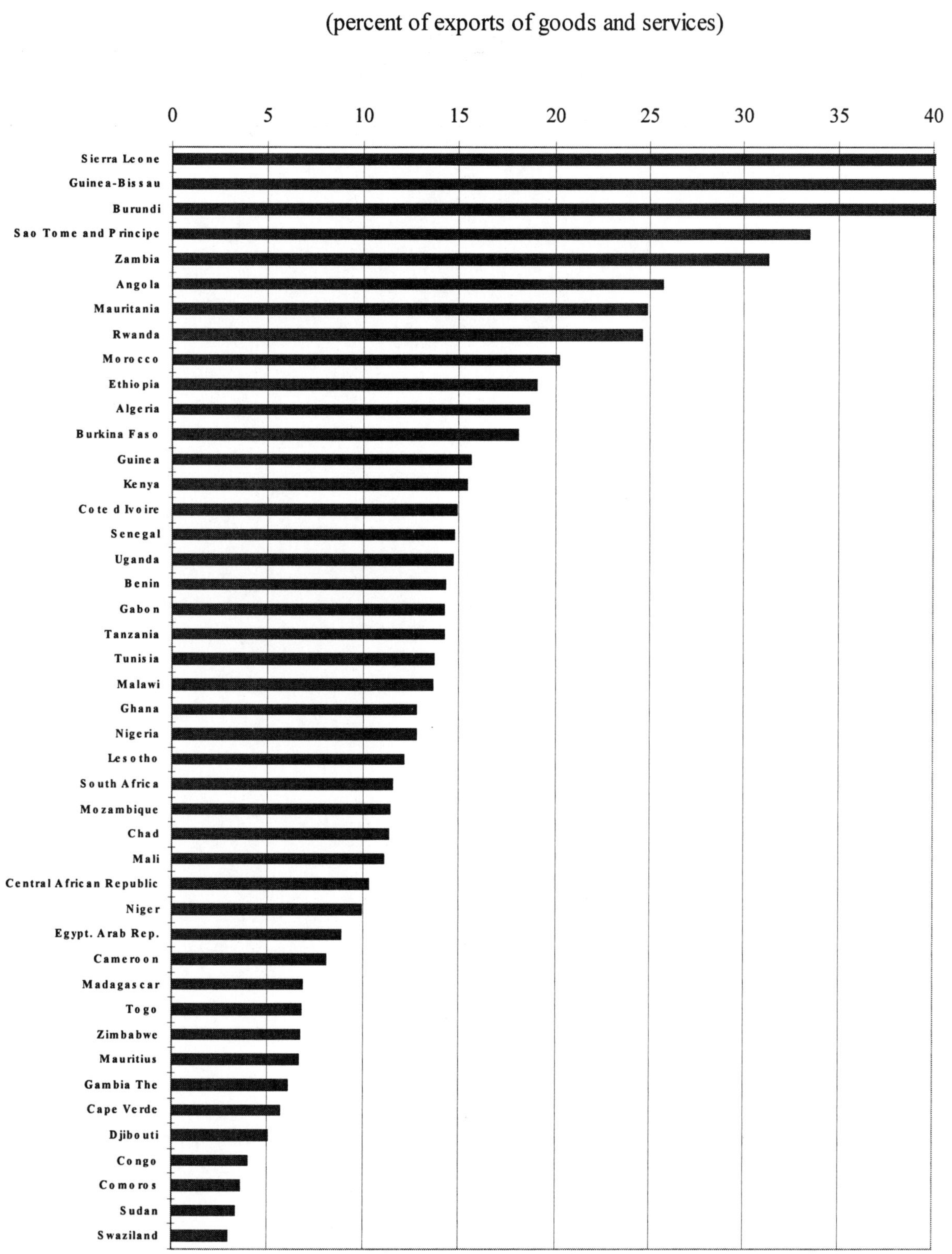

Figure 6-2. Debt to GDP ratio, 2001

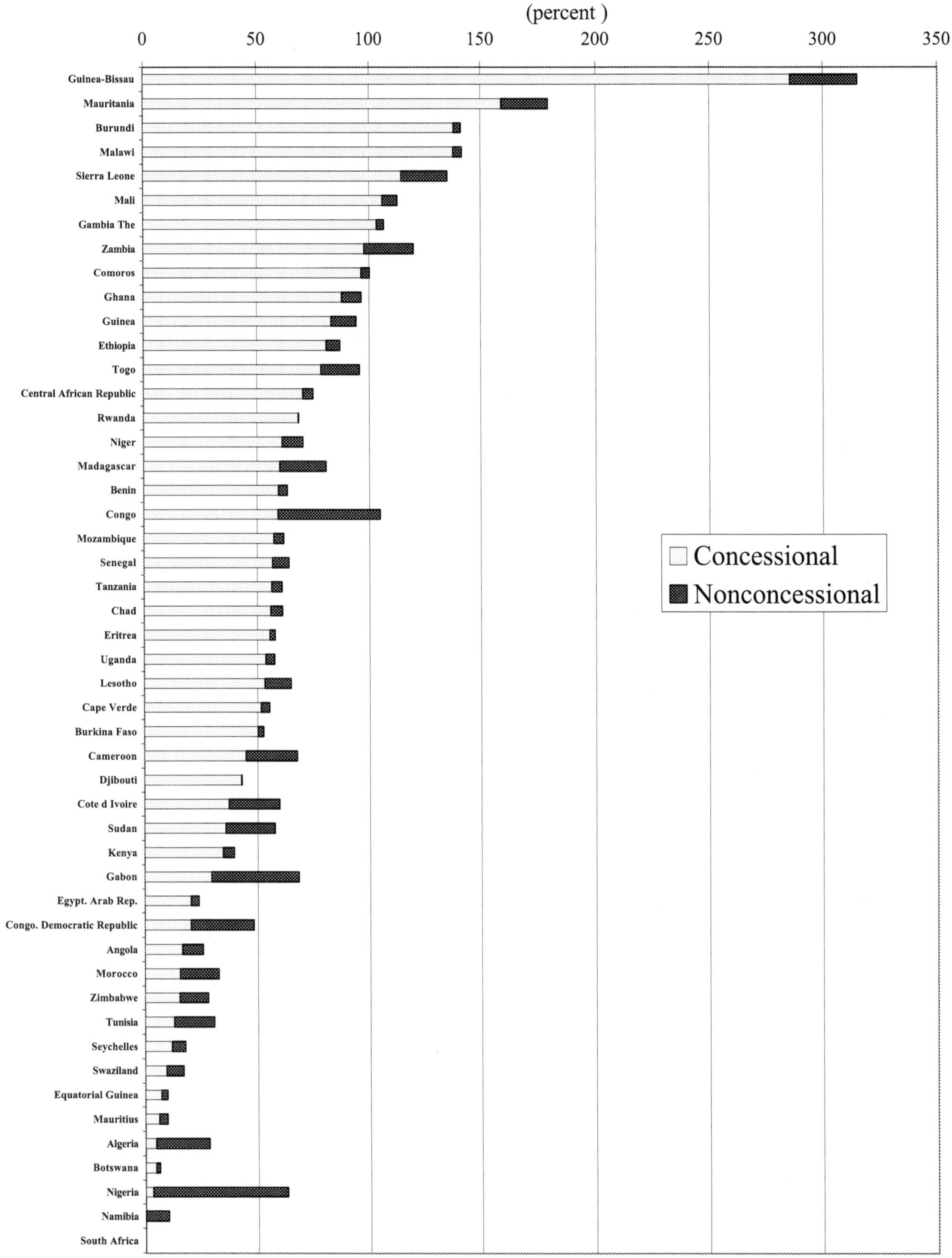

* Sorted by concessional debt.

Technical notes

Tables

Tables 6-1, 6-2, and 6-3. Gross disbursements: official concessional, official nonconcessional, and private long-term loans. Gross disbursements are from commitments of long-term external loans by official concessional, official nonconcessional, and private sources, respectively (World Bank, DRS).

Table 6-4. Disbursements: long-term loans and IMF purchases. This is the sum of tables 6-1 through 6-3, plus IMF purchases.

Tables 6-5, 6-6, and 6-7. Amortization: official concessional, official nonconcessional, and private long-term loans. Amortization is the actual repayment of principal made in foreign currencies, goods, or services on outstanding long-term official concessional, official nonconcessional, and private long-term loans as described above (World Bank, DRS).

Table 6-8. Amortization: long-term loans and IMF repurchases. This is the sum of Tables 6-5 to 6-7, plus repurchases of drawings from the IMF.

Tables 6-9, 6-10, and 6-11. Interest payments: official concessional, official nonconcessional, and private long-term loans. These are actual payments made in foreign currencies, goods, and services to various lenders described above on interest obligations, including IMF charges on drawings due on disbursed debt and on commitment charges due on undisbursed debt (where information is available), that is, on long-term official concessional, official nonconcessional, and private loans (World Bank, DRS).

Table 6-12. Interest payments: long-term loans and IMF charges. This is the sum of Tables 6-9 through 6-11, plus IMF charges on drawings.

Table 6-13. Total external debt service payments: long-term loans and IMF credit. Total external debt service payments include the sum of amortization on long-term loans and IMF credit and interest payments on long-term loans and IMF credit (World Bank, DRS).

Table 6-14. Interest payments: short-term loans. These are estimated for the respective year based on the estimated year-end stock of short-term debt (which may include interest arrears on long-term debt) and the annual average six-month London interbank offered rate (LIBOR) on notes denominated in U.S. dollars as reported in the IFS (with no adjustment for spreads). Actual payments may be different because the LIBOR only approximates actual interest rates on short-term loans, and because not all interest due on short-term loans is actually paid (World Bank, DRS).

Table 6-15. Net flows: long- and short-term loans, including IMF. These flows represent all disbursements of long- and short-term loans net of all repayments of principal on long- and short-term loans and IMF credit (World Bank, DRS).

Table 6-16. Net flows: long-term loans, including IMF. Net flows of long-term loans are as defined above for Table 6-15, but excluding short-term loans (World Bank, DRS).

Table 6-17. Net transfers: long- and short-term loans, including IMF. Net transfers are net flows (Table 6-15) less interest payments (Tables 6-12 and 6-14).

Table 6-18. Net transfers: long-term loans, including IMF. Net transfers include long-term loans and IMF credit only (Table 6-16 less Table 6-12).

Tables 6-19, 6-20, and 6-21. Long-term debt: official concessional, official nonconcessional, and private. This series reflects the total debt outstanding and disbursed of official concessional, official nonconcessional, and private loans (World Bank, DRS). The time series reflects changes in the valuation of year-end debt stocks (because of US dollar exchange rate fluctuation) and debt cancellation, as well as net disbursements. Therefore changes in debt stocks from year to year cannot be used as a measure of net borrowing or vice versa.

Table 6-22. Total external debt. When Tables 6-19 to 6-21 are supplemented with IMF credit and estimates of total short-term debt (which includes interest in arrears on public and publicly guaranteed long-term loans), they sum up to total external debt (World Bank, DRS).

Table 6-23. Structure of external debt. This table summarizes debt structure for 1980 and 2000 (World Bank, DRS). The columns cover the type of creditor and concessionality. The private debt shown includes both the private guaranteed (by an entity of the debtor government) and the private nonguaranteed debt. For each year, all components shown add to the total in Table 6-22.

Table 6-24. Structure of external debt service payments. This summary table compares debt service payments for all types of creditors in 1980 and 2000 (World Bank, DRS). Debt service payments on short-term loans are excluded, to be consistent with Table 6-13. Debt service payments are actual repayments of principal (amortization) and actual payments of interest. The column headings have the same definitions as given above for Table 6-23.

Table 6-25. Terms of long-term external financing, 2000. This table presents the average interest rates, grace periods, maturities, and grant elements shown separately for official concessional and nonconcessional long-term loans (excluding private financing); short-term loans are excluded (World Bank, DRS). Grant elements are calculated using a standard 10 percent discount rate. The indicators are weighted averages (based on amount of commitments) across all loans in each category. For the column on structure of financing (that is, total flows), grants are based on sources for Chapter 12 (Aid Flows) and are not comparable with net official transfers shown in Chapter 5.

Table 6-26. External debt and debt service ratios, 2000. This table includes the ratio of debt outstanding and disbursed to GDP; per capita debt; the ratio of debt outstanding and disbursed to debt outstanding, including undisbursed; the ratio of debt outstanding and disbursed and the ratio of the present value of debt to exports of goods and all services, including receipts of workers' remittances; and the ratio of total debt service paid to exports of goods and all services, more commonly called the debt service ratio (World Bank, DRS). Ratios are shown separately for concessional debt and for all nonconcessional (including private) debt. Both the stock of external debt and debt service payments include short- and long-term loans and IMF credit, except for the ratio of debt outstanding to debt outstanding including undisbursed, which is calculated for public and publicly guaranteed debt only. The data for exports of goods and all services, plus receipts of workers' remittances, are taken from balance of payments data in Chapter 5. The present value of debt is the sum of all future payments discounted to the present (usually with a commercial discount rate similar to LIBOR. The debt service ratio is shown for the ex post category, depicting the amount paid after debt relief and/or arrears.

Figures

The following indicators have been used to derive the figures in this chapter:

Figure 6-1. Debt service ratio (Table 6-26).

Figure 6-2. Debt to GDP ratio (Table 6-26).

Methodology used for regional aggregations and period averages in chapter 6

	Aggregations [a]			Period averages [b]
Table	(1)	(2)	(6)	(1)
6-1	x			x
6-2	x			x
6-3	x			x
6-4	x			x
6-5	x			x
6-6	x			x
6-7	x			x
6-8	x			x
6-9	x			x
6-10	x			x
6-11	x			x
6-12	x			x
6-13	x			x
6-14	x			x
6-15	x			x
6-16	x			x
6-17	x			x
6-18	x			x
6-19	x			x
6-20	x			x
6-21	x			x
6-22	x			
6-23	x			
6-24	x			
6-25			x	
6-26		x		

Note : Regional aggregations are shown in the rows for Sub-Saharan Africa, North Africa, and All Africa. Period averages are shown in the last three columns. This table shows only the methodologies used in this chapter.

a. Regional aggregations: (1) simple total; (2) simple total of the first indicator divided by the simple total of the second indicator (same country coverage); (3) simple total of the gap-filled indicator; (4) simple total of the gap-filled main indicator divided by the simple total of the gap-filled secondary indicator; (5) simple total of the first gap-filled main indicator less the simple total of the second gap-filled main indicator, all divided by the simple total of the secondary indicator; (6) weighted total (by population); (7) median; (8) no aggregation; (9) simple arithmetic mean.

b. Period averages: (1) arithmetic mean (using the same series as shown in the table i.e., ratio if the rest of the table is shown as ratio, level if the rest of the table is shown as level, growth rate if the rest is shown as growth rate); (2) least-squares growth rate (using main indicator); (3) least-squares growth rate (using main indicator in constant terms, with the rest of the table in current terms).

7

Government Finance

The data in this chapter pertain to consolidated government (except when not available) instead of to central government operations, which were reported in previous volumes.

Definitions have been taken from the IMF's Government Finance Statistics (GFS). For this volume, data are taken from country desks. When not available from country desks, data are taken from the GFS and supplemented with data from IMF, World Bank, or staff reports, or from other national government sources. Data from various sources have been harmonized to produce a consistent and comparable time series.

The focus of this chapter is on the principal financial transactions of government—taxing, borrowing, spending, and lending—rather than on the production and consumption of goods and services, the use of labor, or other government activities. Spending covers both current and capital transactions.

The data cover major government finance indicators—fiscal deficit or surplus, expenditure and lending minus repayments, revenue, grants, and domestic and foreign financing—expressed as a percentage of GDP. The chapter also includes information on the major components of revenue and expenditure by economic category, shown as percentages of total revenue and as a percentage of expenditure and lending minus repayments, respectively.

Measures of fiscal deficit or surplus are among the single most important indicators of government fiscal performance. The measure is usually calculated as the difference between total revenue (including grants) and total expenditure (including lending minus repayments). As such, it measures government net financing requirements. *GFS* methodology recommends grouping grants receipt with revenue because they can be spent without incurring an obligation for future payments but lists them separately because grants can sometimes be treated as financing items. Financing includes all government borrowing from others (at home and abroad) minus amortization (government repayment of its borrowing from others and changes in cash balances). Other measures of fiscal balance include the fiscal deficit or surplus without capital grants, which measures the government's ability to operate without foreign capital transfers, and the fiscal deficit or surplus, excluding interest payments from expenditure, referred to as the primary deficit or surplus.

Revenue is divided between taxes—unrequited compulsory payments to government—and nontax revenue. It includes only non-repayable receipts other than grants. Tax revenue is also classified according to the base upon which the tax is levied (for example, income and profits).

Expenditure is classified by economic category (such as wages, purchases, and interest payments). Lending minus repayments—government lending less repayment of past government lending—is grouped with expenditure, except in certain cases (see Technical Notes).

The economic classification of expenditures (for example, on wages) is presented as a percentage of total expenditure and lending minus repayments, because lending minus repayments is itself a separate economic classification.

No attempt was made to reconcile GFS data in this chapter with the System of National Accounts (SNA). The fundamental difference between the two systems is that GFS focuses on government financial transactions, whereas the SNA considers government transactions as part of total demand and value added. (For further discussion, see World Bank 1988b, box 2.1, p. 45.) Indicators calculated as ratios to GDP use GDP at purchaser values or market prices (see Technical Notes to Chapter 1). Because GDP at purchaser values includes import duties (and GDP at market prices includes indirect taxes), ratios for revenues tend to understate tax burdens, especially where such taxes are an important source of government revenue.

Fiscal year data are compared with the calendar year GDP data that correspond either to the second half of the fiscal year or to the calendar year in which most of the fiscal year falls. Fiscal years do not correspond to calendar years in Botswana, Cameroon, Egypt, Ethiopia, The Gambia, and Ghana (before 1982), Kenya, Lesotho, Liberia, Malawi, Mauritius, Niger, Nigeria, Senegal, Sierra Leone, Sudan, Swaziland, Tanzania, Uganda, and Zimbabwe (after 1985).

7-1. Government deficit/surplus (including grants)

	Percentage of GDP											Annual Average		
	1980	*1992*	*1993*	*1994*	*1995*	*1996*	*1997*	*1998*	*1999*	*2000*	*2001*	*75-84*	*85-89*	*90-MR*
SUB-SAHARAN AFRICA	..	-7.1	-7.2	-4.9	-3.3	-3.1	-3.3	-3.5	-3.3	-2.4	-1.9	-4.8	-4.6	-4.1
excluding South Africa	..	-6.7	-5.4	-3.8	-1.6	-1.1	-2.2	-4.2	-4.3	-2.8	-2.1	..	-5.0	-3.7
excl. S.Africa & Nigeria	..	-6.7	-5.4	-5.0	-3.9	-3.1	-2.8	-3.3	-3.7	-3.8	-2.3	-5.3	-5.0	-4.2
Angola	..	-56.9	-21.7	-20.1	-37.5	-16.1	-22.0	-7.9	-16.4	-6.7	0.1	..	-11.1	-21.2
Benin	..	-7.2	-2.9	-4.4	-4.6	-0.4	0.3	2.1	1.9	-1.8	-1.5	..	-5.8	-2.8
Botswana	..	9.3	9.5	5.0	4.1	4.4	5.4	2.1	-2.7	7.0	6.7	10.4	15.2	5.9
Burkina Faso	..	-2.9	-4.4	-3.4	-3.9	-0.6	-3.3	-3.2	-4.0	-4.3	-4.3	..	..	-3.5
Burundi	9.8	-2.7	-3.7	-2.2	-2.2	-7.4	-4.1	-4.7	-6.4	-0.8	-0.9	9.5	-4.4	-3.2
Cameroon	0.4	-6.3	-6.3	-9.2	-3.2	-1.7	-1.2	-1.7	-3.2	1.4	2.4	0.5	-5.2	-3.7
Cape Verde	..	-7.9	-9.3	-14.0	-19.1	-17.2	-6.0	-3.4	-1.8	-18.9	-7.9	-7.2	-5.1	-9.4
Central African Republic	..	-9.0	-8.2	-10.0	-5.1	-3.4	-2.3	-0.8	-1.9	-2.0	-0.2	..	..	-5.0
Chad	..	-8.1	-8.6	-4.7	-4.4	-5.1	-3.9	-2.6	-5.9	-2.0	-1.0	..	-5.3	-4.8
Comoros	..	-9.8	-2.0	-13.8	-6.2	-5.2	-2.1	-3.0	-0.4	-1.9	-3.6	0.0	-4.8	-4.7
Congo, Democratic Rep. of	..	..	..	..	..	-4.2	-10.8	-6.2	-5.3	-5.7	4.2	..	..	-4.7
Congo, Republic of	..	-14.1	-12.6	-13.2	-8.2	-5.0	-9.1	-20.0	-5.9	1.2	-0.7	7.1	-7.9	-8.9
Côte d'Ivoire	..	-11.3	-11.9	-6.4	-3.9	-1.9	-1.3	-1.4	-1.9	-0.7	-0.4	..	-8.2	-5.5
Djibouti	..	-11.7	-13.0	-8.4	-8.0	-3.9	-4.3	0.9	-2.2	-1.8	..	..	..	-5.8
Equatorial Guinea	..	..	..	-5.7	-6.3	-6.3	1.5	-5.7	0.1	9.1	12.1	..	..	-0.2
Eritrea	..	-3.1	15.2	6.9	-12.9	-9.8	0.1	-30.0	-47.7	-28.6	-32.7	..	..	-14.3
Ethiopia	..	-7.0	-5.9	-7.7	-3.9	-5.6	-2.4	-4.4	-9.3	-11.5	-5.0	-6.6	-5.7	-6.7
Gabon	..	-5.2	-5.7	-1.6	3.2	2.7	2.5	-14.4	-1.4	0.6	2.2	-36.9	-7.1	-1.9
Gambia, The	..	1.3	1.3	-1.1	-6.3	-10.0	-6.5	-2.4	-3.5	-1.4	-6.3	-14.7	3.8	-2.8
Ghana	..	-4.0	-3.1	-8.9	-6.4	-9.5	-9.4	-6.5	-7.2	-6.6	-3.8	-2.3	-2.7	-5.4
Guinea	..	-3.1	-3.7	-3.6	-2.7	-3.0	-2.9	-0.7	-3.0	-5.2	-2.7	..	-5.5	-3.2
Guinea-Bissau	0.0	-21.7	-13.0	-8.4	-1.4	-12.2	-18.2	-16.3	-4.4	-10.8	-10.4	-8.3	-14.4	-11.7
Kenya	-8.9	-2.5	-2.3	-0.1	0.0	-0.6	-0.6	0.3	1.1	0.9	-1.3	-6.8	-4.1	-1.4
Lesotho	..	2.3	1.3	4.3	5.0	4.5	2.3	-1.8	-13.2	-5.5	-0.9	-5.4	-5.8	-0.4
Liberia	..	..	..	..	..	..	..	..	..	..	..	..	..	..
Madagascar	..	-6.9	-7.6	-8.7	-5.3	-8.1	-2.4	-5.8	-2.6	-2.6	-4.1	1.7	0.4	-4.7
Malawi	-11.6	-11.1	-6.1	-17.4	-4.7	-3.7	-5.5	-6.6	-4.5	-4.9	-7.3	-8.3	-5.9	-6.6
Mali	-14.9	-3.9	-4.1	-4.6	-3.1	-0.9	-2.1	-5.8	-3.9	-4.2	-6.6	-11.9	-5.4	-3.8
Mauritania	..	-0.7	-7.4	-0.5	1.2	7.4	5.1	3.6	4.7	-1.6	-2.8	..	-9.7	-0.6
Mauritius	-10.9	-2.6	-1.9	-2.4	-3.6	-7.2	-7.4	-3.9	-3.4	-3.8	-6.6	-10.5	-2.8	-3.9
Mozambique	-2.1	-2.7	-3.6	-5.3	-3.2	-2.9	-2.6	-2.3	-1.5	-4.5	-4.9	-8.6	-8.1	-3.6
Namibia	..	-4.6	-4.9	-2.0	-3.3	-5.3	-3.3	-3.6	-3.4	-1.8	-4.4	-4.9	1.3	-3.2
Niger	..	-4.7	-3.8	-6.7	-2.7	-0.2	-2.7	-4.2	-5.1	-2.0	-2.4	-4.9	-4.8	-3.8
Nigeria	..	..	..	1.9	9.9	9.1	1.0	-9.3	-7.5	2.7	-1.2	..	..	0.8
Rwanda	..	-8.1	-8.2	-11.5	-2.4	-5.8	-2.5	-3.0	-3.8	0.1	-1.1	..	..	-4.7
São Tomé and Principe	..	-41.8	-33.6	-43.0	-37.6	-32.3	-26.7	-24.9	-23.2	-16.6	-13.7	..	-3.8	-28.0
Senegal	-4.6	-1.8	-3.1	-1.9	-0.2	2.2	0.5	-0.3	2.2	0.3	-1.9	-6.8	-2.0	-0.4
Seychelles	..	-5.8	-11.4	3.5	1.5	-9.3	-9.0	-23.9	-12.4	-14.8	-9.2	..	..	-8.0
Sierra Leone	..	-9.1	-7.4	-5.5	-9.2	-5.1	-7.0	-10.4	-9.5	-9.3	-9.8	..	-19.3	-8.9
Somalia	..	..	..	..	..	..	..	..	..	..	..	..	..	..
South Africa	-18.0	-7.4	-8.9	-6.2	-5.2	-5.4	-4.5	-2.6	-2.0	-2.0	-1.6	-6.5	-4.3	-4.4
Sudan	..	-18.8	-10.1	-4.4	-1.9	-1.5	-0.5	-0.6	-0.8	-0.8	-1.0	-12.2	-12.1	-5.4
Swaziland	..	-1.6	-4.5	-5.2	-1.7	-1.2	1.8	1.0	-1.2	-1.5	-3.1	..	..	-1.1
Tanzania	..	3.2	-1.4	1.6	-3.4	-1.9	1.8	0.2	0.4	-1.2	-0.7	-9.4	-3.7	0.3
Togo	..	-4.2	-15.5	-11.5	-6.4	-4.5	0.8	-5.2	-3.4	-5.4	-2.1	-2.1	-3.8	-5.6
Uganda	..	-7.3	-3.2	-3.8	-2.6	-1.9	-1.4	-0.5	-1.3	-8.7	-3.0	-2.1	-3.6	-3.5
Zambia	..	-2.5	-5.6	-6.5	-4.3	-0.5	-0.2	-3.2	-2.4	-5.0	-7.2	..	-10.8	-4.4
Zimbabwe	7.6	-6.8	-6.1	-6.7	-10.1	-7.7	-7.6	-2.5	-9.6	-21.4	-11.3	8.0	-7.9	-8.5
NORTH AFRICA	..	-2.4	-4.4	-2.6	-2.1	-0.6	-0.5	-2.2	-2.8	0.2	-0.3	..	-9.0	-2.3
Algeria	-8.4	-1.2	-8.6	-4.4	-1.4	2.9	2.4	-3.9	-0.5	9.9	6.4	-9.5	-9.2	0.6
Egypt, Arab Republic	..	-3.1	-2.3	-0.9	-0.3	-0.7	-0.3	-0.5	-3.6	-3.3	-4.5	..	-14.1	-3.7
Libya	..	..	..	..	..	..	..	..	..	..	..	..	..	..
Morocco	-10.9	-2.3	-2.9	-3.8	-5.4	-3.5	-3.4	-2.7	-4.7	-6.2	-0.8	-0.8	-5.7	-3.1
Tunisia	0.9	-3.0	-2.8	-2.1	-4.2	-4.9	-3.9	-2.5	-2.2	-2.9	-2.7	-1.7	-1.8	-3.4
ALL AFRICA	..	-5.3	-6.2	-4.1	-2.9	-2.3	-2.3	-3.0	-3.1	-1.5	-1.3	-5.8	-6.0	-3.4

Note: 2001 data are preliminary. Nigeria: from 1992 accounts are for consolidated budget; since 1994, ratios are distorted as off. exch. rate used by the Gov. for oil exports oil value added is significantly over-valued.

7-2. Government deficit/surplus (excluding grants)

	Percentage of GDP											Annual Average		
	1980	1992	1993	1994	1995	1996	1997	1998	1999	2000	2001	75-84	85-89	90-MR
SUB-SAHARAN AFRICA	..	-8.6	-8.6	-6.2	-4.4	-4.1	-4.3	-4.6	-4.5	-3.6	-3.2	-5.7	-5.6	-5.3
excluding South Africa	..	-9.4	-8.2	-6.3	-3.7	-3.0	-4.1	-6.2	-6.6	-5.0	-4.5	..	-7.1	-6.0
excl. S.Africa & Nigeria	..	-9.4	-8.2	-7.9	-6.4	-5.4	-5.0	-5.6	-6.4	-6.4	-5.2	-7.3	-7.1	-6.8
Angola	..	-56.9	-21.7	-20.1	-37.5	-19.3	-24.4	-11.3	-35.7	-9.0	-7.5	..	-11.1	-24.3
Benin	..	-11.4	-6.8	-7.0	-7.3	-4.3	-4.2	-1.0	-1.6	-3.5	-4.1	..	-15.5	-6.3
Botswana	..	8.4	8.3	3.6	3.6	4.1	4.9	1.5	-3.3	6.7	6.6	7.8	13.2	5.2
Burkina Faso	..	-9.1	-9.6	-11.2	-11.1	-9.2	-10.6	-10.1	-13.0	-12.5	-12.5	..	..	-10.4
Burundi	6.1	-11.3	-12.7	-4.7	-5.8	-9.7	-7.1	-5.6	-9.2	-4.1	-3.5	5.4	-6.0	-7.8
Cameroon	0.4	-6.3	-6.3	-9.4	-3.3	-1.7	-1.2	-2.0	-3.3	1.4	2.0	0.5	-5.2	-3.8
Cape Verde	..	-25.5	-24.6	-29.2	-27.8	-22.2	-16.1	-19.5	-6.7	-24.6	-8.6	-45.0	-24.5	-19.1
Central African Republic	..	-14.7	-13.5	-15.0	-11.4	-5.0	-6.3	-8.6	-8.7	-9.3	-7.9	..	..	-10.5
Chad	..	-13.0	-13.2	-14.2	-11.9	-11.2	-10.3	-7.7	-10.5	-7.5	-6.4	..	-16.0	-10.9
Comoros	..	-16.6	-11.3	-23.8	-17.9	-14.1	-11.1	-10.7	-7.4	-6.0	-8.0	-19.1	-24.0	-13.3
Congo, Democratic Rep. of	..	..	..	..	..	-4.2	-10.8	-6.2	-5.3	-5.7	4.2	..	..	-4.7
Congo, Republic of	..	-14.1	-12.6	-14.3	-9.2	-5.3	-9.2	-20.3	-6.3	0.9	-0.9	6.2	-8.0	-9.3
Côte d'Ivoire	..	-11.8	-12.4	-7.1	-4.6	-2.6	-2.6	-2.7	-2.9	-1.7	-1.3	..	-8.2	-6.2
Djibouti	..	-24.1	-21.8	-13.4	-10.0	-5.7	-8.1	-7.9	-9.6	-10.4	..	..	..	-12.3
Equatorial Guinea	..	..	..	-9.9	-8.9	-7.2	0.8	-6.4	-0.2	8.9	11.9	..	..	-1.4
Eritrea	..	-11.9	-7.0	-13.3	-26.0	-21.3	-6.0	-39.9	-56.3	-47.8	-51.9	..	..	-28.1
Ethiopia	..	-9.6	-7.6	-11.1	-7.3	-8.5	-6.0	-7.2	-12.9	-14.8	-10.0	-8.7	-9.4	-9.8
Gabon	..	-5.3	-6.0	-2.0	3.2	2.7	2.5	-14.4	-1.4	0.6	2.2	-37.3	-7.6	-2.1
Gambia, The	..	-3.3	-2.4	-4.2	-8.7	-12.2	-7.8	-4.4	-4.9	-3.6	-9.8	-14.7	-10.5	-6.0
Ghana	..	-9.4	-9.8	-12.4	-10.0	-12.1	-11.7	-10.3	-9.8	-10.0	-9.5	-3.1	-5.1	-9.3
Guinea	..	-7.1	-7.3	-7.1	-6.7	-6.2	-5.9	-3.6	-5.3	-7.5	-5.5	..	-8.5	-6.4
Guinea-Bissau	0.0	-37.4	-29.9	-23.1	-17.7	-21.2	-30.9	-19.5	-14.0	-24.9	-23.5	-10.1	-38.4	-25.0
Kenya	-11.4	-5.1	-5.4	-2.9	-2.1	-1.9	-2.0	-1.1	-0.1	-2.7	-5.1	-8.6	-6.1	-3.7
Lesotho	..	-3.8	-0.1	0.7	0.3	-0.3	-1.6	-4.5	-15.5	-7.5	-3.4	-8.9	-11.3	-4.8
Liberia	..	..	..	..	..	..	..	..	..	..	..	..	..	..
Madagascar	..	-10.3	-11.0	-11.7	-8.2	-12.3	-7.7	-9.3	-6.2	-6.2	-7.8	1.0	-1.0	-8.3
Malawi	-15.9	-13.9	-8.8	-29.5	-12.7	-8.3	-9.0	-12.8	-11.0	-14.2	-14.1	-11.1	-9.8	-12.3
Mali	-35.4	-11.0	-9.6	-14.6	-10.7	-8.1	-7.9	-11.7	-9.2	-10.4	-12.5	-38.2	-10.5	-10.5
Mauritania	..	-2.5	-9.6	-3.1	-0.8	5.2	4.3	2.2	2.1	-5.1	-7.6	..	-14.8	-2.9
Mauritius	-10.9	-2.7	-2.1	-2.6	-4.0	-7.5	-7.4	-4.1	-3.5	-4.0	-6.7	-10.8	-3.7	-4.1
Mozambique	-3.9	-16.5	-15.5	-19.2	-13.0	-9.9	-11.9	-10.5	-13.2	-16.1	-17.8	-10.4	-13.4	-14.5
Namibia	..	-5.5	-5.6	-2.4	-3.6	-5.6	-3.6	-3.8	-3.7	-2.1	-5.1	-16.8	-7.6	-3.8
Niger	..	-8.6	-9.4	-12.5	-7.4	-5.1	-7.3	-8.6	-9.0	-6.8	-7.0	-8.3	-9.4	-8.6
Nigeria	..	..	..	1.9	9.9	9.1	1.0	-9.3	-7.5	2.7	-1.2	..	..	0.8
Rwanda	..	-14.2	-14.6	-12.4	-13.7	-13.2	-9.2	-8.3	-9.7	-9.0	-9.5	..	..	-11.3
São Tomé and Principe	..	-50.8	-50.3	-60.5	-60.9	-55.8	-54.5	-34.6	-50.1	-44.5	-53.6	..	-19.1	-50.9
Senegal	-5.3	-3.1	-4.2	-6.1	-3.5	-4.4	-2.0	-3.3	0.1	-1.8	-3.9	-7.7	-3.4	-3.0
Seychelles	..	-7.1	-13.0	2.7	1.0	-9.8	-9.6	-24.3	-13.0	-15.8	-10.8	..	..	-9.0
Sierra Leone	..	-9.1	-7.4	-5.5	-9.2	-6.8	-7.5	-12.8	-14.9	-17.3	-16.2	..	-20.0	-11.0
Somalia	..	..	..	..	..	..	..	..	..	..	..	..	..	..
South Africa	-2.5	-7.8	-9.0	-6.2	-5.2	-5.4	-4.5	-2.7	-2.1	-2.0	-1.6	-4.6	-4.4	-4.5
Sudan	..	-18.8	-10.1	-4.4	-1.9	-1.5	-0.5	-0.6	-0.8	-0.8	-1.0	-12.2	-12.1	-5.4
Swaziland	..	-3.0	-5.4	-5.9	-1.9	-1.5	1.6	0.5	-1.7	-2.5	-4.5	..	..	-1.8
Tanzania	..	0.8	-4.8	-1.7	-5.2	-3.9	-1.4	-2.6	-3.4	-5.4	-4.2	-12.2	-6.7	-2.7
Togo	..	-6.0	-15.8	-12.9	-7.7	-5.1	-0.6	-6.5	-5.1	-5.9	-2.6	-5.6	-6.9	-6.9
Uganda	..	-14.4	-11.3	-10.3	-6.9	-5.9	-5.8	-5.8	-6.3	-14.5	-10.6	-2.7	-4.7	-8.8
Zambia	..	-12.6	-13.6	-11.8	-9.5	-6.6	-5.3	-9.8	-10.3	-10.7	-13.0	..	-12.0	-11.0
Zimbabwe	6.9	-8.4	-8.1	-8.6	-11.9	-9.0	-8.6	-4.2	-10.6	-22.5	-11.6	7.0	-9.0	-9.8
NORTH AFRICA	..	-3.3	-4.9	-3.2	-2.5	-0.9	-0.8	-2.4	-3.0	0.0	-0.5	..	-9.8	-2.8
Algeria	-8.4	-1.2	-8.6	-4.4	-1.4	2.9	2.4	-3.9	-0.6	9.9	6.0	-9.5	-9.2	0.5
Egypt, Arab Republic	..	-5.5	-3.5	-2.1	-1.2	-1.3	-0.9	-1.0	-4.2	-3.6	-4.6	..	-16.0	-4.9
Libya	..	..	..	..	..	..	..	..	..	..	..	..	..	..
Morocco	-11.3	-2.3	-3.3	-4.0	-5.4	-3.5	-3.4	-2.7	-4.7	-6.2	-0.8	-2.6	-6.2	-3.6
Tunisia	0.9	-3.0	-2.8	-2.5	-4.5	-5.1	-4.2	-2.8	-2.6	-3.3	-3.0	-1.7	-1.8	-3.6
ALL AFRICA	..	-6.6	-7.3	-5.2	-3.7	-3.0	-3.1	-3.8	-4.0	-2.4	-2.3	-6.4	-6.8	-4.4

Note: 2001 data are preliminary. Nigeria: from 1992 accounts are for consolidated budget; since 1994, ratios are distorted as off. exch. rate used by the Gov. for oil exports oil value added is significantly over-valued.

7-3. Government primary deficit/surplus (-/+)

	Percentage of GDP											Annual Average		
	1980	1992	1993	1994	1995	1996	1997	1998	1999	2000	2001	75-84	85-89	90-MR
SUB-SAHARAN AFRICA	..	..	..	..	..	..	..	..	..	..	..	..	..	..
excluding South Africa	..	-1.7	-0.9	4.7	2.8	2.7	1.2	-0.8	-0.3	1.4	1.6	..	..	0.7
excl. S.Africa & Nigeria	..	-1.7	-0.9	4.1	0.5	0.8	0.7	0.3	-0.5	-0.2	0.6	..	-1.6	0.1
Angola	..	-48.7	-12.2	219.0	-26.6	-4.5	-16.5	-1.0	-7.3	-1.1	4.8	..	-8.6	5.7
Benin	..	-3.6	-0.2	-1.2	-1.8	2.1	2.0	3.1	2.8	-0.9	-0.7	..	-2.7	-0.7
Botswana	..	9.3	9.5	5.0	4.1	4.4	5.4	2.1	-2.7	7.0	6.7	..	..	5.9
Burkina Faso	..	-1.5	-3.0	-1.9	-2.4	0.3	-2.4	-2.3	-3.1	-3.3	-3.4	..	..	-2.4
Burundi	10.1	-0.8	-2.2	-0.7	-0.4	-5.6	-2.1	-2.3	-3.2	2.2	1.7	10.1	-1.7	-1.1
Cameroon	0.7	-1.2	-1.5	-2.2	3.2	5.0	4.9	4.0	1.9	5.7	6.3	1.6	-3.9	1.4
Cape Verde	..	-4.5	-2.9	-13.0	-15.9	-13.6	-2.1	0.2	-0.5	-16.3	-5.3	-7.2	-4.2	-6.3
Central African Republic	..	-7.0	-6.1	-7.6	-2.8	-1.5	-0.9	0.5	-0.5	-0.1	1.2	..	..	-3.2
Chad	..	-7.4	-7.4	-3.5	-3.4	-4.0	-2.9	-1.8	-5.0	-1.0	-0.2	..	-5.1	-3.9
Comoros	..	-8.9	-1.1	-12.6	-5.2	-4.3	-1.1	-1.9	0.6	-1.5	-2.2	-22.0	-7.3	-3.7
Congo, Democratic Rep. of	..	..	..	..	..	-1.2	-6.1	-2.4	-3.1	-1.8	1.8	..	..	-2.1
Congo, Republic of	..	-6.2	-5.2	-1.1	5.9	7.0	3.0	-5.4	5.7	8.1	6.8	7.1	-3.2	1.5
Côte d'Ivoire	..	-0.9	-3.2	1.5	3.0	3.3	3.1	2.4	2.0	3.4	3.0	..	-0.1	1.1
Djibouti	..	-11.1	-12.5	-8.1	-7.4	-3.2	-3.8	1.3	-1.8	-1.0	..	..	..	-5.3
Equatorial Guinea	..	..	..	1.4	-0.4	-2.4	2.9	-4.1	1.4	9.3	12.3	..	..	2.6
Eritrea	..	-3.1	-7.0	-13.7	-25.3	-9.0	1.2	-28.8	-45.8	-25.7	-29.3	..	..	-18.7
Ethiopia	..	-5.5	-3.9	-4.3	-1.4	-3.2	-0.2	-2.5	-7.3	-9.3	-2.9	-5.7	-4.2	-4.7
Gabon	..	1.1	1.3	5.1	11.3	8.6	8.3	-7.1	5.8	6.1	7.2	-34.5	-2.4	4.4
Gambia, The	..	4.7	5.1	2.6	-2.5	-5.6	-1.3	2.9	1.5	3.2	-1.5	..	8.0	1.5
Ghana	..	-1.8	0.4	-4.4	-2.1	-4.4	-3.1	-1.4	-1.6	0.8	4.1	-1.1	-1.2	-0.9
Guinea	..	-1.5	-2.4	-2.0	-1.3	-1.7	-1.2	0.7	-1.5	-3.5	-1.2	..	-2.8	-1.6
Guinea-Bissau	0.0	-17.0	-7.2	-3.0	5.2	-5.6	-12.7	-9.5	2.0	-5.0	-2.1	-3.2	-10.6	-5.8
Kenya	-3.7	5.1	8.8	8.3	7.3	6.2	4.8	5.2	3.6	1.4	0.7	-2.2	1.3	4.8
Lesotho	..	5.0	3.7	6.2	6.7	6.1	4.1	0.6	-10.1	-1.6	2.3	..	-7.3	2.5
Liberia	..	..	..	..	..	..	..	..	..	..	..	..	..	..
Madagascar	..	-3.5	-3.5	-3.3	-0.2	-3.4	0.6	-3.1	-0.5	-0.3	-2.1	3.2	2.1	-1.5
Malawi	-8.3	-7.9	-3.0	-12.4	1.7	1.6	-2.1	-2.7	-1.1	-0.4	-2.1	-5.2	0.4	-2.4
Mali	-10.5	-2.2	-2.5	-2.1	-1.7	0.2	-1.1	-2.8	-2.9	-3.2	-5.6	-7.7	-3.7	-2.2
Mauritania	..	2.3	-3.3	2.4	4.4	10.6	8.0	7.1	8.3	1.4	0.2	..	-6.5	2.6
Mauritius	..	1.2	0.9	0.3	-0.6	-4.1	-3.9	-0.1	0.1	-0.4	-2.5	-4.6	2.1	-0.3
Mozambique	-2.1	-0.4	-1.1	-4.2	-1.6	-1.4	-1.3	-1.3	-0.8	-4.3	-4.2	-8.5	-7.1	-2.2
Namibia	..	-4.3	-4.3	-1.1	-2.2	-3.8	-1.4	-1.2	-0.9	0.3	-2.0	-2.2	4.0	-1.8
Niger	..	-3.1	-2.1	-4.4	-0.4	1.4	-1.2	-2.6	-3.6	-0.3	-0.6	-2.8	-2.1	-1.9
Nigeria	..	..	..	7.5	13.6	11.4	3.5	-6.3	0.8	10.1	6.1	..	..	5.8
Rwanda	..	-6.2	-6.1	-7.0	0.0	-4.1	-1.2	-2.0	-3.0	1.0	-0.3	..	..	-3.0
São Tomé and Principe	..	-30.8	-22.2	-32.0	-25.5	-22.3	-15.4	-12.5	-11.9	-10.0	-5.8	..	2.5	-17.6
Senegal	-2.5	0.2	-0.8	1.6	2.7	4.6	2.8	1.0	3.6	1.7	-1.1	-4.3	1.2	1.7
Seychelles	..	2.0	-3.5	11.9	11.2	-0.1	0.3	-13.7	-3.0	-6.8	-0.8	..	..	0.7
Sierra Leone	..	-3.3	-3.4	-3.0	-7.3	-3.0	-4.9	-5.6	-3.7	-3.0	-4.9	..	-12.8	-4.4
Somalia	..	..	..	..	..	..	..	..	..	..	..	..	..	..
South Africa	..	..	..	..	..	..	..	..	..	..	..	..	..	..
Sudan	..	..	..	..	..	..	..	0.1	0.0	0.5	..	..	..	0.2
Swaziland	..	-0.8	-3.8	-4.6	-1.1	-0.5	2.5	1.6	-0.4	-0.8	-2.4	..	..	-0.4
Tanzania	..	2.6	-2.5	0.5	-0.4	1.1	4.2	2.3	1.9	0.5	0.9	-7.0	-1.2	1.2
Togo	..	-1.3	-11.2	-6.0	-2.8	-1.8	3.1	-2.6	-0.9	-3.2	-0.1	4.0	1.0	-2.5
Uganda	..	-4.0	-1.4	-2.3	-1.6	-0.9	-0.4	0.5	-0.4	-7.6	-1.7	-0.1	-2.7	-2.2
Zambia	..	6.1	6.7	5.2	3.8	4.2	3.9	0.1	0.5	-1.9	-4.7	..	-1.3	2.1
Zimbabwe	-2.2	-1.1	0.1	0.0	-0.7	0.7	-0.4	7.4	0.7	-4.2	-1.2	-3.2	-3.2	-0.1
NORTH AFRICA	..	2.4	1.1	3.4	3.3	4.7	4.5	2.5	..	4.8	4.4	..	-3.6	2.7
Algeria	..	1.0	-6.3	-1.6	1.7	6.4	6.3	0.1	..	14.0	10.6	..	0.0	3.7
Egypt, Arab Republic	..	3.7	6.1	8.6	6.9	6.2	5.7	4.8	1.8	2.0	0.9	-22.6	-14.3	2.7
Libya	..	..	..	..	..	..	..	..	..	..	..	..	..	..
Morocco	-8.5	3.3	3.0	1.9	0.6	1.9	2.1	2.4	0.8	-1.0	4.0	2.3	0.4	2.4
Tunisia	2.5	0.2	0.7	1.6	-0.2	-0.6	-0.4	0.6	1.1	0.4	0.2	0.1	1.0	0.0
ALL AFRICA	..	..	..	..	..	..	..	..	..	..	..	..	..	..

Note: 2001 data are preliminary. Nigeria: from 1992 accounts are for consolidated budget; since 1994, ratios are distorted as off. exch. rate used by the Gov. for oil exports oil value added is significantly over-valued.

7-4. Government expenditure and lending minus repayments

	Percentage of GDP											Annual Average		
	1980	1992	1993	1994	1995	1996	1997	1998	1999	2000	2001	75-84	85-89	90-MR
SUB-SAHARAN AFRICA	..	29.9	31.6	29.2	28.0	27.0	27.6	25.6	26.7	27.3	27.4	26.9	28.5	28.0
excluding South Africa	..	28.5	27.4	24.9	23.5	21.6	23.3	24.6	27.1	28.5	28.4	..	27.6	25.8
excl. S.Africa & Nigeria	..	28.5	27.4	26.5	25.6	23.7	24.1	24.4	24.9	25.6	24.1	25.1	27.6	25.6
Angola	..	92.5	60.7	62.1	67.6	64.1	64.7	42.8	82.6	60.7	48.6	..	43.4	61.6
Benin	..	20.8	17.8	19.8	22.1	19.5	18.6	16.3	17.6	20.1	20.3	..	20.0	19.3
Botswana	..	39.7	39.2	37.5	32.8	33.9	33.9	37.5	40.0	38.7	39.1	35.8	34.9	37.0
Burkina Faso	..	20.9	21.6	22.8	22.7	21.8	24.2	24.6	28.2	25.9	25.0	..	..	23.2
Burundi	11.9	28.5	30.1	24.7	25.9	27.4	22.2	23.6	28.7	25.0	25.1	12.6	23.9	26.1
Cameroon	16.0	22.1	20.0	19.3	16.2	16.0	16.3	17.9	18.5	17.4	18.6	10.6	23.9	18.9
Cape Verde	..	44.2	48.0	52.6	51.7	42.9	40.4	41.9	33.0	45.0	28.5	67.4	42.2	40.5
Central African Republic	..	23.6	21.2	22.4	20.6	11.0	14.0	17.7	17.9	18.9	18.7	..	19.7	19.3
Chad	..	19.3	20.2	19.1	18.1	18.5	18.1	15.3	18.6	20.3	18.7	..	21.8	18.6
Comoros	..	31.6	25.1	38.3	31.1	26.5	24.9	22.1	19.2	16.1	21.9	36.8	36.9	26.6
Congo, Democratic Rep. of	..	..	..	..	..	9.6	20.2	12.2	10.1	10.2	1.7	..	..	10.7
Congo, Republic of	..	36.6	36.7	36.7	32.8	32.8	37.7	42.9	32.8	25.5	32.0	28.4	33.9	35.0
Côte d'Ivoire	..	31.9	30.0	27.0	26.7	22.4	22.0	21.1	19.4	18.1	18.1	..	35.9	25.2
Djibouti	..	51.0	50.1	43.0	38.7	34.7	35.4	33.3	33.1	32.7	..	..	..	39.1
Equatorial Guinea	..	47.6	55.9	27.1	24.6	24.9	16.6	30.0	16.0	8.6	5.0	..	38.0	30.6
Eritrea	..	35.6	68.2	65.2	77.5	66.0	55.5	81.9	97.9	100.8	96.7	..	..	74.5
Ethiopia	..	20.2	19.6	25.0	24.7	26.9	24.2	25.3	30.8	33.1	29.6	26.1	29.5	26.1
Gabon	..	28.3	28.6	25.5	26.3	23.0	28.8	46.2	27.0	21.5	23.0	36.9	37.6	27.4
Gambia, The	..	26.4	25.4	25.1	27.2	31.1	26.9	23.2	22.7	22.1	26.0	35.9	31.8	25.7
Ghana	18.7	24.6	29.0	31.2	30.4	29.7	29.0	28.6	26.2	27.7	26.2	13.1	18.3	26.7
Guinea	..	19.3	18.5	17.3	17.7	16.5	17.4	14.8	16.1	13.7	14.2	..	22.6	17.1
Guinea-Bissau	0.0	48.1	40.3	35.5	30.4	33.7	46.3	25.0	31.3	44.1	43.0	10.8	52.0	38.9
Kenya	34.3	30.0	35.3	31.1	30.7	29.3	27.2	26.2	24.5	26.0	26.9	27.2	28.5	29.3
Lesotho	..	44.9	45.0	46.3	47.6	48.4	48.1	49.1	56.4	48.4	43.5	37.6	44.7	48.2
Liberia	..	..	..	..	..	..	..	..	..	..	..	..	..	..
Madagascar	..	21.3	21.9	20.4	16.9	21.7	17.4	19.9	17.8	18.1	18.1	13.4	14.6	18.8
Malawi	35.7	34.6	26.0	49.0	31.0	23.3	24.2	29.5	29.1	31.6	31.9	29.2	32.3	30.2
Mali	108.2	24.4	23.4	27.2	23.5	23.5	23.9	27.3	26.4	26.8	31.3	106.8	25.6	26.0
Mauritania	..	24.8	36.8	27.7	24.8	24.0	22.7	25.0	25.8	29.1	25.9	..	39.5	27.8
Mauritius	32.9	25.1	23.1	23.5	23.3	24.6	27.0	23.6	24.0	24.6	24.8	32.5	26.0	24.5
Mozambique	17.4	30.3	29.5	30.9	24.4	20.5	23.5	21.8	25.1	28.8	30.7	26.5	24.5	26.7
Namibia	..	39.4	36.7	32.4	34.4	35.3	35.5	35.8	37.2	35.6	37.5	38.4	35.8	35.3
Niger	..	16.8	16.7	18.6	14.7	12.9	15.7	17.8	17.8	16.1	16.6	19.2	20.1	16.9
Nigeria	..	..	..	16.6	12.7	10.6	19.0	25.5	38.2	43.9	50.5	..	..	27.1
Rwanda	..	24.4	23.7	16.0	20.5	22.5	19.6	18.9	19.6	18.7	20.9	..	..	20.6
São Tomé and Principe	..	71.1	68.3	73.8	77.5	69.3	70.1	59.6	69.5	66.0	76.2	..	43.6	69.0
Senegal	27.4	21.5	20.8	21.0	19.9	20.9	18.9	20.1	17.2	19.9	21.7	26.8	20.6	20.2
Seychelles	..	51.6	64.9	51.0	46.7	52.4	52.9	69.6	59.2	58.0	53.0	..	..	54.9
Sierra Leone	..	21.7	21.3	17.3	18.0	16.9	13.0	20.1	22.0	28.7	30.1	..	29.0	21.5
Somalia	..	..	..	..	..	..	..	..	..	..	..	..	..	..
South Africa	24.1	31.1	35.5	34.0	33.0	33.3	32.6	26.8	26.3	25.8	26.2	26.4	29.3	30.3
Sudan	..	27.6	18.4	13.2	10.6	7.6	7.2	7.4	8.7	12.1	12.4	23.1	20.8	13.6
Swaziland	..	32.7	32.3	32.9	29.7	30.1	27.7	28.7	30.9	30.1	31.6	..	..	30.3
Tanzania	..	14.2	17.7	15.6	16.2	15.8	13.6	13.7	14.1	16.1	15.5	30.9	20.5	15.1
Togo	40.5	22.2	26.7	25.1	22.6	20.0	18.0	22.7	19.5	19.2	16.3	34.9	32.4	22.2
Uganda	..	21.2	18.6	18.6	16.7	16.2	16.8	16.4	18.0	25.8	21.4	13.7	11.0	18.1
Zambia	38.1	31.0	29.4	31.9	29.4	27.3	25.2	28.6	28.0	30.1	32.1	35.1	32.1	30.0
Zimbabwe	4.2	36.1	34.8	33.1	38.6	34.5	37.4	35.7	39.5	49.9	34.9	11.4	35.6	36.8
NORTH AFRICA	..	32.7	33.1	31.9	30.3	29.2	29.1	28.9	30.1	29.4	31.3	..	35.7	30.9
Algeria	46.2	31.4	36.1	33.5	31.6	29.2	31.2	31.7	30.5	29.4	35.4	47.8	39.7	31.3
Egypt, Arab Republic	..	36.6	33.2	32.2	28.6	27.8	26.1	25.3	28.4	27.2	27.8	..	41.3	31.0
Libya	..	..	..	..	..	..	..	..	..	..	..	..	..	..
Morocco	32.2	28.5	29.8	28.2	29.3	28.1	29.8	30.0	31.9	32.4	31.4	24.6	27.3	29.4
Tunisia	27.9	30.2	30.7	33.8	34.5	35.5	32.6	32.0	31.5	31.9	32.0	32.3	31.3	32.3
ALL AFRICA	..	30.9	32.1	30.1	28.8	27.7	28.1	26.8	27.9	28.0	28.7	30.1	31.1	29.0

Note: 2001 data are preliminary. Nigeria: from 1992 accounts are for consolidated budget; since 1994, ratios are distorted as off. exch. rate used by the Gov. for oil exports oil value added is significantly over-valued.

7-5. Government interest payments

	Percentage of GDP											Annual Average		
	1980	*1992*	*1993*	*1994*	*1995*	*1996*	*1997*	*1998*	*1999*	*2000*	*2001*	*75-84*	*85-89*	*90-MR*
SUB-SAHARAN AFRICA	..	..	..	..	..	..	..	..	..	..	..	..	..	..
excluding South Africa	..	5.2	5.3	8.9	4.4	3.8	3.5	3.5	4.2	4.3	3.9	3.4	4.4	4.8
excl. S.Africa & Nigeria	..	4.2	4.6	9.6	4.6	4.1	3.7	3.5	3.4	3.7	3.2	3.2	3.5	4.4
Angola	..	8.2	9.4	239.1	10.9	11.6	5.6	6.9	9.1	5.6	4.7	..	2.5	26.9
Benin	..	3.7	2.7	3.2	2.8	2.4	1.7	1.0	0.9	0.9	0.9	..	2.0	2.1
Botswana	..	0.0	0.0	0.0	0.0	0.0	0.0	0.0	0.0	0.0	0.0	..	..	0.0
Burkina Faso	..	1.4	1.5	1.6	1.5	0.9	0.9	0.9	0.9	1.0	1.0	0.7	1.2	1.2
Burundi	0.2	1.8	1.5	1.5	1.8	1.8	2.0	2.4	3.2	3.1	2.6	0.7	2.0	2.1
Cameroon	0.3	5.2	4.8	7.0	6.4	6.7	6.1	5.7	5.1	4.4	3.9	0.6	1.3	5.1
Cape Verde	..	1.1	1.2	1.0	3.2	3.6	3.9	3.6	1.3	2.7	2.6	0.0	1.1	2.2
Central African Republic	..	1.9	2.1	2.4	2.3	1.9	1.3	1.3	1.4	1.9	1.4	..	1.4	1.7
Chad	..	0.7	1.2	1.2	1.0	1.0	1.0	0.8	0.9	1.0	0.8	..	0.2	0.9
Comoros	..	0.9	0.9	1.2	0.9	1.0	1.0	1.1	1.0	0.4	1.0	0.0	0.3	1.0
Congo, Democratic Rep. of	..	..	..	..	..	3.0	4.7	3.8	2.3	1.8	1.3	..	..	2.8
Congo, Republic of	..	7.9	7.4	12.1	14.1	12.0	12.1	14.6	11.6	6.9	7.5	0.0	4.8	10.4
Côte d'Ivoire	0.0	10.4	8.7	7.9	6.9	5.2	4.4	3.8	3.9	4.1	3.4	1.6	8.1	6.6
Djibouti	..	0.6	0.4	0.3	0.6	0.7	0.5	0.3	0.3	0.7	..	..	..	0.5
Equatorial Guinea	..	8.0	7.6	7.1	5.9	3.9	1.4	1.7	1.4	0.3	0.2	..	5.8	4.2
Eritrea	..	0.0	0.0	0.1	0.5	0.9	1.1	1.3	2.0	2.9	3.4	..	..	1.2
Ethiopia	..	1.5	2.0	3.4	2.5	2.4	2.2	1.9	2.0	2.2	2.1	0.9	1.5	2.1
Gabon	..	6.4	7.0	6.7	8.1	5.9	5.8	7.3	7.2	5.5	5.0	2.4	4.8	6.4
Gambia, The	..	3.4	3.8	3.7	3.8	4.4	5.1	5.3	5.0	4.6	4.8	..	4.2	4.3
Ghana	..	2.2	3.5	4.4	4.2	5.1	6.3	5.1	5.6	7.5	7.9	1.3	1.5	4.6
Guinea	..	1.6	1.3	1.6	1.4	1.3	1.6	1.4	1.6	1.7	1.5	..	2.7	1.7
Guinea-Bissau	0.0	4.6	5.8	5.4	6.7	6.6	5.5	6.8	6.4	5.7	8.4	0.1	3.9	5.9
Kenya	3.5	8.4	14.3	11.2	8.1	7.0	5.9	5.5	4.4	3.5	3.2	3.7	5.1	7.5
Lesotho	..	2.7	2.4	1.9	1.7	1.6	1.8	2.4	3.0	3.9	3.2	..	4.8	2.9
Liberia	..	..	..	..	..	..	..	..	..	..	..	..	..	..
Madagascar	..	3.4	4.0	5.4	5.1	4.7	3.0	2.7	2.1	2.3	2.0	1.0	1.8	3.2
Malawi	3.2	3.2	3.1	5.1	6.4	5.3	3.4	3.8	3.4	4.4	5.2	4.2	6.0	4.2
Mali	4.4	1.8	1.6	2.4	1.4	1.1	1.0	0.8	1.0	1.0	0.9	5.9	1.7	1.4
Mauritania	..	3.0	4.1	2.9	3.2	3.2	3.0	3.5	3.6	3.0	3.1	..	3.2	3.1
Mauritius	..	3.8	2.8	2.7	3.0	3.2	3.4	3.7	3.5	3.4	4.1	5.8	4.9	3.5
Mozambique	0.0	2.4	2.5	1.1	1.6	1.4	1.3	1.0	0.6	0.2	0.6	0.0	1.0	1.3
Namibia	..	0.3	0.6	0.9	1.1	1.5	1.9	2.4	2.4	2.2	2.4	2.6	2.7	1.4
Niger	..	1.6	1.7	2.3	2.3	1.7	1.5	1.6	1.6	1.7	1.8	2.1	2.7	1.8
Nigeria	1.4	9.8	8.2	5.6	3.7	2.3	2.4	3.1	8.3	7.5	7.3	1.7	8.0	6.6
Rwanda	0.2	1.9	2.1	4.5	2.3	1.6	1.2	0.9	0.8	0.9	0.8	0.4	1.0	1.7
São Tomé and Principe	..	11.0	11.5	11.0	12.0	10.0	11.3	12.4	11.3	6.6	7.9	..	6.3	10.4
Senegal	2.0	2.0	2.3	3.5	2.9	2.3	2.3	1.3	1.5	1.5	0.8	2.5	3.2	2.1
Seychelles	1.8	7.9	8.0	8.4	9.7	9.2	9.4	10.2	9.4	8.0	8.4	1.9	6.6	8.7
Sierra Leone	2.0	5.8	4.0	2.4	1.9	2.1	2.1	4.8	5.8	6.3	4.9	2.3	6.4	4.5
Somalia	..	..	..	..	..	..	..	..	..	..	..	..	..	..
South Africa	..	..	..	..	..	..	..	..	..	..	..	..	..	..
Sudan	..	..	..	..	..	..	..	0.7	0.9	1.3	..	..	..	0.9
Swaziland	..	0.8	0.6	0.6	0.6	0.7	0.6	0.6	0.8	0.7	0.7	..	..	0.7
Tanzania	..	1.7	2.3	2.2	3.0	3.0	2.4	2.1	1.5	1.7	1.6	2.4	2.4	2.1
Togo	..	3.0	4.3	5.5	3.5	2.8	2.3	2.6	2.5	2.2	1.9	7.2	4.8	3.1
Uganda	..	3.3	1.8	1.4	1.0	1.0	0.9	1.0	0.9	1.1	1.2	2.0	0.9	1.3
Zambia	4.1	8.5	12.3	11.6	8.1	4.8	4.1	3.4	2.8	3.0	2.5	4.2	9.5	6.5
Zimbabwe	1.2	5.7	6.2	6.7	9.4	8.5	7.1	9.9	10.3	17.2	10.2	2.6	4.8	8.4
NORTH AFRICA	..	4.8	5.6	6.0	5.4	5.3	5.0	4.6	..	4.7	4.6	..	3.6	4.9
Algeria	..	2.2	2.3	2.8	3.1	3.5	4.0	4.0	..	4.0	4.2	..	1.7	3.0
Egypt, Arab Republic	..	6.8	8.5	9.4	7.3	7.0	6.0	5.3	5.4	5.3	5.4	0.0	3.0	6.4
Libya	..	..	..	..	..	..	..	..	..	..	..	..	..	..
Morocco	2.4	5.6	5.9	5.7	6.0	5.4	5.4	5.2	5.5	5.3	4.8	4.1	6.1	5.5
Tunisia	1.6	3.2	3.5	3.7	4.0	4.3	3.4	3.1	3.4	3.3	2.9	1.8	2.8	3.4
ALL AFRICA	..	..	..	..	..	..	..	..	..	..	..	..	..	..

Note: 2001 data are preliminary. Nigeria: from 1992 accounts are for consolidated budget; since 1994, ratios are distorted as off. exch. rate used by the Gov. for oil exports oil value added is significantly over-valued.

7-6. Government revenue (excluding grants)

	Percentage of GDP											Annual Average		
	1980	1992	1993	1994	1995	1996	1997	1998	1999	2000	2001	75-84	85-89	90-MR
SUB-SAHARAN AFRICA	..	22.5	23.2	22.9	23.6	22.9	23.3	21.0	22.2	23.7	24.2	21.0	21.9	22.8
excluding South Africa	..	21.7	20.2	18.6	19.8	18.6	19.2	18.4	20.5	23.6	23.9	18.6	19.1	20.1
excl. S.Africa & Nigeria	..	19.0	19.1	18.6	19.2	18.4	19.0	18.8	18.5	19.2	18.9	18.6	20.2	18.8
Angola	..	35.6	39.1	42.1	30.1	44.8	40.3	31.6	46.8	51.7	41.1	..	32.3	37.3
Benin	..	9.5	11.0	12.8	14.8	15.2	14.5	15.3	16.0	16.6	16.2	14.2	4.5	13.0
Botswana	..	48.1	47.5	41.2	36.4	38.0	38.8	39.0	36.7	45.4	45.7	43.5	48.0	42.2
Burkina Faso	..	11.7	12.0	11.6	11.6	12.6	13.6	14.5	15.2	13.3	12.5	9.7	10.6	12.9
Burundi	18.1	17.2	17.4	20.1	20.1	17.7	15.1	18.0	19.5	20.9	21.6	18.0	17.9	18.3
Cameroon	16.3	15.7	13.7	9.9	12.9	14.3	15.1	15.9	15.2	18.8	20.6	11.1	18.6	15.1
Cape Verde	..	18.7	23.5	23.4	23.9	20.7	24.3	22.4	26.4	20.5	19.9	22.4	16.4	21.4
Central African Republic	..	8.9	7.7	7.5	9.2	6.1	7.7	9.1	9.2	9.7	10.8	..	..	8.8
Chad	..	6.3	7.0	4.9	6.2	7.3	7.8	7.6	8.1	12.8	12.3	3.6	5.4	7.8
Comoros	..	15.0	13.8	14.5	13.2	12.3	13.8	11.4	11.7	10.1	13.9	17.6	12.9	13.3
Congo, Democratic Rep. of	..	..	..	..	..	5.4	9.4	6.0	4.8	4.5	5.9	..	..	6.0
Congo, Republic of	..	22.5	24.1	22.4	23.6	27.5	28.5	22.6	26.5	26.4	31.1	34.6	25.9	25.7
Côte d'Ivoire	..	20.1	17.6	19.9	22.1	19.8	19.4	18.4	16.4	16.4	16.8	30.0	27.7	19.0
Djibouti	..	26.9	28.4	29.5	28.7	28.9	27.3	25.3	23.5	22.3	..	..	..	26.8
Equatorial Guinea	..	..	..	17.3	15.7	17.7	17.4	23.6	15.8	17.6	16.9	..	..	17.7
Eritrea	..	23.6	61.3	52.0	51.5	44.7	49.4	41.9	41.6	53.0	44.8	..	..	46.4
Ethiopia	..	10.6	12.0	13.9	17.4	18.4	18.2	18.1	17.9	18.3	19.6	17.4	20.0	16.3
Gabon	..	22.9	22.6	23.5	29.5	25.7	31.3	31.8	25.6	22.1	25.2	-0.3	30.0	25.4
Gambia, The	..	23.2	23.0	20.9	18.5	18.8	19.1	18.8	17.8	18.5	16.2	21.2	21.3	19.8
Ghana	..	15.2	19.2	18.7	20.4	17.6	17.3	18.3	16.4	17.7	16.7	8.0	13.2	17.3
Guinea	..	12.2	11.2	10.2	11.0	10.3	11.5	11.2	10.8	6.1	8.7	..	14.4	11.1
Guinea-Bissau	0.0	10.7	10.4	12.4	12.7	12.5	15.3	5.4	17.3	19.2	19.6	0.7	13.6	13.9
Kenya	22.9	24.9	29.9	28.1	28.6	27.5	25.2	25.1	24.4	23.4	21.8	18.7	22.4	25.6
Lesotho	..	41.1	45.0	46.9	48.0	48.1	46.5	44.6	40.9	40.8	40.1	31.7	33.5	43.3
Liberia	..	..	..	..	..	..	..	..	..	..	..	..	..	..
Madagascar	..	11.0	10.8	8.8	8.8	9.4	9.7	10.7	11.6	11.9	10.3	14.4	13.6	10.5
Malawi	19.8	20.7	17.1	19.5	18.3	15.1	15.2	16.8	18.1	17.4	17.8	18.1	22.4	17.9
Mali	72.8	13.3	13.8	12.7	12.9	15.4	16.0	15.6	17.2	16.5	18.8	68.6	15.1	15.5
Mauritania	..	22.4	27.2	24.7	24.0	29.2	27.0	27.1	27.9	24.0	18.4	..	24.7	24.9
Mauritius	22.0	22.5	21.0	20.8	19.3	17.1	19.6	19.5	20.5	20.7	18.1	21.8	22.3	20.4
Mozambique	13.4	13.9	14.0	11.8	11.3	10.6	11.6	11.3	12.0	12.7	12.9	16.1	11.1	12.3
Namibia	0.0	33.9	31.1	30.0	30.8	29.7	31.9	32.0	33.5	33.5	32.4	13.0	28.3	31.5
Niger	..	8.2	7.3	6.0	7.2	7.8	8.4	9.1	8.8	9.3	9.6	11.0	10.7	8.4
Nigeria	..	35.1	25.5	18.5	22.6	19.7	20.0	16.2	30.7	46.6	49.4	..	13.6	27.0
Rwanda	..	10.1	9.1	3.6	6.8	9.3	10.4	10.6	9.9	9.7	11.4	9.0	10.5	9.3
São Tomé and Principe	..	20.2	18.0	13.3	16.5	13.4	15.6	25.0	19.3	21.5	22.6	..	24.6	18.1
Senegal	22.1	18.4	16.6	14.9	16.4	16.6	16.9	16.8	17.3	18.1	17.8	19.1	17.2	17.2
Seychelles	..	44.5	51.9	53.7	47.7	42.6	43.4	45.2	46.2	42.3	42.2	40.2	47.0	46.0
Sierra Leone	..	12.6	13.9	11.8	8.9	10.1	5.4	7.3	7.1	11.4	14.0	..	9.0	10.5
Somalia	..	..	..	..	..	..	..	..	..	..	..	..	..	..
South Africa	21.5	23.4	26.5	27.8	27.8	27.9	28.1	24.2	24.3	23.8	24.6	21.9	24.9	25.8
Sudan	..	8.8	8.3	8.8	8.7	6.1	6.6	6.8	7.9	11.3	11.4	10.9	8.7	8.2
Swaziland	..	29.7	26.8	27.0	27.7	28.6	29.3	29.2	29.2	27.6	27.1	..	..	28.5
Tanzania	..	15.1	12.9	13.9	11.0	11.9	12.2	11.1	10.7	10.6	11.4	18.6	13.8	12.5
Togo	..	16.2	10.9	12.2	14.9	14.9	17.4	16.1	14.4	13.3	13.8	28.1	25.5	15.4
Uganda	..	6.8	7.3	8.3	9.8	10.2	11.0	10.7	11.7	11.3	10.8	11.1	6.3	9.4
Zambia	..	18.4	15.9	20.1	19.9	20.7	19.9	18.8	17.7	19.4	19.1	..	20.1	19.1
Zimbabwe	11.1	27.7	26.8	24.5	26.7	25.5	28.7	31.4	28.9	27.4	23.3	18.5	26.6	27.0
NORTH AFRICA	..	29.5	28.2	28.7	27.8	28.3	28.3	26.5	27.0	29.4	30.8	..	25.8	28.1
Algeria	37.9	30.2	27.5	29.1	30.2	32.2	33.5	27.8	29.9	39.3	41.3	38.3	30.4	31.8
Egypt, Arab Republic	..	31.2	29.7	30.0	27.3	26.5	25.2	24.3	24.2	23.6	23.2	..	25.3	26.1
Libya	..	..	..	..	..	..	..	..	..	..	..	..	..	..
Morocco	20.9	26.2	26.6	24.2	23.9	24.6	26.4	27.3	27.2	26.2	30.6	22.0	21.1	25.8
Tunisia	28.8	27.2	27.8	31.3	30.0	30.3	28.4	29.1	28.9	28.6	29.0	30.6	29.5	28.7
ALL AFRICA	..	24.9	24.9	24.9	25.0	24.7	25.0	22.9	23.9	25.6	26.5	23.8	23.4	24.6

Note: 2001 data are preliminary. Nigeria: from 1992 accounts are for consolidated budget; since 1994, ratios are distorted as off. exch. rate used by the Gov. for oil exports oil value added is significantly over-valued.

7-7. Grants to government

	Percentage of GDP											Annual Average		
	1980	*1992*	*1993*	*1994*	*1995*	*1996*	*1997*	*1998*	*1999*	*2000*	*2001*	*75-84*	*85-89*	*90-MR*
SUB-SAHARAN AFRICA	-7.2	1.4	1.3	1.3	1.1	1.0	1.0	1.1	1.2	1.2	1.3	-0.5	1.0	1.2
excluding South Africa	0.7	2.2	2.3	2.4	2.0	1.9	1.9	2.0	2.2	2.2	2.4	0.9	1.8	2.1
excl. S.Africa & Nigeria	0.9	2.7	2.7	2.8	2.4	2.3	2.2	2.4	2.6	2.6	2.9	1.1	2.1	2.5
Angola	..	0.0	0.0	0.0	0.0	3.2	2.4	3.3	19.4	2.3	7.6	..	0.0	3.2
Benin	0.0	4.1	3.9	2.6	2.7	3.9	4.5	3.1	3.5	1.7	2.6	1.1	5.0	3.5
Botswana	0.0	0.9	1.2	1.4	0.5	0.3	0.5	0.6	0.6	0.4	0.1	0.3	2.1	0.7
Burkina Faso	0.0	6.2	5.2	7.7	7.2	8.6	7.3	7.0	9.0	8.2	8.1	0.7	5.5	6.8
Burundi	3.7	8.6	9.1	2.4	3.6	2.2	3.1	0.9	2.8	3.3	2.6	2.0	1.6	4.6
Cameroon	0.0	0.0	0.0	0.1	0.0	0.0	0.0	0.3	0.2	0.0	0.4	0.0	0.0	0.1
Cape Verde	0.0	17.5	15.3	15.2	8.7	5.0	10.1	16.1	4.9	5.6	0.7	3.8	19.3	9.7
Central African Republic	4.4	5.7	5.3	4.9	6.3	1.5	4.0	7.8	6.8	7.3	7.8	1.6	5.1	5.5
Chad	0.0	4.9	4.6	9.5	7.5	6.2	6.4	5.1	4.6	5.5	5.4	0.8	9.8	6.0
Comoros	0.0	6.8	9.2	10.0	11.7	8.9	9.0	7.8	7.0	4.2	4.4	3.8	19.2	8.6
Congo, Democratic Rep. of	0.0	0.0	0.0	0.0	0.0	0.0	0.0	0.0	0.0	0.0	0.0	0.0	0.0	0.0
Congo, Republic of	0.0	0.0	0.0	1.1	1.0	0.3	0.1	0.3	0.4	0.3	0.2	0.2	0.1	0.4
Côte d'Ivoire	0.0	0.5	0.5	0.7	0.7	0.7	1.3	1.3	1.0	1.0	0.9	0.0	0.0	0.8
Djibouti	..	12.4	8.8	5.0	2.0	1.8	3.8	8.8	7.4	8.6	..	..	0.0	5.3
Equatorial Guinea	..	17.1	19.3	4.2	2.6	0.9	0.7	0.7	0.2	0.1	0.2	0.0	4.6	8.7
Eritrea	..	8.8	22.2	20.1	13.1	11.5	6.2	9.9	8.5	19.2	19.2	..	..	13.9
Ethiopia	..	2.6	1.7	3.5	3.3	2.9	3.6	2.8	3.6	3.3	5.1	2.1	3.7	3.1
Gabon	0.0	0.1	0.3	0.4	0.0	0.0	0.0	0.0	0.0	0.0	0.0	0.0	0.5	0.1
Gambia, The	0.0	4.5	3.7	3.1	2.4	2.2	1.3	2.0	1.3	2.3	3.5	0.0	14.2	3.1
Ghana	0.1	5.4	6.8	3.5	3.6	2.6	2.3	3.8	2.6	3.4	5.7	0.1	2.3	3.9
Guinea	..	4.0	3.6	3.5	4.0	3.2	3.1	2.9	2.3	2.3	2.8	..	3.1	3.2
Guinea-Bissau	0.0	15.8	16.9	14.7	16.3	9.0	12.8	3.2	9.6	14.1	13.0	1.8	24.0	13.3
Kenya	2.5	2.6	3.1	2.8	2.1	1.3	1.4	1.4	1.2	3.6	3.8	1.1	2.0	2.3
Lesotho	0.0	6.1	1.3	3.6	4.7	4.8	3.9	2.7	2.3	2.0	2.5	1.0	5.5	4.5
Liberia	0.0	..	..	..	..	..	..	..	..	..	..	0.0	0.0	..
Madagascar	0.0	3.5	3.5	3.0	2.9	4.2	5.3	3.5	3.6	3.6	3.7	0.2	1.3	3.6
Malawi	4.3	2.8	2.8	12.1	8.0	4.5	3.5	6.2	6.5	9.3	6.8	2.2	3.9	5.7
Mali	20.5	7.1	5.5	10.0	7.5	7.2	5.8	5.9	5.3	6.2	5.9	26.3	5.1	6.7
Mauritania	0.0	1.7	2.2	2.6	2.0	2.2	0.8	1.4	2.6	3.5	4.7	0.0	5.1	2.4
Mauritius	0.0	0.1	0.1	0.2	0.4	0.3	0.1	0.2	0.1	0.1	0.2	0.2	0.8	0.2
Mozambique	1.8	13.7	11.9	13.8	9.8	7.0	9.3	8.1	11.7	11.6	12.9	1.9	5.4	10.9
Namibia	0.0	0.9	0.6	0.4	0.3	0.3	0.3	0.2	0.3	0.3	0.8	7.2	8.8	0.6
Niger	0.0	3.9	5.6	5.8	4.7	4.9	4.6	4.4	3.9	4.8	4.7	0.3	4.6	4.8
Nigeria	0.0	0.0	0.0	0.0	0.0	0.0	0.0	0.0	0.0	0.0	0.0	0.0	0.0	0.0
Rwanda	0.0	6.2	6.4	0.9	11.3	7.4	6.8	5.3	6.0	9.0	8.4	1.6	3.5	6.6
São Tomé and Principe	0.0	9.0	16.6	17.5	23.4	23.5	27.8	9.7	27.0	27.9	39.9	0.0	12.2	22.9
Senegal	0.7	1.3	1.1	4.2	3.3	6.6	2.6	3.0	2.1	2.1	1.9	0.5	1.4	2.6
Seychelles	0.0	1.3	1.6	0.8	0.5	0.5	0.5	0.5	0.7	0.9	1.5	1.6	2.2	1.0
Sierra Leone	1.0	0.0	0.0	0.0	0.0	1.7	0.6	2.4	5.4	8.0	6.4	0.4	0.8	2.0
Somalia	0.0	..	..	..	..	..	..	..	..	..	..	0.0	0.0	0.0
South Africa	-15.5	0.3	0.1	0.0	0.0	0.0	0.0	0.1	0.0	0.0	0.0	-2.0	0.1	0.1
Sudan	0.0	0.0	0.0	0.0	0.0	0.0	0.0	0.0	0.0	0.0	0.0	0.0	0.0	0.0
Swaziland	0.0	1.4	1.0	0.7	0.3	0.3	0.3	0.5	0.4	1.0	1.4	0.0	0.0	0.7
Tanzania	..	2.4	3.4	3.3	1.8	2.0	3.2	2.8	3.7	4.2	3.5	2.8	3.0	3.0
Togo	1.5	1.8	0.3	1.4	1.4	0.5	1.4	1.3	1.6	0.5	0.5	1.4	3.1	1.3
Uganda	0.0	7.1	8.1	6.5	4.4	4.1	4.4	5.3	5.0	5.8	7.6	0.1	1.1	5.3
Zambia	0.0	10.2	8.0	5.3	5.2	6.1	5.1	6.6	8.0	5.7	5.7	0.0	1.2	6.6
Zimbabwe	0.7	1.7	2.0	1.9	1.8	1.3	1.1	1.7	1.0	1.1	0.3	0.5	1.0	1.3
NORTH AFRICA	0.1	0.9	0.5	0.6	0.4	0.2	0.3	0.2	0.3	0.2	0.2	0.3	0.5	0.6
Algeria	0.0	0.0	0.0	0.0	0.0	0.0	0.0	0.0	0.1	0.0	0.4	0.0	0.0	0.0
Egypt, Arab Republic	0.0	2.3	1.2	1.3	0.9	0.6	0.6	0.5	0.6	0.4	0.2	0.0	1.2	1.2
Libya	0.0	..	..	..	..	..	..	..	..	..	..	0.0	0.0	..
Morocco	0.5	0.0	0.3	0.2	0.1	0.0	0.0	0.0	0.0	0.0	0.0	1.7	0.5	0.5
Tunisia	0.0	0.0	0.0	0.4	0.3	0.2	0.3	0.4	0.3	0.4	0.3	0.0	0.0	0.2
ALL AFRICA	-4.4	1.2	1.0	1.0	0.9	0.8	0.7	0.8	0.9	0.8	0.9	-0.2	0.8	1.0

Note: 2001 data are preliminary. Nigeria: from 1992 accounts are for consolidated budget; since 1994, ratios are distorted as off. exch. rate used by the Gov. for oil exports oil value added is significantly over-valued.

7-8. Foreign financing

	Percentage of GDP											Annual Average		
	1980	1992	1993	1994	1995	1996	1997	1998	1999	2000	2001	75-84	85-89	90-MR
SUB-SAHARAN AFRICA	1.0	0.1	0.8	2.0	0.9	1.3	0.9	0.3	0.2	0.4	1.6	1.1	1.4	1.0
excluding South Africa	..	0.1	1.5	3.5	1.3	2.3	1.4	0.5	-0.4	0.4	0.6	1.7	2.9	1.4
excl. S.Africa & Nigeria	..	3.4	2.7	5.0	2.2	3.2	1.4	0.9	0.7	1.0	1.8	2.2	3.2	2.4
Angola	..	1.2	-8.7	7.3	17.0	-8.8	7.0	-12.8	2.1	-4.8	-4.9	..	0.6	0.0
Benin	..	7.9	6.9	10.3	8.3	7.6	2.2	2.3	2.7	3.1	4.3	..	27.9	6.4
Botswana	..	0.0	0.0	0.0	-0.1	-0.1	0.4	0.3	-0.1	-0.3	-0.5	..	..	0.0
Burkina Faso	..	9.4	9.6	10.5	13.1	11.2	9.7	-2.9	-4.1	-6.3	-1.7	3.0	1.1	5.0
Burundi	3.3	14.2	10.6	7.4	2.9	3.0	1.6	2.6	1.7	0.5	1.2	5.6	7.5	5.4
Cameroon	2.2	8.4	0.1	20.5	0.1	8.2	-4.0	9.0	3.3	1.3	1.9	1.6	3.0	4.7
Cape Verde	..	2.2	3.2	..	..	..	..	6.5	8.2	-0.1	7.3	11.5	4.8	3.7
Central African Republic	0.4	0.8	0.3	2.3	0.6	-1.6	-1.6	-1.6	-1.9	-1.9	-1.7	1.0	1.9	-0.3
Chad	..	2.0	2.8	2.6	2.8	6.7	5.6	2.7	5.3	3.3	3.8	0.5	4.1	3.9
Comoros	..	-2.4	2.3	4.8	4.1	3.5	2.7	1.8	1.5	-2.6	3.8	0.0	0.7	2.1
Congo, Democratic Rep. of	..	..	..	..	..	0.0	0.0	0.0	0.0	0.0	..	..	..	0.0
Congo, Republic of	11.2	7.0	8.1	5.4	-14.1	75.4	11.0	-13.3	-12.2	-10.4	-4.2	5.7	6.9	7.1
Côte d'Ivoire	7.9	9.8	7.5	11.0	4.2	2.7	0.9	0.6	0.2	4.2	4.5	6.8	6.1	5.7
Djibouti	..	1.7	3.4	2.5	1.6	3.4	1.4	0.7	2.0	3.7	..	..	..	2.3
Equatorial Guinea	..	0.4	0.6	-8.5	-8.0	-0.4	-0.7	-0.9	-0.6	-0.1	-0.1	..	-0.8	-2.1
Eritrea	..	0.0	0.1	5.0	1.3	1.3	4.4	9.2	15.2	19.5	14.0	..	..	7.0
Ethiopia	..	1.4	2.7	6.0	3.7	3.7	1.8	1.7	3.5	1.7	4.0	2.6	3.1	2.9
Gabon	..	-4.2	-5.1	-3.2	-5.7	-3.1	-4.9	-6.2	-6.9	-2.7	-0.9	..	6.8	-4.0
Gambia, The	0.0	4.1	2.0	0.7	2.9	6.6	4.1	1.2	0.6	-0.8	-1.4	1.3	5.6	2.4
Ghana	0.9	3.5	6.2	4.5	4.3	3.7	4.6	3.1	5.8	9.2	2.9	0.7	2.7	4.7
Guinea	..	1.5	3.1	-0.3	1.7	1.2	4.1	1.8	2.4	1.6	3.5	..	4.7	2.0
Guinea-Bissau	0.0	18.8	14.0	9.9	3.3	9.0	20.8	7.8	-0.1	7.4	11.0	0.0	6.7	8.7
Kenya	0.3	1.3	1.2	-0.5	-0.5	-0.6	-1.1	-1.2	-1.9	-0.4	0.4	0.2	1.0	0.0
Lesotho	..	5.8	6.1	4.1	5.3	7.7	7.3	2.0	-0.9	-3.0	-0.5	-0.5	0.9	4.0
Liberia	..	..	..	..	..	..	..	..	..	..	..	..	..	..
Madagascar	5.6	2.7	2.9	1.7	1.9	5.0	3.8	1.9	1.2	2.7	2.1	4.1	3.4	2.7
Malawi	4.0	4.9	4.4	12.9	1.8	4.9	3.4	9.0	3.1	4.3	3.4	4.8	3.5	5.0
Mali	15.2	4.3	3.4	7.8	7.4	6.1	3.4	3.8	3.8	3.9	6.2	20.5	8.1	5.2
Mauritania	..	0.7	23.5	6.8	2.7	3.4	0.1	-3.2	-2.0	0.1	-1.6	0.0	6.8	2.4
Mauritius	5.7	-0.7	-0.6	-0.2	-0.6	3.2	0.2	-0.3	-1.1	-0.5	-2.9	3.0	-0.4	-0.4
Mozambique	2.1	2.1	2.6	5.9	3.8	4.2	5.8	4.6	1.8	2.8	2.3	3.7	4.1	3.8
Namibia	..	0.3	0.6	0.4	0.7	0.8	0.4	0.4	0.1	0.3	0.2	0.0	0.0	0.3
Niger	..	1.5	-0.1	12.5	-0.6	4.1	3.5	4.3	..	..	..	5.4	4.2	3.6
Nigeria	0.5	-15.1	-4.7	-3.7	-2.9	-2.1	1.4	-1.4	-5.9	-2.9	-5.0	0.6	1.9	-3.5
Rwanda	-0.3	4.2	3.0	-1.4	2.2	2.5	2.1	6.3	3.2	2.2	5.2	0.9	3.4	3.0
São Tomé and Principe	..	40.7	23.4	29.8	29.6	24.9	26.7	5.3	16.9	37.6	16.6	..	8.1	23.9
Senegal	2.7	0.8	0.6	9.2	3.6	0.4	1.7	1.5	0.8	0.1	1.7	4.0	3.2	2.0
Seychelles	..	-1.5	0.9	-1.5	0.8	-1.4	0.7	-0.9	-1.3	3.6	1.3	6.6	3.2	0.2
Sierra Leone	7.8	5.5	8.6	4.9	6.9	3.7	1.4	1.4	-1.2	6.1	42.0	5.0	-3.2	7.2
Somalia	..	..	..	..	..	..	..	..	..	..	..	..	..	..
South Africa	-0.1	0.2	0.0	0.4	0.4	0.2	0.5	0.0	0.8	0.4	2.6	0.1	-0.1	0.5
Sudan	..	..	2.0	1.1	1.0	0.2	0.2	0.1	0.3	0.5	0.6	..	..	0.7
Swaziland	..	-0.4	-0.6	-0.9	0.0	0.3	0.5	2.1	-0.2	0.7	1.9	..	..	0.3
Tanzania	..	1.7	1.7	2.1	0.8	-1.1	-0.4	0.9	0.4	1.4	1.1	1.5	0.7	0.8
Togo	..	2.4	0.8	4.9	11.7	5.9	5.4	4.3	2.0	2.3	1.5	..	7.3	4.1
Uganda	..	5.2	5.2	5.5	4.5	3.4	3.2	2.8	3.3	3.5	3.4	0.4	1.3	4.2
Zambia	..	2.3	6.4	4.1	4.1	2.3	..	..	..	-1.0	-1.1	..	4.5	2.8
Zimbabwe	0.4	3.5	2.0	0.5	0.2	0.2	0.3	-2.6	-1.1	-2.5	..	1.8	1.9	0.3
NORTH AFRICA	..	0.2	0.1	1.9	2.0	0.8	0.1	-0.8	-1.4	-1.7	-0.4	1.4	1.0	0.3
Algeria	-0.1	1.3	1.7	8.3	7.6	4.1	2.3	-0.3	-2.3	-2.4	-1.3	-0.1	0.1	1.5
Egypt, Arab Republic	..	-0.2	-1.0	-1.0	-1.1	-1.2	-1.2	-1.0	-1.2	-1.2	-0.9	3.7	3.8	0.1
Libya	..	..	..	..	..	..	..	..	..	..	..	..	..	..
Morocco	4.8	-1.3	-0.7	-1.8	-0.8	-1.5	-1.9	-1.7	-2.0	-1.8	-1.4	4.0	-4.0	-1.7
Tunisia	..	1.0	1.2	1.4	2.9	2.8	2.4	0.0	1.4	..	5.9	2.4	2.8	2.1
ALL AFRICA	..	0.2	0.5	2.0	1.3	1.2	0.7	-0.1	-0.4	-0.3	0.9	1.1	1.3	0.8

Note: 2001 data are preliminary. Nigeria: from 1992 accounts are for consolidated budget; since 1994, ratios are distorted as off. exch. rate used by the Gov. for oil exports oil value added is significantly over-valued.

7-9. Taxes on income and profits

	Percentage of total revenue											Annual Average		
	1980	1992	1993	1994	1995	1996	1997	1998	1999	2000	2001	75-84	85-89	90-MR
SUB-SAHARAN AFRICA	..	37.1	33.2	32.7	33.8	34.3	36.2	41.7	41.0	41.4	41.4	40.9	36.6	37.3
excluding South Africa	..	20.2	19.6	20.3	22.4	22.5	24.5	27.1	25.7	26.6	26.5	23.0	20.5	23.3
excl. S.Africa & Nigeria	..	24.3	23.6	24.4	26.9	26.9	27.3	27.7	27.6	27.4	27.0	23.0	24.9	26.3
Angola	..	65.5	66.4	72.9	91.7	93.3	90.6	84.0	92.5	93.4	89.3	..	47.6	79.2
Benin	..	28.4	29.6	30.9	28.5	26.9	23.5	23.6	21.1	20.7	22.5	26.3	34.1	25.9
Botswana	..	53.4	49.2	56.6	58.0	53.0	58.9	60.3	56.0	64.0	66.4	12.1	8.1	58.5
Burkina Faso	..	22.0	18.9	18.7	23.4	24.7	21.9	20.2	22.7	28.0	24.6	19.7	19.1	22.3
Burundi	18.9	23.4	27.3	18.3	19.1	22.3	23.8	26.1	24.4	19.6	24.9	21.0	17.7	23.0
Cameroon	21.7	18.0	10.9	12.6	10.9	10.0	13.5	15.7	20.8	16.7	16.9	26.9	49.7	17.3
Cape Verde	..	20.4	22.2	25.1	24.4	29.4	24.8	25.7	24.6	29.5	31.8	29.5	23.6	25.0
Central African Republic	..	22.7	23.0	24.4	20.6	24.3	19.4	14.0	19.9	21.2	21.1	..	..	21.5
Chad	..	27.6	23.5	28.7	38.9	37.6	32.7	30.5	32.2	18.7	20.7	7.6	18.1	28.0
Comoros	..	11.1	9.0	12.4	12.2	9.6	11.2	14.7	17.3	17.2	10.4	0.0	12.2	13.2
Congo, Democratic Rep. of	..	..	..	..	..	17.2	25.0	29.9	17.5	12.6	..	..	..	20.4
Congo, Republic of	..	52.0	51.3	67.7	53.4	62.2	78.7	53.6	72.1	78.1	70.5	15.1	29.4	62.8
Côte d'Ivoire	..	20.3	19.4	14.9	18.3	20.5	22.9	23.6	25.3	27.0	25.0	15.8	18.3	21.7
Djibouti	..	38.9	38.7	38.5	37.2	41.0	39.2	39.2	37.4	39.8	38.6	..	..	38.8
Equatorial Guinea	..	..	..	19.6	20.5	52.9	61.7	76.6	77.4	83.4	87.1	..	..	59.9
Eritrea	..	13.1	12.8	19.5	18.8	20.4	19.4	23.2	21.8	14.9	17.0	..	..	18.1
Ethiopia	..	30.1	23.1	24.0	22.2	25.2	25.3	23.1	23.2	24.9	26.9	28.6	28.9	25.7
Gabon	..	13.4	12.8	10.7	10.5	10.6	10.1	13.0	17.0	13.7	14.1	..	23.7	12.8
Gambia, The	..	14.8	16.2	17.7	19.4	19.9	21.1	22.3	23.0	22.5	25.3	14.2	13.8	19.0
Ghana	..	14.6	14.8	17.5	17.4	21.7	24.8	24.0	27.3	29.3	31.1	18.7	22.9	21.7
Guinea	..	6.8	6.9	8.8	9.1	10.9	9.7	9.7	11.2	17.7	15.5	..	1.6	9.4
Guinea-Bissau	..	6.8	7.2	6.7	7.9	7.8	8.3	15.2	3.8	3.5	6.3	21.9	9.7	7.2
Kenya	30.1	28.8	32.9	35.6	34.4	33.2	33.1	31.9	30.1	28.7	27.8	28.3	29.6	31.2
Lesotho	..	16.3	13.8	15.3	16.3	15.1	15.0	17.1	18.1	17.9	20.1	14.2	11.4	15.9
Liberia	..	..	..	..	..	..	..	..	..	..	..	..	..	..
Madagascar	..	11.6	14.9	18.8	14.2	16.9	18.9	15.7	14.6	15.0	19.0	15.3	11.5	15.4
Malawi	83.8	49.2	32.9	32.3	31.7	40.3	38.0	40.7	40.0	41.5	42.1	83.4	70.2	41.1
Mali	15.2	14.3	13.1	15.2	18.4	18.5	18.0	21.2	14.5	12.4	20.0	17.4	12.7	16.0
Mauritania	..	26.5	24.8	24.5	25.3	17.3	19.2	18.5	18.3	19.8	25.1	..	27.0	22.9
Mauritius	19.2	20.2	19.3	17.7	20.3	22.7	19.9	19.2	18.4	17.5	19.4	25.4	15.7	19.7
Mozambique	12.4	15.6	14.3	17.3	16.6	18.2	19.0	18.1	14.0	13.5	15.6	15.5	21.4	16.5
Namibia	..	26.8	31.1	29.0	27.4	28.8	34.1	33.6	32.3	31.9	35.4	18.1	32.9	30.9
Niger	..	33.8	33.7	30.0	30.5	25.4	21.1	21.8	24.0	20.0	23.0	22.0	25.9	26.3
Nigeria	..	..	..	..	..	..	10.0	23.9	15.6	22.5	23.5	..	..	19.1
Rwanda	..	23.4	24.8	25.8	12.5	26.2	25.1	27.7	25.0	27.0	28.4	26.0	25.3	24.4
São Tomé and Principe	..	6.7	8.9	10.7	14.1	21.1	29.3	16.4	18.5	20.9	25.0	..	9.8	16.1
Senegal	26.2	24.2	23.4	21.1	21.9	21.6	21.8	23.3	21.2	22.9	23.9	25.7	23.7	22.7
Seychelles	..	16.9	26.8	29.6	34.8	26.7	28.0	28.3	31.8	33.0	32.5	22.6	18.4	27.7
Sierra Leone	..	23.9	21.7	21.4	15.9	16.5	13.2	17.3	25.8	26.1	26.2	..	25.8	21.3
Somalia	..	..	..	..	..	..	..	..	..	..	..	..	..	..
South Africa	58.2	56.0	48.3	46.6	46.5	48.0	49.8	58.8	58.7	58.5	58.9	57.8	53.8	53.2
Sudan	..	..	..	..	28.7	28.3	19.5	19.9	17.6	11.5	11.2	18.9	14.9	19.3
Swaziland	..	34.2	33.5	32.1	28.1	28.5	26.8	26.1	27.2	25.6	24.9	..	..	29.0
Tanzania	..	27.6	30.9	31.2	41.1	37.4	34.7	39.6	34.3	37.8	29.6	33.6	31.5	32.7
Togo	..	30.5	30.9	40.1	41.4	30.5	22.6	22.3	25.6	23.1	19.1	35.0	34.3	29.0
Uganda	..	12.7	14.5	14.6	14.7	13.2	14.0	15.6	17.9	18.0	20.7	6.7	7.8	14.7
Zambia	..	33.0	28.6	28.7	28.9	30.0	32.0	35.2	36.5	32.5	38.0	..	27.5	31.1
Zimbabwe	0.0	46.0	48.7	47.7	45.9	45.7	47.6	48.0	48.9	50.4	48.2	8.6	45.4	47.3
NORTH AFRICA	..	18.6	19.1	19.8	19.7	20.2	20.8	22.6	20.6	21.4	20.4	..	19.2	20.0
Algeria	11.0	8.9	10.9	9.9	8.9	8.2	8.8	11.4	7.6	5.2	4.7	12.0	19.8	8.9
Egypt, Arab Republic	..	23.0	23.8	22.9	21.8	22.5	22.6	22.5	21.2	24.6	25.4	..	18.0	22.7
Libya	..	..	..	..	..	..	..	..	..	..	..	..	..	..
Morocco	22.8	26.6	23.2	22.5	24.0	25.5	25.8	30.5	28.6	28.9	23.3	22.7	22.7	25.9
Tunisia	16.1	15.1	17.2	31.0	33.3	35.1	38.1	38.9	38.7	40.5	40.4	15.6	14.2	29.8
ALL AFRICA	..	30.7	28.3	28.2	28.9	29.5	30.9	35.2	34.0	34.5	34.2	34.0	31.2	31.3

Note: 2001 data are preliminary (see page 2). Total revenue does not include grants. Nigeria's fiscal data are for consolidated government starting from 1992.

7-10. Taxes on international trade and transactions

	Percentage of total revenue											Annual Average		
	1980	*1992*	*1993*	*1994*	*1995*	*1996*	*1997*	*1998*	*1999*	*2000*	*2001*	*75-84*	*85-89*	*90-MR*
SUB-SAHARAN AFRICA	..	10.0	10.5	11.7	12.9	13.0	13.9	13.9	13.5	12.2	12.4	7.4	10.2	12.2
excluding South Africa	..	16.6	17.4	19.5	21.5	21.2	22.9	22.9	22.2	19.4	19.9	..	15.3	19.8
excl. S.Africa & Nigeria	..	20.0	20.9	23.5	25.9	25.3	25.1	24.6	24.7	22.0	22.2	13.5	18.6	22.9
Angola	..	13.9	6.5	4.6	4.9	4.3	4.8	7.0	2.8	2.7	4.8	..	3.0	4.9
Benin	..	52.8	50.8	39.6	40.6	40.9	45.5	43.3	45.5	47.6	47.4	52.7	80.6	48.8
Botswana	..	..	..	..	..	..	..	..	..	..	..	22.3	13.3	..
Burkina Faso	..	33.3	36.4	54.0	48.4	28.2	27.6	25.7	23.4	17.4	17.2	35.3	45.7	32.2
Burundi	30.5	21.8	21.0	26.6	25.4	15.5	17.5	25.8	21.7	22.3	21.8	22.5	28.3	22.0
Cameroon	..	18.0	16.6	18.3	19.5	19.3	17.0	17.1	16.5	12.9	11.4	..	17.7	16.3
Cape Verde	..	49.0	41.2	40.5	41.6	45.7	36.2	41.1	34.7	47.9	48.1	..	42.1	43.2
Central African Republic	..	34.6	33.0	32.5	42.5	38.7	38.1	44.7	38.0	38.4	35.8	..	..	37.8
Chad	..	15.6	13.6	19.4	27.1	31.1	30.3	36.0	29.5	17.0	19.9	..	26.1	23.3
Comoros	..	32.2	36.6	36.0	32.3	35.2	43.1	33.2	31.7	57.8	58.8	..	48.4	39.8
Congo, Democratic Rep. of	..	..	..	..	..	..	..	..	..	..	..	..	..	..
Congo, Republic of	..	21.2	20.0	13.9	19.2	16.3	9.1	13.4	5.6	5.2	6.9	0.0	4.3	13.7
Côte d'Ivoire	..	25.3	26.3	39.0	38.9	39.6	36.5	34.4	38.4	31.5	31.9	..	34.9	33.3
Djibouti	..	19.7	22.0	24.7	24.7	22.2	21.3	37.6	40.7	39.7	38.9	..	..	29.2
Equatorial Guinea	..	..	..	26.9	30.8	19.0	18.8	8.0	8.2	5.3	3.8	..	..	15.1
Eritrea	..	25.5	13.9	12.3	12.5	14.5	12.9	12.1	11.0	8.5	12.2	..	..	13.5
Ethiopia	..	19.0	22.6	32.9	27.4	26.0	28.7	27.4	27.5	28.2	32.6	24.3	17.9	25.4
Gabon	..	19.4	21.1	16.0	17.6	19.6	17.7	19.6	25.6	20.1	20.8	..	..	19.8
Gambia, The	..	50.4	44.3	37.6	49.4	61.8	0.0	0.0	56.3	57.6	53.5	..	55.2	43.2
Ghana	..	17.7	16.3	28.2	22.7	27.3	25.8	27.5	23.3	20.5	21.3	..	39.1	24.1
Guinea	..	12.8	14.6	15.7	14.4	14.1	15.5	14.5	15.6	36.2	22.6	..	6.4	16.4
Guinea-Bissau	..	18.6	29.5	35.8	27.4	32.9	36.7	34.8	29.3	23.4	27.3	0.0	21.0	29.1
Kenya	0.0	9.5	12.7	14.8	14.9	15.1	15.8	16.0	15.8	14.5	13.5	0.0	0.0	12.3
Lesotho	..	53.3	57.9	58.6	54.8	50.4	51.6	48.8	50.3	44.8	49.5	57.9	57.2	52.3
Liberia	..	..	..	..	..	..	..	..	..	..	..	..	..	..
Madagascar	..	40.2	38.6	41.9	53.7	49.3	54.3	55.2	54.5	51.1	46.3	26.9	38.1	47.2
Malawi	0.0	32.8	15.5	19.9	25.3	22.9	21.9	16.1	14.1	12.9	10.7	0.0	11.7	21.6
Mali	51.6	42.9	45.3	44.4	46.1	45.8	48.7	53.6	49.7	48.6	44.4	46.8	27.2	44.7
Mauritania	..	34.1	33.7	32.4	22.5	16.5	12.0	10.9	9.6	9.8	12.9	..	33.0	21.3
Mauritius	52.0	43.8	45.6	41.8	38.8	38.8	33.9	33.7	28.2	29.7	28.2	46.2	53.5	38.5
Mozambique	18.5	25.5	25.5	21.8	24.0	19.9	17.6	17.6	16.9	17.4	15.4	11.7	12.6	20.6
Namibia	..	..	..	..	..	..	..	..	..	..	..	..	..	..
Niger	..	35.4	41.3	41.5	43.2	46.7	47.7	50.9	46.8	49.3	48.6	36.9	34.7	44.2
Nigeria	..	..	..	..	..	..	11.6	14.0	9.3	5.9	8.4	..	..	9.9
Rwanda	..	31.0	27.8	35.8	38.5	29.2	31.8	23.9	17.3	16.9	16.2	54.7	45.0	27.3
São Tomé and Principe	..	29.0	28.2	30.8	24.1	25.5	21.0	18.6	31.0	22.7	21.4	..	0.0	25.5
Senegal	..	..	27.6	31.5	31.1	33.7	30.7	27.3	24.3	16.0	15.0	..	..	26.4
Seychelles	..	54.2	37.7	30.5	26.2	23.2	25.1	24.3	21.8	24.3	25.5	0.0	0.0	32.9
Sierra Leone	..	37.3	39.2	38.1	45.7	47.2	39.3	52.9	47.7	48.1	45.4	..	46.8	43.2
Somalia	..	..	..	..	..	..	..	..	..	..	..	..	..	..
South Africa	3.6	2.7	2.9	3.0	3.2	3.6	3.4	3.4	3.4	3.7	3.7	4.8	4.8	3.5
Sudan	..	..	..	..	31.2	44.0	49.0	44.2	41.0	21.3	19.5	..	..	35.7
Swaziland	..	..	..	..	..	..	..	..	..	..	..	..	..	..
Tanzania	..	18.7	14.2	15.7	27.6	27.0	30.5	29.2	31.7	28.5	39.1	17.4	19.9	25.1
Togo	..	34.8	35.3	40.8	37.4	40.7	37.4	42.6	41.9	42.5	44.2	35.2	34.4	39.7
Uganda	..	50.3	50.8	53.0	48.6	50.6	51.4	47.7	44.1	42.9	43.0	58.1	57.3	48.9
Zambia	..	32.9	33.3	30.8	27.4	29.7	28.2	25.2	25.5	30.6	33.0	..	29.8	30.4
Zimbabwe	..	..	..	..	..	..	..	..	14.0	9.7	13.2	..	..	12.3
NORTH AFRICA	..	12.3	12.4	13.1	13.9	12.7	11.6	12.0	12.2	10.1	9.8	..	13.1	12.1
Algeria	4.8	8.6	9.4	11.0	12.2	10.2	7.9	9.7	8.5	5.5	7.5	6.0	6.2	8.7
Egypt, Arab Republic	..	10.6	10.7	11.6	12.6	13.0	12.6	13.1	15.1	11.8	12.0	..	14.9	12.3
Libya	..	..	..	..	..	..	..	..	..	..	..	..	..	..
Morocco	22.8	19.3	19.0	17.7	17.6	15.2	14.9	13.6	13.5	13.8	10.8	27.4	17.0	16.3
Tunisia	10.2	15.3	14.9	15.6	16.0	13.5	12.4	11.4	10.2	9.9	6.8	12.9	15.3	13.3
ALL AFRICA	..	10.8	11.2	12.2	13.2	12.9	13.1	13.2	13.1	11.5	11.5	8.5	10.8	12.2

Note: 2001 data are preliminary (see page 2). Total revenue does not include grants. Nigeria's fiscal data are for consolidated government starting from 1992.

7-11. Indirect taxes

	Percentage of total revenue											Annual Average		
	1980	1992	1993	1994	1995	1996	1997	1998	1999	2000	2001	75-84	85-89	90-MR
SUB-SAHARAN AFRICA	..	39.7	40.9	42.0	42.9	42.6	44.5	46.6	45.1	43.7	43.8	44.9	42.6	43.1
excluding South Africa	..	42.4	43.0	44.2	46.3	46.5	50.5	53.0	50.5	47.3	47.5	..	46.7	46.9
excl. S.Africa & Nigeria	..	51.0	51.7	53.2	55.7	55.5	57.0	57.4	57.0	54.4	54.1	57.0	56.7	54.8
Angola	..	32.7	31.9	25.5	7.3	6.2	8.6	14.7	6.9	6.2	10.3	..	19.5	17.3
Benin	..	74.8	72.0	55.6	54.3	56.0	63.8	63.1	64.4	67.2	65.5	67.4	94.7	66.9
Botswana	..	21.8	22.8	19.9	19.4	17.9	17.2	19.4	22.0	20.4	19.3	70.8	72.4	19.3
Burkina Faso	..	49.8	51.2	71.2	66.8	65.6	67.4	69.7	68.3	61.9	66.2	61.9	68.6	62.4
Burundi	53.8	60.1	59.6	64.4	63.3	50.4	60.7	61.6	64.9	68.1	58.1	50.3	58.7	61.4
Cameroon	61.6	46.5	52.7	59.5	61.0	58.9	79.1	76.4	72.9	77.8	78.6	40.4	39.9	63.4
Cape Verde	..	55.4	47.3	45.9	46.6	51.8	40.4	46.6	38.5	59.4	55.2	45.4	46.9	49.5
Central African Republic	..	69.4	70.4	66.4	75.1	74.8	74.8	75.2	68.1	68.9	65.9	..	..	70.9
Chad	..	53.6	54.0	67.5	49.7	49.7	55.0	54.9	49.7	34.3	33.5	71.0	71.5	52.7
Comoros	..	71.5	78.5	76.3	74.0	78.1	82.1	70.7	69.7	71.1	75.3	62.7	71.1	71.9
Congo, Democratic Rep. of	..	..	..	..	..	45.5	45.5	51.6	39.3	32.3	0.0	..	..	35.7
Congo, Republic of	..	46.1	45.7	30.7	41.7	35.7	20.1	43.5	25.5	20.5	27.1	13.8	36.2	34.8
Côte d'Ivoire	..	63.8	64.6	65.2	63.0	64.0	60.9	58.6	65.0	60.1	61.1	48.6	56.2	62.6
Djibouti	..	55.5	55.9	56.6	55.7	51.5	50.5	48.3	54.8	54.5	53.2	..	..	53.6
Equatorial Guinea	..	..	..	61.2	62.4	35.1	32.2	19.4	18.1	11.2	8.2	..	..	31.0
Eritrea	..	47.9	24.2	21.1	20.8	24.2	22.1	21.0	21.0	13.9	18.5	..	..	23.5
Ethiopia	..	43.2	46.0	54.1	43.4	42.6	45.9	42.0	41.4	43.3	46.2	46.7	38.8	44.4
Gabon	..	35.1	37.0	26.7	26.1	25.3	24.2	27.5	37.2	30.1	30.2	..	73.4	30.9
Gambia, The	..	76.5	74.0	70.7	70.6	71.2	68.3	68.1	65.1	64.9	60.9	75.9	77.8	71.0
Ghana	..	56.3	53.7	68.7	54.5	63.9	59.9	62.2	63.5	62.5	63.9	63.8	66.0	61.5
Guinea	..	85.9	86.2	84.1	84.6	82.6	83.5	83.7	82.5	65.9	72.0	..	92.1	82.6
Guinea-Bissau	..	29.0	41.3	48.5	46.8	47.0	43.8	53.0	49.8	55.8	45.3	78.1	46.5	44.7
Kenya	60.9	57.7	57.3	54.1	52.3	52.8	54.4	55.5	55.8	59.4	63.5	60.7	59.4	56.1
Lesotho	..	70.0	73.1	72.7	68.6	62.9	64.0	61.4	62.7	57.8	62.5	63.6	77.2	66.9
Liberia	..	..	..	..	..	..	..	..	..	..	..	..	..	..
Madagascar	..	66.6	60.6	68.9	80.8	73.3	75.4	74.1	78.8	79.1	73.8	50.6	61.5	70.7
Malawi	0.0	32.8	46.4	55.5	56.5	52.2	54.5	50.2	46.9	50.2	49.2	0.0	11.7	46.8
Mali	71.7	63.3	66.9	68.0	64.6	65.3	66.9	72.9	71.8	74.2	67.6	67.3	50.0	65.6
Mauritania	..	47.0	45.3	48.1	45.8	41.3	38.9	39.2	38.2	40.6	53.3	..	49.7	44.3
Mauritius	69.2	68.0	71.4	71.2	65.7	68.3	65.4	66.6	66.0	70.8	70.3	63.4	73.7	69.1
Mozambique	65.7	71.3	76.7	71.3	74.7	73.6	72.6	74.5	78.4	78.4	73.7	53.8	58.1	73.7
Namibia	..	59.3	62.1	58.9	61.7	60.5	56.8	56.3	58.8	59.9	55.4	72.2	54.9	58.7
Niger	..	47.9	56.1	59.1	60.9	61.4	64.9	64.9	67.8	66.7	68.0	65.3	54.9	60.5
Nigeria	..	..	..	..	..	..	17.0	30.0	16.6	10.3	13.8	..	..	17.5
Rwanda	..	64.3	67.5	73.5	81.4	65.8	69.5	67.1	70.1	68.3	63.8	86.9	83.5	68.3
São Tomé and Principe	..	59.3	63.4	64.5	45.1	46.0	38.6	35.7	65.2	60.0	62.7	..	38.7	53.5
Senegal	67.7	60.0	73.0	76.7	74.3	77.2	71.0	72.1	75.7	72.7	71.8	67.8	59.8	70.1
Seychelles	..	60.6	56.7	48.7	46.2	47.0	48.3	46.3	42.4	48.7	51.8	49.1	52.0	50.9
Sierra Leone	..	76.1	69.0	70.7	76.9	76.0	73.1	74.2	66.1	65.8	69.5	..	74.2	72.4
Somalia	..	..	..	..	..	..	..	..	..	..	..	..	..	..
South Africa	29.0	36.6	38.6	39.5	39.1	38.1	37.4	39.1	38.9	39.6	39.5	30.7	38.1	38.7
Sudan	..	..	..	..	50.3	56.3	62.1	60.7	57.0	36.8	39.8	66.7	63.0	51.9
Swaziland	..	55.7	60.2	63.8	68.9	68.0	67.1	65.8	65.8	68.9	69.8	..	..	64.8
Tanzania	..	46.8	35.0	37.8	49.5	48.2	55.2	51.9	55.1	51.8	59.4	59.6	61.1	48.7
Togo	..	45.0	49.8	50.4	50.0	57.2	53.4	63.3	65.7	67.0	65.8	43.4	46.1	56.2
Uganda	..	80.2	77.5	78.5	77.7	80.7	80.1	78.5	75.5	74.0	74.4	86.8	82.5	78.5
Zambia	..	62.5	68.0	64.4	62.7	62.1	62.6	61.5	61.0	56.6	58.7	..	63.9	63.8
Zimbabwe	0.0	44.0	39.1	40.3	42.7	44.6	44.2	44.6	42.7	43.3	45.9	9.2	42.6	43.2
NORTH AFRICA	..	40.0	41.3	41.2	43.3	41.2	40.8	42.2	42.0	38.2	58.7	..	44.4	42.6
Algeria	25.3	25.6	28.5	27.7	29.9	27.0	25.1	31.2	25.6	16.9	90.3	29.6	36.0	32.2
Egypt, Arab Republic	..	32.9	34.7	36.8	39.7	40.3	40.2	42.2	44.4	41.1	43.0	..	34.0	38.5
Libya	..	..	..	..	..	..	..	..	..	..	..	..	..	..
Morocco	66.8	64.4	64.2	65.4	66.5	60.9	60.5	54.4	57.2	57.8	46.6	63.7	69.1	60.7
Tunisia	42.3	60.2	58.2	49.1	50.2	47.4	49.9	50.5	50.7	50.5	50.0	42.6	52.0	53.1
ALL AFRICA	..	39.8	41.1	41.7	43.0	42.1	43.2	45.1	44.1	41.8	48.9	45.1	43.4	42.9

Note: 2001 data are preliminary (see page 2). Total revenue does not include grants. Nigeria's fiscal data are for consolidated government starting from 1992.

7-12. Nontax revenue (excluding grants)

	Percentage of total revenue											Annual Average		
	1980	*1992*	*1993*	*1994*	*1995*	*1996*	*1997*	*1998*	*1999*	*2000*	*2001*	*75-84*	*85-89*	*90-MR*
SUB-SAHARAN AFRICA	..	12.2	13.5	12.8	13.9	13.5	19.1	11.6	13.9	15.8	13.6	13.3	11.0	13.5
excluding South Africa	..	16.6	14.1	12.1	13.8	13.3	24.7	19.8	23.7	27.7	23.8	..	14.0	18.2
excl. S.Africa & Nigeria	..	20.0	17.0	14.5	16.6	15.9	15.3	14.7	15.2	20.2	17.0	19.1	17.0	16.8
Angola	..	1.8	1.8	1.6	1.0	0.5	0.8	1.4	0.6	0.4	0.5	..	32.9	3.5
Benin	..	23.0	18.1	13.7	17.6	17.0	12.7	13.4	14.5	12.1	12.1	6.3	48.6	17.8
Botswana	..	24.8	27.9	23.6	22.6	29.0	23.9	20.3	22.1	15.6	14.2	17.0	19.5	22.3
Burkina Faso	..	25.8	26.8	8.3	8.4	6.9	7.7	7.2	6.7	7.5	6.4	19.9	14.3	11.9
Burundi	6.7	29.9	33.0	9.4	11.6	14.7	17.1	8.5	4.7	4.7	13.8	8.5	13.2	17.5
Cameroon	16.7	35.5	10.5	7.5	8.2	9.3	7.4	7.9	6.3	5.6	4.5	32.7	10.4	11.9
Cape Verde	..	97.9	58.9	60.6	37.5	27.6	8.8	26.9	11.9	11.1	13.0	25.1	97.9	40.2
Central African Republic	..	7.9	6.6	9.2	4.3	0.9	5.7	10.7	12.0	9.9	12.9	..	..	7.5
Chad	..	44.6	35.2	59.4	43.7	39.8	21.9	31.4	19.7	9.4	9.0	21.4	10.5	32.1
Comoros	..	17.4	12.6	11.3	13.7	12.3	6.7	14.6	13.0	11.7	14.4	0.0	20.8	14.9
Congo, Democratic Rep. of	..	..	..	..	..	37.3	29.5	18.5	43.2	55.1	..	..	..	36.7
Congo, Republic of	..	1.9	2.9	6.3	9.2	3.2	1.2	2.9	2.4	1.4	2.4	68.5	34.0	3.2
Côte d'Ivoire	..	15.9	16.0	19.9	18.7	15.5	19.5	21.4	12.8	15.6	16.7	33.6	24.2	17.0
Djibouti	..	5.7	5.4	5.0	7.2	7.5	10.4	..	..	..	..	..	..	6.8
Equatorial Guinea	..	..	..	19.2	21.4	12.0	6.0	4.1	5.5	5.8	5.1	..	..	9.9
Eritrea	..	39.1	26.6	18.1	33.5	29.8	46.0	27.1	25.2	23.8	14.0	..	..	28.3
Ethiopia	..	26.7	30.9	21.9	34.4	32.2	28.8	35.0	35.4	31.8	26.9	24.7	32.4	29.9
Gabon	..	5.3	4.8	3.1	2.9	4.6	4.3	6.7	4.6	56.1	55.7	..	5.2	13.0
Gambia, The	..	21.1	18.6	16.4	9.8	8.9	10.6	9.7	12.0	12.6	13.7	9.5	41.0	13.6
Ghana	..	29.1	31.5	13.8	28.2	14.4	15.2	13.8	9.2	20.2	28.9	17.5	11.0	19.8
Guinea	..	7.3	6.8	7.1	6.3	6.5	6.8	6.6	6.3	16.4	12.5	..	6.3	8.0
Guinea-Bissau	..	93.9	65.6	50.6	98.5	53.7	85.8	90.9	50.2	83.4	69.9	248.0	136.2	75.7
Kenya	16.5	18.2	13.5	11.5	13.3	14.0	12.5	12.6	14.0	13.8	13.5	15.4	12.4	14.2
Lesotho	..	13.7	13.0	12.0	15.2	22.0	20.9	21.5	19.2	24.3	17.4	21.9	12.4	17.2
Liberia	..	..	..	..	..	..	..	..	..	..	..	..	..	..
Madagascar	..	23.1	21.0	15.5	7.5	17.2	27.4	12.8	11.0	10.4	16.0	13.4	13.7	17.4
Malawi	16.2	18.0	20.7	12.2	11.7	7.5	7.5	9.0	13.1	8.2	8.7	16.6	18.0	12.1
Mali	12.9	22.4	20.1	15.4	16.2	16.1	14.5	4.4	10.0	9.3	8.4	15.0	37.3	17.1
Mauritania	..	22.5	27.9	25.9	24.0	38.9	39.6	39.4	41.8	45.3	32.5	..	16.6	31.9
Mauritius	11.5	11.8	9.3	9.9	11.5	5.4	14.7	14.2	13.2	9.5	10.3	11.2	10.5	10.3
Mozambique	24.6	59.5	41.3	62.4	41.3	35.4	46.1	43.5	60.6	48.9	48.7	33.1	36.8	48.3
Namibia	..	13.8	6.8	12.1	10.8	10.6	9.1	10.1	8.9	8.2	9.5	9.7	12.2	10.5
Niger	..	29.3	47.8	46.3	30.1	41.2	34.0	37.1	19.2	24.9	24.0	12.7	21.2	32.7
Nigeria	..	..	..	..	..	..	73.0	46.1	67.8	66.3	58.8	..	..	62.4
Rwanda	..	73.0	77.8	25.7	172.1	87.7	70.5	55.1	65.3	97.8	81.2	12.5	15.3	75.3
São Tomé and Principe	..	34.0	27.7	31.2	63.9	43.7	38.6	25.4	39.0	25.7	20.0	..	86.9	49.7
Senegal	6.0	15.8	3.6	2.2	3.8	1.2	7.2	4.6	3.1	4.4	4.3	6.5	16.5	7.2
Seychelles	..	13.5	8.6	21.7	18.9	26.2	23.7	25.4	25.8	18.3	15.7	28.3	29.6	17.9
Sierra Leone	..	0.0	9.3	7.9	7.2	21.2	23.9	37.7	56.6	66.9	31.9	..	0.0	21.9
Somalia	..	..	..	..	..	..	..	..	..	..	..	..	..	..
South Africa	12.4	7.3	12.8	13.6	13.9	13.6	12.6	2.1	2.4	1.9	1.7	11.2	7.7	7.9
Sudan	..	28.1	22.5	23.6	21.0	15.4	14.7	19.4	25.4	51.8	51.7	14.4	22.1	27.7
Swaziland	..	10.1	6.3	4.1	3.0	3.5	6.1	8.0	7.0	5.5	5.3	..	..	6.2
Tanzania	..	9.8	8.0	6.9	9.5	14.4	10.1	8.6	10.6	10.4	11.0	6.8	7.4	10.0
Togo	..	24.5	17.4	8.3	7.7	11.0	8.4	9.1	8.5	9.9	15.1	22.2	19.7	12.5
Uganda	..	7.1	8.0	6.9	7.7	6.1	5.9	5.9	6.6	8.1	4.9	6.6	9.7	6.8
Zambia	..	4.5	3.4	6.8	8.4	8.0	5.4	3.4	2.6	11.0	3.3	..	8.6	5.1
Zimbabwe	0.0	10.0	12.2	12.0	11.4	9.7	8.2	7.4	4.9	6.3	5.9	2.2	11.9	9.1
NORTH AFRICA	..	17.1	19.6	18.9	17.2	17.6	16.9	16.3	15.5	13.7	14.2	..	18.1	16.7
Algeria	2.6	2.0	2.8	3.1	1.5	1.8	2.2	2.4	4.6	1.0	4.4	6.0	12.4	2.6
Egypt, Arab Republic	..	31.2	35.0	34.3	33.5	32.0	31.4	29.3	26.1	25.2	26.0	..	26.7	30.3
Libya	..	..	..	..	..	..	..	..	..	..	..	..	..	..
Morocco	10.4	9.0	12.6	12.1	9.5	13.6	13.7	15.1	14.2	13.3	9.1	11.6	8.1	11.7
Tunisia	24.8	23.2	23.8	19.8	16.4	17.2	11.8	10.5	10.5	8.9	8.5	25.8	25.9	16.1
ALL AFRICA	..	13.9	15.6	14.9	15.0	14.9	18.3	13.2	14.4	15.1	13.8	13.3	12.9	14.6

Note: 2001 data are preliminary (see page 2). Nigeria's fiscal data are for consolidated government starting from 1992.

7-13. Government expenditure: wages and salaries

	Percentage of total expenditure and lending minus repayments											*Annual Average*		
	1980	*1992*	*1993*	*1994*	*1995*	*1996*	*1997*	*1998*	*1999*	*2000*	*2001*	*75-84*	*85-89*	*90-MR*
SUB-SAHARAN AFRICA	..	30.4	29.0	26.9	27.1	26.6	27.3	30.8	31.0	29.9	31.0	20.9	14.3	28.1
excluding South Africa	..	24.1	24.4	20.9	21.1	21.1	22.1	22.1	22.9	21.6	25.0	..	21.1	22.8
excl. S.Africa & Nigeria	..	24.1	24.4	22.9	22.9	22.6	24.8	24.9	25.2	22.9	27.4	19.9	21.1	24.2
Angola	..	24.4	21.5	8.7	11.1	10.8	15.6	21.0	5.0	9.6	15.0	..	45.5	20.1
Benin	..	33.0	35.5	27.8	24.3	26.4	26.5	28.7	25.6	23.2	22.9	..	38.5	28.9
Botswana	..	..	..	24.9	26.1	23.3	22.6	23.0	23.7	23.4	23.0	..	..	23.8
Burkina Faso	..	30.8	29.0	26.2	24.9	23.4	20.9	19.7	18.8	20.8	21.6	..	..	25.6
Burundi	49.1	23.0	23.7	30.0	28.0	28.7	32.2	29.3	26.0	27.7	28.0	49.0	27.7	27.3
Cameroon	31.4	42.0	43.7	31.4	29.1	25.8	26.5	27.7	26.9	29.0	28.7	24.8	29.0	32.4
Cape Verde	..	20.0	22.1	19.2	20.2	24.1	23.8	22.1	30.0	22.0	34.0	0.0	14.8	24.4
Central African Republic	..	27.2	29.5	24.2	22.5	41.8	32.6	24.2	23.3	21.1	20.4	..	31.3	26.7
Chad	..	21.1	27.1	28.0	28.6	20.3	19.4	20.6	19.0	19.7	20.1	..	15.0	22.4
Comoros	..	27.7	30.8	23.2	28.6	35.4	37.0	34.1	32.6	34.6	36.2	0.0	5.8	31.9
Congo, Democratic Rep. of	..	..	..	..	..	6.8	35.6	43.8	42.1	21.5	89.8	..	..	39.9
Congo, Republic of	..	47.5	48.8	36.3	32.1	24.8	20.4	20.8	21.2	18.3	18.3	0.0	33.3	30.2
Côte d'Ivoire	..	35.5	35.6	28.6	26.0	28.0	27.1	26.1	28.4	32.9	34.8	..	28.1	31.0
Djibouti	..	46.6	48.0	56.4	61.6	60.3	62.2	49.3	47.1	46.1	44.3	..	..	52.2
Equatorial Guinea	..	12.7	10.8	16.4	17.9	17.3	15.3	11.3	17.6	15.6	21.9	..	15.4	14.9
Eritrea	..	18.6	15.0	22.7	24.0	29.0	27.3	19.9	17.5	20.2	16.1	..	..	21.0
Ethiopia	..	28.0	28.3	24.8	22.6	20.6	21.7	23.4	19.7	20.5	23.4	25.1	22.5	24.5
Gabon	..	34.4	34.0	27.9	27.4	27.3	21.4	16.1	29.8	25.8	26.4	16.2	25.1	27.9
Gambia, The	..	19.5	21.1	23.3	21.8	20.3	24.0	27.5	27.0	28.6	21.6	..	17.6	23.0
Ghana	..	24.8	20.2	18.3	18.3	18.2	18.4	19.4	21.6	18.9	20.7	17.6	25.6	20.4
Guinea	..	23.1	24.2	25.1	23.9	27.1	23.8	27.6	25.2	15.1	16.2	..	13.2	22.8
Guinea-Bissau	..	8.0	8.1	7.5	9.2	9.5	6.8	18.8	15.9	15.5	18.0	10.4	13.1	11.4
Kenya	16.8	27.7	23.7	22.8	21.6	16.8	17.6	17.9	18.3	17.4	15.7	19.2	23.6	20.1
Lesotho	..	29.5	29.6	31.4	31.2	29.8	30.5	33.5	26.6	29.8	32.7	32.1	32.7	29.5
Liberia	..	..	..	..	..	..	..	..	..	..	..	..	..	..
Madagascar	..	18.4	17.0	16.4	18.8	14.5	21.3	20.4	24.0	21.9	24.4	40.5	34.1	20.8
Malawi	14.3	18.3	21.6	18.3	22.7	19.6	23.5	17.4	16.7	15.9	17.4	16.4	16.3	18.9
Mali	16.5	22.6	23.0	16.7	16.6	16.1	16.4	14.5	15.6	16.6	15.4	19.8	25.0	18.1
Mauritania	..	23.2	15.4	19.0	20.3	20.3	21.2	19.3	18.6	16.1	18.3	..	16.4	19.0
Mauritius	28.1	27.7	28.9	31.7	32.2	29.1	26.1	29.4	30.0	27.9	26.5	29.0	29.5	29.1
Mozambique	25.8	9.9	10.4	7.9	9.6	10.8	15.4	20.5	23.0	22.7	21.4	19.2	12.2	14.3
Namibia	..	..	..	..	..	..	..	..	..	..	..	..	..	..
Niger	..	37.4	38.3	29.4	36.1	25.5	26.1	20.7	22.8	25.2	21.2	18.8	21.2	28.5
Nigeria	..	..	..	10.8	12.2	13.7	8.2	7.8	11.1	15.2	12.3	..	..	11.4
Rwanda	..	22.1	24.1	25.0	19.5	20.1	26.2	24.6	27.2	27.8	24.6	..	..	24.4
São Tomé and Principe	..	10.1	7.8	7.0	4.3	6.0	8.4	11.3	10.9	11.8	11.4	..	12.0	9.5
Senegal	39.7	40.4	41.4	35.0	35.4	32.7	33.1	29.5	33.0	28.4	24.2	38.8	41.9	35.0
Seychelles	..	27.2	20.9	26.9	32.0	27.7	26.2	21.8	25.0	28.0	31.2	..	..	26.5
Sierra Leone	..	10.1	18.5	20.9	17.3	20.2	25.4	23.8	27.5	23.4	25.0	..	8.6	19.0
Somalia	..	..	..	..	..	..	..	..	..	..	..	..	..	..
South Africa	17.2	36.3	33.4	33.7	33.8	33.1	33.4	41.0	40.4	39.5	38.0	17.7	21.2	34.1
Sudan	..	..	9.3	12.5	13.5	28.1	31.2	33.5	35.4	27.6	34.1	..	..	25.0
Swaziland	..	..	..	..	..	..	..	..	..	..	..	..	..	..
Tanzania	..	19.3	19.0	21.7	22.8	26.2	31.2	28.6	24.4	24.4	24.2	20.9	21.3	23.6
Togo	..	38.8	41.2	36.0	35.5	35.8	36.2	31.1	34.5	34.2	36.7	27.1	25.7	35.4
Uganda	..	8.2	8.7	10.3	15.1	16.9	20.3	20.7	23.3	16.3	20.3	10.9	11.9	14.7
Zambia	..	25.4	17.7	16.1	20.2	20.5	25.1	19.0	19.2	17.8	21.1	..	..	20.5
Zimbabwe	103.4	30.0	29.5	29.1	29.2	32.0	35.5	35.5	34.3	30.6	38.1	75.2	29.0	32.5
NORTH AFRICA	..	26.3	26.3	27.3	27.9	28.0	28.9	29.8	29.4	28.0	31.7	..	27.3	28.2
Algeria	15.5	29.1	27.3	29.1	28.5	28.4	27.3	29.3	28.8	23.9	33.7	15.3	27.0	29.1
Egypt, Arab Republic	..	15.8	18.8	19.7	21.5	22.0	23.0	24.1	22.7	24.0	24.3	..	17.2	20.7
Libya	..	..	..	..	..	..	..	..	..	..	..	..	..	..
Morocco	33.1	37.4	34.4	37.5	38.1	38.1	39.7	39.1	38.7	37.0	40.2	32.0	36.0	38.0
Tunisia	34.7	35.7	35.5	30.1	30.3	29.1	34.1	35.1	37.4	36.8	36.5	31.4	34.0	34.0
ALL AFRICA	..	28.9	28.0	27.0	27.4	27.1	27.8	30.5	30.4	29.2	31.2	21.9	18.7	28.1

Note: 2001 data are preliminary (see page 2). Nigeria's fiscal data are for consolidated government starting from 1992.

7-14. Government expenditure: trends in real wages and salaries

	Index 1987=100											Annual Average		
	1980	*1992*	*1993*	*1994*	*1995*	*1996*	*1997*	*1998*	*1999*	*2000*	*2001*	*75-84*	*85-89*	*90-MR*
SUB-SAHARAN AFRICA	..	157	158	144	119	113	101	128	132	130	132	..	120	137
excluding South Africa	..	141	146	132	117	96	90	104	113	119	129	..	115	125
excl. S.Africa & Nigeria	..	123	131	117	112	92	77	77	92	107	104	..	118	108
Angola	..	..	..	..	..	..	..	..	..	..	..	..	..	..
Benin	..	..	..	..	..	..	..	..	..	..	..	..	..	..
Botswana	..	..	..	..	..	..	..	..	..	..	..	..	..	..
Burkina Faso	..	117	119	106	105	103	106	107	124	134	141	..	104	118
Burundi	..	125	126	117	102	96	82	83	88	80	87	99	101	102
Cameroon	..	105	100	56	48	45	48	57	60	65	72	71	98	72
Cape Verde	..	124	154	163	175	179	174	180	211	232	235	..	98	171
Central African Republic	..	103	100	90	76	71	74	75	78	75	73	..	102	85
Chad	..	160	193	212	207	152	144	131	152	172	170	..	111	168
Comoros	..	..	..	..	..	..	..	..	..	..	..	..	..	..
Congo, Democratic Rep. of	..	..	..	..	..	..	..	..	..	..	..	..	..	..
Congo, Republic of	..	167	161	108	84	73	..	..	..	..	..	..	97	..
Côte d'Ivoire	..	87	80	66	61	67	68	66	67	69	71	0	100	74
Djibouti	..	..	..	..	..	..	..	..	..	..	..	..	..	..
Equatorial Guinea	..	126	131	113	118	176	220	266	414	332	363	..	103	207
Eritrea	..	..	..	..	..	..	..	..	..	..	..	..	..	..
Ethiopia	..	67	81	90	88	103	104	124	127	152	169	106	103	111
Gabon	..	163	168	137	134	138	141	144	156	140	..	86	101	143
Gambia, The	..	..	..	..	..	..	..	..	..	..	..	..	..	..
Ghana	..	162	173	181	164	159	153	170	183	180	195	..	82	161
Guinea	..	223	247	246	248	269	262	263	270	143	165	..	165	232
Guinea-Bissau	..	108	95	85	93	110	103	112	137	192	199	..	104	123
Kenya	..	98	75	69	73	57	59	60	58	57	57	80	90	70
Lesotho	..	..	..	..	..	..	..	..	..	..	..	..	..	..
Liberia	..	..	..	..	..	..	..	..	..	..	..	..	..	..
Madagascar	..	88	86	80	75	74	93	108	119	111	133	122	100	96
Malawi	..	115	117	157	142	114	145	131	127	129	139	92	91	125
Mali	..	..	..	..	..	..	..	..	..	..	..	..	..	..
Mauritania	..	99	97	97	95	97	100	105	107	117	125	..	102	103
Mauritius	110	142	140	167	172	170	178	184	197	197	196	91	111	168
Mozambique	..	159	187	158	154	152	282	403	560	637	745	..	115	312
Namibia	..	..	..	..	..	..	..	..	..	..	..	..	..	..
Niger	..	164	172	149	141	90	116	113	130	129	121	..	103	135
Nigeria	..	180	295	229	183	189	196	218	506	899	814	..	131	344
Rwanda	..	102	104	26	43	56	76	71	87	89	92	..	97	80
São Tomé and Principe	..	69	57	78	65	91	154	165	189	194	221	..	84	120
Senegal	..	119	114	97	95	96	93	93	95	99	97	115	104	102
Seychelles	..	..	..	..	..	..	..	..	..	..	..	..	..	..
Sierra Leone	..	124	234	231	191	209	169	228	247	305	374	415	142	211
Somalia	..	..	..	..	..	..	..	..	..	..	..	..	..	..
South Africa	..	..	..	..	..	..	..	..	..	..	..	..	..	..
Sudan	..	..	..	..	..	..	..	..	..	..	..	..	..	..
Swaziland	..	..	..	..	..	..	..	..	..	..	..	..	..	..
Tanzania	..	119	146	148	164	190	209	204	190	233	239	136	110	174
Togo	..	111	112	103	94	92	90	92	92	88	82	98	100	99
Uganda	..	321	396	486	719	828	1,051	1,184	1,485	1,583	1,801	..	149	856
Zambia	..	..	..	..	..	..	..	..	..	..	..	..	..	..
Zimbabwe	..	116	106	108	113	126	152	147	154	169	130	83	104	133
NORTH AFRICA	..	118	116	126	125	132	142	148	159	161	180	..	104	137
Algeria	56	115	115	113	107	108	112	117	123	124	221	57	95	123
Egypt, Arab Republic	..	96	105	109	107	112	117	124	138	151	163	..	101	118
Libya	..	..	..	..	..	..	..	..	..	..	..	..	..	..
Morocco	36	129	121	134	134	141	154	161	169	165	189	61	106	146
Tunisia	..	125	130	125	130	139	158	167	188	195	206	96	101	149
ALL AFRICA	..	157	150	144	119	113	101	128	132	130	132	..	117	135

Note: 2001 data are preliminary (see page 2). Nigeria's fiscal data are for consolidated government starting from 1992.

7-15. Government expenditure: other goods and services

	Percentage of total expenditure and lending minus repayments											Annual Average		
	1980	*1992*	*1993*	*1994*	*1995*	*1996*	*1997*	*1998*	*1999*	*2000*	*2001*	*75-84*	*85-89*	*90-MR*
SUB-SAHARAN AFRICA	..	-8.4	-6.5	25.4	24.0	25.2	26.2	18.0	18.1	18.7	17.9	-7.0	4.5	12.8
excluding South Africa	..	21.5	22.4	25.7	22.4	22.3	23.9	23.1	22.7	23.0	19.5	..	19.9	22.3
excl. S.Africa & Nigeria	..	21.5	22.4	21.2	23.4	23.7	24.0	23.5	23.5	24.0	17.8	18.2	19.9	22.2
Angola	..	10.9	43.1	41.0	55.0	9.2	27.6	41.7	33.0	43.9	27.5	..	26.4	30.8
Benin	..	7.6	8.4	6.3	5.2	7.6	6.9	7.5	7.1	6.0	5.8	..	7.4	7.0
Botswana	..	..	..	24.2	26.1	24.8	25.8	31.4	32.3	33.1	35.7	..	..	29.2
Burkina Faso	..	8.6	10.7	12.0	10.8	9.8	8.7	9.4	8.6	9.4	8.9	..	..	9.3
Burundi	28.0	12.4	20.4	21.3	24.0	20.9	33.2	27.0	30.1	31.0	25.7	22.6	16.9	23.2
Cameroon	22.9	10.5	10.7	7.5	15.8	16.0	16.1	14.5	16.3	18.9	20.1	20.3	13.7	14.7
Cape Verde	..	2.5	1.8	1.6	1.5	1.6	3.3	1.6	3.3	1.6	2.3	23.4	8.8	2.4
Central African Republic	..	11.7	11.5	13.9	10.0	12.6	15.7	10.3	11.4	10.5	11.3	..	11.5	11.9
Chad	..	26.4	26.3	14.4	11.7	22.1	19.2	22.3	25.2	18.5	22.4	..	18.5	22.0
Comoros	..	19.7	26.4	20.3	22.6	17.7	14.3	14.8	23.5	23.7	20.3	0.0	4.1	20.4
Congo, Democratic Rep. of	..	..	..	..	..	43.8	36.1	23.7	22.6	35.4	..	..	..	32.3
Congo, Republic of	..	10.4	9.1	8.1	7.7	7.2	24.4	36.1	19.2	19.2	15.1	24.5	10.3	14.6
Côte d'Ivoire	..	22.4	22.2	21.7	21.8	23.2	23.0	20.8	25.8	22.6	24.2	..	31.6	23.0
Djibouti	..	29.2	29.2	24.2	22.0	19.0	14.9	21.4	32.6	31.1	31.5	..	..	25.5
Equatorial Guinea	..	14.6	10.1	20.3	25.2	23.8	30.6	16.0	23.9	43.1	22.7	..	18.8	20.8
Eritrea	..	71.0	44.1	49.2	42.7	40.5	26.1	45.2	40.3	49.4	41.3	..	..	45.0
Ethiopia	..	22.1	25.7	25.0	25.3	23.1	25.5	31.8	40.3	50.1	34.0	30.5	32.0	30.6
Gabon	..	20.5	19.4	19.2	17.3	21.1	24.5	36.8	21.9	20.9	21.6	13.8	20.4	22.3
Gambia, The	..	23.5	25.5	25.1	18.9	19.7	17.9	16.0	18.5	-0.1	22.8	..	19.5	19.0
Ghana	..	10.0	12.6	10.5	8.1	7.2	6.9	7.5	9.0	9.3	5.8	34.5	15.4	9.4
Guinea	..	15.6	13.9	13.2	11.3	11.7	11.6	13.6	11.6	13.3	17.5	..	26.5	13.8
Guinea-Bissau	..	10.7	9.4	12.6	11.9	10.0	8.4	18.5	18.5	16.1	10.6	0.0	13.8	12.8
Kenya	27.6	24.4	19.6	13.8	15.8	22.2	22.0	22.0	22.0	23.3	23.7	30.1	28.5	21.0
Lesotho	..	23.6	24.9	22.9	23.3	15.3	13.6	19.0	28.6	31.5	27.6	19.9	23.6	22.2
Liberia	..	..	..	..	..	..	..	..	..	..	..	..	..	..
Madagascar	..	21.6	16.6	15.8	6.4	30.5	23.6	18.9	16.4	15.7	21.0	-11.5	-5.8	16.5
Malawi	0.0	49.1	37.3	41.4	29.1	31.6	36.6	23.7	28.0	24.4	21.1	0.0	0.0	34.8
Mali	13.0	9.8	10.2	10.6	12.2	11.7	13.0	11.4	13.2	7.0	12.1	15.8	4.7	10.1
Mauritania	..	18.9	14.4	17.6	20.1	20.0	21.8	20.8	22.5	18.6	18.3	..	8.8	18.6
Mauritius	8.3	10.5	9.7	9.6	9.4	9.5	9.4	8.7	8.8	8.5	8.9	7.6	8.1	9.1
Mozambique	44.2	31.5	29.3	33.8	22.4	28.3	23.6	27.4	14.8	11.7	12.6	36.0	34.2	24.6
Namibia	..	..	..	..	..	..	..	..	..	..	..	..	..	..
Niger	..	21.3	15.3	18.8	17.9	21.3	22.9	24.3	25.3	22.5	22.5	13.8	14.9	20.2
Nigeria	..	..	..	48.1	17.7	15.1	23.1	20.9	18.5	18.3	28.2	..	..	23.7
Rwanda	..	30.9	24.8	26.4	25.0	26.3	20.3	26.7	27.5	26.7	29.8	..	..	26.3
São Tomé and Principe	..	4.7	3.7	5.0	4.6	5.0	5.0	5.5	5.5	6.6	3.5	..	16.6	4.7
Senegal	22.9	21.1	11.9	11.8	11.4	11.0	10.8	13.0	15.7	15.7	15.2	17.9	15.5	13.5
Seychelles	..	31.5	25.1	30.6	24.6	18.8	22.2	17.2	15.4	16.4	19.9	..	..	23.6
Sierra Leone	..	38.8	31.2	35.4	51.6	35.9	44.1	19.3	23.6	25.2	30.6	..	35.5	34.8
Somalia	..	..	..	..	..	..	..	..	..	..	..	..	..	..
South Africa	..	..	..	25.1	25.7	28.5	28.9	12.2	12.8	13.7	16.2	..	..	20.4
Sudan	..	..	20.3	26.0	53.7	44.8	47.8	38.4	33.1	30.6	28.9	..	..	36.0
Swaziland	..	..	..	..	..	..	..	..	..	..	..	..	..	..
Tanzania	..	36.2	30.7	30.4	28.9	24.2	23.7	21.1	26.0	23.4	30.0	30.5	31.5	28.6
Togo	..	17.0	19.0	16.3	18.9	22.9	21.1	22.6	22.4	21.9	20.4	-27.1	-25.7	20.2
Uganda	..	31.8	26.6	29.7	33.9	33.1	33.8	32.2	31.0	22.1	27.0	35.0	45.2	31.4
Zambia	..	24.5	20.3	22.3	22.5	21.2	18.3	20.3	15.2	12.3	19.5	..	..	19.3
Zimbabwe	-103.4	16.9	19.4	18.1	16.9	16.5	14.1	13.2	14.6	17.9	17.1	-69.3	16.7	16.3
NORTH AFRICA	..	10.5	11.7	10.7	11.1	11.2	11.6	11.8	10.6	10.9	11.9	..	10.9	11.0
Algeria	2.9	3.7	4.0	3.6	4.7	4.6	5.1	5.4	5.5	4.6	6.5	2.9	2.1	4.5
Egypt, Arab Republic	..	13.0	15.3	15.5	16.1	15.9	16.3	16.3	13.8	15.0	15.2	..	15.1	14.9
Libya	..	..	..	..	..	..	..	..	..	..	..	..	..	..
Morocco	17.6	15.9	16.9	14.3	13.7	14.5	15.7	16.0	15.2	14.6	16.7	40.9	14.7	15.0
Tunisia	13.1	10.9	10.7	6.5	6.1	6.9	5.9	5.7	5.0	6.3	6.1	11.7	12.1	7.7
ALL AFRICA	..	-1.4	0.2	20.3	19.5	20.4	21.2	15.9	15.5	16.0	15.9	-1.3	6.3	12.3

Note: 2001 data are preliminary (see page 2). Nigeria's fiscal data are for consolidated government starting from 1992.

7-16. Government expenditure: interest payments

	Percentage of total expenditure and lending minus repayments											Annual Average		
	1980	*1992*	*1993*	*1994*	*1995*	*1996*	*1997*	*1998*	*1999*	*2000*	*2001*	*75-84*	*85-89*	*90-MR*
SUB-SAHARAN AFRICA	..	6.7	7.3	13.6	10.1	9.6	7.9	7.7	8.2	7.9	8.3	3.7	5.8	8.4
excluding South Africa	..	13.8	15.1	25.8	19.1	17.9	14.6	14.3	15.3	14.7	15.5	..	12.7	16.2
excl. S.Africa & Nigeria	..	13.8	15.1	24.1	17.2	17.2	15.0	14.7	14.1	14.3	15.7	11.2	12.7	15.8
Angola	..	8.9	15.5	384.9	16.1	18.2	8.6	16.2	11.1	9.2	9.7	..	5.4	43.6
Benin	..	17.5	15.0	15.9	12.6	12.4	9.0	6.2	5.2	4.4	4.3	..	15.6	11.0
Botswana	..	0.0	0.0	0.0	0.0	0.0	0.0	0.0	0.0	0.0	0.0	..	..	0.0
Burkina Faso	..	6.9	6.9	6.9	6.6	4.2	3.6	3.5	3.1	3.9	3.9	..	..	5.1
Burundi	2.0	6.4	5.0	6.0	6.9	6.7	8.9	10.2	11.2	12.3	10.3	5.3	8.9	8.1
Cameroon	2.0	23.4	24.1	36.5	39.5	41.8	37.2	32.0	27.6	25.1	20.8	2.9	5.7	27.9
Cape Verde	..	2.6	2.5	1.9	6.2	8.4	9.6	8.5	3.9	6.0	9.2	0.0	3.1	5.6
Central African Republic	..	8.2	9.9	10.8	11.1	17.2	9.6	7.6	7.8	10.2	7.4	..	7.2	9.3
Chad	..	3.8	5.8	6.1	5.6	5.6	5.3	5.5	4.8	5.1	4.2	..	1.0	4.8
Comoros	..	2.9	3.7	3.1	3.0	3.6	4.1	4.9	5.2	2.5	4.6	0.0	0.8	3.8
Congo, Democratic Rep. of	..	..	..	..	..	31.1	23.5	31.1	22.6	18.1	74.5	..	..	33.5
Congo, Republic of	..	21.6	20.1	33.0	43.0	36.5	32.2	34.0	35.4	27.2	23.5	0.0	13.0	29.9
Côte d'Ivoire	..	32.7	29.0	29.1	25.8	23.2	20.2	18.0	19.9	22.6	18.7	..	22.7	25.1
Djibouti	..	1.1	0.8	0.8	1.5	2.0	1.4	1.0	0.9	2.3	2.5	..	..	1.4
Equatorial Guinea	..	16.7	13.7	26.0	24.0	15.6	8.7	5.5	8.5	3.4	4.1	..	17.8	12.5
Eritrea	..	0.0	0.1	0.2	0.6	1.3	1.9	1.6	2.0	2.9	3.5	..	..	1.4
Ethiopia	..	7.3	10.2	13.5	10.0	9.0	9.2	7.4	6.4	6.5	7.0	3.4	5.1	8.0
Gabon	..	22.5	24.4	26.4	30.9	25.6	20.1	15.9	26.8	25.4	21.7	6.6	14.1	23.8
Gambia, The	..	12.9	14.8	14.8	14.1	14.2	19.1	23.0	22.2	20.8	18.5	..	13.4	16.9
Ghana	..	8.9	12.0	14.2	13.9	17.2	21.7	17.9	21.4	27.0	30.1	11.4	8.3	16.8
Guinea	..	8.5	7.2	9.0	8.1	8.1	9.3	9.8	9.6	12.3	10.9	..	12.1	9.4
Guinea-Bissau	..	9.7	14.3	15.2	21.9	19.7	11.9	27.4	20.3	13.0	19.5	1.1	7.5	16.2
Kenya	10.1	28.1	40.6	36.2	26.4	23.7	21.7	20.9	17.9	13.3	11.9	13.9	18.0	24.7
Lesotho	..	5.9	5.4	4.2	3.6	3.3	3.7	4.9	5.4	8.0	7.3	..	8.9	5.9
Liberia	..	..	..	..	..	..	..	..	..	..	..	..	..	..
Madagascar	..	15.9	18.3	26.4	30.1	21.6	17.5	13.7	11.8	12.9	10.8	11.2	12.4	16.8
Malawi	9.1	9.3	11.9	10.3	20.5	22.9	14.1	12.9	11.7	14.1	16.3	12.9	18.6	14.1
Mali	4.1	7.3	6.9	9.0	6.1	4.8	4.1	2.8	3.7	3.7	3.0	4.8	6.6	5.6
Mauritania	..	12.2	11.1	10.4	13.0	13.4	13.0	14.0	13.9	10.3	11.9	..	8.2	11.6
Mauritius	..	15.3	12.2	11.7	13.0	12.8	12.7	15.8	14.6	13.9	16.4	18.0	18.9	14.5
Mozambique	0.0	7.9	8.6	3.6	6.6	7.0	5.7	4.5	2.5	0.7	2.1	0.1	3.8	5.1
Namibia	..	0.7	1.7	2.8	3.2	4.2	5.5	6.8	6.6	6.0	6.4	6.8	7.6	3.9
Niger	..	9.8	10.2	12.3	16.0	12.8	9.7	8.8	8.9	10.5	10.7	11.1	13.6	10.9
Nigeria	..	..	..	33.9	28.9	21.8	12.8	12.0	21.7	17.0	14.5	..	..	20.3
Rwanda	..	7.8	9.1	27.9	11.3	7.2	6.2	4.9	4.2	4.9	3.9	..	..	8.4
São Tomé and Principe	..	15.5	16.8	14.9	15.6	14.4	16.1	20.8	16.3	10.0	10.3	..	22.4	15.1
Senegal	7.5	9.3	10.9	16.8	14.5	11.2	12.1	6.3	8.4	7.3	3.9	9.4	15.7	10.5
Seychelles	..	15.2	12.3	16.5	20.7	17.6	17.7	14.7	15.8	13.8	15.9	..	..	16.0
Sierra Leone	..	26.9	18.9	14.0	10.5	12.5	16.3	23.9	26.4	21.9	16.2	..	23.7	20.5
Somalia	..	..	..	..	..	..	..	..	..	..	..	..	..	..
South Africa	..	..	..	..	..	..	..	..	..	..	..	..	..	..
Sudan	..	..	..	..	..	..	..	9.1	9.8	10.9	..	..	..	9.9
Swaziland	..	2.4	2.0	1.8	2.1	2.2	2.3	2.2	2.7	2.4	2.3	..	..	2.3
Tanzania	..	12.2	12.9	14.4	18.4	18.9	17.4	15.2	10.6	10.9	10.1	8.0	12.3	13.9
Togo	..	13.3	16.2	22.0	15.6	13.8	12.6	11.6	13.0	11.7	11.8	20.9	14.8	13.9
Uganda	..	15.5	9.7	7.8	5.9	6.0	5.6	6.1	5.1	4.2	5.8	14.4	7.8	7.1
Zambia	10.9	27.5	41.8	36.5	27.7	17.4	16.4	11.8	10.1	10.1	7.9	12.2	28.6	21.3
Zimbabwe	27.7	15.6	17.9	20.4	24.2	24.5	19.1	27.8	26.0	34.4	29.1	24.8	13.5	22.3
NORTH AFRICA	..	14.5	17.1	19.1	18.2	18.5	17.6	16.5	12.0	16.1	15.2	..	9.7	15.8
Algeria	..	7.0	6.4	8.2	9.9	11.9	12.7	12.6	..	13.8	11.9	..	5.6	9.7
Egypt, Arab Republic	..	18.7	25.5	29.3	25.4	25.1	23.1	21.1	19.1	19.4	19.4	..	9.1	21.0
Libya	..	..	..	..	..	..	..	..	..	..	..	..	..	..
Morocco	7.4	19.5	19.8	20.1	20.3	19.3	18.2	17.2	17.1	16.2	15.3	20.2	22.4	18.9
Tunisia	5.8	10.7	11.5	11.0	11.7	12.2	10.6	9.6	10.7	10.2	9.0	5.5	8.9	10.5
ALL AFRICA	..	9.5	10.9	15.5	12.9	12.7	11.2	10.7	9.5	10.7	10.7	5.4	7.0	11.0

Note: 2001 data are preliminary (see page 2). Nigeria's fiscal data are for consolidated government starting from 1992.

7-17. Government expenditure: subsidies and current transfers

	Percentage of total expenditure and lending minus repayments											Annual Average		
	1980	*1992*	*1993*	*1994*	*1995*	*1996*	*1997*	*1998*	*1999*	*2000*	*2001*	*75-84*	*85-89*	*90-MR*
SUB-SAHARAN AFRICA	..	0.9	1.0	2.8	2.5	2.2	2.3	1.2	1.2	1.4	1.5	1.7	1.2	1.6
excluding South Africa	..	1.8	2.0	1.3	1.5	1.3	1.7	2.3	2.2	2.5	2.9	..	2.6	2.0
excl. S.Africa & Nigeria	..	1.8	2.0	1.6	1.8	1.6	2.0	2.7	2.6	3.0	3.4	2.7	2.6	2.2
Angola	..	8.1	9.1	0.0	0.0	0.0	0.0	0.0	0.0	1.9	7.7	..	5.3	3.2
Benin	..	..	..	..	..	..	..	..	..	..	..	..	..	..
Botswana	..	0.8	0.8	0.8	1.0	1.3	1.2	1.5	1.6	1.1	1.6	..	..	1.2
Burkina Faso	..	..	..	..	..	..	..	..	..	..	..	..	..	..
Burundi	10.9	8.0	5.7	7.5	6.7	5.9	7.6	7.6	7.0	6.5	6.1	10.1	5.8	6.8
Cameroon	11.1	0.0	0.0	0.0	0.0	0.0	4.2	4.8	5.4	5.7	6.8	8.6	0.0	2.3
Cape Verde	..	0.2	0.1	0.0	0.1	0.0	0.0	0.0	0.0	0.0	0.0	1.2	0.9	0.1
Central African Republic	..	..	..	..	..	..	..	..	..	..	..	..	..	..
Chad	..	0.0	0.0	0.0	0.0	0.0	0.0	0.0	0.0	0.0	0.0	..	0.0	0.0
Comoros	..	0.0	0.0	0.0	0.0	0.0	0.0	0.0	0.0	0.0	0.0	0.0	0.0	0.0
Congo, Democratic Rep. of	..	..	..	..	..	0.5	0.3	0.7	0.3	5.5	..	..	..	1.5
Congo, Republic of	..	0.0	0.0	0.0	0.0	0.0	0.0	0.0	0.0	0.0	0.0	0.0	2.4	0.2
Côte d'Ivoire	..	0.0	3.0	3.7	3.9	2.9	3.7	3.5	4.0	6.6	4.6	..	5.4	3.3
Djibouti	..	3.6	3.6	3.6	-9.2	-1.2	-1.7	-2.8	2.7	2.8	2.8	..		0.4
Equatorial Guinea	..	4.1	3.5	4.4	4.4	4.0	4.1	9.0	4.7	6.7	9.4	..	5.3	5.4
Eritrea	..	0.0	0.0	0.0	0.0	0.0	0.0	0.0	0.0	..	..	..	..	0.0
Ethiopia	..	1.4	0.1	1.2	1.8	1.7	1.3	0.0	0.0	0.0	0.0	3.5	1.4	0.9
Gabon	..	0.0	0.0	0.0	0.0	0.0	0.0	0.0	0.0	0.0	0.0	0.0	0.0	0.0
Gambia, The	..	0.5	0.6	0.1	0.0	0.0	0.0	0.0	0.0	0.0	0.0	..	10.4	0.3
Ghana	..	0.0	0.0	0.0	7.9	5.6	4.9	9.3	5.3	5.9	6.7	..	..	3.8
Guinea	..	4.0	3.6	4.3	6.2	6.0	7.5	8.1	9.1	2.2	3.3	..	6.8	5.3
Guinea-Bissau	..	0.0	0.0	0.0	0.0	0.0	0.0	0.0	0.0	0.0	0.0	0.0	0.0	0.0
Kenya	0.1	0.0	0.0	0.0	0.0	0.0	0.0	0.0	0.1	0.1	0.0	0.2	1.5	0.2
Lesotho	..	0.0	0.0	0.0	0.0	0.0	0.0	0.0	0.0	0.0	0.0	..	0.0	0.0
Liberia	..	..	..	..	..	..	..	..	..	..	..	..	..	..
Madagascar	..	..	..	..	..	..	..	..	..	0.0	..	..	..	0.0
Malawi	0.0	0.0	5.1	9.8	3.1	2.0	1.5	12.9	3.0	2.6	5.2	0.0	0.0	3.8
Mali	6.0	2.7	2.7	1.6	1.3	1.4	1.2	5.2	5.6	5.4	4.6	3.7	1.6	3.0
Mauritania	..	..	..	..	..	..	..	..	..	..	..	..	..	..
Mauritius	0.0	4.0	4.6	1.7	1.5	2.7	3.7	3.3	3.0	2.8	2.6	0.0	0.0	2.8
Mozambique	1.4	2.2	1.2	0.9	1.3	1.2	1.0	1.0	0.5	0.4	0.3	7.1	14.3	1.3
Namibia	..	0.0	0.0	0.0	0.0	0.0	0.0	0.0	0.0	0.0	0.0	0.0	0.0	0.0
Niger	..	6.9	12.9	6.6	4.4	6.0	7.6	5.2	5.1	10.2	11.8	9.4	6.6	7.6
Nigeria	..	..	..	0.0	0.0	0.0	0.0	0.0	0.0	0.0	0.0	..	..	0.0
Rwanda	..	8.1	5.0	3.8	4.8	3.3	5.7	7.9	9.1	8.4	9.6	..	..	7.6
São Tomé and Principe	..	..	..	..	..	..	..	..	..	..	..	..	..	..
Senegal	13.9	8.2	13.9	11.4	9.9	7.9	9.6	7.5	12.4	15.0	26.2	12.1	10.1	11.8
Seychelles	..	5.4	4.6	6.3	13.2	-3.7	1.4	1.9	1.8	1.0	1.2	..	..	3.9
Sierra Leone	..	2.4	0.0	0.0	0.0	0.0	0.0	0.0	0.0	0.0	0.0	..	0.5	0.6
Somalia	..	..	..	..	..	..	..	..	..	..	..	..	..	..
South Africa	..	..	..	4.5	3.5	3.2	3.0	0.0	0.0	0.0	0.0	..	..	1.8
Sudan	..	..	..	..	..	..	..	5.1	3.3	2.5	3.4	..	..	3.6
Swaziland	..	1.4	3.3	2.6	6.6	13.8	11.2	9.5	12.0	14.1	14.6	..	..	8.4
Tanzania	..	0.0	0.0	0.0	0.0	0.0	0.0	0.0	0.0	0.0	0.0	0.0	0.0	0.0
Togo	..	5.8	4.6	9.0	6.6	5.4	7.0	6.4	9.4	9.8	11.0	2.3	0.7	7.0
Uganda	..	0.0	0.0	0.0	0.0	0.0	0.0	0.0	0.0	0.0	0.0	0.0	0.0	0.0
Zambia	13.7	2.5	0.6	0.0	0.0	0.0	0.2	0.9	0.8	2.9	2.7	9.9	11.9	2.8
Zimbabwe	29.3	8.3	4.9	1.4	0.5	0.3	0.1	0.0	0.0	0.0	0.0	23.2	8.5	2.4
NORTH AFRICA	..	12.2	9.2	6.6	5.7	5.9	4.9	4.7	4.4	4.9	9.8	..	6.7	6.8
Algeria	..	15.9	13.6	9.4	6.2	4.4	2.1	2.2	2.0	1.9	21.8	..	1.1	6.7
Egypt, Arab Republic	..	14.2	7.7	5.8	6.6	6.8	6.2	5.9	5.2	5.9	6.0	..	10.2	7.8
Libya	..	..	..	..	..	..	..	..	..	..	..	..	..	..
Morocco	6.0	2.3	2.6	4.1	3.3	6.0	6.4	6.0	7.4	8.2	3.4	7.5	4.0	4.4
Tunisia	15.1	13.3	13.9	6.0	5.9	6.2	5.6	4.8	3.0	3.5	2.4	20.3	18.8	8.0
ALL AFRICA	..	5.1	4.0	4.1	3.6	3.5	3.2	2.4	2.3	2.6	4.4	2.8	3.0	3.5

Note: 2001 data are preliminary (see page 2). Nigeria's fiscal data are for consolidated government starting from 1992.

7-18. Government expenditure: capital and net lending

	Percentage of total expenditure and lending minus repayments											Annual Average		
	1980	1992	1993	1994	1995	1996	1997	1998	1999	2000	2001	75-84	85-89	90-MR
SUB-SAHARAN AFRICA	..	16.8	18.3	19.4	19.2	19.5	19.8	20.0	18.3	18.5	18.6	21.7	18.0	18.6
excluding South Africa	..	24.5	24.8	28.1	28.2	29.0	30.1	31.3	29.0	29.7	28.7	..	27.1	27.8
excl. S.Africa & Nigeria	..	24.5	24.8	25.5	25.5	25.1	25.2	25.9	25.2	25.8	25.5	28.6	27.1	25.3
Angola	..	6.4	10.7	5.7	10.3	20.3	7.2	13.8	15.6	10.4	11.1	..	17.3	11.6
Benin	..	21.1	26.8	32.9	36.6	32.9	36.3	36.3	37.7	38.1	38.2	..	27.0	32.7
Botswana	..	44.8	40.6	37.2	31.6	32.8	33.6	32.7	31.1	30.3	27.0	43.3	45.1	36.7
Burkina Faso	..	43.4	34.4	40.8	45.9	51.3	56.5	56.2	58.9	54.3	52.5	..	..	47.2
Burundi	113.6	47.9	43.4	32.6	30.3	35.8	18.0	25.8	25.7	22.5	29.9	119.7	61.9	33.1
Cameroon	32.6	15.5	13.8	17.3	7.1	5.9	10.8	16.8	19.5	16.4	19.0	40.3	43.0	16.0
Cape Verde	..	59.4	58.7	60.9	52.4	47.8	44.7	51.0	19.6	24.5	26.5	67.8	54.3	43.7
Central African Republic	..	40.2	41.1	46.0	50.2	21.9	37.5	54.2	50.9	52.4	55.3	..	41.8	44.4
Chad	..	45.1	38.0	47.5	50.4	49.1	53.8	51.1	50.8	50.8	50.2	..	63.1	47.8
Comoros	..	32.3	15.6	32.1	20.5	21.8	24.0	35.0	28.0	23.4	20.1	0.0	60.0	23.6
Congo, Democratic Rep. of	..	..	..	..	..	0.0	..	..	..	3.1	6.5	..	..	3.2
Congo, Republic of	..	2.1	4.6	7.6	9.1	24.4	9.1	11.1	18.7	27.3	31.8	61.7	27.2	13.0
Côte d'Ivoire	..	9.5	10.3	17.0	21.0	21.9	24.8	28.7	21.9	15.4	17.7	..	12.1	17.0
Djibouti	..	18.3	16.4	12.9	9.4	11.3	12.1	20.0	9.4	9.9	11.2	..	..	13.1
Equatorial Guinea	..	51.6	49.5	32.9	18.0	9.6	20.9	36.4	43.8	31.3	41.9	..	34.0	38.2
Eritrea	..	12.4	29.2	22.4	21.4	31.6	44.3	33.3	40.0	28.1	18.9	..	..	28.2
Ethiopia	..	22.6	34.2	38.0	37.7	45.2	42.9	37.5	32.1	20.0	32.5	27.2	32.9	32.9
Gabon	..	18.9	17.7	22.1	20.9	22.8	31.7	29.2	8.9	24.9	27.0	58.1	35.4	21.7
Gambia, The	..	34.6	29.9	27.4	35.4	36.9	29.3	22.2	20.7	17.3	22.2	36.5	31.2	28.7
Ghana	17.8	41.9	38.3	42.7	46.1	44.8	42.9	39.6	37.3	33.1	31.7	14.5	38.0	40.0
Guinea	..	47.0	49.4	46.3	48.6	45.1	47.8	40.9	44.5	57.2	52.0	..	41.4	47.7
Guinea-Bissau	..	66.8	64.4	59.1	49.6	53.0	66.9	24.4	34.4	23.3	34.6	32.0	62.2	50.1
Kenya	29.5	12.6	10.8	10.8	11.6	11.9	9.9	8.4	9.7	13.0	16.2	23.5	18.7	12.5
Lesotho	..	34.0	33.0	31.4	32.8	40.6	38.3	24.4	29.1	21.6	20.1	37.9	24.1	32.4
Liberia	..	..	..	..	..	..	..	..	..	..	..	..	..	..
Madagascar	..	35.0	35.9	32.2	36.2	32.5	37.5	47.1	47.7	49.4	43.8	39.9	42.1	40.2
Malawi	48.8	23.3	20.3	17.2	21.4	19.9	19.3	26.9	32.9	35.8	26.4	38.0	27.5	23.8
Mali	53.0	53.3	50.4	50.4	53.5	56.2	51.4	46.5	48.3	55.3	54.3	47.9	59.1	53.2
Mauritania	..	24.3	41.3	32.9	27.6	27.8	25.8	29.2	29.3	42.3	35.5	..	26.7	30.5
Mauritius	27.2	18.9	20.3	18.2	15.9	18.7	22.1	12.9	12.1	15.9	14.6	21.8	19.1	17.2
Mozambique	44.0	50.3	49.3	51.1	57.3	55.1	55.8	47.6	49.7	52.5	55.6	40.1	35.6	52.4
Namibia	..	16.8	15.3	12.3	13.2	13.1	13.4	12.4	13.1	12.6	15.9	21.2	17.3	14.1
Niger	..	21.9	21.5	28.6	27.1	29.6	30.6	31.9	30.6	30.7	33.9	46.9	40.8	29.6
Nigeria	..	..	..	41.1	41.3	49.4	55.8	59.4	48.6	49.5	45.1	..	..	48.8
Rwanda	..	30.3	32.1	16.6	39.4	41.3	41.6	35.9	32.0	32.3	32.0	..	..	32.8
São Tomé and Principe	..	57.4	52.3	57.9	69.1	60.7	60.3	51.8	60.9	63.4	59.3	..	43.9	58.7
Senegal	17.6	24.1	20.3	23.6	26.5	35.6	32.9	42.2	28.2	31.3	29.6	16.4	13.5	26.8
Seychelles	..	19.7	22.8	11.0	17.8	17.8	22.3	25.6	24.8	22.9	12.0	..	..	20.2
Sierra Leone	..	21.8	25.2	21.8	13.4	19.6	11.3	24.6	11.2	21.1	17.2	..	24.0	18.8
Somalia	..	..	..	..	..	..	..	..	..	..	..	..	..	..
South Africa	25.8	9.6	12.3	9.6	9.2	8.4	7.8	6.9	6.0	5.6	6.8	23.6	10.3	8.5
Sudan	..	17.0	15.6	14.2	15.1	7.2	7.7	9.1	14.2	21.3	19.6	16.9	14.0	13.9
Swaziland	..	28.7	25.4	24.7	23.8	18.1	17.1	23.0	20.6	20.1	23.0	..	..	22.7
Tanzania	..	16.7	21.2	20.8	17.6	20.4	17.3	25.8	27.4	30.8	22.5	26.2	22.1	20.8
Togo	..	15.9	8.8	9.1	15.5	13.9	11.2	19.2	17.7	15.0	15.6	..	26.0	15.4
Uganda	..	44.5	55.0	52.2	45.1	44.1	40.2	41.0	40.5	51.1	40.8	39.7	35.1	45.7
Zambia	10.5	12.1	10.7	12.5	17.5	32.0	30.1	39.4	44.9	46.9	38.8	11.6	2.2	26.6
Zimbabwe	43.1	18.0	16.8	17.6	14.5	12.7	12.3	6.7	14.2	5.2	2.8	42.7	15.7	13.3
NORTH AFRICA	..	26.2	24.5	22.4	22.0	20.7	20.7	21.4	22.8	24.4	22.0	..	33.7	23.8
Algeria	63.3	28.2	31.3	31.0	29.4	26.6	25.2	24.8	19.9	27.3	23.6	61.6	46.8	27.1
Egypt, Arab Republic	..	29.0	20.9	18.1	18.2	18.7	20.0	21.3	28.9	25.2	21.8	..	39.0	24.6
Libya	..	..	..	..	..	..	..	..	..	..	..	..	..	..
Morocco	33.4	18.4	20.5	18.4	18.8	16.0	14.5	16.2	15.9	18.4	18.6	65.0	19.2	17.8
Tunisia	28.9	24.8	25.6	21.1	20.9	20.7	22.4	21.9	21.4	24.5	24.4	27.7	21.9	23.2
ALL AFRICA	..	20.2	20.6	20.4	20.2	19.9	20.1	20.5	19.9	20.6	19.8	26.3	23.8	20.5

Note: 2001 data are preliminary (see page 2). Nigeria's fiscal data are for consolidated government starting from 1992.

7-19. Government expenditure: trends in real defense spending

	Index 1980=100											Annual Average		
	1980	*1992*	*1993*	*1994*	*1995*	*1996*	*1997*	*1998*	*1999*	*2000*	*2001*	*75-84*	*85-89*	*90-MR*
SUB-SAHARAN AFRICA	..	..	..	..	..	..	..	..	..	..	..	..	..	..
excluding South Africa	..	..	..	..	..	..	..	..	..	..	..	..	..	..
excl. S.Africa & Nigeria	..	..	..	..	..	..	..	..	..	..	..	..	..	..
Angola	..	..	..	..	..	..	..	..	..	..	..	..	..	..
Benin	..	..	..	..	..	..	..	..	..	..	..	..	..	..
Botswana	..	..	..	..	..	..	..	..	..	..	..	..	..	..
Burkina Faso	..	..	..	..	..	..	..	..	..	..	..	..	..	..
Burundi	..	..	..	..	..	..	..	..	..	..	..	..	..	..
Cameroon	..	..	..	..	..	..	..	..	..	..	..	..	..	..
Cape Verde	..	..	..	..	..	..	..	..	..	..	..	..	..	..
Central African Republic	100.0	..	..	249.4	..	..	..	..	..	..	..	100.0	109.2	191.7
Chad	..	..	..	..	..	..	..	..	..	..	..	..	..	..
Comoros	..	..	..	..	..	..	..	..	..	..	..	..	..	..
Congo, Democratic Rep. of	..	..	..	..	..	..	..	..	..	..	..	..	..	..
Congo, Republic of	..	..	..	..	..	..	..	..	..	..	..	..	..	..
Côte d'Ivoire	..	..	..	..	..	..	..	..	..	..	..	..	..	..
Djibouti	..	..	..	..	..	..	..	..	..	..	..	..	..	..
Equatorial Guinea	..	..	..	..	..	..	..	..	..	..	..	..	..	..
Eritrea	..	..	..	..	..	..	..	..	..	..	..	..	..	..
Ethiopia	..	..	..	..	..	..	..	..	..	..	..	..	..	..
Gabon	100.0	..	..	171.9	..	..	..	..	..	..	..	100.0	162.1	144.4
Gambia, The	..	..	..	..	..	..	..	..	..	..	..	..	..	..
Ghana	..	..	..	..	..	..	..	..	..	..	..	..	..	..
Guinea	..	..	..	..	..	..	..	..	..	..	..	..	..	..
Guinea-Bissau	..	..	..	..	..	..	..	..	..	..	..	..	..	..
Kenya	100.0	52.0	43.5	36.2	41.6	48.6	46.2	43.5	41.6	44.4	51.9	77.5	84.0	50.7
Lesotho	..	..	..	..	..	..	..	..	..	..	..	..	..	..
Liberia	..	..	..	..	..	..	..	..	..	..	..	..	..	..
Madagascar	100.0	..	..	..	..	..	..	..	..	..	..	100.0	..	..
Malawi	..	..	..	..	..	..	..	..	..	..	..	..	..	..
Mali	..	..	..	..	..	..	..	..	..	..	..	..	..	..
Mauritania	..	..	..	..	..	..	..	..	..	..	..	..	..	..
Mauritius	..	..	..	..	..	..	..	..	..	..	..	..	..	..
Mozambique	..	..	..	..	..	..	..	..	..	..	..	..	..	..
Namibia	..	..	..	..	..	..	..	..	..	..	..	..	..	..
Niger	100.0	..	..	187.4	..	..	..	..	..	..	..	100.0	83.2	211.5
Nigeria	..	..	..	..	..	..	..	..	..	..	..	..	..	..
Rwanda	..	..	..	..	..	..	..	..	..	..	..	..	..	..
São Tomé and Principe	..	..	..	..	..	..	..	..	..	..	..	..	..	..
Senegal	..	..	..	..	..	..	..	..	..	..	..	..	..	..
Seychelles	..	..	..	..	..	..	..	..	..	..	..	..	..	..
Sierra Leone	..	..	..	..	..	..	..	..	..	..	..	..	..	..
Somalia	..	..	..	..	..	..	..	..	..	..	..	..	..	..
South Africa	..	..	..	..	..	..	..	..	..	..	..	..	..	..
Sudan	..	..	..	..	..	..	..	..	..	..	..	..	..	..
Swaziland	100.0	..	..	..	..	..	..	..	..	..	..	100.0	59.0	100.4
Tanzania	..	..	..	..	..	..	..	..	..	..	..	..	..	..
Togo	100.0	..	..	136.5	..	..	..	..	..	..	..	100.0	124.1	146.3
Uganda	..	..	..	..	..	..	..	..	..	..	..	..	..	..
Zambia	..	..	..	..	..	..	..	..	..	..	..	..	..	..
Zimbabwe	..	..	..	..	..	..	..	..	..	..	..	..	..	..
NORTH AFRICA	..	..	..	..	..	..	..	..	..	..	..	..	..	..
Algeria	100.0	..	..	267.0	..	..	..	..	..	..	..	100.0	111.1	207.6
Egypt, Arab Republic	100.0	..	..	..	..	..	..	..	..	..	..	100.0	108.4	61.9
Libya	100.0	..	..	..	..	..	..	..	..	..	..	100.0	307.4	156.2
Morocco	100.0	..	..	95.5	..	..	..	..	..	..	..	100.0	82.3	90.8
Tunisia	..	..	..	..	..	..	..	..	..	..	..	..	..	..
ALL AFRICA	..	..	..	..	..	..	..	..	..	..	..	..	..	..

Note: Nigeria's fiscal data are for federal level only. Nigeria's fiscal data are for consolidated government starting from 1992.

7-20. Government expenditure: real per capita education spending

	Constant 1995 U.S. dollars											*Annual Average*		
	1980	*1992*	*1993*	*1994*	*1995*	*1996*	*1997*	*1998*	*1999*	*2000*	*2001*	*75-84*	*85-89*	*90-MR*
SUB-SAHARAN AFRICA	..	..	..	..	..	..	..	..	..	..	..	..	..	..
excluding South Africa	..	..	..	..	..	..	..	..	..	..	..	..	..	..
excl. S.Africa & Nigeria	..	..	..	..	..	..	..	12.92	11.26	..	..	..	..	12.09
Angola	..	..	..	..	..	..	..	..	..	..	..	..	..	..
Benin	..	..	..	..	..	12.16	10.02	9.95	10.47	11.82	15.45	11.71	..	11.64
Botswana	..	..	..	..	..	..	..	..	..	..	..	..	161.63	..
Burkina Faso	3.41	6.23	6.19	..	7.21	8.26	8.22	8.96	..	..	..	3.34	4.51	7.05
Burundi	..	4.06	3.53	3.06	2.44	1.83	1.12	1.39	1.35	1.14	..	..	..	2.21
Cameroon	..	..	..	..	..	..	..	..	..	..	..	..	..	..
Cape Verde	..	..	..	..	..	..	..	..	..	..	..	..	..	..
Central African Republic	..	..	..	..	..	..	..	..	..	..	..	15.50	..	..
Chad	..	..	4.46	3.56	3.18	3.13	3.66	3.49	3.98	4.18	5.04	..	..	3.85
Comoros	..	..	..	..	..	18.26	17.76	14.93	9.79	9.49	9.34	..	..	13.26
Congo, Democratic Rep. of	..	..	..	..	..	..	..	..	..	..	..	..	..	..
Congo, Republic of	..	..	..	..	..	..	..	..	..	..	..	..	..	..
Côte d'Ivoire	..	49.30	48.49	36.05	34.11	29.86	31.10	32.86	36.00	40.69	39.30	..	57.51	40.59
Djibouti	..	..	..	..	..	..	..	..	..	..	..	..	..	..
Equatorial Guinea	..	..	..	..	..	..	..	..	..	..	..	..	..	..
Eritrea	..	1.87	3.47	3.47	5.41	4.57	7.89	8.29	8.30	10.52	13.97	..	..	6.78
Ethiopia	..	2.15	2.76	3.49	3.42	4.00	3.96	3.84	4.01	3.63	5.05	2.69	2.53	3.45
Gabon	..	..	..	..	..	..	..	..	..	..	..	..	..	..
Gambia, The	..	10.32	10.87	11.17	11.39	11.83	12.39	10.33	10.27	11.06	15.40	..	..	11.50
Ghana	..	..	..	14.61	14.32	15.57	14.12	15.37	..	..	..	..	..	14.80
Guinea	..	..	..	12.25	12.88	15.88	14.38	10.74	11.59	11.42	11.66	..	..	12.60
Guinea-Bissau	..	3.44	2.01	5.17	7.52	7.56	7.51	2.76	7.24	4.65	4.28	..	4.41	4.89
Kenya	19.52	20.85	22.20	20.64	21.89	21.26	21.93	23.21	21.71	20.04	19.30	15.53	21.36	21.54
Lesotho	..	42.22	41.56	47.55	56.04	59.26	58.68	60.46	64.12	61.07	55.64	..	27.51	51.83
Liberia	..	..	..	..	..	..	..	..	..	..	..	..	..	..
Madagascar	..	..	..	..	..	..	5.29	6.00	7.17	7.35	..	..	..	6.45
Malawi	..	..	0.00	4.57	4.82	6.02	6.61	7.54	6.20	6.42	6.18	..	..	5.37
Mali	..	..	..	..	7.95	8.01	7.81	8.55	11.01	9.18	9.79	6.66	6.66	8.90
Mauritania	..	..	..	..	..	2.40	24.56	23.70	24.84	25.55	25.50	..	..	21.09
Mauritius	..	..	..	..	..	..	..	..	..	..	..	..	..	..
Mozambique	..	3.40	3.01	2.69	2.80	2.83	3.32	4.02	4.87	4.78	4.93	3.21	2.29	3.55
Namibia	..	..	..	..	..	..	..	..	..	..	..	..	..	..
Niger	10.95	..	..	..	..	..	..	..	..	..	..	8.36	..	..
Nigeria	..	..	..	..	..	..	..	..	..	..	..	..	..	..
Rwanda	..	..	..	..	..	..	..	..	..	..	..	..	..	..
São Tomé and Principe	..	..	..	..	..	..	24.24	15.18	..	28.98	32.75	..	..	25.29
Senegal	..	..	23.24	19.53	20.71	22.41	21.18	23.11	20.98	22.04	22.00	..	..	21.69
Seychelles	..	..	..	..	..	..	..	..	..	..	..	..	..	..
Sierra Leone	..	..	..	..	..	..	..	..	..	2.37	3.47	..	..	2.92
Somalia	..	..	..	..	..	..	..	..	..	..	..	..	..	..
South Africa	..	..	..	..	..	..	..	..	..	..	..	..	..	..
Sudan	..	..	..	..	..	..	..	1.42	1.40	1.76	2.44	..	..	1.75
Swaziland	76.92	..	..	..	..	..	..	..	..	..	..	64.25	74.99	..
Tanzania	..	..	..	..	..	..	..	..	3.90	4.74	5.96	..	..	4.87
Togo	..	..	..	..	..	..	..	..	..	..	..	21.20	19.60	..
Uganda	..	..	..	5.21	6.53	6.14	8.46	9.30	11.66	12.63	13.22	..	..	9.15
Zambia	..	10.79	8.98	8.40	5.93	11.31	11.99	9.44	10.51	9.26	..	..	..	10.07
Zimbabwe	..	..	..	..	..	..	..	83.72	54.40	..	..	..	..	69.06
NORTH AFRICA	45.34	55.00	58.39	61.21	61.01	..	..	..	..	..	..	46.78	52.10	57.26
Algeria	..	..	..	..	..	..	..	..	..	..	..	..	..	..
Egypt, Arab Republic	29.88	39.84	43.51	48.16	48.19	..	..	..	..	..	..	32.48	41.19	43.11
Libya	..	..	..	..	..	..	..	..	..	..	..	..	..	..
Morocco	63.78	69.49	72.72	72.03	68.97	..	..	..	..	..	..	61.86	61.37	69.95
Tunisia	88.29	110.16	112.39	113.86	120.82	128.88	..	..	..	..	..	92.78	94.45	113.77
ALL AFRICA	..	..	..	..	..	..	..	..	..	..	..	..	..	..

Note: Nigeria's fiscal data are for consolidated government starting from 1992.

Figure 7-1. Government deficit as percentage of GDP, 1992-2001*

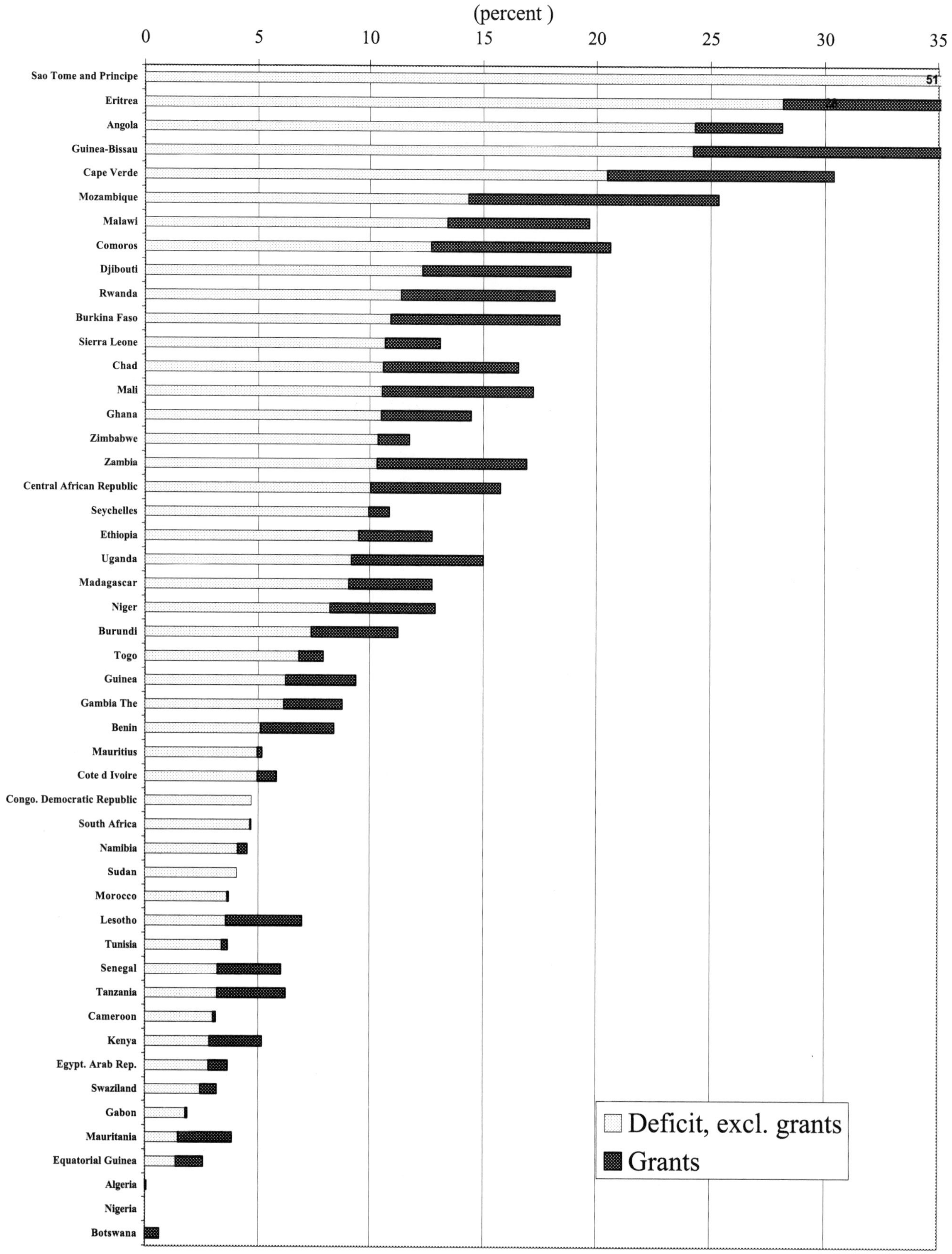

* Or most recent year available.

Technical notes

Tables

Table 7-1. Government deficit/surplus (including grants). Overall surplus/deficit is the difference between total revenue plus grants (as defined in GFS line A-I) and total expenditures and lending minus repayments (as defined in GFS line C-I). It represents the net financing requirement of the consolidated government. This indicator is shown as a percentage of current GDP in national currency (World Bank country desks).

Table 7-2. Government deficit/surplus (excluding grants). This is calculated as above, except that capital grants are excluded from receipts (as defined in *GFS* line A-II, less line C-I). It is a measure of the ability of a government to fund its activities from its own resources. Because some budgetary grants may be tied to certain expenditures that would not otherwise be incurred, excluding grants may overstate the deficit or understate the surplus if no account is taken of the expenditures dependent on these grants. This indicator is shown as a percentage of current GDP in national currency (World Bank country desks).

Table 7-3. Government primary deficit/surplus (–/+). The primary deficit or surplus is the government deficit or surplus including grants (as presented in Table 7-1) excluding interest expenditures on both domestic and foreign debt (Table 7-5). In countries with large government interest payments, this ratio may provide a more reliable indicator for monitoring fiscal stabilization efforts. This indicator is shown as a percentage of current GDP in national currency (World Bank country desks).

Table 7-4. Government expenditure and lending minus repayments. Total expenditure and lending minus repayments (as defined in *GFS* line C-I) represents the government's total outlays for current or capital purposes. Expenditure includes all nonrepayable payments by the government. Lending minus repayments comprises government transactions in debt and equity claims upon others, acquired for purposes of public policy rather than for managing government liquidity or earning a return. It consists of gross lending and acquisition of financial equity minus repayments of past government lending and government sales of equities. (This definition differs from the concept of lending minus repayments adopted in the SNA, which is gross government lending minus repayments of past government lending minus net government borrowing.) In determining a government's deficit or surplus, lending minus repayments is grouped with expenditures rather than with financing. This indicator is shown as a percentage of current GDP in national currency (World Bank country desks).

Table 7-5. Government interest payments. Government interest payments (as defined in *GFS* line C2) include interest on all borrowings, both domestic and foreign, but exclude commission charges paid for assistance in placement of debt (which would be classified as expenditure for the payment of goods and services). This indicator is shown as a percentage of current GDP in national currency (World Bank country desks).

Table 7-6. Government revenue (excluding grants). Government revenue less grants (as defined in *GFS* line A-II) refers to current revenues (tax and nontax) and capital revenues, such as proceeds from the sale of real assets, including land. They do not include grant receipts from other governments or international organizations. This indicator is shown as a percentage of current GDP in national currency (World Bank country desks).

Table 7-7. Grants to government. These are unrequited, nonrepayable, noncompulsory government receipts from other governments or international institutions (as defined in *GFS* line A-II). Grants of goods and services in kind are excluded. This indicator is shown as a percentage of current GDP in national currency (World Bank country desks).

Table 7-8. Foreign financing. Includes all government financing transactions except grants (as defined in *GFS* line D-III) with nonresident individuals, enterprises, governments, international organizations, and other entities. It may be affected by trading in outstanding government securities between residents and nonresidents. The data also reflect changes, resulting from transactions but not revaluations, in government holdings of foreign exchange, deposits in nonresident financial institutions, and securities issued by nonresident entities held by government for liquidity purposes (reserves). This indicator is shown as a percentage of current GDP in national currency (World Bank country desks).

Table 7-9. Taxes on income and profits. These taxes (as defined in *GFS* line A1) are levied on the actual or presumptive net income of individuals and profits of enterprises. Also included are taxes levied on capital gains that are realized on land sales, securities, and other assets. This indicator is shown as a percentage of total revenue (as defined in *GFS* line A-II) (World Bank country desks).

Table 7-10. Taxes on international trade and transactions. Include import duties, export duties, profits of export or import monopolies remitted to government, and monopoly profits of monetary authorities made in foreign exchange transactions as well as taxes levied on the sale of foreign exchange (as defined in *GFS* line A6). This indicator is shown as a percentage of total revenue (as defined in *GFS* line A-II) (World Bank country desks).

Table 7-11. Indirect taxes. These are sales and excise taxes and duties (as defined in GFS line A-IV less A1). This indicator is shown as a percentage of total revenue (as defined in GFS line A-II) (World Bank country desks).

Table 7-12. Nontax revenues (excluding grants). This is all nonrepayable government receipts, other than compulsory unrequited receipts (taxes) and revenue from capital sales or government grants, plus all fines and penalties other than for noncompliance with taxes (as defined in *GFS* line A-V). For some mineral-exporting countries in Africa, this category is quite large, since royalties on the extraction of minerals, such as petroleum in Egypt and Nigeria and bauxite in Guinea, make up significant portions of total government revenues. This indicator is shown as a percentage of total revenue (as defined in *GFS* line A-II) (World Bank country desks).

Table 7-13. Government expenditure: wages and salaries. Are payments in cash, but not in kind, to employees in return for services, before withholding taxes and employee contributions to social security and pension funds are deducted (as defined in GFS line C1.1). Included are basic wages and salaries; pay for overtime, weekends, and nights; cost of living allowances; local allowances and expatriation allowances; and similar compensation. Reimbursement to employees for expenses incurred as part of their employment are excluded. This indicator is shown as a percentage of total expenditure and lending minus repayments (as defined in GFS line C-I) (World Bank country desks).

Table 7-14. Government expenditure: trends in real wages and salaries. Includes expenditure on wages and salaries as discussed above (as defined in *GFS* line C1.1), deflated by the CPI. For most countries the trend is shown in index numbers beginning with 100 in 1987 (World Bank country desks).

Table 7-15. Government expenditure: other goods and services. Includes expenditures for all goods and services (except fixed capital assets and wages and salaries) bought on the market, goods and services to be used to produce fixed capital assets, strategic or emergency stocks, stocks held by market regulatory organizations, and land and intangible assets. This category encompasses purchases of materials, office supplies, fuel and lighting, travel services, and payment of rent, as well as payments in kind to certain civil servants (as defined in *GFS* line C1.3). This indicator is presented as a percentage of total expenditure and lending minus repayments (as defined in *GFS* lines C-I) (World Bank country desks).

Table 7-16. Government expenditure: interest payments. Are payments for the use of all borrowed money, excluding commission charges paid for assistance in placing debt, which would be classified as expenditures for payment of other goods and services (as defined in GFS line C2). This indicator is presented as a percentage of total expenditure and lending minus repayments (as defined in GFS lines C-I) (World Bank country desks).

Table 7-17. Government expenditure: subsidies and current transfers. Are all unrequited, nonrepayable government payments for current purposes (as defined in *GFS* line C3). Transfers for capital purposes (that is, to permit the recipient to acquire capital assets) and transfers in kind are excluded. This indicator is presented as a percentage of total expenditure and lending minus repayments (as defined in *GFS* line C-I) (World Bank country desks).

Table 7-18. Government expenditure: capital and net lending. Represents payments for acquiring land, buildings, and other nonfinancial assets to be used for more than one year in the process of production, including transfers for capital assets as well as net lending (as defined in GFS lines C-IV plus C-V). This indicator is presented as a percentage of total expenditure and lending minus repayments (as defined in GFS line C-I) (World Bank country desks).

Table 7-19. Government expenditure: trends in real defense spending. Real defense spending has been calculated by deflating defense spending in current prices national currency (IMF, as defined in GFS line B2) by the national GDP deflator (Table 3-1). The results are presented in the form of 1980 base indexes.

Table 7-20. Government expenditure: real per capita education spending. Presents education spending (IMF, as defined in *GFS* line B4) deflated by the national GDP deflator (Table 3-1) and divided by total population (Table 2-1). The result is converted into 1995 U.S. dollars by using the 1995 local currency/ US dollar conversion factor (Table 3-6).

Figure

The following indicators have been used to derive the figure in this chapter:

Figure 7-1. Government deficit/surplus (Tables 7-1 and 7-2).

Methodology used for regional aggregations and period averages in chapter 7

	Aggregations [a]		*Period averages* [b]
Table	*(6)*	*(7)*	*(1)*
7-1	x		x
7-2	x		x
7-3	x		x
7-4	x		x
7-5	x		x
7-6	x		x
7-7	x		x
7-8	x		x
7-9	x		x
7-10	x		x
7-11	x		x
7-12	x		x
7-13	x		x
7-14		x	x
7-15	x		x
7-16	x		x
7-17	x		x
7-18	x		x
7-19		x	x
7-20	x		x

Note: Regional aggregations are shown in the rows for Sub-Saharan Africa, North Africa, and All Africa. Period averages are shown in the last three columns. This table shows only the methodologies used in this chapter. For aggregation purposes, all data used in this chapter were converted to U.S. dollars, using the conversion factors shown in Table 3-6.

a. Regional aggregations: (1) simple total; (2) simple total of the first indicator divided by the simple total of the second indicator (same country coverage); (3) simple total of the gap-filled indicator; (4) simple total of the gap-filled main indicator divided by the simple total of the gap-filled secondary indicator; (5) simple total of the first gap-filled main indicator less the simple total of the second gap-filled main indicator, all divided by the simple total of the secondary indicator; (6) weighted total (by population); (7) median; (8) no aggregation; (9) simple arithmetic mean.

b. Period averages: (1) arithmetic mean (using the same series as shown in the table i.e., ratio if the rest of the table is shown as ratio, level if the rest of the table is shown as level, growth rate if the rest is shown as growth rate); (2) least-squares growth rate (using main indicator); (3) least-squares growth rate (using main indicator in constant terms, with the rest of the table in current terms).

8

Agriculture

Agriculture is one of Africa's important sectors. African agriculture has two major components: food production and export commodities. Food production, including meat, is the livelihood for most Africans. Export crops provide many African countries with their main source of foreign exchange and thus the capacity to import, invest, and develop. The information in this chapter provides a basis for assessing recent trends in producer prices, aggregate agricultural production and trade, cereal imports, and food aid in Africa.

The data in this chapter are estimates based on a variety of sources whose quality and reliability vary from country to country and year to year. Furthermore, production and export data are probably underestimated for two reasons. It is difficult to estimate production levels of staple food crops, especially roots and tubers, when much of the output is consumed directly by farmers, rather than marketed. Moreover, parallel market activity, including trade, may not be fully accounted for.

8-1. Nominal producer prices

	Local currency per kilogram										
	1980	*1986*	*1987*	*1988*	*1989*	*1990*	*1991*	*1992*	*1993*	*1994*	*1995*
ALGERIA											
Wheat (hard)	1.2	2.2	2.2	2.7	3.7	4.6	5.4	10.3	10.3	10.3	19.0
Citrus (oranges)	..	..	..	..	..	..	..	..	..	..	..
Dates	4.5	11.3	11.5	..	..	..	..	..	..	..	..
Barley	0.8	1.4	1.7	1.7	2.3	2.3	2.3	4.7	4.7	6.0	14.0
Potatoes	1.3	2.6	2.8	2.7	3.0	3.3	3.3	6.5	6.5	6.5	10.0
ANGOLA											
Coffee	..	67.0	67.0	67.0	67.0	135.0	158.0	..	..	..	..
Maize	..	10.0	10.0	11.5	11.5	11.5	100.0	..	..	..	..
Millet	4.0	10.0	10.0	10.0	10.0	10.0	100.0	..	..	..	..
Wheat	4.5	17.5	17.5	17.5	17.5	17.5	200.0	..	..	..	..
Cassava	..	5.0	5.0	7.7	7.7	7.7	150.0	..	..	..	..
Sweet potatoes	2.5	7.5	7.5	14.0	14.0	14.0	200.0	..	..	..	..
BENIN											
Cotton (seed cotton)	65.0	110.0	100.0	105.0	95.0	100.0	100.0	100.0	94.8	..	..
Palm kernels	35.0	20.0	20.0	30.0	30.0	30.0	35.0	35.0	..	..	..
Maize	40.0	65.0	68.0	64.0	55.0	85.0	58.0	62.0	53.0	..	..
Sorghum	46.0	65.0	72.0	67.0	60.0	60.0	63.0	65.0	55.0	..	..
Cassava	30.0	15.0	20.0	16.0	16.0	16.0	17.0	17.5	18.2	..	..
Yams	32.0	50.0	58.0	49.0	49.0	49.0	49.0	50.0	52.0	..	..
BOTSWANA											
Groundnuts (in shell)	0.2	0.7	0.7	0.7	0.7	0.7	1.1	1.0	1.4	..	..
Sorghum	0.1	0.3	0.3	0.3	0.3	0.3	0.3	0.4	0.4	..	..
Maize	0.1	0.3	0.3	0.3	0.3	0.3	0.3	0.3	0.4	..	..
BURKINA FASO											
Cotton (seed cotton)	55.0	97.2	89.7	94.4	94.6	95.0	..	..	..	..	..
Groundnuts (in shell)	54.0	50.0	60.0	55.0	60.0	60.0	..	..	..	..	..
Sesame seed	70.0	80.0	55.0	65.0	85.0	80.0	..	..	..	..	..
Sorghum	45.0	40.0	45.0	40.0	45.0	60.0	..	..	..	..	..
Millet	45.0	40.0	45.0	40.0	45.0	60.0	..	..	..	..	..
Maize	45.0	45.0	55.0	45.0	50.0	65.0	..	..	..	..	..
BURUNDI											
Coffee (green)	..	..	..	..	..	..	..	..	..	..	..
Tea	..	..	..	..	..	..	..	..	..	..	..
Cotton (seed)	36.1	51.9	52.6	55.3	57.8	60.2	62.4	64.4	..	..	..
Maize	25.0	..	..	..	..	..	..	..	..	..	..
Sorghum	20.0	..	..	..	..	..	..	..	..	..	..
Rice	25.0	..	..	..	..	..	..	..	..	..	..
Millet	20.0	..	..	..	..	..	..	..	..	..	..
Bananas	..	..	..	..	..	..	..	..	..	..	..
Cassava	10.9	..	..	..	..	..	..	..	..	..	..
CAMEROON											
Coffee (Arabica)	320.0	475.0	475.0	475.0	458.0	186.0	165.0	..	..	..	..
Cocoa (grade 1, superior)	300.0	420.0	420.0	42.0	250.0	220.0	200.0	200.0	200.0	..	..
Cotton (seed cotton, nonselected)	70.0	130.0	130.0	140.0	95.0	95.0	95.0	85.0	..	..	..
Maize	60.0	83.2	76.8	82.4	57.0	51.7	..	..	..	..	..
Sorghum	40.0	38.9	60.6	47.2	43.0	77.9	..	..	..	..	..
Millet	40.0	38.9	60.6	47.2	43.0	77.9	..	..	..	..	..
Rice (paddy)	105.0	91.0	64.7	77.5	82.7	53.5	..	..	..	..	..
Cassava	19.0	48.0	46.6	41.7	..	..	..	..	..	..	..
Plantains	25.0	45.3	46.7	47.3	..	54.0	..	..	..	..	..
CENTRAL AFRICAN REPUBLIC											
Coffee (Robusta, cherries)	120.0	135.0	135.0	190.0	110.0	80.0	40.0	40.0	120.0	120.0	240.0
Cotton (seed cotton)	60.0	100.0	100.0	100.0	100.0	..	68.5	60.0	60.0	87.0	117.0
Sorghum	..	103.5	128.3	107.7	92.5	..	..	..	..	136.7	168.9
Maize	40.0	65.3	67.7	104.3	111.6	..	..	..	..	136.0	271.0
Groundnuts (unshelled)	70.0	..	..	171.7	..	..	..	..	..	217.6	526.3
Cassava	30.0	76.2	89.5	57.5	103.7	..	..	..	..	119.2	176.6
Yams	25.0	107.1	91.0	124.5	86.6	..	..	..	..	..	222.5
CHAD											
Cotton (seed cotton, avg. white/yellow)	..	99.0	99.0	97.0	88.0	88.0	88.0	77.0	89.0	..	..
Millet	..	31.0	31.0	48.0	47.0	52.0	62.0	41.0	41.0	..	..
Groundnuts	..	57.0	46.0	44.0	46.0	48.0	70.0	67.0	77.0	..	..

(Table continues on the following page)

8-1. Nominal producer prices (continued)

	Local currency per kilogram										
	1980	*1986*	*1987*	*1988*	*1989*	*1990*	*1991*	*1992*	*1993*	*1994*	*1995*
Vanilla	1150.0	..	..	..	..	..	..	..	..	..	..
Cloves	1250.0	..	..	..	..	..	..	..	..	..	..
Ylang Ylang (flower)	45.0	90.0	65.0	65.0	..	..	..	..	..	..	..
Copra	40.0	..	..	..	..	..	..	..	..	..	..
Bananas	50.0	..	..	..	..	..	..	..	..	..	..
Cassava	40.0	..	..	..	..	..	..	..	..	..	..
Coffee (Arabica, green beans)	4.0	42.6	69.3	107.5	166.9	440.5	13837.3	..	..	..	..
Palm oil	2.1	23.0	37.6	59.4	93.8	247.7	7778.7	..	..	..	..
Rubber (natural)	..	..	..	..	..	..	..	..	..	..	..
Cocoa (beans)	..	30.0	50.0	..	..	..	..	..	..	..	..
Maize	1.2	7.5	10.1	25.8	40.3	106.4	..	..	..	..	..
Rice (paddy)	2.0	11.5	17.0	28.7	45.2	119.4	..	..	..	..	..
Cassava	1.3	3.0	3.9	8.4	13.2	34.7	1090.8	..	..	..	..
Plantains	2.9	..	..	..	..	..	..	..	..	..	..
Coffee	146.0	215.0	215.0	115.0	115.0	115.0	115.0	115.0	115.0	..	..
Cocoa	134.8	190.0	240.0	108.0	108.0	88.0	88.0	88.0	88.0	88.0	88.0
Maize	43.0	73.0	85.0	60.0	60.0	60.0	60.0	100.0	100.0	100.0	100.0
Cassava	..	..	..	..	..	..	..	..	..	..	..
Plantains	..	..	..	..	..	..	..	..	..	..	..
Coffee (Robusta, green)	310.6	399.5	400.0	400.0	404.0	419.0	390.0	232.0	200.0	530.0	700.0
Cocoa (beans)	300.0	400.0	400.0	400.0	400.0	200.0	200.0	200.0	200.0	315.0	320.0
Palm oil	..	..	..	213.8	213.8	213.8	190.0	190.0	190.0	225.0	225.0
Rice (paddy)	50.0	84.0	84.0	60.0	60.0	60.0	60.0	60.0	75.0	75.0	110.0
Maize	68.0	76.0	45.0	45.0	45.0	45.0	45.0	..	..	..	..
Cassava	49.0	46.0	..	..	..	..	..	..	..	..	..
Yams	59.0	99.9	..	..	..	..	..	..	..	..	..
Cotton	0.3	0.6	0.7	0.9	1.3	1.7	2.0	2.4	2.4	2.1	..
Rice (96% humidity)	0.1	0.2	0.2	0.3	0.4	0.4	0.4	0.5	0.5	0.6	..
Wheat (94% humidity)	0.1	0.2	0.2	0.2	0.4	0.5	0.5	0.5	0.5	0.5	..
Sugarcane	0.0	0.0	0.0	0.0	0.1	0.1	0.1	0.1	0.1	0.1	0.1
Broadbeans	0.2	0.5	0.6	0.6	0.6	0.7	0.9	1.1	1.0	1.0	..
Cocoa (first grade dried beans)	..	..	..	..	..	..	..	..	..	..	..
Coffee (Robusta, cherry)	..	..	..	..	..	..	..	..	..	..	..
Cassava	..	..	..	..	..	..	..	..	..	..	..
Plantains	..	..	..	..	..	..	..	..	..	..	..
Coffee (Arabica, beans)	2.6	3.7	4.1	4.2	4.2	4.2	3.1	3.1		..	..
Sesame seed	..	1.1	1.1	1.3	1.3	1.4	1.7	..	..	..	..
Sorghum (mixed)	..	0.5	0.4	0.5	0.5	0.5	0.8	0.8	..	..	..
Maize	..	0.5	0.4	0.4	0.5	0.4	0.6	0.7	..	..	..
Barley (non-white mixed)	..	0.5	0.4	0.5	0.5	0.5	0.7	0.9	..	..	..
Cocoa (first quality)	320.0	430.0	430.0	370.0	210.0	224.0	224.0	269.0	260.0	..	..
Coffee (merchant, processed)	180.0	0.0	260.0	260.0	130.0	130.0	..	150.0	147.0	..	..
Maize	..	..	..	..	..	..	..	..	..	..	..
Cassava	139.5	..	..	..	..	..	..	..	..	..	..
Yams	124.5	..	..	..	..	..	..	..	..	..	..
Groundnuts (unshelled)	0.5	1.8	1.5	1.1	1.5	1.8	..	..	..	..	..
Cotton (seed cotton)	0.5	1.3	1.5	1.6	1.8	1.9	1.9	2.0	2.0	2.2	2.2
Palm kernels	0.3	0.3	..	..	..	..	..	..	..	..	..
Millet	0.5	1.1	1.2	1.2	1.5	1.9	1.9	..	..	..	..
Rice (paddy)	..	..	2.1	2.1	3.4	2.8	2.7	..	..	..	..
Maize	..	0.0	1.2	1.2	1.4	2.1	1.9	..	..	..	..
Sorghum	0.3	0.9	0.0	0.0	1.2	0.0	1.9	..	..	..	..

(Table continues on the following page)

8-1. Nominal producer prices (continued)

	Local currency per kilogram										
	1980	*1986*	*1987*	*1988*	*1989*	*1990*	*1991*	*1992*	*1993*	*1994*	*1995*
Cocoa	4.0	80.3	101.3	153.8	..	..	..	..	..	..	..
Maize	4.1	25.0	42.0	48.0	35.8	86.9	69.5	83.5	93.7	..	..
Millet	5.3	24.2	36.0	83.3	89.7	77.9	113.5	141.4	149.9	..	..
Groundnuts	8.4	..	..	..	..	..	..	..	..	..	..
Cassava	1.5	8.8	10.8	12.9	10.0	10.0	15.8	22.5	25.3	..	..
Plantains	1.9	15.0	18.6	43.0	45.9	27.8	26.8	35.5	91.4	..	..
Coffee (Robusta)	49.0	400.0	400.0	..	..	..	..	..	..	..	..
Palm kernels	6.0	60.0	60.0	..	..	..	..	..	..	..	..
Rice (paddy)	9.0	..	..	..	..	168.0	166.0	..	..	..	..
Maize	7.0	..	..	..	..	130.0	144.0	..	..	..	..
Groundnuts (unshelled)	11.0	..	..	..	250.0	213.0	..	..	..	..	..
Cassava	5.0	..	..	..	..	..	81.0	..	..	..	..
Plantains	4.5	..	..	..	..	..	..	..	..	..	..
Cashew nuts	..	38.5	125.0	230.0	350.0	450.0	550.0	1000.0	3500.0	..	..
Groundnuts (unshelled, grade 1)	..	32.5	40.0	80.0	140.0	225.0	275.0	500.0	1000.0	..	..
Palm kernels	..	..	..	..	..	..	..	..	..	..	..
Rice (paddy, grade 1)	8.5	37.5	50.0	85.0	180.0	225.0	400.0	650.0	1100.0	..	..
Sorghum	..	..	..	..	..	..	..	..	..	..	..
Maize (grade 1)	..	..	..	..	..	..	..	..	740.0	..	..
Coffee (Arabica, washed bean, grade 1-6)	26.4	54.8	34.1	43.0	43.1	36.4	46.5	49.4	98.9	..	..
Tea	15.9	33.8	25.0	26.8	27.2	35.2	38.5	47.5	92.4	..	..
Sugar (cane)	0.1	0.3	0.3	0.4	0.4	0.5	0.5	0.6	0.8	..	..
Sisal	4.2	7.4	7.1	7.4	8.9	9.2	9.4	9.8	9.9	..	..
Maize	1.0	2.1	2.1	2.2	2.7	2.6	3.1	4.7	8.1	..	..
Wheat	1.6	2.9	3.0	3.2	3.4	4.5	5.0	5.6	5.7	..	..
Wheat	0.2	0.4	0.5	0.5	0.6	..	..	0.8	..	..	..
Beans	0.5	1.1	1.3	1.3	1.4	..	..	..	..	..	..
Peas	0.4	0.9	0.9	1.1	1.2	1.2	..	..	..	..	..
Maize	0.1	0.3	0.3	0.4	0.4	0.4	0.5	0.6	0.6	0.6	..
Sorghum	0.2	0.2	0.3	0.3	0.3	0.3	..	0.5	0.6	..	..
Rubber (nonspec. coagul.)	0.8	1.0	1.0	..	..	..	..	..	..	..	..
Coffee (Robusta)	2.1	1.6	1.6	..	..	..	..	..	..	..	..
Cocoa (fair average quality)	2.1	2.3	2.3	..	..	..	..	..	..	..	..
Rice	0.3	0.3	0.3	0.3	..	..	..	..	..	..	..
Cassava	0.0	0.1	0.1	0.1	..	..	..	..	..	..	..
Wheat	0.0	..	..	..	..	..	..	..	..	..	..
Olives	..	..	..	..	..	..	..	..	..	..	..
Oranges	..	..	..	..	..	..	..	..	..	..	..
Barley	..	..	..	..	..	..	..	..	..	..	..
Coffee (Robusta)	215.0	600.0	800.0	950.0	950.0	950.0	..	..	..	..	..
Vanilla (green)	600.0	1100.0	1200.0	1700.0	2000.0	2000.0	2000.0	..	..	..	..
Cloves	395.0	525.0	600.0	600.0	600.0	600.0	..	..	..	..	..
Rice (paddy)	42.5	100.0	127.5	180.0	250.0	250.0	274.0	..	..	..	..
Cassava	7.0	55.0	55.0	..	..	..	124.0	..	..	..	..
Sweet potatoes	..	50.0	60.0	60.0	60.0	..	116.0	..	..	..	..
Tobacco (flue-cured)	..	..	..	..	..	..	..	..	..	..	..
Tobacco (Northen division dark-fired, G2)	0.4	1.0	1.0	1.1	1.7	2.5	2.8	2.8	2.8	3.5	6.0
Tea (dry leaves)	0.7	1.0	1.0	1.5	1.6	2.0	2.0	2.5	2.5	3.0	5.0
Groundnuts (in shell)	0.3	0.5	0.6	0.6	0.6	0.8	0.7	0.9	1.1	1.6	2.5
Cotton (seed cotton)	..	0.5	0.5	0.7	0.8	0.8	0.8	0.9	0.9	1.0	2.5
Maize	0.1	0.1	0.1	0.2	0.2	0.3	0.3	0.3	0.4	0.5	0.7
Sorghum	0.1	0.2	0.1	0.1	0.2	0.2	0.0	0.0	0.7	0.8	1.1
Rice (paddy, grade 1)	0.1	0.2	0.2	0.3	0.3	0.4	0.4	0.5	0.9	1.5	1.8
Cassava	0.0	..	..	0.1	0.1	0.1	..	..	..	..	..

(Table continues on the following page)

8-1. Nominal producer prices (continued)

	Local currency per kilogram										
	1980	*1986*	*1987*	*1988*	*1989*	*1990*	*1991*	*1992*	*1993*	*1994*	*1995*
MALI											
Cotton (seed cotton)	55.0	85.0	85.0	85.0	85.0	85.0	85.0	85.0	..	..	..
Groundnuts (unshelled)	40.0	..	..	..	..	..	..	..	..	..	..
Millet	35.0	55.0	55.0	0.0	0.0	77.0	41.5	42.0	..	..	..
Rice (paddy)	37.5	70.0	70.0	70.0	70.0	70.0	70.0	68.0	..	..	..
Sorghum	35.0	55.0	55.0	58.0	60.0	61.0	..	..	..	..	..
Maize	35.0	55.0	55.0	..	..	54.0	35.0	35.0	..	..	..
MAURITANIA											
Sorghum	11.0	15.4	15.4	16.0	16.0	16.0	16.5	16.5	16.8	17.0	17.2
Millet	11.0	..	..	..	..	..	..	..	..	..	..
Rice (paddy)	10.0	..	..	..	..	..	..	..	..	..	..
Maize	15.0	..	..	..	..	..	..	..	..	..	..
MAURITIUS											
Sugarcane	..	..	..	..	..	..	..	..	..	..	..
Tea	..	9.2	7.4	10.3	10.4	13.5	13.4	16.8	16.4	..	..
Maize (12% moisture)	2.0	4.3	4.3	4.8	4.8	4.8	4.8	5.0	5.0	..	..
Rice (paddy, 14% moisture)	1.4	4.9	4.9	5.0	7.0	..	..	..	..	..	..
Potatoes	2.2	1.9	2.5	2.5	2.8	3.1	3.7	4.1	4.7	..	..
Onions	4.2	4.2	4.8	5.8	5.7	7.1	7.8	7.7	7.6	..	..
MOROCCO											
Citrus (oranges)	1.3	1.6	1.6	1.7	1.8	1.9	2.0	2.1	2.2	2.3	2.4
Cotton	3.2	6.0	6.0	6.0	6.7	0.0	6.7	5.7	5.7	..	..
Wheat (hard)	1.5	2.2	2.2	2.1	2.3	2.5	2.5	2.9	2.9	2.5	..
Sugarbeet (16.5% sugar)	0.1	0.2	0.2	0.2	0.2	0.2	0.3	0.3	0.3	..	..
Barley	1.3	1.3	1.3	1.2	1.3	1.5	1.5	2.0	2.0	2.1	..
MOZAMBIQUE											
Cashew nuts	7.5	13.2	86.0	..	..	..	..	..	..	..	..
Cotton (seed, prime grade)	11.0	16.0	65.0	..	..	..	..	..	..	..	..
Tea	25.6	..	..	..	..	..	..	..	..	..	..
Maize	..	..	..	..	..	..	..	..	..	..	..
Rice	6.2	16.0	48.0	..	..	..	..	..	..	..	..
Cassava	2.0	..	..	..	..	..	..	..	..	..	..
NAMIBIA											
Wheat	..	0.4	0.4	0.4	0.5	0.6	0.6	0.7	0.7	0.7	..
Maize (white)	..	0.3	0.3	0.4	0.4	0.4	0.5	0.5	0.6	0.7	..
NIGER											
Cowpeas	45.0	80.0	80.0	..	..	..	..	..	..	..	..
Cotton (unginned, top grade)	62.0	120.0	120.0	120.0	130.0	110.0	70.0	70.0	77.0	..	..
Groundnuts (in shell)	50.0	130.0	130.0	130.0	132.0	133.0	134.0	135.0	140.0	143.8	146.4
Millet	50.0	..	..	..	..	..	..	..	..	..	..
Sorghum (red)	50.0	..	..	..	..	..	..	..	..	..	..
NIGERIA											
Cocoa (bean)	1.3	3.5	7.5	11.0	10.1	8.5	10.2	12.7	..	..	..
Palm kernels	0.2	0.4	0.9	1.0	1.3	1.2	..	..	..	..	..
Cotton (seed cotton)	0.4	1.0	4.0	4.5	2.4	2.6	4.2	3.8	..	..	..
Groundnuts (in shell)	0.4	1.0	2.3	2.3	4.8	4.3	6.3	6.8	19.7	10.6	..
Sorghum	0.2	0.6	0.8	1.6	2.0	1.7	3.6	4.7	7.0	5.3	..
Millet	0.2	0.6	0.6	1.3	2.1	1.7	3.4	5.7	6.6	6.2	..
Maize	0.2	0.5	0.6	1.6	2.7	2.1	3.3	5.5	7.5	5.6	..
Rice (paddy)	0.3	1.0	2.3	3.8	6.3	6.3	7.5	12.6	18.8	12.3	..
Yams	..	1.0	0.9	2.0	2.4	2.3	2.6	5.9	11.7	14.4	..
Cassava (gari)	..	0.3	0.4	0.8	1.2	2.2	2.1	2.3	4.6	4.5	..
RWANDA											
Coffee	120.0	122.5	125.0	125.0	125.0	99.7	107.4	115.0	..	..	427.0
Tea	75.0	75.0	75.0	..	..	..	..	..	..	..	..
Beans (dry)	20.3	22.3	28.6	30.5	38.4	37.9	40.8	40.2	..	..	90.0
Sorghum	12.7	20.2	20.2	19.3	23.3	24.5	29.3	33.6	..	..	141.0
Maize	11.9	15.6	15.4	13.6	24.7	26.9	32.4	29.0	..	..	45.0
Bananas	..	..	..	10.6	10.7	12.7	15.9	14.9	..	..	..
Sweet potatoes	5.7	6.1	6.2	5.5	9.4	9.8	9.9	6.8	..	..	24.0

(Table continues on the following page)

8-1. Nominal producer prices (continued)

	Local currency per kilogram										
	1980	*1986*	*1987*	*1988*	*1989*	*1990*	*1991*	*1992*	*1993*	*1994*	*1995*
SAO TOME & PRINCIPE											
Cocoa	16.5	24.0	25.0	26.0	27.0	28.0	29.0	30.0	..	..	..
Maize	1.9	2.5	2.6	2.6	2.7	2.7	2.8	2.8	..	..	..
Cassava	2.1	2.7	2.7	2.8	2.8	2.9	2.9	3.0	..	..	..
SENEGAL											
Groundnuts (in shell)	50.0	90.0	90.0	70.0	70.0	70.0	70.0	70.0	100.0	120.0	125.0
Cotton (seed cotton, first quality)	60.0	100.0	100.0	100.0	100.0	100.0	100.0	100.0	115.0	150.0	170.0
Millet	40.0	70.0	70.0	70.0	70.0	70.0	70.0	70.0	70.0	70.0	70.0
Rice (paddy)	41.5	85.0	85.0	85.0	85.0	85.0	85.0	85.0	90.0	..	..
Maize	37.0	70.0	70.0	70.0	70.0	70.0	70.0	70.0	70.0	70.0	70.0
Sorghum	40.0	70.0	70.0	70.0	70.0	70.0	70.0	70.0	70.0	70.0	70.0
SIERRA LEONE											
Cocoa	2.1	17.8	30.2	30.2	..	..	..	..	..	..	..
Coffee (Robusta)	2.0	25.0	40.3	..	..	..	..	..	..	..	..
Palm kernels	0.2	1.1	1.3	..	..	..	..	..	..	..	..
Rice (paddy)	0.4	2.8	7.4	22.2	29.0	37.0	44.4	..	..	..	..
Cassava	0.3	4.9	..	..	..	..	..	..	..	..	..
SOMALIA											
Bananas	..	..	..	..	..	..	..	..	..	..	..
Maize	5.5	21.4	34.5	..	..	..	..	..	..	..	..
Sorghum	5.8	18.9	22.7	..	..	..	..	..	..	..	..
Sesame (seed)	25.2	61.6	76.4	..	..	..	..	..	..	..	..
SOUTH AFRICA											
Maize	0.1	0.2	0.3	0.3	0.3	0.3	0.4	0.5	0.4	0.4	0.6
Wheat	0.2	0.4	0.4	0.4	0.5	0.5	0.6	0.7	0.8	0.8	0.8
Sugar cane	0.0	0.0	0.0	0.0	..	0.1	0.1	0.1	0.1	0.1	0.0
Sorghum	0.1	0.2	0.2	0.2	0.2	0.2	0.3	0.5	0.5	0.4	0.4
Barley	0.2	0.3	0.3	0.3	0.4	0.5	0.5	0.6	0.7	0.7	0.7
SUDAN											
Cotton (seed cotton, long-staple, grade 1)	0.4	1.8	2.5	4.3	4.8	6.7	14.1	37.2	..	..	..
Groundnuts (El-Obeid, in shell)	0.2	1.1	1.2	1.8	4.4	23.5	21.1	22.6	..	..	..
Sesame (El-Obeid, mixed)	0.3	1.3	1.6	5.0	6.5	12.7	30.9	41.6	..	..	..
Gum arabic (El-Obeid)	0.0	6.8	9.0	9.4	10.2	10.3	18.9	17.8	..	..	..
Sorghum	0.1	0.2	0.8	0.9	1.9	11.4	6.6	11.8	..	..	..
Wheat	0.2	0.7	1.0	2.3	2.9	5.7	8.3	11.4	33.3	..	..
SWAZILAND											
Sugarcane (sucrose)	0.0	0.0	0.0	0.0	0.0	..	..	..	..	..	..
Citrus	0.2	0.4	0.2	0.4	0.4	..	..	..	..	..	..
Pineapple	0.0	0.3	0.2	0.2	0.3	0.4	0.5	0.5	0.5	0.6	0.6
Cotton (seed cotton)	0.5	0.9	0.9	1.1	1.1	..	..	..	..	..	..
Maize	0.1	0.3	0.3	0.3	0.4	..	..	..	..	..	..
TANZANIA											
Coffee (Arabica) (parchment)	9.0	50.8	66.0	90.0	..	..	..	..	..	..	..
Cotton (seed cotton, AR)	3.2	16.9	19.5	22.4	28.0	..	..	..	..	..	..
Tea (green leaves)	1.5	7.6	9.9	13.4	..	..	..	..	..	..	..
Maize	1.0	6.3	8.2	9.0	11.0	..	..	..	..	..	..
Sorghum	1.0	4.8	6.0	0.0	0.0	..	..	..	..	..	..
Rice (paddy)	1.8	9.6	14.4	17.3	19.0	..	..	..	..	..	..
Millet	1.5	4.8	6.0	6.6	7.3	..	..	..	..	..	..
Cassava (grade 1, Makopa)	0.7	3.6	4.5	5.0	5.5	..	..	..	..	..	..
TOGO											
Coffee (Robusta)	200.0	365.0	400.0	350.0	175.0	175.0	185.0	140.0	350.0	650.0	..
Cocoa	220.0	330.0	360.0	300.0	225.0	250.0	250.0	225.0	300.0	550.0	..
Cotton (seed cotton)	52.0	105.0	105.0	95.0	95.0	100.0	100.0	90.0	110.0	145.0	..
Maize	68.4	73.0	72.0	79.0	60.0	61.0	58.0	73.0	43.0	62.0	..
Sorghum	68.0	76.0	66.0	98.0	69.0	68.0	67.0	92.0	64.0	68.0	..
Millet	66.7	59.0	61.0	87.0	72.0	58.0	75.0	87.0	61.0	52.0	..
Cassava	20.3	30.0	32.0	26.0	30.0	23.0	28.0	29.0	30.0	31.0	..
Yams	48.5	61.0	63.0	63.0	68.0	68.0	66.0	66.0	63.0	59.0	..

(Table continues on the following page)

8-1. Nominal producer prices

	Local currency per kilogram										
	1980	*1986*	*1987*	*1988*	*1989*	*1990*	*1991*	*1992*	*1993*	*1994*	*1995*
TUNISIA											
Olives	0.1	0.1	0.2	0.2	0.2	0.2	0.3	0.3	0.3	0.3	0.3
Citrus (oranges)	0.1	0.1	0.2	0.2	0.2	0.3	0.3	..	..	..	..
Wheat	0.1	0.2	0.2	0.2	0.2	0.2	0.2	0.3	0.3	0.3	0.3
Barley	0.1	0.1	0.1	0.1	0.1	0.2	0.2	0.2	0.2	0.2	0.2
UGANDA											
Coffee	0.1	8.5	24.0	44.5	60.0	97.5	210.0	190.0	..	..	..
Cotton (seed cotton)	0.2	4.0	19.0	56.0	105.0	175.0	286.7	340.0	..	..	..
Tea (greenleaf)	0.0	5.0	10.0	20.0	35.0	38.3	45.0	70.0	..	..	..
Millet	0.2	7.4	17.6	30.7	109.6	134.8	142.6	294.3	..	..	..
Maize	0.1	4.6	11.3	26.0	82.9	72.0	80.0	225.0	..	..	..
Sorghum	0.1	5.4	18.3	30.5	84.6	104.0	115.3	237.3	..	..	..
Cassava	0.1	2.3	9.3	22.5	35.5	39.5	76.0	163.0	..	..	..
Plantains	0.1	3.9	7.5	13.6	46.9	51.2	64.5	156.7	..	..	..
ZAMBIA											
Cotton (seed cotton)	0.5	1.0	1.6	3.0	3.6	9.7	..	..	..	..	..
Tobacco (Virginia)	1.6	5.1	6.3	14.0	14.4	60.0	94.5	..	..	..	..
Sunflower (seeds)	0.3	0.8	1.4	1.8	3.2	6.4	11.4	..	..	..	..
Maize	0.1	0.6	0.9	0.9	1.2	3.2	5.6	..	..	..	..
Wheat	0.2	1.0	1.2	2.1	..	5.4	8.6	..	..	..	..
Cassava	..	0.6	0.7	1.0	1.4	3.2	5.4	..	..	..	..
ZIMBABWE											
Tobacco	0.8	3.1	2.2	3.9	4.0	6.5	11.6	8.1	6.5	..	..
Cotton (seed cotton)	0.4	0.8	0.8	0.9	1.1	1.4	1.6	1.4	2.6	..	..
Sugarcane	0.0	..	..	..	..	..	..	..	..	..	..
Maize	0.1	0.2	0.2	0.2	0.2	0.2	0.3	0.6	0.9	..	..
Wheat	0.2	0.3	0.3	0.4	0.4	0.5	0.5	1.0	1.5	..	..

Notes: The categories of crops are defined in the technical notes.
Categories are mutually exclusive, and ordering is intended to reflect relative importance of these crops as of 1986-88. In many cases official markets operate simultaneously with parallel or open market activites. Where a large majority of marketed production is believed to pass through the official channels, the official price is also reported as the farmgate price. In most cases, only very rough estimates of the share of marketed production passing through each channel is available.

The CPI is based in 1987 rescaled from price index based in 1980.
For each country one to four export crops (X1,...,X4) are presented in order of importance, in terms of value of total production.
Similarly, up to three traded food crops (F1,...,F3) and two nontraded staples (NT1,NT2) are included.

8-2. Food price index

	Index (average 1995 = 100)											Average annual percentage growth		
	1980	1991	1992	1993	1994	1995	1996	1997	1998	1999	2000	75-84	85-89	90-MR
SUB-SAHARAN AFRICA	12	65	72	76	90	100	108	122	128	127	136	..	13.9	9.7
excluding South Africa	11	66	71	74	90	100	109	123	129	127	133	..	11.8	9.6
excl. S.Africa & Nigeria	14	67	72	76	89	100	108	122	128	127	133	..	12.4	8.9
Angola	..	0	0	0	4	100	..	..	..	..	..	..	..	..
Benin	..	67	73	78	84	100	100	103	111	110	..	..	..	6.8
Botswana	18	61	72	83	90	100	113	125	132	142	148	..	9.6	11.0
Burkina Faso	..	87	81	76	89	100	115	122	136	127	..	..	-2.6	6.0
Burundi	35	74	73	72	85	100	..	..	..	..	..	..	3.3	6.3
Cameroon	63	89	88	91	94	100	106	112	116	117	111	..	0.7	2.5
Cape Verde	..	..	..	..	..	..	..	..	..	..	..	..	..	..
Central African Republic	0	69	68	65	81	100	106	107	104	100	104	..	-2.1	5.1
Chad	..	76	73	63	95	100	114	124	128	112	121	..	..	6.7
Comoros	..	..	..	..	..	..	..	..	..	..	..	..	..	..
Congo, Democratic Rep. of	..	..	..	..	..	..	..	..	..	..	..	..	..	..
Congo, Republic of	42	65	59	63	94	100	114	134	133	140	..	..	-1.0	9.9
Côte d'Ivoire	..	..	..	..	..	..	..	..	..	..	..	..	..	..
Djibouti	..	..	..	..	..	..	..	..	..	..	..	..	..	..
Equatorial Guinea	..	..	..	..	..	..	..	..	..	..	..	..	..	..
Eritrea	..	..	..	..	..	..	..	..	..	..	..	..	..	..
Ethiopia	34	71	80	81	89	100	100	100	102	111	110	..	0.4	7.5
Gabon	..	83	69	70	93	100	101	107	110	109	..	..	0.1	4.5
Gambia, The	14	79	86	93	92	100	101	103	106	110	..	..	24.8	5.1
Ghana	1	36	39	49	62	100	136	164	199	216	242	..	23.1	25.8
Guinea	..	70	81	88	93	100	101	..	..	..	..	..	..	11.2
Guinea-Bissau	..	..	..	..	..	..	..	..	..	..	..	..	..	..
Kenya	0	40	54	78	102	100	108	125	130	132	136	..	..	16.1
Lesotho	15	61	76	84	89	100	111	..	..	..	..	..	12.9	13.4
Liberia	..	..	..	..	..	..	..	..	..	..	..	..	..	..
Madagascar	7	38	44	47	66	100	119	124	131	147	168	..	13.8	18.7
Malawi	5	23	30	37	52	100	145	157	201	287	344	..	21.1	34.3
Mali	..	..	..	..	..	..	..	..	..	..	..	..	..	..
Mauritania	..	78	83	88	94	100	107	113	121	127	131	..	..	6.2
Mauritius	..	74	76	87	95	100	105	113	120	127	129	..	6.7	6.9
Mozambique	..	..	..	..	..	..	..	..	..	..	..	..	..	..
Namibia	..	62	74	79	90	100	107	115	118	..	..	..	14.3	10.3
Niger	68	67	66	76	87	100	115	123	..	..	..	..	-6.4	8.1
Nigeria	4	29	43	68	100	100	224	243	259	..	..	..	23.1	35.0
Rwanda	..	..	..	..	..	..	..	..	..	..	..	..	..	..
São Tomé and Principe	..	..	..	..	..	..	..	..	..	..	..	..	..	..
Senegal	43	68	67	66	91	100	101	102	106	106	105	..	0.6	5.4
Seychelles	..	..	..	..	..	..	..	..	..	..	..	..	..	..
Sierra Leone	..	..	..	..	..	..	..	..	..	..	..	..	..	..
Somalia	..	..	..	..	..	..	..	..	..	..	..	..	..	..
South Africa	12	60	76	81	92	100	106	116	123	129	139	..	17.3	10.8
Sudan	..	..	..	..	..	..	..	..	..	..	..	..	..	..
Swaziland	..	..	..	..	..	..	..	..	..	..	..	..	..	..
Tanzania	3	41	51	64	80	100	125	161	1,829	1,990	2,125	..	31.3	51.3
Togo	..	..	..	..	..	..	..	..	..	..	..	..	..	..
Uganda	..	58	96	92	96	100	107	..	..	..	..	..	..	13.4
Zambia	0	5	17	50	75	100	146	176	219	..	..	..	57.7	80.1
Zimbabwe	6	29	45	62	78	100	127	149	208	349	520	..	11.8	33.4
NORTH AFRICA	23	71	75	85	92	100	106	110	114	119	123	..	10.1	7.3
Algeria	13	35	44	55	78	100	122	127	136	137	135	..	9.7	19.3
Egypt, Arab Republic	11	71	77	83	91	100	108	112	116	124	127	..	21.6	8.1
Libya	..	..	..	..	..	..	..	..	..	..	..	..	..	..
Morocco	32	70	74	87	93	100	101	100	103	102	103	..	3.7	5.3
Tunisia	34	83	86	89	92	100	104	108	111	114	119	..	7.4	4.6
ALL AFRICA	13	67	73	76	90	100	108	119	123	127	131	..	14.5	9.0

8-3. Food production index

	Index (average 1989-91 = 100)											Average annual percentage growth		
	1980	*1992*	*1993*	*1994*	*1995*	*1996*	*1997*	*1998*	*1999*	*2000*	*2001*	*75-84*	*85-89*	*90-MR*
SUB-SAHARAN AFRICA	78	107	112	115	116	124	124	130	133	134	135	0.9	4.1	2.7
excluding South Africa	77	109	113	116	119	125	125	132	135	136	137	0.9	4.1	2.8
excl. S.Africa & Nigeria	81	104	107	110	112	117	116	123	126	125	127	1.0	3.3	2.2
Angola	91	111	109	125	123	128	129	148	142	148	149	-0.7	1.2	3.9
Benin	62	109	111	117	128	136	154	151	154	160	159	3.1	3.7	4.9
Botswana	73	103	103	95	111	106	95	90	94	96	96	0.7	-1.9	-0.5
Burkina Faso	59	115	121	116	119	127	117	137	143	126	137	2.4	6.7	2.9
Burundi	79	108	107	90	97	98	97	92	92	87	96	0.3	3.4	-0.9
Cameroon	80	105	110	114	119	125	122	127	133	128	132	0.7	2.0	2.8
Cape Verde	53	104	121	94	123	114	110	128	154	133	136	1.8	21.6	3.1
Central African Republic	80	107	109	112	115	129	126	130	133	142	143	2.0	4.9	3.4
Chad	82	113	98	112	116	121	136	160	144	135	135	1.3	6.3	3.8
Comoros	83	104	110	109	116	113	116	124	132	121	122	0.7	3.8	2.2
Congo, Democratic Rep. of	73	105	104	106	92	91	89	90	88	85	83	2.3	3.3	-1.8
Congo, Republic of	83	100	102	109	114	119	120	118	126	129	130	2.2	1.6	2.6
Côte d'Ivoire	70	104	106	107	122	132	132	133	136	143	134	4.1	3.7	3.5
Djibouti	53	83	77	83	85	87	88	88	90	90	90	11.0	9.2	-0.7
Equatorial Guinea	71	106	102	104	108	111	111	111	117	116	115	0.0	2.0	1.7
Eritrea	..	..	85	117	108	104	104	150	135	119	127	..	..	4.2
Ethiopia	..	..	107	107	119	138	139	128	136	145	142	..	..	3.8
Gabon	80	103	101	103	105	108	110	113	114	117	117	3.0	3.0	1.6
Gambia, The	72	74	87	91	88	69	90	87	126	140	153	-1.1	3.7	3.0
Ghana	69	117	125	120	138	148	144	157	165	170	174	-1.6	4.1	5.5
Guinea	98	116	118	122	128	132	138	146	149	159	159	0.9	-1.8	4.5
Guinea-Bissau	66	105	106	108	112	116	126	129	135	140	145	3.3	2.2	3.4
Kenya	66	98	93	104	103	104	106	109	109	108	106	2.2	7.4	0.9
Lesotho	89	88	100	108	89	111	115	97	94	128	129	0.9	3.1	1.6
Liberia	..	..	..	..	..	..	..	..	..	..	..	..	..	..
Madagascar	85	102	106	104	108	110	112	111	114	107	107	1.1	1.1	1.0
Malawi	91	77	112	88	105	120	115	142	157	162	163	1.7	1.1	5.3
Mali	74	100	105	110	109	104	105	115	122	112	125	3.2	5.5	1.8
Mauritania	87	95	94	96	101	107	105	107	106	111	112	2.8	3.5	1.2
Mauritius	78	107	105	99	106	108	116	111	87	106	112	-0.3	1.8	0.5
Mozambique	102	81	93	90	108	123	130	139	141	121	124	-1.5	1.1	3.5
Namibia	109	105	108	114	110	118	85	95	123	116	115	-2.6	5.4	0.9
Niger	100	112	97	118	111	122	101	152	136	126	146	2.7	6.4	3.3
Nigeria	58	117	123	127	132	140	143	150	154	157	157	0.6	7.1	4.5
Rwanda	83	108	82	56	66	76	79	85	90	111	110	4.1	0.3	0.2
São Tomé and Principe	112	123	127	131	125	134	139	148	159	166	166	-2.5	0.5	4.6
Senegal	59	91	101	104	116	108	101	100	137	136	137	-3.6	8.5	2.8
Seychelles	132	100	93	116	143	139	143	128	135	138	138	-0.2	-6.0	3.6
Sierra Leone	85	93	92	98	92	97	102	95	85	80	80	0.8	2.1	-1.5
Somalia	..	..	..	..	..	..	..	..	..	..	..	..	..	..
South Africa	89	86	97	102	89	105	106	101	107	111	105	0.6	4.2	1.0
Sudan	102	127	117	139	141	155	157	161	158	160	168	1.3	1.2	5.0
Swaziland	81	99	94	97	88	97	88	90	93	87	87	3.3	1.2	-1.2
Tanzania	74	95	97	96	101	103	97	105	106	101	104	3.6	2.2	0.5
Togo	77	98	116	109	107	129	130	122	135	132	132	1.2	3.8	2.9
Uganda	66	104	110	107	112	103	106	118	127	131	137	-1.8	3.8	2.5
Zambia	74	82	117	102	95	114	99	93	105	105	108	-1.4	8.5	0.5
Zimbabwe	78	64	92	101	75	103	106	94	103	117	110	-1.9	4.0	1.6
NORTH AFRICA	71	113	114	115	117	142	130	141	146	146	150	1.7	4.9	3.5
Algeria	69	119	113	104	120	142	113	129	134	127	139	0.3	4.2	2.8
Egypt, Arab Republic	69	111	114	115	126	137	142	142	152	158	158	2.1	4.4	4.6
Libya	82	102	103	110	120	127	133	160	148	161	163	5.0	0.8	5.1
Morocco	58	83	83	108	73	114	97	112	106	100	106	2.0	10.3	1.1
Tunisia	73	104	116	84	82	143	98	124	136	134	127	0.5	-0.4	3.1
ALL AFRICA	76	109	112	115	117	127	125	132	136	136	138	1.0	4.3	2.9

8-4. Nonfood production index

	Index (average 1989-91 = 100)											Average annual percentage growth		
	1980	*1992*	*1993*	*1994*	*1995*	*1996*	*1997*	*1998*	*1999*	*2000*	*2001*	*75-84*	*85-89*	*90-MR*
SUB-SAHARAN AFRICA	80	98	95	100	100	109	113	104	104	97	109	2.0	1.0	0.6
excluding South Africa	77	100	96	100	100	110	114	105	104	97	110	2.1	1.3	0.7
excl. S.Africa & Nigeria	80	98	96	101	100	109	113	104	104	97	109	2.0	1.0	0.6
Angola	209	89	95	85	90	90	94	97	82	92	92	-19.4	-0.8	-0.8
Benin	12	117	195	174	219	280	261	253	208	257	238	8.1	3.9	9.9
Botswana	100	100	100	100	100	100	81	75	77	81	81	0.0	0.0	-2.5
Burkina Faso	35	100	92	95	91	125	205	194	178	155	162	8.9	10.5	6.5
Burundi	59	113	87	114	80	76	58	59	86	66	81	5.3	3.4	-3.8
Cameroon	86	91	88	98	112	126	100	127	127	133	129	3.5	0.9	3.1
Cape Verde	94	21	21	21	21	21	21	21	21	21	21	-3.0	6.1	-11.6
Central African Republic	89	73	60	94	89	132	125	107	107	83	86	-0.5	-0.5	0.7
Chad	51	115	60	99	99	138	166	103	119	94	113	-4.4	11.2	1.8
Comoros	64	75	59	149	69	79	69	103	79	65	79	-5.0	4.6	-2.1
Congo, Democratic Rep. of	105	94	92	90	87	79	77	65	59	54	49	0.6	-3.6	-5.9
Congo, Republic of	156	93	91	92	94	90	78	61	82	84	86	0.0	-5.1	-2.3
Côte d'Ivoire	77	96	76	80	83	82	114	91	104	148	118	0.2	12.5	2.0
Djibouti	..	..	..	..	..	..	..	..	..	..	..	..	..	..
Equatorial Guinea	92	85	85	78	70	63	54	52	55	55	55	2.2	0.4	-6.2
Eritrea	..	..	96	99	98	99	99	99	99	97	102	..	..	0.3
Ethiopia	..	..	89	101	109	116	110	109	104	110	109	..	..	1.5
Gabon	36	67	93	124	142	209	284	307	307	307	307	19.5	21.2	14.4
Gambia, The	55	123	157	135	84	79	51	25	26	26	26	22.5	3.9	-14.2
Ghana	86	180	243	180	188	248	254	321	274	294	304	-6.0	4.4	11.2
Guinea	48	120	120	117	112	96	105	127	146	177	177	0.9	11.1	4.4
Guinea-Bissau	111	66	83	75	109	109	100	100	126	126	126	25.0	-7.5	3.2
Kenya	62	94	99	99	115	119	104	120	111	115	110	6.1	4.5	1.5
Lesotho	87	176	176	176	180	116	123	85	85	92	92	2.0	-9.1	-2.5
Liberia	..	..	..	..	..	..	..	..	..	..	..	..	..	..
Madagascar	90	86	91	89	83	84	77	83	85	79	79	-1.0	0.9	-2.1
Malawi	59	108	120	93	120	132	141	115	79	101	102	6.3	2.0	0.2
Mali	38	123	92	117	154	172	197	198	179	92	209	5.1	11.8	5.6
Mauritania	..	..	..	..	..	..	..	..	..	..	..	..	..	..
Mauritius	84	103	105	92	73	51	38	33	34	30	32	5.0	-5.6	-12.0
Mozambique	251	116	117	124	120	124	160	192	193	177	177	-6.7	-4.4	6.6
Namibia	276	88	96	123	115	109	121	119	135	135	135	-6.7	-1.0	3.1
Niger	84	131	140	178	275	204	220	181	540	478	298	-5.3	4.4	13.5
Nigeria	41	117	85	86	101	116	122	126	129	129	129	-8.0	23.7	3.1
Rwanda	61	117	90	25	65	63	73	76	80	80	86	6.4	3.5	-2.1
São Tomé and Principe	321	70	107	118	91	113	241	268	311	96	96	1.1	-20.6	7.7
Senegal	51	124	129	121	83	82	110	32	42	58	97	2.0	-2.4	-5.5
Seychelles	21	110	121	121	111	110	133	123	116	116	116	7.6	6.7	1.9
Sierra Leone	44	101	96	106	97	97	114	98	60	60	60	11.2	5.0	-4.0
Somalia	..	..	..	..	..	..	..	..	..	..	..	..	..	..
South Africa	107	80	69	73	66	66	60	63	67	58	58	0.7	0.0	-4.6
Sudan	100	81	84	114	127	128	113	105	103	122	124	-1.6	-7.4	2.2
Swaziland	65	24	41	31	19	41	66	49	60	61	61	-3.4	12.0	-2.1
Tanzania	100	126	106	97	126	134	131	97	95	97	127	-2.2	0.1	0.9
Togo	34	97	100	121	106	140	150	172	130	143	149	5.1	20.5	4.7
Uganda	82	84	107	141	131	199	160	162	195	145	172	-5.8	0.7	6.2
Zambia	49	60	134	68	100	87	126	123	133	125	125	5.1	7.4	3.4
Zimbabwe	77	101	117	106	104	129	137	153	129	153	132	2.1	1.8	3.8
NORTH AFRICA	84	98	97	92	91	95	100	94	95	102	103	4.1	-0.2	0.0
Algeria	84	102	103	98	96	91	91	94	97	104	108	5.1	-0.7	-0.1
Egypt, Arab Republic	171	121	135	86	85	114	114	80	81	74	75	0.6	-6.5	-2.9
Libya	105	98	97	94	100	108	110	99	113	113	113	0.2	-1.6	1.3
Morocco	46	94	89	92	91	95	100	104	95	102	103	0.9	6.2	0.3
Tunisia	73	92	87	74	75	74	74	75	72	81	81	3.8	3.8	-2.4
ALL AFRICA	82	98	96	99	99	109	110	103	103	97	108	2.4	0.7	0.5

8-5. Food production per capita index

	Index (average 1989-91 = 100)											Average annual percentage growth		
	1980	1992	1993	1994	1995	1996	1997	1998	1999	2000	2001	75-84	85-89	90-MR
SUB-SAHARAN AFRICA	106	98	97	96	97	99	95	96	99	97	98	-1.5	0.4	-0.2
excluding South Africa	106	98	98	96	97	99	96	98	100	98	98	-1.6	0.4	-0.1
excl. S.Africa & Nigeria	106	98	97	96	97	99	95	96	99	97	98	-1.7	0.4	-0.2
Angola	124	104	99	110	104	105	103	115	106	108	106	-3.5	-1.5	0.7
Benin	84	102	100	102	109	112	124	119	117	119	115	0.4	0.7	1.9
Botswana	100	98	95	85	97	91	79	75	76	78	77	-2.7	-4.9	-2.7
Burkina Faso	77	109	111	104	105	109	98	113	115	99	104	0.0	3.8	0.4
Burundi	107	104	101	84	90	90	89	83	83	78	83	-2.3	0.2	-2.1
Cameroon	107	99	101	102	104	107	102	104	106	100	101	-2.2	-1.0	0.3
Cape Verde	63	100	113	86	110	100	94	107	125	106	106	0.8	19.4	0.8
Central African Republic	102	101	101	101	101	111	106	107	107	113	111	-0.5	2.7	1.0
Chad	106	107	90	100	100	102	111	126	110	100	97	-0.7	3.3	0.7
Comoros	113	99	101	97	100	95	94	98	101	90	88	-3.0	0.8	-0.7
Congo, Democratic Rep. of	100	97	93	91	76	73	69	69	65	62	59	-0.7	0.1	-4.9
Congo, Republic of	110	94	93	96	98	99	96	92	96	95	93	-0.7	-1.3	-0.5
Côte d'Ivoire	104	98	97	96	107	113	110	109	109	113	103	-0.5	-0.1	1.0
Djibouti	83	78	72	77	78	77	76	74	72	71	70	4.6	1.8	-2.9
Equatorial Guinea	116	101	95	94	96	95	93	91	93	89	86	-2.2	-1.1	-0.9
Eritrea	..	..	84	115	104	99	97	136	119	100	103	..	..	1.7
Ethiopia	..	..	98	95	102	115	113	101	106	110	105	..	..	1.1
Gabon	109	97	93	92	91	91	91	91	89	89	87	0.0	-0.1	-1.2
Gambia, The	103	68	78	78	73	56	69	65	92	100	105	-4.1	-0.5	-0.4
Ghana	96	111	116	108	121	127	121	129	132	134	134	-4.2	1.1	2.9
Guinea	128	108	106	106	107	108	110	114	114	120	118	-1.8	-4.3	1.5
Guinea-Bissau	82	99	98	97	98	100	106	106	109	111	112	0.1	0.0	1.0
Kenya	96	92	85	92	89	88	87	88	86	83	80	-1.6	3.6	-1.7
Lesotho	110	84	94	99	80	97	99	82	79	106	105	-1.3	1.0	-0.3
Liberia	..	..	..	..	..	..	..	..	..	..	..	..	..	..
Madagascar	113	97	98	93	93	92	91	88	88	80	78	-1.6	-1.7	-1.9
Malawi	138	74	107	83	98	110	103	124	134	134	133	-1.4	-4.3	3.4
Mali	95	95	97	100	96	89	88	94	97	87	94	1.0	2.8	-0.8
Mauritania	112	91	87	87	87	89	91	87	85	82	83	81	0.3	1.0	-1.7
Mauritius	86	105	102	95	100	101	108	103	80	96	101	-1.7	1.0	-0.5
Mozambique	118	76	84	78	91	100	104	108	108	90	91	-3.9	0.5	0.5
Namibia	151	98	98	101	95	100	71	77	98	91	88	-4.4	1.1	-1.5
Niger	137	105	88	103	94	100	80	116	100	90	101	-0.4	3.1	-0.2
Nigeria	78	110	113	114	114	118	117	119	119	119	116	-2.4	4.0	1.6
Rwanda	108	121	100	74	89	97	92	88	85	98	93	1.0	-3.3	-1.0
São Tomé and Principe	137	119	120	122	113	120	123	127	135	138	136	-5.0	-1.3	2.7
Senegal	78	87	93	94	102	93	85	82	109	105	104	-6.3	5.5	0.2
Seychelles	146	97	88	109	133	127	129	115	119	120	118	-1.3	-7.0	2.2
Sierra Leone	106	92	91	97	91	96	100	92	81	74	71	-1.2	-0.7	-2.3
Somalia	..	..	..	..	..	..	..	..	..	..	..	..	..	..
South Africa	112	82	92	94	81	94	93	87	91	94	87	-1.8	2.0	-0.8
Sudan	132	121	109	127	125	134	133	134	129	128	131	-1.7	-0.9	2.7
Swaziland	111	95	89	91	81	88	78	78	79	72	71	0.4	-2.4	-3.0
Tanzania	102	88	87	84	85	84	78	82	80	75	76	0.4	-1.0	-2.4
Togo	106	94	109	100	96	112	110	99	106	100	98	-1.4	0.6	0.2
Uganda	92	98	100	95	96	86	86	93	97	97	98	-4.6	0.3	-0.5
Zambia	101	77	108	92	83	97	82	76	83	81	82	-4.5	5.1	-2.0
Zimbabwe	111	61	85	92	66	90	91	79	85	94	88	-5.1	0.3	-0.5
NORTH AFRICA	92	101	106	100	108	122	98	110	119	116	112	-1.5	2.0	1.4
Algeria	92	114	106	96	108	126	98	110	112	104	112	-2.8	1.4	0.8
Egypt, Arab Republic	88	106	107	106	114	122	124	122	128	131	128	-0.3	1.8	2.6
Libya	116	98	97	102	109	113	116	136	123	131	130	0.4	-2.1	2.9
Morocco	74	79	78	100	67	101	84	96	89	82	85	-0.4	7.7	-0.9
Tunisia	92	101	109	78	75	129	87	110	119	116	109	-2.0	-2.6	1.6
ALL AFRICA	106	98	98	96	97	100	96	99	101	99	101	-1.2	0.3	0.0

8-6. Volume of food output, by major food crop

	Thousands of metric tons												Average annual* percentage growth		
	1980	*1992*	*1993*	*1994*	*1995*	*1996*	*1997*	*1998*	*1999*	*2000*	*2001*	*2002*	*75-84*	*85-89*	*90-MR*
ALGERIA															
Wheat	1,511	1,837	1,017	714	1,500	2,983	662	2,280	1,470	760	2,011	2,011	0.1	0.4	0.2
Citrus	422	362	361	376	323	334	351	418	454	433	441	441	-0.3	0.1	0.2
Dates	201	261	262	317	285	361	303	387	428	366	370	370	0.6	0.5	0.3
Barley	794	1,398	408	234	585	1,800	191	700	510	163	574	574	0.5	-0.1	-0.3
Potatoes	591	1,158	1,065	716	1,200	1,150	948	1,100	996	1,208	1,200	1,200	0.0	0.4	0.1
ANGOLA															
Maize	360	320	275	201	211	398	370	505	428	395	429	429	-0.3	0.0	0.4
Millet	57	75	40	60	61	102	62	89	102	105	148	148	-0.3	0.4	0.4
Cassava	1150	1,861	1,861	2,379	2,550	2,500	2,326	3,211	3,130	4,433	5,394	5,394	-0.1	0.1	0.5
Sweet potatoes	165	180	185	180	185	188	189	190	182	224	353	353	0.0	0.0	0.2
BENIN															
Palm oil	34	14	14	9	13	15	9	15	15	15	15	15	-0.4	-0.4	0.0
Maize	271	460	483	492	576	556	701	662	783	750	686	622	0.5	-0.9	0.3
Sorghum	56	110	106	113	117	110	120	138	126	155	165	195	-0.3	0.2	0.2
Cassava	583	1,041	1,147	1,146	1,238	1,457	1,918	1,989	2,113	2,350	2,703	2,452	0.0	-0.6	0.5
Yam	694	1,125	1,185	1,250	1,286	1,346	1,408	1,584	1,647	1,742	1,701	1,875	0.2	0.0	0.2
BOTSWANA															
Livestock (1,000 heads)	149	300	250	238	337	349	360	300	320	350	370	370	-0.4	0.3	0.0
Onions ,dry	1	1	1	1	1	1	1	1	1	1	1	1	-5.2	0.0	-0.1
Sorghum	29	16	38	37	38	78	17	9	13	11	11	11	-1.9	-0.4	-0.5
Maize	12	3	3	11	2	25	12	1	5	9	9	9	-2.2	1.0	-0.1
Millet	2	1	2	4	1	8	2	1	1	1	1	1	-1.3	-4.0	0.1
BURKINA FASO															
Groundnuts	54	143	206	203	181	221	152	215	283	169	301	301	0.1	-0.8	0.4
Sorghum	547	1,292	1,281	973	1,266	1,254	943	1,203	1,178	1,016	1,372	1,350	0.1	-0.3	0.1
Millet	351	784	899	831	734	811	604	973	945	726	1,009	1,000	0.2	-0.3	0.2
Maize	105	343	271	350	212	294	366	378	469	423	606	610	0.6	-0.4	0.3
Rice	40	47	54	61	84	112	90	89	94	103	110	110	0.1	-1.6	0.5
BURUNDI															
Maize	9	14	13	11	14	11	17	11	10	9	9	9	0.0	0.1	-0.2
Sorghum	52	67	65	45	66	66	68	67	60	61	69	69	1.0	0.1	0.0
Rice	10	40	40	38	27	42	65	41	59	52	61	61	0.3	0.8	0.2
Millet	9	14	13	11	14	11	17	11	10	9	9	9	0.0	0.1	-0.2
Bananas	1100	1,626	1,586	1,487	1,421	1,544	1,543	1,399	1,511	1,514	1,549	1,549	-0.1	0.1	0.0
Cassava	400	598	584	527	501	549	603	622	617	657	713	713	0.1	0.1	0.1
CAMEROON															
Maize	414	531	507	524	618	750	760	793	785	850	850	850	-0.1	0.2	0.3
Sorghum	331	380	390	350	460	439	400	500	272	420	450	450	0.3	-2.0	0.0
Millets	100	55	60	50	66	71	71	71	71	71	71	71	0.2	-2.5	0.1
Rice	46	53	29	36	35	36	37	53	67	70	70	70	0.3	-0.8	0.2
Cassava	980	1,636	1,648	1,715	1,780	1,848	1,918	1,966	1,984	1,500	1,700	1,700	0.2	-0.2	0.1
Plantains	1020	1,038	1,120	1,211	1,250	1,290	1,326	1,359	1,332	1,332	1,400	1,400	0.3	-0.5	0.2
CENTRAL AFRICAN REP															
Sorghum	36	21	20	21	22	26	28	29	45	48	50	107	0.2	-1.2	0.5
Maize	41	59	58	63	71	76	83	88	95	101	107	107	0.2	-0.6	0.3
Groundnuts	123	71	72	79	86	91	88	102	110	116	122	122	0.0	-0.2	0.3
Cassava	920	580	575	518	492	526	579	608	559	560	562	562	0.0	-0.3	0.0
Yam	150	260	260	280	320	340	340	360	360	360	360	360	-0.1	0.0	0.2
CHAD															
Sorghum	250	387	243	481	437	353	427	514	457	392	497	428	-0.5	-0.5	0.2
Millet	200	293	212	320	228	258	248	357	361	259	398	369	-0.4	-1.0	0.3
Groundnuts	99	224	190	207	293	305	352	471	372	359	448	448	0.0	0.0	0.5
COMOROS															
Bananas	32	54	55	57	56	57	58	59	59	57	60	60	0.1	0.6	0.1
Cassava	33	51	52	48	49	50	51	52	52	45	54	55	-0.2	1.1	0.1
CONGO															
Maize	9	5	5	5	8	8	9	10	6	6	7	7	-0.7	0.0	0.2
Cassava	628	600	632	723	747	772	780	739	812	828	845	845	0.2	0.1	0.1
Plantains	56	73	75	78	77	76	76	71	68	70	70	70	0.4	0.2	0.0
COTE D'IVOIRE															
Palm oil	189	281	274	276	268	297	249	269	264	278	205	205	0.1	0.3	0.0
Rice	420	660	676	701	764	1,139	1,287	1,197	1,208	1,231	1,212	818	0.0	0.1	0.3
Maize	380	514	517	536	552	569	574	573	815	693	573	600	0.4	0.0	0.2
Cassava	1,010	1,502	1,509	1,564	1,608	1,653	1,699	1,692	1,681	1,691	1,688	1,700	0.1	0.1	0.1
Yams	2,040	2,758	2,771	2,824	2,869	2,924	2,987	2,921	2,944	2,950	2,938	3,000	0.1	0.0	0.0

(Table continues on the following page)

8-6. Volume of food output, by major food crop (continued)

	Thousands of metric tons												*Average annual* percentage growth*		
	1980	*1992*	*1993*	*1994*	*1995*	*1996*	*1997*	*1998*	*1999*	*2000*	*2001*	*2002*	*75-84*	*85-89*	*90-MR*
EGYPT															
Rice	2,382	3,910	4,161	4,583	4,788	4,895	5,480	4,474	5,817	6,000	5,227	5,700	0.1	0.2	0.2
Wheat	1,736	4,618	4,833	4,437	5,722	5,735	5,849	6,093	6,347	6,564	6,255	6,183	0.1	1.0	0.2
Sugarcane	8618	11,708	12,412	13,822	14,105	13,958	13,726	14,353	15,254	15,706	15,572	15,706	0.0	-0.6	0.2
Dry Broadbeans	213	382	438	357	392	442	476	523	307	354	439	439	-0.2	0.5	-0.1
EQUATORIAL GUINEA															
Cassava	32	47	47	47	47	48	45	43	45	45	45	45	0.0	0.1	0.0
Sweet Potatoes	21	35	35	35	35	36	35	34	36	36	36	36	0.1	0.1	0.0
ETHIOPIA															
Sorghum	0	0	628	703	1,141	1,808	2,040	1,083	1,184	1,333	1,538	1,538	..	..	0.3
Maize	0	0	1,456	1,396	1,990	3,164	2,987	2,344	2,685	2,525	3,138	3,138	..	..	0.4
Barley	0	0	787	875	986	1,125	953	983	813	742	845	845	..	..	0.0
Sugarcane	0	0	1,700	1,200	1,200	1,582	1,490	1,650	2,200	2,200	2,400	2,400	..	..	0.3
GABON															
Oil palm	2	7	8	8	7	7	7	6	6	6	6	6	0.0	-0.1	0.0
Maize	10	25	27	28	23	24	24	25	25	26	26	26	0.3	0.5	0.0
Cassava	250	230	207	211	215	214	221	227	224	228	230	230	0.2	0.2	0.0
Yam	79	120	110	125	130	135	140	145	150	155	155	155	0.3	0.2	0.2
Plantains	175	253	238	243	248	258	264	274	265	270	270	270	0.3	-0.1	0.0
GAMBIA,THE															
Groundnuts	60	55	77	81	75	46	78	73	123	138	151	151	-0.2	0.7	0.2
Palm oil	3	3	3	3	3	3	3	3	3	3	3	3	-0.1	0.0	0.0
Millet	15	46	52	53	54	61	66	65	81	95	105	105	0.7	-0.1	0.3
Rice	43	19	12	20	19	18	13	19	32	34	19	19	0.9	-0.7	0.2
Maize	6	18	24	13	14	10	8	13	20	22	29	29	0.6	-0.6	0.1
Sorghum	5	12	9	9	12	14	13	10	18	25	33	33	0.6	-0.6	0.4
GHANA															
Maize	382	731	961	940	1,034	1,008	996	1,035	1,014	1,013	938	1,000	0.3	0.1	0.2
Millet	82	133	198	168	201	193	144	172	160	169	134	160	-0.2	1.4	0.2
Groundnuts	142	100	140	176	168	162	154	212	193	209	258	225	0.3	0.2	0.5
Cassava	1,858	5,662	5,973	6,025	6,612	7,111	7,000	7,227	7,845	8,107	8,966	8,966	0.1	0.1	0.3
Plantains	734	1,082	1,322	1,475	1,638	1,823	1,818	1,893	2,046	1,932	1,932	1,932	-0.4	-0.2	0.4
GUINEA															
Palm oil	40	40	48	50	50	55	55	50	50	50	50	50	0.1	0.1	0.1
Rice	480	512	531	544	631	673	716	764	750	870	870	870	0.0	-0.1	0.3
Maize	90	88	85	83	79	82	85	89	92	95	95	95	0.3	-0.5	0.1
Groundnuts	84	139	128	126	132	145	158	174	190	210	210	210	0.0	-0.1	0.4
Cassava	480	512	550	525	601	667	732	812	900	1,000	1,000	1,000	-0.3	-0.6	0.4
Plantains	350	405	410	420	425	435	430	429	429	430	430	430	0.2	0.0	0.1
GUINEA-BISSAU															
Groundnuts	30	16	18	18	17	17	18	18	19	19	19	19	-0.1	-0.7	0.1
Palm kernels	9	7	7	7	7	7	8	8	8	8	8	8	0.1	-0.2	0.1
Rice	42	124	126	131	133	120	100	87	80	104	100	100	-0.2	0.0	-0.2
Sorghum	18	11	14	14	16	22	12	11	15	11	15	15	0.9	-1.2	0.1
Maize	12	10	13	14	15	9	15	15	27	26	26	26	0.4	0.2	0.3
KENYA															
Sugarcane	4,532	4,180	4,370	3,800	4,550	4,650	4,450	4,900	5,200	4,750	5,150	5,150	0.7	0.2	0.1
Maize	1,620	2,430	2,089	3,060	2,699	2,160	2,214	2,400	2,300	2,200	2,700	2,700	-0.4	-0.4	0.0
Wheat	216	126	150	297	313	290	227	263	190	181	180	180	0.2	-0.4	0.1
LESOTHO															
Wheat	28	12	8	12	11	30	34	29	15	51	51	51	-1.0	1.4	0.5
Dry Beans	4	1	2	3	5	6	14	8	9	8	8	8	-1.3	0.1	0.6
Dry Peas	5	2	1	1	1	4	3	5	3	6	7	7	-0.4	-1.1	0.7
Maize	106	61	92	149	63	188	142	119	125	297	300	300	0.3	0.0	0.5
Sorghum	59	19	52	61	7	36	29	23	33	45	46	46	0.2	-1.0	0.4
LIBERIA															
Rice	243	110	65	50	56	94	168	209	196	183	183	183	0.0	0.1	0.3
Cassava	300	280	245	250	175	213	282	307	361	441	441	441	0.1	0.5	0.1
LIBYA															
Wheat	141	125	126	120	117	124	156	140	130	125	130	130	0.8	0.0	0.0
Olives	161	100	120	140	168	186	186	190	190	190	190	190	0.8	-1.8	0.5
MADAGASCAR															
Rice Paddy	2109	2,450	2,550	2,357	2,450	2,500	2,558	2,447	2,637	2,300	2,300	2,300	0.0	0.0	0.0
Cassava	1683	2,280	2,350	2,360	2,400	2,353	2,418	2,412	2,435	2,228	2,228	2,228	0.2	-0.2	0.0
Sweet potatoes	373	452	500	560	450	500	510	510	520	476	480	480	-0.2	0.1	0.0

(Table continues on the following page)

8-6. Volume of food output, by major food crop (continued)

	Thousands of metric tons												Average annual* percentage growth		
	1980	1992	1993	1994	1995	1996	1997	1998	1999	2000	2001	2002	75-84	85-89	90-MR
MALAWI															
Groundnuts	177	26	55	31	32	40	69	97	125	117	148	158	0.0	-0.5	0.6
Maize	1186	657	2,034	1,040	1,661	1,793	1,226	1,772	2,479	2,501	1,589	1,603	0.1	-0.2	0.2
Sorghum	20	4	22	17	45	55	40	41	41	37	37	39	-2.2	-1.1	0.6
Cassava	292	129	216	250	328	535	714	830	895	2,757	3,313	1,540	0.1	-0.5	1.3
MALI															
Groundnuts	144	127	149	215	157	134	144	152	191	193	196	257	-0.7	-0.2	0.1
Millet	407	582	708	898	707	739	641	814	819	759	793	1,034	0.1	-0.6	0.1
Rice	132	410	428	469	476	627	576	718	727	743	933	926	-0.3	0.3	0.4
Sorghum	356	602	777	746	712	541	560	600	689	565	517	951	0.2	0.3	0.0
Maize	45	193	283	322	266	294	343	393	620	215	299	321	-0.3	-0.2	0.3
MAURITANIA															
Sorghum	28	50	92	147	157	145	58	73	75	95	84	84	0.2	0.3	0.2
Millet	3	2	4	7	8	8	3	3	10	7	3	67	0.3	0.8	0.7
Rice	11	51	65	45	53	67	81	102	52	76	67	67	1.4	1.5	0.2
Maize	5	3	7	6	4	14	12	11	8	6	8	8	0.1	-3.2	0.7
MAURITIUS															
Sugarcane	4564	5,781	5,402	4,813	5,159	5,260	5,787	5,781	3,883	5,109	5,500	5,500	-0.1	0.1	-0.1
Potatoes	12	19	14	18	16	11	18	15	15	14	15	15	0.1	0.1	-0.1
Dry Onions	2	3	4	5	6	6	5	7	9	11	11	11	0.8	-0.7	0.6
MOROCCO															
Citrus	1084	1,111	1,227	1,319	997	1,393	1,229	1,597	1,313	1,423	984	984	0.3	-0.3	0.0
Wheat	1811	1,562	1,573	5,523	1,091	5,916	2,316	4,378	2,154	1,381	3,316	3,357	0.1	-0.9	0.0
Sugarbeet	2241	2,754	3,062	3,144	2,717	2,750	2,613	2,823	3,236	2,883	3,106	3,300	0.3	0.2	0.0
Barley	2,210	1,081	1,027	3,720	608	3,831	1,324	1,970	1,474	467	1,155	1,562	0.1	-2.1	-0.1
MOZAMBIQUE															
Cashew nuts	71	54	24	23	33	67	43	52	59	58	58	58	-0.6	0.6	0.4
Maize	380	132	533	489	734	947	1,042	1,124	1,246	1,019	1,143	1,143	-0.2	-1.2	0.7
Rice	75	33	66	101	113	139	180	191	186	151	167	167	0.3	0.0	0.6
Cassava	3600	3,239	3,511	3,352	4,178	4,734	5,337	5,639	5,353	5,362	5,362	5,362	0.1	0.1	0.2
NAMIBIA															
Wheat	2	3	6	6	3	6	6	3	4	3	6	6	0.8	-0.2	-0.1
Maize	32	11	26	41	18	19	49	18	19	32	28	28	0.1	-2.2	-0.2
NIGER															
Cowpeas	266	402	168	525	184	295	199	787	436	269	350	350	0.3	-0.3	0.3
Groundnuts	126	57	26	67	103	196	88	112	104	113	129	129	0.2	-0.2	0.8
Sorghum	368	387	289	393	266	408	290	503	476	371	656	656	0.1	-0.2	0.2
Millet	1364	1,788	1,658	1,968	1,769	1,761	1,352	2,391	2,296	1,679	2,414	2,414	0.2	-1.2	0.1
NIGERIA															
Groundnuts	471	1,297	1,323	1,453	1,579	2,278	2,531	2,534	2,894	2,901	2,683	2,900	-0.1	-0.5	0.5
Palm oil	650	792	825	837	860	776	810	845	896	899	903	903	0.1	0.3	0.1
Sorghum	3690	5,909	6,051	6,197	6,997	7,084	7,297	7,516	7,520	7,711	7,081	8,194	0.0	0.0	0.2
Millet	2,354	4,501	4,602	4,757	5,563	5,681	5,902	5,956	5,960	6,105	5,530	6,474	-0.1	0.1	0.2
Maize	612	5,840	6,290	6,902	6,931	5,667	5,254	5,127	5,476	4,107	4,620	5,383	-0.3	1.0	-0.1
Rice	1,090	3,260	3,065	2,427	2,920	3,122	3,268	3,275	3,277	3,298	2,752	3,367	1.4	0.9	0.1
Yam	5248	19,781	21,632	23,153	22,818	23,201	23,972	24,768	25,873	26,201	26,374	27,693	-0.2	-0.1	0.2
Cassava	11500	29,184	30,128	31,005	31,404	31,418	32,050	32,695	32,697	32,010	32,586	33,563	0.1	0.4	0.2
RWANDA															
Sorghum	179	113	128	55	77	102	122	121	108	155	175	175	0.2	-0.1	-0.1
Maize	85	98	87	67	56	67	83	59	55	63	92	92	0.2	-0.4	-0.2
Plantains	2063	3,547	2,136	1,489	2,002	2,105	2,248	2,625	2,897	2,212	1,573	1,573	0.2	0.2	-0.1
Sweet potatoes	871	1,055	997	410	551	665	742	751	863	1,033	1,137	1,137	0.3	-0.1	0.0
SENEGAL															
Groundnuts	523	578	628	678	791	646	545	579	1,014	1,062	960	500	0.1	0.7	0.1
Millet	451	446	654	548	667	601	426	428	675	600	470	470	0.4	0.8	0.0
Rice	65	177	193	162	155	149	174	124	240	202	244	244	0.3	0.0	0.1
Maize	57	115	138	108	107	89	60	44	66	79	106	106	0.2	0.0	-0.3
Sorghum	102	117	99	123	127	133	118	120	147	144	140	140	0.4	-0.5	0.1
SIERRA LEONE															
Palm oil	47	48	47	50	45	48	51	40	36	36	36	36	0.1	0.0	-0.2
Palm kernels	30	31	33	32	29	31	32	26	22	22	22	22	-0.2	-0.1	-0.2
Rice	513	479	486	405	356	392	411	328	247	199	199	199	-0.2	-0.1	-0.4
Cassava	95	117	106	244	219	281	310	289	240	241	241	241	0.1	0.1	0.4

(Table continues on the following page)

8-6. Volume of food output, by major food crop

	Thousands of metric tons												Average annual* percentage growth		
	1980	1992	1993	1994	1995	1996	1997	1998	1999	2000	2001	2002	75-84	85-89	90-MR
SOMALIA															
Bananas	60	70	55	43	50	55	55	48	50	55	55	55	-0.2	0.5	-0.2
Maize	110	101	79	150	146	142	128	150	143	210	210	210	0.2	-0.5	0.1
Sorghum	140	92	80	252	136	145	153	79	62	100	100	100	0.2	0.4	-0.3
Sesame	38	15	22	22	25	23	24	21	22	23	23	23	0.2	0.0	-0.2
SOUTH AFRICA															
Maize	11,040	3,277	9,997	13,275	4,866	10,171	10,136	7,693	7,946	11,455	8,040	9,123	0.1	0.2	0.1
Wheat	1,472	1,324	1,984	1,840	1,977	2,712	2,429	1,892	1,733	2,364	2,504	2,400	0.0	0.5	0.1
Sugarcane	14,062	12,955	11,244	15,683	16,714	20,951	22,155	22,930	21,223	23,876	21,157	22,349	-0.1	0.3	0.2
Sorghum	711	118	515	520	291	536	433	358	224	473	211	238	0.3	0.5	0.0
Barley	60	265	230	275	300	176	182	204	92	116	157	142	0.2	1.5	-0.3
SUDAN															
Groundnuts	712	380	428	714	738	815	1,104	776	1,047	1,047	947	990	-0.4	-0.4	0.9
Sesame	221	266	175	170	313	416	281	262	329	329	262	274	-0.3	0.2	0.5
Sorghum	2,084	4,042	2,386	3,648	2,450	4,179	2,870	4,284	2,347	2,488	4,470	3,100	-0.2	-3.3	0.2
Wheat	231	895	453	475	448	527	642	585	172	214	303	247	-0.5	0.2	-0.4
SWAZILAND															
Sugarcane	2,782	3,885	3,647	3,786	3,440	3,846	3,694	3,887	4,323	3,885	3,885	3,885	0.4	0.0	0.0
Citrus (oranges)	45	35	23	48	29	33	33	31	35	36	36	36	0.0	-0.8	0.1
Maize	97	54	73	99	76	151	108	125	113	85	85	85	-0.1	-1.2	0.1
TANZANIA															
Maize	1,726	2,226	2,282	2,159	2,874	2,648	1,831	2,685	2,452	2,551	2,616	2,500	0.1	0.4	0.1
Sorghum	510	587	719	478	839	872	499	563	561	664	736	650	0.7	0.4	0.1
Rice	291	392	641	614	623	807	550	849	506	508	514	514	-0.2	0.7	0.0
Millet	340	263	210	218	342	585	347	236	194	153	170	170	0.6	0.1	0.0
Cassava	4,828	7,112	6,833	7,209	5,969	5,994	5,704	7,033	7,182	5,758	5,650	5,650	0.1	-0.5	-0.1
TOGO															
Maize	138	278	393	348	290	388	452	350	494	482	464	464	0.4	0.4	0.3
Sorghum	95	112	126	110	172	156	152	137	142	151	142	142	-0.4	-0.4	0.1
Millet	43	75	75	58	74	55	49	41	39	37	41	41	-1.2	0.2	-0.2
Cassava	408	452	389	532	602	548	596	579	694	701	652	652	0.2	-0.5	0.1
Yam	484	368	530	484	531	605	683	696	666	563	549	549	0.2	-0.2	0.2
TUNISIA															
Olive oil	115	120	210	70	60	310	90	180	225	110	101	30	-0.4	0.2	-0.1
Citrus	160	226	338	255	235	268	261	279	261	276	295	295	0.2	0.3	0.0
Wheat	869	1,584	1,413	503	531	2,018	885	1,354	1,390	824	1,120	422	0.3	2.8	-0.1
Barley	296	570	478	145	80	835	160	303	420	240	233	90	0.9	3.9	-0.3
UGANDA															
Millet	459	634	610	610	632	440	502	642	606	534	584	584	-0.3	0.4	0.0
Maize	286	657	804	850	913	759	740	924	1,053	1,096	1,174	1,174	-0.5	0.5	0.3
Sorghum	299	375	383	390	399	298	294	420	413	361	423	423	-0.2	0.2	0.0
Cassava	2072	2,896	3,139	2,080	2,224	2,245	2,291	3,204	4,875	4,966	5,265	5,265	-0.4	0.3	0.2
Plantains	5699	7,806	8,222	8,500	9,012	9,144	9,303	9,318	8,949	9,533	9,533	9,533	-0.3	0.2	0.1
ZAIRE															
Palm oil	168	181	182	171	196	186	166	165	168	168	167	170	-0.1	0.1	0.0
Maize	594	1,053	1,130	1,184	1,008	1,101	1,167	1,215	1,199	1,184	1,169	1,155	0.2	0.2	0.1
Rice	234	403	430	426	366	348	322	363	350	338	326	315	0.1	0.2	-0.1
Cassava	13087	19,780	18,890	19,102	16,870	16,887	16,402	17,060	16,500	15,959	15,436	14,930	0.1	0.1	-0.1
Plantains	1563	2,117	2,186	2,262	1,038	948	691	631	577	527	530	530	0.1	0.0	-0.7
ZAMBIA															
Sunflower seeds	28	1	21	10	21	27	8	6	7	7	7	900	0.4	-1.9	0.2
Maize	937	483	1,598	1,021	738	1,409	960	638	856	882	900	900	-0.7	-0.4	-0.1
Wheat	10	58	71	43	50	58	71	64	90	75	75	75	0.9	1.3	0.1
Cassava	315	682	744	744	744	744	702	817	971	815	950	950	0.3	0.4	0.2
ZIMBABWE															
Sugarcane	2528	125	538	3,420	3,773	2,826	4,651	4,811	4,657	4,228	4,100	4,100	0.1	-0.3	0.7
Maize	1511	362	2,012	2,326	840	2,609	2,192	1,418	1,520	2,108	1,467	800	-0.1	-2.3	0.1
Wheat	191	58	276	239	83	280	300	280	320	250	275	213	0.2	-0.2	0.2

Notes: Crops shown represent same major food crops as in Table 8-1, Nominal producer prices, excluding beverages (coffee, tea, cocoa), cotton, and tobacco.

The following commodities are in their least-processed form unless otherwise indicated:

Groundnuts, unshelled

Rice, paddy

Sunflower, seeds

Citrus, total for country

Sesame, seeds

Livestock = combined total head of cattle, sheep, goats, pigs, horses, asses, and mules

Chickens/rabbits = combined total

For South Africa, barley production is for white areas only.

Countries excluded from listing: Cape Verde, Djibouti, Eritrea, São Tomé and Principe, and Seychelles.

* The standard World Bank least square methodology was used to compute the annual percentage growth.

8-7. Value of agricultural exports

	Millions of U.S. dollars (current prices)											Average annual percentage growth		
	1980	*1988*	*1989*	*1990*	*1991*	*1992*	*1993*	*1994*	*1995*	*1996*	*1997*	*75-84*	*85-89*	*90-MR*
SUB-SAHARAN AFRICA	12,212	10,099	10,711	10,358	9,563	9,258	9,317	11,506	13,108	14,312	13,368	1.8	2.0	4.6
excluding South Africa	9,695	8,582	8,699	8,440	7,725	7,467	7,738	9,389	10,823	11,823	10,904	2.0	0.6	4.8
excl. S.Africa & Nigeria	9,249	8,141	8,444	8,210	7,511	7,277	7,462	9,062	10,420	11,281	10,383	2.4	0.6	4.5
Angola	172	22	16	6	5	5	3	1	5	6	6	-12.8	-30.5	-7.6
Benin	55	44	79	84	86	93	83	115	201	188	198	3.0	-4.2	14.2
Botswana	51	74	79	79	90	91	96	97	132	115	115	5.2	2.7	5.9
Burkina Faso	80	87	66	116	94	86	93	80	141	123	119	5.3	5.1	5.6
Burundi	64	127	73	69	88	67	53	113	96	32	82	8.8	-4.0	-1.9
Cameroon	699	510	661	563	341	364	245	393	565	624	504	2.6	5.1	0.5
Cape Verde	0	0	0	0	0	0	0	0	0	0	0	17.7	38.3	-31.8
Central African Republic	60	54	69	45	46	33	36	37	51	28	33	6.8	3.3	-6.4
Chad	115	112	114	134	136	127	84	118	145	127	135	13.2	-7.4	0.9
Comoros	7	18	13	11	20	16	18	8	7	4	4	8.6	13.4	-16.4
Congo, Democratic Rep. of	235	165	182	141	78	83	53	93	135	102	95	-1.7	-8.5	-3.9
Congo, Republic of	13	10	7	15	14	17	9	7	11	16	15	-1.7	-15.1	2.8
Côte d'Ivoire	2,009	1,735	1,807	1,615	1,532	1,434	1,605	1,557	2,216	2,421	2,001	7.0	-2.7	4.2
Djibouti	0	0	0	0	0	0	0	0	0	0	0	96.6	18.8	-7.8
Equatorial Guinea	12	12	8	8	6	6	3	4	4	7	4	-4.0	-10.3	-6.5
Eritrea	..	..	..	..	..	..	4	4	2	2	2	..	..	..
Ethiopia	..	..	..	..	..	..	193	362	409	426	526	..	..	..
Gabon	14	8	7	3	6	7	4	5	8	10	10	13.3	-1.1	8.4
Gambia, The	28	13	10	14	12	11	15	15	16	16	12	-5.0	-22.1	2.9
Ghana	744	482	426	413	369	319	302	358	393	638	616	-5.1	3.2	5.2
Guinea	33	32	31	27	23	31	43	45	61	43	48	5.3	10.7	9.4
Guinea-Bissau	6	13	10	13	16	4	14	32	21	22	22	9.0	2.8	12.4
Kenya	693	735	669	687	641	812	975	1,044	1,153	1,165	1,157	6.5	-1.8	9.1
Lesotho	16	25	21	13	12	13	12	13	12	9	9	7.0	7.7	-7.7
Liberia	151	119	135	23	27	23	32	24	13	13	20	5.7	0.6	-16.5
Madagascar	334	180	206	176	157	143	133	237	200	138	92	2.6	-4.9	-4.8
Malawi	251	274	249	376	462	371	286	288	389	383	359	9.2	-0.6	1.5
Mali	192	208	240	251	267	266	251	239	270	312	271	12.3	3.8	1.8
Mauritania	39	33	34	44	47	48	49	31	38	40	40	7.3	-0.6	-0.6
Mauritius	302	356	346	379	365	402	367	367	420	501	405	-1.1	13.2	2.8
Mozambique	157	47	44	41	45	53	26	64	67	50	50	-8.0	1.4	3.4
Namibia	188	161	170	147	180	200	185	201	199	202	201	-8.0	18.9	3.1
Niger	86	50	54	62	65	55	48	48	45	45	45	8.4	-7.5	-4.1
Nigeria	446	440	255	230	214	189	275	327	403	542	522	-4.4	-2.5	12.9
Rwanda	66	99	113	95	85	60	52	14	42	39	38	5.5	8.6	-15.1
São Tomé and Principe	19	6	5	4	4	4	4	5	2	3	3	0.1	-9.9	-5.5
Senegal	115	153	204	219	135	126	91	126	115	87	58	-5.6	7.7	-12.7
Seychelles	3	1	1	1	1	1	1	1	2	2	2	-1.8	-16.3	16.3
Sierra Leone	59	31	21	18	24	11	9	21	15	16	14	-0.3	-11.6	-3.9
Somalia	125	76	75	74	41	62	60	68	75	76	76	4.9	3.6	2.4
South Africa	2,517	1,517	2,012	1,918	1,838	1,792	1,580	2,118	2,284	2,489	2,464	0.6	10.6	3.7
Sudan	553	507	662	550	381	367	455	471	501	565	556	1.9	5.8	0.3
Swaziland	211	272	253	347	339	306	265	283	291	311	300	6.7	20.8	0.0
Tanzania	406	289	299	279	243	281	303	379	431	496	400	-0.2	-0.6	7.5
Togo	77	100	92	120	101	125	75	76	127	133	128	5.4	4.8	2.7
Uganda	344	284	280	173	167	134	180	425	469	491	405	1.1	-7.4	13.9
Zambia	13	13	20	24	29	36	27	16	32	46	50	-8.1	10.3	8.7
Zimbabwe	453	608	592	750	731	584	617	1,177	895	1,207	1,157	4.4	5.0	9.1
NORTH AFRICA	1,544	1,310	1,296	1,406	1,591	1,396	1,313	1,708	1,892	1,876	1,895	-2.1	1.0	5.0
Algeria	120	30	35	50	54	76	97	35	108	137	91	-12.7	-9.2	13.2
Egypt, Arab Republic	677	514	532	427	391	401	360	553	536	521	442	-1.9	-6.9	1.4
Libya	0	0	0	0	0	0	0	0	0	0	0	-58.1	3.9	26.4
Morocco	606	572	520	647	670	581	509	598	780	896	832	0.4	11.9	5.5
Tunisia	140	193	208	282	477	338	347	523	468	322	530	-2.7	8.0	7.8
ALL AFRICA	13,756	11,408	12,007	11,764	11,154	10,654	10,630	13,214	15,000	16,188	15,263	1.2	1.9	4.6

8-8. Cereal production

	Thousands of metric tons											Average annual percentage growth		
	1980	*1992*	*1993*	*1994*	*1995*	*1996*	*1997*	*1998*	*1999*	*2000*	*2001*	*75-84*	*85-89*	*90-MR*
SUB-SAHARAN AFRICA	49,742	60,609	78,249	83,873	76,333	90,302	85,837	86,141	85,635	89,639	87,894	-0.6	8.0	2.8
excluding South Africa	36,369	55,564	65,456	67,906	68,842	76,655	72,607	75,950	75,600	75,906	78,291	0.0	7.3	3.4
excl. S.Africa & Nigeria	28,581	35,967	45,366	47,533	46,329	54,990	50,754	53,910	53,195	53,015	55,400	-0.3	5.7	4.0
Angola	435	402	322	285	296	525	457	621	550	575	585	-6.0	-1.4	7.4
Benin	346	609	625	645	734	714	906	867	890	878	878	3.0	2.0	4.8
Botswana	44	20	43	52	42	111	31	12	20	22	22	-20.5	60.0	-8.8
Burkina Faso	1,048	2,479	2,527	2,232	2,308	2,482	2,014	2,657	2,700	2,286	2,796	0.3	10.9	2.5
Burundi	217	306	300	225	269	273	305	261	265	245	272	3.9	5.4	-1.2
Cameroon	892	1,019	986	961	1,180	1,296	1,268	1,418	1,196	1,411	1,441	-1.6	3.5	4.7
Cape Verde	9	10	12	8	8	10	5	3	36	21	21	2.1	52.9	5.1
Central African Republic	100	94	94	101	113	126	138	148	173	184	195	1.4	4.0	6.2
Chad	573	977	680	1,073	907	878	986	1,342	1,230	1,156	1,156	-5.2	8.6	5.8
Comoros	18	20	21	21	21	21	21	21	21	21	21	1.4	1.4	0.8
Congo, Democratic Rep. of	889	1,553	1,655	1,708	1,475	1,557	1,584	1,675	1,643	1,616	1,590	3.9	5.8	0.8
Congo, Republic of	12	6	7	7	9	10	10	11	7	8	8	-6.2	8.1	-0.8
Côte d'Ivoire	860	1,262	1,286	1,331	1,409	1,800	1,961	1,878	1,858	1,970	1,808	2.6	1.7	4.9
Djibouti	0	0	0	0	0	0	0	0	0	0	0	..	-5.1	5.2
Equatorial Guinea	..	..	..	..	..	..	..	..	..	..	..	..	..	..
Eritrea	..	..	87	253	..	85	99	458	427	110	219	..	..	8.8
Ethiopia	..	..	5,295	5,245	6,740	9,379	9,473	7,197	8,013	9,691	8,732	..	..	6.8
Gabon	11	26	27	29	24	24	25	26	26	27	27	5.7	12.4	1.2
Gambia, The	70	96	97	95	98	103	100	106	151	176	190	7.0	0.1	5.1
Ghana	674	1,254	1,645	1,594	1,797	1,770	1,669	1,788	1,686	1,711	1,711	-0.6	3.9	4.3
Guinea	725	683	711	718	825	879	927	985	952	1,103	1,103	1.2	-4.6	5.5
Guinea-Bissau	93	169	181	190	201	174	142	137	139	166	166	8.3	-1.6	-0.9
Kenya	2,233	2,849	2,530	3,663	3,275	2,714	2,711	2,962	2,778	2,663	3,167	-2.3	9.8	-0.1
Lesotho	194	94	153	223	81	256	206	171	174	394	398	-4.8	9.5	7.3
Liberia	243	110	65	50	56	94	168	209	196	183	183	2.2	0.2	2.5
Madagascar	2,238	2,591	2,724	2,517	2,642	2,685	2,742	2,610	2,829	2,460	2,460	0.5	1.5	0.1
Malawi	1,252	689	2,137	1,109	1,778	1,943	1,349	1,904	2,635	2,658	2,658	0.6	1.4	6.1
Mali	968	1,809	2,228	2,457	2,173	2,201	2,124	2,529	2,894	2,310	2,866	0.5	12.0	2.5
Mauritania	47	107	169	207	222	234	154	189	146	185	201	1.8	25.5	3.6
Mauritius	1	2	2	1	0	0	0	0	0	1	1	-0.9	-9.5	-17.6
Mozambique	663	242	765	791	1,127	1,379	1,531	1,688	1,822	1,473	1,674	-1.0	-4.7	12.9
Namibia	74	31	75	116	62	89	173	55	72	139	107	3.7	3.5	2.0
Niger	1,775	2,255	2,024	2,430	2,096	2,232	1,725	2,982	2,864	2,127	3,161	3.2	9.7	2.4
Nigeria	7,788	19,597	20,091	20,373	22,513	21,665	21,853	22,040	22,405	22,891	22,891	1.3	11.4	2.3
Rwanda	273	240	234	133	142	183	223	194	179	240	297	4.4	-3.0	-1.5
São Tomé and Principe	0	4	4	4	3	3	1	1	1	2	2	1.5	24.6	-5.2
Senegal	676	856	1,086	943	1,059	976	781	717	1,131	1,026	1,026	-1.6	3.2	-0.2
Seychelles	..	..	..	..	..	..	..	..	..	..	..	..	..	..
Sierra Leone	551	534	542	466	408	444	467	373	280	222	222	-1.0	1.0	-7.7
Somalia	267	209	165	405	285	290	284	232	208	313	313	8.2	5.2	-3.9
South Africa	13,373	5,044	12,792	15,967	7,491	13,648	13,230	10,191	10,035	13,732	9,603	-3.3	10.9	-0.2
Sudan	2,701	5,438	3,102	5,146	3,305	5,202	4,261	5,530	3,108	3,332	3,365	-3.5	4.1	3.2
Swaziland	105	58	75	101	79	152	110	126	114	86	86	-4.2	-6.3	-0.5
Tanzania	2,961	3,533	3,917	3,550	4,629	4,719	3,390	4,495	3,801	3,429	4,131	5.8	6.6	-0.4
Togo	296	495	633	561	550	687	748	620	759	736	740	4.1	6.4	3.9
Uganda	1,078	1,743	1,880	1,936	2,030	1,588	1,625	2,085	2,178	2,112	2,309	-4.5	10.3	2.7
Zambia	984	612	1,758	1,170	882	1,573	1,137	798	1,057	1,037	1,069	-6.3	16.3	-2.6
Zimbabwe	1,989	481	2,498	2,780	987	3,127	2,723	1,829	1,987	2,513	2,027	-4.1	5.6	1.5
NORTH AFRICA	16,445	23,322	21,343	26,455	20,803	34,593	24,318	29,519	27,330	24,350	28,611	-0.3	5.1	1.7
Algeria	2,419	3,330	1,454	965	2,140	4,902	870	3,026	2,021	935	2,502	-2.5	-4.7	-2.0
Egypt, Arab Republic	8,100	14,611	14,961	15,012	16,097	16,542	18,071	17,964	19,401	20,106	19,464	1.0	5.4	4.5
Libya	215	218	180	165	146	160	206	213	213	213	218	4.2	3.8	-2.3
Morocco	4,515	2,950	2,818	9,639	1,783	10,104	4,098	6,632	3,860	2,009	4,607	-2.2	12.2	-4.6
Tunisia	1,197	2,213	1,931	675	637	2,885	1,072	1,684	1,836	1,088	1,820	0.5	-18.2	1.2
ALL AFRICA	66,187	83,931	99,592	110,327	97,136	124,895	110,155	115,661	112,965	113,988	116,505	-0.5	7.3	2.5

8-9. Crop production index

	Index (average 1989-91 = 100)											Average annual percentage growth		
	1980	1992	1993	1994	1995	1996	1997	1998	1999	2000	2001	75-84	85-89	90-MR
SUB-SAHARAN AFRICA	77	106	110	117	117	128	127	132	134	134	136	-0.4	4.8	2.9
excluding South Africa	76	110	113	118	120	130	129	136	137	136	139	-0.4	4.6	3.1
excl. S.Africa & Nigeria	82	104	105	111	112	121	119	126	126	124	128	-0.3	3.2	2.4
Angola	107	111	108	137	132	134	128	158	145	154	155	-6.5	0.9	4.3
Benin	52	111	127	129	146	163	178	174	172	189	185	3.2	4.3	6.5
Botswana	91	68	87	97	81	135	84	72	81	80	80	-6.4	13.1	-1.6
Burkina Faso	55	116	120	113	113	128	125	147	150	124	139	2.2	8.1	3.2
Burundi	77	108	105	90	96	96	96	90	93	87	97	0.8	3.3	-0.9
Cameroon	87	103	108	115	123	132	123	132	137	129	133	0.4	0.6	3.1
Cape Verde	79	73	82	73	70	99	82	86	129	107	107	3.0	22.5	1.3
Central African Republic	103	98	97	107	112	124	129	131	134	133	134	0.0	1.8	3.3
Chad	70	118	88	117	123	133	152	173	154	138	142	-1.2	6.6	4.5
Comoros	80	104	108	111	115	113	116	126	133	120	121	0.8	4.6	2.2
Congo, Democratic Rep. of	74	105	104	106	90	89	86	87	84	82	80	2.4	2.8	-2.2
Congo, Republic of	86	98	100	108	114	119	119	115	124	126	128	1.8	1.3	2.4
Côte d'Ivoire	71	102	99	101	114	123	128	125	130	146	132	3.3	4.8	3.3
Djibouti	66	104	105	108	110	112	116	116	121	122	122	29.6	2.4	2.0
Equatorial Guinea	77	100	97	97	98	98	96	95	101	99	99	0.6	1.5	0.0
Eritrea	..	..	93	158	133	110	109	211	171	129	146	..	..	4.0
Ethiopia	..	..	109	110	128	153	154	135	146	160	154	..	..	4.5
Gabon	79	103	100	103	106	109	113	117	117	121	122	4.6	4.0	2.0
Gambia, The	66	69	85	88	84	63	86	82	129	146	160	-1.0	4.0	3.3
Ghana	68	120	130	123	144	156	152	167	175	178	183	-2.5	4.7	6.1
Guinea	92	118	119	123	126	129	135	143	146	158	158	0.9	-1.1	4.3
Guinea-Bissau	63	104	104	106	113	116	126	130	139	145	150	3.7	1.8	3.8
Kenya	72	98	94	109	112	110	105	115	110	109	112	1.6	6.3	1.2
Lesotho	94	68	88	120	70	136	131	111	113	190	191	-4.2	9.4	5.7
Liberia	..	..	..	..	..	..	..	..	..	..	..	..	..	..
Madagascar	85	100	106	100	102	104	106	104	109	100	100	0.3	1.1	0.3
Malawi	84	83	115	89	111	127	125	139	142	152	154	2.0	1.2	4.7
Mali	51	99	100	115	117	123	128	140	145	107	153	0.1	11.4	3.5
Mauritania	61	89	111	138	149	152	140	136	118	138	145	2.4	17.5	3.5
Mauritius	80	105	101	92	100	98	106	104	75	95	101	0.1	0.1	-0.6
Mozambique	111	79	93	91	113	130	141	155	157	131	135	-2.3	0.5	4.6
Namibia	80	74	88	103	92	104	132	100	111	131	123	1.9	2.2	2.7
Niger	92	113	89	126	103	127	92	173	147	128	158	2.1	9.2	4.0
Nigeria	51	120	126	130	135	144	147	153	157	161	161	-1.0	10.1	4.7
Rwanda	82	110	81	49	64	73	76	82	87	108	107	4.3	0.4	-0.2
São Tomé and Principe	117	123	127	131	124	134	139	148	160	166	166	-2.7	0.4	4.6
Senegal	57	84	94	96	110	97	88	82	132	127	129	-5.1	8.8	2.0
Seychelles	190	86	87	103	118	124	116	107	100	101	101	-2.8	-11.1	0.9
Sierra Leone	81	92	91	98	90	95	102	92	78	70	70	1.0	2.2	-2.5
Somalia	..	..	..	..	..	..	..	..	..	..	..	..	..	..
South Africa	92	68	93	106	81	110	108	99	107	113	101	-0.5	6.9	1.3
Sudan	124	145	112	157	149	180	173	170	157	159	163	-2.4	-0.9	5.1
Swaziland	74	82	77	84	71	87	88	87	95	84	84	3.6	1.9	-0.9
Tanzania	79	94	94	92	99	103	95	99	99	93	100	3.0	1.3	-0.1
Togo	71	98	116	114	114	142	146	141	142	139	141	1.8	5.2	3.9
Uganda	65	100	108	108	112	109	108	120	133	133	141	-3.2	4.4	2.9
Zambia	65	66	119	91	85	110	97	87	102	98	103	-2.5	10.6	0.3
Zimbabwe	76	59	100	106	78	120	126	117	113	134	118	-0.6	4.0	3.1
NORTH AFRICA	78	113	112	110	110	146	124	136	141	137	142	1.0	3.7	3.0
Algeria	81	127	109	93	114	155	104	130	135	114	135	-1.6	2.3	2.5
Egypt, Arab Republic	77	112	116	112	123	135	138	136	148	154	152	2.1	3.3	4.2
Libya	79	100	104	108	116	125	127	130	133	134	135	4.1	1.8	3.2
Morocco	59	73	74	110	62	122	91	111	97	87	95	0.6	9.7	0.4
Tunisia	75	103	114	73	68	144	87	115	128	122	117	0.6	-2.3	2.4
ALL AFRICA	77	108	111	115	115	131	126	133	136	135	137	-0.1	4.6	2.9

8-10. Fertilizer use

	Thousands of metric tons											Average annual percentage growth		
	1980	1991	1992	1993	1994	1995	1996	1997	1998	1999	2000	75-84	85-89	90-MR
SUB-SAHARAN AFRICA	1,973	1,927	1,917	2,169	1,957	1,834	2,100	2,006	2,009	2,074	1,983	4.4	1.4	0.0
excluding South Africa	909	1,186	1,184	1,326	1,204	1,067	1,296	1,245	1,226	1,297	1,225	5.3	5.6	0.0
excl. S.Africa & Nigeria	735	757	744	865	908	884	1,122	1,107	1,062	1,114	1,039	2.4	5.1	3.2
Angola	17	7	9	8	10	8	6	2	3	3	1	-0.5	16.0	-17.2
Benin	1	12	15	17	17	36	31	39	38	57	35	7.5	-15.0	21.7
Botswana	1	1	1	1	1	2	3	4	4	5	5	-5.7	2.7	21.3
Burkina Faso	4	21	21	21	23	24	24	43	50	43	34	23.4	11.1	8.0
Burundi	1	2	5	4	3	3	3	1	4	4	4	11.4	15.1	-1.0
Cameroon	32	18	21	22	30	30	34	39	40	48	48	12.9	-7.8	8.3
Cape Verde	0	0	0	0	0	0	0	0	0	0	0	-0.6	6.3	..
Central African Republic	1	1	1	1	0	0	0	0	1	1	1	-11.1	-17.9	-6.8
Chad	1	9	10	5	7	9	12	8	17	18	18	-4.9	-7.3	11.1
Comoros	0	0	0	0	0	0	0	0	0	0	0	..	..	15.0
Congo, Democratic Rep. of	8	8	2	4	10	9	6	0	3	1	1	0.1	-9.8	-16.1
Congo, Republic of	1	1	2	2	2	2	4	4	5	5	5	4.0	-33.9	18.9
Côte d'Ivoire	53	39	37	54	65	66	71	110	90	71	73	1.4	-6.6	9.5
Djibouti	1	0	0	0	0	0	0	0	0	0	0	-44.2	..	..
Equatorial Guinea	0	0	0	0	0	0	0	0	0	0	0	0.0	..	..
Eritrea	..	..	..	1	1	2	5	6	7	11	11	..	..	50.3
Ethiopia	..	..	..	76	116	134	178	132	164	168	157	..	..	9.0
Gabon	0	1	1	0	0	0	0	0	0	0	0	28.9	-18.8	-11.8
Gambia, The	2	1	1	1	1	1	1	1	3	1	1	7.9	-13.3	1.8
Ghana	12	8	10	8	8	10	17	21	15	15	12	-0.9	1.3	5.8
Guinea	0	2	1	2	4	5	4	2	3	3	3	-15.8	29.7	14.0
Guinea-Bissau	0	1	0	0	0	0	0	0	1	1	2	9.8	..	4.8
Kenya	62	113	102	100	130	78	161	134	127	150	141	6.1	4.8	3.3
Lesotho	5	6	6	6	5	6	6	6	6	5	6	18.1	2.3	1.0
Liberia	3	0	0	0	0	0	0	0	0	0	0	-11.1	24.9	..
Madagascar	9	9	8	11	11	13	17	10	9	8	9	3.1	-1.5	1.1
Malawi	33	70	74	74	21	44	58	57	50	50	33	12.4	8.8	-3.1
Mali	14	15	27	25	25	27	27	48	46	50	52	14.3	-16.4	12.4
Mauritania	1	5	7	5	4	4	5	2	2	2	0	-9.6	28.4	-6.2
Mauritius	27	28	27	26	29	32	38	33	33	35	36	0.7	2.7	2.6
Mozambique	28	5	5	3	6	8	8	7	8	8	14	6.5	-13.1	13.9
Namibia	0	0	0	0	0	0	0	0	0	0	0	..	..	..
Niger	3	1	1	2	6	10	9	1	1	4	5	23.0	-2.8	4.6
Nigeria	174	429	440	461	296	183	174	138	164	183	187	23.8	7.1	-10.1
Rwanda	0	2	1	1	0	0	0	0	0	0	0	11.8	-18.3	-15.2
São Tomé and Principe	..	..	..	..	..	..	..	..	..	..	..	..	..	..
Senegal	19	17	17	24	26	16	22	23	27	41	45	-8.9	-3.7	10.9
Seychelles	0	0	0	0	0	0	0	0	0	0	0	..	..	..
Sierra Leone	2	1	1	3	3	3	3	3	0	0	0	-3.5	-17.8	-16.3
Somalia	1	0	0	0	0	0	1	1	1	1	1	7.3	8.6	-16.5
South Africa	1,064	740	733	843	752	767	804	761	783	777	758	3.6	-3.8	0.0
Sudan	81	56	60	53	58	52	95	77	38	39	38	-1.5	-1.0	-3.3
Swaziland	20	12	12	12	5	5	4	5	6	6	6	4.0	11.8	-9.9
Tanzania	36	50	48	36	36	27	31	40	30	21	22	-1.0	36.5	-13.3
Togo	3	12	12	10	11	16	18	17	17	17	20	8.6	10.8	5.4
Uganda	1	1	1	2	2	1	1	1	4	4	5	-16.2	-5.2	22.8
Zambia	79	62	85	85	59	55	51	57	37	34	30	2.2	6.4	-7.7
Zimbabwe	173	164	114	159	171	145	168	175	175	185	165	2.0	0.1	1.5
NORTH AFRICA	1,221	1,527	1,456	1,660	1,421	1,621	1,645	1,661	1,768	1,847	1,892	6.5	0.8	1.9
Algeria	236	92	97	131	119	46	38	97	108	93	92	1.6	-12.9	-3.1
Egypt, Arab Republic	664	963	877	988	843	1,126	1,158	1,079	1,171	1,197	1,270	7.5	2.7	3.0
Libya	53	85	86	111	75	89	62	62	51	87	57	14.2	-0.6	-3.2
Morocco	207	289	291	334	295	282	290	327	325	359	362	5.4	3.7	0.9
Tunisia	62	99	105	95	89	77	97	97	114	112	111	6.3	3.0	1.4
ALL AFRICA	3,194	3,454	3,373	3,829	3,378	3,455	3,744	3,667	3,777	3,921	3,876	5.3	1.2	0.8

8-11. Fertilizer imports

	Thousands of metric tons											Average annual percentage growth		
	1980	1990	1991	1992	1993	1994	1995	1996	1997	1998	1999	75-84	85-89	90-MR
SUB-SAHARAN AFRICA	971	1,088	1,043	1,154	1,273	1,218	1,005	1,429	1,424	1,443	1,513	5.9	-1.5	3.8
excluding South Africa	742	933	858	950	1,074	1,019	820	1,207	1,155	1,155	1,187	6.8	-1.0	3.2
excl. S.Africa & Nigeria	565	645	651	710	793	729	796	1,130	1,064	1,000	1,070	3.7	2.6	6.0
Angola	17	7	7	9	8	10	8	6	2	5	2	-0.2	19.3	-14.9
Benin	1	11	12	16	18	17	36	30	39	38	57	6.7	-16.1	25.1
Botswana	1	1	1	1	1	1	3	4	4	4	5	-5.7	2.7	22.5
Burkina Faso	5	19	21	21	21	23	24	31	44	50	51	23.7	14.8	10.5
Burundi	1	2	2	6	5	3	3	3	1	4	4	11.9	13.6	-2.9
Cameroon	32	23	18	21	22	47	32	34	39	40	50	13.2	-10.2	8.2
Cape Verde	0	0	0	0	0	0	0	0	0	0	0	-0.6	..	..
Central African Republic	1	1	1	1	1	0	0	0	0	1	1	-11.1	-17.9	-8.9
Chad	1	6	9	10	5	8	8	24	8	17	18	-4.9	-7.3	12.0
Comoros	0	0	0	0	0	0	0	0	0	0	0	..	..	17.9
Congo, Democratic Rep. of	8	6	8	2	4	10	9	6	0	3	1	0.1	-9.8	-12.9
Congo, Republic of	1	2	1	2	2	3	3	4	4	5	5	34.9	-38.7	20.7
Côte d'Ivoire	45	36	41	68	52	79	87	75	181	135	107	6.4	-9.3	15.7
Djibouti	1	0	0	0	0	0	0	0	0	0	0	-44.2	..	..
Equatorial Guinea	0	0	0	0	0	0	0	0	0	0	0	0.0	..	..
Eritrea	..	..	..	..	1	2	2	6	6	7	11	..	..	48.8
Ethiopia	..	..	..	..	115	35	149	251	93	166	168	..	..	14.3
Gabon	0	1	1	1	0	0	0	0	0	0	0	28.0	-18.8	-21.4
Gambia, The	2	1	1	1	1	1	1	1	1	3	1	7.9	-15.0	3.7
Ghana	12	7	8	11	7	8	10	17	22	15	12	-2.3	15.5	3.9
Guinea	0	1	2	1	2	4	5	4	2	3	3	-16.0	29.7	15.9
Guinea-Bissau	0	1	1	0	0	0	0	0	0	1	1	9.8	..	-2.7
Kenya	62	107	113	102	100	131	78	161	134	127	153	5.2	4.6	3.5
Lesotho	5	5	6	6	6	6	6	7	6	6	6	18.1	2.3	2.2
Liberia	3	0	0	0	0	0	0	0	0	0	0	-11.1	24.9	..
Madagascar	9	11	9	8	11	11	13	17	10	9	5	3.1	-1.5	-0.8
Malawi	33	48	76	68	74	21	44	58	57	50	45	13.9	4.8	-2.2
Mali	14	19	13	27	25	25	27	27	48	46	23	14.3	-16.4	8.4
Mauritania	1	5	7	9	7	4	4	5	2	0	0	-9.6	28.4	-4.8
Mauritius	17	29	25	28	22	24	24	38	36	24	28	0.0	5.5	0.7
Mozambique	20	3	5	5	3	6	9	8	7	8	8	24.2	-23.1	12.8
Namibia	0	0	0	0	0	0	0	0	0	0	0	..	..	..
Niger	3	2	1	1	2	5	8	9	1	1	3	23.0	-2.8	0.1
Nigeria	177	288	207	240	281	290	24	77	92	156	118	23.0	-10.1	-10.4
Rwanda	0	1	2	1	1	0	0	0	0	0	0	11.8	1.3	-16.4
São Tomé and Principe	..	..	..	..	..	..	..	..	..	..	..	..	..	..
Senegal	16	29	31	27	35	14	18	16	34	34	35	-7.7	7.0	0.9
Seychelles	0	0	0	0	0	0	0	0	0	0	0	..	..	..
Sierra Leone	2	1	1	2	3	3	3	3	3	0	0	-4.1	-17.7	0.3
Somalia	2	3	0	0	0	0	0	1	1	1	1	0.9	20.5	..
South Africa	229	155	185	204	198	199	185	222	269	287	326	2.9	-4.1	6.4
Sudan	81	82	56	60	53	60	50	95	77	38	92	0.0	-2.6	1.7
Swaziland	18	13	12	12	12	5	5	4	5	6	6	1.2	11.8	-11.4
Tanzania	20	45	53	40	42	31	27	35	39	30	21	4.0	8.3	-5.8
Togo	3	12	7	12	13	13	14	22	17	17	17	7.6	9.6	6.4
Uganda	1	0	1	1	2	2	1	1	1	4	4	-13.1	-5.2	21.2
Zambia	69	62	63	86	68	53	52	47	53	34	51	-1.1	42.3	-6.7
Zimbabwe	56	46	39	44	49	63	33	81	87	70	77	5.9	0.3	7.8
NORTH AFRICA	588	495	390	344	332	312	381	287	432	473	475	-2.2	0.8	0.0
Algeria	189	40	28	19	26	52	19	51	90	90	86	-1.8	-19.9	11.2
Egypt, Arab Republic	182	189	102	107	59	13	76	33	87	131	126	-10.2	6.6	-5.1
Libya	53	68	76	87	107	73	102	62	62	42	58	11.5	4.2	-4.0
Morocco	133	173	169	126	136	167	177	137	187	195	201	3.3	3.4	2.2
Tunisia	30	26	15	6	4	7	7	4	7	15	5	-0.7	5.7	-6.4
ALL AFRICA	1,559	1,583	1,433	1,498	1,605	1,530	1,386	1,716	1,856	1,915	1,988	3.0	-0.8	2.8

8-12. Area under permanent crops

	Thousands of hectares											Average annual percentage growth		
	1980	*1991*	*1992*	*1993*	*1994*	*1995*	*1996*	*1997*	*1998*	*1999*	*2000*	*75-84*	*85-89*	*90-MR*
SUB-SAHARAN AFRICA	123,663	134,344	135,566	149,757	150,549	152,912	153,462	154,296	155,075	155,330	155,692	0.7	0.8	1.7
excluding South Africa	111,223	120,614	121,546	135,447	135,949	137,997	138,587	139,486	140,284	140,577	140,939	0.9	0.8	1.8
excl. S.Africa & Nigeria	83,373	90,814	91,624	105,403	105,784	107,626	109,887	111,286	112,084	112,377	112,739	1.0	0.8	2.5
Angola	2,900	2,950	3,000	3,000	3,000	3,000	3,000	3,000	3,000	3,000	3,000	0.0	0.0	0.3
Benin	1,500	1,620	1,630	1,650	1,680	1,710	1,750	1,800	1,850	1,900	1,950	1.7	0.6	1.8
Botswana	402	417	415	407	397	343	343	343	343	343	370	0.1	0.3	-2.1
Burkina Faso	2,745	3,495	3,470	3,450	3,381	3,400	3,500	3,600	3,700	3,750	3,800	1.8	4.4	0.7
Burundi	930	930	930	930	920	920	920	910	900	900	900	0.0	0.0	-0.4
Cameroon	5,910	5,950	5,960	5,960	5,960	5,960	5,960	5,960	5,960	5,960	5,960	0.8	0.1	0.0
Cape Verde	38	41	41	41	40	39	39	39	39	39	39	0.0	1.2	-0.5
Central African Republic	1,870	1,920	1,930	1,930	1,930	1,930	1,930	1,930	1,930	1,930	1,930	0.5	0.2	0.0
Chad	3,137	3,322	3,342	3,370	3,390	3,420	3,470	3,500	3,520	3,520	3,520	0.5	0.6	0.8
Comoros	75	78	78	78	78	78	78	78	78	78	78	0.0	0.7	0.0
Congo, Democratic Rep. of	6,620	6,680	6,700	6,700	6,700	6,700	6,700	6,700	6,700	6,700	6,700	0.2	0.1	0.0
Congo, Republic of	138	156	155	160	163	165	167	170	173	175	175	1.5	1.0	1.4
Côte d'Ivoire	1,955	2,450	2,600	2,902	2,905	2,920	2,930	2,950	2,950	2,950	2,950	1.9	0.9	2.1
Djibouti	..	..	..	..	..	..	..	..	..	..	..	..	..	..
Equatorial Guinea	130	130	130	130	130	130	130	130	130	130	130	0.0	0.0	0.0
Eritrea	..	..	..	498	437	438	369	391	498	498	498	..	..	1.3
Ethiopia	..	..	..	10,000	9,822	9,850	9,850	9,900	9,950	10,000	10,000	..	..	0.1
Gabon	290	295	295	295	295	325	325	325	325	325	325	2.5	0.0	1.3
Gambia, The	155	191	157	156	175	180	185	195	205	220	230	1.0	2.5	2.4
Ghana	1,900	2,800	2,800	2,800	2,800	2,800	2,800	3,600	3,600	3,600	3,609	2.5	2.6	3.3
Guinea	702	735	755	785	820	883	885	885	885	885	885	0.4	0.3	2.3
Guinea-Bissau	255	300	300	300	300	300	300	300	300	300	300	1.0	1.0	0.0
Kenya	3,800	4,000	4,000	4,000	4,000	4,000	4,000	4,000	4,000	4,000	4,000	0.4	0.7	0.0
Lesotho	292	319	332	330	325	320	322	325	325	325	325	-2.3	1.5	0.4
Liberia	371	390	390	370	370	370	370	370	380	380	380	0.4	1.2	-0.5
Madagascar	2,540	2,750	2,780	2,800	2,800	2,800	2,800	2,820	2,850	2,900	2,900	1.8	0.7	0.6
Malawi	1,518	1,823	1,830	1,837	1,845	1,875	1,900	1,950	2,000	2,050	2,100	3.0	0.7	1.3
Mali	2,010	2,063	2,163	3,060	3,160	3,379	4,606	4,606	4,606	4,606	4,630	1.0	0.4	9.9
Mauritania	210	410	420	431	470	498	488	488	488	488	488	4.0	6.3	2.5
Mauritius	100	100	100	100	100	100	100	100	100	100	100	0.0	0.0	0.0
Mozambique	2,870	3,500	3,520	3,520	3,570	3,650	3,750	3,900	4,000	3,950	3,900	0.7	2.0	1.5
Namibia	655	660	660	698	747	816	816	816	816	816	816	0.1	0.0	2.6
Niger	3,544	3,595	3,990	4,090	4,090	4,190	4,190	4,190	4,490	4,490	4,490	4.3	0.5	2.2
Nigeria	27,850	29,800	29,922	30,044	30,165	30,371	28,700	28,200	28,200	28,200	28,200	0.3	0.7	-0.6
Rwanda	760	880	880	850	700	700	750	800	820	866	900	2.0	0.8	-0.3
São Tomé and Principe	1	2	2	2	3	3	4	4	4	4	4	0.0	10.4	8.9
Senegal	2,341	2,323	2,320	2,318	2,331	2,230	2,250	2,254	2,263	2,313	2,362	0.0	-0.1	-0.1
Seychelles	1	1	1	1	1	1	1	1	1	1	1	0.0	0.0	0.0
Sierra Leone	450	486	486	486	485	485	485	484	484	484	490	1.1	0.7	0.0
Somalia	984	1,022	1,023	1,024	1,030	1,035	1,039	1,043	1,043	1,043	1,043	0.5	0.4	0.2
South Africa	12,440	13,730	14,020	14,310	14,600	14,915	14,875	14,810	14,791	14,753	14,753	-0.2	1.3	1.1
Sudan	12,360	13,000	12,900	14,618	15,000	16,157	16,672	16,600	16,500	16,380	16,233	0.4	0.6	2.8
Swaziland	185	183	179	178	178	178	178	178	178	178	178	-0.9	3.1	-0.4
Tanzania	3,100	3,550	3,600	3,650	3,700	3,748	3,750	3,750	3,750	3,750	4,000	4.8	1.1	1.0
Togo	1,950	2,100	2,100	2,200	2,200	2,200	2,300	2,330	2,410	2,510	2,510	1.2	0.6	1.9
Uganda	4,080	5,020	5,040	5,040	5,060	5,060	5,060	5,060	5,060	5,060	5,060	1.5	0.8	0.1
Zambia	5,094	5,249	5,254	5,254	5,254	5,260	5,260	5,260	5,260	5,260	5,260	0.4	0.4	0.0
Zimbabwe	2,505	2,928	2,966	3,004	3,042	3,080	3,165	3,251	3,220	3,220	3,220	0.8	1.4	1.3
NORTH AFRICA	21,635	22,962	23,668	23,951	23,996	23,969	24,310	24,337	24,222	24,049	23,991	-0.1	0.6	0.6
Algeria	6,875	7,260	7,562	7,533	7,477	7,519	7,521	7,650	7,661	7,673	7,675	0.0	0.7	0.7
Egypt, Arab Republic	2,286	2,267	2,449	2,617	2,740	2,817	2,820	2,834	2,834	2,834	2,825	-1.8	-0.1	2.4
Libya	1,753	1,810	1,815	1,815	1,825	1,870	2,028	2,028	1,815	1,815	1,815	0.2	0.3	0.4
Morocco	7,530	8,717	8,934	8,999	9,124	8,921	9,096	8,980	9,033	8,818	8,767	0.8	1.5	0.3
Tunisia	3,191	2,908	2,908	2,987	2,830	2,842	2,845	2,845	2,879	2,909	2,909	-1.1	-1.4	-0.1
ALL AFRICA	145,298	157,306	159,234	173,708	174,545	176,881	177,772	178,633	179,297	179,379	179,683	0.6	0.8	1.6

8-13. Agricultural yields by major crop

	Thousands of hectograms per hectare												Average annual* percentage growth		
	1980	*1992*	*1993*	*1994*	*1995*	*1996*	*1997*	*1998*	*1999*	*2000*	*2001*	*2002*	*75-84*	*85-89*	*90-MR*
ALGERIA															
Wheat	7.3	9.9	8.1	8.0	8.9	13.1	8.0	8.8	10.7	9.2	11.0	11.0	2.7	3.0	1.6
Citrus	262.9	92.5	87.1	91.4	80.2	86.1	87.2	101.8	111.3	104.6	106.6	106.6	-1.8	-0.8	1.9
Dates	30.0	31.2	31.0	37.2	32.8	37.3	31.4	39.5	42.7	36.5	37.0	37.0	3.7	3.6	3.1
Barley	8.4	9.0	6.3	6.5	7.1	14.0	7.2	7.5	10.9	7.6	11.1	11.1	6.8	2.3	1.0
Potatoes	77.7	107.9	111.2	95.1	136.8	134.6	141.0	160.3	153.5	166.1	160.0	160.0	0.2	-1.5	3.7
ANGOLA															
Coffee(green)	2.2	0.5	0.5	0.3	0.4	0.3	0.3	0.4	0.4	0.4	0.4	0.4	-8.1	-6.5	-0.9
Maize	6.0	3.8	2.6	2.5	3.5	7.0	6.0	7.4	6.4	5.7	6.1	6.1	-2.0	4.0	4.7
Millet	7.1	4.8	2.7	5.4	5.1	4.8	3.8	5.0	5.3	5.3	6.3	6.3	-2.5	0.5	1.3
Wheat	5.8	8.0	8.6	10.0	16.7	16.7	16.7	17.1	17.4	17.4	17.5	17.5	-5.6	-0.7	5.3
Cassava	33.8	42.3	42.3	58.6	51.0	48.1	44.2	55.7	59.8	83.0	94.1	94.1	-0.7	-1.3	4.0
Sweet potatoes	91.7	90.0	88.1	85.7	88.1	85.5	85.9	86.4	82.9	34.9	44.5	44.5	0.1	0.1	-2.1
BENIN															
Seed Cotton	6.6	12.0	17.9	13.9	13.3	12.0	10.1	9.7	10.1	10.6	11.0	11.7	-0.6	-3.2	-1.1
Maize	7.4	9.8	9.8	10.2	11.7	10.8	12.0	11.1	12.5	11.5	11.0	8.8	0.3	-4.0	1.3
Sorghum	6.3	7.7	7.6	7.8	8.2	7.6	8.1	8.2	8.2	8.8	9.1	10.1	-1.2	0.1	0.8
Cassava	65.9	83.8	84.9	81.5	78.4	87.2	103.3	105.0	104.5	107.1	112.6	92.7	-2.4	-2.4	1.5
Yams	97.2	106.0	107.7	108.4	109.7	103.0	107.9	109.5	113.3	111.8	109.2	107.1	0.6	-1.4	-0.1
BOTSWANA															
Sorghum	2.2	2.9	2.9	2.2	2.1	2.6	2.1	1.8	1.9	1.1	1.1	1.1	-15.4	-11.3	-4.5
Maize	2.5	1.9	1.4	1.7	1.2	2.5	3.9	1.4	2.5	1.1	1.1	1.1	-12.7	13.1	-4.1
Millet	1.6	1.3	1.4	3.6	1.0	3.7	2.5	1.7	1.9	1.7	1.7	1.7	-8.0	-21.2	1.8
BURKINA FASO															
Seed Cotton	8.3	10.0	9.6	8.9	10.3	10.1	12.4	9.7	12.1	10.2	11.4	11.4	6.2	-2.7	0.1
Groundnuts	5.1	6.2	9.5	8.4	6.6	10.4	6.5	10.0	10.4	7.1	9.1	9.1	3.1	-3.8	3.3
Sorghum	5.7	9.4	11.0	7.8	8.8	9.1	6.8	8.5	8.9	8.3	9.3	9.3	1.3	-1.3	0.9
Millet	4.9	6.5	7.0	6.3	7.2	7.5	5.2	7.8	7.4	6.4	7.6	7.7	2.8	-1.9	2.0
Maize	9.0	15.2	13.7	16.0	11.4	15.5	15.2	13.9	16.2	17.5	18.1	18.2	0.7	-3.9	0.6
BURUNDI															
Coffee	6.3	9.3	8.2	9.4	7.3	7.9	7.0	6.1	9.4	7.4	7.2	8.3	0.9	2.5	-0.5
Tea	4.0	10.7	9.0	10.4	9.8	7.5	5.6	8.9	9.2	9.7	9.9	9.9	-4.2	3.4	0.9
Maize	10.8	14.2	14.3	12.3	12.8	13.1	12.6	11.5	11.2	10.5	10.8	10.8	0.4	-0.4	-1.6
Sorghum	10.0	11.5	11.3	9.9	13.2	13.2	12.4	12.5	12.0	12.2	12.6	12.6	0.1	1.5	0.5
Rice, paddy	23.5	31.1	30.9	29.4	26.8	27.9	32.6	29.9	32.6	30.4	32.1	32.1	2.1	-6.2	-0.2
Millet	10.0	11.0	10.3	11.1	14.4	11.3	16.7	11.1	11.2	10.5	10.5	10.5	0.5	-0.3	-0.5
Bananas	..	..	..	..	..	..	..	..	..	..	..	..	..	..	..
Cassava	90.9	92.0	89.9	87.9	83.5	85.8	86.2	88.8	88.2	90.0	89.1	89.1	-0.1	0.4	-0.1
CAMEROON															
Coffee	3.0	2.6	2.5	3.0	3.0	3.9	1.8	3.8	3.3	2.9	2.8	2.8	5.8	-8.5	0.3
Cocoa	2.6	2.9	2.9	3.1	3.7	3.5	3.5	3.5	3.1	3.3	3.1	3.1	3.3	-0.4	0.3
Seed Cotton	12.9	12.7	12.3	10.8	10.3	11.7	10.9	11.3	10.9	10.3	11.9	10.0	6.7	-3.1	-0.9
Maize	8.3	14.0	11.3	11.6	15.5	18.8	20.3	18.9	25.9	26.2	24.3	24.3	-0.7	-0.6	1.9
Sorghum	8.7	7.6	7.6	7.3	8.7	8.3	8.9	11.1	11.2	12.0	12.5	12.5	1.2	-4.6	2.5
Millet	7.6	10.0	10.3	10.0	10.2	10.1	10.1	10.1	10.1	10.1	10.1	35.0	0.8	-5.0	0.9
Rice	23.4	35.0	29.0	36.2	35.3	31.4	33.6	35.5	33.1	35.0	35.0	35.0	1.8	-1.7	-1.0
Cassava	59.0	136.3	131.8	127.0	118.7	115.5	106.6	90.0	143.5	108.5	113.3	113.3	-1.3	1.0	-1.9
Plantains	..	..	..	..	..	..	..	..	..	..	..	..	..	..	..
CENTRAL AFRICAN REPUBLIC															
Coffee	3.6	5.0	4.1	8.2	4.7	7.2	6.0	4.8	4.5	5.2	4.9	4.9	-1.1	-2.1	-0.8
Seed Cotton	3.4	6.0	6.6	6.6	7.6	7.3	7.3	7.0	7.0	4.6	7.7	8.6	3.9	3.0	0.7
Sorghum	6.5	12.6	11.6	8.0	7.3	7.8	8.4	8.8	12.9	13.6	14.4	14.4	-1.0	-8.4	1.4
Maize	3.8	9.0	9.0	8.5	8.5	8.5	9.2	9.8	10.6	11.2	11.9	11.9	1.1	-1.2	2.0
Groundnuts	10.1	9.8	9.8	9.4	9.4	9.3	8.8	10.2	11.0	11.6	12.2	12.2	-0.8	-2.0	1.5
Cassava	30.7	34.5	34.5	31.0	28.9	29.2	30.5	30.4	28.0	28.0	28.1	28.1	0.8	-0.6	-0.8
Yams	60.0	68.4	65.0	66.7	66.7	68.0	68.0	67.9	67.9	67.9	67.9	67.9	-1.5	-0.7	0.2
CHAD															
Seed Cotton	5.1	6.3	6.1	7.7	7.6	7.9	6.8	5.4	5.9	6.4	6.3	6.1	3.0	3.6	-0.6
Sorghum	5.1	7.4	4.9	7.8	6.5	6.0	5.8	7.2	7.1	6.0	6.3	6.4	0.9	-1.1	1.1
Millet	4.7	5.2	4.2	4.9	3.6	4.1	3.8	4.5	4.6	3.3	4.7	4.5	2.1	-2.1	1.1
Groundnuts	5.7	8.1	7.1	7.5	9.2	9.6	8.8	11.2	9.7	8.2	9.4	9.4	1.1	-4.9	1.6
COMOROS															
Bananas	..	..	..	..	..	..	..	..	..	..	..	..	..	..	..
Cassava	48.5	56.6	57.9	53.6	53.3	54.0	53.9	54.1	54.1	50.0	54.1	55.0	-2.1	1.3	0.4

(Table continues on the following page)

8-13. Agricultural yields by major crop (continued)

	Thousands of hectograms per hectare												Average annual* percentage growth		
	1980	1992	1993	1994	1995	1996	1997	1998	1999	2000	2001	2002	75-84	85-89	90-MR
CONGO															
Coffee	8.0	4.2	4.3	4.4	4.6	4.7	4.2	2.7	3.0	3.0	3.0	3.0	-5.6	-7.1	-2.3
Cocoa beans	5.6	3.9	3.9	4.0	4.0	3.1	3.2	3.3	3.0	3.0	3.0	3.0	0.2	0.8	-1.8
Maize	8.1	7.1	7.3	7.6	8.0	8.5	8.9	9.8	8.0	8.0	8.0	8.0	-1.8	-1.7	1.8
Cassava	68.8	73.9	65.6	76.1	78.6	81.3	82.1	77.7	90.0	90.0	90.0	90.0	0.5	0.4	1.6
Plantains	..	..	..	..	..	..	..	..	..	..	..	..	..	..	..
COTE D'IVOIRE															
Coffee	2.4	3.2	1.7	1.8	2.1	2.1	3.4	3.9	3.8	4.1	3.1	2.3	-4.6	4.9	2.8
Cocoa	5.0	5.6	5.5	5.4	5.7	5.7	5.6	5.7	5.6	5.9	5.5	4.5	0.1	0.0	0.1
Oil Palm, fruit	..	..	..	..	..	..	..	..	..	..	..	..	..	..	..
Rice	11.7	10.2	13.4	11.2	11.8	23.6	26.7	24.8	23.7	24.1	23.8	16.0	1.3	-0.1	5.0
Maize	8.1	7.8	7.8	7.9	8.1	8.2	8.2	8.2	11.6	9.9	8.2	8.6	3.2	0.0	1.9
Cassava	52.3	50.1	49.5	50.5	51.9	55.6	53.1	56.4	56.0	52.8	52.8	53.1	0.3	-0.1	0.3
Yams	90.7	89.0	88.0	89.6	89.7	88.6	87.9	85.9	84.1	84.3	83.9	85.7	1.2	0.1	-0.7
EGYPT															
Seed Cotton	26.9	27.6	29.2	22.4	21.4	24.8	25.5	18.9	22.8	26.1	17.2	17.2	4.0	2.2	-0.8
Rice, paddy	58.3	76.5	77.2	79.1	81.4	82.9	84.2	86.4	88.8	91.0	92.8	93.0	1.6	-0.7	1.3
Wheat	31.2	52.5	53.0	50.0	54.2	56.4	56.0	59.9	63.5	63.4	63.6	60.1	-0.3	0.9	1.4
Sugarcane	812.5	1,029.1	1,061.7	1,093.4	1,095.3	1,107.4	1,122.5	1,172.0	1,181.7	1,172.2	1,188.1	1,198.4	..	-5.0	1.0
Dry Broadbeans	20.7	21.4	35.1	22.7	31.7	32.0	31.9	32.3	22.9	31.1	31.4	31.4	0.0	-0.5	-1.1
EQUATORIAL GUINEA															
Cocoa	1.1	0.7	0.5	0.6	1.1	0.7	1.0	0.7	0.9	0.8	0.8	0.8	2.4	2.4	-1.1
Coffee(green)	3.4	3.7	3.7	3.7	3.7	3.6	3.6	3.6	3.7	3.7	3.7	3.7	1.0	0.0	-0.1
Cassava	24.6	26.1	26.1	26.1	26.1	25.3	25.0	25.3	25.0	25.0	25.0	25.0	-0.1	0.0	-0.1
ETHIOPIA															
Coffee(green)	2.4	3.9	4.3	4.3	2.7	3.7	2.6	2.4	2.4	2.4	2.4	2.4	..	1.0	-2.7
Sorghum	..	..	..	..	..	..	..	..	..	..	..	..	..	..	..
Maize	16.6	17.6	17.9	17.7	15.2	15.7	15.7	16.1	16.4	16.2	16.3	16.3	..	0.2	-0.2
Barley	..	..	..	..	..	..	..	..	..	..	..	..	..	..	..
GABON															
Coffee(green)	2.4	3.9	4.3	4.3	2.7	3.7	2.6	2.4	2.4	2.4	2.4	2.4	3.0	1.0	-2.7
Sugarcane	497.5	488.9	542.0	568.6	569.5	528.6	519.9	546.8	506.8	591.2	587.5	587.5	15.3	0.3	0.4
Maize	16.6	17.6	17.9	17.7	15.2	15.7	15.7	16.1	16.4	16.2	16.3	16.3	1.5	0.2	-0.2
Cassava	50.0	51.1	49.3	49.1	50.1	49.8	49.1	50.4	49.8	50.7	51.1	51.1	-0.1	-0.1	-0.1
Taro (cocoyam)	58.8	57.6	60.4	61.7	59.6	60.0	60.5	61.1	61.6	62.1	62.1	62.1	0.1	1.4	0.5
Yams	56.4	66.7	64.7	69.4	68.4	67.5	70.0	72.5	75.0	70.5	70.5	70.5	1.0	0.4	0.8
GAMBIA,THE															
Groundnuts	8.7	8.5	12.1	10.8	9.6	7.1	11.1	10.4	12.4	11.7	11.5	11.5	0.7	0.9	1.0
Seed Cotton	6.9	7.5	9.4	5.9	4.2	4.7	4.4	3.0	3.3	3.3	5.1	5.1	4.1	-0.6	-3.7
Oil Palm, fruit	..	..	..	..	..	..	..	..	..	..	..	..	..	..	..
Millet	8.7	11.2	10.3	10.6	9.8	11.0	9.0	9.6	11.2	11.0	10.8	10.8	0.4	0.6	0.7
Rice,paddy	19.7	17.3	14.6	15.4	12.3	10.7	10.2	13.4	21.7	22.1	12.1	12.1	10.8	-3.3	0.8
Maize	10.7	15.1	16.3	12.6	12.9	12.2	11.7	14.3	15.9	16.1	16.9	16.9	3.4	-2.3	1.4
Sorghum	8.0	9.5	11.0	10.6	8.5	10.8	9.6	8.1	11.1	12.7	16.6	16.6	2.9	-5.7	2.5
GHANA															
Cocoa	2.3	4.3	3.6	4.2	4.0	3.8	3.0	3.0	3.1	2.9	3.0	3.0	0.1	-5.4	-1.3
Maize	8.7	12.0	15.1	14.9	15.1	15.2	15.3	14.9	14.6	14.6	13.2	13.0	0.0	-4.1	0.4
Millet	5.9	6.4	9.7	8.8	9.8	10.2	8.4	9.5	8.6	8.1	7.0	7.0	0.4	1.9	2.4
Groundnuts	17.0	7.7	8.8	9.4	9.3	9.0	8.7	10.9	10.4	9.6	10.2	10.0	2.0	-1.9	2.1
Cassava	80.8	102.6	112.3	115.8	119.9	120.4	118.8	114.8	122.5	122.8	123.4	123.4	0.5	-2.0	1.5
Plantains	..	..	..	..	..	..	..	..	..	..	..	..	..	..	..
GUINEA															
Coffee(green)	3.2	5.3	5.2	5.5	5.1	4.1	4.0	4.2	4.2	4.1	4.1	4.1	0.0	-4.1	-1.4
Oil Palm, fruit	..	..	..	..	..	..	..	..	..	..	..	..	..	..	..
Rice, paddy	9.0	13.3	13.8	13.8	14.4	14.7	14.9	15.2	15.0	15.0	15.0	15.0	0.6	-2.4	1.5
Maize	10.0	10.7	10.4	10.3	9.7	9.9	10.1	10.4	10.3	10.3	10.3	10.3	-1.5	0.0	0.0
Groundnuts	6.6	10.1	8.8	9.2	9.1	9.5	9.8	10.3	10.0	10.0	10.0	10.0	0.2	-1.0	1.2
Cassava	70.0	71.7	75.5	71.9	63.0	61.2	59.7	58.0	57.0	62.5	62.5	62.5	0.0	-0.3	-1.6
GUINEA-BISSAU															
Groundnuts	3.5	10.1	10.0	11.7	11.0	11.0	11.6	11.3	11.9	11.9	11.9	11.9	-0.5	-4.6	1.9
Rice, paddy	7.0	19.0	19.7	20.1	19.1	18.4	16.7	14.5	11.8	14.9	18.2	18.2	-2.9	0.5	-2.2
Sorghum	6.4	8.6	9.0	9.2	9.3	9.1	8.3	7.5	9.7	7.5	8.3	8.3	-2.5	-3.5	-0.6
Millet	7.2	8.6	8.6	7.7	9.1	8.6	3.2	8.0	8.3	9.2	9.2	9.2	0.4	-3.6	-0.3
Maize	10.0	9.5	9.3	9.3	10.0	9.4	10.0	10.0	18.1	17.1	9.6	9.6	1.5	-3.2	1.4

(Table continues on the following page)

8-13. Agricultural yields by major crop (continued)

	Thousands of hectograms per hectare												Average annual* percentage growth		
	1980	1992	1993	1994	1995	1996	1997	1998	1999	2000	2001	2002	75-84	85-89	90-MR
KENYA															
Coffee(green)	8.9	5.5	4.7	5.0	5.9	5.5	3.9	3.0	4.0	5.6	4.5	4.5	-2.3	-3.5	-2.4
Tea	11.7	18.2	20.1	19.8	22.0	22.6	19.4	24.7	21.6	19.3	21.2	21.2	1.2	-0.4	0.7
Sugarcane	1,211.8	877.7	841.3	662.1	810.4	815.8	794.6	844.8	866.7	819.0	858.3	858.3	4.0	-3.3	-1.4
Sisal	9.9	11.4	11.7	11.3	13.2	13.4	13.4	9.0	7.0	12.5	12.5	12.5	1.1	0.1	-1.7
Maize	12.0	17.3	16.0	20.4	19.6	14.5	14.7	16.0	14.7	14.0	18.0	18.0	-2.1	-2.8	0.0
Wheat	21.6	12.6	9.7	19.2	19.6	18.5	14.5	17.7	14.8	13.7	13.6	13.6	2.1	-4.2	-0.2
LESOTHO															
Wheat	9.7	8.6	7.3	4.2	6.2	13.3	11.8	11.6	12.3	16.7	16.7	16.7	-2.0	0.9	7.5
Dry Peas	7.8	5.6	5.4	3.1	2.9	9.2	3.5	5.8	7.8	5.2	5.2	5.2	2.1	-6.3	9.9
Dry Beans	5.2	2.9	10.7	3.2	12.4	6.3	10.4	8.4	8.0	6.4	6.6	6.6	0.7	-3.0	-1.1
Maize	9.6	5.8	8.9	8.6	8.1	12.5	9.9	9.5	9.4	16.7	16.9	16.9	0.7	-5.3	3.5
Sorghum	9.7	6.1	13.0	8.8	8.0	8.6	8.1	7.6	11.1	8.6	8.7	8.7	1.7	-8.7	1.4
LIBERIA															
Rubber	7.6	10.7	10.0	6.7	9.3	10.0	9.9	9.4	10.0	10.6	9.6	9.6	-2.0	0.1	-0.4
Coffee(green)	4.6	1.9	2.0	2.0	2.0	2.0	2.0	2.0	2.0	2.0	2.0	2.0	0.3	-3.5	3.7
Cocoa	2.3	0.9	0.8	0.9	1.3	1.3	1.2	1.3	1.3	1.3	1.3	12.8	-1.6	-4.8	3.3
Rice, paddy	12.3	9.2	10.8	11.1	11.2	12.5	12.5	12.9	12.8	12.8	12.8	12.8	0.4	0.3	2.0
Cassava	66.7	66.7	61.3	62.5	60.3	65.0	65.2	65.3	65.1	65.7	65.7	65.7	0.9	0.6	-0.2
LIBYA															
Wheat	5.2	11.9	8.4	7.7	7.3	7.3	10.1	8.8	7.9	7.6	7.9	7.9	1.3	1.5	-3.0
MADAGASCAR															
Coffee	3.7	3.7	3.7	4.2	3.5	3.5	2.9	3.1	3.4	3.3	3.3	3.3	-1.8	-0.8	-0.5
Vanilla	0.4	0.4	0.7	0.6	0.6	0.6	0.6	0.7	0.7	0.7	0.7	0.7	-3.9	7.4	1.4
Cloves	1.7	1.4	2.1	1.8	1.7	1.7	1.8	1.7	1.9	2.0	2.0	2.0	-11.7	-3.8	1.3
Rice	17.6	20.9	20.8	20.7	21.3	21.9	21.7	20.3	21.5	19.1	19.0	19.0	-1.1	0.3	-0.1
Cassava	60.8	67.1	67.7	67.4	68.9	67.4	67.5	67.0	68.0	63.7	63.7	63.7	-1.4	0.8	-0.1
Sweet potatoes	48.6	53.1	51.1	53.8	59.1	58.1	56.0	54.3	55.9	54.2	54.5	54.5	-3.9	-0.4	0.4
MALAWI															
Tobacco leaves	8.6	9.7	10.0	12.5	12.2	12.4	13.8	10.9	7.3	8.3	7.2	5.7	1.7	-1.2	-1.5
Tea	17.1	15.4	21.3	18.7	18.2	19.8	23.4	21.5	22.3	24.6	24.5	25.3	1.1	-4.3	0.6
Groundnuts	7.1	4.0	9.0	3.2	3.6	5.6	6.9	6.9	7.3	6.9	8.1	7.6	-0.3	0.5	-0.7
Seed Cotton	6.9	7.5	9.4	5.9	4.2	4.7	4.4	3.0	3.3	3.3	5.1	5.1	4.1	-0.6	-3.7
Maize	12.2	4.8	15.3	9.2	13.5	14.4	9.9	13.7	18.1	17.4	11.0	10.7	-0.4	-2.3	2.8
Sorghum	6.7	1.4	4.9	3.1	7.3	7.2	4.7	6.1	7.0	6.7	6.8	7.2	-3.5	-7.4	2.6
Cassava	58.4	20.1	28.8	34.7	34.7	45.9	56.7	54.6	53.9	152.5	166.9	149.6	0.8	1.7	8.8
MALI															
Seed Cotton	10.6	13.6	12.8	11.5	12.1	10.7	10.5	10.3	9.5	10.7	10.7	11.5	0.8	0.2	-2.1
Groundnuts	8.9	7.5	7.8	8.4	9.4	9.8	9.5	8.8	7.7	9.7	7.3	8.2	-2.1	-6.3	-0.4
Millet	6.2	5.9	5.4	6.4	5.5	7.9	7.3	8.9	8.8	7.0	5.5	8.3	7.0	0.8	1.5
Rice, paddy	9.7	17.6	17.4	16.5	15.5	19.1	17.6	22.0	22.4	21.1	20.0	20.5	-2.1	2.8	2.1
Sorghum	8.0	6.4	7.5	7.6	8.3	10.0	9.8	9.7	9.4	8.4	7.4	9.3	7.2	0.7	0.8
Maize	11.1	10.1	11.0	11.3	13.0	15.8	17.0	16.4	14.5	13.3	11.5	8.7	9.0	-0.6	0.6
MAURITANIA															
Sorghum	3.2	5.0	5.9	5.8	6.4	6.9	4.1	4.7	4.4	5.0	4.7	4.7	-6.7	3.9	0.0
Rice	32.0	39.9	32.9	27.4	39.4	38.3	37.2	40.6	23.8	42.4	37.3	37.3	2.3	1.5	-0.1
Millet	2.3	2.6	2.6	2.9	3.6	3.4	1.4	1.6	4.1	3.3	3.1	3.1	-2.6	-7.2	1.4
Maize	6.5	7.7	12.3	5.0	8.0	5.9	8.6	8.4	6.4	6.2	7.8	7.8	0.4	-8.5	-0.7
MAURITIUS															
Sugarcane	576.8	770.0	729.7	659.2	716.6	732.6	794.9	781.2	535.5	698.9	705.1	705.1	-1.3	1.7	-1.1
Potatoes	165.6	192.1	200.9	175.7	198.5	195.9	215.8	176.0	239.4	204.9	200.0	200.0	1.7	0.3	0.4
Onions	107.6	151.4	164.6	176.0	184.4	177.9	171.3	220.6	201.5	202.4	210.0	210.0	4.1	-3.1	3.1
MOROCCO															
Wheat	10.6	7.0	6.8	18.1	5.5	18.4	9.3	14.2	8.0	4.8	12.3	12.8	5.7	-9.9	-0.4
Sugarbeet	353.5	528.6	490.6	499.8	467.7	487.1	415.4	577.2	533.2	533.0	545.1	554.6	1.4	-1.7	1.4
Barley	10.3	4.8	4.8	14.4	3.9	15.8	6.6	8.1	7.1	2.1	5.4	7.8	4.3	-14.5	-0.6
MOZAMBIQUE															
Seed Cotton	4.9	5.8	6.1	6.6	6.0	6.8	4.4	4.6	4.8	4.7	4.7	4.7	3.4	4.3	0.4
Tea	10.3	5.1	8.4	10.0	4.9	8.4	7.5	7.5	8.0	18.6	18.6	18.6	1.0	8.1	3.5
Maize	5.4	1.6	6.3	5.2	6.8	9.4	9.0	9.0	10.8	9.4	9.0	9.0	-4.8	-5.5	7.2
Rice, paddy	8.3	3.0	6.2	8.3	8.7	9.7	10.9	10.6	10.0	9.6	9.6	9.6	2.9	-1.1	3.7
Cassava	41.4	33.3	41.7	36.9	42.4	47.7	53.8	55.6	55.9	57.9	57.9	57.9	-0.2	0.5	2.0
NAMIBIA															
Wheat	25.0	51.9	43.8	52.5	40.0	43.8	46.4	60.3	55.5	56.4	80.0	80.0	2.8	-2.4	1.6
Maize	12.3	2.4	7.8	11.5	8.8	6.8	15.7	6.6	5.3	7.2	13.3	13.3	0.5	-11.6	-2.6

(Table continues on the following page)

8-13. Agricultural yields by major crop (continued)

	Thousands of hectograms per hectare												Average annual* percentage growth		
	1980	*1992*	*1993*	*1994*	*1995*	*1996*	*1997*	*1998*	*1999*	*2000*	*2001*	*2002*	*75-84*	*85-89*	*90-MR*
NIGER															
Cowpeas	2.4	1.0	0.5	1.8	0.5	1.0	0.6	2.1	1.1	1.1	1.2	1.2	0.5	-9.4	3.4
Groundnuts	6.7	3.3	2.3	4.5	3.8	4.7	3.8	4.9	4.1	3.1	8.2	8.2	-1.7	-1.1	4.1
Millet	4.4	3.6	3.5	4.0	3.4	3.5	3.0	4.5	4.3	3.3	4.6	4.6	0.4	-6.2	0.9
Sorghum	4.8	1.5	1.3	2.0	1.4	1.9	1.5	2.2	2.3	1.7	2.5	2.5	-1.3	-4.9	3.0
NIGERIA															
Cocoa	2.2	4.0	4.2	4.3	2.6	4.4	4.3	5.0	3.0	3.5	3.5	3.5	-2.3	-7.3	0.2
Oil Palm, fruit	..	..	..	..	..	..	..	..	..	..	..	..	..	..	..
Seed Cotton	1.8	5.3	5.3	5.3	5.8	6.7	8.1	7.3	7.4	7.4	7.4	4.0	-8.8	-2.2	2.1
Groundnuts	8.4	12.4	11.8	9.2	8.9	10.1	11.2	9.7	10.9	10.9	9.8	10.7	1.1	-3.0	-2.0
Sorghum	11.2	10.8	10.8	10.8	11.5	11.4	11.1	11.3	11.3	11.2	10.2	11.3	5.6	0.0	0.7
Millet	8.3	10.3	9.5	9.5	10.9	10.6	10.8	10.6	10.6	10.5	9.4	10.5	3.4	-0.5	0.3
Maize	13.2	11.2	11.8	12.7	12.7	13.3	12.5	13.2	13.8	10.3	11.4	12.7	2.6	-2.1	0.9
Rice, paddy	19.8	19.6	19.6	14.2	16.3	17.5	16.0	16.0	15.0	15.0	12.5	15.0	5.1	3.8	-2.2
Yams	105.4	113.5	113.5	114.0	107.7	106.8	110.5	94.4	95.5	95.6	90.5	97.6	0.4	-5.4	-0.8
Cassava	95.8	105.9	105.9	105.9	106.7	106.6	118.8	107.5	106.4	105.6	95.0	106.5	0.2	-0.9	-0.3
RWANDA															
Coffee(green)	6.9	6.8	5.2	2.8	11.0	7.6	7.4	5.7	7.0	6.0	6.4	6.3	0.3	2.5	-0.2
Tea	7.4	11.1	11.2	4.6	6.0	8.2	11.0	12.2	12.9	12.1	12.5	12.5	-4.9	-0.4	0.1
Sorghum	12.4	7.5	12.8	6.9	11.5	13.6	11.2	10.5	8.3	8.9	10.7	10.7	0.8	2.9	-1.5
Maize	11.8	12.3	17.4	16.8	11.2	11.1	10.9	8.2	7.6	7.0	8.2	8.2	0.2	0.4	-2.5
Plantains	..	..	..	..	..	..	..	..	..	..	..	..	..	..	..
Sweet potatoes	76.3	66.0	60.4	34.1	50.0	51.1	49.7	50.5	47.9	59.1	59.1	59.1	1.1	2.6	-1.0
SENEGAL															
Groundnuts	4.9	6.0	8.5	7.6	9.4	7.0	6.9	10.4	11.1	9.7	9.8	10.0	3.5	4.6	2.0
Seed Cotton	6.9	10.7	11.4	11.0	8.2	7.6	9.7	2.6	10.9	9.2	10.9	10.9	-2.4	1.9	-2.7
Millet	4.7	5.8	6.7	5.9	7.5	6.2	5.2	5.6	6.7	7.1	5.9	5.9	2.9	5.4	0.0
Rice, paddy	9.6	24.1	24.8	20.9	22.5	20.2	23.3	27.2	25.0	23.5	27.7	27.7	1.2	-1.4	0.3
Maize	7.3	10.9	12.7	10.1	10.9	10.4	9.7	8.3	9.4	11.1	12.0	12.0	-5.1	0.3	-1.1
Sorghum	7.7	8.9	7.8	8.7	8.6	8.9	7.7	5.9	6.4	8.7	8.0	8.0	2.1	-0.6	-1.2
SIERRA LEONE															
Cocoa	4.0	2.7	2.7	3.7	3.7	3.7	3.7	3.7	3.6	3.6	3.6	3.6	0.1	-0.7	0.1
Coffee(green)	12.7	23.0	23.0	18.5	17.9	17.9	21.9	18.6	11.0	11.0	11.0	11.0	1.9	-0.9	-4.4
Palm oil	..	..	..	..	..	..	..	..	..	..	..	..	..	..	..
Rice, paddy	12.5	13.5	12.7	12.3	13.0	13.5	13.0	11.5	11.6	10.9	10.9	10.9	-1.4	-1.2	-1.1
Cassava	38.0	53.3	45.8	58.7	58.5	58.6	49.9	51.6	51.8	51.8	51.8	51.8	-3.0	-3.1	-0.2
SOMALIA															
Bananas	..	..	..	..	..	..	..	..	..	..	..	..	..	..	..
Maize	10.1	10.1	9.9	4.1	7.3	7.1	6.4	7.5	7.2	8.4	8.4	8.4	-0.8	-3.1	-2.8
Sorghum	3.1	3.1	2.9	4.1	3.4	3.2	3.1	3.6	3.0	3.3	3.3	3.3	2.0	-1.5	-1.7
Sesame	4.6	3.8	3.1	3.0	3.4	3.3	3.4	3.0	3.1	3.3	3.3	3.3	-3.1	-1.3	-1.9
SOUTH AFRICA															
Maize	24.2	7.9	22.8	28.5	13.8	27.0	25.2	21.6	22.3	30.0	24.9	27.2	3.8	-3.3	2.0
Wheat	9.0	17.7	18.5	17.6	14.5	21.0	17.6	25.3	24.1	27.7	26.1	25.5	-1.6	3.2	4.5
Sugarcane	661.4	471.6	422.9	582.4	612.0	699.2	747.0	724.8	672.1	741.7	657.2	694.3	-2.0	2.0	0.6
Sorghum	26.9	6.2	21.6	22.9	16.1	30.8	26.9	27.3	22.6	33.2	23.4	31.6	4.4	-0.3	3.9
Barley	8.8	19.2	19.8	22.9	24.0	13.9	13.8	18.2	9.1	16.1	19.8	18.3	2.9	8.3	-1.6
SUDAN															
Seed Cotton	8.2	11.4	12.1	14.1	12.4	12.1	14.6	12.3	8.6	13.5	13.7	12.0	3.2	3.0	-1.3
Groundnuts	8.0	7.0	5.5	8.0	6.8	8.6	7.2	5.6	6.9	6.9	6.5	6.5	-1.7	-2.4	0.3
Sesame	2.6	2.0	1.4	1.3	2.1	2.2	1.8	1.9	1.5	1.5	1.4	1.7	0.6	5.5	-0.7
Sorghum	7.1	6.5	5.1	5.7	4.9	6.4	4.4	6.8	5.2	5.9	7.8	21.4	-2.9	-9.9	2.1
Wheat	12.1	23.2	13.8	13.3	16.1	17.7	19.5	22.9	12.1	23.3	25.2	21.4	-0.4	0.8	0.6
SWAZILAND															
Sugarcane	1,077.2	971.2	911.8	946.5	908.4	986.0	953.9	1,009.7	1,080.8	1,064.3	1,064.3	1,064.3	0.3	-0.1	0.4
Seed Cotton	10.2	4.5	9.5	8.8	8.8	13.3	7.9	7.3	6.6	8.0	8.0	8.0	-1.6	2.9	-3.0
Maize	13.6	9.4	12.2	17.6	12.7	24.5	17.8	19.2	17.4	15.4	15.4	15.4	-2.1	-0.9	2.8
TANZANIA															
Coffee	4.2	4.2	4.4	2.8	3.5	4.2	4.0	3.5	4.0	4.0	4.5	4.5	-0.4	3.6	-0.4
Seed Cotton	4.5	7.1	3.1	3.8	6.8	5.8	4.7	4.6	5.4	5.8	5.8	5.8	-1.9	2.1	0.9
Tea	10.9	11.8	12.0	13.2	13.1	13.0	13.4	11.8	13.2	12.4	13.4	13.4	3.1	2.6	0.4
Maize	12.3	11.7	12.5	13.4	16.3	16.2	11.7	12.9	13.9	14.6	18.0	17.2	0.6	1.6	0.9
Rice	11.9	12.8	18.1	17.4	15.8	15.7	11.1	13.0	10.7	10.3	12.8	12.8	-1.2	-0.5	-2.3
Sorghum	6.9	8.6	11.2	7.2	12.2	13.1	8.0	9.5	8.5	10.4	11.9	10.7	10.3	1.3	0.1
Millet	7.6	8.5	6.5	6.4	11.3	12.4	9.8	8.8	9.9	7.5	10.0	10.0	3.0	4.2	0.3
Cassava	107.3	104.0	104.0	104.0	102.1	101.9	86.0	94.4	95.1	67.9	74.2	74.2	0.7	-0.3	-2.2

(Table continues on the following page)

8-13. Agricultural yields by major crop

	Thousands of hectograms per hectare												Average annual* percentage growth		
	1980	1992	1993	1994	1995	1996	1997	1998	1999	2000	2001	2002	75-84	85-89	90-MR
TOGO															
Coffee(green)	4.9	1.6	2.8	2.4	2.5	4.6	2.2	4.1	3.5	3.2	3.5	3.5	2.8	3.2	-1.4
Cocoa	4.5	2.0	2.3	1.8	2.8	6.6	2.7	5.7	3.3	3.1	3.7	3.7	-1.8	4.4	6.2
Seed Cotton	7.7	12.5	12.4	13.9	10.6	13.3	9.7	8.9	8.7	8.3	10.0	10.0	7.2	6.6	-1.6
Maize	9.2	10.1	11.6	9.3	8.6	9.4	10.7	8.7	12.0	12.0	11.4	11.4	3.5	-3.5	0.7
Sorghum	7.5	7.8	6.4	5.4	8.7	6.3	7.3	6.7	8.0	8.3	7.7	7.7	1.3	-2.8	0.2
Millet	2.6	5.6	5.0	3.7	6.7	4.7	5.2	4.5	4.7	4.7	5.2	5.2	-7.9	0.5	0.4
Cassava	103.3	68.9	68.6	58.8	59.2	56.9	62.3	62.2	60.6	56.5	59.8	59.8	-7.9	2.5	-1.7
Yams	86.6	83.3	103.4	98.2	85.8	87.2	109.9	99.1	109.2	110.0	101.8	101.8	0.3	-3.0	0.9
TUNISIA															
Wheat	10.2	17.0	13.7	10.7	12.8	16.2	11.1	14.2	14.2	11.5	20.0	14.1	5.5	13.9	-0.1
Barley	7.7	12.0	9.3	5.9	6.6	11.9	5.2	11.6	9.0	6.5	11.7	9.1	4.1	20.5	-0.5
UGANDA															
Coffee(green)	6.0	4.2	5.5	7.5	6.9	10.3	8.1	7.7	9.2	4.8	7.5	7.5	-0.6	1.2	3.6
Seed Cotton	0.4	1.3	3.0	3.3	3.3	4.5	2.8	2.6	2.6	2.7	2.7	2.7	-10.7	-1.4	1.9
Millet	16.5	16.0	15.1	14.8	16.0	11.0	12.7	16.0	16.1	13.9	15.0	15.0	3.2	2.4	0.0
Maize	11.1	15.0	16.0	15.1	16.0	13.0	12.4	15.0	17.3	17.4	18.0	18.0	0.7	-0.4	1.1
Sorghum	17.9	15.0	15.0	15.0	15.0	11.0	10.7	15.0	15.0	12.9	15.0	15.0	3.2	2.0	-0.1
Cassava	68.6	80.0	85.1	65.0	67.0	67.0	67.0	90.0	130.0	123.8	135.0	135.0	-1.3	0.8	2.4
Plantains	..	..	..	..	..	..	..	..	..	..	..	..	..	..	..
ZAIRE															
Coffee(green)	3.7	3.2	3.6	3.5	3.7	3.2	3.7	3.7	3.2	2.9	2.5	2.7	-1.1	0.9	-0.7
Palm oil	..	..	..	..	..	..	..	..	..	..	..	..	..	..	..
Maize	8.0	8.1	8.3	8.3	7.9	8.0	8.2	8.3	8.0	8.0	8.0	8.0	1.1	1.1	-0.1
Rice	8.0	7.3	7.2	7.3	7.4	7.5	7.6	7.6	7.6	7.6	7.6	7.6	0.1	0.0	-0.3
Cassava	70.0	80.0	78.1	77.2	81.4	81.1	81.1	81.1	81.1	81.1	81.1	81.1	0.1	0.0	0.1
Plantains	..	..	..	..	..	..	..	..	..	..	..	..	..	..	..
ZAMBIA															
Seed Cotton	5.0	4.3	7.3	7.8	6.7	5.6	14.3	13.2	13.3	12.4	12.4	12.4	-5.6	-5.2	5.2
Tobacco leaves	10.4	4.4	5.1	6.7	8.3	10.5	10.8	10.9	12.3	12.1	12.1	12.1	3.6	11.2	1.1
Sunflower	9.2	0.5	5.4	6.6	6.5	5.6	3.8	3.6	5.1	5.4	5.5	5.5	-2.6	5.7	4.4
Maize	16.9	7.3	25.2	15.0	14.2	20.9	14.8	15.6	14.3	15.0	15.0	15.0	0.2	-6.0	0.2
Wheat	40.7	43.3	40.1	43.0	50.0	55.8	66.2	56.7	74.8	62.1	62.0	62.0	-2.9	-4.9	2.7
Cassava	61.8	62.0	62.0	62.0	62.0	62.0	62.0	62.0	57.1	49.4	57.6	57.6	0.0	0.0	-0.5
ZIMBABWE															
Tobacco leaves	19.5	24.3	21.9	24.6	24.2	24.2	22.0	26.3	21.9	25.1	24.6	21.8	1.0	0.7	0.2
Seed Cotton	17.5	2.7	8.6	7.8	4.6	9.2	8.9	9.2	9.1	8.8	8.7	4.8	0.6	-4.0	1.6
Sugarcane	1,031.2	89.3	597.8	1,072.5	1,109.7	905.1	1,081.6	962.2	1,083.0	983.1	976.2	976.2	1.9	-0.7	2.9
Maize	13.4	4.1	16.3	16.6	6.0	17.0	13.4	11.6	10.5	14.9	12.0	8.0	-3.0	-12.9	-0.5
Wheat	49.7	48.3	70.3	56.1	20.8	54.9	51.7	53.8	56.1	58.1	55.0	41.4	1.6	-0.1	0.0

Notes: The following commodities are in their least-processed form unless otherwise indicated:
Cotton, seed cotton
Groundnuts, unshelled
Coffee, green or roasted
Rice, paddy
Cloves, whole
Cocoa, beans
Tobacco, leaves
Sunflower, seeds
1 hectogram = 100 grams = 3.527 oz.

Countries excluded from listing: Cape Verde, Djibouti, Sao Tome and Principe, and Seychelles.

For livestock "yield", see Table 8.6. Food Output by Major Crops.

* The standard World Bank least square methodology was used to compute the annual percentage growth.

8-14. Incidence of drought

	1987	1988	1989	1990	1991	1992	1993	1994	1995	1996	1997	1998	1999	2000
	D=Significant shortage of rain													
SUB-SAHARAN AFRICA	..	..	..	..	..	..	..	..	..	..	..	..	..	..
excluding South Africa	..	..	..	..	..	..	..	..	..	..	..	..	..	..
excluding South Africa & Nigeria	..	..	..	..	..	..	..	..	..	..	..	..	..	..
Angola	..	..	..	..	..	..	..	..	..	..	..	..	..	..
Benin	..	..	..	..	..	..	..	..	..	..	..	..	..	..
Botswana	D	..	..	..	..	D	..	..	D	..	..	..	..	..
Burkina Faso	..	..	..	..	..	..	..	..	..	..	D	..	..	D
Burundi	..	..	..	..	..	..	..	..	..	..	..	D	D	D
Cameroon	..	..	..	..	..	..	..	..	..	D	D	..	..	..
Cape Verde	..	..	..	..	..	..	D	D	..	..	D	D	D	D
Central African Republic	..	..	..	..	..	..	..	..	..	..	..	..	..	..
Chad	..	..	..	..	..	..	D	..	D	D	D	..	D	D
Comoros	..	..	..	..	..	..	..	..	..	..	..	..	..	..
Congo, Democratic Rep. of	..	..	..	..	..	..	..	..	..	..	..	..	..	..
Congo, Republic of	..	..	..	..	..	..	..	..	..	..	..	..	..	..
Côte d'Ivoire	..	..	..	..	..	..	..	..	..	..	D	..	..	..
Djibouti	..	..	..	..	..	..	..	..	..	..	..	..	D	D
Equatorial Guinea	..	..	..	..	..	..	..	..	..	..	..	..	..	..
Eritrea	..	..	..	..	..	..	..	..	..	D	D	..	D	D
Ethiopia	D	D	..	..	D	D	..	D	..	..	D	..	D	D
Gabon	..	..	..	..	..	..	..	..	..	..	..	..	..	..
Gambia, The	..	..	..	..	..	..	..	..	..	..	..	..	..	..
Ghana	..	..	..	..	..	..	..	..	..	..	..	D	..	D
Guinea	..	..	..	..	..	..	..	..	..	..	..	..	..	..
Guinea-Bissau	..	..	..	..	..	..	..	..	..	..	..	..	..	..
Kenya	..	..	..	..	..	D	D	..	..	..	D	D	D	D
Lesotho	..	..	..	..	..	D	..	..	D	..	..	..	..	..
Liberia	..	..	..	..	..	..	..	..	..	..	..	..	..	..
Madagascar	..	..	..	..	..	..	..	..	..	..	..	..	D	D
Malawi	..	..	..	..	..	D	..	D	D	..	D	D	..	..
Mali	..	..	..	..	..	..	..	..	..	..	..	..	..	..
Mauritania	..	..	..	..	..	..	..	..	..	..	..	..	..	..
Mauritius	..	..	..	..	..	..	..	..	..	..	..	..	..	..
Mozambique	..	..	..	..	..	D	..	..	D	..	..	D	..	..
Namibia	..	..	..	..	..	D	..	..	D	..	..	..	..	..
Niger	D	..	..	D	..	..	..	..	D	D	D	..	..	D
Nigeria	..	..	..	..	..	..	..	..	..	..	..	..	..	..
Rwanda	..	..	..	..	..	..	..	..	D	D	..	D	D	D
São Tomé and Principe	..	..	..	..	..	..	..	..	..	..	..	..	..	..
Senegal	..	..	..	..	..	..	..	..	..	..	..	..	..	..
Seychelles	..	..	..	..	..	..	..	..	..	..	..	..	..	..
Sierra Leone	..	..	..	..	..	..	..	..	..	..	..	..	..	..
Somalia	..	..	..	..	..	..	..	..	..	..	..	D	..	..
South Africa	..	..	..	..	..	D	..	..	D	..	D	..	..	..
Sudan	D	..	D	D	..	..	..	..	D	..	D	..	..	D
Swaziland	D	..	..	..	..	D	..	..	D	..	..	..	..	..
Tanzania	..	..	..	..	..	D	..	..	..	..	D	D	D	D
Togo	..	..	..	..	..	..	..	..	..	..	..	..	..	D
Uganda	..	..	..	..	..	..	..	..	..	..	D	..	D	D
Zambia	..	..	..	..	..	D	..	D	D	..	D	D	..	..
Zimbabwe	..	..	..	..	..	D	..	D	D	..	..	..	..	..
NORTH AFRICA	..	..	..	..	..	..	..	..	..	..	..	..	..	..
Algeria	..	D	D	..	..	..	D	D	D	..	D	..	D	D
Egypt, Arab Republic	..	..	..	..	..	..	..	..	..	..	..	..	..	..
Libya	..	..	..	..	..	..	..	..	..	..	..	..	..	..
Morocco	..	..	..	..	..	..	..	..	D	..	D	..	D	D
Tunisia	..	D	D	..	..	..	..	..	D	..	..	..	..	..
ALL AFRICA	..	..	..	..	..	..	..	..	..	..	..	..	..	..

Figure 8-1. Food price index, 2000*

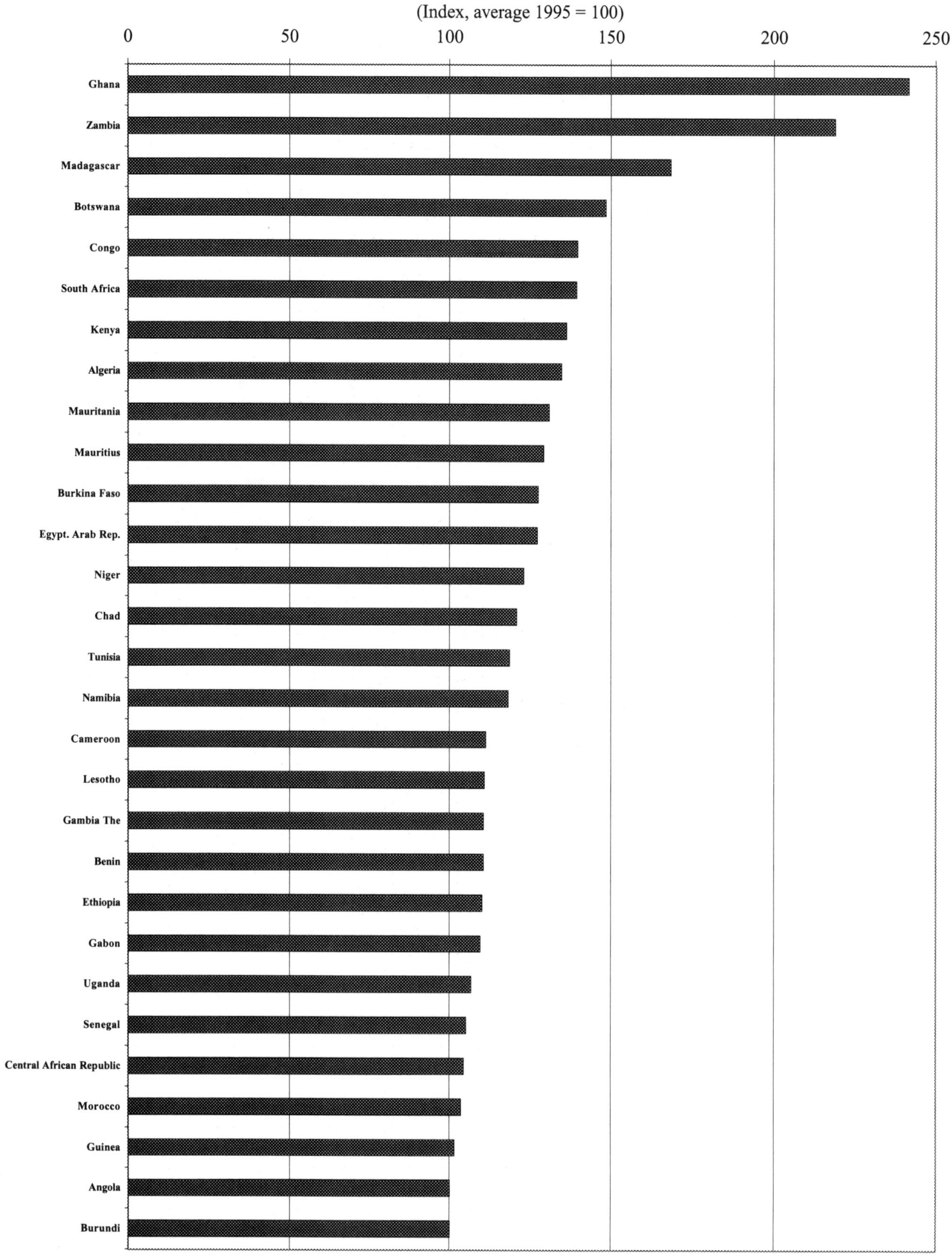

* Or most recent year available.

Figure 8-2. Food production per capita index, 2001*

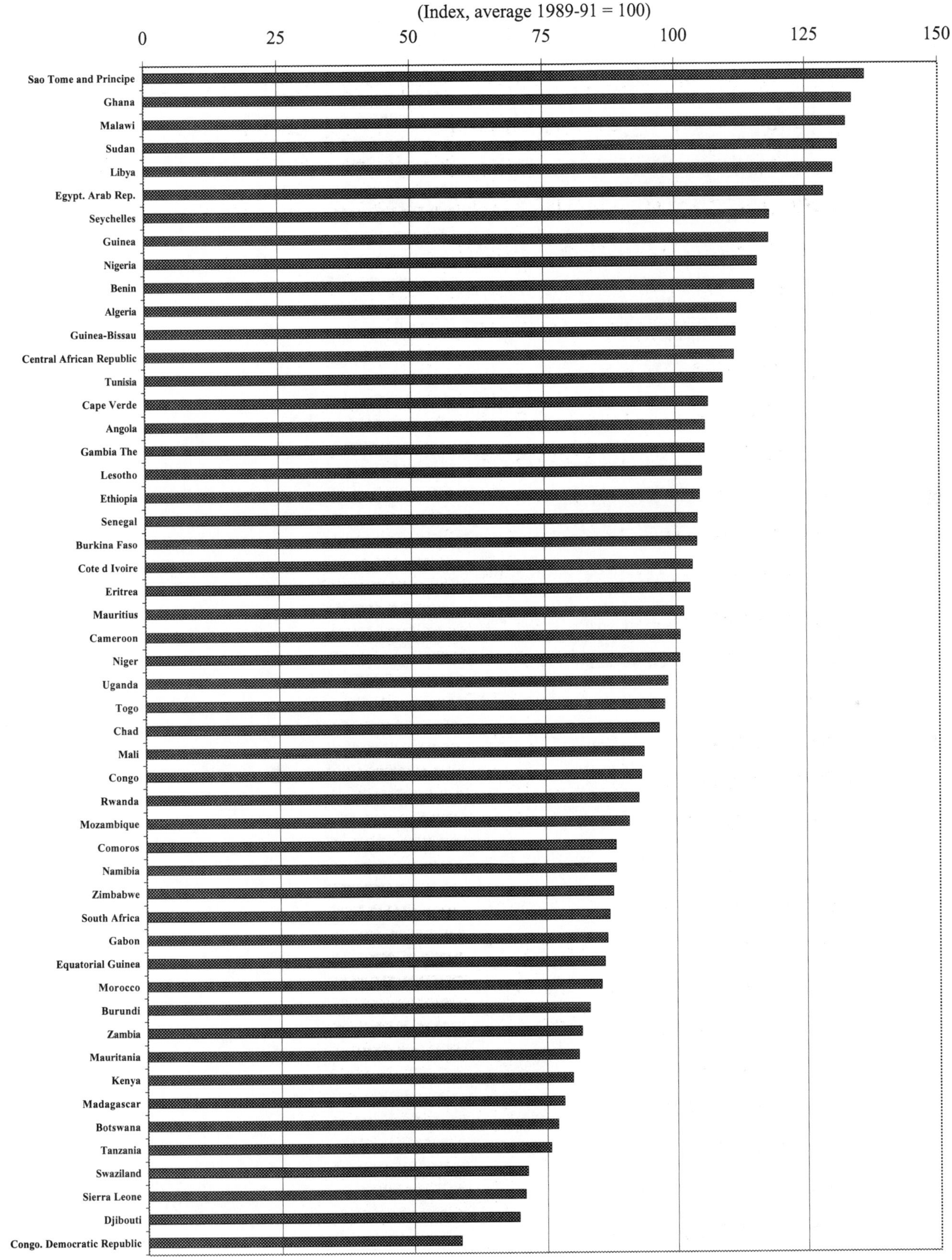

* Or most recent year available.

Figure 8-3. Food and nonfood production index, 2001*

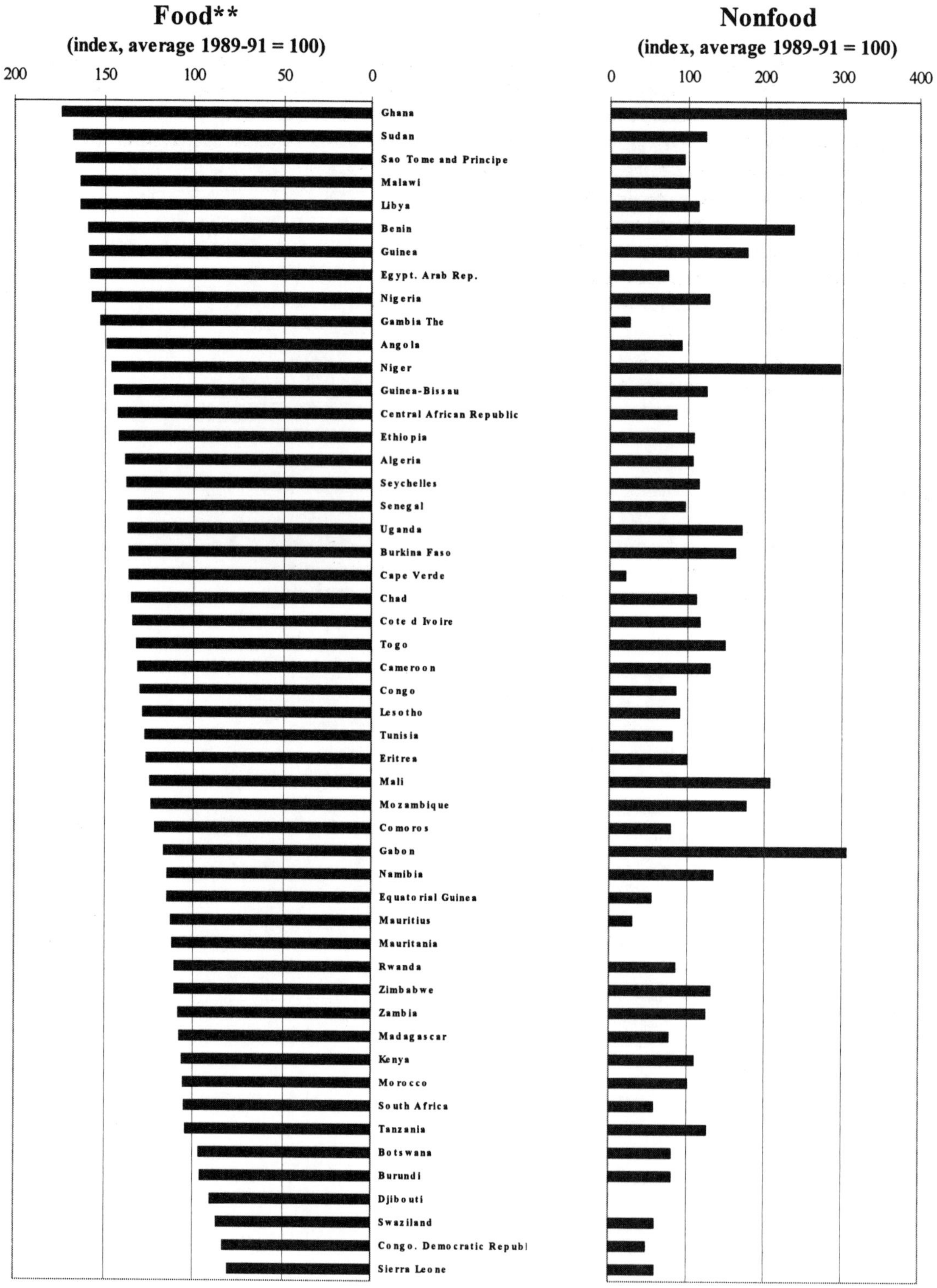

* Or most recent year available.

Figure 8-4. Agriculture exports, 1998*

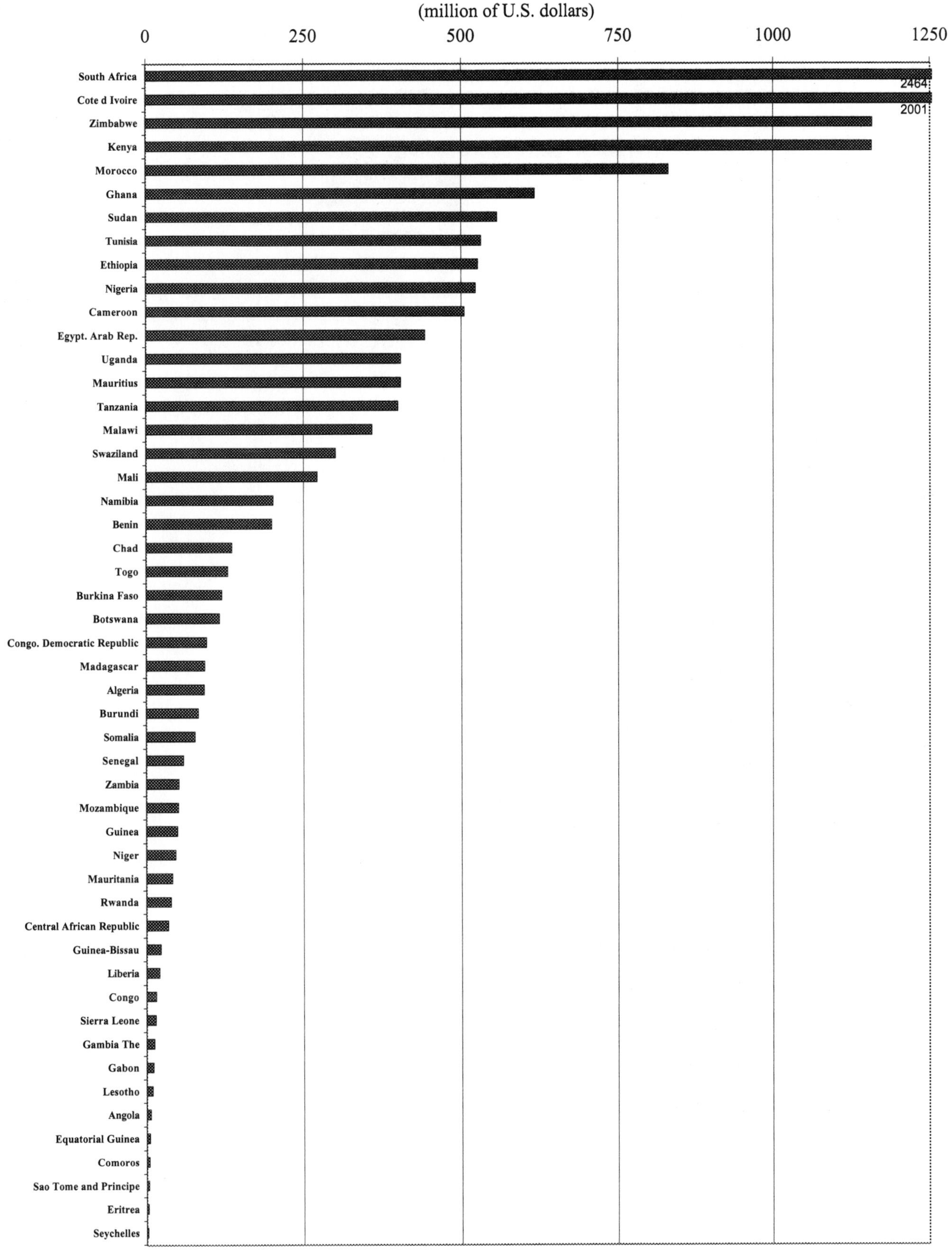

* Or most recent year available.

Figure 8-5. Drought, 1980-2000

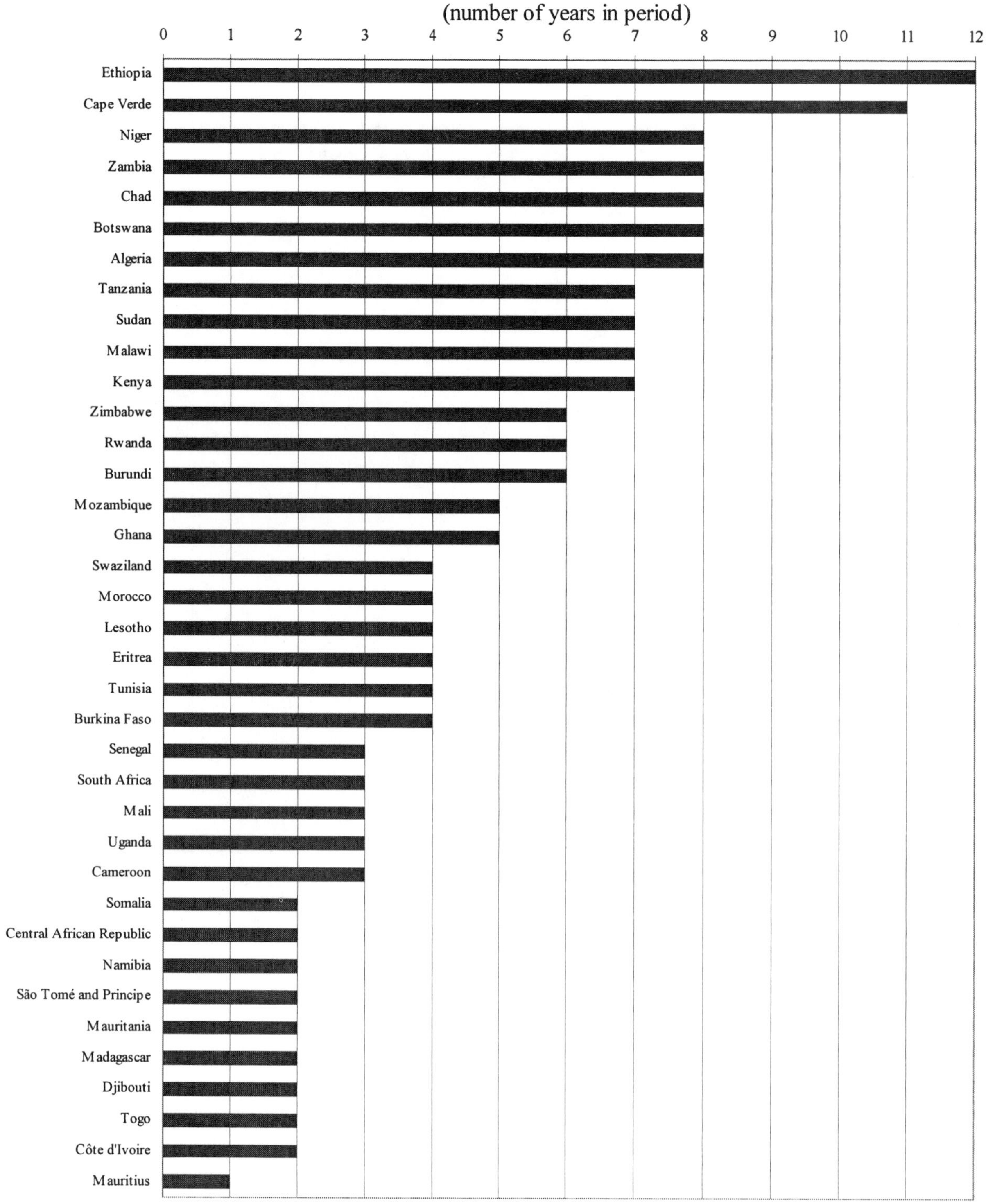

Technical notes

Tables

Table 8-1. Nominal producer prices. Data on nominal producer prices are compiled from the FAO. In general, the figures reflect the average annual price received by farmers in the most important producing regions. But given the wide regional and seasonal variation and the lack of precision in recording specifics about prices quoted, the data should be interpreted only as a rough indication of price levels for an entire country during an entire year.

The data do not differentiate between official producer prices and farmgate prices. In most cases they happen to be the same.

Crop years for most countries span parts of two calendar years; planting takes place in the first calendar year, while harvest and marketing take place at the end of the first and beginning of the second year. For consistency, producer prices are listed corresponding to the calendar year during which planting decisions are made. For example, producer prices for the crop year 1987/88 are listed as 1987.

For each country, up to four export crops and five food crops are included, which represent the most important commodities for that country in terms of value of total production during the early 1980s. The food crops include up to three cereals of "traded" grains (those commonly imported or exported) and up to two "nontraded" staples, generally roots and tubers, which are not normally imported or exported by African countries. In the table, these categories of crops are designated by the following symbols: X1 through X4 for export crops; Fl through F3 for traded food crops; and NT1 and NT2 for nontraded staple food crops. The categorization is consistent across countries, but the numbering of crops within categories in each country depends on which crops are most important.

Where commodities may be marketed in several different forms, the form is generally specified (for instance, shelled or unshelled groundnuts). When not specified, the form of the commodity is the most common (for instance, shelled and dried maize). Where commodities are graded, an average grade has been used unless otherwise specified.

Table 8-2. Food price index. This is a subindex of the consumer price index. It reflects the cost to the average consumer of acquiring a fixed basket of food (IMF, *IFS*).

Table 8-3. Food production index. These indexes are based on 169 commodities that provide calories when consumed (*FAO* data). Some of these (such as cottonseed, cocoa, and vanilla) are not, however, a significant part of African diets, but are produced primarily for export.

Table 8-4. Nonfood production index. Data in this table are derived from 29 products that are not considered nutritious, including coffee, rubber, cotton lint, and tobacco leaves (*FAO* data).

Table 8-5. Food production per capita index. These are derived as the ratio of the food production index (Table 8-3) and estimated total midyear population figures (Table 1-2).

Table 8-6. Volume of food output, by major food crop. The table covers, with only a few differences, the same major food crops as presented in Table 8-1, excluding beverages (coffee, tea, cocoa), cotton, and tobacco. Included also are figures for livestock, which represent the combined total head of cattle, sheep, goats, pigs, horses, asses, and mules, and figures for the total head of rabbits (*FAO* data).

Table 8-7. Value of agricultural exports. Value of agricultural exports is expressed in current U.S. dollars at f.o.b. prices (*FAO* data).

Table 8-8. Cereal production. This refers to crops harvested for dry grain only. Cereal crops harvested for hay or harvested green for food, feed, or silage and those used for grazing are excluded (FAO data).

Table 8-9. Crop production index. Shows agricultural production for each year relative to the base period 1989–91. It includes all crops except fodder crops (*FAO* data).

Tables 8-10 and 8-11. Fertilizer use and imports. Figures are in metric tons and represent the aggregate of nitrogenous, phosphate, and potash fertilizers (FAO database for *Fertilizer Yearbook*).

Table 8-12. Area under permanent crops. Reflects land under permanent crops as defined and reported by the FAO.

Table 8-13. Agricultural yields, by major crop. This table follows closely the selection of commodities of Table 8-1. Units are in thousands of hectograms (which are equivalent to hundreds of kilograms) per hectare. Most of the data come from the database for the *FAO Production Yearbook*, with additional information from World Bank agricultural sector reports.

Table 8-14. Incidence of drought. This is the only indicator in this chapter based on subjective considerations. Data on rainfall levels from other sources are usually presented to suit different purposes, without considering seasonal and regional characteristics of the producing regions. A low rainfall level might not harm agricultural production, if it did not adversely affect the regions where the main crops are produced, whereas an average rainfall level might be associated with difficulties in the producing regions, due to delay, for example. Therefore, simply presenting the annual rainfall levels would not necessarily enrich the agricultural data.

For each country, a binary classification was thus created. A "D" was assigned to a country if a significant shortage of rain unfavorably affected its agricultural production. For normal or average rainfall, the standard sign was given, as in the cases of insufficient information or "not applicable." (Specialists who work on the relevant countries were surveyed, as well as World Bank agricultural and environmental experts. In addition, the Federal Early Warning System project of the U.S. Agency for International Development provided information for 1993–94 for about half of the countries listed.)

Figures

The following indicators have been used to derive the figures in this chapter:

Figure 8-1. Food price index (Table 8-2).

Figure 8-2. Food production per capita index (Table 8-5).

Figure 8-3. Food production index (Table 8-3); non-food production index (Table 8-4).

Figure 8-4. Agriculture exports (Table 8-7).

Figure 8-5. Drought (Table 8-14).

Methodology used for regional aggregations and period averages in chapter 8

	Aggregations [a]				*Period averages* [b]
Table	*(1)*	*(6)*	*(7)*	*(8)*	*(2)*
8-1				x	
8-2			x		x
8-3		x			x
8-4			x		
8-5			x		x
8-6				x	x
8-7	x				x
8-8	x				x
8-9		x			x
8-10	x				x
8-11	x				x
8-12	x				x
8-13				x	x
8-14				x	

Note: Regional aggregations are shown in the rows for Sub-Saharan Africa, North Africa, and All Africa. Period averages are shown in the last three columns. This table shows only the methodologies used in this chapter.

a. Regional aggregations: (1) simple total; (2) simple total of the first indicator divided by the simple total of the second indicator (same country coverage); (3) simple total of the gap-filled indicator; (4) simple total of the gap-filled main indicator divided by the simple total of the gap-filled secondary indicator; (5) simple total of the first gap-filled main indicator less the simple total of the second gap-filled main indicator, all divided by the simple total of the secondary indicator; (6) weighted total (by population); (7) median; (8) no aggregation; (9) simple arithmetic mean.

b. Period averages: (1) arithmetic mean (using the same series as shown in the table i.e., ratio if the rest of the table is shown as ratio, level if the rest of the table is shown as level, growth rate if the rest is shown as growth rate); (2) least-squares growth rate (using main indicator); (3) least-squares growth rate (using main indicator in constant terms, with the rest of the table in current terms).

9

Power, Communications, and Transportation

This chapter provides data on the power, communications, and transportation sectors of the economy.

An adequate and reliable supply of power is a vital ingredient for the economic development of African countries. This chapter presents information on electric power production and distribution losses. Data are from the International Energy Agency's (IEA's) *Energy Statistics and Balances of Non-OECD Countries,* and from the United Nations Statistics Division's *Energy Statistics Yearbook.*

Telecommunications, computers, and the Internet are also essential ingredients of a modern economy. In this chapter, telephone main lines represent the supply side of the system, which in Africa is well short of demand. In fact, waiting time for telephone lines is the highest of any other geographical region. Because of the growing importance of computers on development, a new table on computers and the Internet was added in this chapter. Data on telecommunications are from the International Telecommunications Union's (ITU) *World Telecommunications Development Report* (2000), *Challenges to the Network: Internet for Development* (1999), and the *World Telecommunications Indicators Database* (2000b). The data on Internet hosts are from the Internet Software Consortium (*www.isc.org).*

In addition to power and communications, countries must have a solid transportation sector to underpin expansion of their economies and ensure support to the activities of households, producers, and government. This chapter presents data on vehicle use, roads, and railway traffic. Data are from the World Bank databases and from the International World Road Federation's *World Road Statistics* and from Eurostat (*europa.eu.int/eurostat.html*). The air transport data are from the International Civil Aviation Organization's *Civil Aviation Statistics of the World* and ICAO staff estimates.

9-1. Electric power consumption per capita

	KWH											Annual Average		
	1980	1991	1992	1993	1994	1995	1996	1997	1998	1999	2000	75-84	85-89	90-MR
SUB-SAHARAN AFRICA	426.6	433.1	416.4	431.3	420.2	431.2	436.7	437.9	440.8	436.4	431.6	406.4	446.9	432.5
excluding South Africa	132.6	118.7	119.9	122.9	118.0	119.7	122.1	118.5	109.7	112.8	112.8	127.6	130.9	117.8
excl. S.Africa & Nigeria	156.6	132.6	132.6	133.4	129.1	132.9	136.1	131.0	..	..	..	151.2	148.2	133.0
Angola	66.8	63.0	61.9	60.1	58.4	56.9	59.0	80.3	85.2	83.8	88.2	72.7	63.8	68.9
Benin	29.8	38.9	41.2	41.7	42.1	45.0	42.7	51.8	48.7	56.8	63.6	29.5	35.1	46.3
Botswana	..	..	..	..	..	..	..	..	..	..	..	..	..	..
Burkina Faso	..	..	..	..	..	..	..	..	..	..	..	..	..	..
Burundi	..	..	..	..	..	..	..	..	..	..	..	..	..	..
Cameroon	154.3	195.3	192.0	194.6	170.9	164.0	170.3	180.8	178.3	184.2	182.8	178.4	213.8	183.2
Cape Verde	..	..	..	..	..	..	..	..	..	..	..	..	..	..
Central African Republic	..	..	..	..	..	..	..	..	..	..	..	..	..	..
Chad	..	..	..	..	..	..	..	..	..	..	..	..	..	..
Comoros	..	..	..	..	..	..	..	..	..	..	..	..	..	..
Congo, Democratic Rep. of	147.8	58.7	60.5	66.4	47.2	47.1	44.9	43.5	42.3	43.2	40.2	139.5	137.5	50.0
Congo, Republic of	83.3	168.8	160.3	136.6	129.2	129.1	129.6	104.8	81.1	50.8	86.1	81.4	148.7	121.1
Côte d'Ivoire	191.6	149.6	81.4	139.6	140.3	170.5	174.3	181.3	..	..	..	166.4	164.9	149.4
Djibouti	..	..	..	..	..	..	..	..	..	..	..	..	..	..
Equatorial Guinea	..	..	..	..	..	..	..	..	..	..	..	..	..	..
Eritrea	..	..	..	..	..	..	..	..	..	..	..	..	..	..
Ethiopia	16.2	17.7	17.9	20.1	20.8	21.7	22.3	22.2	22.2	21.4	22.1	16.3	18.0	20.5
Gabon	617.1	806.4	783.1	765.0	769.9	750.5	754.2	762.6	757.3	701.0	696.7	604.8	962.1	761.3
Gambia, The	..	..	..	..	..	..	..	..	..	..	..	..	..	..
Ghana	423.6	303.2	316.2	322.9	299.6	334.8	362.8	281.2	199.4	246.7	288.3	335.9	259.2	295.5
Guinea	..	..	..	..	..	..	..	..	..	..	..	..	..	..
Guinea-Bissau	..	..	..	..	..	..	..	..	..	..	..	..	..	..
Kenya	92.5	117.5	118.1	121.3	123.2	125.1	128.1	126.2	127.4	118.0	105.9	90.1	106.7	120.6
Lesotho	..	..	..	..	..	..	..	..	..	..	..	..	..	..
Liberia	..	..	..	..	..	..	..	..	..	..	..	..	..	..
Madagascar	..	..	..	..	..	..	..	..	..	..	..	..	..	..
Malawi	..	..	..	..	..	..	..	..	..	..	..	..	..	..
Mali	..	..	..	..	..	..	..	..	..	..	..	..	..	..
Mauritania	..	..	..	..	..	..	..	..	..	..	..	..	..	..
Mauritius	..	..	..	..	..	..	..	..	..	..	..	..	..	..
Mozambique	34.0	48.3	46.2	46.2	41.3	44.1	40.7	46.8	54.1	53.0	52.6	42.4	32.8	46.2
Namibia	..	..	..	..	..	..	..	..	..	..	..	..	..	..
Niger	..	..	..	..	..	..	..	..	..	..	..	..	..	..
Nigeria	68.2	81.6	85.5	95.3	88.8	84.8	85.3	85.4	81.9	79.8	80.9	64.6	84.9	84.2
Rwanda	..	..	..	..	..	..	..	..	..	..	..	..	..	..
São Tomé and Principe	..	..	..	..	..	..	..	..	..	..	..	..	..	..
Senegal	96.4	98.5	105.7	101.0	107.1	106.5	108.1	114.6	119.0	114.5	120.6	92.7	97.5	108.5
Seychelles	..	..	..	..	..	..	..	..	..	..	..	..	..	..
Sierra Leone	..	..	..	..	..	..	..	..	..	..	..	..	..	..
Somalia	..	..	..	..	..	..	..	..	..	..	..	..	..	..
South Africa	3,212.9	3,618.2	3,447.4	3,581.3	3,530.7	3,659.8	3,723.2	3,800.2	3,831.9	3,775.5	3,745.2	3,037.2	3,555.5	3,671.8
Sudan	34.2	49.1	49.2	47.2	48.8	48.0	48.7	45.8	44.6	66.6	66.2	36.0	47.5	51.4
Swaziland	..	..	..	..	..	..	..	..	..	..	..	..	..	..
Tanzania	36.8	54.4	53.2	51.4	50.7	54.7	58.8	54.3	53.5	54.1	55.6	35.4	41.7	53.8
Togo	..	..	..	..	..	..	..	..	..	..	..	..	..	..
Uganda	..	..	..	..	..	..	..	..	..	..	..	..	..	..
Zambia	1,015.7	730.0	726.0	723.4	712.4	691.0	668.6	620.9	568.0	574.2	556.3	1,058.2	890.3	666.6
Zimbabwe	973.2	789.8	858.1	751.9	788.8	814.7	858.9	872.3	850.8	883.3	845.2	939.3	891.2	836.5
NORTH AFRICA	362.8	696.9	710.9	713.6	732.7	744.5	757.0	782.6	815.7	846.6	896.1	352.0	606.0	762.2
Algeria	265.3	492.5	521.9	507.9	509.0	516.9	526.3	523.2	550.0	584.6	611.9	259.8	399.9	530.6
Egypt, Arab Republic	379.9	707.1	710.3	726.3	742.7	762.0	781.2	819.9	860.3	899.7	976.0	377.8	606.0	788.7
Libya	1,588.2	3,814.6	3,773.6	3,714.0	3,816.5	3,785.5	3,772.4	3,831.3	3,853.7	3,875.8	3,921.4	1,503.4	3,651.3	3,823.3
Morocco	222.8	355.4	380.9	377.1	398.1	403.7	408.4	422.7	443.0	430.3	447.2	212.1	299.2	400.6
Tunisia	379.2	617.3	651.4	674.1	718.3	734.4	744.8	783.0	824.0	910.9	938.9	323.7	528.8	745.6
ALL AFRICA	411.6	492.6	482.4	494.6	489.9	500.6	507.1	513.2	524.3	527.3	534.0	393.5	483.4	505.8

9-2. Energy production and use

	Energy production (KT oil equivalent)		Commercial energy use (KT oil equivalent)		Electric power transmission and distribution losses (% of output)	
	1980	2000	1980	2000	1980	2000
SUB-SAHARAN AFRICA	322,805	552,297	208,143	341,194	..	..
excluding South Africa	249,636	407,829	142,726	233,599	..	..
excl. S. Africa & Nigeria	101,157	210,103	89,880	143,431	..	..
Angola	11,301	43,669	4,437	7,667	25	15
Benin	1,212	1,821	1,363	2,362	220	72
Botswana	..	..	..	..	..	..
Burkina Faso	..	..	..	..	..	..
Burundi	..	..	..	..	..	..
Cameroon	6,707	12,729	3,676	6,355	7	22
Cape Verde	..	..	..	..	..	..
Central African Republic	..	..	..	..	..	..
Chad	..	..	..	..	..	..
Comoros	..	..	..	..	..	..
Congo, Democratic Rep. of	8,697	15,446	8,706	14,888	8	4
Congo, Republic of	4,024	14,656	862	895	9	60
Côte d'Ivoire	2,419	6,097	3,662	6,928	7	..
Djibouti	..	..	..	..	..	..
Equatorial Guinea	..	..	..	..	..	..
Eritrea	..	..	..	..	..	..
Ethiopia	10,575	17,583	11,145	18,732	8	10
Gabon	9,441	16,800	1,493	1,563	1	10
Gambia, The	..	..	..	..	..	..
Ghana	3,305	5,883	4,063	7,720	0	1
Guinea	..	..	..	..	..	..
Guinea-Bissau	..	..	..	..	..	..
Kenya	7,891	12,260	9,791	15,482	16	22
Lesotho	..	..	..	..	..	..
Liberia	..	..	..	..	..	..
Madagascar	..	..	..	..	..	..
Malawi	..	..	..	..	..	..
Mali	..	..	..	..	..	..
Mauritania	..	..	..	..	..	..
Mauritius	..	..	..	..	..	..
Mozambique	7,413	7,219	8,074	7,126	39	10
Namibia	..	292	..	1,031	..	..
Niger	..	..	..	..	..	..
Nigeria	148,479	197,726	52,846	90,169	36	32
Rwanda	..	..	..	..	..	..
São Tomé and Principe	..	..	..	..	..	..
Senegal	1,046	1,723	1,919	3,086	10	17
Seychelles	..	..	..	..	..	..
Sierra Leone	..	..	..	..	..	..
Somalia	..	..	..	..	..	..
South Africa	73,169	144,469	65,417	107,595	8	8
Sudan	7,089	23,664	8,406	16,216	14	15
Swaziland	..	..	..	..	..	..
Tanzania	9,502	14,601	10,280	15,386	14	22
Togo	562	1,036	715	1,530	..	..
Uganda	..	..	..	..	..	..
Zambia	4,179	5,916	4,719	6,244	7	3
Zimbabwe	5,793	8,708	6,570	10,219	9	21
NORTH AFRICA	205,664	288,706	44,033	110,101	..	..
Algeria	67,103	149,629	12,185	29,060	11	16
Egypt, Arab Republic	34,168	57,599	15,970	46,423	13	12
Libya	96,550	73,904	7,193	16,438	..	..
Morocco	877	572	4,778	10,293	10	6
Tunisia	6,966	7,003	3,907	7,888	12	11
ALL AFRICA	528,469	841,004	252,176	451,296	..	..

9-3. Telephone, radio, and television availability, 1995-2000

	Telephones				Radios	Television
	Mainlines (per 1,000 persons)	Waiting list (Thousands)	Average cost of call US$ per three minutes	Mobile phones (per 1,000 persons)	(per 1,000 persons)	sets (per 1,000 persons)
SUB-SAHARAN AFRICA	14	1,293	..	17	198	59
excluding South Africa	7	1,293	..	5	188	53
excl. S. Africa & Nigeria	8	1,260	..	7	185	49
Angola	5	21	0.05	2	74	19
Benin	8	23	0.09	9	439	45
Botswana	93	12	0.02	123	150	25
Burkina Faso	4	12	0.08	2	35	12
Burundi	3	10	0.02	2	220	30
Cameroon	6	50	0.05	10	163	34
Cape Verde	126	4	0.03	45	182	5
Central African Republic	3	2	0.48	1	80	6
Chad	1	1	0.16	1	236	1
Comoros	10	3	0.14	0	174	4
Congo, Democratic Rep. of	0	6	..	0	386	2
Congo, Republic of	7	..	..	24	123	13
Côte d'Ivoire	18	32	0.05	30	137	60
Djibouti	15	0	0.19	0	87	71
Equatorial Guinea	13	2	0.05	11	427	116
Eritrea	8	20	0.02	0	444	26
Ethiopia	4	197	0.02	0	189	6
Gabon	32	10	0.15	98	501	326
Gambia, The	26	17	0.30	4	396	3
Ghana	12	28	0.03	6	710	118
Guinea	8	2	0.10	5	52	44
Guinea-Bissau	9	5	0.14	0	44	..
Kenya	10	134	0.04	4	223	25
Lesotho	10	19	0.01	10	53	16
Liberia	2	2	..	0	274	25
Madagascar	3	0	0.08	4	216	24
Malawi	4	25	0.03	5	499	3
Mali	3	..	0.07	1	56	14
Mauritania	7	48	0.08	3	149	96
Mauritius	235	19	0.03	151	379	268
Mozambique	4	21	0.06	3	44	5
Namibia	63	2	0.05	47	141	38
Niger	2	1	0.10	0	121	37
Nigeria	4	42	..	0	200	68
Rwanda	2	8	0.03	5	76	0
São Tomé and Principe	31	1	0.05	0	318	228
Senegal	22	25	0.10	26	141	40
Seychelles	235	2	0.14	320	543	203
Sierra Leone	4	25	0.03	2	259	13
Somalia	2	..	..	0	60	14
South Africa	114	116	0.09	190	338	127
Sudan	12	405	0.23	1	464	273
Swaziland	32	17	0.04	33	162	119
Tanzania	5	30	0.08	5	281	20
Togo	9	17	0.09	11	265	32
Uganda	3	9	0.13	8	127	27
Zambia	8	13	0.06	9	145	134
Zimbabwe	18	159	0.04	23	362	30
NORTH AFRICA	72	1,951	..	29	282	165
Algeria	57	646	0.01	3	244	110
Egypt, Arab Republic	8	13	0.06	9	145	189
Libya	18	159	0.04	23	362	137
Morocco	57	646	0.01	3	244	166
Tunisia	86	1,300	0.01	21	339	198
ALL AFRICA	24	3,485	..	19	213	79

9-4. Personal computers and internet use

	Personal computers (per 1,000 people)		*Internet hosts (per 10,000 people)*		*Internet users (Thousands)*	
	1999	*2000*	*1999*	*2000*	*1999*	*2000*
SUB-SAHARAN AFRICA	8.2	9.17	2.32	3.10	2,366	3,696
excluding South Africa	4.3	4.81	0.15	0.32	546	1,296
excl. S. Africa & Nigeria	3.7	4.23	0.18	0.40	446	1,096
Angola	1.0	1.14	0.00	0.01	10	30
Benin	1.5	1.64	0.04	0.04	10	15
Botswana	31.0	36.99	5.79	13.99	12	15
Burkina Faso	1.0	1.26	0.19	0.19	7	10
Burundi	..	..	0.00	0.00	3	3
Cameroon	2.7	3.31	0.00	0.01	20	40
Cape Verde	..	..	0.02	0.05	5	8
Central African Republic	1.4	1.66	0.00	0.02	1	2
Chad	1.3	..	0.00	0.01	1	3
Comoros	3.0	4.32	0.57	0.72	1	2
Congo, Democratic Rep. of	..	..	0.00	0.00	1	..
Congo, Republic of	3.5	..	0.00	0.01	1	..
Côte d'Ivoire	5.5	6.09	0.24	0.37	20	40
Djibouti	9.5	10.19	0.00	0.65	1	1
Equatorial Guinea	2.3	..	0.00	0.00	1	..
Eritrea	1.5	1.61	0.01	0.02	1	5
Ethiopia	0.7	0.95	0.01	0.01	8	10
Gabon	8.4	9.79	0.02	0.21	3	15
Gambia, The	7.9	11.51	0.02	0.12	3	4
Ghana	2.5	2.97	0.06	0.06	20	30
Guinea	3.4	3.67	0.00	0.00	5	8
Guinea-Bissau	..	..	0.13	0.11	2	3
Kenya	4.2	4.89	0.19	0.32	35	200
Lesotho	..	..	0.08	0.42	1	4
Liberia	..	..	0.00	0.00	0	1
Madagascar	1.9	2.20	0.12	0.36	25	30
Malawi	1.0	1.16	0.00	0.00	10	15
Mali	1.0	1.16	0.01	0.05	7	19
Mauritania	7.8	9.43	0.00	0.20	3	5
Mauritius	93.7	100.54	4.55	27.68	55	87
Mozambique	2.6	3.05	0.09	0.10	15	30
Namibia	29.5	34.16	11.61	19.57	6	30
Niger	0.4	0.47	0.03	0.12	3	5
Nigeria	6.4	6.59	0.00	0.01	100	200
Rwanda	..	..	0.00	0.42	5	5
São Tomé and Principe	..	..	17.32	45.00	1	7
Senegal	15.1	16.80	0.28	0.51	30	40
Seychelles	124.4	135.58	0.12	0.49	5	6
Sierra Leone	..	..	0.14	0.16	2	5
Somalia	..	..	0.00	0.00	0	..
South Africa	55.7	61.81	33.36	43.12	1,820	2,400
Sudan	2.9	3.22	0.00	0.00	5	30
Swaziland	..	..	6.28	7.07	5	10
Tanzania	2.4	2.85	0.05	0.16	25	115
Togo	11.1	21.60	0.18	0.35	15	100
Uganda	2.5	2.70	0.06	0.07	25	40
Zambia	7.2	6.72	0.48	0.86	15	20
Zimbabwe	13.0	11.87	1.14	2.50	20	50
NORTH AFRICA	10.6	16.44	0.19	0.47	307	810
Algeria	6.0	6.48	0.01	0.01	20	50
Egypt, Arab Republic	12.0	22.06	0.28	0.85	200	450
Libya	..	..	0.00	0.02	7	10
Morocco	10.8	12.35	0.28	0.33	50	200
Tunisia	15.3	22.86	0.06	0.10	30	100
ALL AFRICA	8.7	10.56	1.95	2.64	2,673	4,506

9-5. Vehicle ownership

	Units per 1000 persons										Annual Average		
	1980	*1990*	*1991*	*1992*	*1993*	*1994*	*1995*	*1996*	*1997*	*1998*	*75-84*	*85-89*	*90-MR*
SUB-SAHARAN AFRICA	..	21	23	24	24	22	23	23	..	..	..	..	23
excluding South Africa	..	9	14	14	15	14	15	15	..	..	..	..	14
excl. S.Africa & Nigeria	..	9	10	10	11	12	12	12	..	..	..	..	11
Angola	..	18	19	19	19	19	20	20	..	..	..	..	19
Benin	..	3	4	5	6	6	7	8	..	..	..	..	5
Botswana	27	18	23	28	32	35	62	48	51	59	27	..	42
Burkina Faso	..	4	4	5	5	5	5	6	..	..	..	..	5
Burundi	..	0	..	..	..	..	..	..	..	..	..	..	0
Cameroon	8	10	10	10	11	11	12	12	..	..	8	..	11
Cape Verde	..	9	9	9	9	10	10	10	..	..	..	..	9
Central African Republic	8	1	1	0	1	1	0	0	0	..	8	..	1
Chad	..	2	3	3	3	3	4	4	..	..	..	..	3
Comoros	..	13	15	17	18	23	24	28	..	..	..	..	20
Congo, Democratic Rep. of	..	22	25	28	28	29	30	31	..	..	..	..	27
Congo, Republic of	..	18	19	19	20	19	20	20	..	..	..	..	19
Côte d'Ivoire	24	24	24	25	27	29	30	32	..	..	24	..	27
Djibouti	..	15	16	16	16	17	18	19	..	..	..	..	17
Equatorial Guinea	..	3	4	4	4	5	5	5	..	..	..	..	4
Eritrea	..	1	1	1	1	1	2	2	..	..	..	..	1
Ethiopia	2	1	1	1	1	1	1	1	1	1	2	1	1
Gabon	..	32	33	35	36	35	37	37	..	..	..	..	35
Gambia, The	..	13	13	13	13	15	15	15	..	..	..	..	14
Ghana	..	..	..	..	..	8	8	8	..	..	..	..	8
Guinea	..	4	4	5	5	5	5	5	..	..	..	..	5
Guinea-Bissau	..	7	7	7	8	10	10	12	..	..	..	..	9
Kenya	8	12	13	13	13	13	13	13	..	..	8	12	13
Lesotho	10	11	12	13	14	17	18	20	..	..	10	..	15
Liberia	1	14	14	14	14	15	14	15	..	..	1	..	14
Madagascar	..	6	5	5	5	7	7	8	..	..	..	..	6
Malawi	5	4	5	5	5	5	6	6	..	..	5	..	5
Mali	..	3	4	4	4	4	4	5	..	..	..	..	4
Mauritania	..	10	10	10	10	12	12	13	..	..	..	..	11
Mauritius	44	59	63	68	71	75	79	83	88	93	44	54	78
Mozambique	..	4	5	5	5	3	2	1	..	..	..	..	3
Namibia	..	71	83	73	78	81	81	84	..	..	..	..	79
Niger	6	6	6	6	6	6	6	6	..	..	6	5	6
Nigeria	4	..	30	29	29	22	25	24	..	..	4	..	26
Rwanda	2	2	3	3	3	4	4	4	..	..	2	1	3
São Tomé and Principe	..	36	37	37	38	40	40	41	..	..	..	..	38
Senegal	19	11	11	12	13	13	13	14	..	..	19	..	13
Seychelles	..	104	104	105	107	116	114	119	118	..	..	..	111
Sierra Leone	..	10	10	11	10	11	9	6	..	..	..	10	10
Somalia	..	2	2	2	2	1	1	1	..	..	..	..	2
South Africa	133	139	140	139	136	141	139	142	..	..	133	160	140
Sudan	..	9	9	10	10	11	11	12	..	..	..	..	10
Swaziland	52	66	71	68	65	62	66	68	67	70	52	63	67
Tanzania	3	5	4	5	5	5	5	5	..	..	3	..	5
Togo	..	24	25	26	26	26	28	28	..	..	..	1	26
Uganda	1	2	3	3	3	3	4	4	5	5	1	..	4
Zambia	..	14	16	18	20	22	24	26	..	..	..	..	20
Zimbabwe	..	..	..	..	32	32	31	30	..	..	..	..	31
NORTH AFRICA	..	33	34	34	35	46	49	49	..	..	..	38	40
Algeria	..	..	..	..	..	55	54	53	..	..	..	54	54
Egypt, Arab Republic	..	29	29	29	28	29	29	30	..	..	..	26	29
Libya	..	..	..	..	..	165	240	241	..	..	..	..	215
Morocco	..	37	38	41	43	47	48	48	49	51	..	..	46
Tunisia	38	48	49	51	52	59	59	64	..	..	38	62	54
ALL AFRICA	..	23	25	25	25	27	28	28	..	..	..	..	26

9-6. Road-to-population ratio

	Road 1000 km/1 million persons											Annual Average		
	1980	1985	1989	1990	1991	1992	1993	1994	1995	1996	1997	75-84	85-89	90-MR
SUB-SAHARAN AFRICA	3.3	3.1	..	2.5	..	..	2.5	2.4	2.9	2.4	..	3.3	3.1	2.5
excluding South Africa	3.1	2.8	..	2.2	..	..	2.5	2.4	2.5	2.4	..	3.1	2.8	2.4
excl. S.Africa & Nigeria	3.5	3.2	..	2.6	..	..	2.8	2.6	2.6	2.6	..	3.5	3.2	2.6
Angola	10.2	8.6	..	7.6	..	7.1	6.8	6.6	6.4	6.2	6.0	11.0	8.6	6.7
Benin	2.1	1.9	1.3	1.8	1.2	1.2	1.3	1.3	1.2	1.2	..	2.1	1.6	1.3
Botswana	9.1	7.6	..	7.0	..	..	13.1	12.6	12.2	12.0	..	11.7	9.8	11.4
Burkina Faso	1.1	1.1	..	..	..	1.4	1.1	1.1	1.3	1.2	..	1.7	1.2	1.2
Burundi	1.2	0.6	..	1.2	..	2.5	2.5	2.4	2.4	2.3	..	1.8	0.6	2.2
Cameroon	7.2	6.5	..	6.0	..	..	2.7	2.6	2.6	..	..	6.5	5.5	3.5
Cape Verde	..	..	..	..	..	..	3.0	3.0	2.9	2.8	..	..	..	2.9
Central African Republic	9.8	7.6	8.2	8.0	7.9	7.7	7.5	7.3	7.1	7.0	..	9.7	7.8	7.5
Chad	6.0	5.3	..	4.7	..	..	5.0	5.0	4.9	4.8	..	6.6	5.3	4.9
Comoros	..	..	..	..	..	..	1.8	1.8	1.8	1.8	..	2.3	..	1.8
Congo, Democratic Rep. of	5.4	4.6	..	..	3.8	3.7	3.6	3.6	3.5	3.5	..	5.5	4.6	3.6
Congo, Republic of	5.0	4.5	..	..	5.5	5.4	5.2	5.1	4.9	4.8	..	5.5	4.5	5.1
Côte d'Ivoire	5.0	4.8	..	4.2	..	..	3.8	3.7	3.6	3.5	..	5.6	4.8	3.8
Djibouti	..	8.2	6.7	6.1	5.7	..	5.2	5.0	5.0	4.9	..	8.1	7.6	5.3
Equatorial Guinea	..	..	..	..	..	..	7.2	7.1	7.1	7.0	..	5.2	..	7.1
Eritrea	..	..	..	..	..	..	1.1	1.1	1.1	1.1	..	..	..	1.1
Ethiopia	1.0	0.9	0.4	0.5	0.5	..	0.5	0.5	0.5	0.5	..	0.9	0.7	0.5
Gabon	10.2	9.5	..	..	7.8	7.6	7.4	7.3	7.1	6.9	..	10.9	9.5	7.3
Gambia, The	3.4	4.1	..	2.6	..	..	2.4	2.4	2.4	2.3	..	3.0	4.1	2.4
Ghana	3.0	2.8	2.6	2.5	..	..	2.2	2.2	2.2	2.1	..	2.8	2.7	2.3
Guinea	5.4	5.8	..	..	..	2.6	0.0	4.7	4.6	4.5	..	4.2	5.8	3.3
Guinea-Bissau	..	..	..	..	..	..	4.1	4.1	4.0	4.0	..	4.9	..	4.1
Kenya	3.1	3.3	2.7	2.6	2.6	..	2.5	2.4	2.4	2.3	..	3.2	3.0	2.5
Lesotho	2.9	2.7	..	..	..	3.0	3.0	2.9	2.7	2.6	..	2.6	2.7	2.8
Liberia	2.9	2.4	..	2.4	..	..	3.8	3.8	3.8	3.8	..	3.9	3.2	3.5
Madagascar	5.7	4.9	1.3	..	2.9	2.8	4.0	3.9	3.7	3.6	..	4.8	4.0	3.5
Malawi	1.7	1.6	1.4	3.2	..	..	1.6	1.6	1.6	1.5	1.7	1.9	1.5	1.9
Mali	2.0	1.8	1.7	1.7	1.7	..	1.6	1.5	1.5	1.5	..	2.1	1.8	1.6
Mauritania	4.7	4.1	..	3.7	..	..	3.5	3.4	3.3	3.3	..	4.7	4.1	3.4
Mauritius	1.8	1.8	1.7	1.7	1.7	..	1.8	1.7	1.7	1.7	1.7	2.2	1.7	1.7
Mozambique	2.9	2.6	1.9	2.5	..	..	1.9	1.9	1.9	1.9	..	3.3	2.0	2.0
Namibia	..	..	..	28.2	..	..	41.2	40.7	39.9	39.1	38.4	..	..	37.9
Niger	2.8	2.7	..	1.5	..	..	1.6	1.1	1.1	1.1	..	2.4	2.8	1.3
Nigeria	1.5	1.3	..	1.2	..	..	1.6	1.6	1.7	1.7	..	1.5	1.3	1.5
Rwanda	2.1	2.0	1.8	1.9	..	..	1.9	2.3	2.3	2.2	..	1.7	1.9	2.1
São Tomé and Principe	..	..	..	..	..	..	2.4	2.3	2.3	2.4	..	..	..	2.4
Senegal	2.5	2.2	..	2.0	..	..	1.8	1.8	1.8	1.7	..	2.4	2.2	1.8
Seychelles	..	..	..	..	..	..	3.6	3.5	3.6	3.7	..	..	..	3.6
Sierra Leone	2.4	2.3	..	..	..	2.8	2.7	2.7	2.5	2.4	2.4	2.5	2.3	2.6
Somalia	2.6	3.2	..	3.0	..	..	2.8	2.9	3.0	2.9	..	3.3	3.2	2.9
South Africa	6.7	5.9	5.3	5.3	5.1	..	..	..	8.5	..	..	7.1	5.5	6.3
Sudan	0.5	0.4	..	0.4	..	..	0.4	0.4	0.4	0.4	..	0.7	0.4	0.4
Swaziland	5.8	5.1	3.8	3.6	3.5	3.6	3.3	3.3	4.1	4.1	..	5.1	4.4	3.7
Tanzania	2.5	3.8	..	..	2.1	2.1	3.1	3.1	3.0	2.9	..	2.5	3.8	2.7
Togo	2.8	2.4	..	2.2	2.1	2.1	2.0	2.0	1.9	1.9	..	2.8	2.4	2.0
Uganda	2.1	2.0	..	1.8	..	1.7	..	..	..	..	..	2.1	2.0	1.7
Zambia	6.3	5.6	5.0	4.8	4.7	4.5	4.4	4.4	7.4	7.2	7.1	6.4	5.3	5.6
Zimbabwe	11.8	9.0	..	..	..	8.4	8.3	1.7	1.6	1.6	..	11.8	9.0	4.3
NORTH AFRICA	2.1	2.0	1.6	..	1.9	1.6	2.5	..	..	..	..	2.1	1.6	2.0
Algeria	3.9	3.6	..	..	3.5	3.6	3.7	3.6	3.7	3.6	..	4.1	3.6	3.6
Egypt, Arab Republic	0.7	0.7	0.9	0.9	0.9	0.9	0.8	..	..	..	..	0.7	0.7	0.9
Libya	..	..	..	..	..	..	17.1	17.2	17.2	5.0	..	..	..	14.1
Morocco	3.0	2.7	2.5	..	2.4	1.1	2.4	2.3	2.3	2.3	2.1	2.9	2.6	2.1
Tunisia	3.7	3.6	3.7	..	..	..	2.4	2.5	2.5	2.5	..	3.4	3.6	2.5
ALL AFRICA	3.1	2.9	..	2.3	..	..	2.5	2.6	3.0	2.5	..	3.1	2.9	2.6

9-7. Paved primary roads

	Percentage of roads									Percent in good condition
	1992	1993	1994	1995	1996	1997	1998	1999	2000	1989
SUB-SAHARAN AFRICA	17.0	17.0	18.0	16.2	16.0	16.6	15.0	13.5	16.2	39
excluding South Africa	17.0	17.0	18.0	16.0	15.7	16.5	14.0	13.3	12.1	39
excl. S. Africa & Nigeria	16.5	16.4	17.1	15.8	15.3	16.3	13.8	13.0	12.1	41
Angola	25.0	25.0	25.0	25.0	25.0	25.0	25.0	10.4	..	..
Benin	20.0	20.0	20.0	20.0	20.0	20.0	20.0	20.0	..	13
Botswana	19.9	21.1	22.2	48.0	52.0	54.0	56.0	55.0	..	94
Burkina Faso	17.6	18.2	18.7	16.0	16.0	16.0	16.0	16.0	..	70
Burundi	..	..	..	..	..	..	7.1	7.1	..	75
Cameroon	11.3	11.7	12.1	12.5	12.5	12.5	12.5	12.5	..	25
Cape Verde	78.0	78.0	78.0	78.0	78.0	78.0	78.0	78.0	..	14
Central African Republic	..	..	2.1	2.1	2.1	2.4	2.7	..	..	30
Chad	0.8	0.8	0.8	0.8	0.8	0.8	0.8	0.8	..	..
Comoros	72.1	73.5	75.0	76.5	..	..	76.5	76.5	..	43
Congo, Democratic Rep. of	..	..	..	..	..	..	..	..	..	20
Congo, Republic of	9.7	9.7	9.7	9.7	9.7	9.7	9.7	9.7	..	50
Côte d'Ivoire	9.1	9.2	9.4	9.6	9.7	9.7	9.7	9.7	..	75
Djibouti	12.6	12.6	12.6	12.6	12.6	12.6	12.6	12.6	..	51
Equatorial Guinea	..	..	..	..	..	..	..	..	..	27
Eritrea	20.2	20.6	21.0	21.4	21.8	21.8	21.8	21.8	..	..
Ethiopia	15.0	15.0	15.0	15.5	15.3	..	14.0	13.3	12.0	47
Gabon	8.2	8.2	8.2	8.2	9.9	..	9.9	9.9	9.9	30
Gambia, The	33.3	34.0	34.6	35.3	35.4	35.4	35.4	35.4	..	22
Ghana	23.5	23.9	24.4	24.9	24.1	..	..	29.6	..	28
Guinea	15.5	15.8	16.1	16.4	16.5	16.5	16.5	16.5	..	50
Guinea-Bissau	9.1	9.4	9.8	10.2	10.3	10.3	10.3	10.3	..	39
Kenya	13.8	14.3	13.6	13.8	12.1	12.1	12.1	12.1	12.1	32
Lesotho	16.0	15.0	15.0	17.9	17.9	16.8	17.3	18.3	..	53
Liberia	5.7	5.9	6.0	6.1	6.2	6.2	6.2	6.2	..	85
Madagascar	15.4	11.5	18.7	11.5	11.6	..	..	11.6	..	56
Malawi	17.0	18.0	18.0	20.0	20.0	19.0	..	18.5	..	56
Mali	11.3	11.5	11.8	12.0	12.1	12.1	12.1	12.1	..	70
Mauritania	11.1	11.1	11.1	11.2	11.3	11.3	11.3	11.3	..	58
Mauritius	93.0	93.0	93.0	93.0	95.0	95.0	96.0	96.0	97.0	95
Mozambique	17.5	17.8	18.2	18.6	18.7	18.7	18.7	18.7	..	19
Namibia	10.9	7.3	7.9	7.9	11.4	13.2	13.5	13.6	..	..
Niger	..	..	7.9	7.9	7.9	7.9	7.9	7.9	..	67
Nigeria	30.0	30.0	21.3	18.8	18.8	30.9	30.9	30.9	..	34
Rwanda	9.4	9.6	9.7	9.9	9.1	..	..	8.3	..	41
São Tomé and Principe	64.1	65.4	66.7	68.0	68.1	68.1	68.1	68.1	..	..
Senegal	28.3	28.3	28.4	28.5	29.3	29.3	29.3	29.3	29.3	28
Seychelles	59.1	60.3	61.5	62.8	80.3	84.5	..	..	..	..
Sierra Leone	11.0	11.0	11.0	8.0	8.0	8.0	8.0	7.9	..	62
Somalia	11.5	11.8	11.8	11.8	11.8	11.8	11.8	11.8	..	52
South Africa	..	..	..	41.5	19.7	19.7	19.7	20.3	20.3	..
Sudan	33.7	34.5	35.4	36.2	36.3	36.3	36.3	36.3	..	27
Swaziland	58.6	59.8	28.2	..	..	..	..	..	..	35
Tanzania	37.0	4.2	4.2	4.2	4.2	4.2	4.2	4.2	..	39
Togo	31.0	31.6	31.6	31.6	31.6	31.6	31.6	31.6	..	75
Uganda	..	..	..	..	..	..	..	6.7	..	10
Zambia	17.3	17.6	18.0	..	..	..	..	..	..	40
Zimbabwe	16.0	17.0	54.9	48.0	47.4	47.4	47.4	47.4	..	70
NORTH AFRICA	66.0	66.7	68.0	68.9	73.5	73.5	66.3	63.8	60.6	..
Algeria	66.0	66.7	68.0	68.9	68.9	68.9	68.9	68.9	..	..
Egypt, Arab Republic	73.0	72.0	75.0	78.0	78.1	78.1	78.1	78.1	..	..
Libya	53.8	54.9	56.0	57.1	..	..	..	57.2	..	..
Morocco	49.5	49.6	50.2	50.2	50.2	52.3	52.3	56.3	56.4	..
Tunisia	74.6	76.0	77.4	78.8	78.9	78.9	63.7	63.8	64.8	..
ALL AFRICA	17.6	17.9	18.5	18.6	17.9	18.9	16.9	16.5	24.8	39

9-8. Rail goods traffic-to-$PPP GDP ratio

	Ton-km per million of $PPP GDP											Annual Average		
	1980	1990	1991	1992	1993	1994	1995	1996	1997	1998	1999	75-84	85-89	90-MR
SUB-SAHARAN AFRICA	..	..	..	..	..	..	..	..	..	..	..	..	..	..
excluding South Africa	..	..	..	..	..	..	..	..	..	..	..	..	..	..
excl. S.Africa & Nigeria	..	..	..	..	..	..	..	..	..	..	..	..	..	..
Angola	..	..	..	..	..	..	..	..	..	..	..	..	..	..
Benin	..	..	..	..	..	..	..	..	..	..	..	..	..	..
Botswana	..	..	..	..	..	..	..	..	..	..	..	..	..	..
Burkina Faso	..	..	..	..	..	..	..	..	..	..	..	..	..	..
Burundi	..	..	..	..	..	..	..	..	..	..	..	..	..	..
Cameroon	55,686	41,749	35,283	37,898	32,795	41,880	42,272	29,833	40,683	..	26,112	59,175	42,138	36,501
Cape Verde	..	..	..	..	..	..	..	..	..	..	..	..	..	..
Central African Republic	..	..	..	..	..	..	..	..	..	..	..	..	..	..
Chad	..	..	..	..	..	..	..	..	..	..	..	..	..	..
Comoros	..	..	..	..	..	..	..	..	..	..	..	..	..	..
Congo, Democratic Rep. of	57,048	34,349	..	..	..	4,489	..	..	..	..	..	52,857	38,112	19,419
Congo, Republic of	..	..	309,706	187,909	140,826	124,747	..	..	..	..	..	402,066	418,562	190,797
Côte d'Ivoire	56,843	15,750	14,837	14,083	8,650	8,983	14,539	..	21,202	..	..	48,440	34,531	14,006
Djibouti	..	..	..	..	..	..	..	..	..	..	..	..	..	..
Equatorial Guinea	..	..	..	..	..	..	..	..	..	..	..	..	..	..
Eritrea	..	..	..	..	..	..	..	..	..	..	..	..	..	..
Ethiopia	..	..	2,057	..	..	..	..	..	..	..	..	8,036	5,318	2,057
Gabon	8,975	..	..	53,511	60,619	58,115	74,061	..	66,351	..	223,237	19,092	44,922	89,316
Gambia, The	..	..	..	..	..	..	..	..	..	..	..	..	..	..
Ghana	10,439	6,228	..	..	..	..	..	..	..	..	..	8,240	6,580	6,228
Guinea	..	..	..	..	..	..	..	..	..	..	..	..	..	..
Guinea-Bissau	..	..	..	..	..	..	..	..	..	..	..	..	..	..
Kenya	220,215	84,134	74,830	59,230	49,719	49,096	..	..	44,948	..	36,787	187,112	104,030	56,963
Lesotho	..	..	..	..	..	..	..	..	..	..	..	..	..	..
Liberia	..	..	..	..	..	..	..	..	..	..	..	..	..	..
Madagascar	..	..	..	..	..	..	..	..	..	..	..	..	..	..
Malawi	104,525	18,408	18,062	13,927	11,512	11,554	12,186	11,172	8,997	12,197	12,669	80,608	27,423	13,138
Mali	40,897	55,439	53,252	48,181	..	..	..	..	35,389	..	27,388	43,487	54,812	43,930
Mauritania	..	..	..	..	..	..	..	..	..	..	..	..	..	..
Mauritius	..	..	..	..	..	..	..	..	..	..	..	..	..	..
Mozambique	..	..	..	..	..	..	..	..	..	..	..	..	..	..
Namibia	..	269,547	181,553	162,417	144,227	131,674	126,605	..	..	..	..	..	..	169,337
Niger	..	..	..	..	..	..	..	..	..	..	..	..	..	..
Nigeria	19,038	3,200	..	601	..	1	..	..	4,917	..	508	27,487	7,987	1,845
Rwanda	..	..	..	..	..	..	..	..	..	..	..	..	..	..
São Tomé and Principe	..	..	..	..	..	..	..	..	..	..	..	..	..	..
Senegal	68,700	64,198	54,001	50,541	41,503	38,739	..	..	37,454	..	32,683	61,780	66,569	45,589
Seychelles	..	..	..	..	..	..	..	..	..	..	..	..	..	..
Sierra Leone	..	..	..	..	..	..	..	..	..	..	..	..	..	..
Somalia	..	..	..	..	..	..	..	..	..	..	..	..	..	..
South Africa	559,760	349,538	321,757	303,021	301,764	294,581	282,612	..	..	..	..	480,587	359,802	308,879
Sudan	162,940	..	30,440	..	..	..	40,886	..	36,877	..	33,151	103,135	45,931	35,339
Swaziland	..	..	..	..	..	..	..	..	..	..	..	..	..	..
Tanzania	..	..	80,047	74,567	97,807	83,363	96,300	82,469	73,082	61,636	72,020	..	64,028	80,144
Togo	..	..	..	..	..	..	..	..	..	..	..	..	..	..
Uganda	..	13,059	10,477	8,313	8,689	12,358	12,243	..	4,724	4,890	7,892	11,493	8,059	9,183
Zambia	345,327	183,792	157,146	147,333	146,163	96,245	64,969	73,702	63,876	64,513	73,721	316,268	223,373	107,146
Zimbabwe	653,437	233,651	208,357	229,162	216,531	153,324	162,486	155,384	145,373	..	..	516,081	323,206	188,033
NORTH AFRICA	..	..	..	..	..	..	..	..	..	..	..	..	..	..
Algeria	41,685	23,792	23,334	20,691	19,105	18,684	..	..	..	..	13,236	38,616	29,109	19,807
Egypt, Arab Republic	39,390	21,490	23,928	20,490	23,740	25,837	..	21,885	20,913	20,223	16,048	36,085	30,151	21,617
Libya	..	..	..	..	..	..	..	..	..	..	..	..	..	..
Morocco	117,019	70,602	56,569	64,450	56,000	53,132	54,999	..	52,242	49,424	48,045	111,247	81,245	56,163
Tunisia	109,555	57,235	53,197	52,074	49,268	52,061	51,765	..	46,095	44,914	41,732	94,933	76,205	49,816
ALL AFRICA	..	..	..	..	..	..	..	..	..	..	..	..	..	..

9-9. Rail load-to-locomotive ratio

	Million rail ton-km/locomotive											Annual Average		
	1980	*1988*	*1989*	*1990*	*1991*	*1992*	*1993*	*1994*	*1995*	*1996*	*1997*	*75-84*	*85-89*	*90-MR*
SUB-SAHARAN AFRICA	..	..	..	20.5	18.5	16.8	..	19.1	..	..	..	14.9	15.2	18.7
excluding South Africa	..	..	..	..	..	..	..	..	..	..	..	..	..	..
excl. S.Africa & Nigeria	..	..	..	..	..	..	..	..	..	..	..	..	..	..
Angola	..	..	..	..	..	..	..	..	..	..	..	..	..	..
Benin	..	..	..	..	..	..	..	..	..	..	..	..	..	..
Botswana	..	..	..	..	..	..	..	..	..	..	19.9	..	..	19.9
Burkina Faso	..	..	..	..	..	..	..	..	..	18.0	24.9	..	..	21.4
Burundi	..	..	..	..	..	..	..	..	..	..	..	..	..	..
Cameroon	10.9	6.5	9.0	10.1	8.9	9.6	8.6	12.4	13.3	10.0	14.2	9.8	8.4	10.9
Cape Verde	..	..	..	..	..	..	..	..	..	..	..	..	..	..
Central African Republic	..	..	..	..	..	..	..	..	..	..	..	..	..	..
Chad	..	..	..	..	..	..	..	..	..	..	..	..	..	..
Comoros	..	..	..	..	..	..	..	..	..	..	..	..	..	..
Congo, Democratic Rep. of	11.7	10.9	..	11.2	..	..	..	1.0	..	..	1.7	12.0	11.5	4.6
Congo, Republic of	..	..	..	..	14.8	9.4	..	5.8	..	..	3.0	11.3	9.4	8.3
Côte d'Ivoire	12.8	..	..	8.0	6.7	6.8	4.5	4.5	5.7	..	17.4	12.3	12.3	7.7
Djibouti	..	..	..	..	..	..	..	..	..	..	..	..	..	..
Equatorial Guinea	..	..	..	..	..	..	..	..	..	..	..	..	..	..
Eritrea	..	..	..	..	..	..	..	..	..	..	..	..	..	..
Ethiopia	..	..	6.1	..	2.3	..	..	..	..	..	..	..	6.1	2.3
Gabon	2.1	7.4	6.1	..	..	4.8	5.2	5.3	7.6	..	30.8	4.2	6.6	10.7
Gambia, The	..	..	..	..	..	..	..	..	..	..	..	..	..	..
Ghana	..	..	..	3.3	..	..	..	..	..	..	..	..	1.6	3.3
Guinea	..	..	..	..	..	..	..	..	..	..	..	..	..	..
Guinea-Bissau	..	..	..	..	..	..	..	..	..	..	..	..	..	..
Kenya	6.9	..	9.2	8.8	9.0	..	..	..	..	..	..	9.2	8.7	8.9
Lesotho	..	..	..	..	..	..	..	..	..	..	..	..	..	..
Liberia	..	..	..	..	..	..	..	..	..	..	..	..	..	..
Madagascar	..	..	..	..	..	..	..	..	..	..	..	..	..	..
Malawi	..	1.4	1.4	1.4	1.5	1.1	1.0	0.9	1.1	..	..	3.5	1.9	1.2
Mali	..	6.7	7.8	7.8	7.8	7.9	..	..	..	..	11.2	6.6	9.0	8.7
Mauritania	..	..	..	..	..	..	..	..	..	..	..	..	..	..
Mauritius	..	..	..	..	..	..	..	..	..	..	..	..	..	..
Mozambique	..	..	..	..	..	..	..	..	..	..	5.9	..	..	5.9
Namibia	..	..	..	27.7	21.4	22.3	19.9	20.3	21.6	..	..	..	..	22.2
Niger	..	..	..	..	..	..	..	..	..	..	..	..	..	..
Nigeria	3.8	..	..	..	..	0.3	..	0.0	..	..	..	5.0	2.5	0.2
Rwanda	..	..	..	..	..	..	..	..	..	..	..	..	..	..
São Tomé and Principe	..	..	..	..	..	..	..	..	..	..	..	..	..	..
Senegal	13.3	18.4	16.7	20.9	18.0	16.4	14.6	16.1	..	..	..	14.3	18.0	17.2
Seychelles	..	..	..	..	..	..	..	..	..	..	..	..	..	..
Sierra Leone	..	..	..	..	..	..	..	..	..	10.8	15.4	..	..	13.1
Somalia	..	..	..	..	..	..	..	..	..	..	..	..	..	..
South Africa	..	19.9	23.2	25.4	23.6	22.6	25.8	26.4	26.9	..	..	18.2	20.5	25.1
Sudan	8.0	..	..	..	4.5	..	..	..	11.1	14.2	12.3	7.0	4.8	10.5
Swaziland	..	..	..	..	..	..	..	..	..	..	..	..	..	..
Tanzania	..	..	8.4	..	11.7	11.4	13.9	12.2	14.9	..	17.4	7.7	8.1	13.6
Togo	..	..	..	..	..	..	..	..	..	..	..	..	..	..
Uganda	..	2.1	1.9	3.1	2.7	2.0	2.3	3.5	4.1	..	8.3	..	1.5	3.7
Zambia	16.1	23.0	22.7	7.5	15.4	14.6	15.1	9.9	6.8	..	7.2	17.2	21.1	10.9
Zimbabwe	21.7	19.3	..	13.6	14.0	16.0	17.5	27.9	27.5	..	..	20.7	20.0	19.4
NORTH AFRICA	9.9	..	..	10.2	10.6	9.7	10.3	10.4	..	..	10.3	9.9	10.3	10.2
Algeria	9.8	15.6	13.3	12.2	12.5	10.7	11.1	10.8	..	..	7.7	10.9	13.6	10.8
Egypt, Arab Republic	3.9	..	..	3.7	6.1	3.6	4.9	4.9	..	..	5.1	3.7	3.8	4.7
Libya	..	..	..	..	..	..	..	..	..	..	..	..	..	..
Morocco	19.5	24.2	18.7	20.4	17.3	19.6	17.4	19.2	19.8	..	22.3	19.1	20.3	19.4
Tunisia	13.9	10.8	10.5	9.3	9.3	10.3	14.0	12.7	13.4	..	13.5	12.7	10.4	11.8
ALL AFRICA	..	..	..	16.0	15.2	13.9	16.4	15.5	..	..	..	12.9	13.9	15.4

9-10. Air transport

	Aircraft departures (Thousands)		Passengers carried (Thousands)		Air freight (million tons per km)	
	1999	2000	1999	2000	1999	2000
SUB-SAHARAN AFRICA	338	360	17,122	18,107	..	..
excluding South Africa	234	249	9,718	10,107	..	..
excl. S. Africa & Nigeria	226	240	9,299	9,692	..	..
Angola	5	4	294	235	52	61
Benin	2	2	84	77	14	12
Botswana	6	7	144	166	0	0
Burkina Faso	3	3	147	144	14	12
Burundi	..	..	..	..	0	..
Cameroon	5	6	293	273	47	51
Cape Verde	12	13	252	264	1	1
Central African Republic	2	2	84	77	14	12
Chad	2	2	84	77	14	12
Comoros	..	..	..	..	..	..
Congo, Democratic Rep. of	..	..	..	..	..	..
Congo, Republic of	6	6	132	128	14	12
Côte d'Ivoire	6	7	260	262	14	12
Djibouti	..	..	..	..	..	..
Equatorial Guinea	..	..	..	..	0	..
Eritrea	..	..	..	..	..	..
Ethiopia	25	27	861	945	102	78
Gabon	7	8	423	442	54	58
Gambia, The	..	..	..	..	..	..
Ghana	5	5	304	314	31	40
Guinea	1	1	59	61	1	1
Guinea-Bissau	..	..	..	..	0	..
Kenya	25	29	1,358	1,557	66	77
Lesotho	0	0	1	1	0	0
Liberia	..	..	..	..	..	..
Madagascar	19	22	640	667	28	33
Malawi	4	5	112	116	1	1
Mali	2	2	84	77	14	12
Mauritania	4	4	187	185	14	13
Mauritius	11	12	823	949	177	183
Mozambique	6	7	235	260	7	7
Namibia	6	6	214	245	37	76
Niger	2	2	84	77	14	12
Nigeria	8	9	420	415	10	9
Rwanda	..	..	..	..	..	..
São Tomé and Principe	1	1	34	35	0	0
Senegal	2	2	103	98	14	0
Seychelles	19	19	347	394	20	20
Sierra Leone	..	0	..	18	..	9
Somalia	..	..	..	..	..	..
South Africa	104	110	7,404	8,000	688	688
Sudan	8	8	390	408	34	37
Swaziland	3	0	83	0	0	0
Tanzania	5	6	190	182	2	3
Togo	2	2	84	77	14	12
Uganda	3	3	179	187	22	21
Zambia	5	6	78	89	0	1
Zimbabwe	15	14	651	606	158	159
NORTH AFRICA	151	155	13,457	13,704	..	..
Algeria	36	37	2,937	2,995	15	13
Egypt, Arab Republic	44	47	4,620	4,522	270	278
Libya	6	7	586	609	0	0
Morocco	44	45	3,392	3,671	58	63
Tunisia	20	20	1,923	1,908	19	21
ALL AFRICA	489	515	30,579	31,811	..	..

Technical notes

Tables

Table 9-1. Electric power consumption per capita. This table refers to per capita electricity consumption, which means the production of power plants and combined heat and power plants, less distribution losses, and own use by heat and power plants (IEA and UN *Energy Statistics Yearbook*).

Table 9-2. Energy production and use, 1980 and 1999. This table presents three indicators. *Energy production* refers to commercial forms of primary energy—petroleum (crude oil, natural gas liquids, and oil from nonconventional sources), natural gas, solid fuels, and primary electricity—all converted into oil equivalent (IEA and UN *Energy Statistics Yearbook*). *Commercial energy use* is indigenous production plus imports and stock changes, minus exports and international marine bunkers (IEA and UN *Energy Statistics Yearbook*). *Electric power transmission* includes losses in transmission between sources of supply and points of distribution and in the distribution to consumers, including pilferage. Production less transmission and distribution losses, own-use, and transformation losses is equal to end-use electricity consumption (IEA and UN *Energy Statistics Yearbook*).

Table 9-3. Telephone, radio, and television availability, 1995–00. This table presents data for six communication indicators. Telephone mainlines (ITU) refer to telephone lines connecting a customer's equipment to the public switched telephone network, where mainline is normally identified by a unique number. Mainlines are presented for every 1,000 people (Table 1.2). *Waiting list* shows the number of applications (in thousands) for a connection to a mainline that have been held up by a lack of technical capacity (ITU). *Cost of local call* is the cost of a three-minute call within the same exchange area using the subscriber's equipment (that is, not from a public phone) (ITU). *Mobile phones* refer to users of portable telephones who subscribe to an automatic public mobile telephone service using cellular technology that provides access to the public switched-telephone network, per 1,000 people (Table 1.2)(ITU). *Radios* are the estimated number of radio receivers in use for broadcast to the general public, per 1,000 people (Table 1.2) (*UNESCO Statistical Yearbook*). *Television sets* are the estimated number of television sets in use, per 1,000 people (Table 1.2) (ITU).

Table 9-4. Personal computers and Internet use. *Personal computers* are self-contained computers designed to be be used by a single individual. *Internet hosts* are computers with active Internet Protocol (IP) addresses connected to the Internet. All hosts without a country code identification are assumed to be located in the United States. *Internet users* are people with access to the worldwide network. The data on personal computers and Internet users are from the ITU. They are reported in the ITU's *World Development Report 2000, Challenges to the Network: Internet for Development* (1999), and the *World Telecommunications Indicators Database* (2000b). The data on Internet hosts are from the Internet Software Consortium (*www.isc.org*).

Table 9-5. Vehicle ownership. Vehicles (International Road Federation) include all forms of road transportation, except buses. They are expressed as a ratio of 1,000 people (Table 1.2).

Table 9-6. Road-to-population ratio. This table presents the ratio of 1,000 kilometers of paved or unpaved road (International Road Federation) per 1 million people (Table 1.2).

Table 9-7. Paved primary roads. This table presents paved primary roads, that is, those that have been sealed with asphalt or similar road-bonding material (International Road Federation) as a ratio to total roads and then shows the percentage that is in good condition (World Bank data).

Table 9-8. Rail goods traffic-to-$PPP GDP ratio. This measures the tonnage of goods per million dollars of GDP measured in PPP terms (World Bank data).

Table 9-9. Rail load-to-locomotive ratio. This is the volume of rail transported goods (measured in millions of metric tons times kilometers traveled) per single locomotive (World Bank data).

Table 9-10. Air transport. *Aircraft departures* are the number of domestic and international takeoffs of air carriers registered in the country. *Air passengers carried* include both domestic and international aircraft passengers of air carriers registered in the country. *Air freight* is the sum of the metric tons of freight, express, and diplomatic bags carried on each flight stage (the operation of an aircraft from takeoff to its next landing) multiplied by the stage distance of air carriers registered in the country. The air transport data are from the International Civil Aviation Organization's (ICAO) *Civil Aviation Statistics of the World* and ICAO staff estimates.

Methodology used for regional aggregations and period averages in chapter 9

	Aggregations [a]				*Period averages* [b]
Table	*(1)*	*(6)*	*(7)*	*(8)*	*(1)*
9-1		x			x
9-2					
Columns 1-4	x				
Columns 5-6				x	
9-3					
Columns 1-2, 4-6		x			
Column 3				x	
9-4					
Columns 1-2		x			
Column 3	x				
9-5		x	x		x
9-6		x	x		x
9-7					
Columns 1-8				x	
Column 9		x			
9-8				x	x
9-9		x	x		x
9-10	x				

Note: Regional aggregations are shown in the rows for Sub-Saharan Africa, North Africa, and All Africa. Period averages are shown in the last three columns. This table shows only the methodologies used in this chapter.

a. Regional aggregations: (1) simple total; (2) simple total of the first indicator divided by the simple total of the second indicator (same country coverage); (3) simple total of the gap-filled indicator; (4) simple total of the gap-filled main indicator divided by the simple total of the gap-filled secondary indicator; (5) simple total of the first gap-filled main indicator less the simple total of the second gap-filled main indicator, all divided by the simple total of the secondary indicator; (6) weighted total (by population); (7) median; (8) no aggregation; (9) simple arithmetic mean.

b. Period averages: (1) arithmetic mean (using the same series as shown in the table i.e., ratio if the rest of the table is shown as ratio, level if the rest of the table is shown as level, growth rate if the rest is shown as growth rate); (2) least-squares growth rate (using main indicator); (3) least-squares growth rate (using main indicator in constant terms, with the rest of the table in current terms).

10

Privatization of Public Enterprises

In the past, the dominance of the public enterprise sector in most African economies warranted the collection and publication of the sector's performance. With its diminishing size and importance due to privatization, it is no longer informative to produce such data. Instead, as privatization programs advance to maturity, it will become important to track the performance of private sector businesses. In the meantime, measurement of the level of privatization activity is a useful gauge of the decreasing role of governments in commercial business; conversely, it indicates how much of state-owned commercial activity has been transferred to the private sector. To the extent that data are available, it is also possible to measure how privatization has, over time, contributed to government revenues and mobilized savings and investment. However, this measurement is by no means easy or precise, partly because of incomplete and inconsistent data but also because of redefinitions of the public enterprise sector. For example, some enterprises, notably those formerly in a monopolistic position, are being split in order to separate their commercial, social, developmental, and regulatory activities. In some cases, separate operating divisions or geographically distinct assets are sold separately. And in yet other cases, commercial and semi-commercial activities are being separated out from government ministries and other agencies to become redefined as "commercial enterprises." These include, for example, business centers, media, and some training institutes. So, the public enterprise sector, as defined several years ago, has changed. Nevertheless, the well over 3,500 privatization transactions that were reported across Africa up to the end of 2000 have brought about fundamental changes:

- The fiscal burden of public enterprises has been reduced or eliminated.
- Privatization receipts have contributed to a reduction in fiscal deficits.
- Privatization has attracted foreign direct investment both to acquire enterprises and for post-privatization investment in those businesses.
- The process has stimulated private sector development by making investment opportunities available, spurring capital market development, and contributing to a more competitive business environment.
- Being a politically sensitive subject, the process has highlighted the need for transparency and public accountability.

The tables presented in this chapter summarize data contained in the World Bank's Africa Privatization Database, which is accessible through the internet at:

http://www.worldbank.org/afr/database/afrpriv/p1query.cfm

10-1. Summary of privatization of public enterprises

	Total no. of trans-actions	Total sales value (US$m)	Transactions completed: Before 1997	1997	1998	1999	2000	2001	Transactions by sector: Agric. prod. & process	Financial	Manu-facturing	Services	Trade	Other
SUB-SAHARAN AFRICA	3,610	7,355	2,543	254	151	112	91	19	788	159	1,106	819	408	330
excluding South Africa	3,594	4,894	2,539	252	147	109	89	19	788	159	1,100	809	408	330
excl. S. Africa & Nigeria	3,513	4,688	2,458	254	151	112	91	19	788	159	1,077	799	408	330
Angola	332	25	56	..	..	..	1	..	9	1	29	9	9	275
Benin	50	63	44	..	..	3	1	..	8	1	18	18	5	..
Botswana	..	..	..	..	..	..	..	..	..	..	..	..	..	..
Burkina Faso	47	24	26	..	2	9	..	1	11	4	17	13	2	..
Burundi	45	14	42	3	..	..	..	..	21	4	7	10	3	..
Cameroon	55	72	39	5	4	1	1	5	24	4	8	18	1	..
Cape Verde	56	172	33	9	1	3	7	1	9	3	20	20	4	..
Central African Republic	37	..	35	..	1	1	..	..	8	6	9	14	..	..
Chad	36	6	31	..	..	2	2	1	11	6	7	9	3	..
Comoros	4	0	..	..	..	..	..	..	..	..	..	..	..	4
Congo, Dem. Rep. of	21	..	21	..	..	..	..	..	3	1	6	10	1	..
Congo, Rep. of	102	50	61	..	..	..	3	1	37	9	22	32	2	..
Côte d'Ivoire	105	811	68	15	11	6	4	..	40	5	34	24	2	..
Djibouti	..	..	..	..	..	..	..	..	..	..	..	..	..	..
Equatorial Guinea	3	0	..	..	..	..	..	..	..	..	..	..	..	3
Eritrea	..	..	..	..	..	..	..	..	..	..	..	..	..	..
Ethiopia	155	203	103	13	18	10	11	..	23	..	34	19	79	..
Gabon	31	..	..	1	1	..	2	2	1	1	3	1	..	25
Gambia, The	34	10	31	..	1	..	1	..	8	4	9	8	5	..
Ghana	236	674	189	27	4	10	4	..	44	10	102	50	30	..
Guinea	117	9	116	1	..	..	..	..	11	7	56	14	29	..
Guinea-Bissau	29	1	29	..	..	..	..	..	4	..	6	14	5	..
Kenya	188	248	157	27	4	..	..	..	71	12	59	39	7	..
Lesotho	33	24	9	1	5	6	10	2	2	6	3	18	4	..
Liberia	..	..	..	..	..	..	..	..	..	..	..	..	..	..
Madagascar	136	43	84	..	..	1	1	..	50	5	47	24	10	..
Malawi	69	57	43	5	5	12	3	..	38	5	14	9	..	3
Mali	77	32	60	..	1	1	8	..	13	3	26	27	8	..
Mauritania	57	10	35	..	..	2	6	1	21	6	7	19	3	1
Mauritius	..	..	..	..	..	..	..	..	..	..	..	..	..	..
Mozambique	579	217	548	31	..	..	..	..	75	2	256	120	126	..
Namibia	..	..	..	..	..	..	..	..	..	..	..	..	..	..
Niger	35	3	34	..	..	..	..	1	2	2	6	4	3	18
Nigeria	81	207	81	..	..	..	..	..	23	24	23	10	1	..
Rwanda	2	..	..	..	..	..	..	..	1	..	1	..	..	..
São Tomé and Principe	9	..	9	..	..	..	..	..	..	..	5	1	3	..
Senegal	66	412	49	4	6	2	2	..	7	11	16	30	2	..
Seychelles	..	..	..	..	..	..	..	..	..	..	..	..	..	..
Sierra Leone	10	..	8	1	..	..	..	..	..	..	4	6	..	..
Somalia	..	..	..	..	..	..	..	..	..	..	..	..	..	..
South Africa	16	2,461	4	2	4	3	2	..	..	..	6	10	..	..
Sudan	32	..	32	..	..	..	..	..	11	1	8	11	1	..
Swaziland	..	..	..	..	..	..	..	..	..	..	..	..	..	..
Tanzania	284	246	154	40	64	23	2	..	98	3	109	46	27	1
Togo	60	39	44	9	3	1	3	..	9	1	25	24	1	..
Uganda	105	149	85	2	..	3	11	4	21	5	33	34	12	..
Zambia	270	906	181	55	16	12	6	..	71	6	70	103	20	..
Zimbabwe	6	166	2	3	..	1	..	..	3	1	1	1	..	..
NORTH AFRICA	186	595	71	30	40	1	..	..	13	..	58	53	2	16
Algeria	..	..	..	..	..	..	..	..	..	..	..	..	..	..
Egypt	59	307	15	8	31	..	..	..	5	..	34	8	1	6
Libya	..	..	..	..	..	..	..	..	..	..	..	..	..	..
Morocco	64	259	29	16	6	1	..	..	4	..	10	28	..	10
Tunisia	63	29	27	6	3	..	..	..	4	..	14	17	1	..
ALL AFRICA	3,796	7,950	2,614	284	191	113	..	..	801	..	1,164	872	410	346

10-2. Divestiture Methods Employed (to end 2001)

	Sales of shares				*Sale of Assets*			*Other methods*							
	Competitive sale	*Direct Sale*	*Preemption rights*	*Public flotation*	*Liquidation*	*Competitive sale*	*Direct sale*	*Debt/ Equity swaps*	*Leases*	*Joint ventures*	*Mgmt./ employee buyouts*	*Mgmt. contracts*	*Trustees*	*Restitution*	*Other*
SUB-SAHARAN AFRICA	971	83	181	104	641	558	40	13	142	37	80	57	19	51	629
excluding South Africa	961	83	181	103	641	558	40	13	142	37	80	57	19	51	625
excl. S. Africa & Nigeria	956	83	181	66	641	558	40	13	142	37	80	57	19	51	629
Angola	..	..	..	..	..	57	..	..	..	..	..	..	..	..	275
Benin	5	2	..	..	23	12	3	..	2	..	..	2	..	1	..
Botswana	..	..	..	..	..	..	..	..	..	..	..	..	..	..	..
Burkina Faso	19	3	..	..	16	..	..	..	1	..	..	1	1	1	4
Burundi	11	3	..	..	13	5	..	..	..	..	1	9	..	..	3
Cameroon	20	..	..	..	19	..	..	..	..	..	..	..	..	..	16
Cape Verde	21	2	5	..	11	1	1	..	..	..	6	1	..	..	8
Central African Republic	2	..	..	..	26	..	..	..	1	1	..	1	..	..	6
Chad	15	2	..	..	11	..	..	..	..	..	..	5	..	..	3
Comoros	..	..	..	..	..	..	..	..	..	..	..	..	..	..	4
Congo, Dem. Rep. of	1	..	..	..	15	..	..	..	..	..	..	5	..	..	..
Congo, Rep. of	2	..	..	..	53	..	..	..	..	..	..	2	..	..	45
Côte d'Ivoire	15	2	23	22	2	24	8	..	3	1	..	..	..	..	3
Djibouti	..	..	..	..	..	..	..	..	..	..	..	..	..	..	..
Equatorial Guinea	..	..	..	..	..	..	..	..	..	..	..	..	..	..	3
Eritrea	..	..	..	..	..	..	..	..	..	..	..	..	..	..	..
Ethiopia	..	..	..	..	..	30	..	..	..	..	44	..	..	..	81
Gabon	4	..	..	..	1	..	..	..	..	..	..	..	..	..	26
Gambia, The	13	7	..	..	3	1	..	..	5	1	1	..	..	..	2
Ghana	10	11	19	13	56	76	12	2	5	13	..	1	..	12	6
Guinea	42	1	..	..	67	1	..	..	4	..	..	2	..	..	..
Guinea-Bissau	7	2	..	..	8	2	..	..	2	1	..	7	..	..	..
Kenya	13	..	96	16	36	17	4	1	..	..	1	1	..	..	3
Lesotho	7	3	..	..	8	3	..	..	1	..	..	1	..	..	10
Liberia	..	..	..	..	..	..	..	..	..	..	..	..	..	..	..
Madagascar	6	14	..	..	29	15	6	..	1	1	..	3	..	8	53
Malawi	22	5	..	2	..	13	..	1	..	..	..	..	3	..	23
Mali	14	1	..	..	31	11	..	..	1	..	..	1	3	..	15
Mauritania	26	..	..	..	17	3	..	..	..	..	..	1	3	..	7
Mauritius	..	..	..	..	..	..	..	..	..	..	..	..	..	..	..
Mozambique	509	..	..	..	..	22	..	..	37	10	..	1	..	..	..
Namibia	..	..	..	..	..	..	..	..	..	..	..	..	..	..	..
Niger	13	..	..	..	17	..	..	..	..	..	..	2	..	..	3
Nigeria	5	5	..	37	2	29	..	..	..	..	1	..	2	..	..
Rwanda	..	..	..	..	..	..	..	..	..	..	..	..	..	..	2
São Tomé and Principe	..	1	..	..	6	..	..	..	..	..	1	1	..	..	..
Senegal	29	1	1	2	23	1	..	1	3	1	..	1	..	..	3
Seychelles	..	..	..	..	..	..	..	..	..	..	..	..	..	..	..
Sierra Leone	..	..	..	..	1	..	..	..	5	..	..	3	..	..	1
Somalia	..	..	..	..	..	..	..	..	..	..	..	..	..	..	..
South Africa	10	..	..	1	..	1	..	..	..	..	..	..	..	..	4
Sudan	7	..	..	..	..	15	..	5	1	..	..	..	..	..	4
Swaziland	..	..	..	..	..	..	..	..	..	..	..	..	..	..	..
Tanzania	61	4	13	1	84	70	3	1	25	3	6	3	2	2	6
Togo	10	7	..	..	20	13	1	..	6	..	..	3	..	..	..
Uganda	14	..	10	2	21	25	..	2	1	4	2	..	5	11	8
Zambia	37	6	14	4	22	111	2	..	38	1	17	..	..	16	2
Zimbabwe	1	1	..	4	..	..	..	..	..	..	..	..	..	..	..
NORTH AFRICA	..	..	..	..	..	..	..	..	..	..	..	..	..	..	..
Algeria	..	..	..	..	..	..	..	..	..	..	..	..	..	..	..
Egypt	..	..	..	..	..	..	..	..	..	..	..	..	..	..	..
Libya	..	..	..	..	..	..	..	..	..	..	..	..	..	..	..
Morocco	..	..	..	..	..	..	..	..	..	..	..	..	..	..	..
Tunisia	..	..	..	..	..	..	..	..	..	..	..	..	..	..	..
ALL AFRICA	971	83	181	104	641	558	40	13	142	37	80	57	19	51	629

10-3. Progress in privatization: ownership and control changes*

	Transfer of majority ownership to private shareholders	*Government retention of majority ownership*	*Government retention of minority interest*	*Sales of minority government interest*	*Total share transactions*	*Total asset sales and liquidation*	*Other transactions*	*Total transactions*
SUB-SAHARAN AFRICA	2,392	219	383	228	1,340	1,240	1,030	3,610
excluding South Africa	2,386	213	382	227	1,329	1,239	1,026	3,594
excl. S. Africa & Nigeria	2,331	212	374	204	1,282	1,208	1,023	3,513
Angola	56	..	..	..	..	57	275	332
Benin	42	3	1	1	7	38	5	50
Botswana	..	..	..	..	..	..	..	..
Burkina Faso	27	..	21	2	22	16	9	47
Burundi	31	..	1	11	14	18	13	45
Cameroon	49	1	1	..	20	19	16	55
Cape Verde	41	2	5	5	28	13	15	56
Central African Republic	29	2	1	2	2	26	9	37
Chad	19	5	6	4	17	11	8	36
Comoros	..	..	..	..	..	..	4	4
Congo, Dem. Rep. of	16	5	..	..	1	15	5	21
Congo, Rep. of	60	1	1	..	2	53	47	102
Côte d'Ivoire	52	9	28	29	63	35	7	105
Djibouti	..	..	..	..	..	..	..	..
Equatorial Guinea	..	..	..	..	..	..	3	3
Eritrea	..	..	..	..	..	..	..	..
Ethiopia	10	..	..	..	..	30	125	155
Gabon	..	1	..	..	4	1	26	31
Gambia, The	20	6	..	6	20	4	10	34
Ghana	183	12	25	24	53	144	39	236
Guinea	108	9	18	..	43	68	6	117
Guinea-Bissau	20	9	..	..	9	10	10	29
Kenya	77	3	53	61	125	57	6	188
Lesotho	15	4	3	1	10	11	12	33
Liberia	..	..	..	..	..	..	..	..
Madagascar	82	4	17	..	20	50	66	136
Malawi	39	..	7	5	29	13	27	69
Mali	56	1	4	3	15	42	20	77
Mauritania	31	3	7	18	26	20	11	57
Mauritius	..	..	..	..	..	..	..	..
Mozambique	536	43	75	..	509	22	48	579
Namibia	..	..	..	..	..	..	..	..
Niger	30	2	4	2	13	17	5	35
Nigeria	55	1	8	23	47	31	3	81
Rwanda	..	..	..	..	..	..	2	2
São Tomé and Principe	8	1	..	..	1	6	2	9
Senegal	49	8	16	6	33	24	9	66
Seychelles	..	..	..	..	..	..	..	..
Sierra Leone	1	9	1	..	..	1	9	10
Somalia	..	..	..	..	..	..	..	..
South Africa	6	6	1	1	11	1	4	16
Sudan	31	1	3	..	7	15	10	32
Swaziland	..	..	..	..	..	..	..	..
Tanzania	241	29	33	3	79	157	48	284
Togo	40	8	1	9	17	34	9	60
Uganda	95	1	9	7	26	46	33	105
Zambia	231	30	28	5	61	135	74	270
Zimbabwe	6	..	5	..	6	..	..	6
NORTH AFRICA	..	..	..	..	..	..	..	..
Algeria	..	..	..	..	..	..	..	..
Egypt	..	..	..	..	..	..	..	..
Libya	..	..	..	..	..	..	..	..
Morocco	..	..	..	..	..	..	..	..
Tunisia	..	..	..	..	..	..	..	..
ALL AFRICA	..	..	..	..	..	..	..	..

* Reflect data to end 2001

Technical notes

Tables

Table 10-1. Summary of privatization of public enterprises. For purposes of monitoring and reporting on privatization activity, all reported transactions involving a sale of assets or shares (however small) or the formal yielding of management control (as through a management contract) are included in the World Bank's Africa Privatization Database. Hence, in the table, "privatization" is used generically to include: the sale or disposal of some or all of the assets of public enterprises, the sale of government-owned shares in enterprises, the reduction in equity percentage held by a government through share dilutions or through transfer of enterprise assets to a new joint venture, liquidations, leases, and management contracts. Sometimes, the process of privatizing an enterprise involves several consecutive transactions (for example, a sale of a block of shares to a core investor and a subsequent initial public offering). The table summarizes the data contained in the Africa Privatization Database which originate from national privatization agencies and other sources. The data are frequently updated and changes to previous entries occur as more information becomes available. There are a few instances where previously reported privatizations are removed from the database because a transaction has been nullified due to non-fulfillment of contractual conditions on the part of one of the parties. For financial data, the term "sale value" is preferred since the use of the term "proceeds" might imply the value of amounts actually paid. In practice, some deals are structured so that new investors may acquire assets or shares on deferred terms. Also, it should be noted that: (i) in the cases of some subsidiary companies, the cash proceeds are not paid to government but instead go to the parent company; and (ii) for official liquidations, the proceeds are paid to the liquidator who first applies them toward settling enterprise debts.

Table 10-2. Divestiture methods employed (to end 2001). The table shows the various privatization methods employed in each country. The methods employed could not be confirmed for all transactions. "Direct sales" refers to transactions which were negotiated directly with one party and which were not the outcome of a competitive bidding process. However, in some cases a direct sale was concluded (on a non-competitive basis) as a result of a failure of an earlier competitive bidding process. "Preemptive rights" refers to transactions whereby a government has sold shares to an existing private shareholder (or shareholders) who exercised preemptive rights to acquire those shares in accordance with specific provisions of the company's charter (Articles of Association). In some cases, the charter specified the amount to be paid per share or the formula for calculating that amount; otherwise it has been the subject of negotiation. "Joint ventures" refer to the type of transaction whereby a government concluded a deal (usually with a foreign investor) involving the formation of a new company in which the government's equity contribution was in the form of the major or all assets of a public enterprise. The remaining shell company would then be maintained only as a book company or be liquidated; if it were liquidated it is not included as a liquidation since this would be double counting. Transactions described as "Trustees" refer to privatizations achieved by transference of shares of a public enterprise to a trustee for onward sale, at a later date or over a period, to the public or to selected segments of the public. "Restitutions" are those transactions whereby a company has been handed back to a previous owner from whom the company had been expropriated. "Other sales" includes sundry methods, such as enterprises donated by governments to local communities, but principally comprises transactions where the method of privatization was not reported.

Table 10-3. Progress in privatization: ownership and control changes (to end 2001). This table presents the inferred outcome of privatization transactions on the ownership and control of enterprises or their assets. Ownership changes are important in indicating the effect that privatization transactions may or may not have on the enterprises and in indicating the extent of a government's willingness and/or ability to exit from equity participation in commercial activity. Although a government's influence is not necessarily restricted by its equity participation, it is generally assumed that once a government owns less than 50 percent of the voting shares of a company, that company is "private" and the private shareholders (except in the instance of exercise of golden share rights) have management control of the company. Ownership control is usually unaffected when government continues to be a majority shareholder or sells a minority interest. Concessions, leases, and management contracts are assumed not to have affected ownership rights but to have transferred management control to the private sector for a defined period. The table shows the number of reported transactions where governments have: fully sold wholly- or majority-owned enterprises, sold shares and transferred ownership control but retained a minority equity interest, sold shares but retained ownership control, sold a proportion of a minority stake, and other transactions where management control has been ceded.

Methodology used for regional aggregations and period averages in chapter 10

	Aggregations [a]		*Period averages* [b]
Table	*(1)*	*(2)*	*(1)*
10-1	x		
10-2	x		
10-3	x		

Note: Regional aggregations are shown in the rows for Sub-Saharan Africa, North Africa, and All Africa. Period averages are shown in the last three columns. This table shows only the methodologies used in this chapter.

a. Regional aggregations: (1) simple total; (2) simple total of the first indicator divided by the simple total of the second indicator (same country coverage); (3) simple total of the gap-filled indicator; (4) simple total of the gap-filled main indicator divided by the simple total of the gap-filled secondary indicator; (5) simple total of the first gap-filled main indicator less the simple total of the second gap-filled main indicator, all divided by the simple total of the secondary indicator; (6) weighted total (by population); (7) median; (8) no aggregation; (9) simple arithmetic mean.

b. Period averages: (1) arithmetic mean (using the same series as shown in the table i.e., ratio if the rest of the table is shown as ratio, level if the rest of the table is shown as level, growth rate if the rest is shown as growth rate); (2) least-squares growth rate (using main indicator); (3) least-squares growth rate (using main indicator in constant terms, with the rest of the table in current terms).

11

Labor Force and Employment

This chapter presents data on the level and structure of the labor force. The distribution of the labor force into various industrial activities is also given, as well as the participation rates of the population in economic activities. Information is also presented on average wages in different sectors.

The treatment of statistics on public sector employment is not consistent among countries. The scope covered often varies. While some countries include education and health sectors, others leave them out. Staff of local, regional, and state or provincial governments are likewise treated differently.

The stipulations on wages take different forms among the countries where such practice exists. While some countries have a minimum wage per hour worked, others stipulate a minimum monthly wage for a worker. To permit some measure of comparability, we have computed and reported the monthly average earnings per wage earner. These earnings are further converted to U.S. dollars at the Atlas exchange rate. These data should be used with caution since some countries have more than one minimum wage rate based on the industry and the occupation within the industry as well as on the region of the country concerned.

The definition of labor force or economically active population is that used by the International Labor Organization (ILO), which follows the UN system of national accounts (SNA). The labor force is measured by dividing economically active persons into two categories: employed and unemployed. Caution in the use of the data is necessary because, as pointed out in the ILO's *World Labor Report 1* (1987), there are many persons who do not clearly come within one of these categories or the other. Many are visibly underemployed in that they work less than full time. Others work full time but earn less than a subsistence income. Some of the unemployed may even be voluntarily idle.

The comparability of the data is further hampered by the fact that practices vary among countries as regards the treatment of such groups as armed forces, inmates of institutions, persons living on reservations, persons seeking their first job, seasonal workers, and persons engaged in part-time economic activities. In some countries, all or part of these groups are included among the economically active, while in others they are treated as inactive. In addition, the extent to which family workers who assist in family enterprises are included among the enumerated economically active population, particularly females, varies considerably from country to country. Further, in some countries the statistics of the economically active relate only to employed and unemployed persons above a specified age, while in others there is no such age provision.

The reference period is also an important factor of difference, especially when it comes to the classification of the labor force according to industry. In some countries, such classification refers to the actual position of each individual on the day of the census or survey date, while in others the data recorded refer to the usual position of each person, generally without reference to any given period of time.

The sources for the tables in this chapter are various issues of the ILO's *Yearbook of Labor Statistics*, and electronic ILO files kept in World Bank SIMA.

11-1. Number and gender structure of the labor force

	Total labor force (thousands)			Percentage of total labor force that is female		
	1980	1990	2001	1980	1990	2001
SUB-SAHARAN AFRICA	171,980	224,619	297,874	42.0	41.7	42.0
excluding South Africa	161,634	211,021	280,661	42.4	42.0	42.3
excl. S. Africa & Nigeria	132,114	172,559	229,035	43.8	43.5	43.5
Angola	3,491	4,484	6,217	47.0	46.5	46.3
Benin	1,657	2,114	2,910	47.0	48.3	48.3
Botswana	395	556	756	50.1	46.8	45.2
Burkina Faso	3,802	4,590	5,683	47.6	46.8	46.5
Burundi	2,269	2,934	3,798	50.2	49.1	48.6
Cameroon	3,649	4,671	6,205	36.8	37.0	38.1
Cape Verde	94	127	186	34.0	38.9	38.9
Central African Republic	1,215	1,447	1,820	..	..	..
Chad	2,233	2,783	3,837	43.4	44.0	44.8
Comoros	152	193	262	43.1	42.9	42.3
Congo, Democratic Rep. of	11,961	15,717	21,638	44.5	43.9	43.4
Congo, Republic of	703	933	1,284	42.4	43.2	43.5
Côte d'Ivoire	3,280	4,465	6,598	32.2	32.4	33.5
Djibouti	..	..	..	..	..	..
Equatorial Guinea	96	150	196	35.1	35.6	35.6
Eritrea	1,218	1,584	2,112	47.4	47.5	47.4
Ethiopia	16,924	22,806	28,261	42.3	40.9	40.9
Gabon	363	455	573	45.0	44.2	44.7
Gambia, The	330	470	678	44.8	44.6	45.1
Ghana	5,088	7,063	9,397	51.0	50.9	50.4
Guinea	2,293	2,821	3,591	47.1	47.5	47.2
Guinea-Bissau	382	453	575	39.9	40.1	40.5
Kenya	7,829	11,184	15,915	46.0	45.9	46.1
Lesotho	571	676	852	37.9	36.5	37.0
Liberia	790	989	1,292	38.4	39.1	39.6
Madagascar	4,323	5,453	7,557	45.2	45.0	44.7
Malawi	3,112	4,189	5,060	50.6	49.5	48.5
Mali	3,393	4,254	5,417	46.7	46.6	46.2
Mauritania	746	904	1,271	45.0	44.3	43.5
Mauritius	343	432	519	25.7	30.3	32.8
Mozambique	6,686	7,492	9,384	49.0	48.4	48.4
Namibia	429	571	739	40.1	40.4	40.9
Niger	2,803	3,746	5,262	44.6	44.1	44.3
Nigeria	29,519	38,462	51,625	36.2	35.4	36.6
Rwanda	2,639	3,628	4,722	49.1	49.0	48.8
São Tomé and Principe	..	..	..	..	..	..
Senegal	2,542	3,269	4,376	42.2	42.4	42.6
Seychelles	..	..	..	..	..	..
Sierra Leone	1,248	1,490	1,917	35.5	35.5	37.0
Somalia	2,968	3,170	3,889	43.4	43.3	43.4
South Africa	10,347	13,598	17,214	35.1	36.9	37.9
Sudan	7,070	9,207	12,716	26.9	27.1	29.8
Swaziland	202	262	394	33.5	37.0	37.8
Tanzania	9,508	13,122	17,731	49.8	49.6	49.0
Togo	1,099	1,447	1,930	39.3	39.8	40.0
Uganda	6,617	8,319	11,175	47.9	47.8	47.6
Zambia	2,398	3,184	4,391	45.4	45.7	44.7
Zimbabwe	3,204	4,755	5,947	44.4	44.2	44.5
NORTH AFRICA	29,265	38,446	52,935	27.2	27.6	31.0
Algeria	4,848	7,046	10,583	21.4	21.1	28.3
Egypt, Arab Republic	14,319	18,313	25,152	26.5	27.0	30.7
Libya	943	1,235	1,551	18.6	18.2	23.6
Morocco	6,968	8,987	11,779	33.5	34.6	34.8
Tunisia	2,187	2,865	3,871	28.9	29.1	31.9
ALL AFRICA	201,245	263,065	350,810	39.8	39.6	40.3

11-2. Children under 14 working in the labor force

	As percentage of population age 10 to 14			
	1970	1980	1990	2001
SUB-SAHARAN AFRICA	36.2	34.5	32.2	29.9
excluding South Africa	39.0	37.0	34.5	31.8
excl. S.Africa & Nigeria	40.9	39.2	36.2	33.5
Angola	31.4	29.7	28.1	25.9
Benin	34.4	30.3	28.6	26.3
Botswana	32.3	25.9	19.4	13.9
Burkina Faso	75.1	70.9	58.7	41.9
Burundi	50.8	50.0	49.4	48.4
Cameroon	38.9	33.9	27.5	22.5
Cape Verde	17.3	16.0	14.7	13.4
Central African Republic	45.0	39.4	33.8	28.6
Chad	41.9	41.6	40.0	36.3
Comoros	45.8	44.7	40.9	37.2
Congo, Democratic Rep. of	36.5	33.2	30.5	28.4
Congo, Republic of	28.3	27.5	26.6	25.3
Côte d'Ivoire	34.6	28.4	22.3	18.3
Djibouti	..	..	..	..
Equatorial Guinea	42.7	40.4	35.8	31.6
Eritrea	46.1	43.8	40.8	38.2
Ethiopia	48.5	46.3	43.5	40.9
Gabon	35.6	29.1	22.7	13.2
Gambia, The	45.9	44.4	40.2	33.2
Ghana	16.3	16.2	14.6	11.7
Guinea	43.3	41.2	37.0	30.5
Guinea-Bissau	45.2	43.4	40.4	36.4
Kenya	45.0	45.0	43.4	38.7
Lesotho	30.9	27.7	23.5	20.5
Liberia	31.1	25.7	21.8	14.7
Madagascar	41.7	40.2	37.6	33.8
Malawi	50.7	45.2	38.9	30.8
Mali	62.5	61.2	57.9	50.5
Mauritania	33.3	29.6	25.8	21.7
Mauritius	5.8	4.8	4.0	1.8
Mozambique	40.7	39.5	35.2	32.1
Namibia	40.2	33.6	26.0	16.5
Niger	48.8	47.8	46.8	43.2
Nigeria	30.8	29.2	27.6	23.5
Rwanda	43.3	42.5	42.1	41.3
São Tomé and Principe	..	..	..	..
Senegal	46.9	42.9	35.4	26.5
Seychelles	..	..	..	..
Sierra Leone	21.7	19.4	17.1	13.6
Somalia	39.9	37.7	34.5	31.0
South Africa	2.7	0.9	0.0	0.0
Sudan	34.1	33.3	31.4	27.0
Swaziland	19.1	17.2	15.3	11.9
Tanzania	45.6	42.8	42.1	36.4
Togo	40.4	36.1	30.4	26.5
Uganda	50.4	48.8	46.8	43.5
Zambia	21.1	19.0	16.9	15.5
Zimbabwe	41.1	36.7	31.8	26.6
NORTH AFRICA	12.7	15.1	8.8	5.8
Algeria	11.4	7.1	3.3	0.0
Egypt, Arab Republic	23.6	18.3	13.2	8.8
Libya	12.8	8.7	0.5	0.0
Morocco	21.5	20.9	10.6	0.6
Tunisia	12.2	5.8	0.0	0.0
ALL AFRICA	31.3	30.9	28.0	25.8

11-3. Unpaid family workers as share of active workers

	Percentage of unpaid family workers in economically active workers (most recent year available between 1980-2000)		
	Female	*Male*	*Total*
SUB-SAHARAN AFRICA	..	..	..
excluding South Africa	..	..	..
excl. S.Africa & Nigeria	..	..	..
Angola	..	..	..
Benin	..	..	..
Botswana	41.8	36.0	77.7
Burkina Faso	..	..	..
Burundi	..	..	..
Cameroon	32.7	9.2	41.9
Cape Verde	..	..	..
Central African Republic	..	..	..
Chad	..	..	..
Comoros	..	..	..
Congo, Democratic Rep. of	..	..	..
Congo, Republic of	..	..	..
Côte d'Ivoire	..	..	..
Djibouti	..	..	..
Equatorial Guinea	..	..	..
Eritrea	..	..	..
Ethiopia	..	..	..
Gabon	..	..	..
Gambia, The	..	..	..
Ghana	0.0	0.0	0.0
Guinea	..	..	..
Guinea-Bissau	..	..	..
Kenya	..	..	..
Lesotho	..	..	..
Liberia	..	..	..
Madagascar	..	..	..
Malawi	..	..	..
Mali	..	..	..
Mauritania	..	..	..
Mauritius	..	..	..
Mozambique	..	..	..
Namibia	..	..	..
Niger	..	..	..
Nigeria	14.9	8.6	23.5
Rwanda	..	..	..
São Tomé and Principe	..	..	..
Senegal	..	..	..
Seychelles	0.4	0.2	0.6
Sierra Leone	..	..	..
Somalia	..	..	..
South Africa	..	..	..
Sudan	..	..	..
Swaziland	..	..	..
Tanzania	..	..	..
Togo	..	..	..
Uganda	..	..	..
Zambia	..	..	..
Zimbabwe	..	..	..
NORTH AFRICA	..	6.9	13.4
Algeria	..	5.6	6.2
Egypt, Arab Republic	1.9	15.0	16.9
Libya	..	..	..
Morocco	..	..	..
Tunisia	18.5	5.1	23.6
ALL AFRICA	..	..	..

11-4. Industrial structure of the labor force

	Percentage of labor force working in								
	Agriculture			*Industry*			*Services*		
	1980	*1990*	*1995-1999*	*1980*	*1990*	*1995-1999*	*1980*	*1990*	*1995-1999*
SUB-SAHARAN AFRICA	..	..	..	..	..	..	..	..	..
excluding South Africa	..	..	..	..	..	..	..	..	..
excl. S.Africa & Nigeria	68	64	..	12	12	..	20	24	..
Angola	76	75	..	8	8	..	16	17	..
Benin	67	64	..	7	8	..	26	28	..
Botswana	5	3	..	33	31	..	62	66	..
Burkina Faso	92	92	..	3	2	..	5	6	..
Burundi	..	..	..	..	..	..	..	..	..
Cameroon	73	70	..	8	9	..	19	22	..
Cape Verde	36	31	..	31	29	..	33	40	..
Central African Republic	85	80	..	3	4	..	12	16	..
Chad	88	83	..	3	4	..	9	13	..
Comoros	81	77	..	8	9	..	12	13	..
Congo, Democratic Rep. of	72	68	..	12	13	..	16	19	..
Congo, Republic of	58	49	..	13	15	..	29	37	..
Côte d'Ivoire	65	60	..	8	10	..	27	31	..
Djibouti	..	..	..	..	..	..	..	..	..
Equatorial Guinea	78	75	..	5	5	..	17	20	..
Eritrea	83	81	..	5	5	..	12	15	..
Ethiopia	..	..	89	..	..	2	..	..	10
Gabon	66	52	..	12	16	..	22	33	..
Gambia, The	84	82	..	7	8	..	9	11	..
Ghana	..	..	..	..	..	..	..	..	..
Guinea	91	87	..	1	2	..	8	11	..
Guinea-Bissau	87	85	..	2	2	..	11	13	..
Kenya	23	19	19	22	20	20	55	61	62
Lesotho	40	40	..	34	28	..	26	32	..
Liberia	77	72	..	6	6	..	18	22	..
Madagascar	82	78	..	6	7	..	13	15	..
Malawi	..	..	..	..	..	..	..	..	..
Mali	89	86	..	2	2	..	9	12	..
Mauritania	71	55	..	7	10	..	22	34	..
Mauritius	29	16	15	25	44	40	43	38	46
Mozambique	84	83	..	8	8	..	8	9	..
Namibia	47	53	38	16	18	14	37	29	47
Niger	6	8	..	67	49	..	26	44	..
Nigeria	..	..	3	..	..	22	..	..	75
Rwanda	93	92	..	3	3	..	4	5	..
São Tomé and Principe	..	..	..	..	..	..	..	..	..
Senegal	81	77	..	6	8	..	13	16	..
Seychelles	..	..	..	..	..	..	..	..	..
Sierra Leone	70	67	..	14	15	..	16	17	..
Somalia	78	75	..	7	8	..	15	16	..
South Africa	..	..	..	..	..	..	..	..	..
Sudan	72	70	..	8	9	..	20	22	..
Swaziland	40	24	..	26	26	..	35	50	..
Tanzania	..	..	..	..	..	..	..	..	..
Togo	69	66	..	10	10	..	22	24	..
Uganda	..	..	..	..	..	..	..	..	..
Zambia	76	75	..	8	8	..	16	17	..
Zimbabwe	32	24	..	27	28	..	40	48	..
NORTH AFRICA	40	27	22	23	27	26	36	46	52
Algeria	36	26	..	27	31	..	37	43	..
Egypt, Arab Republic	42	39	30	20	21	22	36	40	48
Libya	25	11	..	24	23	..	51	66	..
Morocco	..	4	6	..	36	33	..	60	61
Tunisia	39	..	..	30	..	..	31	..	..
ALL AFRICA	..	..	..	..	..	..	..	..	..

Note: Figures may not add up to 100 because of rounding.

11-5. Industrial structure of economically active population

	Percentage of population economically active											
	Agriculture				Industry				Services			
	Male		Female		Male		Female		Male		Female	
	1980	2000*	1980	2000*	1980	2000*	1980	2000*	1980	2000*	1980	2000*
SUB-SAHARAN AFRICA	..	..	..	..	..	..	..	..	..	..	..	..
excluding South Africa	..	..	..	..	..	..	..	..	..	..	..	..
excl. S.Africa & Nigeria	62	58	78	73	15	15	4	5	23	26	18	22
Angola	67	65	87	86	13	14	1	2	20	21	11	13
Benin	66	62	69	65	10	12	4	4	24	27	27	30
Botswana	6	3	3	2	41	38	8	18	53	60	89	80
Burkina Faso	92	91	93	94	3	2	2	2	5	7	5	5
Burundi	88	86	98	98	4	4	1	1	9	10	1	1
Cameroon	65	62	87	83	11	12	2	3	24	26	11	14
Cape Verde	34	30	39	33	38	38	18	16	28	33	42	51
Central African Republic	79	74	90	87	5	6	1	0	15	20	9	13
Chad	82	77	95	91	6	7	0	1	12	16	4	8
Comoros	70	68	93	90	12	13	3	5	17	20	4	5
Congo, Democratic Rep. of	62	58	84	81	18	20	4	5	20	23	12	14
Congo, Republic of	42	33	81	69	20	23	2	4	38	44	17	27
Côte d'Ivoire	60	54	75	72	10	12	5	6	30	34	20	22
Djibouti	..	3	..	0	..	11	..	1	..	78	..	88
Equatorial Guinea	71	66	91	91	7	7	3	2	23	27	6	8
Eritrea	79	77	88	85	7	8	2	2	14	16	11	13
Ethiopia	..	89	..	88	..	2	..	2	..	9	..	11
Gabon	59	46	74	59	18	21	6	10	24	33	21	32
Gambia, The	78	74	93	92	10	12	3	2	13	14	5	6
Ghana	..	66	..	59	..	10	..	10	..	23	..	32
Guinea	86	83	97	92	2	3	1	1	12	15	3	7
Guinea-Bissau	81	78	98	96	3	3	0	1	17	19	3	3
Kenya	23	20	25	16	24	23	9	10	53	57	65	75
Lesotho	26	29	64	59	52	41	5	5	22	30	31	36
Liberia	69	65	89	84	9	9	1	1	22	26	10	16
Madagascar	73	70	93	88	9	10	2	3	19	20	5	9
Malawi	..	50	..	73	..	25	..	7	..	25	..	20
Mali	86	83	92	89	2	2	1	2	12	15	7	9
Mauritania	65	49	79	63	11	16	2	4	25	35	19	34
Mauritius	29	15	30	13	19	39	40	43	47	46	31	45
Mozambique	72	70	97	96	14	15	1	1	14	15	2	3
Namibia	52	38	42	39	22	19	10	8	27	43	47	52
Niger	7	8	6	5	69	51	29	24	25	41	66	71
Nigeria	..	4	..	2	..	30	..	11	..	67	..	87
Rwanda	88	86	98	98	5	6	1	1	7	8	1	2
São Tomé and Principe	..	..	..	..	..	..	..	..	..	..	..	..
Senegal	74	70	90	86	9	10	2	4	17	20	8	11
Seychelles	..	..	..	..	..	..	..	..	..	..	..	..
Sierra Leone	63	60	82	81	20	22	4	4	17	18	14	16
Somalia	69	66	90	87	12	13	2	2	19	21	8	11
South Africa	18	16	16	10	45	42	16	15	37	42	68	76
Sudan	66	64	88	84	9	10	4	5	24	26	8	11
Swaziland	40	..	38	..	29	..	14	..	30	..	48	..
Tanzania	..	78	..	90	..	7	..	1	..	15	..	8
Togo	70	66	67	65	12	12	7	7	19	22	26	29
Uganda	..	91	..	91	..	4	..	6	..	5	..	3
Zambia	69	68	85	83	13	13	3	3	19	19	13	14
Zimbabwe	29	23	50	38	31	32	8	10	40	46	42	52
NORTH AFRICA	38	21	27	24	25	27	13	21	36	51	54	54
Algeria	27	18	69	57	33	38	6	7	40	45	25	36
Egypt, Arab Republic	45	29	10	35	21	25	13	9	33	46	69	56
Libya	16	7	63	28	29	27	3	5	55	66	34	68
Morocco	..	6	..	6	..	32	..	40	..	63	..	54
Tunisia	33	22	53	20	30	32	32	40	37	44	16	38
ALL AFRICA	..	..	..	..	..	..	..	..	..	..	..	..

*or most recent available data.

11-6. Wages in agriculture

	Monthly earnings in current US dollars										
	1980	*1988*	*1989*	*1990*	*1991*	*1992*	*1993*	*1994*	*1995*	*1996*	*1997*
SUB-SAHARAN AFRICA	..	..	..	..	..	..	..	..	..	..	..
excluding South Africa	..	..	..	..	..	..	..	..	..	..	..
excl. S.Africa & Nigeria	..	..	..	..	..	..	..	..	..	..	..
Angola	..	..	..	..	..	..	..	..	..	..	..
Benin	..	..	..	..	..	..	..	..	..	..	..
Botswana	..	54	71	80	97	97	90	90	90	80	80
Burkina Faso	..	..	..	..	..	..	..	..	..	..	..
Burundi	..	..	..	..	..	..	..	..	..	..	..
Cameroon	..	..	..	..	..	..	..	..	..	..	..
Cape Verde	..	..	..	..	..	..	..	..	..	..	..
Central African Republic	..	..	..	..	..	..	..	..	..	..	..
Chad	..	..	..	..	..	..	..	..	..	..	..
Comoros	..	..	..	..	..	..	..	..	..	..	..
Congo, Democratic Rep. of	..	..	..	..	..	..	..	..	..	..	..
Congo, Republic of	..	..	..	..	..	..	..	..	..	..	..
Côte d'Ivoire	..	..	..	..	..	..	..	..	..	..	..
Djibouti	..	..	..	..	..	..	..	..	..	..	..
Equatorial Guinea	..	..	..	..	..	..	..	..	..	..	..
Eritrea	..	..	..	..	..	..	..	..	..	..	..
Ethiopia	..	..	..	..	..	..	..	..	..	..	..
Gabon	..	..	..	..	..	..	..	..	..	..	..
Gambia, The	..	..	..	..	..	..	..	..	..	..	..
Ghana	34	52	73	64	104	..	..	..	..	..	..
Guinea	..	..	..	..	..	..	..	..	..	..	..
Guinea-Bissau	..	..	..	..	..	..	..	..	..	..	..
Kenya	59	53	48	47	45	..	..	..	..	..	39
Lesotho	..	..	..	..	..	..	..	..	..	..	..
Liberia	..	..	..	..	..	..	..	..	..	..	..
Madagascar	..	..	..	..	..	..	..	..	..	..	..
Malawi	20	12	13	15	16	..	..	..	..	..	..
Mali	..	..	..	..	..	..	..	..	..	..	..
Mauritania	..	..	..	..	..	..	..	..	..	..	..
Mauritius	..	..	..	..	..	..	..	..	..	..	..
Mozambique	..	..	..	..	..	..	..	..	..	..	..
Namibia	..	..	..	..	..	..	..	..	..	..	..
Niger	..	..	..	..	..	..	..	..	..	..	..
Nigeria	..	..	..	..	..	..	..	..	..	..	..
Rwanda	..	..	..	..	..	..	..	..	..	..	..
São Tomé and Principe	..	..	..	..	..	..	..	..	..	..	..
Senegal	..	..	..	..	..	..	..	..	..	..	..
Seychelles	139	304	305	348	366	434	442	456	513	..	..
Sierra Leone	..	..	..	..	..	..	..	..	..	..	..
Somalia	..	..	..	..	..	..	..	..	..	..	..
South Africa	..	..	..	..	..	..	..	..	..	..	..
Sudan	..	..	..	..	..	..	..	..	..	..	..
Swaziland	..	..	437	423	496	533	512	550	483	..	..
Tanzania	..	..	..	..	..	..	..	..	..	..	..
Togo	..	..	..	..	..	..	..	..	..	..	..
Uganda	..	..	..	..	..	..	..	..	..	..	..
Zambia	112	..	..	..	..	..	..	..	..	..	..
Zimbabwe	..	76	71	75	56	34	38	35	34	..	..
NORTH AFRICA	..	..	..	..	..	..	..	..	..	..	..
Algeria	..	..	..	..	..	..	..	..	..	..	..
Egypt, Arab Republic	..	154	144	94	53	53	65	69	75	..	..
Libya	..	..	..	..	..	..	..	..	..	..	..
Morocco	..	..	..	..	..	..	..	..	..	..	..
Tunisia	..	82	77	92	89	101	..	..	..	..	..
ALL AFRICA	..	..	..	..	..	..	..	..	..	..	..

11-7. Wages in manufacturing

	Monthly earnings in current US dollars										
	1980	*1988*	*1989*	*1990*	*1991*	*1992*	*1993*	*1994*	*1995*	*1996*	*1997*
SUB-SAHARAN AFRICA	..	..	..	..	..	..	..	..	..	..	..
excluding South Africa	..	..	..	..	..	..	..	..	..	..	..
excl. S.Africa & Nigeria	..	..	..	..	..	..	..	..	..	..	..
Angola	..	..	..	..	..	..	..	..	..	..	..
Benin	..	..	..	..	..	..	..	..	..	..	..
Botswana	..	181	171	206	199	242	250	200	210	186	173
Burkina Faso	..	..	..	..	..	..	..	..	..	..	..
Burundi	..	..	..	..	..	..	..	..	..	..	..
Cameroon	..	..	..	..	..	..	..	..	..	..	..
Cape Verde	..	..	..	..	..	..	..	..	..	..	..
Central African Republic	..	..	..	..	..	..	..	..	..	..	..
Chad	..	..	..	..	..	..	..	..	..	..	..
Comoros	..	..	..	..	..	..	..	..	..	..	..
Congo, Democratic Rep. of	..	..	..	..	..	..	..	..	..	..	..
Congo, Republic of	..	..	..	..	..	..	..	..	..	..	..
Côte d'Ivoire	..	..	..	..	..	..	..	..	..	..	..
Djibouti	..	..	..	..	..	..	..	..	..	..	..
Equatorial Guinea	..	..	..	..	..	..	..	..	..	..	..
Eritrea	..	..	..	..	..	..	..	..	..	..	..
Ethiopia	..	..	..	..	..	..	..	..	..	..	..
Gabon	..	..	..	..	..	..	..	..	..	..	..
Gambia, The	..	..	..	..	..	..	..	..	..	..	..
Ghana	57	106	136	138	93	..	..	..	..	..	..
Guinea	..	..	..	121	113	122	115	133	131	152	..
Guinea-Bissau	..	..	..	..	..	..	..	..	..	..	..
Kenya	169	139	136	134	121	..	..	..	..	..	94
Lesotho	..	..	..	..	..	..	..	..	..	..	..
Liberia	..	..	..	..	..	..	..	..	..	..	..
Madagascar	..	..	..	..	..	..	..	..	..	..	..
Malawi	75	53	53	65	55	47	40	21	13	..	..
Mali	..	..	..	..	..	..	..	..	..	..	..
Mauritania	..	..	..	..	..	..	..	..	..	..	..
Mauritius	..	181	184	209	235	258	250	287	326	333	306
Mozambique	..	..	..	..	..	..	..	..	..	..	..
Namibia	..	..	..	..	..	..	..	..	..	..	..
Niger	..	..	..	..	..	..	..	..	..	..	..
Nigeria	..	..	..	..	..	..	..	..	..	..	..
Rwanda	..	..	..	..	..	..	..	..	..	..	..
São Tomé and Principe	..	..	..	..	..	..	..	..	..	..	..
Senegal	..	..	..	..	..	..	..	..	..	..	..
Seychelles	212	346	350	410	427	459	474	479	528	..	..
Sierra Leone	..	..	..	..	..	..	..	..	..	..	..
Somalia	..	..	..	..	..	..	..	..	..	..	..
South Africa	475	535	548	642	685	770	749	..	..	..	..
Sudan	..	55	..	83	..	12	..	..	..	..	..
Swaziland	571	414	397	533	513	521	351	524	588	556	..
Tanzania	..	..	..	..	..	..	..	..	..	..	..
Togo	..	..	..	..	..	..	..	..	..	..	..
Uganda	..	..	..	..	..	..	..	..	..	..	..
Zambia	..	..	..	..	..	..	..	..	..	..	..
Zimbabwe	..	327	314	325	256	220	192	191	221	230	..
NORTH AFRICA	..	..	..	..	..	..	..	..	..	..	..
Algeria	..	..	..	..	..	..	..	..	..	..	..
Egypt, Arab Republic	..	252	228	150	75	80	90	98	107	..	..
Libya	..	..	..	..	..	..	..	..	..	..	..
Morocco	..	..	..	..	..	..	..	..	..	..	..
Tunisia	..	..	..	..	..	..	..	..	..	..	..
ALL AFRICA	..	..	..	..	..	..	..	..	..	..	..

11-8. Wages in mining and quarrying

	Monthly earnings in current US dollars										
	1980	*1988*	*1989*	*1990*	*1991*	*1992*	*1993*	*1994*	*1995*	*1996*	*1997*
SUB-SAHARAN AFRICA	..	..	..	..	..	..	..	..	..	..	..
excluding South Africa	..	..	..	..	..	..	..	..	..	..	..
excl. S.Africa & Nigeria	..	..	..	..	..	..	..	..	..	..	..
Angola	..	..	..	..	..	..	..	..	..	..	..
Benin	..	..	..	..	..	..	..	..	..	..	..
Botswana	..	287	319	450	424	436	496	430	428	372	371
Burkina Faso	..	..	..	..	..	..	..	..	..	..	..
Burundi	..	..	..	..	..	..	..	..	..	..	..
Cameroon	..	..	..	..	..	..	..	..	..	..	..
Cape Verde	..	..	..	..	..	..	..	..	..	..	..
Central African Republic	..	..	..	..	..	..	..	..	..	..	..
Chad	..	..	..	..	..	..	..	..	..	..	..
Comoros	..	..	..	..	..	..	..	..	..	..	..
Congo, Democratic Rep. of	..	..	..	..	..	..	..	..	..	..	..
Congo, Republic of	..	..	..	..	..	..	..	..	..	..	..
Côte d'Ivoire	..	..	..	..	..	..	..	..	..	..	..
Djibouti	..	..	..	..	..	..	..	..	..	..	..
Equatorial Guinea	..	..	..	..	..	..	..	..	..	..	..
Eritrea	..	..	..	..	..	..	..	..	..	..	..
Ethiopia	..	..	..	..	..	..	..	..	..	..	..
Gabon	..	..	..	..	..	..	..	..	..	..	..
Gambia, The	..	..	..	..	..	..	..	..	..	..	..
Ghana	64	57	64	117	75	..	..	..	..	..	..
Guinea	..	..	..	..	..	..	..	..	..	..	..
Guinea-Bissau	..	..	..	..	..	..	..	..	..	..	..
Kenya	157	104	106	101	93	..	..	..	..	..	96
Lesotho	..	..	..	..	..	..	..	..	..	..	..
Liberia	..	..	..	..	..	..	..	..	..	..	..
Madagascar	..	..	..	..	..	..	..	..	..	..	..
Malawi	36	17	17	20	30	23	59	30	18	..	..
Mali	..	..	..	..	..	..	..	..	..	..	..
Mauritania	..	..	..	..	..	..	..	..	..	..	..
Mauritius	..	245	231	256	272	302	280	374	436	457	415
Mozambique	..	..	..	..	..	..	..	..	..	..	..
Namibia	..	..	..	..	..	..	..	..	..	..	..
Niger	..	..	..	..	..	..	..	..	..	..	..
Nigeria	..	..	..	..	..	..	..	..	..	..	..
Rwanda	..	..	..	..	..	..	..	..	..	..	..
São Tomé and Principe	..	..	..	..	..	..	..	..	..	..	..
Senegal	..	..	..	..	..	..	..	..	..	..	..
Seychelles	212	334	317	348	378	444	455	477	523	..	..
Sierra Leone	..	..	..	..	..	..	..	..	..	..	..
Somalia	..	..	..	..	..	..	..	..	..	..	..
South Africa	330	397	403	477	514	561	541	..	..	..	..
Sudan	..	53	..	99	..	..	..	..	..	..	..
Swaziland	822	483	309	395	367	395	379	387	523	485	..
Tanzania	..	..	..	..	..	..	..	..	..	..	..
Togo	..	..	..	..	..	..	..	..	..	..	..
Uganda	..	..	..	..	..	..	..	..	..	..	..
Zambia	358	..	..	..	..	..	..	..	..	..	..
Zimbabwe	..	254	242	254	204	180	153	153	187	204	..
NORTH AFRICA	..	..	..	..	..	..	..	..	..	..	..
Algeria	..	..	..	..	..	..	..	..	..	..	..
Egypt, Arab Republic	..	375	427	316	174	167	208	210	203	..	..
Libya	..	..	..	..	..	..	..	..	..	..	..
Morocco	..	..	..	..	..	..	..	..	..	..	..
Tunisia	..	..	..	..	..	..	..	..	..	..	..
ALL AFRICA	..	..	..	..	..	..	..	..	..	..	..

11-9. Wages in construction

	Monthly earnings in current US dollars										
	1980	*1988*	*1989*	*1990*	*1991*	*1992*	*1993*	*1994*	*1995*	*1996*	*1997*
SUB-SAHARAN AFRICA	..	..	..	..	..	..	..	..	..	..	..
excluding South Africa	..	..	..	..	..	..	..	..	..	..	..
excl. S.Africa & Nigeria	..	..	..	..	..	..	..	..	..	..	..
Angola	..	..	..	..	..	..	..	..	..	..	..
Benin	..	..	..	..	..	..	..	..	..	..	..
Botswana	..	148	159	182	196	211	220	214	228	197	218
Burkina Faso	..	..	..	..	..	..	..	..	..	..	..
Burundi	..	..	..	..	..	..	..	..	..	..	..
Cameroon	..	..	..	..	..	..	..	..	..	..	..
Cape Verde	..	..	..	..	..	..	..	..	..	..	..
Central African Republic	..	..	..	..	..	..	..	..	..	..	..
Chad	..	..	..	..	..	..	..	..	..	..	..
Comoros	..	..	..	..	..	..	..	..	..	..	..
Congo, Democratic Rep. of	..	..	..	..	..	..	..	..	..	..	..
Congo, Republic of	..	..	..	..	..	..	..	..	..	..	..
Côte d'Ivoire	..	..	..	..	..	..	..	..	..	..	..
Djibouti	..	..	..	..	..	..	..	..	..	..	..
Equatorial Guinea	..	..	..	..	..	..	..	..	..	..	..
Eritrea	..	..	..	..	..	..	..	..	..	..	..
Ethiopia	..	..	..	..	..	..	..	..	..	..	..
Gabon	..	..	..	..	..	..	..	..	..	..	..
Gambia, The	..	..	..	..	..	..	..	..	..	..	..
Ghana	37	43	51	59	71	..	..	..	..	..	..
Guinea	..	84	115	173	159	..	135	132	177	174	..
Guinea-Bissau	..	..	..	..	..	..	..	..	..	..	..
Kenya	133	98	96	99	95	..	..	..	..	..	80
Lesotho	..	..	..	..	..	..	..	..	..	..	..
Liberia	..	..	..	..	..	..	..	..	..	..	..
Madagascar	..	..	..	..	..	..	..	..	..	..	..
Malawi	60	29	29	30	31	34	33	22	17	..	..
Mali	..	..	..	..	..	..	..	..	..	..	..
Mauritania	..	..	..	..	..	..	..	..	..	..	..
Mauritius	..	220	245	255	297	364	324	368	481	507	488
Mozambique	..	..	..	..	..	..	..	..	..	..	..
Namibia	..	..	..	..	..	..	..	..	..	..	..
Niger	..	..	..	..	..	..	..	..	..	..	..
Nigeria	..	..	..	..	..	..	..	..	..	..	..
Rwanda	..	..	..	..	..	..	..	..	..	..	..
São Tomé and Principe	..	..	..	..	..	..	..	..	..	..	..
Senegal	..	..	..	..	..	..	..	..	..	..	..
Seychelles	..	..	..	..	..	..	..	..	..	..	..
Sierra Leone	..	..	..	..	..	..	..	..	..	..	..
Somalia	..	..	..	..	..	..	..	..	..	..	..
South Africa	371	367	348	394	437	475	424	..	..	..	..
Sudan	..	56	..	180	..	13	..	..	..	..	..
Swaziland	525	267	192	247	283	470	211	333	227	246	..
Tanzania	..	..	..	..	..	..	..	..	..	..	..
Togo	..	..	..	..	..	..	..	..	..	..	..
Uganda	..	..	..	..	..	..	..	..	..	..	..
Zambia	172	..	..	..	..	..	..	..	..	..	..
Zimbabwe	..	200	182	179	144	110	102	88	114	124	..
NORTH AFRICA	..	..	..	..	..	..	..	..	..	..	..
Algeria	..	..	..	..	..	..	..	..	..	..	..
Egypt, Arab Republic	..	276	253	153	84	80	96	112	115	..	..
Libya	..	..	..	..	..	..	..	..	..	..	..
Morocco	..	..	..	..	..	..	..	..	..	..	..
Tunisia	..	..	..	..	..	..	..	..	..	..	..
ALL AFRICA	..	..	..	..	..	..	..	..	..	..	..

11-10. Wages in transport, storage, and communication

	Monthly earnings in current US dollars										
	1980	*1988*	*1989*	*1990*	*1991*	*1992*	*1993*	*1994*	*1995*	*1996*	*1997*
SUB-SAHARAN AFRICA	..	..	..	..	..	..	..	..	..	..	..
excluding South Africa	..	..	..	..	..	..	..	..	..	..	..
excl. S.Africa & Nigeria	..	..	..	..	..	..	..	..	..	..	..
Angola	..	..	..	..	..	..	..	..	..	..	..
Benin	..	..	..	..	..	..	..	..	..	..	..
Botswana	..	239	296	346	417	457	434	468	435	376	344
Burkina Faso	..	..	..	..	..	..	..	..	..	..	..
Burundi	..	..	..	..	..	..	..	..	..	..	..
Cameroon	..	..	..	..	..	..	..	..	..	..	..
Cape Verde	..	..	..	..	..	..	..	..	..	..	..
Central African Republic	..	..	..	..	..	..	..	..	..	..	..
Chad	..	..	..	..	..	..	..	..	..	..	..
Comoros	..	..	..	..	..	..	..	..	..	..	..
Congo, Democratic Rep. of	..	..	..	..	..	..	..	..	..	..	..
Congo, Republic of	..	..	..	..	..	..	..	..	..	..	..
Côte d'Ivoire	..	..	..	..	..	..	..	..	..	..	..
Djibouti	..	..	..	..	..	..	..	..	..	..	..
Equatorial Guinea	..	..	..	..	..	..	..	..	..	..	..
Eritrea	..	..	..	..	..	..	..	..	..	..	..
Ethiopia	..	..	..	..	..	..	..	..	..	..	..
Gabon	..	..	..	..	..	..	..	..	..	..	..
Gambia, The	..	..	..	..	..	..	..	..	..	..	..
Ghana	55	89	96	100	106	..	..	..	..	..	..
Guinea	..	..	..	..	..	..	..	119	121	125	..
Guinea-Bissau	..	..	..	..	..	..	..	..	..	..	..
Kenya	237	207	193	187	171	..	..	..	..	..	131
Lesotho	..	..	..	..	..	..	..	..	..	..	..
Liberia	..	..	..	..	..	..	..	..	..	..	..
Madagascar	..	..	..	..	..	..	..	..	..	..	..
Malawi	99	49	62	63	70	66	63	37	25	..	..
Mali	..	..	..	..	..	..	..	..	..	..	..
Mauritania	..	..	..	..	..	..	..	..	..	..	..
Mauritius	..	290	289	307	339	380	353	376	422	453	426
Mozambique	..	..	..	..	..	..	..	..	..	..	..
Namibia	..	..	..	..	..	..	..	..	..	..	..
Niger	..	..	..	..	..	..	..	..	..	..	..
Nigeria	..	..	..	..	..	..	..	..	..	..	..
Rwanda	..	..	..	..	..	..	..	..	..	..	..
São Tomé and Principe	..	..	..	..	..	..	..	..	..	..	..
Senegal	..	..	..	..	..	..	..	..	..	..	..
Seychelles	299	..	..	..	..	..	..	..	..	..	..
Sierra Leone	..	..	..	..	..	..	..	..	..	..	..
Somalia	..	..	..	..	..	..	..	..	..	..	..
South Africa	..	583	577	702	794	1,110	1,075	..	..	..	..
Sudan	..	48	..	79	..	14	..	..	..	..	..
Swaziland	520	242	192	364	442	357	393	480	539	455	..
Tanzania	..	..	..	..	..	..	..	..	..	..	..
Togo	..	..	..	..	..	..	..	..	..	..	..
Uganda	..	..	..	..	..	..	..	..	..	..	..
Zambia	153	..	..	..	..	..	..	..	..	..	..
Zimbabwe	..	425	429	465	334	289	284	258	275	289	..
NORTH AFRICA	..	..	..	..	..	..	..	..	..	..	..
Algeria	..	..	..	..	..	..	..	..	..	..	..
Egypt, Arab Republic	..	283	248	147	78	84	121	112	117	..	..
Libya	..	..	..	..	..	..	..	..	..	..	..
Morocco	..	..	..	..	..	..	..	..	..	..	..
Tunisia	..	..	..	..	..	..	..	..	..	..	..
ALL AFRICA	..	..	..	..	..	..	..	..	..	..	..

11-11. Wages in community, social, and personal services

	Monthly earnings in current US dollars										
	1980	*1988*	*1989*	*1990*	*1991*	*1992*	*1993*	*1994*	*1995*	*1996*	*1997*
SUB-SAHARAN AFRICA	..	..	..	..	..	..	..	..	..	..	..
excluding South Africa	..	..	..	..	..	..	..	..	..	..	..
excl. S.Africa & Nigeria	..	..	..	..	..	..	..	..	..	..	..
Angola	..	..	..	..	..	..	..	..	..	..	..
Benin	..	..	..	..	..	..	..	..	..	..	..
Botswana	..	195	189	231	239	249	265	254	280	243	250
Burkina Faso	..	..	..	..	..	..	..	..	..	..	..
Burundi	..	..	..	..	..	..	..	..	..	..	..
Cameroon	..	..	..	..	..	..	..	..	..	..	..
Cape Verde	..	..	..	..	..	..	..	..	..	..	..
Central African Republic	..	..	..	..	..	..	..	..	..	..	..
Chad	..	..	..	..	..	..	..	..	..	..	..
Comoros	..	..	..	..	..	..	..	..	..	..	..
Congo, Democratic Rep. of	..	..	..	..	..	..	..	..	..	..	..
Congo, Republic of	..	..	..	..	..	..	..	..	..	..	..
Côte d'Ivoire	..	..	..	..	..	..	..	..	..	..	..
Djibouti	..	..	..	..	..	..	..	..	..	..	..
Equatorial Guinea	..	..	..	..	..	..	..	..	..	..	..
Eritrea	..	..	..	..	..	..	..	..	..	..	..
Ethiopia	..	..	..	..	..	..	..	..	..	..	..
Gabon	..	..	..	..	..	..	..	..	..	..	..
Gambia, The	..	..	..	..	..	..	..	..	..	..	..
Ghana	..	59	81	68	98	..	..	..	..	..	..
Guinea	..	..	..	..	..	..	..	..	..	..	..
Guinea-Bissau	..	..	..	..	..	..	..	..	..	..	..
Kenya	..	128	118	114	104	..	..	..	..	..	75
Lesotho	..	..	..	..	..	..	..	..	..	..	..
Liberia	..	..	..	..	..	..	..	..	..	..	..
Madagascar	..	..	..	..	..	..	..	..	..	..	..
Malawi	..	..	..	..	59	50	43	24	12	..	..
Mali	..	..	..	..	..	..	..	..	..	..	..
Mauritania	..	..	..	..	..	..	..	..	..	..	..
Mauritius	..	235	245	262	278	307	278	357	392	394	404
Mozambique	..	..	..	..	..	..	..	..	..	..	..
Namibia	..	..	..	..	..	..	..	..	..	..	..
Niger	..	..	..	..	..	..	..	..	..	..	..
Nigeria	..	..	..	..	..	..	..	..	..	..	..
Rwanda	..	..	..	..	..	..	..	..	..	..	..
São Tomé and Principe	..	..	..	..	..	..	..	..	..	..	..
Senegal	..	..	..	..	..	..	..	..	..	..	..
Seychelles	..	..	..	..	..	..	..	..	..	..	..
Sierra Leone	..	..	..	..	..	..	..	..	..	..	..
Somalia	..	..	..	..	..	..	..	..	..	..	..
South Africa	..	532	563	679	735	937	..	..	..	..	..
Sudan	..	..	..	..	..	..	..	..	..	..	..
Swaziland	..	..	223	446	276	412	238	455	352	352	..
Tanzania	..	..	..	..	..	..	..	..	..	..	..
Togo	..	..	..	..	..	..	..	..	..	..	..
Uganda	..	..	..	..	..	..	..	..	..	..	..
Zambia	..	..	..	..	..	..	..	..	..	..	..
Zimbabwe	..	255	240	259	206	161	139	128	143	192	..
NORTH AFRICA	..	..	..	..	..	..	..	..	..	..	..
Algeria	..	..	..	..	..	..	..	..	..	..	..
Egypt, Arab Republic	..	203	179	128	64	65	67	80	112	..	..
Libya	..	..	..	..	..	..	..	..	..	..	..
Morocco	..	..	..	..	..	..	..	..	..	..	..
Tunisia	..	..	..	..	..	..	..	..	..	..	..
ALL AFRICA	..	..	..	..	..	..	..	..	..	..	..

Technical notes

Tables

Table 11-1. Number and gender structure of the labor force. This table (ILO data) provides the total number of persons in the labor force and the percentage that is female. Labor force refers to "economically active" persons, including the armed forces and the unemployed but excluding housewives and students. The "economically active" population comprises all persons of either gender who furnish the labor to produce economic goods and services, as defined by the SNA, during a specified period. The production of economic goods and services should include all production and processing of primary products, whether for the market, for barter, or for own consumption; the production of all other goods and services for the market; and, for households that produce such goods and services for the markets, the corresponding production for own consumption.

Table 11-2. Children under 14 working in the labor force. This table (ILO data) shows the percentage of children between the ages of 10 to 14 that participate in the labor force.

Table 11-3. Unpaid family workers as share of active workers. This table (ILO data) shows the percentage of family members—male and female—that are active workers but receive no compensation for their services.

Table 11-4. Industrial structure of the labor force. The industrial structure of the labor force can often indicate the relative level of development of the economy. This table (ILO data) shows the distribution of the labor force among the various sectors of economic activities. The agriculture sector includes farming, animal husbandry, hunting, forestry, and fishing. The industry sector includes mining and quarrying, manufacturing, construction and public works, electricity, water, and gas. All other branches of activity are included in services.

Table 11-5. Industrial structure of economically active population. This is the percentage of the economically active population working in agriculture, industry, or services. Data are shown for males and females (ILO data).

Table 11-6. Wages in agriculture. Data are from ILO, *Yearbook of Labor Statistics* (1988, 1993, 1994, 1995, and 1998) and show the monthly earnings at the average wage converted to U.S. dollars at the *Atlas* exchange rates in the countries concerned. Earnings here are limited to wages and salaries of employees only unless otherwise specified. They include remuneration for time not worked, such as for annual vacation, other paid leave or holidays, bonuses and gratuities, and housing and family allowances paid by the employer to the employee. They exclude employers' contributions to social security and pension schemes and the benefits received by employees under these schemes, as well as severance and termination pay.

It should be remembered that these earnings do not reflect workers' disposable or net earnings since they include gross wages before deductions, such as taxes or social security contributions.

International comparisons of wages in agriculture should be interpreted with caution because they entail wide coverage variations mainly as a result of the form of remuneration, the nature of the work, and the length of the working day.

For the following countries wages are paid entirely in cash: Botswana, Burundi, Egypt, Malawi, Mauritius, Seychelles, Swaziland, Tanzania, Tunisia, and Zambia.

For the following countries, wages shown are cash portion only, although the workers receive other payments-in-kind in addition: Ghana, Kenya, and Zimbabwe. Wages for these three countries include the value of food and lodging allowances.

Data for Burundi include family allowances. Data for Egypt are for establishments with 10 or more persons employed. Data for Ghana include forestry and fishing. Data for Kenya include the value of payments in kind. Data for Malawi include forestry and fishing. Data for Mauritius include sugar and tea factories. Data for Seychelles exclude hunting. Data for Swaziland include forestry and refer to skilled male workers only. Data for Zimbabwe include forestry and refer to all persons engaged.

Figures for Egypt were converted from weekly to monthly earnings using a rate of 4.3 weeks per month. Figures for Mauritius and Tunisia were converted from daily to monthly earnings using a rate of 22 days per month.

Table 11-7. Wages in manufacturing. Data are from ILO, *Yearbook of Labor Statistics* (1988, 1993, 1994, 1995, and 1998). Refer to the definitions in Table 11-6.

Data for Burundi include family allowances. Data for Egypt are for establishments with 10 or more persons employed. Data for the Gambia are for establishments with five or more persons employed. Data for Mauritius exclude sugar and tea factories. Data for Seychelles include electricity and water before 1992, and beginning in 1988 earnings are exempted from income tax. Data for Swaziland refer to skilled male workers only. Data for Zimbabwe include the value of payments-in-kind and refer to all persons engaged.

Figures for Egypt and Sierra Leone were converted from weekly to monthly earnings using a rate of 4.3 weeks per month. Figures for The Gambia were converted from daily to monthly earnings using a rate of 22 days per month.

Table 11-8. Wages in mining and quarrying. Data are from ILO, *Yearbook of Labor Statistics* (1988, 1993, 1994, 1995, and 1998). Refer to the definitions in Table 11-6.

Data for Burundi include family allowances. Data for Egypt are for establishments with 10 or more persons employed. Data for Kenya include the value of payments-in-kind. Data for Swaziland refer to skilled male workers only. Data for Seychelles include construction, and beginning in 1988 earnings are exempted from income tax. Data for South Africa exclude salt and iron works. Data for Swaziland refer to skilled male workers only. Data for Zimbabwe include the value of payments-in-kind and refer to all persons engaged.

Figures for Egypt and Sierra Leone were converted from weekly to monthly earnings using a rate of 4.3 weeks per month.

Table 11-9. Wages in construction. Data are from ILO, Yearbook of Labor Statistics (1988, 1993, 1994, 1995, and 1998). Refer to the definitions in Table 11-6.

Data for Burundi include family allowances. Data for Egypt are for establishments with 10 or more persons employed. Data for The Gambia are for establishments with five or more persons employed. Data for Kenya include the value of payments-in-kind. Data for Swaziland refer to skilled male workers only. Data for South Africa include private construction. Data for Swaziland refer to skilled male workers only. Data for Zimbabwe include the value of payments-in-kind and refer to all persons engaged.

Figures for Egypt and Sierra Leone were converted from weekly to monthly earnings using a rate of 4.3 weeks per month. Figures for The Gambia were converted from daily to monthly earnings using a rate of 22 days per month.

Table 11-10. Wages in transport, storage, and communications. Data are from ILO, *Yearbook of Labor Statistics* (1988, 1993, 1994, 1995, and 1998). Refer to the definitions in Table 11-6.

Data for Burundi include family allowances. Data for Egypt are for establishments with 10 or more persons employed. Data for The Gambia are for establishments with five or more persons employed. Data for Kenya include the value of payments-in-kind. Data for Swaziland refer to skilled male workers only. Data for Zimbabwe include the value of payments-in-kind and refer to all persons engaged.

Figures for Egypt and Sierra Leone were converted from weekly to monthly earnings using a rate of 4.3 weeks per month. Figures for The Gambia were converted from daily to monthly earnings using a rate of 22 days per month.

Table 11-11. Wages in community, social, and personal services. Data are from ILO *Yearbook of Labor Statistics* (1998). Refer to the definitions in Table 11-6. This sector comprises public administration and defense; sanitary and similar services; educational services; research and scientific institutes; medical, dental, and other health services; welfare institutions; business, professional, and labor associations; and other social and community services. Data for Egypt refer to wage earners. Figures for Egypt were converted from weekly to monthly earnings using a rate of 4.3 weeks per month.

Methodology used for regional aggregations and period averages in chapter 11

	Aggregations[a]		
Table	*(1)*	*(6)*	*(8)*
11-1			
Columns 1-3	x		
Columns 4-6		x	
11-2		x	
11-3			x
11-4		x	
11-5		x	
11-6			x
11-7			x
11-8			x
11-9			x
11-10			x
11-11			x

Note: Regional aggregations are shown in the rows for Sub-Saharan Africa, North Africa, and All Africa. Period averages are shown in the last three columns. This table shows only the methodologies used in this chapter.

a. Regional aggregations: (1) simple total; (2) simple total of the first indicator divided by the simple total of the second indicator (same country coverage); (3) simple total of the gap-filled indicator; (4) simple total of the gap-filled main indicator divided by the simple total of the gap-filled secondary indicator; (5) simple total of the first gap-filled main indicator less the simple total of the second gap-filled main indicator, all divided by the simple total of the secondary indicator; (6) weighted total (by population); (7) median; (8) no aggregation; (9) simple arithmetic mean.

12

Aid Flows

Official development assistance (ODA) consists of concessional financial flows that aim to promote economic development and welfare. ODA disbursements from bilateral and multilateral sources became increasingly important to Africa in the second half of the 1980s. For many countries, the foreign savings made available through ODA flows are equivalent to a sizable share of GDP and to the bulk of their domestic investment. Thus, monitoring aid flows is of special importance because of their significance to the economic performance of the region.

The tables in this chapter show data on net ODA flows and their relative importance to key economic and demographic indicators in recipient countries, real growth in net ODA flows to Sub-Saharan Africa from major donors or donor groups, and the share of each donor's worldwide aid portfolio allocated to Sub-Saharan Africa.

These flows are concessional in character and contain a grant element of at least 25 percent (based on a standard 10 percent discount rate). Net ODA disbursements equal gross ODA disbursements less principal repayments (amortization) of previous ODA loans.

ODA includes both grants (inflows of unrequited transfers from official sources) for current and capital expenditures and disbursements of concessional loans. However, because of different sources and definitions of data, the ODA flows shown in this chapter will not necessarily equal those that could be calculated by adding net disbursements of official concessional long-term loans (Table 6-1 less Table 6-4) and net official transfers (Tables 5-6 and 5-9). For example, one of the reasons for differences is that the flows shown here include "off-shore" disbursements of grants, primarily for technical cooperation, which are generally excluded from transfers as recorded in the balance of payments (Tables 5-6 and 5-9). Other reasons include possible differences in the timing of the recording of disbursements and in the recording of multilateral ODA.

The data on net ODA disbursements are taken from the most recent electronic version of OECD, *Geographical Distribution of Financial Flows to Developing Countries.* The tables include only those flows for which the recipient is specified in creditor reports.

To determine growth rates (based on constant price series), import price deflators (from the World Bank) have been used to deflate the current price series, regardless of the type of donor, to indicate the volume of imports that aid can finance over time.

12-1. Net ODA from all donors, nominal

	Millions of U.S. dollars (current prices)											Annual Average		
	1980	*1992*	*1993*	*1994*	*1995*	*1996*	*1997*	*1998*	*1999*	*2000*	*2001*	*75-84*	*85-89*	*90-MR*
SUB-SAHARAN AFRICA	7,665	19,514	17,595	19,438	18,877	16,519	14,958	14,504	13,226	13,397	13,868	6,167	12,848	16,515
excluding South Africa	7,665	19,514	17,320	19,143	18,488	16,155	14,461	13,991	12,684	12,909	13,440	6,167	12,848	16,199
excl. S.Africa & Nigeria	7,629	19,252	17,030	18,953	18,276	15,965	14,261	13,787	12,532	12,725	13,255	6,122	12,722	15,983
Angola	53	346	291	450	418	473	355	335	388	307	268	51	138	348
Benin	90	270	288	256	280	288	221	205	211	239	273	72	158	255
Botswana	106	112	130	86	90	75	122	106	61	31	29	83	133	93
Burkina Faso	212	434	467	434	491	420	368	400	398	336	389	165	264	407
Burundi	117	311	217	312	288	111	56	67	74	93	131	96	188	182
Cameroon	265	716	545	731	444	412	499	499	434	380	398	187	261	502
Cape Verde	64	119	117	122	117	117	111	130	137	94	76	42	89	113
Central African Republic	111	179	173	168	169	170	91	120	118	75	76	80	163	147
Chad	35	239	225	213	236	296	228	168	188	131	179	79	214	223
Comoros	43	48	49	39	42	39	27	35	21	19	28	30	49	38
Congo, Democratic Rep. of	428	269	179	246	196	166	158	125	132	184	251	317	537	273
Congo, Republic of	92	114	123	362	125	429	270	66	142	33	75	82	101	174
Côte d'Ivoire	210	757	764	1,594	1,213	965	446	967	448	352	187	136	271	751
Djibouti	73	113	134	129	105	97	85	81	75	71	55	60	94	104
Equatorial Guinea	9	62	53	30	34	31	24	22	20	21	13	7	39	36
Eritrea	..	..	67	157	149	159	123	167	149	176	280	..	..	159
Ethiopia	212	1,178	1,090	1,071	883	818	579	660	643	693	1,080	208	738	900
Gabon	56	69	101	181	144	127	39	45	48	12	9	50	92	87
Gambia, The	55	111	85	70	47	37	39	39	34	49	51	38	88	63
Ghana	192	615	624	548	651	651	494	702	609	609	652	136	452	633
Guinea	90	448	408	359	417	299	381	359	238	153	272	68	226	334
Guinea-Bissau	59	107	94	175	119	181	124	96	52	80	59	49	92	111
Kenya	397	886	910	678	734	597	448	415	310	512	453	319	667	671
Lesotho	94	145	144	116	114	104	92	61	31	37	54	72	107	97
Liberia	98	120	123	64	124	173	76	72	94	68	37	77	78	102
Madagascar	230	363	363	289	301	357	834	481	359	322	354	148	295	406
Malawi	143	578	498	471	435	492	344	435	447	446	402	115	279	467
Mali	267	432	363	441	541	491	429	347	354	360	350	194	398	420
Mauritania	176	200	325	267	230	272	238	165	219	212	262	177	214	237
Mauritius	33	46	26	14	23	20	43	42	42	20	22	36	52	38
Mozambique	169	1,463	1,179	1,200	1,064	888	948	1,040	805	877	935	141	626	1,039
Namibia	..	143	154	138	192	188	166	181	179	153	109	0	24	159
Niger	170	365	344	377	274	255	333	292	187	211	249	165	333	305
Nigeria	36	262	290	190	212	190	200	204	152	185	185	44	126	216
Rwanda	155	351	356	716	702	467	230	350	373	322	291	131	222	401
São Tomé and Principe	4	56	47	50	84	47	33	28	28	35	38	7	22	46
Senegal	263	670	500	640	666	580	423	501	535	423	419	254	569	568
Seychelles	22	19	20	13	13	19	17	24	13	18	14	16	23	19
Sierra Leone	91	133	208	276	206	184	119	106	74	182	334	51	85	166
Somalia	433	654	893	537	189	88	81	80	115	104	149	283	462	297
South Africa	..	..	275	295	389	364	496	514	541	488	428	..	..	421
Sudan	623	541	454	412	242	220	139	209	243	225	172	540	936	379
Swaziland	50	57	55	58	58	33	28	35	29	13	29	33	34	42
Tanzania	679	1,339	950	966	877	877	945	1,000	990	1,022	1,233	513	797	1,038
Togo	91	223	97	125	192	157	125	128	71	70	47	81	162	141
Uganda	114	725	610	752	835	676	813	647	590	819	783	85	304	715
Zambia	318	1,036	872	718	2,034	610	610	349	624	795	374	204	411	782
Zimbabwe	164	792	498	560	492	371	336	262	245	178	159	114	259	385
NORTH AFRICA	2,719	5,364	3,729	3,901	2,970	3,340	2,921	3,057	2,674	2,168	2,350	2,694	2,587	3,886
Algeria	183	406	348	419	312	304	250	394	89	162	182	140	177	289
Egypt, Arab Republic	1,385	3,603	2,395	2,690	2,015	2,199	1,985	1,955	1,582	1,328	1,255	1,774	1,640	2,622
Libya	17	6	4	4	6	8	7	7	7	..	..	9	9	9
Morocco	899	946	712	631	495	650	464	530	679	419	517	537	494	694
Tunisia	232	390	227	106	71	124	194	150	253	223	378	223	252	239
ALL AFRICA	10,384	24,878	21,324	23,339	21,847	19,860	17,878	17,562	15,900	15,565	16,218	8,860	15,435	20,401

Note: Regional aggregates for ODA include data for economies not specified elsewhere. Thus sum of countries may not add up to the regional totals.

12-2. Net ODA from DAC donors, nominal

	Millions of U.S. dollars (current prices)											Annual Average		
	1980	1992	1993	1994	1995	1996	1997	1998	1999	2000	2001	75-84	85-89	90-MR
SUB-SAHARAN AFRICA	4,547	11,837	10,818	11,339	10,707	10,052	9,277	9,133	8,380	8,592	8,244	3,632	8,177	10,107
excluding South Africa	4,547	11,837	10,634	11,125	10,389	9,740	8,862	8,712	7,994	8,238	7,931	3,632	8,177	9,864
excl. S.Africa & Nigeria	4,530	11,699	10,563	11,078	10,316	9,693	8,810	8,678	7,941	8,154	7,824	3,605	8,074	9,776
Angola	36	194	151	224	242	294	227	214	252	189	179	30	94	208
Benin	36	171	148	142	177	165	148	144	119	191	144	36	88	153
Botswana	83	93	80	57	54	68	56	73	41	24	24	63	102	66
Burkina Faso	151	268	255	265	252	269	218	227	232	228	221	112	182	245
Burundi	60	149	126	108	108	68	38	44	52	41	55	50	85	89
Cameroon	171	579	528	397	346	280	330	303	254	213	275	130	205	352
Cape Verde	39	80	81	82	77	77	68	85	89	70	49	28	61	76
Central African Republic	75	107	117	94	122	121	61	57	59	53	48	52	92	86
Chad	20	148	146	104	127	122	96	75	64	53	73	44	119	111
Comoros	13	23	29	18	22	22	15	19	13	11	10	11	28	20
Congo, Democratic Rep. of	317	163	99	97	118	106	105	80	87	103	143	221	336	173
Congo, Republic of	55	102	116	253	105	395	260	60	121	23	30	49	88	149
Côte d'Ivoire	152	527	708	820	727	449	233	490	366	250	159	105	191	474
Djibouti	32	92	94	94	80	71	62	62	55	42	28	35	61	71
Equatorial Guinea	1	36	28	17	22	23	18	18	15	18	13	4	22	24
Eritrea	..	..	48	96	95	128	81	98	80	112	151	..	..	99
Ethiopia	91	457	417	567	526	448	374	365	325	379	367	86	413	433
Gabon	49	65	97	161	136	113	30	37	34	-12	-8	42	80	77
Gambia, The	17	50	50	38	25	17	17	13	13	15	13	16	50	30
Ghana	107	333	312	332	359	349	292	375	356	385	396	75	187	350
Guinea	33	233	185	186	220	135	126	148	111	93	120	20	126	156
Guinea-Bissau	34	57	56	124	77	125	59	65	32	42	30	29	46	67
Kenya	277	520	426	401	459	346	301	276	254	293	270	244	477	407
Lesotho	64	69	74	45	62	49	45	33	26	22	29	44	63	51
Liberia	60	26	25	35	31	112	31	31	45	24	16	53	54	40
Madagascar	91	216	228	190	195	230	549	334	192	139	138	77	169	246
Malawi	76	208	159	251	221	264	174	204	228	269	196	63	134	216
Mali	131	239	221	243	285	298	257	236	237	300	209	104	248	260
Mauritania	54	116	196	128	126	99	97	64	89	82	81	45	116	108
Mauritius	25	35	27	8	11	-1	3	20	5	12	8	23	43	22
Mozambique	115	1,007	813	733	698	552	622	713	593	624	720	104	476	716
Namibia	..	98	123	113	148	136	123	129	117	97	77	0	16	108
Niger	105	262	254	261	194	163	181	145	120	106	114	97	209	193
Nigeria	17	138	71	47	73	47	52	34	53	84	108	27	103	88
Rwanda	97	187	201	487	339	252	179	209	181	175	149	83	127	231
São Tomé and Principe	1	26	28	26	62	29	21	18	19	18	22	2	9	27
Senegal	182	454	364	475	399	392	292	289	416	288	224	157	355	384
Seychelles	18	15	7	7	11	8	6	17	5	3	8	14	17	11
Sierra Leone	57	74	106	54	60	67	41	53	60	116	167	28	50	75
Somalia	139	497	688	438	119	40	46	42	76	56	88	93	299	206
South Africa	..	..	183	214	319	312	415	421	386	354	313	..	..	324
Sudan	272	188	164	174	131	118	86	150	159	90	108	211	499	180
Swaziland	33	27	33	27	38	21	16	17	15	3	4	22	21	22
Tanzania	524	816	650	570	587	605	569	769	613	779	944	383	617	709
Togo	52	135	77	63	118	97	76	66	47	52	28	46	93	87
Uganda	42	255	348	344	423	370	439	384	357	578	386	31	112	368
Zambia	234	699	511	434	439	354	367	257	340	486	274	156	326	429
Zimbabwe	112	536	310	280	348	281	222	216	219	193	149	86	226	284
NORTH AFRICA	1,663	4,411	2,643	3,084	2,406	2,643	1,989	1,967	1,789	1,630	1,659	1,437	2,205	2,816
Algeria	118	376	265	373	290	263	193	122	37	27	25	116	123	209
Egypt, Arab Republic	1,187	2,996	1,824	2,311	1,690	1,933	1,497	1,472	1,298	1,139	1,090	959	1,533	2,048
Libya	10	1	2	2	3	2	2	4	3	..	..	4	5	3
Morocco	188	734	422	318	347	391	215	251	333	293	342	189	354	404
Tunisia	158	298	127	73	52	42	70	102	102	150	184	160	178	140
ALL AFRICA	6,210	16,247	13,461	14,424	13,113	12,695	11,266	11,100	10,168	10,221	9,903	5,069	10,382	12,923

Note: Regional aggregates for ODA include data for economies not specified elsewhere. Thus sum of countries may not add up to the regional totals.

12-3. Net ODA from non-DAC bilateral donors, nominal

	Millions of U.S. dollars (current prices)											Annual Average		
	1980	*1992*	*1993*	*1994*	*1995*	*1996*	*1997*	*1998*	*1999*	*2000*	*2001*	*75-84*	*85-89*	*90-MR*
SUB-SAHARAN AFRICA	684	73	80	46	45	73	116	80	125	165	115	560	321	129
excluding South Africa	684	73	80	46	42	67	116	79	123	163	113	560	321	128
excl. S.Africa & Nigeria	684	70	69	46	43	68	116	80	120	163	115	560	321	126
Angola	1	1	3	0	0	0	0	0	0	6	-1	0	1	1
Benin	2	0	0	4	7	6	0	-1	-2	-1	1	1	2	1
Botswana	0	-2	7	1	0	-2	-3	-3	-1	-1	1	2	0	0
Burkina Faso	0	2	1	1	8	6	3	6	9	4	14	2	5	6
Burundi	4	-1	-2	-3	-3	-1	0	-1	0	0	0	4	7	-1
Cameroon	23	0	1	0	2	-2	-2	-2	-3	-3	-3	7	0	-1
Cape Verde	2	0	1	1	0	3	0	0	0	0	0	1	1	0
Central African Republic	2	3	3	2	3	5	0	0	0	0	0	1	3	2
Chad	0	0	3	1	1	3	5	5	7	1	0	3	0	2
Comoros	16	0	0	0	0	0	0	0	0	0	2	6	1	0
Congo, Democratic Rep. of	5	2	0	0	0	3	9	2	0	0	0	3	0	8
Congo, Republic of	15	0	0	0	0	0	0	0	0	0	0	10	0	0
Côte d'Ivoire	0	0	0	1	1	0	1	1	2	1	0	0	0	1
Djibouti	33	-1	11	12	3	5	5	2	1	10	0	17	14	11
Equatorial Guinea	0	0	0	0	0	0	0	0	0	0	-1	0	0	0
Eritrea	..	..	1	12	5	3	17	32	19	9	3	..	..	11
Ethiopia	0	1	1	0	1	1	7	13	15	15	28	11	3	13
Gabon	0	0	0	0	-1	-2	-3	-1	0	0	0	3	3	0
Gambia, The	7	-2	-2	-2	-1	-2	-2	1	1	2	2	5	-1	0
Ghana	25	-2	2	-4	-6	-1	13	3	4	2	3	7	1	2
Guinea	0	-2	-4	-2	6	20	34	24	18	3	-1	11	10	8
Guinea-Bissau	1	6	4	3	3	4	0	0	0	0	0	3	5	2
Kenya	0	-3	-3	-3	5	3	2	1	3	5	5	4	7	2
Lesotho	0	3	3	1	0	4	7	-1	-1	-1	-1	1	0	1
Liberia	9	1	1	1	1	2	1	0	0	0	0	3	0	1
Madagascar	48	0	0	0	0	0	0	0	0	-1	-1	12	-2	0
Malawi	0	6	3	4	3	0	-1	1	5	6	11	0	1	5
Mali	33	4	-4	-11	-14	-8	-6	-5	0	-1	13	17	16	-1
Mauritania	86	-7	-6	-10	-16	-11	-13	-7	5	0	-1	83	26	-3
Mauritius	0	-1	0	-1	-1	-1	10	-1	0	1	7	1	2	1
Mozambique	20	3	4	3	2	3	-1	-2	-2	0	4	3	5	1
Namibia	..	1	0	1	0	0	1	1	1	1	1	0	0	1
Niger	2	0	2	5	1	1	10	1	1	0	1	17	5	3
Nigeria	0	3	11	0	0	-1	0	-1	3	0	-1	0	0	2
Rwanda	1	0	2	3	0	1	1	0	0	0	0	2	5	2
São Tomé and Principe	0	0	0	0	0	0	0	0	0	0	0	0	0	0
Senegal	2	17	14	2	13	11	9	1	4	-5	-1	19	27	7
Seychelles	0	0	1	0	0	3	5	1	2	7	0	0	1	1
Sierra Leone	4	0	0	0	1	4	1	3	0	0	2	2	4	1
Somalia	128	11	14	0	0	0	1	0	0	0	14	81	7	10
South Africa	..	..	0	1	3	6	0	1	2	2	1	..	..	2
Sudan	158	20	3	3	4	1	0	1	26	99	10	183	148	16
Swaziland	0	4	3	2	3	3	2	4	0	0	3	0	1	2
Tanzania	27	-2	0	6	5	-2	3	3	1	-3	-5	12	3	0
Togo	0	-2	0	0	0	-2	-1	1	3	1	4	1	3	0
Uganda	1	15	1	13	12	9	3	0	1	6	2	6	7	13
Zambia	23	0	0	0	0	0	0	-1	0	0	1	11	0	0
Zimbabwe	5	-3	-1	-3	-3	-3	-3	-1	0	-1	-4	6	-2	-1
NORTH AFRICA	745	456	390	111	102	49	124	233	123	123	151	798	176	458
Algeria	49	4	1	2	-12	7	12	19	31	71	54	10	28	17
Egypt, Arab Republic	2	409	380	95	117	54	100	214	73	54	61	453	14	354
Libya	0	0	0	0	0	0	0	0	0	..	..	0	0	0
Morocco	645	53	18	29	20	26	32	30	29	-4	34	300	111	91
Tunisia	49	-10	-9	-15	-22	-38	-20	-31	-11	1	1	35	23	-4
ALL AFRICA	1,429	529	469	158	147	122	240	312	248	288	265	1,358	497	588

Note: Regional aggregates for ODA include data for economies not specified elsewhere. Thus sum of countries may not add up to the regional totals.

12-4. Net ODA from multilateral donors, nominal

	Millions of U.S. dollars (current prices)											Annual Average		
	1980	*1992*	*1993*	*1994*	*1995*	*1996*	*1997*	*1998*	*1999*	*2000*	*2001*	*75-84*	*85-89*	*90-MR*
SUB-SAHARAN AFRICA	2,430	7,603	6,695	8,052	8,125	6,394	5,564	5,291	4,720	4,629	5,496	1,915	4,317	6,276
excluding South Africa	2,430	7,603	6,603	7,972	8,058	6,347	5,483	5,199	4,566	4,497	5,382	1,915	4,317	6,204
excl. S.Africa & Nigeria	2,412	7,482	6,395	7,829	7,918	6,204	5,335	5,029	4,470	4,396	5,304	1,898	4,294	6,078
Angola	16	152	137	226	176	179	128	121	136	112	90	20	42	140
Benin	53	98	140	111	96	118	73	63	93	49	127	34	68	102
Botswana	23	21	43	28	35	8	69	36	21	8	4	17	31	27
Burkina Faso	61	164	212	168	231	144	147	167	157	104	154	52	77	156
Burundi	54	163	94	207	182	44	18	23	22	52	76	42	95	94
Cameroon	71	137	16	334	97	134	171	198	183	169	126	51	56	151
Cape Verde	23	39	36	40	40	36	43	45	48	25	28	13	27	36
Central African Republic	34	70	54	72	43	45	30	63	59	22	28	27	68	59
Chad	15	91	76	109	109	171	126	88	116	77	106	33	95	110
Comoros	13	25	20	21	20	17	12	16	8	8	16	12	20	18
Congo, Democratic Rep. of	106	105	79	148	78	57	44	43	45	81	107	93	201	92
Congo, Republic of	22	12	7	109	20	35	10	6	20	10	45	23	13	26
Côte d'Ivoire	58	229	55	773	486	515	213	477	81	101	28	31	80	276
Djibouti	9	22	29	23	22	21	19	17	19	20	27	9	19	21
Equatorial Guinea	8	26	25	13	12	8	6	4	6	3	1	4	17	12
Eritrea	..	..	18	49	49	29	26	38	50	55	126	..	..	49
Ethiopia	120	720	671	504	357	369	198	282	303	298	685	111	322	455
Gabon	7	4	4	20	9	15	11	9	13	23	17	5	9	11
Gambia, The	31	62	37	34	23	22	23	25	19	32	35	17	39	33
Ghana	59	284	309	220	298	303	189	325	250	222	253	55	264	281
Guinea	57	217	228	174	191	143	222	187	109	58	153	36	90	170
Guinea-Bissau	24	45	34	48	39	52	66	31	20	39	28	18	41	42
Kenya	120	370	487	280	270	248	145	138	53	214	177	71	183	261
Lesotho	31	73	68	70	52	51	40	30	7	16	26	27	44	45
Liberia	29	93	97	28	91	58	44	41	49	44	21	21	24	61
Madagascar	91	147	135	99	106	127	284	148	166	185	217	59	128	161
Malawi	68	365	336	216	211	228	171	230	214	171	195	52	144	245
Mali	103	189	146	209	270	201	178	117	117	61	128	73	134	162
Mauritania	36	91	135	150	120	185	154	108	125	129	182	49	72	133
Mauritius	8	11	-1	7	14	22	30	23	37	7	6	12	7	15
Mozambique	34	454	363	464	364	333	328	330	213	254	210	34	145	322
Namibia	..	45	31	25	44	51	42	51	60	55	30	..	8	50
Niger	64	103	88	111	80	91	141	146	66	105	134	50	118	109
Nigeria	18	121	208	143	140	143	149	170	96	100	79	17	23	126
Rwanda	57	164	152	226	363	213	50	141	192	146	141	46	90	168
São Tomé and Principe	3	30	18	24	23	19	12	10	8	17	16	5	13	19
Senegal	79	200	122	164	254	177	122	211	115	140	196	78	187	176
Seychelles	3	4	12	6	2	8	6	6	6	8	5	2	5	6
Sierra Leone	30	59	102	222	146	113	76	51	13	67	165	21	31	89
Somalia	166	146	191	99	70	49	34	38	39	47	46	109	157	81
South Africa	..	..	92	80	67	46	81	92	153	132	114	..	..	95
Sudan	192	333	287	235	108	101	52	59	58	36	54	147	289	184
Swaziland	17	26	19	28	18	10	10	14	14	10	22	12	12	18
Tanzania	128	525	300	389	286	274	373	228	376	246	295	118	177	328
Togo	39	89	19	62	74	62	51	61	21	16	15	34	65	54
Uganda	70	455	261	394	400	297	371	263	232	236	394	49	186	335
Zambia	62	336	361	284	1,594	255	243	93	283	309	98	37	85	352
Zimbabwe	47	259	189	283	147	93	116	46	26	-14	14	28	34	102
NORTH AFRICA	311	498	696	705	462	648	808	857	762	416	540	459	206	611
Algeria	17	26	82	44	34	35	45	253	21	64	104	15	26	63
Egypt, Arab Republic	196	198	192	285	208	212	389	268	211	136	104	363	93	220
Libya	7	4	2	2	3	6	5	3	4	..	..	6	4	6
Morocco	66	160	273	285	128	233	217	249	316	130	140	48	30	198
Tunisia	25	102	109	49	41	121	144	78	161	72	193	28	51	103
ALL AFRICA	2,741	8,100	7,391	8,757	8,587	7,042	6,372	6,149	5,482	5,044	6,037	2,374	4,523	6,887

Note: Regional aggregates for ODA include data for economies not specified elsewhere. Thus sum of countries may not add up to the regional totals.

12-5. Net ODA from all donors, real

	Millions of U.S. dollars (constant 2000 prices)											Average annual percentage growth		
	1980	1992	1993	1994	1995	1996	1997	1998	1999	2000	2001	75-84	85-89	90-MR
SUB-SAHARAN AFRICA	12,047	17,902	16,869	18,018	15,808	13,977	13,770	13,564	12,394	13,397	14,206	7.4	2.1	-3.2
excluding South Africa	12,047	17,902	16,593	17,730	15,462	13,658	13,308	13,085	11,892	12,909	13,771	7.4	2.1	-3.6
excl. S.Africa & Nigeria	11,993	17,649	16,314	17,551	15,281	13,490	13,117	12,891	11,747	12,725	13,582	7.7	1.8	-3.5
Angola	78	297	280	425	355	393	322	312	363	307	273	40.5	1.5	2.7
Benin	140	249	269	231	224	244	202	191	196	239	278	2.8	11.2	-1.9
Botswana	164	102	128	82	78	66	110	104	57	31	31	5.4	0.8	-11.5
Burkina Faso	320	386	432	386	393	338	329	360	366	336	398	4.1	-2.3	0.3
Burundi	179	283	204	285	242	92	51	62	71	93	132	10.4	-2.3	-11.6
Cameroon	393	611	482	643	340	326	441	456	401	380	410	1.9	6.7	-2.4
Cape Verde	99	107	111	110	94	95	100	117	125	94	78	13.9	-5.2	-0.8
Central African Republic	156	163	158	150	135	140	83	108	108	75	79	6.9	0.3	-8.7
Chad	55	218	209	189	188	241	204	150	174	131	182	-4.2	4.1	-5.1
Comoros	67	43	45	35	34	31	24	32	19	19	28	4.2	-9.2	-7.8
Congo, Democratic Rep. of	649	250	168	223	153	133	142	114	122	184	255	3.0	7.8	-12.2
Congo, Republic of	132	97	108	315	96	335	227	58	127	33	77	3.3	-9.9	-5.5
Côte d'Ivoire	294	656	675	1,414	966	805	406	902	412	352	188	-0.1	18.6	-5.6
Djibouti	112	96	125	114	85	80	77	75	69	71	57	6.8	-14.2	-5.9
Equatorial Guinea	15	53	49	27	27	24	22	20	18	21	13	17.3	20.5	-12.2
Eritrea	..	..	67	148	124	134	116	161	139	176	285	..	..	11.9
Ethiopia	336	1,076	1,073	1,001	762	705	539	614	609	693	1,112	5.4	1.8	-3.2
Gabon	75	58	89	152	110	96	34	38	42	12	9	2.7	1.0	-18.2
Gambia, The	90	106	84	65	41	33	37	36	32	49	53	13.9	3.4	-9.9
Ghana	312	590	612	517	556	573	471	700	585	609	667	6.5	18.0	-1.7
Guinea	146	410	387	329	342	254	353	343	221	153	280	16.3	12.9	-4.6
Guinea-Bissau	87	98	91	161	96	151	115	91	48	80	59	16.8	5.8	-5.6
Kenya	639	845	890	632	620	519	420	396	297	512	466	9.9	10.1	-9.9
Lesotho	151	137	141	108	98	89	85	57	29	37	55	11.0	-3.1	-11.8
Liberia	179	116	122	62	107	142	71	67	92	68	37	17.5	-19.6	-6.1
Madagascar	377	325	341	260	246	303	743	442	336	322	364	8.4	4.9	-0.1
Malawi	241	553	487	450	385	450	326	418	421	446	412	5.8	13.8	-2.8
Mali	422	395	344	402	444	407	393	322	332	360	358	4.7	-4.6	-2.8
Mauritania	284	175	301	238	185	224	217	151	201	212	270	0.0	-6.9	-1.3
Mauritius	49	39	23	12	20	17	39	37	38	20	22	0.6	4.1	-7.7
Mozambique	258	1,304	1,137	1,124	899	759	880	965	752	877	952	41.6	17.6	-1.8
Namibia	..	127	148	127	153	154	149	162	162	153	111	..	42.5	3.0
Niger	260	330	318	334	224	205	301	266	172	211	255	-0.8	0.9	-5.0
Nigeria	55	253	278	179	181	168	191	194	145	185	189	-11.6	42.5	-6.1
Rwanda	236	315	336	698	617	393	206	326	351	322	296	5.8	-2.9	-0.2
São Tomé and Principe	6	52	45	46	69	39	30	26	25	35	38	14.9	16.3	-5.6
Senegal	398	611	466	566	537	488	381	455	490	423	430	7.0	5.7	-5.1
Seychelles	33	19	18	12	11	16	15	22	12	18	14	-0.8	-8.0	-4.5
Sierra Leone	162	122	200	257	176	162	112	101	71	182	340	15.1	-0.2	4.7
Somalia	724	667	945	563	172	74	73	74	107	104	150	9.8	-6.4	-15.4
South Africa	..	..	276	288	347	318	462	479	502	488	434	..	..	7.9
Sudan	1,016	508	443	391	204	190	128	196	233	225	174	10.0	-8.3	-14.3
Swaziland	83	56	57	55	51	29	28	35	27	13	30	0.8	-5.8	-7.4
Tanzania	1,051	1,236	921	899	731	758	871	938	929	1,022	1,291	8.6	2.9	-0.4
Togo	139	198	88	112	153	132	117	120	66	70	48	4.7	1.8	-11.0
Uganda	185	671	604	714	714	588	757	612	557	819	802	19.6	12.3	1.4
Zambia	505	980	839	681	1,749	532	582	331	587	795	385	10.2	-1.2	-2.1
Zimbabwe	264	756	480	528	419	316	314	248	238	178	165	63.2	-9.9	-7.1
NORTH AFRICA	4,628	5,127	3,653	3,592	2,502	2,846	2,649	2,837	2,491	2,168	2,393	-6.0	-8.6	-7.8
Algeria	268	333	311	357	234	232	214	337	81	162	185	-6.1	-7.6	-4.3
Egypt, Arab Republic	2,535	3,651	2,446	2,540	1,779	1,970	1,849	1,879	1,518	1,328	1,259	-9.0	-9.3	-9.5
Libya	27	5	3	4	5	7	7	7	7	..	..	-9.1	4.5	-10.8
Morocco	1,452	807	652	563	383	509	400	467	606	419	536	7.6	-10.9	-5.3
Tunisia	341	319	203	87	47	85	162	130	224	223	394	-4.0	1.5	-3.5
ALL AFRICA	16,675	23,029	20,522	21,610	18,310	16,823	16,418	16,401	14,886	15,565	16,598	2.8	0.1	-4.2

Note: Regional aggregates for ODA include data for economies not specified elsewhere. Thus sum of countries may not add up to the regional totals.

12-6. Net ODA from DAC donors, real

	Millions of U.S. dollars (constant 2000 prices)											Average annual percentage growth		
	1980	*1992*	*1993*	*1994*	*1995*	*1996*	*1997*	*1998*	*1999*	*2000*	*2001*	*75-84*	*85-89*	*90-MR*
SUB-SAHARAN AFRICA	6,816	10,714	10,306	10,522	8,927	8,462	8,532	8,542	7,880	8,592	8,421	8.4	4.4	-3.1
excluding South Africa	6,816	10,714	10,114	10,305	8,635	8,186	8,141	8,143	7,516	8,238	8,103	8.4	4.4	-3.5
excl. S.Africa & Nigeria	6,791	10,575	10,042	10,260	8,575	8,145	8,092	8,115	7,466	8,154	7,994	8.8	3.8	-3.4
Angola	49	156	145	216	210	245	208	203	237	189	183	43.1	2.1	4.3
Benin	48	158	133	124	136	138	135	135	110	191	146	2.9	13.7	0.0
Botswana	126	85	80	55	49	60	54	75	40	24	25	3.7	6.7	-11.9
Burkina Faso	218	232	229	230	193	210	192	200	212	228	225	7.1	1.9	-0.7
Burundi	82	134	116	96	90	55	34	40	50	41	55	11.7	-7.2	-10.6
Cameroon	235	493	466	336	260	214	281	269	230	213	283	5.1	3.8	-4.3
Cape Verde	56	71	76	73	60	62	61	76	80	70	49	28.2	-1.9	-1.4
Central African Republic	96	96	103	82	96	98	56	52	55	53	51	10.1	-0.8	-6.7
Chad	30	131	131	88	97	91	82	64	57	53	73	-2.9	4.5	-8.5
Comoros	17	20	26	15	17	16	13	17	12	11	10	1.3	2.8	-9.6
Congo, Democratic Rep. of	463	149	89	83	88	83	92	71	79	103	145	2.3	4.9	-12.4
Congo, Republic of	71	86	101	213	79	305	218	52	108	23	30	4.0	-4.3	-8.6
Côte d'Ivoire	196	448	622	694	552	359	207	442	334	250	161	3.6	7.9	-5.7
Djibouti	43	77	85	82	63	57	55	58	50	42	29	0.6	-4.2	-6.6
Equatorial Guinea	2	28	25	14	17	18	16	16	13	18	13	125.3	26.4	-8.4
Eritrea	..	..	48	90	79	106	76	94	74	112	152	..	..	8.7
Ethiopia	134	410	418	537	461	383	348	340	311	379	376	-0.2	1.2	-2.3
Gabon	64	55	85	135	104	86	26	32	31	-12	-8	4.4	2.7	-13.5
Gambia, The	26	49	50	36	22	15	16	13	13	15	14	14.2	2.4	-15.0
Ghana	170	323	309	316	309	313	281	385	344	385	402	2.8	19.3	0.2
Guinea	50	207	169	170	178	115	113	144	104	93	123	18.2	21.9	-4.8
Guinea-Bissau	45	49	54	114	62	102	55	62	29	42	30	40.6	7.0	-5.5
Kenya	438	500	417	374	389	301	284	266	244	293	280	8.8	6.3	-9.0
Lesotho	99	65	73	44	55	43	42	31	24	22	30	12.2	-4.0	-10.8
Liberia	115	25	26	36	29	90	30	30	45	24	15	23.5	-21.3	-5.3
Madagascar	143	188	211	168	157	195	479	307	181	139	141	13.2	3.6	-1.8
Malawi	127	200	156	245	208	252	167	203	218	269	200	-1.5	21.8	0.2
Mali	194	216	208	219	231	242	233	218	221	300	213	7.2	-5.7	-1.8
Mauritania	79	99	177	110	99	82	91	62	83	82	86	12.2	3.0	-5.0
Mauritius	36	29	23	7	10	1	3	19	5	12	8	3.9	6.1	-18.5
Mozambique	167	871	781	690	591	467	575	657	557	624	732	44.7	18.4	-1.5
Namibia	..	86	118	103	118	112	112	116	107	97	79	..	57.3	6.2
Niger	150	235	233	228	159	128	160	129	110	106	116	0.4	1.2	-7.9
Nigeria	24	138	73	46	61	41	49	28	50	84	110	-16.9	64.8	-11.9
Rwanda	138	166	186	485	306	208	162	192	170	175	151	6.3	-3.3	-1.0
São Tomé and Principe	2	23	27	23	49	23	19	16	17	18	22	38.1	24.3	-4.0
Senegal	262	405	335	415	314	326	260	260	380	288	228	10.0	6.8	-6.2
Seychelles	27	15	6	7	9	6	6	16	5	3	9	-2.6	-6.0	-10.9
Sierra Leone	105	66	101	51	53	60	40	51	58	116	168	17.4	11.6	3.8
Somalia	230	520	746	471	113	33	42	39	72	56	89	29.6	-1.1	-16.3
South Africa	..	..	191	217	291	276	391	399	364	354	318	..	..	7.5
Sudan	427	173	160	169	110	102	80	140	154	90	108	23.7	-6.5	-12.2
Swaziland	54	28	37	27	35	19	17	19	14	3	5	-0.2	-14.0	-12.4
Tanzania	791	741	630	532	486	522	519	719	575	779	993	7.3	3.2	0.0
Togo	74	116	69	55	90	80	71	60	43	52	29	4.5	7.0	-10.2
Uganda	65	232	348	334	370	323	405	362	339	578	392	27.1	22.2	6.3
Zambia	364	664	493	416	382	309	353	244	322	486	284	7.7	2.9	-3.6
Zimbabwe	177	510	298	270	300	243	208	207	214	193	154	57.3	-9.3	-5.7
NORTH AFRICA	2,853	4,222	2,613	2,854	2,043	2,283	1,818	1,869	1,697	1,630	1,691	8.7	-7.7	-8.5
Algeria	158	305	232	316	217	198	163	103	32	27	25	-3.7	-15.2	-15.9
Egypt, Arab Republic	2,204	3,070	1,886	2,191	1,507	1,745	1,403	1,433	1,258	1,139	1,090	17.3	-9.3	-9.0
Libya	15	1	2	1	2	2	2	3	3	..	..	-11.1	-5.6	-7.2
Morocco	256	606	381	281	265	304	182	224	299	293	360	3.0	-1.5	-6.3
Tunisia	216	235	109	58	33	25	58	92	91	150	198	-2.3	-1.2	-5.7
ALL AFRICA	9,669	14,936	12,919	13,376	10,969	10,745	10,350	10,411	9,577	10,221	10,112	8.4	1.4	-4.3

Note: Regional aggregates for ODA include data for economies not specified elsewhere. Thus sum of countries may not add up to the regional totals.

12-7. Net ODA from non-DAC bilateral donors, real

	Millions of U.S. dollars (constant 2000 prices)											Average annual percentage growth		
	1980	1992	1993	1994	1995	1996	1997	1998	1999	2000	2001	75-84	85-89	90-MR
SUB-SAHARAN AFRICA	895	78	88	51	45	73	122	89	140	180	121	2.0	-27.7	-2.8
excluding South Africa	895	78	88	50	42	67	122	89	138	178	120	2.0	-27.7	-2.9
excl. S.Africa & Nigeria	895	75	76	50	43	68	122	89	135	178	122	2.0	-27.8	-2.6
Angola	1	1	4	0	0	0	0	0	0	7	-1	..	17.6	-17.3
Benin	2	0	0	4	7	6	0	-2	-2	-1	2	1.9	-3.4	-5.1
Botswana	0	-2	8	1	0	-2	-4	-3	-1	-1	1	..	..	..
Burkina Faso	0	3	1	1	8	6	4	7	11	4	15	8.9	-52.2	17.4
Burundi	5	-2	-2	-3	-3	-1	0	-1	0	0	0	28.0	-21.4	..
Cameroon	30	0	1	0	2	-2	-2	-2	-4	-3	-3	4.6	-72.8	..
Cape Verde	3	0	1	1	0	3	0	0	0	0	0	-3.2	-21.2	-18.1
Central African Republic	3	3	3	2	3	5	0	0	0	0	0	-17.0	106.7	-42.1
Chad	0	0	3	1	1	3	5	5	8	1	0	-27.6	..	3.8
Comoros	22	0	0	0	0	0	0	0	0	0	2	6.9	-62.7	7.6
Congo, Democratic Rep. of	7	2	0	0	0	3	9	3	0	0	0	-63.9	..	-22.3
Congo, Republic of	20	0	0	0	0	0	0	0	0	0	0	11.0	..	1.4
Côte d'Ivoire	0	0	0	1	1	0	1	1	2	1	0	..	..	5.2
Djibouti	43	-1	12	13	3	5	5	2	1	10	0	-13.1	-47.8	-8.9
Equatorial Guinea	0	0	0	0	0	0	0	0	0	0	-1	..	43.8	-25.2
Eritrea	..	..	1	13	5	3	18	35	21	10	3	..	..	16.4
Ethiopia	0	1	2	1	1	1	8	15	17	16	30	6.8	..	19.4
Gabon	0	0	0	0	-1	-2	-3	-2	0	0	0	-21.6	..	..
Gambia, The	9	-2	-2	-2	-1	-2	-2	1	1	3	3	-2.9	..	..
Ghana	33	-2	3	-4	-6	-1	14	3	4	3	3	113.9	..	3.1
Guinea	0	-2	-4	-2	6	20	36	27	20	3	-1	10.4	7.8	1.0
Guinea-Bissau	2	6	4	3	3	4	0	0	0	0	0	-6.7	4.6	-36.5
Kenya	0	-4	-4	-3	5	3	2	1	3	5	6	166.1	-47.8	-2.1
Lesotho	0	4	3	1	0	4	7	-1	-1	-1	-1	81.9	..	..
Liberia	12	1	1	1	1	2	1	0	0	0	0	-69.9	64.9	-27.6
Madagascar	63	0	0	0	0	0	0	0	0	-1	-1	54.7	..	1.1
Malawi	0	6	3	5	3	0	-1	1	5	7	11	..	215.7	6.1
Mali	43	4	-5	-12	-14	-8	-6	-6	0	-1	14	3.5	-33.1	..
Mauritania	113	-8	-6	-11	-16	-11	-13	-8	6	0	-2	-5.9	-33.2	..
Mauritius	0	-1	0	-1	-1	-1	11	-1	0	1	8	..	1.7	..
Mozambique	27	3	4	3	2	3	-1	-2	-2	0	4	51.0	-8.2	17.7
Namibia	..	1	0	1	0	0	1	1	2	1	1	..	..	14.0
Niger	2	0	2	6	1	1	11	1	1	0	1	16.3	-8.5	-14.0
Nigeria	0	4	12	0	0	-1	0	-1	3	0	-1	..	41.4	-7.9
Rwanda	2	0	3	4	0	1	1	0	0	0	0	-3.9	-9.3	-28.8
São Tomé and Principe	0	0	0	0	0	0	0	0	0	0	0	..	..	-11.1
Senegal	3	18	16	2	13	11	10	1	5	-5	-1	18.1	-27.0	-10.6
Seychelles	0	0	1	0	0	3	5	1	2	7	0	..	-39.0	17.6
Sierra Leone	6	0	0	0	1	4	1	3	0	0	2	3.5	-23.6	13.4
Somalia	167	11	15	0	0	0	1	0	0	0	15	-12.3	-44.0	-15.6
South Africa	..	..	0	1	3	6	0	1	2	2	1	..	..	0.3
Sudan	207	22	3	3	3	4	1	0	1	30	109	10	0.7	-27.5	-3.9
Swaziland	0	4	3	2	3	3	2	5	0	0	3	..	..	-0.9
Tanzania	36	-2	0	7	5	-2	3	3	1	-3	-6	45.4	-48.3	-1.2
Togo	0	-2	0	0	0	-2	-1	1	4	2	4	-7.2	2.2	42.3
Uganda	2	16	1	14	12	9	3	0	1	6	2	-19.5	205.0	-22.8
Zambia	29	0	0	0	0	0	0	-1	0	0	1	19.3	..	4.4
Zimbabwe	7	-3	-1	-3	-3	-3	-3	-1	0	-1	-4	15.6	..	..
NORTH AFRICA	976	488	430	121	102	49	130	260	139	134	160	-28.5	-23.8	-11.7
Algeria	64	5	1	3	-12	7	12	21	35	78	57	-47.3	222.2	22.8
Egypt, Arab Republic	3	438	419	103	117	54	105	239	83	59	65	-61.8	..	-23.2
Libya	0	0	0	0	0	0	0	0	0	..	..	..	..	13.6
Morocco	845	56	19	31	20	26	33	34	33	-4	37	16.3	-38.7	-18.0
Tunisia	64	-11	-10	-16	-22	-38	-21	-34	-12	1	1	-9.3	14.7	..
ALL AFRICA	1,871	566	518	172	147	122	252	349	280	315	281	-14.2	-27.6	-9.8

Note: Regional aggregates for ODA include data for economies not specified elsewhere. Thus sum of countries may not add up to the regional totals.

12-8. Net ODA from multilateral donors, real

	Millions of U.S. dollars (constant 2000 prices)											Average annual percentage growth		
	1980	1992	1993	1994	1995	1996	1997	1998	1999	2000	2001	75-84	85-89	90-MR
SUB-SAHARAN AFRICA	4,076	7,117	6,484	7,453	6,844	5,451	5,127	4,943	4,393	4,629	5,652	6.6	4.4	-3.4
excluding South Africa	4,076	7,117	6,400	7,382	6,791	5,414	5,057	4,863	4,257	4,497	5,537	6.6	4.4	-3.6
excl. S.Africa & Nigeria	4,045	7,005	6,204	7,249	6,671	5,286	4,915	4,696	4,164	4,396	5,455	6.7	4.4	-3.7
Angola	27	140	131	209	145	148	115	109	126	112	91	42.2	-0.2	0.5
Benin	89	91	135	104	81	102	66	57	87	49	131	2.3	8.3	-5.1
Botswana	38	20	41	26	28	7	59	31	18	8	4	5.9	-6.7	-11.6
Burkina Faso	103	152	203	155	192	122	134	155	146	104	159	-0.2	-7.4	2.2
Burundi	90	151	91	192	155	38	17	23	21	52	77	8.2	5.2	-12.9
Cameroon	119	118	15	307	79	113	161	189	174	169	129	-4.7	21.1	3.7
Cape Verde	39	37	34	37	34	31	39	42	46	25	29	2.9	-10.0	0.4
Central African Republic	57	65	52	66	36	38	27	56	53	22	29	3.0	1.6	-11.0
Chad	25	87	75	100	91	147	117	82	110	77	109	-3.2	3.8	-2.2
Comoros	22	23	19	19	17	15	11	15	7	8	17	22.6	-18.2	-5.9
Congo, Democratic Rep. of	177	100	78	139	65	48	41	41	43	81	110	4.6	12.3	-10.9
Congo, Republic of	36	11	7	103	16	30	9	6	19	10	47	-3.0	-23.2	2.2
Côte d'Ivoire	98	208	53	720	414	446	199	460	77	101	27	-11.8	66.6	-6.2
Djibouti	14	20	29	21	19	18	17	15	17	20	28	35.7	-20.2	1.4
Equatorial Guinea	14	25	25	12	10	7	6	3	5	3	1	28.3	14.4	-20.3
Eritrea	..	..	18	46	40	25	24	36	47	55	130	..	..	16.6
Ethiopia	202	666	653	463	301	322	184	260	284	298	708	8.6	3.2	-4.4
Gabon	11	4	3	17	8	12	10	8	12	23	17	3.5	-1.1	10.0
Gambia, The	52	59	36	31	20	19	22	23	18	32	36	13.5	6.6	-6.3
Ghana	100	269	301	205	252	260	178	313	237	222	262	12.3	15.3	-4.1
Guinea	95	204	222	161	158	120	208	176	101	58	158	29.0	10.2	-5.2
Guinea-Bissau	40	43	33	44	32	44	60	29	18	39	29	19.0	5.0	-5.5
Kenya	201	349	477	262	227	215	134	129	50	214	181	11.3	26.8	-12.1
Lesotho	51	69	65	64	43	43	36	28	6	16	26	8.8	0.5	-13.1
Liberia	48	90	95	25	77	51	40	37	46	44	22	7.4	-15.9	-5.3
Madagascar	153	137	130	92	89	108	263	135	155	185	224	2.9	3.4	1.5
Malawi	114	348	328	201	175	198	160	215	198	171	200	16.1	8.6	-5.4
Mali	173	175	140	193	225	172	165	109	111	61	132	1.4	1.0	-5.0
Mauritania	60	84	129	138	100	152	139	96	113	129	185	1.1	1.0	2.6
Mauritius	13	10	-1	7	11	18	26	20	33	7	7	-7.0	6.9	2.9
Mozambique	57	431	352	431	306	289	305	311	197	254	216	37.6	16.1	-2.7
Namibia	..	40	30	23	36	42	37	45	54	55	31	..	25.3	-0.8
Niger	107	95	83	101	65	76	131	136	62	105	138	-6.0	1.7	-0.6
Nigeria	31	111	196	133	120	127	143	167	93	100	81	-1.3	1.2	3.2
Rwanda	96	150	148	210	311	183	43	134	181	146	145	5.9	-1.6	1.2
São Tomé and Principe	5	29	18	22	19	16	11	9	8	17	16	12.1	11.9	-7.6
Senegal	133	190	117	149	212	152	112	194	106	140	202	1.2	15.8	-2.6
Seychelles	6	4	11	5	2	6	5	5	6	8	5	25.0	-7.1	1.9
Sierra Leone	50	56	99	207	122	98	71	47	12	67	170	10.0	-8.7	5.3
Somalia	279	137	186	91	59	41	30	35	35	47	47	11.4	-11.4	-13.0
South Africa	..	..	85	71	53	37	70	80	136	132	115	..	..	10.1
Sudan	322	315	281	220	91	87	48	55	54	36	56	8.2	-2.8	-20.7
Swaziland	29	25	18	26	15	8	9	12	13	10	22	3.6	0.8	-4.8
Tanzania	214	497	291	361	241	238	349	217	354	246	303	11.3	3.3	-1.7
Togo	65	83	19	58	62	54	48	59	20	16	15	5.1	-1.7	-13.4
Uganda	117	424	254	368	335	258	349	250	218	236	407	24.0	5.7	-2.2
Zambia	103	316	346	265	1,366	223	229	88	265	309	101	18.7	-14.3	2.2
Zimbabwe	79	249	183	260	122	76	109	42	24	-14	15	128.4	-11.8	-7.9
NORTH AFRICA	522	462	656	634	371	520	713	741	676	416	545	-4.6	-4.7	3.1
Algeria	28	24	78	39	28	29	40	216	19	64	104	-11.6	11.2	7.5
Egypt, Arab Republic	329	184	185	259	171	177	351	237	190	136	105	-3.4	-12.2	-0.6
Libya	11	4	2	2	3	5	5	3	4	..	..	-4.3	14.6	-12.4
Morocco	111	150	254	255	101	182	187	213	278	130	141	6.6	-3.5	5.3
Tunisia	43	94	103	43	33	94	124	67	142	72	195	-4.6	6.1	4.2
ALL AFRICA	4,598	7,578	7,140	8,087	7,215	5,971	5,840	5,684	5,069	5,044	6,197	4.3	3.8	-2.9

Note: Regional aggregates for ODA include data for economies not specified elsewhere. Thus sum of countries may not add up to the regional totals.

12-9. Net ODA from all donors as share of recipient GDP

	Percentage of GDP											*Annual Average*		
	1980	*1992*	*1993*	*1994*	*1995*	*1996*	*1997*	*1998*	*1999*	*2000*	*2001*	*75-84*	*85-89*	*90-MR*
SUB-SAHARAN AFRICA	4.0	11.0	5.8	6.8	5.9	4.9	4.4	4.5	4.0	4.0	4.4	4.2	7.9	6.3
excluding South Africa	4.0	11.0	10.5	13.1	11.1	8.5	7.5	7.4	6.4	6.2	6.7	4.2	7.9	9.0
excl. S.Africa & Nigeria	6.6	13.4	12.0	15.5	13.3	10.4	9.1	8.8	7.7	7.7	8.4	6.1	9.2	10.8
Angola	..	6.0	5.5	11.1	8.3	6.3	4.6	5.2	6.4	3.5	2.8	..	1.8	5.4
Benin	6.4	16.6	13.7	17.1	14.0	13.1	10.2	8.8	8.8	10.6	11.5	7.0	11.1	12.8
Botswana	10.0	2.7	3.1	2.0	1.9	1.6	2.3	2.2	1.2	0.6	0.6	10.8	7.0	2.1
Burkina Faso	12.4	21.7	21.8	24.7	22.5	16.9	16.1	15.9	15.7	14.5	15.6	12.4	13.1	17.7
Burundi	12.8	28.7	23.1	33.7	28.8	12.3	5.9	7.7	10.4	13.7	19.0	11.9	16.6	19.1
Cameroon	3.9	6.3	4.6	9.3	5.6	4.5	5.5	5.7	4.6	4.3	4.6	3.6	2.4	5.3
Cape Verde	60.3	30.2	32.3	29.6	23.9	23.2	22.0	24.1	23.3	16.9	13.0	47.2	42.2	25.0
Central African Republic	13.9	12.5	13.3	19.7	15.0	15.9	9.1	11.5	11.2	7.9	7.9	12.8	14.0	12.8
Chad	3.4	12.7	15.4	18.1	16.4	18.4	15.1	9.9	12.0	9.3	11.2	8.6	17.2	14.2
Comoros	35.1	17.1	17.6	20.9	18.0	17.1	12.9	16.3	9.6	9.2	12.5	36.9	29.0	16.1
Congo, Democratic Rep. of	3.0	3.3	2.0	4.2	3.5	2.7	4.8	2.0	1.1	1.2	..	2.6	6.5	3.6
Congo, Republic of	5.4	3.9	6.4	20.5	5.9	16.9	11.6	3.4	6.0	1.0	2.7	6.4	4.6	7.6
Côte d'Ivoire	2.1	6.8	7.3	20.8	12.1	7.9	3.8	7.6	3.6	3.3	1.8	1.9	2.8	7.3
Djibouti	..	24.0	28.5	26.4	21.1	19.6	17.0	15.7	14.0	12.9	..	..	23.5	22.7
Equatorial Guinea	..	40.1	34.8	23.7	20.5	11.9	4.9	4.8	2.3	1.6	0.7	1.1	35.1	19.9
Eritrea	..	..	18.0	33.5	28.7	25.8	19.0	23.4	21.2	28.1	40.7	..	..	26.5
Ethiopia	..	21.2	17.4	21.9	15.3	13.6	9.1	10.1	10.0	10.9	17.3	5.1	10.0	15.2
Gabon	1.3	1.2	2.3	4.3	2.9	2.2	0.7	1.0	1.1	0.2	0.2	1.6	2.5	1.8
Gambia, The	22.6	31.8	23.2	19.2	12.2	9.5	9.5	9.3	7.8	11.6	12.4	19.6	38.4	17.5
Ghana	4.3	9.6	10.5	10.1	10.1	9.4	7.2	9.4	7.9	12.2	12.3	3.6	8.7	10.1
Guinea	..	13.7	12.5	10.5	11.3	7.7	10.1	10.0	6.9	5.0	9.1	..	11.2	10.0
Guinea-Bissau	53.7	47.5	39.9	74.2	46.7	66.8	46.3	46.6	23.4	37.3	29.4	37.3	55.4	46.3
Kenya	5.5	11.1	18.3	9.5	8.1	6.4	4.2	3.6	2.9	4.9	4.0	5.5	8.6	8.2
Lesotho	21.9	17.6	17.6	13.9	12.2	11.0	9.0	6.9	3.4	4.1	6.8	22.5	26.3	12.0
Liberia	8.8	..	..	..	..	..	..	..	..	..	..	7.4	6.9	..
Madagascar	5.7	12.0	10.8	9.7	9.5	8.9	23.5	12.9	9.6	8.3	7.7	4.6	11.0	11.9
Malawi	11.6	32.1	24.0	39.8	30.4	20.2	13.6	25.0	24.7	26.1	23.0	11.1	20.9	25.9
Mali	15.0	15.2	13.6	25.0	22.0	18.8	17.3	13.4	13.8	15.7	15.1	15.0	22.8	17.4
Mauritania	24.8	16.8	34.4	26.0	21.6	24.4	21.7	16.4	22.8	21.7	25.4	27.8	25.1	22.8
Mauritius	2.9	1.5	0.8	0.4	0.6	0.5	1.0	1.0	1.0	0.5	0.5	3.7	3.2	1.2
Mozambique	4.8	78.9	59.5	55.1	46.1	31.3	27.9	26.9	20.2	23.0	25.9	5.8	24.5	39.9
Namibia	..	5.0	5.4	4.2	5.5	5.4	4.6	5.3	5.3	4.5	3.5	0.0	1.2	5.0
Niger	6.8	15.6	21.4	24.1	14.6	12.8	18.0	14.0	9.3	11.7	12.7	9.9	16.9	15.5
Nigeria	0.1	0.8	1.4	0.8	0.8	0.5	0.6	0.6	0.4	0.4	0.4	0.1	0.5	0.7
Rwanda	13.4	17.2	18.1	95.0	54.3	33.8	12.4	17.6	19.3	17.8	17.1	12.5	10.5	27.7
São Tomé and Principe	8.4	124.0	98.0	101.0	185.2	105.7	76.0	68.8	58.7	75.2	80.8	15.9	44.6	96.6
Senegal	8.8	11.1	9.2	17.6	14.9	12.5	9.6	10.8	11.3	9.7	9.1	10.5	13.7	11.8
Seychelles	14.7	4.4	4.2	2.7	2.6	3.5	2.9	4.0	2.1	3.1	2.4	13.1	10.1	4.0
Sierra Leone	8.3	19.6	27.0	27.7	22.2	19.6	14.0	15.8	11.0	28.7	44.5	5.0	11.2	21.1
Somalia	71.8	..	..	..	..	..	..	..	..	..	..	42.1	46.8	53.8
South Africa	..	..	0.2	0.2	0.3	0.3	0.3	0.4	0.4	0.4	0.4	..	..	0.3
Sudan	8.2	8.5	5.8	5.0	3.4	2.7	1.3	1.8	2.4	2.0	1.4	6.6	6.1	4.0
Swaziland	9.2	5.6	5.1	5.1	4.3	2.5	2.0	2.6	2.1	0.9	2.3	7.9	6.3	3.7
Tanzania	..	29.1	22.3	21.4	16.7	13.5	12.3	11.9	11.5	11.3	13.2	11.4	18.9	17.7
Togo	8.0	13.1	7.8	12.8	14.7	10.7	8.3	9.1	5.0	5.7	3.7	10.0	14.0	10.0
Uganda	9.1	25.4	18.9	18.8	14.5	11.2	13.0	9.9	9.9	13.9	13.8	4.0	5.9	15.4
Zambia	8.2	32.5	26.6	21.5	58.6	18.6	15.6	10.8	19.9	24.6	10.3	6.3	16.5	23.3
Zimbabwe	2.5	11.7	7.6	8.1	6.9	4.3	4.0	4.6	4.5	2.5	1.8	1.6	3.8	5.4
NORTH AFRICA	2.1	4.0	2.7	2.8	1.9	2.0	1.7	1.6	1.4	1.1	1.1	3.1	1.7	2.6
Algeria	0.4	0.8	0.7	1.0	0.7	0.6	0.5	0.8	0.2	0.3	0.3	0.5	0.3	0.6
Egypt, Arab Republic	6.0	8.6	5.1	5.2	3.3	3.3	2.6	2.4	1.8	1.3	1.3	10.3	4.4	5.1
Libya	0.0	..	..	..	..	..	..	..	..	..	..	0.0	0.0	..
Morocco	4.8	3.3	2.7	2.1	1.5	1.8	1.4	1.5	1.9	1.3	1.5	3.8	2.9	2.3
Tunisia	2.7	2.5	1.6	0.7	0.4	0.6	1.0	0.8	1.2	1.1	1.9	3.5	2.6	1.5
ALL AFRICA	3.2	7.9	4.8	5.4	4.6	3.9	3.4	3.4	3.0	2.9	3.0	3.6	5.0	4.9

Note: Regional aggregates for ODA include data for economies not specified elsewhere.

12-10. Net ODA from DAC donors as share of recipient GDP

	Percentage of GDP											Annual Average		
	1980	1992	1993	1994	1995	1996	1997	1998	1999	2000	2001	75-84	85-89	90-MR
SUB-SAHARAN AFRICA	2.4	6.6	3.5	3.9	3.4	3.0	2.7	2.8	2.5	2.6	2.6	2.4	5.0	3.8
excluding South Africa	2.4	6.6	6.4	7.5	6.3	5.1	4.6	4.6	4.0	4.0	3.9	2.4	5.0	5.5
excl. S.Africa & Nigeria	3.8	8.1	7.4	9.0	7.5	6.3	5.6	5.5	4.9	4.9	4.9	3.5	5.8	6.6
Angola	..	3.4	2.9	5.5	4.8	3.9	3.0	3.3	4.1	2.1	1.9	..	1.2	3.2
Benin	2.5	10.5	7.0	9.5	8.8	7.5	6.9	6.2	5.0	8.4	6.1	3.6	6.1	7.6
Botswana	7.9	2.3	1.9	1.3	1.1	1.4	1.1	1.5	0.8	0.4	0.5	8.3	5.2	1.5
Burkina Faso	8.8	13.4	11.9	15.1	11.6	10.9	9.5	9.0	9.2	9.9	8.9	8.3	8.9	10.6
Burundi	6.5	13.7	13.4	11.7	10.8	7.5	4.0	5.1	7.3	6.0	7.9	6.3	7.5	9.3
Cameroon	2.5	5.1	4.4	5.1	4.3	3.1	3.6	3.5	2.7	2.4	3.2	2.5	1.9	3.6
Cape Verde	36.5	20.3	22.4	19.8	15.7	15.4	13.4	15.8	15.1	12.5	8.3	30.6	28.0	17.0
Central African Republic	9.4	7.4	9.0	11.0	10.9	11.3	6.1	5.4	5.6	5.6	5.0	8.2	8.0	7.6
Chad	2.0	7.9	10.0	8.8	8.8	7.6	6.4	4.4	4.1	3.8	4.5	4.7	9.6	7.0
Comoros	10.9	8.2	10.4	9.6	9.4	9.5	7.2	8.6	5.9	5.3	4.3	14.0	15.6	8.5
Congo, Democratic Rep. of	2.2	2.0	1.1	1.7	2.1	1.8	3.2	1.3	0.7	0.7	..	1.8	4.1	2.3
Congo, Republic of	3.2	3.5	6.1	14.3	5.0	15.5	11.2	3.1	5.2	0.7	1.1	3.8	4.0	6.4
Côte d'Ivoire	1.5	4.7	6.8	10.7	7.3	3.7	2.0	3.8	2.9	2.4	1.5	1.5	2.0	4.6
Djibouti	..	19.6	19.9	19.3	16.0	14.3	12.4	12.1	10.3	7.6	..	..	15.8	15.5
Equatorial Guinea	..	23.3	18.2	13.1	13.2	9.0	3.6	4.0	1.7	1.4	0.7	..	19.7	12.3
Eritrea	..	..	13.0	20.4	18.2	20.6	12.5	13.7	11.4	17.9	22.0	..	..	16.6
Ethiopia	..	8.2	6.7	11.6	9.1	7.5	5.9	5.6	5.0	6.0	5.9	1.9	5.6	7.3
Gabon	1.1	1.2	2.2	3.8	2.7	2.0	0.6	0.8	0.8	-0.2	-0.2	1.3	2.2	1.5
Gambia, The	6.8	14.5	13.6	10.5	6.6	4.4	4.2	3.2	3.1	3.5	3.3	8.7	21.8	8.5
Ghana	2.4	5.2	5.2	6.1	5.6	5.0	4.2	5.0	4.6	7.7	7.5	2.0	3.6	5.6
Guinea	..	7.1	5.6	5.4	6.0	3.5	3.3	4.1	3.2	3.0	4.0	..	6.3	4.7
Guinea-Bissau	31.1	25.1	23.8	52.4	30.3	46.1	21.8	31.5	14.3	19.3	15.3	21.9	27.6	27.9
Kenya	3.8	6.5	8.6	5.6	5.1	3.7	2.8	2.4	2.4	2.8	2.4	4.3	6.2	4.9
Lesotho	14.8	8.4	9.0	5.4	6.6	5.2	4.4	3.7	2.8	2.4	3.7	13.7	15.5	6.3
Liberia	5.4	..	..	..	..	..	..	..	..	..	..	5.1	4.8	..
Madagascar	2.2	7.1	6.8	6.4	6.2	5.8	15.5	8.9	5.2	3.6	3.0	2.4	6.3	7.3
Malawi	6.1	11.6	7.7	21.2	15.5	10.9	6.9	11.7	12.6	15.8	11.2	6.3	10.2	12.2
Mali	7.3	8.4	8.3	13.8	11.6	11.4	10.4	9.1	9.2	13.0	9.0	8.0	14.2	10.7
Mauritania	7.6	9.8	20.8	12.5	11.8	8.9	8.8	6.3	9.3	8.4	7.9	6.7	13.4	10.4
Mauritius	2.2	1.2	0.8	0.2	0.3	0.0	0.1	0.5	0.1	0.3	0.2	2.4	2.7	0.7
Mozambique	3.3	54.3	41.0	33.7	30.2	19.4	18.3	18.4	14.9	16.4	20.0	4.3	18.7	27.4
Namibia	..	3.4	4.3	3.5	4.2	3.9	3.4	3.8	3.5	2.8	2.5	0.0	0.8	3.4
Niger	4.2	11.2	15.8	16.7	10.3	8.2	9.8	7.0	6.0	5.9	5.8	5.9	10.7	9.9
Nigeria	0.0	0.4	0.3	0.2	0.3	0.1	0.1	0.1	0.2	0.2	0.3	0.1	0.4	0.3
Rwanda	8.3	9.2	10.2	64.7	26.2	18.2	9.7	10.5	9.3	9.7	8.7	7.9	6.0	16.3
São Tomé and Principe	2.6	57.3	59.5	53.2	135.2	64.3	48.2	44.4	40.7	38.1	46.7	4.6	18.1	57.0
Senegal	6.1	7.5	6.7	13.0	8.9	8.4	6.7	6.2	8.8	6.6	4.8	6.5	8.6	8.0
Seychelles	12.4	3.6	1.4	1.5	2.2	1.4	1.1	2.9	0.8	0.5	1.4	11.1	7.2	2.5
Sierra Leone	5.2	10.9	13.7	5.4	6.4	7.1	4.9	7.9	8.9	18.2	22.3	2.6	6.6	10.0
Somalia	23.1	..	..	..	..	..	..	..	..	..	..	13.4	30.1	29.4
South Africa	..	..	0.1	0.2	0.2	0.2	0.3	0.3	0.3	0.3	0.3	..	..	0.2
Sudan	3.6	2.9	2.1	2.1	1.8	1.4	0.8	1.3	1.5	0.8	0.9	2.5	3.3	1.8
Swaziland	6.0	2.7	3.1	2.4	2.8	1.6	1.1	1.2	1.1	0.2	0.3	5.2	4.1	2.0
Tanzania	..	17.7	15.3	12.6	11.2	9.3	7.4	9.2	7.1	8.6	10.1	8.1	14.6	12.0
Togo	4.6	8.0	6.3	6.5	9.0	6.6	5.0	4.7	3.3	4.3	2.3	5.7	8.0	6.1
Uganda	3.4	8.9	10.8	8.6	7.4	6.1	7.0	5.9	6.0	9.8	6.8	1.6	2.1	7.6
Zambia	6.0	22.0	15.6	13.0	12.7	10.8	9.4	7.9	10.9	15.0	7.5	4.8	12.9	12.9
Zimbabwe	1.7	7.9	4.7	4.1	4.9	3.3	2.6	3.8	4.0	2.7	1.6	1.2	3.3	3.9
NORTH AFRICA	1.3	3.3	1.9	2.2	1.6	1.5	1.1	1.1	0.9	0.8	0.8	1.4	1.5	1.9
Algeria	0.3	0.8	0.5	0.9	0.7	0.6	0.4	0.3	0.1	0.1	0.0	0.4	0.2	0.4
Egypt, Arab Republic	5.2	7.2	3.9	4.5	2.8	2.9	2.0	1.8	1.5	1.2	1.1	4.6	4.1	3.9
Libya	0.0	..	..	..	..	..	..	..	..	..	..	0.0	0.0	..
Morocco	1.0	2.6	1.6	1.0	1.1	1.1	0.6	0.7	0.9	0.9	1.0	1.4	1.9	1.3
Tunisia	1.8	1.9	0.9	0.5	0.3	0.2	0.4	0.5	0.5	0.8	0.9	2.5	1.9	0.9
ALL AFRICA	1.9	5.2	3.0	3.3	2.8	2.5	2.2	2.2	1.9	1.9	1.9	2.0	3.3	3.1

Note: Regional aggregates for ODA include data for economies not specified elsewhere.

12-11. Net ODA from multilateral donors as share of recipient GDP

	Percentage of GDP											*Annual Average*		
	1980	*1992*	*1993*	*1994*	*1995*	*1996*	*1997*	*1998*	*1999*	*2000*	*2001*	*75-84*	*85-89*	*90-MR*
SUB-SAHARAN AFRICA	1.3	4.3	2.2	2.9	2.5	1.9	1.6	1.6	1.4	1.4	1.7	1.3	2.7	2.4
excluding South Africa	1.3	4.3	4.1	5.5	4.8	3.3	2.8	2.7	2.3	2.2	2.7	1.3	2.7	3.5
excl. S.Africa & Nigeria	2.1	5.3	4.6	6.5	5.7	4.0	3.4	3.2	2.7	2.6	3.3	1.9	3.1	4.1
Angola	..	2.6	2.6	5.6	3.5	2.4	1.7	1.9	2.2	1.3	0.9	..	0.6	2.2
Benin	3.8	6.1	6.6	7.4	4.8	5.3	3.4	2.7	3.9	2.2	5.4	3.3	4.8	5.1
Botswana	2.1	0.5	1.0	0.6	0.7	0.2	1.3	0.7	0.4	0.2	0.1	2.2	1.7	0.6
Burkina Faso	3.6	8.2	9.9	9.6	10.6	5.8	6.4	6.6	6.2	4.5	6.2	3.9	3.9	6.8
Burundi	5.9	15.1	10.0	22.3	18.2	4.9	1.9	2.7	3.1	7.6	11.0	5.2	8.4	9.8
Cameroon	1.1	1.2	0.1	4.2	1.2	1.5	1.9	2.3	2.0	1.9	1.5	1.0	0.5	1.7
Cape Verde	22.0	10.0	9.8	9.6	8.2	7.3	8.5	8.3	8.2	4.4	4.7	15.6	13.5	8.0
Central African Republic	4.2	4.9	4.1	8.4	3.8	4.2	3.0	6.1	5.6	2.4	2.9	4.4	5.8	5.0
Chad	1.5	4.8	5.2	9.2	7.6	10.7	8.4	5.2	7.4	5.5	6.6	3.6	7.6	7.0
Comoros	10.8	8.9	7.2	11.3	8.6	7.5	5.6	7.6	3.7	3.8	7.5	14.1	12.4	7.5
Congo, Democratic Rep. of	0.7	1.3	0.9	2.5	1.4	0.9	1.4	0.7	0.4	0.5	..	0.8	2.5	1.2
Congo, Republic of	1.3	0.4	0.4	6.2	1.0	1.4	0.4	0.3	0.9	0.3	1.6	1.9	0.6	1.2
Côte d'Ivoire	0.6	2.1	0.5	10.1	4.9	4.2	1.8	3.7	0.6	1.0	0.3	0.5	0.8	2.7
Djibouti	..	4.6	6.2	4.7	4.5	4.3	3.7	3.3	3.5	3.6	..	..	5.0	4.3
Equatorial Guinea	..	16.8	16.5	10.6	7.3	2.9	1.3	0.8	0.6	0.2	0.1	0.7	15.3	7.2
Eritrea	..	..	4.8	10.5	9.5	4.6	4.0	5.3	7.1	8.8	18.3	..	..	8.1
Ethiopia	..	12.9	10.7	10.3	6.2	6.1	3.1	4.3	4.7	4.7	11.0	2.8	4.4	7.7
Gabon	0.2	0.1	0.1	0.5	0.2	0.3	0.2	0.2	0.3	0.5	0.4	0.2	0.2	0.2
Gambia, The	12.8	17.9	10.1	9.2	6.0	5.6	5.6	5.9	4.4	7.6	8.6	8.5	16.9	9.0
Ghana	1.3	4.4	5.2	4.0	4.6	4.4	2.7	4.3	3.2	4.5	4.8	1.4	5.1	4.5
Guinea	..	6.6	6.9	5.1	5.2	3.7	5.9	5.2	3.1	1.9	5.1	..	4.4	5.1
Guinea-Bissau	21.4	19.7	14.3	20.5	15.2	19.1	24.4	15.1	9.1	18.0	14.2	13.1	24.8	17.6
Kenya	1.6	4.6	9.8	3.9	3.0	2.7	1.4	1.2	0.5	2.1	1.6	1.2	2.3	3.3
Lesotho	7.1	8.8	8.3	8.4	5.6	5.4	3.9	3.4	0.7	1.8	3.2	8.7	10.7	5.5
Liberia	2.6	..	..	..	..	..	..	..	..	..	..	2.1	2.1	..
Madagascar	2.3	4.9	4.0	3.3	3.4	3.2	8.0	3.9	4.5	4.8	4.7	1.9	4.8	4.6
Malawi	5.5	20.3	16.2	18.2	14.8	9.4	6.7	13.3	11.8	10.0	11.2	4.8	10.7	13.4
Mali	5.8	6.6	5.5	11.8	10.9	7.7	7.2	4.5	4.6	2.7	5.5	5.6	7.5	6.7
Mauritania	5.1	7.7	14.3	14.6	11.3	16.6	14.1	10.8	13.0	13.2	17.7	7.6	8.2	12.7
Mauritius	0.7	0.4	0.0	0.2	0.4	0.5	0.7	0.5	0.9	0.2	0.1	1.2	0.4	0.4
Mozambique	1.0	24.5	18.3	21.3	15.7	11.7	9.6	8.5	5.4	6.6	5.8	1.3	5.6	12.5
Namibia	..	1.6	1.1	0.8	1.3	1.5	1.1	1.5	1.8	1.6	1.0	..	0.4	1.6
Niger	2.5	4.4	5.5	7.1	4.2	4.6	7.7	7.0	3.3	5.8	6.8	3.1	6.0	5.5
Nigeria	0.0	0.4	1.0	0.6	0.5	0.4	0.4	0.5	0.3	0.2	0.2	0.0	0.1	0.4
Rwanda	4.9	8.0	7.7	29.9	28.1	15.4	2.7	7.1	10.0	8.1	8.3	4.3	4.2	11.3
São Tomé and Principe	5.8	66.7	38.5	47.8	49.9	41.4	27.7	24.3	18.0	37.2	34.0	11.3	26.5	39.5
Senegal	2.6	3.3	2.2	4.5	5.7	3.8	2.8	4.5	2.4	3.2	4.2	3.2	4.4	3.7
Seychelles	2.3	1.0	2.6	1.2	0.5	1.5	1.0	1.0	1.0	1.4	0.9	1.6	2.5	1.2
Sierra Leone	2.7	8.7	13.3	22.3	15.7	12.0	9.0	7.5	2.0	10.5	22.0	2.1	4.1	10.9
Somalia	27.5	..	..	..	..	..	..	..	..	..	..	15.9	16.0	15.5
South Africa	..	..	0.1	0.1	0.0	0.0	0.1	0.1	0.1	0.1	0.1	..	..	0.1
Sudan	2.5	5.2	3.6	2.9	1.5	1.2	0.5	0.5	0.6	0.3	0.4	1.8	1.9	2.0
Swaziland	3.2	2.6	1.8	2.5	1.3	0.7	0.7	1.0	1.0	0.7	1.7	2.8	2.1	1.5
Tanzania	..	11.4	7.0	8.6	5.4	4.2	4.9	2.7	4.4	2.7	3.2	2.9	4.1	5.7
Togo	3.4	5.3	1.6	6.3	5.7	4.2	3.4	4.3	1.5	1.3	1.2	4.2	5.7	3.8
Uganda	5.6	15.9	8.1	9.9	7.0	4.9	5.9	4.0	3.9	4.0	6.9	2.2	3.7	7.4
Zambia	1.6	10.6	11.0	8.5	45.9	7.8	6.2	2.9	9.0	9.5	2.7	1.1	3.6	10.4
Zimbabwe	0.7	3.8	2.9	4.1	2.1	1.1	1.4	0.8	0.5	-0.2	0.2	0.4	0.5	1.4
NORTH AFRICA	0.2	0.4	0.5	0.5	0.3	0.4	0.5	0.5	0.4	0.2	0.3	0.5	0.1	0.4
Algeria	0.0	0.1	0.2	0.1	0.1	0.1	0.1	0.5	0.0	0.1	0.2	0.1	0.0	0.1
Egypt, Arab Republic	0.9	0.5	0.4	0.5	0.3	0.3	0.5	0.3	0.2	0.1	0.1	2.2	0.2	0.4
Libya	0.0	..	..	..	..	..	..	..	..	..	..	0.0	0.0	..
Morocco	0.4	0.6	1.0	0.9	0.4	0.6	0.6	0.7	0.9	0.4	0.4	0.3	0.2	0.6
Tunisia	0.3	0.7	0.7	0.3	0.2	0.6	0.8	0.4	0.8	0.4	1.0	0.4	0.5	0.6
ALL AFRICA	0.8	2.6	1.7	2.1	1.8	1.4	1.2	1.2	1.0	0.9	1.1	1.0	1.4	1.6

Note: Regional aggregates for ODA include data for economies not specified elsewhere.

12-12. Net ODA from all donors as share of recipient GDI

	Percentage of GDI											Annual Average		
	1980	1992	1993	1994	1995	1996	1997	1998	1999	2000	2001	75-84	85-89	90-MR
SUB-SAHARAN AFRICA	20.2	66.1	36.4	39.7	32.6	27.1	24.6	24.0	21.7	22.8	22.9	21.8	49.4	36.4
excluding South Africa	20.2	66.1	61.1	72.0	62.5	44.4	39.3	35.4	30.5	32.5	31.2	21.8	49.4	49.5
excl. S.Africa & Nigeria	35.0	88.1	74.3	87.5	73.6	51.1	46.9	43.6	37.6	42.1	42.3	32.8	57.3	60.9
Angola	..	165.6	49.3	66.8	29.5	18.1	18.2	14.6	13.6	9.8	8.3	..	12.7	36.2
Benin	42.4	120.6	88.9	108.6	71.2	76.3	55.7	51.7	50.5	55.9	60.1	40.9	91.4	78.3
Botswana	25.0	8.9	10.8	7.5	7.7	6.2	8.3	6.4	4.5	3.4	2.5	29.9	32.2	7.2
Burkina Faso	72.9	103.0	110.2	113.6	87.3	61.8	56.5	52.7	59.6	57.0	61.7	64.1	60.5	74.6
Burundi	91.9	191.3	141.8	319.4	300.1	102.3	72.9	87.5	114.2	150.2	274.3	89.3	108.0	172.3
Cameroon	18.7	43.9	27.7	60.6	38.4	29.4	33.9	32.7	25.3	26.0	26.0	15.0	11.3	32.6
Cape Verde	116.9	87.8	81.4	68.3	56.3	96.4	99.9	121.7	111.3	87.3	73.1	95.0	131.5	94.7
Central African Republic	198.7	102.6	131.0	168.5	111.3	369.9	92.6	84.6	78.0	72.9	56.0	129.1	115.2	125.4
Chad	..	170.2	157.4	108.5	159.4	123.7	102.0	56.8	95.5	54.8	26.2	159.7	219.0	115.2
Comoros	105.7	88.1	96.1	101.1	92.6	88.1	81.1	90.7	64.4	70.2	95.6	114.1	120.1	96.2
Congo, Democratic Rep. of	29.8	47.6	112.8	53.5	37.0	9.8	17.2	10.2	5.0	28.7	..	23.1	47.1	47.4
Congo, Republic of	15.1	17.9	21.8	65.5	16.2	62.7	52.0	12.6	21.7	4.9	10.0	19.5	22.2	29.9
Côte d'Ivoire	7.8	98.0	88.5	165.7	89.7	65.6	26.4	56.7	27.2	31.3	18.2	8.9	25.3	70.4
Djibouti	..	..	..	..	250.3	216.2	180.3	103.1	157.3	100.3	..	..	..	167.9
Equatorial Guinea	..	165.7	158.2	32.0	26.8	10.5	7.4	5.3	4.2	4.2	4.8	7.8	..	64.8
Eritrea	..	..	25.3	162.1	103.0	76.0	49.4	63.5	49.4	78.8	115.2	..	..	80.3
Ethiopia	..	230.1	122.6	144.4	93.0	80.6	53.3	59.1	61.3	71.3	95.9	37.2	70.6	112.1
Gabon	4.7	5.5	10.3	19.8	12.3	9.4	2.4	2.6	3.9	0.9	0.6	4.1	7.7	7.3
Gambia, The	84.7	143.6	110.5	106.0	60.5	44.1	55.1	50.5	43.6	68.5	69.4	100.5	225.0	86.4
Ghana	76.7	74.9	47.1	42.1	50.3	32.2	28.9	40.7	37.6	51.7	51.2	60.7	78.4	50.6
Guinea	..	78.3	69.8	67.9	68.2	44.6	57.1	55.7	29.8	22.6	41.3	..	69.1	55.3
Guinea-Bissau	190.7	98.1	129.2	340.7	209.2	290.0	212.4	409.5	139.2	233.2	135.6	158.2	161.6	209.8
Kenya	22.3	80.8	103.2	57.7	46.3	38.4	27.5	23.8	20.1	35.9	31.1	26.8	42.0	49.4
Lesotho	59.0	26.7	32.2	25.1	20.2	18.9	16.6	14.6	7.9	10.3	18.4	72.7	61.5	21.9
Liberia	32.1	..	..	..	..	..	..	..	..	..	..	44.5	94.0	..
Madagascar	38.1	107.0	94.0	89.1	87.1	76.7	183.5	87.1	64.7	55.2	49.6	47.1	101.1	98.2
Malawi	46.8	161.2	158.4	136.9	179.0	174.9	111.3	186.0	166.5	208.4	210.2	49.5	112.0	161.0
Mali	96.7	69.4	62.2	91.5	95.9	81.9	84.1	64.0	65.1	69.3	67.8	103.7	117.1	76.6
Mauritania	94.3	87.1	166.8	125.6	111.9	131.3	123.5	86.7	128.4	71.6	95.2	106.9	97.3	112.7
Mauritius	11.3	5.3	2.6	1.4	2.1	1.9	3.6	3.6	3.8	1.8	2.0	15.5	13.0	4.0
Mozambique	80.8	506.0	467.3	278.1	201.6	143.2	135.6	110.9	54.7	58.1	62.3	99.7	215.4	212.6
Namibia	..	23.1	32.9	19.6	25.2	23.3	22.0	20.2	21.6	18.6	14.4	..	16.0	22.9
Niger	24.1	225.0	334.4	232.2	199.4	132.7	166.1	124.7	90.7	108.8	111.0	84.2	127.1	178.1
Nigeria	0.3	3.7	5.8	4.1	4.6	3.8	3.2	2.6	1.9	2.0	1.6	0.6	3.2	3.6
Rwanda	82.8	110.3	107.8	952.2	404.8	234.9	89.9	118.8	112.1	101.4	92.7	85.9	68.5	211.4
São Tomé and Principe	49.8	319.9	277.4	242.9	271.9	188.3	154.7	192.1	150.4	173.0	161.9	115.6	286.9	249.0
Senegal	75.1	75.0	65.4	94.7	89.0	67.5	53.6	57.9	59.2	48.9	45.3	81.6	116.5	70.8
Seychelles	..	20.9	14.5	10.5	8.4	7.0	9.5	10.6	6.9	10.0	6.4	48.3	59.2	14.3
Sierra Leone	51.0	236.5	351.1	355.5	423.2	195.5	-575.6	297.9	3,750.4	358.5	563.8	43.0	126.2	516.1
Somalia	169.3	..	..	..	..	..	..	..	..	..	..	156.0	166.2	347.2
South Africa	..	..	1.5	1.4	1.4	1.5	2.1	2.5	2.8	2.6	2.5	..	..	2.0
Sudan	55.8	..	..	..	..	12.1	6.6	11.5	14.5	11.3	7.8	44.2	52.5	10.6
Swaziland	24.6	22.3	22.3	23.5	21.3	7.8	9.6	11.5	11.2	4.8	12.5	25.2	31.2	17.4
Tanzania	..	106.8	88.8	86.8	84.4	81.2	82.5	86.2	73.8	63.9	77.7	..	122.0	85.0
Togo	28.1	83.7	105.0	84.8	91.1	57.1	51.3	43.7	26.6	27.3	17.9	39.6	82.3	60.1
Uganda	148.3	159.2	124.2	128.2	88.3	69.6	77.2	61.0	50.9	70.3	68.9	58.4	59.9	96.0
Zambia	35.2	273.6	177.0	260.3	367.3	145.1	107.0	65.7	113.4	131.5	51.2	34.1	112.2	167.9
Zimbabwe	14.5	57.9	33.3	34.3	35.2	23.4	22.0	26.6	27.6	19.6	22.5	9.3	22.5	29.0
NORTH AFRICA	7.2	15.6	11.5	12.1	8.5	9.5	7.3	6.3	5.3	4.4	4.6	9.4	7.2	10.3
Algeria	1.1	2.7	2.4	3.2	2.4	2.6	2.2	2.9	0.7	1.3	1.2	1.2	1.0	2.1
Egypt, Arab Republic	22.0	47.3	31.3	31.3	19.5	19.6	12.1	9.2	7.0	5.6	5.7	33.9	15.9	24.7
Libya	0.2	..	..	..	..	..	..	..	..	..	..	0.2	..	..
Morocco	19.7	14.3	11.8	9.7	7.2	9.1	6.7	6.7	8.2	5.2	6.1	14.5	12.1	10.1
Tunisia	9.1	7.3	5.3	2.8	1.6	2.5	3.9	2.8	4.5	4.2	6.7	11.3	10.9	5.0
ALL AFRICA	13.2	38.0	25.8	28.3	23.4	20.6	17.7	16.2	14.3	14.3	14.4	14.2	24.3	23.9

Note: Regional aggregates for ODA include data for economies not specified elsewhere.

12-13. Net ODA from DAC donors as share of recipient GDI

	Percentage of GDI											Annual Average		
	1980	*1992*	*1993*	*1994*	*1995*	*1996*	*1997*	*1998*	*1999*	*2000*	*2001*	*75-84*	*85-89*	*90-MR*
SUB-SAHARAN AFRICA	11.8	40.3	22.4	23.0	18.5	16.5	15.3	15.2	13.8	14.7	13.6	12.6	31.1	22.5
excluding South Africa	11.8	40.3	37.6	41.5	35.2	26.8	24.1	22.1	19.2	20.8	18.4	12.6	31.1	30.2
excl. S.Africa & Nigeria	20.5	53.8	46.2	50.8	41.7	31.0	29.0	27.5	23.8	27.1	25.0	18.9	36.0	37.4
Angola	..	92.8	25.6	33.2	17.1	11.3	11.6	9.4	8.8	6.0	5.6	..	8.7	20.4
Benin	16.8	76.6	45.6	60.2	45.0	43.6	37.3	36.3	28.5	44.6	31.8	21.0	50.1	46.4
Botswana	19.6	7.4	6.7	4.9	4.6	5.7	3.8	4.4	3.0	2.6	2.1	23.0	24.3	5.2
Burkina Faso	51.9	63.5	60.1	69.4	44.9	39.6	33.5	29.8	34.7	38.6	35.0	43.3	41.5	44.8
Burundi	46.8	91.6	82.1	111.0	113.1	62.5	49.5	57.7	79.9	66.3	114.7	48.1	49.4	83.1
Cameroon	12.1	35.5	26.9	33.0	29.9	20.0	22.4	19.9	14.8	14.6	18.0	10.1	8.7	22.5
Cape Verde	70.7	58.9	56.4	45.8	36.9	64.0	61.0	79.7	72.2	64.7	46.8	58.6	89.1	64.2
Central African Republic	134.5	61.2	88.4	94.4	80.8	262.7	62.4	39.9	39.1	51.3	35.3	84.4	65.2	77.2
Chad	..	105.6	102.0	52.7	85.7	50.9	43.2	25.3	32.8	22.3	10.7	86.5	122.1	59.1
Comoros	32.8	42.3	56.6	46.2	48.1	49.1	45.4	48.1	39.6	40.4	33.2	43.0	67.4	50.4
Congo, Democratic Rep. of	22.1	28.7	62.6	21.2	22.2	6.3	11.4	6.5	3.3	16.1	..	16.1	29.5	29.2
Congo, Republic of	9.1	16.1	20.5	45.8	13.6	57.6	50.1	11.5	18.6	3.4	4.0	11.8	19.5	25.6
Côte d'Ivoire	5.6	68.3	82.0	85.3	53.7	30.6	13.8	28.7	22.1	22.2	15.4	7.0	18.0	46.0
Djibouti	..	..	..	..	189.5	157.9	131.2	79.4	116.1	59.2	..	..	..	122.2
Equatorial Guinea	..	96.1	83.0	17.7	17.3	7.9	5.5	4.4	3.1	3.6	4.7	..	..	40.5
Eritrea	..	..	18.2	98.7	65.4	60.9	32.4	37.1	26.8	50.1	62.3	..	..	50.2
Ethiopia	..	89.3	46.9	76.4	55.3	44.2	34.4	32.7	31.0	39.1	32.6	13.6	39.5	52.7
Gabon	4.2	5.2	9.9	17.6	11.6	8.5	1.9	2.2	2.8	-0.9	-0.6	3.4	6.7	6.5
Gambia, The	25.6	65.5	64.9	58.1	32.6	20.3	24.7	17.6	17.2	20.4	18.2	46.6	128.1	41.6
Ghana	42.8	40.5	23.6	25.5	27.7	17.3	17.1	21.7	22.0	32.6	31.1	32.8	32.1	27.8
Guinea	..	40.8	31.6	35.2	36.0	20.1	18.8	23.0	13.9	13.7	18.3	..	38.8	25.9
Guinea-Bissau	110.3	51.9	77.3	240.8	135.7	200.1	100.0	276.7	85.2	120.6	70.3	92.8	81.4	128.3
Kenya	15.6	47.4	48.4	34.1	28.9	22.3	18.5	15.8	16.5	20.5	18.6	20.7	30.4	29.4
Lesotho	39.9	12.7	16.5	9.8	10.9	8.9	8.1	7.8	6.5	6.1	10.1	43.4	36.2	11.7
Liberia	19.7	..	..	..	..	..	..	..	..	..	..	32.5	66.7	..
Madagascar	15.0	63.6	59.0	58.5	56.4	49.4	120.8	60.4	34.7	23.8	19.3	25.0	57.7	60.2
Malawi	24.7	58.0	50.5	73.0	90.9	93.9	56.4	87.1	84.9	125.7	102.5	26.2	54.8	76.6
Mali	47.5	38.4	37.8	50.4	50.5	49.6	50.3	43.5	43.5	57.7	40.4	55.7	73.4	47.4
Mauritania	28.7	50.6	100.6	60.1	61.2	47.6	50.1	33.4	52.0	27.9	29.6	25.5	53.1	51.7
Mauritius	8.6	4.0	2.7	0.7	1.0	-0.1	0.2	1.7	0.5	1.1	0.7	10.3	10.8	2.5
Mozambique	54.8	348.2	322.1	169.9	132.3	89.0	88.9	76.0	40.3	41.3	48.0	74.1	164.0	145.6
Namibia	..	15.8	26.2	15.9	19.4	16.9	16.3	14.3	14.2	11.8	10.2	..	9.8	15.5
Niger	14.9	161.3	247.0	160.9	140.9	85.0	90.4	61.8	58.3	54.6	50.7	51.1	80.2	115.8
Nigeria	0.1	1.9	1.4	1.0	1.6	0.9	0.8	0.4	0.7	0.9	0.9	0.4	2.6	1.5
Rwanda	51.5	58.8	61.0	647.8	195.6	126.9	69.9	70.9	54.2	55.2	47.5	54.3	39.2	126.9
São Tomé and Principe	15.4	147.7	168.3	127.9	198.6	114.5	98.1	124.1	104.2	87.6	93.6	30.6	110.1	143.8
Senegal	51.9	50.8	47.5	70.3	53.4	45.6	37.0	33.4	46.0	33.3	24.2	50.5	73.0	48.0
Seychelles	..	16.8	5.1	5.9	7.1	2.9	3.5	7.5	2.5	1.8	3.9	42.7	37.7	9.4
Sierra Leone	31.8	131.4	178.5	69.4	122.2	71.1	-201.0	149.0	3,049.7	227.2	281.9	24.2	73.9	352.8
Somalia	54.4	..	..	..	..	..	..	..	..	..	..	49.5	107.6	189.7
South Africa	..	..	1.0	1.0	1.2	1.3	1.7	2.0	2.0	1.9	1.8	..	..	1.6
Sudan	24.4	..	..	..	..	6.5	4.1	8.3	9.4	4.5	4.9	17.0	28.3	6.3
Swaziland	16.1	10.5	13.6	11.1	13.8	4.9	5.5	5.5	5.8	1.0	1.8	16.1	20.4	9.3
Tanzania	..	65.1	60.8	51.3	56.4	56.0	49.7	66.3	45.7	48.7	59.4	..	93.3	57.8
Togo	16.1	50.7	83.7	42.9	55.8	35.4	31.0	22.5	17.5	20.4	10.9	21.5	46.6	37.7
Uganda	55.2	56.0	70.8	58.7	44.8	38.1	41.7	36.2	30.8	49.6	34.0	24.1	21.2	46.8
Zambia	25.9	184.7	103.7	157.3	79.4	84.3	64.4	48.3	61.8	80.4	37.6	26.1	88.8	94.2
Zimbabwe	9.9	39.2	20.7	17.1	24.9	17.7	14.6	22.0	24.8	21.2	21.0	7.2	19.8	22.0
NORTH AFRICA	4.4	12.9	8.1	9.6	6.9	7.5	5.0	4.1	3.6	3.3	3.3	4.5	6.1	7.6
Algeria	0.7	2.5	1.8	2.8	2.2	2.2	1.7	0.9	0.3	0.2	0.2	0.9	0.7	1.5
Egypt, Arab Republic	18.8	39.4	23.8	26.9	16.3	17.2	9.1	7.0	5.7	4.8	4.9	15.3	14.9	19.5
Libya	0.1	..	..	..	..	..	..	..	..	..	..	0.1	..	..
Morocco	4.1	11.1	7.0	4.9	5.1	5.5	3.1	3.2	4.0	3.6	4.1	5.5	8.3	5.9
Tunisia	6.1	5.6	3.0	1.9	1.2	0.8	1.4	1.9	1.8	2.8	3.3	8.0	7.7	2.9
ALL AFRICA	7.8	25.0	16.3	17.5	14.1	13.2	11.2	10.2	9.1	9.4	8.8	7.8	16.3	15.3

Note: Regional aggregates for ODA include data for economies not specified elsewhere.

12-14. Net ODA from multilateral donors as share of recipient GDI

	Percentage of GDI											Annual Average		
	1980	*1992*	*1993*	*1994*	*1995*	*1996*	*1997*	*1998*	*1999*	*2000*	*2001*	*75-84*	*85-89*	*90-MR*
SUB-SAHARAN AFRICA	6.5	25.6	13.9	16.6	14.0	10.5	9.1	8.7	7.7	7.8	9.0	6.8	16.8	13.6
excluding South Africa	6.5	25.6	23.3	30.4	27.2	17.4	14.9	13.1	10.9	11.2	12.5	6.8	16.8	18.9
excl. S.Africa & Nigeria	11.1	34.0	27.9	36.6	31.7	19.8	17.5	15.8	13.4	14.4	16.9	10.2	19.6	23.1
Angola	..	72.5	23.1	33.5	12.4	6.8	6.5	5.3	4.8	3.6	2.8	..	3.9	15.6
Benin	24.8	44.0	43.2	46.8	24.5	31.1	18.4	15.8	22.3	11.5	28.0	19.5	39.7	31.7
Botswana	5.3	1.6	3.6	2.4	3.0	0.7	4.7	2.2	1.5	0.9	0.3	6.2	7.7	2.1
Burkina Faso	21.0	38.9	50.0	43.9	41.1	21.2	22.5	22.0	23.5	17.7	24.5	20.1	17.9	28.6
Burundi	42.2	100.6	61.2	211.4	189.9	41.0	23.8	30.5	34.2	83.8	159.4	39.0	54.8	90.2
Cameroon	5.0	8.4	0.8	27.7	8.4	9.6	11.6	13.0	10.7	11.6	8.2	4.3	2.6	10.2
Cape Verde	42.5	29.1	24.6	22.2	19.3	30.1	38.8	41.9	39.3	23.0	26.6	34.3	40.5	30.3
Central African Republic	60.5	39.9	40.7	72.1	28.2	96.7	30.2	44.7	38.9	21.7	20.7	42.9	48.1	46.4
Chad	..	64.5	53.4	55.3	73.4	71.5	56.6	29.9	59.2	32.1	15.5	69.7	96.9	54.9
Comoros	32.7	45.8	39.1	54.7	44.3	38.8	35.6	42.3	24.8	29.1	57.0	43.1	49.0	45.2
Congo, Democratic Rep. of	7.4	18.5	50.0	32.2	14.7	3.4	4.8	3.5	1.7	12.6	..	6.8	17.7	17.3
Congo, Republic of	3.6	1.9	1.2	19.8	2.6	5.1	1.9	1.1	3.1	1.5	6.0	5.7	2.8	4.2
Côte d'Ivoire	2.2	29.7	6.4	80.4	35.9	35.0	12.6	28.0	4.9	9.0	2.7	1.9	7.3	24.3
Djibouti	..	..	..	..	53.1	47.3	39.4	21.5	39.3	27.7	..	..	..	38.0
Equatorial Guinea	..	69.6	75.2	14.3	9.5	2.6	2.0	0.9	1.2	0.7	0.5	5.3	..	23.5
Eritrea	..	..	6.8	50.8	33.9	13.7	10.3	14.5	16.5	24.6	51.8	..	..	24.8
Ethiopia	..	140.7	75.5	67.9	37.6	36.4	18.2	25.3	28.9	30.7	60.8	20.4	30.6	58.0
Gabon	0.6	0.3	0.4	2.1	0.8	1.1	0.7	0.5	1.1	1.8	1.2	0.5	0.7	0.9
Gambia, The	48.0	80.8	48.3	50.9	29.9	25.8	32.6	32.2	24.8	44.7	47.9	43.2	98.4	45.0
Ghana	23.7	34.6	23.3	16.9	23.1	15.0	11.1	18.8	15.4	18.8	19.9	24.9	46.2	22.7
Guinea	..	37.8	38.9	33.0	31.2	21.4	33.2	29.0	13.6	8.5	23.2	..	27.1	28.2
Guinea-Bissau	75.9	40.8	46.4	94.0	68.1	83.0	111.9	132.6	54.0	112.6	65.2	54.6	71.6	78.8
Kenya	6.7	33.7	55.2	23.8	17.0	15.9	8.9	7.9	3.5	15.0	12.1	5.7	11.2	19.9
Lesotho	19.1	13.4	15.1	15.1	9.2	9.3	7.2	7.2	1.7	4.5	8.8	28.8	24.9	10.1
Liberia	9.4	..	..	..	..	..	..	..	..	..	..	10.9	27.3	..
Madagascar	15.1	43.4	35.0	30.6	30.7	27.3	62.6	26.7	29.9	31.6	30.4	19.9	44.3	38.1
Malawi	22.1	101.6	107.0	62.7	87.0	81.1	55.3	98.5	79.9	79.8	102.2	23.3	57.0	82.6
Mali	37.4	30.4	25.0	43.3	47.8	33.6	34.9	21.5	21.5	11.8	24.8	38.7	38.1	29.4
Mauritania	19.3	39.7	69.1	70.2	58.4	89.1	80.1	56.9	73.3	43.7	66.1	30.4	32.4	62.6
Mauritius	2.7	1.3	-0.1	0.7	1.3	2.1	2.5	2.0	3.4	0.7	0.6	4.7	1.6	1.4
Mozambique	16.3	156.9	143.7	107.6	68.9	53.8	46.9	35.1	14.5	16.8	14.0	22.5	49.6	66.7
Namibia	..	7.2	6.7	3.5	5.8	6.4	5.5	5.7	7.3	6.7	4.0	..	6.2	7.3
Niger	9.0	63.6	85.4	68.1	57.8	47.3	70.5	62.4	32.1	54.2	59.8	26.4	45.2	60.8
Nigeria	0.1	1.7	4.2	3.1	3.0	2.9	2.4	2.2	1.2	1.1	0.7	0.2	0.6	2.1
Rwanda	30.6	51.4	46.1	300.0	209.4	107.4	19.7	47.9	57.8	46.1	45.1	29.7	27.7	83.6
São Tomé and Principe	34.4	172.2	109.0	114.9	73.3	73.7	56.4	67.9	46.2	85.5	68.2	85.0	176.9	105.1
Senegal	22.6	22.4	15.9	24.2	33.9	20.6	15.4	24.4	12.7	16.1	21.1	25.0	36.9	21.9
Seychelles	..	4.5	9.0	4.7	1.6	3.0	3.4	2.7	3.3	4.6	2.5	5.3	18.0	4.2
Sierra Leone	16.7	104.9	172.3	285.9	299.7	119.8	-369.6	141.5	683.0	131.3	278.4	16.3	45.7	160.7
Somalia	65.0	..	..	..	..	..	..	..	..	..	..	58.5	56.2	99.9
South Africa	..	..	0.5	0.4	0.2	0.2	0.3	0.4	0.8	0.7	0.7	..	..	0.5
Sudan	17.2	..	..	..	..	5.6	2.5	3.2	3.5	1.8	2.5	12.0	14.7	3.2
Swaziland	8.6	10.4	7.6	11.5	6.5	2.3	3.5	4.5	5.4	3.7	9.4	9.1	10.4	7.3
Tanzania	..	41.9	28.1	35.0	27.5	25.4	32.6	19.7	28.0	15.4	18.6	..	28.7	27.1
Togo	12.0	33.6	21.0	41.7	35.1	22.5	20.7	20.8	7.9	6.4	5.6	17.2	33.4	22.3
Uganda	91.3	100.0	53.1	67.2	42.3	30.6	35.3	24.8	20.0	20.2	34.7	32.2	37.4	46.9
Zambia	6.8	88.8	73.3	102.9	287.9	60.8	42.6	17.6	51.5	51.0	13.5	6.2	23.4	73.6
Zimbabwe	4.2	18.9	12.6	17.3	10.5	5.9	7.6	4.7	2.9	-1.5	2.0	2.1	2.9	7.1
NORTH AFRICA	0.8	1.4	2.1	2.2	1.3	1.8	2.0	1.8	1.5	0.8	1.1	1.6	0.6	1.6
Algeria	0.1	0.2	0.6	0.3	0.3	0.3	0.4	1.9	0.2	0.5	0.7	0.1	0.1	0.5
Egypt, Arab Republic	3.1	2.6	2.5	3.3	2.0	1.9	2.4	1.3	0.9	0.6	0.5	7.2	0.9	1.9
Libya	0.1	..	..	..	..	..	..	..	..	..	..	0.1	..	..
Morocco	1.4	2.4	4.5	4.4	1.9	3.2	3.1	3.1	3.8	1.6	1.7	1.3	0.7	2.8
Tunisia	1.0	1.9	2.6	1.3	0.9	2.5	2.9	1.5	2.9	1.3	3.4	1.4	2.2	2.1
ALL AFRICA	3.4	12.2	8.9	10.7	9.1	7.3	6.3	5.6	4.9	4.6	5.3	3.7	7.1	7.8

Note: Regional aggregates for ODA include data for economies not specified elsewhere.

12-15. Net ODA per capita from all donors

	U.S. dollars (current prices)											Annual Average		
	1980	*1992*	*1993*	*1994*	*1995*	*1996*	*1997*	*1998*	*1999*	*2000*	*2001*	*75-84*	*85-89*	*90-MR*
SUB-SAHARAN AFRICA	22	39	32	34	33	28	24	23	21	20	21	17	30	29
excluding South Africa	22	39	34	36	34	29	25	24	21	21	21	17	30	30
excl. S.Africa & Nigeria	27	49	42	45	43	36	31	30	26	26	26	22	37	37
Angola	7	34	27	41	37	40	29	27	30	23	20	7	15	30
Benin	26	54	56	48	51	51	38	35	35	38	42	21	36	47
Botswana	117	82	92	59	60	48	77	66	37	18	17	91	114	64
Burkina Faso	30	47	49	44	49	41	35	37	36	30	34	24	32	40
Burundi	28	54	37	52	47	18	9	10	11	14	19	23	37	30
Cameroon	30	58	43	56	33	30	36	35	30	26	26	22	24	38
Cape Verde	223	335	323	326	307	298	277	315	323	216	171	144	276	292
Central African Republic	48	58	55	52	50	49	26	33	32	20	20	34	58	45
Chad	8	39	36	33	35	43	32	23	25	17	23	18	40	34
Comoros	129	106	105	81	85	78	53	66	39	34	48	119	123	79
Congo, Democratic Rep. of	16	7	4	6	4	4	3	3	3	4	5	12	16	7
Congo, Republic of	55	48	50	144	48	160	98	23	48	11	24	49	49	68
Côte d'Ivoire	26	60	59	118	87	67	30	64	29	22	11	17	25	55
Djibouti	244	211	241	225	181	165	143	133	121	113	85	206	245	187
Equatorial Guinea	43	168	140	77	84	75	58	51	45	47	28	27	116	93
Eritrea	..	..	20	45	42	43	33	43	37	43	67	..	..	41
Ethiopia	6	21	20	20	16	14	10	11	10	11	16	5	16	16
Gabon	81	69	99	173	134	114	34	38	40	10	7	73	107	84
Gambia, The	85	110	81	65	42	32	33	32	27	38	38	58	108	59
Ghana	18	38	38	32	38	37	27	38	32	32	33	13	33	37
Guinea	20	74	65	56	63	44	55	51	33	21	36	15	42	51
Guinea-Bissau	78	107	92	166	110	164	110	83	45	67	48	66	103	104
Kenya	24	36	36	26	28	22	16	14	11	17	15	19	31	26
Lesotho	69	83	81	64	61	55	47	31	16	18	26	52	67	53
Liberia	52	47	47	24	45	62	26	24	31	22	11	40	34	38
Madagascar	26	30	29	22	23	26	59	33	24	21	22	16	27	30
Malawi	23	66	56	52	47	52	36	44	44	43	38	19	35	50
Mali	41	48	40	47	56	50	43	34	33	33	32	29	51	44
Mauritania	113	96	151	121	101	116	99	66	85	80	95	115	115	103
Mauritius	34	42	24	13	21	17	38	36	36	17	18	37	51	34
Mozambique	14	100	79	78	67	55	57	61	47	50	52	11	45	66
Namibia	..	97	101	89	121	116	101	108	104	87	61	0	19	100
Niger	30	45	40	43	30	27	34	29	18	19	22	30	47	34
Nigeria	1	3	3	2	2	2	2	2	1	1	1	1	1	2
Rwanda	30	48	47	115	110	69	29	43	45	38	33	26	34	56
São Tomé and Principe	44	464	373	389	638	351	241	198	190	236	251	72	208	353
Senegal	47	88	64	79	80	68	48	55	58	44	43	45	84	69
Seychelles	337	268	269	174	172	248	221	308	163	225	164	242	338	254
Sierra Leone	28	32	48	63	46	40	25	22	15	36	65	16	23	36
Somalia	67	85	115	70	26	12	10	10	14	12	16	46	71	39
South Africa	..	..	7	8	10	9	12	12	13	11	10	..	..	10
Sudan	32	21	17	15	9	8	5	7	8	7	5	28	40	14
Swaziland	89	69	65	66	65	36	29	35	28	13	27	60	49	48
Tanzania	37	49	34	34	30	29	30	31	30	30	36	28	34	35
Togo	36	62	26	33	49	39	30	30	16	15	10	32	51	37
Uganda	9	42	34	40	43	34	40	31	27	37	34	7	20	37
Zambia	55	125	103	82	226	66	65	36	63	79	36	35	58	88
Zimbabwe	23	73	45	50	43	32	28	22	20	14	12	15	28	34
NORTH AFRICA	31	45	31	31	24	26	22	23	20	16	17	31	24	32
Algeria	10	15	13	15	11	11	9	13	3	5	6	8	8	10
Egypt, Arab Republic	34	66	43	47	35	37	33	32	25	21	19	44	34	46
Libya	5	1	1	1	1	2	1	1	1	..	..	3	2	2
Morocco	46	38	28	24	19	24	17	19	24	15	18	28	22	27
Tunisia	36	46	26	12	8	14	21	16	27	23	39	36	33	27
ALL AFRICA	24	40	32	34	31	27	24	23	20	20	20	20	29	30

Note: Regional aggregates for ODA include data for economies not specified elsewhere.

12-16. Net ODA per capita from DAC donors

	U.S. dollars (current prices)											Annual Average		
	1980	1992	1993	1994	1995	1996	1997	1998	1999	2000	2001	75-84	85-89	90-MR
SUB-SAHARAN AFRICA	13	24	20	20	18	17	15	15	13	13	12	10	19	18
excluding South Africa	13	24	21	21	19	18	15	15	13	13	13	10	19	18
excl. S.Africa & Nigeria	16	29	26	26	24	22	19	19	17	17	16	13	23	23
Angola	5	19	14	20	21	25	19	17	20	14	13	4	10	18
Benin	10	34	28	27	32	29	26	24	20	30	22	11	20	28
Botswana	92	69	57	39	36	44	35	45	25	14	14	69	87	46
Burkina Faso	22	29	27	27	25	26	21	21	21	20	19	16	22	24
Burundi	14	26	21	18	18	11	6	7	8	6	8	12	17	15
Cameroon	20	47	42	31	26	21	24	21	17	14	18	15	19	27
Cape Verde	135	225	224	219	201	198	169	207	210	160	110	95	188	198
Central African Republic	32	35	37	29	37	35	17	16	16	14	13	22	33	26
Chad	5	25	23	16	19	18	14	10	9	7	9	10	22	17
Comoros	40	51	62	37	44	44	30	35	24	19	17	45	69	42
Congo, Democratic Rep. of	12	4	2	2	3	2	2	2	2	2	3	8	10	4
Congo, Republic of	33	43	48	100	40	147	94	21	41	8	10	30	43	58
Côte d'Ivoire	19	42	54	61	52	31	16	32	23	16	10	13	18	35
Djibouti	107	172	169	164	137	120	104	102	89	67	44	122	158	127
Equatorial Guinea	5	97	73	42	54	57	42	42	33	40	28	14	66	61
Eritrea	..	..	14	27	26	35	21	25	20	27	36	..	..	26
Ethiopia	2	8	8	10	9	8	6	6	5	6	6	2	9	8
Gabon	71	65	95	154	126	102	27	32	29	-9	-6	61	93	75
Gambia, The	26	50	48	35	23	15	15	11	10	11	10	25	61	29
Ghana	10	21	19	20	21	20	16	20	19	20	20	7	13	20
Guinea	7	38	30	29	33	20	18	21	15	13	16	4	23	24
Guinea-Bissau	45	57	55	117	71	113	52	56	27	35	25	38	51	63
Kenya	17	21	17	15	17	13	11	10	9	10	9	15	22	16
Lesotho	47	39	41	25	33	26	23	16	13	11	14	32	39	28
Liberia	32	10	9	13	11	40	11	11	15	8	5	27	24	14
Madagascar	10	18	18	15	15	17	39	23	13	9	9	8	16	18
Malawi	12	24	18	28	24	28	18	21	23	26	19	10	17	23
Mali	20	27	24	26	30	30	25	23	22	28	19	16	32	27
Mauritania	35	56	91	58	55	42	40	25	34	31	30	29	62	47
Mauritius	26	32	24	7	10	-1	2	17	4	10	7	24	42	20
Mozambique	9	69	54	48	44	34	37	42	34	35	40	8	34	45
Namibia	..	66	81	72	93	84	75	77	68	55	43	0	12	67
Niger	19	32	30	30	21	17	19	14	11	10	10	17	30	22
Nigeria	0	1	1	0	1	0	0	0	0	1	1	0	1	1
Rwanda	19	26	27	78	53	37	23	26	22	21	17	16	20	32
São Tomé and Principe	14	214	226	205	466	213	153	128	132	120	145	22	84	206
Senegal	33	59	46	59	48	46	33	32	45	30	23	28	52	47
Seychelles	284	215	94	98	145	102	82	218	60	40	100	213	247	155
Sierra Leone	18	18	25	12	13	14	9	11	12	23	32	8	13	16
Somalia	21	64	89	57	16	5	6	5	9	6	10	15	46	27
South Africa	..	..	5	6	8	8	10	10	9	8	7	..	..	8
Sudan	14	7	6	6	5	4	3	5	5	3	3	11	21	7
Swaziland	58	33	39	31	42	22	17	17	15	3	4	39	31	26
Tanzania	28	30	23	20	20	20	18	24	19	23	27	21	26	24
Togo	21	37	21	17	30	24	18	16	11	11	6	18	29	23
Uganda	3	15	19	18	22	19	21	18	17	26	17	2	7	19
Zambia	41	85	60	50	49	38	39	27	34	48	27	27	46	48
Zimbabwe	16	50	28	25	30	24	19	18	18	15	12	11	24	25
NORTH AFRICA	19	37	22	25	19	21	15	15	13	12	12	16	21	23
Algeria	6	14	10	14	10	9	7	4	1	1	1	6	5	8
Egypt, Arab Republic	29	55	33	40	29	33	25	24	21	18	17	23	31	36
Libya	3	0	0	0	1	0	0	1	1	..	..	1	1	1
Morocco	10	29	17	12	13	15	8	9	12	10	12	10	16	16
Tunisia	25	35	15	8	6	5	8	11	11	16	19	25	23	16
ALL AFRICA	14	26	20	21	19	18	15	15	13	13	12	11	19	19

Note: Regional aggregates for ODA include data for economies not specified elsewhere.

12-17. Net ODA per capita from multilateral donors

	U.S. dollars (current prices)											*Annual Average*		
	1980	*1992*	*1993*	*1994*	*1995*	*1996*	*1997*	*1998*	*1999*	*2000*	*2001*	*75-84*	*85-89*	*90-MR*
SUB-SAHARAN AFRICA	7	15	12	14	14	11	9	8	7	7	8	5	10	11
excluding South Africa	7	15	13	15	15	11	10	9	8	7	9	5	10	12
excl. S.Africa & Nigeria	9	19	16	19	18	14	12	11	9	9	11	7	12	14
Angola	2	15	13	21	16	15	11	10	11	8	7	3	5	12
Benin	15	20	27	21	18	21	13	11	15	8	20	10	16	19
Botswana	25	15	30	19	24	5	44	22	13	5	2	19	27	18
Burkina Faso	9	18	22	17	23	14	14	16	14	9	13	7	9	15
Burundi	13	28	16	34	30	7	3	4	3	8	11	10	19	16
Cameroon	8	11	1	26	7	10	12	14	13	11	8	6	5	11
Cape Verde	81	111	98	106	105	93	108	109	114	57	62	46	84	94
Central African Republic	15	23	17	22	13	13	8	18	16	6	7	12	24	18
Chad	3	15	12	17	16	25	18	12	16	10	13	7	18	16
Comoros	40	55	43	44	41	34	23	31	15	14	29	45	50	36
Congo, Democratic Rep. of	4	3	2	3	2	1	1	1	1	2	2	3	6	2
Congo, Republic of	13	5	3	43	8	13	4	2	7	3	15	14	7	10
Côte d'Ivoire	7	18	4	57	35	36	14	31	5	6	2	4	7	20
Djibouti	29	40	53	40	38	36	31	28	30	31	42	30	50	37
Equatorial Guinea	37	70	66	34	30	18	15	8	12	7	3	17	50	31
Eritrea	..	..	5	14	14	8	7	10	12	13	30	..	..	13
Ethiopia	3	13	13	9	6	6	3	5	5	5	10	3	7	8
Gabon	10	4	3	19	9	14	10	7	11	19	13	8	10	10
Gambia, The	48	62	36	31	21	19	19	20	15	25	26	26	47	30
Ghana	6	18	19	13	17	17	10	18	13	12	13	5	19	16
Guinea	13	36	36	27	29	21	32	26	15	8	20	8	17	26
Guinea-Bissau	31	45	33	46	36	47	58	27	17	32	23	23	46	39
Kenya	7	15	19	11	10	9	5	5	2	7	6	4	8	10
Lesotho	22	42	38	38	28	27	21	15	3	8	12	19	28	25
Liberia	15	37	37	10	33	21	15	14	16	14	7	11	10	23
Madagascar	10	12	11	8	8	9	20	10	11	12	14	7	12	12
Malawi	11	42	38	24	23	24	18	23	21	17	19	8	18	26
Mali	16	21	16	22	28	20	18	11	11	6	12	11	17	17
Mauritania	23	43	63	68	53	79	64	43	48	49	66	31	39	57
Mauritius	8	11	-1	7	12	20	26	20	31	6	5	12	7	13
Mozambique	3	31	24	30	23	21	20	19	12	14	12	3	10	20
Namibia	..	30	20	16	28	32	25	31	35	31	17	..	7	32
Niger	11	13	10	13	9	10	14	14	6	10	12	9	17	12
Nigeria	0	1	2	1	1	1	1	1	1	1	1	0	0	1
Rwanda	11	22	20	36	57	32	6	17	23	17	16	9	14	23
São Tomé and Principe	30	250	146	184	172	137	88	70	58	117	106	50	125	147
Senegal	14	26	16	20	31	21	14	23	12	15	20	14	28	21
Seychelles	53	58	166	78	33	107	79	77	77	104	63	25	79	81
Sierra Leone	9	14	24	50	32	24	16	10	3	13	32	7	8	19
Somalia	26	19	25	13	9	6	4	5	5	5	5	18	24	10
South Africa	..	..	2	2	2	1	2	2	4	3	3	..	..	2
Sudan	10	13	11	9	4	4	2	2	2	1	2	8	12	7
Swaziland	31	32	22	33	20	11	11	14	14	10	21	21	17	20
Tanzania	7	19	11	14	10	9	12	7	11	7	9	6	8	11
Togo	15	25	5	16	19	15	12	14	5	4	3	13	20	14
Uganda	5	26	14	21	21	15	18	13	11	11	17	4	12	17
Zambia	11	41	42	32	178	28	26	10	29	31	10	6	12	39
Zimbabwe	7	24	17	25	13	8	10	4	2	-1	1	4	4	9
NORTH AFRICA	4	4	6	6	4	5	6	6	6	3	4	5	2	5
Algeria	1	1	3	2	1	1	2	9	1	2	3	1	1	2
Egypt, Arab Republic	5	4	3	5	4	4	6	4	3	2	2	9	2	4
Libya	2	1	0	0	1	1	1	1	1	..	..	2	1	1
Morocco	3	6	11	11	5	9	8	9	11	5	5	2	1	7
Tunisia	4	12	13	6	5	13	16	8	17	8	20	4	7	11
ALL AFRICA	6	13	11	13	12	10	9	8	7	6	7	5	8	10

Note: Regional aggregates for ODA include data for economies not specified elsewhere.

Figure 12-1. Total net ODA as a share of recipient GDP, 2001*

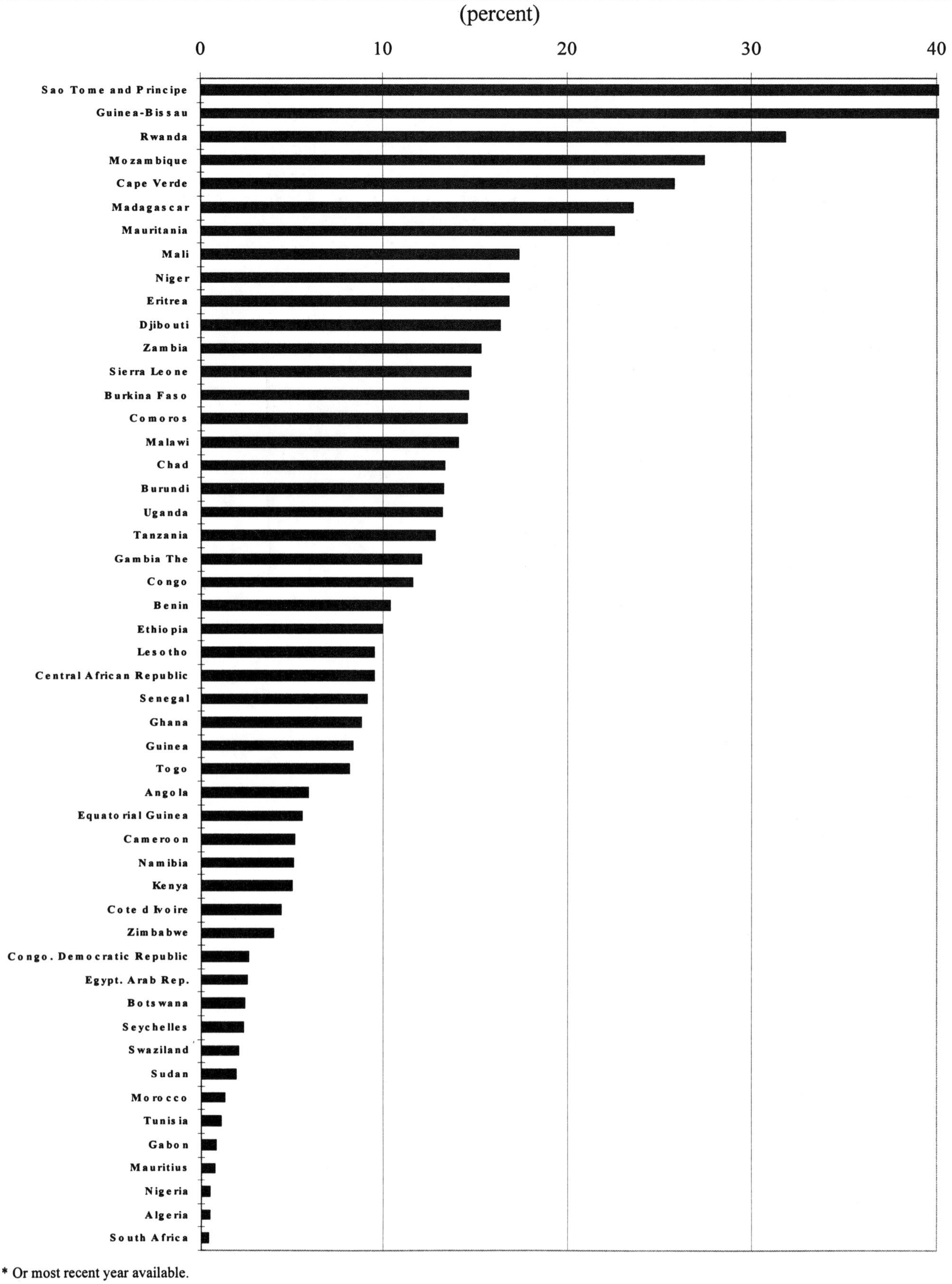

* Or most recent year available.

Figure 12-2. Total net ODA per capita, 2001*

(U.S. dollars)

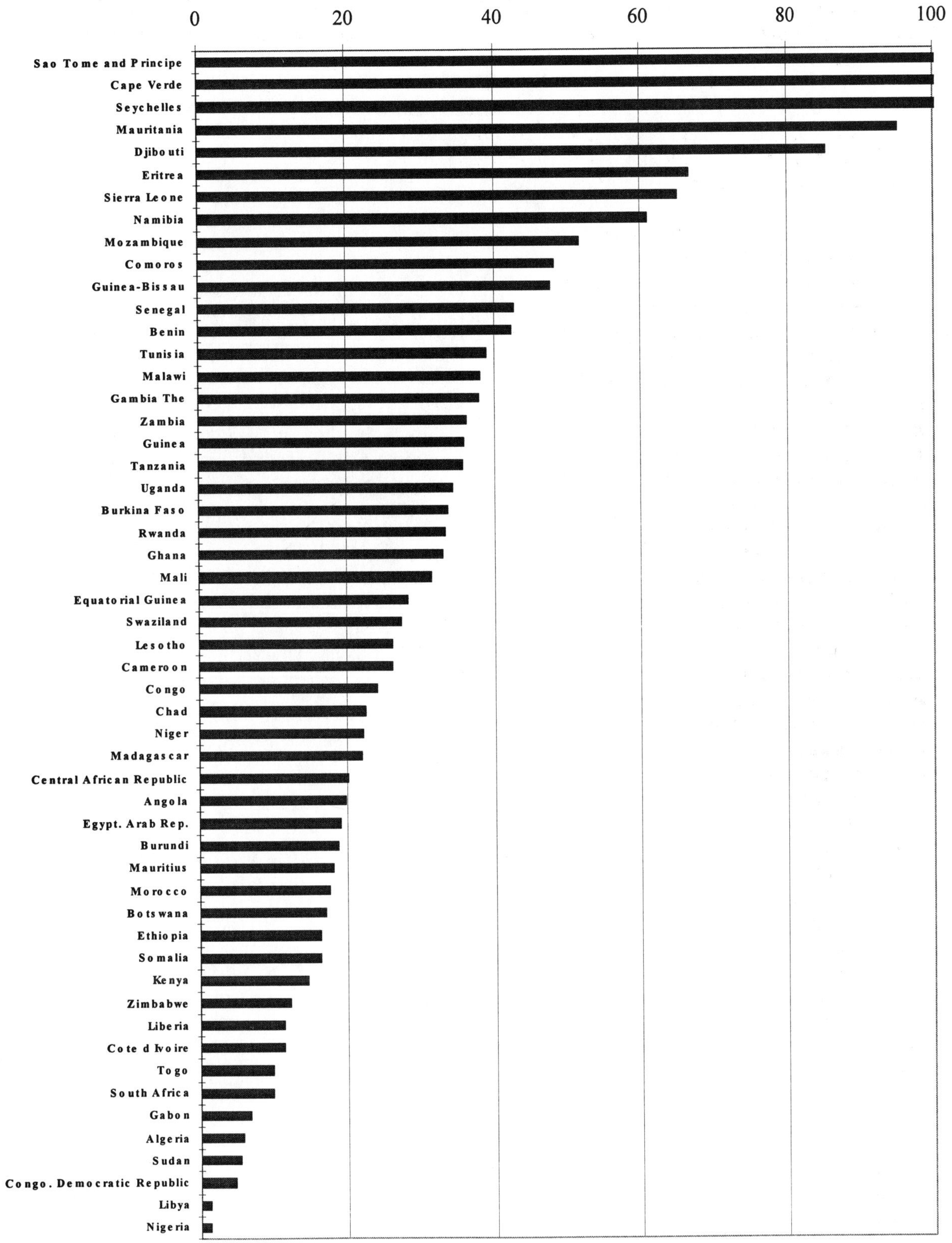

* Or most recent year available.

Technical notes

Tables

Table 12-1. Net ODA from all donors, nominal. This table represents the total of Tables 12-2 through 12-4.

Table 12-2. Net ODA from DAC donors, nominal. This table (OECD data) includes net ODA from Australia, Austria, Belgium, Canada, Denmark, Finland, France, the Federal Republic of Germany before reunification, Italy, Japan, the Netherlands, Norway, Sweden, Switzerland, the United Kingdom, and the United States (OECD data). (Ireland and New Zealand have been excluded in compilation because their ODA to Africa is negligible.)

Table 12-3. Net ODA from non-DAC bilateral donors, nominal. This is net ODA from Organization of Petroleum Exporting Countries (OPEC), the former Council for Mutual Economic Assistance (CMEA) countries, and China (OECD data). OPEC countries are Algeria, Iran, Iraq, Kuwait, Libya, Nigeria, Qatar, Saudi Arabia, the United Arab Emirates, and Venezuela. The former CMEA countries are Bulgaria, Czechoslovakia, the former German Democratic Republic, Hungary, Poland, Romania, and the former Soviet Union.

Table 12-4. Net ODA from multilateral donors, nominal. This includes net ODA (OECD data), most notably from the African Development Fund, the European Development Fund for the Commission of the European Communities, the International Development Association (IDA), the International Fund for Agricultural Development, Arab/OPEC-financed multilateral agencies, and UN programs and agencies (OECD data). The UN programs and agencies include mainly the UN regular program of Technical Assistance, the UN Development Programme (UNDP), the UN High Commissioner for Refugees, the UN Children's Fund (UNICEF), and the World Food Programme. Arab/OPEC-financed multilateral agencies include the Arab Bank for Economic Development in Africa, the Arab Fund for Economic and Social Development (AFESD), the Islamic Development Bank, the OPEC Fund for International Development, the Arab Authority for Agricultural Investment and Development, the Arab Fund for Technical Assistance to African and Arab Countries, and the Islamic Solidarity Fund. ODA flows from the IMF Trust Fund and Structural Adjustment Facility (SAF) are also included.

Tables 12-5, 12-6, 12-7, and 12-8. Net ODA from all donors, from DAC donors, from non-DAC bilateral donors, and from multilateral donors, real (OECD data).

Tables 12-9, 12-10, and 12-11. Net ODA from all donors, from DAC donors, and from multilateral donors as a share of recipient GDP. These tables show the relative importance of these aid flows to recipients' economies. They are obtained by dividing figures in Tables 12-1, 12-2, and 12-4 by GDP data from Table 2-5, which reflect current prices and exchange rates. For a given level of aid flows, devaluation of a recipient's currency may inflate the ratios shown in the table. Thus, trends for a given country and comparisons across countries that have implemented different exchange rate policies should be interpreted carefully.

Tables 12-12, 12-13, and 12-14. Net ODA from all donors, from DAC donors, and from multilateral donors as a share of recipient GDI. These tables are obtained by dividing figures in Tables 12-1, 12-2, and 12-4 by GDI (World Bank country desks). These tables highlight the relative importance of the indicated aid flows in maintaining and increasing investment in these economies. The same caveats mentioned above apply to their interpretation. Furthermore, aid flows do not exclusively finance investment (for example, food aid finances consumption), and the share of ODA going to investment varies across countries.

Tables 12-15, 12-16, and 12-17. Net ODA per capita from all donors, from DAC donors, and from multilateral donors. These are calculated by dividing figures in Tables 12-1, 12-2, and 12-4 by midyear population (Table 1-2). These ratios offer some indication of the importance of aid flows in sustaining per capita income and consumption levels (shown in Tables 2-19 and 2-20, respectively), although comparisons must be done carefully because exchange rate fluctuations, the actual rise of ODA flows, and other factors vary across countries and over time.

Figures

The following indicators have been used to derive the figures in this chapter.

Figure 12-1. Total net ODA as a share of recipient GDP (Table 12-9).

Figure 12-2. Total net ODA per capita (Table 12-15).

Methodology used for regional aggregations and period averages in chapter 12

	Aggregations [a]		*Period averages* [b]	
Table	*(1)*	*(2)*	*(1)*	*(2)*
12-1	x		x	
12-2	x		x	
12-3	x		x	
12-4	x		x	
12-5	x			x
12-6	x			x
12-7	x			x
12-8	x			x
12-9		x	x	
12-10		x	x	
12-11		x	x	
12-12		x	x	
12-13		x	x	
12-14		x	x	
12-15		x	x	
12-16		x	x	
12-17		x	x	

Note: Regional aggregations are shown in the rows for Sub-Saharan Africa, North Africa, and All Africa. Period averages are shown in the last three columns. This table shows only the methodologies used in this chapter.

a. Regional aggregations: (1) simple total; (2) simple total of the first indicator divided by the simple total of the second indicator (same country coverage); (3) simple total of the gap-filled indicator; (4) simple total of the gap-filled main indicator divided by the simple total of the gap-filled secondary indicator; (5) simple total of the first gap-filled main indicator less the simple total of the second gap-filled main indicator, all divided by the simple total of the secondary indicator; (6) weighted total (by population); (7) median; (8) no aggregation; (9) simple arithmetic mean.

b. Period averages: (1) arithmetic mean (using the same series as shown in the table i.e., ratio if the rest of the table is shown as ratio, level if the rest of the table is shown as level, growth rate if the rest is shown as growth rate); (2) least-squares growth rate (using main indicator); (3) least-squares growth rate (using main indicator in constant terms, with the rest of the table in current terms).

13

Social Indicators

This chapter provides indicators in the areas of demography, health, education, and gender issues in development. These indicators can be useful in evaluating and monitoring the social impact of development progress, aid flows, and structural adjustment policies.

The chapter presents such indicators as dependency ratio, urbanization, crude death rate, life expectancy at birth, infant mortality rate, child mortality rate, immunization rates for children, maternal death rate, and number of population per physician. These indicators are an indirect measure of the physical well being of the population. In the same vein, such indicators as literacy rate among adults, school enrollment ratios by gender, and pupil-teacher ratio give some picture of the progress being made in education and training. Social indicators refer to phenomena that are inherently more qualitative than macroeconomic variables and thus need to be interpreted cautiously. Further caution is called for because of the particular limitations of the data. One of these limitations is the paucity—or even nonexistence—of data on certain indicators in many of the countries covered. This is especially true of indicators dealing with gender issues. Many countries have no data showing the gender breakdown of several social indicators.

Even when data are available, comparison among countries is limited due to varied practices in data gathering and reporting. Often the countries report survey data that cover different portions of the nation. Sometimes surveys are limited to just the urban areas to cover only the largest cities or the capital city alone. This is especially true of the health indicators. Such indicators as immunization rates for children under one year of age, percentage of births attended by health personnel, infant mortality rate, child mortality rate, and maternal death rate are often based on surveys of a handful of hospitals in the urban areas.

Another source of limitation is the definition of terms, which may differ from country to country. Some countries, for example, consider an institution as a "private school" only if it receives no form of financial support from the government, while others classify as "private" all schools not run by the government, whether or not they receive financial support from the government. In like manner, some countries include personnel other than doctors and trained nurses in the term "medical personnel."

Cultural norms may also affect the reported data. This is especially true for gender issues. In some countries, it is assumed that no woman can be the head of any household that also contains an adult male. In population censuses, therefore, enumerators and respondents simply take such assumptions for granted, reporting a male rather than a female as head of the household or family (see United Nations, The World's Women, 1970–90). This distorts the true picture of the percentage of households headed by women.

The main source for this chapter is the *World Development Indicators* in the World Bank Statistical Information Management Analysis Database (SIMA), which contains electronic information as reported by a number of institutions and agencies in the socioeconomic field, such as the United Nations, UNICEF, UNESCO, World Health Organization (WHO), the UNDP, UNAIDS, and the ECA. Other sources of data also include reports and publications on children, health, human development, education, and population from various agencies including the World Bank.

In this chapter, columns headed by a period (for example, 1995–99) show data for the latest available year within the period.

13-1. Age and gender structure of the population

	Females as percentage of total population		*Age groups as percentage of total population*						*Age dependency ratio*	
			1980			*2001*				
	1980	*2001*	*0-14*	*15-64*	*65+*	*0-14*	*15-64*	*65+*	*1980*	*2000*
SUB-SAHARAN AFRICA	50.4	50.1	45.5	51.6	2.9	44.0	52.8	2.9	0.9	0.9
excluding South Africa	50.4	50.0	45.8	51.3	2.9	44.8	52.1	2.9	1.0	0.9
excl. S.Africa & Nigeria	50.6	50.1	45.9	51.2	2.9	44.8	52.1	2.9	1.0	0.9
Angola	50.8	50.5	44.6	52.4	2.9	47.9	49.3	2.8	0.9	1.0
Benin	50.7	50.7	45.1	50.8	4.1	45.8	51.4	2.7	1.0	0.9
Botswana	52.2	50.9	48.7	49.3	2.0	39.8	52.9	2.5	1.0	0.8
Burkina Faso	51.7	51.4	48.6	48.3	3.1	48.3	48.5	3.0	1.0	1.0
Burundi	51.9	51.3	44.7	51.8	3.5	46.8	50.4	2.7	0.9	0.9
Cameroon	50.6	50.2	44.3	52.1	3.6	43.2	53.2	3.6	0.9	0.9
Cape Verde	54.1	53.2	46.0	47.9	6.1	39.7	57.3	4.5	1.1	0.8
Central African Republic	51.9	51.2	41.7	54.4	4.0	42.7	53.6	3.8	0.8	0.9
Chad	50.9	50.5	44.3	52.2	3.4	46.6	50.4	3.0	0.8	1.2
Comoros	50.3	50.0	48.2	49.3	2.6	42.5	54.7	2.7	1.0	0.9
Congo, Democratic Rep. of	51.1	50.4	46.0	51.2	2.8	48.5	48.7	2.8	1.0	1.0
Congo, Republic of	51.2	51.0	45.1	51.5	3.4	46.2	50.6	3.2	0.9	1.0
Côte d'Ivoire	48.5	48.9	45.8	51.8	2.4	41.7	54.8	2.9	1.0	0.8
Djibouti	53.3	52.8	41.9	56.2	1.9	42.4	54.2	3.2	0.9	0.8
Equatorial Guinea	51.0	50.6	41.1	54.8	4.2	43.4	52.6	3.9	0.8	0.9
Eritrea	50.4	50.3	44.2	53.1	2.6	44.1	53.0	2.8	..	0.9
Ethiopia	50.5	50.2	44.5	52.8	2.7	45.3	51.8	2.8	0.9	1.0
Gabon	50.8	50.5	34.3	59.4	6.3	40.0	54.0	5.7	0.7	0.8
Gambia, The	50.7	50.5	42.6	54.5	2.8	40.6	55.7	3.1	0.8	0.9
Ghana	50.4	50.2	45.8	51.4	2.8	40.5	55.8	3.2	0.9	0.8
Guinea	50.1	49.7	45.3	52.0	2.6	43.7	53.5	2.7	0.9	0.9
Guinea-Bissau	50.8	50.7	41.1	55.3	3.7	43.2	53.2	3.7	0.8	0.9
Kenya	50.3	50.1	50.1	47.0	2.9	42.7	54.2	2.7	1.1	0.9
Lesotho	51.3	50.4	41.4	54.9	3.7	39.0	56.6	4.1	0.9	0.8
Liberia	49.5	49.7	44.3	52.0	3.7	43.0	54.1	2.8	0.9	0.9
Madagascar	50.3	50.2	44.7	52.2	3.0	44.4	52.4	3.0	0.9	0.9
Malawi	51.6	50.4	47.5	50.2	2.3	45.9	51.2	2.8	1.0	0.9
Mali	51.2	50.5	46.8	50.7	2.6	46.2	49.9	3.7	1.0	1.0
Mauritania	50.7	50.4	43.7	53.2	3.0	43.6	52.8	3.1	0.9	0.9
Mauritius	50.7	50.2	35.6	60.8	3.6	25.2	68.3	6.3	0.6	0.5
Mozambique	50.8	50.7	44.1	52.7	3.2	43.1	53.4	3.2	0.9	0.9
Namibia	51.4	50.5	45.6	50.8	3.6	42.9	52.9	3.7	0.9	0.8
Niger	50.1	49.8	49.2	48.6	2.2	49.7	48.2	2.1	1.0	1.1
Nigeria	50.0	49.8	45.2	51.9	2.9	44.7	52.2	2.9	1.0	0.9
Rwanda	50.6	50.5	48.8	48.8	2.4	44.3	53.3	2.4	1.0	0.8
São Tomé and Principe	..	..	0.0	0.0	0.0	39.1	54.3	6.6	..	0.8
Senegal	50.0	50.2	45.3	51.8	2.8	44.2	53.1	2.5	0.9	0.9
Seychelles	..	..	0.0	0.0	0.0	28.1	64.3	7.3	..	0.6
Sierra Leone	51.0	50.8	43.0	53.9	3.1	44.1	53.2	2.8	0.9	0.9
Somalia	50.6	50.4	46.7	50.4	2.9	48.0	49.5	2.4	1.0	1.0
South Africa	50.3	50.9	41.8	55.1	3.1	33.1	62.7	3.7	0.7	0.6
Sudan	49.9	49.7	44.3	52.8	2.9	39.9	57.0	3.4	0.9	0.7
Swaziland	50.9	50.8	45.9	51.1	2.9	41.3	54.8	3.3	1.0	0.8
Tanzania	50.8	50.4	47.6	50.1	2.3	44.7	52.7	2.4	1.0	0.9
Togo	50.6	50.3	45.7	51.2	3.0	44.0	52.3	3.0	0.9	0.9
Uganda	50.3	50.1	47.9	49.6	2.5	49.0	48.5	2.3	1.0	1.0
Zambia	50.4	49.8	47.5	49.8	2.6	45.7	51.1	2.7	1.1	0.9
Zimbabwe	50.3	49.9	48.4	48.6	3.0	43.1	52.8	3.0	1.0	0.8
NORTH AFRICA	49.5	49.4	42.2	53.9	3.9	34.0	61.7	4.3	0.9	0.6
Algeria	50.4	49.3	46.5	49.6	3.9	34.9	61.5	4.1	1.0	0.7
Egypt, Arab Republic	49.2	49.3	39.5	56.5	4.0	34.4	61.2	4.2	0.8	0.6
Libya	47.1	48.2	46.7	51.1	2.2	34.1	62.4	3.4	1.0	0.7
Morocco	49.9	49.9	43.2	52.7	4.1	33.8	61.9	4.2	0.9	0.6
Tunisia	49.3	49.5	41.6	54.6	3.8	29.4	64.8	5.9	0.8	0.6
ALL AFRICA	50.3	49.9	44.9	52.0	3.1	42.3	54.3	3.2	0.9	0.8

Note: Some age groups may not add up to 100 due to rounding up error.

13-2. Poverty

	GDP per capita, based on PPP, 2001	Percentage of population living under US$ 1 a day, 1985-1999	National poverty headcount as % of population, 1984-2000	% of the population below 2/3 of national mean per capita income, 1991-1999		Gini coefficients, 1991-1997		Percentage of household income spent on food, 1991-1999
				Urban	Rural	Urban	Rural	
SUB-SAHARAN AFRICA	..	..	..	22	37	..	..	64
excluding South Africa	..	..	..	22	37	..	..	64
excl. S. Africa & Nigeria	..	..	..	22	37	..	..	64
Angola	1,866	..	..	..	..	..	..	..
Benin	1,041	..	33	..	..	..	..	..
Botswana	8,196	33	..	..	..	..	..	..
Burkina Faso	1,025	61	45	13	65	38	46	57
Burundi	598	..	36	..	..	..	..	..
Cameroon	1,772	33	40	..	..	..	..	55
Cape Verde	4,902	..	..	..	..	..	..	..
Central African Republic	1,184	67	..	33	77	51	63	60
Chad	938	..	64	..	..	..	..	..
Comoros	1,607	..	..	..	..	..	..	..
Congo, Democratic Rep. of	..	..	..	..	..	..	..	..
Congo, Republic of	767	..	..	..	..	..	..	..
Côte d'Ivoire	1,568	12	37	29	51	39	33	48
Djibouti	2,077	..	45	38	84	38	39	43
Equatorial Guinea	22,901	..	..	..	..	..	..	..
Eritrea	803	..	53	..	..	..	..	..
Ethiopia	717	31	44	21	50	56	40	72
Gabon	6,310	..	..	..	..	..	..	..
Gambia, The	1,730	59	64	21	73	43	35	60
Ghana	2,054	45	31	22	37	34	36	39
Guinea	2,052	..	40	18	57	..	..	56
Guinea-Bissau	771	..	49	30	65	55	56	..
Kenya	1,032	27	42	14	53	51	52	71
Lesotho	2,093	43	49	..	..	..	..	..
Liberia	..	..	..	..	..	..	..	..
Madagascar	889	49	71	21	57	..	..	70
Malawi	631	..	65	..	..	..	57	..
Mali	935	73	..	8	64	53	55	75
Mauritania	1,783	29	46	18	56	34	33	70
Mauritius	10,400	..	11	..	..	..	..	..
Mozambique	1,110	38	69	..	..	..	..	..
Namibia	6,650	35	..	..	..	..	..	..
Niger	776	61	63	14	55	39	31	60
Nigeria	898	70	34	32	52	44	46	67
Rwanda	1,007	36	51	..	..	..	..	..
São Tomé and Principe	..	..	..	..	..	..	..	..
Senegal	1,583	26	33	14	66	..	..	61
Seychelles	..	..	..	..	..	..	..	..
Sierra Leone	474	57	68	..	..	..	50	..
Somalia	..	..	..	..	..	..	..	..
South Africa	9,565	12	..	40	86	..	..	56
Sudan	1,878	..	..	..	..	..	..	..
Swaziland	4,586	..	40	36	70	..	..	65
Tanzania	545	20	42	20	51	..	..	70
Togo	1,449	..	32	..	..	..	..	..
Uganda	1,255	..	55	16	46	35	44	63
Zambia	820	64	73	28	70	40	46	64
Zimbabwe	2,406	36	35	..	..	..	..	..
NORTH AFRICA	..	..	..	..	..	..	..	..
Algeria	5,319	2	23	..	..	..	..	..
Egypt, Arab Republic	3,750	3	17	..	..	..	..	..
Libya	..	..	..	..	..	..	..	..
Morocco	3,787	2	19	..	..	..	..	..
Tunisia	6,769	2	8	..	..	..	..	..
ALL AFRICA	..	..	..	22	37	..	..	64

13-3. Income distribution

	Share of income held by population groups			
	Richest 10%	*Richest 20%*	*Poorest 10%*	*Poorest 20%*
	1986-99	*1986-99*	*1986-99*	*1986-99*
SUB-SAHARAN AFRICA	..	..	..	..
excluding South Africa	..	..	..	..
excl. S. Africa & Nigeria	..	..	..	..
Angola	..	..	..	..
Benin	..	..	..	..
Botswana	42.9	58.9	1.4	2.2
Burkina Faso	46.8	60.4	2.0	4.5
Burundi	32.9	48.0	1.8	5.1
Cameroon	36.6	53.1	1.9	4.6
Cape Verde	..	..	..	..
Central African Republic	47.7	65.0	0.7	2.0
Chad	..	..	..	..
Comoros	..	..	..	..
Congo, Democratic Rep. of	..	..	..	..
Congo, Republic of	..	..	..	..
Côte d'Ivoire	28.8	44.3	3.1	7.1
Djibouti	29.9	45.4	2.3	6.3
Equatorial Guinea	..	..	..	..
Eritrea	..	..	..	..
Ethiopia	33.8	47.7	3.0	..
Gabon	..	..	..	..
Gambia, The	38.2	55.3	1.6	4.0
Ghana	30.1	46.7	2.2	5.6
Guinea	32.0	47.2	2.6	6.4
Guinea-Bissau	42.3	58.9	0.5	5.2
Kenya	36.1	51.2	2.4	5.6
Lesotho	44.1	62.2	1.0	1.4
Liberia	..	..	..	..
Madagascar	28.6	44.8	2.6	6.4
Malawi	..	..	..	4.9
Mali	40.4	56.2	1.8	4.6
Mauritania	28.4	44.1	2.5	6.4
Mauritius	..	..	..	..
Mozambique	31.7	46.5	2.5	6.5
Namibia	65.0	78.3	0.6	1.4
Niger	35.4	53.3	0.8	2.6
Nigeria	40.8	55.7	1.6	4.4
Rwanda	..	..	..	..
São Tomé and Principe	..	..	..	..
Senegal	33.5	48.2	2.6	6.4
Seychelles	..	..	..	..
Sierra Leone	43.5	63.4	0.5	1.1
Somalia	..	..	..	..
South Africa	45.9	64.8	1.1	2.0
Sudan	..	..	..	..
Swaziland	50.2	64.4	1.0	2.7
Tanzania	30.1	45.5	2.8	6.8
Togo	..	..	..	..
Uganda	29.8	44.9	3.0	7.1
Zambia	41.0	56.6	1.1	3.3
Zimbabwe	40.4	55.7	2.0	4.6
NORTH AFRICA	..	..	..	..
Algeria	26.8	42.6	2.8	7.0
Egypt, Arab Republic	25.0	39.0	4.4	8.6
Libya	..	..	..	..
Morocco	30.9	46.6	2.6	6.5
Tunisia	31.8	47.9	2.3	5.7
ALL AFRICA	..	..	..	..

13-4. Urbanization

	Total population (millions)			Average annual percentage growth of total population			Urban population as percentage of total population			Average annual percentage growth of urban population		
	1980	1990	2001	1975-1979	1980-1990	1990-2001	1980	1990	2001	1975-1979	1980-1990	1990-2001
SUB-SAHARAN AFRICA	382.0	509.1	674.5	2.9	2.9	2.6	23.0	27.9	34.8	5.0	4.9	4.7
excluding South Africa	354.5	473.9	631.3	3.0	2.9	2.7	21.1	26.3	33.2	5.5	5.3	4.9
excl. S. Africa & Nigeria	283.3	377.7	501.4	3.0	2.9	2.6	19.6	24.1	30.2	5.4	5.1	4.8
Angola	7.1	9.6	13.5	2.5	3.2	3.1	20.9	27.6	34.8	5.9	6.1	5.4
Benin	3.5	4.7	6.4	2.5	3.1	2.9	27.3	34.5	43.0	7.3	5.6	5.0
Botswana	0.9	1.3	1.7	3.6	3.5	2.8	18.5	42.3	49.4	11.7	12.5	4.0
Burkina Faso	7.0	8.9	11.6	2.3	2.5	2.4	8.5	13.6	16.9	7.8	7.6	4.5
Burundi	4.1	5.5	6.9	2.1	2.8	2.2	4.3	6.3	9.3	8.4	6.8	5.9
Cameroon	8.7	11.6	15.2	2.9	2.9	2.5	31.4	40.3	49.7	6.6	5.5	4.5
Cape Verde	0.3	0.3	0.4	0.7	1.6	2.5	23.5	44.2	63.3	2.6	8.1	6.2
Central African Republic	2.3	2.9	3.8	2.3	2.5	2.4	35.1	37.5	41.7	3.3	3.2	3.4
Chad	4.5	5.7	7.9	2.0	2.6	3.0	18.8	21.0	24.2	6.2	3.8	4.3
Comoros	0.3	0.4	0.6	0.0	0.6	2.6	23.2	27.9	33.8	0.0	0.6	4.4
Congo, Democratic Rep. of	26.9	37.0	52.4	3.0	3.2	3.3	28.7	27.9	30.8	2.4	3.0	4.1
Congo, Republic of	1.7	2.2	3.1	2.9	2.9	3.1	42.0	55.7	66.0	6.3	6.0	4.7
Côte d'Ivoire	8.2	11.8	16.4	4.0	3.7	3.1	34.7	39.8	44.0	5.9	5.2	4.0
Djibouti	0.3	0.5	0.6	7.9	4.2	2.9	74.2	81.0	84.2	9.6	5.1	3.3
Equatorial Guinea	0.2	0.4	0.5	-2.7	5.3	2.6	27.4	35.7	49.2	-2.5	8.0	5.7
Eritrea	2.4	3.1	4.2	2.7	2.8	2.7	13.8	15.8	19.1	4.3	4.2	4.5
Ethiopia	37.7	51.2	65.8	2.7	3.0	2.3	10.5	12.7	15.9	4.8	5.0	4.4
Gabon	0.7	0.9	1.3	3.2	3.0	2.8	49.6	68.1	82.2	7.9	6.5	4.6
Gambia, The	0.6	0.9	1.3	3.2	3.7	3.4	19.6	24.9	31.3	6.2	6.2	5.6
Ghana	10.7	15.1	19.7	1.7	3.5	2.4	31.2	33.5	36.4	2.5	4.2	3.2
Guinea	4.5	5.8	7.6	1.3	2.5	2.6	19.1	23.4	28.0	4.6	4.7	4.2
Guinea-Bissau	0.8	0.9	1.2	3.7	2.3	2.3	17.3	23.8	32.3	5.3	5.5	5.3
Kenya	16.6	23.4	30.7	3.8	3.5	2.6	16.1	24.0	34.3	8.4	7.8	6.0
Lesotho	1.4	1.7	2.1	2.2	2.2	1.9	13.4	20.1	28.7	6.7	6.4	5.4
Liberia	1.9	2.4	3.2	3.1	2.7	2.5	35.0	42.0	45.5	6.1	4.7	3.3
Madagascar	8.9	11.6	16.0	2.6	2.7	3.0	18.5	23.6	30.1	5.2	5.2	5.3
Malawi	6.2	8.5	10.5	3.3	3.3	2.0	9.1	11.6	15.1	7.1	5.8	4.5
Mali	6.6	8.5	11.1	2.2	2.5	2.5	18.5	23.8	30.9	4.8	5.1	5.0
Mauritania	1.6	2.0	2.7	2.5	2.5	2.9	27.7	44.0	59.0	9.3	7.5	5.8
Mauritius	1.0	1.1	1.2	1.6	0.9	1.2	42.4	40.5	41.6	1.3	0.5	1.3
Mozambique	12.1	14.2	18.1	2.8	1.7	2.2	13.1	21.1	33.2	11.6	6.8	6.6
Namibia	1.0	1.4	1.8	2.0	3.2	2.4	22.8	26.6	31.4	4.0	4.9	4.0
Niger	5.6	7.7	11.2	3.1	3.2	3.5	12.6	16.1	21.1	6.8	5.8	6.0
Nigeria	71.1	96.2	129.9	3.0	3.1	2.8	26.9	35.0	44.9	5.9	5.9	5.2
Rwanda	5.2	7.0	8.7	3.3	3.1	2.0	4.7	5.3	6.3	6.9	4.5	3.5
São Tomé and Principe	0.1	0.1	0.2	1.2	2.5	2.6	30.8	39.1	47.6	4.0	5.0	4.5
Senegal	5.5	7.3	9.8	2.9	2.8	2.7	35.7	40.0	48.1	3.7	4.0	4.4
Seychelles	0.1	0.1	0.1	1.7	0.8	1.5	40.8	53.5	64.5	6.0	3.7	3.3
Sierra Leone	3.2	4.0	5.1	2.0	2.1	2.3	24.1	30.0	37.3	4.7	4.4	4.4
Somalia	6.5	7.2	9.1	10.1	0.4	2.0	22.2	24.2	27.9	11.1	1.3	3.3
South Africa	27.6	35.2	43.2	2.2	2.5	2.0	48.1	48.8	57.6	2.2	2.6	3.5
Sudan	19.3	24.8	31.7	3.0	2.6	2.3	20.0	26.6	37.0	4.3	5.5	5.5
Swaziland	0.6	0.8	1.1	3.2	3.1	3.1	17.8	23.8	26.7	8.7	6.3	4.2
Tanzania	18.6	25.5	34.4	3.1	3.2	2.8	14.8	21.7	33.2	11.4	7.4	7.0
Togo	2.5	3.5	4.7	1.8	3.3	2.7	22.9	28.5	33.9	8.6	5.8	4.4
Uganda	12.8	16.3	22.8	2.8	2.3	3.1	8.8	11.2	14.5	3.8	4.8	5.6
Zambia	5.7	7.8	10.3	3.4	3.1	2.6	39.8	39.4	39.8	6.3	3.1	2.7
Zimbabwe	7.1	10.2	12.8	3.1	3.7	2.1	22.3	28.4	36.0	5.9	6.3	4.4
NORTH AFRICA	88.4	114.0	140.3	2.6	2.6	1.9	44.6	48.8	52.2	3.6	3.5	2.6
Algeria	18.7	25.0	30.8	3.1	3.0	2.0	43.5	51.4	57.7	4.5	4.8	3.1
Egypt, Arab Republic	40.9	52.4	65.2	2.3	2.5	2.0	43.8	43.6	42.7	2.6	2.5	1.8
Libya	3.0	4.3	5.4	4.4	3.8	2.0	69.3	81.8	87.9	7.7	5.6	2.7
Morocco	19.4	24.0	29.2	2.3	2.2	1.8	41.3	48.4	56.1	4.1	3.8	3.2
Tunisia	6.4	8.2	9.7	2.5	2.5	1.6	51.5	57.9	66.1	3.4	3.7	2.9
ALL AFRICA	470.4	623.1	814.8	2.8	2.9	2.5	27.1	31.7	37.8	4.5	4.5	4.2

13-5. Components of population change

	Total fertility rate			*Crude birth rate*			*Crude death rate*		
	1982	*1992*	*2000*	*1982*	*1992*	*2000*	*1982*	*1992*	*2000*
SUB-SAHARAN AFRICA	6.6	5.9	5.2	46.5	43.3	39.5	17.0	15.4	16.8
excluding South Africa	6.8	6.1	5.4	47.3	44.2	40.4	17.5	15.9	16.8
excl. S. Africa & Nigeria	6.8	6.2	5.4	46.8	44.4	40.6	17.6	16.4	17.0
Angola	7.0	7.2	6.6	50.8	50.8	47.5	22.8	19.2	18.8
Benin	7.0	6.5	5.5	49.3	43.9	39.4	18.1	15.3	13.0
Botswana	6.0	4.8	4.0	44.1	36.8	32.0	9.5	8.0	19.9
Burkina Faso	7.5	6.9	6.5	46.9	47.3	43.8	19.9	18.3	19.2
Burundi	6.8	6.8	6.0	46.2	46.2	40.2	17.9	21.5	19.9
Cameroon	6.4	5.7	4.8	43.9	40.6	37.0	15.7	12.8	14.2
Cape Verde	6.1	5.2	3.7	38.4	36.0	34.0	11.3	7.6	5.8
Central African Republic	5.7	5.3	4.7	42.4	39.6	36.1	18.6	17.4	19.5
Chad	7.1	6.9	6.4	44.2	47.0	44.9	21.4	18.2	16.3
Comoros	7.2	5.2	4.3	45.5	37.0	33.2	16.8	10.2	8.2
Congo, Democratic Rep. of	6.7	6.7	6.1	47.9	47.7	45.7	15.2	15.0	16.6
Congo, Republic of	6.3	6.3	6.0	43.9	44.6	42.5	15.6	14.9	14.1
Côte d'Ivoire	7.4	5.7	4.8	50.1	38.9	36.9	16.0	14.9	16.8
Djibouti	6.6	5.8	5.3	44.2	39.0	36.7	19.1	16.2	17.8
Equatorial Guinea	5.8	5.9	5.7	43.3	43.5	40.8	21.1	18.0	15.5
Eritrea	7.5	6.1	5.4	..	42.4	38.7	..	16.4	12.9
Ethiopia	7.0	6.8	5.6	48.0	49.0	43.8	22.1	20.2	20.1
Gabon	4.5	5.2	4.2	33.1	36.6	35.5	18.1	16.1	15.5
Gambia, The	6.5	6.0	5.0	48.2	43.5	39.3	23.1	19.2	13.2
Ghana	6.5	5.3	4.2	45.0	36.6	29.6	13.1	10.2	11.1
Guinea	6.2	5.7	5.2	46.8	45.0	39.0	23.5	19.0	16.9
Guinea-Bissau	6.0	6.0	5.8	45.2	45.0	41.5	24.8	21.7	20.0
Kenya	7.7	5.2	4.4	49.7	36.1	34.5	12.1	9.4	14.2
Lesotho	5.3	5.0	4.4	38.9	36.4	32.7	13.8	11.3	17.0
Liberia	6.8	6.8	6.0	47.0	48.2	44.0	16.7	24.8	17.2
Madagascar	6.6	6.0	5.4	46.5	45.9	40.0	15.5	12.6	12.1
Malawi	7.6	6.7	6.3	53.5	50.2	45.8	21.6	22.1	24.2
Mali	7.1	6.8	6.3	49.0	51.1	46.2	21.6	18.8	20.0
Mauritania	6.3	6.1	5.7	42.3	43.9	41.6	18.5	16.2	14.5
Mauritius	2.5	2.3	2.0	22.2	20.4	17.0	6.0	6.7	6.7
Mozambique	6.5	6.3	5.1	45.7	44.9	40.3	20.1	18.6	20.5
Namibia	5.8	5.3	5.0	40.3	38.5	35.6	13.5	11.8	17.1
Niger	8.0	7.4	7.2	56.5	55.3	50.6	24.2	22.0	19.3
Nigeria	6.9	5.9	5.3	49.6	43.3	39.6	17.1	14.2	16.2
Rwanda	8.1	6.6	5.9	50.4	40.0	44.5	18.6	26.6	21.6
São Tomé and Principe	..	4.9	4.5	38.7	43.0	31.4	10.2	9.0	9.2
Senegal	6.7	6.0	5.1	47.2	41.4	36.6	19.5	14.8	12.7
Seychelles	3.5	2.7	2.1	24.1	22.9	18.5	7.4	7.2	6.9
Sierra Leone	6.5	6.5	5.8	48.9	49.1	44.4	28.5	29.8	23.4
Somalia	7.3	7.3	7.1	51.8	52.1	50.9	22.0	25.1	17.5
South Africa	4.2	3.2	2.9	35.5	31.2	25.8	11.1	8.8	16.0
Sudan	6.0	5.3	4.6	41.5	37.9	34.3	15.8	13.4	11.5
Swaziland	6.0	5.1	4.4	43.1	40.2	35.8	13.7	10.7	14.9
Tanzania	6.7	6.1	5.3	46.5	42.8	39.4	14.8	13.5	17.2
Togo	6.9	6.6	5.0	45.0	41.6	36.7	15.8	15.5	15.0
Uganda	7.3	6.9	6.2	49.1	50.2	45.4	17.6	18.2	19.2
Zambia	6.9	6.2	5.3	49.0	44.6	40.0	14.8	15.1	21.4
Zimbabwe	6.2	4.3	3.8	43.0	35.5	29.8	11.8	10.9	17.7
NORTH AFRICA	5.4	3.8	3.1	38.9	28.1	24.2	11.6	7.4	6.1
Algeria	6.3	4.0	3.2	40.6	28.2	24.8	10.7	6.0	5.4
Egypt, Arab Republic	5.1	3.8	3.3	39.1	28.5	25.0	12.7	8.6	6.5
Libya	7.2	4.1	3.5	45.6	28.8	26.6	10.9	4.6	4.6
Morocco	5.1	3.8	2.9	37.3	28.2	23.8	11.4	7.5	6.4
Tunisia	4.9	3.2	2.1	33.7	24.9	17.1	8.4	5.5	5.6
ALL AFRICA	6.4	5.5	4.8	45.1	40.5	36.8	16.0	14.0	14.9

13-6. Survival prospects

	Life expectancy at birth (years)		*Infant mortality (per thousand)*		*Mortality of children under 5 years (per thousand)*	*Maternal mortality (per 100,000 live births)*
	1985	*2000*	*1985*	*2000*	*2000*	*1999 or MR available*
SUB-SAHARAN AFRICA	49	47	107	91	162	1086
excluding South Africa	48	46	110	92	165	1149
excl. S. Africa & Nigeria	49	46	115	95	169	1163
Angola	43	47	142	128	208	1300
Benin	50	53	114	87	143	880
Botswana	60	39	61	58	99	480
Burkina Faso	45	44	117	104	206	1400
Burundi	47	42	116	102	176	1900
Cameroon	52	50	88	76	155	720
Cape Verde	63	69	78	37	48	55
Central African Republic	47	43	108	96	152	1200
Chad	44	48	118	101	188	1500
Comoros	52	61	96	60	80	950
Congo, Democratic Rep. of	51	46	104	85	163	940
Congo, Republic of	51	51	87	68	106	1100
Côte d'Ivoire	51	46	101	111	180	1200
Djibouti	46	46	126	115	178	570
Equatorial Guinea	45	51	131	102	167	820
Eritrea	46	52	94	60	103	1100
Ethiopia	44	42	143	98	179	1800
Gabon	50	53	88	58	89	620
Gambia, The	45	53	137	73	..	1100
Ghana	55	57	85	58	112	590
Guinea	42	46	137	95	161	1200
Guinea-Bissau	41	45	156	126	211	910
Kenya	57	47	64	78	120	1300
Lesotho	56	44	111	91	143	530
Liberia	53	47	139	111	185	560
Madagascar	52	55	117	88	144	580
Malawi	46	39	147	103	193	580
Mali	45	42	158	120	218	630
Mauritania	48	52	116	101	164	870
Mauritius	68	72	26	16	20	45
Mozambique	44	42	135	129	200	980
Namibia	55	47	74	62	112	370
Niger	44	46	137	114	248	920
Nigeria	47	47	90	84	153	1100
Rwanda	48	40	119	123	203	2300
São Tomé and Principe	..	65	77	46	62	..
Senegal	47	52	98	60	129	1200
Seychelles	69	72	19	9	14	..
Sierra Leone	36	39	185	154	267	2100
Somalia	44	48	136	117	195	1600
South Africa	59	48	60	63	79	340
Sudan	50	56	107	81	..	1500
Swaziland	54	46	88	89	119	560
Tanzania	51	44	108	93	149	1100
Togo	51	49	91	75	142	980
Uganda	48	42	116	83	161	1100
Zambia	50	38	103	115	186	870
Zimbabwe	56	40	60	69	116	610
NORTH AFRICA	61	69	79	39	49	205
Algeria	64	71	67	33	39	150
Egypt, Arab Republic	59	67	91	42	52	170
Libya	65	71	41	26	32	120
Morocco	61	67	79	47	60	390
Tunisia	65	72	55	26	30	70
ALL AFRICA	51	50	103	85	148	916

13-7. HIV/AIDS estimates and data, end 2001

	Estimated number of people living with HIV/AIDS					*AIDS Orphans*	*Estimated AIDS deaths*
	Adults and children	*Adults (15-49)*	*Adult rate (%)*	*Women (15-49)*	*Children (0-14)*	*Orphans (0-14), currently living*	*Adults and Children*
SUB-SAHARAN AFRICA	28,459,000	25,626,100	8.4	14,784,050	2,613,280	10,909,900	2,189,920
excluding South Africa	23,459,000	20,926,100	7.4	12,084,050	2,363,280	10,249,900	1,829,920
excl. S. Africa & Nigeria	19,959,000	17,726,100	7.7	10,384,050	2,093,280	9,249,900	1,659,920
Angola	350,000	320,000	5.5	190,000	37,000	100,000	24,000
Benin	120,000	110,000	3.6	67,000	12,000	34,000	8,100
Botswana	330,000	300,000	38.8	170,000	28,000	69,000	26,000
Burkina Faso	440,000	380,000	6.5	220,000	61,000	270,000	44,000
Burundi	390,000	330,000	8.3	190,000	55,000	240,000	40,000
Cameroon	920,000	860,000	11.8	500,000	69,000	210,000	53,000
Cape Verde	..	..	..	..	..	..	..
Central African Republic	250,000	220,000	12.9	130,000	25,000	110,000	22,000
Chad	150,000	130,000	3.6	76,000	18,000	72,000	14,000
Comoros	..	..	..	..	..	..	..
Congo, Democratic Rep. of	1,300,000	1,100,000	4.9	670,000	170,000	930,000	120,000
Congo, Republic of	110,000	99,000	7.2	59,000	15,000	78,000	11,000
Côte d'Ivoire	770,000	690,000	9.7	400,000	84,000	420,000	75,000
Djibouti	..	..	..	..	..	..	..
Equatorial Guinea	5,900	5,500	3.4	3,000	420	..	370
Eritrea	55,000	49,000	2.8	30,000	4,000	24,000	350
Ethiopia	2,100,000	1,900,000	6.4	1,100,000	230,000	990,000	160,000
Gabon	..	..	..	..	..	..	..
Gambia, The	8,400	7,900	1.6	4,400	460	5,300	400
Ghana	360,000	330,000	3.0	170,000	34,000	200,000	28,000
Guinea	..	..	..	..	..	..	..
Guinea-Bissau	17,000	16,000	2.8	9,300	1,500	4,300	1,200
Kenya	2,500,000	2,300,000	15.0	1,400,000	220,000	890,000	190,000
Lesotho	360,000	330,000	31.0	180,000	27,000	73,000	25,000
Liberia	..	..	..	..	..	..	..
Madagascar	22,000	21,000	0.3	12,000	1,000	6,300	..
Malawi	850,000	780,000	15.0	440,000	65,000	470,000	80,000
Mali	110,000	100,000	1.7	54,000	13,000	70,000	11,000
Mauritania	..	..	..	..	..	..	..
Mauritius	700	700	0.1	350	..	..	..
Mozambique	1,100,000	1,000,000	13.0	630,000	80,000	420,000	60,000
Namibia	230,000	200,000	22.5	110,000	30,000	47,000	13,000
Niger	..	..	..	..	..	..	..
Nigeria	3,500,000	3,200,000	5.8	1,700,000	270,000	1,000,000	170,000
Rwanda	500,000	430,000	8.9	250,000	65,000	260,000	49,000
São Tomé and Principe	..	..	..	..	..	..	..
Senegal	27,000	24,000	0.5	14,000	2,900	15,000	2,500
Seychelles	..	..	..	..	..	..	..
Sierra Leone	170,000	150,000	7.0	90,000	16,000	42,000	11,000
Somalia	43,000	43,000	1.0	..	..	..	..
South Africa	5,000,000	4,700,000	20.1	2,700,000	250,000	660,000	360,000
Sudan	450,000	410,000	2.6	230,000	30,000	62,000	23,000
Swaziland	170,000	150,000	33.4	89,000	14,000	35,000	12,000
Tanzania	1,500,000	1,300,000	7.8	750,000	170,000	810,000	140,000
Togo	150,000	130,000	6.0	76,000	15,000	63,000	12,000
Uganda	600,000	510,000	5.0	280,000	110,000	880,000	84,000
Zambia	1,200,000	1,000,000	21.5	590,000	150,000	570,000	120,000
Zimbabwe	2,300,000	2,000,000	33.7	1,200,000	240,000	780,000	200,000
NORTH AFRICA	..	41,000	0.05	..	..	..	..
Algeria	..	13,000	..	..	..	..	..
Egypt, Arab Republic	8,000	8,000	<0.1	780	..	..	..
Libya	7,000	7,000	0.2	1,100	..	..	..
Morocco	13,000	13,000	0.1	2,000	..	..	..
Tunisia	..	..	..	..	..	..	..
ALL AFRICA	28,487,000	25,667,100	6.7	14,787,930	2,613,280	10,909,900	2,189,920

13-8. Immunization and ORT use

	Percentage of children (0-1 year) immunized against						*ORT use among the under five (percent)*
	DPT			*Measles*			
	1986	*1995*	*1999**	*1986*	*1995*	*1999**	*1992-93*
SUB-SAHARAN AFRICA	32	54	49	39	54	54	..
excluding South Africa	29	53	47	38	53	52	50
excl. S. Africa & Nigeria	31	59	54	40	55	55	..
Angola	10	24	22	44	46	46	48
Benin	17	67	79	21	65	79	28
Botswana	85	80	90	88	68	86	64
Burkina Faso	19	34	42	40	43	53	15
Burundi	55	73	74	59	80	75	49
Cameroon	39	46	48	44	46	62	84
Cape Verde	..	..	..	..	66	61	5
Central African Republic	19	53	33	24	46	39	24
Chad	10	18	21	12	26	30	15
Comoros	..	..	..	71	69	69	70
Congo, Democratic Rep. of	..	..	..	39	27	15	46
Congo, Republic of	71	50	29	69	38	23	67
Côte d'Ivoire	30	52	62	30	57	62	16
Djibouti	24	41	23	19	41	21	56
Equatorial Guinea	2	79	40	17	81	24	40
Eritrea	..	58	93	..	58	88	..
Ethiopia	7	57	21	10	38	27	68
Gabon	59	70	37	66	57	55	25
Gambia, The	..	..	..	62	91	88	51
Ghana	35	70	72	31	70	73	44
Guinea	15	54	46	28	61	52	82
Guinea-Bissau	47	45	38	59	45	70	26
Kenya	72	94	79	65	83	79	69
Lesotho	82	88	85	73	82	77	78
Liberia	..	..	..	..	..	..	15
Madagascar	22	57	55	11	55	55	26
Malawi	57	89	84	60	90	83	50
Mali	11	49	52	27	54	57	41
Mauritania	32	55	40	40	67	62	54
Mauritius	86	93	85	71	89	79	..
Mozambique	32	57	61	39	61	57	60
Namibia	..	76	72	..	69	66	75
Niger	5	23	28	27	40	36	17
Nigeria	22	34	26	28	44	41	80
Rwanda	87	83	85	79	84	87	36
São Tomé and Principe	..	..	..	58	74	64	50
Senegal	54	80	60	71	80	60	27
Seychelles	94	97	99	95	97	99	..
Sierra Leone	..	..	46	..	..	62	60
Somalia	17	22	18	25	34	26	78
South Africa	70	72	76	64	76	82	..
Sudan	14	48	50	11	51	53	47
Swaziland	74	82	99	74	94	82	85
Tanzania	..	..	..	97	78	72	83
Togo	37	58	41	43	53	43	33
Uganda	21	59	55	27	57	53	45
Zambia	66	86	84	58	86	90	90
Zimbabwe	75	88	81	83	87	79	..
NORTH AFRICA	73	86	89	71	86	91	24
Algeria	69	76	83	67	77	83	27
Egypt, Arab Republic	80	88	94	78	89	95	34
Libya	..	..	..	78	92	92	80
Morocco	63	91	91	58	88	90	14
Tunisia	72	94	96	67	91	84	22
ALL AFRICA	39	58	54	44	58	58	48

Notes: ORT = Oral re-hydration therapy; DPT = diphtheria, pertussis (whooping cough), and tetanus. *or most recent available data.

13-9. Child malnutrition

	Percentage of children (1990-00)			Percentage of infants with low birth weight		Percentage of under-five (1990-00) suffering from moderate to severe		
	Exclusively breastfed, (0-3 months)	Breastfed, plus other food, (6-9 months)	Still breastfeading, (20-23 months)	1988	1993-99	Underweight	Wasting	Stunting
SUB-SAHARAN AFRICA	29	63	47	..	..	..	..	..
excluding South Africa	29	63	47	..	..	..	..	..
excl. S. Africa & Nigeria	37	67	49	..	..	..	..	..
Angola	12	70	49	..	..	41	6	53
Benin	15	97	65	8	9	29	14	25
Botswana	39	82	23	8	..	13	11	29
Burkina Faso	12	44	81	..	..	34	13	29
Burundi	89	66	73	..	16	45	9	43
Cameroon	7	77	35	..	..	22	6	29
Cape Verde	18	..	..	..	..	14	6	16
Central African Republic	23	93	52	15	..	23	7	34
Chad	2	81	62	..	..	28	..	40
Comoros	5	87	45	..	..	25	8	34
Congo, Democratic Rep. of	32	40	64	..	20	34	10	45
Congo, Republic of	43	95	27	..	..	..	..	..
Côte d'Ivoire	3	65	45	..	..	21	8	24
Djibouti	..	..	..	11	..	18	13	26
Equatorial Guinea	..	..	..	..	..	..	..	..
Eritrea	66	45	60	..	..	44	16	38
Ethiopia	74	..	35	..	9	47	8	64
Gabon	57	..	..	..	..	12	..	..
Gambia, The	..	8	58	..	..	17	6	14
Ghana	19	63	48	17	8	25	11	26
Guinea	52	..	15	25	13	33	12	29
Guinea-Bissau	..	..	..	..	..	25	5	..
Kenya	17	90	54	..	..	22	6	34
Lesotho	54	47	52	..	..	18	5	44
Liberia	15	17	25	..	..	..	..	..
Madagascar	61	93	49	10	15	40	7	48
Malawi	11	78	68	20	..	25	7	48
Mali	13	33	60	17	..	27	23	30
Mauritania	90	64	59	..	9	32	7	44
Mauritius	16	29	..	9	..	15	14	10
Mozambique	37	..	..	20	..	26	8	36
Namibia	22	65	23	..	..	26	9	29
Niger	1	67	52	..	..	40	21	41
Nigeria	2	52	43	20	..	31	9	43
Rwanda	90	68	85	..	..	24	4	42
São Tomé and Principe	..	..	..	..	..	..	..	26
Senegal	16	69	50	..	..	18	7	23
Seychelles	..	..	..	..	..	..	..	..
Sierra Leone	..	94	41	17	..	27	9	35
Somalia	..	..	..	..	16	26	..	30
South Africa	..	..	..	..	..	9	3	23
Sudan	14	45	44	15	15	11	17	34
Swaziland	37	51	20	..	..	10	..	..
Tanzania	41	93	53	13	..	29	7	43
Togo	15	25	99	20	..	25	..	34
Uganda	70	64	40	..	..	23	5	38
Zambia	27	88	43	..	10	24	4	42
Zimbabwe	16	93	26	..	11	13	6	21
NORTH AFRICA	45	34	..	..	..	14	..	..
Algeria	48	29	21	9	..	6	9	18
Egypt, Arab Republic	53	37	..	..	..	4	5	30
Libya	..	..	..	..	..	5	3	15
Morocco	31	33	20	..	4	10	2	24
Tunisia	12	53	16	8	16	4	4	23
ALL AFRICA	32	59	45	..	..	..	..	..

13-10. Access to sanitation facilities

	Percentage of population with access to sanitation facilities					
	1990			*2000*		
	Total	*Urban*	*Rural*	*Total*	*Urban*	*Rural*
SUB-SAHARAN AFRICA	55	80	46	55	81	41
excluding South Africa	55	80	46	53	79	39
excl. S. Africa & Nigeria	54	81	45	50	76	38
Angola	..	..	..	44	70	30
Benin	20	46	6	23	46	6
Botswana	61	84	44	..	..	..
Burkina Faso	24	88	14	29	88	16
Burundi	89	67	90	..	79	..
Cameroon	87	99	79	92	99	85
Cape Verde	..	..	..	71	95	32
Central African Republic	30	43	23	31	43	23
Chad	18	70	4	29	81	13
Comoros	98	98	98	98	98	98
Congo, Democratic Rep. of	..	..	..	20	53	6
Congo, Republic of	..	..	..	..	14	..
Côte d'Ivoire	49	78	30	..	..	..
Djibouti	..	..	..	91	99	50
Equatorial Guinea	..	..	..	53	60	46
Eritrea	..	..	..	13	66	1
Ethiopia	13	58	6	15	58	6
Gabon	..	..	..	21	25	4
Gambia, The	..	..	..	37	41	35
Ghana	60	59	61	63	62	64
Guinea	55	94	41	58	94	41
Guinea-Bissau	..	..	..	47	88	34
Kenya	84	94	81	86	96	81
Lesotho	..	..	..	92	93	92
Liberia	..	..	..	..	..	..
Madagascar	36	70	25	42	70	30
Malawi	73	96	70	77	96	70
Mali	70	95	62	69	93	58
Mauritania	30	44	19	33	44	19
Mauritius	100	100	100	99	100	99
Mozambique	..	..	..	43	69	26
Namibia	33	84	14	41	96	17
Niger	15	71	4	20	79	5
Nigeria	60	77	51	63	85	45
Rwanda	..	..	..	8	12	8
São Tomé and Principe	..	39	7	..	..	..
Senegal	57	86	38	70	94	48
Seychelles	..	..	..	..	..	..
Sierra Leone	..	..	..	28	23	31
Somalia	..	..	..	..	..	..
South Africa	..	..	..	86	99	73
Sudan	58	87	48	62	87	48
Swaziland	..	..	..	..	..	..
Tanzania	88	97	86	90	98	86
Togo	37	71	24	34	69	17
Uganda	84	96	82	75	96	72
Zambia	63	86	48	78	99	64
Zimbabwe	64	98	51	68	99	51
NORTH AFRICA	80	96	65	85	96	72
Algeria	..	..	..	73	90	47
Egypt, Arab Republic	87	96	80	94	98	91
Libya	97	97	96	97	97	96
Morocco	62	95	31	75	100	42
Tunisia	76	97	48	..	..	..
ALL AFRICA	60	84	49	60	85	45

13-11. Access to safe water

	Percentage of population with access to safe water					
	1990			2000		
	Total	Urban	Rural	Total	Urban	Rural
SUB-SAHARAN AFRICA	49	81	37	55	82	41
excluding South Africa	49	81	37	53	81	39
excl. S. Africa & Nigeria	49	83	38	52	80	39
Angola	..	..	..	38	34	40
Benin	..	..	..	63	74	55
Botswana	95	100	91	..	100	..
Burkina Faso	53	74	50	..	84	..
Burundi	65	94	63	..	96	..
Cameroon	52	76	36	62	82	42
Cape Verde	..	..	..	74	64	89
Central African Republic	59	80	46	60	80	46
Chad	..	..	..	27	31	26
Comoros	88	97	84	96	98	95
Congo, Democratic Rep. of	..	..	..	45	89	26
Congo, Republic of	..	..	..	51	71	17
Côte d'Ivoire	65	89	49	77	90	65
Djibouti	..	..	..	100	100	100
Equatorial Guinea	..	..	..	43	45	42
Eritrea	..	..	..	46	63	42
Ethiopia	22	77	13	24	77	13
Gabon	..	..	..	70	73	55
Gambia, The	..	..	..	62	80	53
Ghana	56	83	43	64	87	49
Guinea	45	72	36	48	72	36
Guinea-Bissau	..	..	..	49	29	55
Kenya	40	89	25	49	87	31
Lesotho	..	..	..	91	98	88
Liberia	..	..	..	..	..	..
Madagascar	44	85	31	47	85	31
Malawi	49	90	43	57	95	44
Mali	55	65	52	65	74	61
Mauritania	37	34	40	37	34	40
Mauritius	100	100	100	100	100	100
Mozambique	..	..	..	60	86	43
Namibia	72	98	63	77	100	67
Niger	53	65	51	59	70	56
Nigeria	49	78	33	57	81	39
Rwanda	..	..	..	41	60	40
São Tomé and Principe	..	100	61	..	..	..
Senegal	72	90	60	78	92	65
Seychelles	..	..	..	..	..	..
Sierra Leone	..	..	..	28	23	31
Somalia	..	..	..	..	..	..
South Africa	..	..	..	86	92	80
Sudan	67	86	60	75	86	69
Swaziland	..	..	..	..	..	..
Tanzania	50	80	42	54	80	42
Togo	51	82	38	54	85	38
Uganda	44	80	40	50	72	46
Zambia	52	88	28	64	88	48
Zimbabwe	77	99	68	85	100	77
NORTH AFRICA	86	94	80	91	96	85
Algeria	..	..	..	94	98	88
Egypt, Arab Republic	94	97	91	95	96	94
Libya	71	72	68	72	72	68
Morocco	75	94	58	82	100	58
Tunisia	80	94	61	..	..	..
ALL AFRICA	56	85	43	61	85	47

*or most recent available data.

13-12. Health expenditure

	Public expenditure	Private expenditure	Total expenditure		
	as % of GDP, 1995-00	as % of GDP, 1995-00	as % of GDP, 1995-00	per capita, US$, 1995-00	per capita PPP, international $, 1995-00
SUB-SAHARAN AFRICA	2.5	3.3	5.8	29	89
excluding South Africa	1.7	2.2	4.0	13	40
excl. S.Africa & Nigeria	2.0	2.4	4.4	15	46
Angola	2.0	1.6	3.6	24	..
Benin	1.6	1.6	3.2	11	29
Botswana	3.8	2.2	6.0	191	267
Burkina Faso	3.0	1.2	4.2	8	36
Burundi	1.6	1.5	3.1	3	21
Cameroon	1.1	3.2	4.3	24	77
Cape Verde	1.8	0.8	2.6	30	119
Central African Republic	1.4	1.5	2.9	8	33
Chad	2.5	0.6	3.1	6	25
Comoros	3.2	1.2	4.4	13	69
Congo, Democratic Rep. of	1.1	0.4	1.5	9	..
Congo, Republic of	1.5	0.7	2.2	22	46
Côte d'Ivoire	1.0	1.7	2.7	16	62
Djibouti	4.2	2.8	7.0	56	..
Equatorial Guinea	2.3	1.1	3.4	54	163
Eritrea	2.8	1.5	4.3	9	..
Ethiopia	1.8	2.8	4.6	5	25
Gabon	2.1	0.9	3.0	120	198
Gambia, The	3.4	0.7	4.1	10	56
Ghana	2.2	2.0	4.2	11	85
Guinea	1.9	1.5	3.4	13	68
Guinea-Bissau	2.6	1.3	3.9	9	..
Kenya	1.8	6.5	8.3	28	79
Lesotho	5.2	1.1	6.3	28	..
Liberia	3.0	1.0	4.0	2	..
Madagascar	2.5	1.0	3.5	9	16
Malawi	3.6	4.0	7.6	11	36
Mali	2.2	2.7	4.9	10	30
Mauritania	3.4	0.9	4.3	14	74
Mauritius	1.9	1.5	3.4	134	302
Mozambique	2.7	1.6	4.3	9	28
Namibia	4.2	2.9	7.1	136	417
Niger	1.8	2.1	3.9	5	20
Nigeria	0.5	1.7	2.2	8	23
Rwanda	2.7	2.5	5.2	12	34
São Tomé and Principe	1.6	0.7	2.3	8	..
Senegal	2.6	2.0	4.6	22	61
Seychelles	4.1	2.1	6.2	440	..
Sierra Leone	2.6	1.7	4.3	6	27
Somalia	0.9	0.4	1.3	19	..
South Africa	3.7	5.1	8.8	255	623
Sudan	1.0	3.7	4.7	13	48
Swaziland	3.0	1.2	4.2	56	148
Tanzania	2.8	3.1	5.9	12	15
Togo	1.5	1.3	2.8	8	36
Uganda	1.5	2.4	3.9	10	65
Zambia	3.5	2.1	5.6	18	52
Zimbabwe	3.1	4.2	7.3	43	186
NORTH AFRICA	2.0	1.8	3.9	62	140
Algeria	3.0	0.6	3.6	64	216
Egypt, Arab Republic	1.8	2.0	3.8	51	119
Libya	1.6	1.7	3.3	246	..
Morocco	1.3	3.2	4.5	50	134
Tunisia	2.9	2.6	5.5	110	287
ALL AFRICA	2.3	2.8	5.1	34	95

13-13. Health care

	Population per physician		*Population per hospital bed*		*Percentage of births attended by trained health personnel*	*Percentage of population with access to health services*
	1981	*1990-2000*	*1981*	*1990-2000*	*1990-2000*	*1990-2000*
SUB-SAHARAN AFRICA	..	..	..	1,304	..	..
excluding South Africa	..	..	..	1,304	..	..
excl. S.Africa & Nigeria	..	..	..	1,523	..	..
Angola	..	12,981	..	774	23	24
Benin	16,943	17,546	884	4,280	60	42
Botswana	7,452	4,274	..	635	99	..
Burkina Faso	55,744	26,315	..	706	27	..
Burundi	..	17,684	..	1,508	25	80
Cameroon	..	13,515	..	392	56	..
Cape Verde	..	5,845	..	634	53	..
Central African Republic	22,831	28,607	..	1,145	44	..
Chad	..	30,347	..	1,389	16	26
Comoros	..	13,622	..	362	62	..
Congo, Democratic Rep. of	..	14,494	..	701	70	59
Congo, Republic of	..	3,986	..	298	50	..
Côte d'Ivoire	..	11,115	..	1,232	47	..
Djibouti	4,471	7,176	277	394	..	..
Equatorial Guinea	..	4,058	..	..	5	..
Eritrea	..	33,364	..	..	21	..
Ethiopia	88,119	35,096	..	4,141	10	55
Gabon	2,187	4,319	..	313	86	..
Gambia, The	..	28,244	..	1,637	51	..
Ghana	..	16,132	..	685	44	25
Guinea	45,463	7,691	..	1,816	35	45
Guinea-Bissau	..	6,025	507	677	35	..
Kenya	10,098	7,576	..	607	44	..
Lesotho	..	18,505	..	..	60	..
Liberia	9,454	43,671	..	..	..	..
Madagascar	10,060	9,344	..	1,068	47	..
Malawi	54,000	35,976	..	746	56	..
Mali	25,987	15,993	..	4,167	24	..
Mauritania	..	7,245	..	1,503	58	..
Mauritius	1,813	1,176	..	325	97	99
Mozambique	36,970	..	..	1,153	44	..
Namibia	..	3,390	..	..	76	..
Niger	..	30,591	..	8,574	16	30
Nigeria	..	5,208	..	599	42	67
Rwanda	32,318	24,967	677	605	31	..
São Tomé and Principe	2,388	2,148	..	211	..	..
Senegal	12,687	10,529	..	2,490	51	40
Seychelles	..	757	..	..	..	99
Sierra Leone	18,972	13,706	..	..	42	..
Somalia	24,382	24,967	..	1,327	34	..
South Africa	..	1,776	..	..	84	..
Sudan	9,917	11,112	1,149	919	86	70
Swaziland	..	6,636	..	..	..	55
Tanzania	..	24,400	..	1,123	35	93
Togo	20,592	13,165	..	662	51	..
Uganda	21,405	25,000	661	1,091	38	..
Zambia	7,913	14,484	287	..	47	..
Zimbabwe	7,221	7,194	..	1,959	84	..
NORTH AFRICA	5,936	1,120	570	620	..	88
Algeria	..	1,000	..	476	92	..
Egypt, Arab Republic	733	625	483	476	61	99
Libya	612	781	207	233	94	100
Morocco	18,558	2,174	814	1,020	40	62
Tunisia	3,642	1,428	..	588	90	90
ALL AFRICA	..	..	..	1,133	..	..

13-14. Illiteracy rate

	Percentage of population 15 years of age and above that is illiterate								
	1985			*1990*			*2001*		
	Total	*Male*	*Female*	*Total*	*Male*	*Female*	*Total*	*Male*	*Female*
SUB-SAHARAN AFRICA	56	45	66	50	40	60	37	29	45
excluding South Africa	59	48	70	53	42	64	39	31	48
excl. S. Africa & Nigeria	59	48	70	53	42	64	41	32	50
Angola	..	..	..	..	..	..	..	..	..
Benin	78	68	87	74	62	85	61	47	75
Botswana	37	39	35	32	34	30	22	25	19
Burkina Faso	87	79	94	84	75	92	75	65	85
Burundi	68	55	79	63	51	73	51	43	58
Cameroon	45	34	56	38	28	47	23	17	29
Cape Verde	43	29	53	36	24	46	25	15	33
Central African Republic	72	58	85	67	53	79	52	39	63
Chad	78	69	87	72	63	81	56	47	64
Comoros	47	39	55	46	39	54	44	37	51
Congo, Democratic Rep. of	59	45	73	53	39	66	37	26	48
Congo, Republic of	41	29	52	33	23	42	18	12	24
Côte d'Ivoire	72	63	82	67	57	77	52	44	60
Djibouti	53	38	68	47	33	60	35	24	44
Equatorial Guinea	33	18	48	27	14	39	16	7	24
Eritrea	58	46	70	54	42	65	43	32	54
Ethiopia	76	67	85	71	62	80	60	52	68
Gabon	..	..	..	..	..	..	..	..	..
Gambia, The	79	74	85	74	68	80	62	55	69
Ghana	49	36	61	42	30	53	27	19	36
Guinea	..	..	..	..	..	..	..	..	..
Guinea-Bissau	77	63	91	73	57	87	60	44	75
Kenya	36	24	48	29	19	39	17	11	23
Lesotho	25	38	13	22	35	11	16	27	6
Liberia	66	51	82	61	45	77	45	29	61
Madagascar	47	38	56	42	34	50	33	26	39
Malawi	52	34	68	48	31	64	39	25	52
Mali	81	74	87	74	67	81	57	50	64
Mauritania	68	56	79	65	54	76	59	49	69
Mauritius	23	17	29	20	15	25	15	12	18
Mozambique	71	56	85	67	51	82	55	39	70
Namibia	29	25	33	25	23	28	17	17	18
Niger	90	84	96	89	82	95	84	76	91
Nigeria	59	48	70	51	40	62	35	26	43
Rwanda	53	43	64	47	37	56	32	25	38
São Tomé and Principe	..	..	..	..	..	..	..	..	..
Senegal	76	66	85	72	62	81	62	52	71
Seychelles	..	..	..	..	..	..	..	..	..
Sierra Leone	..	..	..	..	..	..	..	..	..
Somalia	..	..	..	..	..	..	..	..	..
South Africa	21	20	22	19	18	20	14	14	15
Sudan	60	45	75	54	40	68	41	30	52
Swaziland	34	31	36	28	26	30	20	19	21
Tanzania	44	29	57	37	24	49	24	15	32
Togo	62	46	77	56	39	71	42	27	56
Uganda	49	35	63	44	31	57	32	22	42
Zambia	37	25	47	32	21	41	21	14	27
Zimbabwe	24	17	31	19	13	25	11	7	14
NORTH AFRICA	57	44	71	52	39	65	40	30	52
Algeria	56	44	67	47	36	59	32	23	42
Egypt, Arab Republic	57	43	71	53	40	66	44	33	55
Libya	39	22	59	32	17	49	19	9	31
Morocco	67	53	80	61	47	75	50	37	63
Tunisia	47	34	61	41	28	53	28	18	38
ALL AFRICA	56	45	67	51	40	61	38	29	47

13-15. Primary school gross enrollment ratio

	Total			Males			Females		
	1980	*1990*	*1998-99*	*1980*	*1990*	*1998-99*	*1980*	*1990*	*1998-99*
SUB-SAHARAN AFRICA	80	74	79	88	82	85	67	67	73
excluding South Africa	80	71	75	88	79	82	67	63	69
excl. S. Africa & Nigeria	72	66	81	78	72	88	59	59	74
Angola	175	92	64	..	95	69	..	88	60
Benin	67	58	86	91	78	103	43	39	69
Botswana	91	113	108	83	109	109	100	117	109
Burkina Faso	17	33	43	22	41	51	13	26	35
Burundi	26	73	62	32	79	69	21	66	56
Cameroon	98	101	91	107	109	98	89	93	84
Cape Verde	114	121	122	119	125	145	110	118	143
Central African Republic	71	65	56	92	80	68	51	51	45
Chad	..	54	70	..	75	87	..	34	53
Comoros	86	75	84	100	87	91	72	63	76
Congo, Democratic Rep. of	92	70	47	108	81	49	77	60	44
Congo, Republic of	141	133	84	148	141	88	134	124	79
Côte d'Ivoire	75	67	77	90	79	88	60	56	66
Djibouti	37	38	37	..	45	43	..	32	31
Equatorial Guinea	..	..	125	..	..	137	..	..	112
Eritrea	..	..	61	..	..	67	..	..	55
Ethiopia	37	33	71	48	39	85	27	26	57
Gabon	..	..	151	..	..	152	..	..	151
Gambia, The	53	64	75	70	76	79	36	52	71
Ghana	79	75	78	88	82	82	71	68	74
Guinea	36	37	63	48	50	75	25	24	51
Guinea-Bissau	68	56	83	94	72	99	43	39	66
Kenya	115	95	91	120	97	91	110	93	90
Lesotho	103	112	104	85	100	99	122	123	108
Liberia	48	29	118	61	35	137	34	23	99
Madagascar	130	103	102	131	103	104	129	103	100
Malawi	60	68	158	72	74	158	48	62	158
Mali	26	26	55	34	34	65	19	19	45
Mauritania	37	49	84	47	56	87	26	41	82
Mauritius	93	109	108	94	109	108	91	109	109
Mozambique	99	67	85	114	77	98	84	57	73
Namibia	..	129	113	..	123	112	..	135	114
Niger	25	29	32	33	37	39	18	21	26
Nigeria	109	91	..	123	104	..	95	79	..
Rwanda	63	70	122	66	70	124	60	69	121
São Tomé and Principe	..	..	..	..	..	..	..	..	..
Senegal	46	59	73	55	68	78	37	50	68
Seychelles	..	..	..	..	..	..	..	..	..
Sierra Leone	52	50	65	61	60	68	43	41	63
Somalia	21	11	..	28	14	..	15	7	..
South Africa	90	122	119	..	123	121	..	121	117
Sudan	50	53	55	59	60	59	41	45	51
Swaziland	103	111	125	104	114	128	102	109	121
Tanzania	93	70	63	99	70	63	86	69	63
Togo	118	109	124	144	132	139	93	86	109
Uganda	50	71	141	56	79	146	43	63	136
Zambia	90	99	79	97	102	81	83	95	76
Zimbabwe	85	116	97	..	117	98	..	115	95
NORTH AFRICA	84	91	103	97	100	107	69	83	98
Algeria	94	100	114	108	108	119	81	92	110
Egypt, Arab Republic	73	94	100	84	101	104	61	86	96
Libya	125	105	117	129	108	118	121	102	116
Morocco	83	67	90	102	79	98	63	54	83
Tunisia	102	113	118	117	120	121	87	107	115
ALL AFRICA	81	78	89	90	85	95	67	70	83

13-16. Pupil progression

	Pecentage of cohort reaching grade 5 (1992-98)			Progression to secondary school 1993		
	Total	Male	Female	Total	Male	Female
SUB-SAHARAN AFRICA	..	..	..	52	..	..
excluding South Africa	..	..	..	46	..	..
excl. S. Africa & Nigeria	..	..	..	..	..	..
Angola	4	3	4	..	..	..
Benin	61	64	57	..	..	..
Botswana	88	84	91	84	84	85
Burkina Faso	68	67	70	27	27	27
Burundi	..	..	..	11	12	11
Cameroon	..	..	..	..	..	..
Cape Verde	..	..	..	..	..	..
Central African Republic	..	..	..	..	..	..
Chad	55	58	50	47	..	..
Comoros	79	..	..	39	..	..
Congo, Democratic Rep. of	64	73	54	27	25	30
Congo, Republic of	55	40	78	..	..	..
Côte d'Ivoire	75	77	71	33	..	..
Djibouti	77	71	85	38	..	..
Equatorial Guinea	16	14	19	..	..	..
Eritrea	95	97	93	80	85	74
Ethiopia	51	51	50	80	82	77
Gabon	59	58	61	..	..	..
Gambia, The	80	78	83	..	..	..
Ghana	..	..	..	..	..	..
Guinea	87	92	79	50	51	47
Guinea-Bissau	..	..	..	..	..	..
Kenya	..	..	..	41	..	..
Lesotho	68	61	76	71	..	..
Liberia	33	..	..	..	..	..
Madagascar	51	51	52	35	35	35
Malawi	34	36	32	15	..	..
Mali	84	92	70	63	64	60
Mauritania	64	61	68	32	34	28
Mauritius	99	98	99	51	49	54
Mozambique	46	49	42	39	39	39
Namibia	83	80	87	74	76	72
Niger	61	62	60	..	..	..
Nigeria	..	..	..	52	..	..
Rwanda	45	48	43	15	..	..
São Tomé and Principe	..	..	..	..	..	..
Senegal	87	89	85	..	..	..
Seychelles	100	98	99	100	..	..
Sierra Leone	..	..	..	..	..	..
Somalia	..	..	..	..	..	..
South Africa	76	75	77	90	87	91
Sudan	74	75	73	61	..	..
Swaziland	76	70	81	79	79	79
Tanzania	81	79	83	12	..	..
Togo	52	54	48	38	40	35
Uganda	45	44	46	32	..	..
Zambia	78	83	73	..	..	..
Zimbabwe	79	78	79	66	..	..
NORTH AFRICA	..	..	..	79	77	81
Algeria	95	94	96	80	77	82
Egypt, Arab Republic	..	..	..	83	82	85
Libya	..	..	..	..	..	..
Morocco	82	82	82	81	79	84
Tunisia	92	91	93	62	62	63
ALL AFRICA	..	..	..	56	..	..

Notes: In Seychelles a policy of automatic promotion is practiced at the primary level of education. Tanzanian figures refer to mainland only.

13-17. Net primary enrollment ratio

	Total			Males			Females		
	1985	1993	1998-99	1985	1993	1998-99	1985	1993	1998-99
SUB-SAHARAN AFRICA	..	..	54	..	..	57	..	..	51
excluding South Africa	..	..	..	..	..	..	..	..	..
excl. S. Africa & Nigeria	..	..	54	..	..	57	..	..	51
Angola	..	..	27	..	..	29	..	..	25
Benin	53	54	70	71	70	83	36	38	57
Botswana	89	94	84	84	91	82	94	96	85
Burkina Faso	23	29	35	29	36	41	17	23	28
Burundi	41	52	44	47	56	49	36	48	40
Cameroon	..	..	..	..	..	..	..	..	..
Cape Verde	95	..	92	97	..	98	93	..	99
Central African Republic	61	53	53	75	64	63	47	42	42
Chad	..	..	57	..	..	69	..	..	45
Comoros	61	52	55	..	57	60	..	47	50
Congo, Democratic Rep. of	..	54	33	..	60	33	..	47	32
Congo, Republic of	96	..	..	99	..	..	93	..	..
Côte d'Ivoire	..	47	58	..	..	67	..	..	50
Djibouti	31	30	31	37	34	35	26	26	26
Equatorial Guinea	..	..	79	..	..	88	..	..	70
Eritrea	..	28	40	..	29	43	..	26	37
Ethiopia	..	20	31	..	24	34	..	16	28
Gabon	..	..	..	..	..	..	..	..	..
Gambia, The	62	55	70	77	64	75	48	46	65
Ghana	..	..	50	..	..	51	..	..	50
Guinea	27	37	49	36	..	56	18	..	41
Guinea-Bissau	47	..	54	63	..	63	31	..	45
Kenya	91	..	..	92	..	..	89	..	..
Lesotho	72	72	58	62	65	55	82	79	62
Liberia	..	..	83	..	..	103	..	..	64
Madagascar	..	..	66	..	..	66	..	..	67
Malawi	43	68	69	46	66	66	41	71	71
Mali	20	27	43	..	33	51	..	21	36
Mauritania	..	47	61	..	52	63	..	43	59
Mauritius	100	94	94	100	94	94	101	94	94
Mozambique	51	39	50	56	44	55	47	34	46
Namibia	..	89	80	..	86	77	..	93	82
Niger	25	23	21	32	29	21	17	17	22
Nigeria	..	..	..	..	..	..	..	..	..
Rwanda	60	75	97	61	76	97	59	75	97
São Tomé and Principe	..	..	..	..	..	..	..	..	..
Senegal	48	50	62	57	55	66	39	41	58
Seychelles	..	..	..	..	..	..	..	..	..
Sierra Leone	..	..	65	..	..	68	..	..	63
Somalia	10	..	..	13	..	..	7	..	..
South Africa	..	103	95	..	101	95	..	104	96
Sudan	..	..	45	..	..	49	..	..	41
Swaziland	79	91	93	78	91	92	80	91	94
Tanzania	56	49	47	55	49	46	56	50	48
Togo	61	69	91	72	80	101	49	58	82
Uganda	..	..	109	..	..	110	..	..	108
Zambia	77	..	66	81	..	67	73	..	66
Zimbabwe	..	..	80	..	..	80	..	..	80
NORTH AFRICA	..	86	90	..	92	93	..	79	87
Algeria	86	95	97	94	100	99	78	90	96
Egypt, Arab Republic	..	88	92	..	94	95	..	82	90
Libya	..	96	..	..	97	..	..	96	..
Morocco	61	66	74	73	76	79	48	56	70
Tunisia	93	97	98	99	100	99	87	94	97
ALL AFRICA	..	..	63	..	..	66	..	..	60

13-18. Number of school teachers

	Primary						Secondary					
	Total teaching staff			Percentage females			Total teaching staff			Percentage females		
	1980	1990-90	1996-98	1980	1990-90	1996-98	1980	1990	1996-98	1980	1990	1996-98
SUB-SAHARAN AFRICA	..	..	..	30	35	..	..	..	..	..	..	..
excluding South Africa	..	..	..	30	35	..	..	..	..	..	..	..
excl. S. Africa & Nigeria	..	..	..	28	32	39	..	..	..	..	..	..
Angola	..	31,062	..	..	..	..	..	..	18,035	..	..	32
Benin	7,994	13,556	16,335	23	25	23	..	..	10,691	..	..	13
Botswana	5,316	8,956	11,654	72	80	82	1,137	3,716	8,469	37	40	46
Burkina Faso	3,700	8,903	16,660	20	27	25	..	..	6,215	..	..	..
Burundi	4,805	9,465	12,350	47	46	54	..	2,026	4,230	..	21	..
Cameroon	26,763	38,430	41,142	20	30	36	8,926	19,820	19,515	..	..	28
Cape Verde	1,436	..	3,190	..	..	62	184	..	1,665	..	..	..
Central African Republic	4,130	4,004	3,320	25	25	220	724	..	..	16	..	..
Chad	..	7,980	12,373	..	6	9	..	..	3,619	..	..	5
Comoros	1,292	1,995	2,381	7	..	26	449	..	..	20	..	..
Congo, Democratic Rep. of	..	114,000	154,618	..	24	21	..	..	89,461	..	..	10
Congo, Republic of	7,186	7,578	4,515	25	32	42	5,117	6,851	..	..	..	..
Côte d'Ivoire	26,460	39,002	44,731	15	19	20	..	..	20,124	..	..	..
Djibouti	419	742	966	..	37	28	278	..	680	..	..	22
Equatorial Guinea	647	..	1,322	..	..	28	..	..	958	..	..	6
Eritrea	..	2,895	5,576	..	45	35	..	..	2,278	..	..	12
Ethiopia	33,322	68,370	92,775	22	24	28	..	23,319	..	..	10	..
Gabon	3,441	..	6,022	27	..	42	1,587	..	3,078	24	..	16
Gambia, The	1,932	2,757	4,578	32	31	29	620	756	1,949	25	..	15
Ghana	47,921	66,946	71,340	42	36	36	31,636	..	..	21	..	..
Guinea	7,165	8,699	15,512	14	22	25	..	5,976	5,756	..	12	11
Guinea-Bissau	3,257	..	..	24	..	..	462	..	..	21	..	..
Kenya	102,489	172,117	192,306	..	37	42	17,081	..	44,335	..	..	35
Lesotho	5,097	6,448	14,555	75	80	80	1,299	..	3,126	..	..	51
Liberia	..	..	10,047	..	..	19	..	..	6,621	..	..	16
Madagascar	39,474	38,933	42,678	..	..	58	..	..	20,386	..	..	44
Malawi	12,540	22,942	..	..	31	..	953	..	..	..	..	..
Mali	6,862	8,156	15,447	20	23	23	..	5,748	7,663	..	14	14
Mauritania	2,183	3,741	7,366	9	18	26	..	..	2,419	..	..	10
Mauritius	6,379	6,507	5,065	43	44	53	..	..	4,737	..	..	45
Mozambique	17,030	23,107	31,512	22	..	24	..	4,657	9,555	..	..	17
Namibia	..	..	11,992	..	..	67	..	..	..	..	..	..
Niger	5,518	8,835	12,901	30	33	31	1,284	2,775	4,303	21	18	18
Nigeria	343,551	331,915	416,745	34	43	48	41,581	141,377	..	29	33	..
Rwanda	11,912	19,183	23,730	38	46	55	1,454	2,802	..	16	20	..
São Tomé and Principe	588	..	660	..	..	..	..	..	..	..	..	..
Senegal	9,175	13,394	21,277	24	..	..	4,302	..	8,499	..	..	16
Seychelles	658	..	656	80	..	88	127	328	555	37	..	53
Sierra Leone	9,528	10,850	..	..	..	..	..	5,969	..	..	18	..
Somalia	8,122	..	..	29	..	..	2,089	..	..	7	..	..
South Africa	160,286	..	216,040	..	..	78	..	..	143,804	..	..	50
Sudan	43,451	60,047	94,125	31	51	68	18,831	33,628	37,032	..	35	57
Swaziland	3,278	5,083	6,425	79	79	75	..	..	3,416	..	..	46
Tanzania	81,386	96,850	106,329	37	41	44	3,837	7,944	12,751	..	24	26
Togo	9,201	11,105	23,107	21	19	13	..	4,492	6,595	..	12	13
Uganda	38,422	84,149	109,733	30	30	33	3,833	..	24,982	..	..	21
Zambia	21,455	33,200	34,810	40	..	47	4,882	..	10,000	..	..	26
Zimbabwe	28,118	59,154	63,718	..	39	44	3,782	24,547	28,254	..	29	36
NORTH AFRICA	..	..	..	..	45	48	..	..	..	..	..	40
Algeria	88,481	151,262	169,519	37	39	46	41,137	127,024	154,628	..	39	47
Egypt, Arab Republic	..	558,630	345,981	..	52	52	121,999	286,797	453,967	31	..	41
Libya	36,591	85,537	97,334	47	..	53	24,323	..	90,737	24	..	25
Morocco	56,908	91,680	123,021	30	37	39	36,526	159,314	87,932	..	29	33
Tunisia	27,375	50,609	60,470	29	45	50	14,328	33,058	56,466	29	32	39
ALL AFRICA	..	..	..	30	37	45	..	..	..	..	..	..

Note: Figures include both part-time and full-time teachers.

13-19. Pupil/teacher ratio

	Number of pupils per teacher					
	Primary			*Secondary*		
	1980	*1990*	*1998-99*	*1980*	*1990*	*1998-99*
SUB-SAHARAN AFRICA	38	39	..	..	..	..
excluding South Africa	40	39	..	..	..	..
excl. S. Africa & Nigeria	43	38	40	..	..	..
Angola	..	32	..	..	..	18
Benin	48	36	53	..	..	20
Botswana	32	32	28	18	17	17
Burkina Faso	54	57	49	..	..	28
Burundi	37	67	46	..	22	17
Cameroon	52	51	52	26	25	24
Cape Verde	40	..	29	18	..	24
Central African Republic	60	77	99	62	..	..
Chad	..	66	68	..	..	34
Comoros	46	37	35	31	..	..
Congo, Democratic Rep. of	..	40	26	..	..	14
Congo, Republic of	54	65	61	37	27	..
Côte d'Ivoire	39	36	43	..	..	29
Djibouti	40	43	40	18	..	23
Equatorial Guinea	69	..	57	..	..	21
Eritrea	..	38	47	..	..	51
Ethiopia	64	36	..	..	37	..
Gabon	45	..	44	19	..	28
Gambia, The	24	31	33	16	27	24
Ghana	29	29	..	22	..	..
Guinea	36	40	47	..	14	30
Guinea-Bissau	23	..	..	10	..	..
Kenya	38	31	28	25	..	26
Lesotho	48	55	25	19	..	23
Liberia	..	..	39	..	..	17
Madagascar	44	40	47	..	..	17
Malawi	65	61	..	27	..	..
Mali	42	48	62	..	15	28
Mauritania	41	45	47	..	..	26
Mauritius	20	21	26	..	..	..
Mozambique	81	55	61	..	34	29
Namibia	..	..	32	..	..	..
Niger	41	42	41	30	28	24
Nigeria	35	41	..	45	21	..
Rwanda	59	57	54	14	25	..
São Tomé and Principe	28	..	36	..	..	..
Senegal	46	53	49	22	..	28
Seychelles	22	..	15	7	13	14
Sierra Leone	33	34	..	..	17	..
Somalia	33	..	..	21	..	..
South Africa	27	..	37	..	..	30
Sudan	34	34	26	20	22	27
Swaziland	34	33	33	..	..	18
Tanzania	41	35	38	21	21	..
Togo	55	58	41	..	28	35
Uganda	34	29	60	..	..	19
Zambia	49	44	45	21	..	29
Zimbabwe	44	36	..	20	27	..
NORTH AFRICA	..	17	23	22	16	16
Algeria	35	28	28	25	17	18
Egypt, Arab Republic	..	12	23	24	19	17
Libya	18	14	8	12	..	7
Morocco	38	27	28	22	7	17
Tunisia	39	28	24	20	17	19
ALL AFRICA	38	30	33	..	..	..

Note: Figures include both part-time and full-time teachers.

13-20. Secondary school gross enrollment ratio

	Total			Males			Females		
	1980	*1990*	*1998-99*	*1980*	*1990*	*1998-99*	*1980*	*1990*	*1998-99*
SUB-SAHARAN AFRICA	15	23	..	20	26	..	10	20	..
excluding South Africa	15	19	..	20	23	..	10	16	..
excl. S. Africa & Nigeria	14	18	22	18	21	25	9	14	19
Angola	21	12	15	..	15	18	..	10	13
Benin	16	12	22	24	17	30	8	7	14
Botswana	19	43	82	17	41	78	20	45	85
Burkina Faso	3	7	10	4	9	12	2	5	8
Burundi	3	6	7	4	7	8	2	4	6
Cameroon	18	28	20	24	33	22	13	23	17
Cape Verde	8	21	69	9	21	..	7	20	..
Central African Republic	14	12	..	21	17	..	7	7	..
Chad	..	8	11	..	13	18	..	3	5
Comoros	22	18	21	30	21	23	15	14	18
Congo, Democratic Rep. of	24	22	18	35	29	24	13	14	13
Congo, Republic of	74	53	..	89	62	..	60	44	..
Côte d'Ivoire	19	22	22	26	30	28	11	14	15
Djibouti	12	12	15	15	14	13	9	9	17
Equatorial Guinea	..	..	31	..	..	43	..	..	19
Eritrea	..	..	28	..	..	33	..	..	23
Ethiopia	9	14	5	12	16	6	7	13	4
Gabon	..	..	54	..	..	58	..	..	51
Gambia, The	11	19	27	16	25	31	7	12	23
Ghana	41	36	37	50	45	42	31	28	33
Guinea	17	10	14	24	15	20	10	5	7
Guinea-Bissau	6	9	20	10	13	26	2	6	14
Kenya	20	24	30	23	28	31	16	21	28
Lesotho	18	25	28	14	20	24	21	30	32
Liberia	22	14	23	31	20	27	12	8	18
Madagascar	..	18	14	..	18	15	..	18	14
Malawi	5	8	45	7	11	50	3	5	40
Mali	8	7	15	12	9	20	5	5	10
Mauritania	11	14	18	17	19	21	4	9	15
Mauritius	50	53	107	51	53	108	49	53	106
Mozambique	5	8	14	8	10	17	3	6	11
Namibia	..	44	60	..	39	56	..	49	63
Niger	5	7	7	7	9	8	3	4	5
Nigeria	18	25	..	24	29	..	12	21	..
Rwanda	3	8	12	4	9	12	3	7	12
São Tomé and Principe	..	..	..	..	..	..	..	..	..
Senegal	11	16	20	15	21	24	7	11	15
Seychelles	..	..	..	..	..	..	..	..	..
Sierra Leone	14	17	24	20	22	26	8	13	22
Somalia	9	6	..	13	8	..	5	4	..
South Africa	..	74	90	..	69	133	..	80	48
Sudan	16	24	29	20	27	22	12	21	36
Swaziland	38	44	60	39	45	60	37	43	60
Tanzania	3	5	5	4	6	6	2	4	5
Togo	33	24	36	50	35	50	16	12	22
Uganda	5	13	..	7	17	..	3	10	..
Zambia	16	24	25	22	30	29	11	18	22
Zimbabwe	8	50	45	9	53	48	6	46	43
NORTH AFRICA	41	62	69	49	69	71	31	56	68
Algeria	33	61	67	40	67	65	26	54	69
Egypt, Arab Republic	50	76	84	61	84	86	39	68	81
Libya	76	86	79	89	85	75	63	87	84
Morocco	26	35	39	32	41	44	20	30	35
Tunisia	27	45	75	34	50	73	20	40	76
ALL AFRICA	20	30	..	26	34	..	15	27	..

Note: "Secondary" refers to secondary general education.

13-21. Public expenditure on education

	As percentage of Total public expenditure			*As percentage of GDP*		
	1980	*1990*	*1993-97*	*1980*	*1990*	*1993-98*
SUB-SAHARAN AFRICA	..	..	..	..	..	..
excluding South Africa	..	..	..	..	..	..
excl. S. Africa & Nigeria	..	..	..	..	..	..
Angola	..	..	..	..	..	2.6
Benin	..	..	..	..	..	2.6
Botswana	..	..	..	5.3	6	9.1
Burkina Faso	15.5	18	17.9	2.2	3	3.0
Burundi	..	..	3.2	..	3	3.9
Cameroon	..	..	..	3.2	3	2.6
Cape Verde	..	..	..	..	..	4.4
Central African Republic	..	..	..	..	2	1.9
Chad	..	..	..	..	..	1.7
Comoros	..	..	..	..	..	..
Congo, Democratic Rep. of	..	..	..	..	..	..
Congo, Republic of	..	..	..	6.4	5	4.7
Côte d'Ivoire	..	30	..	6.9	..	3.7
Djibouti	..	..	..	..	4	..
Equatorial Guinea	..	..	..	..	..	1.8
Eritrea	..	..	..	..	..	4.8
Ethiopia	10.2	10	14.0	..	3	4.3
Gabon	..	..	..	2.5	..	3.3
Gambia, The	..	..	14.5	3.1	4	4.8
Ghana	..	..	..	3.1	3	4.0
Guinea	..	..	..	..	..	1.8
Guinea-Bissau	..	..	..	..	..	0.0
Kenya	22.9	23	21.4	6.5	7	6.6
Lesotho	..	15	27.8	7.5	6	13.0
Liberia	11.9	..	..	5.5	..	..
Madagascar	..	..	..	4.3	2	1.9
Malawi	..	..	..	3.1	3	4.6
Mali	..	..	..	3.4	..	2.9
Mauritania	..	..	..	..	..	4.3
Mauritius	..	..	..	5.5	4	4.2
Mozambique	..	..	..	2.5	3	2.9
Namibia	..	..	..	..	7	8.1
Niger	18.0	..	..	3.1	3	2.7
Nigeria	..	..	..	..	1	0.6
Rwanda	..	..	..	2.7	..	..
São Tomé and Principe	..	..	..	..	..	3.6
Senegal	..	..	..	..	4	3.5
Seychelles	..	..	..	5.6	8	6.0
Sierra Leone	..	..	..	3.7	..	1.0
Somalia	..	..	..	1.0	..	..
South Africa	..	..	..	..	6	6.1
Sudan	..	..	..	41.8	6	3.3
Swaziland	24.6	..	..	5.7	6	6.1
Tanzania	13.3	..	..	..	3	2.1
Togo	..	..	..	5.4	6	4.5
Uganda	..	..	..	1.2	1	1.6
Zambia	..	8	13.1	4.1	2	2.3
Zimbabwe	..	..	..	5.2	8	10.8
NORTH AFRICA	15.0	17	15.5	..	..	..
Algeria	..	..	..	7.6	5	6.0
Egypt, Arab Republic	8.1	14	13.8	..	4	4.7
Libya	..	..	..	3.4	..	..
Morocco	17.3	18	16.6	5.9	5	4.9
Tunisia	17.0	17.0	18.7	5.2	6.0	7.6
ALL AFRICA	..	..	..	..	..	..

13-22. Economic opportunities of women

	Female / male ratio of participation in economic activity 1995	Female as percentage of male in occupational group, 1996*			
		Administrative and managerial	Professional and technical	Clerical and sales	Services
SUB-SAHARAN AFRICA	73	10	28	..	..
excluding South Africa	74	10	26	..	..
excl. S.Africa & Nigeria	78	..	..	..	..
Angola	87	..	..	..	..
Benin	93	..	..	..	..
Botswana	85	36	61	60	70
Burkina Faso	87	14	26	63	22
Burundi	97	13	30	..	..
Cameroon	60	10	24	37	31
Cape Verde	64	23	48	63	57
Central African Republic	88	9	19	59	12
Chad	80	..	..	..	..
Comoros	74	..	29	..	..
Congo, Democratic Rep. of	77	9	17	..	..
Congo, Republic of	77	6	40	..	..
Côte d'Ivoire	49	29	..	..	..
Djibouti	..	2	20	..	..
Equatorial Guinea	55	2	27	..	..
Eritrea	90	17	30	48	43
Ethiopia	69	11	24	..	..
Gabon	80	..	..	..	..
Gambia, The	81	16	24	28	14
Ghana	103	9	36	59	68
Guinea	90	..	..	..	..
Guinea-Bissau	67	..	..	..	..
Kenya	85	..	..	..	..
Lesotho	58	33	57	144	209
Liberia	66	..	..	..	..
Madagascar	81	..	..	..	..
Malawi	96	5	35	33	28
Mali	87	20	19	57	41
Mauritania	77	8	21	25	45
Mauritius	46	23	38	49	28
Mozambique	94	11	20	..	..
Namibia	68	21	41	54	72
Niger	79	9	8	30	0
Nigeria	56	6	26	58	11
Rwanda	93	9	47	48	35
São Tomé and Principe	..	..	..	..	..
Senegal	74	..	..	..	..
Seychelles	..	29	58	59	59
Sierra Leone	57	8	32	66	15
Somalia	75	..	..	..	..
South Africa	60	17	47	..	196
Sudan	40	2	29	..	..
Swaziland	60	26	60	42	82
Tanzania	98	..	..	..	..
Togo	67	8	21	..	..
Uganda	91	..	..	..	..
Zambia	83	6	32	58	22
Zimbabwe	80	15	40	34	30
NORTH AFRICA	41	14	30	28	14
Algeria	32	6	28	11	19
Egypt, Arab Republic	40	12	30	35	10
Libya	26	..	..	..	..
Morocco	53	26	31	28	17
Tunisia	44	13	36	33	17
ALL AFRICA	67	11	28	..	..

*or most recent available data.

13-23. Household and economic participation of women

	Percentage of households headed by women (latest available between 1991-99)	Percentage of women in occupational group 1991-99					
		Agriculture	Mining	Utilities & manufacturing	Construction, transport, storage & communications	Service industries	Community, social & personal services
SUB-SAHARAN AFRICA	..	..	..	..	..	..	..
excluding South Africa	..	..	..	..	..	..	..
excl. S.Africa & Nigeria	..	..	..	..	..	..	..
Angola	..	..	..	..	..	..	..
Benin	..	..	..	..	..	..	..
Botswana	..	2	1	12	9	35	41
Burkina Faso	6	..	..	..	..	..	..
Burundi	..	..	..	..	..	..	..
Cameroon	18	..	..	..	..	..	..
Cape Verde	..	..	..	..	..	..	..
Central African Republic	16	..	..	..	..	..	..
Chad	..	14	0	14	14	14	43
Comoros	..	..	..	..	..	..	..
Congo, Democratic Rep. of	..	..	..	..	..	..	..
Congo, Republic of	..	..	..	..	..	..	..
Côte d'Ivoire	12	..	..	..	..	..	..
Djibouti	17	..	..	..	..	..	..
Equatorial Guinea	..	..	..	..	..	..	..
Eritrea	..	..	..	..	..	..	..
Ethiopia	18	10	0	24	6	10	50
Gabon	..	..	..	..	..	..	..
Gambia, The	1	..	..	..	..	..	..
Ghana	14	..	..	..	..	..	..
Guinea	8	..	..	..	..	..	..
Guinea-Bissau	10	..	..	..	..	..	..
Kenya	15	20	0	8	5	11	57
Lesotho	..	..	..	..	..	..	..
Liberia	..	..	..	..	..	..	..
Madagascar	18	..	..	..	..	..	..
Malawi	..	73	0	7	2	4	14
Mali	6	..	..	..	..	..	..
Mauritania	24	..	..	..	..	..	..
Mauritius	..	11	0	61	2	9	17
Mozambique	..	..	..	..	..	..	..
Namibia	..	..	..	..	..	..	..
Niger	6	5	5	20	25	25	25
Nigeria	13	..	..	..	..	..	..
Rwanda	..	..	..	..	..	..	..
São Tomé and Principe	..	..	..	..	..	..	..
Senegal	8	..	..	..	..	..	..
Seychelles	..	..	..	..	..	..	..
Sierra Leone	..	..	..	..	..	..	..
Somalia	..	..	..	..	..	..	..
South Africa	27	..	..	..	..	..	..
Sudan	..	..	..	..	..	..	..
Swaziland	26	23	1	16	4	20	36
Tanzania	11	..	..	..	..	..	..
Togo	..	..	..	..	..	..	..
Uganda	2	..	..	..	..	..	..
Zambia	19	..	..	..	..	..	..
Zimbabwe	..	38	1	7	4	9	..
NORTH AFRICA	..	36	0	21	2	8	32
Algeria	..	..	..	..	..	..	..
Egypt, Arab Republic	..	47	0	7	2	8	36
Libya	..	..	..	..	..	..	..
Morocco	..	3	0	45	2	11	39
Tunisia	..	..	..	..	..	..	..
ALL AFRICA	..	..	..	..	..	..	..

Figure 13-1. Life expectancy, 2000

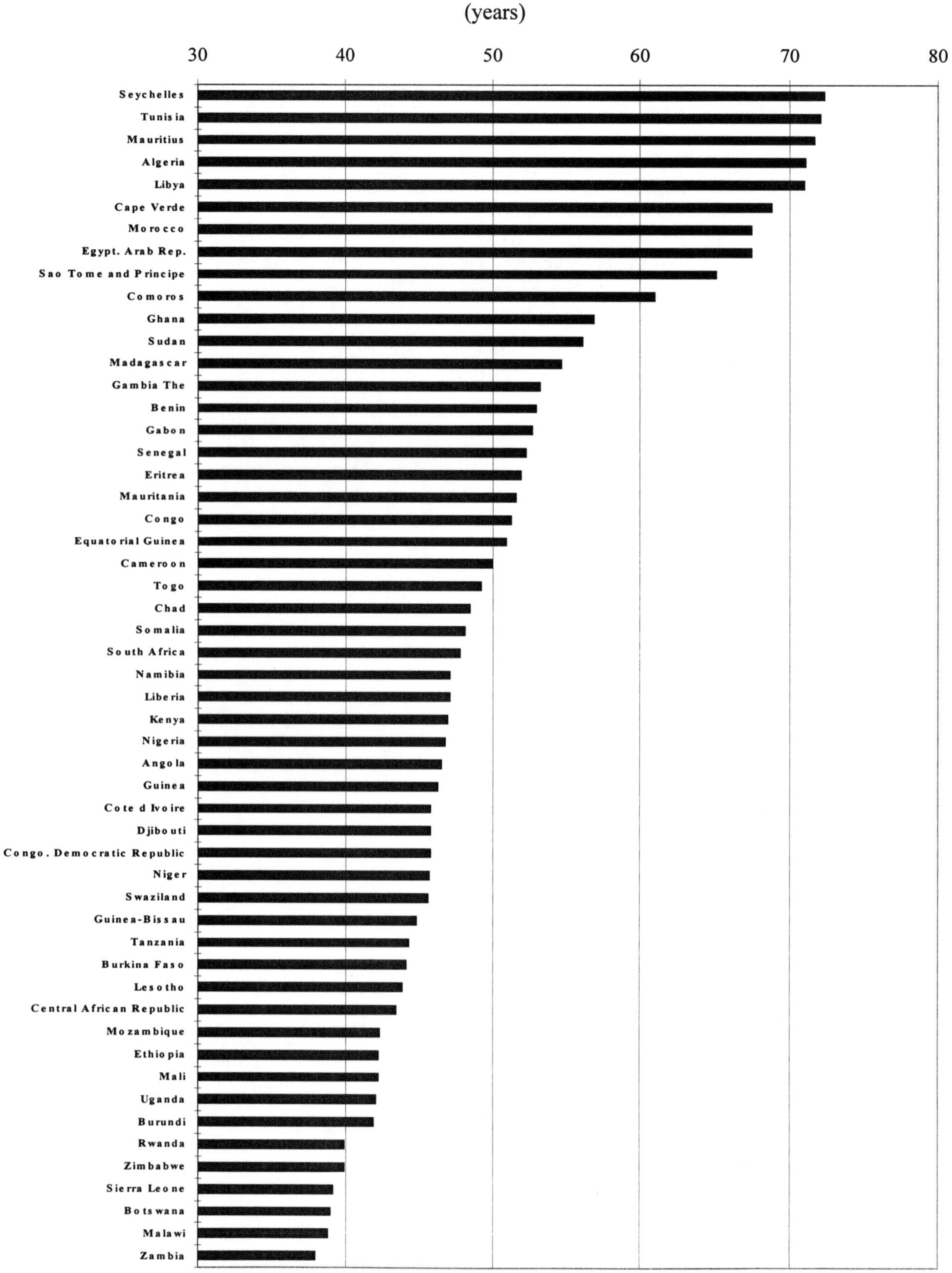

Figure 13-2. GDP per capita based on PPP, 2001

(U.S. dollars)

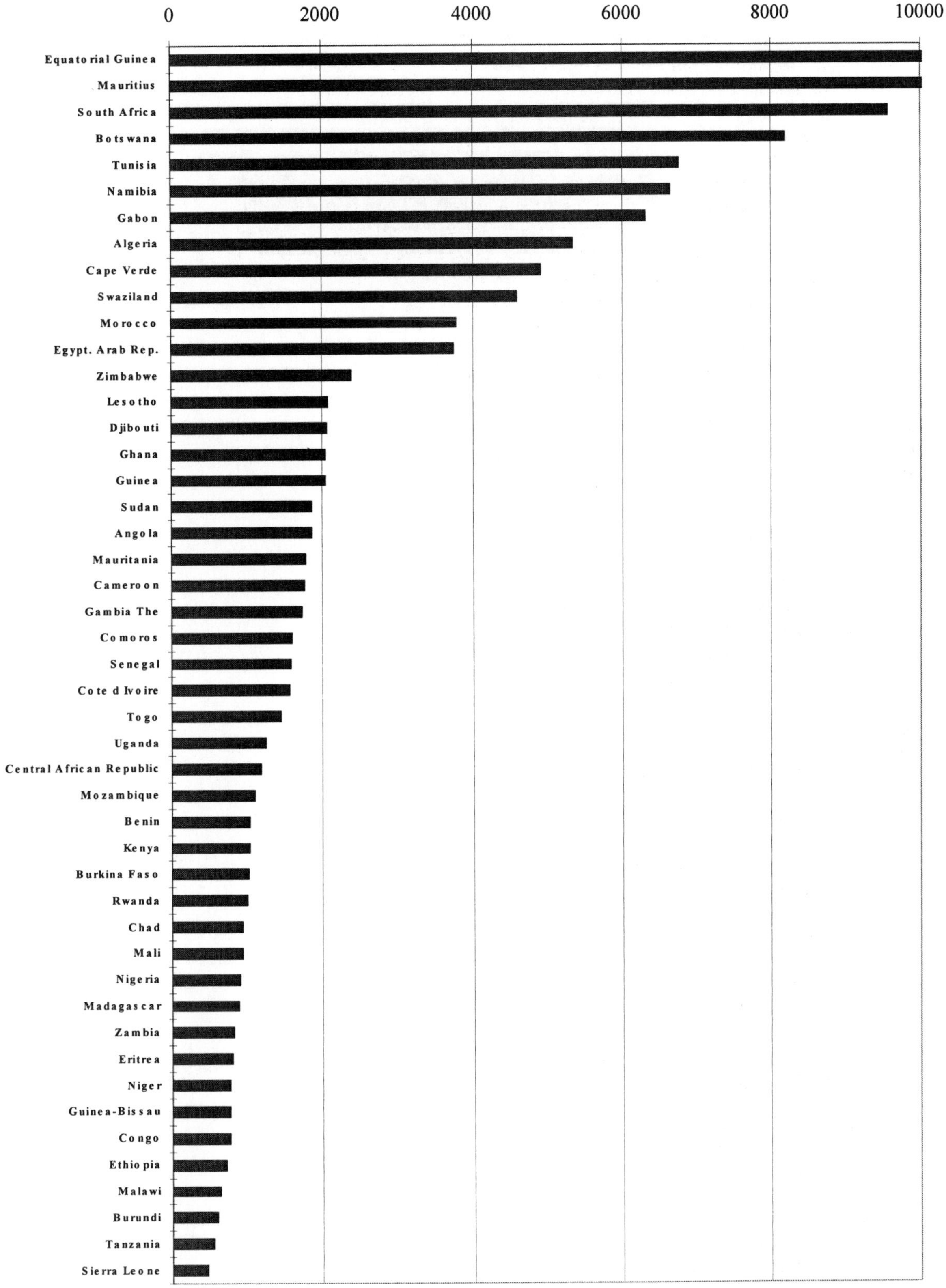

Figure 13-3. Urban population as a percentage of total population, 2001*

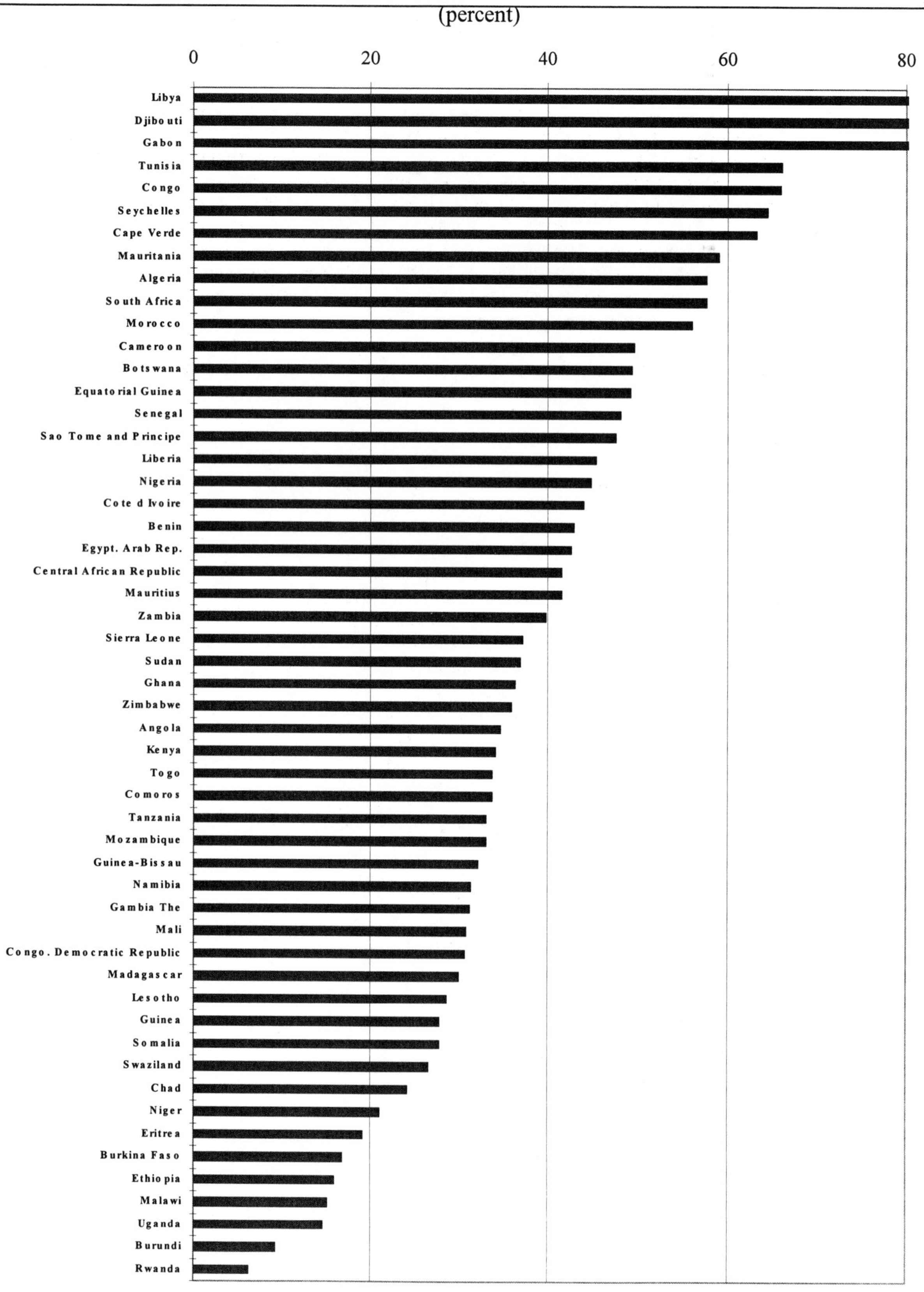

* Or most recent year available.

Figure 13-4. Primary school gross enrollement ratio, 1999*

(percent)

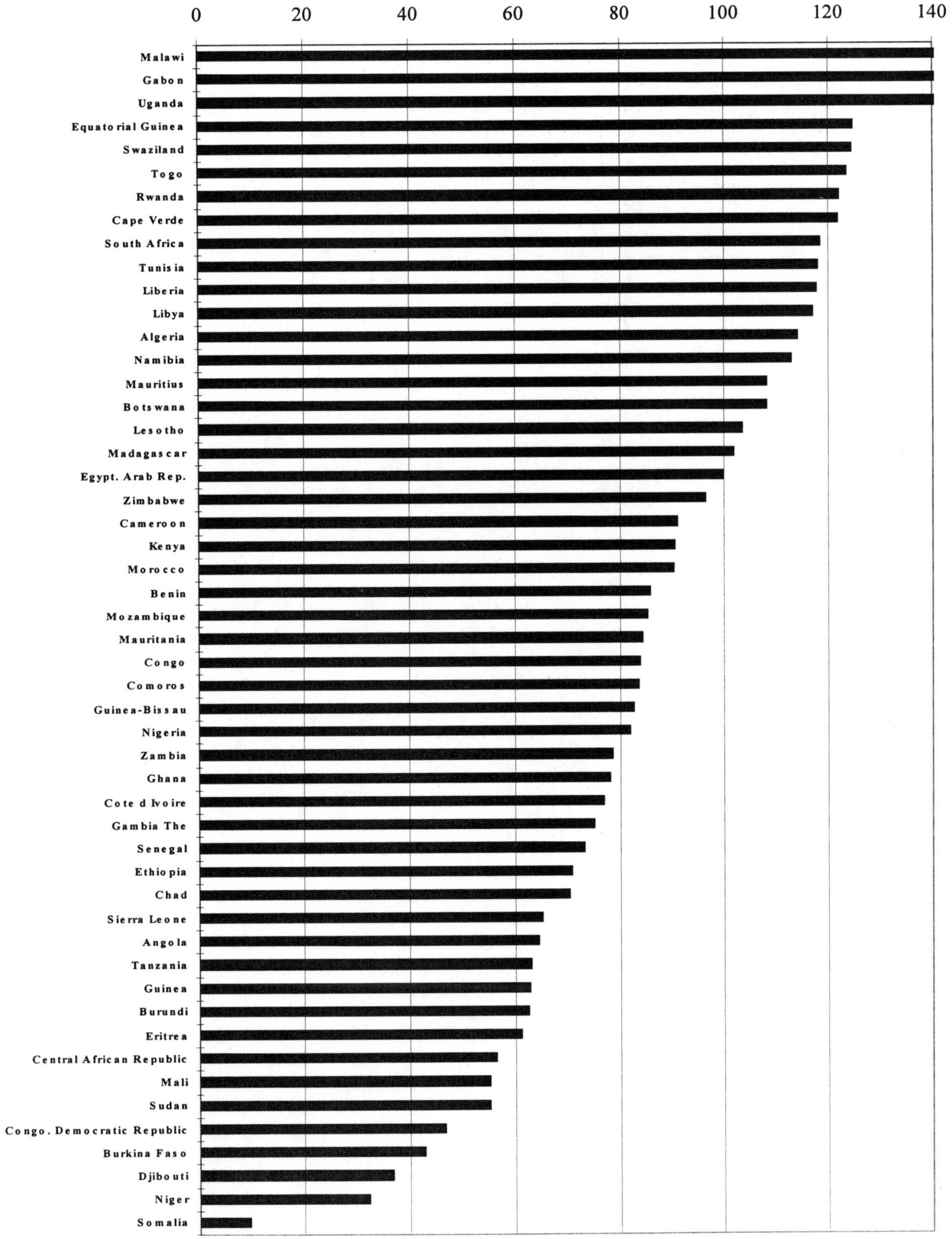

* Or most recent year available.

Figure 13-5. Maternal mortality, 2000*

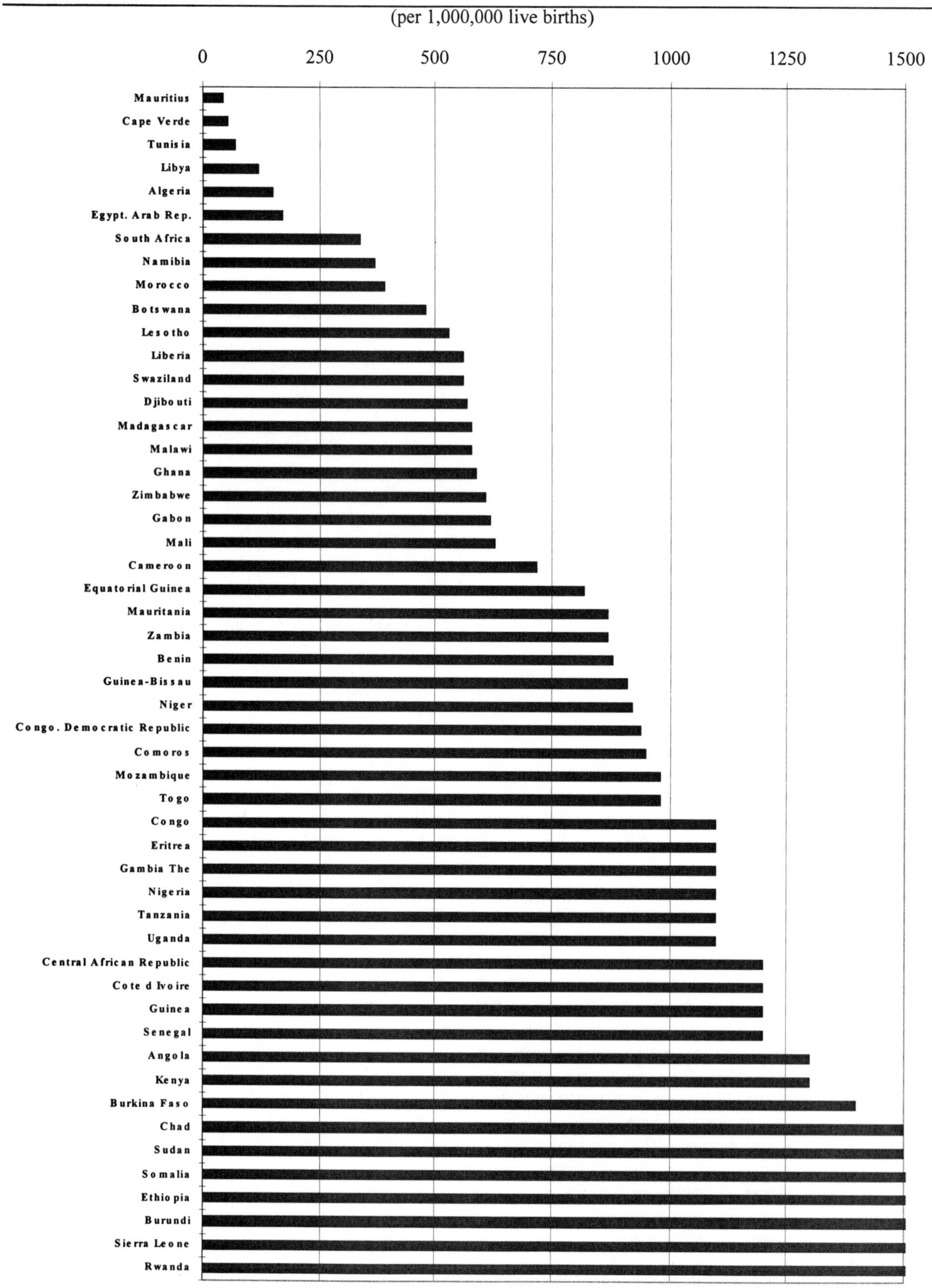

* Or most recent year available.

Technical notes

Tables

Table 13-1. Age and gender structure of the population. Age and gender structure of the population (UN and World Bank data) is the distribution of the total population according to age and gender. Only the female composition of the population is presented, as the male composition can easily be figured as the residual. Figures relate to midyear populations as estimated from the latest censuses. Age dependency ratio is calculated as the ratio of dependents—population under age 15 and above age 65—to the working age population—those aged 15 to 64.

Table 13-2. Poverty. This table presents selected indicators for comparing the incidence and extent of urban and rural poverty. The first indicator uses purchasing power parities rather than official exchange rates to calculate GDP per capita: a measure of the overall mean level of poverty at the national level. The next indicator is the national poverty headcount, which shows the percentage of the population living below the poverty line deemed appropriate for the country by its authorities. The poverty line is defined as the below which adequate standards of nutrition, shelter, and personal amenities cannot be assured. Since these levels are country specific, cross-country comparisons cannot be made. The next indicator, however, uses a relative concept of poverty, which does allow such comparisons. It shows the percentage of the urban and rural populations living on less than two-thirds of the mean national per capita income. Associated with these indicators are the urban and rural Gini coefficients, which describe the level of inequality in urban and rural income distributions. The last indicator shows the percentage of household income spent on food (UNDP, World Bank, Penn World Tables, and National Household Surveys).

Table 13-3. Income distribution. This table presents the share of income held by the richest and poorest population groups in a country (World Bank data and national household surveys).

Table 13-4. Urbanization. This table presents the number of persons living in urban areas as a percentage of the total population. Average annual percentage growth rates are shown separately for the urban population and the total population. The urban population percentages are based on the number of persons living in areas defined as "urban" according to national definitions of this concept. Since national definitions differ, cross-country comparisons should be made with caution (World Bank data).

Table 13-5. Components of population change. This table presents three determinants of population change: total fertility rate, crude birth rate, and crude death rate. Crude birth rate is the number of births per 1,000 population in a given year. Crude death rate is the number of deaths per 1,000 population in a given year. Total fertility rate is the average number of children that would be born alive to a woman during her lifetime, if she were to bear children at each age in accordance with prevailing age-specific fertility rates (World Bank data).

Table 13-6. Survival prospects. This table shows four health-related indicators: life expectancy at birth, infant mortality rate, child mortality rate and maternal mortality rate.

Life expectancy at birth is the number of years a newborn infant would live if prevailing patterns of mortality at the time of its birth were to stay the same throughout its life. Infant mortality rate is the number of deaths of infants under one year of age per 1,000 live births in a given year. Child mortality rate is the number of deaths of children under five years of age per 1,000 live births in a given year. Maternal mortality rate is the annual number of deaths of women from pregnancy-related causes per 100,000 live births.

Table 13-7. HIV/AIDS estimates and data, end 2001. Data reported on this table give the estimated number of people living with HIV/AIDS. The data are broken down to adults aged 15 and above, and children below the age of 15. Adult rate is the total number of adults (men and women) living with HIV/AIDS divided by the corresponding mid-year population. Orphans are defined as children who lost their mother or both parents to AIDS when they were under the age of 15 (UNAIDS data).

Table 13-8. Immunization and ORT use. This is the percentage of children under one year of age immunized against tuberculosis, DPT, polio, and measles. It also gives the use rate of oral rehydration therapy (ORT) among children under five years of age. DPT refers to diphtheria, pertussis (whooping cough), and tetanus. ORT use is the percentage of all cases of diarrhea in children under five years of age treated with oral rehydration salts or an appropriate household solution (WHO data).

Table 13-9. Child malnutrition. Data reported on this table give the percentage of children and babies suffering from nutrition-related problems of low birthweight, underweight, wasting, and stunting. Figures are also given on the extent of breastfeeding among nursing mothers.

Low birthweight refers to babies born weighing less than 2,500 grams. Underweight refers to children under the age of five weighing two standard deviations below the median weight for age of the reference population. Wasting refers to children of ages 12 through 23 months weighing two standard deviations below the median weight for height of the reference population. Stunting refers to children of ages 24 through 59 months standing two standard deviations below the median height-for-age of the reference population (UNDP various years, WHO and World Bank data).

Table 13-10. Access to sanitation facilities. Table 13-10 shows the percentage of the population with access to sanitation facilities (WHO data). Urban areas with access to sanitation facilities are defined as urban populations served by connections to public sewers or household systems, such as pit privies, pour-flush latrines, septic tanks, communal toilets, and other such facilities. Rural populations with access were defined as those with adequate disposal, such as pit privies and pour-flush latrines. Application of these definitions may vary, and comparisons can therefore be misleading.

Table 13-11. Access to safe water. This table refers to the percentage of the population with reasonable access to safe water supply, which includes treated surface waters or untreated, but uncontaminated water, such as that from springs, sanitary wells, and protected boreholes. In an urban area, this may be a public fountain or standpost located not more than 200 meters away. In rural areas, it implies that members of the household do not have to spend a disproportionate part of the day fetching water. Data are presented separately for total, urban and rural population (WHO data).

Table 13-12. Health expenditure. This table shows total health expenditure as percentage of GDP and on a per capita basis—both in current $ and PPP terms. The ratio to GDP is also shown for public and private expenditure. *Total health expenditure* is the sum of public and private health expenditures. It covers the provision of health services (preventive and curative), family planning activities, nutrition activities, and emergency aid designated for health but does not include provision of water and sanitation. *Public health* *expenditure* consists of recurrent and capital spending from government (central and local) budgets, external borrowings and grants (including donations from international agencies and nongovernmental organizations, and social (or compulsory) health insurance funds. *Private health expenditure* includes direct household (out-of-pocket) spending, private insurance, charitable donations, and direct service payments by private corporations (WHO, IMF, and World Bank data).

Table 13-13. Health care. Indicators presented here are population per physician, population per hospital bed, the percentage of births attended by trained health personnel, and access to health services. The figure for physicians includes, in addition to the total number of registered practitioners in the country, medical assistants whose medical training is less than that of qualified physicians, but who nevertheless dispense similar medical services, including simple surgical operations. The definition of recognized medical practitioners differs among countries. Hospital beds include inpatient beds available in public, private, general, and specialized hospitals and in rehabilitation centers. In most cases acute and chronic care are included. Births attended refers to births attended by physicians, nurses, midwives, trained primary healthcare workers, or trained traditional birth attendants. Access to health services refers to the percentage of the population that can reach appropriate local health services by the local transport in no more than one hour (WHO and World Bank data).

Table 13-14. Illiteracy rate. This table shows the share of illiterate adults in total adult population aged 15 years and over. Literacy is defined as the ability to read and write. A person who can, with understanding, both read and write a short, simple statement about his everyday life is literate. Persons who can read, but cannot write, are included with illiterates. Figures are shown separately for males, females, and both genders combined (UNESCO data).

Tables 13-15. Primary school gross enrollment ratio. This is the total number of pupils enrolled at the primary level of education, regardless of age, expressed as a percentage of the population corresponding to the official school age of primary education in a given country. Data are given separately for males, females, and both genders combined. Figures shown may be more than 100 percent since total enrollment includes pupils above and pupils below the primary school age, as well as repeaters (UNESCO data).

Tables 13-16. Pupil progression. This table provides two education indicators. *Percentage of cohort reaching grade 5 of primary school* shows the percentage of children starting primary school, who eventually attain grade 4. The estimate is based on the Reconstructed Cohort Method, which uses data on enrollment and repeaters for two consecutive years. Progression to secondary school (general) is the number of new children in the first grade of secondary school (general) divided by the number of children enrolled in the final grade of primary school in the previous year (according to the country's duration of primary education (UNESCO and World Bank data).

Table 13-17. Net primary enrollment ratio. This is the ratio of the number of children of official school age enrolled in school to the number of children of official school age in the population (UNESCO data).

Table 13-18. Number of schoolteachers. Teachers in both public and private schools are covered in this table. Data refer to both full-time and part-time teachers, excluding other instructional personnel without teaching functions. Figures are shown here separately for primary and secondary schools. Percentage females means the number of female teachers expressed as a percentage of total teaching staff (UNESCO data).

Table 13-19. Pupil/teacher ratio. This ratio gives the average number of pupils per teacher. Figures are given separately for primary and secondary schools. As teaching staff includes both full-time and part-time teachers, comparability of this ratio between countries may be affected as the proportion of part-time teachers varies greatly from one country to another (UNESCO data).

Table 13-20. Secondary school gross enrollment ratio. This is the secondary school equivalent of the data presented in Table 13-15. It gives the total number of students enrolled at the secondary level of education, regardless of age, expressed as a percentage of the population corresponding to the official school age of secondary education. Data are presented separately for males, females, and both genders combined. Second level, general refers to education in secondary schools that provides general or specialized instruction based upon at least four years of previous instruction at the first or primary level, which do not specifically aim at preparing the pupils directly for a given trade or occupation. Such schools may be called high schools, middle schools, or lyceums and offer courses of study whose completion is a minimum condition for admission into universities. In some countries, some of these schools provide both academic and vocational training. These composite secondary schools are considered as equivalent to the academic type of secondary school and are thus classified as second level, general (UNESCO data).

Table 13-21. Public expenditure on education. This table presents the public expenditure on education (UNESCO) first as a percentage of total public expenditure (IMF/GFS) and then as a percentage of current GDP (Table 2-5).

Table 13-22. Economic opportunities of women. This table shows two indicators. Female/male ratio of participation in economic activity shows the number of female workers in relation to the number of male workers. Females as percentage of males in occupational group show the breakdown of the first indicator for occupational categories (UNDP data).

Table 13-23. Household and economic participation of women. This table presents indicators on gender issues in development. Households headed by women (World Bank data) refers to families in which a woman is acknowledged as the head by the other members. The occupational statistics are based on UN, *Statistical Yearbook.*

Figures

The following indicators have been used to derive the figures in this chapter:

Figure 13-1. Life expectancy (Table 13-6).

Figure 13-2. GDP per capita, based on PPP, 1997 (Table 13-2).

Figure 13-3. Urban population as a percentage of total population (Table 13-4).

Figure 13-4. Primary school gross enrollment ratio (Table 13-15).

Figure 13-5. Maternal mortality (Table 13-6).

Methodology used for regional aggregations and period averages in chapter 13

	Aggregations [a]					*Period averages* [b]	
Table	*(1)*	*(2)*	*(6)*	*(7)*	*(8)*	*(1)*	*(2)*
13-1							
Columns 1-8		x					
Columns 9-10			x				
13-2							
Columns 1, 3			x				
Columns 4, 5, 8				x			
Columns 2, 6-7					x		
13-3					x		
13-4							
Columns 1-3	x						
Columns 4-6							x
Columns 7-9			x				
Columns 10-12							x
13-5							
Columns 1-3			x				
Columns 4-6		x					
Columns 7-9		x					
13-6			x				
13-7	x						
13-8			x				
13-9			x				
13-10			x				
13-11			x				
13-12							
Columns 1-4			x				
Column 5					x		
13-13			x				
13-14			x				
13-15			x				
13-16			x				
13-17			x				
13-18							
Columns 1-3, 7-9					x		
Columns 4-6, 10-12			x				
13-19			x				
13-20			x				
13-21			x				
13-22			x				
13-23					x		

Note: Regional aggregations are shown in the rows for Sub-Saharan Africa, North Africa, and All Africa. Period averages are shown in the last three columns. This table shows only the methodologies used in this chapter.

a. Regional aggregations: (1) simple total; (2) simple total of the first indicator divided by the simple total of the second indicator (same country coverage); (3) simple total of the gap-filled indicator; (4) simple total of the gap-filled main indicator divided by the simple total of the gap-filled secondary indicator; (5) simple total of the first gap-filled main indicator less the simple total of the second gap-filled main indicator, all divided by the simple total of the secondary indicator; (6) weighted total (by population); (7) median; (8) no aggregation; (9) simple arithmetic mean.

b. Period averages: (1) arithmetic mean (using the same series as shown in the table i.e., ratio if the rest of the table is shown as ratio, level if the rest of the table is shown as level, growth rate if the rest is shown as growth rate); (2) least-squares growth rate (using main indicator); (3) least-squares growth rate (using main indicator in constant terms, with the rest of the table in current terms).

14

Environmental Indicators

This chapter was drawn entirely from the World Resources Institute and reflects tables published in their *World Resources 2001*. It includes data on natural resources—their use by sector and the trends in their use—protected resources and those in danger of extinction, commercial energy production and its components, globally threatened species and protection and management programs.

Until the early 1970s, environmental issues were mainly focused on problems of industrial countries and on such issues as water and air pollution, acid rain, and greenhouse gas emissions. Since the publication of the Club of Rome's *The Limit to Growth* in 1972, however, issues of natural resource depletion and degradation have received considerable attention in assessing environmental factors and their impacts on the development prospects of developing nations. At the national level, environmental concerns revolve around population expansion, desertification, deforestation, and the by-products of energy consumption.

Environmental destruction is not, however, confined by geographic borders. For instance, global warming, said to be caused by greenhouse gas emissions, has become a major global environmental concern. The issue of the greenhouse effect may be subject to controversy at the theoretical level and difficult to prove at the practical level. The fact that industrial wastes generated in one country cross-frontiers and cause environmental damage to other nations is, however, widely acknowledged. Common interests, therefore, compel the international community to jointly work toward a common goal of preserving the environment.

Increasing emphasis on the links between the environment and development, both at the national and international levels, is reflected in the growing number of scientific and analytical studies. Challenging the hegemony of the SNA national income accounting convention, numerous scholarly endeavors are under way to internalize environmental consequences in national income calculations. The argument is made that the SNA methodology overstates national income levels for two reasons. First, it does not account for both the direct and indirect costs of drawing down natural resources. Second, it counts expenditure on resources for environmental protection activities as income. The changes both in methodology and emphasis have created an urgent demand for physical data. The information in this chapter aims to meet this growing demand, notwithstanding the limitations in data coverage and reliability.

The rate of deforestation is of particular concern because the cost of deforestation goes far beyond the loses of forest products, such as timber and fuelwood. There are equally significant indirect costs, including soil erosion; the substitution of animal and agricultural residues for cooking, which would otherwise be used for fertilizer; and climate changes. Deforestation is caused by many factors, including increased demand for settlement area, cultivation, fuelwood, or a combination thereof. The information in this chapter provides an empirical framework for assessing policy alternatives in reversing the continuing depletion of natural resources.

Data on roundwood production and consumption are important in monitoring the causes of deforestation. In addition, since roundwood is a primary source of energy in developing nations, data on roundwood consumption is essential in analyzing air pollution. For instance, for 1985–87, Africa used close to 88 percent of its roundwood production for fuel and charcoal production, while approximately 12 percent of the roundwood production went to industrial uses. To put these figures in perspective, the corresponding figures for Europe are 16 and 84 percent.

Information on fresh water resources available and on the extent and the methods of their uses can provide a partial basis for analyzing Africa's agricultural performance, its potential hydroelectric power, and its populations' health conditions. Almost all Sub-Saharan African countries use a very small fraction of their internal renewable water resources. For instance, Ethiopia, a nation that has suffered from repeated droughts, uses only 2 percent of its water resources. The major problem rests in the uneven geographic distribution of water resources with respect to population density and the state of freshwater drawing technology. The quality of water is as important as the quantity of water available. Water-related disease accounts for 80 percent of all sicknesses and for 90 percent of the 15 million deaths in developing countries each year.

Data on energy production are shown because of related environmental consequences. Biomass fuel, comprising woodfuel and animal and agricultural residues, accounts for 40 to 90 percent of total energy used in Sub-Saharan Africa.

Data on protected areas and endangered species indicate the intentions of countries to safeguard the environment and protect the use of natural resources for future generations.

14-1. Forest resources, 1990-2000

	Forest area								
	Total forest			Natural forest			Plantation		
	Extent (000 ha)		Annual % change	Extent (000 ha)		Annual % change	Extent (000 ha)		Annual % change
	1990	2000	1990-2000	1990	2000	1990-2000	1990	2000	1990-2000
SUB-SAHARAN AFRICA	..	..	..	..	..	..	..	..	..
excluding South Africa	..	..	..	..	..	..	..	..	..
excl. S. Africa & Nigeria	..	..	..	..	..	..	..	..	..
Angola	70,998	69,756	-0.2	70,858	69,615	-0.2	140	141	0.1
Benin	3,349	2,650	-2.3	3,248	2,538	-2.5	101	112	1.0
Botswana	13,611	12,427	-0.9	13,610	12,426	-0.9	1	1	4.1
Burkina Faso	7,241	7,089	-0.2	7,220	7,023	-0.3	22	67	11.3
Burundi	241	94	-9.0	189	21	-21.9	52	73	3.4
Cameroon	26,076	23,858	-0.9	25,998	23,778	-0.9	78	80	0.3
Cape Verde	35	85	9.3	0	0	..	35	85	8.9
Central African Republic	23,207	22,907	-0.1	..	22,903	..	..	4	..
Chad	13,509	12,692	-0.6	13,498	12,678	-0.6	11	14	2.5
Comoros	12	8	-4.3	11	7	-5.3	1	2	3.9
Congo, Dem. Rep. of	140,531	135,207	-0.4	140,435	135,110	-0.4	96	97	0.1
Congo, Rep. of	22,235	22,060	-0.1	22,209	21,977	-0.1	26	83	11.5
Côte d'Ivoire	9,766	7,117	-3.1	9,629	6,933	-3.3	137	184	2.9
Djibouti	6	6	0.0	..	..	..	..	..	..
Equatorial Guinea	1,858	1,752	-0.6	1,826	..	..	..	..	..
Eritrea	1,639	1,585	-0.3	1,639	1,563	-0.5	0	22	..
Ethiopia	4,996	4,593	-0.8	4,800	4,377	-0.9	196	216	1.0
Gabon	21,927	21,826	0.0	..	21,790	..	..	36	..
Gambia, The	436	481	1.0	..	479	..	..	2	..
Ghana	7,535	6,335	-1.7	7,476	6,259	-1.8	59	76	2.5
Guinea	7,276	6,929	-0.5	7,264	6,904	-0.5	12	25	7.4
Guinea-Bissau	2,403	2,187	-0.9	..	2,186	..	..	2	..
Kenya	18,027	17,096	-0.5	17,816	16,865	-0.5	212	232	0.9
Lesotho	14	14	0.0	14	0	..	0	14	..
Liberia	4,241	3,481	-2.0	4,124	3,363	-2.0	118	119	0.1
Madagascar	12,901	11,727	-0.9	12,608	11,378	-1.0	294	350	1.7
Malawi	3,269	2,562	-2.4	3,173	2,450	-2.6	96	112	1.5
Mali	14,179	13,186	-0.7	14,172	13,172	-0.7	8	15	6.6
Mauritania	415	317	-2.7	415	293	-3.5	0	25	..
Mauritius	17	16	-0.6	4	3	-3.4	13	13	0.2
Mozambique	31,238	30,601	-0.2	31,195	30,551	-0.2	43	50	1.5
Namibia	8,774	8,040	-0.9	..	8,040	..	..	0	..
Niger	1,945	1,328	-3.7	1,898	1,256	-4.1	48	73	4.2
Nigeria	17,501	13,517	-2.6	17,038	12,824	-2.8	463	693	4.0
Rwanda	457	307	-3.9	..	68	-15.2	246	261	0.6
São Tomé and Principe	27	27	0.0	211	46	..	..	..	..
Senegal	6,655	6,205	-0.7	6,501	5,942	-0.9	154	263	5.3
Seychelles	30	30	0.0	..	25	..	5	..	..
Sierra Leone	1,416	1,055	-2.9	..	1,049	..	..	6	..
Somalia	8,284	7,515	-1.0	..	7,512	..	..	3	..
South Africa	8,997	8,917	-0.1	7,563	7,363	-0.3	1,434	1,554	0.8
Sudan	71,216	61,627	-1.4	70,876	60,987	-1.5	341	641	6.3
Swaziland	464	522	1.2	..	362	..	..	161	..
Tanzania	39,724	38,811	-0.2	..	38,676	..	..	135	..
Togo	719	510	-3.4	687	472	-3.8	32	38	1.7
Uganda	5,103	4,190	-2.0	5,073	4,147	-2.0	30	43	3.6
Zambia	39,755	31,246	-2.4	39,699	31,171	-2.4	56	75	2.9
Zimbabwe	22,239	19,040	-1.5	22,120	18,899	-1.6	119	141	1.7
NORTH AFRICA	..	..	..	..	..	..	..	..	..
Algeria	1,879	2,145	1.3	1,493	1,376	-0.2	424	718	5.3
Egypt	52	72	3.3	0	0	0.0	52	72	3.3
Libya	311	358	1.4	190	190	0.0	122	168	3.3
Morocco	3,037	3,025	0.0	3,573	3,514	-0.4	438	534	2.0
Tunisia	499	510	0.2	369	354	-3.5	63	202	11.7
ALL AFRICA	702,272	649,641	-0.7	590,720	640,910	0.8	5,771	8,026	3.9

Sources: Food and Agriculture Organization of the United Nations and the United Nations Economic Commission for Europe.

Notes: 0 = zero or less than half the unit of measure; negative numbers indicate reduction in forest area; .. = not available.

14-2. Forest ecosystems, 1990-99

	Land area (000 ha) 1998	Closed forests: Original Forest as a % of land area a/	Closed forests: Forests as a % of original forest: Current forests b/ 1996	Closed forests: Forests as a % of original forest: Frontier forests c/ 1996	Percent frontier forests c/ threatened 1996	Forest ecosystems (1990-99): Mangroves: Area (000 ha)	Mangroves: Percent protected	Tropical forests: Area (000 ha)	Tropical forests: Percent protected	Nontropical forests: Area (000 ha)	Nontropical forests: Percent protected	Sparse trees and parkland: Area (000 ha)	Sparse trees and parkland: Percent protected
SUB-SAHARAN AFRICA	..	..	..	..	..	..	..	..	..	..	..	..	..
excluding South Africa	..	..	..	..	..	..	..	..	..	..	..	..	..
excl. S. Africa & Nigeria	..	..	..	..	..	..	..	..	..	..	..	..	..
Angola	124,670	20	15	0	111	0	0	37,564	3	0	0	0	0
Benin	11,262	16	4	0	0	0	0	1,516	18	0	0	585	2
Botswana	58,173	2	100	0	0	0	0	12,123	2	0	0	0	0
Burkina Faso	27,400	0	0	0	0	0	0	0	0	0	0	5,667	16
Burundi	2,783	46	3	0	0	0	0	219	18	0	0	139	3
Cameroon	47,544	80	42	8	97	227	2	20,009	6	0	0	2,416	22
Cape Verde	403	..	..	..	..	..	..	..	..	..	..	..	..
Central African Republic	62,298	52	16	4	100	0	0	17,101	20	0	0	1,451	48
Chad	128,400	0	0	0	0	0	0	3,516	4	0	0	2,857	1
Comoros	223	50	0	0	0	..	..	..	..	..	..	..	..
Congo, Dem. Rep. of	234,486	83	60	16	70	22	0	135,071	7	0	0	172	40
Congo, Rep. of	34,200	100	68	29	65	19	76	24,321	4	0	0	0	0
Côte d'Ivoire	32,246	75	10	2	100	0	0	2,702	23	0	0	625	18
Djibouti	2,320	2	0	0	0	0	0	33	0	0	0	0	0
Equatorial Guinea	2,805	96	38	0	0	25	0	1,749	0	0	0	0	0
Eritrea	11,760	..	..	..	..	0	0	1	0	0	0	0	0
Ethiopia	110,430	25	17	0	0	0	0	11,937	19	0	0	4,804	21
Gabon	26,767	100	90	32	100	147	3	21,481	4	0	0	0	0
Gambia, The	1,130	39	62	0	0	51	5	188	5	0	0	244	2
Ghana	23,854	66	9	0	0	0	0	1,694	7	0	0	336	17
Guinea	24,586	76	5	0	0	316	0	3,073	1	0	0	2,723	1
Guinea-Bissau	3,612	100	34	0	0	317	0	1,141	0	0	0	550	0
Kenya	58,037	17	19	0	0	0	0	3,423	8	0	0	2,754	3
Lesotho	3,035	2	0	0	0	0	0	89	9	0	0	0	0
Liberia	11,137	100	44	0	0	0	0	3,149	3	0	0	1	0
Madagascar	58,704	93	13	0	0	310	0	6,940	6	0	0	0	0
Malawi	11,848	12	0	0	0	0	0	3,830	9	0	0	0	0
Mali	124,019	0	0	0	0	0	0	6,132	2	0	0	336	0
Mauritania	102,552	0	0	0	0	..	..	..	..	..	..	..	..
Mauritius	204	..	..	..	..	..	..	..	..	..	..	..	..
Mozambique	80,159	33	14	0	0	565	4	20,863	7	0	0	14,414	7
Namibia	82,429	0	95	0	0	0	0	3,436	11	0	0	0	0
Niger	126,700	0	0	0	0	0	0	27	16	0	0	0	0
Nigeria	92,377	45	11	1	100	1,145	0	11,634	7	0	0	10,588	4
Rwanda	2,634	36	16	0	0	0	0	291	77	0	0	162	2
São Tomé and Principe	96	33	71	0	0	0	0	30	0	0	0	0	0
Senegal	19,672	14	16	0	0	158	3	2,076	7	0	0	8,816	13
Seychelles	45	..	..	..	..	..	..	..	..	..	..	..	..
Sierra Leone	7,174	100	10	0	0	176	1	260	20	0	0	104	0
Somalia	63,766	4	0	0	0	0	0	11,800	1	0	0	1,530	1
South Africa	122,104	13	0	0	0	0	0	10,333	5	52	26	0	0
Sudan	250,581	1	0	0	0	0	0	12,288	12	0	0	5,870	9
Swaziland	1,736	22	0	0	0	0	0	286	3	0	0	0	0
Tanzania	94,509	22	9	0	0	323	0	14,356	16	0	0	583	3
Togo	5,679	33	7	0	0	0	0	224	3	0	0	91	9
Uganda	24,104	70	4	0	0	0	0	3,772	17	0	0	1,850	65
Zambia	75,261	7	70	0	0	0	0	21,989	32	0	0	39	14
Zimbabwe	39,076	7	67	0	0	0	0	15,397	12	0	0	0	0
NORTH AFRICA	..	..	..	..	..	..	..	..	..	..	..	..	..
Algeria	238,174	5	12	0	0	0	0	0	0	2,694	4	1	83
Egypt	100,145	1	0	0	0	0	0	134	0	4	0	0	0
Libya	175,954	1	0	0	0	0	0	0	0	53	0	0	0
Morocco	44,655	22	7	0	0	0	0	0	0	1,862	3	0	0
Tunisia	16,361	18	5	0	0	0	0	0	0	300	2	0	0
ALL AFRICA	3,004,279	23	34	8	77	3,801	1	448,197	9	8,249	2	69,710	11

Source: Food and Agriculture Organization of the United Nations.

Notes:
a. Original forest is that estimated to have covered the planet 8000 years ago given current climate conditions.
b. Includes frontier and nonfrontier forests.
c. Frontier forests are large, relatively undisturbed forest ecosystems.
0 = zero or less than half of the unit of measure; .. = not available.

14-3. Wood production and trade, 1986-98

	Average annual roundwood production						Average annual forest products production				Trade in forest products		
	Total roundwood		Wood fuel		Industrial roundwood		Wood-based panels		Paper and paperboard		Import	Export	
	Cubic meters (000) 1996-98	Percent change since 1986-88	Cubic meters (000) 1996-98	Percent change since 1986-88	Cubic meters (000) 1996-98	Percent change since 1986-88	Cubic meters (000) 1996-98	Percent change since 1986-88	Metric tons (000) 1996-98	Percent change since 1986-88	Value (million US$) 1996-98	Value (million US$) 1996-98	Percent of total exports 1998
SUB-SAHARAN AFRICA	..	..	..	..	..	..	..	..	..	..	..	..	..
excluding South Africa	..	..	..	..	..	..	..	..	..	..	..	..	..
excl. S. Africa & Nigeria	..	..	..	..	..	..	..	..	..	..	..	..	..
Angola	6,272	37	5,220	38	1,052	32	11	-55	0	0	5	1	0
Benin	5,839	32	5,507	32	332	36	0	0	0	0	2	2	0
Botswana	1,641	33	1,540	33	101	33	0	0	0	0	0	0	..
Burkina Faso	10,506	32	10,022	32	484	32	0	0	0	0	2	0	0
Burundi	1,669	37	1,487	27	182	287	0	0	0	0	3	0	0
Cameroon	15,191	29	11,869	32	3,323	20	124	42	2	-67	22	427	17
Cape Verde	..	..	..	..	..	..	..	..	..	..	3	1	..
Central African Republic	3,388	-1	2,660	-12	728	80	1	-67	0	0	0	27	13
Chad	1,871	37	1,147	36	724	38	0	0	0	0	2	0	0
Comoros	..	..	..	..	..	..	..	..	..	..	2	0	..
Congo, Dem. Rep. of	3,985	30	2,456	33	1,529	25	54	-5	0	0	1	147	8
Congo, Rep. of	48,372	41	44,814	42	3,557	28	21	-47	3	13	6	63	4
Côte d'Ivoire	12,983	21	9,970	33	3,013	-6	306	42	0	0	37	280	6
Djibouti	..	..	..	..	..	..	..	..	..	..	2	0	..
Equatorial Guinea	811	27	447	0	364	92	9	13	0	0	1	57	13
Eritrea	2,107	..	2,110	..	..	..	0	0	0	0	9	0	0
Ethiopia	48,990	..	46,522	..	2,468	..	13	..	9	..	16	0	0
Gabon	5,144	62	2,491	33	2,653	104	36	-80	0	0	4	288	9
Gambia, The	813	29	700	18	113	208	0	0	0	0	1	0	0
Ghana	21,931	61	20,678	64	1,253	23	136	112	0	0	16	145	9
Guinea	8,643	138	7,977	154	666	32	0	0	0	0	6	9	1
Guinea-Bissau	586	4	422	0	164	18	0	0	0	0	0	3	6
Kenya	28,813	33	26,879	34	1,934	19	52	26	129	41	30	1	0
Lesotho	1,556	27	1,556	27	0	0	0	0	0	0	0	0	0
Liberia	2,936	-19	2,700	0	236	-75	45	644	0	0	1	12	..
Madagascar	9,254	20	8,878	28	376	-53	5	20	4	-62	9	6	1
Malawi	9,449	25	8,950	24	499	45	18	213	0	0	4	2	0
Mali	6,284	24	5,890	24	394	21	0	0	0	0	5	1	0
Mauritania	15	29	9	29	6	29	0	0	0	0	2	0	0
Mauritius	15	-54	7	-68	8	-28	..	..	..	..	55	0	..
Mozambique	17,973	18	16,724	17	1,249	37	3	-64	0	-100	1	10	2
Namibia	..	..	..	..	..	..	..	..	..	..	0	0	0
Niger	6,260	39	5,873	39	386	39	0	0	0	0	2	0	0
Nigeria	95,993	18	87,001	18	8,992	14	38	-80	59	-28	80	30	0
Rwanda	3,020	-48	3,000	-46	20	-92	0	-100	0	0	2	0	0
São Tomé and Principe	9	13	..	..	..	..	..	..	..	..	0	0	..
Senegal	4,785	30	4,029	30	756	28	0	0	0	0	24	0	0
Seychelles	..	..	..	..	..	..	..	..	..	..	1	0	..
Sierra Leone	3,215	16	3,092	18	124	-12	0	0	0	0	2	1	1
Somalia	7,616	8	7,513	8	102	5	0	-100	0	0	0	0	..
South Africa	32,906	46	14,467	36	18,439	55	653	64	1988	19	482	1025	3
Sudan	9,289	23	7,207	23	2,082	23	2	0	3	-69	34	0	0
Swaziland	1,494	60	560	0	934	150	8	0	..	..	0	60	..
Tanzania	38,193	35	35,947	35	2,246	28	4	-67	25	32	6	5	0
Togo	1,156	41	872	33	284	73	0	0	0	0	3	2	0
Uganda	15,236	30	13,080	30	2,156	33	5	47	3	50	3	0	0
Zambia	8,051	31	7,219	29	832	58	18	-20	3	-2	5	1	0
Zimbabwe	8,192	8	6,260	2	1,932	34	68	148	74	-7	29	22	1
NORTH AFRICA	..	..	..	..	..	..	..	..	..	..	..	..	..
Algeria	2,676	34	2,239	27	437	79	50	0	62	-48	337	0	0
Egypt	2,776	24	2,647	24	129	23	81	27	263	70	949	8	0
Libya	650	2	536	0	114	11	0	0	6	0	46	0	..
Morocco	1,324	-7	539	-31	785	21	35	-75	108	2	336	60	1
Tunisia	2,770	23	2,559	20	211	65	104	16	97	58	203	17	0
ALL AFRICA	..	..	..	..	..	..	..	..	..	..	..	..	..

Source: Food and Agriculture Organization of the United Nations.

Notes: 0 = zero or less than half of the unit of measure; .. = not available.

14-4. Freshwater resources and withdrawals, 1977-2001

	Annual internal renewable water resources		Annual river flows		Annual withdrawals				Sectoral withdrawals (percent)		
	Total (cubic km)	Per capita 2001 (cubic meters)	From other countries (cubic km)	To other countries (cubic km)	Year of data	Total (cubic km)	Percentage of water resources	Per capita (cubic meters)	Domestic	Industrial	Agricultural
SUB-SAHARAN AFRICA	..	..	..	..	..	..	..	..	..	..	..
excluding South Africa	..	..	..	..	..	..	..	..	..	..	..
excl. S. Africa & Nigeria	..	..	..	..	..	..	..	..	..	..	..
Angola	184	14,288	..	..	1987	0.48	0.3	57	14	10	76
Benin	10	1,689	15.5	..	1994	0.15	1.4	28	23	10	67
Botswana	3	1,788	11.8	..	1992	0.11	3.8	81	32	20	48
Burkina Faso	13	1,466	..	..	1992	0.38	2.1	39	19	0	81
Burundi	4	538	..	..	1987	0.10	2.8	20	36	0	64
Cameroon	273	17,766	0.0	0.0	1987	0.40	0.1	38	46	19	35
Cape Verde	0	..	..	..	..	..	..	..	..	..	..
Central African Republic	141	39,001	..	..	1987	0.07	0.0	26	21	6	73
Chad	15	1,961	28.0	..	1990	0.19	1.3	33	16	2	82
Comoros	1	..	..	..	..	..	..	..	..	..	..
Congo, Dem. Rep. of	900	18,101	84.0	..	1994	0.36	0.0	8	61	16	23
Congo, Rep. of	222	75,387	610.0	..	1987	0.04	0.0	20	62	27	11
Côte d'Ivoire	77	5,187	1.0	..	1987	0.70	0.9	66	22	11	67
Djibouti	0	..	..	..	..	..	..	..	..	..	..
Equatorial Guinea	26	66,275	0.0	..	1987	0.01	0.0	30	81	13	6
Eritrea	3	727	6.0	..	..	..	..	..	..	..	..
Ethiopia	110	1,758	0.0	..	1987	2.20	2.0	50	11	3	86
Gabon	164	133,754	0.0	..	1987	0.06	0.0	70	72	22	6
Gambia, The	3	2,298	5.0	..	1990	0.03	1.0	33	7	2	91
Ghana	30	1,499	22.9	..	1970	0.30	1.0	35	35	13	52
Guinea	226	30,416	0.0	..	1987	0.74	0.3	141	10	3	87
Guinea-Bissau	16	13,189	11.0	..	1991	0.02	0.1	17	60	4	36
Kenya	20	672	10.0	..	1990	2.05	10.1	87	20	4	76
Lesotho	5	2,430	0.0	..	1987	0.05	1.0	31	22	22	56
Liberia	200	63,412	32.0	..	1987	0.13	0.1	54	27	13	60
Madagascar	337	21,139	0.0	..	1990	19.70	5.8	1694	1	0	99
Malawi	16	1,605	1.1	..	1994	0.94	5.4	98	10	3	86
Mali	60	5,341	40.0	..	1987	1.36	2.3	164	2	1	97
Mauritania	0	150	11.0	..	1990	16.30	4,075.0	8046	6	2	92
Mauritius	2	..	..	..	..	..	..	..	..	..	..
Mozambique	99	5,081	116.0	..	1992	0.61	0.6	40	9	2	89
Namibia	6	3,592	39.3	..	1990	0.25	4.0	185	29	3	68
Niger	4	326	29.0	..	1990	0.50	14.3	65	16	2	82
Nigeria	221	1,982	59.0	..	1990	4.00	1.8	46	31	15	54
Rwanda	5	815	..	..	1993	0.77	12.2	134	5	1	94
São Tomé and Principe	2	..	..	..	..	..	..	..	..	..	..
Senegal	26	2,784	13.0	..	1990	1.50	5.7	205	5	3	92
Seychelles	..	..	..	..	..	..	..	..	..	..	..
Sierra Leone	160	32,960	0.0	..	1987	0.37	0.2	98	7	4	89
Somalia	6	594	9.7	..	1987	0.81	13.5	115	3	0	97
South Africa	45	1,110	5.2	..	1990	13.30	29.7	391	17	11	72
Sudan	30	1,187	119.0	..	1995	17.80	50.9	669	5	1	94
Swaziland	3	..	..	..	..	..	..	..	..	..	..
Tanzania	82	2,387	9.0	..	1994	1.17	1.5	40	9	2	89
Togo	12	2,484	0.5	..	1987	0.09	0.8	28	62	13	25
Uganda	39	1,791	27.0	..	1970	0.20	0.5	20	32	8	60
Zambia	80	8,747	35.8	..	1994	1.71	2.1	214	16	7	77
Zimbabwe	14	1,208	5.9	..	1987	1.22	8.7	136	14	7	79
NORTH AFRICA	..	..	..	..	..	..	..	..	..	..	..
Algeria	14	442	0.4	0.4	1990	4.50	32.4	180	25	15	60
Egypt	2	34	56.0	0.0	1993	55.10	2,395.7	920	6	8	86
Libya	1	143	0.0	0.0	1995	3.89	486.3	783	9	4	87
Morocco	29	1,058	0.0	0.2	1991	11.05	36.8	454	5	3	92
Tunisia	4	367	0.6	0.0	1996	2.83	80.4	312	13	2	86
ALL AFRICA	..	..	..	..	..	..	..	..	..	..	..

Source: Food and Agriculture Organization of the United Nations.

Notes: 0 = zero or less than half of the unit of measure; .. = not available.

14-5. Marine and freshwater catches, aquaculture, balance of trade, and fish consumption

	Average annual marine catch a/ (000 metric tons) 1995-97	*% change since 1985-87*	*Average annual freshwater catch a/ (000 metric tons) 1995-97*	*% change since 1985-87*	*Average annual aquaculture production 1995-97 (metric tons): Marine fish*	*Diadromous fish*	*Fresh-water fish*	*Molluscs & Crustaceans*	*Average annual balance of trade b/ 1995-97 (million US$): Fish*	*Molluscs & crustaceans*	*Fish meal*	*Per capita annual food supply from fish and seafood: Total 2000 (kg)*
SUB-SAHARAN AFRICA	..	..	..	..	..	..	..	..	..	..	..	..
excluding South Africa	..	..	..	..	..	..	..	..	..	..	..	..
excl. S. Africa & Nigeria	..	..	..	..	..	..	..	..	..	..	..	..
Angola	73	15	6.0	-23	..	..	..	..	-7.9	3.1	..	12.5
Benin	9	2	25.0	-6	..	..	..	..	-5.3	1.8	..	7.1
Botswana	..	..	2.0	20	..	..	..	..	-4.9	-0.3	-0.1	6.3
Burkina Faso	..	..	8.0	5	..	..	25	..	-3.1	0.0	..	1.7
Burundi	..	..	14.8	26	..	..	23	..	-0.1	0.0	..	1.5
Cameroon	64	24	23.0	15	..	..	55	..	-22.3	1.8	-0.3	12.0
Cape Verde	..	..	..	..	..	..	..	..	..	..	..	22.3
Central African Republic	..	..	12.7	-2	..	..	370	..	..	..	..	4.2
Chad	..	..	91.7	49	..	..	..	..	..	0.0	..	6.7
Comoros									..	..	..	18.6
Congo, Dem. Rep. of	4	93	157.4	3	..	..	750	..	-26.6	7.0	..	6.2
Congo, Rep. of	19	-1	23.9	67	..	..	115	..	-50.4	..	..	19.9
Côte d'Ivoire	56	-28	11.3	-54	..	..	655	..	35.4	4.5	0.1	15.4
Djibouti	..	..	..	..	..	..	..	..	..	..	..	2.1
Equatorial Guinea	3	9	0.7	76	..	..	..	..	0.2	0.1	..	
Eritrea	3	..	0.0	..	..	..	..	..	0.1	0.0	..	1.8
Ethiopia	0	..	8.5	..	..	..	46	..	-0.1	..	..	0.3
Gabon	33	89	8.8	365	..	..	53	..	-8.9	6.5	..	50.3
Gambia, The	26	211	2.5	-7	..	..	3	..	0.9	2.6	..	22.3
Ghana	352	29	67.9	35	..	..	500	..	64.4	2.1	..	31.2
Guinea	77	154	3.2	26	..	..	3	..	8.4	4.7	0.0	12.5
Guinea-Bissau	5	94	0.3	188	..	..	..	..	5.7	2.9	..	3.4
Kenya	4	-20	172.1	53	..	71	506	0	33.2	5.1	-0.5	6.0
Lesotho	..	..	0.0	..	..	4	10	..	..	..	..	0.0
Liberia	4	-62	4.0	0	..	..	0	..	-1.9	-0.1	..	6.5
Madagascar	71	101	30.0	-21	..	0	4,153	2,146	13.4	76.8	0.4	7.5
Malawi	..	..	57.9	-22	..	..	227	2	0.0	0.1	-0.4	4.1
Mali	..	..	114.8	102	..	..	73	..	-0.6	..	..	8.2
Mauritania	52	14	5.8	-3	..	..	..	..	22.1	104.6	..	9.3
Mauritius	..	..	..	..	..	..	..	..	..	..	..	23.6
Mozambique	13	-47	8.0	129	..	..	14	..	-5.4	73.5	..	2.8
Namibia	282	1,466	1.3	51	..	..	5	43	..	..	..	11.5
Niger	..	..	4.7	112	..	..	20	..	-0.9	0.0	..	1.1
Nigeria	224	46	106.0	14	..	24	17,014	..	-208.4	19.6	..	8.8
Rwanda	..	..	3.1	134	..	..	47	..	..	..	..	0.9
São Tomé and Principe	..	..	..	..	..	..	..	..	..	..	..	14.0
Senegal	352	66	54.4	262	..	..	49	22	205.9	73.2	3.4	28.1
Seychelles	..	..	..	..	..	..	..	..	..	..	..	57.5
Sierra Leone	48	38	14.7	-9	..	..	28	..	13.1	9.9	..	12.0
Somalia	15	-9	0.3	-26	..	..	..	..	4.1	..	..	2.6
South Africa	497	-50	0.8	4	3	870	101	2,616	101.8	42.7	-37.1	6.4
Sudan	5	382	40.8	64	..	..	1,000	24	0.0	0.0	..	1.6
Swaziland	..	..	..	..	..	..	..	..	..	..	..	9.0
Tanzania	43	5	310.7	13	..	..	217	..	51.7	8.9	0.0	7.8
Togo	9	-24	5.0	43	..	..	21	..	-22.5	4.8	..	12.1
Uganda	..	..	207.3	11	..	..	205	..	38.5	..	..	8.7
Zambia	..	..	64.6	-2	..	..	4,550	1	-0.3	0.1	-0.2	7.0
Zimbabwe	..	..	16.9	-8	..	100	63	15	-14.7	-1.2	-0.9	2.1
NORTH AFRICA	..	..	..	..	..	..	..	..	..	..	..	..
Algeria	99	42	0.0	-100	37	18	256	27	-7.2	2.1	..	3.8
Egypt	82	99	215.1	67	19,799	..	50,569	..	-108.4	-0.5	..	12.8
Libya	34	108	0.0	0	..	..	100	..	21.4	-0.1	..	6.1
Morocco	663	39	1.7	30	972	155	767	229	269.6	437.0	2.2	8.4
Tunisia	70	-10	0.7	..	886	138	380	111	7.5	76.9	-0.1	9.9
ALL AFRICA	..	..	..	..	..	..	..	..	..	..	..	..

Source: Food and Agriculture Organization of the United Nations.

Notes: a. Aquaculture production is included in country totals.

b. Exports minus imports.

0 = zero or less than half of the unit of measure; .. = not available.

14-6. Energy production by source

	Energy production: From all sources (000 metric toe) (a) 1997	% change since 1987	Per capita (kg oil equivalent) 1997	From non-renewable energy sources: Solid fuels (000 metric toe) (a) 1997	Liquid fuels (000 metric toe) (a) 1997	Gaseous fuels (000 metric toe) (a) 1997	Nuclear fuels (000 metric toe) (a) 1997	Other sources (000 metric toe) (a) 1997	Total electricity generated (000 metric toe) (a) 1997	% change since 1987
SUB-SAHARAN AFRICA	..	..	..	..	..	..	..	..	..	..
excluding South Africa	..	..	..	..	..	..	..	..	..	..
excl. S. Africa & Nigeria	..	..	..	..	..	..	..	..	..	..
Angola	41,430	89	3,537	0	35,700	465	0	0	95	37
Benin	1,897	8	337	0	67	0	0	0	4	92
Botswana	..	..	..	..	..	..	..	..	..	..
Burkina Faso	..	..	..	..	..	..	..	..	..	..
Burundi	..	..	..	..	..	..	..	..	..	..
Cameroon	11,250	-7	808	0	6,357	0	0	0	269	25
Cape Verde	..	..	..	..	..	..	..	..	..	..
Central African Republic	..	..	..	..	..	..	..	..	..	..
Chad	..	..	..	..	..	..	..	..	..	..
Comoros	..	..	..	..	..	..	..	..	..	..
Congo, Dem. Rep. of	14,364	29	299	56	1,315	0	0	0	517	11
Congo, Rep. of	13,540	89	4,998	0	12,638	3	0	0	37	53
Côte d'Ivoire	4,908	31	349	0	803	0	0	0	276	55
Djibouti	..	..	..	..	..	..	..	..	..	..
Equatorial Guinea	..	..	..	..	..	..	..	..	..	..
Eritrea	..	..	..	..	..	..	..	..	..	..
Ethiopia	16,316	27	280	0	0	0	0	0	115	50
Gabon	19,786	129	17,403	0	18,794	68	0	0	87	13
Gambia, The	..	..	..	..	..	..	..	..	..	..
Ghana	5,843	48	313	0	361	0	0	0	529	26
Guinea	..	..	..	..	..	..	..	..	..	..
Guinea-Bissau	..	..	..	..	..	..	..	..	..	..
Kenya	11,651	20	410	0	0	0	0	0	364	60
Lesotho	..	..	..	..	..	..	..	..	..	..
Liberia	..	..	..	..	..	..	..	..	..	..
Madagascar	..	..	..	..	..	..	..	..	..	..
Malawi	..	..	..	..	..	..	..	..	..	..
Mali	..	..	..	..	..	..	..	..	..	..
Mauritania	..	..	..	..	..	..	..	..	..	..
Mauritius	..	..	..	..	..	..	..	..	..	..
Mozambique	6,994	-1	379	0	0	0	0	0	86	199
Namibia	..	..	..	..	..	..	..	..	..	..
Niger	..	..	..	..	..	..	..	..	..	..
Nigeria	191,034	55	1,839	86	117,249	4,429	0	0	1,305	35
Rwanda	..	..	..	..	..	..	..	..	..	..
São Tomé and Principe	..	..	..	..	..	..	..	..	..	..
Senegal	1,654	32	189	0	0	20	0	0	108	52
Seychelles	..	..	..	..	..	..	..	..	..	..
Sierra Leone	..	..	..	..	..	..	..	..	..	..
Somalia	..	..	..	..	..	..	..	..	..	..
South Africa (a)	142,139	27	3,667	124,678	401	1,543	3,296	0	17,866	38
Sudan	9,881	18	356	0	259	0	0	0	169	43
Swaziland	..	..	..	..	..	..	..	..	..	..
Tanzania	13,529	23	431	3	0	0	0	0	166	52
Togo	..	..	..	..	..	..	..	..	..	..
Uganda	..	..	..	..	..	..	..	..	..	..
Zambia	5,556	16	647	106	0	0	0	0	689	-8
Zimbabwe	8,152	9	727	2,712	0	0	0	0	628	15
NORTH AFRICA	..	..	..	..	..	..	..	..	..	..
Algeria	125,576	37	4,272	0	61,670	63,381	0	0	1,865	70
Egypt	57,997	9	896	0	44,640	11,070	0	0	4,958	52
Libya	78,942	43	15,151	0	73,067	5,750	0	0	1,563	17
Morocco	836	3	31	211	242	23	0	231	1,129	64
Tunisia	6,655	2	723	0	4,013	1,466	0	0	686	75
ALL AFRICA	..	..	..	..	..	..	..	..	..	..

Source: International Energy Agency (IEA)

Notes: a. Tons of oil equivalent. See technical notes for more information on toe.
0 = zero or less than half of the unit of measure; .. = not available or indeterminate.

14-7. Energy consumption by economic sector

	Energy Consumption by Economic Sector (% of total consumption)															
	Industry				Transportation											
	All industries		Iron and steel		Total		Air		Road		Agriculture		Commercial and public services		Residential	
	1987	1997	1987	1997	1987	1997	1987	1997	1987	1997	1987	1997	1987	1997	1987	1997
SUB-SAHARAN AFRICA	..	..	..	..	..	..	..	..	..	..	..	..	..	..	..	..
excluding South Africa	..	..	..	..	..	..	..	..	..	..	..	..	..	..	..	..
excl. S. Africa & Nigeria	..	..	..	..	..	..	..	..	..	..	..	..	..	..	..	..
Angola	..	11.6	..	0.0	..	12.3	..	6.1	..	6.2	..	..	..	0.0	..	75.6
Benin	..	17.1	..	0.0	..	12.6	..	2.4	..	10.1	..	..	..	0.0	..	70.3
Botswana	..	..	..	..	..	..	..	..	..	..	..	..	..	..	..	..
Burkina Faso	..	..	..	..	..	..	..	..	..	..	..	..	..	..	..	..
Burundi	..	..	..	..	..	..	..	..	..	..	..	..	..	..	..	..
Cameroon	..	17.0	..	0.0	..	11.6	..	1.0	..	10.6	..	..	..	0.5	..	69.7
Cape Verde	..	..	..	..	..	..	..	..	..	..	..	..	..	..	..	..
Central African Republic	..	..	..	..	..	..	..	..	..	..	..	..	..	..	..	..
Chad	..	..	..	..	..	..	..	..	..	..	..	..	..	..	..	..
Comoros	..	..	..	..	..	..	..	..	..	..	..	..	..	..	..	..
Congo, Dem. Rep. of	..	21.8	..	0.1	..	5.4	..	1.2	..	4.2	..	..	..	0.0	..	70.9
Congo, Rep. of	..	14.2	..	0.0	..	18.4	..	6.3	..	12.1	..	..	..	0.0	..	65.7
Côte d'Ivoire	..	7.0	..	0.0	..	16.0	..	3.1	..	12.5	..	1.2	..	12.1	..	62.0
Djibouti	..	..	..	..	..	..	..	..	..	..	..	..	..	..	..	..
Equatorial Guinea	..	..	..	..	..	..	..	..	..	..	..	..	..	..	..	..
Eritrea	..	..	..	..	..	..	..	..	..	..	..	..	..	..	..	..
Ethiopia	..	..	..	..	..	..	..	..	..	..	..	..	..	..	..	..
Gabon	..	23.2	..	0.0	..	19.6	..	6.7	..	11.0	..	..	..	0.9	..	51.5
Gambia, The	..	..	..	..	..	..	..	..	..	..	..	..	..	..	..	..
Ghana	16.0	14.1	0.0	0.0	11.0	13.2	1.4	1.2	9.0	11.4	0.7	1.0	0.5	0.7	69.8	69.9
Guinea	..	..	..	..	..	..	..	..	..	..	..	..	..	..	..	..
Guinea-Bissau	..	..	..	..	..	..	..	..	..	..	..	..	..	..	..	..
Kenya	..	11.4	..	0.0	..	12.6	..	4.5	..	7.7	..	6.5	..	0.7	..	67.7
Lesotho	..	..	..	..	..	..	..	..	..	..	..	..	..	..	..	..
Liberia	..	..	..	..	..	..	..	..	..	..	..	..	..	..	..	..
Madagascar	..	..	..	..	..	..	..	..	..	..	..	..	..	..	..	..
Malawi	..	..	..	..	..	..	..	..	..	..	..	..	..	..	..	..
Mali	..	..	..	..	..	..	..	..	..	..	..	..	..	..	..	..
Mauritania	..	..	..	..	..	..	..	..	..	..	..	..	..	..	..	..
Mauritius	..	..	..	..	..	..	..	..	..	..	..	..	..	..	..	..
Mozambique	..	7.8	..	0.0	..	1.5	..	0.4	..	1.1	..	0.6	..	3.4	..	85.0
Namibia	..	..	..	..	..	..	..	..	..	..	..	..	..	..	..	..
Niger	..	..	..	..	..	..	..	..	..	..	..	..	..	..	..	..
Nigeria	..	10.9	..	0.1	..	6.7	..	0.7	..	5.9	..	..	..	0.3	..	79.7
Rwanda	..	..	..	..	..	..	..	..	..	..	..	..	..	..	..	..
São Tomé and Principe	..	..	..	..	..	..	..	..	..	..	..	..	..	..	..	..
Senegal	..	17.0	..	0.0	..	24.0	..	10.0	..	12.6	..	2.3	..	0.6	..	55.3
Seychelles																
Sierra Leone	..	..	..	..	..	..	..	..	..	..	..	..	..	..	..	..
Somalia	..	..	..	..	..	..	..	..	..	..	..	..	..	..	..	..
South Africa	48.4	36.6	17.6	7.8	21.0	23.5	1.3	2.5	17.9	19.2	2.6	3.4	4.1	5.2	19.3	21.3
Sudan	..	7.4	..	0.0	..	17.8	..	1.0	..	16.9	..	0.1	..	2.0	..	70.9
Swaziland	..	..	..	..	..	..	..	..	..	..	..	..	..	..	..	..
Tanzania	..	11.7	..	0.0	..	1.7	..	0.3	..	1.4	..	3.2	..	0.3	..	79.1
Togo	..	..	..	..	..	..	..	..	..	..	..	..	..	..	..	..
Uganda	..	..	..	..	..	..	..	..	..	..	..	..	..	..	..	..
Zambia	..	23.6	..	0.1	..	5.1	..	0.9	..	4.2	..	0.7	..	2.0	..	66.6
Zimbabwe	..	12.2	..	2.0	..	10.0	..	1.5	..	8.3	..	9.2	..	3.6	..	61.8
NORTH AFRICA	..	..	..	..	..	..	..	..	..	..	..	..	..	..	..	..
Algeria	21.2	20.6	4.3	2.3	39.1	18.7	3.3	2.2	34.9	12.2	0.3	0.0	1.5	0.0	23.0	29.2
Egypt	49.6	47.8	0.7	0.5	19.8	20.6	2.9	3.6	16.9	16.9	0.5	0.6	0.0	0.0	23.2	22.9
Libya	32.5	33.8	0.0	0.0	36.8	38.0	6.1	3.4	30.7	34.6	0.0	0.0	0.0	0.0	7.2	9.5
Morocco	31.4	23.7	0.1	0.0	28.0	11.8	5.2	3.7	19.7	5.7	4.9	0.7	6.5	2.4	25.7	24.7
Tunisia	31.7	22.7	1.2	0.6	33.1	28.0	5.8	5.7	21.9	21.9	5.5	6.2	7.5	7.7	22.0	32.9
ALL AFRICA	..	..	..	..	..	..	..	..	..	..	..	..	..	..	..	..

Source: International Energy Agency (IEA)

Notes: 0 = zero or less than half of the unit of measure; .. = not available or indeterminate.

14-8. CO_2 emissions from industrial processes, 1998

	CO_2 emissions (000 metric tons)								Per capita carbon emissions (kilograms)
	Solid fuels 1998	Liquid fuels 1998	Gaseous fuels 1998	Gas flaring 1998	Cement manufact-uring 1998	Total 1990	Total 1998	Total contribution Since 1950	1996
SUB-SAHARAN AFRICA	..	..	..	..	..	..	..	..	..
excluding South Africa	..	..	..	..	..	..	..	..	..
excl. S. Africa & Nigeria	..	..	..	..	..	..	..	..	..
Angola	0	2,928	1,085	1,738	174	4,650	5,925	145,552	450
Benin	0	473	0	0	259	564	732	14,762	120
Botswana	2,510	1,268	4	9	0	2,415	3,778	51,505	13,035
Burkina Faso	0	989	0	0	20	1,008	1,009	14,682	90
Burundi	18	213	0	0	0	194	231	3,975	35
Cameroon	4	1,535	0	0	224	1,488	1,763	86,507	260
Cape Verde	0	121	0	0	0	84	121	..	..
Central African Republic	0	249	0	0	0	198	249	5,866	70
Chad	0	110	0	0	0	143	110	5,027	14
Comoros	0	70	0	0	0	66	70	..	..
Congo, Dem. Rep. of	865	1,510	0	0	60	4,096	2,434	142,475	49
Congo, Rep. of	0	1,645	7	167	0	2,037	1,820	40,161	1,884
Côte d'Ivoire	0	12,875	0	0	324	9,907	13,199	185,109	946
Djibouti	0	366	0	0	0	352	366	..	..
Equatorial Guinea	0	253	0	0	0	117	253	2,862	349
Eritrea		..	..	..	..	..	1,990	..	..
Ethiopia	0	1,579	0	0	411	2,964	2,820	66,509	59
Gabon	0	1,466	1,257	0	98	6,112	227	135,432	3,333
Gambia, The	0	227	0	0	0	191	4,357	4,481	188
Ghana	7	3,353	0	0	997	3,539	1,225	109,271	223
Guinea	0	1,096	0	0	130	1,011	231	32,445	150
Guinea-Bissau	0	231	0	0	0	209	9,131	4,477	208
Kenya	176	8,358	0	0	598	5,822	353	180,020	243
Lesotho	..	..	..	..	..	..	1,251	..	..
Liberia	0	348	0	0	5	465	747	33,189	148
Madagascar	48	1,143	0	0	60	945	485	37,860	84
Malawi	44	616	0	0	87	601	2,916	18,184	75
Mali	0	480	0	0	5	421	1,726	12,025	46
Mauritania	15	2,876	0	0	25	2,634	1,332	40,648	1,232
Mauritius	180	1,546	0	0	0	1,151	10	..	..
Mozambique	92	1,096	0	0	144	997	1,110	89,149	56
Namibia	0	0	0	0	10	..	78,455	..	..
Niger	462	630	0	0	18	1,048	2,231	20,863	119
Nigeria	172	25,410	11,325	40,203	1,345	88,665	511	1,944,327	822
Rwanda	0	502	0	2	7	528	7	9,167	90
São Tomé and Principe	0	77	0	0	0	66	77	..	..
Senegal	0	2,799	0	0	498	2,895	3,298	76,142	358
Seychelles	0	198	0	0	0	114	198	..	..
Sierra Leone	0	473	0	0	50	333	523	19,844	104
Somalia	0	0	0	0	0	18	0	13,747	2
South Africa (a)	275,232	61,094	2,656	0	4,734	291,108	343,716	8,541,575	7,678
Sudan	0	3,448	0	0	150	3,459	3,597	137,001	128
Swaziland	399	0	0	0	0	425	399	..	..
Tanzania	15	2,063	0	0	150	2,272	2,227	61,694	80
Togo	0	601	0	0	281	689	882	17,023	180
Uganda	0	1,176	0	0	105	846	1,281	32,837	53
Zambia	454	905	0	0	199	2,444	1,559	111,151	291
Zimbabwe	12,161	1,363	0	0	548	16,646	14,072	369,232	1,667
NORTH AFRICA	..	..	..	..	..	..	..	..	..
Algeria	1,726	33,027	54,641	13,332	3,887	80,443	106,613	1,725,913	3,283
Egypt	2,510	69,957	23,717	0	9,569	75,434	105,753	1,856,890	1,541
Libya	15	20,910	10,508	3,520	1,495	37,772	36,448	855,830	7,978
Morocco	9,277	19,100	70	0	3,588	23,486	32,035	558,859	1,055
Tunisia	209	14,374	5,236	259	2,287	13,260	22,364	318,035	1,782
ALL AFRICA	..	..	..	..	..	..	..	..	..

Sources: Carbon Dioxide Information Analysis Center.

Notes: Estimates are of the carbon dioxide emitted, 3.664 times the carbon it contains.
0 = zero or less than half the unit of measure, .. = not available.

14-9. Globally threatened species: mammals, birds, and higher plants, late 1990s

	Mammals				*Birds*				*Higher plants*			
	Total number of known species			*No. of species*	*Total number of known species*			*No. of species*	*Total number of known species*			*No. of species*
	All species	*Endemic species*	*Threatened species*	*per 10,000 km² a/*	*Breeding species*	*Endemic species*	*Threatened species*	*per 10,000 km² a/*	*All species b/*	*Endemic species*	*Threatened species*	*per 10,000 km² a/*
SUB-SAHARAN AFRICA	..	..	..	..	..	..	..	..	..	..	..	..
excluding South Africa	..	..	..	..	..	..	..	..	..	..	..	..
excl. S. Africa & Nigeria	..	..	..	..	..	..	..	..	..	..	..	..
Angola	276	7	17	56	765	12	13	156	5,185	1,260	20	1,055
Benin	188	0	9	85	307	0	1	138	2,201	..	2	990
Botswana	164	0	5	43	386	1	7	101	2,151	17	0	563
Burkina Faso	147	0	6	49	335	0	1	112	1,100	..	..	369
Burundi	107	0	5	76	451	0	6	322	2,500	..	0	1,783
Cameroon	409	14	32	114	690	8	14	193	8,260	156	67	2,310
Cape Verde	5	..	1	7	38	4	3	51	774	86	..	..
Central African Republic	209	2	11	53	537	1	2	137	3,602	100	1	921
Chad	134	1	14	27	370	0	3	75	1,600	..	5	322
Comoros	12	..	3	20	50	14	6	82	721	136	..	..
Congo, Dem. Rep. of	450	28	38	74	929	24	26	153	6,000	1,100	69	1,818
Congo, Rep. of	200	2	10	62	449	0	3	140	11,007	1,200	2	1,870
Côte d'Ivoire	230	0	16	73	535	2	12	170	3,660	62	42	1,163
Djibouti	61	..	3	46	126	1	3	96	826	6	..	..
Equatorial Guinea	184	1	12	131	273	3	4	194	3,250	66	6	2,312
Eritrea	112	0	6	50	319	0	3	140	..	..	..	..
Ethiopia	255	31	35	54	626	28	20	133	6,603	1,000	125	1,398
Gabon	190	3	12	64	466	1	4	157	6,651	..	78	2,248
Gambia, The	117	0	4	112	280	0	1	269	974	..	0	935
Ghana	222	1	13	78	529	0	10	186	3,725	43	22	1,308
Guinea	190	1	11	66	409	0	12	142	3,000	88	29	1,043
Guinea-Bissau	108	0	4	71	243	0	1	159	1,000	12	..	655
Kenya	359	23	43	94	847	9	24	221	6,506	265	130	1,703
Lesotho	33	0	2	23	58	0	5	40	1,591	2	0	1,103
Liberia	193	0	11	87	372	1	13	168	2,200	103	1	993
Madagascar	141	93	46	37	202	105	28	53	9,505	6,500	255	2,479
Malawi	195	0	7	86	521	0	9	230	3,765	49	46	1,665
Mali	137	0	13	28	397	0	6	81	1,741	11	5	355
Mauritania	61	1	14	13	273	0	3	59	1,100	..	2	239
Mauritius	4	..	4	7	27	8	10	46	878	325	..	..
Mozambique	179	2	13	42	498	0	14	117	5,692	219	57	1,340
Namibia	250	3	11	58	469	3	8	109	4,040	687	14	942
Niger	131	0	11	27	299	0	2	60	1,178	..	..	238
Nigeria	274	4	26	62	681	2	9	153	4,715	205	16	1,059
Rwanda	151	0	9	110	513	0	6	373	2,290	26	0	1,664
São Tomé and Principe	8	..	3	17	63	25	9	137	895	134	..	..
Senegal	192	0	13	72	384	0	6	144	2,086	26	15	780
Seychelles	6	..	2	17	38	11	9	106	1,230	182	..	..
Sierra Leone	147	0	9	77	466	1	12	243	2,090	74	8	1,091
Somalia	171	12	18	43	422	11	8	107	3,028	500	57	768
South Africa	255	35	33	52	596	8	16	122	23,420	..	1,875	4,797
Sudan	267	11	21	43	680	1	9	110	3,137	50	2	507
Swaziland	47	..	5	39	364	0	6	303	2,715	4	..	..
Tanzania	316	15	33	70	827	24	30	183	10,008	1,122	326	2,231
Togo	196	0	8	110	391	0	1	220	3,085	..	0	1,739
Uganda	338	6	18	118	830	3	10	290	5,406	..	8	1,891
Zambia	233	3	11	56	605	2	10	145	4,747	211	5	1,141
Zimbabwe	270	0	9	81	532	0	9	159	4,440	95	73	1,325
NORTH AFRICA	..	..	..	..	..	..	..	..	..	..	..	..
Algeria	92	2	15	15	192	1	8	32	3,164	250	125	520
Egypt	98	7	15	21	153	0	11	33	2,076	70	59	454
Libya	76	5	11	14	91	0	2	17	1,825	134	41	331
Morocco	105	4	18	30	210	0	11	60	3,675	625	182	1,049
Tunisia	78	1	11	31	173	0	6	69	2,196	..	6	873
ALL AFRICA	..	..	..	..	..	..	..	..	..	..	..	..

Source: World Conservation Monitoring Centre (WCMC).

Notes: a. Values are standardized using a species-area curve.

b. Flowering plants only.

.. = not available.

14-10. Globally threatened species: reptiles, amphibians, and fish, late 1990s

	Reptiles				*Amphibians*				*Freshwater fish*	
	Total number of known species			*No. of species per 10,000 km² a/*	*Total number of known species*			*No. of species per 10,000 km² a/*	*Total number of known species*	
	All species	*Endemic species*	*Threatened species*		*All species*	*Endemic species*	*Threatened species*		*All species*	*Threatened species b/*
SUB-SAHARAN AFRICA	..	..	..	..	..	..	..	..	..	..
excluding South Africa	..	..	..	..	..	..	..	..	..	..
excl. S. Africa & Nigeria	..	..	..	..	..	..	..	..	..	..
Angola	..	19	5	..	..	22	0	..	..	0
Benin	..	1	2	..	..	0	0	..	150	0
Botswana	157	2	0	41	38	0	0	10	92	0
Burkina Faso	..	3	1	..	..	0	0	..	..	0
Burundi	..	0	0	..	..	2	0	..	..	0
Cameroon	183	21	3	51	190	66	1	53	354	26
Cape Verde	12	9	3	16	0	0	0	0	..	1
Central African Republic	129	0	1	33	47	0	0	12	..	0
Chad	5	1	1	1	..	0	0	..	..	0
Comoros	22	7	2	36	2	0	0	3	15	1
Congo, Dem. Rep. of	377	35	3	62	80	53	0	13	..	1
Congo, Rep. of	..	1	2	..	..	1	0	..	..	0
Côte d'Ivoire	..	3	4	..	..	3	1	..	..	0
Djibouti	36	0	2	27	3	0	0	2	1	0
Equatorial Guinea	..	4	2	..	..	2	1	..	..	0
Eritrea	85	1	3	38	19	2	0	8	..	0
Ethiopia	188	9	1	40	62	24	0	13	150	0
Gabon	..	3	3	..	..	4	0	..	..	0
Gambia, The	47	1	1	45	30	0	0	29	79	0
Ghana	..	1	4	..	..	4	0	..	..	0
Guinea	..	3	3	..	..	3	1	..	..	0
Guinea-Bissau	..	2	3	..	..	1	0	..	..	0
Kenya	190	18	5	50	88	10	0	23	..	20
Lesotho	..	2	0	..	..	0	0	..	8	1
Liberia	62	2	3	28	38	4	1	17	..	0
Madagascar	363	259	17	95	179	155	2	47	121	13
Malawi	124	7	0	55	69	3	0	31	..	0
Mali	16	4	1	3	..	1	0	..	..	0
Mauritania	..	1	3	..	..	0	0	..	..	0
Mauritius	11	11	6	19	..	0	0	0	..	0
Mozambique	167	5	5	39	62	1	0	15	..	2
Namibia	250	25	3	58	51	2	1	12	114	3
Niger	..	0	1	..	..	0	0	..	..	0
Nigeria	135	7	4	30	109	1	0	24	260	0
Rwanda	..	1	0	..	..	1	0	..	..	0
São Tomé and Principe	16	7	2	35	9	8	0	20	..	0
Senegal	100	1	7	37	2	1	0	1	79	0
Seychelles	37	14	4	103	12	11	4	33	..	0
Sierra Leone	..	1	3	..	..	2	0	..	..	0
Somalia	193	49	2	49	27	3	0	7	..	3
South Africa	315	97	19	65	108	49	9	22	94	27
Sudan	..	8	3	..	..	1	0	..	..	0
Swaziland	102	0	0	85	40	0	0	33	40	0
Tanzania	289	61	4	64	133	49	0	30	..	19
Togo	..	1	3	..	..	3	0	..	..	0
Uganda	149	2	1	52	50	1	0	17	291	28
Zambia	145	3	0	35	65	1	0	16	106	0
Zimbabwe	153	2	0	46	120	3	0	36	112	0
NORTH AFRICA	..	..	..	..	..	..	..	..	..	..
Algeria	81	4	1	13	10	0	0	2	..	1
Egypt	83	0	6	18	6	0	0	1	70	0
Libya	56	1	3	10	3	0	0	1	..	0
Morocco	90	11	2	26	11	1	0	3	..	1
Tunisia	62	1	2	25	7	0	0	3	..	0
ALL AFRICA	..	..	..	..	..	..	..	..	..	..

Source: World Conservation Monitoring Centre (WCMC).

Notes: a. Values are standardized using a species-area curve.

b. Threatened species include a few marine species.

..= not available.

14-11. National protection of natural areas, 2001

	All protected areas (IUCN categories I-V)					Number of Marine Protected Areas (a) (IUCN Categories I-VI)		
			Percent	No. of Areas at least:				
		Area	of land	100,000	1 million			
	Number	(000 ha)	area	ha in Size	ha in Size	Total	Littoral	Marine
SUB-SAHARAN AFRICA	..	..	..	..	..	..	..	..
excluding South Africa	..	..	..	..	..	..	..	..
excl. S. Africa & Nigeria	..	..	..	..	..	..	..	..
Angola	13	8,181	6.6	9	2	4	4	3
Benin	2	778	6.9	2	0	..	..	..
Botswana	12	10,499	18.0	7	3	..	..	..
Burkina Faso	12	2,855	10.4	6	1	..	..	..
Burundi	13	146	5.3	0	0	1	1	1
Cameroon	18	2,098	4.4	8	0	2	1	2
Cape Verde	..	..	..	..	..	..	2	..
Central African Republic	13	5,110	8.2	11	2	..	..	..
Chad	9	11,494	9.0	9	2	..	..	..
Comoros	..	..	..	..	..	..	..	..
Congo, Dem. Rep. of	15	10,191	4.3	9	4	1	1	0
Congo, Rep. of	9	1,545	4.5	5	0	1	1	1
Côte d'Ivoire	11	1,986	6.2	4	1	3	3	1
Djibouti	..	..	..	..	..	..	2	..
Equatorial Guinea	0	0	0.0	0	0	4	4	0
Eritrea	3	501	4.3	2	0	..	..	..
Ethiopia	21	5,518	5.0	14	0	..	..	..
Gabon	5	723	2.7	1	0	4	4	1
Gambia, The	6	23	2.0	0	0	5	5	3
Ghana	10	1,104	4.6	3	0	..	..	..
Guinea	3	164	0.7	1	0	1	0	1
Guinea-Bissau	0	0	0.0	0	0	2	2	1
Kenya	50	3,507	6.0	7	1	14	13	10
Lesotho	1	7	0.2	0	0	..	..	..
Liberia	1	129	1.2	1	0	..	..	..
Madagascar	40	1,121	1.9	1	0	3	3	1
Malawi	9	1,059	8.9	3	0	..	..	..
Mali	13	4,532	3.7	8	2	..	..	..
Mauritania	9	1,746	1.7	3	1	5	5	2
Mauritius	..	..	..	..	..	15	14	..
Mozambique	11	4,779	6.0	7	1	7	7	6
Namibia	20	10,616	12.9	7	3	4	4	0
Niger	6	9,694	7.7	4	2	..	..	..
Nigeria	27	3,021	3.3	9	0	..	..	..
Rwanda	6	362	13.8	1	0	..	..	..
São Tomé and Principe	..	..	..	..	..	..	..	..
Senegal	12	2,181	11.1	3	0	7	6	6
Seychelles	..	..	..	..	..	16	15	..
Sierra Leone	2	82	1.1	0	0	..	..	..
Somalia	2	180	0.3	1	0	2	2	2
South Africa	390	6,619	5.4	6	1	20	17	8
Sudan	11	8,642	3.4	6	2	2	0	2
Swaziland	..	..	..	..	..	..	..	..
Tanzania	39	13,817	14.6	19	3	9	8	8
Togo	9	429	7.6	2	0	1	0	1
Uganda	37	1,913	7.9	6	0	..	..	..
Zambia	35	6,366	8.5	11	1	..	..	..
Zimbabwe	48	3,071	7.9	6	1	..	..	..
NORTH AFRICA	..	..	..	..	..	..	..	..
Algeria	18	5,891	2.5	2	2	8	6	3
Egypt	16	794	0.8	1	0	18	16	6
Libya	8	173	0.1	1	0	5	2	3
Morocco	12	317	0.7	1	0	10	9	3
Tunisia	7	45	0.3	0	0	7	5	4
ALL AFRICA	..	..	..	..	..	..	..	..

Source: World Conservation Monitoring Centre (WCMC).

Notes: a. Includes areas with substantial terrestrial components that reach the shore. An area can be both, marine and littoral (see technical notes).

0 = zero or less than half the unit of measure. .. = not available or indeterminate.

14-12. International protected areas, 2001

	International protection systems					
	Biosphere reserves		World heritage sites		Wetlands of international importance	
	Number	Area (000 ha)	Number	Area (000 ha)	Number	Area (000 ha)
SUB-SAHARAN AFRICA	..	..	..	..	..	..
excluding South Africa	..	..	..	..	..	..
excl. S. Africa & Nigeria	..	..	..	..	..	..
Angola	0	..	0	0	0	..
Benin	1	623	0	0	2	139
Botswana	0	..	0	0	1	6,864
Burkina Faso	1	186	0	0	3	299
Burundi	0	..	0	0	0	..
Cameroon	3	850	1	526	0	..
Cape Verde	..	..	..	..	..	..
Central African Republic	2	1,640	1	1,740	0	..
Chad	0	..	0	0	1	195
Comoros	..	..	..	..	..	..
Congo, Dem. Rep. of	3	283	5	6,855	2	866
Congo, Rep. of	2	246	0	0	1	439
Côte d'Ivoire	2	1,480	3	1,484	1	19
Djibouti	..	..	..	..	..	..
Equatorial Guinea	0	..	0	0	0	..
Eritrea	0	..	0	0	0	..
Ethiopia	0	..	1	22	0	..
Gabon	1	15	0	0	3	1,080
Gambia, The	0	..	0	0	1	20
Ghana	1	8	0	0	6	178
Guinea	2	133	1	13	6	225
Guinea-Bissau	1	110	0	0	1	39
Kenya	5	891	2	300	2	49
Lesotho	0	..	0	0	0	..
Liberia	0	..	0	0	0	..
Madagascar	1	140	1	152	2	53
Malawi	0	..	1	9	1	225
Mali	1	2,349	1	400	3	162
Mauritania	0	..	1	1,200	2	1,216
Mauritius	1	4	0	0	0	..
Mozambique	0	..	0	0	0	..
Namibia	0	..	0	0	4	630
Niger	1	25,128	2	7,957	1	220
Nigeria	1	0	0	0	0	..
Rwanda	1	15	0	0	0	..
São Tomé and Principe	..	..	..	..	..	..
Senegal	3	1,094	2	929	4	100
Seychelles	..	..	..	..	..	..
Sierra Leone	0	..	0	0	1	295
Somalia	0	..	0	0	0	..
South Africa	0	104	0	0	16	493
Sudan	2	1,901	0	0	0	..
Swaziland	0	..	0	0	0	..
Tanzania	2	2,338	4	6,860	0	..
Togo	0	..	0	0	2	194
Uganda	1	220	2	132	1	15
Zambia	0	..	1	7	2	333
Zimbabwe	0	..	2	733	0	..
NORTH AFRICA	..	..	..	..	..	..
Algeria	3	7,294	1	8,000	3	5
Egypt	2	2,456	0	0	2	106
Libya	0	..	0	0	0	..
Morocco	1	2,569	0	0	4	14
Tunisia	4	32	1	13	1	13
ALL AFRICA	. 48	52,109	33	37,332	79	14,486

Source: World Conservation Monitoring Centre (WCMC), United Nations Educational, Scientific, and Cultural Organization (UNESCO), and Ramsar Convention Bureau, Switzerland.

Notes: 0 = zero or less than half the unit of measure. .. = not available or indeterminate.

Technical notes

Tables

These notes are based on technical notes for each table as presented in WRI 2001. They have been edited and shortened for this volume. Readers are urged to consult the original source for details.

Table 14-1. Forest resources, 1990–2000. Total forest consists of all forest area for temperate countries and the sum of natural forest and plantation area categories.

FAO defines a *natural forest* as a forest composed primarily of indigenous (native) tree species. Natural forests include closed forest, where trees cover a high proportion of the ground and where grass does not form a continuous layer on the forest floor (e.g., broadleaved forests, coniferous forests, and bamboo forests), and open forest, which FAO defines as mixed forest/grasslands with at least 10 percent tree cover and a continuous grass layer on the forest floor. Natural forests encompass all stands except plantations and include stands that have been degraded to some degree by agriculture, fire, logging, and other factors.

Plantations refer to forest stands established artificially by afforestation and reforestation for industrial and nonindustrial usage. Reforestation does not include regeneration of old tree crops (through either natural regeneration or forest management), although some countries may report regeneration as reforestation. Many trees are also planted for nonindustrial uses, such as village wood lots. Reforestation data often exclude this component. The data presented here reflect plantation survival rates as estimated by FAO.

Average annual percent change is shown as a percentage of the exponential growth rate. If negative (in parentheses), these figures reflect net deforestation, which is defined as the clearing of forest lands for all forms of agricultural uses (shifting cultivation, permanent agriculture, and ranching) and for other land uses such as settlements, other infrastructure, and mining. In tropical countries, this entails clearing that reduces tree crown cover to less than 10 percent. Deforestation, as defined here, does not reflect changes within the forest stand or site, such as selective logging (unless the forest cover is permanently reduced to less than 10 percent).

Table 14-2. Forest ecosystems, 1990–99. *Closed forests* exclude some woodlands and wooded savanna.

Original forest as a percentage of land area refers to the estimate of the percentage of land that would have been covered by closed forest about 8,000 years ago, assuming current climatic conditions, before large-scale disturbance by human society began.

Current forests refer to estimated closed forest cover within the past 10 years or so (this varies by country). Only closed moist forests are given for Africa.

Frontier forests are large, relatively intact forest ecosystems. They represent undisturbed forest areas that are large enough to maintain all of their biodiversity, including viable populations of wide-ranging species associated with each forest type.

Percentage of frontier forests threatened refers to frontier forests where ongoing or planned human activities such as logging, mining, and other large-scale disturbances will eventually degrade the ecosystem through species decline or extinction, drastic changes in the forest's age structure, etc., and would result, if continued, in the violation of one of the above-mentioned criteria.

Tropical forests include all forests located between the Tropics of Cancer and Capricorn. All other forests are put into the *nontropical* category.

Percentage protected includes forest areas that fall within the protected areas in the world that are listed as the World Conservation Union's (IUCN) management categories I-V.

Table 14-3. Wood production and trade, 1986–98. *Total roundwood production* refers to all wood in the rough, whether destined for industrial or fuelwood uses.

Industrial roundwood production comprises all roundwood products other than fuelwood and charcoal.

Processed wood production includes sawnwood and panels.

Paper and paper board includes newsprint, printing and writing paper, and other paper and paperboard.

Trade in forest products is the balance of imports minus exports.

Table 14-4. Freshwater resources and withdrawals, 1977–2001. Annual internal renewable water resources refer to the average annual flow of rivers and groundwater generated from endogenous precipitation. Caution should be used when comparing different countries because these estimates are based on differing sources and dates. These annual averages also disguise large seasonal, inter-annual, and long-term variations. When data for annual river flows from and to other countries are not shown, the internal renewable water resources figure may include these flows. Per capita annual internal renewable water resource data were calculated using 2001 population estimates.

Annual withdrawals as a percentage of water resources refer to total water withdrawals, not counting evaporative losses from storage basins, as a percentage of internal renewable water resources and river flows from other countries. Water withdrawals also include water from desalination plants in countries where that source is a significant part of all water withdrawals.

Per capita annual withdrawals were calculated using national population data for the year of data shown for withdrawals.

Sectoral withdrawals are classified as domestic (drinking water, homes, commercial establishments, public services [for example, hospitals], and municipal use or provision); industry (including water withdrawn to cool thermoelectric plants); and agriculture (irrigation and livestock).

Table 14-5. Marine and freshwater catches, aquaculture, balance of trade, and fish consumption. *Marine and freshwater catch* data refer to marine and freshwater fish, killed, caught, trapped, collected, bred, or cultivated for commercial, industrial, and subsistence use (catches from recreational activities are included where available). Crustaceans and mollusks are included. Statistics for mariculture, aquaculture, and other kinds of fish farming are included in the country totals. Figures are the national totals averaged over a 3-year period; they include fish caught by a country's fleet anywhere in the world. Catches of freshwater species caught in low-salinity seas are included in the statistics of the appropriate marine area. Marine catch includes catches of diadromous (migratory between saltwater and freshwater) species.

Data are represented as nominal catches, which are the landings converted to a live-weight basis, that is, the weight when caught.

Landings for some countries are identical to catches.

Aquaculture is defined by FAO as "the farming of aquatic organisms, including fish, mollusks, crustaceans, and aquatic plants. Farming implies some form of intervention in the rearing process to enhance production, such as regular stocking, feeding, and protection from predators, etc. [It] also implies ownership of the stock being cultivated. . . ." Aquatic organisms that are exploitable by the public as a common property resource are included in the harvest of fisheries.

Marine fish include a variety of species groups such as mullets, sea basses, groupers, snappers, tunas, mackerels, etc. *Diadromus fish* include surgeons, river eels, salmons, trouts, etc. *Freshwater fish* include carps, perches, catfish, and tilapias, among others. Mollusks include freshwater molluscs, oysters, mussels, scallops, clams, abalones, and cephalopods. *Crustaceans* include, among others, freshwater crustaceans, crabs, lobsters, shrimps, and prawns. Data on whales and other marine mammals are excluded from this table.

Balance of trade is defined as exports minus imports. Figures are the national totals averaged over a 3-year period in millions of U.S. dollars. Imports are usually on a cost, insurance, and freight basis (c.i.f.) (i.e., insurance and freight costs added in). Exports are generally on a free-on-board basis (FOB) (i.e., not including insurance or freight costs). A surplus of imports over exports is shown in parentheses. Trade in *fish* includes fish that is fresh, frozen, chilled, salted, or smoked as well as fish products and preparations. Trade in *mollusks and crustaceans* includes mollusks and crustaceans that are fresh, chilled, smoked, derived products, etc. Trade in *fish meal* includes meals, solubles, etc.

Per capita annual food supply from fish and seafood is the quantity of both freshwater and marine fish, seafood, and derived products available for human consumption. Data on aquatic plants and whale meat are excluded from the totals. The amount of fish and seafood actually consumed may be lower than the figures provided, depending on how much is lost during storage, preparation, and cooking, and on how much is discarded. Data are presented in kilograms per capita. Years shown are 3-year averages.

Table 14-6. Energy production by source. All energy data in a common unit of 1,000 metric tons of oil equivalent (toe) to facilitate comparisons of energy sourcing, consumption, substitution, and conservation. A toe is defined as 41.868 gigajoules.

Energy production from all sources is the amount of energy from all sources produced by each country in the year specified. In addition to solid, liquid, and gaseous fuels and nuclear electricity, the total also includes hydropower, geothermal, solar, wind, tidal, wave, combustible renewables and waste, and indigenous heat production from heat pumps. *Per capita* shows the amount produced per person for that country.

Energy production from *solid fuels* is the energy produced from all types of primary coal (i.e., hard coal or lignite). Peat is also included in the category.

Energy production from *liquid fuels* is energy produced from liquid fuels such as crude oil or natural gas liquids.

Energy production from *gaseous fuels* is the amount of energy produced from natural gas.

Energy production from *nuclear fuels* shows the primary heat equivalent of the electricity produced by nuclear power plants. Heat-to-electricity conversion efficiency is assumed to be 33 percent.

Total electricity generated is the toe equivalent of the electrical energy produced by thermal, nuclear, geothermal, hydropower (excluding pumped storage production), and other power plants. Electricity generated is not a primary energy source and should not be mistakenly added to the energy production from primary sources presented in this table. These data were converted from gigawatt-hours to toe using a conversion rate of 1Gwh = 86 toe.

Table 14-7. Energy consumption by economic sector. *Industry* sector includes energy consumption by the iron and steel industry, chemical industry, nonferrous metals basic industries, nonmetallic mineral products (glass, ceramic, cement, etc.), transport equipment, machinery, mining and quarrying, food and tobacco, paper, pulp and print, wood and wood products, construction, textile and leather, and any nonspecified industry.

Iron and steel consumption is the energy consumed by the iron and steel industry as a percentage of the total energy consumed by the country.

Transportation sector includes all fuel for air, road, and water transport except fuel used for international marine bunkers and for ocean, coastal, and inland fishing. *Air* transportation includes both international and domestic civil aviation. *Road* transportation includes all human and cargo transport along national road networks.

Agriculture refers to all agricultural and forestry activity, including ocean, coastal, and inland fishing.

Commercial and public services refer to service sectors such as stores, repair shops, and restaurants.

Residential sector includes household energy use.

The IEA reports that it can be difficult to distinguish accurately between the agriculture, commercial, and public services sectors and that a figure for "total energy use" is more accurate than totals for the individual sectors.

Table 14-8. CO_2 emissions from industrial processes, 1998. This table includes data on industrial additions to the carbon dioxide flux from solid fuels, liquid fuels, gas fuels, gas flaring, and cement manufacture. The Carbon Dioxide Information Analysis Center (CDIAC) annually calculates emissions of CO_2 from the burning of fossil fuels and the manufacture of cement for most of the countries of the world. Estimates of total and per capita national emissions do not include bunker fuels used in international transport because of the difficulty of apportioning these fuels among countries benefiting from that transport. Emissions from bunker fuels are shown separately for the country where the fuel was delivered.

Emissions of CO_2 are often calculated and reported in terms of their content of elemental carbon. CDIAC reports them that way. For this table, CDIAC's figures were converted to the actual mass by 3.664 (the ratio of the mass of carbon to that of CO_2).

Solid, liquid, and gas fuels are primarily, but not exclusively, coals, petroleum products, and natural gas. Gas flaring is the practice of burning off gas released in the process of petroleum extraction, a practice that is declining. During cement manufacture, cement is calcined to produce calcium oxide. In the process, 0.498 metric ton of CO_2 is released for each metric ton of cement produced. Total emissions consist of the sum of the CO_2 produced during the consumption of solid, liquid, and gas fuels, and from gas flaring and the manufacture of cement.

Combustion of different fossil fuels releases CO_2 at different rates for the same level of energy production. Burning oil releases about 1.5 times the amount of CO_2 released from burning natural gas; burning coal releases about twice as much CO_2 as natural gas.

Table 14-9. Globally threatened species: mammals, birds, and higher plants, late 1990s. The total number of known species may include introductions in some instances. Data on mammals exclude cetaceans (whales and porpoises), except where otherwise indicated. Threatened bird species are listed for countries included within their breeding or wintering ranges. Higher plants refer to numbers of native vascular plant species, as totals are of full species only, rather than of species and subspecies. The number of endemic species refers to those species known to be found only within the countries listed. Figures are not necessarily comparable among countries because taxonomic concepts and the extent of knowledge vary (for the latter reason, country totals of species and endemics may be underestimates). In general, numbers of mammals and birds are fairly well known, while plants have not been as well inventoried.

The World Conservation Union classifies threatened and endangered species in six categories.

Endangered. "Taxa in danger of extinction and whose survival is unlikely if the causal factors continue operating."

Vulnerable. "Taxa believed likely to move into the endangered category in the near future if the causal factors continue operating."

Rare. "Taxa with world populations that are not at present endangered or vulnerable, but are at risk."

Indeterminate. "Taxa known to be endangered, vulnerable, or rare but where there is not enough information to say which of the three categories is appropriate."

Out of danger. "Taxa formerly included in one of the above categories, but which are now considered relatively secure because effective conservation measures have been taken or the previous threat to their survival has been removed."

Insufficiently known. "Taxa that are suspected but not definitely known to belong to any of the above categories."

The number of threatened species listed for all countries includes full species that are endangered, vulnerable, rare, indeterminate, and insufficiently known, but excludes introduced species or those known to be extinct.

Number of species per 10,000 square kilometers provides a relative estimate for comparing numbers of species among countries of differing size. Because the relationship between area and species number is nonlinear (that is, as the area sampled increases, the number of new species located decreases), a species-area curve has been used to standardize these species numbers.

Table 14-10. Globally threatened species: reptiles, amphibians, and fish, late 1990s. Threatened marine turtles and marine fish are excluded from country totals. Endangered fish species numbers do not include approximately 250 haplochromine and 2 tilapiine species of Lake Victoria cichlids, since the ranges of these species are undetermined.

The number of species per 10,000 square kilometers provides a relative estimate for comparing numbers of species among countries of differing size.

Table 14-11. National protection of natural areas, 2001. All protected areas combine natural areas in five World Conservation Union (formerly the International Union for Conservation of Nature and Natural Resources, IUCN), management categories (areas at least 1,000 hectares).

Totally protected areas are maintained in a natural state and are closed to extractive uses. They encompass the following three management categories: *category I,* scientific reserves and strict nature reserves; *category II*, national parks and provincial parks; and *category III*, natural monuments and natural landmarks.

Partially protected areas are areas that may be managed for specific uses, such as recreation or tourism, or areas that provide optimum conditions for certain species or communities of wildlife. Some extractive use within these areas is allowed. They encompass two management categories: *category IV*, managed nature reserves wildlife sanctuaries; and *category V*, protected landscapes and seascapes.

Protected areas between at least 100,000 hectares and 1 million hectares in size refer to all IUCN category I–V protected areas that fall within these two classifications.

IUCN has an additional management category, category VI, which includes areas "managed mainly for the sustainable use of natural ecosystems." These areas contain predominantly unmodified natural systems, managed to ensure long-term protection and maintenance of biological diversity, while also providing a sustainable flow of natural products and services to meet community needs.

Marine protected areas include protected areas in any of the IUCN categories (I–VI) that are marine or have a marine component. IUCN defines a "marine protected area" as "any area of intertidal or subtidal terrain, together with its overlying water and associated flora and fauna, historical and cultural features, which has been reserved by law or other effective means to protect part or all of the enclosed environment." Marine protected areas (MPAs) include areas that are fully marine as well as areas that have only a small area of intertidal land. Many of these MPAs have large terrestrial areas. The extent of the marine portion of most protected areas is rarely documented. The degree of protection varies from one country to another, and it may bear little relationship to the legal status of any site. The categories of *marine* and *littoral* are not exclusive. One protected area can be littoral and marine, therefore adding numbers under these two different categories may produce a higher number than the total for MPAs. Littoral is defined as any site that is known to incorporate at least some intertidal area. Such sites can also include marine and/or terrestrial elements. All sites with mangrove and saltmarsh communities are recorded as littoral. Marine is defined as any site that is known to incorporate at least some subtidal area permanently submerged under the ocean. Such sites can also include littoral and terrestrial elements. All sites with coral reefs and seagrasses are recorded as marine.

The values in this table do not include locally or provincially protected sites, or privately owned areas.

Table 14-12. International protected areas, 2001. Internationally protected areas usually include sites that are listed under national protection systems.

Biosphere reserves are representative of terrestrial and coastal environments that have been internationally recognized under the Man and the Biosphere Programme of UNESCO.

World heritage sites represent areas of "outstanding universal value" for their natural features, their cultural value, or for both natural and cultural values. The table includes only natural and mixed natural and cultural sites.

Any party to the Convention on Wetlands of International Importance, especially as it pertains to waterfowl habitat, agrees to respect the site's integrity and to establish wetland reserves can designate wetlands of international importance.

Marine and coastal protected areas refer to all protected areas greater than 1,000 hectares with littoral, coral, island, marine, or estuarine components. The area given is the whole protected area.

15

The Heavily Indebted Poor Countries (HIPC) Initiative

The Heavily Indebted Poor Countries (HIPC) debt initiative was proposed by the World Bank and IMF, and agreed to by governments around the world in the fall of 1996. It was the first comprehensive approach to reduce the external debt of the world's poorest, most heavily indebted countries, and represented an important step forward in placing debt relief within an overall framework of poverty reduction. While the initiative yielded significant early progress, multilateral organizations, bilateral creditors, HIPC governments, and civil society have been engaged in an intensive dialogue about the strengths and weaknesses of the program. A major review in 1999 has resulted in a significant enhancement of the original framework, and has produced a HIPC Initiative which is "deeper, broader, and faster."

Which countries qualify?

- The poorest countries, those that are only eligible for highly concessional assistance from the International Development Association (IDA)—the part of the World Bank that lends on highly concessional terms—and from the IMF's Poverty Reduction and Growth Facility (previously the Enhanced Structural Adjustment Facility).
- Those that also face an unsustainable debt situation even after the full application of traditional debt relief mechanisms (such as application of Naples terms under the Paris Club Agreement).

How the HIPC Initiative works

Under the enhanced framework, countries for which existing mechanisms would not achieve debt sustainability at the decision point will now receive assistance under the HIPC Initiative starting at the decision point.

In contrast to the original framework, where debt reduction was calculated on projections of debt stock at the completion point, relief under the new framework will be committed based on actual data at the decision point. This modification not only adds greater certainty to the calculations, but will in most cases increase the amount of relief actually provided, since most countries will reduce their NPV debt-to-export and debt-to-revenue ratios between the decision and completion points.

In short, under the enhanced framework, the benefits of export and central government revenue will accrue fully to the country, allowing for greater investment in poverty reduction strategies.

Creditors participation
All creditors participate in providing exceptional assistance beyond current mechanisms as required to reach debt sustainability. Creditors share the costs of HIPC assistance based on broad and equitable burden sharing, and provide relief that is proportional to their share of the debt after the full application of traditional forms of debt relief; these forms include Naples terms from Paris Club creditors, which provide a 67 percent NPV reduction on eligible debt.

HIPC Eligible Countries (42 countries)

Africa (34 countries)
Angola
Benin
Burkina Faso
Burundi
Cameroon
Central African Republic
Chad
Comoros
Congo, Rep. of
Congo, Dem. Rep.
Côte d'Ivoire
Ethiopia
The Gambia
Ghana
Guinea
Guinea-Bissau
Kenya
Liberia
Madagascar
Malawi
Mali
Mauritania
Mozambique
Niger
Rwanda
São Tomé and Príncipe
Senegal
Sierra Leone
Somalia
Sudan
Tanzania
Togo
Uganda
Zambia

Latin America (4 countries):
Bolivia
Guyana
Honduras
Nicaragua

Asia (3 countries)
Lao, People's Dem. Rep.
Myanmar
Vietnam

Middle East (1 country):
Yemen, Rep. of

15-1. HIPC DEBT INITIATIVE: Flow Chart

First Stage
Eligibility Requirements

- Paris Club provides flow rescheduling as per current Naples terms, i.e. rescheduling of debt service on eligible debt falling due during the three-year consolidation period (up to 67 percent reduction on eligible maturities on a net present value basis).
- Other bilateral and commercial creditors provide at least comparable treatment.
- Multilateral institutions continue to provide concessional financing in the framework of World Bank and IDMF-supported adjustement program.
- Country establishes three-year track record of good performance and develops together with civil society a Poverty Reduction Strategy Paper (PRSP); in early cases, an interim PRSP may be sufficient to reach the decision point.

Decision Point

EITHER EXIT

Paris Club stock-of- debt operation under Naples terms (67% net present value reduction of eligible debt) and comparable treatment by other bilateral and commercial creditors **is adequate** for the country to reach sustainability by the decision point.

Sustainability targets: 150 percent of NPV of debt-to exports ratio; or 250 percvent NPV of debt-to revenue eatio for country reaching qualifying threshold for the fiscal openess/window (30 percent exports-to-GDP ratio and 15 percent revenue-to-GDP ratio).

====> Exit

(Country is not eligible for HIPC assistance.)

OR QUALIFICATION FOR ASSISTANCE

Hypothetical Paris Club stock-of-debt operation under Naples terms and comparable treatment by other bilateral and commercial creditors **is not sufficient** for the country to reach sustainability by the decision point. Countries request additional support under the HIPC Initiative. IMF and World Bank determine eligibility.

====> Decision Point

The International community commits sufficient assistance to reach sustainability targets. This relief can be deleivred at the decision point and the remainder at the completeion point when the country has implemented pre-agreed key structural ans social reforms (triggers) provided the macroeconomic program remains on track.

Second Stage
The interim period

- Paris Club creditors provide interim relief (Cologne terms flows, i.e., 90% NPV of debt reduction on eligible debt) and other bilateral and commercial creditors provide at least comparable treatment.
- Some multilateral institutions, of which World Bank and IMF, provide interim assistance (e.g., debt service reduction).
- Donors support interim assistance.
- Country establishes a second track record by implementing the Bank/IMF-supported programs, including the one-year implemementation of a full PRSP (triggers). Length of this stage is determined by the speed by which country implement the triggers.
- Country also take steps to strengthen debt management.

"Floating" Completion Point

- Timing of completion point is tied to the implemention of policies determined at the decision point.
- All creditors provide the assistance determined at the decision point; interim debt relief provided between decision and completion points counts towards this assistance. Assistance is provided without further policy conditionality.

15-2. Grouping of African HIPC countries: status as of February 1, 2003

African Heavily Indebted Poor Countries (32)[1/]			
Benin	Congo, Rep. of *	Madagascar	Senegal
Burkina Faso	Cote d'Ivoire	Malawi	Sierra Leone*
Burundi *	Ethiopia	Mali	Somalia *
Cameroon	The Gambia	Mauritania	Sudan *
Central African Republic*	Ghana	Mozambique	Tanzania
Chad	Guinea	Niger	Togo
Comoros	Guinea-Bissau *	Rwanda*	Uganda
Congo, Dem. Rep.*	Liberia *	Sao Tome and Principe	Zambia

COUNTRIES THAT HAVE REACHED COMPLETION POINT (5)	HIPC RELIEF APPROVED AT DECISION POINT (17)		COUNTRIES TO BE CONSIDERED (10)	
Burkina Faso	Benin	Madagascar	Burundi	Togo
Mauritania	Cameroon	Malawi	Central African Rep	
Mozambique	Chad	Mali	Comoros	
Tanzania	Ethiopia	Niger	Congo, Dem. Rep.	
Uganda	The Gambia	Rwanda	Congo, Rep. of	
	Ghana	Sao Tome and Principe	Cote d'Ivoire	
	Guinea	Senegal	Liberia	
	Guinea-Bissau	Sierra Leone	Somalia	
		Zambia	Sudan	

Sources: HIPC documents; and IMF and World Bank staff estimates.

* Conflict-affected countries

1/ Comoros has been added to the group as a preliminary assessment of its debt situation showed a potential need for HIPC debt.

2/ Preliminary documents considered by the Boards

15-3. External debt service for individual African HIPCs that reached decision points, by country, 1998-2005

	(In million of US dollars, unless otherwise indicated)							
	1998	*1999*	*2000*	*2001*	*2002*	*2003*	*2004*	*2005*
Benin								
Debt service paid	64	66	55	36				
Debt service due after enhanced HIPC Initiative relief 1/					32	30	30	34
Debt service/exports (in percent)	16	17	16	10	9	7	7	7
Debt service/government revenue (in percent)	17	17	15	9	7	6	6	6
Debt service/GDP (in percent)	3	3	2	2	1	1	1	1
Burkina Faso								
Debt service paid	60	53	47	29				
Debt service due after enhanced HIPC Initiative relief 1/					21	16	17	18
Debt service/exports (in percent)	16	20	19	11	7	4	4	4
Debt service/government revenue (in percent)	18	15	15	9	5	4	3	3
Debt service/GDP (in percent)	2	2	2	1	1	1	1	1
Cameroon 2/ 3/								
Debt service paid	401	401	437	271				
Debt service due after enhanced HIPC Initiative relief 1/ 5/					267	261	284	313
Debt service/exports (in percent)	18	15	16	10	11	10	11	12
Debt service/government revenue (in percent)	28	24	26	15	16	16	16	16
Debt service/GDP (in percent)	4	4	5	3	3	3	3	3
Chad 3/								
Debt service paid	38	30	32	17				
Debt service due after enhanced HIPC Initiative relief 1/					28	21	23	23
Debt service/exports (in percent)	12	12	14	7	12	8	1	1
Debt service/government revenue (in percent)	29	23	29	14	18	12	7	6
Debt service/GDP (in percent)	2	2	2	1	1	1	1	1
Ethiopia 2/ 3/								
Debt service paid	101	127	112	197				
Debt service due after enhanced HIPC Initiative relief 1/					118	51	78	100
Debt service/exports (in percent)	10	14	11	21	12	5	9	10
Debt service/government revenue (in percent)	9	11	10	16	9	4	5	6
Debt service/GDP (in percent)	2	2	2	3	2	1	1	1
Gambia, The 3/ 4/								
Debt service paid	26	20	13	16				
Debt service due after enhanced HIPC Initiative relief 1/					16	9	10	11
Debt service/exports (in percent)	12	15	11	14	10	5	6	6
Debt service/government revenue (in percent)	12	25	16	26	23	12	12	13
Debt service/GDP (in percent)	6	5	3	4	4	2	2	2
Ghana 3/								
Debt service paid	560	521	560	215				
Debt service due after enhanced HIPC Initiative relief 1/					129	115	104	112
Debt service/exports (in percent)	22	21	23	9	5	4	3	3
Debt service/government revenue (in percent)	41	53	57	19	13	10	7	7
Debt service/GDP (in percent)	7	7	11	4	2	2	1	1
Guinea 3/								
Debt service paid	128	132	172	100				
Debt service due after enhanced HIPC Initiative relief 1/					80	73	60	50
Debt service/exports (in percent)	15	18	23	12	9	8	6	4
Debt service/government revenue (in percent)	34	35	51	29	20	17	12	9
Debt service/GDP (in percent)	4	4	6	3	3	2	2	1
Guinea-Bissau 3/								
Debt service paid	7	6	13	0				
Debt service due after enhanced HIPC Initiative relief 1/					6	8	5	4
Debt service/exports (in percent)	23	11	19	1	9	11	6	4
Debt service/government revenue (in percent)	63	15	31	1	15	17	9	7
Debt service/GDP (in percent)	3	3	6	0	2	3	2	1
Madagascar 3/ 6/								
Debt service paid	166	106	87	63				
Debt service due after enhanced HIPC Initiative relief 1/					68	62	70	79
Debt service/exports (in percent)	21	12	7	5	5	4	4	5
Debt service/government revenue (in percent)	42	25	19	12	11	9	9	9
Debt service/GDP (in percent)	4	3	2	1	1	1	1	1
Malawi 3/								
Debt service paid	90	65	98	69				
Debt service due after enhanced HIPC Initiative relief 1/					44	46	35	46
Debt service/exports (in percent)	16	13	22	15	9	9	7	8
Debt service/government revenue (in percent)	22	21	33	22	14	13	9	11
Debt service/GDP (in percent)	5	4	6	4	2	2	2	2

Sources: HIPC country document; and staff estimates.

Note: the footnotes for this table are in the technical notes at the end of this chapter.

(Table continues on the following page)

The HIPC Initiative

15-3. External debt service for individual African HIPCs that reached decision points, by country, 1998-2005 (continued)

(In million of US dollars, unless otherwise indicated)

	1998	1999	2000	2001	2002	2003	2004	2005
Mali								
Debt service paid	74	84	65	37				
Debt service due after enhanced HIPC Initiative relief 1/					45	69	73	81
Debt service/exports (in percent)	11	12	10	4	5	7	7	8
Debt service/government revenue (in percent)	17	20	17	8	8	12	11	12
Debt service/GDP (in percent)	3	3	3	1	2	2	2	2
Mauritania 7/								
Debt service paid	88	81	95	84				
Debt service due after enhanced HIPC Initiative relief 1/					39	35	35	37
Debt service/exports (in percent)	22	22	25	22	11	9	8	8
Debt service/government revenue (in percent)	35	30	39	40	17	15	14	14
Debt service/GDP (in percent)	10	8	10	8	4	3	3	3
Mozambique								
Debt service paid	104	60	18	27				
Debt service due after enhanced HIPC Initiative relief 1/					38	46	47	53
Debt service/exports (in percent)	41	9	2	3	4	4	2	2
Debt service/government revenue (in percent)	23	12	4	6	8	8	7	7
Debt service/GDP (in percent)	3	1	0	1	1	1	1	1
Niger 3/								
Debt service paid	17	19	18	21				
Debt service due after enhanced HIPC Initiative relief 1/					28	23	19	22
Debt service/exports (in percent)	5	6	6	8	10	8	6	7
Debt service/government revenue (in percent)	9	11	12	12	13	10	7	8
Debt service/GDP (in percent)	1	1	1	1	1	1	1	1
Rwanda 3/ 5/								
Debt service paid	14	47	37	19				
Debt service due after enhanced HIPC Initiative relief 1/					22	16	12	11
Debt service/exports (in percent)	13	40	25	12	15	10	7	6
Debt service/government revenue (in percent)	7	25	21	10	10	7	5	4
Debt service/GDP (in percent)	1	2	2	1	1	1	1	0
São Tomé and Príncipe 3/								
Debt service paid	7	2	5	2				
Debt service due after enhanced HIPC Initiative relief 1/					1	1	1	1
Debt service/exports (in percent)	55	12	33	12	5	5	3	4
Debt service/government revenue (in percent)	84	21	53	19	11	10	6	6
Debt service/GDP (in percent)	16	4	12	4	2	2	1	1
Senegal								
Debt service paid	222	146	143	113				
Debt service due after enhanced HIPC Initiative relief 1/					116	88	82	84
Debt service/exports (in percent)	14	10	11	8	8	6	5	5
Debt service/government revenue (in percent)	27	18	18	14	13	9	8	7
Debt service/GDP (in percent)	5	3	3	2	2	2	1	1
Sierra Leone								
Debt service paid	9	37	32	90				
Debt service due after enhanced HIPC Initiative relief 1/					21	26	41	11
Debt service/exports (in percent)	9	40	29	74	17	19	22	5
Debt service/government revenue (in percent)	18	77	44	89	18	20	28	7
Debt service/GDP (in percent)	1	5	5	12	3	3	4	1
Tanzania 2/ 8/								
Debt service paid	224	193	154	103				
Debt service due after enhanced HIPC Initiative relief 1/					131	125	142	146
Debt service/exports (in percent)	21	16	13	8	9	8	9	8
Debt service/government revenue (in percent)	29	20	15	10	12	9	10	10
Debt service/GDP (in percent)	3	2	2	1	1	1	1	1
Uganda 2/								
Debt service paid	110	98	90	71				
Debt service due after enhanced HIPC Initiative relief 1/					66	68	83	89
Debt service/exports (in percent)	15	12	14	11	10	9	10	10
Debt service/government revenue (in percent)	16	13	13	12	9	9	10	9
Debt service/GDP (in percent)	2	2	2	1	1	1	1	1
Zambia 3/								
Debt service paid	147	126	148	149				
Debt service due after enhanced HIPC Initiative relief 1/					158	161	221	202
Debt service/exports (in percent)	16	15	17	15	15	14	19	16
Debt service/government revenue (in percent)	24	23	24	21	23	21	27	23
Debt service/GDP (in percent)	5	4	5	4	4	4	5	4

Sources: HIPC country document; and staff estimates.

Note: the footnotes for this table are in the technical notes at the end of this chapter.

15-4. Committed debt relief and outlook for African HIPCs, status as of February 2003

(In million of US dollars) 1/

	Reduction in NPV Terms			Nominal Debt Service Relief			
	Original HIPC Initiative	Enhanced HIPC Initiative	Total	Original HIPC Initiative	Enhanced HIPC Initiative	Total	Date of Approval
	AFRICAN COUNTRIES THAT HAVE REACHED THEIR COMPLETION POINTS (5)						
TOTAL	**2,292**	**3,934**	**6,226**	**4,750**	**6,530**	**11,280**	
Burkina Faso	229	324	553	400	530	930	Apr-02
Mauritania	0	622	622	0	1,100	1,100	Jun-02
Mozambique	1,716	306	2,022	3,700	600	4,300	Sep-01
Tanzania	0	2,026	2,026	0	3,000	3,000	Nov-01
Uganda	347	656	1,003	650	1,300	1,950	May-00
	AFRICAN COUNTRIES THAT HAVE REACHED THEIR DECISION POINTS (17)						
TOTAL	**121**	**12,699**	**12,820**	**220**	**20,730**	**20,950**	
Benin	..	265	265	..	460	460	Jul-00
Cameroon	..	1,260	1,260	..	2,000	2,000	Oct-00
Chad	..	170	170	..	260	260	May-01
Ethiopia	..	1,275	1,275	..	1,930	1,930	Nov-01
The Gambia	..	67	67	..	90	90	Dec-00
Ghana	0	2,186	2,186	0	3,700	3,700	Feb-02
Guinea	..	545	545	..	800	800	Dec-00
Guinea-Bissau	..	416	416	..	790	790	Dec-00
Madagascar	..	814	814	..	1,500	1,500	Dec-00
Malawi	..	643	643	..	1,000	1,000	Dec-00
Mali	121	401	522	220	650	870	Sep-00
Niger	..	521	521	..	900	900	Dec-00
Rwanda	..	452	452	..	800	800	Dec-00
São Tomé and Príncipe	..	97	97	..	200	200	Dec-00
Senegal	..	488	488	..	850	850	Jun-00
Sierra Leone	0	600	600	0	950	950	Mar-02
Zambia	..	2,499	2,499	..	3,850	3,850	Dec-00
	AFRICAN COUNTRIES STILL TO BE CONSIDERED (10)						
Côte d'Ivoire 2/	345	2,519	2,519	800	3,950	3,950	Mar-02 3/
Burundi	..	..	..	..	..	..	
Central African Republ	..	..	..	..	..	..	
Comoros	..	..	..	..	..	..	
Congo, Dem. Rep. of	0	5,773	5,773	0	9,800	9,800	Jun-02 3/
Congo, Rep. of	..	..	..	..	..	..	
Liberia	..	..	..	..	..	..	
Somalia	..	..	..	..	..	..	
Sudan	..	..	..	..	..	..	
Togo	..	..	..	..	..	..	
Memorandum item:							
Debt relief committed under original and enhanced frameworks 4/	**2,758**	**16,633**	**19,391**	**5,770**	**27,260**	**33,030**	

Source: HIPC country documents; and World Bank and IMF staff estimates.

1/ In net present value (NPV) terms of the decision point year.

2/ It is suggested that debt relief under the original framework be overtaken by HIPC relief under the enhanced framework.

15-5. Social Expenditure for African HIPCs that Reached Decision Points1/

(In million of US dollar

	1999	2000	2001	2002	2003	2004	2005
Benin							
Social Expenditure	115	110	161	160	...	...	...
Social Expenditure/Government Revenue (in percent)	30	29	42	38	...	...	...
Social Expenditure/GDP (in percent)	5	5	7	6	...	...	...
Burkina Faso							
Social Expenditure	141	121	117	120	...	...	...
Social Expenditure/Government Revenue (in percent)	36	43	38	31	...	...	...
Social Expenditure/GDP (in percent)	5	6	5	5	...	...	...
Cameroon 2/							
Social Expenditure	264	287	336	307	328	361	389
Social Expenditure/Government Revenue (in percent)	16	17	19	18	20	20	20
Social Expenditure/GDP (in percent)	3	3	4	3	3	4	4
Chad 2/							
Social Expenditure	190	186	231	298	309	420	396
Social Expenditure/Government Revenue (in percent)	150	165	185	199	180	122	95
Social Expenditure/GDP (in percent)	12	13	14	16	14	11	10
Ethiopia 2/							
Social Expenditure	268	534	692	1,000	1,209	1,307	1,370
Social Expenditure/Government Revenue (in percent)	23	44	57	77	85	83	79
Social Expenditure/GDP (in percent)	4	8	11	17	18	18	18
The Gambia 2/							
Social Expenditure	24	22	22	23	28	32	34
Social Expenditure/Government Revenue (in percent)	30	27	37	34	38	40	41
Social Expenditure/GDP (in percent)	5	5	6	6	7	7	8
Ghana 2/							
Social Expenditure 3/	345	246	286	368	...	...	...
Social Expenditure/Government Revenue (in percent)	35	52	25	26	...	...	...
Social Expenditure/GDP (in percent)	4	7	5	6	...	...	...
Guinea 2/							
Social Expenditure	85	73	83	158	167	178	192
Social Expenditure/Government Revenue (in percent)	23	22	24	40	38	37	35
Social Expenditure/GDP (in percent)	2	2	3	5	5	5	5
Guinea-Bissau 2/							
Social Expenditure	70	89	82	92	100	107	114
Social Expenditure/Government Revenue (in percent)	182	215	207	221	216	210	205
Social Expenditure/GDP (in percent)	32	40	41	34	34	34	34
Madagascar 2/							
Social Expenditure	156	188	230	298	376	416	456
Social Expenditure/Government Revenue (in percent)	37	41	42	46	52	53	52
Social Expenditure/GDP (in percent)	4	5	5	6	7	7	7
Malawi 2/							
Social Expenditure	208	160	170	207	224	250	277
Social Expenditure/Government Revenue (in percent)	66	54	55	64	65	67	68
Social Expenditure/GDP (in percent)	12	9	10	11	11	12	12
Mali							
Social Expenditure	103	105	123	136	122	128	134
Social Expenditure/Government Revenue (in percent)	24	28	28	26	21	20	19
Social Expenditure/GDP (in percent)	4	4	5	5	4	4	4

(Table continues on the following page)

Sources: HIPC country documents; and staff estimates.

1/ Data refer to pro-poor expenditure comprising health, non-university education, basic sanitation, and certain rural development and urban development programs.

2/ The figures for 2000 largely reflect social expenditure before HIPC relief because these countries reached their decision points in late 2000 or in 2001. Thus, the full impact of HIPC relief for them will not be felt until 2001 and thereafter.

15-5. Social Expenditure for African HIPCs that Reached Decision Points1/

(In million of US dollars)

	1999	2000	2001	2002	2003	2004	2005
Mauritania							
Social Expenditure	85	95	84	117	118	127	141
Social Expenditure/Government Revenue (in percent)	35	38	40	30	37	38	41
Social Expenditure/GDP (in percent)	9	10	9	11	11	11	11
Mozambique							
Social Expenditure	259	331	342	342	357	405	451
Social Expenditure/Government Revenue (in percent)	53	70	74	68	65	60	59
Social Expenditure/GDP (in percent)	6	9	9	9	9	9	9
Niger 2/							
Social Expenditure	104	95	122	150	159	164	170
Social Expenditure/Government Revenue (in percent)	58	61	68	70	69	65	61
Social Expenditure/GDP (in percent)	5	5	6	7	7	7	7
Rwanda 2/							
Social Expenditure	75	73	91	112	126	140	157
Social Expenditure/Government Revenue (in percent)	40	41	47	52	52	53	56
Social Expenditure/GDP (in percent)	4	4	5	6	7	7	7
São Tomé and Príncipe 2/							
Social Expenditure	8	8	9	10	11	13	12
Social Expenditure/Government Revenue (in percent)	88	79	83	82	83	89	73
Social Expenditure/GDP (in percent)	17	17	18	18	19	20	16
Senegal							
Social Expenditure	254	213	206	220	266	281	293
Social Expenditure/Government Revenue (in percent)	31	27	25	24	27	27	26
Social Expenditure/GDP (in percent)	5	5	4	5	5	5	5
Sierre Leone 2/							
Social Expenditure	15	15	25	46	...	...	...
Social Expenditure/Government Revenue (in percent)	32	21	25	40	...	...	...
Social Expenditure/GDP (in percent)	2	2	4	7	...	...	...
Tanzania							
Social Expenditure 4/	289	352	622	837	1,025	1,090	...
Social Expenditure/Government Revenue (in percent)	30	34	58	75	88	88	...
Social Expenditure/GDP (in percent)	3	4	7	9	11	11	...
Uganda							
Social Expenditure	306	401	438	559	614	682	756
Social Expenditure/Government Revenue (in percent)	40	60	71	78	79	80	81
Social Expenditure/GDP (in percent)	5	7	8	9	10	10	11
Zambia 2/							
Social Expenditure	166	149	181	264	285	314	347
Social Expenditure/Government Revenue (in percent)	30	24	26	38	38	39	40
Social Expenditure/GDP (in percent)	5	5	5	7	7	7	7

Sources: HIPC country documents; and staff estimates.

Note: The coverage of social expenditure varies across countries. All social data includes spending on health and education.

In 11 countries, social spending refers exclusively to public expenditure on health and education. In addition, social spending includes new programs to be financed partly with HIPC assistance in Benin, basic sanitary infrastructure in Bolivia, rural development and water supply in Burkina Faso, social affairs in Chad, poverty-related activities such as de-mining and rural development in Gu funding for the Social Impact Amelioration Program and Basic Needs Trust Fund in Guyana, social safety net and rural development programs in Honduras, poverty reduction programs in Mauritania, other spending including promotion of women in Senegal, water supply in both Tanzania and Uganda, and social safety nets, water and sanitation and disaster relief in Zambia.

1/ Data refer to pro-poor expenditure comprising health, non-university education, basic sanitation, and certain rural development and urban development programs.

2/ The figures for 2000 largely reflect social expenditure before HIPC relief because these countries reached their decision points in late 2000 c in 2001. Thus, the full impact of HIPC relief for them will not be felt until 2001 and thereafter.

Figure 15-1. Nominal Debt Service Relief for African Decision Point Countries*

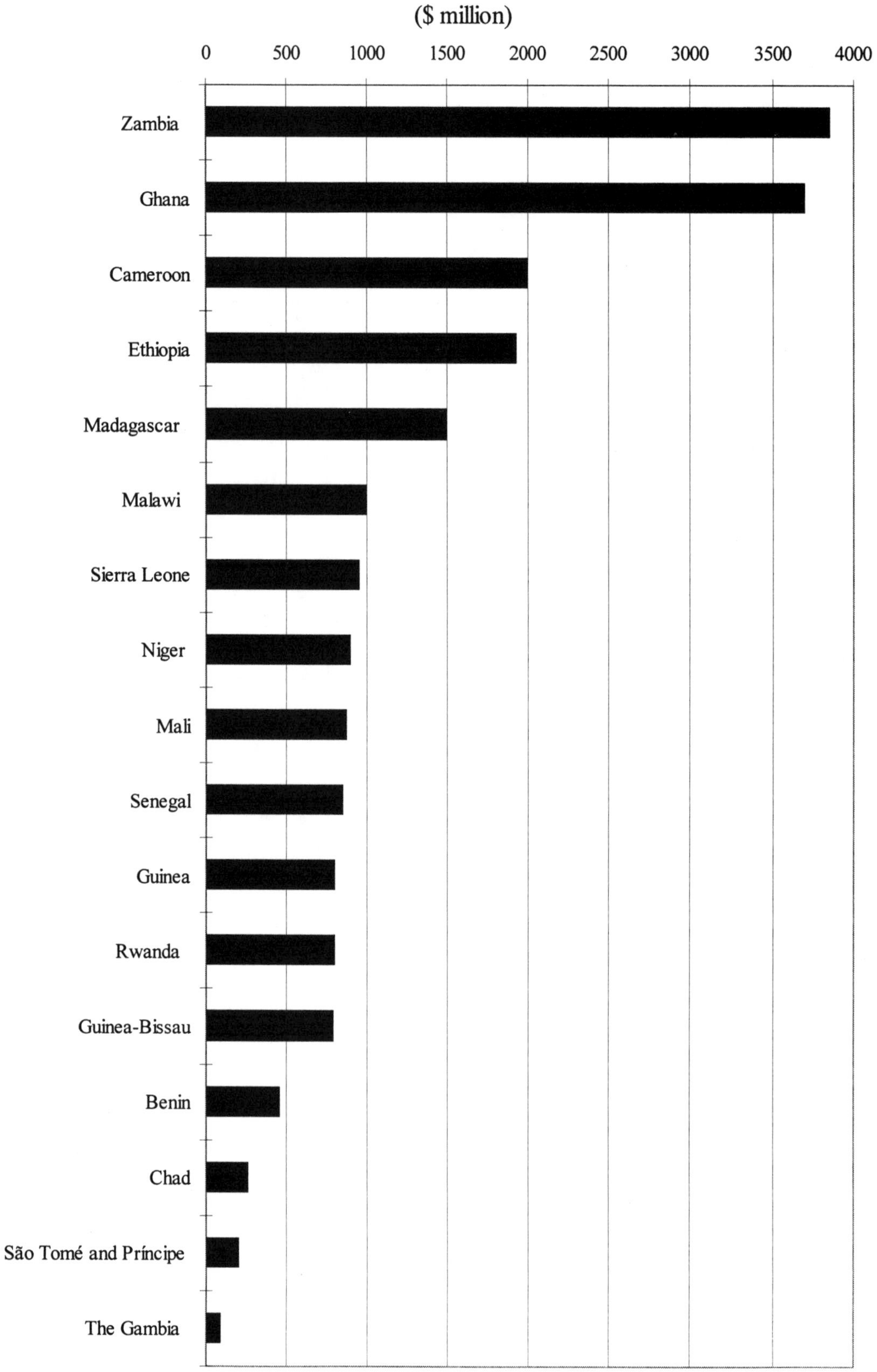

Technical notes

Tables

Table 15.3 Debt Service for Individual African HIPCs that Reached Decision Points, by Country, 1998-2005

1/ Debt service due after the full use of traditional debt relief mechanism and assistance under the enhanced HIPC initiative. For Mozambique, these figures are also after additional bilateral assistance beyond HIPC.
2/ On fiscal year basis, i.e., 2000 column shows FY 1999/2000.
3/ The debt service figures for 2000 largely reflect pre-HIPC relief debt service because these countries did not reach their decision point until late in 2000 or later. Thus, the full impact of relief for did not take effect until 2001 and thereafter.
4/ Debt service is higher than anticipated at the decision point due to higher new borrowing than previously projected.
5/ Debt service is lower than anticipated at the decision point due to lower financing needs than previously projected.
6/ The relief for Madagascar is indicative and subject to change. The Madagasy authorities and Paris Club creditors would need to revisit the outstanding bilateral debt numbers. Also, minor adjustments need to be incorporated in the case of three multilateral creditors. Consequently, the IMF Board approved US$790 million in HIPC relief with the the understanding that Madagascar's exact level of HIPC assistance will be determined once such revisions are made.
7/ Debt service figures differ from those in the decision point document due to exchange rate changes.
8/ Debt service reflects some payments to commercial creditors and payments on moratorium interest not reflected in the completion point document.

Note: Debt service figures for 1998 and 1999 reflect debt relief already provided to Mozambique, and Uganda under the original framework.

The source for this table is HIPC country documents, and World Bank and IMF staff estimates.

16

Household Welfare

While macroeconomic data about many African countries are published often, more disaggregated data are not frequently reported in statistical abstracts such as the *African Development Indicators*. This chapter addresses that issue by presenting statistics on poverty and some of its correlates at a sub-national level. These statistics are based upon household surveys rather than ministry-level data. The presentation of indicators is linked to the Millennium Development Goals to help in understanding the statistics. The tables that follow contain data for fourteen countries of Sub-Saharan Africa: Burundi, Burkina Faso, Côte d'Ivoire, Cameroon, Ethiopia, The Gambia, Ghana, Kenya, Madagascar, Mozambique, Malawi, São Tomé and Principe, Uganda, and Zambia.

This chapter is similar to one published in the 2000 Africa Development Indicators, but the underlying set of definitions and variables has changed. In addition, the presentation of this new set of indicators has been organized along the Millennium Development Goals. The definitions used in this presentation (see below) reflect the work of an ongoing project in the Africa Region's Operational Quality and Knowledge Services Unit: the Standardized Files and Standardized Indicators. The project, which builds upon earlier work, takes national statistical agencies' raw data files, as stored in the Africa Household Survey Databank, and performs consistency checks prior to harmonizing the data, using a common dictionary. This process may include the computation of expenditure aggregates when they are not available to the unit. For more information on this, please see the technical notes at the end of the chapter.

The definitions presented herein may diverge from those used in other publications, whether by the World Bank or a country's National Statistical Organization. This means that certain statistics may differ from those previously published. An example of this is enrollment rates; if the country bases them upon one definition of the age at which children should attend primary school, while this report uses another, it is unlikely that the two statistics will be identical. Neither statistic is wrong; they are just different metrics and cannot be necessarily compared.

Selected definitions

Household National definitions are used, although most definitions do not differ markedly from those set forth by the United Nations. Additional information is available in the technical notes.

Expenditure quintiles are derived by ranking weighted sample individuals according to annual deflated per capita expenditure. When regional deflators are available, they are used, otherwise nominal expenditure is used. Individuals are used as the basis for estimating quintiles. Quintiles are constructed such that the first quintile represents the poorest 20 percent of the population, the second quintile the next poorest 20 percent (less poor), and so on; the fifth quintile represents the richest 20 percent of the population. The definition of expenditure varies from survey to survey. Please consult the technical notes for each survey for more details. The following surveys' data are presented with deflated expenditure quintiles: Côte d'Ivoire, Cameroon, Ghana, Kenya, Madagascar, Mozambique, and Malawi.

Demographic indicators

Number of households in each quintile varies due to differences in household size, although the total number of individuals in each quintile is the same.

Total population. Sampled population weighted by the cluster weights to give an estimate of the actual population size.

Education and literacy indicators (drawn from UNESCO definitions)

Net primary enrollment rate. The total number of children of primary school age enrolled in primary school as a proportion of the total number of children of primary school age. The age range varies by country. Please consult the technical notes for details.

Net secondary enrollment rate. The total number of children of secondary school age enrolled in secondary school as a proportion of the total number of children of secondary school age. The age range varies by country. Please consult the technical notes for details.

Literacy (adult). The percentage of people aged 15 and above who can read and write a short, simple statement on their everyday life. The survey may have tested individuals to verify this, or may have used other methods. Please consult the technical notes for details.

Head of household indicators

Polygamous male-headed. Male-headed household with more than one spouse. However, differences exist in the way in polygamous households are defined. Please consult the technical notes for details on each country's definition of a household.

De facto female-headed. Defined as either a (1) household without a resident male head or where the husband is not present and the wife is the head by default and the main decision-maker in his absence; or (2) household where the resident male head has lost most of his functions as the economic provider due to infirmity, inability to work, etc.

De jure female-headed. Single female-headed household where the head has never been married, or is divorced or separated or widowed.

Household expenditure indicators

These indicators provide information on per capita expenditure in local currency (including the value of own-produced food consumed in the household and the imputed rent of homeowners when possible) and the share of food in household expenditures. These are computed as weighted averages of each household's per-capita expenditure, or as weighted ratios in the case of the shares.

Employment indicators

Employment ratio. Includes only persons who are employed and the unemployed aged 15–64 (inclusive), excluding the following categories: homemakers, retired, dependent, student, and other.

Formal employment. Defined as wage employees in the government or formal private sector.

Informal employment. Defined as those whose employment status is "informal" or "self-employed."

Anthropometric indicators

All three indicators are calculated for children who are less than 60 months old. Z-scores two standard deviations below the mean of reference population indicate that a child is *stunted* (height-for-age), *wasted* (weight-for-height), or *underweight* (weight-for-age). The reference is defined jointly by the National Center for Health Statistics and Centers for Disease Control (both United States).

16-1. Burkina Faso

			Expenditure Quintile											
			Rural						*Urban*					
	Unit of Measure	*National total*	*All*	*Q1*	*Q2*	*Q3*	*Q4*	*Q5*	*All*	*Q1*	*Q2*	*Q3*	*Q4*	*Q5*
Indicators														
Demographic Indicators														
Sample size (households)	Number	8,478	5,885.0	913.0	993.0	1,048.0	1,280.0	1,651.0	2,593.0	354.0	450.0	511.0	540.0	738.0
Total Population	000s	10,597	8,830.0	1,766.3	1,765.3	1,766.8	1,765.7	1,765.9	1,767.4	352.9	354.1	353.2	353.2	353.9
Age dependency ratio	Number	1.0	1.1	1.2	1.2	1.1	1.1	0.9	0.7	1.0	0.8	0.7	0.6	0.5
Average household size	Number	7.6	8.2	10.3	10.1	9.1	7.6	5.7	5.6	8.0	6.5	5.7	5.4	4.0
Head Of Household Characteristics														
Age Dependency by household structure														
Monogamous male	Number	0.9	1.0	1.1	1.1	1.0	1.0	0.8	0.7	1.0	0.9	0.8	0.7	0.5
Polygamous male	Number	1.1	1.2	1.3	1.2	1.2	1.1	1.0	0.8	1.0	0.8	0.7	0.6	0.6
Single male	Number	0.6	0.8	1.2	1.2	0.9	0.7	0.5	0.2	0.4	0.3	0.2	0.1	0.1
De facto female	Number	1.1	1.4	2.7	1.2	1.4	1.6	0.9	0.8	1.3	1.2	0.9	0.6	0.6
De jure female	Number	0.8	1.1	1.1	1.5	1.4	1.0	0.8	0.6	1.0	0.8	0.6	0.5	0.3
Education level of head														
No level	Percent	82.3	91.5	97.3	94.9	94.7	94.0	82.4	50.6	81.8	73.7	58.2	43.0	21.5
Primary, not completed	Percent	8.7	5.4	2.4	4.8	4.4	5.3	8.1	20.1	15.2	17.2	24.7	26.2	16.6
Primary completed, no secondary	Percent	0.7	0.2	..	..	..	..	0.6	2.4	..	0.7	1.2	2.6	5.4
Secondary not completed	Percent	5.1	..	..	..	..	..	..	..	..	..	..	..	..
Secondary completed	Percent	1.4	0.7	..	..	..	..	2.3	3.8	0.5	0.2	1.9	3.9	8.8
Tertiary	Percent	1.8	0.4	..	..	..	0.1	1.2	6.7	..	0.7	1.2	3.2	20.2
Pre-school	Percent	0.1	0.0	..	..	..	..	0.2	0.1	0.6	..	..	..	..
Undefined	Percent	..	..	..	..	..	..	..	..	..	..	..	..	..
Marital Status of head														
Monogamous male	Percent	53.1	51.2	44.5	44.3	49.8	55.0	56.7	59.7	53.1	59.2	62.4	65.9	56.8
Polygamous male	Percent	31.0	36.7	46.4	49.1	42.1	33.3	23.4	11.5	26.6	17.8	11.3	6.1	4.6
Single male	Percent	7.3	5.2	4.1	2.3	3.1	4.9	9.1	14.2	8.3	7.6	10.7	14.3	23.6
De facto female	Percent	2.2	1.9	1.4	0.8	1.0	2.0	3.2	3.4	2.9	3.3	3.3	3.3	3.8
De jure female	Percent	6.4	..	..	..	..	..	..	..	..	..	..	..	..
Labor Market														
Proportion aged 15-64 in population	Percent	49.7	47.9	44.5	45.8	47.0	48.8	53.7	58.8	51.0	55.2	57.2	62.1	68.6
Proportion employed (aged 15 to 64)	Percent	86.3	93.0	95.0	94.7	94.1	93.7	88.3	59.0	72.8	65.7	55.8	51.3	53.1
Females among employed (aged 15 to 64)	Percent	52.0	54.1	57.2	55.7	54.5	53.2	50.3	38.7	45.0	44.3	37.2	34.1	32.1
Employment Ratios (among labor force)														
Employment Ratio	Percent	97.0	99.0	99.1	99.1	99.0	99.2	98.8	85.8	89.1	87.5	84.9	81.4	85.7
Formal Employment among Employed	Percent	5.4	1.0	0.1	0.1	0.3	0.5	3.6	34.0	12.6	20.6	32.4	41.9	63.4
Public Employed among Formal Employment	Percent	42.4	71.7	28.0	40.5	25.5	49.6	79.6	37.1	9.7	17.9	31.4	35.8	52.1
Informal Employment among Employed	Percent	94.1	98.6	99.7	99.5	99.3	99.2	95.8	64.9	86.7	79.0	66.7	57.0	34.3
Self-Employed among Informal Employed	Percent	27.8	..	..	..	..	..	..	..	..	..	..	..	..
Employers among Employed	Percent	0.4	0.3	0.3	0.4	0.4	0.3	0.3	0.7	0.3	0.3	0.1	0.8	1.8
Proportion Employed in Agriculture	Percent	88.2	96.5	98.6	98.4	97.9	97.3	90.7	35.1	67.5	52.3	28.6	18.1	5.2
MDG1: Eradicate Extreme Poverty and Hunger														
Mean monthly per capita expenditure	CFA francs	12,318	8,418.5	2,522.8	3,917.9	5,097.2	6,913.9	17,433.8	25,685.3	4,361.5	7,578.0	11,746.0	18,675.2	62,084.7
Mean monthly share on food	Percent	57.7	63.1	64.1	67.7	66.1	65.5	56.3	39.1	48.0	48.1	43.4	37.7	27.4
Mean monthly share on health	Percent	3.1	2.7	1.6	2.0	2.4	2.8	3.8	4.4	2.3	3.4	4.2	5.7	5.4
Mean monthly share on education	Percent	1.3	0.7	0.8	0.8	0.6	0.6	0.6	3.6	3.4	3.4	4.1	3.7	3.3
MDG2: Education and Literacy; MDG3: Promote Gender Equality														
Access to primary school (within 30 minutes)	Percent	59	52	47	48	50	49	59	84	75	84	85	84	89
Net primary enrollment rate														
Total	Percent	26	20	14	18	17	19	32	67	52	64	70	76	75
Male	Percent	30	23	18	24	20	22	37	69	53	70	70	77	81
Female	Percent	22	15	10	12	13	16	28	64	52	59	69	75	68
Net secondary enrollment rate														
Total	Percent	12	5	2	5	3	6	11	38	13	29	38	50	58
Male	Percent	13	7	4	5	4	7	15	41	13	33	39	58	68
Female	Percent	10	4	1	4	2	4	7	34	13	25	37	42	51
Tertiary enrolment rate per 10,000														
Total	per 10,000	8	..	..	..	..	..	..	..	..	..	..	..	..
Adult literacy rate														
Total	Percent	18	10	5	8	9	10	18	51	23	34	48	62	78
Male	Percent	25	15	8	12	14	14	25	59	30	44	56	69	84
Female	Percent	13	6	3	5	5	6	12	42	15	25	40	54	71
Youth literacy rate														
Total	Percent	26	15	9	12	11	16	24	65	40	50	68	77	81
Male	Percent	32	20	13	17	15	21	32	72	49	62	76	81	89
Female	Percent	20	10	5	7	8	12	18	57	31	40	60	72	74

Enquête Prioritaire Auprès des Menages II 1998

(Table continues on the following page)

16-1. Burkina Faso (continued)

Indicators	Unit of Measure	National total	Expenditure Quintile: Rural All	Rural Q1	Rural Q2	Rural Q3	Rural Q4	Rural Q5	Urban All	Urban Q1	Urban Q2	Urban Q3	Urban Q4	Urban Q5
MDG4: Reduce Child Mortality; MDG5: Improve Maternal Health														
Proportion with distance to Health Center less than 5 km	Percent	63	53	49	51	52	50	58	96	92	95	96	98	98
Morbidity	Percent	7	6	4	5	6	7	10	11	7	9	11	12	15
Action taken when sick	Percent	41	39	29	29	34	37	51	49	35	45	45	52	57
Health provider ownership														
Public	Percent	83	85	84	85	85	82	86	79	75	87	81	78	75
Private - Modern Medicine	Percent	3	1	1	0	..	1	1	10	6	5	11	7	18
Private - Traditional Healers	Percent	11	12	12	10	14	16	10	4	16	3	4	4	2
Other	Percent	3	2	3	4	1	1	2	6	2	5	5	11	5
Child survival and malnutrition														
Birth assisted by trained staff	Percent	..	..	..	..	..	..	..	..	..	..	..	..	..
1-year-olds immunisation coverage	Percent	..	..	..	..	..	..	..	..	..	..	..	..	..
1-year-olds immunized against measles	Percent	..	..	..	..	..	..	..	..	..	..	..	..	..
Stunting (6-59 months)	Percent	43	46	46	44	46	50	43	28	32	37	27	22	17
Wasting (6-59 months)	Percent	24	24	24	22	25	24	25	23	19	15	21	35	26
Underweight (6-59 months)	Percent	50	52	53	49	54	56	50	34	38	37	30	38	26
MDG7: Ensure Environmental Sustainability														
Owner occupancy rate	Percent	85	94	98	97	96	95	86	58	79	71	58	56	41
Access to sanitation facilities	Percent	32	16	7	11	13	14	26	89	71	82	89	95	97
Proportion with distance to Water Source less than 2 km	Percent	78	73	67	72	74	72	77	96	88	94	97	98	99
Proportion with distance distance to Market less than 5 km	Percent	78	72	73	72	71	69	75	97	93	97	97	98	99
Access to improved water source														
Pipe (own tap)	Percent	5	0	..	0	0	..	0	24	3	6	14	27	50
Pipe borne	Percent	16	5	4	3	4	4	8	53	56	61	58	56	41
Well (Protected)	Percent	42	52	50	53	55	52	51	9	17	12	11	5	4
Total	Percent	63	57	54	56	58	55	59	86	76	79	82	88	95
Access to unimproved water source														
Surface Water	Percent	10	12	14	13	12	13	11	0	..	1	1	1	0
Other	Percent	27	31	32	31	29	31	30	14	24	20	17	12	4
Total	Percent	37	43	46	44	42	45	41	14	24	21	18	12	5
Traditional Fuel Use														
Firewood	Percent	87	91	95	94	93	92	85	74	88	92	87	78	46
Charcoal	Percent	5	5	3	4	4	4	7	6	1	2	3	7	11
Total	Percent	92	96	98	97	97	97	92	80	90	94	89	84	57
Nontraditional Fuel Use														
Kerosene	Percent	1	1	0	1	1	1	2	2	2	1	2	1	3
Electricity	Percent	0	0	..	..	..	..	0	1	..	0	..	1	1
Gas	Percent	3	1	..	..	..	..	2	10	..	0	3	4	29
Other	Percent	4	3	2	2	2	3	4	8	9	5	6	9	10
Total	Percent	8	4	2	3	3	3	8	20	10	6	11	16	43

Enquête Prioritaire Auprès des Menages II 1998

16-2. Burundi

	Unit of Measure	National total	Expenditure Quintile: Rural All	Rural Q1	Rural Q2	Rural Q3	Rural Q4	Rural Q5	Urban All	Urban Q1	Urban Q2	Urban Q3	Urban Q4	Urban Q5
Indicators														
Demographic Indicators														
Sample size (households)	Number	6,668	3,908.0	740.0	649.0	723.0	817.0	979.0	2,760.0	473.0	494.0	562.0	541.0	690.0
Total Population	000s	6,026	5,717.1	1,142.7	1,152.8	1,135.0	1,143.0	1,143.6	308.6	61.7	61.7	61.7	61.7	61.7
Age dependency ratio	Number	1.1	1.1	1.4	1.2	1.2	1.0	0.9	0.7	1.1	0.9	0.7	0.6	0.4
Average household size	Number	4.9	4.9	5.5	5.5	5.1	4.7	4.0	4.8	6.4	6.1	5.0	4.7	3.3
Head Of Household Characteristics														
Age Dependency by household structure														
Monogamous male	Number	1.0	1.0	1.3	1.2	1.1	1.0	0.8	0.8	1.1	0.9	0.7	0.7	0.5
Polygamous male	Number	1.1	1.1	2.7	0.0	1.0	0.9	0.8	1.1	1.5	0.4	..	..	..
Single male	Number	0.9	1.0	1.8	1.0	1.0	1.1	0.5	0.2	0.7	0.4	0.2	0.1	0.1
De facto female	Number	1.6	1.6	1.8	1.7	2.5	1.0	1.4	1.0	1.1	1.5	1.0	0.6	0.7
De jure female	Number	1.2	1.3	1.5	1.3	1.2	1.0	1.0	0.8	1.3	0.9	0.6	0.5	0.5
Education level of head														
No level	Percent	..	..	..	..	..	..	..	..	..	..	..	..	..
Primary, not completed	Percent	25.2	25.4	21.9	22.2	27.2	26.8	27.8	21.5	31.8	36.1	29.2	14.8	7.6
Primary completed, no secondary	Percent	4.3	4.1	0.9	4.1	3.6	3.6	7.2	7.7	7.9	13.0	9.5	6.4	4.5
Secondary not completed	Percent	3.4	..	..	..	..	..	..	..	..	..	..	..	..
Secondary completed	Percent	0.4	0.2	..	..	..	0.1	0.6	4.2	0.6	1.8	4.6	5.6	6.1
Tertiary	Percent	1.3	0.0	..	..	..	..	0.2	24.3	0.1	2.1	9.0	35.5	51.5
Pre-school	Percent	..	..	..	..	..	..	..	..	..	..	..	..	..
Undefined	Percent	65.4	68.0	76.8	72.7	68.0	66.0	59.8	18.6	51.7	27.6	18.3	7.9	4.1
Marital Status of head														
Monogamous male	Percent	68.3	68.4	56.5	67.3	71.1	71.0	73.6	65.9	62.0	72.5	67.8	68.3	61.2
Polygamous male	Percent	0.3	0.3	0.4	0.3	0.1	0.3	0.2	0.1	0.5	0.1	..	..	..
Single male	Percent	5.4	4.9	4.1	4.3	3.7	6.3	5.6	13.9	4.6	5.5	10.5	14.4	25.3
De facto female	Percent	3.0	3.0	2.3	0.9	4.9	2.7	3.9	3.4	4.0	3.3	3.7	3.8	2.6
De jure female	Percent	23.1	..	..	..	..	..	..	..	..	..	..	..	..
Labor Market														
Proportion aged 15-64 in population	Percent	48.2	47.6	41.9	45.6	46.3	50.6	53.9	58.2	46.8	52.5	59.6	63.1	69.3
Proportion employed (aged 15 to 64)	Percent	86.0	88.5	92.5	88.5	88.4	85.2	88.5	48.4	42.6	42.0	42.9	48.6	61.9
Females among employed (aged 15 to 64)	Percent	55.8	56.4	58.7	56.3	57.6	55.1	54.6	39.5	49.8	40.4	32.2	40.1	38.1
Employment Ratios (among labor force)														
Employment Ratio	Percent	98.8	99.6	99.5	99.9	99.5	99.5	99.6	81.3	73.4	76.7	78.9	83.4	88.5
Formal Employment among Employed	Percent	4.8	2.9	1.6	1.6	2.6	3.3	4.9	57.6	23.6	34.2	56.0	72.5	75.7
Public Employed among Formal Employment	Percent	57.0	58.0	18.4	34.6	57.0	78.0	63.3	55.6	26.5	41.1	57.5	64.1	56.5
Informal Employment among Employed	Percent	94.8	96.9	98.1	98.4	97.1	96.6	94.8	37.6	70.5	57.8	39.3	23.7	20.7
Self-Employed among Informal Employed	Percent	46.1	..	..	..	..	..	..	..	..	..	..	..	..
Employers among Employed	Percent	0.1	0.1	0.1	0.0	0.2	0.0	0.1	1.5	0.4	0.7	0.5	1.8	2.6
Proportion Employed in Agriculture	Percent	84.4	87.1	93.8	89.7	83.5	85.3	84.2	8.9	34.7	15.8	5.0	1.6	1.0
MDG1: Eradicate Extreme Poverty and Hunger														
Mean monthly per capita expenditure	Burundi francs	6,574	5,438.1	1,437.8	2,924.5	4,221.2	5,909.8	10,764.5	27,313.6	4,453.9	9,137.2	15,444.1	26,007.1	58,137.1
Mean monthly share on food	Percent	73.6	75.0	69.3	76.6	76.9	76.9	74.8	48.0	58.7	57.9	51.9	44.5	36.7
Mean monthly share on health	Percent	2.2	2.2	3.3	2.3	2.0	2.0	1.6	2.7	3.1	3.1	3.2	2.4	2.0
Mean monthly share on education	Percent	1.4	1.2	1.7	1.4	1.2	1.5	0.6	3.4	3.8	4.0	3.5	3.8	2.4
MDG2: Education and Literacy; MDG3: Promote Gender Equality														
Access to primary school (within 30 minutes)	Percent	72	70	63	73	70	73	73	97	94	96	98	99	98
Net primary enrollment rate														
Total	Percent	56	55	40	50	59	63	66	83	67	84	90	93	94
Male	Percent	60	59	44	56	62	69	67	83	67	84	89	93	94
Female	Percent	51	50	36	44	55	57	65	83	66	83	91	93	94
Net secondary enrollment rate														
Total	Percent	9	7	2	4	7	13	11	48	14	34	56	74	74
Male	Percent	10	8	3	6	6	15	11	48	16	33	56	71	73
Female	Percent	9	7	1	3	8	12	11	48	13	35	56	76	74
Tertiary enrolment rate per 10,000														
Total	per 10,000	11	..	..	..	..	..	..	..	..	..	..	..	..
Adult literacy rate														
Total	Percent	49	47	33	45	47	52	54	84	58	76	87	95	97
Male	Percent	58	56	43	55	55	61	62	90	70	85	90	97	98
Female	Percent	42	39	26	37	40	44	47	79	50	68	83	93	97
Youth literacy rate														
Total	Percent	71	70	55	71	66	77	77	90	72	88	91	98	99
Male	Percent	72	71	56	72	66	78	79	92	75	91	93	99	98
Female	Percent	71	70	55	70	66	77	76	89	69	86	90	97	100

Étude Nationale sur les Conditions de Vie au Burundi

(Table continues on the following page)

16-2. Burundi (continued)

Expenditure Quintile

	Unit of Measure	National total	Rural						Urban					
			All	*Q1*	*Q2*	*Q3*	*Q4*	*Q5*	*All*	*Q1*	*Q2*	*Q3*	*Q4*	*Q5*
Indicators														
MDG4: Reduce Child Mortality; MDG5: Improve Maternal Health														
Proportion with distance to Health Center less than 5 km	Percent	66	65	64	66	59	66	67	98	94	97	99	99	99
Morbidity	Percent	21	21	22	18	19	21	25	15	18	17	17	13	11
Action taken when sick	Percent	60	59	51	54	59	62	69	72	52	69	77	86	87
Health provider ownership														
Public	Percent	..	..	..	..	..	..	..	..	..	..	..	..	..
Private - Modern Medicine	Percent	..	..	..	..	..	..	..	..	..	..	..	..	..
Private - Traditional Healers	Percent	..	..	..	..	..	..	..	..	..	..	..	..	..
Other	Percent	..	..	..	..	..	..	..	..	..	..	..	..	..
Child survival and malnutrition														
Birth assisted by trained staff	Percent	..	..	..	..	..	..	..	..	..	..	..	..	..
1-year-olds immunisation coverage	Percent	..	..	..	..	..	..	..	..	..	..	..	..	..
1-year-olds immunized against measles	Percent	..	..	..	..	..	..	..	..	..	..	..	..	..
Stunting (6-59 months)	Percent	56	59	62	64	56	59	52	30	47	31	23	22	23
Wasting (6-59 months)	Percent	8	8	8	8	9	9	9	7	5	6	6	5	11
Underweight (6-59 months)	Percent	44	47	48	50	54	44	38	15	25	19	12	9	9
MDG7: Ensure Environmental Sustainability														
Owner occupancy rate	Percent	94	97	97	98	99	98	95	40	50	41	33	39	40
Access to sanitation facilities	Percent	..	..	..	..	..	..	..	..	..	..	..	..	..
Proportion with distance to Water Source less than 2 km	Percent	88	87	84	88	87	87	89	97	98	96	98	97	96
Proportion with distance distance to Market less than 5 km	Percent	77	76	76	80	72	77	76	100	100	100	100	100	100
Access to improved water source														
Pipe (own tap)	Percent	4	1	1	1	0	1	2	57	11	28	50	76	88
Pipe borne	Percent	16	14	14	17	14	12	14	40	80	66	48	23	11
Well (Protected)	Percent	66	69	65	66	71	71	71	1	3	2	1	0	1
Total	Percent	85	84	80	83	85	84	87	98	94	96	98	99	100
Access to unimproved water source														
Surface Water	Percent	15	16	20	17	15	16	13	2	6	4	2	1	0
Other	Percent	..	..	..	..	..	..	..	..	..	..	..	..	..
Total	Percent	15	16	20	17	15	16	13	2	6	4	2	1	0
Traditional Fuel Use														
Firewood	Percent	94	98	99	100	98	100	95	15	54	23	11	4	2
Charcoal	Percent	5	1	0	..	0	0	4	82	46	77	88	94	91
Total	Percent	99	99	100	100	98	100	98	97	99	100	99	98	93
Nontraditional Fuel Use														
Kerosene	Percent	1	1	0	..	2	0	2	0	0	..	..	0	0
Electricity	Percent	0	..	..	..	..	..	..	2	..	..	1	2	6
Gas	Percent	0	..	..	..	..	..	..	0	..	0	..	1	1
Other	Percent	0	0	0	0	0	..	..	0	0	..	0	0	0
Total	Percent	1	1	0	0	2	0	2	3	1	0	1	2	7

Étude Nationale sur les Conditions de Vie au Burundi

16-3. Cameroon

			Expenditure Quintile: Rural						Expenditure Quintile: Urban					
	Unit of Measure	*National total*	*All*	*Q1*	*Q2*	*Q3*	*Q4*	*Q5*	*All*	*Q1*	*Q2*	*Q3*	*Q4*	*Q5*
Indicators														
Demographic Indicators														
Sample size (households)	Number	1,731	628.0	119.0	89.0	113.0	120.0	187.0	1,103.0	132.0	171.0	181.0	284.0	335.0
Total Population	000s	12,573	8,814.0	1,747.5	1,773.2	1,768.1	1,735.1	1,790.2	3,758.9	744.9	756.1	751.8	750.2	755.9
Age dependency ratio	Number	0.9	1.0	1.2	1.2	1.0	0.9	0.6	0.7	1.0	0.9	0.7	0.6	0.5
Average household size	Number	5.9	6.3	7.6	8.5	7.3	6.2	4.1	5.2	7.3	6.4	6.0	4.2	3.8
Head Of Household Characteristics														
Age Dependency by household structure														
Monogamous male	Number	0.9	1.0	1.1	1.2	1.1	0.9	0.7	0.8	1.0	0.9	0.8	0.7	0.5
Polygamous male	Number	1.1	1.1	1.3	1.2	1.1	1.1	0.7	1.2	1.4	1.5	1.0	0.9	1.8
Single male	Number	0.4	0.6	1.2	1.2	0.8	0.3	0.4	0.2	0.5	0.1	0.1	0.2	0.1
De facto female	Number	0.7	0.9	1.1	1.1	0.8	1.4	0.5	0.5	0.9	0.6	0.4	0.5	0.3
De jure female	Number	..	..	..	..	..	..	..	..	..	..	..	..	..
Education level of head														
No level	Percent	..	..	..	..	..	..	..	..	..	..	..	..	..
Primary, not completed	Percent	32.1	36.2	34.1	39.6	37.4	43.2	30.3	24.2	41.4	20.5	31.6	20.8	15.9
Primary completed, no secondary	Percent	..	..	..	..	..	..	..	..	..	..	..	..	..
Secondary not completed	Percent	26.8	..	..	..	..	..	..	..	..	..	..	..	..
Secondary completed	Percent	..	..	..	..	..	..	..	..	..	..	..	..	..
Tertiary	Percent	6.2	1.2	0.6	0.6	..	1.6	2.3	15.9	0.9	14.0	14.9	14.1	26.9
Pre-school	Percent	..	..	..	..	..	..	..	..	..	..	..	..	..
Undefined	Percent	35.0	44.8	49.8	44.4	50.3	43.9	39.7	15.8	19.1	29.3	18.0	12.3	8.0
Marital Status of head														
Monogamous male	Percent	52.2	51.9	65.5	52.0	46.7	57.7	43.7	52.7	70.0	57.9	49.6	46.2	48.3
Polygamous male	Percent	15.7	21.0	19.0	30.7	26.9	21.4	14.0	5.3	5.7	10.3	12.5	0.6	1.8
Single male	Percent	14.9	12.5	6.6	4.5	10.0	9.5	23.0	19.7	4.7	9.0	17.5	24.6	30.7
De facto female	Percent	17.2	14.5	8.9	12.9	16.5	11.5	19.3	22.4	19.6	22.9	20.3	28.6	19.2
De jure female	Percent	..	..	..	..	..	..	..	..	..	..	..	..	..
Labor Market														
Proportion aged 15-64 in population	Percent	53.3	50.8	46.4	45.5	49.4	51.6	61.1	59.0	49.5	53.7	59.5	63.5	68.8
Proportion employed (aged 15 to 64)	Percent	67.2	76.5	78.4	71.4	77.2	76.4	78.2	48.4	43.0	45.3	45.7	48.1	56.9
Females among employed (aged 15 to 64)	Percent	48.2	52.0	55.5	55.8	54.9	45.8	49.4	36.2	43.3	38.2	32.0	38.2	32.5
Employment Ratios (among labor force)														
Employment Ratio	Percent	91.0	95.2	96.6	91.5	95.3	96.0	96.0	79.9	67.8	74.5	83.6	82.8	87.0
Formal Employment among Employed	Percent	13.9	6.3	2.3	7.1	6.5	5.8	8.5	35.6	28.0	31.3	25.7	33.2	50.5
Public Employed among Formal Employment	Percent	43.2	50.1	61.6	64.0	28.8	44.5	55.5	39.8	43.4	29.3	39.7	50.5	37.2
Informal Employment among Employed	Percent	81.5	89.5	92.6	91.5	89.9	89.8	85.6	59.0	69.8	60.2	71.2	60.2	43.5
Self-Employed among Informal Employed	Percent	81.1	..	..	..	..	..	..	..	..	..	..	..	..
Employers among Employed	Percent	4.6	4.3	5.0	1.3	3.6	4.4	5.9	5.4	2.1	8.4	3.0	6.6	6.0
Proportion Employed in Agriculture	Percent	64.8	83.0	88.3	83.2	85.1	81.6	78.2	6.8	8.6	7.2	8.2	5.5	5.6
MDG1: Eradicate Extreme Poverty and Hunger														
Mean monthly per capita expenditure	CFA francs	20,115	14,519.0	4,447.5	6,858.7	8,913.7	12,665.7	28,017.0	31,043.7	5,983.2	11,066.0	15,986.0	25,458.3	70,161.8
Mean monthly share on food	Percent	53.5	55.2	61.1	54.9	54.0	54.8	53.0	50.2	60.7	54.2	52.4	49.9	41.2
Mean monthly share on health	Percent	7.4	6.9	5.0	5.4	7.2	5.4	9.6	8.3	9.4	9.1	7.5	9.7	6.4
Mean monthly share on education	Percent	4.2	2.8	3.4	4.1	2.7	2.8	2.0	6.8	10.6	10.5	6.4	6.4	3.3
MDG2: Education and Literacy; MDG3: Promote Gender Equality														
Access to primary school (within 30 minutes)	Percent	...	..	..	..	..	..	..	..	..	..	..	..	..
Net primary enrollment rate														
Total	Percent	74	72	61	78	77	71	74	78	79	66	81	89	79
Male	Percent	76	76	66	88	82	69	74	77	77	62	84	88	79
Female	Percent	71	68	58	68	72	73	73	79	80	70	78	90	78
Net secondary enrollment rate														
Total	Percent	26	16	8	10	21	20	24	49	37	41	45	62	62
Male	Percent	27	18	9	10	27	20	24	47	37	44	37	62	59
Female	Percent	26	14	6	9	14	20	24	50	36	38	50	63	64
Tertiary enrolment rate per 10,000														
Total	per 10,000	65	..	..	..	..	..	..	..	..	..	..	..	..
Adult literacy rate														
Total	Percent	62	51	48	57	48	49	53	84	82	74	81	90	90
Male	Percent	72	64	59	70	59	64	67	88	87	82	84	93	93
Female	Percent	52	41	40	46	40	35	42	79	77	65	79	87	86
Youth literacy rate														
Total	Percent	79	72	68	80	73	68	72	91	89	85	89	94	96
Male	Percent	84	79	74	84	77	77	81	92	89	91	88	97	96
Female	Percent	74	66	63	75	70	58	65	89	89	80	90	91	96

Enquête Camerounaise Auprès des Menages 1996

(Table continues on the following page)

16-3. Cameroon (continued)

			Expenditure Quintile											
			Rural						*Urban*					
	Unit of Measure	*National total*	*All*	*Q1*	*Q2*	*Q3*	*Q4*	*Q5*	*All*	*Q1*	*Q2*	*Q3*	*Q4*	*Q5*
Indicators														
MDG4: Reduce Child Mortality; MDG5: Improve Maternal Health														
Proportion with distance to Health Center less than 5 km	Percent	..	..	..	..	..	..	..	..	..	..	..	..	..
Morbidity	Percent	21	18	16	17	16	18	22	28	31	27	26	30	27
Action taken when sick	Percent	51	45	27	47	46	44	57	60	50	61	57	61	74
Health provider ownership														
Public	Percent	42	42	24	32	46	45	53	41	40	36	45	43	40
Private - Modern Medicine	Percent	43	37	40	42	28	37	39	50	43	54	46	52	52
Private - Traditional Healers	Percent	15	20	36	26	26	18	9	10	17	10	9	6	8
Other	Percent	..	..	..	..	..	..	..	..	..	..	..	..	..
Child survival and malnutrition														
Birth assisted by trained staff	Percent	..	..	..	..	..	..	..	..	..	..	..	..	..
1-year-olds immunisation coverage	Percent	64	58	64	57	72	41	40	80	88	57	88	93	86
1-year-olds immunized against measles	Percent	69	63	71	68	77	41	40	83	88	62	95	100	86
Stunting (6-59 months)	Percent	36	38	36	40	42	37	34	31	41	27	40	16	23
Wasting (6-59 months)	Percent	10	11	16	14	7	7	5	9	9	12	5	14	6
Underweight (6-59 months)	Percent	24	27	30	26	29	24	24	17	25	17	20	10	7
MDG7: Ensure Environmental Sustainability														
Owner occupancy rate	Percent	71	87	86	98	93	86	78	42	61	57	43	40	24
Access to sanitation facilities	Percent	93	90	85	92	88	87	93	99	98	100	100	97	100
Proportion with distance to Water Source less than 2 km	Percent	..	..	..	..	..	..	..	..	..	..	..	..	..
Proportion with distance distance to Market less than 5 km	Percent	..	..	..	..	..	..	..	..	..	..	..	..	..
Access to improved water source														
Pipe (own tap)	Percent	10	3	3	..	2	5	4	23	3	10	20	23	41
Pipe borne	Percent	6	1	1	..	..	2	2	15	16	14	18	15	13
Well (Protected)	Percent	33	38	31	42	30	37	44	24	38	25	15	30	18
Total	Percent	49	42	34	42	32	44	50	62	57	49	54	68	72
Access to unimproved water source														
Surface Water	Percent	37	51	58	53	60	50	42	9	16	9	8	9	6
Other	Percent	15	7	7	5	8	7	9	29	28	42	38	23	22
Total	Percent	51	58	66	58	68	56	50	38	43	51	46	32	28
Traditional Fuel Use														
Firewood	Percent	76	94	99	97	94	92	92	42	70	64	50	34	16
Charcoal	Percent	4	1	1	..	1	2	1	9	1	5	6	13	15
Total	Percent	80	95	99	97	95	93	93	51	71	68	56	47	31
Nontraditional Fuel Use														
Kerosene	Percent	6	1	1	..	1	1	2	17	8	8	18	24	21
Electricity	Percent	0	0	..	..	..	1	..	0	..	..	2	0	0
Gas	Percent	6	0	..	..	..	..	1	17	2	6	7	17	36
Other	Percent	7	3	..	3	4	4	4	14	19	17	17	11	12
Total	Percent	20	5	1	3	5	7	7	49	29	32	44	53	69

Enquête Camerounaise Auprès des Menages 1996

16-4. Côte d'Ivoire

Indicators	Unit of Measure	National total	Rural All	Rural Q1	Rural Q2	Rural Q3	Rural Q4	Rural Q5	Urban All	Urban Q1	Urban Q2	Urban Q3	Urban Q4	Urban Q5
Demographic Indicators														
Sample size (households)	Number	4,200	2,280.0	470.0	453.0	457.0	453.0	447.0	1,920.0	400.0	382.0	386.0	376.0	376.0
Total Population	000s	16,816	9,225.4	2,552.0	2,135.3	1,915.2	1,484.8	1,138.1	7,590.2	2,128.8	1,780.8	1,504.4	1,250.7	925.4
Age dependency ratio	Number	0.8	1.0	1.2	1.1	0.9	0.8	0.7	0.7	1.0	0.8	0.6	0.6	0.4
Average household size	Number	5.7	5.9	8.3	6.9	5.9	4.7	3.6	5.6	8.0	6.8	5.5	4.5	3.2
Head Of Household Characteristics														
Age Dependency by household structure														
Monogamous male	Number	0.9	1.0	1.2	1.2	0.9	0.8	0.7	0.8	1.0	0.9	0.7	0.7	0.4
Polygamous male	Number	0.9	1.0	1.1	1.0	0.8	0.9	0.8	0.8	0.9	0.7	0.5	0.9	0.6
Single male	Number	0.5	0.6	1.1	0.9	0.7	0.4	0.2	0.3	0.6	0.5	0.3	0.2	0.1
De facto female	Number	1.0	1.4	1.9	2.0	1.5	1.1	0.6	0.8	1.2	0.9	0.9	0.9	0.3
De jure female	Number	0.8	1.0	1.4	1.0	0.8	1.1	0.5	0.6	0.9	0.7	0.6	0.4	0.3
Education level of head														
No level	Percent	57.1	67.6	76.7	71.1	67.4	64.6	58.1	44.8	69.5	51.0	42.8	34.0	26.6
Primary, not completed	Percent	11.1	12.1	12.7	11.7	13.1	11.1	11.8	9.9	8.7	12.0	11.2	10.7	7.1
Primary completed, no secondary	Percent	7.8	7.4	5.0	8.8	7.7	7.4	8.1	8.2	7.7	9.7	10.5	7.3	6.0
Secondary not completed	Percent	16.8	..	..	..	..	..	..	..	..	..	..	..	..
Secondary completed	Percent	2.8	1.2	0.5	0.2	1.2	2.0	2.0	4.7	2.0	3.9	4.3	6.3	6.9
Tertiary	Percent	4.2	1.3	..	0.2	0.7	1.3	4.1	7.8	1.0	3.2	4.3	10.1	20.2
Pre-school	Percent	0.1	0.1	..	..	..	0.1	0.3	0.0	..	..	..	0.2	..
Undefined	Percent	0.1	0.0	..	..	..	..	0.2	0.1	..	..	0.3	0.2	..
Marital Status of head														
Monogamous male	Percent	58.2	58.0	49.1	62.3	62.5	58.2	58.0	58.3	51.5	63.2	67.5	58.7	50.7
Polygamous male	Percent	13.0	18.1	30.0	19.1	17.8	16.3	7.3	6.9	17.2	10.4	3.2	2.6	1.4
Single male	Percent	13.5	11.6	7.4	8.1	8.7	14.1	19.5	15.9	8.2	8.9	12.4	21.4	28.6
De facto female	Percent	3.4	2.2	1.4	2.4	2.9	2.6	1.8	4.8	5.8	4.9	4.5	4.6	4.3
De jure female	Percent	11.9	..	..	..	..	..	..	..	..	..	..	..	..
Labor Market														
Proportion aged 15-64 in population	Percent	54.3	50.8	45.8	47.3	52.7	54.7	60.6	58.6	50.7	55.5	61.7	62.0	73.3
Proportion employed (aged 15 to 64)	Percent	67.2	82.3	87.5	85.8	81.0	79.0	74.4	51.3	55.2	48.9	49.8	52.3	49.9
Females among employed (aged 15 to 64)	Percent	47.5	50.5	54.5	51.3	49.3	48.2	45.8	42.6	49.8	43.6	42.9	36.7	34.9
Employment Ratios (among labor force)														
Employment Ratio	Percent	90.7	97.6	98.2	98.4	97.7	97.1	95.6	81.0	82.6	78.1	80.7	81.2	82.7
Formal Employment among Employed	Percent	..	..	..	..	..	..	..	..	..	..	..	..	..
Public Employed among Formal Employment	Percent	..	..	..	..	..	..	..	..	..	..	..	..	..
Informal Employment among Employed	Percent	..	..	..	..	..	..	..	..	..	..	..	..	..
Self-Employed among Informal Employed	Percent	..	..	..	..	..	..	..	..	..	..	..	..	..
Employers among Employed	Percent	..	..	..	..	..	..	..	..	..	..	..	..	..
Proportion Employed in Agriculture	Percent	56.1	83.5	89.8	88.9	82.5	77.6	71.0	9.7	18.0	11.9	6.9	4.6	1.8
MDG1: Eradicate Extreme Poverty and Hunger														
Mean monthly per capita expenditure	CFA francs	35,387	28,540.6	7,484.3	13,577.5	19,516.2	28,702.9	73,472.4	43,452.4	11,162.2	19,023.4	28,312.6	42,885.3	116,049.2
Mean monthly share on food	Percent	56.7	64.8	65.3	66.2	65.0	65.2	62.1	47.3	54.4	50.4	49.6	45.0	36.9
Mean monthly share on health	Percent	6.1	5.7	4.9	5.6	5.8	5.7	6.7	6.5	5.3	6.6	6.4	6.7	7.7
Mean monthly share on education	Percent	2.4	1.9	2.1	2.5	1.7	1.6	1.4	3.1	3.8	3.5	2.7	3.0	2.4
MDG2: Education and Literacy; MDG3: Promote Gender Equality														
Access to primary school (within 30 minutes)	Percent	..	..	..	..	..	..	..	..	..	..	..	..	..
Net primary enrollment rate														
	Percent	52	43	33	43	46	53	59	64	54	62	65	75	89
Male	Percent	55	47	38	46	48	55	65	67	57	68	67	83	89
Female	Percent	49	40	28	39	43	51	54	61	51	57	63	69	89
Net secondary enrollment rate														
Total	Percent	21	10	5	9	13	15	14	31	18	33	37	34	46
Male	Percent	26	14	7	11	18	21	21	40	23	42	50	44	60
Female	Percent	16	6	3	6	8	9	8	24	14	22	27	27	37
Tertiary enrolment rate per 10,000														
Total	per 10,000	62	..	..	..	..	..	..	..	..	..	..	..	..
Adult literacy rate														
Total	Percent	48	33	24	31	35	38	43	64	50	61	65	74	79
Male	Percent	61	46	36	45	49	51	55	77	64	77	79	85	87
Female	Percent	35	21	15	18	21	25	31	51	38	46	52	62	70
Youth literacy rate														
Total	Percent	61	47	39	47	51	49	56	73	65	76	71	78	80
Male	Percent	72	59	49	59	61	62	67	86	75	89	88	89	92
Female	Percent	50	36	30	33	39	38	47	61	55	62	59	66	70

Expenditure Quintile columns: Rural (All, Q1–Q5); Urban (All, Q1–Q5).

Enquête Niveau de Vie des Ménages en Côte d'Ivoire 1998

(Table continues on the following page)

16-4. Côte d'Ivoire (continued)

Indicators	Unit of Measure	National total	Rural All	Rural Q1	Rural Q2	Rural Q3	Rural Q4	Rural Q5	Urban All	Urban Q1	Urban Q2	Urban Q3	Urban Q4	Urban Q5
			Expenditure Quintile											
MDG4: Reduce Child Mortality; MDG5: Improve Maternal Health														
Proportion with distance to Health Center less than 5 km	Percent	..	..	..	..	..	..	..	..	..	..	..	..	..
Morbidity	Percent	15	14	11	11	15	18	17	16	13	15	17	20	20
Action taken when sick	Percent	54	48	36	51	49	50	58	60	49	62	62	61	72
Health provider ownership														
Public	Percent	..	..	..	..	..	..	..	..	..	..	..	..	..
Private - Modern Medicine	Percent	..	..	..	..	..	..	..	..	..	..	..	..	..
Private - Traditional Healers	Percent	..	..	..	..	..	..	..	..	..	..	..	..	..
Other	Percent	..	..	..	..	..	..	..	..	..	..	..	..	..
Child survival and malnutrition														
Birth assisted by trained staff	Percent	..	..	..	..	..	..	..	..	..	..	..	..	..
1-year-olds immunisation coverage	Percent	..	..	..	..	..	..	..	..	..	..	..	..	..
1-year-olds immunized against measles	Percent	..	..	..	..	..	..	..	..	..	..	..	..	..
Stunting (6-59 months)	Percent	..	..	..	..	..	..	..	..	..	..	..	..	..
Wasting (6-59 months)	Percent	..	..	..	..	..	..	..	..	..	..	..	..	..
Underweight (6-59 months)	Percent	..	..	..	..	..	..	..	..	..	..	..	..	..
MDG7: Ensure Environmental Sustainability														
Owner occupancy rate	Percent	50	70	81	79	71	63	58	25	37	27	24	18	19
Access to sanitation facilities	Percent	67	42	34	42	39	43	52	96	92	96	96	98	97
Proportion with distance to Water Source less than 2 km	Percent	..	..	..	..	..	..	..	..	..	..	..	..	..
Proportion with distance distance to Market less than 5 km	Percent	..	..	..	..	..	..	..	..	..	..	..	..	..
Access to improved water source														
Pipe (own tap)	Percent	19	6	4	4	5	8	12	35	21	31	33	40	48
Pipe borne	Percent	7	2	1	2	2	2	3	13	7	10	14	15	18
Well (Protected)	Percent	51	73	79	77	74	68	69	25	47	31	22	16	11
Total	Percent	78	82	84	83	82	77	84	72	75	71	69	70	77
Access to unimproved water source														
Surface Water	Percent	7	13	14	14	12	16	10	0	..	..	..	..	0
Other	Percent	15	5	2	3	6	7	6	27	25	29	31	30	23
Total	Percent	22	18	16	17	18	23	16	28	25	29	31	30	23
Traditional Fuel Use														
Firewood	Percent	64	90	96	96	94	86	79	32	65	41	29	16	9
Charcoal	Percent	25	3	0	1	2	4	8	51	28	52	60	63	49
Total	Percent	89	93	96	98	96	91	87	83	93	94	89	80	58
Nontraditional Fuel Use														
Kerosene	Percent	0	0	..	..	..	..	0	0	0	..	..	0	0
Electricity	Percent	0	0	..	..	..	..	0	..	..	..	..	..	..
Gas	Percent	4	0	0	0	0	0	2	8	1	2	4	8	23
Other	Percent	8	6	4	2	4	9	11	9	6	5	6	12	18
Total	Percent	11	7	4	2	4	9	13	17	7	6	11	20	42

Enquête Niveau de Vie des Ménages en Côte d'Ivoire 1998

16-5. Ethiopia

			Expenditure Quintile											
			Rural						*Urban*					
Indicators	*Unit of Measure*	*National total*	*All*	*Q1*	*Q2*	*Q3*	*Q4*	*Q5*	*All*	*Q1*	*Q2*	*Q3*	*Q4*	*Q5*
Demographic Indicators														
Sample size (households)	Number	16,672	8,459.0	1,469.0	1,382.0	1,519.0	1,678.0	2,411.0	8,213.0	1,118.0	1,358.0	1,506.0	1,883.0	2,348.0
Total Population	000s	54,756	47,531.2	9,501.7	9,513.1	9,503.8	9,507.2	9,505.4	7,224.9	1,446.0	1,443.3	1,445.9	1,444.9	1,444.7
Age dependency ratio	Number	1.0	1.1	1.3	1.2	1.1	1.0	0.8	0.7	1.0	0.9	0.8	0.6	0.5
Average household size	Number	4.9	4.9	5.9	5.4	5.2	4.8	3.8	4.5	5.6	5.1	4.7	4.3	3.5
Head Of Household Characteristics														
Age Dependency by household structure														
Monogamous male	Number	1.0	1.1	1.3	1.2	1.1	1.0	0.8	0.8	1.0	0.9	0.8	0.7	0.5
Polygamous male	Number	1.0	1.0	1.4	1.0	1.1	1.1	0.5	0.6	0.5	0.6	1.9	0.7	0.5
Single male	Number	0.6	0.6	1.0	0.6	0.8	0.8	0.4	0.5	1.0	0.8	0.6	0.4	0.3
De facto female	Number	0.8	0.8	1.1	0.7	0.9	1.3	0.5	0.7	0.8	0.8	0.9	0.5	0.5
De jure female	Number	1.0	1.1	1.4	1.2	1.2	1.0	0.8	0.7	1.0	0.8	0.8	0.6	0.5
Education level of head														
No level	Percent	70.9	75.7	83.3	79.7	77.3	70.3	71.2	41.7	60.3	54.3	44.6	36.1	24.0
Primary, not completed	Percent	10.8	10.5	6.9	8.4	9.5	14.0	12.0	12.9	13.4	17.5	16.5	13.1	6.8
Primary completed, no secondary	Percent	2.7	2.3	1.7	1.5	2.1	3.0	2.9	4.6	4.5	2.7	5.9	5.2	4.6
Secondary not completed	Percent	5.2	..	..	..	..	..	..	..	..	..	..	..	..
Secondary completed	Percent	1.9	0.6	0.1	0.2	0.1	0.8	1.6	9.7	2.1	3.1	8.2	11.6	18.4
Tertiary	Percent	1.7	0.4	..	..	0.1	0.3	1.3	9.5	1.1	3.7	5.7	9.5	21.6
Pre-school	Percent	6.0	6.3	5.5	7.0	6.0	8.0	5.2	4.1	5.9	5.0	3.5	4.4	2.7
Undefined	Percent	0.8	0.8	0.7	0.9	1.0	0.6	0.6	1.1	1.2	1.2	0.8	2.0	0.7
Marital Status of head														
Monogamous male	Percent	67.8	71.1	74.8	72.3	74.3	73.5	63.5	47.8	52.5	50.0	50.0	49.0	40.9
Polygamous male	Percent	0.6	0.7	0.7	0.9	0.9	0.4	0.6	0.1	0.2	0.1	0.0	0.1	0.0
Single male	Percent	5.9	5.0	3.4	4.4	3.2	4.1	8.5	11.1	5.9	3.9	7.1	10.1	23.1
De facto female	Percent	0.9	0.6	0.6	0.6	0.9	0.3	0.7	3.0	2.3	3.6	4.1	2.8	2.4
De jure female	Percent	24.8	..	..	..	..	..	..	..	..	..	..	..	..
Labor Market														
Proportion aged 15-64 in population	Percent	49.8	48.6	42.9	46.2	47.6	49.3	57.0	58.1	49.8	53.4	56.6	62.5	68.1
Proportion employed (aged 15 to 64)	Percent	43.0	41.9	42.9	39.9	40.1	41.4	44.9	48.9	46.8	46.1	46.8	47.9	55.3
Females among employed (aged 15 to 64)	Percent	28.5	24.5	30.4	24.1	21.3	21.9	25.1	47.5	49.6	50.1	45.1	47.1	46.3
Employment Ratios (among labor force)														
Employment Ratio	Percent	89.1	91.4	90.9	90.2	91.3	91.7	92.4	79.7	81.4	78.3	76.2	79.5	82.3
Formal Employment among Employed	Percent	71.3	79.1	73.0	79.4	81.9	81.5	79.4	34.4	22.0	26.8	30.1	39.3	46.1
Public Employed among Formal Employment	Percent	6.9	1.8	0.5	0.5	1.9	1.0	4.4	61.7	44.4	62.0	63.2	63.0	65.1
Informal Employment among Employed	Percent	24.2	17.4	24.2	17.6	14.6	14.8	16.6	56.5	73.7	67.7	64.6	49.8	38.3
Self-Employed among Informal Employed	Percent	24.8	..	..	..	..	..	..	..	..	..	..	..	..
Employers among Employed	Percent	2.5	2.7	2.0	2.4	3.1	3.0	3.0	1.5	0.7	1.4	1.1	1.3	2.6
Proportion Employed in Agriculture	Percent	..	..	..	..	..	..	..	..	..	..	..	..	..
MDG1: Eradicate Extreme Poverty and Hunger														
Mean monthly per capita expenditure	Ethiopian birr	103	93.1	41.8	59.9	75.3	95.0	161.4	161.6	49.4	75.5	102.7	146.9	346.0
Mean monthly share on food	Percent	66.1	67.9	71.8	70.7	69.2	68.3	61.9	55.2	65.9	62.0	58.9	53.1	42.9
Mean monthly share on health	Percent	0.9	0.8	0.7	0.8	0.7	0.8	1.1	1.2	0.8	0.8	1.1	1.5	1.4
Mean monthly share on education	Percent	0.6	0.4	0.4	0.5	0.4	0.3	0.3	1.6	1.6	1.5	1.5	1.6	1.8
MDG2: Education and Literacy; MDG3: Promote Gender Equality														
Access to primary school (within 30 minutes)	Percent	..	..	..	..	..	..	..	..	..	..	..	..	..
Net primary enrollment rate														
Total	Percent	30	25	19	23	29	25	32	75	66	70	76	84	85
Male	Percent	32	27	20	25	30	27	35	75	68	68	75	85	86
Female	Percent	29	22	18	20	28	21	29	75	64	71	77	82	84
Net secondary enrollment rate														
Total	Percent	9	3	2	3	3	3	5	40	30	36	41	50	47
Male	Percent	10	4	4	3	3	5	7	43	29	38	47	54	54
Female	Percent	8	2	1	2	2	2	3	38	30	35	36	46	42
Tertiary enrolment rate per 10,000														
Total	per 10,000	10	..	..	..	..	..	..	..	..	..	..	..	..
Adult literacy rate														
Total	Percent	28	21	15	19	20	23	25	67	54	59	66	71	79
Male	Percent	41	34	26	32	33	39	39	81	70	75	80	86	91
Female	Percent	17	9	6	8	8	9	11	56	43	47	56	61	69
Youth literacy rate														
Total	Percent	39	29	24	32	29	30	31	84	80	81	86	87	86
Male	Percent	50	43	35	47	43	45	42	90	84	86	91	95	95
Female	Percent	28	17	12	17	16	16	20	80	76	78	82	81	81

Welfare Monitoring Survey, 2000

(Table continues on the following page)

16-5. Ethiopia (continued)

	Unit of Measure	National total	Expenditure Quintile: Rural All	Rural Q1	Rural Q2	Rural Q3	Rural Q4	Rural Q5	Urban All	Urban Q1	Urban Q2	Urban Q3	Urban Q4	Urban Q5
Indicators														
MDG4: Reduce Child Mortality; MDG5: Improve Maternal Health														
Proportion with distance to Health Center less than 5 km	Percent	47	47	38	37	39	40	37	37	98	97	98	99	98
Morbidity	Percent	26	26	27	27	27	27	26	31	20	20	20	20	20
Action taken when sick	Percent	41	41	39	30	36	40	41	46	67	60	65	68	71
Health provider ownership														
Public	Percent	45	45	44	44	49	45	42	41	52	56	59	52	43
Private - Modern Medicine	Percent	45	45	45	46	40	46	46	48	42	36	36	41	51
Private - Traditional Healers	Percent	1	1	1	0	0	1	1	1	1	0	0	1	1
Other	Percent	6	6	7	6	7	5	9	7	4	4	3	4	4
Child survival and malnutrition														
Birth assisted by trained staff	Percent	..		..	..	..	..	..	..	..	..	..	..	..
1-year-olds immunisation coverage	Percent	45		41	35	48	42	38	45	85	81	81	84	88
1-year-olds immunized against measles	Percent	51		47	44	50	47	49	46	90	84	88	90	94
Stunting (6-59 months)	Percent	59	59	61	64	60	61	61	55	47	56	51	49	29
Wasting (6-59 months)	Percent	11	11	11	12	11	11	9	11	7	8	9	6	7
Underweight (6-59 months)	Percent	45	45	46	53	46	48	41	43	27	36	30	27	14
MDG7: Ensure Environmental Sustainability														
Owner occupancy rate	Percent	86	86	92	94	92	94	93	90	48	46	49	49	47
Access to sanitation facilities	Percent	18	18	9	8	8	8	10	11	73	49	64	74	87
Proportion with distance to Water Source less than 2 km	Percent	90	90	89	90	89	88	90	87	98	97	98	98	99
Proportion with distance distance to Market less than 5 km	Percent	58	58	52	54	52	52	52	50	98	98	98	99	97
Access to improved water source														
Pipe (own tap)	Percent	0	0	0	0	0	0	0	0	1	1	1	1	2
Pipe borne	Percent	17	17	7	7	7	6	6	8	82	74	79	84	88
Well (Protected)	Percent	11	11	12	8	11	12	13	13	8	9	11	8	6
Total	Percent	29	29	19	15	18	18	19	21	92	83	91	93	96
Access to unimproved water source														
Surface Water	Percent	34	34	39	42	39	37	39	36	5	8	5	4	2
Other	Percent	37	37	43	43	43	44	42	43	4	8	4	3	2
Total	Percent	71	71	81	85	82	82	81	79	8	17	9	7	4
Traditional Fuel Use														
Firewood	Percent	75	75	78	82	78	77	78	77	58	75	67	61	40
Charcoal	Percent	1	1	0	0	..	..	..	0	8	5	7	9	11
Total	Percent	77	77	78	82	78	77	78	77	66	80	74	70	51
Nontraditional Fuel Use														
Kerosene	Percent	3	3	0	0	0	0	0	1	21	7	13	20	36
Electricity	Percent	0	0	0	0	0	..	0	0	2	0	1	2	4
Gas	Percent	0	0	0	..	..	0	0	0	1	0	0	1	3
Other	Percent	19	19	21	17	22	23	21	22	9	13	12	7	6
Total	Percent	23	23	22	18	22	23	22	23	34	20	26	30	49

Welfare Monitoring Survey, 2000

16-6. The Gambia

Indicators	Unit of Measure	National total	Rural: All	Rural: Q1	Rural: Q2	Rural: Q3	Rural: Q4	Rural: Q5	Urban: All	Urban: Q1	Urban: Q2	Urban: Q3	Urban: Q4	Urban: Q5
			Expenditure Quintile											
Demographic Indicators														
Sample size (households)	Number	1,958	933.0	138.0	158.0	166.0	191.0	280.0	1,025.0	119.0	148.0	177.0	230.0	351.0
Total Population	000s	1,699	941.8	189.8	188.6	188.2	186.8	188.4	757.4	150.6	152.3	150.8	151.0	152.6
Age dependency ratio	Number	0.9	1.1	1.1	1.2	1.2	1.1	0.9	0.7	0.9	0.9	0.8	0.6	0.6
Average household size	Number	7.8	9.2	13.6	11.2	10.2	8.6	6.1	6.5	11.3	8.8	7.4	5.8	3.9
Head Of Household Characteristics														
Age Dependency by household structure														
Monogamous male	Number	0.9	1.0	1.1	1.0	1.1	1.1	0.9	0.7	0.8	0.8	0.8	0.6	0.6
Polygamous male	Number	1.0	1.1	1.1	1.3	1.1	1.1	1.0	0.9	1.0	1.0	0.9	0.8	0.7
Single male	Number	0.4	0.8	1.5	0.9	0.9	0.5	0.3	0.2	0.4	0.1	0.3	0.3	0.1
De facto female	Number	0.8	1.1	1.1	1.3	1.2	1.0	0.7	0.8	0.8	1.0	0.8	0.7	0.7
De jure female	Number	0.7	1.2	1.0	1.2	2.0	1.2	0.8	0.6	1.0	0.6	0.6	0.5	0.5
Education level of head														
No level	Percent	70.7	87.9	95.1	95.2	90.4	91.0	76.4	55.5	78.2	72.8	63.6	58.5	33.7
Primary, not completed	Percent	3.0	2.1	2.1	0.6	2.1	0.5	4.3	3.8	4.3	4.8	3.8	4.8	2.5
Primary completed, no secondary	Percent	2.7	1.4	..	1.4	..	3.3	1.4	3.9	3.6	4.2	4.5	3.3	4.1
Secondary not completed	Percent	2.5	..	..	..	..	..	..	..	..	..	..	..	..
Secondary completed	Percent	13.2	5.4	0.7	0.9	4.4	3.8	12.0	20.2	4.6	7.0	13.8	18.0	36.1
Tertiary	Percent	3.3	0.9	..	..	..	0.7	2.6	5.5	1.2	0.6	2.9	3.2	12.0
Pre-school	Percent	..	..	..	..	..	..	..	..	..	..	..	..	..
Undefined	Percent	1.1	0.1	..	..	..	..	0.3	2.1	0.8	0.6	2.0	2.2	3.2
Marital Status of head														
Monogamous male	Percent	50.1	49.5	36.1	39.4	45.7	57.3	57.8	50.6	42.7	48.2	56.5	55.5	48.2
Polygamous male	Percent	27.1	38.2	54.6	48.3	42.3	30.5	28.1	17.4	37.8	27.1	17.4	13.7	8.5
Single male	Percent	7.2	4.0	3.8	4.4	2.4	2.1	6.1	10.1	6.1	3.4	5.6	8.4	18.0
De facto female	Percent	8.6	5.1	4.8	5.0	5.5	6.1	4.2	11.7	9.2	11.9	13.4	12.4	11.1
De jure female	Percent	6.9	..	..	..	..	..	..	..	..	..	..	..	..
Labor Market														
Proportion aged 15-64 in population	Percent	52.6	48.4	47.6	46.5	46.5	48.0	53.5	57.8	53.2	53.7	56.4	61.4	64.5
Proportion employed (aged 15 to 64)	Percent	58.7	75.9	82.2	76.5	76.2	72.7	72.2	40.8	38.0	37.0	40.0	42.7	45.2
Females among employed (aged 15 to 64)	Percent	48.7	53.8	54.1	58.2	57.2	52.8	47.4	38.7	51.4	38.9	38.4	36.5	32.2
Employment Ratios (among labor force)														
Employment Ratio	Percent	92.7	97.9	98.7	98.3	97.2	98.1	97.2	84.0	79.4	80.0	82.6	85.5	90.5
Formal Employment among Employed	Percent	16.4	4.2	0.9	3.0	2.6	7.3	7.5	40.1	23.9	31.4	35.3	44.2	57.4
Public Employed among Formal Employment	Percent	35.8	45.4	53.4	40.3	38.7	33.9	58.6	33.9	21.6	31.1	36.3	32.1	38.5
Informal Employment among Employed	Percent	82.4	95.1	98.8	96.4	97.1	91.6	91.2	57.9	75.1	66.1	63.1	53.5	40.5
Self-Employed among Informal Employed	Percent	74.8	..	..	..	..	..	..	..	..	..	..	..	..
Employers among Employed	Percent	0.7	0.4	0.1	0.5	0.3	0.1	1.0	1.2	0.7	0.6	0.9	2.1	1.3
Proportion Employed in Agriculture	Percent	66.1	88.7	98.0	90.0	93.0	83.3	79.0	22.3	42.7	31.1	23.8	14.6	8.1
MDG1: Eradicate Extreme Poverty and Hunger														
Mean monthly per capita expenditure	Gambian dalasis	393	203.5	50.9	84.5	118.7	165.7	414.9	559.8	121.4	195.5	284.5	422.7	1,110.9
Mean monthly share on food	Percent	66.1	72.8	69.6	71.1	72.9	74.9	73.6	60.3	67.8	65.5	65.4	60.9	52.4
Mean monthly share on health	Percent	1.0	1.1	1.3	1.1	1.1	1.0	1.0	1.0	0.7	1.0	1.0	1.1	0.9
Mean monthly share on education	Percent	3.0	2.7	2.5	3.8	3.0	2.6	2.0	3.3	4.4	3.7	3.8	3.4	2.5
MDG2: Education and Literacy; MDG3: Promote Gender Equality														
Access to primary school (within 30 minutes)	Percent	..	..	..	..	..	..	..	..	..	..	..	..	..
Net primary enrollment rate														
Total	Percent	49	44	30	49	44	50	48	57	44	49	56	64	75
Male	Percent	51	47	37	50	45	50	53	59	46	58	57	62	75
Female	Percent	46	41	23	47	42	50	44	54	42	42	54	67	75
Net secondary enrollment rate														
Total	Percent	18	8	1	8	10	10	14	30	16	20	31	35	54
Male	Percent	22	11	1	11	15	12	18	36	21	28	34	40	57
Female	Percent	14	5	..	4	3	7	9	24	12	12	27	30	50
Tertiary enrolment rate per 10,000														
Total	per 10,000	7	..	..	..	..	..	..	..	..	..	..	..	..
Adult literacy rate														
Total	Percent	..	..	..	..	..	..	..	..	..	..	..	..	..
Male	Percent	..	..	..	..	..	..	..	..	..	..	..	..	..
Female	Percent	..	..	..	..	..	..	..	..	..	..	..	..	..
Youth literacy rate														
Total	Percent	..	..	..	..	..	..	..	..	..	..	..	..	..
Male	Percent	..	..	..	..	..	..	..	..	..	..	..	..	..
Female	Percent	..	..	..	..	..	..	..	..	..	..	..	..	..

The Gambia 1998 Household Poverty Survey

(Table continues on the following page)

16-6. The Gambia (continued)

			Expenditure Quintile											
			Rural						*Urban*					
	Unit of Measure	*National total*	*All*	*Q1*	*Q2*	*Q3*	*Q4*	*Q5*	*All*	*Q1*	*Q2*	*Q3*	*Q4*	*Q5*
Indicators														
MDG4: Reduce Child Mortality; MDG5: Improve Maternal Health														
Proportion with distance to Health Center less than 5 km	Percent	..	..	..	..	..	..	..	..	..	..	..	..	..
Morbidity	Percent	7	8	8	7	8	9	9	6	4	5	6	7	5
Action taken when sick	Percent	75	72	72	69	79	75	65	81	78	85	86	81	78
Health provider ownership														
Public	Percent	82	82	84	80	82	80	87	82	77	88	90	78	75
Private - Modern Medicine	Percent	14	13	10	18	18	15	6	16	17	9	9	21	24
Private - Traditional Healers	Percent	3	4	6	2	1	6	7	2	6	3	1	1	1
Other	Percent	..	..	..	..	..	..	..	..	..	..	..	..	..
Child survival and malnutrition														
Birth assisted by trained staff	Percent	..	..	..	..	..	..	..	..	..	..	..	..	..
1-year-olds immunisation coverage	Percent	..	..	..	..	..	..	..	..	..	..	..	..	..
1-year-olds immunized against measles	Percent	..	..	..	..	..	..	..	..	..	..	..	..	..
Stunting (6-59 months)	Percent	24	28	34	21	27	29	31	17	27	21	15	10	12
Wasting (6-59 months)	Percent	7	8	8	6	9	7	8	7	3	7	5	10	13
Underweight (6-59 months)	Percent	21	26	33	22	23	26	27	13	14	14	17	11	9
MDG7: Ensure Environmental Sustainability														
Owner occupancy rate	Percent	..	..	..	..	..	..	..	..	..	..	..	..	..
Access to sanitation facilities	Percent	96	93	96	93	92	94	91	99	99	99	97	99	99
Proportion with distance to Water Source less than 2 km	Percent	..	..	..	..	..	..	..	..	..	..	..	..	..
Proportion with distance distance to Market less than 5 km	Percent	..	..	..	..	..	..	..	..	..	..	..	..	..
Access to improved water source														
Pipe (own tap)	Percent	21	2	1	..	1	2	3	39	15	16	26	39	64
Pipe borne	Percent	38	25	19	23	32	24	25	50	60	65	63	52	31
Well (Protected)	Percent	20	40	54	51	40	31	34	2	4	4	1	1	1
Total	Percent	79	66	74	74	73	56	63	90	78	85	89	92	96
Access to unimproved water source														
Surface Water	Percent	..	..	..	..	..	..	..	..	..	..	..	..	..
Other	Percent	21	34	26	26	27	44	37	10	22	15	11	8	4
Total	Percent	21	34	26	26	27	44	37	10	22	15	11	8	4
Traditional Fuel Use														
Firewood	Percent	..	..	..	..	..	..	..	..	..	..	..	..	..
Charcoal	Percent	..	..	..	..	..	..	..	..	..	..	..	..	..
Total	Percent	..	..	..	..	..	..	..	..	..	..	..	..	..
Nontraditional Fuel Use														
Kerosene	Percent	..	..	..	..	..	..	..	..	..	..	..	..	..
Electricity	Percent	..	..	..	..	..	..	..	..	..	..	..	..	..
Gas	Percent	..	..	..	..	..	..	..	..	..	..	..	..	..
Other	Percent	..	..	..	..	..	..	..	..	..	..	..	..	..
Total	Percent	..	..	..	..	..	..	..	..	..	..	..	..	..

The Gambia 1998 Household Poverty Survey

16-7. Ghana

			Expenditure Quintile											
			Rural						Urban					
	Unit of Measure	National total	All	Q1	Q2	Q3	Q4	Q5	All	Q1	Q2	Q3	Q4	Q5
Indicators														
Demographic Indicators														
Sample size (households)	Number	5,998	3,799.0	568.0	625.0	665.0	776.0	1,165.0	2,199.0	310.0	343.0	403.0	435.0	708.0
Total Population	000s	18,239	11,493.4	2,295.4	2,190.8	2,266.7	2,240.6	2,499.9	6,745.8	1,150.2	1,265.3	1,331.0	1,440.3	1,559.0
Age dependency ratio	Number	0.9	1.0	1.2	1.2	1.1	1.0	0.7	0.8	1.1	0.9	0.8	0.7	0.5
Average household size	Number	4.4	4.7	6.3	5.7	5.3	4.7	3.1	4.0	5.7	5.2	4.5	4.3	2.6
Head Of Household Characteristics														
Age Dependency by household structure														
Monogamous male	Number	0.9	1.0	1.2	1.1	1.1	0.9	0.8	0.8	1.1	0.9	0.8	0.7	0.6
Polygamous male	Number	1.0	1.1	1.1	1.2	1.1	1.0	1.1	0.8	0.6	0.9	1.3	0.9	0.6
Single male	Number	0.4	0.5	0.8	1.0	0.6	0.7	0.2	0.2	1.1	0.5	0.5	0.2	0.1
De facto female	Number	1.1	1.2	1.8	1.2	1.3	1.1	1.0	0.9	1.3	0.8	1.0	0.8	0.7
De jure female	Number	1.0	1.1	1.5	1.3	1.3	1.0	0.7	0.9	1.3	1.1	0.8	0.8	0.6
Education level of head														
No level	Percent	32.0	39.1	65.3	47.4	32.9	32.5	30.1	21.8	44.3	31.6	25.7	19.8	9.5
Primary, not completed	Percent	15.2	17.7	10.7	16.6	21.1	21.6	17.2	11.7	14.7	12.8	14.0	10.8	9.8
Primary completed, no secondary	Percent	29.4	26.4	13.9	23.7	30.2	29.1	29.8	33.8	25.9	29.4	36.6	37.9	34.6
Secondary not completed	Percent	4.0	..	..	..	..	..	..	..	..	..	..	..	..
Secondary completed	Percent	5.9	2.9	0.8	2.2	2.2	3.7	4.1	10.3	1.1	7.7	4.9	10.5	16.9
Tertiary	Percent	8.4	5.0	0.9	2.4	4.5	3.9	9.0	13.4	4.7	9.3	10.5	14.7	18.7
Pre-school	Percent	3.3	4.0	4.7	4.0	4.3	4.6	3.1	2.4	6.1	3.6	3.2	1.5	0.9
Undefined	Percent	0.2	0.1	..	..	..	0.1	0.3	0.4	..	..	0.4	1.1	0.3
Marital Status of head														
Monogamous male	Percent	52.8	56.2	63.4	57.0	63.2	56.9	48.3	48.0	48.9	54.3	54.3	56.9	37.0
Polygamous male	Percent	2.8	3.8	7.4	5.1	3.4	3.7	1.7	1.3	3.8	2.1	0.8	1.4	0.2
Single male	Percent	11.8	9.6	4.5	6.4	4.1	8.0	17.2	15.0	6.1	6.9	7.2	10.6	27.6
De facto female	Percent	11.6	10.1	8.3	10.4	12.9	9.0	9.9	13.8	20.0	12.0	14.9	14.4	11.6
De jure female	Percent	21.0	..	..	..	..	..	..	..	..	..	..	..	..
Labor Market														
Proportion aged 15-64 in population	Percent	52.1	49.5	44.5	46.2	47.4	51.0	57.5	56.6	47.4	52.0	55.4	58.5	66.7
Proportion employed (aged 15 to 64)	Percent	57.4	58.0	46.9	50.6	57.5	59.4	70.4	56.6	50.3	52.7	55.1	57.0	63.3
Females among employed (aged 15 to 64)	Percent	51.1	49.2	42.6	48.5	51.8	51.8	49.3	54.0	57.3	57.0	58.2	55.5	47.2
Employment Ratios (among labor force)														
Employment Ratio	Percent	66.1	70.8	69.3	65.2	70.0	68.0	77.8	59.9	56.5	57.2	58.0	59.3	65.0
Formal Employment among Employed	Percent	18.7	11.7	3.6	5.0	10.7	11.1	20.1	29.3	12.9	22.1	28.6	33.0	37.8
Public Employed among Formal Employment	Percent	43.1	45.1	36.4	44.9	48.0	52.7	42.2	41.9	56.9	52.6	41.5	41.3	36.9
Informal Employment among Employed	Percent	78.6	86.2	95.2	93.3	87.4	86.4	77.3	67.0	85.6	74.2	68.6	63.3	57.0
Self-Employed among Informal Employed	Percent	100.0	..	..	..	..	..	..	..	..	..	..	..	..
Employers among Employed	Percent	2.4	1.8	1.2	1.3	1.7	1.8	2.4	3.3	1.3	3.7	1.9	3.4	4.8
Proportion Employed in Agriculture	Percent	43.4	61.6	82.4	68.8	63.1	61.7	47.1	15.5	40.6	20.6	15.5	10.9	5.5
MDG1: Eradicate Extreme Poverty and Hunger														
Mean monthly per capita expenditure	Ghanaian cedis	119,877	91,523.9	23,106.8	39,131.6	55,065.0	77,592.2	176,149.1	161,066.8	38,435.6	66,819.4	96,992.2	136,525.6	286,033.0
Mean monthly share on food	Percent	59.2	62.4	62.9	64.0	62.9	62.0	61.3	54.6	59.5	56.4	55.2	53.2	52.8
Mean monthly share on health	Percent	3.7	3.8	3.3	3.5	3.8	4.0	4.0	3.5	3.2	3.5	3.5	3.6	3.5
Mean monthly share on education	Percent	3.9	3.1	3.5	3.7	3.7	3.4	2.0	5.0	5.8	5.4	5.3	6.6	3.6
MDG2: Education and Literacy; MDG3: Promote Gender Equality														
Access to primary school (within 30 minutes)	Percent	..	..	..	..	..	..	..	..	..	..	..	..	..
Net primary enrollment rate														
Total	Percent	61	54	39	48	53	68	68	74	67	70	73	81	79
Male	Percent	61	53	38	50	50	70	64	77	68	76	73	87	79
Female	Percent	61	56	40	46	58	67	71	71	65	65	74	75	80
Net secondary enrollment rate														
Total	Percent	10	7	3	6	6	8	12	16	7	12	19	21	19
Male	Percent	11	8	3	6	10	10	12	16	5	10	22	21	23
Female	Percent	10	6	3	6	3	7	12	15	9	13	17	21	16
Tertiary enrolment rate per 10,000														
Total	per 10,000	13	..	..	..	..	..	..	..	..	..	..	..	..
Adult literacy rate														
Total	Percent	53	43	24	35	44	50	55	67	45	59	64	75	82
Male	Percent	67	59	36	50	63	66	72	79	60	75	76	84	91
Female	Percent	40	29	13	23	28	36	39	57	34	47	54	67	73
Youth literacy rate														
Total	Percent	66	57	42	48	56	66	68	78	67	74	79	80	86
Male	Percent	73	65	47	56	69	77	77	85	74	80	86	87	91
Female	Percent	59	47	34	39	42	55	58	72	59	67	70	75	81

Ghana Living Standards Survey 4 1998/1999

(Table continues on the following page)

16-7. Ghana (continued)

			Expenditure Quintile											
			Rural						*Urban*					
	Unit of Measure	*National total*	*All*	*Q1*	*Q2*	*Q3*	*Q4*	*Q5*	*All*	*Q1*	*Q2*	*Q3*	*Q4*	*Q5*
Indicators														
MDG4: Reduce Child Mortality; MDG5: Improve Maternal Health														
Proportion with distance to Health Center less than 5 km	Percent	..	..	..	..	..	..	..	..	..	..	..	..	..
Morbidity	Percent	26	28	24	26	27	28	34	23	23	22	21	22	27
Action taken when sick	Percent	44	40	33	37	39	39	47	53	42	49	53	56	62
Health provider ownership														
Public	Percent	47	47	47	39	59	47	45	46	50	49	38	52	45
Private - Modern Medicine	Percent	44	42	43	52	33	42	44	45	35	37	51	42	52
Private - Traditional Healers	Percent	5	6	8	6	4	7	5	5	9	6	7	3	2
Other	Percent	4	4	2	3	4	4	6	4	6	7	4	3	2
Child survival and malnutrition														
Birth assisted by trained staff	Percent	..	..	..	..	..	..	..	..	..	..	..	..	..
1-year-olds immunisation coverage	Percent	..	..	..	..	..	..	..	..	..	..	..	..	..
1-year-olds immunized against measles	Percent	..	..	..	..	..	..	..	..	..	..	..	..	..
Stunting (6-59 months)	Percent	..	..	..	..	..	..	..	..	..	..	..	..	..
Wasting (6-59 months)	Percent	..	..	..	..	..	..	..	..	..	..	..	..	..
Underweight (6-59 months)	Percent	..	..	..	..	..	..	..	..	..	..	..	..	..
MDG7: Ensure Environmental Sustainability														
Owner occupancy rate	Percent	41	51	62	55	54	52	41	26	33	32	25	22	24
Access to sanitation facilities	Percent	79	70	37	63	74	81	81	91	78	87	91	94	95
Proportion with distance to Water Source less than 2 km	Percent	98	97	98	97	97	98	97	98	97	96	97	99	99
Proportion with distance distance to Market less than 5 km	Percent	100	100	100	100	100	100	100	100	100	100	100	100	100
Access to improved water source														
Pipe (own tap)	Percent	4	1	..	..	0	1	2	8	0	2	4	8	14
Pipe borne	Percent	40	19	7	15	15	19	29	70	60	70	71	72	72
Well (Protected)	Percent	17	28	38	28	32	29	22	1	2	3	2	2	1
Total	Percent	61	48	44	43	47	48	54	79	62	74	77	81	86
Access to unimproved water source														
Surface Water	Percent	23	35	31	38	40	38	31	7	19	12	6	4	2
Other	Percent	16	16	24	19	12	14	15	14	18	14	17	15	12
Total	Percent	39	52	56	57	53	52	46	21	38	26	23	19	14
Traditional Fuel Use														
Firewood	Percent	57	81	93	91	89	83	65	23	64	37	24	17	6
Charcoal	Percent	35	16	2	7	10	16	31	62	35	61	65	66	68
Total	Percent	92	97	95	98	99	99	96	85	99	98	89	83	74
Nontraditional Fuel Use														
Kerosene	Percent	1	0	0	0	0	0	1	2	..	..	2	2	4
Electricity	Percent	0	0	..	..	..	0	0	1	..	..	2	0	1
Gas	Percent	5	1	..	..	0	0	2	11	..	1	6	14	19
Other	Percent	1	1	5	2	1	0	0	1	1	0	1	1	2
Total	Percent	8	3	5	2	1	1	4	15	1	2	11	17	26

Ghana Living Standards Survey 4 1998/1999

16-8. Kenya

Indicators	Unit of Measure	National total	Rural All	Rural Q1	Rural Q2	Rural Q3	Rural Q4	Rural Q5	Urban All	Urban Q1	Urban Q2	Urban Q3	Urban Q4	Urban Q5
			Expenditure Quintile											
Demographic Indicators														
Sample size (households)	Number	10,874	8,963.0	1,339.0	1,521.0	1,646.0	1,813.0	2,644.0	1,911.0	273.0	262.0	327.0	514.0	535.0
Total Population	000s	25,468	21,490.3	4,297.7	4,298.9	4,292.9	4,302.9	4,297.9	3,978.0	797.2	792.5	798.2	795.0	795.0
Age dependency ratio	Number	0.9	1.0	1.3	1.1	1.0	0.9	0.7	0.6	1.0	0.8	0.5	0.4	0.3
Average household size	Number	4.6	4.9	6.4	5.8	5.4	4.8	3.3	3.5	5.3	4.3	3.8	2.9	2.5
Head Of Household Characteristics														
Age Dependency by household structure														
Monogamous male	Number	0.9	1.0	1.3	1.1	1.0	0.9	0.7	0.6	1.1	0.7	0.6	0.4	0.3
Polygamous male	Number	1.0	1.0	1.2	1.0	1.0	0.9	0.8	0.8	1.0	0.8	0.9	0.5	0.2
Single male	Number	0.4	0.5	1.0	0.8	0.9	0.7	0.1	0.0	0.1	0.1	0.0	0.1	0.0
De facto female	Number	1.3	1.3	1.7	1.5	1.4	1.1	0.9	0.8	1.5	1.3	0.6	0.4	0.7
De jure female	Number	0.9	1.0	1.4	1.1	1.0	0.9	0.8	0.6	0.9	1.2	0.2	0.5	0.2
Education level of head														
No level	Percent	27.5	32.5	41.1	36.3	35.7	29.5	26.1	8.0	14.7	11.2	4.6	7.5	5.6
Primary, not completed	Percent	27.8	29.7	36.0	33.4	29.4	29.4	24.7	20.2	28.9	22.7	23.1	22.8	10.6
Primary completed, no secondary	Percent	14.9	14.6	10.9	14.3	14.8	17.3	14.8	16.1	17.3	17.2	20.4	16.5	11.6
Secondary not completed	Percent	10.4	..	..	..	..	..	..	..	..	..	..	..	..
Secondary completed	Percent	14.4	10.8	3.5	5.5	7.7	11.5	19.0	28.3	16.0	26.9	21.9	32.2	35.9
Tertiary	Percent	2.8	1.3	0.5	0.8	0.3	0.5	3.1	8.5	0.9	5.2	6.3	3.3	19.8
Pre-school	Percent	0.1	0.1	0.0	0.1	0.1	0.3	0.1	..	..	..	..	..	..
Undefined	Percent	2.2	2.3	2.3	2.2	2.5	2.2	2.4	1.8	2.7	2.1	2.3	1.2	1.3
Marital Status of head														
Monogamous male	Percent	58.0	56.0	56.9	55.3	57.5	58.7	53.3	65.8	76.3	63.1	58.4	64.5	68.5
Polygamous male	Percent	7.2	8.1	11.0	11.6	7.5	7.5	5.4	3.8	6.2	6.0	4.3	2.1	2.4
Single male	Percent	6.5	5.6	1.8	3.2	4.0	3.5	11.4	10.0	1.7	1.9	11.5	12.4	15.6
De facto female	Percent	11.6	13.7	16.0	14.5	14.3	14.8	11.0	3.6	5.6	2.5	5.4	3.9	1.7
De jure female	Percent	16.6	..	..	..	..	..	..	..	..	..	..	..	..
Labor Market														
Proportion aged 15-64 in population	Percent	52.0	49.8	42.6	46.9	49.1	51.7	58.8	64.1	48.8	55.5	67.4	71.6	76.9
Proportion employed (aged 15 to 64)	Percent	43.9	39.7	34.4	33.7	38.2	38.6	50.5	61.5	48.1	59.9	58.7	63.3	71.9
Females among employed (aged 15 to 64)	Percent	37.9	39.2	38.7	39.3	42.0	39.6	37.3	34.4	30.5	40.7	35.4	33.3	32.4
Employment Ratios (among labor force)														
Employment Ratio	Percent	85.4	86.3	84.0	82.9	85.6	87.1	89.3	83.2	75.2	78.6	78.1	86.3	92.0
Formal Employment among Employed	Percent	26.9	21.7	12.1	15.8	15.8	22.5	32.6	41.2	28.7	34.8	37.2	43.6	51.2
Public Employed among Formal Employment	Percent	48.5	52.8	38.0	42.5	50.1	53.8	58.5	42.6	41.2	33.3	47.4	47.4	40.8
Informal Employment among Employed	Percent	72.4	77.9	87.6	83.7	84.1	76.9	66.7	57.4	70.9	63.9	61.9	55.8	46.0
Self-Employed among Informal Employed	Percent	67.0	..	..	..	..	..	..	..	..	..	..	..	..
Employers among Employed	Percent	0.7	0.5	0.2	0.4	0.1	0.5	0.7	1.4	0.4	1.3	0.9	0.6	2.8
Proportion Employed in Agriculture	Percent	43.4	56.9	64.7	62.3	61.2	56.9	47.6	6.9	8.1	6.8	6.0	6.7	7.2
MDG1: Eradicate Extreme Poverty and Hunger														
Mean monthly per capita expenditure	Kshs.	2,244	1,716.4	454.8	710.7	998.1	1,431.2	3,568.8	4,298.6	1,048.4	1,636.9	2,255.1	3,541.5	9,396.2
Mean monthly share on food	Percent	70.4	73.9	76.8	75.8	76.9	74.9	68.8	56.9	65.3	64.4	58.4	56.6	47.9
Mean monthly share on health	Percent	0.2	0.2	0.1	0.2	0.1	0.2	0.2	0.2	0.1	0.2	0.1	0.2	0.3
Mean monthly share on education	Percent	3.5	3.3	2.8	3.2	3.3	3.6	3.5	4.0	1.9	3.5	3.8	4.2	5.3
MDG2: Education and Literacy; MDG3: Promote Gender Equality														
Access to primary school (within 30 minutes)	Percent	69	63	57	63	62	64	66	91	88	89	93	90	95
Net primary enrollment rate														
Total	Percent	73	73	65	73	72	77	82	78	69	81	83	82	80
Male	Percent	72	71	64	71	69	77	82	77	66	87	81	78	74
Female	Percent	75	74	66	74	74	78	81	78	72	74	85	85	86
Net secondary enrollment rate														
Total	Percent	12	10	4	6	9	13	18	29	10	14	22	38	62
Male	Percent	12	9	3	5	8	13	19	36	18	13	34	42	73
Female	Percent	11	10	4	7	10	13	17	22	3	14	14	33	49
Tertiary enrolment rate per 10,000														
Total	per 10,000	28	..	..	..	..	..	..	..	..	..	..	..	..
Adult literacy rate														
Total	Percent	78	75	67	72	74	78	79	92	87	91	94	93	95
Male	Percent	86	83	77	80	82	86	88	96	92	93	98	96	98
Female	Percent	71	67	59	64	67	71	71	89	83	89	89	90	91
Youth literacy rate														
Total	Percent	94	93	91	91	94	94	95	95	92	98	95	95	96
Male	Percent	95	94	92	93	96	95	96	98	95	99	99	98	98
Female	Percent	92	92	90	90	92	93	94	93	90	98	90	93	93

Kenya Welfare Monitoring Survey III 1997

(Table continues on the following page)

16-8. Kenya (continued)

	Unit of Measure	National total	Rural All	Rural Q1	Rural Q2	Rural Q3	Rural Q4	Rural Q5	Urban All	Urban Q1	Urban Q2	Urban Q3	Urban Q4	Urban Q5
			Expenditure Quintile											
Indicators														
MDG4: Reduce Child Mortality; MDG5: Improve Maternal Health														
Proportion with distance to Health Center less than 5 km	Percent	72	65	56	62	61	66	73	98	98	99	98	98	99
Morbidity	Percent	16	15	12	15	14	17	18	17	14	13	22	17	21
Action taken when sick	Percent	90	90	86	89	87	93	92	92	88	93	96	96	88
Health provider ownership														
Public	Percent	32	31	34	30	38	28	27	36	54	35	31	39	28
Private - Modern Medicine	Percent	51	49	48	46	41	53	55	59	41	56	65	54	69
Private - Traditional Healers	Percent	3	3	3	4	4	3	1	2	3	1	2	2	0
Other	Percent	7	8	7	12	11	7	6	1	0	1	2	2	1
Child survival and malnutrition														
Birth assisted by trained staff	Percent	47	42	30	37	40	50	61	75	62	71	76	88	94
1-year-olds immunisation coverage	Percent	72	68	52	74	69	72	80	86	73	96	83	97	92
1-year-olds immunized against measles	Percent	83	80	69	80	83	83	91	92	87	96	91	100	92
Stunting (6-59 months)	Percent	38	40	50	40	34	35	35	32	44	31	26	28	21
Wasting (6-59 months)	Percent	6	6	7	5	8	6	6	5	5	7	8	2	2
Underweight (6-59 months)	Percent	22	24	32	26	21	19	19	13	20	12	14	7	8
MDG7: Ensure Environmental Sustainability														
Owner occupancy rate	Percent	72	87	96	93	93	91	74	11	17	9	4	9	14
Access to sanitation facilities	Percent	86	83	73	80	82	86	89	95	88	89	95	99	97
Proportion with distance to Water Source less than 2 km	Percent	68	62	53	59	61	61	68	92	89	96	90	92	94
Proportion with distance distance to Market less than 5 km	Percent	82	78	77	79	78	77	79	99	99	98	99	99	100
Access to improved water source														
Pipe (own tap)	Percent	17	10	3	6	8	9	17	44	32	33	38	45	59
Pipe borne	Percent	19	14	10	15	10	14	17	40	42	46	44	45	30
Well (Protected)	Percent	13	16	16	18	17	18	12	2	6	3	1	1	1
Total	Percent	49	39	29	39	34	41	46	86	81	82	83	91	90
Access to unimproved water source														
Surface Water	Percent	32	39	47	37	42	39	35	2	3	2	1	2	2
Other	Percent	20	22	24	24	24	20	19	12	17	17	16	7	8
Total	Percent	51	61	71	61	66	59	54	14	19	18	17	9	10
Traditional Fuel Use														
Firewood	Percent	73	91	99	97	97	93	78	5	16	5	2	4	2
Charcoal	Percent	8	5	1	2	2	4	11	21	32	21	26	22	12
Total	Percent	82	96	100	99	99	97	89	26	48	26	28	26	13
Nontraditional Fuel Use														
Kerosene	Percent	15	3	..	0	0	2	9	62	51	72	69	65	54
Electricity	Percent	1	0	..	0	0	0	0	3	0	1	0	2	7
Gas	Percent	2	0	0	..	0	0	1	9	..	0	2	6	25
Other	Percent	1	1	0	0	1	1	0	0	..	..	1	0	0
Total	Percent	18	4	0	1	1	3	11	74	52	74	72	74	87

Kenya Welfare Monitoring Survey III 1997

16-9. Madagascar

Indicators	Unit of Measure	National total	Rural: All	Rural: Q1	Rural: Q2	Rural: Q3	Rural: Q4	Rural: Q5	Urban: All	Urban: Q1	Urban: Q2	Urban: Q3	Urban: Q4	Urban: Q5
			Expenditure Quintile											
Demographic Indicators														
Sample size (households)	Number	5,120	2,880.0	452.0	495.0	554.0	622.0	757.0	2,240.0	298.0	367.0	415.0	487.0	673.0
Total Population	000s	14,631	11,377.0	2,276.9	2,275.0	2,277.3	2,272.5	2,275.4	3,253.6	652.3	649.4	650.9	650.2	650.8
Age dependency ratio	Number	0.9	1.0	1.3	1.2	1.0	0.9	0.7	0.7	1.1	0.9	0.7	0.6	0.5
Average household size	Number	5.1	5.2	6.7	6.1	5.4	4.9	3.8	4.9	6.8	5.5	5.1	4.5	3.5
Head Of Household Characteristics														
Age Dependency by household structure														
Monogamous male	Number	0.9	1.0	1.3	1.2	1.0	0.9	0.7	0.7	1.0	0.9	0.7	0.6	0.6
Polygamous male	Number	..	..	..	..	..	..	..	..	..	..	..	..	..
Single male	Number	0.8	0.8	1.5	1.0	1.0	0.6	0.6	0.6	1.3	0.7	0.4	0.7	0.3
De facto female	Number	1.0	1.1	1.6	1.0	1.3	0.9	0.8	0.9	1.1	1.2	0.8	0.8	0.4
De jure female	Number	0.8	0.9	1.3	1.2	0.9	0.9	0.6	0.7	1.2	0.8	0.8	0.7	0.4
Education level of head														
No level	Percent	23.8	27.3	38.1	26.8	32.1	23.8	20.7	12.4	25.8	15.7	17.6	7.3	4.0
Primary, not completed	Percent	30.5	34.4	38.6	37.8	36.2	34.7	28.2	17.8	29.4	25.1	17.2	13.9	10.6
Primary completed, no secondary	Percent	16.4	16.3	12.2	16.9	14.6	19.1	17.1	16.8	20.5	22.3	16.4	16.1	12.3
Secondary not completed	Percent	21.2	..	..	..	..	..	..	..	..	..	..	..	..
Secondary completed	Percent	4.8	3.0	0.8	2.1	2.0	2.2	6.0	11.0	5.1	6.7	8.6	12.8	16.8
Tertiary	Percent	2.8	1.1	..	0.4	0.5	0.5	3.1	8.4	1.4	2.5	4.0	8.7	18.4
Pre-school	Percent	0.5	0.6	1.0	0.4	0.9	0.4	0.6	0.1	..	..	0.1	0.1	0.2
Undefined	Percent	..	..	..	..	..	..	..	..	..	..	..	..	..
Marital Status of head														
Monogamous male	Percent	75.6	76.8	76.7	81.3	81.1	79.6	69.0	71.5	74.3	73.0	72.9	73.2	67.1
Polygamous male	Percent	..	..	..	..	..	..	..	..	..	..	..	..	..
Single male	Percent	6.5	6.5	5.4	3.9	3.5	5.7	11.6	6.5	3.1	5.0	2.5	6.7	11.7
De facto female	Percent	7.9	7.9	10.3	6.8	8.0	6.8	8.1	7.8	9.9	11.3	7.2	8.0	4.8
De jure female	Percent	10.0	..	..	..	..	..	..	..	..	..	..	..	..
Labor Market														
Proportion aged 15-64 in population	Percent	51.7	50.0	43.2	45.9	49.8	52.5	58.9	57.5	48.4	52.1	59.8	60.6	66.7
Proportion employed (aged 15 to 64)	Percent	78.0	83.5	83.9	82.5	84.7	85.7	81.0	61.2	66.1	62.5	58.0	58.9	61.6
Females among employed (aged 15 to 64)	Percent	46.9	47.3	48.8	45.0	46.9	48.1	47.4	45.4	47.6	43.7	46.5	45.0	44.6
Employment Ratios (among labor force)														
Employment Ratio	Percent	97.7	98.0	98.2	98.2	98.1	98.3	97.6	96.1	95.3	96.5	97.3	95.5	95.8
Formal Employment among Employed	Percent	14.2	8.5	3.5	7.3	6.2	7.9	15.8	38.0	22.8	30.1	37.8	45.2	50.0
Public Employed among Formal Employment	Percent	20.9	18.1	12.2	10.9	14.5	19.2	22.5	23.5	16.4	25.2	23.7	23.1	25.2
Informal Employment among Employed	Percent	85.1	91.1	96.4	92.5	93.3	91.6	83.4	60.1	74.2	68.5	60.2	54.1	47.7
Self-Employed among Informal Employed	Percent	58.5	..	..	..	..	..	..	..	..	..	..	..	..
Employers among Employed	Percent	0.5	0.3	0.0	0.2	0.5	0.2	0.7	1.4	2.3	0.8	1.3	0.4	2.0
Proportion Employed in Agriculture	Percent	52.5	57.6	55.2	60.1	57.3	61.2	54.3	31.1	46.1	43.9	30.7	22.9	16.9
MDG1: Eradicate Extreme Poverty and Hunger														
Mean monthly per capita expenditure	Malagasy francs	67,747	54,210.1	15,779.9	26,141.9	36,507.4	51,866.3	108,172.9	112,000.6	26,008.5	47,759.3	72,120.9	107,535.4	226,089.9
Mean monthly share on food	Percent	72.4	75.2	75.1	76.7	75.5	76.5	73.1	63.0	68.5	65.2	62.8	62.3	59.5
Mean monthly share on health	Percent	3.0	2.8	2.9	3.1	2.7	2.8	2.6	3.8	3.7	3.8	4.3	3.7	3.6
Mean monthly share on education	Percent	1.9	1.5	2.0	1.7	1.6	1.2	1.3	3.2	3.0	3.8	3.8	3.4	2.2
MDG2: Education and Literacy; MDG3: Promote Gender Equality														
Access to primary school (within 30 minutes)	Percent	..	..	..	..	..	..	..	..	..	..	..	..	..
Net primary enrollment rate														
Total	Percent	67	64	52	66	64	64	77	82	67	78	84	94	97
Male	Percent	67	63	55	63	65	63	74	82	66	74	91	97	95
Female	Percent	68	64	50	68	64	65	81	82	68	81	79	92	98
Net secondary enrollment rate														
Total	Percent	10	6	2	4	4	6	16	24	6	18	24	34	46
Male	Percent	9	6	1	3	3	8	14	23	5	20	18	30	53
Female	Percent	11	6	2	4	5	4	19	25	8	16	28	37	40
Tertiary enrolment rate per 10,000														
Total	per 10,000	8	..	..	..	..	..	..	..	..	..	..	..	..
Adult literacy rate														
Total	Percent	67	61	44	58	58	66	74	84	66	81	85	90	94
Male	Percent	71	66	49	64	62	71	77	87	68	86	87	93	95
Female	Percent	63	57	40	52	54	61	70	82	63	76	83	87	93
Youth literacy rate														
Total	Percent	70	64	47	60	63	72	78	87	69	89	91	91	95
Male	Percent	70	65	47	62	64	74	76	87	66	92	89	92	96
Female	Percent	70	64	48	58	63	71	79	88	72	86	93	91	94

Enquête Prioritaire 1999

(Table continues on the following page)

16-9. Madagascar (continued)

			Expenditure Quintile											
			Rural						*Urban*					
	Unit of Measure	*National total*	*All*	*Q1*	*Q2*	*Q3*	*Q4*	*Q5*	*All*	*Q1*	*Q2*	*Q3*	*Q4*	*Q5*
Indicators														
MDG4: Reduce Child Mortality; MDG5: Improve Maternal Health														
Proportion with distance to Health Center less than 5 km	Percent	..	..	..	..	..	..	..	..	..	..	..	..	..
Morbidity	Percent	11	11	10	10	11	12	13	9	9	11	8	9	9
Action taken when sick	Percent	46	42	29	39	41	48	52	61	56	58	61	64	68
Health provider ownership														
Public	Percent	59	61	76	69	68	59	47	53	62	70	56	39	39
Private - Modern Medicine	Percent	32	30	20	22	23	32	42	36	23	21	36	48	53
Private - Traditional Healers	Percent	4	4	3	6	6	2	5	4	4	5	4	5	2
Other	Percent	2	3	1	2	2	3	4	1	1	2	1	1	1
Child survival and malnutrition														
Birth assisted by trained staff	Percent	..	..	..	..	..	..	..	..	..	..	..	..	..
1-year-olds immunisation coverage	Percent	61	57	45	57	51	63	76	76	70	78	63	84	91
1-year-olds immunized against measles	Percent	..	..	..	..	..	..	..	..	..	..	..	..	..
Stunting (6-59 months)	Percent	49	50	50	48	50	52	49	44	48	51	44	42	32
Wasting (6-59 months)	Percent	14	15	16	15	16	13	10	14	17	17	11	15	11
Underweight (6-59 months)	Percent	35	35	40	33	40	33	29	31	36	36	27	34	18
MDG7: Ensure Environmental Sustainability														
Owner occupancy rate	Percent	..	..	..	..	..	..	..	..	..	..	..	..	..
Access to sanitation facilities	Percent	52	43	32	36	39	46	54	80	60	70	81	84	93
Proportion with distance to Water Source less than 2 km	Percent	..	..	..	..	..	..	..	..	..	..	..	..	..
Proportion with distance distance to Market less than 5 km	Percent	..	..	..	..	..	..	..	..	..	..	..	..	..
Access to improved water source														
Pipe (own tap)	Percent	4	1	..	..	..	1	2	15	1	3	7	16	32
Pipe borne	Percent	19	8	3	5	6	8	15	52	40	51	60	54	51
Well (Protected)	Percent	1	1	0	1	0	1	2	3	2	3	4	6	2
Total	Percent	24	10	3	6	6	10	19	70	43	57	71	76	85
Access to unimproved water source														
Surface Water	Percent	57	70	77	79	73	74	55	14	32	22	14	10	4
Other	Percent	19	20	19	15	21	17	26	16	25	20	15	13	11
Total	Percent	76	90	97	94	94	90	81	30	57	43	29	24	15
Traditional Fuel Use														
Firewood	Percent	80	92	99	98	96	92	80	40	84	63	39	28	14
Charcoal	Percent	18	7	0	1	3	6	18	55	14	35	59	69	75
Total	Percent	98	99	99	99	99	98	98	95	98	98	97	96	89
Nontraditional Fuel Use														
Kerosene	Percent	..	..	..	..	..	..	..	..	..	..	..	..	..
Electricity	Percent	0	..	..	..	..	..	..	1	..	..	0	1	2
Gas	Percent	1	0	..	..	..	1	1	2	..	0	1	1	6
Other	Percent	1	1	1	1	1	1	1	2	2	2	1	2	3
Total	Percent	2	1	1	1	1	2	2	5	2	2	3	4	11

Enquête Prioritaire 1999

16-10. Malawi

			Expenditure Quintile											
			Rural						*Urban*					
Indicators	*Unit of Measure*	*National total*	*All*	*Q1*	*Q2*	*Q3*	*Q4*	*Q5*	*All*	*Q1*	*Q2*	*Q3*	*Q4*	*Q5*
Demographic Indicators														
Sample size (households)	Number	6,586	5,657.0	902.0	1,024.0	1,106.0	1,198.0	1,427.0	929.0	200.0	184.0	174.0	194.0	177.0
Total Population	000s	9,795	8,795.0	1,759.5	1,759.4	1,758.0	1,759.1	1,758.9	1,000.0	200.3	199.9	199.8	199.5	200.4
Age dependency ratio	Number	0.9	0.9	1.2	1.0	0.9	0.8	0.7	0.6	0.9	0.7	0.6	0.5	0.4
Average household size	Number	4.4	4.4	5.3	4.8	4.5	4.2	3.6	4.1	5.4	4.5	4.2	3.5	3.6
Head Of Household Characteristics														
Age Dependency by household structure														
Monogamous male	Number	0.9	0.9	1.1	1.0	0.9	0.8	0.7	0.7	1.0	0.7	0.6	0.6	0.5
Polygamous male	Number	0.9	0.9	1.1	1.5	0.9	0.9	0.7	..	..	..	..	..	..
Single male	Number	0.4	0.5	0.6	1.2	0.6	0.5	0.2	0.2	0.5	0.3	0.4	0.2	0.0
De facto female	Number	1.1	1.2	1.3	1.3	1.1	1.1	0.8	0.7	0.7	1.1	0.9	0.3	0.6
De jure female	Number	1.1	1.1	1.4	1.2	1.2	1.0	0.7	0.7	0.8	1.0	0.7	0.6	0.4
Education level of head														
No level	Percent	25.7	28.3	41.0	31.9	28.7	24.7	19.6	3.9	12.8	6.4	1.0	1.7	0.5
Primary, not completed	Percent	58.2	61.3	53.6	61.1	64.5	64.1	61.9	31.8	60.5	48.3	29.9	24.9	8.1
Primary completed, no secondary	Percent	6.1	4.7	1.8	3.6	3.3	5.9	7.5	17.5	10.9	26.4	19.4	16.2	14.4
Secondary not completed	Percent	0.4	..	..	..	..	..	..	..	..	..	..	..	..
Secondary completed	Percent	6.1	3.2	0.7	0.7	1.2	2.8	8.4	30.7	10.8	13.9	37.5	44.9	37.4
Tertiary	Percent	1.1	0.2	0.3	..	..	0.2	0.7	8.6	0.8	3.1	7.5	3.9	23.8
Pre-school	Percent		..	..	..	..	..	..	..	..	..	..	..	..
Undefined	Percent	2.4	1.9	2.6	2.4	2.1	1.7	1.2	6.7	3.3	1.2	3.8	7.8	14.8
Marital Status of head														
Monogamous male	Percent	68.1	67.9	65.1	67.9	70.5	69.7	66.2	69.6	78.1	79.9	75.0	65.2	55.7
Polygamous male	Percent	0.7	0.8	0.5	0.9	1.0	0.7	0.9	..	..	..	..	..	..
Single male	Percent	6.2	5.3	1.7	2.7	3.3	5.6	10.8	13.8	4.1	4.4	9.4	21.4	23.9
De facto female	Percent	7.1	7.6	9.7	8.2	7.6	6.3	6.6	3.1	4.9	3.1	2.3	2.3	3.6
De jure female	Percent	17.9	..	..	..	..	..	..	..	..	..	..	..	..
Labor Market														
Proportion aged 15-64 in population	Percent	53.0	52.1	46.4	48.8	51.6	54.9	58.7	61.5	51.8	58.1	61.1	65.5	70.9
Proportion employed (aged 15 to 64)	Percent	43.3	43.0	36.5	40.6	43.9	44.3	48.0	45.8	38.3	41.6	46.3	48.1	52.2
Females among employed (aged 15 to 64)	Percent	37.7	39.1	43.8	42.4	41.7	37.3	33.2	28.0	23.9	21.2	25.8	28.2	36.3
Employment Ratios (among labor force)														
Employment Ratio	Percent	96.8	97.1	97.1	96.8	96.7	97.2	97.6	95.0	96.8	96.8	94.1	91.2	97.0
Formal Employment among Employed	Percent	23.2	16.5	10.7	10.4	13.3	17.7	25.7	72.8	59.7	63.9	75.1	78.2	78.2
Public Employed among Formal Employment	Percent	39.4	37.7	17.4	25.5	32.3	38.0	48.0	42.3	35.3	38.3	37.2	48.3	45.3
Informal Employment among Employed	Percent	73.6	80.6	84.5	87.6	83.5	79.2	72.2	21.7	35.2	27.8	20.0	15.8	17.7
Self-Employed among Informal Employed	Percent	92.8	..	..	..	..	..	..	..	..	..	..	..	..
Employers among Employed	Percent	1.1	1.2	0.9	0.7	1.7	1.3	1.0	0.8	0.5	0.2	2.0	0.7	0.4
Proportion Employed in Agriculture	Percent	55.8	63.4	61.8	69.3	69.1	62.8	56.1	2.2	6.6	3.2	1.5	1.9	0.0
MDG1: Eradicate Extreme Poverty and Hunger														
Mean monthly per capita expenditure	Malawi kwacha	431	307.7	91.0	154.6	218.1	310.3	637.0	1,456.4	297.9	509.9	759.4	1,212.1	3,820.4
Mean monthly share on food	Percent	70.9	74.3	77.9	77.3	76.9	75.2	67.0	42.5	55.8	51.9	46.2	39.7	25.9
Mean monthly share on health	Percent	0.7	0.6	0.5	0.6	0.7	0.6	0.7	1.5	1.3	1.6	1.5	1.5	1.6
Mean monthly share on education	Percent	0.5	0.3	0.2	0.2	0.2	0.3	0.6	1.7	0.5	0.7	1.1	1.4	4.3
MDG2: Education and Literacy; MDG3: Promote Gender Equality														
Access to primary school (within 30 minutes)	Percent	..	..	..	..	..	..	..	..	..	..	..	..	..
Net primary enrollment rate														
Total	Percent	57	56	57	53	54	55	63	69	65	58	72	80	71
Male	Percent	56	55	54	56	49	52	66	68	57	54	78	85	72
Female	Percent	59	58	59	50	60	59	61	69	76	61	66	74	70
Net secondary enrollment rate														
Total	Percent	4	2	1	2	1	2	5	16	8	11	14	17	30
Male	Percent	4	2	1	3	1	2	6	16	9	9	18	17	30
Female	Percent	4	2	0	2	2	2	4	15	7	13	10	17	30
Tertiary enrolment rate per 10,000														
Total	per 10,000	4	..	..	..	..	..	..	..	..	..	..	..	..
Adult literacy rate														
Total	Percent	51	47	35	44	44	50	58	85	74	80	93	91	86
Male	Percent	62	58	47	55	55	61	68	89	83	88	96	90	86
Female	Percent	41	37	26	33	35	40	48	82	65	73	90	92	87
Youth literacy rate														
Total	Percent	63	59	50	57	57	63	66	88	79	84	96	94	87
Male	Percent	69	66	58	62	64	68	73	90	85	88	98	93	87
Female	Percent	58	54	42	53	51	58	61	87	75	81	95	95	87

Malawi Integrated Household Survey 1997/1998

(Table continues on the following page)

16-10. Malawi (continued)

	Unit of Measure	National total	Rural All	Rural Q1	Rural Q2	Rural Q3	Rural Q4	Rural Q5	Urban All	Urban Q1	Urban Q2	Urban Q3	Urban Q4	Urban Q5
Indicators														
MDG4: Reduce Child Mortality; MDG5: Improve Maternal Health														
Proportion with distance to Health Center less than 5 km	Percent	52	48	46	45	46	48	52	90	78	85	92	96	96
Morbidity	Percent	28	29	24	27	30	31	34	15	16	18	15	15	13
Action taken when sick	Percent	..	..	..	..	..	..	..	..	..	..	..	..	..
Health provider ownership														
Public	Percent	..	..	..	..	..	..	..	..	..	..	..	..	..
Private - Modern Medicine	Percent	..	..	..	..	..	..	..	..	..	..	..	..	..
Private - Traditional Healers	Percent	..	..	..	..	..	..	..	..	..	..	..	..	..
Other	Percent	..	..	..	..	..	..	..	..	..	..	..	..	..
Child survival and malnutrition														
Birth assisted by trained staff	Percent	..	..	..	..	..	..	..	..	..	..	..	..	..
1-year-olds immunisation coverage	Percent	87	86	89	85	83	90	84	97	91	100	100	100	100
1-year-olds immunized against measles	Percent	89	89	91	89	87	91	85	99	96	100	100	100	100
Stunting (6-59 months)	Percent	56	56	58	56	57	58	51	57	54	47	67	68	55
Wasting (6-59 months)	Percent	11	11	11	12	11	9	11	10	14	17	7	4	..
Underweight (6-59 months)	Percent	25	26	33	22	27	23	25	17	27	18	11	3	5
MDG7: Ensure Environmental Sustainability														
Owner occupancy rate	Percent	86	92	98	97	95	90	86	37	49	42	34	29	35
Access to sanitation facilities	Percent	..	..	..	..	..	..	..	..	..	..	..	..	..
Proportion with distance to Water Source less than 2 km	Percent	..	..	..	..	..	..	..	..	..	..	..	..	..
Proportion with distance distance to Market less than 5 km	Percent	68	64	63	63	63	65	66	98	96	98	99	98	99
Access to improved water source														
Pipe (own tap)	Percent	6	1	0	0	1	1	3	43	13	22	44	49	72
Pipe borne	Percent	21	19	20	21	18	18	20	39	52	51	45	35	19
Well (Protected)	Percent	23	25	27	24	25	25	24	8	14	11	3	11	2
Total	Percent	50	45	47	46	43	43	46	89	79	83	92	96	93
Access to unimproved water source														
Surface Water	Percent	11	12	12	12	11	13	12	5	9	9	4	1	5
Other	Percent	39	43	41	42	46	44	42	5	12	8	3	3	3
Total	Percent	50	55	53	54	57	57	54	11	21	17	8	4	7
Traditional Fuel Use														
Firewood	Percent	92	97	99	99	97	97	96	49	76	68	56	40	18
Charcoal	Percent	2	0	0	0	..	1	1	18	18	20	22	18	12
Total	Percent	94	98	99	99	97	97	96	67	94	88	78	59	29
Nontraditional Fuel Use														
Kerosene	Percent	1	0	..	0	0	0	1	5	3	5	3	7	9
Electricity	Percent	3	0	0	..	..	0	0	27	3	5	18	35	61
Gas	Percent	0	..	..	..	..	..	..	0	..	1	..	..	1
Other	Percent	2	2	1	1	2	2	2	0	..	1	0	0	..
Total	Percent	6	2	1	1	3	3	4	33	6	12	22	41	71

Malawi Integrated Household Survey 1997/1998

16-11. Mozambique

			Expenditure Quintile											
			Rural						*Urban*					
	Unit of Measure	*National total*	*All*	*Q1*	*Q2*	*Q3*	*Q4*	*Q5*	*All*	*Q1*	*Q2*	*Q3*	*Q4*	*Q5*
Indicators														
Demographic Indicators														
Sample size (households)	Number	8,250	5,811.0	987.0	948.0	1,059.0	1,215.0	1,602.0	2,439.0	337.0	383.0	463.0	519.0	737.0
Total Population	000s	15,867	12,634.4	2,526.6	2,518.5	2,535.6	2,526.6	2,527.2	3,232.8	646.0	646.9	646.6	647.3	645.9
Age dependency ratio	Number	0.9	0.9	1.2	1.1	1.0	0.9	0.6	0.9	1.3	1.1	0.9	0.8	0.6
Average household size	Number	4.8	4.7	6.6	5.8	5.1	4.3	3.2	5.5	6.2	6.1	5.7	5.2	4.5
Head Of Household Characteristics														
Age Dependency by household structure														
Monogamous male	Number	0.9	0.9	1.2	1.1	1.0	0.9	0.6	0.9	1.2	1.1	0.8	0.8	0.7
Polygamous male	Number	1.0	1.0	1.2	1.1	1.1	1.0	0.7	1.1	0.9	1.7	1.0	0.7	0.9
Single male	Number	0.6	0.6	0.9	0.8	0.9	0.6	0.3	0.5	1.3	0.8	0.6	0.5	0.3
De facto female	Number	1.0	1.0	1.3	1.3	1.1	0.9	0.6	1.2	1.7	1.7	1.4	1.3	0.5
De jure female	Number	1.0	1.0	1.4	1.1	1.2	0.9	0.7	1.1	1.6	1.3	1.0	0.9	0.5
Education level of head														
No level	Percent	71.7	78.2	84.1	79.9	78.7	77.7	74.5	41.8	65.0	53.4	43.3	33.5	22.6
Primary, not completed	Percent	18.2	15.8	11.7	14.4	16.8	17.1	16.9	29.5	25.4	26.7	34.0	34.4	26.7
Primary completed, no secondary	Percent	6.8	4.9	3.7	5.0	3.5	4.4	6.6	15.4	6.6	13.3	11.8	20.1	21.8
Secondary not completed	Percent	1.7	..	..	..	..	..	..	..	..	..	..	..	..
Secondary completed	Percent	0.6	0.1	..	..	..	0.2	0.1	3.0	0.3	0.8	2.2	2.3	7.6
Tertiary	Percent	0.6	0.2	..	0.1	..	0.1	0.5	2.6	..	0.1	1.7	2.7	6.8
Pre-school	Percent	..	..	..	..	..	..	..	..	..	..	..	..	..
Undefined	Percent	0.4	0.4	0.4	0.2	0.4	0.4	0.4	0.7	0.8	0.3	2.1	0.3	0.4
Marital Status of head														
Monogamous male	Percent	65.0	64.8	65.5	67.8	67.0	66.2	60.3	66.3	63.4	70.8	66.9	65.5	65.4
Polygamous male	Percent	8.0	9.0	14.6	9.6	10.1	7.6	6.5	3.3	1.8	5.0	4.7	3.7	1.8
Single male	Percent	5.5	4.9	2.0	2.0	3.6	4.2	9.2	8.1	2.5	5.5	5.9	10.0	14.0
De facto female	Percent	6.3	6.5	5.0	8.6	5.8	6.1	6.8	5.3	6.9	3.6	4.7	5.1	6.0
De jure female	Percent	15.2	..	..	..	..	..	..	..	..	..	..	..	..
Labor Market														
Proportion aged 15-64 in population	Percent	51.5	51.4	45.7	47.0	49.3	52.8	62.1	51.9	43.9	46.6	53.0	54.9	61.4
Proportion employed (aged 15 to 64)	Percent	45.9	45.5	38.6	43.3	43.7	47.1	52.3	47.5	41.0	49.8	48.4	49.4	47.8
Females among employed (aged 15 to 64)	Percent	34.7	34.0	34.2	36.1	33.0	32.8	34.0	37.3	40.1	37.7	38.2	38.4	33.6
Employment Ratios (among labor force)														
Employment Ratio	Percent	81.5	88.5	84.4	89.6	89.4	87.7	90.4	62.9	56.5	64.2	64.5	63.9	63.9
Formal Employment among Employed	Percent	17.8	9.6	10.4	9.9	9.0	9.6	9.2	48.5	31.8	40.2	50.5	52.0	60.1
Public Employed among Formal Employment	Percent	62.1	56.9	56.2	55.5	56.5	53.9	60.8	66.0	63.1	66.3	60.6	60.3	75.2
Informal Employment among Employed	Percent	81.3	89.9	89.3	89.7	90.7	89.4	90.2	48.9	63.3	58.3	48.6	45.0	36.6
Self-Employed among Informal Employed	Percent	99.8	..	..	..	..	..	..	..	..	..	..	..	..
Employers among Employed	Percent	0.4	0.2	0.1	0.2	0.2	0.3	0.4	1.1	1.4	1.1	0.2	0.9	1.8
Proportion Employed in Agriculture	Percent	..	..	..	..	..	..	..	..	..	..	..	..	..
MDG1: Eradicate Extreme Poverty and Hunger														
Mean monthly per capita expenditure	Mozambican meticais	192,481	182,572.4	53,117.5	86,604.1	119,027.5	164,442.1	350,673.8	237,860.6	52,180.1	93,179.4	132,225.9	203,190.9	592,973.1
Mean monthly share on food	Percent	68.3	70.3	68.4	71.1	71.6	71.4	69.2	59.1	62.5	64.6	60.5	60.4	50.6
Mean monthly share on health	Percent	0.3	0.2	0.3	0.2	0.2	0.2	0.2	0.5	0.7	0.6	0.5	0.4	0.3
Mean monthly share on education	Percent	0.5	0.4	0.7	0.5	0.4	0.3	0.2	1.0	1.7	1.0	1.0	0.7	0.6
MDG2: Education and Literacy; MDG3: Promote Gender Equality														
Access to primary school (within 30 minutes)	Percent	...	..	..	..	..	..	..	..	..	..	..	..	..
Net primary enrollment rate														
Total	Percent	36	32	25	30	33	36	39	54	34	48	60	68	71
Male	Percent	38	35	27	32	36	39	42	54	34	53	63	70	66
Female	Percent	33	29	22	27	31	33	35	53	34	43	57	67	76
Net secondary enrollment rate														
Total	Percent	10	5	3	3	6	7	7	26	11	15	23	34	44
Male	Percent	10	6	4	3	7	8	9	26	14	19	22	37	40
Female	Percent	9	4	2	3	4	5	5	25	8	11	24	31	47
Tertiary enrolment rate per 10,000														
Total	per 10,000	7	..	..	..	..	..	..	..	..	..	..	..	..
Adult literacy rate														
Total	Percent	41	33	28	33	35	33	35	72	52	62	73	79	86
Male	Percent	58	51	44	51	53	52	53	84	70	80	84	88	94
Female	Percent	25	17	14	16	19	16	20	60	36	45	63	70	78
Youth literacy rate														
Total	Percent	51	42	35	42	47	39	45	82	71	75	83	86	90
Male	Percent	64	56	42	56	61	57	63	88	79	87	89	91	93
Female	Percent	40	29	28	28	34	25	32	76	61	65	78	82	88

Inquérito Nacional aos Agregados Familiares Sobre as Condições de Vida 1996

(Table continues on the following page)

16-11. Mozambique (continued)

			Expenditure Quintile											
			Rural						*Urban*					
	Unit of Measure	*National total*	*All*	*Q1*	*Q2*	*Q3*	*Q4*	*Q5*	*All*	*Q1*	*Q2*	*Q3*	*Q4*	*Q5*
Indicators														
MDG4: Reduce Child Mortality; MDG5: Improve Maternal Health														
Proportion with distance to Health Center less than 5 km	Percent	..	..	..	..	..	..	..	..	..	..	..	..	..
Morbidity	Percent	11	12	9	10	11	13	15	11	11	10	10	12	11
Action taken when sick	Percent	60	57	54	58	55	59	59	74	64	71	73	83	76
Health provider ownership														
Public	Percent	78	74	68	76	73	82	72	88	90	83	94	85	89
Private - Modern Medicine	Percent	6	5	3	6	6	4	6	9	10	13	4	13	7
Private - Traditional Healers	Percent	14	18	23	16	18	13	21	2	0	4	2	2	4
Other	Percent	2	2	6	2	2	1	1	0	..	0	0	0	0
Child survival and malnutrition														
Birth assisted by trained staff	Percent	..	..	..	..	..	..	..	..	..	..	..	..	..
1-year-olds immunisation coverage	Percent	..	..	..	..	..	..	..	..	..	..	..	..	..
1-year-olds immunized against measles	Percent	86	82	76	77	90	80	89	95	96	94	94	98	93
Stunting (6-59 months)	Percent	55	61	61	62	62	59	58	34	49	36	30	27	24
Wasting (6-59 months)	Percent	9	9	11	7	7	11	8	9	13	11	6	6	7
Underweight (6-59 months)	Percent	37	40	49	38	39	36	37	25	38	27	20	18	19
MDG7: Ensure Environmental Sustainability														
Owner occupancy rate	Percent	70	69	77	72	68	68	66	71	72	75	73	72	66
Access to sanitation facilities	Percent	35	29	26	29	28	29	29	67	44	55	70	76	81
Proportion with distance to Water Source less than 2 km	Percent	94	93	92	94	92	93	94	99	99	98	99	98	100
Proportion with distance distance to Market less than 5 km	Percent	..	..	..	..	..	..	..	..	..	..	..	..	..
Access to improved water source														
Pipe (own tap)	Percent	2	0	0	0	0	0	1	9	0	2	5	9	25
Pipe borne	Percent	16	11	9	8	10	10	14	41	41	38	43	44	40
Well (Protected)	Percent	..	..	..	..	..	..	..	..	..	..	..	..	..
Total	Percent	18	11	9	8	10	10	14	51	42	40	48	53	65
Access to unimproved water source														
Surface Water	Percent	32	39	44	40	37	40	35	5	11	6	2	3	2
Other	Percent	50	51	46	52	53	50	51	45	47	54	50	43	32
Total	Percent	82	89	91	92	90	90	86	49	58	60	52	47	35
Traditional Fuel Use														
Firewood	Percent	90	99	99	99	99	98	98	50	70	66	51	41	31
Charcoal	Percent	7	0	0	0	0	0	1	37	27	30	44	45	38
Total	Percent	97	99	99	99	99	98	99	87	97	96	94	86	70
Nontraditional Fuel Use														
Kerosene	Percent	..	..	..	..	..	..	..	..	..	..	..	..	..
Electricity	Percent	2	0	..	..	..	0	0	8	0	1	3	8	23
Gas	Percent	1	1	0	1	0	1	0	3	2	1	2	4	7
Other	Percent	0	0	0	0	0	1	0	1	1	2	0	1	1
Total	Percent	3	1	1	1	1	2	1	13	3	4	6	14	30

Inquérito Nacional aos Agregados Familiares Sobre as Condições de Vida 1996

16-12. São Tomé and Principe

			Expenditure Quintile											
			Rural						*Urban*					
	Unit of Measure	*National total*	*All*	*Q1*	*Q2*	*Q3*	*Q4*	*Q5*	*All*	*Q1*	*Q2*	*Q3*	*Q4*	*Q5*
Indicators														
Demographic Indicators														
Sample size (households)	Number	2,416	1,173.0	179.0	197.0	215.0	244.0	338.0	1,243.0	187.0	202.0	242.0	264.0	348.0
Total Population	000s	128	56.6	11.3	11.3	11.3	11.3	11.3	70.9	14.2	14.2	14.2	14.2	14.2
Age dependency ratio	Number	0.9	1.0	1.3	1.1	1.0	1.0	0.6	0.8	1.1	1.0	0.8	0.8	0.6
Average household size	Number	4.6	4.5	6.3	5.7	4.9	4.2	3.0	4.6	6.2	5.5	4.9	4.4	3.3
Head Of Household Characteristics														
Age Dependency by household structure														
Monogamous male	Number	0.9	0.9	1.2	1.1	1.0	0.9	0.6	0.8	1.0	1.0	0.8	0.8	0.6
Polygamous male	Number	..	..	..	..	..	..	..	..	..	..	..	..	..
Single male	Number	0.7	0.8	1.5	0.8	1.0	1.0	0.6	0.6	1.2	0.7	0.6	0.6	0.5
De facto female	Number	0.9	0.9	1.2	1.0	0.7	1.0	0.7	0.9	1.2	1.0	0.9	0.8	0.6
De jure female	Number	1.0	1.1	1.6	1.1	1.2	1.1	0.6	0.9	1.2	1.1	0.8	0.8	0.6
Education level of head														
No level	Percent	..	..	..	..	..	..	..	..	..	..	..	..	..
Primary, not completed	Percent	11.1	10.6	15.6	10.3	11.9	8.7	8.9	11.4	16.7	13.9	10.7	10.9	7.9
Primary completed, no secondary	Percent	31.7	35.2	32.1	43.6	35.0	35.3	32.3	28.8	34.6	30.8	27.0	30.5	24.6
Secondary not completed	Percent	19.0	..	..	..	..	..	..	..	..	..	..	..	..
Secondary completed	Percent	19.0	14.0	4.4	5.3	12.6	13.6	24.5	23.1	10.1	14.2	15.3	26.5	38.5
Tertiary	Percent	..	..	..	..	..	..	..	..	..	..	..	..	..
Pre-school	Percent	0.3	..	..	..	..	..	..	0.5	..	0.7	0.4	0.5	0.7
Undefined	Percent	19.0	22.3	27.8	22.0	20.7	26.4	17.7	16.2	25.0	21.0	20.5	11.8	9.1
Marital Status of head														
Monogamous male	Percent	51.0	52.7	61.6	65.8	65.6	48.4	36.6	49.6	51.2	50.5	45.6	56.2	46.0
Polygamous male	Percent	..	..	..	..	..	..	..	..	..	..	..	..	..
Single male	Percent	16.4	18.3	9.0	5.5	10.1	16.3	36.2	14.9	4.5	9.4	12.5	14.4	26.1
De facto female	Percent	7.5	6.3	4.5	4.8	5.0	8.5	7.3	8.4	7.5	11.3	11.7	4.5	7.9
De jure female	Percent	25.1	..	..	..	..	..	..	..	..	..	..	..	..
Labor Market														
Proportion aged 15-64 in population	Percent	53.4	51.1	43.4	48.4	50.4	50.9	62.4	55.2	48.6	50.8	56.6	56.3	63.9
Proportion employed (aged 15 to 64)	Percent	51.9	55.8	52.4	52.7	56.0	54.9	61.2	49.1	44.8	48.1	46.2	49.0	55.8
Females among employed (aged 15 to 64)	Percent	35.4	35.4	38.1	40.7	32.7	39.2	29.3	35.5	35.7	35.5	34.0	37.3	34.8
Employment Ratios (among labor force)														
Employment Ratio	Percent	88.1	86.5	77.0	81.5	90.9	88.7	92.2	89.5	83.8	86.4	89.7	90.0	95.0
Formal Employment among Employed	Percent	58.3	54.6	55.0	52.0	53.4	52.8	58.4	61.5	62.7	58.0	59.6	62.5	63.6
Public Employed among Formal Employment	Percent	33.7	31.2	28.6	31.2	34.0	29.4	32.0	35.6	24.4	33.6	27.7	38.8	46.5
Informal Employment among Employed	Percent	38.9	43.3	43.7	43.5	45.3	44.3	40.5	35.3	30.0	39.0	37.1	35.4	34.7
Self-Employed among Informal Employed	Percent	..	..	..	..	..	..	..	..	..	..	..	..	..
Employers among Employed	Percent	0.1	0.1	0.0	0.4	0.4	0.0	0.0	0.1	0.0	0.4	0.0	0.2	0.0
Proportion Employed in Agriculture	Percent	27.2	42.2	60.8	45.1	47.9	33.8	31.2	14.6	22.4	17.5	16.0	8.6	11.5
MDG1: Eradicate Extreme Poverty and Hunger														
Mean monthly per capita expenditure	Sao Tome and Principe dobras	451,490	318,312.9	80,362.2	128,371.4	175,195.7	243,054.0	679,373.3	560,829.2	108,471.0	179,365.7	252,849.6	359,040.7	1,403,365.5
Mean monthly share on food	Percent	71.7	75.3	78.1	76.8	77.9	75.9	71.2	68.7	76.0	73.7	68.6	67.9	62.3
Mean monthly share on health	Percent	3.3	2.8	3.0	3.2	2.0	3.0	3.0	3.8	2.8	3.3	4.1	3.3	4.8
Mean monthly share on education	Percent	2.2	1.8	2.0	2.3	1.7	1.8	1.5	2.6	2.5	2.5	3.1	3.3	1.8
MDG2: Education and Literacy; MDG3: Promote Gender Equality														
Access to primary school (within 30 minutes)	Percent	34	33	46	44	37	35	16	35	51	39	35	38	23
Net primary enrollment rate														
Total	Percent	70	67	68	68	63	68	67	73	71	73	78	73	74
Male	Percent	71	70	67	75	62	71	70	73	72	71	75	80	66
Female	Percent	69	64	68	60	63	64	63	73	69	75	81	65	79
Net secondary enrollment rate														
Total	Percent	43	29	13	26	23	34	50	52	32	39	64	62	64
Male	Percent	43	29	15	24	24	42	47	52	30	41	65	66	66
Female	Percent	42	28	11	28	22	25	51	52	35	37	62	59	63
Tertiary enrolment rate per 10,000														
Total	per 10,000	..	..	..	..	..	..	..	..	..	..	..	..	..
Adult literacy rate														
Total	Percent	83	80	76	82	79	77	85	86	78	83	85	89	91
Male	Percent	92	89	87	89	89	87	92	94	90	92	92	95	97
Female	Percent	76	72	67	76	70	69	77	79	68	75	80	84	84
Youth literacy rate														
Total	Percent	94	92	90	92	91	91	95	96	91	94	98	98	96
Male	Percent	95	93	95	91	90	94	96	96	94	96	97	98	98
Female	Percent	93	91	86	92	92	88	95	95	88	92	98	98	95

Enquête Nationale sur les Conditions de Vie des Ménages

(Table continues on next page)

16-12. São Tomé and Principe (continued)

			Expenditure Quintile											
			Rural						*Urban*					
	Unit of Measure	*National total*	*All*	*Q1*	*Q2*	*Q3*	*Q4*	*Q5*	*All*	*Q1*	*Q2*	*Q3*	*Q4*	*Q5*
Indicators														
MDG4: Reduce Child Mortality; MDG5: Improve Maternal Health														
Proportion with distance to Health Center less than 5 km	Percent	84	81	77	74	81	82	85	87	86	90	85	89	87
Morbidity	Percent	18	15	12	14	14	17	20	19	12	19	19	22	24
Action taken when sick	Percent	48	45	41	45	40	50	47	50	38	44	50	56	57
Health provider ownership														
Public	Percent	70	81	94	88	78	83	68	64	80	78	68	62	53
Private - Modern Medicine	Percent	25	14	4	9	16	10	27	31	15	18	29	32	43
Private - Traditional Healers	Percent	3	2	..	3	..	3	4	4	5	1	3	6	2
Other	Percent	1	2	2	..	6	3	1	1	..	3	..	..	2
Child survival and malnutrition														
Birth assisted by trained staff	Percent	..	..	..	..	..	..	..	..	..	..	..	..	..
1-year-olds immunisation coverage	Percent	..	..	..	..	..	..	..	..	..	..	..	..	..
1-year-olds immunized against measles	Percent	..	..	..	..	..	..	..	..	..	..	..	..	..
Stunting (6-59 months)	Percent	..	..	..	..	..	..	..	..	..	..	..	..	..
Wasting (6-59 months)	Percent	..	..	..	..	..	..	..	..	..	..	..	..	..
Underweight (6-59 months)	Percent	..	..	..	..	..	..	..	..	..	..	..	..	..
MDG7: Ensure Environmental Sustainability														
Owner occupancy rate	Percent	67	69	66	69	69	74	66	66	72	65	72	63	62
Access to sanitation facilities	Percent	31	23	21	16	23	21	30	37	15	30	38	42	49
Proportion with distance to Water Source less than 2 km	Percent	88	93	93	94	93	95	92	84	82	80	87	86	85
Proportion with distance distance to Market less than 5 km	Percent	87	81	74	73	80	86	86	92	90	88	91	93	94
Access to improved water source														
Pipe (own tap)	Percent	20	10	7	9	7	13	12	27	12	20	26	29	40
Pipe borne	Percent	8	13	19	15	15	11	10	4	4	3	5	5	4
Well (Protected)	Percent	49	44	48	46	42	46	41	53	65	56	49	56	43
Total	Percent	77	67	74	70	64	70	63	84	82	79	81	89	88
Access to unimproved water source														
Surface Water	Percent	20	29	24	26	33	24	34	13	18	17	14	9	10
Other	Percent	3	4	2	4	3	6	3	3	0	4	5	2	1
Total	Percent	23	33	26	30	36	30	37	16	18	21	19	11	12
Traditional Fuel Use														
Firewood	Percent	73	91	98	96	97	90	82	59	88	74	63	50	36
Charcoal	Percent	11	4	1	2	2	4	6	16	8	9	18	22	20
Total	Percent	84	95	100	98	99	94	88	75	96	83	81	72	57
Nontraditional Fuel Use														
Kerosene	Percent	15	5	0	1	1	5	11	23	4	16	18	26	40
Electricity	Percent	0	0	..	..	..	..	0	0	..	..	..	1	1
Gas	Percent	1	0	..	1	..	..	..	1	..	..	1	1	2
Other	Percent	0	0	..	0	..	1	0	0	..	1	0	..	0
Total	Percent	16	5	0	2	1	6	12	25	4	17	19	28	43

Enquête Nationale sur les Conditions de Vie des Ménages

16-13. Uganda

Indicators	Unit of Measure	National total	Rural All	Rural Q1	Rural Q2	Rural Q3	Rural Q4	Rural Q5	Urban All	Urban Q1	Urban Q2	Urban Q3	Urban Q4	Urban Q5
			Expenditure Quintile											
Demographic Indicators														
Sample size (households)	Number	10,696	8,344.0	1,241.0	1,459.0	1,594.0	1,832.0	2,218.0	2,352.0	554.0	463.0	466.0	437.0	432.0
Total Population	000s	22,035	19,067.4	3,812.9	3,813.6	3,810.0	3,812.1	3,818.8	2,968.1	593.1	594.0	593.5	593.4	594.0
Age dependency ratio	Number	1.2	1.3	1.5	1.5	1.4	1.2	0.9	0.9	1.3	1.1	1.0	0.7	0.5
Average household size	Number	5.4	5.5	6.5	6.3	5.9	5.2	4.3	4.6	5.8	5.2	4.6	4.4	3.6
Head Of Household Characteristics														
Age Dependency by household structure														
Monogamous male	Number	1.2	1.3	1.5	1.5	1.3	1.2	0.9	0.9	1.2	1.1	1.1	0.8	0.5
Polygamous male	Number	1.5	1.5	1.7	1.6	1.6	1.4	1.1	1.4	1.4	1.3	1.7	..	0.2
Single male	Number	0.6	0.7	1.0	1.1	1.4	0.9	0.4	0.3	1.0	0.6	0.5	0.1	0.1
De facto female	Number	1.5	1.6	2.0	1.9	1.6	1.3	0.9	1.0	1.6	1.5	0.9	1.1	0.5
De jure female	Number	1.2	1.3	1.5	1.5	1.4	1.2	0.9	0.9	1.5	1.1	0.9	0.6	0.4
Education level of head														
No level	Percent	25.4	28.5	44.2	29.0	25.5	26.5	21.5	8.9	23.7	12.2	6.8	5.7	1.9
Primary, not completed	Percent	40.0	42.6	40.1	46.8	45.3	43.4	38.9	25.7	33.1	31.6	32.8	20.7	15.5
Primary completed, no secondary	Percent	10.9	10.6	8.4	11.3	12.2	9.9	10.9	12.9	12.9	14.0	16.5	17.7	5.5
Secondary not completed	Percent	12.6	..	..	..	..	..	..	..	..	..	..	..	..
Secondary completed	Percent	1.3	1.0	0.5	0.5	0.7	1.0	1.9	3.0	1.7	4.0	1.1	2.4	4.9
Tertiary	Percent	7.9	5.4	1.2	2.3	3.9	6.5	10.6	21.4	5.1	10.0	12.8	26.6	41.6
Pre-school	Percent	1.1	1.2	1.2	1.7	0.9	1.0	1.3	0.5	0.4	1.0	0.2	0.6	0.5
Undefined	Percent	0.7	0.4	0.4	0.2	0.6	0.6	0.4	1.9	2.1	1.9	1.3	1.8	2.2
Marital Status of head														
Monogamous male	Percent	62.0	63.0	60.1	68.0	67.5	66.7	55.2	56.9	60.6	60.1	53.2	59.8	53.1
Polygamous male	Percent	2.2	2.5	3.2	2.9	2.8	2.0	1.9	0.4	0.8	0.4	0.7	..	0.1
Single male	Percent	8.6	8.1	2.6	4.1	4.2	6.5	18.7	11.4	3.3	5.4	10.3	12.6	20.3
De facto female	Percent	8.9	9.1	17.7	7.2	8.4	6.7	7.1	7.8	8.3	9.7	9.7	6.4	6.0
De jure female	Percent	18.3	..	..	..	..	..	..	..	..	..	..	..	..
Labor Market														
Proportion aged 15-64 in population	Percent	45.3	44.0	39.3	40.1	42.3	45.6	52.9	53.4	43.8	48.1	49.6	57.3	68.2
Proportion employed (aged 15 to 64)	Percent	46.8	45.3	38.4	42.7	45.0	47.1	51.1	54.6	48.6	49.9	54.2	58.9	58.3
Females among employed (aged 15 to 64)	Percent	36.4	34.8	34.7	32.9	34.8	36.6	34.8	43.3	46.5	46.1	45.9	41.2	40.0
Employment Ratios (among labor force)														
Employment Ratio	Percent	98.6	99.3	99.5	98.9	99.7	99.2	99.1	95.8	95.7	94.8	94.1	97.9	96.0
Formal Employment among Employed	Percent	22.0	15.3	7.8	11.7	12.9	15.6	23.2	51.5	38.1	47.9	39.7	57.4	63.7
Public Employed among Formal Employment	Percent	25.4	29.4	19.3	24.8	26.7	35.3	30.6	20.3	16.2	10.7	18.5	23.4	24.3
Informal Employment among Employed	Percent	0.1	0.0	0.0	0.0	0.0	0.0	0.1	0.6	0.2	0.1	0.1	0.9	1.1
Self-Employed among Informal Employed	Percent	100.0	..	..	..	..	..	..	..	..	..	..	..	..
Employers among Employed	Percent	77.9	84.7	92.2	88.3	87.1	84.4	76.7	48.0	61.7	52.0	60.2	41.7	35.2
Proportion Employed in Agriculture	Percent	66.5	79.3	88.6	85.6	82.4	77.1	69.6	10.4	28.1	12.0	10.3	7.6	2.3
MDG1: Eradicate Extreme Poverty and Hunger														
Mean monthly per capita expenditure	Ugandan shillings	32,946	24,953.3	7,718.8	12,717.3	17,409.9	24,052.4	50,929.9	75,763.4	17,524.3	30,565.5	45,654.5	70,290.1	170,608.3
Mean monthly share on food	Percent	57.9	59.9	63.1	61.1	60.7	60.0	56.2	47.2	54.8	50.1	48.2	46.1	40.8
Mean monthly share on health	Percent	3.8	3.9	3.0	3.7	4.0	3.9	4.8	2.9	3.5	3.1	3.3	2.6	2.3
Mean monthly share on education	Percent	3.2	2.8	1.5	2.3	2.5	3.2	3.7	5.5	4.4	5.7	5.8	6.7	5.0
MDG2: Education and Literacy; MDG3: Promote Gender Equality														
Access to primary school (within 30 minutes)	Percent	..	..	..	..	..	..	..	..	..	..	..	..	..
Net primary enrollment rate														
Total	Percent	63	61	50	60	63	67	70	74	63	73	79	78	82
Male	Percent	63	61	54	59	63	65	69	76	62	78	82	77	86
Female	Percent	62	61	46	61	63	69	71	72	65	67	75	79	76
Net secondary enrollment rate														
Total	Percent	13	10	3	6	8	11	23	29	18	19	30	36	40
Male	Percent	12	10	3	7	8	10	21	31	16	11	30	45	52
Female	Percent	14	11	3	4	9	13	24	28	19	27	31	31	31
Tertiary enrolment rate per 10,000														
Total	per 10,000	17	..	..	..	..	..	..	..	..	..	..	..	..
Adult literacy rate														
Total	Percent	67	63	44	58	65	69	75	88	73	83	90	93	95
Male	Percent	79	76	64	74	78	79	82	93	83	90	94	97	96
Female	Percent	56	51	29	43	53	60	68	83	64	78	86	89	94
Youth literacy rate														
Total	Percent	79	76	56	72	78	83	87	92	87	86	91	96	95
Male	Percent	85	83	67	82	85	86	88	96	92	93	95	97	98
Female	Percent	74	70	45	61	73	79	85	89	84	82	89	94	93

Uganda National Household Survey 1999/2000

(Table continues on next page)

16-13. Uganda (continued)

	Unit of Measure	National total	Rural All	Rural Q1	Rural Q2	Rural Q3	Rural Q4	Rural Q5	Urban All	Urban Q1	Urban Q2	Urban Q3	Urban Q4	Urban Q5
Indicators														
MDG4: Reduce Child Mortality; MDG5: Improve Maternal Health														
Proportion with distance to Health Center less than 5 km	Percent	..	..	..	..	..	..	..	..	..	..	..	..	..
Morbidity	Percent	28	28	26	27	29	28	30	26	26	26	25	25	26
Action taken when sick	Percent	92	92	83	93	92	94	95	96	92	95	98	98	98
Health provider ownership														
Public	Percent	14	15	13	14	14	16	15	14	18	15	15	14	8
Private - Modern Medicine	Percent	17	17	14	16	18	16	20	16	17	9	17	24	13
Private - Traditional Healers	Percent	1	1	1	1	1	1	1	1	1	1	0	1	1
Other	Percent	68	67	72	69	67	67	63	69	64	75	68	61	79
Child survival and malnutrition														
Birth assisted by trained staff	Percent	..	..	..	..	..	..	..	..	..	..	..	..	..
1-year-olds immunisation coverage	Percent	58	57	47	55	52	68	67	70	73	56	69	70	84
1-year-olds immunized against measles	Percent	66	66	57	62	62	75	76	73	77	58	72	71	84
Stunting (6-59 months)	Percent	35	36	38	39	37	33	33	23	34	19	24	8	19
Wasting (6-59 months)	Percent	5	6	7	6	6	5	5	3	6	1	4	..	1
Underweight (6-59 months)	Percent	21	22	28	22	22	19	19	9	16	9	10	3	0
MDG7: Ensure Environmental Sustainability														
Owner occupancy rate	Percent	82	91	96	94	93	91	83	35	50	38	34	28	30
Access to sanitation facilities	Percent	86	84	59	82	88	91	92	99	94	99	100	100	100
Proportion with distance to Water Source less than 2 km	Percent	94	93	93	93	93	94	93	98	97	98	99	98	98
Proportion with distance distance to Market less than 5 km	Percent	..	..	..	..	..	..	..	..	..	..	..	..	..
Access to improved water source														
Pipe (own tap)	Percent	2	1	0	1	1	1	1	7	1	2	3	6	17
Pipe borne	Percent	10	3	1	2	2	3	4	49	27	44	49	58	58
Well (Protected)	Percent	45	48	48	48	46	50	48	31	53	40	35	22	16
Total	Percent	57	51	49	51	49	54	53	87	81	86	87	87	91
Access to unimproved water source														
Surface Water	Percent	7	8	9	7	8	7	8	1	2	2	1	1	0
Other	Percent	36	40	42	41	42	38	38	11	15	11	13	12	7
Total	Percent	43	49	51	49	51	46	47	13	19	14	13	13	9
Traditional Fuel Use														
Firewood	Percent	83	95	99	98	97	96	88	20	50	25	19	12	4
Charcoal	Percent	14	4	1	1	2	3	10	70	47	72	77	78	72
Total	Percent	98	99	100	99	99	99	98	90	97	97	96	90	75
Nontraditional Fuel Use														
Kerosene	Percent	1	0	..	0	0	0	1	5	1	1	2	5	14
Electricity	Percent	1	0	..	0	0	0	0	3	1	1	1	3	7
Gas	Percent	0	0	..	..	..	..	0	1	..	..	..	..	3
Other	Percent	1	0	0	0	0	0	1	1	2	1	1	1	1
Total	Percent	2	1	0	1	1	1	2	10	3	3	4	10	25

Expenditure Quintile columns: Rural (All, Q1–Q5) and Urban (All, Q1–Q5).

Uganda National Household Survey 1999/2000

16-14. Zambia

Indicators	Unit of Measure	National total	Rural All	Rural Q1	Rural Q2	Rural Q3	Rural Q4	Rural Q5	Urban All	Urban Q1	Urban Q2	Urban Q3	Urban Q4	Urban Q5
Demographic Indicators														
Sample size (households)	Number	16,422	8,317.0	1,414.0	1,461.0	1,561.0	1,655.0	2,226.0	8,105.0	1,298.0	1,384.0	1,518.0	1,752.0	2,153.0
Total Population	000s	9,989	6,276.5	1,239.5	1,252.3	1,265.2	1,259.9	1,259.6	3,712.0	712.0	742.8	752.0	751.8	753.4
Age dependency ratio	Number	0.9	0.9	1.0	1.0	0.9	0.9	0.8	0.8	1.0	0.9	0.8	0.7	0.5
Average household size	Number	5.4	5.3	6.0	5.7	5.5	5.2	4.3	5.5	6.9	6.3	6.0	5.2	4.2
Head Of Household Characteristics														
Age Dependency by household structure														
Monogamous male	Number	0.9	0.9	1.0	1.0	1.0	0.9	0.8	0.8	1.0	1.0	0.9	0.7	0.6
Polygamous male	Number	..	..	..	..	..	..	..	..	..	..	..	..	..
Single male	Number	0.5	0.6	0.9	1.0	0.7	0.5	0.4	0.4	0.7	0.6	0.5	0.3	0.2
De facto female	Number	1.0	1.1	1.3	1.0	0.9	1.2	1.0	0.8	1.3	1.6	0.6	0.5	0.5
De jure female	Number	0.8	0.9	1.0	0.9	1.0	0.8	0.7	0.7	1.0	0.8	0.8	0.6	0.4
Education level of head														
No level	Percent	..	..	..	..	..	..	..	..	..	..	..	..	..
Primary, not completed	Percent	30.2	41.7	50.6	49.1	42.6	35.4	35.9	13.2	28.3	14.9	13.0	9.6	6.9
Primary completed, no secondary	Percent	23.1	27.6	29.6	30.4	29.0	26.9	24.1	16.5	24.5	23.3	17.2	15.3	8.2
Secondary not completed	Percent	26.1	..	..	..	..	..	..	..	..	..	..	..	..
Secondary completed	Percent	12.7	5.9	3.7	2.0	4.0	8.0	9.3	22.8	9.8	15.8	22.7	27.8	30.4
Tertiary	Percent	7.9	2.8	0.4	0.9	1.9	3.5	5.4	15.5	4.8	7.7	9.4	14.7	30.9
Pre-school	Percent	0.1	0.1	..	0.3	..	..	0.1	0.0	..	0.1	..	..	0.1
Undefined	Percent	0.0	0.0	0.0	..	..	..	..	..	..	..	..	..	..
Marital Status of head														
Monogamous male	Percent	70.1	70.1	66.1	69.0	75.2	72.8	67.4	70.1	68.4	74.3	76.0	72.3	62.3
Polygamous male	Percent	..	..	..	..	..	..	..	..	..	..	..	..	..
Single male	Percent	7.4	6.2	3.4	4.8	3.9	7.0	10.6	9.6	6.1	6.1	6.5	8.6	17.1
De facto female	Percent	3.4	4.2	4.4	5.1	4.0	3.3	4.1	2.1	2.4	2.0	1.6	3.1	1.6
De jure female	Percent	19.0	..	..	..	..	..	..	..	..	..	..	..	..
Labor Market														
Proportion aged 15-64 in population	Percent	53.8	52.3	49.4	50.9	51.3	53.4	56.7	56.2	50.4	52.1	54.3	59.3	64.5
Proportion employed (aged 15 to 64)	Percent	60.3	72.0	70.0	72.9	73.0	71.9	72.1	42.0	35.4	39.4	40.1	42.8	49.8
Females among employed (aged 15 to 64)	Percent	47.0	50.9	54.8	51.0	51.0	49.6	48.6	36.6	42.0	36.0	34.5	35.1	36.7
Employment Ratios (among labor force)														
Employment Ratio	Percent	87.9	94.4	92.5	93.9	96.4	93.9	95.0	74.3	61.9	72.9	74.1	75.6	82.9
Formal Employment among Employed	Percent	18.5	5.7	2.3	2.4	4.8	7.6	10.6	53.2	35.1	47.3	54.5	55.6	63.5
Public Employed among Formal Employment	Percent	51.2	49.7	19.5	46.3	46.6	49.9	57.0	51.6	40.7	45.9	54.3	53.8	54.3
Informal Employment among Employed	Percent	80.6	93.8	97.3	97.1	94.7	92.1	88.8	44.6	63.9	49.3	43.0	42.9	33.9
Self-Employed among Informal Employed	Percent	67.5	..	..	..	..	..	..	..	..	..	..	..	..
Employers among Employed	Percent	0.4	0.2	0.3	0.3	0.2	0.2	0.2	1.0	0.4	1.5	1.0	0.7	1.1
Proportion Employed in Agriculture	Percent	67.0	87.8	92.9	91.5	87.9	85.2	82.5	10.7	26.8	12.0	9.1	7.0	5.2
MDG1: Eradicate Extreme Poverty and Hunger														
Mean monthly per capita expenditure	Zambian kwacha	46,798	32,947.7	5,267.6	11,112.8	17,218.4	27,740.1	85,707.9	71,511.5	13,061.2	25,361.1	37,361.5	56,295.0	174,264.2
Mean monthly share on food	Percent	67.5	73.7	75.7	77.2	74.8	72.3	69.8	56.5	66.9	63.2	59.0	55.7	44.8
Mean monthly share on health	Percent	1.4	1.3	1.1	1.1	1.4	1.3	1.5	1.7	1.5	1.5	1.6	1.5	2.0
Mean monthly share on education	Percent	2.4	1.8	3.0	2.1	1.6	1.4	1.1	3.6	4.2	3.5	3.5	3.5	3.5
MDG2: Education and Literacy; MDG3: Promote Gender Equality														
Access to primary school (within 30 minutes)	Percent	..	..	..	..	..	..	..	..	..	..	..	..	..
Net primary enrollment rate														
Total	Percent	66	59	46	55	60	67	70	77	65	75	78	84	86
Male	Percent	65	59	49	56	59	66	70	77	64	77	77	82	87
Female	Percent	66	59	44	55	60	68	69	77	65	73	79	84	86
Net secondary enrollment rate														
Total	Percent	23	14	8	10	14	18	21	38	21	31	36	45	55
Male	Percent	25	16	10	11	16	20	24	40	21	33	38	52	58
Female	Percent	22	12	5	8	12	17	18	36	21	28	34	40	53
Tertiary enrolment rate per 10,000														
Total	per 10,000	34	..	..	..	..	..	..	..	..	..	..	..	..
Adult literacy rate														
Total	Percent	..	..	..	..	..	..	..	..	..	..	..	..	..
Male	Percent	..	..	..	..	..	..	..	..	..	..	..	..	..
Female	Percent	..	..	..	..	..	..	..	..	..	..	..	..	..
Youth literacy rate														
Total	Percent	..	..	..	..	..	..	..	..	..	..	..	..	..
Male	Percent	..	..	..	..	..	..	..	..	..	..	..	..	..
Female	Percent	..	..	..	..	..	..	..	..	..	..	..	..	..

Expenditure Quintile columns: Rural (All, Q1–Q5); Urban (All, Q1–Q5).

Zambia Living Conditions Monitoring Survey II, 1998

(Table continues on next page)

Household Welfare 401

16-14. Zambia (continued)

	Unit of Measure	National total	Rural All	Rural Q1	Rural Q2	Rural Q3	Rural Q4	Rural Q5	Urban All	Urban Q1	Urban Q2	Urban Q3	Urban Q4	Urban Q5
			Expenditure Quintile											
Indicators														
MDG4: Reduce Child Mortality; MDG5: Improve Maternal Health														
Proportion with distance to Health Center less than 5 km	Percent	67	50	47	49	51	50	52	97	96	97	97	98	98
Morbidity	Percent	11	12	9	12	12	14	15	10	10	9	8	10	11
Action taken when sick	Percent	37	33	30	31	31	34	38	46	38	43	43	45	56
Health provider ownership														
Public	Percent	..	..	..	..	..	..	..	..	..	..	..	..	..
Private - Modern Medicine	Percent	..	..	..	..	..	..	..	..	..	..	..	..	..
Private - Traditional Healers	Percent	..	..	..	..	..	..	..	..	..	..	..	..	..
Other	Percent	..	..	..	..	..	..	..	..	..	..	..	..	..
Child survival and malnutrition														
Birth assisted by trained staff	Percent	..	..	..	..	..	..	..	..	..	..	..	..	..
1-year-olds immunisation coverage	Percent	59	56	46	54	56	57	67	64	64	68	58	61	70
1-year-olds immunized against measles	Percent	89	87	79	88	88	90	92	94	95	92	93	92	95
Stunting (6-59 months)	Percent	62	66	70	65	65	62	65	57	64	64	55	54	45
Wasting (6-59 months)	Percent	6	6	8	5	6	5	5	5	6	5	5	5	5
Underweight (6-59 months)	Percent	27	30	37	30	32	26	24	23	31	27	20	20	14
MDG7: Ensure Environmental Sustainability														
Owner occupancy rate	Percent	74	90	95	95	92	88	84	45	63	50	45	40	33
Access to sanitation facilities	Percent	81	71	61	68	72	73	77	99	98	99	100	99	100
Proportion with distance to Water Source less than 2 km	Percent	98	98	98	97	98	98	98	100	100	100	100	100	100
Proportion with distance distance to Market less than 5 km	Percent	60	38	35	36	34	40	43	99	97	99	99	99	99
Access to improved water source														
Pipe (own tap)	Percent	16	1	0	0	1	1	4	41	27	35	39	42	55
Pipe borne	Percent	17	4	3	3	3	4	5	40	41	42	43	43	32
Well (Protected)	Percent	23	32	29	31	34	31	33	8	11	9	8	7	6
Total	Percent	56	37	33	35	38	36	42	89	79	87	91	91	93
Access to unimproved water source														
Surface Water	Percent	43	62	66	65	61	63	56	10	21	12	9	8	5
Other	Percent	1	1	1	1	1	1	2	1	1	1	1	1	2
Total	Percent	44	63	67	65	62	64	58	11	21	13	9	9	7
Traditional Fuel Use														
Firewood	Percent	62	90	95	93	91	89	84	12	29	11	9	6	8
Charcoal	Percent	23	9	5	7	9	9	13	48	57	63	56	47	29
Total	Percent	85	99	100	100	99	99	97	60	85	74	65	54	37
Nontraditional Fuel Use														
Kerosene	Percent	0	0	0	0	0	0	0	0	0	0	0	0	0
Electricity	Percent	15	1	0	0	0	1	3	40	14	26	35	46	63
Gas	Percent	0	0	..	0	0	..	0	0	..	..	..	0	0
Other	Percent	0	0	..	0	0	0	0	0	..	0	0	0	..
Total	Percent	15	1	0	0	1	1	3	40	15	26	35	46	63

Zambia Living Conditions Monitoring Survey II, 1998

Technical notes

Burkina Faso

Data source. Burkina Faso's Institut National de la Statistique et de la Démographie carried out the Enquête Prioritaire II sur les Conditions de Vie des Ménages au Burkina. Data were collected between May 1998 and August 1998. The project was funded by the Government of Burkina Faso, the World Bank, the African Development Bank (ADB), and the United Nations through the UNDP.

Household. Defined as the basic socio-economic unit in which the different members, related or, live in the same house or property, put together their resources and jointly meet their basic needs, including food, under the authority of one person who is recognized as the head.

Literacy. Household members aged five and up who could both read and write a simple sentence in any language were considered literate.

The survey had no information on the following topics: birth assistance and immunization.

Burundi

Data source. The Institut de Statistiques et d'Études économiques of Burundi, in conjunction with the UNDP, carried out the Enquête Prioritaire—Étude nationale sur les conditions de vie des populations.

Household. Defined as those people who habitually live and eat their meals in the same compound. One member is recognized as the head.

Literacy. Household members aged five and up who could both read and write were considered literate.

The survey had no information on the following topics: birth assistance, health provider ownership, and immunizations.

Cameroon

Data source. Cameroon's Bureau Central des Recensements et des Enquêtes of the Direction de la Statistique et de la Comptabilité carried out the Enquête Nationale auprès des Ménages.

Household. Defined by the survey to be those people who live under the same roof, take their meals together or in little groups, put some or all of their incomes together for the group's spending purposes, at the head of household's discretion.

Literacy. Household members aged five and up who could both read and write were considered literate.

The survey had no information on the following topics: access to primary services.

Côte d'Ivoire

Data source. The Institut National de la Statistique carried out the Enquête Niveau de Vie, a priority survey, in 1998.

Household This was defined as a person or a group of people who live under the same roof, share the same meals, and recognize one person as the head.

Literacy. Household members aged five and up who could both read and write a simple sentence in any language were considered literate.

The survey had no information on the following topics: access to primary services, child survival and malnutrition, employment categories and job types, and health provider ownership.

Ethiopia

Data source. The 1999/2000 Household Income, Consumption, and Expenditure Survey (HICES) was carried out by the Central Statistical Office. The data collection process was spread over six months, from June 1999 to February 2000.

Household. This was defined as a person or a group of people who live under the same roof, share the same meals, and recognize one person as the head.

Literacy. Persons were considered as literate if they could read and write a sentence in the national language.

The survey had no information on the following topics: access to primary school, and birth assisted by trained staff..

The Gambia

Data source. The Central Department of Statistics of the Ministry of Economic Planning and Industrial Development of the Gambia carried out the 1998 National Household Poverty Survey, an integrated survey. Data was collected between April 1998 and May 1998.

Household. This was defined as the set of people who normally ate and lived together for six out of the twelve months prior to the survey.

Literacy. Such information is not reliably available for this survey; less than one in 1,100 who could have answered this question did so.

The survey had no information on the following topics: access to primary services, birth assisted by trained staff, cooking fuel, and immunization.

Ghana

Data source. The Ghana Statistical Service carried out the Ghana Living Standards Survey IV, an integrated survey. Data collection was done between April 1988 and March 1989.

Household. In this survey, a household was defined as a group of people who have usually slept in the same dwelling and taken their meals together for at least nine of the twelve months preceding the interview.

Literacy. Household members aged 5 and up who could both read and write a simple sentence in English or any local language were considered literate.

The survey had no information on the following topics: access to health center and primary school, and child survival and malnutrition.

Kenya

Data source. The Kenya Central Bureau of Statistics carried out data collection for the 1997 Welfare Monitoring Survey III, a priority survey, in March and April 1997.

Sample. Due to logistical and financial constraints, the survey did not adequately cover the North Eastern and parts of the Eastern Provinces.

Household. This was defined as the set of people who normally ate and lived together for six out of the twelve months prior to the survey.

Literacy. Literacy was defined as the ability to read and write.

Madagascar

Data source. The Institut National de la Statistique carried out the Enquête Prioritaire auprès des ménages in 1999. The project was funded by the Government of Madagascar and the World Bank (IDA).

Household. Defined as the set of people who have or do not have family links between them, who live and sleep in the same housing, and take their meals together regularly. The housing may be an individual house, an apartment, or one or more rooms in a larger building. The household is headed by one individual whose authority is recognized by all in the household.

Literacy. Household members aged 5 and up who had completed at least four years of primary school or could read and write were considered to be literate.

The survey had no information on the following topics: access to primary services, birth assisted by trained staff, immunization against measles, and owner occupancy rates.

Malawi

Data source. The Malawi National Statistics Office carried out the Integrated Household Survey from November 1997 to October 1998.

Household. Defined by the survey as either a person living alone or a group of people , either related or unrelated, who lived together as a single unit in the sense that they have common housekeeping arrangements (that is, shared or were supported by a common budget). Someone who did not live with the household during the survey period was not counted as a current member of the household.

Literacy. Defined as the ability to read and write a simple sentence for those who had not attended school in the past two months, and defined based upon educational attainment for those who had attended school in the past two months.

The survey had no information on the following topics: access to primary school, access to a water source, access to sanitation facilities, birth assisted by trained staff, and health provider ownership.

Mozambique

Data source. The Instituto Nacional de Estatistiqua carried out the Inquérito Nacional aos Agregados Familiares sobre as Condições de Vida, an integrated survey.

Household. This was defined as the set of people who partly or totally shared their expenditures, had not been absent for more than six months out of the previous year, and were not domestic help. In the case of polygamous households, each wife and her children were considered to be a separate household.

Literacy. Literacy was defined as the ability to read and write in Portuguese.

The survey had no information on the following topics: access to a health center, access to market, access to primary school, birth assisted by trained staff, immunization coverage, and expenditure on health or education.

São Tomé and Principe

Data source. The Instituto Nacional de Estatistica of the Ministério de Planomento, Finanças e Cooperaçao carried out the Enquête sur les Conditions de Vie des Ménages in 2000. The project was financed by the Government of São Tomé and Principe with assistance from the African Development Bank and the United Nations Development Program. Technical assistance was provided by the International Labor Organization.

Household. Defined by the survey as the set of people, related or not, who live together under the same roof, put their resources together, and address as a unit their primary needs, under the authority of one person whom they recognize as the head of the household.

Literacy. Defined as the ability to read and write a simple sentence.

The survey had no information on the following topics: child survival and malnutrition, and self-employment.

Uganda

Data source. The Uganda Bureau of Statistics carried out the National Household Survey. Data collection occurred between August 1999 and July 2000. The project was funded by the Government of Uganda and the World Bank. Statistics Denmark and the World Bank provided consultants for technical support.

Sample. The survey did not collect data in the Kitgum, Gulu, Kasese, and Bundibugio districts.

Household. Defined by the survey as those individuals who normally eat and live together.

Literacy. If individuals had answered questions about the ability to read and write, they were considered to be literate if they could do both. Otherwise, the level of education was used to make this determination.

The survey had no information on the following topics: access to primary school, access to a health center, access to market, and birth assisted by trained staff.

Zambia

Data source. The Zambian Central Statistical Office carried out the Living Conditions Monitoring Survey II. Data collection was done between November 1998 and December 1998.

Household. A household was defined as a group of persons who normally cooked, ate, and lived together.

These people may or may not have been related by blood, but make common provision for food or other essentials for living, and they have one person whom they all regarded as the head of the household.

Literacy. No information on literacy is available in the survey.

The survey had no information on the following topics: access to primary school, health provider ownership, and birth assisted by trained staff.

UNESCO class cohorts for the net enrollment statistics in Chapter 16

	Primary school		*Secondary school*	
Country	*Entrance age*	*Duration*	*Entrance age*	*Duration*
Benin	6	6	12	7
Burkina Faso	7	6	13	7
Burundi	7	6	13	7
Cameroon	6	6	12	7
Côte d'Ivoire	6	6	12	7
Ethiopia	7	4	11	8
Gambia	6	6	12	6
Ghana	6	6	12	6
Kenya	6	7	13	5
Madagascar	6	5	11	7
Malawi	6	4	10	8
Mozambique	6	5	11	7
São Tomé and Principe	7	6	13	6
Uganda	6	7	13	6
United Republic of Tanzania	7	7	14	6
Zambia	7	7	14	5

Source: "Sub-Saharan Africa: Regional Report," UNESCO Institute for Statistics, 2001.

Sample size and expenditure details for surveys covered in Chapter 16

		*Number of Households**		*Expenditure details*			
Country	*Survey year*	*Rural*	*Urban*	*Items*	*Visits*	*Deflated*	*Aggregation***
Burkina Faso	1998	5,885	2,593	65	1	no	WB
Burundi	1998	3,908	2,760	41	1	no	NSO
Cameroon	1996	628	1,103	74	7	yes	NSO
Côte d'Ivoire	1998	2,280	1,920	73	1	yes	WB
Ethiopia	1999/2000	8,459	8,213	852	16	no	WB
Gambia, The	1998	933	1,025	165	2	no	NSO
Ghana	1998	3,799	2,199	127	6	yes	NSO
Kenya	1997	18,134	3,597	168	1	yes	WB**
Madagascar	1999	4,920	5,280	111	1	yes	WB
Malawi	1997	5,657	929	131	1	yes	NSO
Mozambique	1996	6,087	2,163	125	2	yes	WB
São Tomé and Principe	2000	1,173	1,243	161	1	no	WB**
Uganda	1999	8,344	2,352	131	1	no	WB
Zambia	1998	13,551	14,619	155	1	No	NSO

*N*otes:
(*) These are the sample sizes for the Standardized Files; the original sample size may be different.
(**) The symbol "WB" means that the data was aggregated at the World Bank; the symbol "NSO" means that the aggregation was done by the country's national statistical office. Rent was imputed for Kenya and São Tomé and Principe.

Bibliography

Association for the Development of African Education. 1995. *A Statistical Profile of Education in Sub-Saharan Africa, 1990–93*. Paris.

Candoy-Sekse, Rebecca. 1988. *Techniques of Privatization of State-Owned Enterprises. Volume III. Inventory of Country Experience and Reference Materials*. World Bank Technical Paper 90. Washington, D.C.

Central African Republic, Division of Statistics and Economic Studies. 1994. "Enquete prioritaire sur les conditions de vie des menages." Bangui.

Club of Rome. 1972. The Limit to Growth. Rome.

Côte d'Ivoire, Institut National de Statistique. 1994. "Enquete prioritaire." Abidjan.

Currency Data & Intelligence Inc. Monthly. *Global Currency Report*. New York.

Floyd, Robert, Clive Gray, and R. P. Short. 1984. *Public Enterprise in Mixed Economies: Some Macro-economic Aspects*. Washington, D.C.: International Monetary Fund.

Food and Agriculture Organization (FAO). 1987. *Agrostat Code Book*. Rome.

___. annual. *Fertilizer Yearbook*. Rome.

___. annual. *Food and Agriculture Organization Production Yearbook*. Rome.

___. annual. *Food Aid in Figures*. Rome.

___. annual. *Trade Yearbook*. Rome.

___. annual. *Yearbook of Forest Products*. Rome.

Galal, Ahmed. 1990. "Public Enterprise Reform: A Challenge for the World Bank." PRE Working Paper 407. World Bank, Country Economics Department, Washington, D.C. Processed

___. 1991. Public Enterprise Reform: Lessons from the Past and Issues for the Future. World Bank Discussion Paper 119. Washington, D.C.

The Gambia, Ministry of Finance. 1993. "Report on the 1992 Priority Survey." Banjul.

Grootaert, Christian, and Timothy Marchant. 1991. *The Social Dimensions of Adjustment Priority Survey: An Instrument for the Rapid Identification and Monitoring of Policy Targeting Groups.* SDA Working Paper 12. Washington, D.C.: World Bank.

Guinea, Ministry of Planning and Finance. 1991. "Rapport Final: Enquete sur les informations prioritaire: Dimensions Sociales de l'Adjustment Structurel." Conakry.

Guinea-Bissau, National Institute of Statistics and Census. 1992. "Relatorio Final: Inquerito Ligeiro Junto as Familias." Bissau.

Hemming, Richard, and Ali M. Mansoor. 1988. *Privatization and Public Enterprises*. IMF Occasional Paper 56. Washington, D.C.

International Energy Agency (IEA). 1996. *Energy Statistics and Balances of Non-OECD Countries, 1993–94*. Paris.

International Labour Organization (ILO). annual. *Yearbook of Labor Statistics*. Geneva.

___. 1968. *International Standard Classification of Occupations*. Geneva.

___. 1987. *World Labor Report* 1. Oxford: Oxford University Press.

International Monetary Fund (IMF). 1986. Manual on Government Finance Statistics. Washington, D.C.

___. 1993. *Balance of Payments Manual*, Fifth ed. Washington, D.C.

___. annual. *Balance of Payments Yearbook.*Washington, D.C.

___. annual. *Government Finance Statistics Yearbook*. Washington, D.C.

___. monthly. *International Financial Statistics*. Washington, D.C.

___. various issues. *Recent Economic Development*. Washington, D.C.

International Road Federation. 1995. *World Road Statistics, 1990–94*. Geneva.

International Telecommunication Union (ITU). 1995. *World Telecommunication Development Report*. Geneva.

Jager, William, and Charles Humphreys. 1988. "The Effect of Policy Reforms on Africa." *American Journal of Agricultural Economics* 70 (50): 1036–43.

Kenya, Central Bureau of Statistics. 1993. "Welfare Monitoring Survey." Nairobi.

Metallgesellschaft AG. annual. *Metallstatistik*. Frankfurt am Main.

Mukui, John Thinguri. 1994. "Kenya: Poverty Profiles, 1982–92." Prepared for the Office of the Vice-President and Ministry of Planning and National Development, Nairobi, Kenya.

Nair, Govindan, and Anastosios Filppides. 1988. "How Much Do State-Owned Enterprises Contribute to Public Sector Deficits in Developing Countries?" PPR Working Paper 45. World Bank, Development Economics Vice Presidency, Washington, D.C. Processed.

Organisation for Economic Cooperation and Development (OECD). Various issues. Geographical Distribution of Financial Flows to Developing Countries. Paris.

Republic of South Africa. 1990. *South Africa Statistics*. Pretoria: Government Printer.

Swanson, Daniel, and Teferra Wolde-Semait. 1989. *Africa's Public Enterprise Sector and Evidence of Reforms*. World Bank Technical Paper 95. Washington, D.C.

Uganda, Ministry of Finance and Economic Planning. 1993. "Report on the Uganda National Integrated Household Survey 1992–93." Entebbe.

United Nations. 1950. *Index Numbers of Industrial Production*. New York.

___. 1989. *Compendium of Statistics and Indicators on the Situation of Women*. New York.

___. 1992. *The World's Women, 1970–90*. New York.

___. annual. *Population and Vital Statistics Report*. New York.

___. annual. *Yearbook. G., International Trade Statistics*. New York.

United Nations Children's Fund (UNICEF). annual. *The State of the World's Children*. New York.

United Nations Development Programme (UNDP). 1994. Human Development Report 1994. New York.

United Nations Development Programme and the World Bank. 1989. *African Economic and Financial Data*. Washington, D.C.

___. 1992. *African Development Indicators*. Washington, D.C.

United Nations Program on HIV/AIDS (UNAIDS). June 2000. "Report on the Global HIV/AIDS Epidemic." Geneva.

United Nations Statistical Office (UNSO). 1975, 1986. "United National Standard International Trade Classification," revisions 2 and 3 (SITC, rev. 2 and 3). Statistical Papers, series M. no. 34, rev. 2 and 3. New York.

___. *United Nations International Standard Classification of All Economic Activities*, revision 2 (ISIC, rev. 2). New York.

___. annual. *Energy Statistics Yearbook*. New York.

United Nations Educational, Scientific, and Cultural Organization (UNESCO). 1982. Conferences of Ministers of Education and Those Responsible for Economic Planning in African Member States. Paris.

___. 1986. *Regional Bulletin of Education Statistics BREDA – STAT*. Regional Office for Education in Africa. Paris.

___. 1989. *Trends and Projections of Enrollment by Level of Education and by Age, 1960–2025 (as assessed in 1989)*. Division of Statistics on Education. Paris.

___. 1990. *Basic Education and Literacy: World Statistical Indicators*. Paris.

___. annual. *Statistical Yearbook*. Paris.

Wadda, Rohey, and Russel Craig. 1993. "Report on the 1992 Priority Survey." Central Statistics, Ministry of Finance and Economic Affairs, Banjul, The Gambia.

World Bank. 1988. *Education in Sub-Saharan Africa: Policies for Adjustment, Revitalization, and Expansion*. Washington, D.C.

___. 1993a. "Africa Adjustment Study P.E. Sector Reform: Case Studies." Washington, D.C. Processed.

___. 1993b. "Public Enterprise Reform and Privatization in Africa." Washington, D.C. Processed.

___. 1994a. "Kenya Poverty Assessment." Eastern Africa Department, Africa Region. Washington, D.C.

___. 1994b. "A Statistical Profile of Education in Sub-Saharan Africa in the 1980s." Africa Technical Department. Washington, D.C. Processed.

___. 1994c. *World Population Projections, 1994-95*. Washington, D.C.

___. 1994d. "Zambia Poverty Assessment." Southern Africa Department. Washington D.C.

___. 1995. *Bureaucrats in Business*. New York: Oxford University Press.

___. annual. *Commodity Trade and Price Trends.* Washington, D.C.

___. annual. *Global Development Finance* (was *World Debt Tables* up to 1996).

___. annual. *World Bank Atlas*. Washington, D.C.

___. annual. World Debt Tables (until 1996; now Global Development Finance). Washington, D.C.

___. annual. *World Development Indicators*. Washington, D.C.

___. annual. *World Development Report.* New York: Oxford University Press.

World Resources Institute. 2000. *World Resources 2000*. Washington, D.C.

World Resources Institute. 1998. *World Resources, 1998–99*. Washington, D.C.

___. 1996. *World Resources 1996–97.* Washington, D.C.

World Bureau of Metal Statistics. monthly. *World Metal Statistics*. London.

World Health Organization (WHO). annual. *World Health Statistics Annua*l. Geneva.

___. various issues. *World Health Statistics Quarterly*. Geneva.

Zambia, Central Statistical Office. 1993. "Social Dimensions of Adjustment: Priority Survey I, 1991." Lusaka.